OBJECTIVE VERBAL & NON-VERBAL REASONING

For All Competitive Examinations

SSC - CGL, CHSL, MTS/RRB - Group 'D', ALP, NTPC/NDA/CDS/IBPS PO & Clerk

Get the #OswaalEdge

100% Exam Readiness	Cognitive Learning	Valuable Exam Insights	Extensive Practice	Examination Analysis
with Concise theory & Previous Years Questions for Practice	with Smart Mind Maps	with Learning Objectives & Exercises with 3 levels of difficulties	with more than 2000+ Questions	with Exam-wise & Topic-wise Trend Analysis

Powered by

oswaal.ai LEARNING MADE SMARTER

Smart guidance that helps you learn, practise and improve.

This Edition: 2026

ISBN: 9789357287258

Disclaimer

This publication has been prepared by qualified subject matter experts with rigorous editorial review. Despite our best efforts, errors may exist. Readers are encouraged to report any by scanning the QR code on the Table of Contents page so corrections can reach all users.

This book is a study aid. Examination results depend on multiple factors including individual preparation and the specific examination conducted. No particular outcome is guaranteed.

Links in this book provide access to supplementary content. Accessibility depends on internet connectivity and device compatibility. Third-party content linked herein was verified at the time of printing; however, the Publisher does not guarantee that such content will remain accurate, available, or appropriate over time.

Views expressed by individual contributors are their own and do not represent the Publisher's position. The Publisher does not endorse personal opinions or political statements contained herein.

All maps, boundaries, and diagrams are artistic representations for educational reference only and are not geographically or politically authoritative.

For details on personal data processing, see our Privacy Policy at www.oswaalbooks.com/privacy. This publication is governed by the laws of India. Disputes shall be subject to the exclusive jurisdiction of courts in Agra, Uttar Pradesh.

Published by: Oswaal Books and Learning Private Limited, Oswaal House, 1/11, Sahitya Kunj, M.G. Road, Agra-282002 (U.P.), India

contact@oswaalbooks.com

+91-562-2857671

Printed at: Alankar Graphics, G.Noida

Contents

Preface

Welcome to the world of reasoning, where logic and deduction merge to unravel the mysteries behind verbal and non-verbal reasoning. This book **'Objective Verbal & Non-Verbal Reasoning'** is meticulously crafted to serve as a comprehensive guide and an exhaustive question bank for mastering the intricate realms of reasoning.

In today's dynamic and competitive world, the ability to reason effectively stands as a fundamental skill. Whether you're preparing for competitive exams, aiming to enhance your cognitive abilities, or simply seeking to sharpen your logical thinking, this book is designed to be your trusted companion.

The verbal reasoning sections delve into the intricacies of language, testing your ability to decipher complex information, draw inferences, and discern patterns within the context of words and sentences. On the other hand, the non-verbal reasoning sections challenge your visual acumen, spatial awareness, and logical thinking through an assortment of figures, diagrams, and patterns.

Some unique features of this book are:

- **Crisp Revision:** Concepts Review & Mind Maps offer bite-sized and just-in-time revision tools.
- **Extensive Practice:** with More than 2000 Previous year questions from various competitive exams segregated based on difficulty level.
- **Concept Clarity:** Easy to Grasp theory complemented by Solved examples.
- **Expert Tips:** Helps you get expert knowledge to master the Reasoning Ability on your first attempt.
- **Learning Objectives:** Outlines what aspirant should understand or be able to achieve after the course
- **To-the-point theory:** The book provides concise and clear explanations of Verbal & Non-Verbal Reasoning concepts without overwhelming readers with too much information.
- **Quick and easy techniques:** The book offers shortcuts and easy-to-follow techniques to help readers solve typical exam questions quickly and efficiently.

In conclusion, this book aims to provide a one-stop solution for all the aspirants who are preparing for competitive exams.

Our books have always been well received by our readers and this is a testament to our research-oriented approach. Our learning pedagogy supplements our editorial research and makes our book current and relevant. We hope our resources will help students to supplement their examination preparation strategy and help them secure high scores.

We wish our readers great success ahead!

Happy learning!

Team Oswaal

Deciphering Verbal & Non-Verbal Reasoning

In competitive examinations, a balanced proficiency in both verbal and non-verbal reasoning is essential. These tests aim to gauge an individual's overall cognitive aptitude, including analytical skills, logical reasoning, problem-solving abilities, and adaptability to various question formats.

1. **Verbal Reasoning:**
   - **Reading Comprehension:** Understand and analyze passages, extracting key information, and inferring implied meanings.
   - **Critical Reasoning:** Evaluate arguments, identify assumptions, draw conclusions, and assess the validity of statements.
   - **Syllogisms and Logical Deductions:** Apply logical rules to assess the validity of conclusions drawn from given statements.
   - **Analogies and Relationships:** Recognize patterns, similarities, and relationships between words or concepts.
   - **Coding-Decoding:** Decipher coded language or symbols based on given patterns or rules.
   - **Word Problems:** Solve problems involving verbal statements, equations, and logical deductions.
2. **Non-Verbal Reasoning:**
   - **Spatial Reasoning:** Understand and manipulate shapes, figures, and spatial arrangements.
   - **Pattern Recognition:** Identify and continue sequences, analogies, and patterns among shapes, images, or symbols.
   - **Classification:** Grouping or categorizing elements based on shared characteristics or rules.
   - **Series and Sequences:** Recognize and predict sequences or patterns in non-verbal elements like figures, symbols, or shapes.
   - **Mirror and Water Images:** Visualize and understand how objects or shapes appear in mirrors or when reflected in water.
   - **Cube and Dice Problems:** Analyze and solve problems based on rotations or arrangements of three-dimensional objects.
3. **Strategies for Preparation:**
   - **Practice Regularly:** Solve a variety of problems regularly to improve speed and accuracy.
   - **Understand Concepts:** Grasp the underlying principles and rules governing different types of reasoning problems.
   - **Time Management:** Practice time-bound solving to manage the limited time available in exams effectively.
   - **Review Mistakes:** Learn from errors to understand the reasoning behind correct solutions.
   - **Mock Tests:** Take simulated exams to simulate real test conditions and assess your readiness.

Contd....

4. **Effective Techniques:**
   - **Elimination Method:** Eliminate improbable choices to increase the probability of selecting the correct answer.
   - **Backtracking:** Revisit questions if time permits, but avoid excessive dwelling on a single problem.
   - **Visualization:** Develop visual methods or mental imagery to tackle non-verbal reasoning problems effectively.
   - **Keyword Analysis:** Pay attention to keywords or cues in verbal reasoning questions to derive accurate answers.
   - **Relate to Real Life:** Relate problems to real-life scenarios to understand and solve them efficiently.
   - Understanding and practicing both verbal and non-verbal reasoning concepts extensively can significantly enhance performance in competitive examinations..

Importance of Verbal & Non-Verbal Reasoning

Verbal and non-verbal reasoning play crucial roles in various competitive examinations by assessing different cognitive abilities:

1. **Verbal Reasoning:**
   - **Critical Thinking:** Verbal reasoning assesses your ability to comprehend and evaluate written information, draw conclusions, and think critically about the presented material.
   - **Language Skills:** It evaluates vocabulary, grammar, and reading comprehension, which are fundamental in most competitive exams.
   - **Logical Deduction:** Tests often include questions related to syllogisms, logical reasoning, and argument analysis, checking your ability to follow and draw logical conclusions from written information.

2. **Non-verbal Reasoning:**
   - **Visual-Spatial Skills:** This section assesses your ability to understand and analyze visual information, such as patterns, sequences, and relationships between shapes or objects.
   - **Abstract Thinking:** Non-verbal reasoning evaluates your capability to recognize and manipulate abstract concepts and patterns.
   - **Problem-Solving:** Questions may involve series completion, analogies, classifications, and spatial reasoning, which are crucial for problem-solving skills.

In competitive examinations, both verbal and non-verbal reasoning sections aim to gauge different aspects of intelligence and cognitive abilities. They help examiners assess candidates' logical thinking, problem-solving capabilities, and ability to interpret information accurately, making them significant parts of such assessments. Strong performances in these sections often indicate a candidate's adaptability, quick thinking, and overall intellectual aptitude, which are valued across various professions and academic pursuits.

Tips to Crack Verbal & Non-Verbal Reasoning in the First Attempt

The Reasoning Ability is a crucial section in many competitive exams in India, such as bank exams, UPSC, SSC, CAT, and other MBA entrance exams. Reasoning Ability has a major role in competitive exams in India as it tests essential knowledge and skills required for various fields & evaluates analytical and logical thinking skills. Cracking the Reasoning Ability section of a competitive exam in the first attempt requires hard work, dedication, and a strategic approach. Here are some tips that can help you achieve success in your first attempt:

1 Think Right

Calming yourself and thinking positive is the first and the best course of action that one is required to take. Think and believe that the exam goal is achievable if worked upon smartly.

2 Start studying from the beginning

All the aspirants are aware of how vast, comprehensive and detailed the syllabus of the Reasoning Ability Section is. To crack the exam in the first attempt you have to start preparing for the exam from the beginning of your 12th class. It is only then that you will be able to complete the entire syllabus. Following this approach will also allow you plenty of time to revise.

3 Respect the syllabus and arrange the materials accordingly

While preparing for the Reasoning Ability nothing can be labelled as less important. Questions can come from the most unexpected topics too. Laying down your whole syllabus in front of you will help you to decide on the study material you require.

4 Get the right tools and study material

Gathering and preparing from the appropriate study material is something you cannot be ignorant towards. You can refer to Oswaal 'Objective Verbal & Non-Verbal Reasoning to enhance your preparation. the is on the lines of the current syllabus and can be entrusted upon before the examination.

5 Schedule total me for each subject

Creating a schedule which gives due time to all the subjects is a must. Giving proper time to all the subjects daily will help you cover the syllabus on time, giving you enough time for revision.

6 Understand the concepts

No one can crack the Reasoning Ability exam just by mugging up all the concepts and topics. The syllabus of the exam is in-depth such that you need to understand every concept.

7 Practice a lot of Sample Papers

Oswaal 'Objective Verbal & Non-Verbal Reasoning' will not only help you in understanding the examination pattern, but they will also help you in figuring out the questons that come up every year and this might give you an edge over other students. The includes all the typologies of Questons asked in the Examination, Previous Years Papers with solutions, Mind Maps, etc. Referring to various sample papers might also help you in comprehending the areas which require more work.

8 Revise whenever you get me

Make sure you revise as much as possible. The revision will help you in keeping the concepts fresh in your mind.

9 Analysing your performance

While you are solving papers, make sure you keep a track of time i.e. how much time does it take to solve one section or one question? Make a report of the sections and type of questions which take minimum and maximum time.

Syllabus for major Competitive Examinations

SSC - CHSL (Combined Higher Secondary Level)

A. Verbal Reasoning

1. Number Series
2. Classification
3. Venn Diagrams
4. Problems on Figural Pattern
5. Statements and Arguments
6. Statements and Assumptions
7. Puzzles
8. Coding and Decoding
9. Alphabet Series
10. Analogy
11. Paper folding
12. Syllogism
13. Statements and Conclusions
14. Assertions and Reasoning
15. Seating Arrangements (Circular and Linear)
16. Word building
17. Blood Relations

B. Non-Verbal Reasoning

1. Analogy
2. Pattern Matching
3. Classifications
4. Mirror Images & Reflection
5. Rotations & Symmetry
6. Grouping of Identical Figures
7. Figure Matrix
8. Paper Folding
9. Cube and Dice
10. Water Images
11. Rule Detection
12. Series
13. Embedded Figures

SSC - CGL (Combined Graduate Level)

- Analogies
- Similarities and differences
- Space visualization
- Spatial orientation
- Problem-solving
- Analysis
- Judgment
- Blood Relations
- Decision making
- Visual memory
- Discrimination
- Observation
- Relationship concepts
- Arithmetical reasoning
- Figural classification
- Arithmetic number series
- Non-verbal series
- Coding and decoding
- Statement conclusion
- Syllogistic reasoning

Contd....

LIC - AAO (Assistant Administrative Officer)	
➢ Puzzles	➢ Coding-Decoding
➢ Seating Arrangements	➢ Machine Input-Output
➢ Direction Sense	➢ Inequalities
➢ Blood Relation	➢ Alpha-Numeric Symbol Series
➢ Syllogism	➢ Data Sufficiency
➢ Order and Ranking	➢ Logical Reasoning

IBPS PO – Probationary Officer	IBPS – Clerk
➢ Verbal Reasoning	➢ Verbal Reasoning
➢ Alphabet Test	➢ Analogy
➢ Blood Relations	➢ Classification
➢ Calendars	➢ Word formation
➢ Clock Reasoning	➢ Statement and conclusions Syllogism
➢ Data Sufficiency	➢ Statement and assumptions
➢ Decision Making	➢ Statement and arguments
➢ Distance & Directions	➢ Coding-Decoding
➢ Input Output	➢ Blood Relations
➢ Puzzle	➢ Passage and conclusions
➢ Seating Arrangement	➢ Alphabet test
➢ Non-verbal Reasoning	➢ Series Test
➢ Analogy	➢ Number, Ranking and time sequence
➢ Classification	➢ Direction sense Test
➢ Number Series	➢ Decision-making test
➢ Mixed Series	➢ Figure series
➢ Counting Figures	➢ Input/output
➢ Mirror Image & Water Image	➢ Assertion and reasoning
➢ Cube and Dice	➢ Sitting Arrangement
	➢ Non-Verbal Reasoning
	➢ Series test
	➢ Odd figure Out
	➢ Analogy
	➢ Miscellaneous Test

Common Admission Test (CAT)
Verbal Ability: Para Jumbles, Summary, Sentence Completion, Odd Sentence Out, Antonyms & Synonyms, Error Detection, Phrase Modifiers, Idioms, Analogies, Cloze Test, Word Usage

Exam-wise & Topic-wise Trend Analysis

Chapters	SSC-CHSL	SSC-CGL	IBPO PO	IBPS Clerk	CAT	LIC AAO	RRB	Airforce Group X & Y
A. Verbal Reasoning								
Series Completion	2-4	2-3				3-5	4-6	6-8
Analogy	2-4	2-3	3-5	2-4	1-2		3-5	4-6
Classification	1-3	1-2					2-4	4-6
Coding-Decoding	2-4	2-3	3-5	3-5		2-3	3-5	4-6
Blood Relations	1-3	1-2	3-5	2-4		2-4	2-4	2-4
Puzzles	2-3		5-10	5-10		5-7		
Sequence Output Tracing								
Direction Sense Test	1-2	1-2	3-5	1-3		2-3	1-3	2-4
Logical Venn Diagrams	1-2	1-2						2-4
Alphabet Test		1						
Alpha Numeric								
Ranking and Time Sequence Test		1-2						
Mathematical Operations								
Inserting the Missing Characters								

Contd....

Chapters	SSC-CHSL	SSC-CGL	IBPO PO	IBPS Clerk	CAT	LIC AAO	RRB	Airforce Group X & Y
B. Non-Verbal Reasoning								
Series	2-4	2-3	5-10	3-5	4-5	3-5	4-6	6-8
Analogy	1-2	1-2	3-5	2-4	3-4	2-4	3-5	4-6
Classification	1-2	1	3-5	2-4	3-4	2-3	2-4	4-6
Mirror and Water Images	1-3	2-4	3-5	1-3		2-4	2-4	2-4
Embedded figures	1-2	1		1-3		2-3	2-4	2-4
Completion of Incomplete Pattern	2-4	1	2-3	2-5	2-3		3-5	2-4
Grouping of Identical Figures and Figure matrix		3-5		3-4	1-2		2-4	5
Paper Folding and Cutting	1-3	1-2	2-3	1-3		1-2	1-3	2-4
Cubes and Dice		1						2-4
Dot Situations								

Be mindful. Be grateful. Be positive. Be true. Be kind

01 Three things that make you special

02 Three people you are grateful for and why

03 Three simple things you are grateful for

04 A challenging experience that made you stronger

05 Three ways to inject gratitude into a current challenge

06 Describe the last time you did something nice for someone

07 A fear you have overcome

08 Three activities you enjoy most and why

09 What made you smile today?

10 Three things you love about your family

11 What is your favorite place, and why?

12 Three things you love most about yourself

13 The last time you were overcome with joy

14 A risk you are grateful you took and why

15 Three everyday items you are grateful for

16 Three songs that bring you joy

17 What skill do you have that you are grateful for and why?

18 One luxury you are thankful for

19 Describe a rejection you are grateful for

20 Three things about your body you are grateful for

21 What are you most grateful for in your daily life?

22 Three things you are grateful for about where you live

23 Three items in your home you are grateful for

24 Say thank you to someone

25 Something in nature you are grateful for

26 A person in your past you are grateful for

27 Something at school you're grateful for

28 Describe the last time you laughed so hard you cried

29 What is your proudest accomplish-ment?

30 Three things you want to manifest

Positive Affirmations

An affirmation is a positive statement or phrase that individuals repeat to themselves with the intention of fostering a positive mindset, self-confidence, or personal development. The practice involves affirming desired beliefs or qualities, often in the present tense, to reinforce a positive self-image and encourage a more optimistic outlook.

" EMBRACE YOUR UNIQUENESS, NOURISH SELF-CARE, AND PRESS FORWARD RELENTLESSLY. TO ACHIEVE FLIGHT, UNLOAD THE BAGGAGE THAT SLOWS YOUR ASCENT."

I strongly trust in my vision and work diligently towards making it a reality.

I am capable of learning and growing everyday.

I am not defined by grades & test scores. My true worth lies in my character, compassion and positive impact I have on others.

I celebrate my quirks, for they make me beautifully unique.

I embrace my mistakes, learn from them and use them to fuel my growth & resilience.

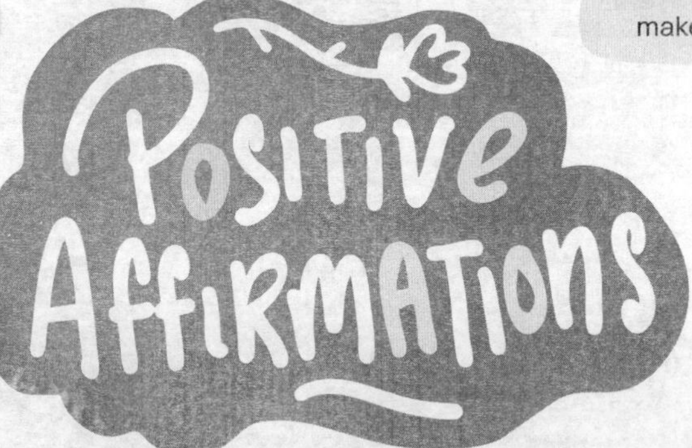

My voice matters and I believe in the power of my words to shape the world around me.

I am not the product of circumstances, I am the product of my own choices.

I face challenges with courage and determination.

I celebrate the achievements of others without diminishing my journey.

I believe that the twists & turns of my life lead me to an extraordinary destinations.

Exclusive School Books Suppliers

	KARNATAKA
BENGALURU	Pride Book World, 9448685507, Tanwer Books and Garments, 9916049273, Jipsy, 9620325985
MYSORE	Ragavendra Book Agency, 9591911489
	TELANGANA
HYDERABAD	Shri Sharada store Books & Stationers, 9700768789, Sri Balaji Book Depot, 9676996199, Vishal Book Distributors, 9246333166, Pranavi Publishers, 919948853126, Shri Sharada store Books & Stationers, 9700768789
	TAMIL NADU
CHENNAI	M.K. Stores, 9840030099, Sivaa Book Centre, 9952933315, Kamal Book House, 9841077369
ERODE	Selvam Book Centre, 919843199697
MADURAI	Selvi Book Shoppe, 9345037977, Madurai Book Shop, 9751937519
COIMBATORE CUDDALORE	Indian Book Centre, 9443093053
	MAHARASHTRA
PUNE	Madhusheela Books & Stationers, 7875899892, Pravin Sales, 8888038889
NANDED	Vijay Book Centre, 9822994436
JALNA	Anil Paper Mart, 919422722522
CHHATRAPATI SAMBHAJINAGAR	AARTI BOOK CENTRE, 919422203836
NAGPUR	Sandeep Book Depot, 9371078789
VASAI	Dinvin Books Excellence PVT. LTD. , 9867561128
MUMBAI	New Student Agencies LLP, 8355965098, Ravechi Book Stationery, 9769002371
	ANDHRA PRADESH
VISAKHAPATNAM	VKML Books, 8125168946
NANDYAL	Sathyam Book Store & Fancy, 9052439300
NELLORE	S V S Book Centre, 9347100774
VIJAYAWADA	VKML Books, 9966639957
	HARYANA
ROHTAK	Babu Ram Pradeep Kumar, 9813214692
VIZIANAGARAM	Himamsu Book Distributor, 9493434777
	MADHYA PRADESH
INDORE	Mahesh Book Depot, 9893855543
SHAHDOL	Anjali Book Centre, 917067572992
	JHARKHAND
DEOGHAR	Navyug Sahitya Mandir, 919031917035
BOKARO STEEL CITY	Bokaro Student Friends Pvt. Ltd, 919234628152
	MEGHALAYA
SHILLONG	New Book Centre, 9774088719
	WEST BENGAL
KOLKATA	Oriental Pub. Dist. Pvt. Ltd., 919903879153, United Book House, 9831344622
COOCH BEHAR	S.B. Book Distributors, 9002670771
	UTTAR PRADESH
PRAYAGRAJ	Saraswati book depot, 7706855403
KANPUR	Raj Book, 9235616506
MATHURA	Sapra Traders, 9410076716, Agrawal Book House, 7906527213
GHAZIABAD	Vani Enterprises, 919891276834
	DELHI
DELHI	Mittal Books, 919810133323, Prakash Brothers, 919811179840, R.D. Chawla & Sons, 9810045752, Ameen Global Services, 919716028892, Need Prakashan Pvt Ltd, 9968383261
	GUJARAT
VADODARA	Career Skills Education and Research Foundation, 8469149288
BHARUCH	J.D. Agency, 9099944480
	KERALA
ERNAKULAM	Novel House School Supplies, 8792342807
	ASSAM
GUWAHATI	Central Book Agency, 9954707165
SILCHER	New Book Stall, 919435712617
JORHAT	Bajrang stationery, 9706978968
	RAJASTHAN
ANUPGARH	City Pride Departmental Store, 919414095677
BARMER	Dev Indra Enterprises, 7073282106
	MANIPUR
IMPHAL	Global Agencies, 917641814494
	PUNJAB
TARN TARAN	Sital Di Hatti, 919988206890
KHAMMAM	Sri Nivasa Book Stall, 919948247838
	CHHATTISGARH
RAIPUR	Central Book House, 9406016308

Our Distributors

	ANDHRA PRADESH
VISAKHAPA-THAM	Sri Rajeshwari Book Link, 9848036014,
VIJAYAWADA	Sree Vidya Book Depot, 9491830839
	ANDAMAN & NICOBAR ISLAND
PORTBLAIR	Krishna Book Centre, 9474205570, Andaman Book Centre, 9434264521
	ARUNACHAL PRADESH
NAHARLAGUN	New Pothi Ghar, 8731832947
	ASSAM
SILCHAR	Book Emporium, 9675972993, 6000763186,
	New Book Stall, 9435712617
GUWAHATI	Kayaan Enterprises, (0361) 2630443,
	BIHAR
PATNA	Nova Publisher & Distributors, (0612) 2666404, Gyan Ganga Limited, 9304826651,
	Rishu Pustak Bhandar, 8294576789, Sri Durga Pustak Mandir, 9334477386,
	Vikas Book Depot, 919504780402,
	Bokaro Student Friends Pvt. Ltd, 7277931285
BIHAR SHARIF	Good Books , 8210685462
MUZAFFARPUR	Pustak Bhandar, 7870834225
	CHATTISGARH
AMBIKAPUR	M.P Department Stores, 9425254264
BOKARO	Bokaro Student Friends Pvt. Ltd, Bokaro, 7277931285
DURG	Bhagwati Bhawani Book Depot, 0788-2327620, 9827473100
RAIPUR	Gupta Pustak Mandir, 7974220323, Anil Publication, 7999078802
BILASPUR	Pustak Bhawan, 9300667909, Agrawal Book Depot, 9711088843
	DELHI
DELHI	Mittal Books, (011) 23288887, 9899037390, A One Books, New Delhi, 8800497047,
	Batheja Super Store, 9871833924, 9811182352, Zombozone, 9871274082,
	LDS Marketing, 9811182352/9999353491, R.D. Chawla & Sons, 9810045752,
	Janta Book Depot, 9313046321
	Bokaro Student Friends Pvt. Ltd, 7004074900
	GUJARAT
AHMEDABAD	Patel Book Agencies, 9898184248, 9824386112, 9825900335,
	Shalibhadra Stationers, 9904477855, Hardik Book Agency, 9904659821
VAPI	Goutam Book Sellers, 9081790813
VADODARA	Shree ji Book Depot, 9824649375, Nilesh Book Centre, 9924458748
	Umakant Book Sellers & Stationer, 6359396370
	Sagar Book Suppliers, 9879402375
AHMEDNAGAR	Hira Stationers, 9970150300
	HARYANA
ROHTAK	Swami Kitab Ghar, 9355611088, Babu Ram Pradeep Kumar, 9813214692
	Dhruv Book Depot, 8901352187
GURGAON	Book Care Centre Venture, 9654564783
REWARI	Repro Books Ltd, 8657315914, Annu book depot, 9053246268
	JHARKHAND
BOKARO	Bokaro Student Friends Pvt. Ltd. (0654) 2233094, 7360021503,
	Bharati Bhawan Agencies, 06542-265302, 9431740797
HAZARIBAGH	Khandelwal Book Depot, 9708607489
DEOGHAR	Navyug Sahitya Mandir, 9031917035
RANCHI	Pustak Mandir, 9431115138, Agarwal Book Depot, 9334869210, Jayshree Book House, 8434430311
	Bokaro Student Friends Pvt. Ltd, 7360021508
DHANBAD	Bokaro Student Friends Pvt. Ltd, 6202834756
	KARNATAKA
HUBLI	Renuka Book Distributor, (0836) 2244124,
	Vidyamandir Book Distributors, 9980773976
BENGALURU	Krishna book house, 9739847334,
	Sapna Book House Pvt. Ltd., 9980513242,
	Sree Sai Ram Book Traders, 9738881088
	MADHYA PRADESH
INDORE	Pustak Bhawan, 8982150100, Bhaiya Store, 9425318103
	S.P. & Publication, 7000025933
UJJAIN	Shreenath Book Depot, 9827544045
GWALIOR	Agarwal Book Depot, 9425116210
JABALPUR	Vinay Pustak Sadan, 8962362667,
	Anand Books and Stationers, 9425323508
	Akash Book Distributor, 8989111444, Bharat Book House, 9826541542
KATNI	Shri Mahavir Agency, 9425363412
	MAHARASHTRA
AMRAVATI	Delta Pen House, 9890350073

15/05/26

Our Distributors

PUNE	Vikas Book House, 9921331187, Pravin Sales, 9890683475,
	New Saraswati Granth Bhandar, 9422323859
	Sai Book Collection, 9623224343
	Yash Agencies, 9850956542
MUMBAI	New Student Agencies, 7045065799,
	Shivam Books & Stationery, 8619805332
KOLHAPUR	Jai Book Co. 9404671543
NAGPUR	Laxmi Pustakalay and Stationers, (0712) 2727354, Vijay Book Depot, 9860122094
	Renuka Book Distributor, 9765406133, Novelty Book Depot, 9657690220,
	Shree Mahalaxmi Pustakalaya, 7507099360
DHULE	Navjeevan Book Stall, 7020525561
YAVATMAL	Shri Ganesh Pustkalaya, 9423131275
NASHIK	Vishal Book Centre, Nashik - 8208249434
VASAI	Prime Book Centre, Vasai, 9890293662
LATUR	Tara Book Stall, 9657709101
	ODISHA
CUTTACK	A. K. Mishra Agencies, 9437025991, 9437081319
BHUBANESHWAR	M/s Pragnya, 8847888616, 9437943777, Padmalaya, 9437026922,
KEONJHAR	Students Corner, 7008435418
KORAPUT	Ambica Book Centre, 7008585008
	PUNJAB
AMBALA	Bharat Book Depot, 7988455354
PATIALA	Goel Sons, 9463619978,
	Adarsh Enterprises, 9814347613
JALANDHAR	Cheap Book Store, 9872223458, 9878258592, City Book Shop, 9417440753,
	Subhash Book Depot, 9876453625, B.P. Publishers and Distributors, 7009571805
	Gaurav Book world, 9478821183
LUDHIANA	Amit Book Depot, 9815807871,
	Bhatia Book Centre, 9815277131, Gupta Brothers, 9888200206
CHANDIGARH	Mohindra Book Depot, 9814920226
BATHINDa	Goyal Sons , 9464478362, Bhagwati Book Depot, 9463120564
BARNALA	Nav Chetan Book Depot, 9417906880
	RAJASTHAN
AJMER	Laxmi General Store, Ajmer, 0145- 2428942 9460652197
KOTA	Raj Traders, 9309232829, A J Book Seller, 9571365020
BHILWARA	Nakoda Book Depot, (01482) 243653, 9214983594,
JAIPUR	Saraswati Book House, (0141) 2610823, 9829811155,
	Goyal Book Distt., 9460983939, 9414782130,
JODHPUR	Kitab Mahal, 9460957875
BHIWADI	Alankar Book Depot, 9414707462
	TRIPURA
AGARTALA	Books Corner, 8794894165, 8984657146
	TAMIL NADU
COIMBATORE	Majestic Book House, 9791966665
CHENNAI	M.R. Book Store (044) 25364596,
	Kalaimagal Store, (044) 5544072, 9940619404, Vijaya Stores, 9381037417,
	Bookmark It-Books & Stat. Store, 7305151653,
	M.K. Stores, 9840030099, Tiger Books Pvt. Ltd., 9710447000,
MADURAI	Selvi Book Shoppe, 9843057435
	KERALA
ERNAKULAM	Academic Book House, (0484) 2376613, H & C Store, 9864196344
KOTTAYAM	Asad Book Centre, (0481) 2566992
CALICUT	Aman Book Stall, (0495) 2721282,

KOZHIKODE	T.B.S. Publishers Distributors, 7559822223
	TELANGANA
HYDERABAD	Sri Balaji Book Depot, (040) 27613300, 9866355473
	Vishal Book Distributors, 9246333166, Aditya Navneet Book World, 6281055905
	Insta Book Store, 9866589298
	UTTARAKHAND
DEHRADUN	Inder Book Agencies, 9634045280
	Brothers Pustak Bhandar, 9897833882
ROORKEE	Universal Book Depot, 9897503504
	UTTAR PRADESH
AGRA	Sparsh Book Agency, 9412257817,
	Sanjay Publication, 8126699922 Arti book centre, 8630128856,
	Om Pustak Mandir, (0562) 2464014, 9319117771
	Panchsheel Books, 9412257962, 9412257961
	Manav Book World, 9760316933
DEORIA	Kanodia Book Depot, 9415277835
MATHURA	Sapra Traders, 9410076716
PRAYAGRAJ	Mehrotra Book Agency, (0532) 2266865, 9415636890
AZAMGARH	Sasta Sahitya Bhandar, 9450029674
ALIGARH	K.B.C.L. Agarwal, 9897124960,
NAJIBABAD	Gupta News Agency, 8868932500
KANPUR	Radha News Agency, 8957247427,
	Raj Book Dist., 9235616506,
	H K Book Distributors, 9506033137/9935146730
GORAKHPUR	Vidyarthi Sahitya Bhandar, 6394026706
LUCKNOW	Om Book Depot, 7705871398, Azad Book Depot Pvt. Ltd., 7317000250,
	Ashirwad Book Depot, 9235501197, Book.com, 7458922755, Universal Books,
	9450302161, Sheetla Book Agency, 9235832418, Vidyarthi Kendra Publisher & Distributor Pvt Ltd, 9554967415, Tripathi Book House, 9415425943,
	Navyug Book Agencies, 8073564410, Pustak Vatika, 7905317119
	Book Sadan, 8318643277
MEERUT	Ideal Book Depot, (0121) 4059252, 9837066307
NOIDA	Goyal Books Overseas Pvt.Ltd., 1204655555, 9873387003
PRAYAGRAJ	Kanhaiya Pustak Bhawan, 9415317109
RENUKOOT	Om Stationers, 7007326732
VARANASI	Bokaro Student Friends Pvt. Ltd , 9798050654, Gupta Books, 8707225564
	WEST BENGAL
KOLKATA	Oriental Publishers & Distributor (033) 40628367, Katha 'O' Kahini, (033)
	22196313, 22419071, Saha Book House, (033), 22193671, 9333416484,
	United Book House, 9831344622, Bijay Pustak Bhandar, 8961260603,
	Shawan Books Distributors, 8336820363
PUDUCHERRY	Sri Lakshmi Book Stall, 7871555145
SILIGURI	Agarwal Book House, 9832038727
NORTH DINAJPUR	Sarkar Book Suppliers, 9830949359
COOCH BEHAR	S.B. Book Distributor, 9002670771
KHARAGPUR	Subhani Book Store, 9046891334
SINGRAULI	Ambedkar Book Depot, 9826115292
KANPUR	Lamba Book Stall, 9839024277
KARNAL	Chopra Book Store, 8950322681
JAMMU	Harnamdass & Bros Agency, 9419180999
	MANIPUR
IMPHAL	P.C. Jain & Company, 9856084649

15/05/26

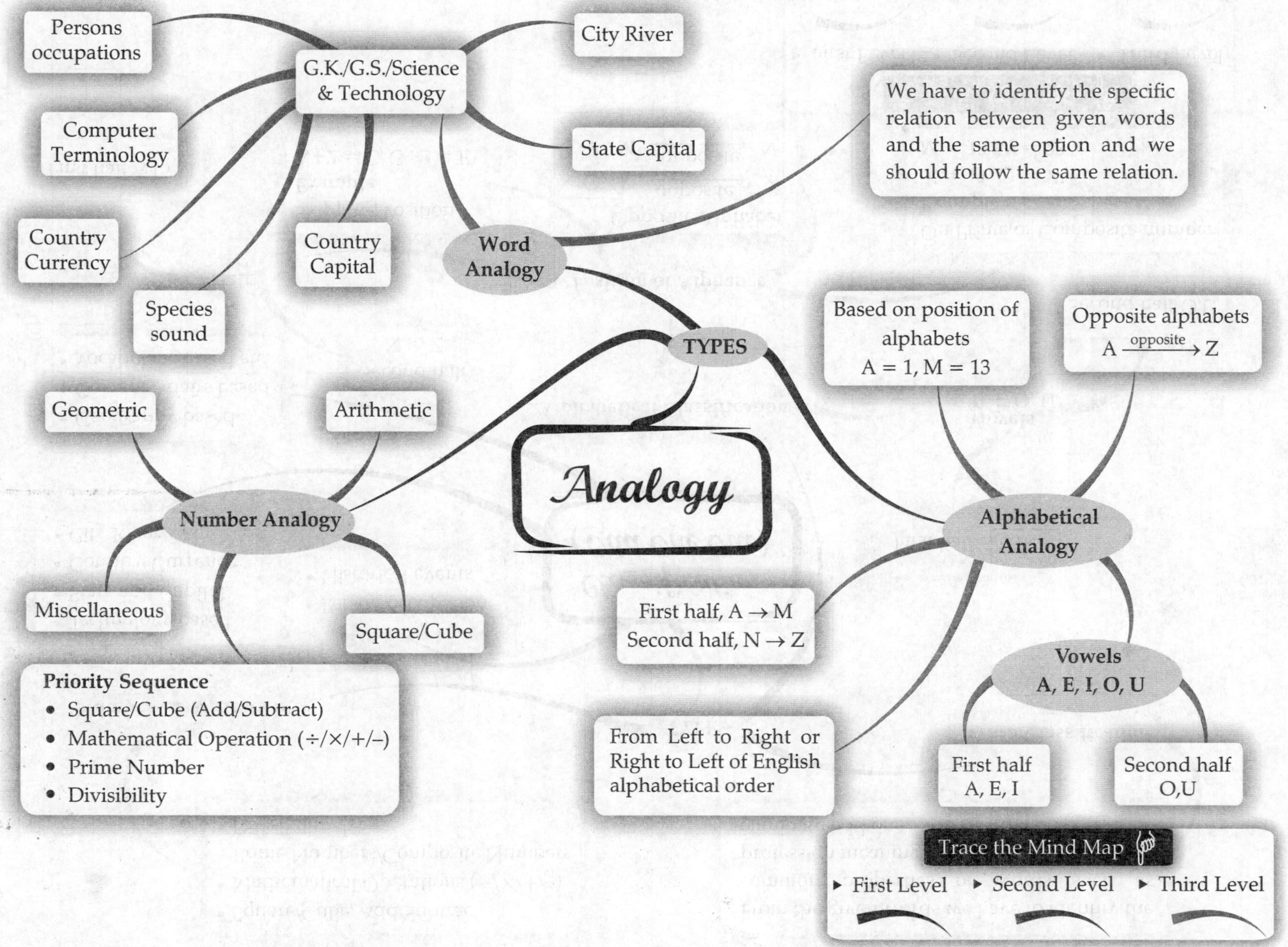
Analogy
TYPES
Word Analogy
We have to identify the specific relation between given words and the same option and we should follow the same relation.
G.K./G.S./Science & Technology
Persons occupations
Computer Terminology
Country Currency
Species sound
Country Capital
City River
State Capital
Number Analogy
Geometric
Arithmetic
Miscellaneous
Square/Cube
Priority Sequence
• Square/Cube (Add/Subtract)
• Mathematical Operation (÷/×/+/–)
• Prime Number
• Divisibility
Alphabetical Analogy
Based on position of alphabets A = 1, M = 13
Opposite alphabets A —opposite→ Z
First half, A → M Second half, N → Z
From Left to Right or Right to Left of English alphabetical order
Vowels A, E, I, O, U
First half A, E, I
Second half O,U
Trace the Mind Map
First Level
Second Level
Third Level

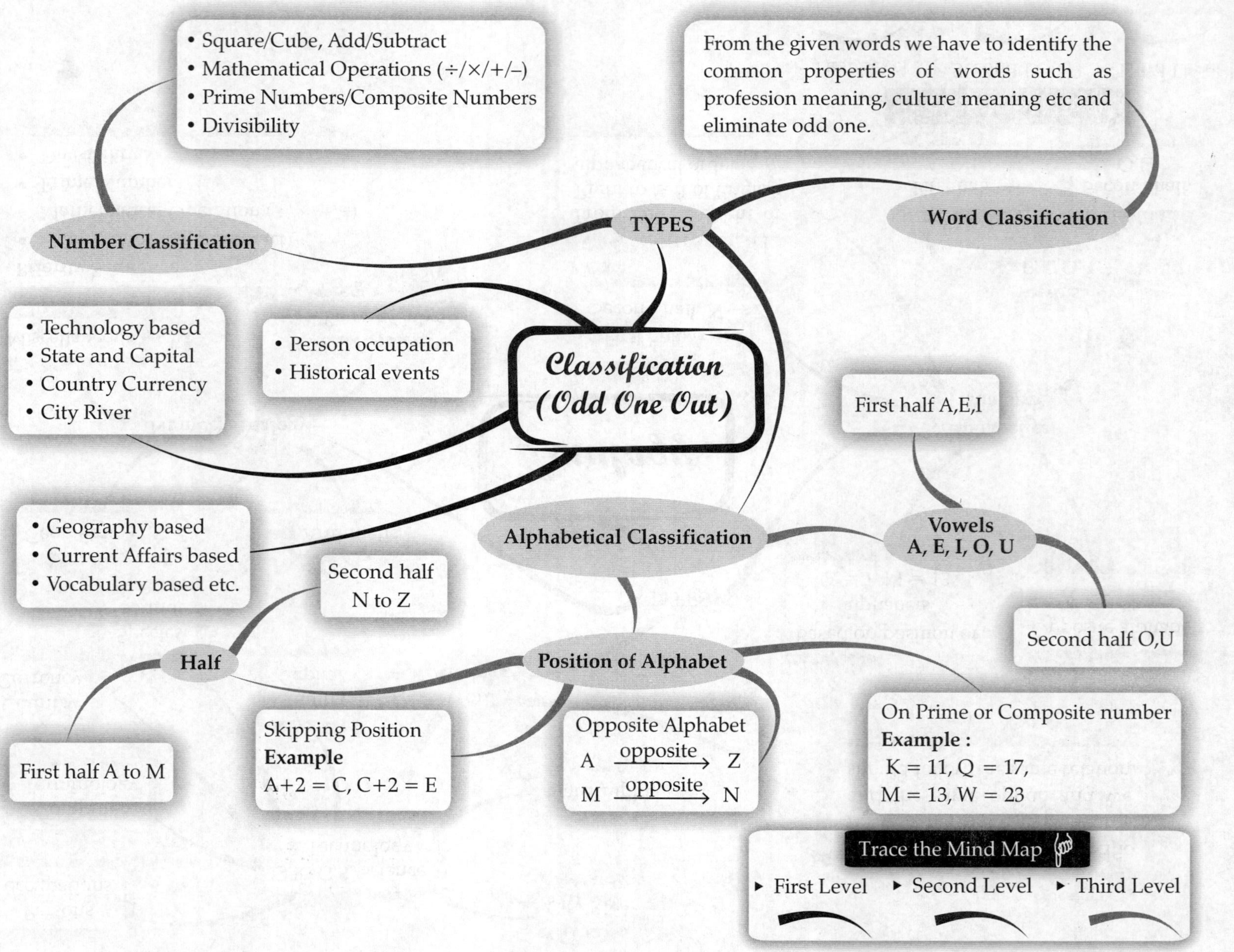
Classification (Odd One Out)
TYPES
Number Classification
• Square/Cube, Add/Subtract
• Mathematical Operations (÷/×/+/–)
• Prime Numbers/Composite Numbers
• Divisibility
Word Classification
From the given words we have to identify the common properties of words such as profession meaning, culture meaning etc and eliminate odd one.
• Technology based
• State and Capital
• Country Currency
• City River
• Person occupation
• Historical events
• Geography based
• Current Affairs based
• Vocabulary based etc.
Alphabetical Classification
Vowels A, E, I, O, U
First half A,E,I
Second half O,U
Position of Alphabet
Half
First half A to M
Second half N to Z
Skipping Position
Example
A+2 = C, C+2 = E
Opposite Alphabet
A opposite Z
M opposite N
On Prime or Composite number
Example :
K = 11, Q = 17,
M = 13, W = 23
Trace the Mind Map
First Level
Second Level
Third Level

Direction and Distance

Shadow Concept

1. Sunrise- in east then shadow forms towards west.
2. Sunset- in west direction then shadow forms in towards east direction.
3. Morning time - Sunrise
4. Evening time - Sunset
5. At the time of sunrise
   a. if a man is facing east then his shadow will form towards the west/towards his back.
   b. If a man is facing the west direction then his shadow will form towards his front/in front of him.
   c. if a man is facing north direction then his shadow will form towards his left hand/left.
   d. if a man is facing south direction then his shadow will form towards his right hand/right.
6. At the time of sunset -
   a. If a man facing towards sun the shadow will be towards his back or in the east.
   b. If a man facing towards the north the shadow will be towards his right.
   c. If a man facing towards the east, the shadow will be towards his front.
   d. If a man facing towards south, the shadow will be towards his left.
7. During 12 pm at noon, there will be no shadow because at that time the rays of the sun are vertically downward.

General Steps to solve question

1. Take reference axis and denote all four directions.
2. Move always from the origin of the reference axis and follow the steps according to questions.
3. Finally draw a line between initial point and final point.

If someone move towards left or right side, we assume that the movement is at an angle of 90 degrees.

Movement & Turn

- A person facing north, on taking left will face towards the west and no taking the right turn towards the east.
- A person facing west, on taking left will face towards the south and on taking right turn towards the north.
- A person facing east, on taking left will face towards the north and on taking the right turn towards the south.
- A person facing south, on taking left will face towards the east and on taking the right turn towards the west.

- Moving left means moving anticlockwise
- Moving right means moving clockwise

Pythagoras Theorem

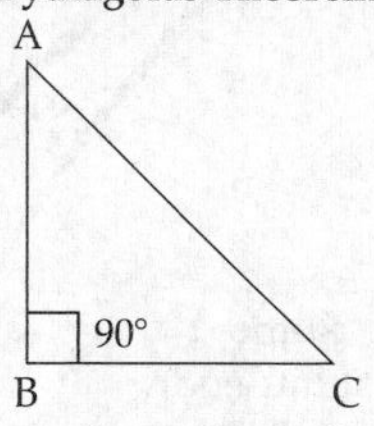

A, B, C; 90°

$AC^2 = AB^2 + BC^2$

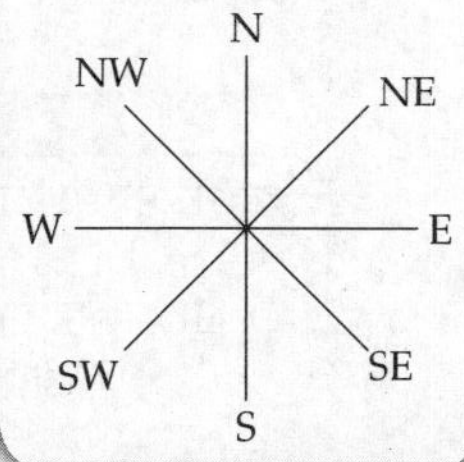

When a person moves left or right side, the movement is 90°.

Cardinal Direction

North → N
South → S
East → E
West → W
Remember - NEWS

Type of Questions

1. Based on Turns
2. Based on rotations
3. Based on turns and rotations
4. Based on shadow concept-sunrise and sunset
5. Based on finding the-shortest distance
6. Based on the orientation of one point to another
7. Based on coding
8. Based on seating arrangement
9. Based on clock timing

Representation of Directions

N, NE, E, SE, S, SW, W, NW

Opposite pair means = 180° difference
NE - SW ; SW - NE
NW - SE ; SE - NW

Intermediate Direction

North-East → NE
North-West → NW
South-East → SE
South-West → SW

Trace the Mind Map

▸ First Level ▸ Second Level ▸ Third Level

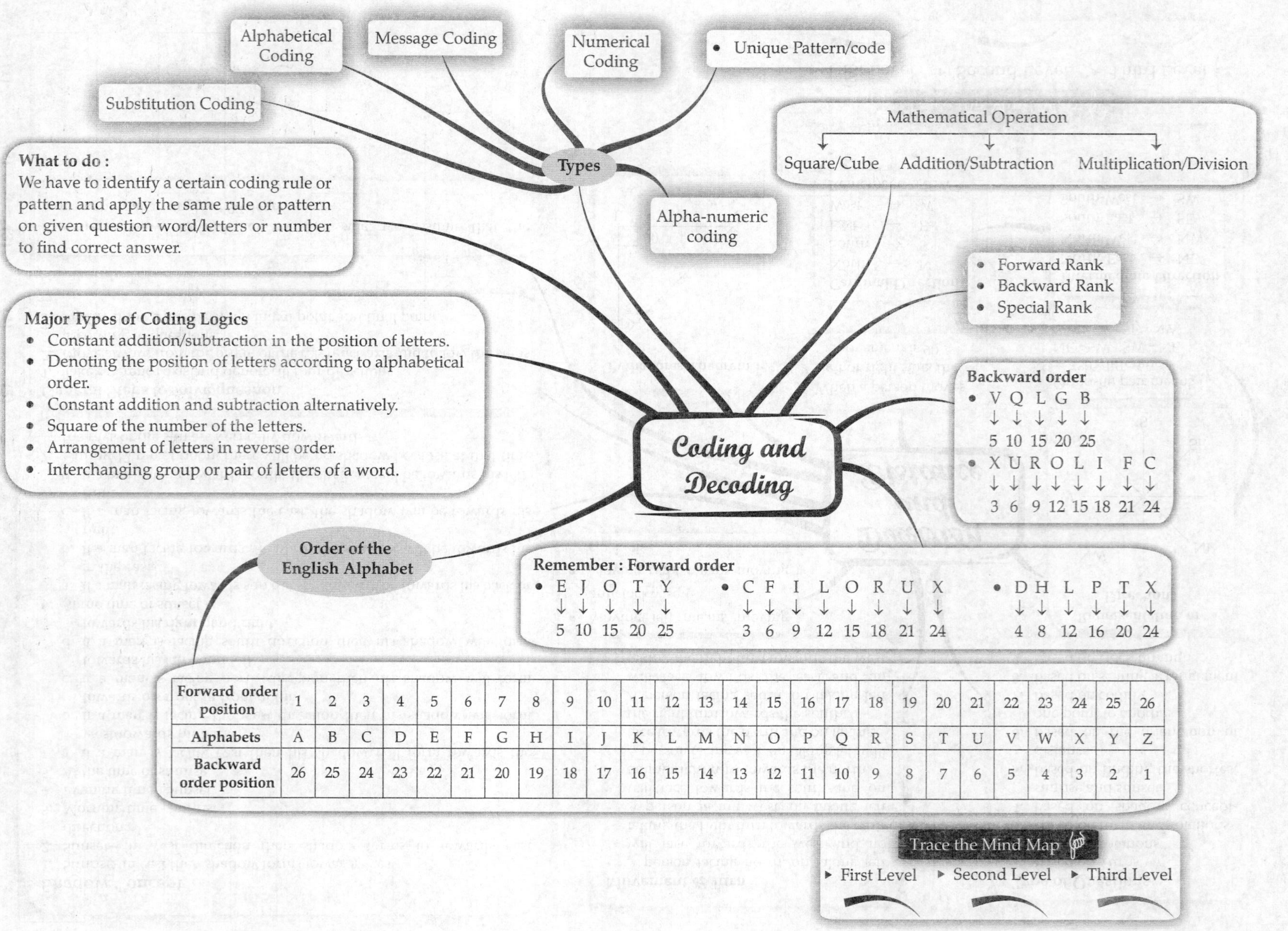

Forward order position	1	2	3	4	5	6	7	8	9	10	11	12	13	14	15	16	17	18	19	20	21	22	23	24	25	26
Alphabets	A	B	C	D	E	F	G	H	I	J	K	L	M	N	O	P	Q	R	S	T	U	V	W	X	Y	Z
Backward order position	26	25	24	23	22	21	20	19	18	17	16	15	14	13	12	11	10	9	8	7	6	5	4	3	2	1

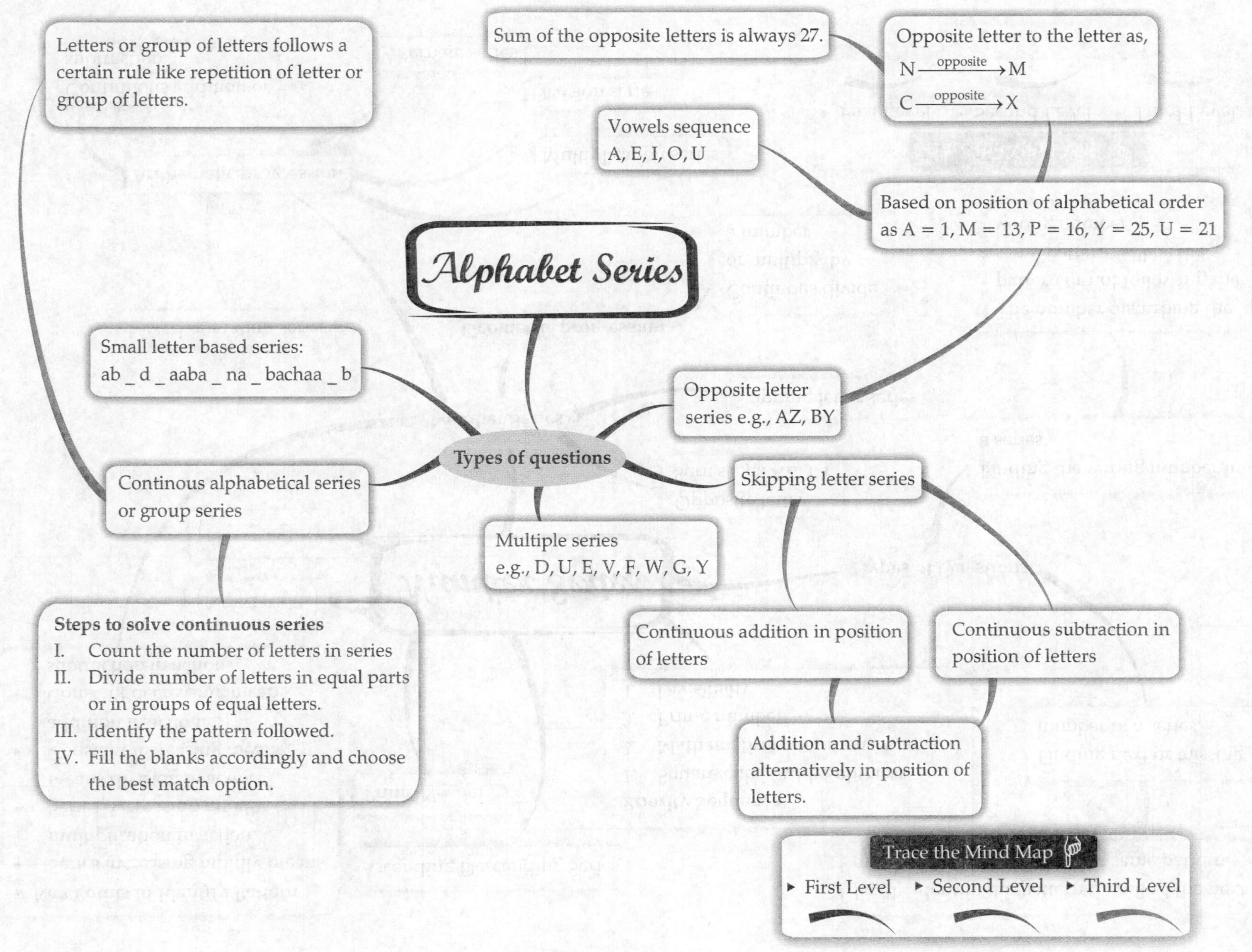
Alphabet Series
Types of questions
Letters or group of letters follows a certain rule like repetition of letter or group of letters.
Sum of the opposite letters is always 27.
Opposite letter to the letter as,
N —opposite→ M
C —opposite→ X
Vowels sequence A, E, I, O, U
Based on position of alphabetical order as A = 1, M = 13, P = 16, Y = 25, U = 21
Small letter based series: ab _ d _ aaba _ na _ bachaa _ b
Opposite letter series e.g., AZ, BY
Continous alphabetical series or group series
Skipping letter series
Multiple series e.g., D, U, E, V, F, W, G, Y
Steps to solve continuous series
I. Count the number of letters in series
II. Divide number of letters in equal parts or in groups of equal letters.
III. Identify the pattern followed.
IV. Fill the blanks accordingly and choose the best match option.
Continuous addition in position of letters
Continuous subtraction in position of letters
Addition and subtraction alternatively in position of letters.
Trace the Mind Map
First Level
Second Level
Third Level

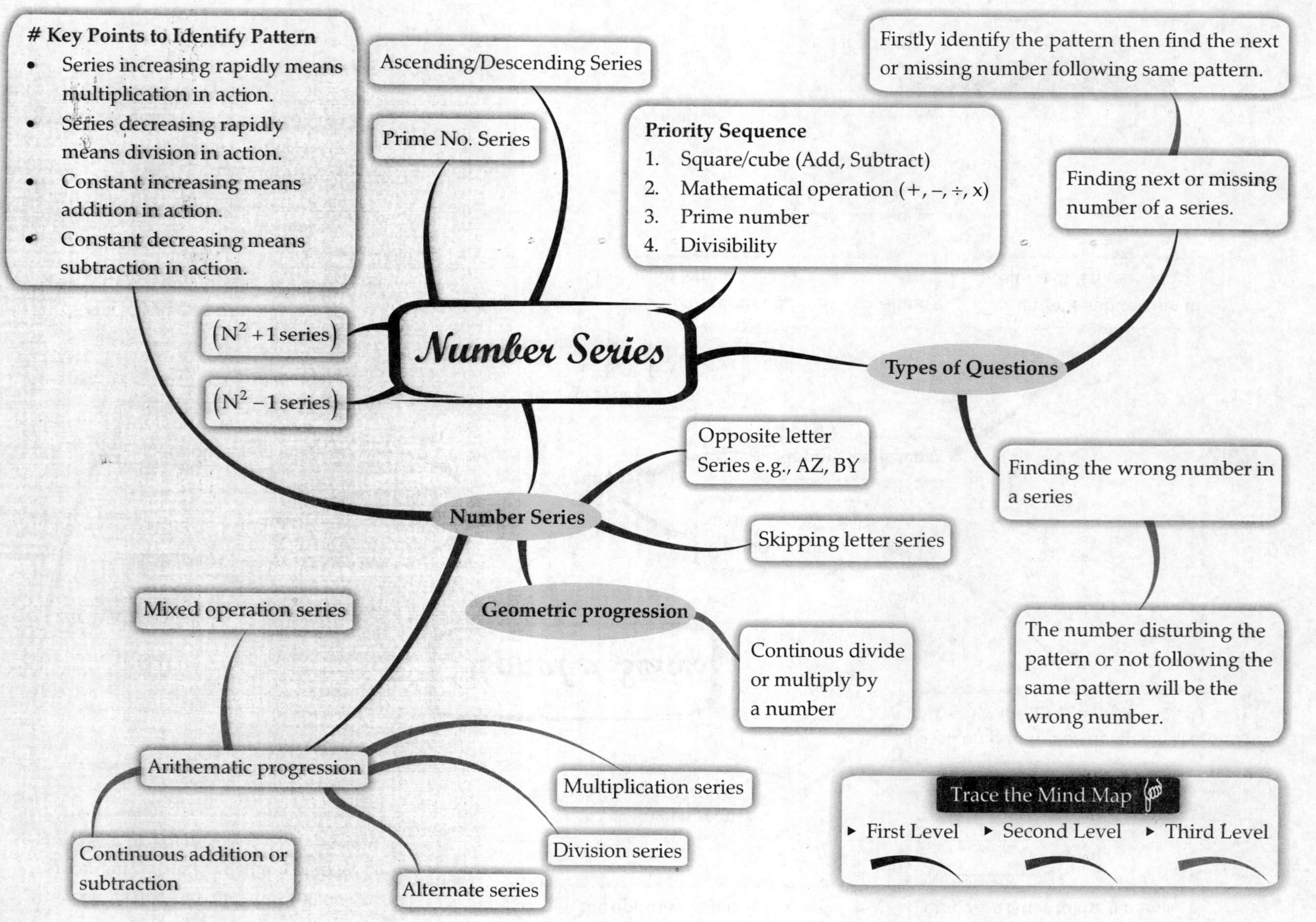
Number Series
Key Points to Identify Pattern
• Series increasing rapidly means multiplication in action.
• Series decreasing rapidly means division in action.
• Constant increasing means addition in action.
• Constant decreasing means subtraction in action.
Ascending/Descending Series
Prime No. Series
Priority Sequence
1. Square/cube (Add, Subtract)
2. Mathematical operation (+, −, ÷, x)
3. Prime number
4. Divisibility
Firstly identify the pattern then find the next or missing number following same pattern.
Finding next or missing number of a series.
Types of Questions
(N² +1 series)
(N² −1 series)
Opposite letter Series e.g., AZ, BY
Finding the wrong number in a series
Number Series
Skipping letter series
Mixed operation series
Geometric progression
Continous divide or multiply by a number
The number disturbing the pattern or not following the same pattern will be the wrong number.
Arithematic progression
Multiplication series
Division series
Alternate series
Continuous addition or subtraction
Trace the Mind Map
▸ First Level ▸ Second Level ▸ Third Level

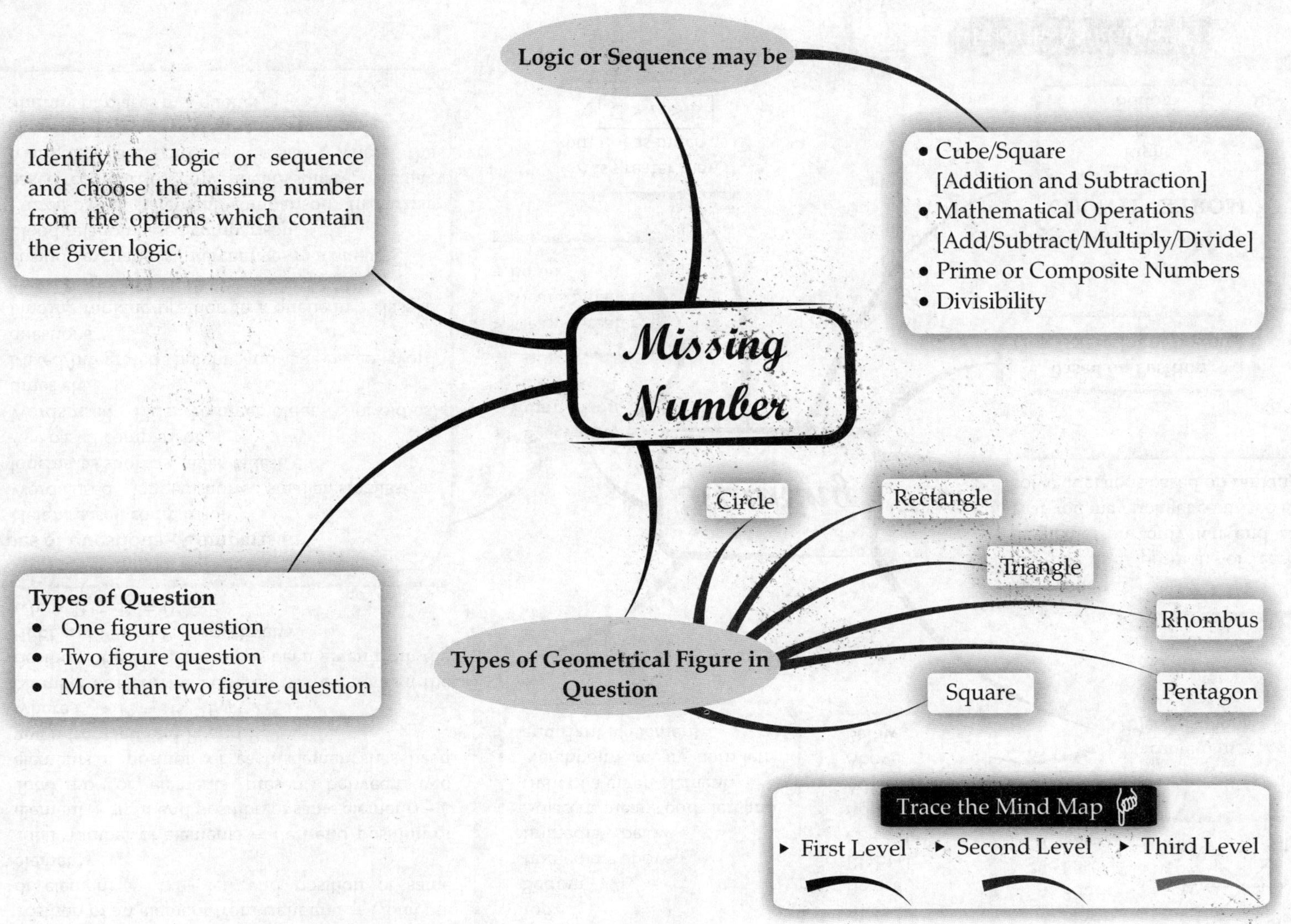
Logic or Sequence may be
Identify the logic or sequence and choose the missing number from the options which contain the given logic.
• Cube/Square
[Addition and Subtraction]
• Mathematical Operations
[Add/Subtract/Multiply/Divide]
• Prime or Composite Numbers
• Divisibility
Missing Number
Circle
Rectangle
Triangle
Rhombus
Types of Question
• One figure question
• Two figure question
• More than two figure question
Types of Geometrical Figure in Question
Square
Pentagon
Trace the Mind Map
First Level
Second Level
Third Level

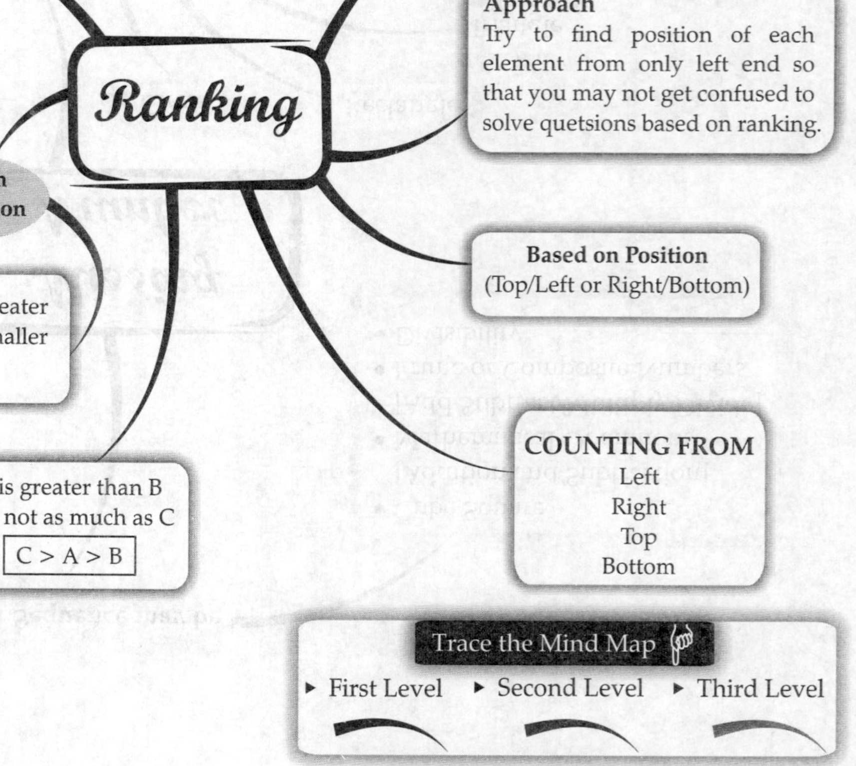

FACING
North
South
East
West

N, N-E, E, S-E, S, S-W, W, N-W

POSITIONS
Ahead
Before
Right side
Left side
Adjacent right
Adjacent left
Above
Below

Immediate right
Immediate left
Top
Bottom
Immediate above
Immediate below
Adjacent means both left and right of a given element.
Neighbours means both left and right of element

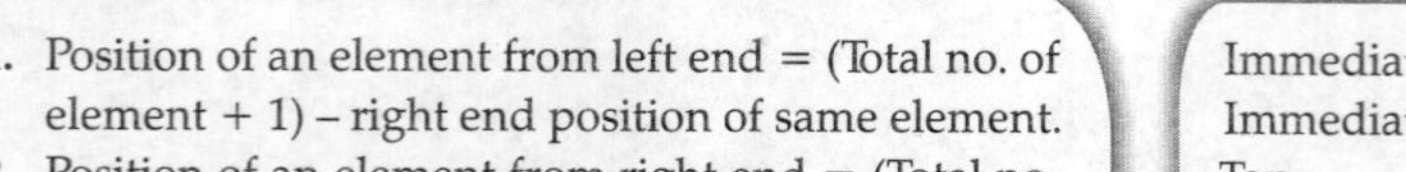

1. Position of an element from left end = (Total no. of element + 1) – right end position of same element.
2. Position of an element from right end = (Total no. of element + 1) – left end position of same element.
3. Total number of elements = (left end position of element + right end position of same element) – 1.
4. Total no. of elements present between two elements if position of each element has been given from left end P_1 and P_2 where $P_2 > P_1 = (P_2 - P_1) - 1$.
5. Number of elements between two elements if the position of each element has been given from the right end P_1 and P_2 respectively, where $P_2 > P_1 = (P_2 - P_1) - 1$.

Types of questions - Comparison

1. Height based comparison
   Words used - longer, shorter, smaller, smallest, as long as, as short as, taller, tallest, etc.
2. Age based comparison
   Words used - Elder, Younger, older, As of old as, times etc.
3. Mixed/Integrated height and age-based word questions.
4. Finding ranking/position in a queue/in a class/in an arrangement.
5. Position exchanges/interchanges in a queue.
6. Blood relation based comparison.
7. Puzzle-based statement comparison. In puzzle based comparison any linear, square, circular, triangular, etc. can be possible where the element's direction of facing is given.
8. Shifting of places in a queue.

> Means Greater
< Means Smaller
= Equal

A is greater than B but not as much as C

C > A > B

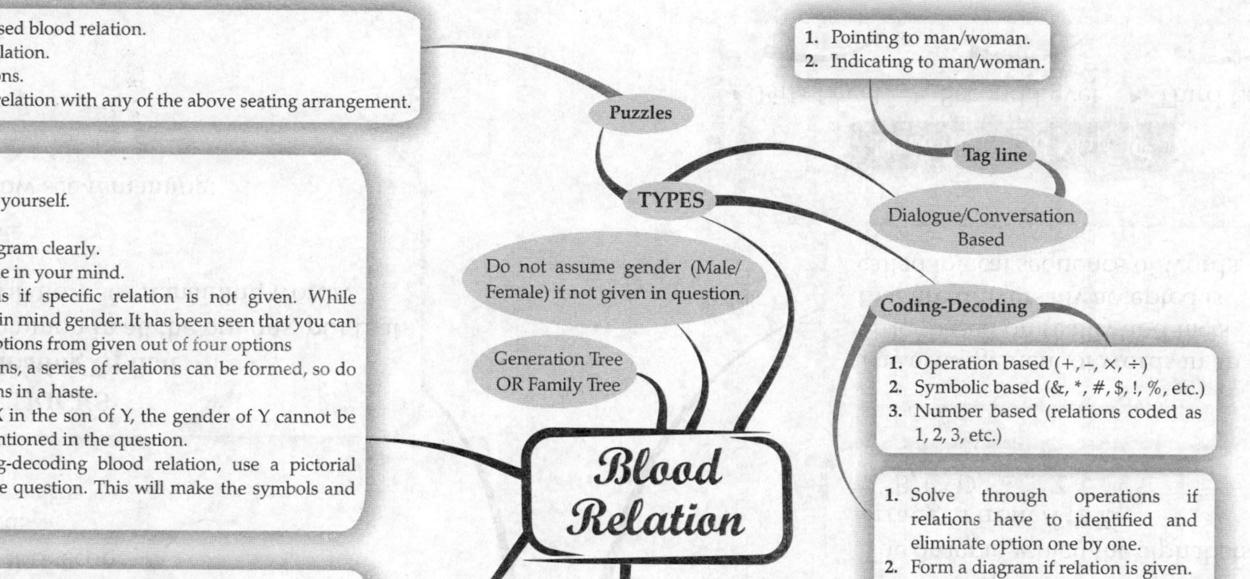

Blood Relation

TYPES

Puzzles

1. Linear arrangement based blood relation.
2. Circular based blood relation.
3. Age based blood relations.
4. Combination of blood relation with any of the above seating arrangement.

Dialogue/Conversation Based

Tag line

1. Pointing to man/woman.
2. Indicating to man/woman.

Coding-Decoding

1. Operation based (+, –, ×, ÷)
2. Symbolic based (&, *, #, $, !, %, etc.)
3. Number based (relations coded as 1, 2, 3, etc.)

1. Solve through operations if relations have to identified and eliminate option one by one.
2. Form a diagram if relation is given.

Do not assume gender (Male/Female) if not given in question.

Generation Tree OR Family Tree

TIPS/TRICKS

1. Apply the question in yourself.
2. Do not assume gender.
3. Draw a family tree diagram clearly.
4. Keep all relation's name in your mind.
5. Solve through options if specific relation is not given. While checking options keep in mind gender. It has been seen that you can eliminate maximum options from given out of four options
6. In puzzle-based qustions, a series of relations can be formed, so do not solve such questions in a haste.
7. If the statement says X in the son of Y, the gender of Y cannot be determined unless mentioned in the question.
8. In the case of coding-decoding blood relation, use a pictorial description to solve the question. This will make the symbols and relation more clear.

Following standard symbols can be used to draw a family diagram.

S.No.	Symbols	Meaning	S.No.	Symbols	Meaning
1.	⊕	Male	7.	⊕ Father | ⊕ Son	Father–Son
2.	⊖	Female	8.	⊕ Father | ⊖ Daughter	Father–Daughter
3.	⊕←→⊖	Husband–Wife	9.	⊖ Mother | ⊕ Son	Mother–Son
4.	⊕——⊕	Brother-Brother	10.	⊕ Mother | ⊖ Daughter	Mother–Daughter
5.	⊖——⊖	Sister–Sister	11.	?	Unknown Gender
6.	⊕——⊖	Brother–Sister			

Some of the blood relations are summarised below :

Father's or Mother's only Son/Daughter	One self
Mother's or Father's Son	Brother
Mother's or Father's Daughter	Sister
Mother's or Father's Brother	Uncle
Mother's or Father's Sister	Aunt
Mother's or Father's Father	Grandfather
Mother's or Father's Mother	Grandmother
Son's Wife	Daughter-in-law
Daughter's Husband	Son-in-law
Husband's or Wife's Sister	Sister-in-law
Husband's or Wife's Brother	Brother-in-law
Brother's Wife	Sister-in-law
Sister's Husband	Brother-in-law
Brother's or Sister's Son	Nephew
Brother's or Sister's Daughter	Niece

Trace the Mind Map

▸ First Level ▸ Second Level ▸ Third Level

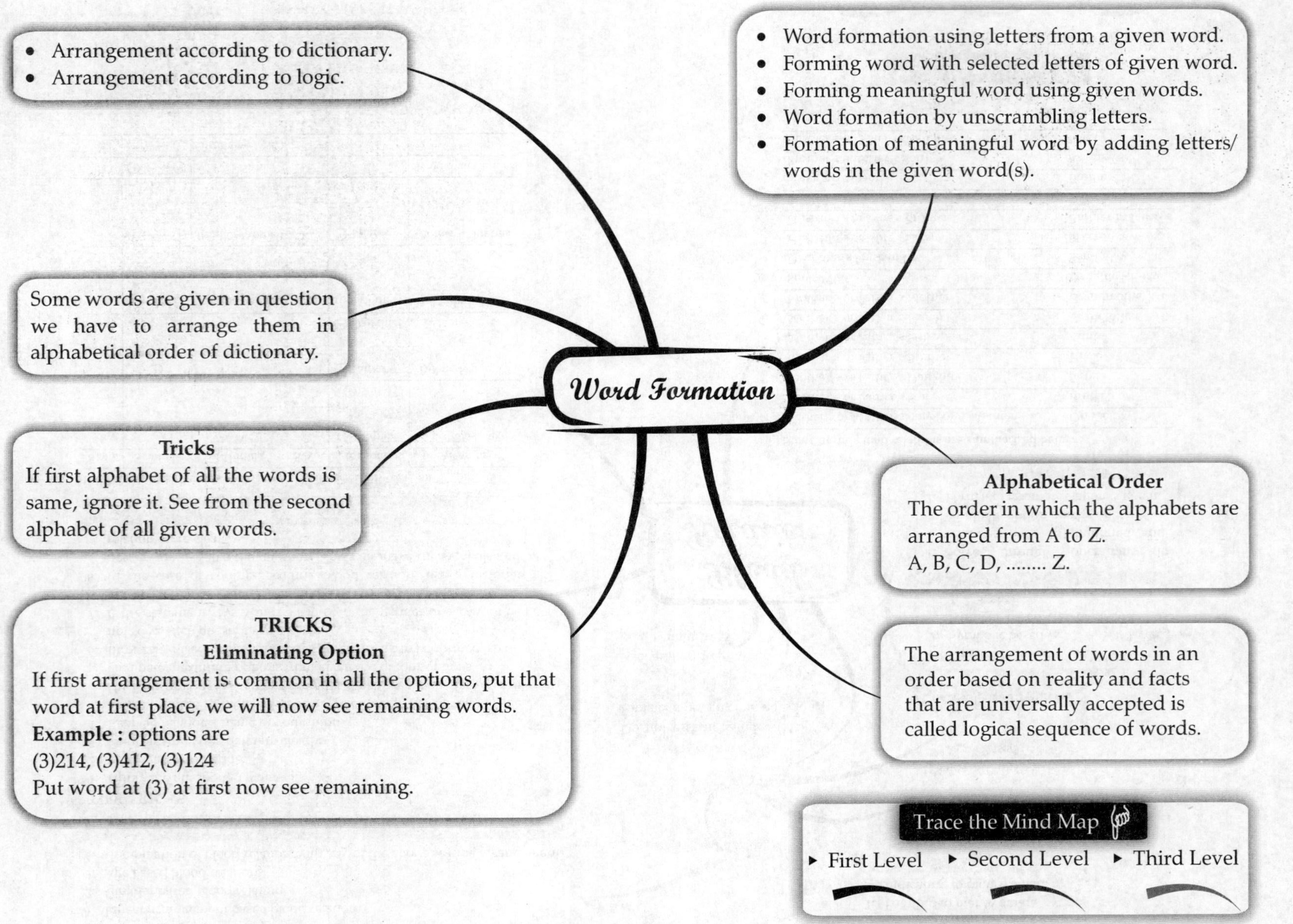
Word Formation
• Word formation using letters from a given word.
• Forming word with selected letters of given word.
• Forming meaningful word using given words.
• Word formation by unscrambling letters.
• Formation of meaningful word by adding letters/ words in the given word(s).
• Arrangement according to dictionary.
• Arrangement according to logic.
Some words are given in question we have to arrange them in alphabetical order of dictionary.
Tricks
If first alphabet of all the words is same, ignore it. See from the second alphabet of all given words.
TRICKS
Eliminating Option
If first arrangement is common in all the options, put that word at first place, we will now see remaining words.
Example : options are
(3)214, (3)412, (3)124
Put word at (3) at first now see remaining.
Alphabetical Order
The order in which the alphabets are arranged from A to Z.
A, B, C, D, ... Z.
The arrangement of words in an order based on reality and facts that are universally accepted is called logical sequence of words.
Trace the Mind Map
First Level
Second Level
Third Level

Mathematical Operations

- Symbol substitution
- Interchange of signs and Numbers
- Balancing the equation
- Trick based Mathetical Operations

Balancing the Expression

$8 \times 8 \times 1 \times 7 = 8$

↓ ↓ ↓

$\div$ $\times$ $+$

Interchange of sign

$4 \times 3 - 2 + 6 = 4$

↓ ↓

$-$ $\times$

Trick based operations

$9 \times 5 \times 2 = 529$

$7 \times 8 \times 3 = 837$

$4 \times 7 \times 6 = 764$

Question based on symbol substitution

Example :

P ⟶ +

Q ⟶ –

R ⟶ ×

S ⟶ ÷

VBODMAS RULE

- V means Vinculum or Bar... (The bar you see on the top of the value $\bar{X}$)
- B means Bracket – () {} [ ]
- O means 'of' (multiplication).
- D means Division [÷]
- M means Multiplication [×]
- A means Addition [+]
- S means Subtraction [–].

- Symbols, notations, mathematical signs.
- Miscellaneous patterns.

We have to follow the relationship given through these sign, symbols given in the question.

Question based on interchanging mathematical signs.

Example :

+ ⟷ –

× ⟶ ÷

We have that option of interchanging which will satisfy the given equation in the question.

Trace the Mind Map

▸ First Level ▸ Second Level ▸ Third Level

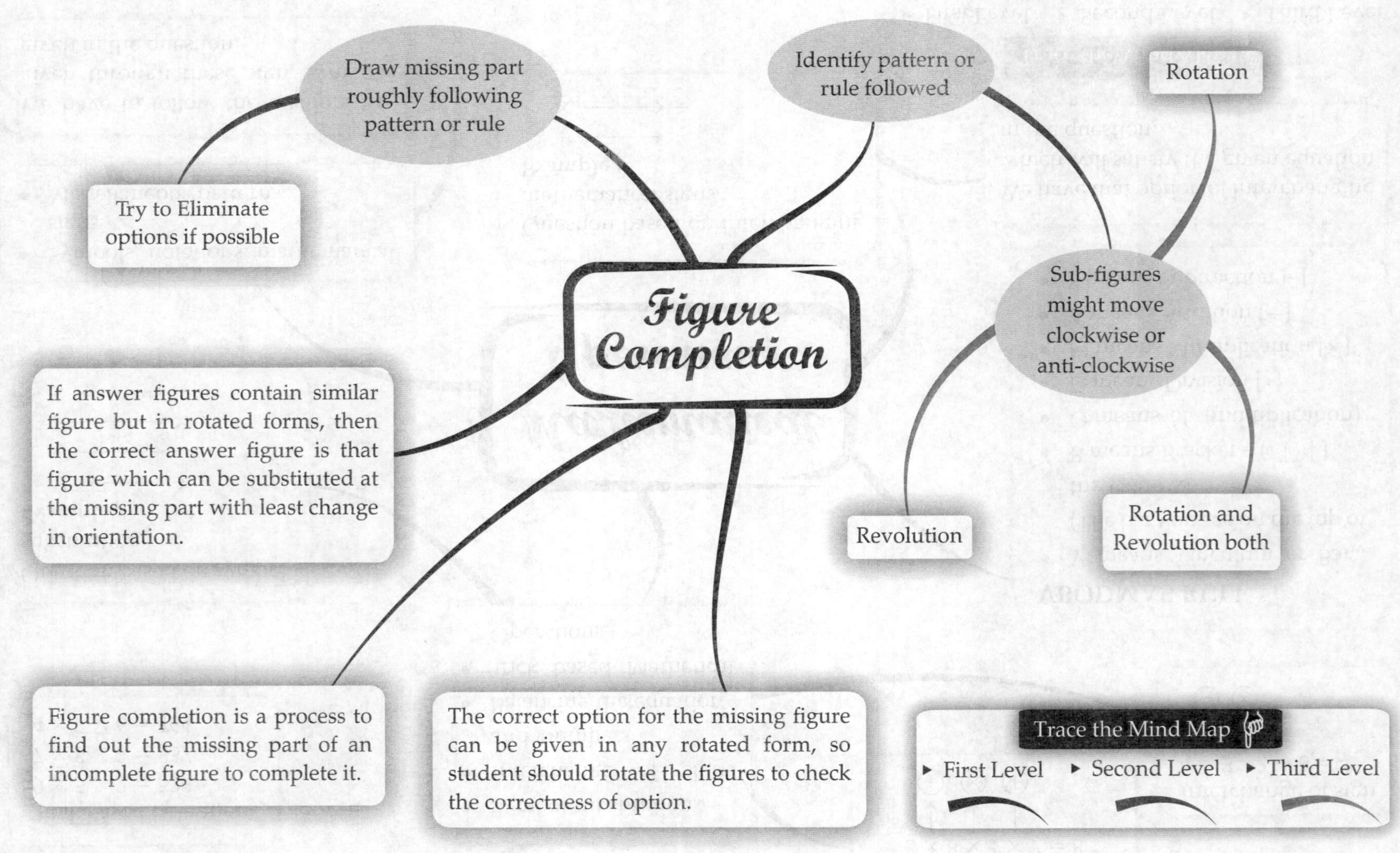
Figure Completion
Draw missing part roughly following pattern or rule
Try to Eliminate options if possible
Identify pattern or rule followed
Rotation
Sub-figures might move clockwise or anti-clockwise
Revolution
Rotation and Revolution both
If answer figures contain similar figure but in rotated forms, then the correct answer figure is that figure which can be substituted at the missing part with least change in orientation.
Figure completion is a process to find out the missing part of an incomplete figure to complete it.
The correct option for the missing figure can be given in any rotated form, so student should rotate the figures to check the correctness of option.
Trace the Mind Map
First Level
Second Level
Third Level

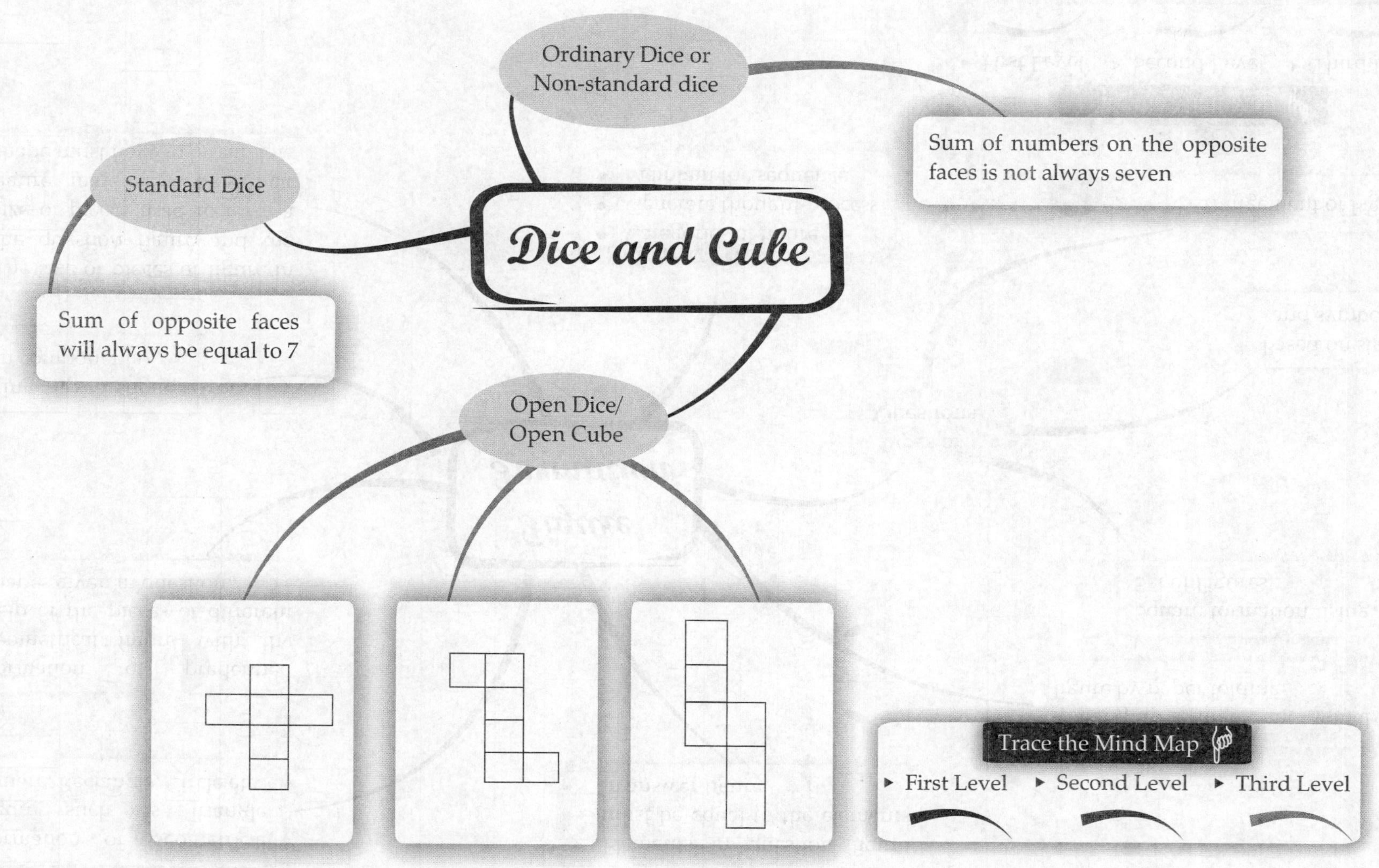

Dice and Cube
Ordinary Dice or Non-standard dice
Sum of numbers on the opposite faces is not always seven
Standard Dice
Sum of opposite faces will always be equal to 7
Open Dice/ Open Cube
Trace the Mind Map
First Level
Second Level
Third Level

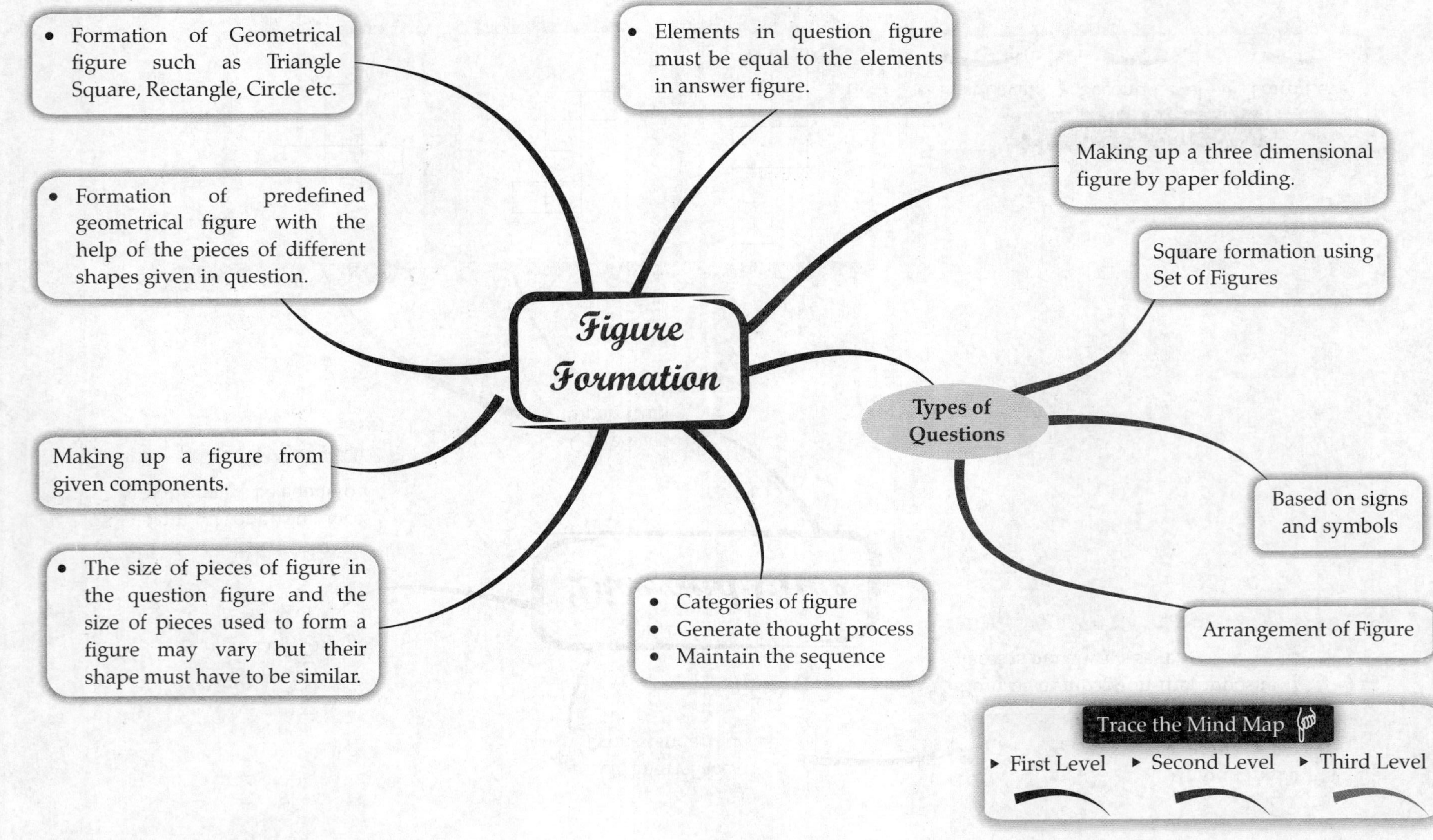
Figure Formation
• Formation of Geometrical figure such as Triangle Square, Rectangle, Circle etc.
• Elements in question figure must be equal to the elements in answer figure.
Making up a three dimensional figure by paper folding.
• Formation of predefined geometrical figure with the help of the pieces of different shapes given in question.
Square formation using Set of Figures
Types of Questions
Making up a figure from given components.
Based on signs and symbols
• The size of pieces of figure in the question figure and the size of pieces used to form a figure may vary but their shape must have to be similar.
• Categories of figure
• Generate thought process
• Maintain the sequence
Arrangement of Figure
Trace the Mind Map
First Level
Second Level
Third Level

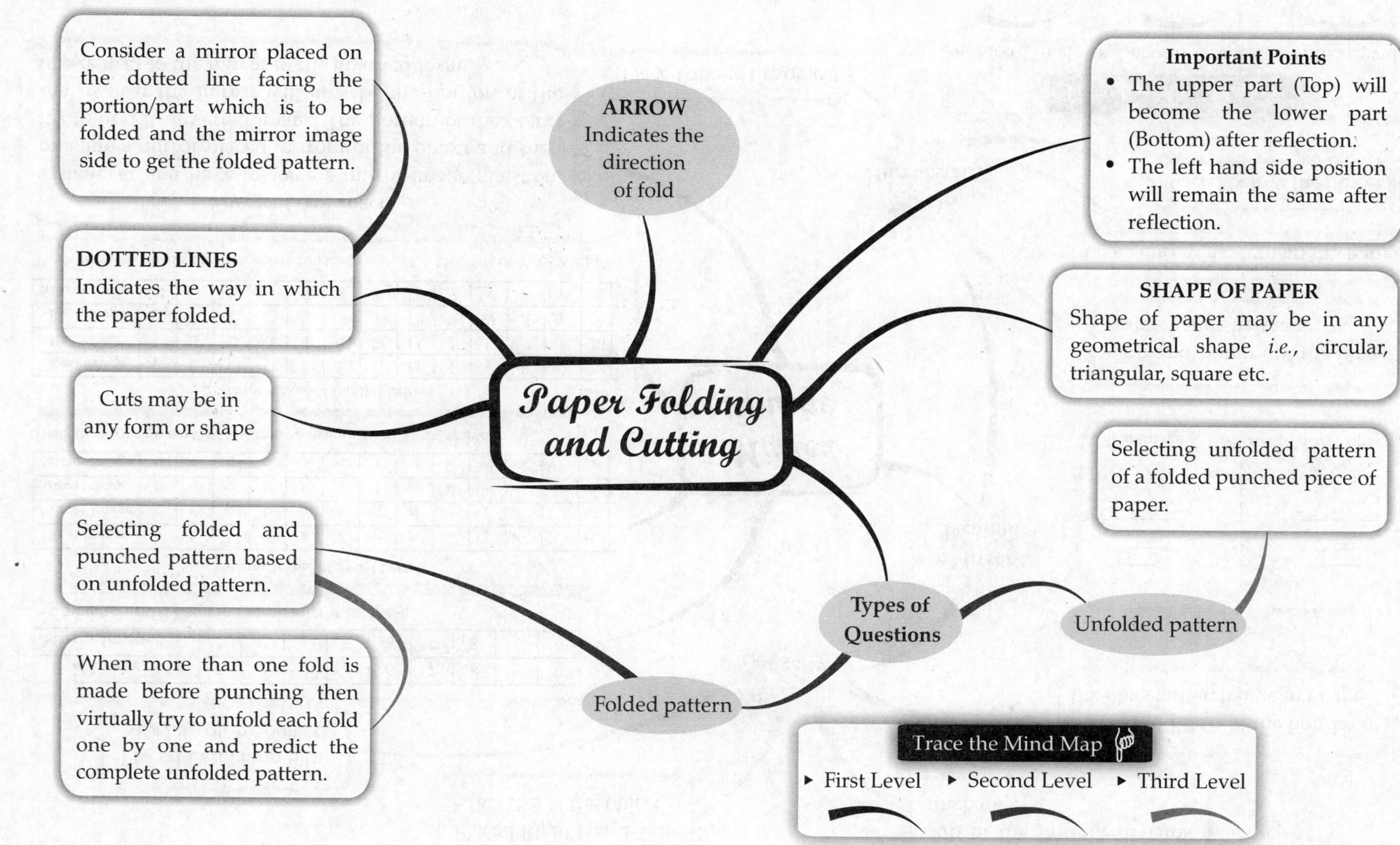
Paper Folding and Cutting
ARROW
Indicates the direction of fold
Important Points
• The upper part (Top) will become the lower part (Bottom) after reflection.
• The left hand side position will remain the same after reflection.
SHAPE OF PAPER
Shape of paper may be in any geometrical shape i.e., circular, triangular, square etc.
Types of Questions
Unfolded pattern
Selecting unfolded pattern of a folded punched piece of paper.
Folded pattern
Selecting folded and punched pattern based on unfolded pattern.
When more than one fold is made before punching then virtually try to unfold each fold one by one and predict the complete unfolded pattern.
DOTTED LINES
Indicates the way in which the paper folded.
Consider a mirror placed on the dotted line facing the portion/part which is to be folded and the mirror image side to get the folded pattern.
Cuts may be in any form or shape
Trace the Mind Map
First Level
Second Level
Third Level

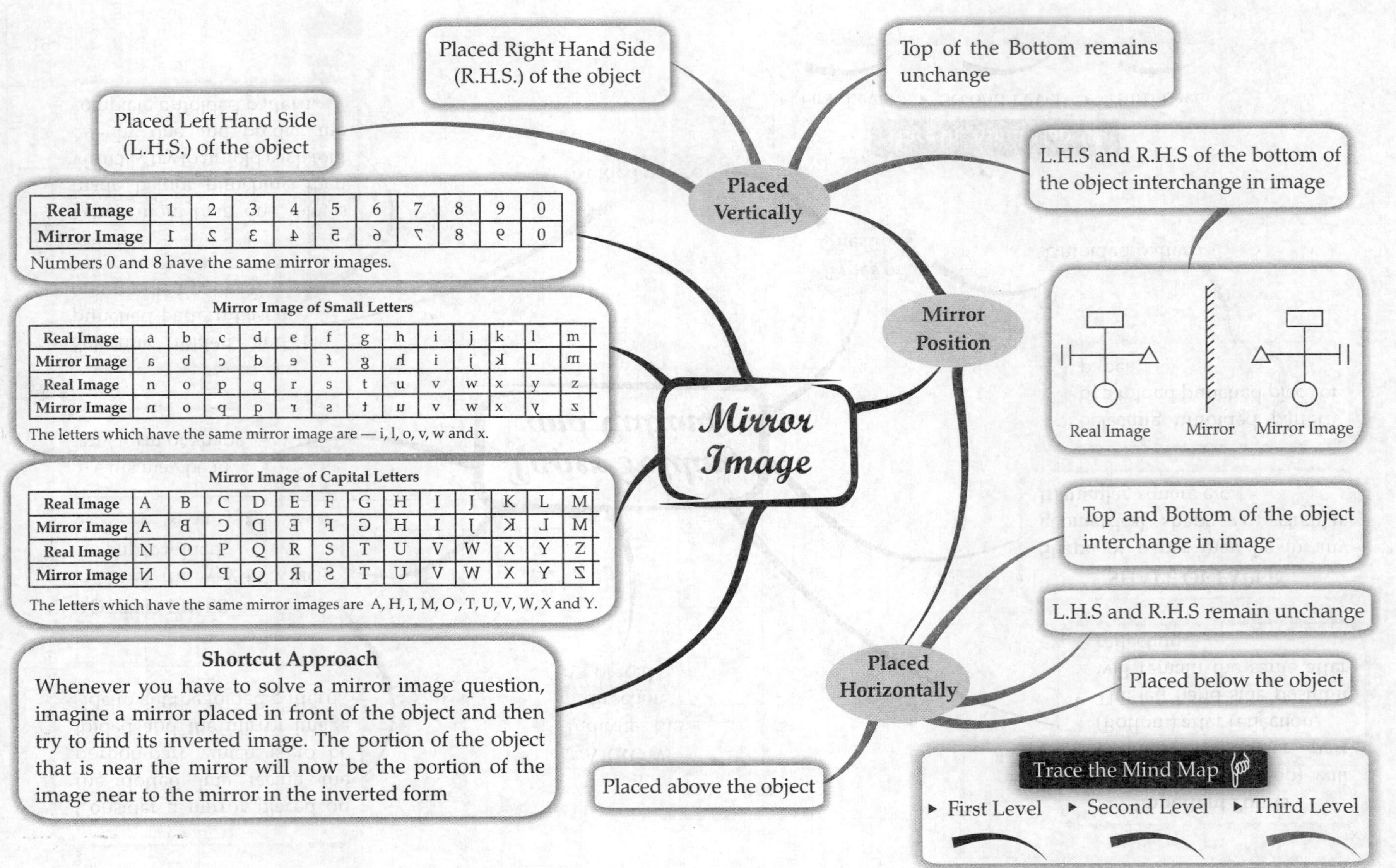

Real Image	1	2	3	4	5	6	7	8	9	0
Mirror Image	I	Ƨ	Ɛ	ᔭ	ꙅ	∂	Ꞁ	8	୧	0

Numbers 0 and 8 have the same mirror images.

Mirror Image of Small Letters

Real Image	a	b	c	d	e	f	g	h	i	j	k	l	m
Mirror Image	ɒ	d	ɔ	b	ɘ	ʇ	ϱ	ʜ	i	ꞁ	ʞ	l	m
Real Image	n	o	p	q	r	s	t	u	v	w	x	y	z
Mirror Image	n	o	q	p	ɿ	ƨ	ƚ	u	v	w	x	γ	ƹ

The letters which have the same mirror image are — i, l, o, v, w and x.

Mirror Image of Capital Letters

Real Image	A	B	C	D	E	F	G	H	I	J	K	L	M
Mirror Image	A	ꓭ	Ɔ	ꓷ	Ǝ	ꟻ	Ꭾ	H	I	Ⴑ	ꓘ	⅃	M
Real Image	N	O	P	Q	R	S	T	U	V	W	X	Y	Z
Mirror Image	И	O	ꟼ	Ϙ	Я	Ƨ	T	U	V	W	X	Y	Ƹ

The letters which have the same mirror images are A, H, I, M, O, T, U, V, W, X and Y.

Shortcut Approach

Whenever you have to solve a mirror image question, imagine a mirror placed in front of the object and then try to find its inverted image. The portion of the object that is near the mirror will now be the portion of the image near to the mirror in the inverted form

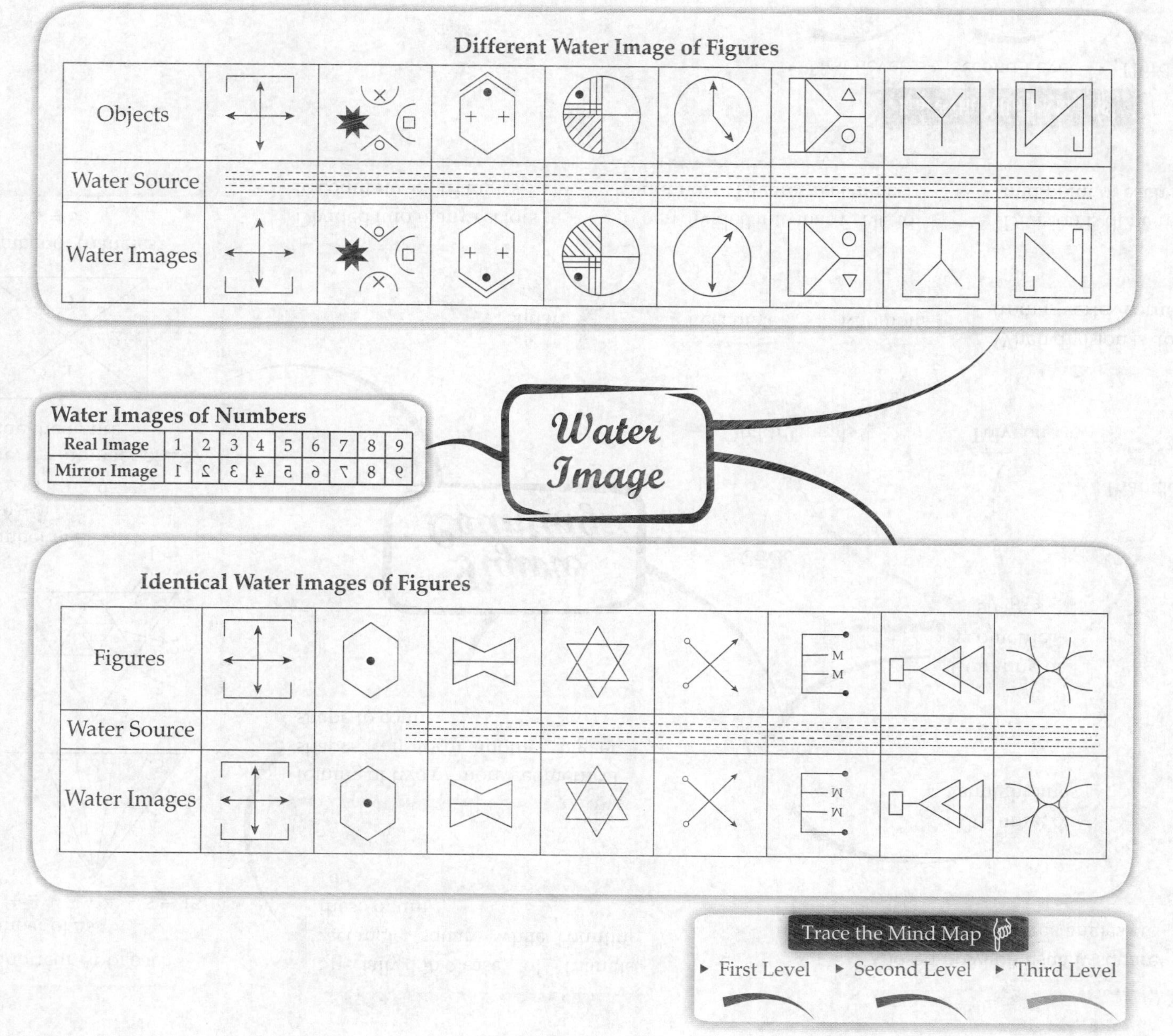
Different Water Image of Figures
Objects
Water Source
Water Images
Water Image
Water Images of Numbers
Real Image 1 2 3 4 5 6 7 8 9
Mirror Image
Identical Water Images of Figures
Figures
M
M
Water Source
Water Images
Trace the Mind Map
First Level
Second Level
Third Level

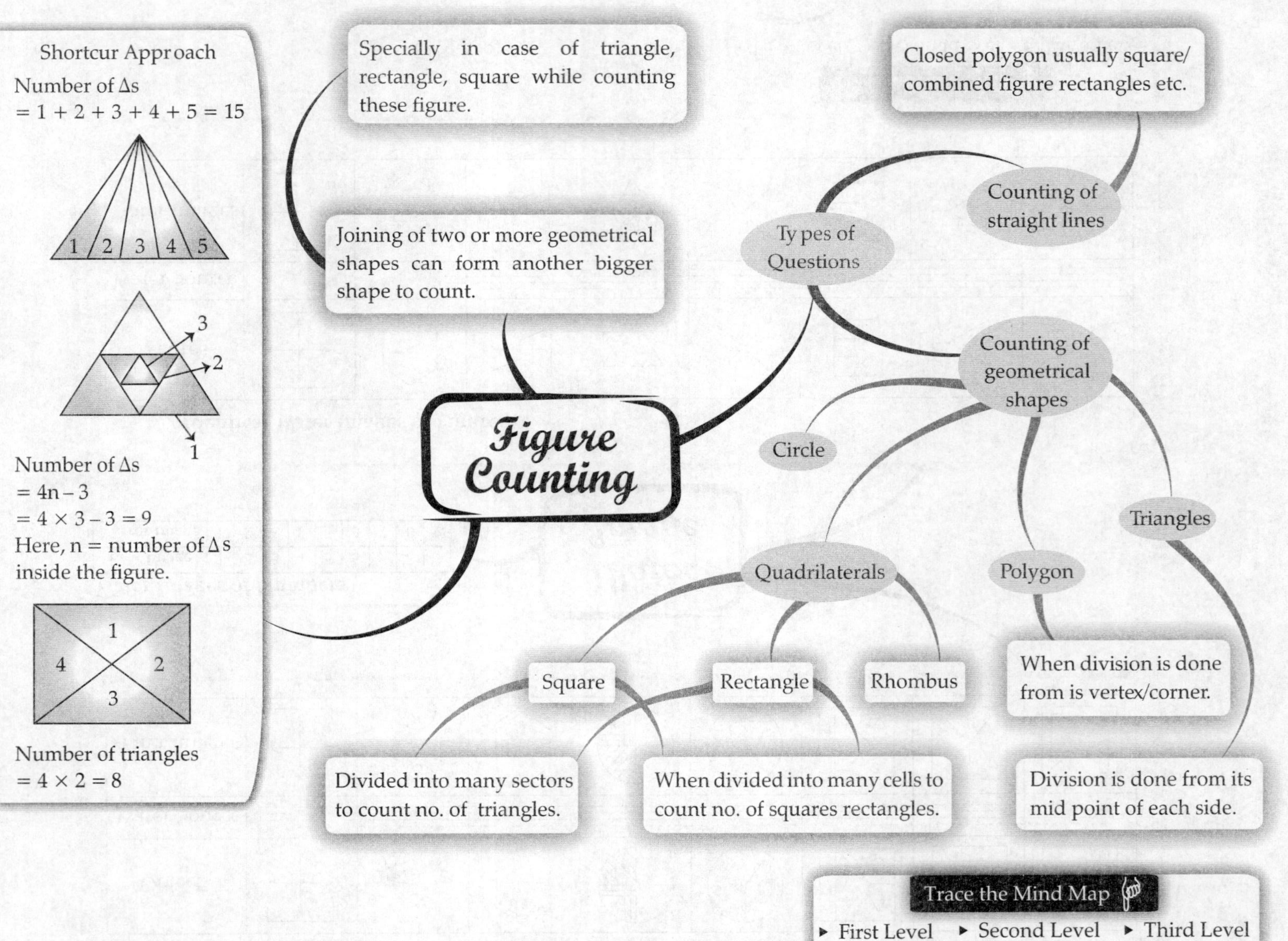
Shortcur Approach
Number of Δs
= 1 + 2 + 3 + 4 + 5 = 15
1 2 3 4 5
3
2
1
Number of Δs
= 4n – 3
= 4 × 3 – 3 = 9
Here, n = number of Δs
inside the figure.
1
4
2
3
Number of triangles
= 4 × 2 = 8
Specially in case of triangle, rectangle, square while counting these figure.
Joining of two or more geometrical shapes can form another bigger shape to count.
Figure Counting
Types of Questions
Counting of straight lines
Closed polygon usually square/ combined figure rectangles etc.
Counting of geometrical shapes
Circle
Triangles
Polygon
Quadrilaterals
Square
Rectangle
Rhombus
When division is done from is vertex/corner.
Division is done from its mid point of each side.
Divided into many sectors to count no. of triangles.
When divided into many cells to count no. of squares rectangles.
Trace the Mind Map
First Level
Second Level
Third Level

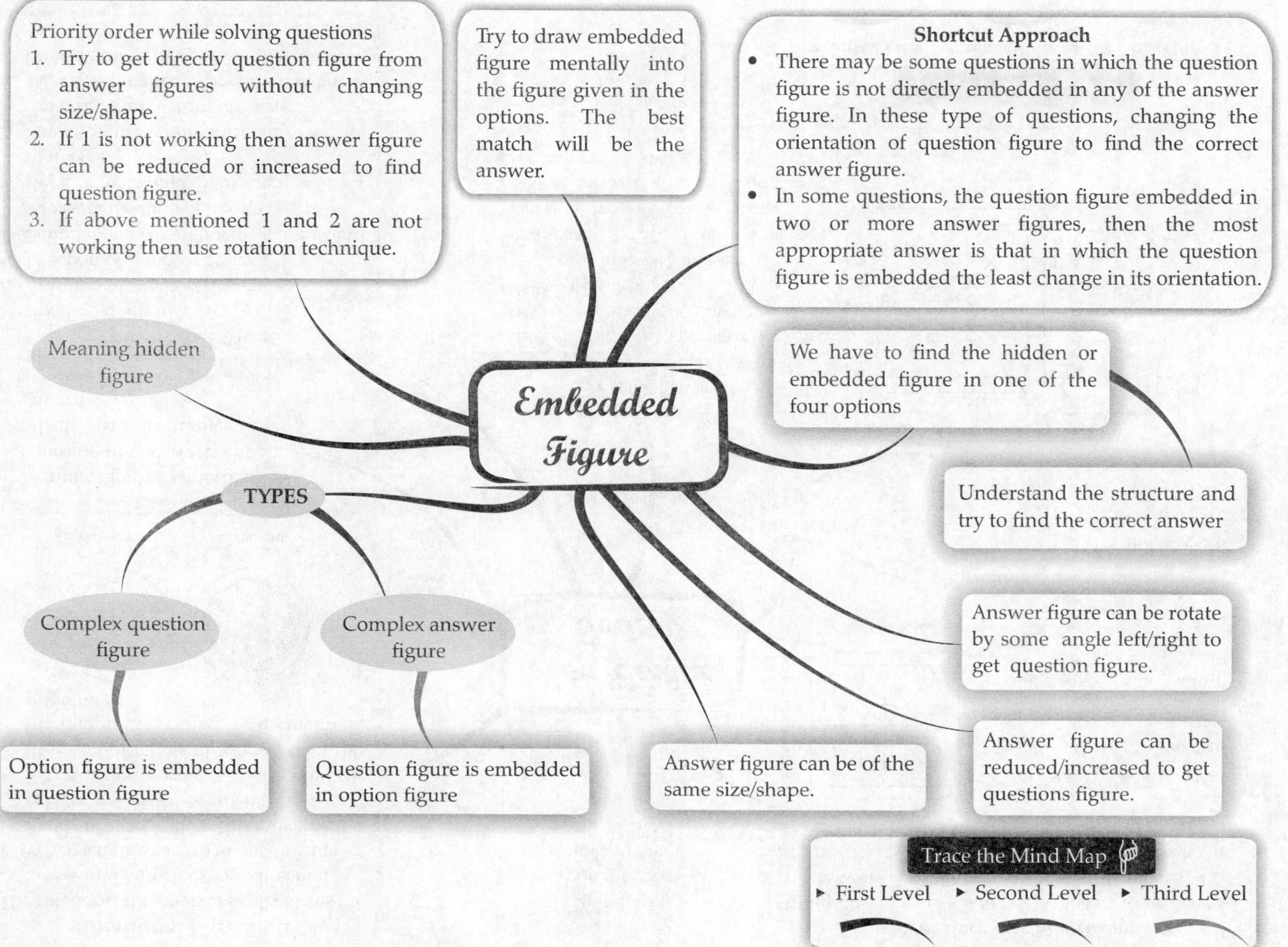
Embedded Figure
Priority order while solving questions
1. Try to get directly question figure from answer figures without changing size/shape.
2. If 1 is not working then answer figure can be reduced or increased to find question figure.
3. If above mentioned 1 and 2 are not working then use rotation technique.
Try to draw embedded figure mentally into the figure given in the options. The best match will be the answer.
Shortcut Approach
• There may be some questions in which the question figure is not directly embedded in any of the answer figure. In these type of questions, changing the orientation of question figure to find the correct answer figure.
• In some questions, the question figure embedded in two or more answer figures, then the most appropriate answer is that in which the question figure is embedded the least change in its orientation.
Meaning hidden figure
We have to find the hidden or embedded figure in one of the four options
Understand the structure and try to find the correct answer
TYPES
Complex question figure
Complex answer figure
Option figure is embedded in question figure
Question figure is embedded in option figure
Answer figure can be rotate by some angle left/right to get question figure.
Answer figure can be of the same size/shape.
Answer figure can be reduced/increased to get questions figure.
Trace the Mind Map
First Level
Second Level
Third Level

Non Verbal Series

Rotational Direction

The rotational direction basically states the clockwise and anti-clockwise direction.

- When a figure rotates in the direction of hands of a clock, then this movement is called clockwise movement.
- When a figure rotates in the opposite direction of hands of a clock, then this movement is called anti-clockwise movement.

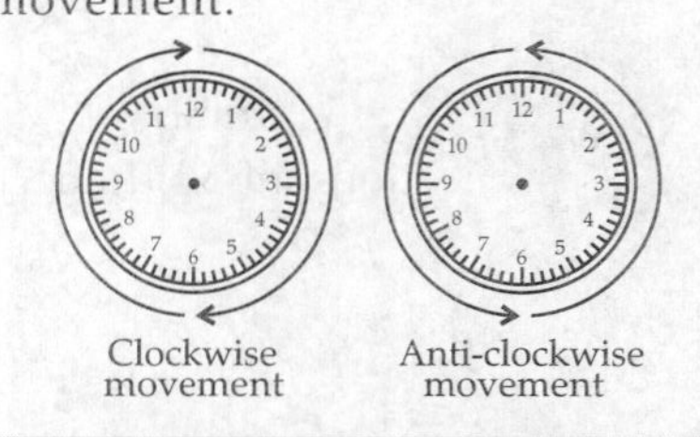

Identification of pattern, and choosing the correct option which will continues the pattern.

Types of questions

1. Rotation of figures
2. Addition of symbols/designs.
3. Deletion of symbols/designs
4. Simultaneous operation of rotation and addition/ deletion of designs.
5. Replacement and rearrangement of figures.
6. Similar figure within the series.
7. Reverse figure within the series.
8. Mixed simultaneous operation in terms of addition, replacement and rotation, etc.

Series based upon different, shapes, symbols, signs, etc.

Anti-clockwise Movement

Suppose the element at position A moves to position H, then we can say it moves 45° anti-clockwise. If it moves to position G, then we can say it moves 90° anti-clockwise and so on.

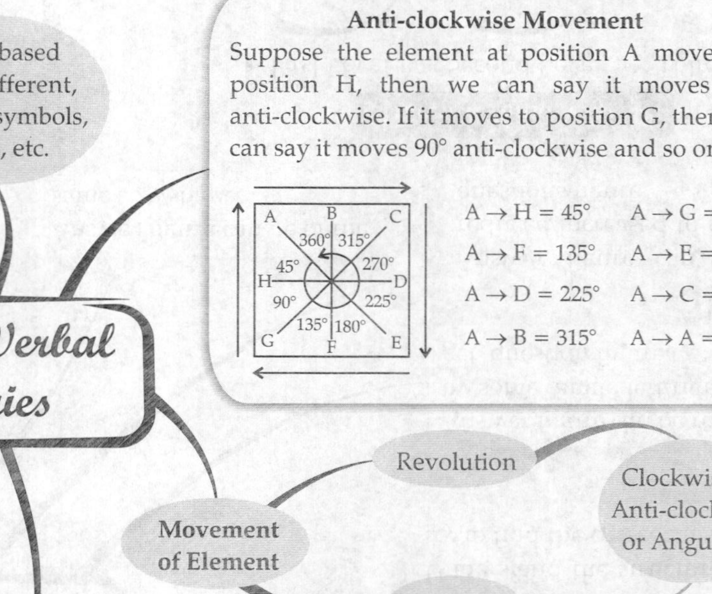

A → H = 45° A → G = 90°
A → F = 135° A → E = 180°
A → D = 225° A → C = 270°
A → B = 315° A → A = 360°

Movement of Element

Revolution

Rotation

Clockwise or Anti-clockwise or Angularly

Angular Movement

In some type of questions the whole figure is not rotated to obtain another figure but some elements inside the figure move to obtain the subsequent figures.

Clockwise Movement

Suppose the element at position A moves to position B, then we can say it moves 45° clockwise, if it moves to position C, then we can say it moves 90° clockwise and so on.

A → B= 45°
A → C= 90°
A → D= 135°
A → E= 180°
A → F= 225°
A → G= 270°

Chapter 1

Verbal Reasoning

Series Completion

LEARNING OBJECTIVES:

- Questions based on number series
- Questions based on alphabet series
- Questions based on mixed series
- Different types of questions asked in competitive exams

Series completion in verbal reasoning is a type of logical reasoning task that involves identifying the pattern or rule followed in a given series of words or phrases and determining the missing element that completes the series. It is commonly used in aptitude tests, entrance exams, and assessments to assess an individual's ability to recognise and understand patterns and sequences.

In series completion, you are typically given a sequence of words or phrases that follow a specific pattern. Your task is to identify the underlying rule or relationship between the elements and then applying that rule to determine the missing element or elements in the series.

NUMBER SERIES

➤ Number series is a type of verbal reasoning task that involves identifying the pattern or rule followed in a given series of numbers and determining the missing number(s) that complete the series. It is a common component of aptitude tests, entrance exams, and assessments used to assess an individual's numerical reasoning and logical thinking abilities.

In number series, you are presented with a sequence of numbers, and your goal is to determine the underlying pattern or relationship between the numbers. By identifying the pattern, you can predict the missing number(s) and complete the series.

Example 1: Which number would replace the question mark in the series?

3, 8, 13, ?, 23

(a) 15 (b) 18

(c) 16 (d) 21

Sol. (b) Clearly, the given sequence follows the pattern

$3+5=8, 8+5=13$

So, the missing number = $13+5=18$

Example 2: Which is the number that comes next in the sequence?

3, 10, 29, 66, 127, ?

(a) 215 (b) 196

(c) 218 (d) 225

Sol. (c) Clearly, the given series is,

$1^3+2, 2^3+2, 3^3+2, 4^3+2, 5^3+2.$

So, next number = $6^3+2=216+2=218$

ALPHABET SERIES

➤ In verbal reasoning, alphabet series entail identifying the pattern or rule followed in a given series of letters or alphabets and determining the missing letter(s) to complete the series. It is a common component of aptitude tests, entrance exams, and assessments used to evaluate a person's logical thinking, pattern recognition, and reasoning abilities.

In alphabet series, you are shown a series of letters and your task is to figure out the underlying pattern or relationship between the letters. By recognising the pattern, you can predict the missing letter(s) and complete the series.

Example 3: Find the next two terms in the series.

A, C, F, J, ?, ? **(CBI 2003)**

(a) L, P (b) M, O

(c) O, U (d) R, V

Sol. (c) We have the following sequence,

$A \xrightarrow{+2} C \xrightarrow{+3} F \xrightarrow{+4} J \xrightarrow{+5} O \xrightarrow{+6} U$

So, missing terms are O and U.

Example 4: In the following letter series, some of the letters are missing which are given in that order as one of the alternatives below it. Choose the correct alternative.

_ xy _ _ yyx _ yxy

(a) xyxy (b) yxyx

(c) yyxy (d) xxyy

Sol. (c) The pattern is yxy/yxy/yxy/yxy

The missing terms are y, y, x and y.

MIXED SERIES

- A mixed series is a type of reasoning task in which multiple patterns or rules are combined within a single series. It entails recognising and analysing various patterns, relationships, or sequences within a given series of numbers, letters, or other elements, as well as determining the missing element(s) that complete the series.
Mixed series may contain a mix of number sequences, alphabetical sequences, or patterns involving symbols or other elements. The series may include alternating patterns, overlapping patterns, or a pattern change after a certain number of elements.

Example 5: Find the next term in the alpha-numeric series:

Z1A, W3D, T5G, Q7J, N9M, K11P, ?

(a) H13S (b) L13P
(c) H15N (d) L13S

Sol. (a) Clearly, the pattern follow by the letters are given:

I[st] Letter:

$Z \xrightarrow{-3} W \xrightarrow{-3} T \xrightarrow{-3} Q \xrightarrow{-3} N \xrightarrow{-3} K \xrightarrow{-3} \textcircled{H}$

IInd Letter:

$A \xrightarrow{+3} D \xrightarrow{+3} G \xrightarrow{+3} J \xrightarrow{+3} M \xrightarrow{+3} P \xrightarrow{+3} \textcircled{S}$

Follow the pattern

$1 \xrightarrow{+2} 3 \xrightarrow{+2} 5 \xrightarrow{+2} 7 \xrightarrow{+2} 9 \xrightarrow{+2} 11 \xrightarrow{+2} \textcircled{13}$

Hence, H13S is the right answer.

Example 6: In the following question, a series of letters and numbers is given the terms of which follow certain definite pattern in groups. However, some terms in the series are missing, which are given in the same order as one of the alternatives below the series. Choose the correct alternative.

Z_A X _ C _ 17ET13_

(a) 2521VG (b) 2421TM
(c) 2127UH (d) 2520UM

Sol. (a) Here, the pattern is:

Z – A = 26 – 1 = 25, X – C = 24 – 3 = 21
V – E = 22 – 5 = 17, T – G = 20 – 7 = 13

1 Beginner Level

Directions (Qs. 1–10): There is a number series with one term missing in each of the following questions:
Select the right answer to replace the question mark in the provided series with one that follows the same pattern.

1. 141, 120, 101, 84, 69, ?
(A) 45 (B) 50
(C) 56 (D) 52

2. 11, 13, 17, 19, 23, 25, ? [RRB 2004]
(A) 26 (B) 27 (C) 29 (D) 37

3. 2315, 3420, 4525, 5630, ?
(A) 6150 (B) 6735
(C) 5950 (D) 6045

4. 2, 5, 9, ? 20, 27 [RRB 2002]
(A) 14 (B) 16 (C) 18 (D) 24

5. 0, 4, 8, 16, 24, 36, 48, ?
(A) 64 (B) 72
(C) 50 (D) 68

6. 0, 2, 8, 14, ?, 34 [BBS 2004]
(A) 20 (B) 23 (C) 24 (D) 25

7. 1, 9, 25, 49, ?, 121 [SSC 2002]
(A) 64 (B) 81 (C) 91 (D) 100

8. 1, 6, 16, 31, 51, 76, ?
(A) 106 (B) 115
(C) 95 (D) 118

9. 4, 7, 12, 19, 28, ? [MCA 2005]
(A) 30 (B) 36 (C) 39 (D) 49

10. 6, 12, 21, ?, 48 [RRB 2003]
(A) 33 (B) 38 (C) 40 (D) 45

Directions (Qs. 11–12): Select the number or letter that can replace the question mark (?) in the following series.

11. 87, 89, 92, 97, 104, 115, ?, 145 [SSC CGL 2021]
(A) 125 (B) 128 (C) 133 (D) 132

12. BTC, DSF, FRI, HQL, ?
(A) IPT (B) JPS (C) IRQ (D) JPO

13. Select the set of letters that when sequentially placed in the blanks of the given letter series will complete the series. [SSC CGL 2020]
_ swws _ wwws _ swwww_ sss
(A) w, s, w, s (B) w, s, s, s
(C) w, w, s, s (D) w, s, s, w

Directions (Qs. 14–16): Select the number or letter that can replace the question mark (?) in the following series.

14. 17, 20, 15, 22, 13 ? [SSC CGL 2020]
(A) 2 (B) 22 (C) 4 (D) 24

15. MVG, OSJ, QPM, SMP, ?
(A) UJS (B) THQ
(C) UKP (D) TJP

16. O, B, L, C, I, D, F, E ? [SSC CGL 2021]
(A) K (B) C (C) H (D) N

17. Select the set of letters that can sequentially placed in the blanks of the given letter series will complete the series.
cb_db_cba_bc_bad_c
(A) acdcb (B) cabdc
(C) acbcd (D) dcbcb

18. Which number will complete the given series?
1, 3, 7, 15, 31, 63, ... [SSC CPO 2019]
(A) 139 (B) 127 (C) 125 (D) 126

19. Identify the number that does not belong in the given series.
1, 8, 27, 64, 125, 216, 344, 512, 729 [SSC CPO 2019]
(A) 512 (B) 729 (C) 64 (D) 344

20. Which number will replace the question mark in the following series?
2, 5, 11, 23, 47, ?
(A) 92 (B) 98 (C) 94 (D) 95

Directions (Qs. 21–25): In each of the following questions, various terms of an alphabet series are given with one or more terms missing as shown by (?). Choose the missing terms out of the given alternatives.

21. R, U, X, A, D,? **[BTM 2006]**
(A) F (B) G (C) H (D) I

22. B, D, F, I, L, P ? **[SSC 2003]**
(A) R (B) S (C) T (D) U

23. V, ?, N, ?, F, ?
(A) P, H, C (B) R, K, D
(C) R, J, B (D) P, T, M

24. T, R, P, N, L, ?,? **[SSC CPO 2004]**
(A) J, G (B) J, H (C) K, H (D) K, I

25. Z, X, S, I, R, R,?, ? **[BTM 2006]**
(A) G, I (B) J, I (C) J, K (D) K, M

2 Level Intermediate

Directions (Qs. 1–10): There is a number series with one term missing in each of the following questions: Select the right answer to replace the question mark in the provided series with one that follows the same pattern.

1. 165, 195, 255, 285, 345, ?
(A) 375 (B) 390 (C) 420 (D) 435

2. 5, 6, 14, 45, 184, ?
(A) 845 (B) 715 (C) 925 (D) 995

3. 8, 28, 116, 584, ? **[RRB 2004]**
(A) 1752 (B) 3502 (C) 3504 (D) 3508

4. 4, 9, 29, 109, 429, ?
(A) 1709 (B) 785 (C) 1818 (D) 1518

5. 2, 8, 16, 128, ? **[SSC CGL 2020]**
(A) 2042 (B) 2046 (C) 2048 (D) 2056

6. 8, 12, 20, 32, 52, 84, ?
(A) 152 (B) 136 (C) 82 (D) 116

7. 24, 60, 120, 210, ? **[PGDTM 2006]**
(A) 300 (B) 336 (C) 420 (D) 525

8. 1, 2, 6, 7, 21, 22, 66, 67, ? **[MCA 2005]**
(A) 70 (B) 134 (C) 201 (D) 301

9. 11, 27, 59, 123, 251, ?
(A) 507 (B) 611 (C) 391 (D) 415

10. $4, 6, 9, 13\frac{1}{2}, ?$ **[PGDTM 2006]**
(A) $17\frac{1}{2}$ (B) 19 (C) $20\frac{1}{4}$ (D) $22\frac{3}{4}$

Directions (Qs. 11–15): In each of the following questions, various terms of an alphabet series are given with one or more terms missing as shown by (?). Choose the missing terms out of the given alternatives.

11. Y, B, T, G, O, ? **[MCA 2005]**
(A) N (B) M (C) L (D) K

12. Z, S, W, O, T, K, Q, G, ?, ?
(A) N, C (B) N, D (C) O, C (D) O, D

13. A, B, N, C, D, O, E, F, P, ?, ?, ? **[MAT 2002]**
(A) G, H, I (B) G, H, J
(C) G, H, Q (D) J, K, L

14. AI, BJ, CK, ?
(A) DL (B) DM (C) GH (D) LM

15. b, e, d, f, ?, h, j, ?, l **[RRB 2008]**
(A) i, m (B) m, l (C) l, n (D) j, m

Directions (Qs. 16–20): In each of the following letter series, some of the letters are missing which are given in that order as one of the alternatives below it. Choose the correct alternative.

16. _ _ aba _ _ ba _ ab
(A) abbba (B) abbab
(C) baabb (D) bbaba

17. xx __ y __ y x __ xyy __ xxx
(A) xxyx (B) xxxy
(C) yxyx (D) xyxy

18. a_ ba _ b _ b _ a _b **[Hotel Management 2004]**
(A) abaab (B) abbab
(C) aabba (D) bbabb

19. r __ prqp __ q __ rq __ rqp
(A) qrpq (B) qrpp
(C) rqqr (D) qprq

20. _ nmmn _ mmnn_ mnnm _ **[CPO 2017]**
(A) nmmn (B) mnnm
(C) nnmm (D) nmnm

21. Which letter-cluster will replace the question mark (?) in the following series?
XCA, WDZ, UFX, RIU, NMQ, ? **[SSC CPO 2019]**
(A) IJK (B) JKO (C) JFU (D) IRL

22. Which letter will come next in the following series?
Z, T, O, K, H, ?
(A) F (B) G (C) E (D) M

23. Which of the following element should come in a place of?
AB3, CE6, FI10, JN15?
(A) OT20 (B) TO21 (C) OT21 (D) TS21

24. In the following question select the missing number from the given series.
19, 38, ?, 228, 684, 1368 **[SSC CGL 2017]**
(A) 108 (B) 113 (C) 114 (D) 138

25. Which letter will come next in the following series?
A, C, E, G, ? **[SSC CGL 2017]**
(A) H (B) I (C) J (D) F

3 Level Expert

Directions (Qs. 1–5): In each of the following questions, one term in the number jerks is wrong. Find out the wrong term.

1. 6, 9, 14, 21, 30, 41, 54, 65
   (A) 41 (B) 19 (C) 30 (D) 65
2. 80, 86, 96, 104, 116, 130
   (A) 86 (B) 96 (C) 104 (D) 130
3. 125, 126, 124, 127, 123, 129 [SSC CGL 2013]
   (A) 126 (B) 124 (C) 123 (D) 129
4. 130, 120, 105, 85, 60, 30, 0, –45
   (A) 105 (B) 60 (C) 0 (D) –45
5. 542, 286, 158, 98, 62, 46
   (A) 46 (B) 158 (C) 98 (D) 542

Directions (Qs. 6–10): In each of the following questions, various terms of an alphabet series are given with one or more terms missing as shown by (?). Choose the missing terms out of the given alternatives.

6. AZ, GT, MN, ?, YB [RRB 2002]
   (A) JH (B) SH (C) SK (D) TS
7. ajs, gpy, ?, sbk, yhq [MBA 2004]
   (A) dmv (B) mve (C) oua (D) qzi
8. UPI, ? ODP, MBQ, IAW [BANK PO 2004]
   (A) RHJ (B) SHJ (C) SIJ (D) THK
9. JSD, KPF, LLH, ?, NAL
   (A) TIJ (B) MGJ (C) GKJ (D) JIM
10. A, CD, GHI, ?, UVWXY [RRB 2004]
    (A) LMNO (B) MNO
    (C) MNOP (D) NOPQ

Directions (Qs. 11–15): A series is given, with one term missing. Choose the correct alternatives from the given ones that will complete the series:

11. AFI, JOR, MRU, ? [SSC CGL 2013]
    (A) GJU (B) HMP (C) PMO (D) RJL
12. gh, hij, jk, klm, mn, ?
    (A) nop (B) npo (C) pqr (D) no
13. C-1, E-4, G-9, I-16, ?
    (A) X-20, M-25 (B) K-25, M-36
    (C) O-16, X-25 (D) M-9, K-18
14. 5, 16, 51, 158, ? [SSC CGL 2013]
    (A) 1452 (B) 483 (C) 481 (D) 1454
15. 6, 47, 340, 2397, ?
    (A) 21500 (B) 16802 (C) 12284 (D) 15400

ANSWER KEY

Level-1: Beginner

1.	(C)	2.	(C)	3.	(B)	4.	(A)	5.	(A)	6.	(C)	7.	(B)	8.	(A)	9.	(C)	10.	(A)
11.	(B)	12.	(D)	13.	(B)	14.	(D)	15.	(A)	16.	(B)	17.	(A)	18.	(B)	19.	(D)	20.	(D)
21.	(B)	22.	(C)	23.	(C)	24.	(B)	25.	(A)										

Level-2: Intermediate

1.	(D)	2.	(C)	3.	(D)	4.	(A)	5.	(C)	6.	(B)	7.	(B)	8.	(C)	9.	(A)	10.	(C)
11.	(C)	12.	(A)	13.	(C)	14.	(A)	15.	(A)	16.	(B)	17.	(D)	18.	(D)	19.	(B)	20.	(C)
21.	(D)	22.	(A)	23.	(C)	24.	(C)	25.	(B)										

Level-3: Expert

1.	(D)	2.	(B)	3.	(D)	4.	(C)	5.	(C)	6.	(B)	7.	(B)	8.	(B)	9.	(B)	10.	(C)
11.	(B)	12.	(A)	13.	(B)	14.	(C)	15.	(B)										

Solutions with Detailed Explanations

Level-1: BEGINNER

1. **Option (C) is correct.**
   Explanation: The pattern is:
   $141 \xrightarrow{-21} 120 \xrightarrow{-19} 101 \xrightarrow{-17} 84 \xrightarrow{-15} 69 \xrightarrow{-13} 56$
   So, the missing number is 56.
2. **Option (C) is correct.**
   Explanation: We can see,
   The pattern is: +2, +4, +2, +4 ....
   So, the missing term= 25 + 4 = 29

3. **Option (B) is correct.**
Explanation: The pattern is :
$2315 \xrightarrow{+1105} 3420 \xrightarrow{+1105} 4525 \xrightarrow{+1105} 5630 \xrightarrow{+1105} 6735$
So, the missing number is 6735.

4. **Option (A) is correct.**
Explanation: We can see,
The pattern is: +3, +4, +5, +6, +7
So, missing term= 9 + 5 = 14

5. **Option (A) is correct.**
Explanation: The pattern is:
$0 \xrightarrow{+4} 4 \xrightarrow{+4} 8 \xrightarrow{+8} 16 \xrightarrow{+8} 24 \xrightarrow{+12} 36 \xrightarrow{+12} 48 \xrightarrow{+16} \boxed{64}$
So, the missing number is 64.

6. **Option (C) is correct.**
Explanation: We can see,
The pattern is: +2, +6, +6, +10, +10, ...
So, the missing term = 14 + 10 = 24

7. **Option (B) is correct.**
Explanation: We can see,
The pattern is square of consecutive odd numbers i.e., $1^2, 3^2, 5^2, 7^2$,....
So, the missing term = $9^2 = 81$

8. **Option (A) is correct.**
Explanation: The pattern is :
$1 \xrightarrow{+5} 6 \xrightarrow{+10} 16 \xrightarrow{+15} 31 \xrightarrow{+20} 51 \xrightarrow{+25} 76 \xrightarrow{+30} \boxed{106}$
So, the missing number is 106.

9. **Option (C) is correct.**
Explanation: We can see,
The pattern is: +3, +5, +7, +9, +11, +13, +15....
So, missing term = 28 + 11 = 39

10. **Option (A) is correct.**
Explanation: We can see,
The pattern is: +6, +9, +12, +15....
So, the missing term = 21 + 12 = 33

11. **Option (B) is correct.**
Explanation: We can see,
There are successive prime numbers added to each number in the given series.
87 + 2 = 89
89 + 3 = 92
92 + 5 = 97
97 + 7 = 104
104 + 11 = 115
115 + 13 = 128
128 + 17 = 145
So, the missing term = 128

12. **Option (D) is correct.**
Explanation: The pattern is:
$B \xrightarrow{+2} D \xrightarrow{+2} F \xrightarrow{+2} H \xrightarrow{+2} \boxed{J}$
$T \xrightarrow{-1} S \xrightarrow{-1} R \xrightarrow{-1} Q \xrightarrow{-1} \boxed{P}$
$C \xrightarrow{+3} F \xrightarrow{+3} I \xrightarrow{+3} L \xrightarrow{+3} \boxed{O}$
So, the missing term is JPO.

13. **Option (B) is correct.**
Explanation: We can see,
The correct pattern is:
w/s/ww/ss/www/sss/wwww/ssss
So, the missing letters are w, s, s and s.

14. **Option (D) is correct.**
Explanation: We can see,
Every number in the given series is the addition and subtraction of the prime number in the next terms, respectively.
17 + 3 = 20
20 – 5 = 15
15 + 7 = 22
22 – 9 = 13
13 + 11 = 24

15. **Option (A) is correct.**
Explanation: We can see the pattern is:
$M \xrightarrow{+2} O \xrightarrow{+2} Q \xrightarrow{+2} S \xrightarrow{+2} \boxed{U}$
$V \xrightarrow{-3} S \xrightarrow{-3} P \xrightarrow{-3} M \xrightarrow{-3} \boxed{J}$
$G \xrightarrow{+3} J \xrightarrow{+3} M \xrightarrow{+3} P \xrightarrow{+3} \boxed{S}$
So, the missing term is UJS.

16. **Option (B) is correct.**
Explanation: We can see,
Two series were combined to create the series.
O, L, I, F, ? and B, C, D, E
So, O – 3 = L
L – 3 = I
I – 3 = F
F – 3 = C

17. **Option (A) is correct.**
Explanation: We can see,
The pattern is:
cbadbc/cbadbc/cbadbc
So, the missing terms are a, c, d, c and b.

18. **Option (B) is correct.**
Explanation: We can see,
The pattern is:
$2^n - 1$, where $n = 1, 2, 3, 4, ...$
Next term will be: $2^7 - 1 = 128 - 1 = 127$

19. **Option (D) is correct.**
Explanation: We can see,
The pattern is:
$1^3, 2^3, 3^3, 4^3, 5^3, 6^3, 7^3, 8^3, 9^3$
But $7^3 = 343 \neq 344$
So, 344 is the wrong term.

20. **Option (D) is correct.**
Explanation: The pattern is:
$2 \xrightarrow{\times 2+1} 5 \xrightarrow{\times 2+1} 11 \xrightarrow{\times 2+1} 23 \xrightarrow{\times 2+1} 47 \xrightarrow{\times 2+1} (95)$
So, the missing number is 95.

21. **Option (B) is correct.**
Explanation: The relationship is:
+3, +3, +3, +3, +3,....
We can see, the pattern is,
R + 3 = U
U + 3 = X

X + 3 = A
A + 3 = D
D + 3 = G

So, the missing term is G.

22. Option (C) is correct.

Explanation: The pattern is: +2, +2, +3, +3, +4, +4,
B + 2 = D, D + 2 = F, F + 3 = I, I + 3 = L, L + 4 = P, P + 4 = T

23. Option (C) is correct.

Explanation: The pattern is :

$V \xrightarrow{-4} \underline{R} \xrightarrow{-4} N \xrightarrow{-4} \underline{J} \xrightarrow{-4} F \xrightarrow{-4} \underline{B}$

So, the missing terms are R, J, B

24. Option (B) is correct.

Explanation: We can see:
The pattern is: T – 2 = R, R – 2 = P, P – 2 = N, N – 2 = L, L – 2 = J, J – 2 = H
So, the missing terms are J and H.

25. Option (A) is correct.

Explanation: We can see,
The pattern is:
Z – 2 = X, X – 5 = S, S – 10 = I, I – 17 = R, R – 26 = R, R – 37 = G, G – 50 = I
Note that the numbers that indicate the intervals between the terms of the series again form the series 2, 5, 10, 17, 26, 37, 50 with the pattern being +3, +5, +7, +9, +11, +13.
So, the missing terms are G and I.

Level-2: INTERMEDIATE

1. Option (D) is correct.

Explanation: We can see,
The pattern is:
15 × 11, 15 × 13, 15 × 17, 15 × 19, 15 × 23,....
So, the missing term = 15 × 29 = 435

2. Option (C) is correct.

Explanation: The pattern is :

$5 \xrightarrow{\times 1+1} 6 \xrightarrow{\times 2+2} 14 \xrightarrow{\times 3+3} 45 \xrightarrow{\times 4+4} 184 \xrightarrow{\times 5+5} \boxed{925}$

So, the missing number is 925.

3. Option (D) is correct.

Explanation: We can see,
The pattern is: ×3 + 4, ×4 + 4, ×5 + 4, ×6 + 4, ...
So, the missing term = 584 × 6 + 4 = 3508

4. Option (A) is correct.

Explanation: We can see,
The pattern is: +5, +20, +80, +320, ...
or + (5×1^2), + (5×2^2), + (5×4^2), + (5×8^2).....
So, the missing term 429 + (5×16^2)
= 429 + 1280 = 1709

5. Option (C) is correct.

Explanation: We can see, every term in the series, with the exception of the first two, is the result of the multiplication of previous two terms.
So, the missing term = 16 × 128 = 2048

6. Option (B) is correct.

Explanation: We can see,
Except for the first two terms, every term in the series is the sum of the two terms that came before it.
So, the missing term = 52 + 84 = 136

7. Option (B) is correct.

Explanation: We can see,
The pattern is: +36, +60, +90,....
= +[6 × (6 + 0)], [6 × (6 + 4)], [6 × (6 + 9)]........
So, missing term = 210 + [6 × (6 + 15)]
= 210 + 126 = 336

8. Option (C) is correct.

Explanation: We can see,
The pattern is:
+1, ×3, +1, ×3, +1, ×3, +1, ×3,....
So, the missing term = 67 × 3 = 201

9. Option (A) is correct.

Explanation: The pattern is:

$11 \xrightarrow{\times 2+5} 27 \xrightarrow{\times 2+5} 59 \xrightarrow{\times 2+5} 123 \xrightarrow{\times 2+5} 251 \xrightarrow{\times 2+5} \boxed{507}$

So, the missing number is 507.

10. Option (C) is correct.

Explanation: We can see,

The pattern is: $\left[\times \frac{3}{2}\right]$

So, missing number = $13\frac{1}{2} \times \frac{3}{2} = \frac{27}{2} \times \frac{3}{2} = \frac{81}{4} = 20\frac{1}{4}$

11. Option (C) is correct.

Explanation: A combination of the two series:
Y, T, O and B, G, ?
The provided sequence is composed of I is made up of the second, seventh, and twelfth letters from the end of the English alphabet, while II is made up of the second, seventh, and twelfth letters from the beginning. L, the 12th letter from the start of the English alphabet, thereby fills the gap in II.

12. Option (A) is correct.

Explanation: The present series can be classified into two groups:
First: Z, W, T, Q, and Second: S, O, K, G
First pattern: Z – 3 = W, W – 3 = T, T – 3 = Q, Q – 3 = (N)
Second pattern: S – 4 = O, O – 4 = K, K – 4 = G, G – 4 = (C)

13. Option (C) is correct.

Explanation: The present series can be classified into two groups:
I. A, B, C, D, E, F, ? and II. N, O, P, ?
Clearly, the provided series consists of two terms of I and one term of II. G and H are the omitted terms in I, while Q is the omitted term in the II.

14. Option (A) is correct.

Explanation: We can see,
First letter: A + 1 = B, B + 1 = C, C + 1 = (D)
Second letter: I + 1 = J, J + 1 = K, K + 1 = (L)

15. **Option (A) is correct.**
Explanation: We can see, the pattern is
bed/f?h/j?l
Clearly, the second and third letters in the first group are three and two steps ahead of the first letter, respectively. In the second and third groups, a comparable alphabets would come next.
So, the missing terms are i and m.

16. **Option (B) is correct.**
Explanation: We can see,
The pattern is = ab/ab/ab/ab/ab/ab
Thus, the pattern (ab) is repeated

17. **Option (D) is correct.**
Explanation: We can see,
The pattern is: xxx/yyy/xxx/yyy/xxx
Thus, the pattern (xxxyyy) is repeated.

18. **Option (D) is correct.**
Explanation: We can see,
The pattern is: abb/abb/abb/abb
Thus, the pattern (abb) is repeated.

19. **Option (B) is correct.**
Explanation: We can see,
The pattern is: rqp/rqp/rqp/rqp/rqp
Thus, the pattern (rqp) is repeated.

20. **Option (C) is correct.**
Explanation: We can see,
The pattern is: nnmm/nnmm/nnmm/nnmm
Thus, the pattern (nnmm) is repeated.

21. **Option (D) is correct.**
Explanation: The pattern is:

$X \xrightarrow{-1} W \xrightarrow{-2} U \xrightarrow{-3} R \xrightarrow{-4} N \xrightarrow{-5} \boxed{I}$

$C \xrightarrow{+1} D \xrightarrow{+2} F \xrightarrow{+3} I \xrightarrow{+4} M \xrightarrow{+5} \boxed{R}$

$A \xrightarrow{-1} Z \xrightarrow{-2} X \xrightarrow{-3} U \xrightarrow{-4} Q \xrightarrow{-5} \boxed{L}$

22. **Option (A) is correct.**
Explanation: The pattern is :

$Z \xrightarrow{-6} T \xrightarrow{-5} O \xrightarrow{-4} K \xrightarrow{-3} H \xrightarrow{-2} F$

23. **Option (C) is correct.**
Explanation: The pattern is:

$A \xrightarrow{+2} C \xrightarrow{+3} F \xrightarrow{+4} J \xrightarrow{+5} (O)$

$B \xrightarrow{+3} E \xrightarrow{+4} I \xrightarrow{+5} N \xrightarrow{+6} (T)$

$3 \xrightarrow{+3} 6 \xrightarrow{+4} 10 \xrightarrow{+5} 15 \xrightarrow{+6} (21)$

24. **Option (C) is correct.**
Explanation: The pattern is:
×2, ×3, ×2, ×3
$19 \times 2 = 38$
$38 \times 3 = 114$
$114 \times 2 = 228$
$228 \times 3 = 684$
$684 \times 2 = 1368$
So, the missing number of the given series is 144.

25. **Option (B) is correct.**
Explanation: The pattern is:

$A \xrightarrow{+2} C;\ C \xrightarrow{+2} E;\ E \xrightarrow{+2} G;\ G \xrightarrow{+2} \boxed{I}$

Level-3: EXPERT

1. **Option (D) is correct.**
Explanation: The terms of the series are
$(1^2 + 5), (2^2 + 5), (3^2 + 5), (4^2 + 5), (5^2 + 5), (6^2 + 5), (7^2 + 5), (8^2 + 5)$
So, 65 is wrong and must be replace by $(8^2 + 5) = 69$

2. **Option (B) is correct.**
Explanation: The pattern is:
+6, +8, +10, +12, +14,
So, 96 is wrong and must be replace by $(86 + 8) = 94$

3. **Option (D) is correct.**
Explanation: The pattern is:
+1, –2, +3, –4, +5
So, 129 is wrong and must be replace by $(123 + 5) = 128$

4. **Option (C) is correct.**
Explanation: The pattern is:
–10, –15, –20, –25, –30, –35, –40
So, 0 is wrong and must be replace by $(30 – 35) = –5$

5. **Option (C) is correct.**
Explanation: The pattern is:
–256, –128, –64, –32, –16
So, 98 is wrong and must be replace by $(158 – 64) = 94$

6. **Option (B) is correct.**
Explanation: We can see,
The pattern is:

1st letter: $A \xrightarrow{+6} G \xrightarrow{+6} M \xrightarrow{+6} (S) \xrightarrow{+6} Y$

2nd letter: $Z \xrightarrow{-6} T \xrightarrow{-6} N \xrightarrow{-6} (H) \xrightarrow{-6} B$

7. **Option (B) is correct.**
Explanation: The pattern is:

1st letter: $a \xrightarrow{+6} g \xrightarrow{+6} (m) \xrightarrow{+6} s \xrightarrow{+6} y$

2nd letter: $j \xrightarrow{+6} p \xrightarrow{+6} (v) \xrightarrow{+6} b \xrightarrow{+6} h$

3rd letter: $s \xrightarrow{+6} y \xrightarrow{+6} (e) \xrightarrow{+6} k \xrightarrow{+6} q$

8. **Option (B) is correct.**
Explanation: The pattern is:

1st letter: $U \xrightarrow{-2} (S) \xrightarrow{-4} O \xrightarrow{-2} M \xrightarrow{-4} I$

2nd letter: $P \xrightarrow{-8} (H) \xrightarrow{-4} D \xrightarrow{-2} B \xrightarrow{-1} A$

3rd letter: $I \xrightarrow{+1} (J) \xrightarrow{+6} P \xrightarrow{+1} Q \xrightarrow{+6} W$

9. **Option (B) is correct.**
Explanation: The correct pattern is,

1st letter : $J \xrightarrow{+1} K \xrightarrow{+1} L \xrightarrow{+1} (M) \xrightarrow{+1} N$

2nd letter : $S \xrightarrow{-3} P \xrightarrow{-4} L \xrightarrow{-5} (G) \xrightarrow{-6} A$

3rd letter : $D \xrightarrow{+2} F \xrightarrow{+2} H \xrightarrow{+2} (J) \xrightarrow{+2} L$

10. **Option (C) is correct.**
Explanation: Each term consists of consecutive letters in order. The number of letters in the terms goes on increasing by one at each step. Also, there is a gap of one letter between the last letter of the first term and the first letter of the second term; a gap of two letters between the last letter of the second term and the first letter of the third term; and so on. So, there should be a gap of three letters between the last letter of the third term and the first letter of the desired term.
So, the missing term is MNOP.

11. Option (B) is correct.

Explanation: The pattern is:

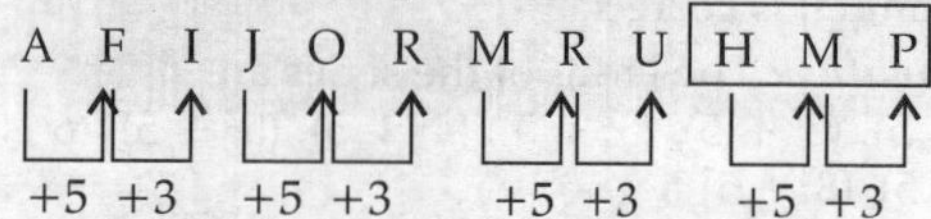

12. Option (A) is correct.

Explanation: The series begins with the final letter of the word, and the following two letters are added to the term.

So, nop is the missing term.

13. Option (B) is correct.

Explanation: Every letter in this series has been given an alphabetical series number, with one letter skipped in between.

14. Option (C) is correct.

Explanation: The pattern is:

$5 \times 3 + 1 = 16$

$16 \times 3 + 3 = 51$

$51 \times 3 + 5 = 158$

$158 \times 3 + 7 = 481$

15. Option (B) is correct.

Explanation: We can see,

$7^1 - 1, 7^2 - 2, 7^3 - 3, 7^4 - 4$

So, the missing term $= 7^5 - 5 = 16807 - 5 = 16802$

■ ■ ■

Chapter 2

Analogy

LEARNING OBJECTIVES:

- Question based on number analogy
- Questions based on alphabet analogy
- Questions based on mixed analogy
- Different types of questions asked in competitive exams

'ANALOGY' MEANS 'CORRESPONDENCE'.

In questions based on analogy, a particular relationship is given and another similar relationship has to be identified from the alternative provided. Analogy tests are therefore meant to test a candidate's overall knowledge, power of reasoning and ability to think concisely and accurately. Below are given some common relationships which will help you detect most analogies better.

NUMBER ANALOGY

This section deals with two types of questions:

I. Choosing a similarly related pair as the given number pair on the basis of the relation between the numbers in each pair.

II. Choosing a number similar to a number on the basis of certain common properties that they possess.

Example 1: 4 : 21 :: 9: ?

(a) 70 (b) 86
(c) 78 (d) 65

Sol. (b) Clearly,

$4^2 + 5 = 21$

Now,

$9^2 + 5 = 86$

So, if the first number is a, the second number is $a^2 + 5$.

Hence, the answer is (b).

Example 2: 216 : 6 : : 343 : ?

(a) 9 (b) 10
(c) 5 (d) 7

Sol. (d) Clearly, the relationship is: $a = a^{1/3}$

Now, the correct answer is (d).

ALPHABET ANALOGY

In this type of questions, two of alphabets related to each other in the same way, are given. The candidate is required to find out this relationship and choose a group of alphabets which is related in the same way to a third group provided in the question.

Example 3: ABCD : KLMN :: WXYZ : ?

(a) RSTU (b) GHIJ
(c) DEFG (d) MNOP

Sol. (b) Clearly, each letter of the first group is moved ten steps forward to obtain the corresponding letter of the second group.

A similar relationship will exist between the third and fourth groups.

Hence, the correct answer is (b).

Example 4: OKQI : KOMM :: WCYA : ?

(a) EGSU (b) ESVU
(c) GAUS (d) SGUE

Sol. (d) The first and third letters of the groups are each moved four steps backward to obtain the corresponding letters of the second group. The second and fourth letters of the first group are each moved four steps forward to obtain the corresponding letters of the second group.

A similar relationship will exist between the third and the fourth groups.

Hence, the correct answer is (d).

MIXED ANALOGY

An incompatible or confusing combination of two or more dissimilar metaphors is known as a mixed analogy. A senseless or illogical expression is the result of this. When a speaker or writer tries to compare two distinct items or concepts, but the comparison falls apart because the analogies are not coherent with one another, this is known as a mixed analogy.

Example 5: D H : 4 8 :: MQ : ? **(SSC CGL 2015)**

(a) 12 17 (b) 13 17
(c) 12 16 (d) 14 18

Sol. (b) Position of D and H in alphabetical series is 4 and 8.

So, the missing term will be 13 17.

Example 6: B : 16 :: D : ? (SSC CGL 2003)

(a) 120 (b) 150
(c) 200 (d) 256

Sol. (d) B is 2nd letter of the English alphabet.
Here, 2nd term = $2^4 = 16$
Now, D is 4th letter of English alphabet.
So, 4th term $4^4 = 256$

Level 1 Beginner

Directions (Qs. 1–25): Select the option that is related to the third number/ term/ word in the same way as the second number/ term/ word is related to the first.

1. 256 : 14 : : 441 : ?
(A) 18 (B) 25
(C) 19 (D) 21

2. 7528 : 5306 : : 4673 : ? **[RRB 2006]**
(A) 2367 (B) 2451
(C) 2531 (D) None of these

3. 12 : 144 : : 20 : ? **[RRB 2006]**
(A) 464 (B) 400
(C) 135 (D) 140

4. 18 : 59 : : 27 : ?
(A) 89 (B) 86
(C) 81 (D) 78

5. 6 : 18 : : 4 :? **[SSC CGL 2021]**
(A) 2 (B) 6 (C) 12 (D) 16

6. 21 : 3 : : 574 : ? **[RRB 2004]**
(A) 23 (B) 82 (C) 97 (D) 113

7. 25 : 125 : : 81 : ?
(A) 180 (B) 706 (C) 729 (D) 625

8. 8 : 81 : : 7 : ? **[CPO 2004]**
(A) 125 (B) 64 (C) 525 (D) 625

9. 25 : 37 : : 49 : ? **[MBA 2004]**
(A) 41 (B) 56 (C) 60 (D) 65

10. 1 : 1 : : 5 : ? **[MTS 2021]**
(A) 26 (B) 125 (C) 240 (D) 625

11. LOGIC : BHFNK : : CLERK : ? **[AFCAT 2016]**
(A) XVRPA (B) QBKJA
(C) LPRTU (D) JQDKB

12. MNO : NML : : TUV : ? **[CPO 2006]**
(A) JHI (B) GFE (C) WVU (D) ABC

13. PALE : LEAP : : POSH : ? **[SNAP 2004]**
(A) HSOP (B) POHS
(C) SHOP (D) None of these

14. GIK : LNP : : BDF : ?
(A) GIK (B) HJL
(C) CEG (D) MOR

15. CIRCLE is related to RICELC in the same way as SQUARE is related to .... ? **[SSC 2015]**
(A) QSUERA (B) UQSREA
(C) UQSAER (D) UQSERA

16. EVTG is related to HSQJ in the same way as CXVE is related to ....? **[CBI 2003]**
(A) EVUF (B) FSUH
(C) FUSH
(D) FUTG

17. PRTV : QSUW : : DFHJ : ?
(A) GIKM (B) KLMN
(C) CEGI (D) EGIK

18. EGI : VTR : : KMO : ? **[SSC 2005]**
(A) WUS (B) PNL (C) JHF (D) DBZ

19. BAG : CCJ : : PEN : ?
(A) QGQ (B) OFO
(C) RGP (D) OCK

20. BCF : HHL : : MNQ : ?
(A) WXY (B) WTX (C) WTV (D) TTX

21. KMF : LLH : : RMS : ? **[AAO Exam 2004]**
(A) SLR (B) SLU (C) SSU (D) SUS

22. BYCX : DWEV : : FUGT : ?**[Hotel Management 2002]**
(A) EHU (B) GHU
(C) HSIR (D) SRHS

23. BUCKET : ACTVBDJLDFSU : : BONUS : ?
(A) ACMNMOTVRT (B) SUNOB
(C) ACNPMOTVRT (D) ACMNMOTURT

24. ACEG : DFHJ : : QSUW : ? **[MBA 2003]**
(A) KMNP (B) MNPR
(C) TOST (D) TVXZ

25. AG : IO : : PV : ?
(A) TU (B) XD (C) XY (D) SV

Level 2 Intermediate

1. EGIK is related to WUSQ in the same way as DFHJ is related to .... ? **[Tax & Central Excise 2002]**
(A) BDFH (B) ECGI
(C) SQOM (D) XVTR

2. STM is related to TSN in the same way as GKL is related to .... ?
(A) KGO (B) KGM (C) GKO (D) HIO

3. RATIONAL is to RATNIOLA as TRIBAL is to.......? **[NMIMS 2005]**
(A) TIRLAB (B) TRIALB
(C) TIRLBA (D) TRILBA

4. BENEFIT is to YVMVURG as POPULAR is to:
(A) KLKFOZI (B) OPUPALR
(C) HZOEKLK (D) RQRWNCT

5. CFED is related to PSQR in the same way as JMKL is related to .... ? **[SSC CGL 2015]**
(A) YXZW (B) YUZX
(C) WZWZ (D) UVXZ

6. USPL is to KMPT as LJGC is to.... ? **[Section Officer 2004]**
(A) BDGK (B) CEHL
(C) GHIJ (D) QSUW

7. ACFJ is related to ZXUQ in the same way as EGJN is related to .... ? **[RRB 2018]**
(A) DBYU (B) VTQM
(C) VTRP (D) VUSQ

8. AEROPLANE is to ARPAENLOE as TELEVISION is to .... ?
(A) CGNCXGUGQL (B) VELETNOSIV
(C) ETELIVISNO (D) TLVSONIIEE

9. As COUNSEL is to BITIRAK so also GUIDANCE is to .... ? **[AIMATS 2002]**
(A) EOHYZKBB (B) FOHYZJBB
(C) FPHZZKAB (D) HOHYBJBA

10. Given set : (9, 15, 21) **[SSC 2017]**
(A) (10, 14, 16) (B) (7, 21, 28)
(C) (5, 10, 25) (D) (4, 8, 12)

11. Given set : (8, 3, 2) **[RRB 2004]**
(A) (10, 6, 5) (B) (63, 8, 3)
(C) (95, 24, 5) (D) (168, 15, 4)

12. Given set : (21, 51, 15) **[SSC CGL 2014]**
(A) (21, 30, 51) (B) (21, 35, 41)
(C) (21, 51, 42) (D) (21, 91, 35)

13. Given set : (6561, 729, 81)
(A) (150, 90, 10) (B) (181, 97, 9)
(C) (144, 243, 9) (D) (2187, 243, 27)

14. Given set : (49, 25, 9) **[UGC 2004]**
(A) (36, 16, 4) (B) (36, 25, 16)
(C) (39, 26, 13) (D) (64, 27, 8)

15. Given set : (6, 13, 22) **[SSC CPO 2019]**
(A) (6, 13, 27) (B) (10, 16, 28)
(C) (11, 18, 27) (D) (13, 19, 32)

16. Given set : (28, 8, 6) **[RRB 2005]**
(A) (13, 7, 2) (B) (21, 12, 10)
(C) (17, 6, 3) (D) (34, 32, 6)

17. Given set : (12, 20, 4) **[MBA 2006]**
(A) (5, 10, 5) (B) (13, 18, 5)
(C) (17, 27, 5) (D) (20, 15, 25)

18. Given set : (14, 23, 32) **[Bank PO 2006]**
(A) (15, 23, 31) (B) (14, 19, 24)
(C) (13, 21, 29) (D) (12, 21, 30)

19. Given set : (246, 345, 417)
(A) (245, 275, 425) (B) (243, 253, 256)
(C) (273, 435, 831) (D) (433, 743, 845)

20. Given set : (99, 77, 55)
(A) (108, 84, 60) (B) (56, 49, 35)
(C) (88, 50, 77) (D) (65, 78, 91)

21. Given set: 992, 733, 845, 632 **[SSC 2017]**
(A) 114 (B) 326 (C) 425 (D) 947

22. Given set: 363, 489, 579 **[AAO 2005]**
(A) 562 (B) 471 (C) 382 (D) 281

23. Given set: 494, 584, 674
(A) 575 (B) 978 (C) 777 (D) 783

24. Given set : 256, 367, 478
(A) 589 (B) 158
(C) 275 (D) 356

25. Given set: 538, 725, 813 **[SSC CGL 2021]**
(A) 814 (B) 712 (C) 328 (D) 219

3 Level Expert

1. Which of the following has the same relationship as Cell : Cytology :: ? **[RRB ASM 2009]**
(A) Worms : Ornithology
(B) Insects : Entomology
(C) Diseases : Physiology
(D) Tissues : Morphology

2. Which of the following has the same relationship as Carpenter : Wood :: ? **[SSC 10+2 2013]**
(A) Teacher : Cloth (B) Tailor : Cloth
(C) Cobbler : Book (D) Cook : Shoes

3. Which of the following has the same relationship as Surgeon : Scalpel :: ? **[MAT 2012]**
(A) Musician : Instrument
(B) Carpenter : Cabinet
(C) Sculptor : Chisel
(D) Baker: Oven

4. Which of the following has the same relationship as (8, 88, 160)?
(A) (8, 70, 99) (B) (9, 90, 150)
(C) (9, 99, 180) (D) (10, 90, 170)

5. Which of the following has the same relationship as Horse : Hoof :: ? **[SSC DEO & LDC 2012]**
(A) Man : Foot
(B) Carpenter : Cabinet
(C) Sculptor : Chisel
(D) Baker : Oven

6. Which of the following has the same relationship as Book : Author :: ? **[CLAT 2013]**
(A) Rain : Flood (B) Light : Switch
(C) Symphony : Composer (D) Song : Music

7. Which of the following has the same relationship as Sailor : Compass :: ? **[PNB Clerk 2011]**
(A) Student : Exam
(B) Doctor : Stethoscope
(C) Pen : Officer
(D) Painter : Artist
(E) Bricks : Plumber

8. Which of the following has the same relationship as Nuts: Bolts :: ? **[CLAT 2013]**

(A) Nitty : Gritty (B) Bare : Feet
(C) Naked : Clothes (D) Hard : Soft

9. Given set: (63, 8, 3)
(A) (10, 6, 5) (B) (575, 24, 5)
(C) (95, 24, 5) (D) (168, 15, 4)

10. Given set: (60, 56, 40)
(A) (90, 85, 60) (B) (85, 70, 40)
(C) (60, 80, 90) (D) (45, 55, 65)

11. Given set: (32, 24, 8) [SSC CPO 2005]
(A) (26, 32, 42) (B) (34, 24, 14)
(C) (24, 16, 0) (D) (42, 34, 16)

12. Peat, Bituminous, Lignite. [RRB 2004]
(A) Coke (B) Granite
(C) Basalt (D) Anthracite

13. Haryana, Goa, Gujarat
(A) Amritsar (B) Allahabad
(C) Punjab (D) Baroda

14. Violet, Blue, Green
(A) Black (B) Orange
(C) White (D) Paint

15. Yuan, Kyat, Lira
(A) Dirham (B) Turkey
(C) Madrid (D) Mass

ANSWER KEY

Level-1: Beginner

1.	(C)	2.	(B)	3.	(B)	4.	(B)	5.	(C)	6.	(B)	7.	(C)	8.	(B)	9.	(D)	10.	(B)
11.	(D)	12.	(B)	13.	(C)	14.	(A)	15.	(D)	16.	(C)	17.	(D)	18.	(B)	19.	(A)	20.	(D)
21.	(B)	22.	(C)	23.	(C)	24.	(D)	25.	(B)										

Level-2: Intermediate

1.	(D)	2.	(A)	3.	(D)	4.	(A)	5.	(C)	6.	(A)	7.	(B)	8.	(D)	9.	(B)	10.	(D)
11.	(B)	12.	(D)	13.	(D)	14.	(A)	15.	(C)	16.	(D)	17.	(B)	18.	(D)	19.	(C)	20.	(A)
21.	(C)	22.	(B)	23.	(A)	24.	(A)	25.	(D)										

Level-3: Expert

1.	(B)	2.	(B)	3.	(C)	4.	(C)	5.	(A)	6.	(C)	7.	(B)	8.	(C)	9.	(B)	10.	(A)
11.	(C)	12.	(D)	13.	(C)	14.	(B)	15.	(A)										

Solutions with Detailed Explanations

Level-1: BEGINNER

1. **Option (C) is correct.**
Explanation: The given pattern is :
$14 + 2 = 16 \Rightarrow 16^2 = 256$
So, $\sqrt{441} - 2 = 21 - 2 = 19$

2. **Option (B) is correct.**
Explanation: The relationship is: $a : (a - 2222)$
Here, we can see: $7528 - 2222 = 5306$
So, 4th term $= 4673 - 2222 = 2451$

3. **Option (B) is correct.**
Explanation: The relationship is: $a : a^2$
We can see,
$12 : 12^2 = 12 : 144$
So, $20 : 20^2 = 20 : 400$

4. **Option (B) is correct.**
Explanation: The given pattern is :
$18 \times 3 + 5 = 59$
So, $27 \times 3 + 5 = 81 + 5 = 86$

5. **Option (C) is correct.**
Explanation: Here we can see,
2nd term $= 6 \times 3 = 18$
Similarly, 4th term $= 4 \times 3 = 12$

6. **Option (B) is correct.**
Explanation: Here we can see, 1st term
$= 2^{nd}$ term $\times 7 = 21$
Similarly, the pattern between 3rd and 4th term
$= 82 \times 7 = 574$

7. **Option (C) is correct.**
Explanation: The relationship is: $a^2 : a^3$
Here we can see
$5^2 : 5^3 = 25 : 125$
Similarly, $9^2 : 9^3 = 81 : 729$

8. **Option (B) is correct.**
Explanation: The relationship is: $a : (a + 1)^2$
Here, we can see,
$(8 + 1)^2 = 81$
Similarly, $(7 + 1)^2 = 8^2 = 64$

9. Option (D) is correct.
Explanation: The relationship is: $a^2 : (a + 1)^2 + 1$
Here, we can see,
$5^2 : (5 + 1)^2 + 1 = 25 : 37$
So, missing term = $(7 + 1)^2 + 1 = 65$

10. Option (B) is correct.
Explanation: Here, $1^3 = 1$
Similarly, $5^3 = 125$

11. Option (D) is correct.
Explanation: The given pattern, letters coming just before the letters of first word, i.e., letter before L is K, before O is N, before G is F, before I is H and before C is B and they are arranged in reverse order.
Applying the same rule on letters of the third word. Letter coming before C is B, before L is K, before E is D, before R is Q and before K is J.
Now arranging in reverse order, we get JQDKB.

12. Option (B) is correct.
Explanation: The relationship between each letter of the first group is moved opposite letter forward to obtain the corresponding letter of the second group.
So, the missing term = GFE

13. Option (C) is correct.
Explanation: The first, second, third and fourth letters of the second group are respectively the third, fourth, second and first letter of the first group.
So, the missing term = SHOP

14. Option (A) is correct.
Explanation: The pattern is :

G	I	K
+5 ↓	+5 ↓	+5 ↓
L	N	P

So,

B	D	F
+5 ↓	+5 ↓	+5 ↓
G	I	K

15. Option (D) is correct.
Explanation: The first three letters and the last three letters of the first group are written in a reverse order to obtain the second group.
So, the missing term = UQSERA

16. Option (C) is correct.
Explanation: The first and fourth letters of the group are each moved three steps forward and the second and third letters are each moved three steps backward to obtain the corresponding letters of the second group.
So, the missing term
= (C+3)(X–3)(V–3)(E+3) = FUSH

17. Option (D) is correct.
Explanation: The second group is obtained by adding 1 letter to the first group.

18. Option (B) is correct.
Explanation: The relationship between each letter of the first group is moved opposite letter forward to obtain the corresponding letter of the second group.
So, the missing term = PNL

19. Option (A) is correct.
Explanation: The pattern is

B	A	G
+1 ↓	+2 ↓	+3 ↓
C	C	J

So,

P	E	N
+1 ↓	+2 ↓	+3 ↓
Q	G	Q

20. Option (D) is correct.
Explanation: BCF forms a sequence of alternate letters while in HHL the first two letters are consecutive and there is a gap of two letters between the second and third letters.
Similarly, MNQ forms a sequence of alternate letters, the group having properties similar to HHL is TTX.

21. Option (B) is correct.
Explanation: The first letter of the first group is moved one step forward, the second letter is moved one steps backward and the third letter is moved two steps forward to obtain the corresponding letter of the second group.
So, the missing term = (R+1)(M–1)(S+2) = SLU

22. Option (C) is correct.
Explanation: The first and third letter of the first group are each moved two steps forward, the second and fourth letter are each moved two steps backward obtained the corresponding letters of the second group.
So, the missing term=(F+2)(U–2)(G+2)(T–2) = HSIR

23. Option (C) is correct.
Explanation: Each letter of the first group is replaced by two letter, one that come, after it and one that comes before it in the second group.
So, the missing term = ACNPMOTVRT

24. Option (D) is correct.
Explanation: The relationship between each letter of the first group is moved three steps forward to obtain the corresponding letter of the second group.
So, missing term = (Q+3)(S+3)(U+3)(W+3) = TVXZ

25. Option (B) is correct.
Explanation: The relationship between each letter of the first group is moved eight steps forward to obtain the corresponding letter of the second group.
So, the 4th term = (P+8)(V+8) = XD

Level-2: INTERMEDIATE

1. Option (D) is correct.
Explanation: E, G, I, K are fifth, seventh, ninth and eleventh letters from the beginning of the alphabet and W, U, S, Q are fourth, sixth, eighth and tenth letters from the end of the alphabet.
Similarly, D, F, H, J are fourth, sixth, eighth and tenth letters from the beginning of the alphabet. So, the required group will consist of letters which are third, fifth, seventh and ninth from the end of the alphabet.

2. **Option (A) is correct.**
Explanation: The first two letters of the first group are written in a reverse order in the second group. 'The third letter is replaced by a letter occupying the same position from the end of the English alphabet, as it occupies from the beginning.
3. **Option (D) is correct.**
Explanation: The first three letters do not shift their positions. The next three letters show a cyclic movement.
So, TRIBAL will be written as TRILBA.
4. **Option (A) is correct.**
Explanation: All the letters of the first group are replaced by the corresponding letters from the other end of the alphabet in the second group.
5. **Option (C) is correct.**
Explanation: The first and second letters in the first group are each moved 13 steps forward, the third letters is moved 12 steps forward and the fourth letters is moved 14 steps forward to obtain the corresponding letters of the second group.
So, the missing term = (J+13)(M+13)(K+12)(L+14) = WZWZ
6. **Option (A) is correct.**
Explanation: The letters of the first group are first written in a reverse order. Then, first and fourth letters of the group are each moved one step backward and the second and third letters are each moved three steps backward to obtain the corresponding letters of the second group.
7. **Option (B) is correct.**
Explanation: A, C, F and J are first, third, sixth and tenth letters from the beginning of English alphabet and are replaced by corresponding letters from the end of the alphabet in the second group. A similar relationship exists between the third and fourth groups.
So, the missing term = VTQM
8. **Option (D) is correct.**
Explanation: The alternate letters of the first group, starting from the first letter are first written, and then the remaining letters are written in the reverse order to obtain the second group.
So, TELEVISION will be written as TLVSONIIEE.
9. **Option (B) is correct.**
Explanation: The first, third, fifth and seventh letters of the first group are each moved one step backward to obtain the corresponding letters of the second group. The movement of other letters is not required to find the answer.
10. **Option (D) is correct.**
Explanation: The relationship is $(3 \times 3, 3 \times 5, 3 \times 7)$
Hence, $(2 \times 2, 2 \times 4, 2 \times 6)$ is the correct answer.
11. **Option (B) is correct.**
Explanation: Here, (8, 3, 2)
$3^2 - 1 = 8, 2^2 - 1 = 3$
Now, $8^2 - 1 = 63, 3^2 - 1 = 8$
(63, 8, 3)
12. **Option (D) is correct.**
Explanation: In each set, 2nd number = 2 (3rd number) + 1st number
13. **Option (D) is correct.**
Explanation: All the numbers in each set can be expressed in terms of powers of 3 i.e., $6561 = 3^8$, $729 = 3^6$, $81 = 3^4$.
So, correct answer is (2187, 243, 27)
14. **Option (A) is correct.**
Explanation: Each set contains squares of three consecutive alternate numbers in reverse order.
Thus, $3^2 = 9, 5^2 = 25, 7^2 = 49$.
So, the correct answer is (36, 16, 4)
15. **Option (C) is correct.**
Explanation: In each, 2nd number = 1st number + 7; 3rd number = 2nd number +9.
16. **Option (D) is correct.**
Explanation: The relationship is each set consists of only even numbers.
17. **Option (B) is correct.**
Explanation: The sum of numbers in each set is 36.
18. **Option (D) is correct.**
Explanation: In each set, Second number – first number = 9
Third number – second number = 9
19. **Option (C) is correct.**
Explanation: The sum of digits of the numbers in the set is 12.
20. **Option (A) is correct.**
Explanation: Each set consists of numbers which are obtained by multiplying a certain number by 9, 7 and 5 respectively.
Here, in the given set, $11 \times 9 = 99, 11 \times 7 = 77, 11 \times 55$.
Similarly, $12 \times 9 = 108, 12 \times 7 = 84, 12 \times 5 = 60$.
21. **Option (C) is correct.**
Explanation: : In all the numbers, the middle digit is the sum of the digits of the product of other two digits.
Now, $9 \times 2 = 18, 1 + 8 = 9$ (middle digit in 992);
$7 \times 3 = 21, 2 + 1 = 3$ (Middle digit in 733);
$8 \times 5 = 40, 4 + 0 = 4$ (Middle digit in 845)find so on.
So, in option (C), $4 \times 5 = 20, 2 + 0 = 2$ (middle digit in 425)
22. **Option (B) is correct.**
Explanation:

Number	Sum of digits	New sum of digits
363	$3 + 6 + 3 = 12$	$1 + 2 = 3$
489	$4 + 8 + 9 = 21$	$2 + 1 = 3$
579	$5 + 7 + 9 = 21$	$2 + 1 = 3$
471	$4 + 7 + 1 = 12$	$1 + 2 = 3$

23. **Option (A) is correct.**
Explanation: In all the numbers, the sum of digits is 17 and the largest digit lies in the middle.
$494 = 4 + 9 + 4 = 17$
$584 = 5 + 8 + 4 = 17$
$674 = 6 + 7 + 4 = 17$
Now, $575 = 5 + 7 + 5 = 17$
24. **Option (A) is correct.**
Explanation: The first digits of the numbers form the series 2, 3, 4, 5

The second digits of the numbers form the series 5, 6, 7, 8.

The last digits of the numbers form the series 6, 7, 8, 9.

So, the correct answer is 589.

25. Option (D) is correct.

Explanation: In all the numbers, (first digit + third digit) – Middle digit = 10.

Thus, $5 + 8 - 3 = 10, 7 + 5 - 2 = 10, 8 + 3 - 1 = 10$.

Level-3: EXPERT

1. Option (B) is correct.

Explanation: Cytology is the science of study of Cells. In the same way, Entomology is the science of study of Insects.

2. Option (B) is correct.

Explanation: As, a carpenter uses wood. Similarly, a tailor uses cloth.

3. Option (C) is correct.

Explanation: A scalpel is used by a surgeon during an operation, in the same way, a sculptor uses his chisel for carting sculptures.

4. Option (C) is correct.

Explanation:

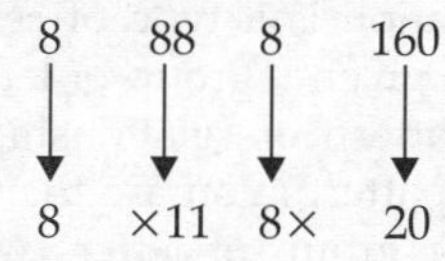

Similarly,

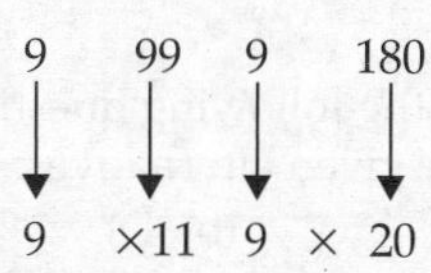

5. Option (A) is correct.

Explanation: The hoofs of an animal such as a Horse are the hard lower parts of its feet. In the same way, foot is the lower part of a man.

6. Option (C) is correct.

Explanation: A book is written by an author. Similarly, symphony is composed by a composer.

7. Option (B) is correct.

Explanation: Sailor judges the direction through Compass. A doctor checks the breathing and heart beats through a Stethoscope.

8. Option (C) is correct.

Explanation: As, Nuts are covered with Bolts. Similarly, Naked is covered with Clothes.

9. Option (B) is correct.

Explanation: Here,

$8^2 - 1 = 63$

$3^2 - 1 = 8$

Similarly,

$24^2 - 1 = 575$

$5^2 - 1 = 24$

10. Option (A) is correct.

Explanation: Given,

$60 - 4 = 56, 56 - 4^2 = 40$

Then, $90 - 5 = 85, 85 - 5^2 = 60$

11. Option (C) is correct.

Explanation: $32 - 24 = 8, 24 - 16 = 8$

Similarly,

$24 - 8 = 16$

$16 - 16 = 0$

12. Option (D) is correct.

Explanation: Anthracite is a type of a coal.

13. Option (C) is correct.

Explanation: All are the Indian states.

14. Option (B) is correct.

Explanation: All are the colours of the rainbow.

15. Option (A) is correct.

Explanation: All are the currencies of different countries.

■ ■ ■

Chapter 3

Classification

LEARNING OBJECTIVES:

- Questions based on number classification
- Questions based on letter classification
- Different types of questions asked in competitive exams

NUMBER CLASSIFICATION

Number classification is a type of reasoning question that involves analysing a set of numbers and identifying the pattern or rule that governs their arrangement. In these type of questions, a series of numbers is given, and the task is to classify them into different groups based on some specific criteria or logic.

Example 1: Select the odd one out.

(a) 34 (b) 36
(c) 40 (d) 44

Sol. (a) Except 34, all others are multiples of 4.

Example 2: Choose the one which is different from the rest four.

(a) 2 (b) 32
(c) 56 (d) 128

Sol. (c) Each of the numbers except 56, can be expressed in terms of power of 2.

LETTER CLASSIFICATION

Letter classification is a type of reasoning question where you are given a group of letters and asked to identify the pattern or relationship between them. Based on this pattern, you are then asked to choose which letter or group of letters would fit into the same category.

Example 3: In the following question, select the odd letters from the given alternatives.

(a) KQ (b) DJ
(c) SZ (d) RX

Sol. (c) Here, Q is 6 alphabets ahead of K, J is 6 alphabets ahead of D, and X is 6 alphabets ahead of R. So, the 6 alphabet ahead of S will be Y not Z.

Example 4: Choose the group of letters which is different from others.

(a) H (b) Q
(c) T (d) Z

Sol. (b) All the other alphabets are at even number positions.

Level 1 Beginner

Direction: Find the odd one out that does not belong to the group in the given question.

1. **(A)** Zinc **(B)** Bronze
   (C) Silver **(D)** Platinum
   [SSC CGL 2013]
2. **(A)** Huge **(B)** Tiny
   (C) Heavy **(D)** Small
   (E) Big
3. **(A)** Swimming **(B)** Sailing
   (C) Diving **(D)** Driving
   (E) Boating [EPEO 2011]
4. **(A)** Gallon **(B)** Ton
   (C) Quintal **(D)** Kilogram
   [SSC CPO 2021]
5. **(A)** Hexagon **(B)** Pentagon
   (C) Circle **(D)** Triangle
   (E) Octagon
6. **(A)** Walk **(B)** Pull
   (C) Hear **(D)** Jump
   (E) Run [RBI 2003]
7. **(A)** Monitor **(B)** Pencil
   (C) Keyboard **(D)** Mouse

8. (A) Indigo (B) Violet
(C) Yellow (D) Pink
(E) Blue

9. (A) Herd (B) Flight
(C) Hound (D) Swarm
[SSC Steno 2013]

10. (A) Ring (B) Tyre
(C) Plate (D) Bangle
(E) Rubber tube
[SBI Clerk 2011]

11. (A) Frequency (B) Rectangle
(C) Bar (D) Pi
[SSC Steno 2013]

12. (A) Carpenter (B) Goldsmith
(C) Blacksmith (D) Driver
[SSC Constable 2013]

13. (A) Rigveda (B) Yajurveda
(C) Atharveda (D) Ayurveda
(E) Samaveda

14. (A) Grapes (B) Apple
(C) Pineapple (D) Onion

15. (A) 9, 49 (B) 13, 121
(C) 10, 61 (D) 7, 25
[SSC CPO 2013]

16. (A) 14, 17, 23 (B) 19, 22, 28
(C) 17, 20, 26 (D) 21, 23, 30
[SSC Steno 2013]

17. (A) 257 (B) 369 (C) 426 (D) 356

18. (A) 24 (B) 60 (C) 124 (D) 210
[SSC CGL 2019]

19. (A) 4867 (B) 5555 (C) 6243 (D) 6655
[RRB Group D 2011]

20. (A) 729 (B) 130 (C) 145 (D) 40

21. (A) 227 (B) 201 (C) 240 (D) 340

22. (A) 25 (B) 36 (C) 9 (D) 18

23. (A) 65 (B) 45 (C) 81 (D) 20

24. (A) 11 (B) 44 (C) 19 (D) 13

25. (A) 46, 57 (B) 38, 49 (C) 41, 52 (D) 64,73
[SSC CGL 2020]

Level 2 Intermediate

Direction: Find the odd one that does not belong to the group in the given questions.

1. (A) Mountain (B) Hill
(C) Plateau (D) Plane

2. (A) Cholera (B) Aids
(C) Cancer (D) Health
(E) Jaundice
[LIC AAO 2011]

3. (A) Pellagra (B) Beriberi
(C) Anemia (D) Influenza

4. (A) Cube (B) Cuboid
(C) Sphere (D) Circle

5. (A) Brass (B) Gun metal
(C) Bronze (D) Germanium
[SSC Steno 2013]

6. (A) Barter (B) Purchase
(C) Sale (D) Borrow
[SSC 10+2 2013]

7. (A) Table (B) Stool
(C) Chair (D) Blackboard

8. (A) Moon (B) Venus
(C) Mars (D) Jupiter

9. (A) Coat (B) Sweater
(C) Cap (D) Shorts
[SSC Multitaksing 2012]

10. (A) Sweetness (B) Grassful
(C) Bright (D) Pretty

11. (A) Ship (B) Cruise
(C) Boat (D) Car

12. (A) Guitar (B) Flute
(C) Piano (D) Sexophone

13. (A) Graph (B) Chart
(C) Model (D) Drawing
(E) Figure
[IBPS Clerk 2012]

14. (A) Asia (B) South America
(C) Australia (D) Africa
(E) England
[SSC 10+2 2013]

15. (A) PQXZ (B) BCQN
(C) MNPR (D) GHJL
[Corporation Bank PO 2012]

16. (A) 35:1221 (B) 21:437
(C) 11:118 (D) 33:1085
[SSC CGL 2020]

17. (A) A (B) E
(C) I (D) Z
(E) U
[SSC 10+2 2013]

18. (A) GMS (B) EKQ
(C) JOU (D) LRX
(E) BHN
[SSC CPO 2019]

19. (A) A (B) M
(C) D (D) J
(E) L

20. (A) 5 : 25 : 125 (B) 7 : 49 : 343
(C) 4 : 16 : 64 (D) 9 : 81 : 729

21. (A) 2-8 (B) 3-27
(C) 4-32 (D) 5-125
(E) 6-216
[SBI Clerk 2012]

22. (A) 121 (B) 81
(C) 49 (D) 729
(E) 225

23. (A) 36 (B) 144 (C) 196 (D) 27 (E) 728 [SSC Multitasking 2013]
24. (A) 120 (B) 168 (C) 290 (D) 380
25. (A) 2316 (B) 3238 (C) 2305 (D) 3015

Level 3 Expert

1. Three of the following four numbers are alike in a certain way and one is different. Identify the different one.
   (A) 215 (B) 121 (C) 324 (D) 625
2. Select the odd one out.
   (A) Lion-Roar (B) Snake-Hiss
   (C) Bees-Hum (D) Frog-Bleat
   (E) Dog-Bark [IBPS Clerk 2011]
3. Select the odd one out.
   (A) Dim : Bright (B) Wrong : Right
   (C) Shallow : Deep (D) Genuine : Real
   (E) Involvement : Indifference [IBPS Clerk 2011]
4. Select the odd one out.
   (A) Needle-prick (B) Gun-fire
   (C) Auger-Bore (D) Chisel-carve
   [SSC (LDC & DEO), 2012]
5. Select the odd one out.
   (A) Petrol-Car
   (B) Electricity-Television
   (C) Ink-Pen
   (D) Dust-Vacuum cleaner [LIC AAO 2012]
6. Three of the following four words are alike in a certain way and one is different. Find the odd one out.
   [SSC CPO Exam 2019]
   (A) Cairo (B) Paris (C) Ottawa (D) Kyat
7. Select the odd one out.
   (A) Captain : Team (B) Boss : Gang
   (C) Prime-Minister : Cabinet (D) Artist : Troupe
   [RRB Group D 2012]
8. Select the odd one out.
   (A) Morning : Evening (B) Inside : Outside
   (C) Across : Along (D) Small : Big
9. Select the odd one out.
   (A) Circle : Arc (B) Line : Dot
   (C) Hexagon : Angle (D) Square : Line
   [SSC 10+2 201]
10. Select the odd one out.
    (A) Hard : Soft (B) Pointed : Blunt
    (C) Sweet : Sour (D) Long : High
    (E) Day : Night [LIC ADO 2012]
11. Select the odd one out.
    (A) 339 (B) 326 (C) 428 (D) 338
    [SSC CGL 2015]
12. In the following question, select the odd number from the given alternatives. [SSC CGL 2017]
    (A) 253 (B) 473 (C) 143 (D) 633
13. Select the odd one out.
    (A) 9-12 (B) 5-8 (C) 6-9 (D) 3-5
14. In the following question, select the odd word pair from the given alternatives. [SSC CGL Exam 2017]
    (A) Venus : Planet (B) Moon : Satellite
    (C) Jupiter : Black Hole (D) Sun : Star
15. Select the odd one out.
    (A) 25-16 (B) 61-36 (C) 58-22 (D) 44-30

ANSWER KEY

Level-1: Beginner

1.	(A)	2.	(C)	3.	(D)	4.	(A)	5.	(C)	6.	(C)	7.	(B)	8.	(D)	9.	(C)	10.	(C)
11.	(B)	12.	(D)	13.	(D)	14.	(D)	15.	(C)	16.	(D)	17.	(D)	18.	(C)	19.	(D)	20.	(A)
21.	(C)	22.	(D)	23.	(C)	24.	(B)	25.	(D)										

Level-2: Intermediate

1.	(D)	2.	(D)	3.	(D)	4.	(D)	5.	(D)	6.	(D)	7.	(D)	8.	(A)	9.	(D)	10.	(A)
11.	(D)	12.	(B)	13.	(C)	14.	(E)	15.	(B)	16.	(B)	17.	(D)	18.	(C)	19.	(A)	20.	(C)
21.	(C)	22.	(D)	23.	(D)	24.	(D)	25.	(D)										

Level-3: Expert

1.	(A)	2.	(D)	3.	(D)	4.	(A)	5.	(D)	6.	(D)	7.	(D)	8.	(C)	9.	(C)	10.	(D)
11.	(D)	12.	(D)	13.	(D)	14.	(C)	15.	(D)										

Solutions with Detailed Explanations

Level-1: BEGINNER

1. **Option (A) is correct.**
Explanation: Zinc is the only metal in the group that is not a precious metal.
2. **Option (C) is correct.**
Explanation: All the other words are related to size or dimensions. But "heavy" is related to weight.
3. **Option (D) is correct.**
Explanation: The practise of "driving" on a street or highway. But all others are related to water.
4. **Option (A) is correct.**
Explanation: "Gallon' is used for liquids. But others are used for weight measurements.
5. **Option (C) is correct.**
Explanation: Except circle, all others are polygons.
6. **Option (C) is correct.**
Explanation: Except hearing, all others are activities done physically.
7. **Option (B) is correct.**
Explanation: Only pencil is a stationery item.
8. **Option (D) is correct.**
Explanation: Except pink, all others are colours of rainbow.
9. **Option (C) is correct.**
Explanation: The other three options are all used to describe groups of animals. But "Hound" is related to a single breed of dogs.
10. **Option (C) is correct.**
Explanation: A "plate" is typically round but it is not a circular shape. The other options are all circular in shape. So, the right answer is a plate.
11. **Option (B) is correct.**
Explanation: Other options are related to graph. But rectangle is a geometrical figure.
12. **Option (D) is correct.**
Explanation: All the other options are professions that involve working with tools and materials to create, "driver" serve his work.
13. **Option (D) is correct.**
Explanation: The other option is related to Veda. But Ayurveda is branch of medicine.
14. **Option (D) is correct.**
Explanation: Except onion, all others are fruits.
15. **Option (C) is correct.**
Explanation:
Here, $9 - 2 = 7; 7^2 = 49$
$13 - 2 = 11; 11^2 = 121$
$10 - 2 = 8; 8^2 \neq 61$
$7 - 2 = 5; 5^2 = 25$
16. **Option (D) is correct.**
Explanation:
Here, $14 + 3 = 17 \rightarrow 17 + 6 = 23$
$19 + 3 = 22 \rightarrow 22 + 6 = 28$
$17 + 3 = 20 \rightarrow 20 + 6 = 26$
$21 + (2) = 23 \rightarrow 23 + (7) = 30$
17. **Option (D) is correct.**
Explanation: Here,
Sum of the first and second digit = last digit
But, $3 + 5 = 8 \neq 6$
18. **Option (C) is correct.**
Explanation:
Here, 124 is not a multiple of 3. All other numbers are multiple of 3.
19. **Option (D) is correct.**
Explanation:
Here, $4867 = 4 + 8 + 6 + 7 = 25$ (Divisible by 5)
$5555 = 5 + 5 + 5 + 5 = 20$ (Divisible by 5)
$6243 = 6 + 2 + 4 + 3 = 15$ (Divisible by 5)
$6655 = 6 + 6 + 5 + 5 = 22$ (Not divisible by 5)
20. **Option (A) is correct.**
Explanation: Here,
$9^3 = 729$ {Perfect cube}.
21. **Option (C) is correct.**
Explanation:
Here, $227 = 2 + 2 + 7 = 11$ (Prime number)
$201 = 2 + 0 + 1 = 3$ (Prime number)
$240 = 2 + 4 + 0 = 6$ (Not a prime number)
$340 = 3 + 4 + 0 = 7$ (Prime number)
22. **Option (D) is correct.**
Explanation: Here, 18 is not a perfect square number.
23. **Option (C) is correct.**
Explanation:
Here, $81 = 9^2$ [square of root]
All other options are common numbers.
24. **Option (B) is correct.**
Explanation: Here,
44 is not a prime number.
But other options are prime number.
25. **Option (D) is correct.**
Explanation:
Here, $46 + 11 = 57$
$38 + 11 = 49$
$41 + 11 = 52$
$64 + 11 = 75 \neq 73$

Level-2: INTERMEDIATE

1. **Option (D) is correct.**
Explanation: All three options have height.
2. **Option (D) is correct.**
Explanation: Except health, all are different types of disorders.
3. **Option (D) is correct.**
Explanation: Influenza is the right answer. Other diseases are causes by any vitamins.
4. **Option (D) is correct.**
Explanation: Here, circle is the right answer. Other options are 3-D shapes.
5. **Option (D) is correct.**
Explanation: Germanium is an element. Brass, gun metal, bronze are alloy.
6. **Option (D) is correct.**
Explanation: Except "Borrow", all are business words.
7. **Option (D) is correct.**
Explanation: Here, other three options are use for sitting.
8. **Option (A) is correct.**
Explanation: Except moon, all others are planets.
9. **Option (D) is correct.**
Explanation: Except shorts, all others are winter wears.
10. **Option (A) is correct.**
Explanation: All with the exception of sweetness are connected to beauty. While sweetness is connected to taste.
11. **Option (D) is correct.**
Explanation: Here, Car is the only mode of transportation i.e., road transport.
12. **Option (B) is correct.**
Explanation: Only flute is played with mouth.
13. **Option (C) is correct.**
Explanation: Other options are made on paper.
14. **Option (E) is correct.**
Explanation: England is the right answer. Other are continents.
15. **Option (B) is correct.**
Explanation: All other three alternatives final two letters have a one-letter gap, hence they are all the same.
16. **Option (B) is correct.**
Explanation:

Option (A): $35 = (3 + 5 = 8)$
$1221 = (1 + 2 + 2 + 1) = 6$
Option (B): $21 = (2 + 1 = 3)$
$437 = (4 + 3 + 7) = 14$
Option (C): $11 = (1 + 1 = 2)$
$118 = (1 + 1 + 8 = 10)$
Option (D): $33 = (3 + 3 = 6)$
$1085 = (1 + 0 + 8 + 5) = 14$

Except option (B), all others option have even sum.

17. **Option (D) is correct.**
Explanation: Other four options are vowels but Z is not a vowel.
18. **Option (C) is correct.**
Explanation: Every other group's first and third letters are similarly spaced apart from the central letter in relation to their positions in the English alphabet.
19. **Option (A) is correct.**
Explanation: Other four options are consonants but A is not a consonant.
20. **Option (C) is correct.**
Explanation: Three options are arranged like $= [a : a^2 : a^3]$
21. **Option (C) is correct.**
Explanation: Second number is cube of the first number.
22. **Option (D) is correct.**
Explanation: Only number in option (D) is a perfect cube.
23. **Option (D) is correct.**
Explanation: 27 is not a perfect square number.
24. **Option (D) is correct.**
Explanation: Except 380, every other integer is either one less than or one greater than the square of a number.
25. **Option (D) is correct.**
Explanation:

$$2316 = 2 + 3 + 6 - 1 = 10$$
$$3238 = 3 + 2 + 8 - 3 = 10$$
$$2305 = 2 + 3 + 5 - 0 = 10$$
$$3015 = 3 + 0 + 5 - 1 = 7$$

Level-3: EXPERT

1. **Option (A) is correct.**
Explanation: All the three options are perfect square but 215 is not a perfect square.
2. **Option (D) is correct.**
Explanation: Frogs do not bleat.
3. **Option (D) is correct.**
Explanation: In option (D), two words are synonyms .
4. **Option (A) is correct.**
Explanation: Needle-Prick is the right answer. This is not an instrument action pair.
5. **Option (D) is correct.**
Explanation: A car needs petrol to run. Television needs electricity to run. A pen needs ink for writing. A vacuum cleaner is used for dust cleaning. So, option (D) is correct.
6. **Option (D) is correct.**
Explanation: Ottawa is the capital of Canada, Paris is the capital of France, Cairo is the capital of Egypt. But Kyat is currency of Myanmar. So, option (D) is correct.
7. **Option (D) is correct.**
Explanation: In other, the first one is head of second.

8. **Option (C) is correct.**
Explanation: Pairs like Small-Big, Inside-Outside, and Morning-Evening signify the inverse relationship between them. Conversely, across and along are synonyms.

9. **Option (C) is correct.**
Explanation: Hexagon is not made from an angle.

10. **Option (D) is correct.**
Explanation: All options contain the opposite of the second words.

11. **Option (D) is correct.**
Explanation:
Here,
$$339 = 3 \times 3 = 9$$
$$326 = 3 \times 2 = 6$$
$$428 = 4 \times 2 = 8$$
$$338 = 3 \times 3 = 9 \neq 8.$$

12. **Option (D) is correct.**
Explanation: Here, all other numbers are divisible by 11. But 633 is not divisible by 11.

13. **Option (D) is correct.**
Explanation:
$$9 + 3 = 12$$
$$5 + 3 = 8$$
$$6 + 3 = 9$$
But
$$3 + 2 = 5$$

14. **Option (C) is correct.**
Explanation: Venus is a planet. Moon is a satellite. Sun is a star. Where Jupiter is not a black hole. So, option (C) is correct.

15. **Option (D) is correct.**
Explanation:
Here,
$$25 - 16 = 9 = 3^2$$
$$61 - 36 = 25 = 5^2$$
$$58 - 22 = 36 = 6^2$$
$$44 - 30 = 14$$
14 is not a square of any number.

■ ■ ■

Coding-Decoding

LEARNING OBJECTIVES:

- Questions based on letter coding
- Questions based on number coding
- Questions based on mixed coding
- Different types of questions asked in competitive exams

The individuals in charge of transmitting and receiving a code or signal are commonly referred to as the sender and receiver, respectively. Decoding refers to the action taken by the receiver to interpret the transmitted codes or signals. Coding-decoding questions typically involve encoding a word, usually a fundamental term, in a specific way and then requiring test takers to encode other words using the same rule. The goal of coding and decoding exams is to assess a candidate's understanding of the encoding rule applied to a specific word or message, as well as their ability to decipher the code and decode the message.

LETTER CODING -DECODING

In this category, we deal with the questions where the letters of a word are swapped out particularly for other letters in accordance with a predetermined pattern or rule to create a code. You must recognise the coding pattern and, using that coding pattern, answer the subsequent question(s).

Example 1: If in a certain language MYSTIFY is coded as NZTUJGZ, how is NEMESIS coded in that language?

(a) MDLHRDR (b) OFNFTJT
(c) ODNHTDR (d) PGOKUGU

Sol. (b) It is obvious that each letter in the term MYSTIFY is advanced one space to correspond to a letter in the code.

M Y S T I F Y
N Z T U J G Z

So, NEMESIS will be coded as OFNFTJT.

Example 2: In a certain code, SIKKIM is written as THLJJL. How is TRAINING written in that code?

(a) SQBHOHOH (b) UQBHOHOF
(c) UQBJOHHO (d) UQBJOHOH

Sol. (b) Clearly, it is obvious that to obtain the letters of the code, the letters in the word SIKKIM are alternately moved one step forward and one step backward.

We can see in this figure

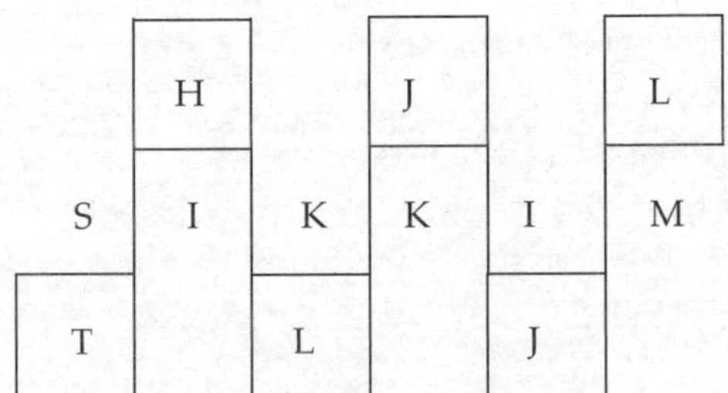

So, TRAINING will be coded as UQBHOHOF.

NUMBER CODING–DECODING

➢ In these questions, either a word is given a numerical code value or the numbers are given alphabetical code letters. The candidate must analyses the code in accordance with the instructions.

Example 3: If in a certain language A is coded as 1, B is coded as 2, and so on, how is BIDDIC coded in that code?

(a) 294493 (b) 284563
(c) 375582 (d) 394492

Sol. (a) As given, the letters are coded as

A	B	C	D	E	F	G	H	I
1	2	3	4	5	6	7	8	9

So, in BIDDIC, B is coded as 2, I as 9, D as 4, and C as 3. So, BIDDIC=294493

Example 4: If D = 4 and COVER = 63, then BASIS = ?

(a) 49 (b) 50
(c) 54 (d) 55

Sol. (b) Clearly, in the given code,

A = 1, B = 2, C = 3, D = 4 .....

So,that COVER = 3 + 15 + 22 + 5 + 18 = 63

Now, BASIS = 2 + 1 + 19 + 9 + 19 = 50

MIXED CODING-DECODING

- In mixed coding-decoding problems, you are typically given a set of rules or patterns that govern the coding and decoding of information. These rules define how certain elements or attributes of the information are represented or transformed using symbols. Your task is to analyse the given information and apply the rules to decode or encode new pieces of information.

Example 5: In a certain code, 2 is coded as P, 3 as N, 9 as Q, 5 as R, 4 as A and 6 as B. How is 599423 coded in that code?

(a) EIIDBC (b) RQPANB
(c) EIMDBC (d) RQQAPN

Sol. (d) Clearly, as given 5 is coded as R, 9 as Q, 4 as A, 2 as P and 3 as N. So, RQQAPN = 599423

Example 6: In a certain code, 3456 is coded as ROPE, 15526 is coded as APPLE, then how is 54613 coded?

(a) RPPEO (b) ROPEA
(c) POEAR (d) PAREO

Sol. (c) We can see, the number are coded as

3	4	5	6	1	2
R	O	P	E	A	L

So, 54613 = POEAR

1 Level Beginner

1. If in a certain code, BAT =23 and CAT =24, then how will you code BALL? **[BBS 2004]**
(A) 27 (B) 28
(C) 32 (D) 120

2. In a certain code, ROAD is written as URDG. How is SWAN written in that code? **[BTM 2006]**
(A) VXDQ (B) VZDQ
(C) VZCP (D) UXDQ

3. If A = 2, M = 26, Z = 52, then RATE = ?
(A) 78 (B) 88
(C) 64 (D) 50

4. If FLOWER is coded as 14 and DISTASTE is coded as 18, then how will BUREAUCRAT be coded as? **[SSC CGL Exam, 2019]**
(A) 22 (B) 18
(C) 20 (D) 28

5. If DEER = 12215 and HIGH = 5645, how will you code HEEL? **[MAT 2002]**
(A) 2328 (B) 3449
(C) 4337 (D) 5229

6. If A = 26, RUN = 28, Then RAT = ?
(A) 24 (B) 40
(C) 42 (D) 38

7. In a certain code language, STRAIGHT is written as TSARGITH. How will THURSDAY be written as in that language? **[SSC CGL Exam, 2020]**
(A) UHTDRSYA (B) HTRUDSYA
(C) HTRUDSAY (D) AYSDURTH

8. If in a certain code, LUTE is as MUTE and FATE is written as GATE, then how will BLUE be written in that code? **[Bank PO 2004]**
(A) CLUE (B) GLUE (C) FLUE (D) SLUE

9. In a certain code, RUMOUR is written as QVLPTS. How is DANGER written in that code?
(A) EBDHFS (B) CBMHDS
(C) BEHOSF (D) BCHMSD

10. If each of the letters in the English alphabet is assigned odd numerical value beginning A = 1, B = 3 and so on, what will be the total value of the letters of the word INDIAN? **[RBI 2002]**
(A) 86 (B) 88
(C) 89 (D) 96
(E) None of these

11. In a certain code language, SERVANT is coded as 195182211420. How will MAGNIFY be coded as in that language? **[SSC CGL Exam, 2020]**
(A) 1426693625 (B) 1316143522
(C) 1317149625 (D) 1417139625

12. In a certain code, PRODUCTIONS is written as QQPCVEUHPMT. How is ORIENTATION written in that code? **[MBA 2002]**
(A) PQJDOVBSJNO (B) PQJDOUBUJPO
(C) PSJFOVBSJNO (D) NSHFMVBSJNO
(E) None of these

13. If FISH is written as EHRG in a certain code, how would JUNGLE be written in that code? **[SSC 2000]**
(A) ITMFKD (B) ITNFKD
(C) KVOHMF (D) TIMFKD

14. If AT = 20, CAT = 60, then MAT will be equal to?
(A) 300 (B) 500
(C) 260 (D) 270

15. In a certain code language, LARVAE is coded as 3-1-9-4-1-5, how will INSECT be coded as in that language? **[SSC CGL Exam, 2020]**
(A) 9-4-8-4-6-7 (B) 3-4-8-2-6-8
(C) 9-4-8-2-6-7 (D) 9-5-10-5-3-2

16. In code language 43720 is coded as 52811. What will be the code for 75163 in that language?
(A) 75340 (B) 85643
(C) 84254 (D) 85374

17. If SUMMER is coded as RUNNER, the code for WINTER will be? **[UPSC 2004]**
(A) SUITER (B) VIOUER
(C) WALKER (D) SUFFER

18. If, in a code, MODE becomes KMBC and RIGHT becomes PGEFR, then what will CREATE be in that code?

(A) APCYRC (B) PAYARC
(C) DSFBUF (D) BQDZSD

19. If REQUEST is written as S2R52TU, then how will ACID be written? **[Bank PO, 2003]**
(A) 1394 (B) IC94
(C) BDJE (D) B3J4
(E) None of these

20. In certain code, TWINKLE is written as SVHOJKD, then how would FILTERS be written in the same code? **[Agriculture Officers' 2005]**
(A) EHKSDQR (B) EHKUDQR
(C) EGKUDQR (D) GJMSFST
(E) None of these

21. In a certain code, the word DIAL is coded as 4 – 9 – 1 – 12. Following the same rule of coding, what should be the code for the word CODE?
(A) 10 – 4 – 3 – 25 (B) 3 – 15 – 4 – 5
(C) 9 – 1 – 5 – 23 (D) 3 – 14 – 4 – 5

22. If GO = 32, SHE = 49, then SOME will be equal to? **[RRB 2004]**
(A) 56 (B) 58
(C) 62 (D) 64

23. If TIP = 234 and TAP = 282, then how will you code MAP?
(A) 198 (B) 324
(C) 250 (D) 300

24. If in a certain language, MADRAS is coded as NBESBT, how is BOMBAY coded in that language? **[MAT 2004]**
(A) CPNCBX (B) CPNCBZ
(C) CPOCBZ (D) CQOCBZ

25. In a certain 'code language, OPERATION is written as NODQBUJPO. How is INVISIBLE written in that code? **[RBI 2003]**
(A) JOWJTJCMF (B) JOWJTHAKD
(C) HMUHTJCMF (D) HMUHTHAKD
(E) None of these

26. In a certain code language, 'STORED' is written as 'URQPGB', What is the code for 'POINTA' in that code language? **[SSC MTS 2019]**
(A) SNMLWZ (B) SNLMWZ
(C) RMLKVY (D) RMKLVY

27. In a certain code language, if CARE is written as 270, then how will DARE be written in that code language?
(A) 360 (B) 305
(C) 280 (D) 310

28. In a certain code language GREAT is coded as RGETA. How will MERIT be coded in that language?
(A) EIMRT (B) TIREM
(C) EMRTI (D) TEMRI

29. In a certain code language, 'PANKIL' is written as 'SDQNLO'. What is the code for 'ROHANS' in that code languge? **[SSC MTS 2019]**
(A) VRKDQU (B) VRKDQV
(C) URKDQU (D) URKDQV

30. In a certain code language, 'MONKEY' is written as 'NQOMFA'.Then how will HORSE be coded in that language?
(A) IPSTF (B) ESROH
(C) IQSUF (D) JQTUG

31. In a certain code language, 'KAVERI' is written as 'VAKIRE'. How is 'MYSORE' written in that code? **[RBI 2003]**
(A) EROSYM (B) SYMROE
(C) SYMEOR (D) SMYERP
(E) None of these

32. If FIELD is coded as EMFJG, then how will TREAT be coded in that language?
(A) RTETA (B) UBFSU
(C) VTGCV (D) USFBU

33. In a certain code language if MOUSE is coded as EMOSU, then how will MIECE be coded in the same code language?
(A) EIEMC (B) MEIEC
(C) ECEIM (D) CEEIM

Direction (Qs. 34–39): In a certain code language, some digits are coded as follows :

Digits	0	1	2	3	4	5	6	7	8	9
Codes	M	@	#	T	©	*	%	R	S	J

34. Find the code for 51430.
(A) * @ © TM (B) * @ © % *
(C) @ * % MT (D) * @ % T S

35. Find the code for 88772.
(A) RRSS# (B) SSRR#
(C) TTRR# (D) MMSS@

36. Find the code for 15879.
(A) * @ © RJ (B) * @ R S J
(C) @ * S R J (D) @ * S R %

37. Find the code for 74312.
(A) M © R S T (B) R T © @ %
(C) @ # * % M (D) R © T @ #

38. Find the code for 99315.
(A) M M S @ © (B) J J T @ *
(C) J J @ S @ (D) T T @ # %

39. Find the code for 43198.
(A) © T @ J S (B) © @ # T S
(C) © M S @ T (D) T @ S M ©

40. In a certain code language, 'GUD' is written as '31'. 'PUH' is written as '44'. What is the code for 'FAR' in that language? **[SSC MTS 2019]**
(A) 25 (B) 23
(C) 24 (D) 26

2 Level Intermediate

1. In a code language if FRIDGE is written as GTLHLK, then in the same language, how will you write the word KETTLE? **[SSC CGL Exam, 2019]**
(A) WQLGXK (B) LGWXQK
(C) GLXWQK (D) XKWQLG
2. If DRIVER = 12, PEDESTRIAN = 20, ACCIDENT = 16, then CAR =? **[MAT 2002]**
(A) 3 (B) 6
(C) 8 (D) 10
3. If 'pencil' is called 'book', 'book' is called 'sharpener', 'sharpener' is called 'bag' and 'bag' is called 'eraser', then what is used to sharp a pencil?
(A) book (B) eraser
(C) bag (D) sharpener
4. If D = 4 and SAND = 38, how will you code BULB?
(A) 37 (B) 15
(C) 26 (D) 28
5. If in a certain language, MIRACLE is coded as NKUEHRL, then how is GAMBLE coded in that language? **[PGDTM, 2006]**
(A) JDOCMF (B) CLEMNK
(C) HCPFQK (D) AELGMN
6. If WORK is coded as 4 – 12 – 9 – 16, then how will you code WOMAN? **[RRB 2002]**
(A) 4 – 12 – 14 – 26 – 13
(B) 4 – 26 – 14 – 13 – 12
(C) 23 – 12 – 26 – 14 – 13
(D) 23 – 15 – 13 – 1 – 14
7. In a certain language, RIGHT is written as EVTUG, how is DEVIL written in the same language?
(A) LIVED (B) CDUHK
(C) PQHUZ (D) QRIVY
8. If B is coded as 8, F is coded as 6, Q is coded as 4, T is coded as 2, M is coded as 3 and K is coded as 5, then what is the coded form of QKTBFM? **[RBI 2002]**
(A) 425783 (B) 452683
(C) 452783 (D) 472683
(E) None of these
9. If 'Oranges' are 'Apples', 'Bananas' are 'Apricots', 'Apples' are 'Chilies', 'Apricots' are 'Oranges' and 'Chilies' are 'Bananas', then which of the following are green in colour? **[SCMHRD, 2002]**
(A) Apricots (B) Apples
(C) Chilies (D) Bananas
(E) Oranges
10. If RESIGN is coded as 5 and BELOVED as 6, then what is the code for PARLIAMENT?
(A) 6 (B) 8
(C) 9 (D) 5
11. If BE QUICK is coded as ZCOSGAI, then the code of the last letter of the third word in the sentence I LOVE MY COUNTRY is **[CPO 2004]**
(A) A (B) T
(C) U (D) W
12. If BIHAR can be coded as CKICS, how would you code GUJARAT?
(A) UGAJTAR (B) HWKCSCU
(C) FTIZQZS (D) HVKBSBU
13. If TRUTH is coded as SUQSTVSUGI, then the code for FALSE will be **[ATMA 2004]**
(A) EGZBKMRDE (B) EGZKMRTDE
(C) EGZBKMRTDF (D) FGZBKNRTDF
14. If 'black' is called red', 'red' is called 'green', 'green' is called 'orange', 'orange' is called 'white', 'white ' is called 'pink', 'pink' is called 'violet' and 'violet' is called 'blue', what would be the colour of egg?
(A) Red (B) White
(C) Pink (D) Orange
15. In a certain code, BASIC is written as DDULE. How is LEADER written in that code? **[MBA 2005]**
(A) NGCFGT (B) NHCGGU
(C) OGDFHT (D) OHDGHU
16. If in a certain code, GLAMOUR is written as IJCNMWP and MISRULE is written as OGUSSNC, then how will TOPICAL be written in that code? **[RBI 2005]**
(A) VMRJECN (B) VMRHACJ
(C) VMRJACJ (D) VNRJABJ
(E) None of these
17. If ROSE is coded as SOTF, DOME is coded as EONF and BIRD is coded as CISE, how would you code DIED?
(A) IDDE (B) EIFE
(C) EJGF (D) CHDC
18. In a certain code, SPRING is written as UNUFRC. How will the word MOBILE be written in that code? **[Bank PO 2004]**
(A) KQEFPA (B) OMDGNC
(C) OMDGPA (D) OMEFPA
(E) None of these
19. If DEFENCE is coded as 45651435, then how will ARMY be coded?
(A) 4181220 (B) 1181325
(C) 1171225 (D) 2151325
20. If ACNE can be coded as 3, 7, 29, 11, then BOIL will be coded as: **[RRB 2006]**
(A) 5, 29, 19, 27 (B) 5, 29, 19, 25
(C) 5, 31, 21, 25 (D) 5, 31, 19, 25
21. If O = 16, FOR = 42, then what is FRONT equal to? **[MCA 2005]**
(A) 61 (B) 65
(C) 73 (D) 78
22. If TEMPLE is code as ELPMET, then how will CHURCH be coded as? **[SSC CPO Exam, 2019]**
(A) HCURCH (B) HCRUHC
(C) HCRUCH (D) HCURHC

23. If TOTALITY is coded as 26213927, then EXAMINATION is coded as?
(A) 45038401854 (B) 56149512965
(C) 57159413955 (D) 67250623076

24. If MASTER is coded as 411259, then POWDER is coded as? **[RRB 2004]**
(A) 765439 (B) 765449
(C) 765459 (D) 765549

25. If in a certain code, BELIEF is written as AFKKDI. How is SELDOM written in that code? **[Hotel Management 2004]**
(A) RDKCNL (B) RFKENM
(C) RFKFNP (D) TFKENP
(E) None of these

26. In a code language 'TORCH' is written as 'UNPSDI' and 'BEST' is written as 'CDFTU'. How will MARKS be written in that language? **[RRB 2018]**
(A) NZBSLT (B) OZBSMT
(C) NABSLU (D) NZCSLT

27. In a certain code language, 'GOLF' is coded as "44" and 'BALL' is coded as '31'. How will 'PLAY' be coded in that language? **[SSC CGL 2022]**
(A) 60 (B) 58
(C) 62 (D) 56

28. In a code language, 'PLACARD' is written as 'TPEYEVH'. How will 'MONSTER' be written in that language? **[RRB 2018]**
(A) QSROXIV (B) RTSOXIV
(C) QSRRXIV (D) PSSOXJV

Direction (Qs. 29–33): Study the following information carefully and answer the questions given below:
In a certain code language:
"work is worship" is coded as "jk rt pq".
"work hard always" is coded as "jk mn uv",
"always do worship" is coded as "uv st pq"
"hard time passes" is coded as "mn ab ef". **[IBPS 2020]**

29. What is the code of "time passes" as per the given code language?
(A) ab uv
(B) ef jk
(C) cannot be determined
(D) ab ef
(E) ef rt

30. What is the code of "worship" as per the given code language?
(A) pq (B) ab
(C) mn (D) ef
(E) None of these

31. Which among the following words is coded as "rt"?
(A) work (B) is
(C) hard (D) time
(E) None of these

32. Which among the following words is coded as "ab"?
(A) time (B) passes
(C) is (D) can't be determined
(E) None of these

33. Which of the following words is correctly matched with its code?
(A) work–rt (B) is–gk
(C) worship–mn (D) do–rt
(E) hard–mn

34. In a certain code language, 'DENTIST' is written as 'CDMSHRS' and 'TOOTH' is written as 'SNNSG', how will 'HEALING' be written in that language? **[SSC CGL 2022]**
(A) IFBMJOH (B) GDZMJOH
(C) IFBKHMF (D) GDZKHMF

35. In a certain code language, '587' is written as 'see good pictures', '539' is written as 'good and beautiful' and '967' is written as 'pictures are beautiful', what is the code for the word 'see' in that language? **[MTS 2022]**
(A) 8 (B) 7
(C) 6 (D) 5

Level 3 Expert

1. If MADRAS can be written as ARSMDA, How can ARKONAM be written in that code?
(A) ROAAKNM (B) ROAKANM
(C) ROAKNNM (D) ROAKNAM

2. In a certain code language, STRING is written as $\% = * - \$ \div$ and PRAISE as $?*@-\%\times$. How will the word GRAPES be written in that code language? **[Bank PO 2004]**
(A) $\div * @ \times ?\%$ (B) $\div @ * ? \times \%$
(C) $\div * @ ? \times \%$ (D) $\div * - ? \times \%$

3. If CAPACITY is written as DKWCDCSE, then ORDINARY is written as
(A) OBSZPSEJ (B) OCUCPTGM
(C) VQCHMZQX (D) DNHCZMZQ

4. In a certain code, POETRY is written as QONDSQX and OVER is written as PNUDQ. How is MORE written in that code language? **[Bank PO 2008]**
(A) LNNQD (B) NNNQD
(C) NLNQD (D) NLPQD
(E) None of these

5. If in a certain code language, PREMONITION is written as 68530492904, how will the word MONITOR be written in that code language? **[Bank PO 2003]**
(A) 1234567 (B) 3029408
(C) 3049208 (D) 3049258
(E) None of these

6. If MUMBAI is written as UMBMIA, how will PUNJAB be written in that code?
(A) NBAUPJ (B) UPJNBA
(C) NUPBAJ (D) QVOKBC
(E) None of these

7. In a certain code MOUSE is written as PRUQC. How is SHIFT written in that code? **[SSC 10+2 2012]**
(A) VJIDR (B) VKIDR
(C) RKIVD (D) VIKRD

8. If ROME is written as MORE, then DARE is written as **[SSC CGL Tier 1 Exam, 2015]**
(A) RDAE (B) RDEA
(C) RAED (D) RADE

9. If SOLD is coded as XYQN, how is RATE written in that code?
(A) OYKW (B) WFYJ
(C) WKYO (D) UDWH
(E) None of these

10. In a certain code, DRAIN is written as *%÷#× and LIAR is written as $#÷%. How is LAND written in that code?
(A) % × # $ (B) % # × $
(C) $ ÷ × * (D) + × % $
(E) None of these

11. In a certain code language, BORN is written as APQON and LACK is written as KBBLK. How will the word GRID be written in that code language? **[Bank PO 2002]**
(A) FSHCD (B) HSJED
(C) FOHCD (D) FSHED
(E) None of these

12. If ENGLAND is written as 1234526 and FRANCE is written as 785291, how is GREECE coded? **[MAT 2000]**
(A) 381171 (B) 381191
(C) 832252 (D) 835545

13. If the word TERMINATION is coded as 12345671586, what should be the code for the word MOTION? **[RRB 2004]**
(A) 438586 (B) 458586
(C) 481586 (D) 485186

14. In a certain code SCIENCE is written as ISCNEEC. How will FOREIGN be written in that code?
(A) OFRFGIN (B) GPSFJHO
(C) RFOIENG (D) OHJFSPG

15. A certain language FASHION is coded as FOIHSAN. How is PROBLEM coded in that code? **[SSC CGL Tier 1 Exam, 2015]**
(A) PELBORM (B) ROBLEMP
(C) PRBOELM (D) RPBOELM

Direction (Qs. 16–20): Study the information and answer the following questions.
In a certain code language
Get details for venue .... fe wi mo rs
Venue book required details .... rs gt rd wi
Details required book guest .... wi gt rd ra
Guest get more venue .... ra fe gk rs **[IPBS PO 2018]**

16. What is the code for 'details' in the given code language?
(A) fe (B) mo
(C) wi (D) ra
(E) None of these

17. What is the code for the word 'guest venue' in the given code language?
(A) gt gk (B) fe mo
(C) rs ra (D) gt ra
(E) None of these

18. What is the code for the word 'get' in the given code language?
(A) gt (B) fe
(C) rs (D) rd
(E) None of these

19. If the code for the words 'for _____' is coded as 'mo gk in the coded language, then what will be the missing word?
(A) book (B) required
(C) guest (D) more
(E) Either (A) or (D)

20. What is the code for 'book' in the given code language?
(A) rs (B) gt
(C) rd (D) kl
(E) Either (B) or (C)

Direction (Qs. 21–25): Study the given information carefully and answer the question given below.
In a certain code language;
"Never talk between others" is coded as "sm nt ro fi".
"Others should be helpful" is coded as "ro el ac jq".
"Never be time specific" is coded as "fi dg el pa".
"Focus between specific hours" is coded as "hy dg nt ks". **[IPBS 2019]**

21. What is the code for "Never together" in the given code language?
(A) nt ro (B) ro fi
(C) fi uy (D) jq nt
(E) None of these

22. What is the code for "specific' in the given code language?
(A) dg (B) ac
(C) jq (D) fi
(E) None of these

23. What is the code for "others" in the given code language?
(A) sm (B) ro
(C) el (D) pa
(E) None of these

24. The code 'el' is coded as which of the following word?
(A) never (B) time
(C) focus (D) be
(E) None of these

25. What may be the possible code for "focus real" in the given code language?
(A) ks ze (B) ro hy
(C) hy tr (D) Either (A) or (C)
(E) nt me

ANSWER KEY

Level-1: Beginner

1.	(A)	2.	(B)	3.	(B)	4.	(A)	5.	(D)	6.	(C)	7.	(B)	8.	(A)	9.	(B)	10.	(D)
11.	(C)	12.	(A)	13.	(A)	14.	(C)	15.	(D)	16.	(C)	17.	(B)	18.	(A)	19.	(E)	20.	(B)
21.	(B)	22.	(A)	23.	(B)	24.	(B)	25.	(C)	26.	(D)	27.	(A)	28.	(C)	29.	(D)	30.	(C)
31.	(E)	32.	(B)	33.	(D)	34.	(A)	35.	(B)	36.	(C)	37.	(D)	38.	(B)	39.	(A)	40.	(C)

Level-2: Intermediate

1.	(B)	2.	(B)	3.	(C)	4.	(A)	5.	(C)	6.	(A)	7.	(D)	8.	(E)	9.	(D)	10.	(C)
11.	(D)	12.	(B)	13.	(C)	14.	(C)	15.	(B)	16.	(C)	17.	(B)	18.	(D)	19.	(B)	20.	(D)
21.	(D)	22.	(B)	23.	(B)	24.	(C)	25.	(C)	26.	(A)	27.	(B)	28.	(A)	29.	(D)	30.	(A)
31.	(B)	32.	(D)	33.	(E)	34.	(D)	35.	(A)										

Level-3: Expert

1.	(A)	2.	(C)	3.	(B)	4.	(C)	5.	(C)	6.	(B)	7.	(B)	8.	(D)	9.	(C)	10.	(C)
11.	(D)	12.	(B)	13.	(C)	14.	(C)	15.	(A)	16.	(C)	17.	(C)	18.	(B)	19.	(D)	20.	(E)
21.	(E)	22.	(A)	23.	(B)	24.	(D)	25.	(D)										

Solutions with Detailed Explanations

Level-1: BEGINNER

1. **Option (A) is correct.**
Explanation: The code for CAT is one more than the code for BAT, and C is one step ahead of B. As a result, the letters of the English alphabet are coded using numbers. A = 1, B = 2, Z = 26.
So, BALL = B + A + L + L = 2 + 1 + 12 + 12 = 27

2. **Option (B) is correct.**
Explanation: To obtain the corresponding letter of the code, the word's fetch letter is advanced three steps.

3. **Option (B) is correct.**
Explanation: Clearly, each letter is given a numerical value that is twice the number indicating its place in the English alphabet.
So, RATE = R + A + T + E
= (2 × 18) + (2 × 1) + (20 × 2) + (5× 2) = 88

4. **Option (A) is correct.**
Explanation: The number of letters in the code is two times greater than the number of letters in the specified word.
FLOWER → 6 × 2 + 2 = 14
DISTASTE → 8 × 2 + 2 = 18
So, BUREAUCRAT → 10 × 2 + 2 = 22

5. **Option (D) is correct.**
Explanation: Each letter is replaced by a number that is three less than the letter's designation. The integer codes for the individual letters are physically combined to create the word's code. As a result, the code for HEEL is now 5229.

6. **Option (C) is correct.**
Explanation: Letters are replaced by the place value of their reverse letters i.e., Z = 1, Y = 2, B =25, A = 26, M = 14.
Then, RUN = R + U + N = 9 + 6 + 13 = 28
So, RAT = R + A + T = 9 + 26 + 7 = 42

7. **Option (B) is correct.**
Explanation: The term given has interchangeable letter pairs.
S T R A I G H T
T S A R G I T H
Similarly
T H U R S D A Y
H T R U D S Y A

8. **Option (A) is correct.**
Explanation: We can see, the word's initial letter is advanced one space to create the first letter of the code, but the other letters are unchanged.

9. **Option (B) is correct.**
Explanation: To get the corresponding letters of the code, the first, third, and fifth letters are each moved one step backward, while the second, fourth, and sixth letters are each moved one step ahead.

10. **Option (D) is correct.**
Explanation: Clearly, we have

Letter	A	B	C	D	E	F	G	H	I	J	K	L	M	N
Value	1	3	5	7	9	11	13	15	17	19	21	23	25	27

So, INDIAN = I + N + D + I + A + N
= 17 + 27 + 7 + 17 + 1 + 27 = 96

11. **Option (C) is correct.**
Explanation: According to their position in the English alphabet, the letters of the given word are coded. So, the code for "MAGNIFY" will be "1317149625."

12. Option (A) is correct.
Explanation: The middle (sixth) letter is moved two steps forward to obtain the matching letters of the code. The first, third, fifth, seventh, ninth, and eleventh letters in the word are all moved one step forward. The second, fourth, eighth, and tenth letters are all moved one step backward.

13. Option (A) is correct.
Explanation: The code letter for each letter in the word is obtained by moving that letter one step backward in the word.

14. Option (C) is correct.
Explanation:
Taking, A = 1, B = 2, ..., T = 20, ..., Z = 26
We have,
AT = A × T = 1 × 20 = 20
CAT = C × A × T = 3 × 1 × 20 = 60
So, MAT = M × A × T = 13 × 1 × 20 = 260

15. Option (D) is correct.
Explanation: The provided word's letters are classified according to their position in the alphabet. The sum of the digits is written if the number has two digits:
L → 12 = 1 + 2 = 3
A → 1
R → 18 = 1 + 8 = 9
V → 22 = 2 + 2 = 4
A → 1
E → 5
Similarly,
I → 9
N → 14 = 1 + 4 = 5
S → 19 = 1 + 9 = 10
E → 5
C → 3
T → 20 = 2 + 0 = 2
So, INSECT will be coded as 9 – 5 – 10 – 5 – 3 – 2

16. Option (C) is correct.
Explanation:
We can see,
The pattern is forming,

4	3	7	2	0
+1↓	−1↓	+1↓	−1↓	+1↓
5	2	8	1	1

Similarly,

7	5	1	6	3
+1↓	−1↓	+1↓	−1↓	+1↓
8	4	2	5	4

17. Option (B) is correct.
Explanation: Moving the word's first letter to get the appropriate letters of the code, take one step back while moving the two middle letters each one step forward.

18. Option (A) is correct.
Explanation: To get the corresponding letter of the code, each letter in the word is two steps backward.

19. Option (E) is correct.
Explanation: Vowels A, E, I, O, and U are clearly coded as 1, 2, 3, 4 and 5, respectively. Each of the word's consonants is shifted forward one position to provide the matching letter of the code. The ACID code is 1D3E.

20. Option (B) is correct.
Explanation: Every letter in the word is shifted one position backward, with the exception of the centre letter. To get the relevant letter of the code, move forward one step.

21. Option (B) is correct.
Explanation:
Each letter's numerical position in the English alphabet clearly serves as a code for that letter. Thus, A is coded as 1, B as 2, C as 3, D as 4, L as 12, M as 13, Y as 25, and Z as 26.
So, the code for CODE is 3 – 15 – 4 – 5.

22. Option (A) is correct.
Explanation: In the given code,
Z = 1, Y = 2, X = 3,..., C = 24, B = 25, A = 26
So, GO = 20 + 12 = 32 and SHE = 8 + 19 + 22 = 49
Similarly, SOME = S + O + M + E = 8 + 12 + 14 + 22 = 56

23. Option (B) is correct.
Explanation:
Taking Z = 2, Y = 3, ..., N = 14, B = 26, A = 27
We have,
TIP = (T + I + P) × 6 = (8 + 19 + 12) × 6
= 39 × 6 = 234
So, MAP = (M + A + P) × 6 = (15 + 27 + 12) × 6
= 54 × 6 = 324

24. Option (B) is correct.
Explanation: The word's letters have each been moved one position forward to get the relevant code letter.

25. Option (C) is correct.
Explanation: The code letter is obtained by moving the first four letters of the word one step backward and the last five letters one step forward, respectively.

26. Option (D) is correct.
Explanation: We have

S	T	O	R	E	D
+2↓	−2↓	+2↓	−2↓	+2↓	−2↓
U	R	Q	P	G	B

So,

P	O	I	N	T	A
+2↓	−2↓	+2↓	−2↓	+2↓	−2↓
R	M	K	L	V	Y

27. Option (A) is correct.
Explanation: We have,
C × A × R × E = 3 × 1 × 18 × 5 = 270
Now, D × A × R × E = 4 × 1 × 18 × 5 = 360

28. Option (C) is correct.
Explanation: We have,

So,

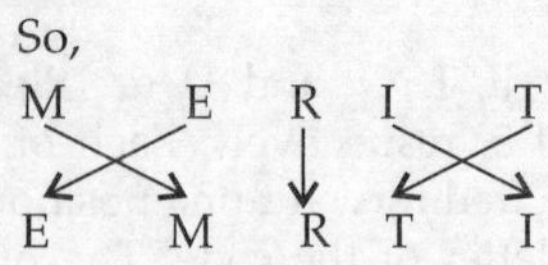

29. Option (D) is correct.
Explanation: We have,

P A N K I L
+3 +3 +3 +3 +3 +3
S D Q N L O

So,

R O H A N S
+3 +3 +3 +3 +3 +3
U R K D Q V

30. Option (C) is correct.
Explanation: We have

M O N K E Y
+1 +2 +1 +2 +1 +2
N Q O M F A

So,

H O R S E
+1 +2 +1 +2 +1
I Q S U F

31. Option (E) is correct.
Explanation: We have

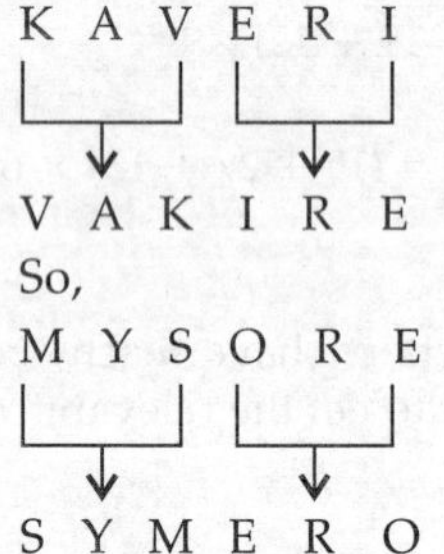

32. Option (B) is correct.
Explanation: Here,

FIELD $\xrightarrow{\text{reverse}}$ D L E I F
+1 +1 +1 +1 +1
E M F J G

So,

TREAT $\xrightarrow{\text{reverse}}$ T A E R T
+1 +1 +1 +1 +1
U B F S U

33. Option (D) is correct.
Explanation: The alphabets are arranged in alphabetical order.

34. Option (A) is correct.
Explanation: The code for 51430 is * @ © TM

35. Option (B) is correct.
Explanation: The code for 88772 is SSRR#

36. Option (C) is correct.
Explanation: The code for 15879 is @ * S R J

37. Option (D) is correct.
Explanation: The code for 74312 is R © T @ #

38. Option (B) is correct.
Explanation: The code for 99315 is J J T @ *

39. Option (A) is correct.
Explanation: The code for 43198 is © T @ J S

40. Option (C) is correct.
Explanation: Here, GUD $\rightarrow$ G + U + D
= 7 + 21 + 4 = 32
So, 32 – 1 = 31
and PUH $\rightarrow$ P + U + H = 16 + 21 + 8 = 45
So, 45 – 1 = 44
Now, FAR $\rightarrow$ F + A + R = 6 + 1 + 18 = 25
So, 25 – 1 = 24

Level-2: INTERMEDIATE

1. Option (B) is correct.
Explanation:
The pattern is,

F R I D G E
+1↓ +2↓ +3↓ +4↓ +5↓ +6↓
G T L H L K

Similarly,

K E T T L E
+1↓ +2↓ +3↓ +4↓ +5↓ +6↓
L G W X Q K

2. Option (B) is correct.
Explanation: Clearly, each word is coded by the numeral which is twice the number of letters in the word.
CAR = (CAR × 2) = 6

3. Option (C) is correct.
Explanation: A sharpener is used to sharp a pencil, although it is actually referred to as a bag.

4. Option (A) is correct.
Explanation: We have,
A = 1, B = 2, C = 3, D = 4, ..., Y = 25, Z = 26
The code for a word is clearly determined by the sum of each letter's separate values. Hence, SAND
= 19 + 1 + 14 + 4 = 38
So, BULB = 2 + 21 + 12 + 2 = 37

5. Option (C) is correct.
Explanation: The first, second, third, fourth, fifth, sixth, and seventh letters of the word are each advanced one, two, three, four, five, and six steps respectively in order to obtain the matching letters of the code.

6. Option (A) is correct.
Explanation: Each letter is, without a doubt, coded by the number that results from deducting the letter's English alphabet position from 27, which is represented by the number. W, O, M, A, and N are the 23rd, 15th, 13th, 1st, and 14th letters, respectively. Consequently, their codes are
(27 – 23), (27 – 15), (27 – 13), (27 – 1), (27 – 14)
= 4, 12, 14, 26, 13

7. **Option (D) is correct.**
Explanation: To get the corresponding letter of the code, each letter in the word is advanced by thirteen spaces.

8. **Option (E) is correct.**
Explanation: We can see,
The code for QKTBFM = 452863

9. **Option (D) is correct.**
Explanation: Chilies are described as being "bananas" and are green in appearance. Bananas are hence green in colour.

10. **Option (C) is correct.**
Explanation: There is no doubt that each word is coded by a number that is one less than the word's total number of letters. The word "PARLIAMENT" contains 10 letters; hence, the needed code is 10 – 1 = 9.

11. **Option (D) is correct.**
Explanation: The code letter for each letter in the message is obtained by moving that letter two steps backward. Y, the word's final letter, must be coded as W in the example sentence.

12. **Option (B) is correct.**
Explanation: The pattern is:

B	I	H	A	R
+1↓	+2↓	+1↓	+2↓	+1↓
C	K	I	C	S

Similarly,

G	U	J	A	R	A	T
+1↓	+2↓	+1↓	+2↓	+1↓	+2↓	+1↓
H	W	K	C	S	C	U

13. **Option (C) is correct.**
Explanation: Each letter in the word is changed to a pair of letters in the code, one coming before it and the other after it i.e., T is thus changed to SU, R to QS, and so fourth.

14. **Option (C) is correct.**
Explanation: The colour of egg is "white," and when given that name, "white" is referred to as "pink." Therefore, colour of egg is "pink."

15. **Option (B) is correct.**
Explanation: To get the corresponding letters of the code, the letters in the word at the odd and even numbered locations are each advanced by two steps, and three steps.

16. **Option (C) is correct.**
Explanation: The first, third, and sixth letters of the word are each moved two steps forward; the second, fifth, and seventh letters are each moved two steps backward; and the fourth letter is moved one step ahead to produce the matching letters of the code.

17. **Option (B) is correct.**
Explanation: To get the appropriate letter of the code, move each letter one step forward except the second letter.

18. **Option (D) is correct.**
Explanation: To get the letters of the code, the first, third, and fifth letters of the word are moved two, three, and four steps forward while the second, fourth, and sixth letters of the word are moved two, three, and four steps backward.
So, code for 'MOBILE' will be 'OMEFPA'.

19. **Option (B) is correct.**
Explanation: Putting A = 1, B = 2, C = 3 .....X = 24, Y = 25, Z = 26
DEFENCE → 45651435
So, ARMY → 1181325

20. **Option (D) is correct.**
Explanation: Given coding system, we have

Letter	A	B	C	D	E	F	G	H	I	J	K	L	M	N	O
Code	3	5	7	9	11	13	15	17	19	21	23	25	27	29	31

So, the code of BOIL is 5, 31, 19, 25.

21. **Option (D) is correct.**
Explanation: We have
A = 2, B = 3, C = 4 .....X = 25, Y = 26, Z = 27
Then,
FOR = F + O + R = 7 + 16 + 19 = 42
FRONT = F + R + O + N + T
= 7 + 19 + 16 + 15 + 21 = 78

22. **Option (B) is correct.**
Explanation: The letters in the word "TEMPLE" were coded in the opposite direction of "ELPMET." The code for CHURCH will be HCRUHC.

23. **Option (B) is correct.**
Explanation: We have
A = 1, B = 2, C = 3, ..., X = 24, Y = 25, Z = 26
Then,
T = 20 = 2 + 0 = 2
O = 15 = 1 + 5 = 6
T = 20 = 2 + 0 = 2
A = 1
L = 12 = 1 + 2 = 3
I = 9
T = 20 = 2 + 0 = 2
Y = 25 = 2 + 5 = 7
So,
MOBILITY = 46293927
In the same way, 'EXAMINATION' will be coded as '56149512965'.

24. **Option (C) is correct.**
Explanation: A = 1, B = 2, C = 3, ..., X= 24, Y = 25, Z = 26
Now, M =13 =4 (remainder obtained after dividing by 9);
S = 19 = 1 (remainder obtained after dividing by 9);
T = 20 = 2 (remainder obtained after dividing by 9);

R = 18 = 9 (remainder obtained after dividing by 9).
So, MASTER = 411259
Similarly,
POWDER = 765459

25. Option (C) is correct.
Explanation: The first, third, and fifth letters of the word are each shifted back one step, and the second, fourth, and sixth letters are each moved forward one, two, and three steps to produce the letters of the code.

26. Option (A) is correct.
Explanation: We have

T O R C H
+1 −1 +1 +1 +1 +1
U N P P D I

So,

M A R K S
+1 −1 +1 +1 +1 +1
N Z B S L T

27. Option (B) is correct.
Explanation: As, G + O + L + F = 7 + 15 + 12 + 6 = 40
So, 40 + 4 = 44
So, BALL = B + A + L + L = 2 + 1 + 12 + 12 = 27
So, 27 + 4 = 31
Hence, PLAY = P + L + A + Y = 16 + 12 + 1 + 25 = 54
So, 54 + 4 = 58

28. Option (A) is correct.
Explanation: We have,

P L A C A R D
+4 +4 +4 −4 +4 +4 +4
T P E Y E V H

So,

M O N S T E R
+4 +4 +4 −4 +4 +4 +4
Q S R O X I V

(29-33).
(i) work is worship → jk rt pq
(ii) work hard always → jk mn uv
(iii) always do worship → uv st pq
(iv) hard time passes → mn ab ef

29. Option (D) is correct.
Explanation:
From (ii) and (iv)
hard → mn
Hence, from (iv)
time passes → ab ef

30. Option (A) is correct.
Explanation:
From (i) and (iii)
worship → pq

31. Option (B) is correct.
Explanation:
From (i) and (ii)
work → jk
Hence, from (i)
is → rt

32. Option (D) is correct.
Explanation:
From (iv), ab is the code for either time or passes.

33. Option (E) is correct.
Explanation:
From (i) and (ii)
work → jk
From (i)
is → rt
From (i) and (ii)
worship → pq
From (ii) and (iii)
do → st
From (iv)
hard → mn

34. Option (D) is correct.
Explanation: We have,

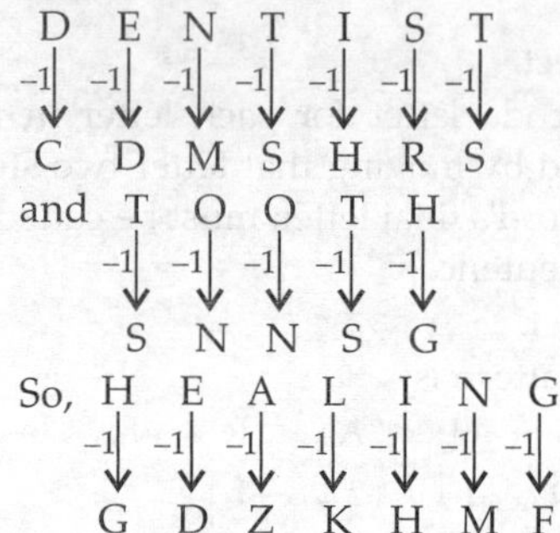

35. Option (A) is correct.
Explanation: We have,
(i) 587 → see good pictures
(ii) 539 → good and beautiful
(iii) 967 → pictures are beautiful
From (i) and (ii)
5 → good
From (i) and (iii)
7 → pictures
So, 8 → see

Level-3: EXPERT

1. Option (A) is correct.
Explanation: In order to create the code, the word is first written with the letters placed in even locations and then write the rest of the letters.

2. Option (C) is correct.
Explanation: Given coding system, we have

Letter	S	T	R	I	N	G	P	A	E
Code	%	=	*	–	$	÷	?	@	×

The code for GRAPES: ÷ * @ ? × %

3. Option (B) is correct.
Explanation: The pattern is:
CAPACITY → CITYCAPA
Now,

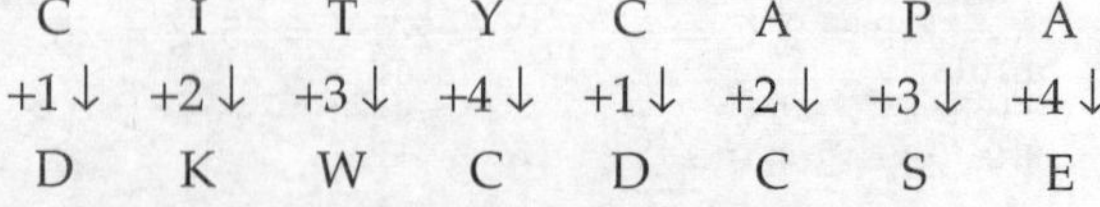

Similarly, ORDINARY → NARYORDI

N	A	R	Y	O	R	D	I
+1↓	+2↓	+3↓	+4↓	+1↓	+2↓	+3↓	+4↓
O	C	U	C	P	T	G	M

4. **Option (C) is correct.**
Explanation: The word's first letter is changed in the code to a pair of letters, one coming after it and the other before it. To get the remaining letters of the code in order, the remaining letters of the word are each moved one step backward.

5. **Option (C) is correct.**
Explanation: Given coding system, we have

Letter	P	R	E	M	T	I	O	N
Code	6	8	5	3	2	9	0	4

The code for MONITOR = 3049208

6. **Option (B) is correct.**
Explanation: The pattern is:
M U M B A I
U M B M I A
So, P U N J A B
U P J N B A

7. **Option (B) is correct.**
Explanation: The pattern is,

M	O	U	S	E
+3↓	+3↓	+0↓	−2↓	−2↓
P	R	U	Q	C

Similarly,

S	H	I	F	T
+3↓	+3↓	+0↓	−2↓	−2↓
V	K	I	D	R

8. **Option (D) is correct.**
Explanation: The pattern is,

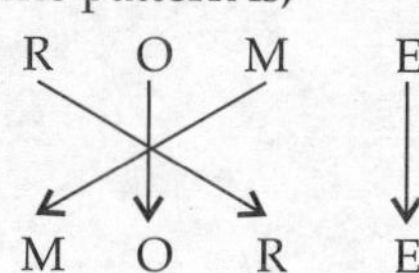

Similarly,

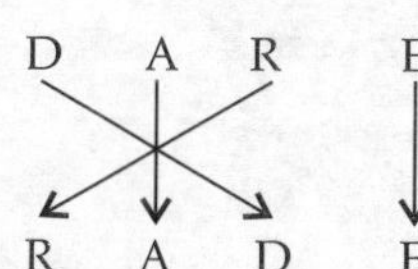

9. **Option (C) is correct.**
Explanation: The pattern is:

S	O	L	D
+5↓	+10↓	+5↓	+10↓
X	Y	Q	N

Similarly,

R	A	T	E
+5↓	+10↓	+5↓	+10↓
W	K	Y	O

10. **Option (C) is correct.**
Explanation: Given coding system, we have

Letter	D	R	A	I	N	L
Code	*	%	÷	#	×	$

The code for LAND = $ ÷ × *

11. **Option (D) is correct.**
Explanation: The first and third letters are each shifted one step backward, while the second and fourth letters are each moved one step forward, to produce the matching letters of the code. Finally, the final letter of the word is added at the conclusion of the code that was thusly generated.

12. **Option (B) is correct.**
Explanation: Given coding system, we have

Letter	E	N	G	L	A	D	F	R	C
Code	1	2	3	4	5	6	7	8	9

The code for GREECE = 381191

13. **Option (C) is correct.**
Explanation: Given coding system, we have

Letter	T	E	R	M	I	N	A	O
Code	1	2	3	4	5	6	7	8

The code for MOTION = 481586

14. **Option (C) is correct.**
Explanation: The pattern is,

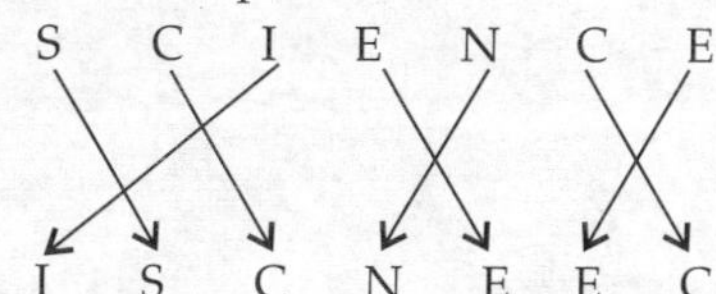

Similarly,

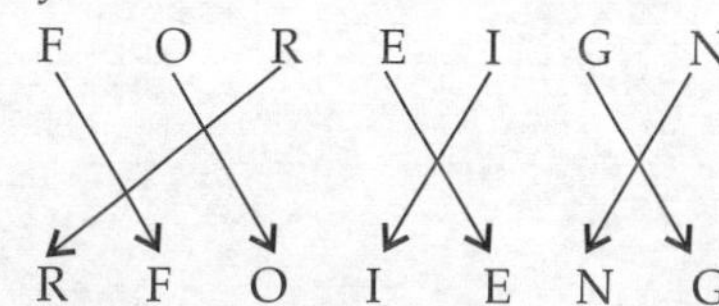

15. **Option (A) is correct.**
Explanation: The pattern is,

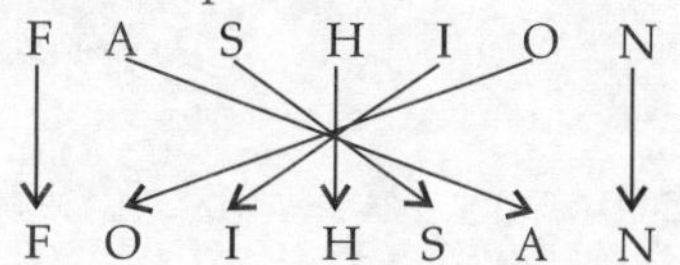

Similarly, PROBLEM is coded as PELBORM

16-20.

(i) Get details for venue .... fe wi mo rs
(ii) Venue book required details .... rs gt rd wi
(iii) Details required book guest .... wi gt rd ra
(iv) Guest get more venue .... ra fe gk rs

16. **Option (C) is correct.**
Explanation: From (i), (ii) and (iii), details is coded as wi

17. **Option (C) is correct.**
Explanation: From (iii) and (iv) guest is coded as ra

From (i), (ii) and (iv),
Venue is coded as rs
So, 'guest venue' ra rs

18. Option (B) is correct.
Explanation: As using solution (17), (i) and (iv), get is coded as fe.

19. Option (D) is correct.
Explanation: more is coded as gk

20. Option (E) is correct.
Explanation: As details → wi
Venue → rs
So, book is coded as either gt or rd.

(21-25):

(i) "Never talk between others" → sm nt ro fi
(ii) "Others should be helpful" → ro el ac jq
(iii) "Never be time specific" → fi dg el pa
(iv) "Focus between specific hours" → hy dg nt ks

21. Option (E) is correct.
Explanation: From (i) and (iii)
Never → fi
Code for together is not given here.

22. Option (A) is correct.
Explanation: From (iii) and (iv)
Specific → dg

23. Option (B) is correct.
Explanation: From (i) and (ii),
others → ro

24. Option (D) is correct.
Explanation: From (ii) and (iii)
el is the code of be

25. Option (D) is correct.
Explanation: From (iv)
Focus → either hy or ks

■ ■ ■

Chapter 5

Blood Relations

LEARNING OBJECTIVES:

- Methods of finding a relation using the family tree
- Methods of solving the questions based on coded blood relations
- Different types of question asked in competitive exams

A person is said to be related to another by blood when they are born into the same family rather than through marriage.

This chapter's questions concern "blood relations." To answer these questions, you should be sufficiently knowledgeable about "blood relations." The relationships can be classified into two broad categories.

Relations on the mother's side are referred to as maternal, while those on the father's side are referred to as paternal.

FAMILY TREE

➢ A "family tree" is a visual diagram that depicts the logical connections between concepts or categories in the realm of reasoning and logic. It is a method of organising and presenting information that demonstrates the relationships between various ideas or categories. In this context, a family tree can be viewed as a hierarchical structure in which more specific or narrower concepts or categories are represented at lower levels and broader or more general concepts or categories are represented at higher levels. Arrows or lines are commonly used to depict the connections or relationships between the nodes in the tree. Family trees in reasoning are widely used to analyse and understand concepts in many fields, including philosophy, cognitive science, and artificial intelligence.

Example 1: Pointing towards a person, a man said to a woman, "His mother is the only daughter of your father." How is the woman related to that person? **[RRB 2005]**

(a) Daughter (b) Sister
(c) Mother (d) Wife

Sol. (c) This woman is the father's only daughter. The lady is therefore the person's mother, and the person is the woman's son.

Example 2: Anuj introduces Rishi as the son of the only brother of his father. How is Rishi related to Anuj?

(a) Cousin (b) Son
(c) Uncle (d) Son-in-law

Sol. (a) The relationships can be broken down into the following categories: Father's brother – uncle, uncle's son – cousin.

CODED BLOOD RELATION

➢ In this case, we have provided certain codes but not actual relationships. We first obtain these codes, after which we extract crucial data and lastly respond to inquiries.
+, –, ×, ÷, *, $, @, etc.

Example 3: If 'A $ B' means 'A is the father of B', 'A * B' means 'A is the mother of B', 'A@B' means 'A is the wife of B', then which of the following means M is the grandmother of N? **[EPFOSSA 2004]**

(a) M*T$N@R (b) M*T$R@N
(c) M*R$T@N (d) M*R@T@N
(e) None of these

Sol. (a) 'M is the grandmother of N' means 'M is the mother of the father (say T) of N' that is M*T$N@R.

Example 4: If 'P + Q' means 'P is the father of Q, P × Q means 'P is the brother of Q; 'P – Q' means 'P is the mother of Q', then which of the following is definitely true about C – A + B?

(a) B is the son of A.
(b) A is the son of C.
(c) B is the father of A.
(d) C is the mother of B.

Sol. (b) The phrase "C – A + B" denotes that A is the father of B and C is the mother of A. It is obvious from this that A is a male and hence the son of C.

1 Level Beginner

Directions (Qs. 1–8): Read the following information carefully and answer the questions given below it:

A+B means 'A is the father of B'; 'A – B' means 'A is the wife of B'; 'A × B means A is the brother of B'; 'A ÷ B' means 'A is the daughter of B'.

1. If P ÷ R + S + Q, which of the following is true? **[NTPC 2016]**
   (A) P is the daughter of Q.
   (B) Q is the aunt of P.
   (C) P is the aunt of Q.
   (D) P is the mother of Q
2. If P – R + Q, which of the following statements is true?
   (A) P is the mother of Q.
   (B) Q is the daughter of P.
   (C) P is the aunt of Q.
   (D) P is the sister of Q.
3. If P × R ÷ Q, which of the following statements is true?
   (A) P is the uncle of Q.
   (B) P is the father of Q.
   (C) P is the brother of Q.
   (D) P is the son of Q.
4. If P × R – Q, which of the following is true?
   (A) P is the brother-in-law of Q.
   (B) P is the brother of Q.
   (C) P is the uncle of Q.
   (D) P is the father of Q.
5. If P + R ÷ Q, which of the following is true?
   (A) P is the brother of Q.
   (B) P is the son of Q.
   (C) P is the husband of Q.
   (D) P is the father of Q.
6. If P ÷ R + Q, which of the following is true?
   (A) P is the father of Q.
   (B) P is the brother of Q.
   (C) P is the mother of Q.
   (D) P is the sister of Q
7. If P × R + Q, which of the following is true?
   (A) P is the uncle of Q.
   (B) P is the father of Q.
   (C) P is the brother-in-law of Q.
   (D) P is the grandfather of Q.
8. If P – R × Q, which of the following is true?
   (A) P is the sister of Q.
   (B) Q is the husband of P.
   (C) P is the sister-in-law of Q.
   (D) Q is the son of P.
9. V is married to W. R is the only sister of W. A is the mother of R. A has three children. G is the niece of R and P. V has no sibling, R is unmarried. Then, how is P related to V? **[SBI PO Exam 2018]**
   (A) Mother-in-law (B) Sister
   (C) Brother-in-law (D) Brother
   (E) None of these
10. P is the father of Q and R is the son of S. T is the brother of P. Q is the sister of R. How is S related to T? **[SSC CGL, Exam, 2019]**
   (A) Brother-in-law (B) Daughter
   (C) Sister-in-law (D) Brother
11. Pointing to a girl, Amit said, "She is the daughter of the only child of my grandfather." How is Amit related to the girl?
   (A) Brother (B) Nephew
   (C) Cousin (D) Data inadequate
12. Introducing a boy to her friend, Kirti said that he is the son of the only daughter of her father. How is Kirti related to the boy?
   (A) Mother-in-law (B) Mother
   (C) Sister (D) Aunt
13. Vinod introduces, Vishal as the son of the only brother of his father's wife. How is Vinod related to Vishal? **[SSC CGL 2011]**
   (A) Cousin (B) Brother
   (C) Son (D) Uncle
14. Looking at a portrait of a man, Harsh said, "His mother is the wife of my father's son. Brothers and sisters I have none." At whose portrait was Harsh looking? **[MBA 2016]**
   (A) His son (B) His cousin
   (C) His uncle (D) His nephew
   (E) None of these
15. Pointing to a boy, Sakshi said, "His mother's brother is my husband". How is that boy related to Sakshi?
   (A) Brother (B) Nephew
   (C) Husband (D) None of these

Directions (Qs. 16–18): Study the following information carefully and answer the questions given below it:

Seven members are living in the family. Q is the daughter of P. B is the brother of R. G is the mother-in-law of A. B is married to A. B is the uncle of Q. D is the father of B. **[IBPS PO Exam 2019]**

16. What is the relation of B with respect to P?
   (A) Brother (B) Sister-in-law
   (C) Brother-in-law (D) Mother
   (E) Aunt
17. If C is the brother of B, then what is the relation of C with respect to Q?
   (A) Father (B) Uncle
   (C) Aunt (D) Sister
   (E) Mother

18. If P is the father of Q, then what is the relation of R with respect to P?

(A) Wife (B) Husband
(C) Father (D) Father-in-law
(E) Mother

Directions (Qs. 19–20): Read the following information carefully and answer the questions given below it.

All the given members belong to the same family. J is the brother of L. J is the only son of R. W is the father-in-law of L. D is the maternal grandfather of P, who is a male. Q is the only son of W. W is the grandfather of N and C is the daughter of N. **[SBI Clerk 2018]**

19. How L is related to C?

(A) Mother (B) Grand mother
(C) Brother (D) Father
(E) None of these

20. How is P related to N?

(A) Mother (B) Son
(C) Brother (D) Father
(E) None of these

21. Introducing a woman, a man said, "Her husband is the only son of my father." How is that woman related to the man?

(A) Sister (B) Mother-in-law
(C) Maternal aunt (D) Wife

22. Introducing a man to her husband, a woman said, "His brother's father is the only son of my grandfather." How is the woman related to this man?"**[IITTM 2005]**

(A) Mother (B) Aunt
(C) Sister (D) Daughter
(E) Grandmother

23. Pointing towards a girl in the picture, Sarita said, "She is the mother of Neha whose father is my son." How is Sarita related to the girl in the picture? **[Bank PO 2005]**

(A) Mother (B) Aunt
(C) Cousin (D) Data inadequate
(E) None of these

Directions (Qs. 24–27): Refer to the details given below and answer the questions following it:

A family has 6 people living in the same house. There are two couples in the family.

- The Doctor is the eldest among the family and has only two sons – Rahul and Kashish and both are teachers.
- Mrs Kirti and her mother-in-law both are doctors.
- Rahul's wife is a lawyer and they have a son, Manish.

24. What is the profession of Rahul's wife?

(A) Doctor
(B) Teacher
(C) Lawyer
(D) Cannot be determined

25. How is Manish related to Kirti?

(A) Son (B) Grandson
(C) Nephew (D) Brother

26. What is the profession of Kashish's wife?

(A) Lawyer (B) Teacher
(C) Doctor (D) None of these

27. Which of the given statement is correct with respect to the blood relation given here?

(A) The head of the family is male
(B) Kirti is Rahul's wife
(C) Manish is the grandson of a doctor
(D) None of the above

28. Deepak said to Nitin, "That boy playing football is the younger of the two brothers of the daughter of my father's wife." How is the boy playing football related to Deepak? **[MBA 2004]**

(A) Son (B) Brother
(C) Cousin (D) Nephew
(E) Brother-in-law

29. Introducing a woman, a man said, "She is the only daughter of my mother's mother." How is the woman related to the man?

(A) Mother (B) Aunt
(C) Sister (D) Niece

30. Showing the picture of Shikha, Parul said, "She is the grandmother of my father's only son". How is Shikha related to Parul? **[SSC CHSL 2020]**

(A) Grandmother (B) Mother
(C) Sister (D) Daughter-in-law

31. Pointing towards Arti, Sukanya said, "She is my husband's mother-in-law's husband's daughter." How is Arti related to Sukanya? **[SSC Steno 2021]**

(A) Maternal aunt (B) Mother
(C) Sister-in-law (D) Sister

32. When Sumit saw Manish, he recalled, "He is the father of my daughter's mother." Who is Manish to Sumit?

(A) Father-in-law (B) Brother
(C) Cousin (D) Uncle

33. Pointing to a man in a photograph, Kanika said, "His mother's only sister is my mother." How is Kanika related to that man?

(A) Nephew (B) Sister
(C) Wife (D) Cousin

34. When Amit saw Mohit, he recalled, "He is the only son of the father of my daughter". Who is Mohit to Amit?

(A) Son (B) Brother
(C) Cousin (D) Uncle

35. Pointing to a lady Anita said, "She is the sister of my father." Who is the lady to Anita?

(A) Mother (B) Sister
(C) Aunt (D) Niece
(E) None of these

2 Level Intermediate

Directions (Qs. 1–3): Study the information carefully and answer the questions given below.

Eight persons in three generations of a family. K is the daughter-in-law of G. M is the father of L who is the daughter-in-law of P. H is the brother-in-law of G and only son of F. T is the grandson of F. H is unmarried and G is male. M has two children. **[SBI PO 2021]**

1. How is M related to G?
(A) Father (B) Brother
(C) Father-in-law (D) Brother-in-law
(E) None of these

2. How is K related to L?
(A) Daughter (B) Mother-in-law
(C) Daughter-in-law (D) Sister
(E) None of these

3. Who among the following is the son of M?
(A) H (B) G
(C) T (D) L

4. A, B and C are sisters. D is the brother of E and E is the daughter of B. How is A related to D? **[SSC 2003]**
(A) Sister (B) Cousin
(C) Niece (D) Aunt

5. Kanika has a brother Rohan. Kanika is the daughter of Mohit. Manish is Mohit's father. In terms of relationship, who is Rohan of Manish?
(A) Son (B) Grandson
(C) Brother (D) Grandfather

6. In a joint family, there are father, mother, 3 married sons and one unmarried daughter. Of the sons, two have 2 daughters each, and one has a son. How many female members are there in the family? **[SSC 2005]**
(A) 2 (B) 3
(C) 6 (D) 9

7. Pointing to a lady, a man said, "The son of her only brother is the brother of my wife." How is the lady related to the man? **[IITTM 2005]**
(A) Mother's sister
(B) Grandmother
(C) Mother-in-law
(D) Sister of father-in-law
(E) Maternal aunt

8. If 'P x Q' means 'P is the daughter of Q; 'P + Q' means 'P is the father of Q'; 'P ÷ Q' means 'P is the mother of Q' and 'P – Q means P is the brother of Q, then in the expression A ÷ B + C – E × F, how is A related to F ? **[SBI PO 2001]**
(A) Mother (B) Aunt
(C) Daughter-in-law (D) Sister-in-law
(E) None of these

Direction (Qs. 9–10): Read the information given below and answer the questions.

All the given members belong to the same family. J is the brother of L. J is the only son of R. W is the father-in-law of L. D is the maternal grandfather of P, who is a male. Q is the only son of W. W is the grandfather of N and C is the daughter of N. **[SBI 2018]**

9. How L is related to C?
(A) Mother (B) Son
(C) Brother (D) Father
(E) None of these

10. How is P related to N?
(A) Mother (B) Son
(C) Brother (D) Father
(E) None of these

11. Pointing to a man, a woman said, "His mother is the only daughter of my mother." How is the woman related to the man? **[MBA 2003]**
(A) Mother (B) Daughter
(C) Sister (D) Grandmother
(E) None of these

Directions (Qs. 12–14): Read the following information and answer the questions given below it:
'A + B' means 'A is the daughter of B';
'A × B' means 'A is the son of B';
'A – B' means 'A is the wife of B'.

12. If P + Q – S, which of the following is true?
(A) S is wife of Q (B) S is father of P
(C) P is son of Q (D) Q is father of P

13. If T + S × B + M, which of the following is true?
(A) B is mother of S (B) M is husband of B
(C) T is wife of S (D) S is daughter of B

14. If Z + T × S + U × P, then what is U to T?
(A) Mother
(B) Grandmother
(C) Father
(D) None of these

15. If X is the brother of son of Y's son, then how is X related to Y? **[RRB 2005]**
(A) Brother (B) Cousin
(C) Grandson (D) Son

16. Arsh is Shivam's father and Dhruva is the son of Bimla. Eshwar is the father of Arsh. If Shivam is the brother of Dhruv, how is Bimla related to Eshwar? **[SSC CGL 2020]**
(A) Wife (B) Daughter-in-law
(C) Mother (D) Sister-in-law

17. **(i)** B is the daughter of A
(ii) A is the son of C
(iii) D is the brother of E
(iv) E is the daughter of B
The maternal grandfather of D is:
(A) A (B) B
(C) C (D) E

Direction (Qs. 18–20): Study the following information carefully and answer the questions given below:

Seven members are living in the family. Q is the daughter of P. B is the brother of R. G is the mother-in-law of A. B is married to A. B is the uncle of Q. D is the father of B.

[IBPS 2019]

18. What is the relation of B with respect to P?
    (A) Brother (B) Sister-in-law
    (C) Brother-in-law (D) Mother
    (E) Aunt
19. If C is the brother of B, then what is the relation of C with respect to Q?
    (A) Aunt (B) Uncle
    (C) Father (D) Mother
    (E) Sister
20. If P is the father of Q, then what is the relation of R with respect to P?
    (A) Wife (B) Husband
    (C) Father (D) Father-in-law
    (E) Mother
21. Pointing towards a boy, Veena said, "He is the son of the only son of my grandfather." How is that boy related to Veena? **[Bank Clerical 2005]**
    (A) Uncle (B) Brother
    (C) Cousin (D) Data inadequate
    (E) None of these
22. Pointing toward Rita, Nikhil said, "I am the only son of her mother's son." How is Rita related to Nikhil? **[IGNOU 2003]**
    (A) Aunt (B) Niece
    (C) Mother (D) Cousin
23. A man introduces a woman as the daughter of the brother of her father. How is the woman related to the man?
    (A) Nephew (B) Son
    (C) Cousin (D) Uncle
24. A and B are a married couple. X and Y are brothers. X is the brother of A. How is Y related to B? **[RRB 2004]**
    (A) Brother-in-law (B) Brother
    (C) Cousin (D) None of these
25. Pointing to Ketan, Namrata said, "He is the son of my father's only son." How is Ketan's mother related to Namrata? **[Bank PO 2004]**
    (A) Daughter (B) Aunt
    (C) Sister (D) Sister-in-law
    (E) None of these

Directions (Qs. 26–29): Study the following information carefully and answer the questions given below:

R has 2 children of different genders. A is the brother-in-law of T who is unmarried. D is the cousin of M who is the granddaughter of R. B is the aunt of L who is the only daughter of K. Q is the mother of B. A is the spouse of K. T is the aunt of L and has only one sibling. C is the son-in-law of R. **[RRB 2022]**

26. Who is the grandson of Q?
    (A) M (B) T
    (C) L (D) D
    (E) None of these
27. How many females are there in the family?
    (A) Four (B) More than five
    (C) Five (D) Three
    (E) None of these
28. Who is the brother-in-law of A?
    (A) D (B) L
    (C) M (D) C
    (E) None of these
29. Who is the mother-in-law of K?
    (A) Q (B) B
    (C) M (D) T
    (E) None of these
30. If P $ Q means 'P is the father of Q; 'P # Q means 'P is the mother of Q; 'P * Q means 'P is sister of Q', then how is D related to N in N # A $ B * D? **[SBI PO 2000]**
    (A) nephew (B) grandson
    (C) grand daughter (D) data inadequate
    (E) None of these
31. Introducing Rina, Monika said, "She is the only daughter of my father's only daughter." How is Monika related to Rina? **[RBI 2002]**
    (A) Aunt (B) Niece
    (C) Cousin (D) Data inadequate
    (E) None of these
32. Pointing to a man Kirti said, "He is the brother of the daughter of my husband." How is the man related to Kirti?
    (A) Son (B) Husband
    (C) Cousin (D) Nephew
    (E) Brother-in-law
33. If Rahul is the brother of the son of Kartik's son, how is Rahul related to Kartik?
    (A) Son (B) Brother
    (C) Cousin (D) Grandson
34. Pointing to a photograph, a woman said, "I have no brother or sister but that woman's mother is my mother's daughter." Whose photograph was it?
    (A) Daughter (B) Father's
    (C) Son (D) None of these
35. A # B means 'A is the sister of B'
    A @ B means 'A is the daughter of B'
    A & B means 'A is the husband of B'
    A % B means 'A is the father of B'
    If A % B & C # D @ E, then how is B related to E?
    [SSC CGL 2022]
    (A) Brother (B) Son-in-law
    (C) Father (D) Son

3 Level Expert

Directions (Qs. 1–5): Read the following information carefully and answer the questions given below it:

There are six persons A, B, C, D, E and F. C is the sister of F. B is the brother of E's husband. D is the father of A and grandfather of F. There are two fathers, three brothers and a mother in the group.

1. Who is the mother? **[MAT 2005]**
   (A) A (B) B
   (C) D (D) E
2. Who is E's husband?
   (A) B (B) C
   (C) A (D) F
3. How many male members are there in the group?
   (A) 1 (B) 2
   (C) 3 (D) 4
4. How is F related to E?
   (A) Uncle (B) Husband
   (C) Son (D) Daughter
5. Which of the following is a group of brother?
   (A) ABF (B) ABD
   (C) BFC (D) BDF
6. A man showed a boy next to him and said "He is the son of my wife's sister but I am the only child of my parents." How is my son related to him? **[SSC CGL Exam 2013]**
   (A) Cousin (B) Brother
   (C) Uncle (D) Nephew
7. Six members of a family namely A, B, C, D, E, F are travelling together, B is the son of C but C is not the mother of B. A and C are a married couple. E is the brother of C. D is the daughter of A. F is the brother of B. How many male members are there in the family? **[SSC CGL Exam 2015]**
   (A) 2 (B) 3
   (C) 4 (D) 1

Directions (Qs. 8–9): Read the following information carefully to answer the given questions.

R is the sister of Q. M is the father of R. V is the son of Q. C is the maternal grandfather of V. M does not have a married daughter. **[IBPS 2017]**

8. How is R related to V?
   (A) Uncle
   (B) Aunt
   (C) Mother
   (D) Can't be determined
   (E) Nephew
9. If B is married to Q, then how is B related to M?
   (A) Grandson (B) Son-in-law
   (C) Son (D) Daughter-in-law
   (E) Can't be determined
10. If Nayra says, "Kanika's father Rahul is the only son of my father-in-law Amit", then how is Bhawna, who is the sister of Kanika, related to Amit?
    (A) Niece (B) Daughter
    (C) Wife (D) Daughter-in-law
    (E) None of these
11. A girl introduced a boy as the son of the only daughter of the father of her maternal uncle. The boy is girl's:
    (A) Brother (B) Son
    (C) Uncle (D) Son-in-law
    (E) Nephew
12. Arun said, "This girl is the wife of the grandson of my mother." Who is Arun to the girl? **[IITTM 2005]**
    (A) Father (B) Grandfather
    (C) Husband (D) Father-in-law
13. Sunil is the son of Keshav. Simran, Keshav's sister, has a son Maruti and daughter Sita. Prem is the maternal uncle of Maruti. How is Sunil related to Maruti? **[SSC CGL Exam 2015]**
    (A) Cousin (B) Maternal uncle
    (C) Brother (D) Nephew
14. If 'A + B' means 'A is the father of B', 'A -B' means 'A is the mother of B, 'A* B' means 'A is the brother of B' and 'A % B' means 'A is the sister of B', then how is Q related to S in "P + Q * R – S"? **[SSC CGL Exam 2017]**
    (A) Husband (B) Uncle
    (C) Brother (D) Father
15. If A × B means that A is the brother of B, A – B means that A is the sister of B, A + B means that A is the father of B, then which of the following expression shows that P is the paternal aunt of R? **[SSC CGL 2022]**
    (A) P – Q × R (B) P – Q + R
    (C) P × Q + R (D) P + Q – R
16. A + B means 'A is the wife of B'
    A - B means 'B is the daughter of A
    A x B means 'B is the brother of A
    A ÷ B means 'A is the father of B'.
    If P + R × T – Q + S ÷ U, then how is P related to the mother of U? **[SSC CGL 2020]**
    (A) Aunt
    (B) Mother
    (C) Maternal grandmother
    (D) Paternal grandmother
17. Pointing to a gentleman, Deepak said, "His only brother is the father of my daughter's father." How is the gentleman related to Deepak? **[RRB 2002]**
    (A) Grandfather (B) Father
    (C) Brother-in-law (D) Uncle
    (E) None of these
18. A is the brother of B, B is the daughter of C and D is the father of A. Then, how is C related to D? **[SSC CGL Exam 2014]**
    (A) Husband (B) Wife
    (C) Granddaughter (D) Grandfather

19. Pointing to the woman in the picture, Rajiv said, "Her mother has only one grandchild whose mother is my wife." How is the woman in the picture related to Rajiv? **[Bank PO 2005]**

(A) Cousin **(B)** Wife
(C) Sister **(D)** Data inadequate
(E) None of these

20. 'A # B' means 'A is the brother of B'.
'A @ B' means 'A is the daughter of B'.
'A & B' means 'A is the husband of B'.
'A % B' means 'A is the wife of B'.
If D @ N @ H & Y @ F % V, then how is N related to F? **[SSC CGL Tier 2 2022]**

(A) Son's wife **(B)** Daughter
(C) Daughter's daughter **(D)** Sister's daughter

Direction (Qs. 21–25): Read the following information carefully to answer these questions:

(i) 'A $ B' means A is mother of B.
(ii) 'A # B' means A is father of B.
(iii) 'A @ B' means A is husband of B.
(iv) 'A % B' means A is daughter of B. **[SBI PO 2005]**

21. P @ Q $ M # T indicates what relationship of P with T?

(A) Paternal grandmother
(B) Maternal grandmother
(C) Paternal grandfather
(D) Maternal grandfather
(E) None of these

22. Which of the following expression indicates 'R is the sister of H'?

(A) H $ D @ F # R **(B)** R % D @ F $ H
(C) R $ D @ F # H **(D)** H % D @ F $ R
(E) None of these

23. If F @ D % K # H, then how is F related to H?

(A) Brother-in-law
(B) Sister
(C) Sister-in-law
(D) Cannot be determined
(E) None of these

24. Which of the following expression indicates 'H is the brother of N'?

(A) H # R $ D $ N **(B)** N% F @ D $ H # R
(C) N % F @ D $ H **(D)** N % F @ D % H
(E) None of these

25. If G $ M @ K, how is K related to G?

(A) Daughter-in-law **(B)** Mother-in-law
(C) Daughter **(D)** Aunt
(E) None of these

ANSWER KEY

Level-1: Beginner

1.	(C)	2.	(A)	3.	(D)	4.	(A)	5.	(C)	6.	(D)	7.	(A)	8.	(C)	9.	(C)	10.	(C)
11.	(A)	12.	(B)	13.	(A)	14.	(A)	15.	(B)	16.	(C)	17.	(B)	18.	(A)	19.	(E)	20.	(C)
21.	(D)	22.	(C)	23.	(E)	24.	(C)	25.	(C)	26.	(D)	27.	(C)	28.	(B)	29.	(A)	30.	(A)
31.	(D)	32.	(A)	33.	(D)	34.	(A)	35.	(C)										

Level-2: Intermediate

1.	(C)	2.	(C)	3.	(A)	4.	(D)	5.	(B)	6.	(D)	7.	(D)	8.	(E)	9.	(E)	10.	(C)
11.	(A)	12.	(B)	13.	(A)	14.	(D)	15.	(C)	16.	(B)	17.	(A)	18.	(A)	19.	(B)	20.	(A)
21.	(B)	22.	(A)	23.	(C)	24.	(A)	25.	(D)	26.	(E)	27.	(B)	28.	(D)	29.	(A)	30.	(D)
31.	(E)	32.	(A)	33.	(D)	34.	(A)	35.	(B)										

Level-3: Expert

1.	(D)	2.	(C)	3.	(D)	4.	(C)	5.	(A)	6.	(A)	7.	(C)	8.	(B)	9.	(D)	10.	(E)
11.	(A)	12.	(D)	13.	(A)	14.	(B)	15.	(B)	16.	(A)	17.	(D)	18.	(B)	19.	(B)	20.	(C)
21.	(C)	22.	(B)	23.	(A)	24.	(B)	25.	(A)										

Solutions with Detailed Explanations

Level-1: BEGINNER

1. **Option (C) is correct.**

   Explanation: P is the daughter of R, who is the father of S, who is the father of Q, which implies that P is the sister of S, who is the father of Q, and thus P is the aunt of Q.

2. **Option (A) is correct.**

   Explanation: $P - R \div Q$ means P is the wife of R, who is the father of Q i.e. P is the mother of Q.

3. **Option (D) is correct.**

   Explanation: $P \times R$ denotes that P is the brother of R. $R \div Q$ denotes that R is the daughter of Q. So, P is the son of Q. So, option (D) is correct.

4. **Option (A) is correct.**

   Explanation: $P \times R - Q$ means P is the brother of R, who is the wife of Q. So, P is the brother-in-law of Q.

5. **Option (C) is correct.**

   Explanation: $P + R$ denotes that P is R's father and $R \div Q$ denotes that R is the daughter of Q. So, Q's husband is P.

6. **Option (D) is correct.**

   Explanation: P is the sister of Q since she is the daughter of R, who is Q's father, according to the formula $P \div R + Q$.

7. **Option (A) is correct.**

   Explanation: $P \times R$ denotes that P is brother of R. $R + Q$ denotes that R is the father of Q. So, here P is Q's father's brother or Q's uncle.

8. **Option (C) is correct.**

   Explanation: $P - R \times Q$ means P is the wife of R who is the brother of Q. So, here P is the sister-in-law of Q.

9. **Option (C) is correct.**

   Explanation: We can see in this figure

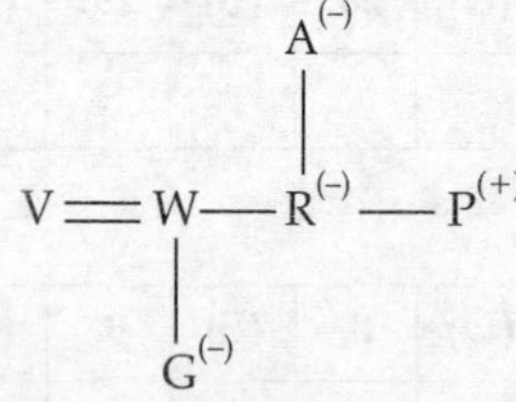

   P is the brother-in-law of V.

10. **Option (C) is correct.**

    Explanation: We can see in this figure

    $T^{(+)}$—$P^{(+)}$═$S^{(-)}$

    $Q^{(-)}$—$R^{(+)}$

    Therefore, S is the sister-in-law of T.

11. **Option (A) is correct.**

    Explanation: Only child of Amit's grandfather is his father and the daughter of Amit's father is his sister, So, Amit is the brother of that girl.

12. **Option (B) is correct.**

    Explanation: Only daughter of Kirti's father is Kirti herself. So, Kirti is the mother of that boy.

13. **Option (A) is correct.**

    Explanation: Only brother of Vinod's father's wife is Vinod's maternal uncle. Hence, Vinod is the cousin of Vishal.

14. **Option (A) is correct.**

    Explanation: Wife of Harsh's father's only son - Harsh's wife. Harsh's wife is the mother of that man. So, that man in the portrait is Harsh's son.

15. **Option (B) is correct.**

    Explanation: Boy's mother's brother is his maternal uncle. So, Sakshi is the maternal aunt of the boy.

16. **Option (C) is correct.**

    Explanation: We can see in this figure,

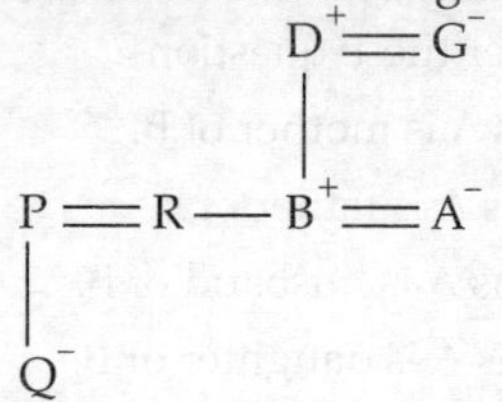

    B is the brother-in-law of P.

17. **Option (B) is correct.**

    Explanation: We can see in this figure,

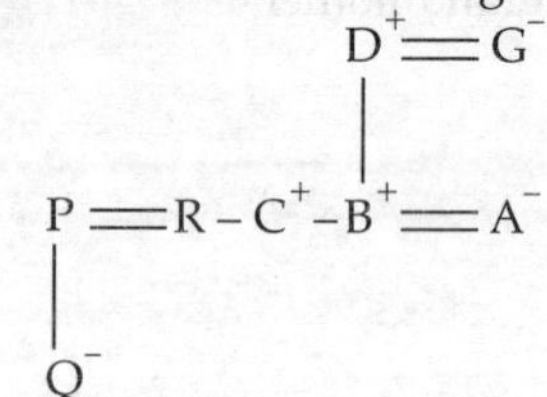

    C is the uncle of Q.

18. **Option (A) is correct.**

    Explanation: We can see in this figure,

    D^{+}═G^{-}

    P^{+}═R—B^{+}═A^{-}

    Q^{-}

    If P is the father of Q, then R is the wife of P.

19. **Option (E) is correct.**

    Explanation: We can see in this figure

    $D^{(+)}$═$R^{(-)}$ $W^{(+)}$

    $J^{(+)}$—$L^{(-)}$═$Q^{(+)}$

    $P^{(+)}$ N

    $C^{(-)}$

    L is the grandmother of C.

20. Option (C) is correct.
Explanation: We can see in this figure

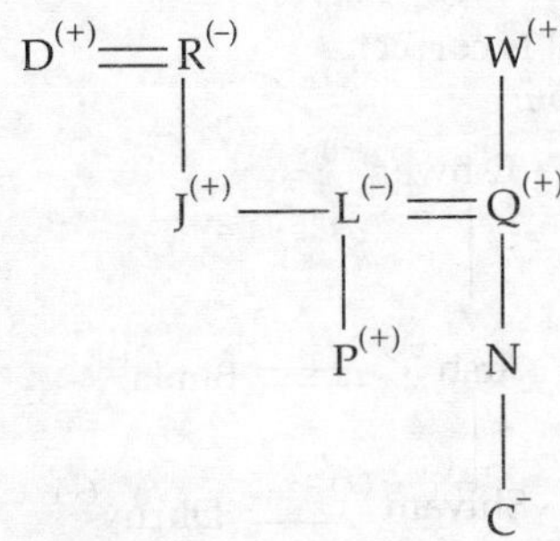

P is the brother of N.

21. Option (D) is correct.
Explanation: Only son of the man's father—man himself. So, the woman is man's wife.

22. Option (C) is correct.
Explanation: Woman's grandfather's only son - woman's father. The woman's father is also that man's brother's father. So, the woman is sister of that man.

23. Option (E) is correct.
Explanation: Neha's mother is the girl, who is also the wife of Sarita's son. The girl is therefore Sarita's son's wife, making Sarita the girl's mother-in-law.

(24–27):

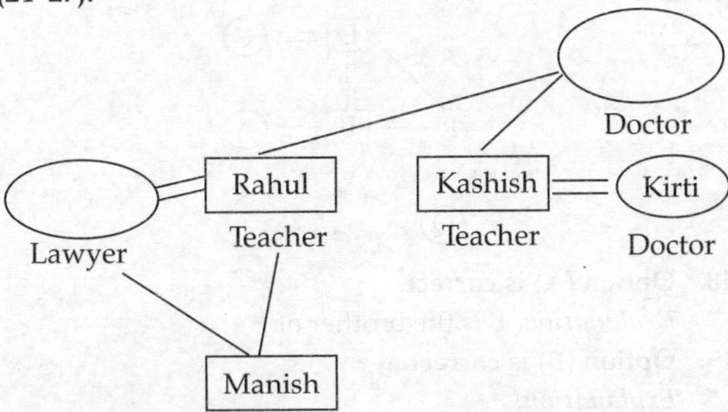

24. Option (C) is correct.
Explanation: Rahul's wife is a lawyer.

25. Option (C) is correct.
Explanation: Manish is the nephew of Kirti.

26. Option (D) is correct.
Explanation: Kashish's wife Kirti is a doctor.

27. Option (C) is correct.
Explanation: Manish is the grandson of a doctor.

28. Option (B) is correct.
Explanation: Father's wife—Mother. Mother's daughter–Sister; Deepak's sister's younger brother–Deepak's younger brother. So, the boy is Deepak's brother.

29. Option (A) is correct.
Explanation: We can see, Mother's mother–maternal grandmother:
Maternal grandmother only daughter's mother
So, the woman is the man's mother.

30. Option (A) is correct.
Explanation: Parul's father's only son is Parul himself. So, Shikha is the grandmother of Parul.

31. Option (D) is correct.
Explanation: Sukanya's husband's mother-in-law is Sukanya's mother. So, Sukanya's mother's husband is her father. Hence, Sukanya's father's daughter is her sister. So, Arti is the sister of Sukanya.

32. Option (A) is correct.
Explanation: Sumit's daughter's mother is Sumit's wife. So, the father of Sumit's wife is his father-in-law. Hence, Manish is the father-in-law of Sumit.

33. Option (D) is correct.
Explanation: Kanika mother's sister is the man's mother i.e., Kanika is the cousin of that man.

34. Option (A) is correct.
Explanation: Father of Amit's daughter is Amit himself. So, Mohit is the son of Amit.

35. Option (C) is correct.
Explanation: Anita's father's sister is Anita's paternal aunt.

Level-2: INTERMEDIATE

1. Option (C) is correct.
Explanation: M is the father-in-law of G

$P \qquad F^{(-)} = M^{(+)}$

$G^{(+)} = L^{(-)} — H^{(+)}$

$T^{(+)} = K^{(-)}$

2. Option (C) is correct.
Explanation: K is the daughter-in-law of L

$P \qquad F^{(-)} = M^{(+)}$

$G^{(+)} = L^{(-)} \quad H^{(+)}$

$T^{(+)} = K^{(-)}$

3. Option (A) is correct.
Explanation: We can see,

$P \qquad F^{(-)} = M^{(+)}$

$G^{(+)} = L^{(-)} — H^{(+)}$

$T^{(+)} = K^{(-)}$

H is the son of M.

4. Option (D) is correct.
Explanation: D is the brother of E, who is the daughter of B. Hence, D is B's son. A and C are also sisters of B. A is thus D's aunt.

5. Option (B) is correct.
Explanation:

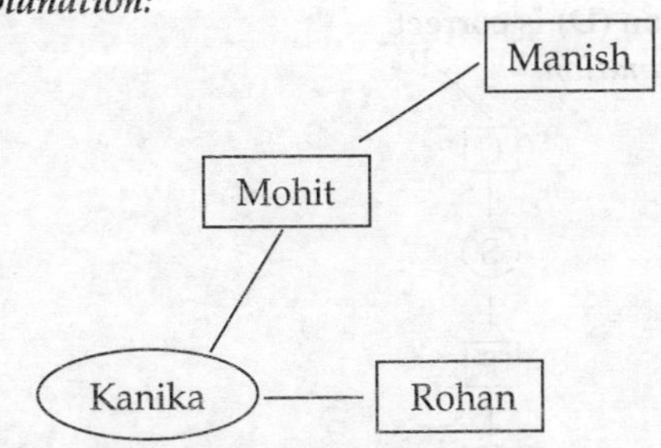

So, Rohan is grandson of Manish.

6. **Option (D) is correct.**
Explanation: The family's female members are the mothers of three married sons, wives of all three son's, one unmarried daughter and two have 2 daughters each.
So, number of females in the family
$= (1 + 3 + 1 + 2 \times 2) = 9$
7. **Option (D) is correct.**
Explanation: Brother of man's wife → brother-in-law of the man. So, the son of the woman's brother is brother-in-law of the man. Therefore, the brother of the woman is the father-in-law of the man.
Hence, the woman is the sister of the man's father-in-law.
8. **Option (E) is correct.**
Explanation: $A \div B + C - E \times F$ means A is the mother of B, who is the father of C, who is the brother of E, who is the daughter of F. Thus, C and E are the children of B and F. Since B is the father, so F is the mother of C and E i.e. F is the wife of B. A is the mother of F's husband i.e. A is the mother-in-law of F.

(9–10):

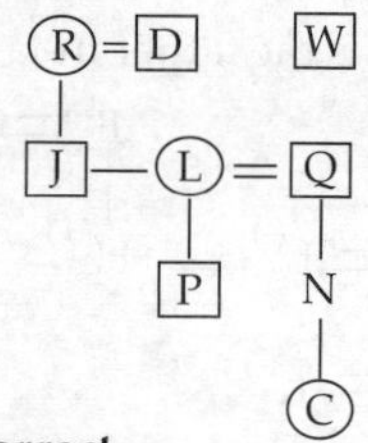

9. **Option (E) is correct.**
10. **Option (C) is correct.**
Explanation: P is brother of N.
11. **Option (A) is correct.**
Explanation: I am my mother's only daughter. The man's mother is hence the woman.
12. **Option (B) is correct.**
Explanation: P + Q – S means

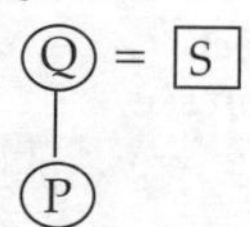

So, S is father of P.
13. **Option (A) is correct.**
Explanation:

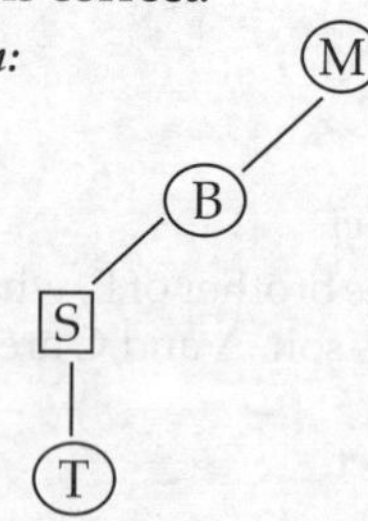

14. **Option (D) is correct.**
Explanation:

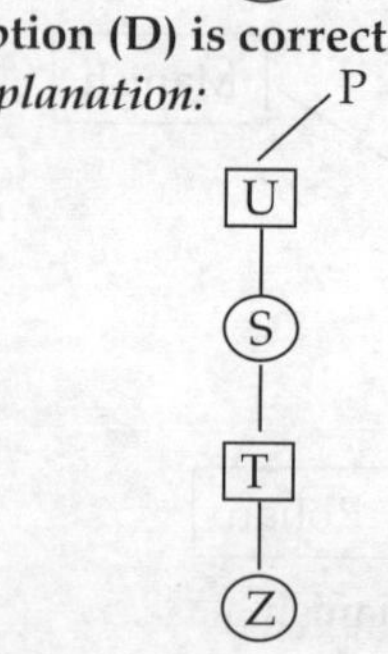

15. **Option (C) is correct.**
Explanation: As X is the brother of son of Y's son. So, clearly X is the grandson of Y.
16. **Option (B) is correct.**
Explanation:

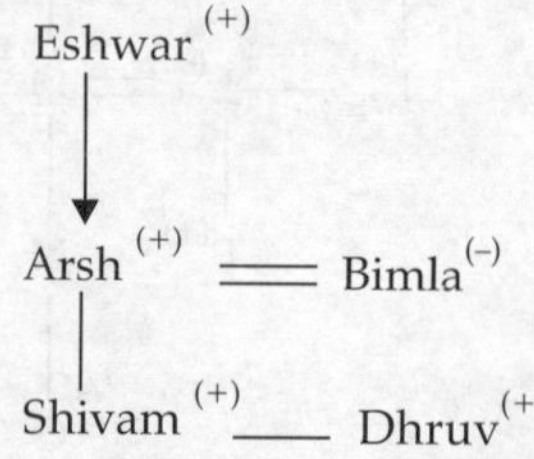

So, Bimla is the daughter-in-law of Eshwar.
17. **Option (A) is correct.**
Explanation:

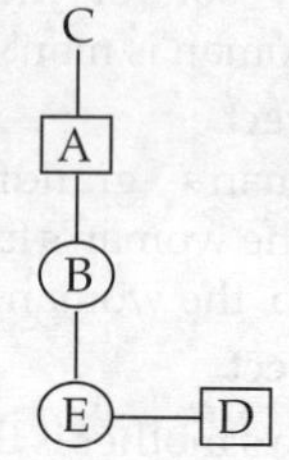

Here, B is the mother of D. So, A is the maternal grandfather of D.

(18–20):

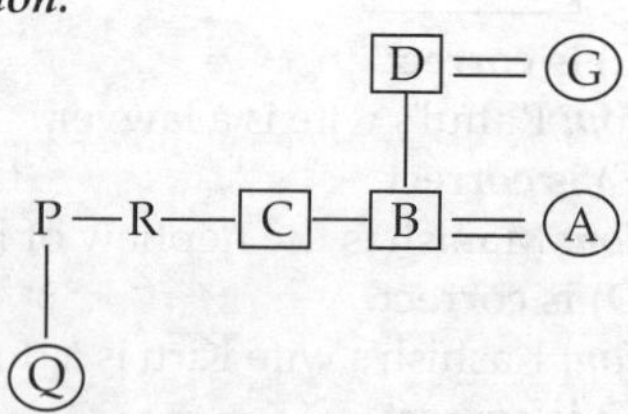

18. **Option (A) is correct.**
Explanation: B is the brother of P.
19. **Option (B) is correct.**
Explanation:

So, C is the uncle of Q.
20. **Option (A) is correct.**
Explanation:
So, R is the wife of P.

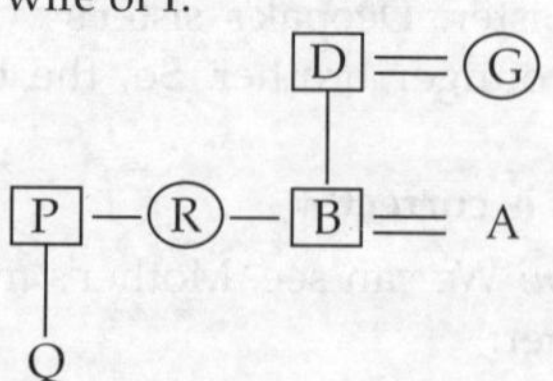

21. **Option (B) is correct.**
Explanation: Only son of the grandfather—Father; only son of the father—Brother. Therefore, the boy is Veena's brother.

22. **Option (A) is correct.**
Explanation: Brother of Rita; son of Rita's mother. Nikhil is thus Rita's brother's son. So, Rita is the aunt of Nikhil.

23. **Option (C) is correct.**
Explanation: Brother of father --- uncle,
Daughter of uncle --- cousin.

24. **Option (A) is correct.**
Explanation: A and B are married couples. X and Y are brothers, and since X is A's brother, Y is likewise A's brother. Y is therefore the brother-in-law of B.

25. **Option (D) is correct.**
Explanation: Namrata's father's only son—Namrata's brother.
So, Ketan is the son of Namrata's brother.
Thus, Ketan's mother is the wife of Namrata's brother.
So, she is Namrata's sister-in-law.

(26–29):

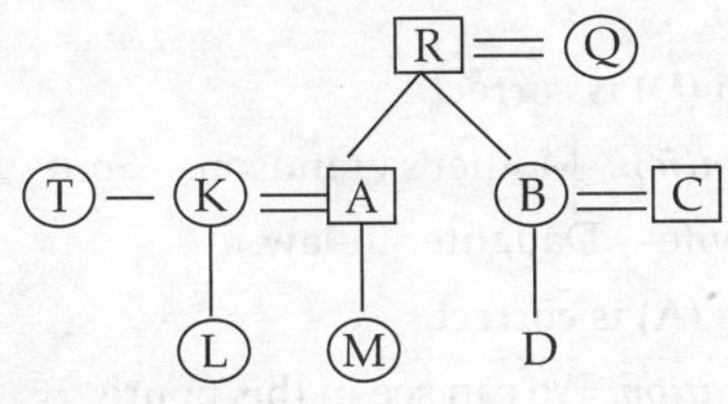

26. **Option (E) is correct.**
27. **Option (B) is correct.**
28. **Option (D) is correct.**
Explanation: C is the brother-in-law of A.
29. **Option (A) is correct.**
30. **Option (D) is correct.**
Explanation: N is the mother of A, who is the father of B, and B is the sister of D. So, D may be son or daughter of A.
31. **Option (E) is correct.**
Explanation: Only daughter of Monika's father, Monika. Consequently, Rina is Monika's child, making Monika, Rina's mother.
32. **Option (A) is correct.**
Explanation: Daughter of Kirti's husband - Kirti's daughter. So, the man is Kirti's son.
33. **Option (D) is correct.**
Explanation:

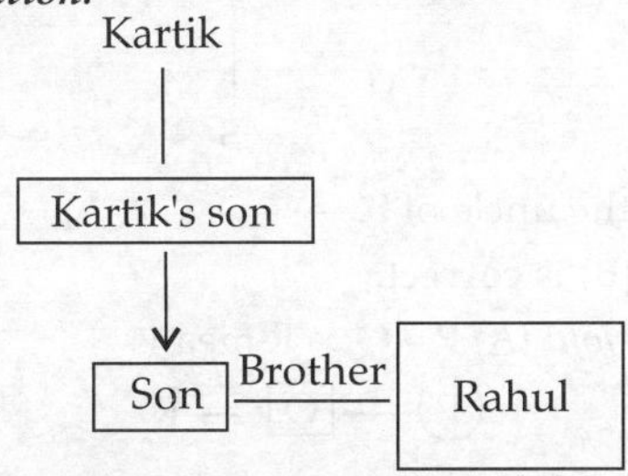

So, Rahul is the grandson of Kartik.

34. **Option (A) is correct.**
Explanation: We can see, the narrator is her mother's daughter, as she does not have a brother. Therefore, the woman speaking is the mother of the woman in the picture. So, the woman in the picture is her daughter.

35. **Option (B) is correct.**
Explanation: A % B & C # D @ E means

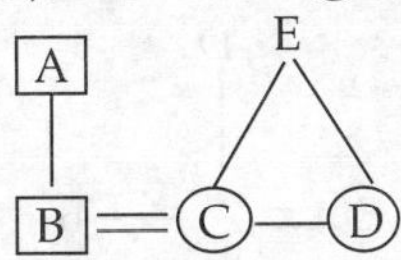

As, C is the daughter of E, so B is the son-in-law of E.

Level-3: EXPERT

1. **Option (D) is correct.**
Explanation:

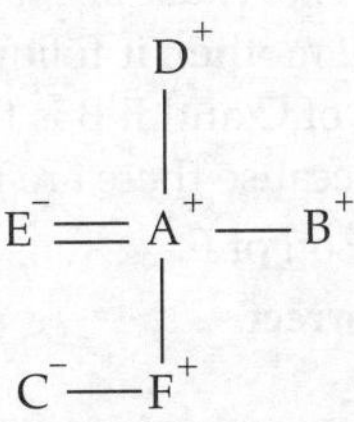

A is the father of F because F's grandfather, D, is the father of A. D and A are the fathers as a result. C is the daughter of A because she is F's sister. Given that there is just one mother, it follows that E is A's wife and the mother of C and F. B is therefore A's brother. F is C's sibling because there are three brothers.
Clearly, E is the mother.

2. **Option (C) is correct.**
Explanation:

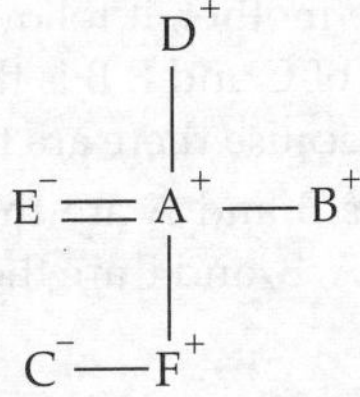

A is the father of F because F's grandfather, D, is the father of A. D and A are the fathers as a result. C is the daughter of A because she is F's sister. Given that there is just one mother, it follows that E is A's wife and the mother of C and F. B is therefore A's brother. F is C's sibling because there are three brothers.
Clearly, A is husband of E.

3. **Option (D) is correct.**
Explanation:

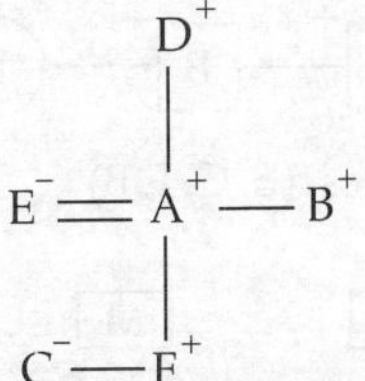

A is the father of F because F's grandfather, D, is the father of A. D and A are the fathers as a result. C is the daughter of A because she is F's sister. Given that there is just one mother, it follows that E is A's wife and the mother of C and F. B is therefore A's brother. F is C's sibling because there are three brothers.
There are four male members.

4. **Option (C) is correct.**
Explanation:

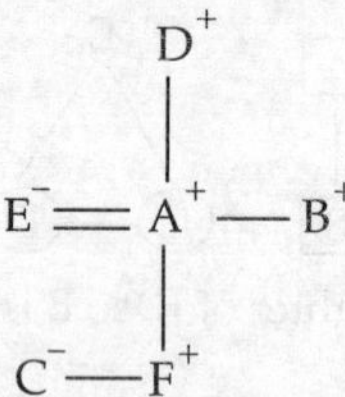

A is the father of F because F's grandfather, D, is the father of A. D and A are the fathers as a result. C is the daughter of A because she is F's sister. Given that there is just one mother, it follows that E is A's wife and the mother of C and F. B is therefore A's brother. F is C's sibling because there are three brothers.

Clearly, F is the son of E.

5. **Option (A) is correct.**
Explanation:

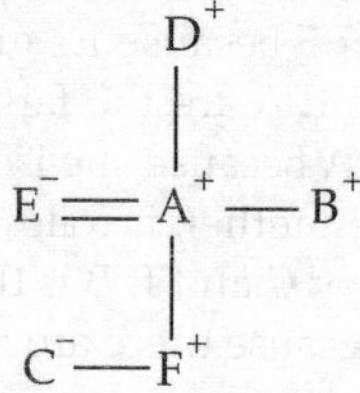

A is the father of F because F's grandfather, D, is the father of A. D and A are the fathers as a result. C is the daughter of A because she is F's sister. Given that there is just one mother, it follows that E is A's wife and the mother of C and F. B is therefore A's brother. F is C's sibling because there are three brothers. Clearly, brothers B and A are the siblings. Also, the sibling of C is F. A, B, and F are the names of the three brothers.

6. **Option (A) is correct.**
Explanation: The boy is the son of the man's sister-in-law. Therefore, the man's son is the cousin of that boy.

7. **Option (C) is correct.**
Explanation: We can see in this figure

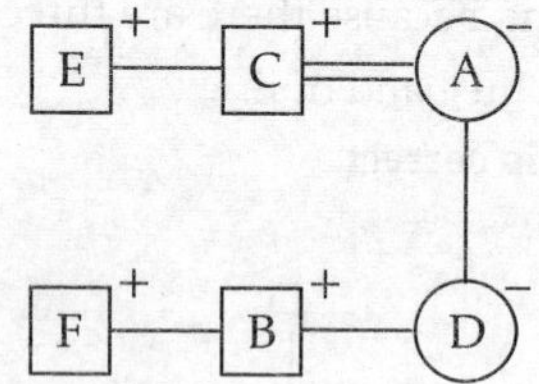

There are 4 males. (E, C, F, B)

(8–9):

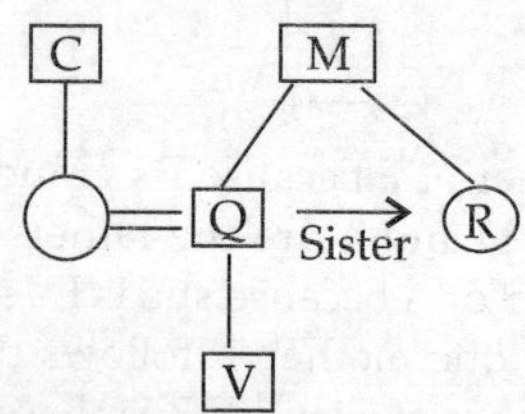

8. **Option (B) is correct.**
Explanation: R is the aunt of V.

9. **Option (D) is correct.**
Explanation:

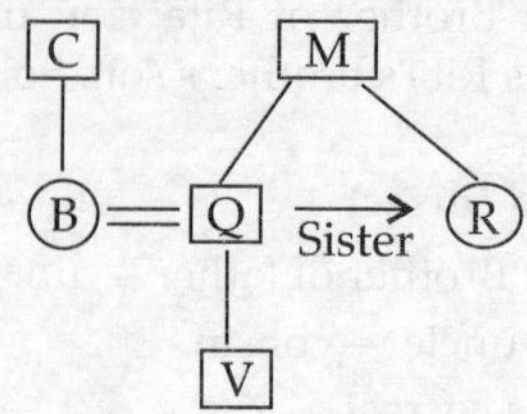

So, B is the daughter-in-law of M.

10. **Option (E) is correct.**
Explanation: Amit, Nayra's father-in-law, is a single parent. Rahul is Nayra's spouse, and as Kanika and Bhawna are his daughters. So, Bhawna is Amit's granddaughter.

11. **Option (A) is correct.**
Explanation: Only daughter of maternal uncle's father— Uncle's sister— Mother, so Mother's son— Brother.

12. **Option (D) is correct.**
Explanation: Mother's grandson— Son;
Son's wife— Daughter-in-law.

13. **Option (A) is correct.**
Explanation: We can see in this figure

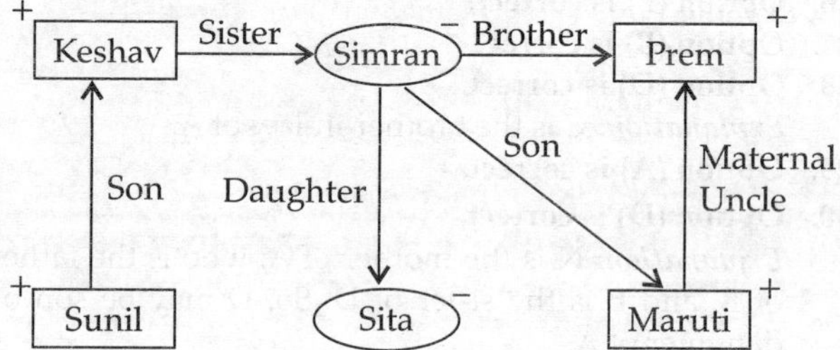

It is clear from the figure, that Sunil is the cousin of Maruti .

14. **Option (B) is correct.**
Explanation: We can see in this figure

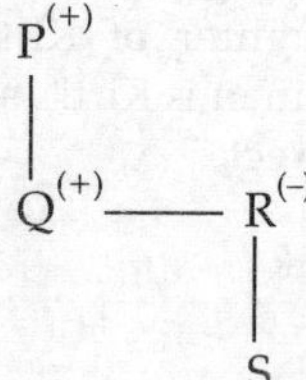

So, Q is the uncle of S.

15. **Option (B) is correct.**
Explanation: (A) P – Q × R means

So, P is the sister of R.

(B) P – Q + R means

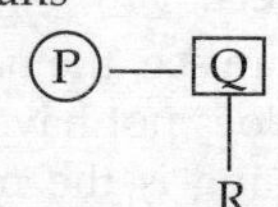

So, P is the paternal aunt of R.

(C) P × Q + R means

So, P is the paternal uncle of R.

(D) P + Q – R means

So, P is the father of R

16. Option (A) is correct.

Explanation: Here, P + R × T – Q + S ÷ U means

So, P is the aunt of Q, who is the mother of U.

17. Option (D) is correct.

Explanation: The father of Deepak's daughter is Deepak himself. Thus, the father of Deepak is the man's brother. The man will be Deepak's uncle, who is also his father's sibling.

18. Option (B) is correct.

Explanation: We can see in this figure.

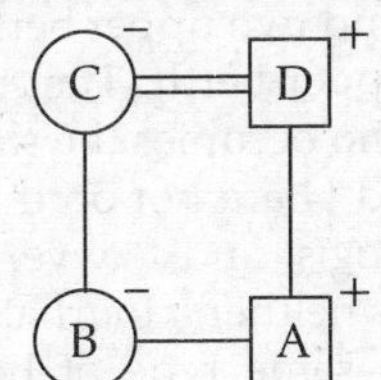

B is the daughter of C, A is B's brother, and D is A's father; hence, C is wife of D.

19. Option (B) is correct.

Explanation: Child of Rajiv and his wife also his own. The child of Rajiv and the woman is the grandchild of the lady. So, the woman in the picture is Rajiv's wife.

20. Option (C) is correct.

Explanation: Here, D @ N @ H & Y @ F % V means

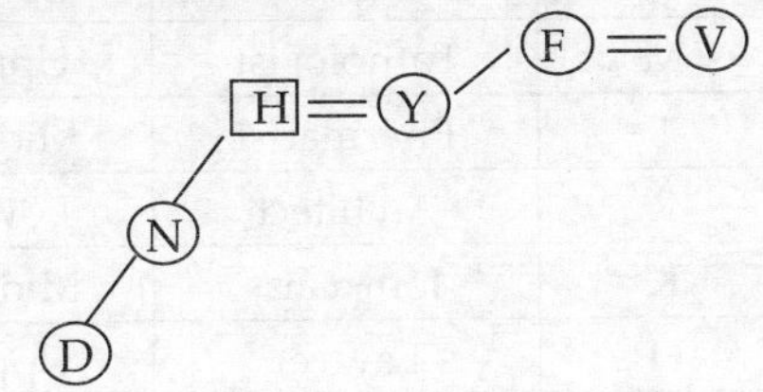

So, N is F's daughter's daughter.

21. Option (C) is correct.

Explanation: P @ Q $ M # T means

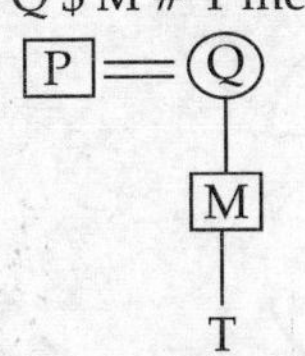

So, P is paternal grandfather of T.

22. Option (B) is correct.

Explanation: R % D @ F $ H means

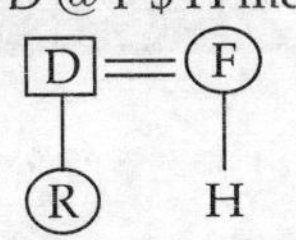

So, R is the sister of H.

23. Option (A) is correct.

Explanation: F @ D % K # H, means

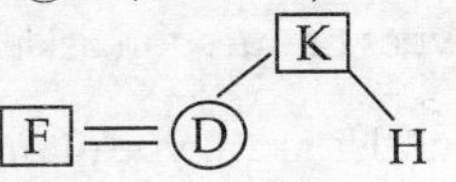

So, F is the brother-in-law of H.

24. Option (B) is correct.

Explanation: N % F @ D $ H # R means

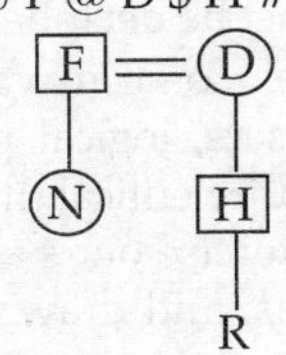

So, H is the brother of N.

25. Option (A) is correct.

Explanation: G $ M @ K means

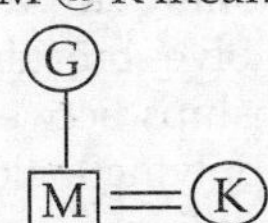

So, K is the daughter-in-law of G.

■ ■ ■

Chapter 6

Puzzles

LEARNING OBJECTIVES:

- Solving questions based on different types of puzzles
- Different types of question asked in competitive exams

Reasoning puzzles are a type of problem or challenge that necessitate logical thinking, analysis, and deduction in order to find a solution. These puzzles often involve presenting clues, information, or situations that must be deciphered and understood.

Reasoning puzzles come in various forms, such as riddles, brain teasers, logical problems, or complex scenarios that require critical thinking. Their purpose is to assess and exercise one's ability to reason, make logical connections, and draw conclusions based on the provided information.

Solving reasoning puzzles entails working with limited data or constraints and employing deductive or inductive reasoning to reach a solution. The process usually involves breaking down the problem, examining relationships between different elements or variables, and applying logical rules or patterns to narrow down possibilities.

The challenge of reasoning puzzles lies in the ability to think analytically, outside the box, and consider multiple perspectives to find the correct solution. They offer both enjoyment and difficulty, providing a stimulating mental exercise that enhances problem-solving skills, critical thinking abilities, and cognitive flexibility.

This category of analytical reasoning comprises puzzles involving a specific number of items, such as individuals or objects. Candidates are required to analyse the given information, condense it appropriately, and answer the questions based on the puzzle.

The questions on Puzzle Test may be any of the following types:

I. Classification Type Questions
II. Seating/Placing Arrangements
III. Comparison Type Questions
IV. Sequential Order of Things
V. Selection Based on Given Conditions
VI. Family-Based Problems
VII. Jumbled Problems

Example 1: Study the following information carefully and answer the given question:

B, M, T, R, K, H and D are travelling in a train compartment with a III-tier sleeper berth. Each of them has a different profession of Engineer, Doctor, Architect, Pharmacist, Lawyer, Journalist and Pathologist. They occupied two lower berths, three middle berths and two upper berths. B, the Engineer, is not on the upper berth. The Architect is the only other person who occupies the same type of berth as that of B. M and H are not on the middle berth and they are Pathologist and Lawyer respectively. T is a Pharmacist. D is neither a Journalist nor an Architect. K occupies the same type of berth as that of the Doctor.

Who is the Architect?

(a) D
(b) H
(c) R
(d) Data inadequate
(e) None of these

Sol. (c)

Persons	Professions	Berth
B	Engineer	Lower
M	Pathologist	Upper
T	Pharmacist	Middle
R	Architect	Lower
K	Journalist	Middle
H	Lawyer	Upper
D	Doctor	Middle

R is the Architect.

Example 2: There are six persons A, B, C, D, E and F in a school. Each of the teachers teaches two subjects, one compulsory subject and the other optional subject. D's optional subject was History while three others have it as compulsory subject. E and F have Physics as one of their subjects. F's compulsory subject is Mathematics which is an optional subject of both C and E. History and English are A's subjects but in terms of compulsory and optional subjects, they are just reverse of those of D's. Chemistry is an optional subject of only one of them. The only female teacher in the school has English as her compulsory subject.

What is C's compulsory subject?

(a) History (b) Physics
(c) Chemistry (d) English
(e) Mathematics

Sol. (a)

Teachers	Compulsory Subject	Optional Subject
A	History	English
B	History	Chemistry
C	History	Mathematics
D	English	History
E	Physics	Mathematics
F	Mathematics	Physics

C's compulsory subject is History.

1 Level Beginner

1. Three persons A, B and C wore shirts of black, blue and orange colours (not necessarily in that order) and pants of green, yellow and orange colours (not necessarily in that order). No person wore pant and shirt of the same colour. Further, it is given that
   1. A did not wear shirt of black colour.
   2. B did not wear shirt of blue colour.
   3. C did not wear shirt of orange colour.
   4. A did not wear pant of green colour.
   5. B wore pant of orange colour.

   What were the colours of pant and shirt worn by C, respectively? **[UPSC 2005]**

   (A) Yellow and Black **(B)** Yellow and Blue
   (C) Green and blue **(D)** Orange and Black
   (E) Green and Blue

Directions (Qs. 2–6): Study the following information carefully and answer the given questions. **[IBPS RRB Clerk, 2016]**

A, B, C, D, E, F and G are seven friends. They play three types of games, viz Snooker, Ice hockey and Table tennis. Each game is played by at least two players. Each one of them has a favourite car, viz Honda, Fiat, Ferrari, Benz, Etios, Swift and Beleno, but not necessarily in the same order.

B likes Etios and does not play Table tennis. The one who likes Beleno plays the same game as E. C likes Fiat and plays the same game as G. D plays Ice hockey only with the one who likes Honda. G plays neither Ice hockey nor Table tennis. F does not like Beleno. G likes neither Benz nor Ferrari. D does not like Benz. E does not like Honda.

2. Which of the following groups play Snooker?

   (A) B, G **(B)** A, B, C
   (C) B, C, G **(D)** D, G, B
   (E) None of these

3. Who likes the Ferrari Car?

   (A) A **(B)** G
   (C) F **(D)** D
   (E) None of these

4. Which of the following cars does A like?

   (A) Ferrari
   (B) Beleno
   (C) Honda
   (D) Either Beleno or Swift
   (E) None of these

5. Which of the following combination is true?

   (A) A-Beleno-Table tennis
   (B) G-Honda-Table tennis
   (C) B-Etios-Ice hockey
   (D) D-Ferrari-Snooker
   (E) None of these

6. Who likes Honda?

   (A) G **(B)** A
   (C) E **(D)** C
   (E) F

7. A ate grapes and pineapple; B ate grapes and oranges; C ate oranges, pineapple and apple; D ate grapes, apple and pineapple. After taking fruits, B and C fell sick. In the light of the above facts, it can be said that the cause of sickness was **[UPSC Pre 2016]**

   (A) apple **(B)** pineapple
   (C) grapes **(D)** oranges

Directions (Qs. 8–12): Study the following information carefully and answer the questions given below.

There are seven persons i.e. A, B, C, D, E, F and G. They all belongs to different cities i.e. Kolkata, Mumbai, Chennai, Pune, Lucknow, Ahmedabad and Delhi, but not necessarily in the same order. D belongs to Pune. Neither A nor F belongs to Kolkata. B belongs to Ahmedabad. C does not belong to Kolkata and Lucknow. G belongs to Mumbai. A does not belongs to Lucknow and Chennai. **[IBPS Clerk 2018]**

8. Who among the following belongs to Kolkata?

   (A) A **(B)** D
   (C) F **(D)** G
   (E) None of these

9. Which of the following statements is true?

   (A) A belongs to Chennai.
   (B) G belongs to Delhi.
   (C) E belongs to Kolkata.
   (D) F belongs to Pune.
   (E) None of these

10. F belongs to which of the following city?

(A) Chennai (B) Mumbai
(C) Delhi (D) Lucknow
(E) None of these

11. Which of the following combination is true?

(A) A-Delhi (B) D-Pune
(C) E-Kolkata (D) All are correct
(E) All are Incorrect

12. A belongs to which of the following city?

(A) Delhi (B) Mumbai
(C) Kolkata (D) Chennai
(E) None of these

Directions (Qs. 13–17): Study the following information carefully and answer the questions given below.

Eight persons have different designations i.e., Chairman (CHM), General Manager (GM), Assistant General Manager (AGM), Deputy General Manager (DGM), Manager, Assistant Manager, Probationary Officer, Clerk in a company. The order of seniority is the same as given above i.e., CHM is the senior-most designation and Clerk is the junior-most designation. Only two persons are junior than J. Only one designation is there between J and O. Only two designations are there between O and M. M is senior than O. Number of persons who are senior than O is same as the number of persons who are junior than P. N is senior than P but junior than L. K is not in the junior-most post. Q is not the PO. **[SBI Clerk 2020]**

13. How many persons are junior than O?

(A) Three (B) One
(C) Two (D) None
(E) Four

14. How many designations are there between N and M?

(A) One (B) Two
(C) Three (D) Four
(E) Five

15. Number of persons who are junior than J is the same as the number of persons who are senior than.........?

(A) M (B) L
(C) K (D) N
(E) O

16. Which of the following designations is exactly between the designations of Q and O?

(A) Assistant Manager (B) Manager
(C) PO (D) CGM
(E) AGM

17. Who among the following is the Manager of the company?

(A) O (B) P
(C) J (D) L
(E) N

Directions (Qs. 18–22): Study the following information carefully and answer the questions given below.

A, B, C, D, E, F and G are seven boys looking for three different types of shoes i.e., Canvas, Formal and Sports with at least two but not more than three for each type of shoe. Each of them has a liking for different shoe brands i.e. Nike, Adidas, Spark, Reebok, Woodland, Bata & Puma but not necessarily in the same order. C is looking for Sports shoes and his choice is Puma. F does not like Adidas and Bata and looking for same type of shoe only as of G among them. B is looking for same type of shoe as that of A but neither Sports nor Canvas. E is not looking for Sports shoes and he likes Reebok. The one who likes Nike is not looking for Canvas and Formal Shoes. A likes Spark. The one who likes Bata is not looking for formal shoes. **[IBPS Clerk Pre 2015]**

18. Which is B's favourite brand?

(A) Nike (B) Puma
(C) Bata (D) Adidas
(E) None of these

19. Which brand does D like?

(A) Bata (B) Spark
(C) Nike (D) Data inadequate
(E) None of these

20. Which types of shoe does three of them have?

(A) Canvas (B) Formal
(C) Sports (D) Data inadequate
(E) None of these

21. Which is F's favourite brand?

(A) Adidas (B) Reebok
(C) Bata (D) Nike
(E) None of these

22. What type of shoe does F like?

(A) Canvas (B) Formal
(C) Sports (D) Data inadequate
(E) None of these

Directions (Qs.23–25): Consider the following information and answer the questions based on it.

Y, R, M, J and B pursue five professions, namely, Designer, Technician, Teacher, Engineer, and Accountant and have five gadgets, namely Mobile, Laptop, Calculator, Tablet and Computer, in random order. A person can pursue only one profession and have only one gadget. **[RRB Non-Technical 2016]**

(i) M has a calculator and is neither a teacher nor a Technician.
(ii) The designer has a tablet.
(iii) The person who has a mobile is neither an accountant nor a teacher.
(iv) Y is an engineer who has neither computer nor mobile.
(v) J is a technician and B is not a teacher.

23. Which gadget does the accountant have?

(A) Tablet (B) Calculator
(C) Mobile (D) Laptop

24. Which among the following is a right combination?

(A) Teacher-Laptop (B) Accountant-Tablet
(C) Technician-Computer (D) Engineer-Laptop

25. Who has a computer?

(A) B (B) J
(C) R (D) Y

Directions (Qs. 26–30): Study the given information carefully and answer the questions that follow:

(i) A, B, C, D, E, F and G are sitting in a circle facing at the centre and playing cards.

(i) E is neighbour of A and D.
(iii) G is not between F and C.
(iv) F is to the immediate right of A. **[Bank PO 2005]**

26. Which of the following does not have the pair of persons sitting adjacent to each other?
(A) BA (B) CB
(C) DE (D) GD
(E) None of these

27. Which of the following pairs has the second person sitting immediately to the right of the first?
(A) AB (B) CB
(C) EA (D) DG
(E) None of these

28. What is the position of F?
(A) Third to the left of C.
(B) Second to the right of C.
(C) To the immediate left of A.
(D) To the immediate right of B.
(E) None of these

29. Who are the neighbours of B?
(A) A and F (B) C and D
(C) F and C (D) Data inadequate
(E) None of these

30. Which of the following persons are sitting to each other from left to right in the order as shown?
(A) BGC (B) FBC
(C) CDG (D) EDG
(E) None of these

Directions (Qs. 31–35): Read the following information carefully and answer the following questions.

Seven persons A, B, C, D, E, F and G were born on different months viz. January, February, March, April, June, August and October of the same year, but not necessarily in the same order. Only three persons were born before E and D is not one of them. F was not born immediately after E. B was born after F. A was born immediately before the month in which G was born. Only two persons were born between G and F. **[RBI PO 2017]**

31. How many persons were born between C and E?
(A) Three (B) Two
(C) Four (D) Five
(E) None of these

32. Who amongst the following is the oldest?
(A) A (B) C
(C) E (D) B
(E) F

33. Who amongst the following was born between the months in which A and D were born?
(A) E (B) G
(C) C (D) B
(E) Both E and G

34. How many persons were born after D?
(A) One (B) Three
(C) Four (D) Two
(E) None of these

35. Who amongst the following is the person who was born in the month which has less than 30 days?
(A) F (B) B
(C) G (D) C
(E) A

2 Intermediate Level

Directions (Qs. 1–5): Study the following information carefully and answer the questions given below.

Seven boxes J, K, L, M, N, O and P are kept one above the other, but not necessarily in the same order. Each box contains different elements—Cookies, Pencils, Spoons, Diaries, Colours, Jewellery and Watches, but not necessarily in the same order. Only two boxes are kept between M and N. The pencil box is kept immediately below M. Only two boxes are kept between the pencil box and the Watch box. N is kept above the Watch box. The Diary box is kept immediately below the Watch box. Only three boxes are kept between the Diary box and J. The jewellery box is kept immediately above the J. O is kept immediately above K. O is not a pencil box. P is kept immediately below the Cookies box. Only one box is kept between P and the Spoon box.

1. Which of the following boxes is kept immediately above M?
(A) P (B) O
(C) L (D) Diary box
(E) Jewellery box

2. What is the position of O in the given stack of boxes?
(A) First from top (B) Second from top
(C) Third from bottom (D) Fifth from bottom
(E) Fourth from top

3. Which of the following boxes contains Spoons?
(A) Other than those given as options
(B) K
(C) M
(D) N
(E) L

4. Four of the following five are alike in a certain way and hence form a group. Which of the following does not belong to the group?
(A) N-Diaries (B) P-Spoons
(C) O-Colours (D) K-Pencils
(E) M-Jewellery

5. How many boxes are kept between K and the Watch box?
(A) More than three (B) None
(C) Three (D) One
(E) Two

Directions (Qs. 6–10): Study the following information carefully and answer the questions given below.

Eight people E, F, G, H, W, X, Y and Z are sitting in two parallel rows containing four people each. E, F, G and H are sitting in Row-I facing North and W, X, Y and Z are sitting in Row 2 facing South. (But not necessarily in the same order). Thus, each person sitting in Row-I faces another person sitting in Row 2. Each of the two rows consists of one Professor, one Leader, one Technician and one Doctor (but not necessarily in the same order). The Doctor of Row 1 sits second to the right of H. E is an immediate neighbour of H. E faces the Leader of Row 2. X sits to the immediate right of the Leader. X faces one of the immediate neighbours of the Professor of Row 1. The Professor of Row 1 does not sit at any of the extreme ends of the line.W sits second to the left of Y. Z does not face G. F faces the Professor of Row 2. In both the rows, only one person sits between the Professor and the Technician. W is not a Doctor.

6. Which of the following represent both the immediate neighbours of W?
   (A) X and Leader of Row 2
   (B) Y and Technician of Row 2
   (C) Y and Doctor of Row 2
   (D) X and Professor of Row 2
   (E) Z and Doctor of Row 2
7. Who amongst the following sits to the immediate left of the Leader of Row 1?
   (A) Professor of Row 1 **(B)** F
   (C) H **(D)** G
   (E) Professor of Row 1
8. Which of the given statements is true with respect to the given arrangement?
   (A) None of the given statements is true.
   (B) Y sits to the immediate right of Z.
   (C) H is a Teacher.
   (D) Technician of one row faces the Doctor of another row.
   (E) Y and H face each other.
9. If E and X interchange their places and so do G and Z, then who amongst the following will face W?
   (A) Z
   (B) Other than those given as options.
   (C) A
   (D) X
   (E) H
10. Which of the following represent the people sitting at extreme ends of both the lines?
    (A) F, H and Z, W **(B)** F, H and X, Y
    (C) E, H and Y, Z **(D)** G, F and Z, Y
    (E) G, F and W, Y

Directions (Qs. 11–16): Study the given information carefully to answer the given questions.

Seven athletes M, N, O, P, Q, R and S live on seven different floors of a building but not necessarily in the same order. The lowermost floor of the building is numbered 1, the one above that is numbered 2 and so on till the topmost floor is numbered 7. Each one of them runs for a different distance in marathon — 850 m, 1300 m, 2200 m, 2800 m, 3300 m, 4000 m, and 4700 m, but not necessarily in the same order. The one who runs for 2200 m lives on floor numbered 3. Only one person lives between O and the one who runs for 2200 m. The one who runs for 4000m lives immediately above O. Only one person lives between the one who runs for 4000 m and the one who runs for 1300 m. The number of people living between O and the one who runs for 1300 m is same as that between the one who runs for 4000 m and R. N lives on an odd numbered floor. N ran for 2000 m more than the one who lives on floor number 4. Only two people live between Q and the one who runs for 3300 m. The one who runs for 2800 m lives on one of the floors below Q but not on the floor number 2, only two people live between M and S. The one who runs for 850 m lives immediately below M.

11. How many people live between S and N?
    (A) Three **(B)** One
    (C) Five **(D)** Four
    (E) Two
12. Who amongst the following live(s) between P and the one who runs for 1300 m?
    (A) Both Q and R
    (B) Only S
    (C) Both R and the one who runs for 850 m.
    (D) Only the one who runs for 4000 m.
    (E) Both R and the one who runs for 2200 m.
13. As per the given arrangement, four of the following five are alike in a certain way and so form a group. Which one of the following does not belong to the group?
    (A) Q-3300 m **(B)** O-1300 m
    (C) Floor number 4-S **(D)** Floor number 2-R
    (E) Floor number 7–1300 m
14. Which of the following statements is true with respect to the given arrangement?
    (A) Only two people live between P and O.
    (B) Q runs for 4000 m.
    (C) N lives on floor number 7.
    (D) The one who runs for 850 m lives immediately above P.
    (E) None of the above
15. If the total distance covered by B and M is 5300 m, then how much did B run alone?
    (A) 2000 m **(B)** 4000 m
    (C) 3100 m **(D)** 1300 m
    (E) 600 m
16. Who amongst the following runs for 2200 m?
    (A) P **(B)** N
    (C) Q **(D)** R
    (E) S

Directions (Qs. 17–22): Study the following information carefully and answer the questions asked.

Seven friends A, B, C, D, E, F and G are sitting around a circular table facing either the center or outside. Each one of them belongs to a different department viz. Finance, Marketing, Sales, HR, Corporate Finance, Investment Banking and Operations but not necessarily in the same order.

C sits third to the right of G. G faces the centre. Only one person sits between C and the person working in the HR department. Immediate neighbours of C face outside. Only one person sits between F and D. Both F and D face the center. D does not work in the HR department. A works in

Investment Banking Department. A faces the centre. Two people sit between the person who work in Investment Banking and Marketing Departments. The person who works in Corporate Finance sits to the immediate left of E. C faces same direction as E. The person who works in Sales department sits to the immediate left of the person who works for Operations department.

17. For which of the following departments does B works?

(A) Finance **(B)** Marketing
(C) HR **(D)** Corporate Finance
(E) Operations

18. What is the position of B with respect to the person who works for the Sales department?

(A) Immediate right **(B)** Third to the left
(C) Second to the right **(D)** Second to the left
(E) Fourth to the right

19. Who sits to the immediate right of E?

(A) The person who works for the marketing department.
(B) C
(C) B
(D) F
(E) A

20. Who amongst the following sits exactly between C and the person who works for the HR department?

(A) B
(B) The person who works for marketing department.
(C) The person who works Operations department.
(D) D
(E) G

21. Who amongst the following sit between the persons who work for Marketing and Investment Banking departments when counted for the left hand side of the person working for the Marketing department?

(A) F and G **(B)** E and C
(C) C and B **(D)** F and D
(E) B and D

22. How many people sit between the person who works for the Operations department and A, when counted from the right hand side of A?

(A) One **(B)** Two
(C) Three **(D)** Four
(E) More than four

Directions (Qs. 23–25): Study the following information carefully and answer the questions given below.

Seven square boxes of different areas are placed on seven shelves of different widths from bottom to top (such as bottom shelf is numbered as 1 and top is numbered as 7). Seven boxes of different areas contain different chocolates viz. 5-Star, Dairy milk, KitKat, Perk, Bournville, Silk and Munch. Each box is of different colour viz. Blue, Black, Green, Orange, Purple, Pink and White. The width of each shelf is different viz. 5, 9, 11, 15, 17, 21, 35, but not necessarily in the same order. The area of the box placed immediately below the top shelf is equal to the square of the width (which is a prime number) of the corresponding shelf. The area of the box of KitKat is equal to the addition of the areas of the box of Silk and the one which is placed on the bottom shelf. The shelf which contain green box has highest width. There are only two boxes between the box of Orange colour and box of Perk, which is placed at an even numbered shelf but below 5th shelf. Box of Bourneville and Dairy milk are not of Blue colour and Pink colour. The box of dairy milk has its side, equal to the width of the corresponding shelf minus 1 and has equal number of shelf above and below it.The sides of the boxes of Silk is 12 and Munch is 5. The ratio of the widths of shelf on which Pink and White box is equal to the ratio of the widths of shelf on which Green and Black box is kept. No box is placed above the Pink box and it is neither Silk nor Munch. The area of the box of 5-star is equal to the square of the width of the shelf on which White colour box is kept.

The box of Bourneville is placed immediately above the box of KitKat. The width of the shelf on which Pink box is kept is multiple of seven and width of the shelf on which White box is kept is a perfect square. The width of the shelf on which box of KitKat is placed is least. Green box is placed at the bottom and it does not contain Silk. There are three boxes in between Purple and Blue box, which is not placed above the box of Silk. No two boxes have equal areas. The width of the shelf on which the Blue box is kept is less than the width of the shelf on which Black box is kept. The box which has its area equal to the square of seven is placed immediately below the Black box.

23. What is the colour of the box, which is placed immediately above the box, whose side is equal to the width of the corresponding shelf minus 1?

(A) White **(B)** Orange
(C) Blue **(D)** Pink
(E) None of these

24. What will be the area of the box of Bourneville?

(A) 25 **(B)** 144
(C) 81 **(D)** 64
(E) 289

25. Which of the following combination is true regarding Silk in pattern of 'Shelves-Colour-Area-Width'?

(A) 2-Blue-144-11 **(B)** 3-B1ue-144-11
(C) 3-B1ack-144-15 **(D)** 6-White-169-17
(E) None of the above

Directions (Qs. 26–30): Study the following information carefully to answer these questions.

Eight friends A, B, C, D, E, F, G and H are sitting around a circle facing the center. A sits third to the left of B, while second to the right of F. D does not sit next to A or B. C and G always sit next to each other. H never sits next to D and C does not sit next to B. **[SBI Clerk 2016]**

26. Which of the following pairs sits between H and E?

(A) F, D **(B)** H, B
(C) C, G **(D)** E, G
(E) None of these

27. Starting from A's position, if all the eight were arranged in alphabetical order in clockwise direction, the seating position of how many members (excluding A) would not change?

(A) None **(B)** One
(C) Two **(D)** Three
(E) None of these

28. Which of the following pairs has only one person sitting between them, if the counting is done in clockwise direction?
(A) A, B (B) C, D
(C) F, E (D) G, H
(E) None of these

29. Who sits to the immediate right of E?
(A) A (B) D
(C) F (D) H
(E) None of these

30. What is the position of B with respect to C?
(A) Second to the left
(B) Third to the right
(C) Third to the left
(D) Can't be determined
(E) None of these

Directions (Qs.31–33): Read the information carefully and answer the questions:

A company ABC printed different number of books in different years 1947, 1956, 1987, 1998, 2002 such that number of books printed are not same in any year. 66 books were printed in an odd numbered year which is not 1947. The number of books printed in 1947 is 10 less than that printed in 1987. 59 books were printed in an year before the year in which 61 books are printed but not immediate before. The number of books printed in 2002 is 2 more than that printed in 1998. **[SBI Clerk 2018]**

31. How many books were printed in 1947 ?
(A) 56 (B) 66
(C) 63 (D) 61
(E) None of these

32. What is the difference between the number of books printed in 1956 and 2002?
(A) 7 (B) 10
(C) 8 (D) 4
(E) None of these

33. In how many years the number of books printed are more than that printed in 1998?
(A) Two (B) One
(C) None (D) Three
(E) Four

Directions (Qs. 34–35): These questions are based on the following information:

Five men A, B, C, D and E read a newspaper. The one who reads first gives it to C. The one who reads last had taken from A. E was not the first or last to read. There were two readers between B and A. **[SSC 1999]**

34. B passed the newspaper to whom?
(A) A (B) C
(C) D (D) E
(E) None of these

35. Who read the newspaper last?
(A) A (B) B
(C) C (D) D
(E) None of these

3 Level Expert

1. Eight boxes i.e., M, N, O, P, Q, R, S and T are placed one above the another but not necessarily in the same order. Three boxes are placed between M and T. M is placed either at the top most or bottom most position. Box O is placed just above to the box N. Box S is placed just below to the box T. There are two boxes placed between R and S. Not more than two boxes are placed between M and R. More than three boxes are placed between O and P.
Which of the following box is placed third from the bottom? **[SBI PO 2021]**
(A) S (B) Q
(C) O (D) R
(E) None of these

2. Eight persons A, B, C, D, E, F, G and H are buying some products one after another but not necessarily in the same order. At most two persons are buying products before F. Only one person is buying between D and F. C is buying just before H. One person is buying between C and D. A is buying just before E. B is buying before G and after E.
How many persons are buying their products after D? **[SBI Clerk Exam 2020]**
(A) None (B) Two
(C) More than three (D) One
(E) None of these

3. There are eight persons namely S, T, U, V, W, X, Y and Z living on eight different floors from one to eight. Ground floor is number one and top floor is number eight but not necessarily in the same order, X lives on odd number floor but does not live on the 3rd floor. Z lives immediate below X. More than two person live between Z and Y. There are six persons who live between S and Y. V lives immediate above W but below T. U does not live above X. W does not live immediate above U.
Who lives on floor number five? **[IBPS Clerk Exam 2017]**
(A) U (B) S
(C) Z (D) T
(E) None of these

4. More than 10 persons were sitting in a circular row facing the centre. B is 3rd to the left of C. Two person are sitting between D and B. A sits immediate right of E. One person is sitting between C and E. Less than two people are sitting between D and A. A does not sit second to the right of B.
How many persons are sitting in the circular arrangement? **[IBPS PO Mains Exam 2017]**
(A) 14 (B) 11
(C) 12 (D) 13
(E) None of these

Direction (Qs. 5–6): Eight friends A, B, C, D, W, X, Y and Z are sitting around a square table in such a way that four of them sit at four corners of the square while the other four sit in the middle of each sides. The ones who sit at the four corners face outside while those who sit in the middle of the sides face inside. C is an immediate neighbour of A, who faces center. W sits second to the left of C. Y sits fourth to the left of W. Two persons sit between Y and D (either from left or right). C is not an immediate neighbour of D. B sits second to the right of D. X sits second to the right of B. **[IBPS PO 2017]**

5. How many persons sits between Z and C when counted from left of Z?
   (A) None **(B)** One
   (C) Two **(D)** Three
   (E) More than three
6. What is the position of Y with respect to D?
   (A) Third to the right **(B)** Second to the right
   (C) Fourth to the left **(D)** Third to the left
   (E) None of these

Direction (Qs. 7–10): Five friends P, Q, R, S and T travel from Goa individually for five cities i.e. Chennai, Kolkata, Delhi, Hyderabad and Mangalore by different means of transport i.e. bus, train, airplane, car and boat. The one who travelled for Delhi did not use boat. R travelled for Mangalore by car and S travelled by boat. Q travelled by airplane for Kolkata and T travelled by train. Delhi and Chennai is not connected with bus route with Goa. **[SBI Clerk Exam 2011]**

7. Which combination of place and transport of the following is true?
   (A) Kolkata — bus **(B)** Delhi — airplane
   (C) Mangalore — train **(D)** Chennai — boat
   (E) Hyderabad — car
8. Kolkata : Aeroplane. Similarly, S:
   (A) Hyderabad
   (B) Chennai
   (C) Mangalore
   (D) Delhi
   (E) Cannot be determined.
9. Who of the following travelled to Delhi?
   (A) T **(B)** R
   (C) S **(D)** P
   (E) Q
10. Which combination of the following is true for P?
    (A) travelled by bus for Kolkata
    (B) travelled by train for Delhi
    (C) travelled by boat for Chennai
    (D) travelled by bus for Hyderabad
    (E) None of these

Direction (Qs. 11–15): Eight people P, Q, R S, T, U, V and W were born in three different months (of the same year) but not necessarily in the same order, namely March, June and December. Such that not less than two people and not more than three people were born in a month, each of them likes a different fruit, namely, Guava, Peach, Banana Cherry, Mango, Orange, Kiwi and Apple not necessarily in the same order. Only Q and W were born in March, R likes Apple and was born in the same month as T. R was not born in December. The one who likes Mango was born in June. T does not like Mango. U was not born in the same month as T. V does not like Mango. The one who likes kiwi and the one who likes Banana were born in the same month. The one who likes kiwi was not born in same month as W. U does not like kiwi. The one who likes Guava was born in the same month as P. Q does not like peach. **[Andhra Bank PO 2015]**

11. As per the given arrangement, which of the following combinations represents only the people who were born in December?
    (A) T, V **(B)** U, P, T
    (C) V, U **(D)** P, T
    (E) U, V, S
12. As per the given arrangement, which of the following person represent the one who was born in the same month as the one who likes orange?
    (A) U **(B)** P
    (C) R **(D)** T
    (E) W
13. Which of the following fruits does T like, as per the given arrangement?
    (A) Orange **(B)** Peach
    (C) Guava **(D)** Banana
    (E) Other than those given as options
14. Which of the following combination is correct, as per the given arrangement?
    (A) December — Peach **(B)** June — Orange
    (C) June — Banana **(D)** March — Guava
    (E) None of these
15. Who amongst the following likes Peach, as per the given arrangement?
    (A) P **(B)** V
    (C) U **(D)** W
    (E) T

Directions (Qs. 16–20): Study the following information carefully and answer the questions given below:

Eight persons sit around a square table and four of them face inside while four of them face outside. Four persons sit at the corner and rest four sit at the edges of the table. O and N face each other. P sits 2nd to the right of N. L sits just left Q who sits at corner of table. Q faces outside. M and Q are immediate neighbours and face opposite direction to each other. P face opposite direction as R and S face. S does not sit just left of P. **[RRB PO 2022]**

16. Who sits 4th to the left of L?
    (A) P **(B)** S
    (C) O **(D)** M
    (E) None of these
17. Who among the following persons face outside?
    (A) M, O **(B)** N, L
    (C) R, L **(D)** O, P
    (E) None of these
18. Who among the following is the immediate neighbour of R?
    (A) P **(B)** M
    (C) S **(D)** Q
    (E) O

19. Which of the following statement is true?

I. P and Q sit diagonally opposite to each other

II. S does not face outside

III. N and R are immediate neighbours

(A) Both I and II are true
(B) Only III is true
(C) Both II and III are true
(D) Both I and III are true
(E) None is true

20. What is the position of S with respect to M?

(A) 2nd to the right **(B)** Immediate left
(C) 2nd to the left **(D)** 3rd to the right
(E) None of these

Directions (Qs. 21–25): Study the following information carefully and answer the given questions.

Nine persons A, B, C, D, E, F, G, H, I like different flowers tulip, lily, rose, lotus, sunflower, orchid, iris, Tithonia and Cosmos also each of them live in three different cities Patna, Surat and Mumbai. Not less than two and not more than four live in same cities. G lives with only the one who likes tulip. B lives with H and the one who likes Lotus. D and F lives with the one who likes Sunflower. The one who likes Tithonia does not lives in Surat. The one who likes Lily and the one who likes Orchid live in the same city but not in Patna. Neither A nor H likes Tithonia. The one who likes Iris lives with A and I. E lives in Surat but does not like Lily. G does not live in Patna. H does not like Iris. A does not like Rose and Lotus. D does not like Orchid. The one who like Rose and the one who like Cosmos live in same city. Neither A nor I likes Sunflower. **[IBPS PO 2018]**

21. Who among the following like Tulip?

(A) C **(B)** H
(C) B **(D)** F
(E) None of these

22. In which of the following city D and E live respectively?

(A) Mumbai and Surat **(B)** Both in Patna
(C) Patna and Surat **(D)** Both in Surat
(E) None of these

23. A likes which of the following flower?

(A) Lily **(B)** Tithonia
(C) Cosmos **(D)** Orchid
(E) None of these

24. Four of the following are alike in a certain way so form a group. Which of the following does not belong to that group?

(A) B **(B)** H
(C) A **(D)** F
(E) I

25. C lives with which among the following?

(A) B, I and H **(B)** D, F and E
(C) A, I and E **(D)** Only G
(E) None of these

ANSWER KEY

Level-1: Beginner

1.	(C)	2.	(C)	3.	(D)	4.	(B)	5.	(A)	6.	(E)	7.	(D)	8.	(E)	9.	(C)	10.	(D)
11.	(D)	12.	(A)	13.	(E)	14.	(A)	15.	(D)	16.	(A)	17.	(B)	18.	(D)	19.	(C)	20.	(B)
21.	(E)	22.	(A)	23.	(B)	24.	(A)	25.	(D)	26.	(A)	27.	(C)	28.	(E)	29.	(C)	30.	(B)
31.	(B)	32.	(B)	33.	(E)	34.	(D)	35.	(E)										

Level-2: Intermediate

1.	(D)	2.	(B)	3.	(A)	4.	(C)	5.	(B)	6.	(D)	7.	(D)	8.	(D)	9.	(D)	10.	(D)
11.	(A)	12.	(B)	13.	(C)	14.	(C)	15.	(E)	16.	(E)	17.	(A)	18.	(D)	19.	(D)	20.	(B)
21.	(C)	22.	(A)	23.	(B)	24.	(E)	25.	(C)	26.	(A)	27.	(D)	28.	(C)	29.	(B)	30.	(E)
31.	(A)	32.	(D)	33.	(A)	34.	(B)	35.	(D)										

Level-3: Expert

1.	(A)	2.	(E)	3.	(D)	4.	(B)	5.	(D)	6.	(A)	7.	(D)	8.	(B)	9.	(A)	10.	(D)
11.	(E)	12.	(E)	13.	(C)	14.	(E)	15.	(D)	16.	(B)	17.	(C)	18.	(A)	19.	(D)	20.	(C)
21.	(A)	22.	(D)	23.	(C)	24.	(D)	25.	(D)										

Solutions with Detailed Explanations

Level-1: BEGINNER

1. **Option (C) is correct.**
Explanation: B wore pant of orange colour. Now, A didn't wear pant of green or orange colour. so, A wore pant of yellow colour. Thus, C wore pant of green colour. B wore the pant of orange colour and so, didn't wear shirt of orange colour. Also, B didn't wear shirt of blue colour. So, B wore shirt of black colour. Thus, C didn't wear shirt of black or orange colour. Hence, C wore shirt of blue colour.

Sol. (2–6):

Cars	Person	Game
Beleno	A	Table tennis
Etios	B	Snooker
Fiat	C	Snooker
Ferrari	D	Ice hockey
Benz	E	Table tennis
Honda	F	Ice hockey
Swift	G	Snooker

2. **Option (C) is correct.**
Explanation: B, C, G play snooker.
3. **Option (D) is correct.**
Explanation: D likes Ferrari car.
4. **Option (B) is correct.**
Explanation: A likes Beleno car.
5. **Option (A) is correct.**
Explanation: A Beleno table tennis is true.
6. **Option (E) is correct.**
Explanation: F likes Honda.
7. **Option (D) is correct.**
Explanation:

Fruit/ Person	Apple	Pineapple	Grapes	Orange
A		√	√	
B			√	√
C	√	√		√
D	√	√	√	

Since, B and C fell sick, so the cause of sickness is oranges which is eaten by both of them.

Sol. (8–12):

Person	Cities
A	DELHI
B	AHMEDABAD
C	CHENNAI
D	PUNE
E	KOLKATA
F	LUCKNOW
G	MUMBAI

8. **Option (E) is correct.**
Explanation: E belongs to Kolkata.
9. **Option (C) is correct.**
Explanation: E belongs to Kolkata is true.
10. **Option (D) is correct.**
Explanation: F belong to Lucknow.
11. **Option (D) is correct.**
Explanation: All of the given combinations are true.
12. **Option (A) is correct.**
Explanation: A belong to Delhi.

Sol. (13–17):

Designation	Person
Chairman CHM	M
General manager GM	L
Assistant general manager AGM	N
Deputy general manager DGM	O
Manager	P
Assistant manager	J
Probationary officer	K
Clerk	Q

13. **Option (E) is correct.**
Explanation: Four persons are junior than O.
14. **Option (A) is correct.**
Explanation: Only one designation that is general manager is there between N and M.
15. **Option (D) is correct.**
Explanation: There are two people who are junior to J and two people who are seniors to N.
16. **Option (A) is correct.**
Explanation: Assistant Manager falls exactly in the middle of Q and O.
17. **Option (B) is correct.**
Explanation: P is the manager of the company.

Sol. (18–22):

Brand	Boy	Types of Shoes
Puma	C	Sport
Woodland	F	Canvas
Bata	G	Canvas
Adidas	B	Formal
Spark	A	Formal
Reebok	E	Formal
Nike	D	Sport

18. Option (D) is correct.
Explanation: Adidas is B′s favourite shoes.

19. Option (C) is correct.
Explanation: D likes Nike.

20. Option (B) is correct.
Explanation: Three of them have formal shoes.

21. Option (E) is correct.
Explanation: F′s favourite brand is woodland.

22. Option (A) is correct.
Explanation: F likes canvas.

Sol. (23–25):

Person	Gadget	Profession
M	Calculator	Accountant
B	Tablet	Designer
R	Computer	Teacher
Y	Laptop	Engineer
J	Mobile	Technician

23. Option (B) is correct.
Explanation: The accountant has calculator.

24. Option (A) is correct.
Explanation: Engineer—laptop is the correct combination.

25. Option (D) is correct.
Explanation: R has a computer.

Sol. (26–30):
The sitting arrangement is :

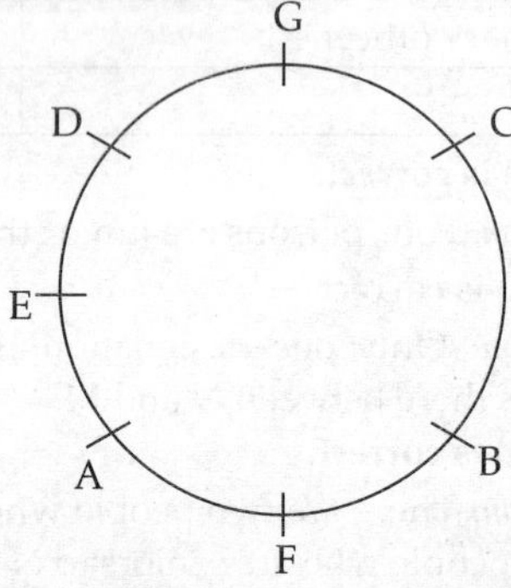

26. Option (A) is correct.
Explanation: B and A are not sitting adjacent to each other.

27. Option (C) is correct.
Explanation: A is sitting to the immediate right of E

28. Option (E) is correct.

29. Option (C) is correct.
Explanation: F and C are the neighbours of B.

30. Option (B) is correct.
Explanation: F, B and C are sitting to each other from left to right in the order.

Sol. (31–35):

Months of birth	Person
January	C
February	A
March	G
April	E
June	D
August	F
October	B

31. Option (B) is correct.
Explanation: Two persons were born between C and E.

32. Option (B) is correct.
Explanation: C is the oldest.

33. Option (E) is correct.
Explanation: Both E and G were born between the months in which A and D were born.

34. Option (D) is correct.
Explanation: Two persons were born after D.

35. Option (E) is correct.
Explanation: A was born in February.

Level-2: INTERMEDIATE

Sol. (1–5):

Box	Item
N	colour
O	Watches
K	Diaries
M	Cookies
P	Pencils
L	Jewellery
J	Spoons

1. **Option (D) is correct.**
Explanation: Diary box is kept immediately above M.

2. **Option (B) is correct.**
Explanation: O is second from the top.

3. **Option (A) is correct.**
Explanation: Box J contains spoon.

4. **Option (C) is correct.**
Explanation: O-colours follows different pattern, so it does not belong to the group.

5. **Option (B) is correct.**
Explanation: None

Sol. (6-10):

Doctor Technician Leader Professor

Row 2 Y X W Z ↓ Facing South

G H E F ↑ Facing North

Row 1

Technician Leader Professor Doctor

6. **Option (D) is correct.**
Explanation: X and the professor of row 2 are immediate neighbours of W.

7. **Option (D) is correct.**
Explanation: Technician G sits to the immediate left of the leader of row 1.
8. **Option (D) is co rrect.**
Explanation: The technician of row 1 faces the doctor of row 2.
9. **Option (D) is correct.**
Explanation: The new arrangement is

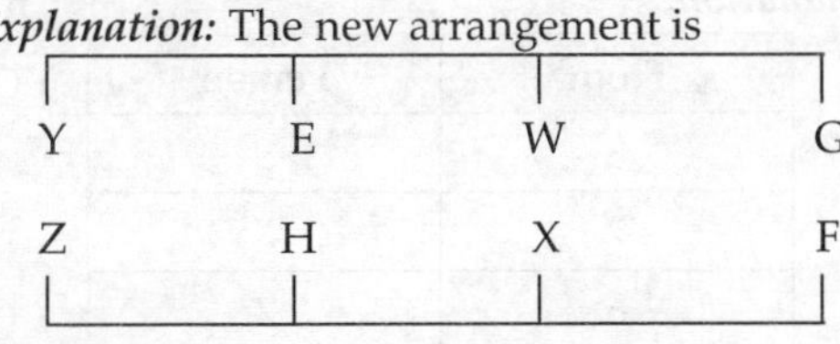

X will face W.
10. **Option (D) is correct.**
Explanation: G, F and Z, Y are sitting extreme ends of both the lines.

Sol. (11–16):

Person	Floor number	Distance
N	7	3300 m
M	6	4700 m
R	5	850 m
Q	4	1300 m
S	3	2200 m
P	2	4000 m
O	1	2800 m

11. **Option (A) is correct.**
Explanation: Three people live between N and S.
12. **Option (B) is correct.**
Explanation: Only S lives between P and the people who runs 1300 m.
13. **Option (C) is correct.**
Explanation: All other pairs have three places of difference between the elements, with the exception of pair, floor number 4-S.
14. **Option (C) is correct.**
Explanation: N lives on floor number 7.
15. **Option (E) is correct.**
Explanation: Here, M covered the distance = 4700 m
Distance covered by B and M = 5300 m
So, B runs alone = 5300 – 4700 = 600 m
16. **Option (E) is correct.**
Explanation: S runs for 2200 m.

Sol. (17–22):

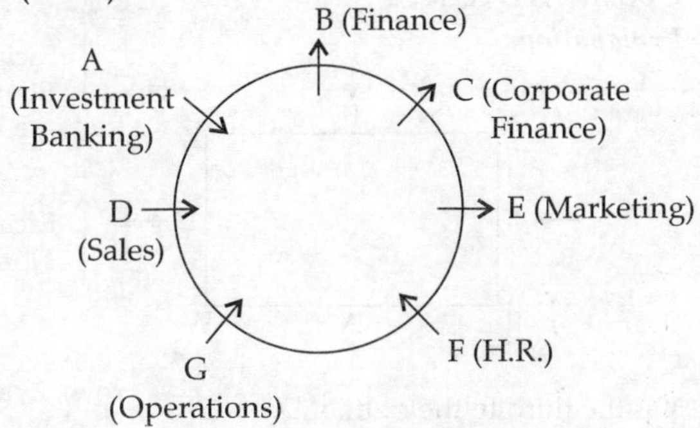

17. **Option (A) is correct.**
Explanation: B works in finance department.
18. **Option (D) is correct.**
Explanation: B is the 2nd to the left of D.
19. **Option (D) is correct.**
Explanation: F, a member of the HR Department, is seated directly to E's right.
20. **Option (B) is correct.**
Explanation: It is obvious that E, who works in the marketing department, is seated between C and F.
21. **Option (C) is correct.**
Explanation: Counting from the left of E, the individuals who work in the departments of marketing and investment banking are E and A, respectively, and the individuals who sit between them are C and B.
22. **Option (A) is correct.**
Explanation: G is the employee who works in the operations department.
As a result, there is just one person—D—sitting between G and A when counting from the right side of A.

Sol. (23–25):

Shelves	Boxes	Area of the box	Colour	Width of the shelf
7	5 star	81	Pink	21
6	Bournville	289	Purple	17
5	Kit kat	169	Orange	5
4	Dairy milk	64	White	9
3	Silk	144	Black	15
2	Perk	49	Blue	11
1	Munch	25	green	35

23. **Option (B) is correct.**
Explanation: The colour of required box is orange.
24. **Option (E) is correct.**
Explanation: The area of the box Bournville is 289.
25. **Option (C) is correct.**
Explanation: Silk: black, 3-144-15 is the correct combination.

Sol. (26–30):
The sitting arrangement is :

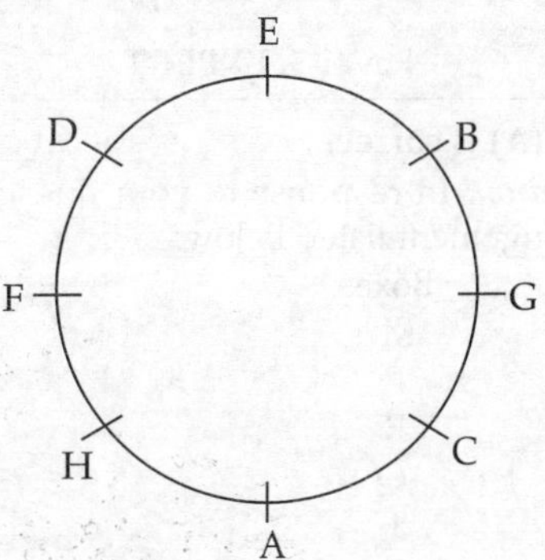

26. **Option (A) is correct.**
Explanation: D and F sits between H and E.

27. Option (D) is correct.

Explanation: The new sitting arrangement is

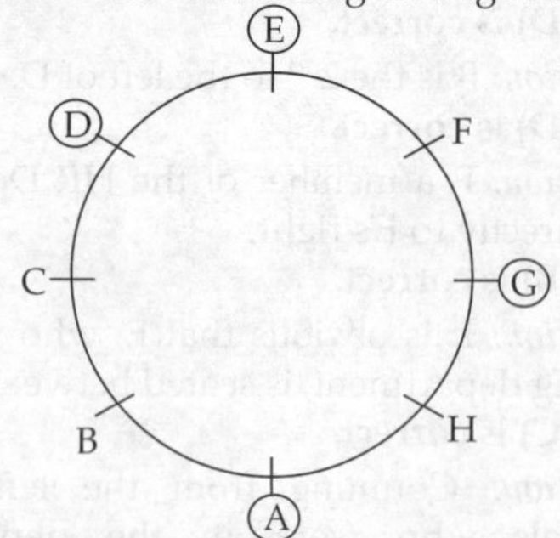

28. Option (C) is correct.

Explanation: D sits between F and E

29. Option (B) is correct.

Explanation: D sits to the immediate right of E.

30. Option (E) is correct.

Explanation: B sits second to the right of C.

Sol. (31–33):

Years	Number of books printed
1947	56
1956	59
1987	66
1998	61
2002	63

31. Option (A) is correct.

Explanation: Number of books printed in 1947 = 56

32. Option (D) is correct.

Explanation: Required difference = 63 – 59 = 4

33. Option (A) is correct.

Explanation: In two years, the number of books printed are more than printed is 1998.

Sol. (34–35):

Men	Newspaper reading order
A	Fourth
B	First
C	Second
D	Fifth
E	Third

34. Option (B) is correct.

Explanation: B passed the newspaper to C.

35. Option (D) is correct.

Explanation: D reads the newspaper last.

Level-3: EXPERT

1. Option (A) is correct.

Explanation: In response to your question, we have the arrangement listed below:

Boxes
M
P
R
Q
T
S
O
N

Box 'S' is placed third from the bottom.

2. Option (E) is correct.

Explanation: Based on the evidence provided, we arrive at the following chronology:

A > E > F > B > D > G > C >H

Three other people are purchasing the goods after D.

3. Option (D) is correct.

Explanation:

Floor	Person
8	S
7	X
6	Z
5	T
4	V
3	W
2	U
1	Y

T lives on the fifth floor.

4. Option (B) is correct.

Explanation:

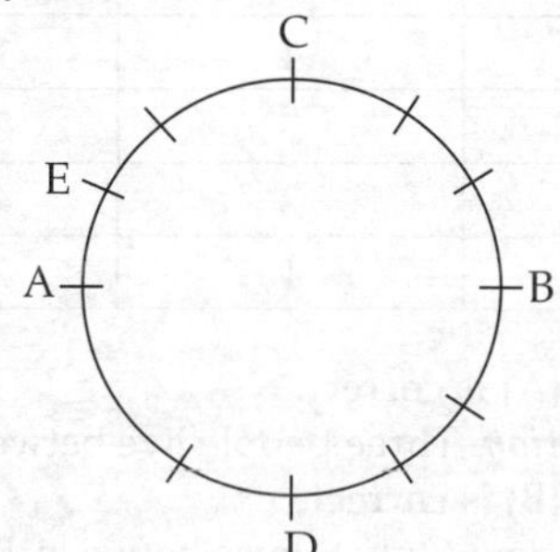

There are a total of 11 people seated in a circle.

5. Option (D) is correct.

Explanation:

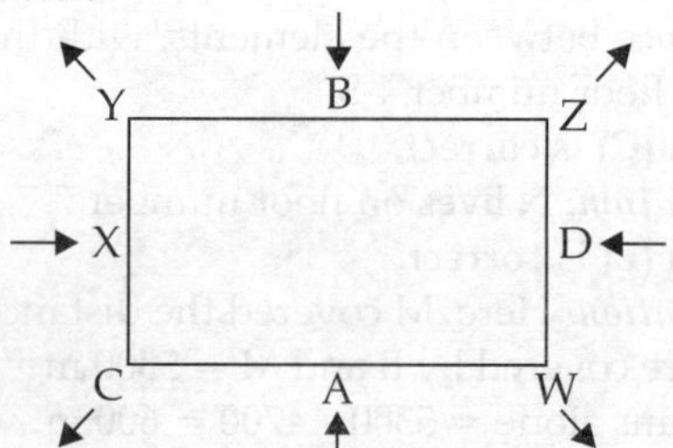

When counting from the left of Z, three people (B, Y, and X) are seated between Z and C.

6. Option (A) is correct.

Explanation:

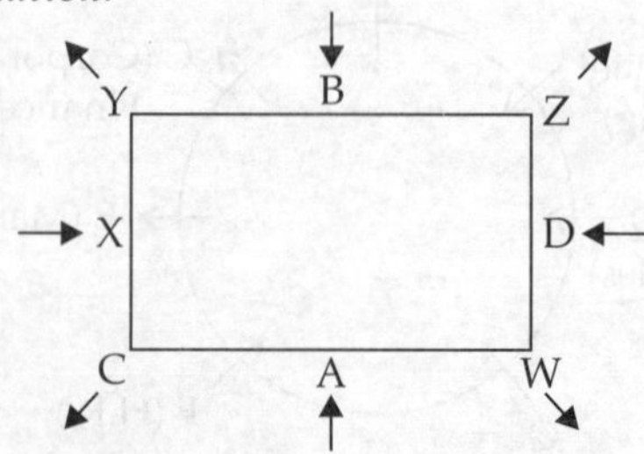

Y is the third to the right of D.

Sol. (7–10):

P	Hyderabad	Bus
Q	Kolkata	Aeroplane
R	Mangalore	Car
S	Chennai	Boat
T	Delhi	Train

7. **Option (D) is correct.**
Explanation: Chennai - Boat is correct.
8. **Option (B) is correct.**
Explanation: Chennai
9. **Option (A) is correct.**
Explanation: T travelled for Delhi.
10. **Option (D) is correct.**
Explanation: P travelled to Hyderabad by bus.

Sol. (11–15):

Person	Month	Fruit
P	JUNE	MANGO
Q	MARCH	ORANGE
R	JUNE	APPLE
S	DECEMBER	CHERRY
T	JUNE	GUAVA
U	DECEMBER	BANANA
V	DECEMBER	KIWI
W	MARCH	PEACH

11. **Option (E) is correct.**
Explanation: U, V, S
12. **Option (E) is correct.**
Explanation: W is the correct answer.
13. **Option (C) is correct.**
Explanation: Guava is the answer.
14. **Option (E) is correct.**
Explanation: None of the given combinations is correct.
15. **Option (D) is correct.**
Explanation: W likes Peach.

Sol. (16–20):

The sitting arrangement is

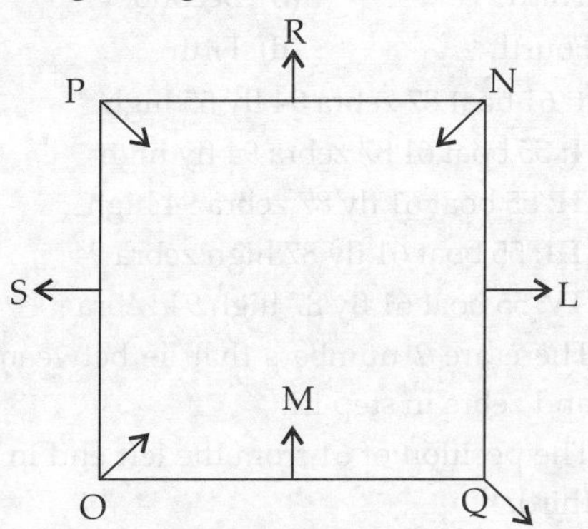

16. **Option (B) is correct.**
Explanation: S sits 4th to the left of C.
17. **Option (C) is correct.**
Explanation: R and L face outside
18. **Option (A) is correct.**
Explanation: P is the immediate neighbour of R.
19. **Option (D) is correct.**
Explanation: Both I and III are true
20. **Option (C) is correct.**
Explanation: S is 2nd to the left of M.

Sol. (21–25):

Person	City	Flower
A	Patna	Cosmos
B	Patna	Iris
C	Mumbai	Tulip
D	Surat	Lily
E	Surat	Sunflower
F	Surat	Orchid
G	Mumbai	Titaonia
H	Patna	Rose
I	Patna	Lotus

21. **Option (A) is correct.**
Explanation: C likes tulip.
22. **Option (D) is correct.**
Explanation: D and E lives in Surat.
23. **Option (C) is correct.**
Explanation: A likes cosmos.
24. **Option (D) is correct.**
Explanation: Except F, all others lives in same city Patna.
25. **Option (D) is correct.**
Explanation: C lives with G in Mumbai.

■ ■ ■

Sequential Output Tracing

LEARNING OBJECTIVES:

- Methods of finding a particular step using the given step
- Different types of question asked in competitive exams

In these types of questions, a message will be given to us as an input which consists of combinations of numbers, words or combination of both followed by some steps. In these steps, a particular rule is followed in each step. These rules can be as follows:

1. Numbers are arranged in ascending order
2. Numbers are arranged in descending order
3. Words are arranged in alphabetical order
4. Words are arranged in reverse alphabetical order

Note that some rules are the combinations of above four rules.

Example 1: Study the following information carefully to answer the given questions.

A number arrangement machine when given an input line of numbers rearranges them by following a particular rule in each step. The following is an illustration of an input and its rearrangement.

Input: 84 93 19 37 42

Step I: 93 84 19 37 42

Step II: 93 84 42 19 37

Step III: 93 84 42 37 19

And step III is the last step of the above input. As per the rules followed in the above step, find the solutions for the following input.

Input: 55 08 31 77 29

(i) What will be the last step for the above input?

(a) II (b) III
(c) IV (d) V

(ii) Which of the following numbers will be second from the right end in step II?

(a) 08 (b) 77
(c) 29 (d) 55

Sol. Input: 55 08 31 77 29

Step I: 77 55 08 31 29

Step II: 77 55 31 08 29

Step III: 77 55 31 29 08

(i) **(b)** The last step for the given input is III.

(ii) **(a)** Second number from the right end in step II is 08.

Example 2: Study the following information carefully to answer the given questions.

A word and number arrangement machine when given an input line of words and numbers rearranges them by following a particular rule in each step. The following is an illustration of an input and its rearrangement.

Input: 74 shape 15 pot 36 door 21 table

Step I: 15 door 74 shape pot 36 21 table

Step II: 15 door 21 pot 74 shape 36 table

Step III: 15 door 21 pot 36 shape 74 table

And step III is the last step of the above input. As per the rules followed in the above step, find the solutions for the following input.

Input: 61 boat 87 zebra 94 fly 55 high

(i) How many numbers lie between the boat and zebra in step III?

(a) 1 (b) 2
(c) 3 (d) 4

(ii) The position of 61 from the left end in step IV is ________.

(a) Third (b) Second
(c) Fourth (d) Fifth

Sol. Input: 61 boat 87 zebra 94 fly 55 high

Step I: 55 boat 61 87 zebra 94 fly high

Step II: 55 boat 61 fly 87 zebra 94 high

Step III: 55 boat 61 fly 87 high zebra 94

Step IV: 55 boat 61 fly 87 high 94 zebra

(i) **(b)** There are 2 numbers that lie between the boat and zebra in step III.

(ii) **(a)** The position of 61 from the left end in step IV is third.

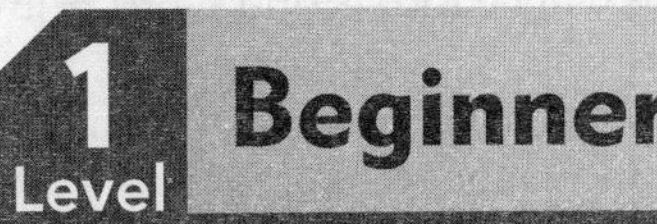

Level 1 Beginner

Directions (Qs. 1–5): Study the following information carefully to answer the given questions.

A word arrangement machine when given an input line of words rearranges them by following a particular rule in each step. The following is an illustration of an input and its rearrangement.

Input: place done with car apple
Step I: apple place done with car
Step II: apple car place done with
Step III: apple car done place with

And step III is the last step of the above input. As per the rules followed in the above step, find the solutions for the following input.

Input: Great blind dear fox horse.

1. What will be the last step for the above input?
   (A) II (B) III (C) IV (D) V
2. Which of the following word will be third from the left end in last step?
   (A) blind (B) great
   (C) fox (D) horse
3. Which of the following will be in exactly in the middle step II?
   (A) horse (B) dear
   (C) fox (D) great
4. The word which is fourth from the right end in step III is
   (A) dear (B) blind
   (C) great (D) fox
5. The last word in step II is
   (A) blind (B) horse
   (C) great (D) fox

Directions (Qs. 6–10): Study the following information carefully to answer the given questions.

A number arrangement machine when given an input line of numbers rearranges them by following a particular rule in each step. The following is an illustration of an input and its rearrangement.

Input: 25 97 38 15 45 76
Step I: 97 25 38 15 45 76
Step II: 97 76 25 38 15 45
Step III: 97 76 45 25 38 15
Step IV: 97 76 45 38 25 15

And step IV is the last step of the above input. As per the rules followed in the above step, find the solutions for the following input.

Input: 88 54 12 31 64 49

6. The position of 12 from the left end in step III is ______.
   (A) 6th (B) 5th (C) 3rd (D) 2nd
7. Which of the following will be fifth from the left end in last step?
   (A) 88 (B) 31 (C) 64 (D) 49
8. Which of the following will be the last number in second last step?
   (A) 31 (B) 64 (C) 88 (D) 49
9. How many numbers lie between 88 and 49 in step II?
   (A) 2 (B) 3 (C) 1 (D) 4
10. The second last number in step I is
   (A) 88 (B) 49 (C) 31 (D) 64

Directions (Qs. 11–15): A word and number arrangement machine, when given an input line of words and numbers, rearranges them by following a particular rule in each step. The following is an illustration of input and rearrangement.

Input: develop 76 create 53 dancer 61 pot 24 straight 38
Step 1: 78 develop create 53 dancer 61 pot 24 38 straight
Step 2: 78 63 develop create 53 dancer 24 38 straight pot
Step 3: 78 63 55 create dancer 24 38 straight pot develop
Step 4: 78 63 55 40 create 24 straight pot develop dancer
Step 5: 78 63 55 40 26 straight pot develop dancer create

Step 5 is the final output.

Find the different steps of output using the above mentioned logic for the following input.

Input: fly 64 challenge 37 internal 29 phone 71 compress 55

11. In which of the following steps " 29 phone" is seen in the same sequence for the first time?
   (A) Step III (B) Step II
   (C) Step IV (D) Step V
12. How many words are to the right of '29' in step 4?
   (A) 4 (B) 3 (C) 5 (D) 2
13. What is the difference between the highest and the lowest numbers of step 3?
   (A) 45 (B) 26 (C) 35 (D) 44
14. Which of the following elements is fourth to the left of phone in step 5?
   (A) 66 (B) 73
   (C) 57 (D) None of these
15. Which of the following elements is/are between compress and internal in step 3?
   (A) 37 (B) 29 (C) phone (D) fly

Directions (Qs. 16–20): Study the following information carefully to answer the given questions.

A word arrangement machine when given an input iine of words rearranges them by following a particular rule in each step. The following is an illustration of an input and its rearrangement.

Input: curd mango carrot potato ginger orange
Step I: carrot curd mango potato ginger orange
Step II: carrot curd mango ginger orange potato
Step III: carrot curd ginger mango orange potato
Step IV: carrot curd ginger orange mango potato

And step IV is the last step of the above input. As per the rules followed in the above step, find the solutions for the following input.

Input: goat lion tiger monkey crow fox

16. What will be the second last step for the above input?
(A) crow fox goat lion tiger monkey
(B) crow fox goat lion monkey tiger
(C) crow fox lion tiger goat monkey
(D) None of these

17. Which of the following will be the fourth element from the left end in third step?
(A) crow **(B)** tiger **(C)** lion **(D)** fox

18. Which of the following will be the second word from left end in step I?
(A) lion **(B)** monkey **(C)** crow **(D)** goat

19. The word which is second to the right of second word from the left end in step II is:
(A) monkey **(B)** tiger **(C)** crow **(D)** fox

20. The third last word in step III is
(A) tiger **(B)** lion **(C)** crow **(D)** goat

2 Level Intermediate

Directions (Qs. 1–5): An electronic device rearranges step by step in a particular order according to a set of rules. The device stops when the final result is obtained. In this case, the device stops at Step V.

Input: 85 16 36 04 19 97 63 09
Step I: 97 85 16 36 04 19 63 09
Step II: 97 85 63 16 36 04 19 09
Step III: 97 85 63 36 16 04 19 09
Step IV: 97 85 63 36 19 16 04 09
Step V: 97 85 63 36 19 16 09 04

Study the above arrangement carefully and then answer the following questions. **[SNAP 2005]**

1. Which of the following will be Step III for the input below?
Input: 09 25 16 30 32 18 17 06
(A) 32 30 25 09 16 18 17 06
(B) 32 30 09 25 16 18 17 06
(C) 32 09 05 16 30 18 17 06
(D) 32 30 09 25 16 19 17 06

2. Which is the last step for the input below?
Input: 16 09 25 27 06 05
(A) Step II **(B)** Step III
(C) Step IV **(D)** None of these

3. What is the output of Step V for the input below?
Input: 25 08 35 11 88 67 23
(A) 08 11 23 25 35 67 88 **(B)** 88 67 35 25 23 11 08
(C) 88 67 35 25 23 08 11 **(D)** None of these

4. Which one of the following would be the last step for the input below?
Input: 03 31 43 22 11 09
(A) Step II **(B)** Step III
(C) Step IV **(D)** None of these

5. If the output of Step IV is as given below, what was the input?
Step IV: 92 86 71 69 15 19 06 63 58
(A) 15 19 06 63 58 86 92 69 71
(B) 15 86 19 92 06 69 63 58 71
(C) 86 92 69 71 15 19 06 63 58
(D) Cannot be determined

Directions (Qs. 6–10): A word and number arrangement machine, when given an input line of words and numbers, rearranges them by following a particular rule in each step. The following is an illustration of input and rearrangement.

Input: fire 86 foil 53 fast 24 favour 27 free 32
Step 1: 88 fast fire foil 53 24 favour 27 free 32
Step 2: 51 favour 88 fast fire foil 24 27 free 32
Step 3: 34 fire 51 favour 88 fast foil 24 27 free
Step 4: 25 foil 34 fire 51 favour 88 fast 24 free
Step 5: 26 free 25 foil 34 fire 51 favour 88 fast

Find the different steps of output using the above mentioned logic for the following input.
Input: name 24 noble 61 nerve 70 narrator 53 noise 17

6. Which of the following steps is the step 3 of the given input?
(A) 72 noise 59 noble 55 nerve name 24 narrator 17
(B) 59 noble 72 noise 55 nerve name 24 narrator 17
(C) 72 noise noble 55 nerve 59 name 24 narrator 17
(D) None of these

7. Which of the following is third from the left end in step 1?
(A) Noble **(B)** Name **(C)** 70 **(D)** 24

8. Which of the following comes exactly between noble and nerve in step 4?
(A) 55 **(B)** 72 **(C)** 17 **(D)** 24

9. In which of the following steps '55 nerve name' is seen in the same sequence for the first time?
(A) Step 2 **(B)** Step 1
(C) Step 3 **(D)** Step 5

10. What is the sum of all the prime numbers in step 5?
(A) 76 **(B)** 75 **(C)** 84 **(D)** 94

Directions (Qs. 11–15): Study the following information carefully to answer the given questions.

When a word and number arrangement machine is given an input line of words and numbers, it arranges them by following a particular rule. The following is an illustration of input and rearrangement.

Input: 41 sprain 10 early 97 noble 26 65 ankle death
Step I: 97 41 10 early noble 26 65 ankle death sprain
Step II: noble 97 41 10 early 26 ankle death sprain 65
Step III: 41 noble 97 10 26 ankle death sprain 65 early
Step IV: death 41 noble 97 10 ankle sprain 65 early 26
Step V: 10 death 41 noble 97 sprain 65 early 26 ankle

Step V is the last step of the above arrangement.

As per the rules followed in the given steps, find out the appropriate steps for the given input.

Input: omits 36 59 yards 41 elect train 12 lakes 85

[Andhra Bank, PO, 2015]

11. Which element comes exactly between '85' and 'lakes' in step III of the given input?
(A) 59 (B) Yards
(C) Train (D) Omits
(E) Elect

12. If in the first step, '59' interchanges its position with 'lakes' and 'omits' also interchanges its position with '12', then which element will be to the immediate left of '41'?
(A) 59 (B) Omits (C) 12 (D) Elect
(E) Lakes

13. Which of the following combinations represents the first two and last two elements in the step V of the given input?
(A) 41, train and omits, 36
(B) 12, lakes and 36, elect
(C) 12, lakes and omits, 36
(D) Lakes, 41 and 36, elect
(E) Lakes, 41 and 59, omits

14. Which element is 4th to the right of the one which is 9th from the right end is Step V of the given input?
(A) 36 (B) Yards (C) 85 (D) Elect
(E) 12

15. In which step are the elements 'train 85 yards 59' found in the same order?
(A) Third (B) Fourth (C) Second (D) Fifth
(E) The given order of elements is not found in any step

Directions (Qs. 16–20): Study the following information carefully to answer the given questions.

Number arrangement machine when given an input line of numbers rearranges them following a particular rule in each step. The following is an illustration of input and rearrangement.

Input: 91 53 72 14 39 24 85 76 61 67
Step I: 15 91 53 72 39 85 76 61 67 25
Step II: 40 15 91 72 85 76 61 67 25 54
Step III: 62 40 15 91 72 85 76 25 54 68
Step IV: 73 62 40 15 91 85 25 54 68 77
Step V: 86 73 62 40 15 25 54 68 77 92
Step V, is the last step.

Input: 58 40 99 28 63 84 16 34 71 87 **[SBI PO 2018]**

16. How many numbers are there between 59 and the one which 3rd to left of 85 in step V?
(A) One (B) More than three
(C) Three (D) None
(E) Two

17. How many numbers are there between the one which is 2nd from the left end and 99 in step II?
(A) One (B) More than three
(C) Three (D) None
(E) Two

18. What is the position of 35 from the left end in second last step?
(A) First (B) Fifth (C) Second
(D) Third (E) Sixth

19. Which of the following number is 6th to the left of 29 in the III step?
(A) 35 (B) 59 (C) 17 (D) 99
(E) None of these

20. Which of the following number is 5th from the right end in step V?
(A) 35 (B) 59 (C) 17 (D) 29
(E) None of these

3 Level Expert

Directions (Qs. 1–5): Study the following information to answer the given questions:

A word and number arrangement machine when given an input line of words and numbers rearranges them by following a particular rule. The following is an illustration of input and rearrangement.

Input: 78 former 44 quicker colder 65 taller outer 27 8
Step I: cold former 44 quicker 65 taller outer 27 8 79
Step II: 9 cold former 44 quicker 65 outer 27 79 tall
Step III: form 9 cold 44 quicker outer 27 79 tall 66
Step IV: 28 form 9 cold 44 quicker 79 tall 66 out
Step V: quick 28 form 9 cold 79 tall 66 out 45

Step V is the last step of the rearrangement. As per the rules followed in the above steps, find out in each of the following questions the appropriate steps for the given input.

Input: warmer 76 94 scraper locker 11 greater 52 39 adopter **[IBPS RRB 2018]**

1. How many steps would be needed to complete the arrangement?
(A) IV (B) V (C) VII (D) VI
(E) None of these

2. What will the addition of the numbers which is third from the right end in step II and 2nd from the right end in step IV?
(A) 112 (B) 210 (C) 151 (D) 116
(E) None of these

3. Which of the following would be the difference of the numbers which is 3rd from left end in step IV and 2nd from right end in Step II?
(A) 90 (B) 83 (C) 25 (D) 10
(E) None of these

4. Which of the following element will be 6th to the left of 3rd from the right end in step V?
(A) 95 (B) Adopt
(C) 40 (D) Scrap
(E) None of these

5. In which of the following step '39 95 warm' would be find in the same order?
(A) Step V (B) Step II and III
(C) Step II (D) Step III and IV
(E) None of these

Directions (Qs. 6–10): A word and number arrangement machine when given an input line of words and numbers, rearranges them by following a particular logic. Below is the illustration of the same.

Input: Destiny 14 Faster 17 Produce 09 Brain 12

Step I: Brain 18 Destiny 14 Faster 17 Produce 12

Step II: Destiny 24 Brain 18 Faster 14 17 Produce

Step III: Faster 28 Destiny 24 Brain 18 17 Produce

Step IV: Produce 34 Faster 28 Destiny 24 Brain 18

Step IV is the last step.

On the basis of above illustration find the output for the input given below.

Input: Crawling 24 Mind 07 Wicket 13 Distract 06

6. What is the sum of the even numbers in step II?
   (A) 40 (B) 50 (C) 35 (D) 48
7. What is the 5th term from the left end in step III for the given input?
   (A) Crawling (B) Mind (C) 14 (D) 48
8. Which of the following element is third from the right end in step IV?
   (A) Wicket (B) Distract (C) 26 (D) 14
9. Find the odd one out keeping step III for the given input in mind.
   (A) Mind (B) Distract
   (C) Crawling (D) Wicket
10. Which of the following steps is- Mind 26 Distract 14 Crawling 12 24 Wicket?
    (A) Step III (B) Step II
    (C) Step IV (D) Step V

Directions (Qs. 11–15): Study the following information carefully to answer the given questions:

A word and number arrangement machine when given an input line of words and numbers rearranges them by following a particular rule. The following is an illustration of input and rearrangement.

Input: 97 nosy 21 snow cold 32 asian 46 65 viral 83 high

Step I: 211 97 nosy snow cold asian 46 65 viral 83 high 322

Step II: asian 211 97 nosy snow 46 65 viral 83 high 322 cold

Step III: 463 asian 211 97 nosy snow viral 83 high 322 cold 654

Step IV: high 463 asian 211 97 snow viral 83 322 cold 654 nosy

Step V: 835 high 463 asian 211 snow viral 322 cold 654 nosy 976

Step VI: snow 835 high 463 asian 211 322 cold 654 nosy 976 viral

Step VI is the last step of the rearrangement. As per the rules followed in the above steps, find out in each of the following questions the appropriate steps for the given input.

Input: peak 18 utility 76 emerge 27 beautiful 37 51 visible 86 know **[IBPS RRB 2017]**

11. How many steps would be needed to complete the arrangement?
    (A) X (B) VIII (C) V (D) VI
    (E) None of these
12. What will the addition of the numbers which is fifth from the left end in step II and 5th from the right end in step IV?
    (A) 312 (B) 210 (C) 162 (D) 165
    (E) None of these
13. Which of the following would be the difference of the numbers which is 2nd from left end in step IV and 2nd from right end in Step II?
    (A) 290 (B) 83 (C) 193 (D) 101
    (E) None of these
14. Which of the following element will be 6th from the left of 3rd from the right end in step V?
    (A) 181 (B) Beautiful
    (C) 373 (D) Know
    (E) None of these
15. In Step IV, which of the following word /number would be on 4th position (from the left end)?
    (A) Visible (B) 181
    (C) 97 (D) Utility
    (E) None of these

ANSWER KEY

Level-1: Beginner

1.	(B)	2.	(C)	3.	(D)	4.	(A)	5.	(B)	6.	(A)	7.	(B)	8.	(A)	9.	(A)	10.	(C)
11.	(C)	12.	(A)	13.	(D)	14.	(A)	15.	(C)	16.	(D)	17.	(C)	18.	(D)	19.	(A)	20.	(B)

Level-2: Intermediate

1.	(A)	2.	(A)	3.	(B)	4.	(D)	5.	(D)	6.	(A)	7.	(B)	8.	(A)	9.	(C)	10.	(A)
11.	(E)	12.	(E)	13.	(B)	14.	(B)	15.	(D)	16.	(E)	17.	(B)	18.	(D)	19	(A)	20	(D)

Level-3: Expert

1.	(B)	2.	(D)	3.	(B)	4.	(C)	5.	(B)	6.	(B)	7.	(A)	8.	(D)	9.	(D)	10.	(A)
11.	(D)	12.	(C)	13.	(D)	14.	(B)	15.	(B)										

Solutions with Detailed Explanations

Level-1: BEGINNER

(1–5). Here, the words are arranged alphabetically in each step.

Input: great blind dear fox horse
Step I: blind great dear fox horse
Step II: blind dear great fox horse
Step III: blind dear fox great horse

1. **Option (B) is correct.**
Explanation: The last step is Step III.
2. **Option (C) is correct.**
Explanation: Third word from the left end in last step is fox.
3. **Option (D) is correct.**
Explanation: The word great is exactly middle in step II.
4. **Option (A) is correct.**
Explanation: The word which is fourth from the right end in step III is dear.
5. **Option (B) is correct.**
Explanation: The last word in step II is horse.

(6–10). Here, the numbers are arranged in descending order in each step.

Input: 88 54 12 31 64 49
Step I: 88 64 54 12 31 49
Step II: 88 64 54 49 12 31
Step III: 88 64 54 49 31 12

6. **Option (A) is correct.**
Explanation: The position of 12 from the left end in step III is sixth.
7. **Option (B) is correct.**
Explanation: Fifth from the left end in last step is 31.
8. **Option (A) is correct.**
Explanation: The last number in second last step is 31.
9. **Option (A) is correct.**
Explanation: There are 2 numbers lie between 88 and 49 in step II.
10. **Option (C) is correct.**
Explanation: The second last number in step I is 31.

(11–15). Here, the numbers are arranged in descending order after adding it by 2 in each step and words are arranged in reverse alphabetical order.

Input: fly 64 challenge 37 internal 29 phone 71 compress 55
Step 1: 73 fly 64 challenge 37 internal 29 compress 55 phone
Step 2: 73 66 fly challenge 37 29 compress 55 phone internal
Step 3: 73 66 57 challenge 37 29 compress phone internal fly
Step 4: 73 66 57 39 challenge 29 phone internal fly compress
Step 5: 73 66 57 39 31 phone internal fly compress challenge

11. **Option (C) is correct.**
Explanation: 29 phone" is seen in the same sequence for the first time in step IV.
12. **Option (A) is correct.**
Explanation: There are 4 words to the right of '29' in step 4.
13. **Option (D) is correct.**
Explanation: Difference = 73 – 29 = 44
14. **Option (A) is correct.**
Explanation: Fourth to the left of 'phone' in step 5 is 66.
15. **Option (C) is correct.**
Explanation: The element which is between compress and internal in step 3 is phone.

(16–20). Here the words are arranged alphabetically in each step.

Input: goat lion tiger monkey crow fox
Step I: crow goat lion tiger monkey fox
Step II: crow goat lion monkey fox tiger
Step III: crow fox goat lion monkey tiger

16. **Option (D) is correct.**
Explanation: The second last step for the given input is: crow goat lion fox monkey tiger
17. **Option (C) is correct.**
Explanation: The fourth element from the right end in third step is lion.
18. **Option (D) is correct.**
Explanation: The second word from left end in step is goat.
19. **Option (A) is correct.**
Explanation: The second word from the left end in step II is goat and second to the right of goat is monkey.
20. **Option (B) is correct.**
Explanation: The third last word in step III is lion.

Level-2: INTERMEDIATE

(1–5). Here, the numbers are arranged in decreasing order in each step.

1. **Option (A) is correct.**
Explanation:
Input: 09 25 16 30 32 18 17 06
Step I: 32 09 25 16 30 18 17 06
Step II: 32 30 09 25 16 18 17 06
Step III: 32 30 25 09 16 18 17 06
2. **Option (A) is correct.**
Explanation:
Input: 16 09 25 27 06 05
Step I: 27 16 09 25 06 05
Step II: 27 25 16 09 06 05
So, Step II is the last step.
3. **Option (B) is correct.**
Explanation:
Input: 25 08 35 11 88 67 23
Step I: 88 25 08 35 11 67 23

Step II: 88 67 25 08 35 11 23

Step III: 88 67 35 25 08 11 23

Step IV: 88 67 35 25 23 08 11

Step V: 88 67 35 25 23 11 08

4. **Option (D) is correct.**

Explanation:

Input: 03 31 43 22 11 09

Step I: 43 03 31 22 11 09

Step II: 43 31 03 22 11 09

Step III: 43 31 22 03 11 09

Step IV: 43 31 22 11 03 09

Step V: 43 31 22 11 09 03

So, Step V is the last step.

5. **Option (D) is correct.**

Explanation: Input for the given step can't be determined.

(6–10). Here, the numbers are arranged in descending order by adding and subtracting 2 alternatively in each step. The words are arranged in reverse alphabetical order.

Input: name 24 noble 61 nerve 70 narrator 53 noise 17

Step 1: 72 noise name 24 noble 61 nerve narrator 53 17

Step 2: 72 noise 59 noble name 24 nerve narrator 53 17

Step 3: 72 noise 59 noble 55 nerve name 24 narrator 17

Step 4: 72 noise 59 noble 55 nerve 22 name narrator 17

Step 5: 72 noise 59 noble 55 nerve 22 name 17 narrator

6. **Option (A) is correct.**

Explanation: Third step is: 72 noise 59 noble 55 nerve name 24 narrator 17

7. **Option (B) is correct.**

Explanation: Third from the left end in step 1 is name.

8. **Option (A) is correct.**

Explanation: 55 comes exactly between noble and nerve in step 4

9. **Option (C) is correct.**

Explanation: '55 nerve name' is seen in the same sequence for the first time in Step 3.

10. **Option (A) is correct.**

Explanation: Required sum = 59 + 17 = 76

(11–15).

Input: omits 36 59 yards 41 elect train 12 lakes 85

Step I: 85 omits 36 59 41 elect train 12 lakes yards

Step II: train 85 omits 36 41 elect 12 lakes yards 59

Step III: 41 train 85 36 elect 12 lakes yards 59 omits

Step IV: lakes 41 train 85 elect 12 yards 59 omits 36

Step V: 12 lakes 41 train 85 yards 59 omits 36 elect

11. **Option (E) is correct.**

Explanation: elect comes exactly between '85' and 'lakes' in step III of the given input.

12. **Option (E) is correct.**

Explanation: The new step is:

85 12 36 lakes 41 elect train omits 59 yards

13. **Option (B) is correct.**

Explanation: 12 & lakes are the first two words and 36 & elect are last two words in step V.

14. **Option (B) is correct.**

Explanation: 9th element from the right end in Step V of the given input is lakes and 4th to the right of lakes is yards.

15. **Option (D) is correct.**

Explanation: 'train 85 yards 59' found in the same order is in Step V.

(16–20):

Input: 58 40 99 28 63 84 16 34 71 87

Step I: 17 58 40 99 63 84 34 71 87 29

Step II: 35 17 58 99 63 84 71 87 29 41

Step III: 59 35 17 99 84 71 87 29 41 64

Step IV: 72 59 35 17 99 87 29 41 64 85

Step V: 88 72 59 35 17 29 41 64 85 100

16. **Option (E) is correct.**

Explanation: Third to the left of 85 is 29. So, there are two numbers between 59 and 29.

17. **Option (B) is correct.**

Explanation: 2nd from the left end in step II is 87. So, there are four numbers between 99 and 87.

18. **Option (D) is correct.**

Explanation: The position of 35 from the left end in second last step is third.

19. **Option (A) is correct.**

Explanation: 6th to the left of 29 in the III step is 35.

20. **Option (D) is correct.**

Explanation: 5th from the right end in step V is 29.

Level-3: EXPERT

(1–5):

Input: warmer 76 94 scraper locker 11 greater 52 39 adopter

Step I: adopt warmer 76 scraper locker 11 greater 52 39 95

Step II: 12 adopt 76 scraper locker greater 52 39 95 warm

Step III: great 12 adopt scraper locker 52 39 95 warm 77

Step IV: 40 great 12 adopt locker 52 95 warm 77 scrap

Step V: lock 40 great 12 adopt 95 warm 77 scrap 53

1. **Option (B) is correct.**

Explanation: Five steps are needed.

2. **Option (D) is correct.**

Explanation: Third from the right end in step II is 39 and 2nd from the right end in step IV is 77.

So, required sum = 39 + 77 = 116.

3. **Option (B) is correct.**

Explanation: 3rd from left end in step IV is 12 and 2nd from right end in Step II is 95.

So, required difference = 95 – 12 = 83

4. **Option (C) is correct.**

Explanation: 3rd from the right end in step V is 77. So, 6th to the left of 77 is 40.

5. **Option (B) is correct.**

Explanation: 39 95 warm occurs in step II and III.

(6–10). Here, all the words are arranged in reverse alphabetical order and Numbers are arranged in descending order after multiplying it by 2.

Input: Crawling 24 Mind 07 Wicket 13 Distract 06

Step I: Crawling 12 24 Mind 07 Wicket 13 Distract

Step II: Distract 14 Crawling 12 24 Mind Wicket 13

Step III: Mind 26 Distract 14 Crawling 12 24 Wicket

Step IV: Wicket 48 Mind 26 Distract 14 Crawling 12

6. **Option (B) is correct.**
Explanation: Sum of the even numbers in step II = 14 + 12 + 24 = 50

7. **Option (A) is correct.**
Explanation: 5th term from the left end in step III for the given input is Crawiing.

8. **Option (D) is correct.**
Explanation: Third element from the right end in step IV is 14.

9. **Option (D) is correct.**
Explanation: Except wicket, all other words are alternative elements.

10. **Option (A) is correct.**
Explanation: Mind 26 Distract 14 Crawling 12 24 Wicket is the step III.

(11–15):

Input: peak 18 utility 76 emerge 27 beautiful 37 51 visibie 86 know

Step I: 181 peak utility 76 emerge beautiful 37.51 visible 86 know 272

Step II: beautiful 181 peak utility 76 37 51 visible 86 know 272 emerge

Step III: 373 beautiful 181 peak utility 76 visible 86 know 272 emerge 514

Step IV: know 373 beautiful 181 utility 76 visible 86 272 emerge 514 peak

Step V: 765 know 373 beautiful 181 utility visible 272 emerge 514 peak 866

Step VI: utility 765 know 373 beautiful 181 272 emerge 514 peak 866 visible

11. **Option (D) is correct.**
Explanation: Number of steps needed to complete the arrangement = VI

12. **Option (C) is correct.**
Explanation: Fifth from the left end in step II = 76 and 5th from the right end in step IV = 86
So, required sum = 76 + 86 = 162

13. **Option (D) is correct.**
Explanation: 2nd from left end in step IV = 373 and 2nd from right end in Step II = 272
So, required difference = 373 – 272 = 101

14. **Option (B) is correct.**
Explanation: 3rd element from the right end in step V is 514 and 6th from the left of 514 is beautiful.

15. **Option (B) is correct.**
Explanation: 4th position (from the left end) is 181.

■ ■ ■

Direction Sense Test

LEARNING OBJECTIVES:

- Methods of evaluating the distance between the starting and final position
- Questions based on Pythagoras theorem
- Different types of question asked in competitive exams

The Direction Sense Test is a type of question that is frequently used in verbal reasoning assessments. It assesses a person's ability to understand and interpret directions or spatial relationships.

In a typical direction sense question, you are given a series of instructions involving the movement of a person or an object in a specific direction. The task is to determine the final direction or position based on the given instructions.

To help the candidates with directions, the adjacent figure displays the four major directions (North N, South S, East E, and West W) as well as the four cardinal directions (Northeast NE, Northwest NW, Southeast SE, and Southwest SW).

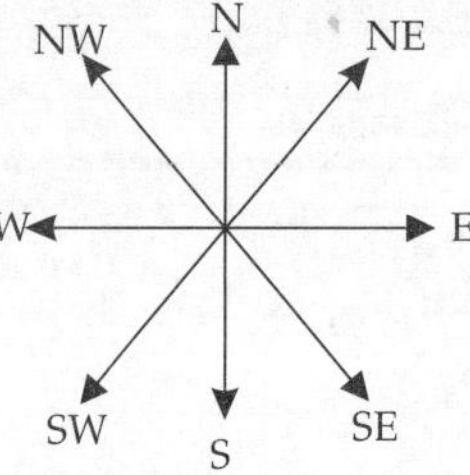

DIRECTION AND DISTANCE

- The orientation or movement between two points or objects is what is commonly meant by direction. It denotes a position's or an angle's relation to an axis or other point of reference. The terms left, right, up, down, north, south, east, and west are just a few that can be used to define direction. It reveals details regarding how one point or item is situated or aligned in reference to another.

  On the other hand, distance refers to the quantitative measurement of the length or space that separates two places or things. The degree of the space between the two entities' physical separation is quantified. In addition to metres, kilometres, and miles, any other length unit that is appropriate can be used to measure distance.

Example 1: One day, Navya left home and cycled 10 km east, turned right and cycled 10 km and turned left and cycled 5 km and turned left and cycled 10 km. How many kilometres will she have to cycle to reach her home straight?

(a) 10 km (b) 15 km
(c) 20 km (d) 25 km

Sol. (b) Navya starts from E, her home, travels 10 km east to B, turns right and travels 10 km to C, then again goes left and travels 5 km to D, and again goes left for 10 km to E.

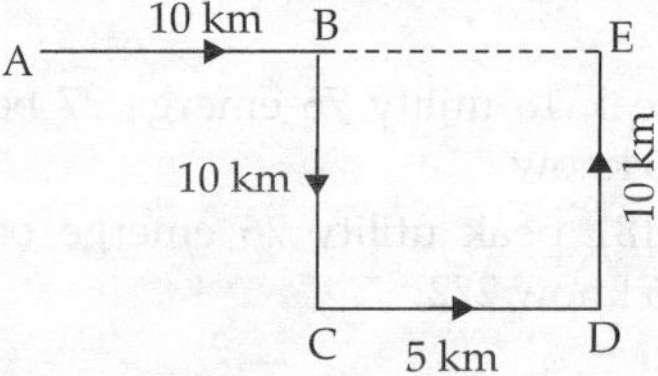

Her distance from position A
= AE = AB + BE = (10 + 5) = 15 km

Example 2: Kailash faces towards north. Turning to his right, he walks 25metres. He then turns to his left and walks 30 metres. Next, he moves 25 metres to his right. He then turns to his right again and walks 55 metres. Finally, he turns to the right and moves 40 metres. In which direction is he now from his starting point? **(MBA 2006)**

(a) South-west (b) South
(c) North-west (d) South-east

Sol. (d) Kailash makes a right turn as he travels north. In order to get to B, he proceeds 25 metres eastward, turns left and moves 30 metres up to C, then turns right and moves 25 metres up to D. He makes a right turn to the south at D and proceeds 55 metres up to E. He then makes a right turn once more and moves 40 metres up to point F. He is therefore south-east of where he started.

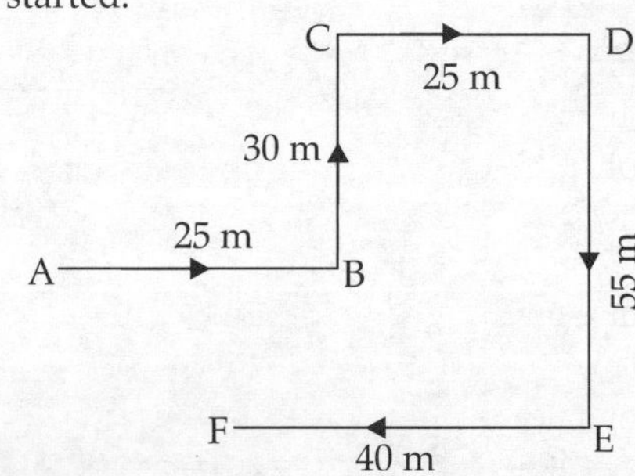

Level 1 Beginner

1. Rishi starts walking straight towards North. After walking 25 metres, he turns to the left and walks 40 metres straight. Again he turns to the left, walks a distance of 25 metres straight, again he turns to the right and walks a distance of 35 metres. How far is he from the starting point?
   (A) 75 metres **(B)** 80 metres
   (C) 115 metres **(D)** 140 metres
2. Rohan walks a distance of 3 kilometres towards North, then turns to his left and walks for 2 kilometres. He again turns left and walks for 3 kilometres. At this point, he turns to his left and walks for 3 kilometres. How many kilometres is he from the starting point? **[SSC 2005]**
   (A) 1 kilometres **(B)** 2 kilometres
   (C) 3 kilometres **(D)** 5 kilometres
3. You go North, turn right, then right again go to the left. In which direction are you? **[SSC 2002]**
   (A) North **(B)** South
   (C) East **(D)** West
4. A man is facing towards west and turns through 45° clockwise, again 180° clockwise and then turns through 270° anti-clockwise. In which direction is he facing now? **[RRB 2005]**
   (A) West **(B)** South
   (C) North-west **(D)** South-west
5. Kunal walks 10 km towards North. From there, he walks 6 km towards South. Then, he walks 3 km towards East. How far and in which direction is he with reference to his starting point? **[MBA 2004]**
   (A) 5 km West **(B)** 5 km North-east
   (C) 7 km East **(D)** 7 km West

Directions (Qs. 6–8): Study the following information carefully and answer the questions given below.

Point A is in 8 m north of point B. Point C is in 4 m east of point B. Point D is in 5 m south of point C. Point F is in 5 m north of Point E, which is 8 m east of point D. Point F is in 4m west of point G. Point H is in 8 m north of Point G. **[SBI Clerk 2021]**

6. What is the shortest distance between Point A and Point H?
   (A) 12 m **(B)** 14 m
   (C) 16 m **(D)** 18 m
   (E) None of these
7. What is the direction of Point H with respect to Point D?
   (A) North-east **(B)** North
   (C) South-east **(D)** North-west
   (E) None of these
8. What is the shortest distance between Point F and Point C?
   (A) 5 m **(B)** 8 m
   (C) 10 m **(D)** 12 m
   (E) None of these
9. A person walks 9 km to the South. From there, he walks 5 km to the North. After this, he walks 3 km to the West. In which direction and how far is he now from the starting point? **[SSC SI 2012]**
   (A) 4 km South **(B)** 4 km North
   (C) 5 km North West **(D)** 5 km South West
10. One evening, Raja started to walk towards the Sun. After walking a while, he turned to his right and again to his right. After walking a while, he again turned right. In which direction is he facing? **[SSC CGL 2011]**
    (A) South **(B)** East
    (C) West **(D)** North

Directions (Qs. 11–12): Study the following information carefully and answer the questions given below:

Point E is in 15 m north of Point D. Point F is in 20 m north of Point C. Point A is in 35 m east of Point F. Point P is in 25 m south of Point A. Point E is in 20 m east of Point P. **[SBI Clerk Exam, 2020]**

11. What is the direction of point F with respect to point P?
    (A) North-west **(B)** North-east
    (C) South-west **(D)** South-east
    (E) North
12. Four of the following five are alike in a certain way and hence they form a group. Which one of the following does not belong to that group?
    (A) C-P **(B)** A-E
    (C) A-C **(D)** P-D
    (E) F-E
13. Raj is standing in the middle of a square field. He starts walking diagonally to north-east. Then, he turns right and reaches the far end of the field. Then, he turns right and starts walking. In the midway, he again turns right and starts walking. In halfway, he turns to his left and reaches a new far end. In what direction is Raj now? **[SSC CGL Tier 1 Exam, 2013]**
    (A) North **(B)** South
    (C) North- west **(D)** South- west
14. Raju drives 25 km north and turns left and travels 5 km and reaches point O. He then turns right and covers another 5 km. Afterwards, he turns to East and drives 5 km. How much distance he has to travel to go back to the starting point? **[SSC CGL Tier 1 Exam, 2015]**
    (A) 30 km **(B)** 20 km
    (C) 25 km **(D)** 35 km
15. Varun travelled 12 km northwards, then turned right and travelled 10 km, then turned right and travelled 12 km. How far was Vijay from the starting point?
    (A) 22 km **(B)** 44 km
    (C) 12 km **(D)** 10 km

Direction (Qs. 16–18): Study the following information carefully and answer the questions given below:

Point S is 15 m West of point R. Point R is 30 m South of point Q. Point P is 20 m West of point Q. Point U is 15 m South of point P. Point T is 35 m North of point S. **[SBI Clerk 2019]**

16. If point V is exactly between point Q and R, then how far and in which direction is point U with respect to V?

(A) 15 m, North-East **(B)** 15 m, East
(C) 10 m, North-West **(D)** 20 m, West
(E) 20 m, North-East

17. Four of the following are alike in a certain way, so form a group. Which of the following does not belong to that group?

(A) P, T **(B)** U, Q
(C) R, P **(D)** S, Q
(E) U, T

18. If point W is in 5 m East of point U, then what is the distance between point W and point S?

(A) 5 m **(B)** 15 m
(C) 25 m **(D)** 10 m
(E) 20 m

Direction (Qs. 19–21): Study the information and answer the following questions.

Point R is 5 metres West of point Q. Point P is 16 metres North of point Q. Point R is 23 metres South of point T. Point T is 10 metres West of point V. Point V is 9 metres North of point J. **[SBI PO Exam, 2019]**

19. Point J is at how much distance and in which direction with respect to point P?

(A) 10 metres southeast
(B) 5 metres south
(C) 5 metres east
(D) 10 metres northwest
(E) 5 metres west

20. If point W is West of point J and North of point R, then what is the distance between T and W?

(A) 15 metres **(B)** 9 metres
(C) 12 metres **(D)** 10 metres
(E) 5 metres

21. What is the direction of point V with respect to point R?

(A) North **(B)** South-west
(C) North-east **(D)** South
(E) North-west

Direction (Qs. 22–24): Read the information carefully and answer the questions:

Point U is 10 m North of point Q. Point T is 10 m East of point U. Point S is 15 m South of point T. Point P is 20 m South of point Q. Point R is 25 m East of point P. Point L is 15 m East of point S. Point M is the midpoint of point U and P. **[SBI 2018]**

22. What is the distance between point L and R?

(A) 10 m **(B)** 15 m
(C) 5 m **(D)** 20 m
(E) 25 m

23. In which direction is point T with respect to P?

(A) North-west **(B)** South-west
(C) South-east **(D)** North-east
(E) None of these

24. Which of the following points are in line?

(A) P, R, S **(B)** Q, M, L
(C) U, S,T **(D)** M, S, L
(E) Q, S, L

25. A man is facing North-east. He turns 180° in the clockwise direction and then 135° in the clockwise direction. Which direction is he facing now?

(A) North-east **(B)** West
(C) South-east **(D)** East

26. I am standing at the centre of a circular field. I go down South to the edge of the field and then turning left, I walk along the boundary of the field equal to three-eighths of its length. Then, I turn West and go right across to the opposite point on the boundary. In which direction am I from the starting point? **[Hotel Management, 2005]**

(A) North-west **(B)** North
(C) South-west **(D)** West

27. A man is facing North-west. He turns 45° in the anti-clockwise direction and then 135° in the anti-clockwise direction. Which direction is he facing now?

(A) South-east **(B)** North-east
(C) North **(D)** South-west

Directions (Qs. 28-30): Study the information carefully and answer the questions given below.

Point P is 8 m West of point G. Point G is 16 m East of point T. Point H is East of point E. Point E is 5 m North-west of point L. Point A is 12 m South of point F and point P is the midpoint between them. Point L is 8 m South of point S. Point H is midpoint between point L and S. Point T is 14 m South of point E.

28. If point B is West of point A and South of point S, then what is the distance between point A and point B? **[SBI Clerk Exam, 2020]**

(A) 13 m **(B)** 7 m
(C) 6 m **(D)** 5 m
(E) None of these

29. In which direction point L is with respect to point F?

(A) South **(B)** Southeast
(C) Northeast **(D)** East
(E) None of these

30. What is the distance between point E and point H?

(A) 7 m **(B)** 3 m
(C) 4 m **(D)** 5 m
(E) None of these

31. Pratap starts from school and walks 7 km towards East. He takes a left and walks 4 km, then takes a right and walks 2 km, again takes a right and walks 3 km. Which direction is he facing now? **[SSC CGL Tier 1 Exam, 2014]**

(A) South **(B)** North
(C) East **(D)** West

32. I am facing East. I turn 100° in the clockwise direction and then 145° in the anti-clockwise direction. Which direction am I facing now? **[Hotel Management 2005]**
(A) East (B) North-east
(C) North (D) South-west

Directions (Qs. 33–35): Study the information and answer the following questions:
Point U is 20 m North of point Q. Point T is 20 m East of point U. Point S is 25 m South of point T. Point P is 30 m South of point Q. Point R is 45 m East of point P. Point L is 25 m East of point S. Point M is the midpoint of point U and P.

33. What is the distance between point L and S?
(A) 10 metres (B) 15 metres
(C) 5 metres (D) 20 metres
(E) 25 metres

34. In which direction is point T with respect to M?
(A) North-west (B) South-west
(C) South-east (D) North-east
(E) None of these

35. Which of the following points are in line?
(A) P, R, S (B) Q, M, L
(C) U, S, T (D) U, M, P
(E) Q, S, L

Level 2 Intermediate

Directions (Qs. 1–2): Study the following information carefully to answer these questions.
A vehicle starts from point P and run 10 km towards North. It takes a right turn and runs 15 km. Now, it runs 6 km after taking a left turn. Finally, It takes a left turn, runs 15 km and stops at point Q. **[SBI 2016]**

1. How far is point Q with respect to point P?
(A) 16 km (B) 25 km
(C) 4 km (D) 0 km
(E) None of these

2. Towards which direction was the vehicle moving before it stopped at point Q?
(A) North (B) East
(C) South (D) West
(E) North-West

3. A rat runs 20 m towards East and turns to right, runs 10 m and turns to right, runs 9 m and again turns to left, runs 5 m and then turns to left, runs 12 m and finally turns to left and runs 6 m. Now, which direction is the rat facing? **[CPO 2005]**
(A) East (B) West
(C) North (D) South

4. A person starts from a point A and travels 3 km eastwards to B and then turns left and travels thrice that distance to reach C. He again turns left and travels five times the distance he covered between A and B and reaches his destination D. The shortest distance between the starting point and the destination is: **[Civil Services 2000]**
(A) 12 km (B) 15 km
(C) 16 km (D) 18 km

5. Rashmi moves towards North-west distance of 7 m, then she moves towards East and travels a distance of 14 m. From here, she moves towards South-west a distance of 7 m and finally, she moves distance of 10 m towards East and stood at that point. How far is the starting point from where she stood?
(A) 3 metres (B) 8 metres
(C) 4 metres (D) 10 metres

6. If the clock is turned through an angle of 135 degrees in an anti-clockwise direction, in which direction will its minute hand point at 8.45 p.m.?
(A) North (B) South
(C) East (D) None of these

7. A clock is so placed that at 12 noon its minute points towards North-east. In which direction its hour hand point at 1:30 p.m.? **[MBA 2004]**
(A) North (B) South
(C) East (D) West

Direction (Qs. 8–10): Study the information and answer the following questions:
D is 20 m South of A. C is 5 m East of D. E is 10 m North of C. F is 10 m East of E. G is 15 m South of F. X is 15 m West of G. B is 10 m to the East of A. Z is 10 m to the South of B. L is 10 m to east of C. **[IBPS 2018]**

8. In which direction is point A with respect to point G?
(A) North-west (B) South-east
(C) North (D) South-west
(E) North-east

9. Four of the following are alike in a certain way so form a group, which of the following does not belong to that group?
(A) EF (B) EC
(C) LG (D) BZ
(E) FL

10. What is distance between point F and L?
(A) 10 m (B) 5 m
(C) 15 m (D) 20 m
(E) 25 m

Directions (Qs. 11–13): Study the following information carefully and answer the questions below:
Point O is 20 m West of point N. Point N is 40 m south of Point M. Point L is 25 m west of point M. Point Q is 20 m South of point L. Point P is 45 m north of point O.

11. If point R is exactly between point M and N, then how far and in which direction is point R with respect to Q?
(A) 20 m, Northeast (B) 15 m, West
(C) 10 m, Northwest (D) 25 m, West
(E) 25 m, Northeast

12. Four of the following are alike in a certain way to form a group. Which of the following does not belong to that group?
(A) L, Q (B) M, R
(C) O, N (D) R, N
(E) O, P

13. If point J is in 5 m East of point Q, then what is the distance between point J and point P?
(A) 40 m (B) 30 m
(C) 25 m (D) 10 m
(E) 20 m

14. Raghu starts from his house in his car and travels 8 km towards the North, then 6 km towards East, then 10 km towards his right, 4 km towards his left, 10 km towards North and finally 4 km towards his right. In which direction is he now with respect to the starting point?
(A) South (B) North East
(C) South East (D) North

15. A cyclist goes 30 km to the North and then turning East he goes 40 km. Again he turns to his right and goes 20 km. After this, he turns to his right and goes 40 km. How far is he from his starting point? **[SSC CHSL 2013]**
(A) 25 km (B) 40 km
(C) 6 km (D) 10 km

16. Namita walks 14 metres towards west, then turns to her right and walks 14 metres and then turns to her left and walks 10 metres. Again turning to her left she walks 14 metres. What is the shortest distance between her starting point and the present position? **[SSC Exam 2002]**
(A) 10 metres (B) 24 metres
(C) 28 metres (D) 38 metres
(E) None of these

17. Maya starts at point T, walks straight to point U which is 4 feet away. She turns left at 90 degrees and walks to W which is 4 feet away, turns 90 degrees right and goes 3 feet to P, turns 90 degrees right and walks 1 feet to Q, turns left at 90 degrees and goes to V, which is 1 feet away and once again turns 90 degrees right and goes to R, 3 feet away. What is the distance between T and R? **[SSC 2003]**
(A) 4 feet (B) 5 feet
(C) 7 feet (D) 8 feet

18. Manick walked 40 metres towards North, took a left turn and walked 20 metres. He again took a left turn and walked 40 metres. How far and in which direction is he from the starting point? **[Assistant Manager Exam, 2005]**
(A) 20 metres East (B) 20 metres North
(C) 20 metres South (D) 100 metres South
(E) None of these

19. A direction pole was situated on the crossing. Due to an accident, the pole turned in such a manner that the pointer, which was showing East, started showing South. One traveller went to the wrong direction thinking it to be west. In what direction actually he was travelling? **[MBA 2004]**
(A) North (B) South
(C) East (D) West

Directions (Qs. 20–24): Read the following information carefully and answer the questions given below it:
(i) Six flats on a floor in two rows facing North and South are allotted to P, Q, R, S, T and U.
(ii) Q gets a North facing flat and is not next to S.
(iii) S and U get diagonally opposite flats.
(iv) R, next to U, gets a South facing flat and T gets a North facing flat. **[IBPS PO Exam, 2018]**

20. Which of the following combinations get South facing flats?
(A) QTS (B) UPT
(C) URP (D) Data inadequate
(E) None of these

21. Whose flat is between Q and S?
(A) T (B) U
(C) R (D) P
(E) Data inadequate

22. If the flats of T and P are interchanged, who's flat will be next to that of U?
(A) P (B) Q
(C) R (D) T
(E) None of these

23. The flats of which of the pairs other than SU are diagonally opposite to each other?
(A) QP (B) QR
(C) PT (D) TS
(E) None of these

24. To arrive at the answers to the above questions, which of the following statements can be dispensed with?
(A) None (B) (i) only
(C) (ii) only (D) (iii) Only
(E) None of these

25. A man leaves for his office from his house. He walks towards East. After moving a distance of 20 m, he turns South and walks 10 m. Then he walks 35 m towards the West and further 5 m towards the destination North. He then turns towards East and walks 15 m. What is the straight distance (in metres) between his initial and final positions? **[MAT 2005]**
(A) 0 m
(B) 5 m
(C) 10 m
(D) Cannot be determined
(E) None of these

26. Rachel starts walking towards North. After walking 15 metres, she turns towards South and walks 20 metres. She then turns towards East and walks 10 metres. Then, again, she walks 5 metres towards North. How far is she from her starting point and in which direction? **[SSC CGL 2013]**
(A) 10 metres, West (B) 5 metres, East
(C) 5 metres, North (D) 10 metres, East

27. Amit walked 30 metres towards East, took a right turn and walked 40 metres. Then, he took a left turn and walked 30 metres. In which direction is he now from the starting point? **[Bank PO 2005]**

(A) North-east (B) East
(C) South-east (D) South
(E) None of these

28. Sunita rode her scooty northwards, then turned left and then again rode to her left 4 km. She found herself exactly 2 km West of her starting point. How far did she ride northwards initially? **[SSC CGL 2014]**
(A) 2 km (B) 4 km
(C) 5km (D) 6 km

29. Rahul starts from his house towards South. After walking a distance of 30 metres, he turned towards left and walked 5 metres. He then turned right and moving a distance of 40 metres, turned to his right again and walked 10 metres. He now turns to the right and walks 20 metres. Finally, he turns to his left. In which direction is he walking now?
(A) North (B) South
(C) East (D) South-west
(E) West

30. Ratan walks 15 m towards the north and then turns right and walks 23 m. Then, he turns left and walks 16 m. After that, he turns left and walks 11 m. Then, he turns right and walks 17 m. Then, he turns left and walks 12 m. He finally turns right and walks 19 m. In which direction and how far is he now with reference to the starting point? **[SSC SI 2021]**
(A) South, 51 m (B) North, 52 m
(C) North, 48 m (D) North, 67 m

31. It is 3 o'clock in a watch. If the minute hand points towards the North-east, then the hour hand will point towards **[RRB 2004]**
(A) South (B) South-west
(C) North-west (D) South-east

32. A villager went to meet his uncle in another village situated 5 km away in the North-east direction of his own village. From there he came to meet his father-in-law living in a village situated 4 km in the South of his uncle's village. How far away and in which direction is he now? **[ATMA 2004]**
(A) 3 km in the North (B) 3 km in the East
(C) 4 km In the East (D) 4 km in the West

33. A watch reads 4:30. If the minute hand points east, then in which direction will the hour hand point? **[MAT 2005]**
(A) North (B) North-west
(C) South-east (D) North-east
(E) None of these

34. If South-east becomes North, North-east becomes west and so on, what will West become? **[SNAP 2004]**
(A) North-east (B) North-west
(C) South-east (D) South-west
(E) South

35. If 'South-east' is called 'East', 'North-west' is called 'West', 'South-west' is called 'South' and so on. What will 'North' be called?
(A) East (B) North-east
(C) North-west (D) South
(E) None of these

Level 3 Expert

1. A girl starts from home and walks straight for 10 km towards East. Then, she takes a right turn and walks for 5 km. Then, she turns right again and walks for 3 km and then turns left walks for 1 km. Then, she turns right and travels 1 km and then turns right and travels for 6 km straight. How far is she from the starting point?
(A) 5 km (B) 6 km
(C) 2 km (D) 4 km

2. Kartik goes 50 metres north, then turns right and walks 30 metres, then again turns right and walks 30 metres, then again turns right and walks 30 metres. How many metres is he from his original position?
(A) 0 m (B) 10 m
(C) 20 m (D) 40 m
(E) None of these

Directions (Qs. 3–5): Study the following information carefully and answer the questions given below:

Point A is 6 m to the north of point H which is 8 m to the east of point B. Point B is 5 m to the north of point F. Point E is 9 m to the north of point D and 8 m to the east of point F. Point G is 5 m to the north of point J. Point D is 4 m to the east of point G. **[RRB 2022]**

3. In which direction is point E with respect to point A?
(A) South (B) North
(C) North west (D) South east
(E) East

4. What is the shortest distance between point D and point J?
(A) $\sqrt{33}$ m (B) $\sqrt{41}$ m
(C) 41 m (D) 35 m
(E) None of these

5. What is the total distance from point E to point J?
(A) 23 m (B) 20 m
(C) 18 m (D) 25 m
(E) 19 m

Directions (Qs. 6–7): Study the following information carefully and answer the given questions.

Point Q is 15 m south of point P. Point R is 10 m east of point Q. Point S is 5 m north of point R. Point T is 5 m west of point S. **[SBI PO Exam, 2018]**

6. If Point U is 10 m east of point P, then point S is how far and in which direction from point U?
(A) 10 m, North (B) 5 m, South
(C) 15 m, North (D) 10 m, South
(E) 5 m, North

7. Point P is in which direction from point T?
(A) Northwest (B) Southeast
(C) North (D) Southwest
(E) Northeast

8. A man walks 30 metres towards West. Then turning to his right, he walks 20 metres. Then, turning to his right, he walks 30 metres. Again, he turns to his left and walks 30 metres. How far is he from his initial position?
(A) 20 metres (B) 30 metres
(C) 60 metres (D) 80 metres
(E) 50 metres

9. Sanjeev walks 10 metres towards the South. Turning to the left, he walks 20 metres and then moves to right. After moving a distance of 20 metres, he turn, to the right and walks 20 metres. Finally, he turns to the right and moves a distance of 10 metres. How far and in which direction is he from the starting point? **[MAT 2004]**
(A) 10 metres North (B) 20 metres South
(C) 20 metres North (D) 10 metres South
(E) None of these

10. I am facing south. I turn right and walk 20 m. Then, I turn right again and walk 10 m. Then I turn left and walk 10 m and then turning right and walk 20 m. Then, I turn right again and walk 60 m. In which direction am I from the starting point? **[Hotel Management, 2004]**
(A) North (B) North west
(C) East (D) North east

Directions (Qs. 11–13): Study the information carefully and answer the questions given below.

Point P is 26 m west of point S. Point G is 52 m north of point P. Point M is 39 m east of point G and point K is 13 m south of point G. Point H is 39 m north of point S. **[RRB 2020]**

11. In which direction point P with respect to point M?
(A) South (B) South-east
(C) North-east (D) East
(E) None of these

12. What is the shortest distance between point K and point H?
(A) 13 m (B) 26 m
(C) 39 m (D) 25 m
(E) None of these

13. If Point Z is 13 m north of point H, then what is the distance between point M and point Z?
(A) 13 m (B) 26 m
(C) 39 m (D) 25 m
(E) None of these

14. Pinky walks a distance of 500 m towards North. Turns right and moves 600 m then turns right and walks 500 m and then turns right again and moves 600 m and halts. At what distance (in m) is she from the starting point?
(A) 0 (B) 600
(C) 500 (D) 2200

15. Kailash walks 3 km to East and turns South and walks 4 km. Again turns West and walks 6 km. How far is he from the starting point? **[SSC CGL Tier 1 Exam, 2015]**
(A) 7 km (B) 5 km
(C) 6 km (D) 3 km

16. A girl leaves from her home. She first walks 30 metres in South-West direction and then 30 metres in North-West direction. Next, she walks in 30 metres in North-East direction. Finally, she turns towards her home. In which direction is she moving?
(A) North-east (B) North-west
(C) South-east (D) South-west

17. A nurse moved 90 metres in the East in a hospital to look for her duty doctor. Then, she turned right and went 20 metres. After this, she turned right and after going 30 metres she reached I.C.U. but the Doctor was not there. From there, she went 100 metres to her North and meet her doctor. What distance did she move to meet her duty doctor from the starting point. **[SSC CPO Exam, 2019]**
(A) 100 metres (B) 120 metres
(C) 80 metres (D) 140 metres

18. Sunita rode her scooty Northwards. Then, turned left and then again rode to her left 4 km. She found herself exactly 2 km West of her starting point. How far did she ride Northwards initially? **[SSC CGL Tier 1 Exam, 2015]**
(A) 2 km (B) 4 km
(C) 6 km (D) 5 km

Directions (Qs. 19–21): Study the information and answer the following questions:

D is 20 metres in south of A. C is 5 metres east of D. E is 10 metres north of C. F is 10 metres east of E. G is 15 metres south of F. X is 15 metres west of G. B is 10 metres to the east of A. Z is 10 metres to the south of B. L is 10 metres to east of C. **[IBPS PO Exam, 2018]**

19. In which direction is point A with respect to point G?
(A) North-west (B) South-east
(C) North (D) South-west
(E) North-east

20. Four of the following are alike in a certain way so form a group, which of the following does not belong to that group?
(A) EF (B) EC
(C) LG (D) BZ
(E) CL

21. What is distance between point F and L?
(A) 10 metres (B) 5 metres
(C) 15 metres (D) 20 metres
(E) 25 metres

Directions (Qs. 22–24): These questions are based on the following information:

Seven villages A, B, C, D, E, F and G are situated are as follows:

E is 2 km to the West of B.
F is 2 km to the North of A.
C is 1 km to the West of A.
D is 2 km to the South of G.
G is 2 km to the East of C.
D is exactly in the middle of B and E. **[NIFT 2003]**

22. A is in the middle of:
(A) E and C (B) E and G
(C) F and G (D) G and C

23. Which two villages are the farthest from one another?

(A) D and C (B) F and E
(C) F and B (D) G and E

24. How far is E from F (in km) as the crow flies?

(A) 4 (B) $\sqrt{20}$
(C) 5 (D) $\sqrt{26}$

25. A river flows west to east and on the way turns left and goes in a semi-circle round a hillock, and then turns left at right angles. In which direction is the river finally flowing? [MAT 2005]

(A) West (B) North
(C) East (D) South

ANSWER KEY

Level-1: Beginner

1.	(A)	2.	(A)	3.	(C)	4.	(D)	5.	(B)	6.	(C)	7.	(A)	8.	(B)	9.	(D)	10.	(A)
11.	(A)	12.	(C)	13.	(D)	14.	(A)	15.	(D)	16.	(D)	17.	(C)	18.	(B)	19.	(C)	20.	(B)
21.	(C)	22.	(B)	23.	(D)	24.	(D)	25.	(D)	26.	(C)	27.	(B)	28.	(D)	29.	(E)	30.	(B)
31.	(A)	32.	(B)	33.	(E)	34.	(D)	35.	(D)										

Level-2: Intermediate

1.	(A)	2.	(D)	3.	(C)	4.	(B)	5.	(C)	6.	(D)	7.	(C)	8.	(A)	9.	(C)	10.	(A)
11.	(D)	12.	(D)	13.	(C)	14.	(B)	15.	(D)	16.	(B)	17.	(D)	18.	(E)	19.	(B)	20.	(C)
21.	(A)	22.	(C)	23.	(A)	24.	(A)	25.	(B)	26.	(D)	27.	(C)	28.	(B)	29.	(C)	30.	(D)
31.	(D)	32.	(B)	33.	(D)	34.	(C)	35.	(C)										

Level-3: Expert

1.	(B)	2.	(C)	3.	(A)	4.	(B)	5.	(C)	6.	(D)	7.	(A)	8.	(E)	9.	(B)	10.	(D)
11.	(E)	12.	(B)	13.	(A)	14.	(A)	15.	(B)	16.	(C)	17.	(A)	18.	(B)	19.	(A)	20.	(C)
21.	(A)	22.	(D)	23.	(C)	24.	(A)	25.	(C)										

Solutions with Detailed Explanations

Level-1: BEGINNER

1. Option (A) is correct.

Explanation: The movements of Rishi are as shown in figure.

Clearly, AD = CD = 40 m

So, AE = AD + DE = 40 + 35 = 75 m

2. Option (A) is correct.

Explanation: The movements of Rohan are as shown in figure.

Clearly, we can see,

AB = CD = 3 km and BC = AD = 2 km

So, required distance=AE

= (DE – AD) = (3 – 2) = 1 km

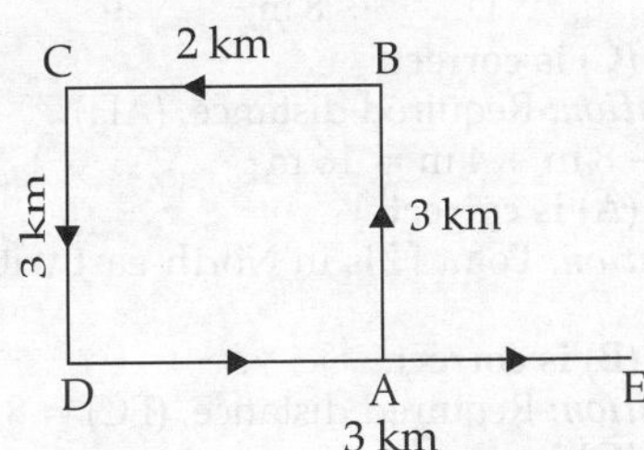

3. Option (C) is correct.

Explanation: The movements listed are from A to B, B to C, C to D, and D to E, as shown in the figure. Finally, I'm facing towards east.

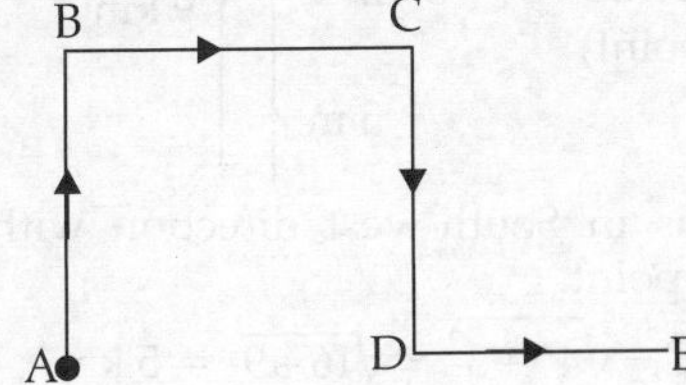

4. **Option (D) is correct.**
Explanation: As depicted in figure, the man faces OA at first. The man turns 45 degrees clockwise and faces OB. He turns to face OC after rotating another 180 degrees clockwise. He finally faces the direction of OD, or south-west, after rotating 270 degrees anti-clockwise.

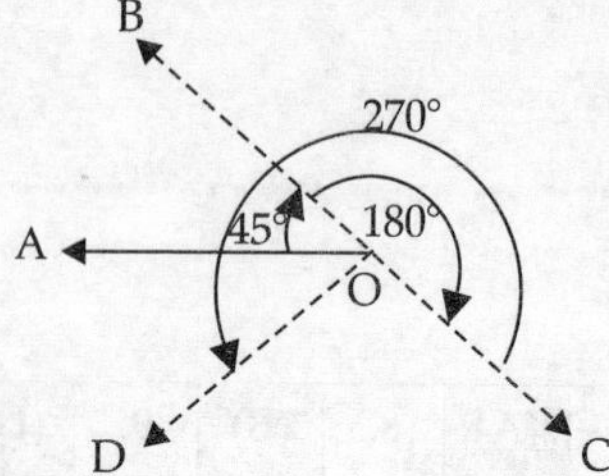

5. **Option (B) is correct.**
Explanation: The movements of Kunal are as shown in figure.

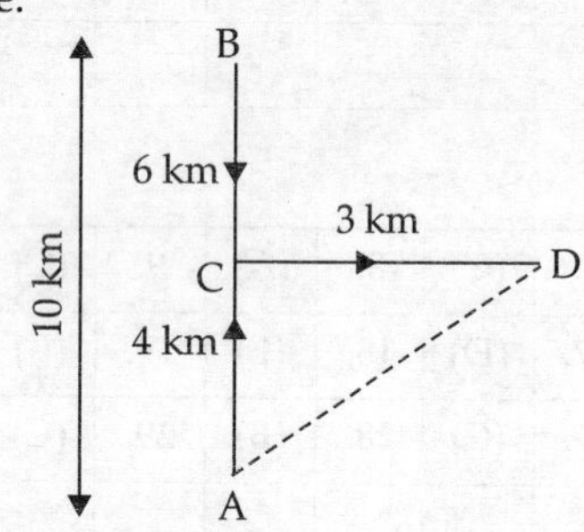

AC = (AB – BC) = (10 – 6) = 4 km
Clearly, D is to the North-East of A.
$AD = \sqrt{AC^2 + CD^2} = \sqrt{4^2 + 3^2} = \sqrt{25} = 5 \text{ km}$

6-8. According to the information

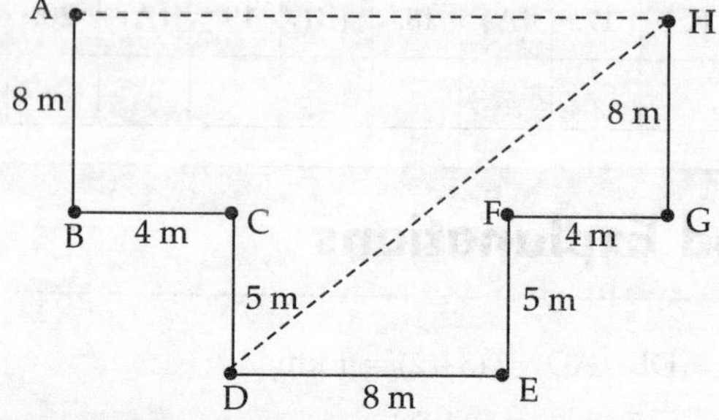

6. **Option (C) is correct.**
Explanation: Required distance, (AH)
= 4 m + 8 m + 4 m = 16 m
7. **Option (A) is correct.**
Explanation: Point H is in North-east with respect to point D.
8. **Option (B) is correct.**
Explanation: Required distance, (FC) = 8 m
9. **Option (D) is correct.**
Explanation:

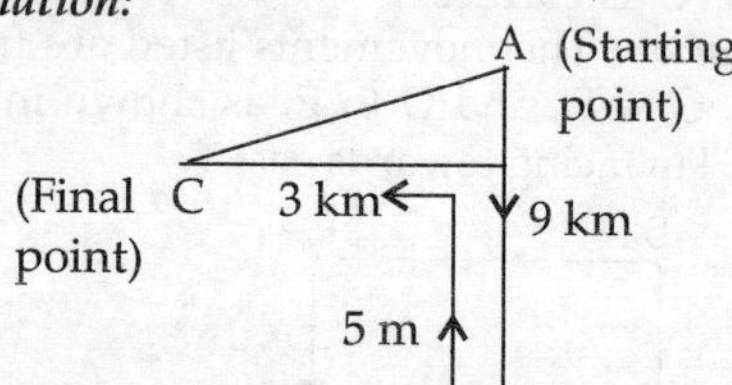

So, he is in South-west direction with respect to starting point.
Also, $AC = \sqrt{4^2 + 3^2} = \sqrt{16 + 9} = 5 \text{ km}$

10. **Option (A) is correct.**
Explanation:

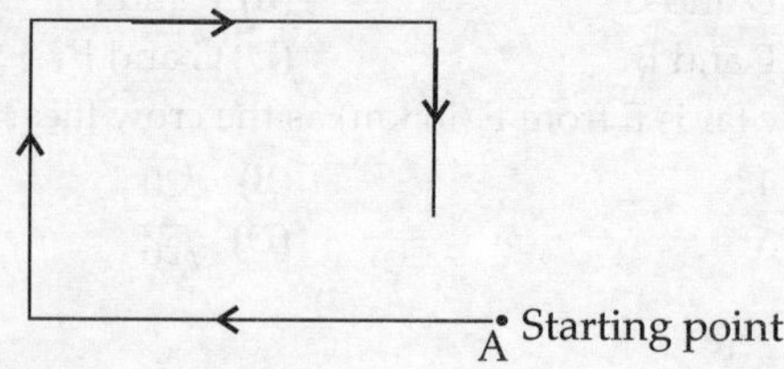

So, Raja is facing towards South now.
11. **Option (A) is correct.**
Explanation: We can see in this figure,

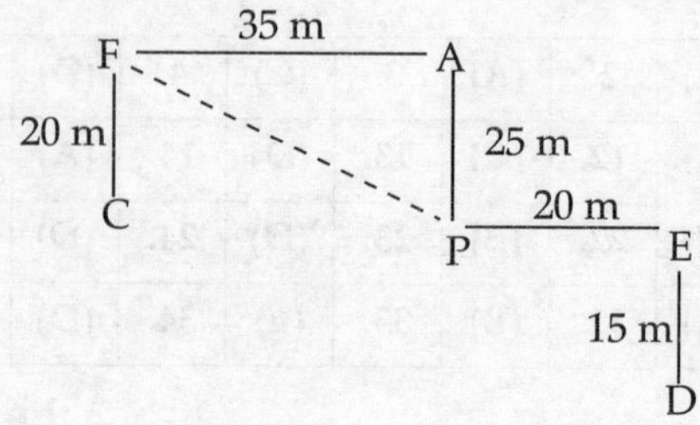

In relation to point P, F is to the North-west.
12. **Option (C) is correct.**
Explanation: We can see according to figure,

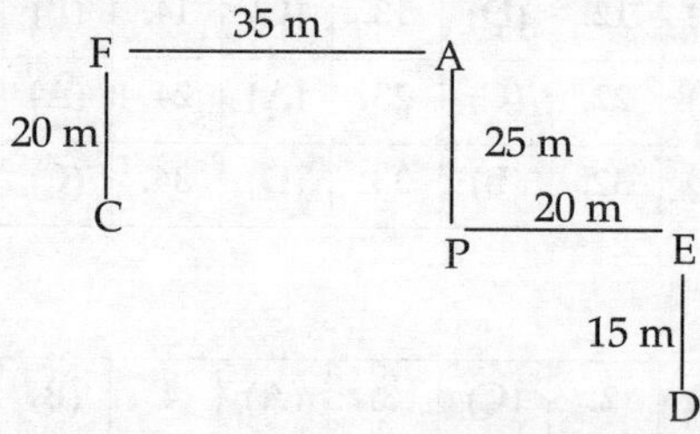

While other options followed a North-west to South-west route, option C went in the other direction.
13. **Option (D) is correct.**
Explanation: We can see according to the given figure,

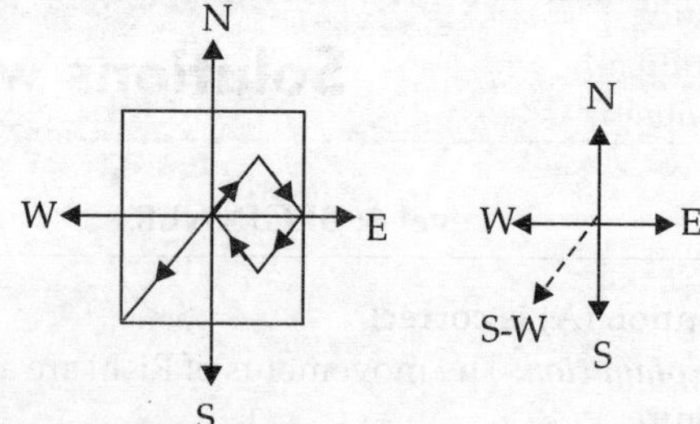

Raj is moving South-west.
14. **Option (A) is correct.**
Explanation: We can see according to the given figure,

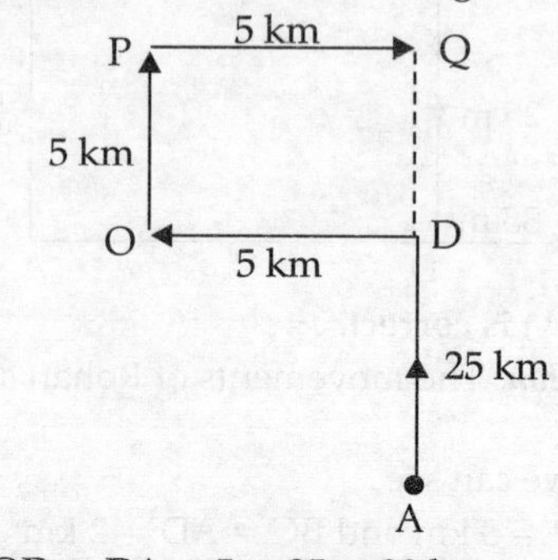

QA = QD + DA = 5 + 25 = 30 km

15. Option (D) is correct.
Explanation: As shown in the figure, the distance between A and D = AD = BC = 10 km

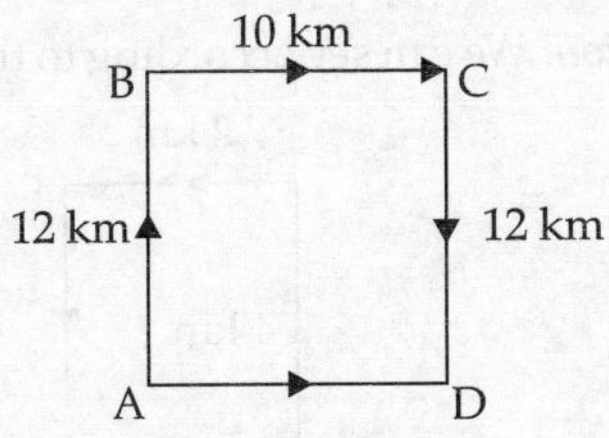

(16-18): According to the information, we have

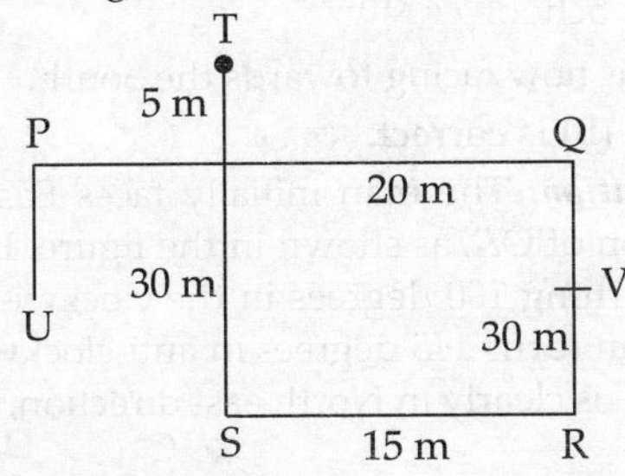

16. Option (D) is correct.
Explanation: Point U is 20 m West of point V.

17. Option (C) is correct.
Explanation: Except R and P, all other combinations are in same direction.

18. Option (B) is correct.
Explanation:

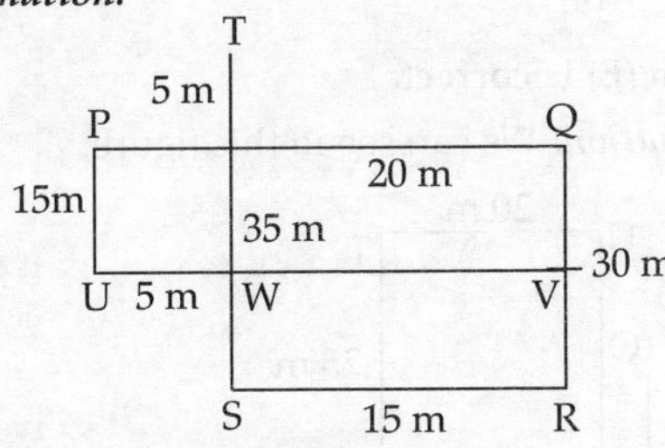

Required distance, WS = 15 m

19. Option (C) is correct.
Explanation: We can see in this figure,

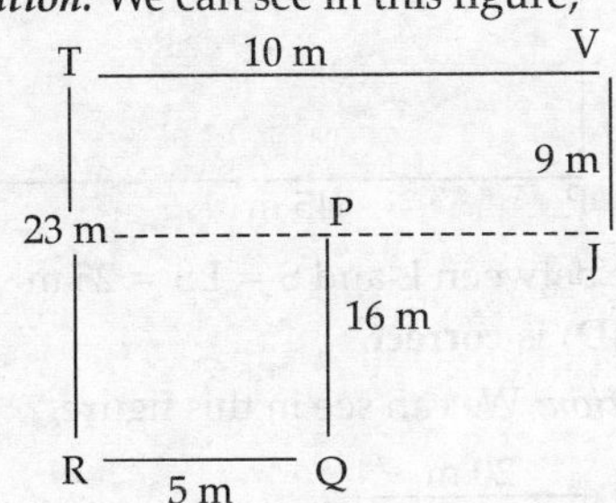

Point J is 5m far from point P in East direction.

20. Option (B) is correct.
Explanation: We can see in this figure,

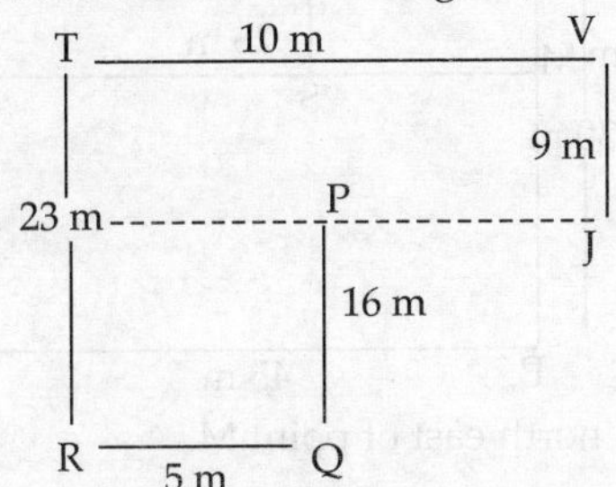

Distance between T and W = TW = VJ = 9 m

21. Option (C) is correct.
Explanation: We can see in this figure,

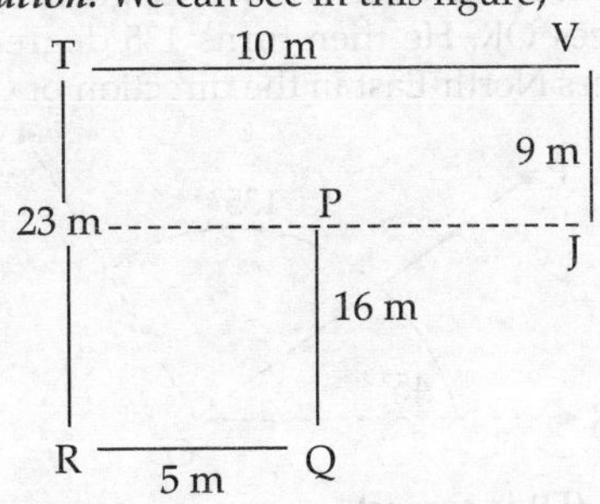

V is in north east direction from point R.

Sol. (22-24): According to the information, we have

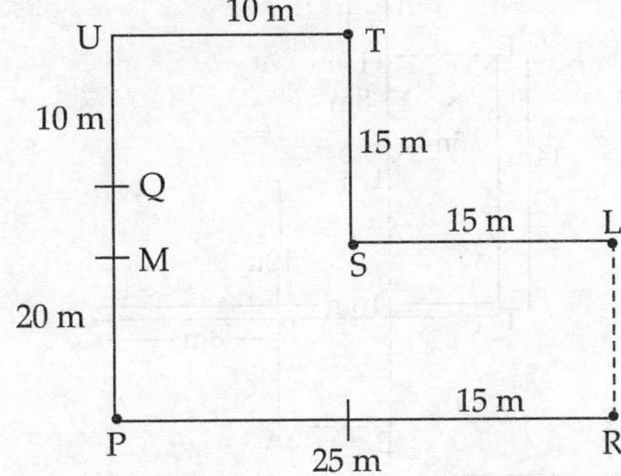

22. Option (B) is correct.
Explanation: Required distance, LR = 15 m

23. Option (D) is correct.
Explanation: Point T is in North-east direction with respect to point P.

24. Option (D) is correct.
Explanation: M, S and L are in a line.

25. Option (D) is correct.
Explanation: According to figure, the man is facing towards B in starting. He turns to face OC after turning 180 degrees clockwise. He again turns 135 degrees anti-clockwise and faces East in the direction of OM.

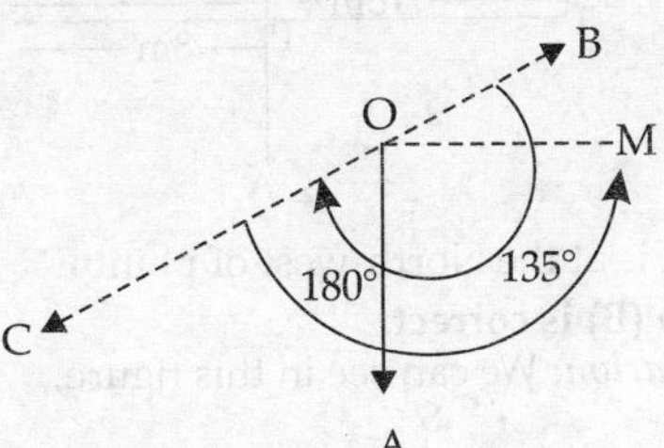

26. Option (C) is correct.
Explanation: The movements (O to A, A to B, and B to C) are shown in figure. It is obvious that C is southwest of O.

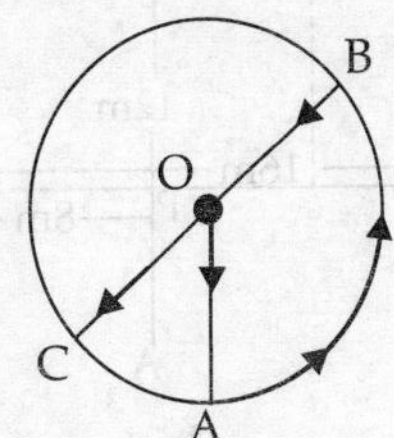

27. Option (B) is correct.

Explanation: According to the figure, the man faces OP at first. The man turns 45 degrees anticlockwise and faces OR. He then turns 135 degrees clockwise and faces North-East in the direction of OQ.

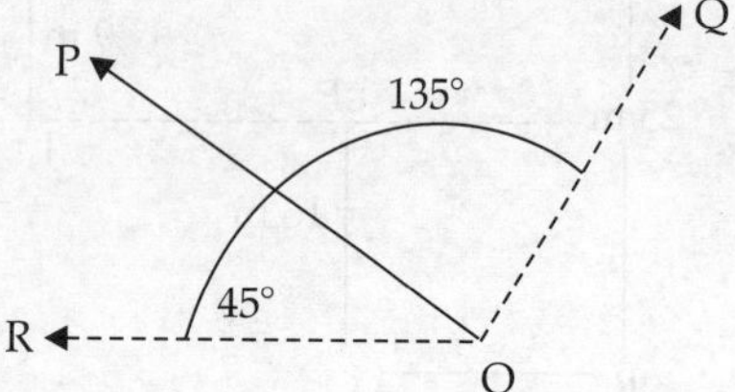

28. Option (D) is correct.

Explanation: We can see in this figure,

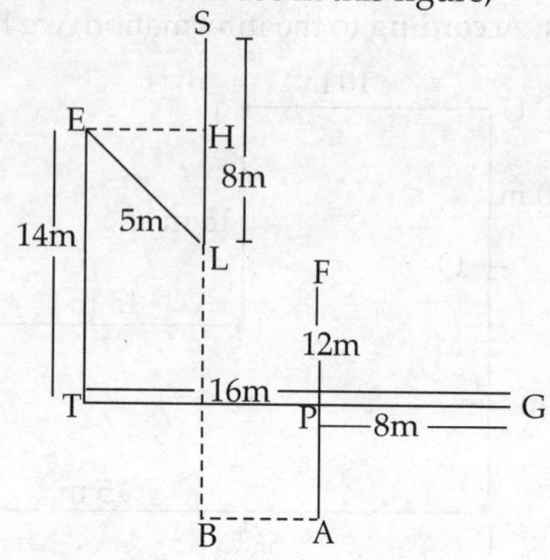

$EH = \sqrt{5^2 - 4^2} = 3$ m

So, AB = TP – EH = 8 – 3 = 5 m

29. Option (E) is correct.

Explanation: We can see in this figure,

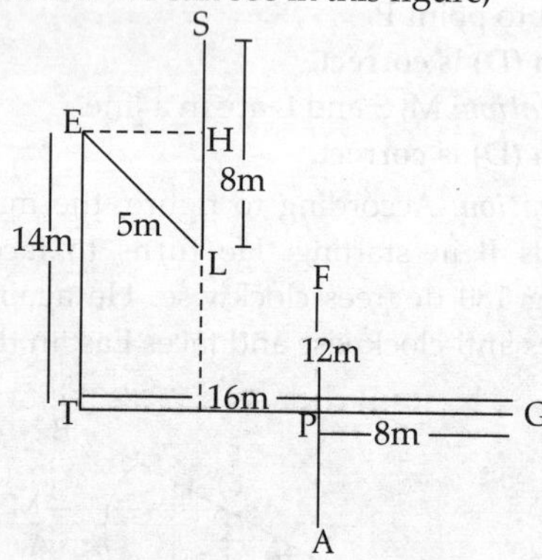

Point L is at the North-west of point F.

30. Option (B) is correct.

Explanation: We can see in this figure,

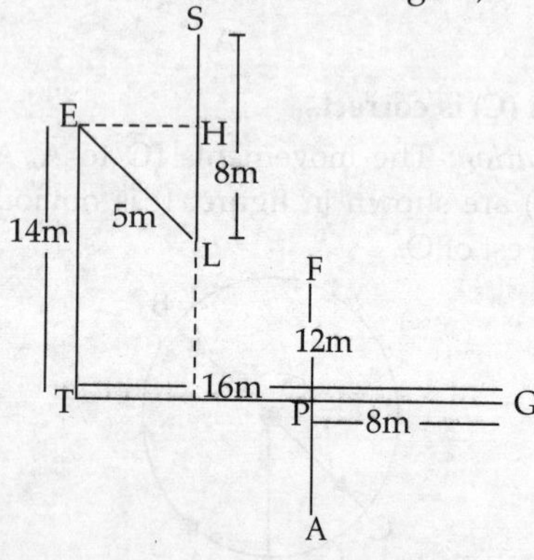

$EH = \sqrt{EL^2 - HL^2} = \sqrt{5^2 - 4^2} = \sqrt{9} = 3$ m

31. Option (A) is correct.

Explanation: We can see according to the given figure,

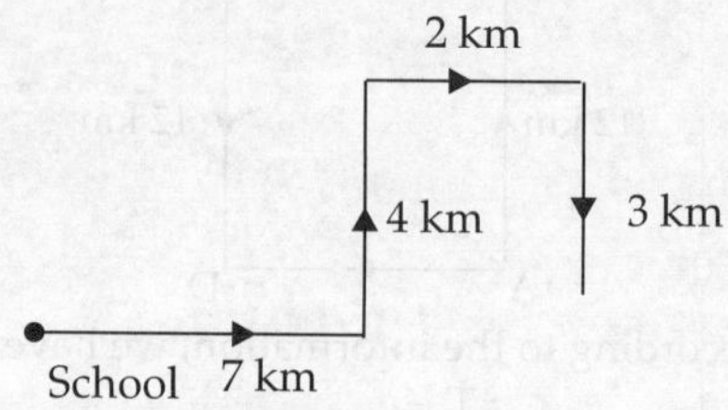

Pratap is now facing towards the South.

32. Option (B) is correct.

Explanation: The man initially faces East, or in the direction of OA, as shown in the figure. He faces OB after turning 100 degrees in the clockwise direction. He again turns 145 degrees in anti-clockwise faces to OC. OC is clearly in North east direction.

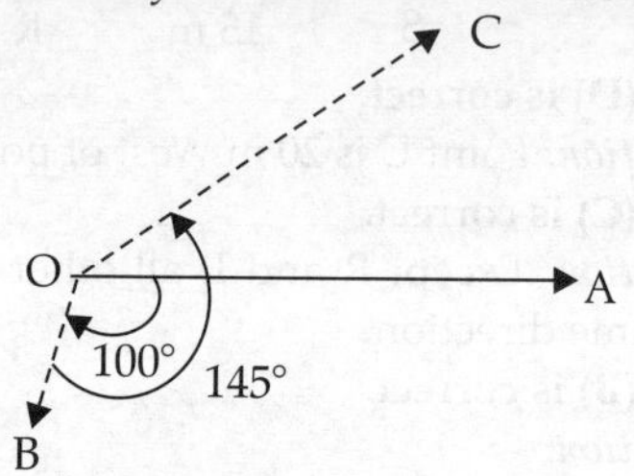

33. Option (E) is correct.

Explanation: We can see in this figure,

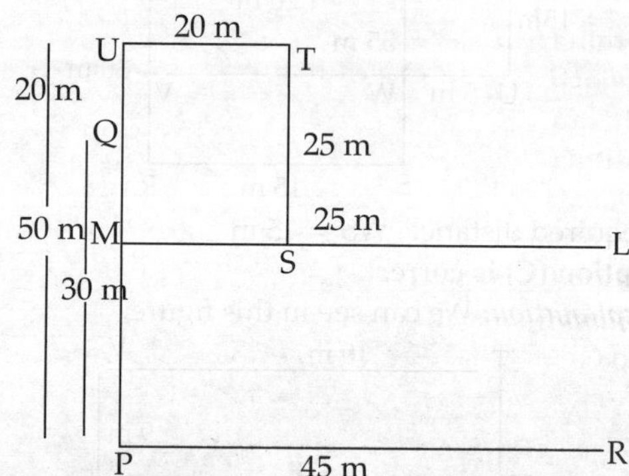

Distance between L and S = LS = 25 m

34. Option (D) is correct.

Explanation: We can see in this figure,

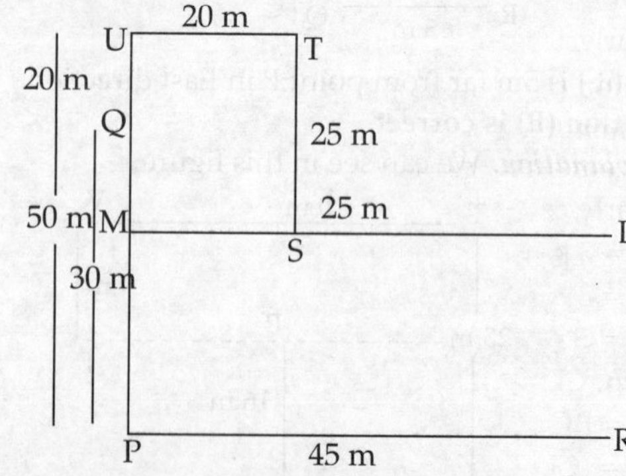

T is in north east of point M.

35. Option (D) is correct.

Explanation: We can see in this figure,

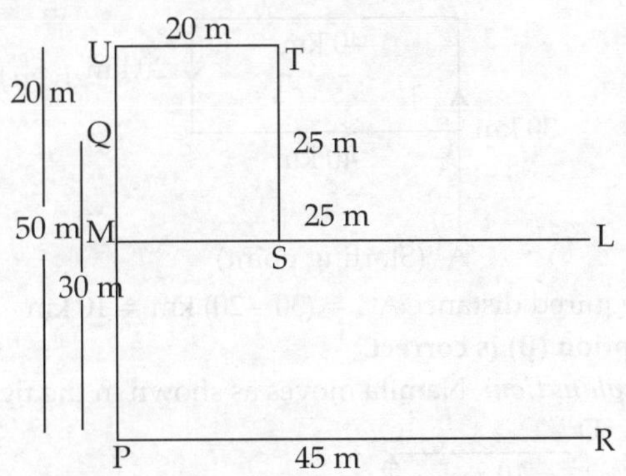

Point U, M, P are in line.

Level-2: INTERMEDIATE

(1-2).

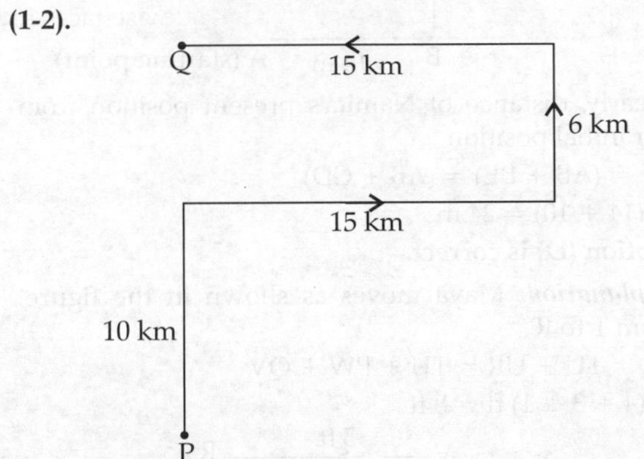

1. Option (A) is correct.

Explanation: Required distance, QP = (10 + 6) km = 16 km

2. Option (D) is correct.

Explanation: The vehicle was moving towards west direction before it stopping at point Q.

3. Option (C) is correct.

Explanation: A rat moves as shown in the figure, from A to G.

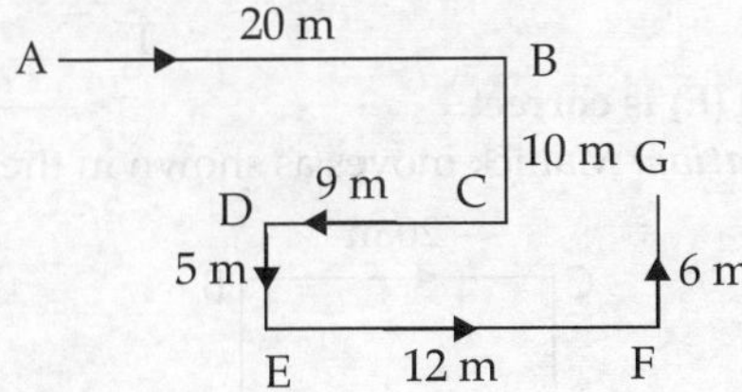

Clearly, it is finally walking in the North direction.

4. Option (B) is correct.

Explanation: According to the figure, the person's movements are depicted.

Clearly,

AB = 3 km

BC = 3 AB = (3 × 3) = 9 km

CD = 5 AB = (5 × 3) = 15 km

Then, CE = AB = 3 km

AE = BC = 9 km

DE = (CD – CE) = (15 – 3) = 12 km

So, $AD^2 = AE^2 + DE^2$

$\Rightarrow AD = \sqrt{9^2 + 12^2} = \sqrt{225} = 15$ km

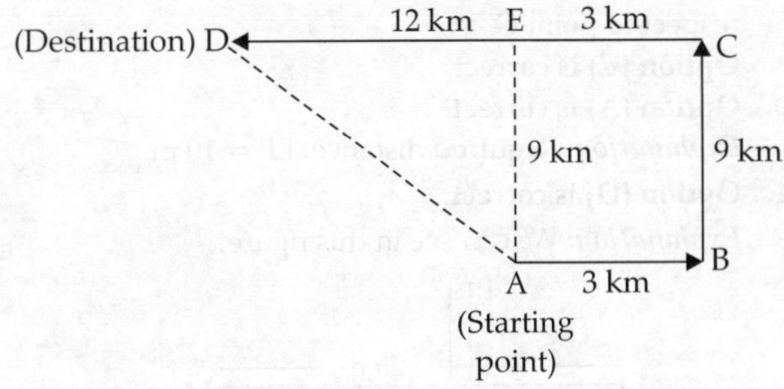

5. Option (C) is correct.

Explanation: Radha moves as shown in the figure. Clearly, distance of Radha from her initial position,

OD = (OC – CD) = (AB – CD)

= (14 – 10) m = 4 m

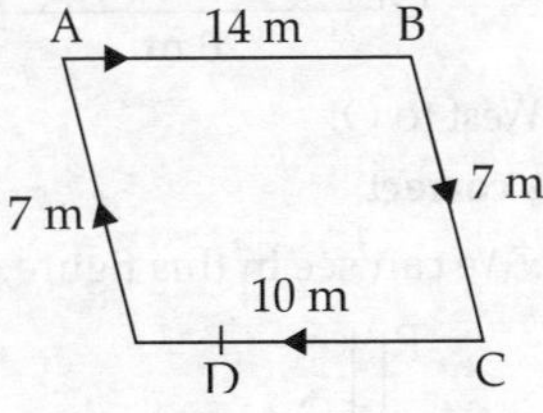

6. Option (D) is correct.

Explanation: The below diagram shows the clock after rotating the standard clock by 135 degrees anti-clockwise. The minute hand clearly indicates a direction South-East.

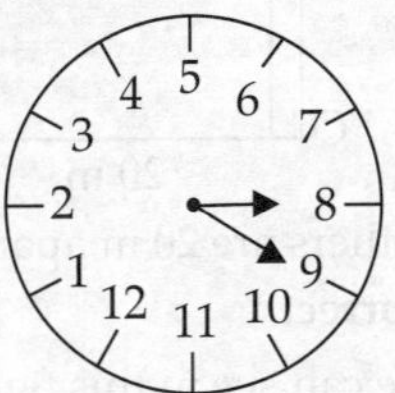

7. Option (C) is correct.

Explanation: Clearly, the minute and hour hands are in the locations indicated in the diagrams at 12 noon and 1.30 p.m. As can be seen, the hour hand at 1:30 p.m. is pointing eastward.

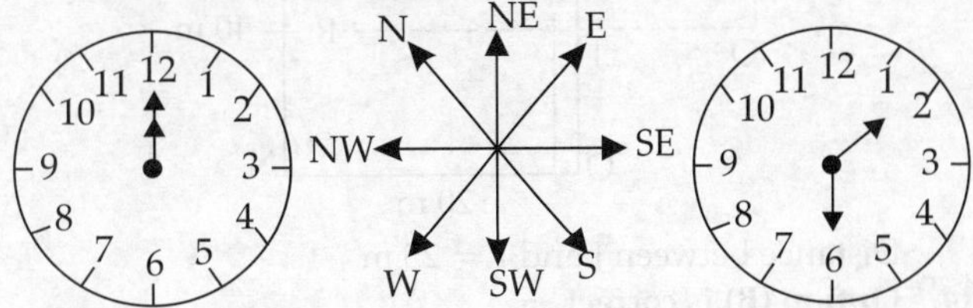

Sol. (8-10): According to the information, we have

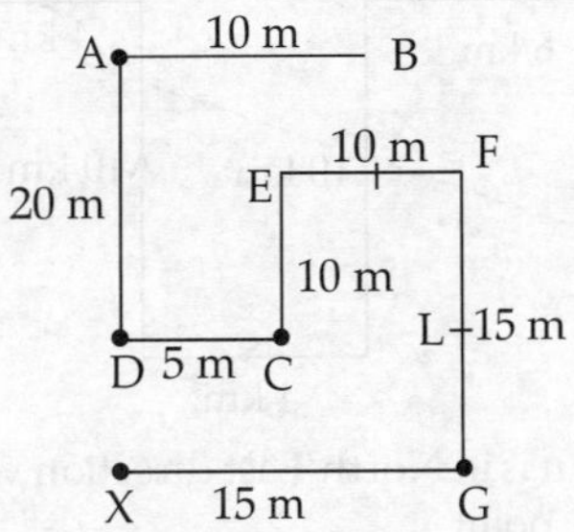

8. **Option (A) is correct.**
Explanation: Point A is in North-west direction with respect to point G.
9. **Option (C) is correct.**
10. **Option (A) is correct.**
Explanation: Required distance, LF = 10 m
11. **Option (D) is correct.**
Explanation: We can see in this figure,

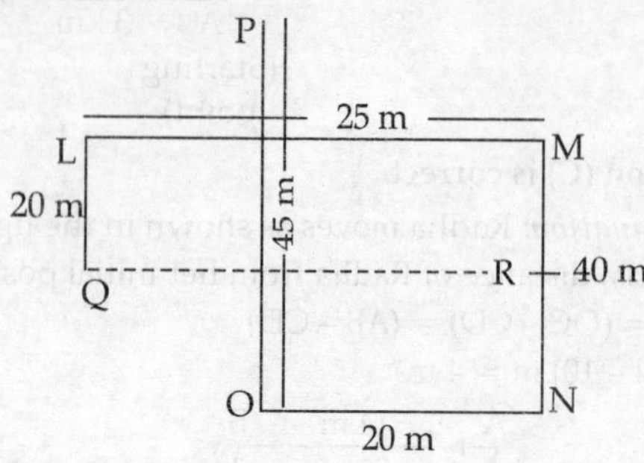

R is at 25 m West to Q.
12. **Option (E) is correct.**
Explanation: We can see in this figure,

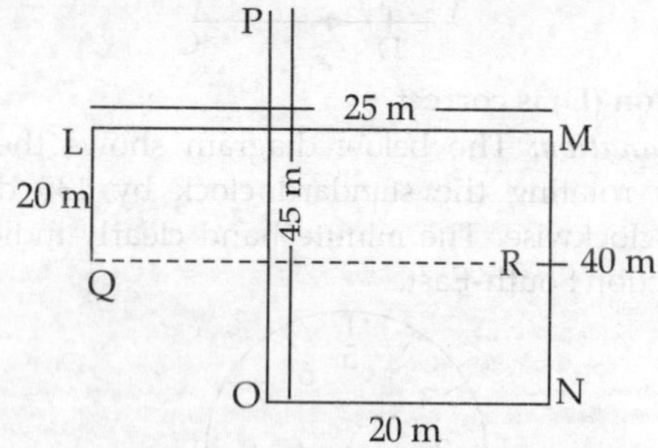

All except OP, others are 20 m apart from each other.
13. **Option (C) is correct.**
Explanation: We can see in this figure,

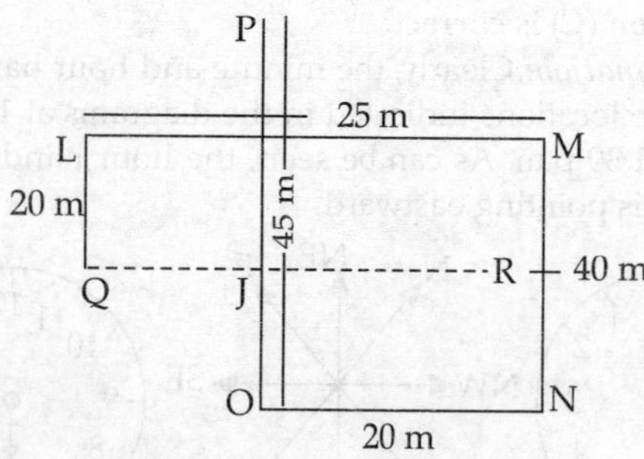

Distance between J and P = 25 m
14. **Option (B) is correct.**
Explanation:

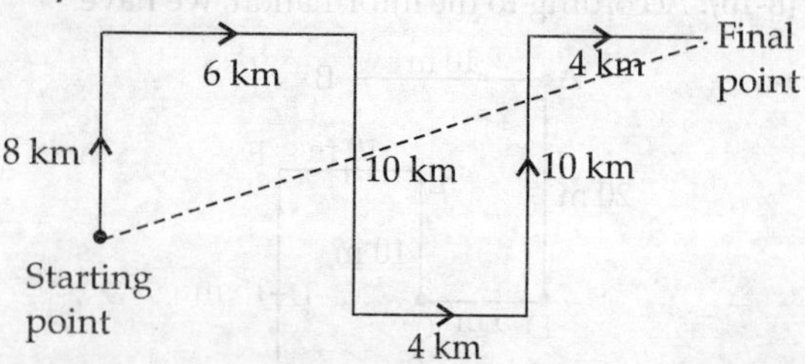

Now, Raghu is in North-East direction with respect to his starting point.

15. **Option (D) is correct.**
Explanation:

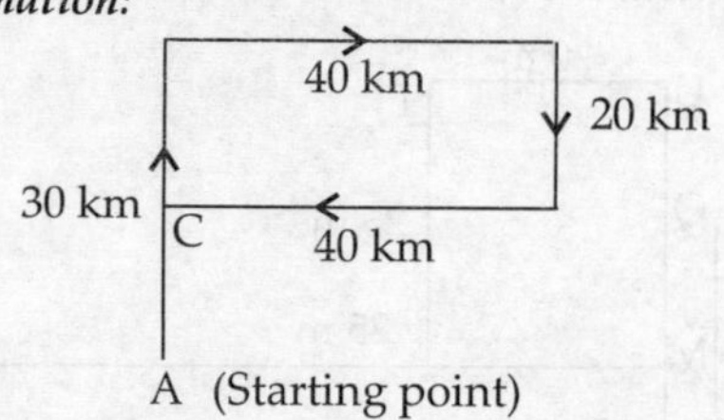

Required distance AC = (30 – 20) km = 10 km
16. **Option (B) is correct.**
Explanation: Namita moves as shown in the figure.

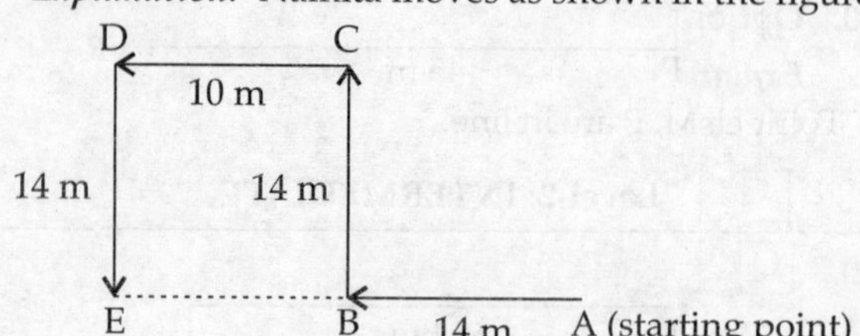

Clearly, distance of Namita's present position from her initial position
AE = (AB + BE) = (AB + CD)
= (14 + 10) = 24 m
17. **Option (D) is correct.**
Explanation: Maya moves as shown in the figure, from T to R
TR = TU + UR = TU + PW + QV
= (4 + 3 + 1) ft = 8 ft

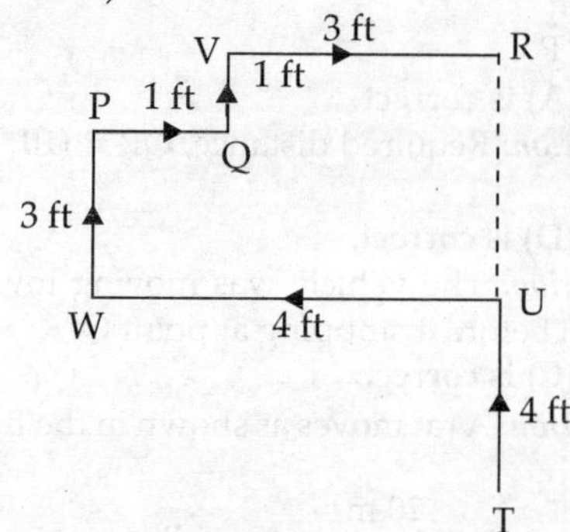

18. **Option (E) is correct.**
Explanation: Manick moves as shown in the figure.

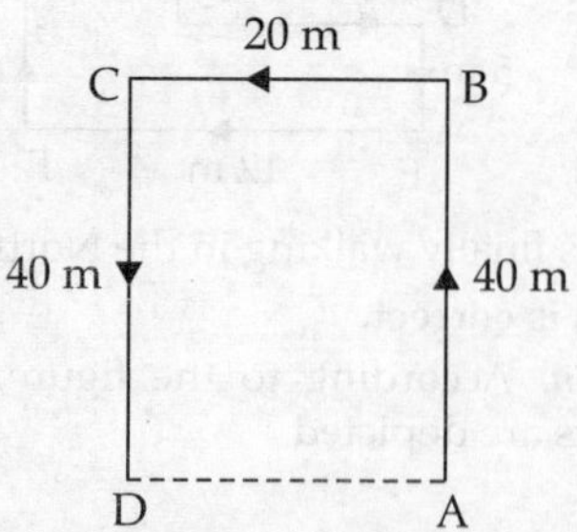

Clearly, ABCD is a rectangle and so
AD = BC = 20 m
So, D is 20 m to the west of A.
19. **Option (B) is correct.**
Explanation: The actual positions of the directions are depicted in (i) and (ii) can be used to explain how the pointer's positions have changed. It is obvious

that the incorrectly positioned pointer in Figure (ii) is actually pointing south instead of west.

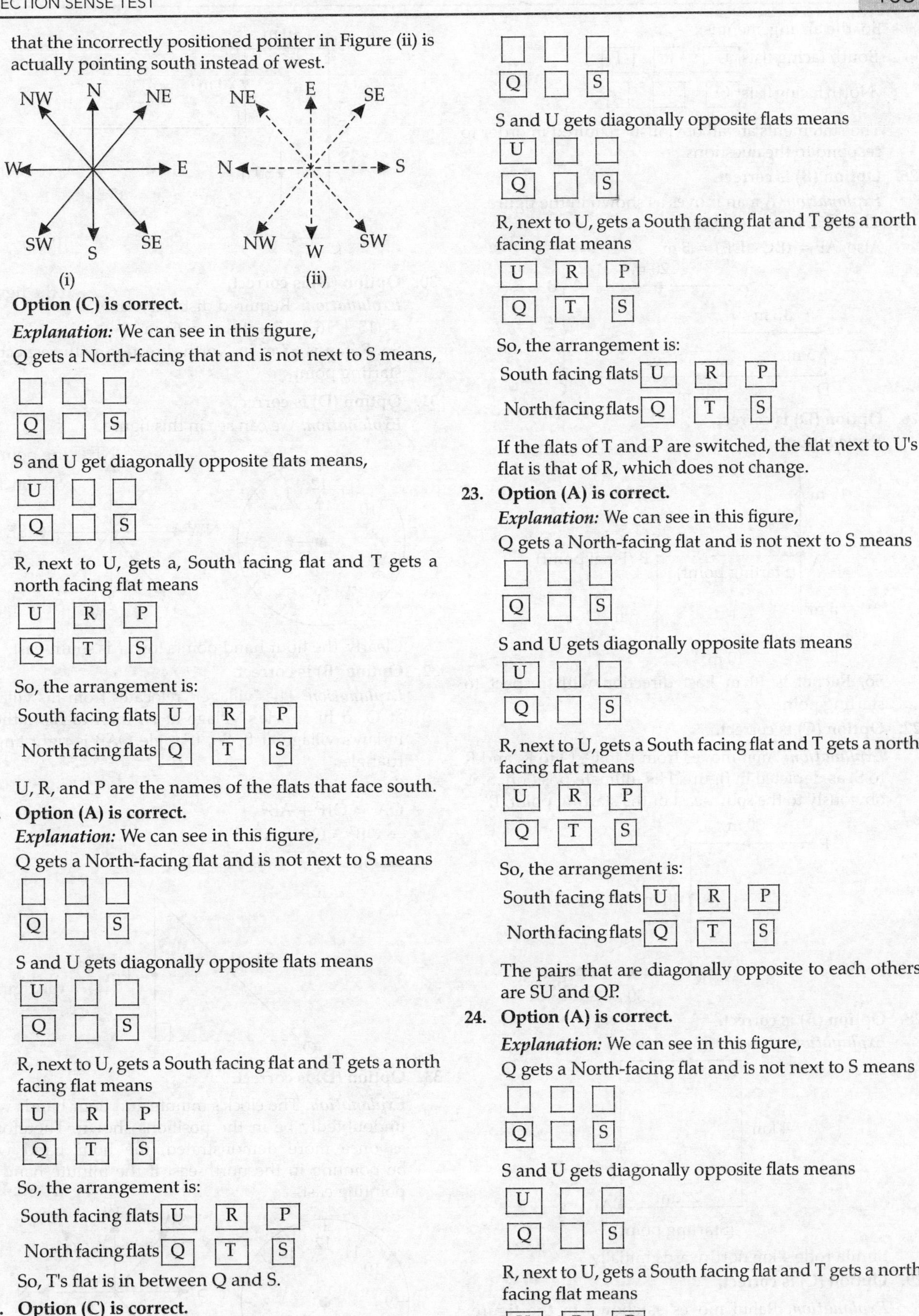

20. Option (C) is correct.

Explanation: We can see in this figure,

Q gets a North-facing that and is not next to S means,

Q		S

S and U get diagonally opposite flats means,

U		
Q		S

R, next to U, gets a, South facing flat and T gets a north facing flat means

U	R	P
Q	T	S

So, the arrangement is:

South facing flats	U	R	P
North facing flats	Q	T	S

U, R, and P are the names of the flats that face south.

21. Option (A) is correct.

Explanation: We can see in this figure,

Q gets a North-facing flat and is not next to S means

Q		S

S and U gets diagonally opposite flats means

U		
Q		S

R, next to U, gets a South facing flat and T gets a north facing flat means

U	R	P
Q	T	S

So, the arrangement is:

South facing flats	U	R	P
North facing flats	Q	T	S

So, T's flat is in between Q and S.

22. Option (C) is correct.

Explanation: We can see in this figure,

Q gets a North-facing flat and is not next to S means

Q		S

S and U gets diagonally opposite flats means

U		
Q		S

R, next to U, gets a South facing flat and T gets a north facing flat means

U	R	P
Q	T	S

So, the arrangement is:

South facing flats	U	R	P
North facing flats	Q	T	S

If the flats of T and P are switched, the flat next to U's flat is that of R, which does not change.

23. Option (A) is correct.

Explanation: We can see in this figure,

Q gets a North-facing flat and is not next to S means

Q		S

S and U gets diagonally opposite flats means

U		
Q		S

R, next to U, gets a South facing flat and T gets a north facing flat means

U	R	P
Q	T	S

So, the arrangement is:

South facing flats	U	R	P
North facing flats	Q	T	S

The pairs that are diagonally opposite to each others are SU and QP.

24. Option (A) is correct.

Explanation: We can see in this figure,

Q gets a North-facing flat and is not next to S means

Q		S

S and U gets diagonally opposite flats means

U		
Q		S

R, next to U, gets a South facing flat and T gets a north facing flat means

U	R	P
Q	T	S

So, the arrangement is:

South facing flats	U	R	P
North facing flats	Q	T	S

The statements are all obviously required in order to respond to the questions.

25. Option (B) is correct.

Explanation: A man moves as shown in the figure.

Clearly, F is in line with A

Also, AF = (BC – DE) = 5 m

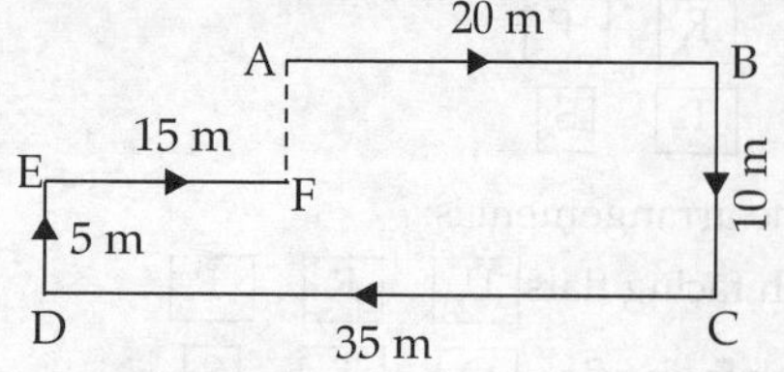

26. Option (D) is correct.

Explanation:

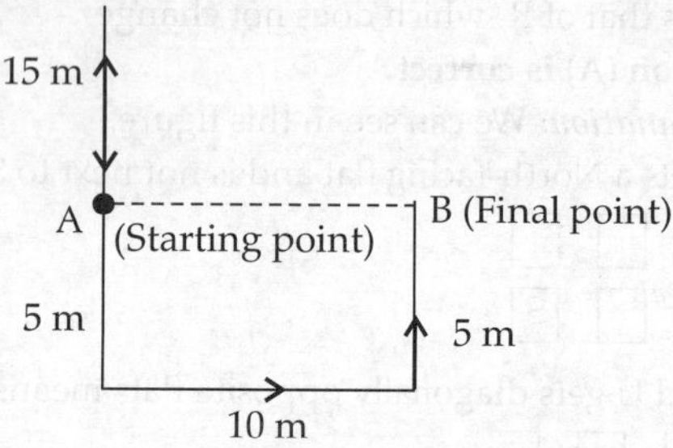

So, Rachel is 10 m East direction with respect to starting point.

27. Option (C) is correct.

Explanation: Amit moves from P to Q, Q to R, and R to S, as depicted in figure. His ultimate position, S, is obviously to the south-east of the starting point, P.

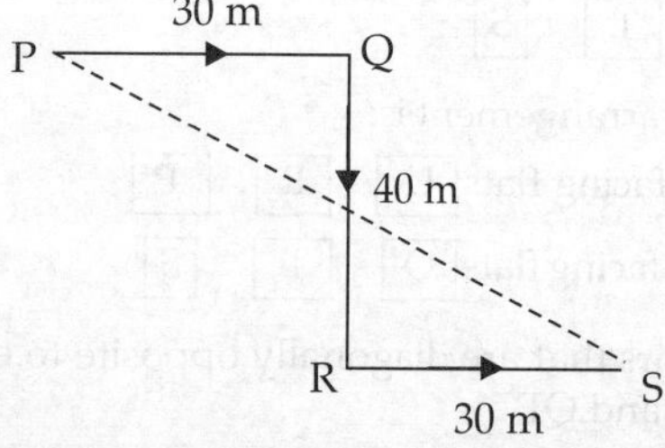

28. Option (B) is correct.

Explanation:

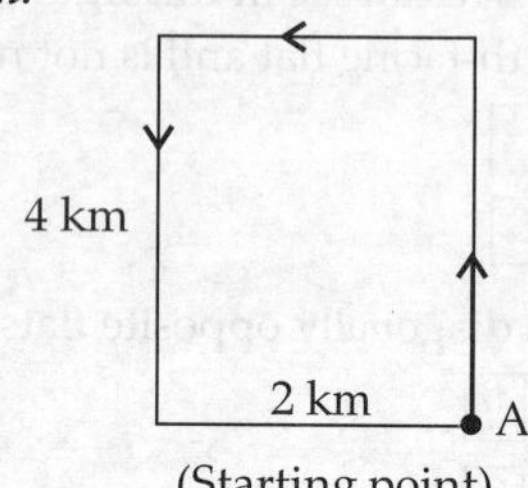

Sunita rode 4 km northwards initially.

29. Option (C) is correct.

Explanation: Rahul moves as shown in the figure, from A to G.

Clearly, Rahul is finally walking in the east direction.

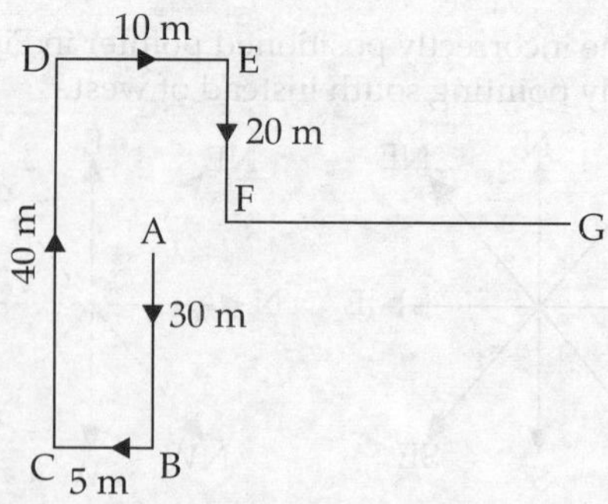

30. Option (D) is correct.

Explanation: Required distance, AB

= (15 + 16 + 17 + 19) m = 67 m

So, Ratan is 67 m in North direction with respect to starting point.

31. Option (D) is correct.

Explanation: We can see in this figure,

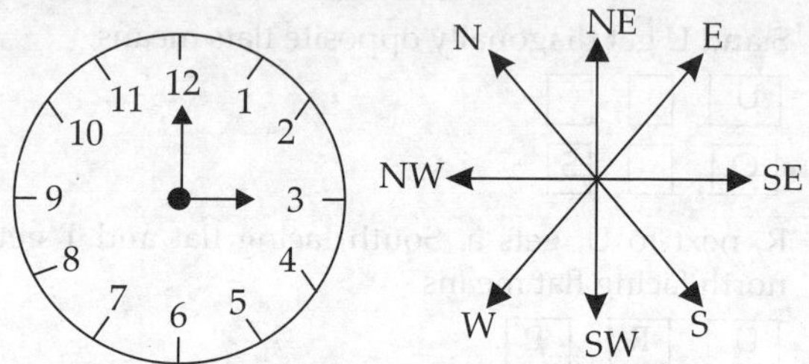

Clearly, the hour hand points towards south-east.

32. Option (B) is correct.

Explanation: The "villager" relocates from his village at O to his uncle's village at A, then to his father-in-law's village at B. So, triangle OAB is right angle triangle.

So,

$OA^2 = OB^2 + AB^2$

$\Rightarrow OB^2 = OA^2 - AB^2$

$\Rightarrow OB = \sqrt{25-16} = \sqrt{9} = 3$ km

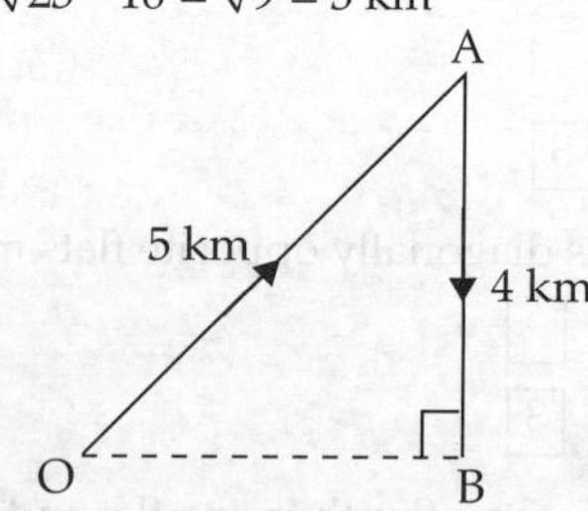

33. Option (D) is correct.

Explanation: The clock's minute and hour hands will undoubtedly be in the positions shown. Therefore, as once more demonstrated, the hour hand will be pointing in the north-east if the minute hand is pointing east.

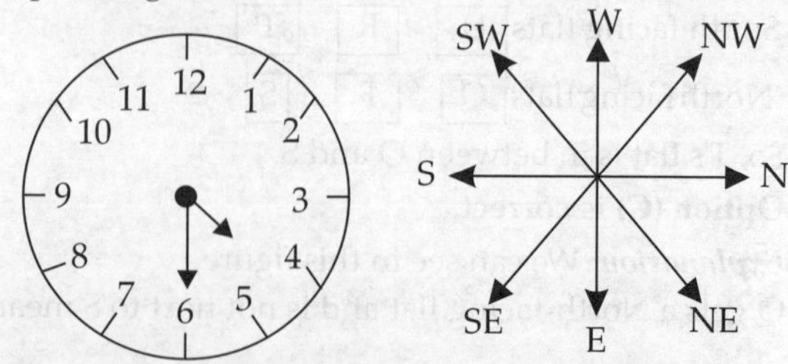

34. **Option (C) is correct.**
Explanation: We can see in this figure,

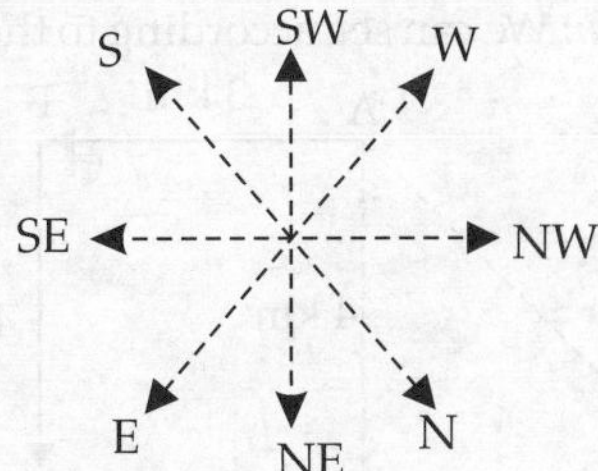

As shown in above, West will become South East.

35. **Option (C) is correct.**
Explanation: The directions are shown exactly as they are in diagram (i). According to the provided information, diagram (ii) north will therefore be referred to as being in the north-west when comparing the direction of North in (i) with that in (ii).

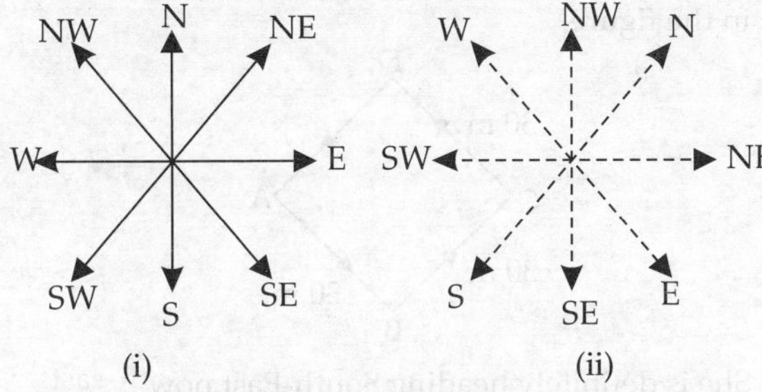

So, the right answer will be north-west.

Level-3: EXPERT

1. **Option (B) is correct.**
Explanation: We can see according to the given figure,

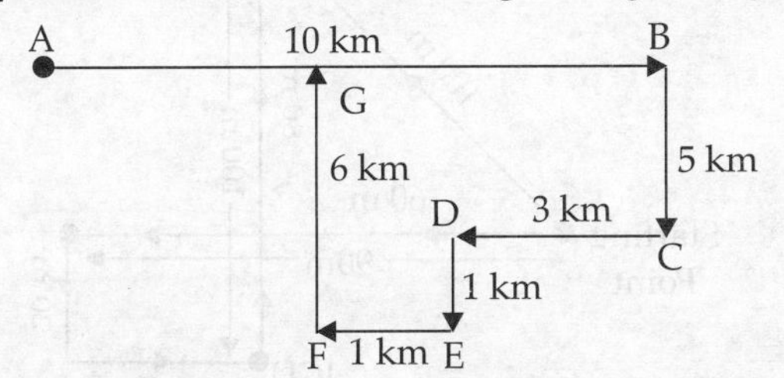

AG = AB – BG
= 10 – 4 = 6 km

2. **Option (C) is correct.**
Explanation: We can see according to the given figure,

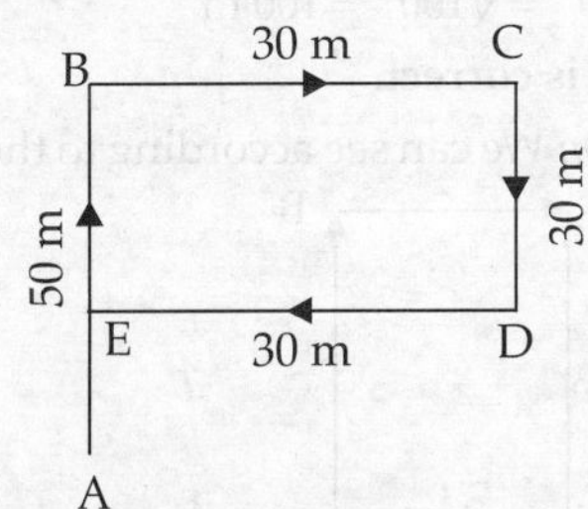

AE = (AB – BE) = (AB – CD)
= (50 – 30) m = 20 m

Sol. (3-5).
According to the information, we have

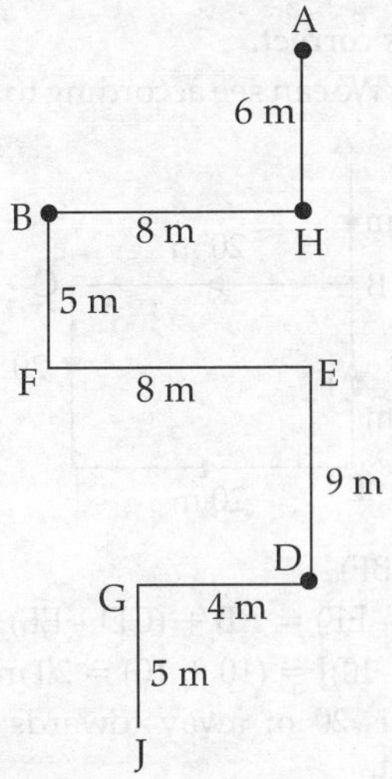

3. **Option (A) is correct.**
Explanation: Point E is in South direction with respect to point A

4. **Option (B) is correct.**
Explanation: Required distance,

$$DJ = \sqrt{4^2 + 5^2} = \sqrt{16 + 25} = \sqrt{41} \text{ m}$$

5. **Option (C) is correct.**
Explanation: Required distance = ED + DG + GJ
= 9 m + 4 m + 5 m = 18 m

6. **Option (D) is correct.**
Explanation: We can see in this figure,

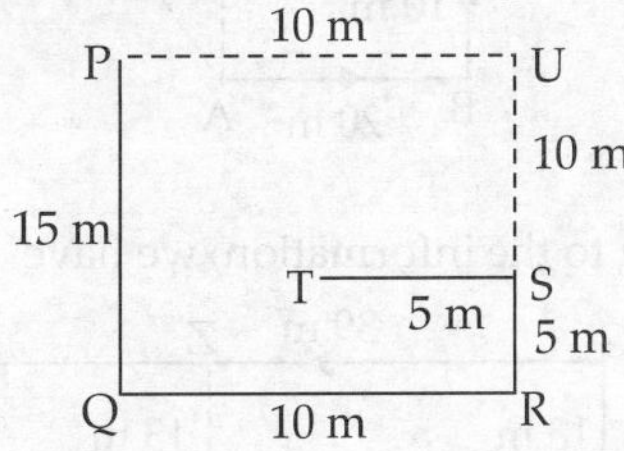

Clearly, point U is 10 metres to the south of point S.

7. **Option (A) is correct.**
Explanation: We can see in this figure,

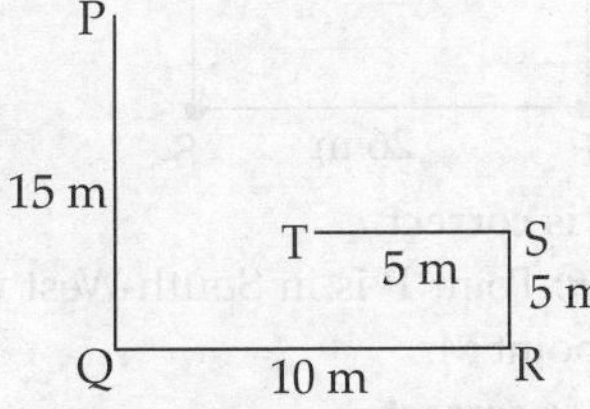

So, the northwest of point T is point P.

8. **Option (E) is correct.**
Explanation: We can see according to the given figure,

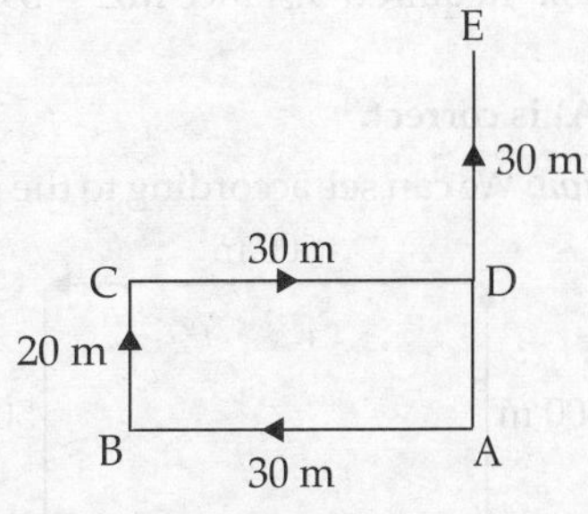

AE = (AD + DE) = (AB + CD) = (20 + 30) = 50 m

9. Option (B) is correct.

Explanation: We can see according to the given figure,

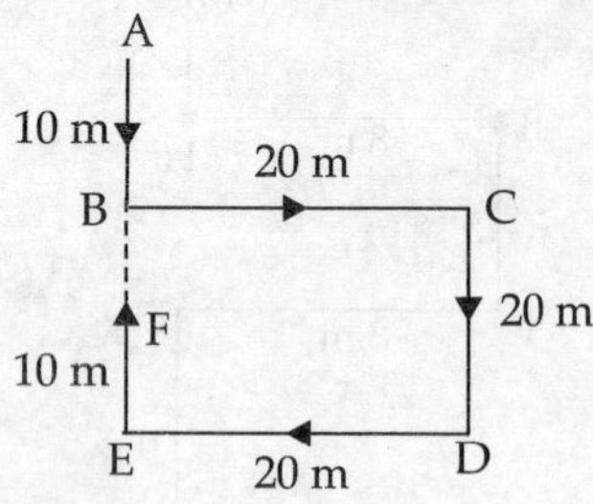

AF = (AB + BF)
= AB + (BE – EF) = AB + (CD – EF)
= [10 + (20 – 10)] = (10 + 10) = 20 m

So, Sanjeev is 20 m away towards south from the starting point.

10. Option (D) is correct.

Explanation: According to the figure, the person's movements range from A to F. Clearly, the destination is at location F, which is northeast of the beginning point A.

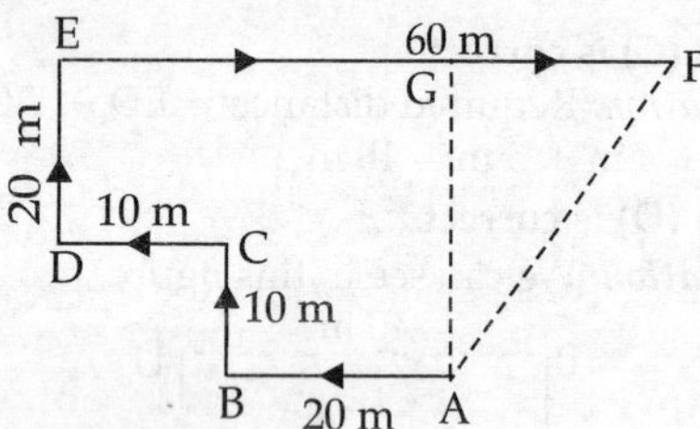

Sol. (11–13):

According to the information, we have

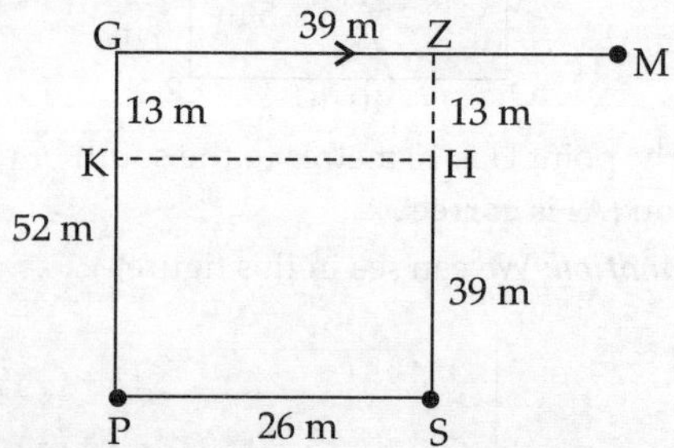

11. Option (E) is correct.

Explanation: Point P is in South-West direction with respect to point M.

12. Option (B) is correct.

Explanation: Required distance, KH = 26 m

13. Option (A) is correct.

Explanation: Required distance MZ = 39 m – 26 m = 13 m

14. Option (A) is correct.

Explanation: We can see according to the given figure,

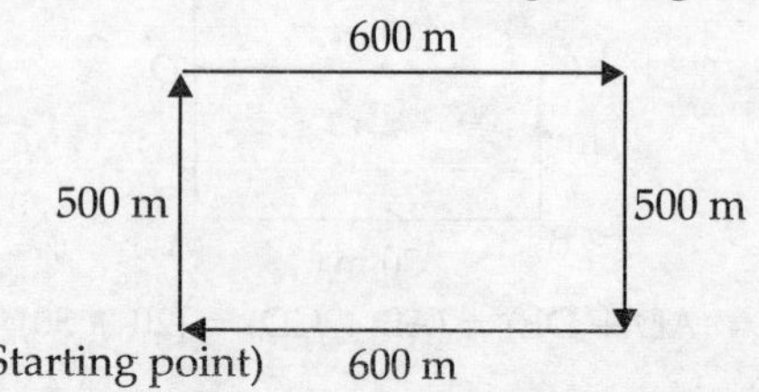

Pinky is reached at starting point.

15. Option (B) is correct.

Explanation: We can see according to the given figure,

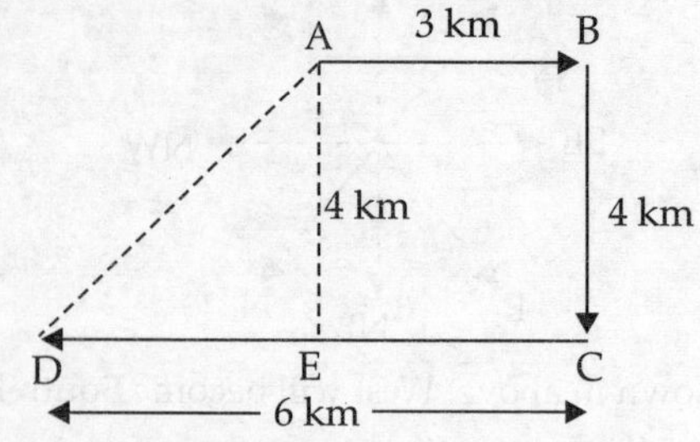

$(AD)^2 = (AE)^2 + (DE)^2$

$\Rightarrow AD^2 = (4)^2 + (3)^2 = 16 + 9 = 25$

$\Rightarrow AD = \sqrt{25} = 5$ km

16. Option (C) is correct.

Explanation: The movements of the girl are as shows in the figure.

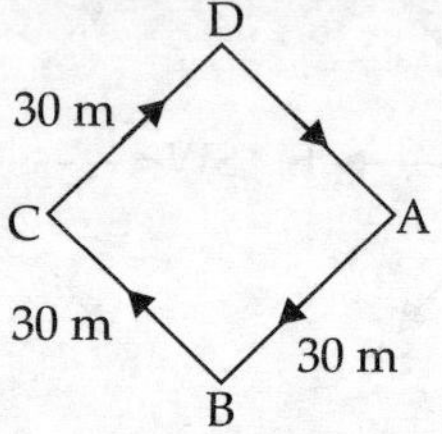

She is definitely heading South-East now.

17. Option (A) is correct.

Explanation: We can see in this figure,

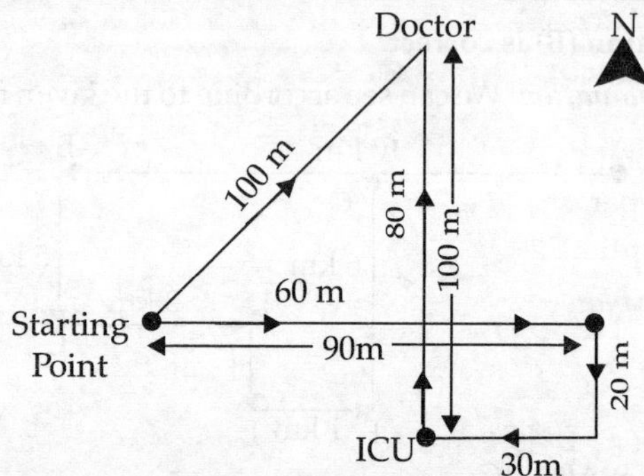

The distance between the starting point and the meeting place of the nurse and doctor

$= \sqrt{60^2 + 80^2} = \sqrt{100^2} = 100$ m

18. Option (B) is correct.

Explanation: We can see according to the given figure,

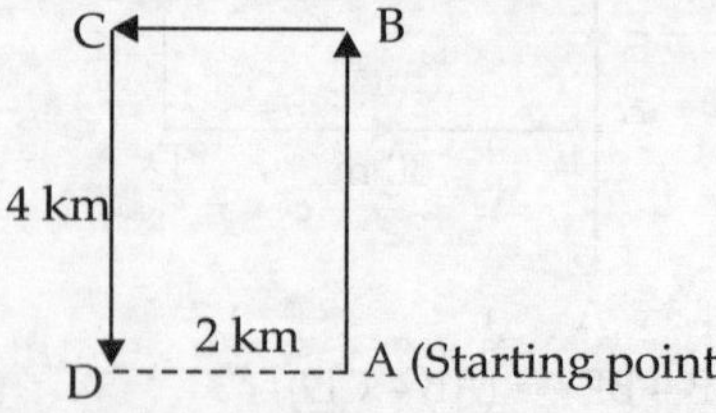

Required distance = AB = CD = 4 km

19. Option (A) is correct.

Explanation: We can see in this figure,

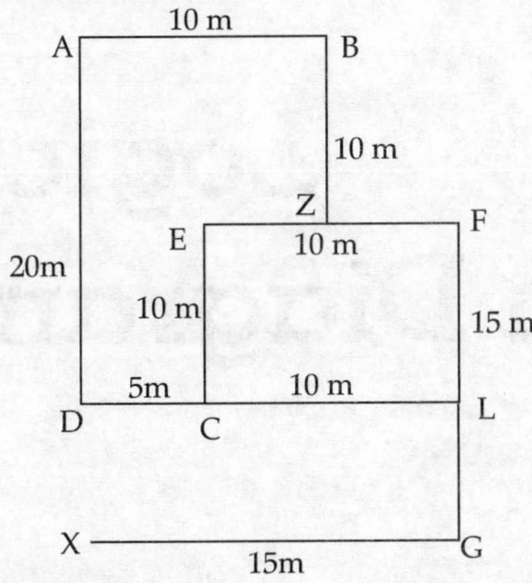

In relation to point G, point A is to the northwest.

20. Option (C) is correct.

Explanation: We can see in this figure,

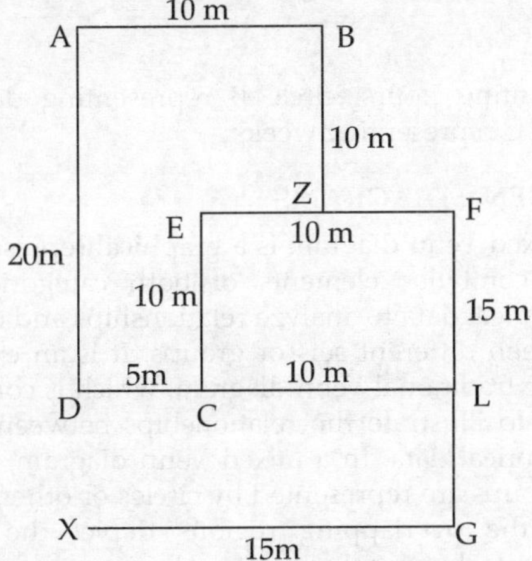

While others have a distance of 10 m, LG is only separated by 5 m.

21. Option (A) is correct.

Explanation: We can see in this figure,

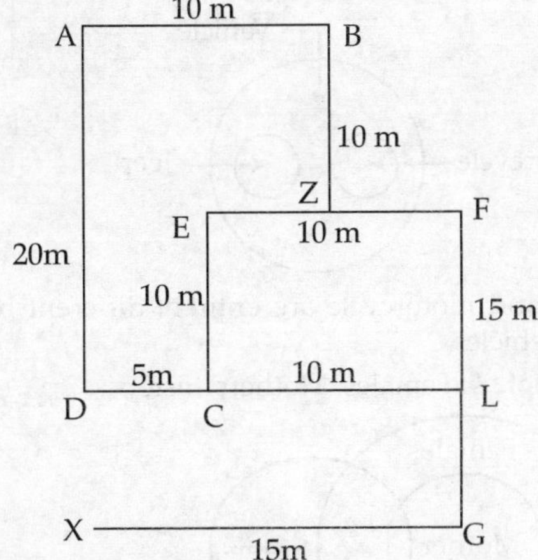

Distance between F and L = EC = 10 m

Sol. (22-24): According to the given information,

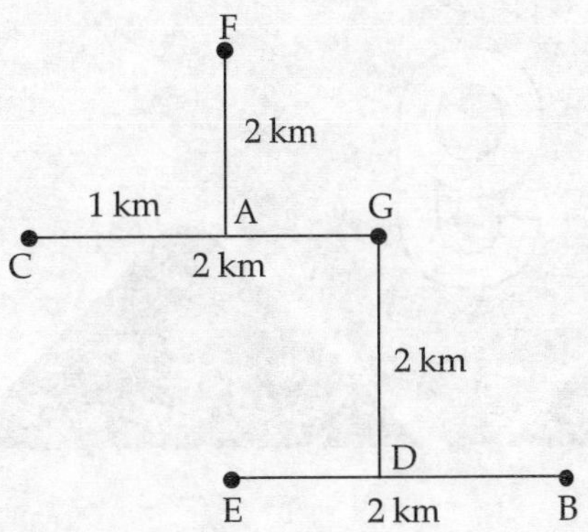

22. Option (D) is correct.

Explanation: A is in the middle of C and G.

23. Option (C) is correct.

Explanation: DC = $\sqrt{4+4} = 2\sqrt{2}$ km

FE = 2 + 2 = 4 km

FB = $\sqrt{16+4} = 2\sqrt{5}$ km

GE = $\sqrt{4+1} = \sqrt{5}$ km

So, B and F are farthest from each other.

24. Option (A) is correct.

Explanation: FE = 2 + 2 = 4 km

25. Option (C) is correct.

Explanation: According to the figure, the river travels eastward from A towards B before turning left and travelling in a semicircle until it reaches C, where it then turns left and flows towards D.

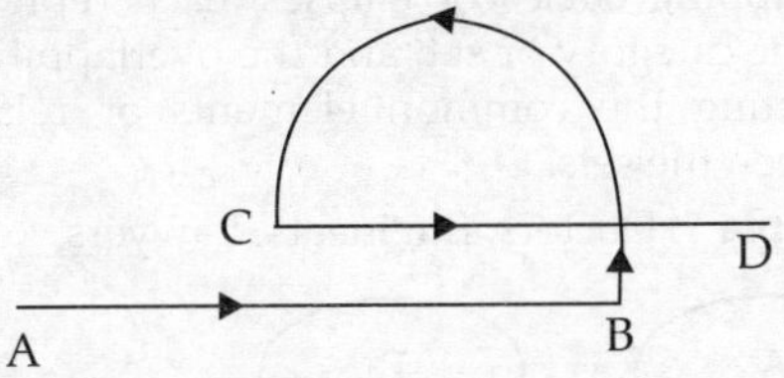

■ ■ ■

Chapter

9

Logical Venn Diagrams

LEARNING OBJECTIVES:

- Method of finding missing number in Simple Venn Diagrams
- Method of finding missing number in Mixed Venn Diagrams
- Different types of question asked in competitive exams

This segment consists of inquiries meant to assess a candidate's aptitude for relating a certain set of objects and diagrammatically illuminating them. Here are a few distinct sorts of Venn diagrams and their explanations of their consequences: Consider receiving a trio of goods.

SIMPLE VENN DIAGRAM S

- A simple Venn diagram is a graphical representation of sets or groups, used in reasoning to depict relationships and overlapping elements between different categories or concepts. It consists of overlapping circles or ellipses, each representing a specific category or set, and the overlapping regions indicating the common elements or relationships between the sets.

Example 1: Doctors, Engineers, Lawyers

Sol. A B C

There is no connection between these three products. Thus, as seen, they are represented by three separate figures.

Example 2: Hours, Days, Week

Sol.

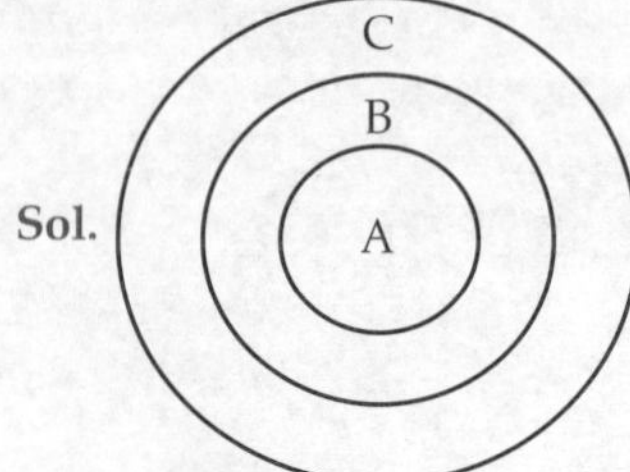

If one item belongs to the class of the second and the second belongs to the class of third, then the representation is in the form of three concentric circles, clearly, hours are a part of days and days are a part of week. So, the Venn diagram would be as shown in the adjoining figure with circle A representing hours, circle B representing days and circle C representing weeks.

MIXED VENN DIAGRAMS

- A mixed Venn diagram is a graphical representation that combines elements of both categorical and numerical data to analyze relationships and overlaps between different sets or groups. It is an extension of the traditional Venn diagram, which is commonly used to illustrate the relationships between sets of categorical data. In a mixed Venn diagram, the sets or groups are represented by circles or other shapes, and the overlapping regions depict the shared elements between the sets. However, in addition to representing categorical data, the mixed Venn diagram also incorporates numerical data, such as proportions or percentages, to provide further insights into the relationships between the sets.

Example 3: Vehicle, Motorcycle, Jeep.

Sol.

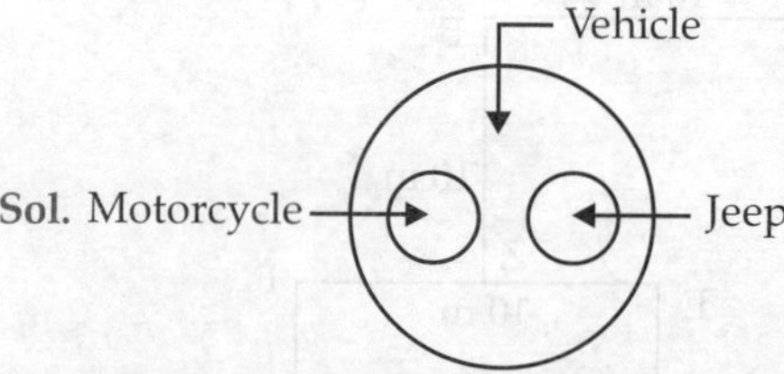

Jeep and motorcycle are entirely different but both are vehicles.

Example 4: Females, Mothers, Sisters

Sol.

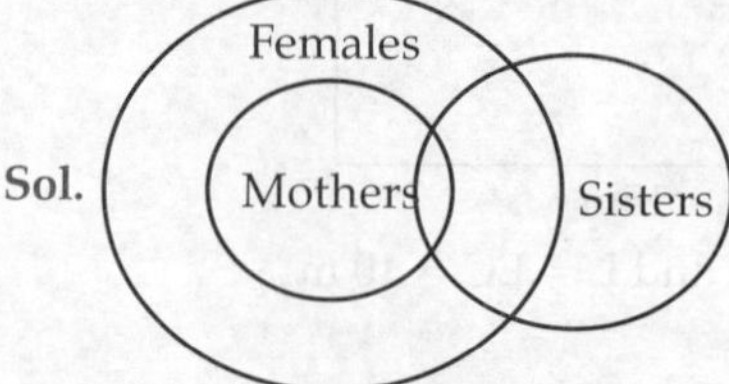

All mothers are females. This would be two concentric circles but some females are sisters.

Level 1 Beginner

Directions (Qs. 1–10): Each of these questions below contains three groups of things. You have to choose from the following five lettered diagrams, the one that depicts the correct relationship among the groups of things in each question.

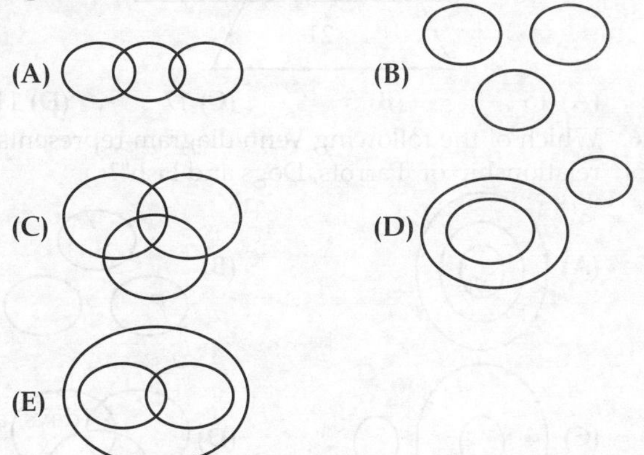

1. Dogs, Elephants, Fishes
2. Anti-social elements, Pickpockets, Blackmailers **[MBA 2006]**
3. Volleyball fans, Cricket players, Girls
4. Human beings, Teachers, Graduates **[MAT 2001]**
5. Sun, Moon, Earth
6. Flowers, Clothes, White **[RRB 2004]**
7. Chapters, Book, Notebook
8. Smokers, Men, Lawyers
9. Males, Fathers, Doctors
10. Musicians, Adults, Teenagers

Directions (Qs. 11–14): In the figure given below, there are three intersecting circles each representing certain section of people. Different regions are marked p to v. Read the statements in each of the following questions and choose the letter of the region which correctly represents the statement.

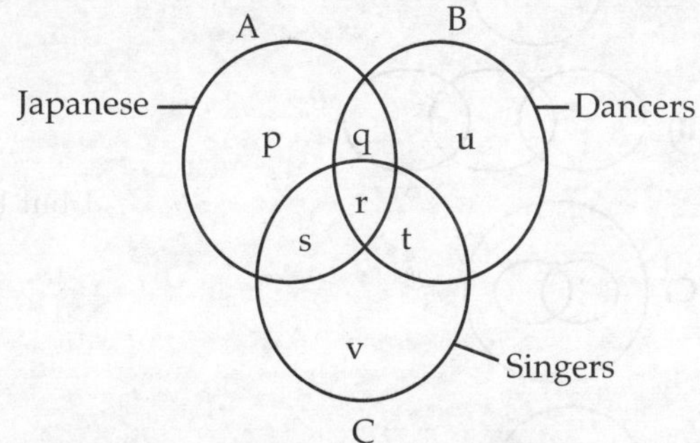

11. Japanese who are dancers but not singers.
(A) q (B) s (C) r (D) v

12. Dancers who are neither Japanese nor singers.
(A) q (B) r (C) u (D) v

13. Japanese who are singers but not dancers.
(A) s (B) q (C) p (D) r

14. Japanese who are dancers as well as singers.
(A) q (B) p (C) r (D) v

Directions (Qs. 15–19): Read the statements in each of the following questions and choose the letter of the region which correctly represents the statement.

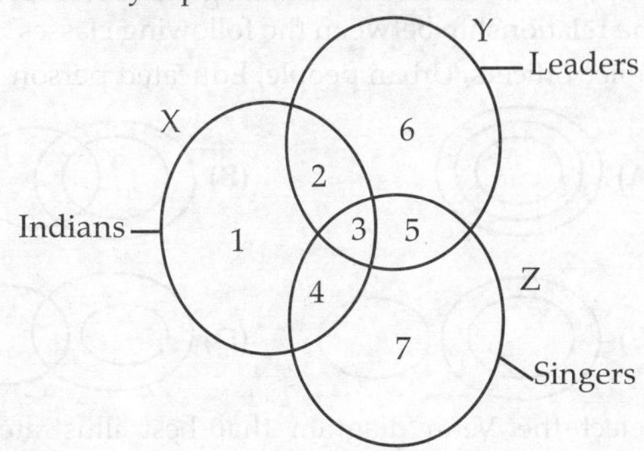

[CBI 2003]

15. Which region denotes Indian leaders who are not singers?
(A) 2 (B) 3 (C) 4 (D) 5

16. Which region represents Indian leaders who are singers?
(A) 2 (B) 3 (C) 4 (D) 5

17. Which region represents leaders who are neither singers nor Indians?
(A) 2 (B) 3 (C) 6 (D) 7

18. Which region represents Indian singers who are not leaders?
(A) 1 (B) 2 (C) 3 (D) 4

19. Which region represents singers who are neither Indians nor leaders?
(A) 2 (B) 4 (C) 6 (D) 7

20. Select the Venn diagram that best illustrates the relationship between the following three classes.
School, Teacher, Student

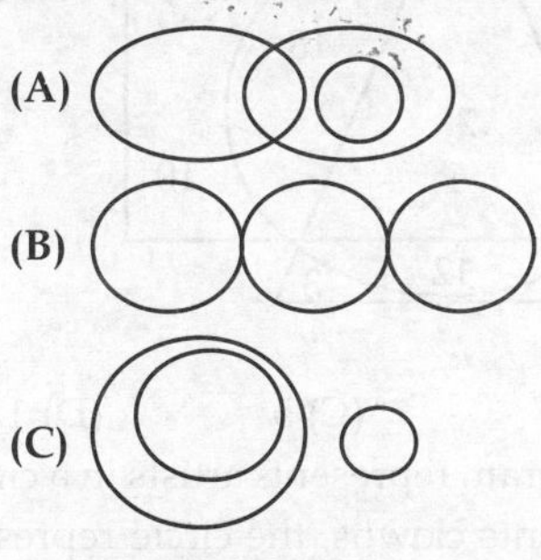

21. Select the Venn diagram that best illustrates the relationship between the following classes.
Graduates, Literates, Hardworking

[SSC CGL Exam 2019]

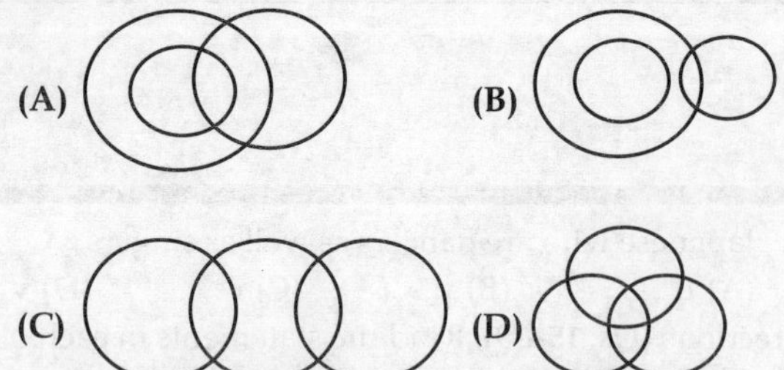

22. Which of the following Venn diagrams best represents the relationship between the following classes?
Police officers, Urban people, Educated person

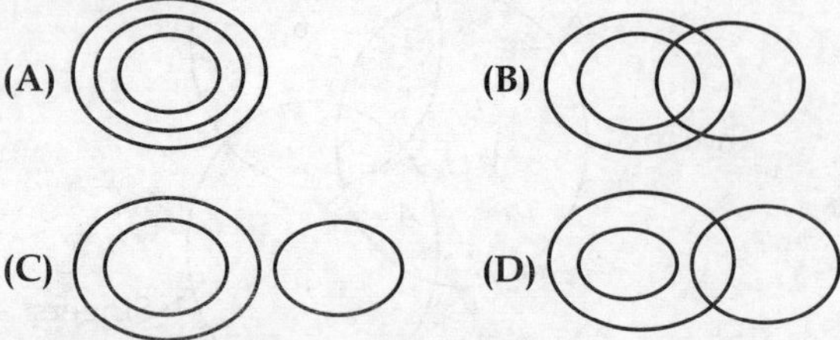

23. Select the Venn diagram that best illustrates the relationship between the following three classes.
Fruits, Eraser, Apple

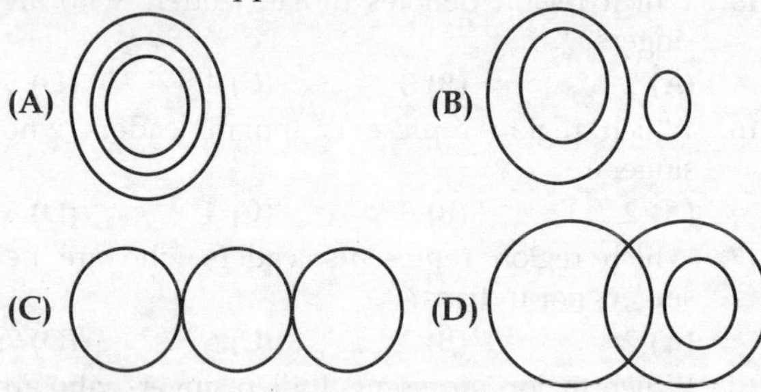

24. In the following diagram, the rectangle represents doctors, the triangle represents players and circle represents philosophers. The numbers for different segments show the number of persons.
According to the given diagram, how many players are philosophers but not doctors?

[SSC CPO Exam 2019]

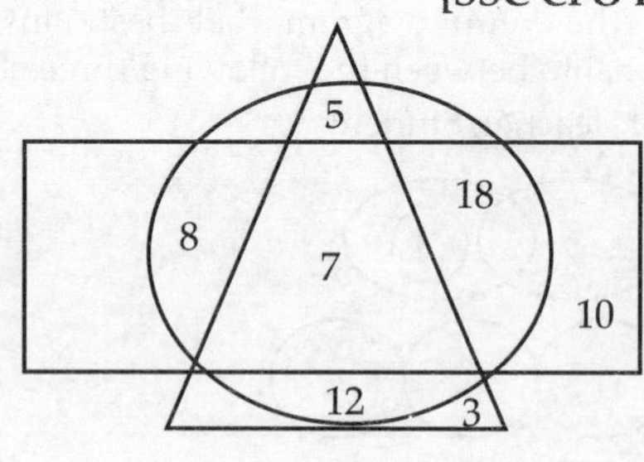

(A) 17 (B) 7 (C) 5 (D) 12

25. The given Venn diagram represents artists in a circus: The triangle represents clowns, the circle represents acrobats, the rectangle represents males and the square represents ringmasters. The numbers given in the diagram represent the number of persons in that particular category. How many male clowns are also ringmasters, but NOT acrobats?

[SSC CGL Exam 2020]

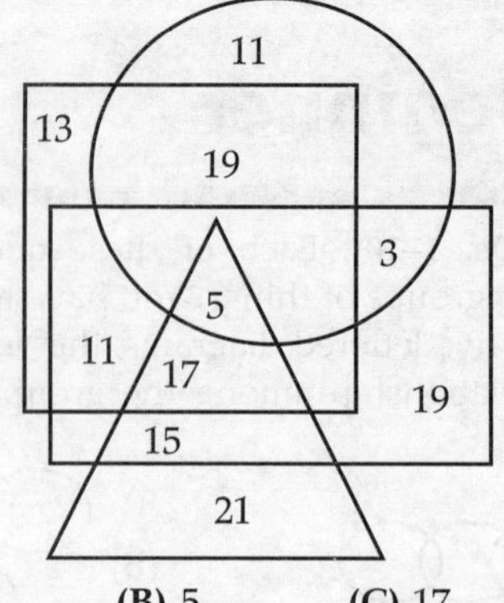

(A) 15 (B) 5 (C) 17 (D) 11

26. Which of the following Venn diagram represents the relationship of "Parrots, Dogs and Fish"?

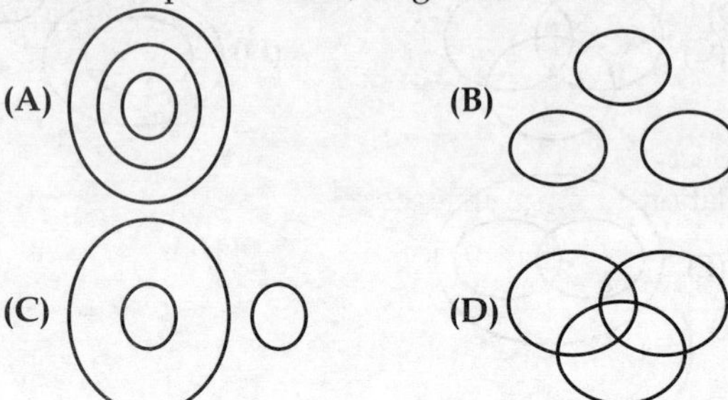

27. Which of the following diagram represents the relationship of "India, Haryana and Gurugram"?

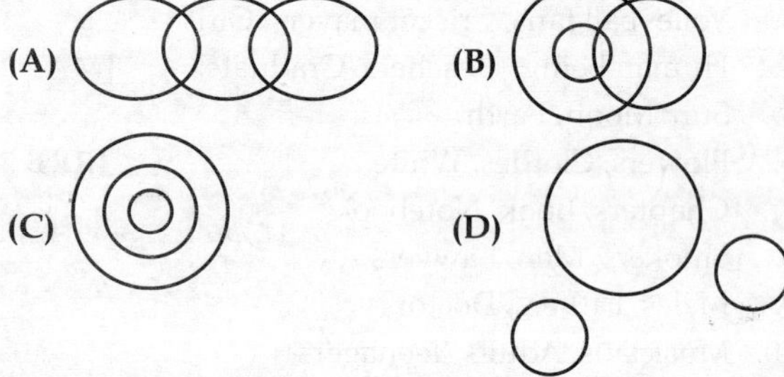

28. Select the Venn diagram that best illustrates the relationship among the following classes.
Women, Researchers, Introverts **[SSC CGL 2021]**

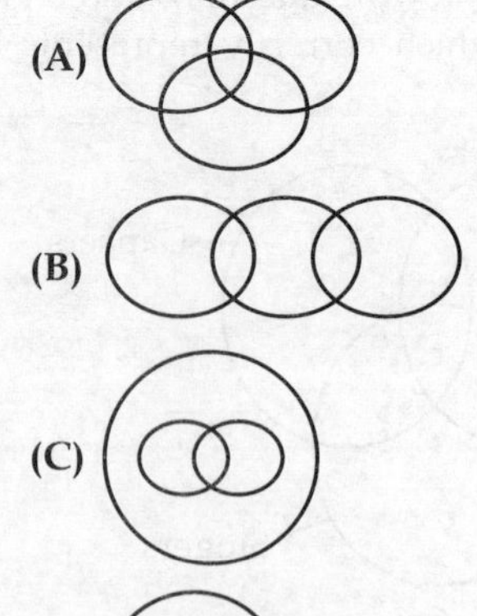

29. Select the Venn diagram that best represents the relationship between the following classes.
Reptile, Mammal, Lizard **[SSC CHSL 2020]**

(A)

(B)

(C)

(D)

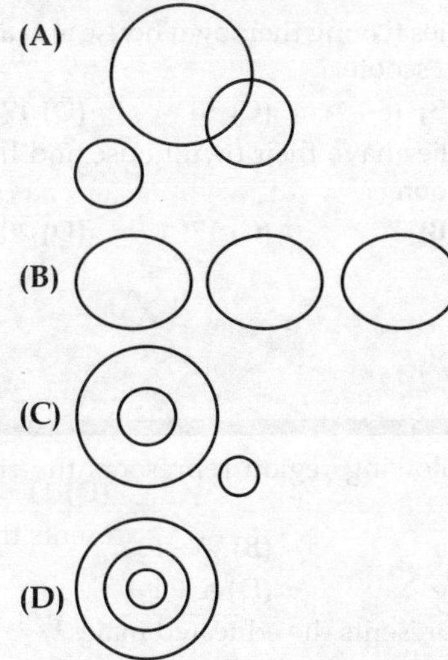

30. Select the Venn diagram that best represents the relationship of "Circle, Polygon and Rectangle". **[SSC CHSL 2020]**

(A)

(B)

(C)

(D)

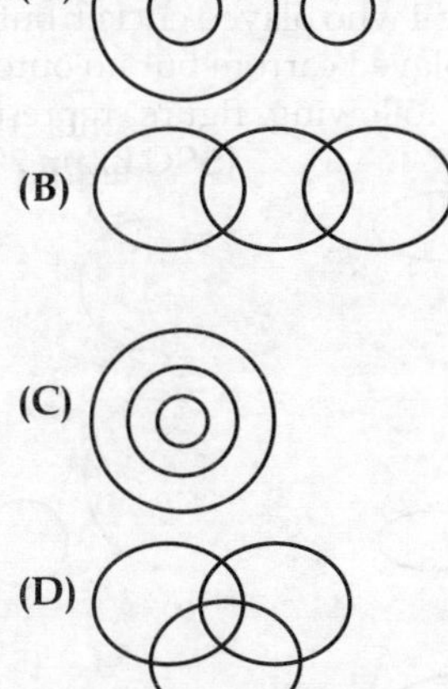

31. Which of the following diagram represents the relationship of "Vowels, Alphabets and Numbers"?

(A) 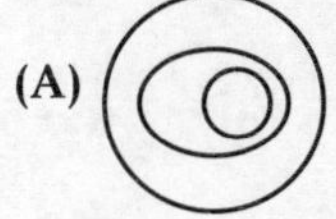

(B) 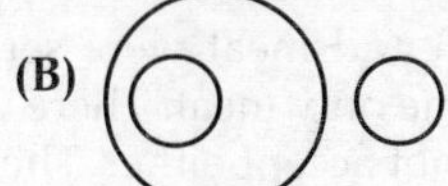

(C) 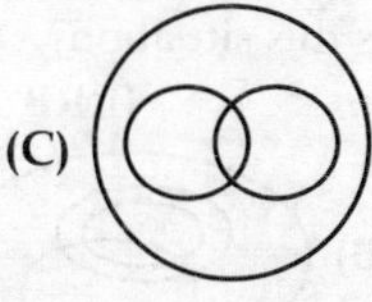

(D) 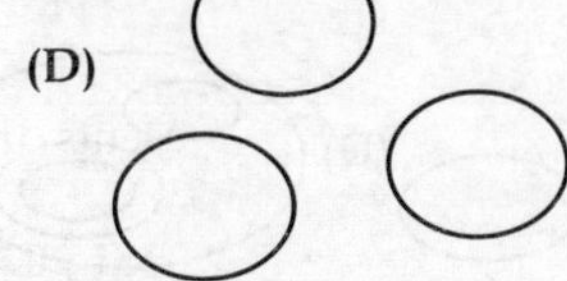

32. Which of the following diagram represents the relationship of "Drinks, Coffee and Mango juice"?

(A) 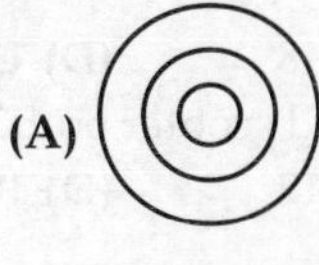

(B) 

(C) 

(D) 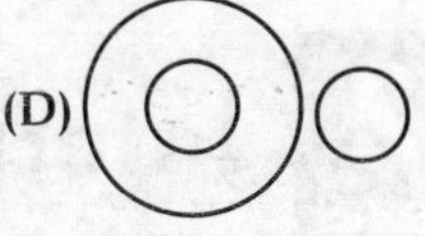

33. Select the Venn diagram that best represents the relationship of "Languages, Hindi, Telugu".

(A) 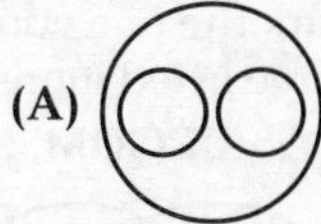

(B) 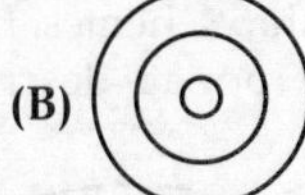

(C) 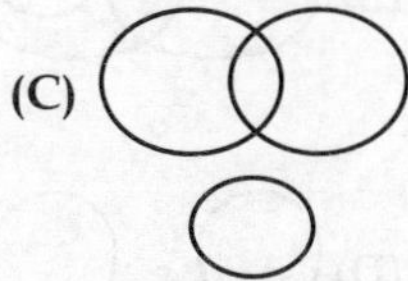

(D) 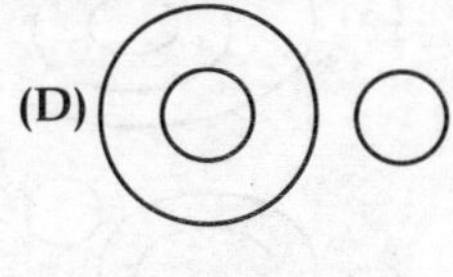

34. Select the Venn diagram that best represents the relationship of "Chartered Accountant, Female and Actors".

(A) 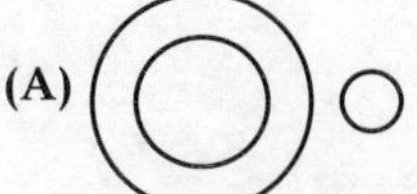

(B) 

(C) 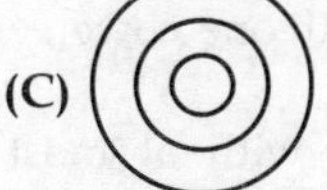

(D) 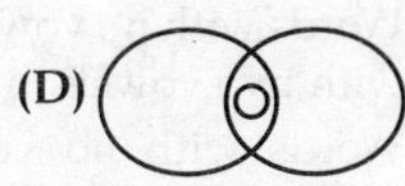

35. Which of the following Venn diagram represents the relationship among the following classes?
Earth, Mountains, Jupiter **[SSC CHSL 2020]**

(A)

(B) 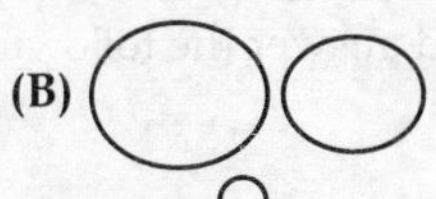

(C) 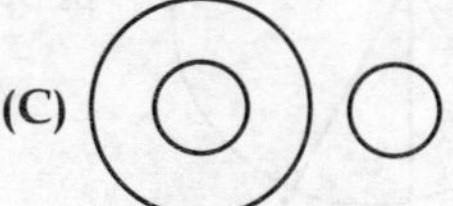

(D) 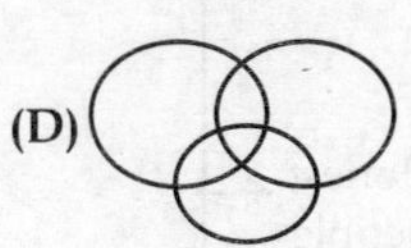

Directions (Qs. 36–40): Study the given Venn diagram carefully and answer the following questions.

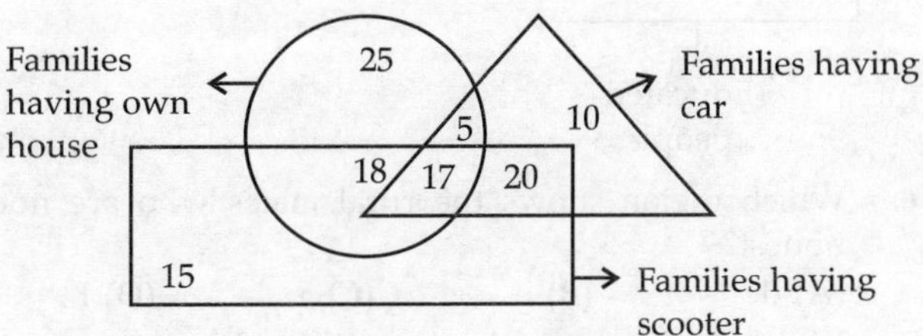

36. How many families have a car only?
(A) 15 **(B)** 5 **(C)** 10 **(D)** 20

37. How many families have their own house as well as scooter both?
(A) 25 (B) 17 (C) 18 (D) 15

38. How many families having car and scooter both?
(A) 20 (B) 10 (C) 17 (D) 18

39. How many families having their own house and a car but do not have a scooter?
(A) 5 (B) 18 (C) 10 (D) 17

40. How many families have their own house and have both a car and scooter?
(A) 25 (B) 5 (C) 17 (D) 20

2 Level Intermediate

Directions (Qs. 1–5): Given below are five possible membership schemes. In each case, mark the one you feel is the appropriate description of the three listed items. **[PGDM, 2002]**

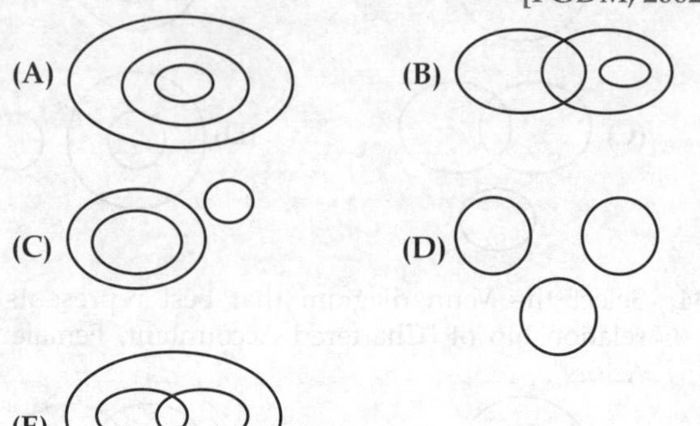

1. Apples, Golden apples, Fruits
2. Triangles, Scalene triangles, Right-angled triangles
3. Words with no vowels, words with one vowel, words with two vowels
4. Words with no vowels, words with at most one vowel, words with at least two vowels
5. Names beginning with a vowel, names beginning with E, names beginning with either A or P

Directions (Qs. 6–10): Study the given figure carefully and answer the following questions.

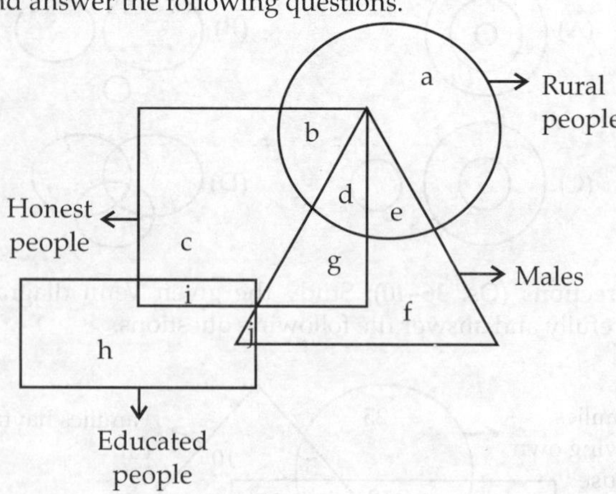

6. Which region shows the rural males who are not honest?
(A) d (B) e (C) g (D) f

7. Which region shows that honest females who are not rural and uneducated?
(A) i (B) g (C) c (D) f

8. Which of the following region represents the rural people?
(A) b + c + d + e (B) g + f
(C) a + b + d + e (D) h + i + j

9. Which region represents the educated males?
(A) h (B) i (C) j (D) f

10. Which region shows the honest rural males who are not educated?
(A) d (B) e (C) g (D) c

11. In a class of 46 students, 18 played football, 17 played cricket, including 6 who played football. 16 students played hockey including 4 who played cricket, but not football. Five students played carrom but no outdoor games. Which of the following figure represents these facts? **[SSC Exam 2003]**

(A)
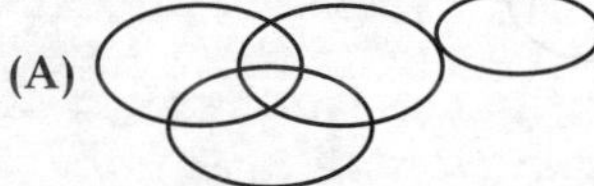

(B)
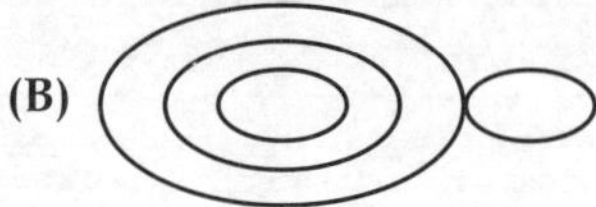

(C)

(D)
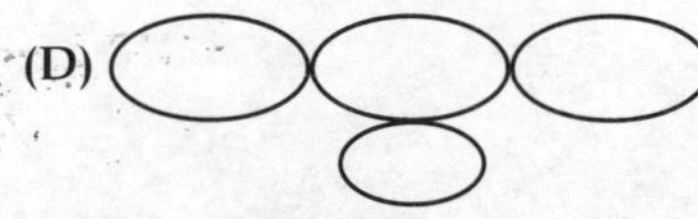

12. In a dinner party, both fish and meat were served. Some took only fish and some only meat. There were some vegetarians who did not accept either. The rest accepted both fish and meat. Which of the following logic diagrams correctly reflects this situation? **[RRB 2006]**

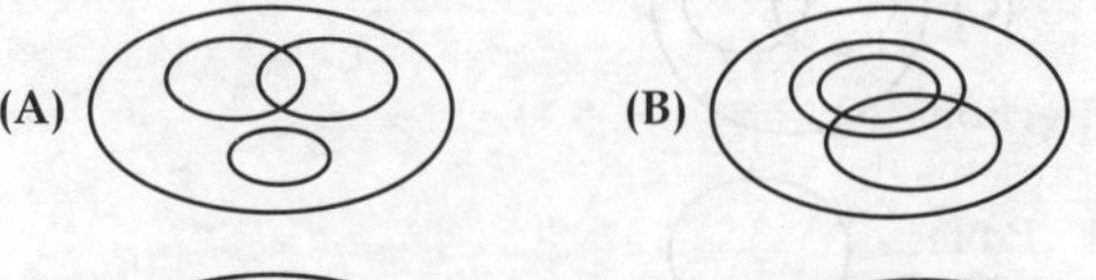

13. Which of the following sets is best represented in the given diagram? **[RRB 2004]**

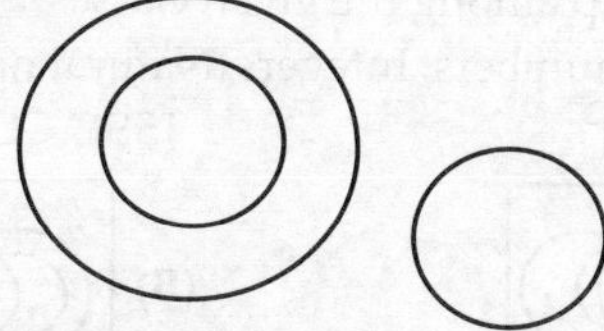

(A) Animals, Insects, Cockroaches
(B) Animals, Males, Females and Hermaphrodites
(C) States, Districts, Union Territories
(D) Country, States, Districts

14. In the Accounts Department of a company, there are some who are only chartered accountants and some who are only cost accountants. A few hold both chartered and cost accountancy qualifications. Besides these, there are others who hold Management Accountancy qualifications. Some of these Management Accountants have also done either Chartered or Cost Accountancy or both. Which of the following figures represents these facts? **[SSC Exam 2003]**

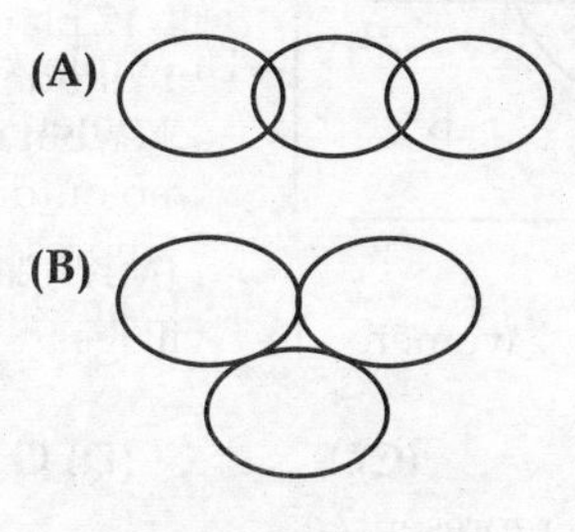

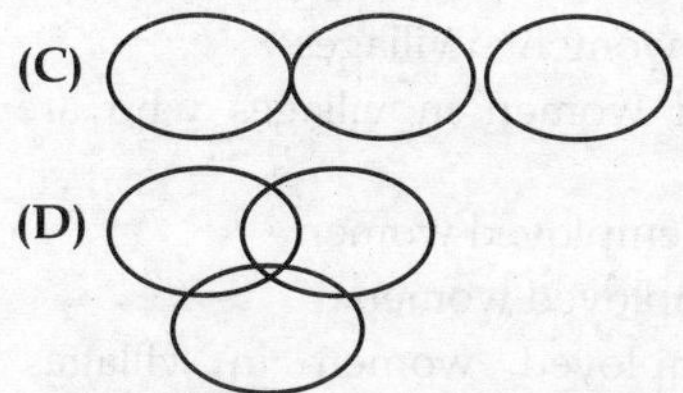

15. Some of the Cricket players are tennis players, some tennis players are hockey players, and no cricket player is a hockey player. Which of the following diagram correctly represents the above statements? **[SSC Exam 2002]**

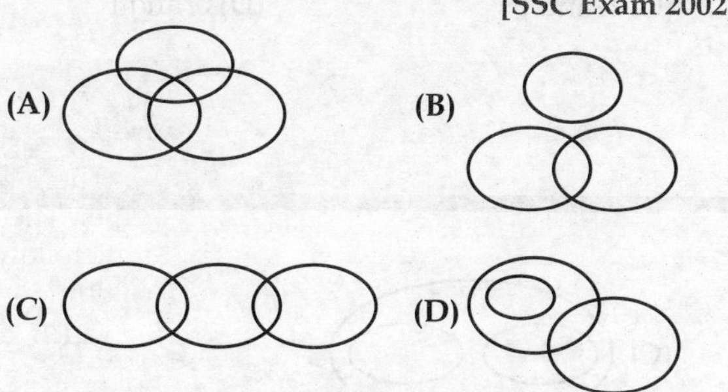

Directions (Qs. 16–19): Identify the diagram that best represents the relationship among the given classes.

16. Professors, Researchers, Scientists **[SSC CGL Exam 2015]**

(A) 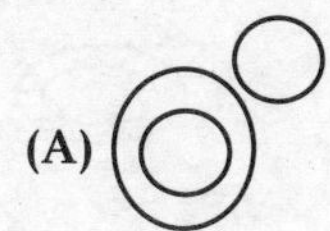 **(B)** 

(C) 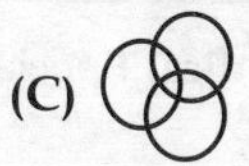 **(D)** 

17. Science, Biology, SST

(A)  **(B)** 

(C) 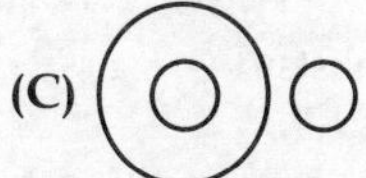 **(D)** 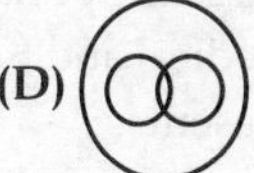

18. Tigers, Cats, Animals

(A) 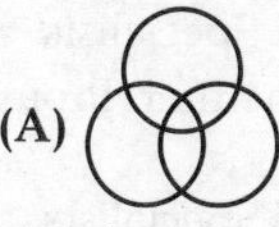 **(B)** 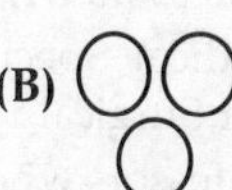

(C) 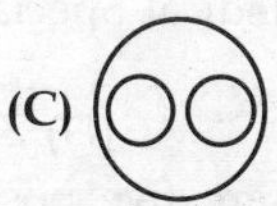 **(D)** 

19. Animals, Land animals, Sea animals

(A)  **(B)** 

(C) 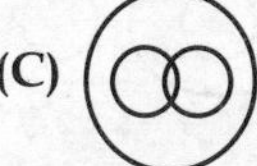 **(D)** 

20. In the given figure, how many people like English and Mathematics both?

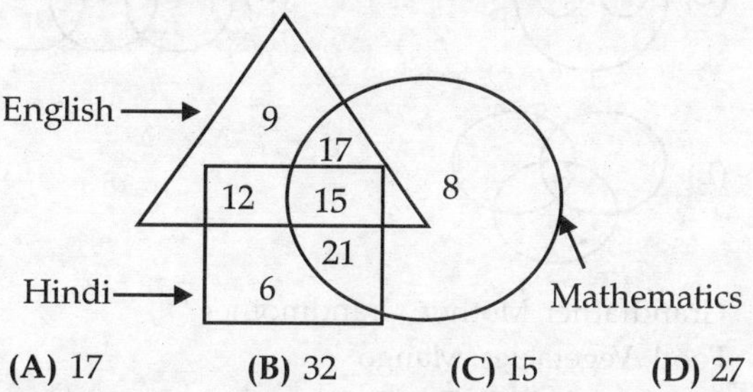

(A) 17 **(B)** 32 **(C)** 15 **(D)** 27

Directions (Qs. 21–25): In the following diagram, the circle represents College Professors, the triangle stands for Surgical Specialists, and Medical Specialists are represented by the rectangle.

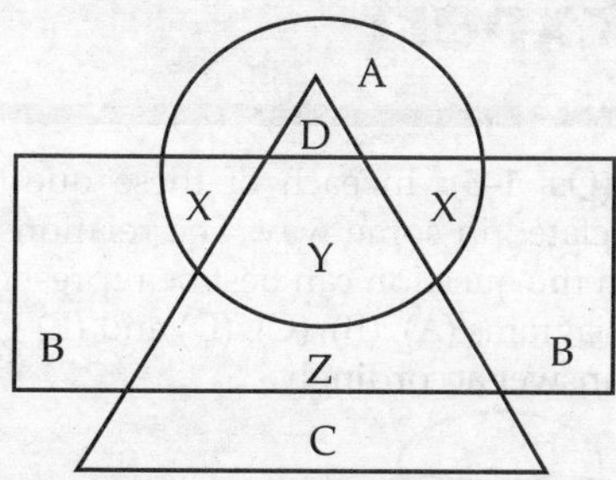

[MBA 2002]

21. College Professors who are also Surgical specialists only are represented by:

(A) A **(B)** B
(C) C **(D)** D

22. Surgical Specialists who are also Medical Specialists but not Professors are represented by:
(A) B (B) C (C) X (D) Z

23. C represents:
(A) Medical Specialists
(B) College Professors
(C) Surgical Specialists
(D) Medical and Surgical Specialists

24. B represents:
(A) Professors who are neither Medical nor Surgical Specialists
(B) Professors who are not Surgical Specialists
(C) Medical Specialists who are neither Professors nor Surgical Specialists
(D) Professors who are not Medical Specialists

25. College Professors who are also Medical Specialists are represented by :
(A) A (B) X (C) Y (D) Z

Directions (Qs. 26—30): Given below are five possible membership schemes. In each case, mark the one you feel is the appropriate description of the three listed items.

(A) 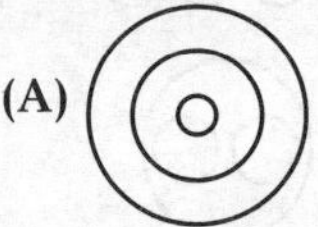
(B) 
(C) 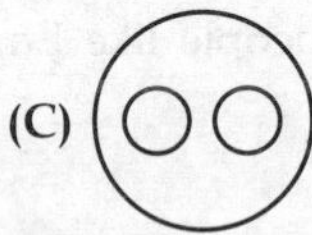
(D) 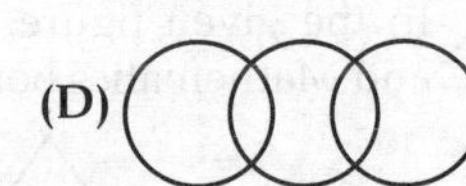
(E) 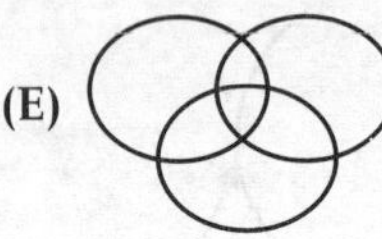

26. Grandfather, Mother, Grandmother
27. Food, Vegetables, Mango
28. Sea animals, Fish, Eagle
29. Asia, Ganga river, India
30. Rainbow colours, Blue, White

31. Identify the diagram that best represents the relationship among the given classes.
Complex numbers, Integers, Natural numbers
[SSC CGL Exam 2017]

(A) 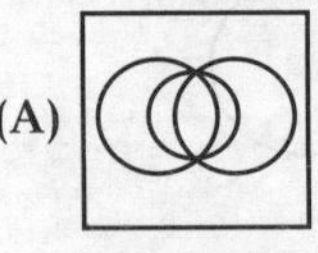
(B) 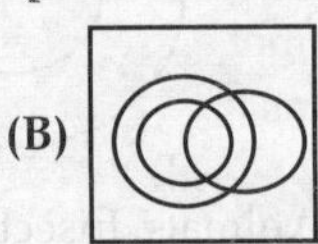
(C) 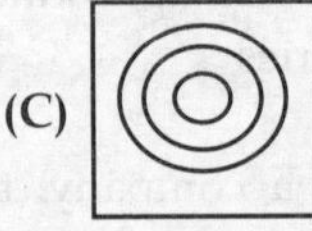
(D) 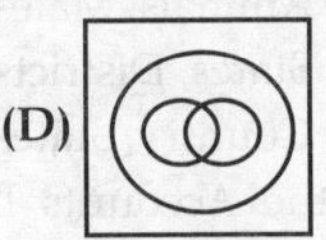

Directions (Qs. 32–35): Study the diagram given below to answer these questions:

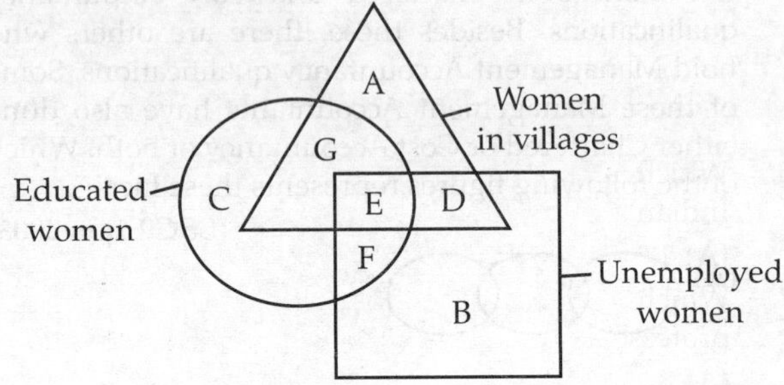

[MAT 2002]

32. Educated employed women in villages are represented by:
(A) D (B) E (C) F (D) G

33. What does the letter D represent?
(A) Uneducated women in villages
(B) Unemployed women in villages who are not educated
(C) Educated unemployed women
(D) Educated employed women

34. Educated unemployed women in villages are represented by:
(A) A (B) B (C) D (D) E

35. Educated unemployed women are represented by:
(A) B and C (B) D and E
(C) E and F (D) G and E

3 Level Expert

Directions (Qs. 1–5): In each of these questions, three words are related in some way. The relationship among the words in the question can best be represented by one of the five diagrams (A), (B), (C), (D) and (E) given below. Mark your answer accordingly.

(A) (B) 

(C) 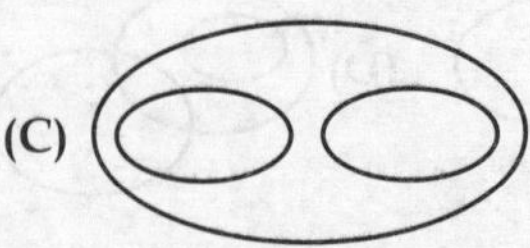
(D) 
(E) 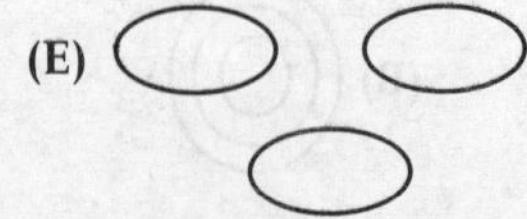

1. Iron, Lead, Nitrogen [Bank PO 2005]
2. Father, Homosapien, Men
3. Singers, Dancers, Swimmers
4. Sparrows, Bird, Rat
5. Cabinet, Home Minister, Minister

Directions (Qs. 6–10): In the following questions, answers are to be based on the diagram given below, where the triangle represents scientists, the circle represents professors and the rectangle represents Indians.

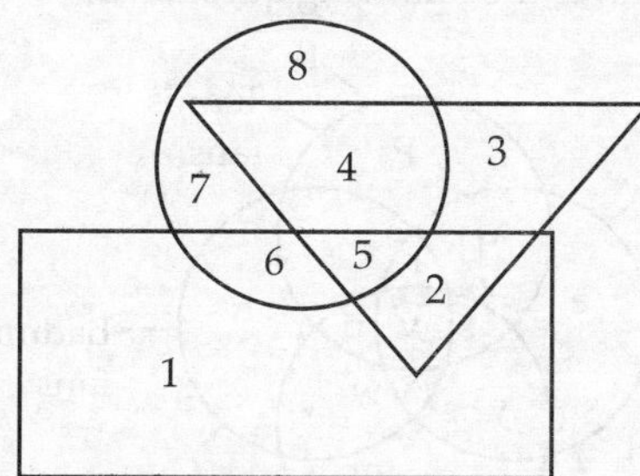

6. Which numbered space in the diagram represents Indian scientists who are also professors?
(A) 1 (B) 8 (C) 4 (D) 5
7. Which number represents Indians who are also professors only?
(A) 8 (B) 6 (C) 5 (D) 2
8. Which number represents Indians who are neither scientists nor professors?
(A) 1 (B) 4 (C) 7 (D) 6
9. Which number represents scientists who are neither Indians nor professors?
(A) 8 (B) 3 (C) 4 (D) 7
10. Which numbers represent professors who are neither Indians nor scientists?
(A) 1, 2 (B) 3, 4 (C) 6, 7 (D) 7, 8

Directions (Qs. 11–15): Each of these questions given below contains three elements. These elements may or may not have some inter-linkage. Each group of elements may fit into one of these diagrams at (A), (B), (C) and (D) You have to indicate the group of elements which correctly fits the diagrams. **[AFCAT 2016]**

11. Which of the following diagram indicates the best relation between Teachers, Poet and Graduate?

(A) (B) 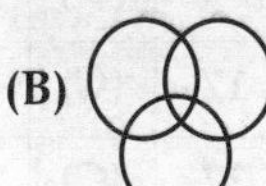

(C)  (D) 

12. Which of the following diagram indicates the best relation between Teachers, Men and Authors?

(A) 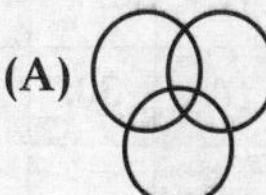 (B) 

(C)  (D) 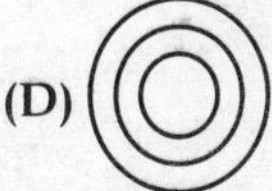

13. Which of the following diagram indicates the best relation between Tennis fans, Cricket players and Students?

(A) 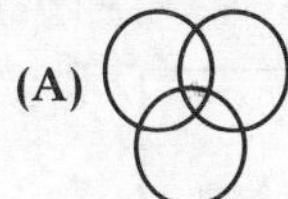 (B) 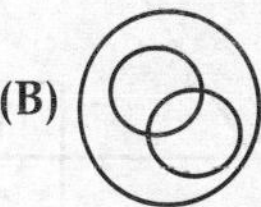

(C) (D) 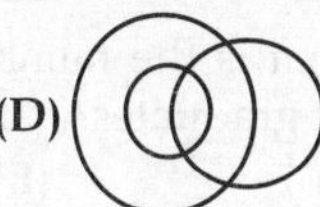

14. Which of the following diagram indicates the best relation between Rose, Flower and Lotus?

(A)  (B) 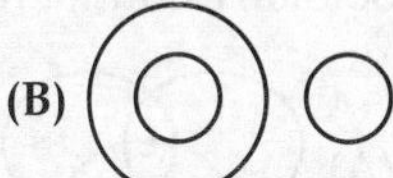

(C) (D) 

15. Which of the following diagram indicates the best relation between Goat, Four-footed and Donkey?

(A) 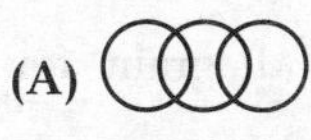 (B) 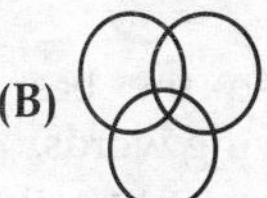

(C) (D) 

16. Identify the diagram that best represents the relationship among the classes given below:
Soda water, Mineral water, Liquid **[SSC CGL 2015]**

(A) 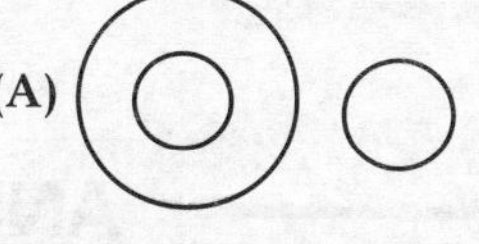 (B) 

(C)  (D) 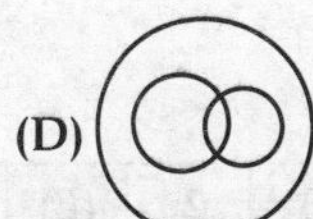

17. Select the diagram which represents the relationship between "Mathematics, History and Geography"?

(A) 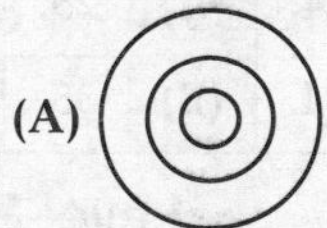 (B) 

(C) 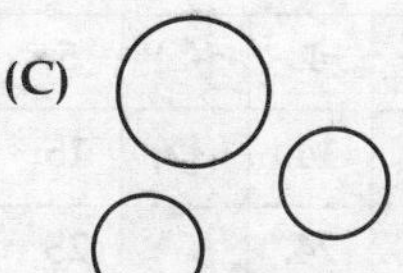 (D) 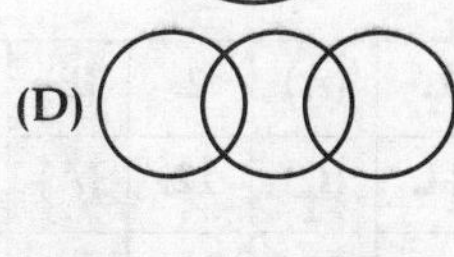

18. In the following diagram, the circle represents 'rural folk', the triangle represents 'businessmen' and the rectangle represents 'graduates', Study the diagram carefully and answer the question that follows:
[SSC CGL 2021]

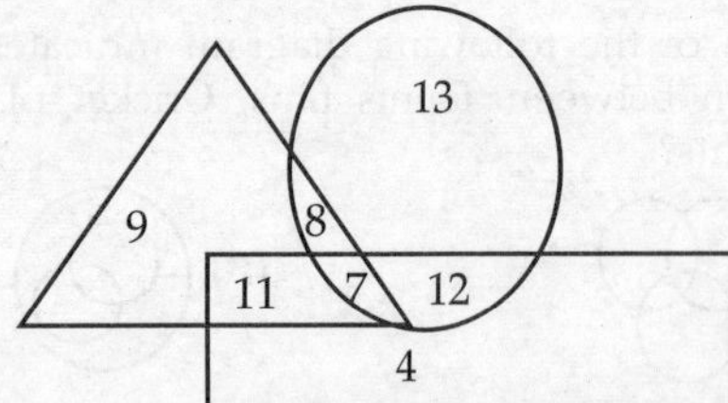

What is the number of rural businessmen, who are not graduates?

(A) 7 **(B)** 8 **(C)** 15 **(D)** 11

19. Which of the following Venn diagram best represents the relationship between the following classes?
Soldier, Dentist, Engineer

(A) 

(B) 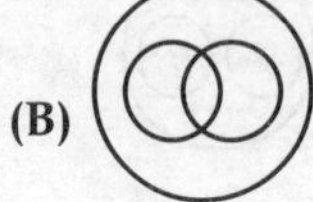

(C) 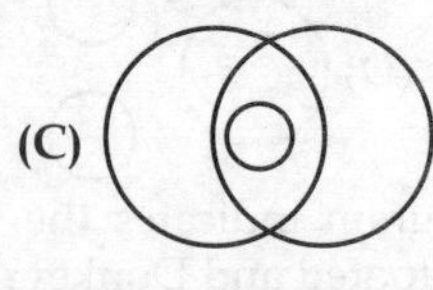

(D) 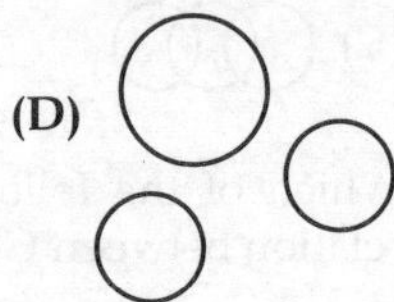

20. Choose the best suitable Venn diagram for the following words.
Capsicum, Mat, Rat **[RBI 2018]**

(A) 

(B) 

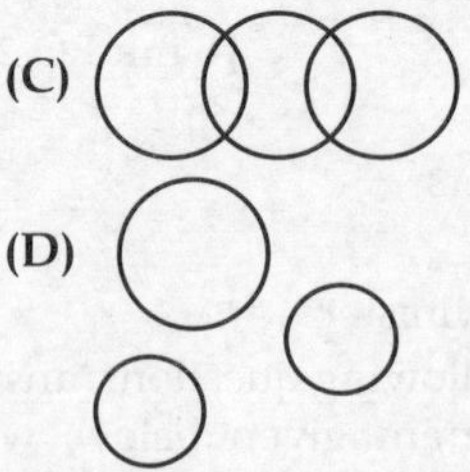

Directions (Qs. 21–25): Refer to the following Venn diagram, answer the following questions.

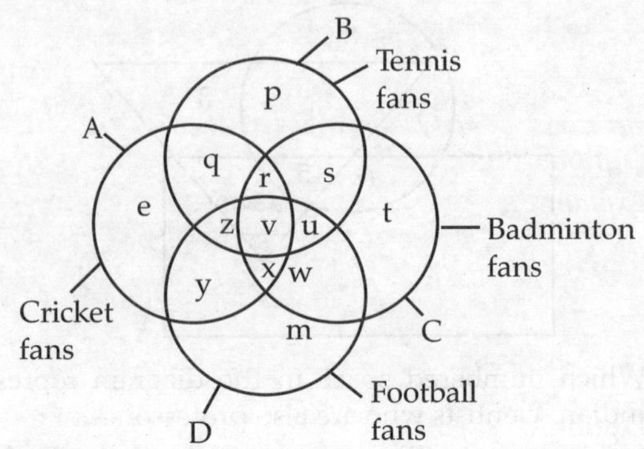

21. The region which shows the cricket and football fans only is ______.

(A) l **(B)** z **(C)** y **(D)** v

22. The region which shows the tennis and cricket fans but neither badminton nor football fans is ______.

(A) z **(B)** q **(C)** p **(D)** r

23. The region which shows all the fans is ______.

(A) u **(B)** y **(C)** s **(D)** v

24. The region which shows only football fans is ______.

(A) m **(B)** l **(C)** x **(D)** u

25. The region which show the badminton and cricket fans but neither tennis fans nor football fans is ______.

(A) x **(B)** w
(C) s **(D)** None of these

ANSWER KEY

Level-1: Beginner

1.	(B)	2.	(E)	3.	(C)	4.	(E)	5.	(B)	6.	(A)	7.	(D)	8.	(C)	9.	(D)	10.	(A)
11.	(A)	12.	(C)	13.	(A)	14.	(C)	15.	(A)	16.	(B)	17.	(C)	18.	(D)	19.	(D)	20.	(D)
21.	(A)	22.	(B)	23.	(B)	24.	(A)	25.	(C)	26.	(B)	27.	(C)	28.	(A)	29.	(C)	30.	(A)
31.	(B)	32.	(B)	33.	(A)	34.	(B)	35.	(C)	36.	(C)	37.	(C)	38.	(A)	39.	(A)	40.	(C)

Level-2: Intermediate

1.	(A)	2.	(E)	3.	(D)	4.	(C)	5.	(B)	6.	(B)	7.	(A)	8.	(C)	9.	(C)	10.	(A)
11.	(C)	12.	(A)	13.	(C)	14.	(D)	15.	(C)	16.	(C)	17.	(C)	18.	(C)	19.	(C)	20.	(B)
21.	(D)	22.	(D)	23.	(C)	24.	(C)	25.	(B)	26.	(B)	27.	(C)	28.	(B)	29.	(A)	30.	(B)
31.	(C)	32.	(D)	33.	(B)	34.	(D)	35.	(C)										

Level-3: Expert

1.	(E)	2.	(B)	3.	(A)	4.	(D)	5.	(B)	6.	(D)	7.	(B)	8.	(A)	9.	(B)	10.	(D)
11.	(B)	12.	(A)	13.	(A)	14.	(A)	15.	(C)	16.	(C)	17.	(C)	18.	(B)	19.	(D)	20.	(D)
21.	(C)	22.	(B)	23.	(D)	24.	(A)	25.	(D)										

Solutions with Detailed Explanations

Level-1: BEGINNER

1. **Option (B) is correct.**
Explanation: : According to the Venn diagram,

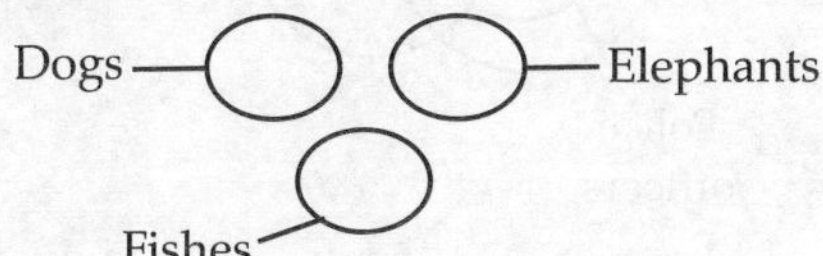

2. **Option (E) is correct.**
Explanation: According to the Venn diagram,

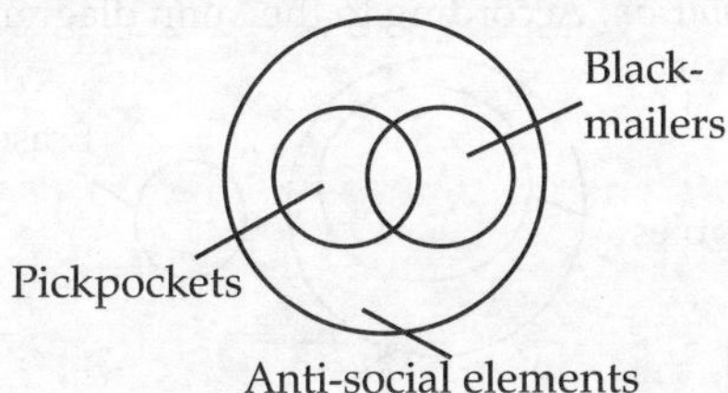

Blackmailers and pickpockets are both anti-social people. However, some pickpockets might also be blackmailers, and vice versa.

3. **Option (C) is correct.**
Explanation: : According to the Venn diagram,

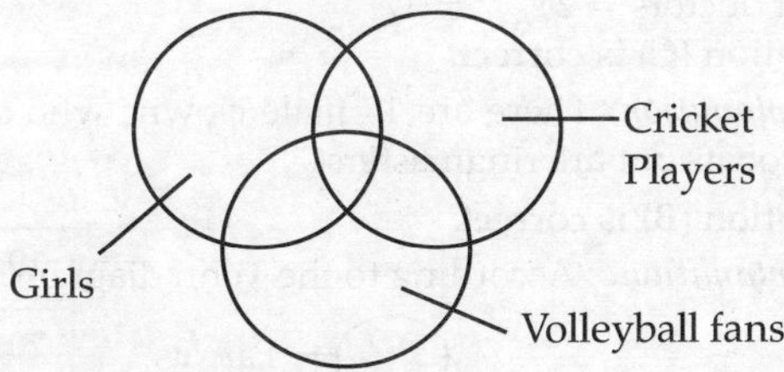

Some girls are cricket players.
Some cricket players may be volleyball fans.
Some girls may be volleyball fans. So, the given items are partly related to each other.

4. **Option (E) is correct.**
Explanation: According to the Venn diagram,

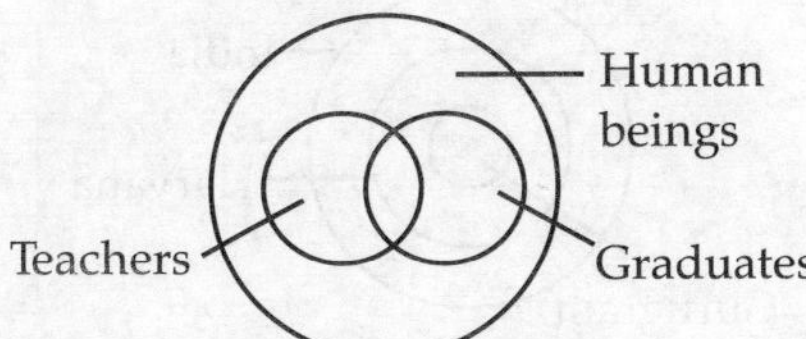

All teachers and graduates are human beings.
But, some teachers may be graduates and some graduates may be teachers.

5. **Option (B) is correct.**
Explanation: According to the Venn diagram,

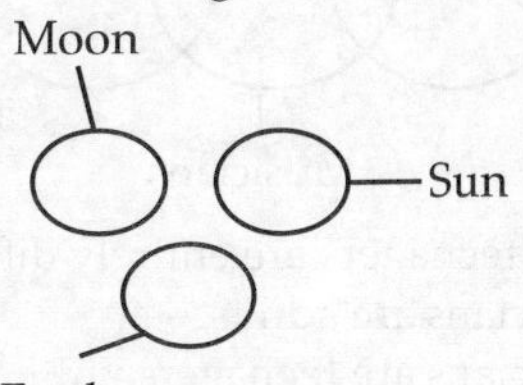

All are different from each other.

6. **Option (A) is correct.**
Explanation: According to the Venn diagram,

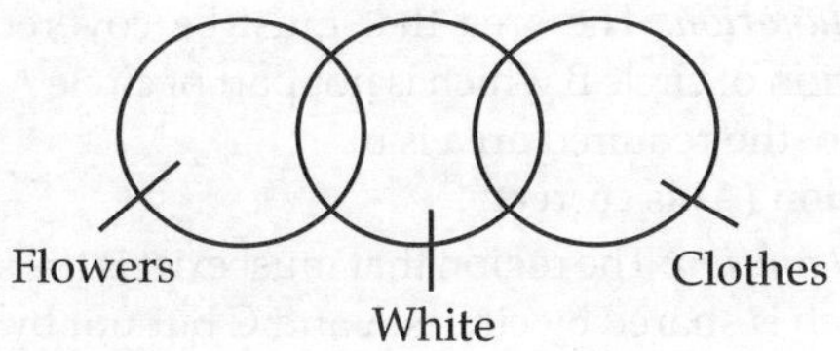

Some flowers are white.
Some clothes are white.
Flowers and clothes are entirely different.

7. **Option (D) is correct.**
Explanation: According to the Venn diagram,

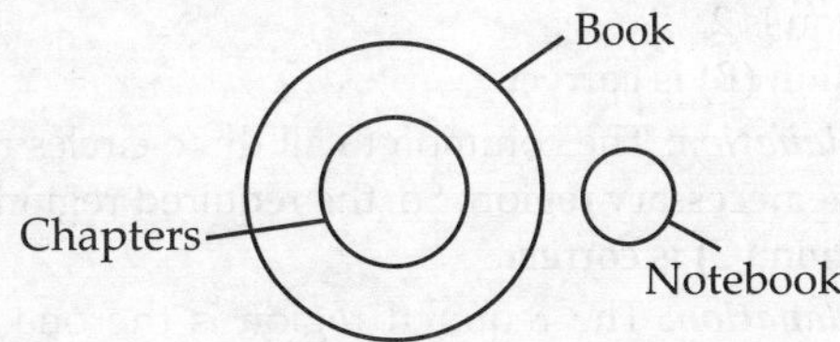

8. **Option (C) is correct.**
Explanation: According to the Venn diagram,

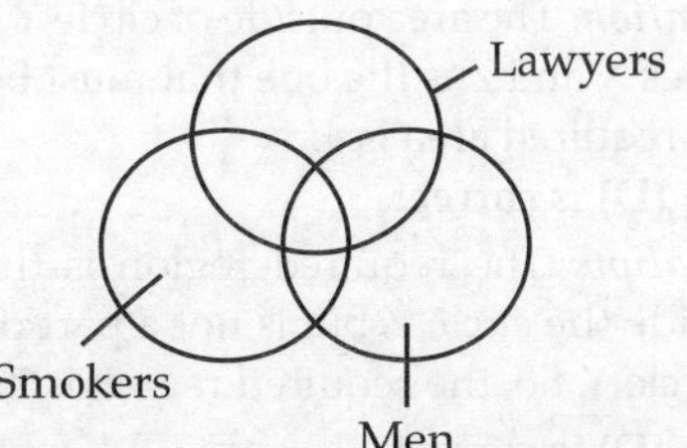

Some men may be smokers. Some men may be lawyers. Some lawyers may be smokers.

9. **Option (D) is correct.**
Explanation: According to the Venn diagram,

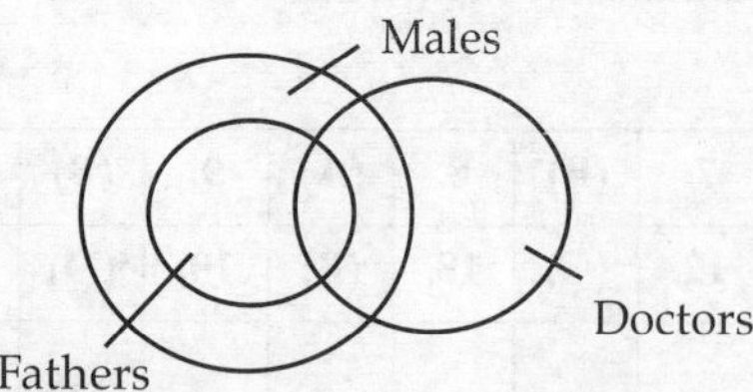

All fathers are males.
Some fathers and some men may be doctors.

10. **Option (A) is correct.**
Explanation: According to the Venn diagram,

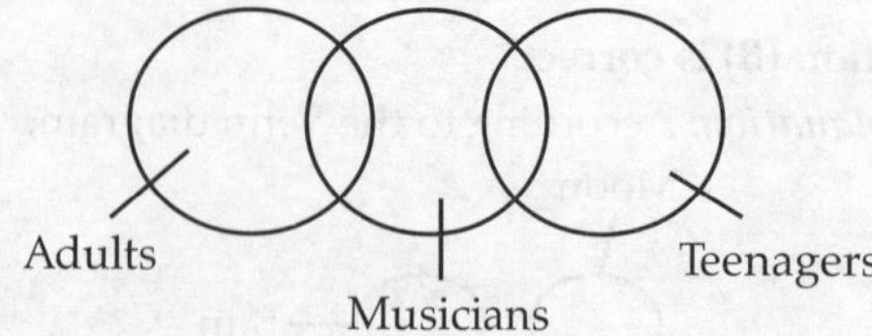

Adults and teenagers are entirely different.
Some musicians are adults.
Some musicians are teenagers.

11. **Option (A) is correct.**
Explanation: The region which is shared by circles A and B but outside of circle C, is region q.
12. **Option (C) is correct.**
Explanation: The area that must be covered is that portion of circle B which is not part of circle A or circle C. So, the required area is u.
13. **Option (A) is correct.**
Explanation: The region that must exist is the s-region, which is shared by circles A and C but not by circle B.
14. **Option (C) is correct.**
Explanation: The required region is the one common to all the three circles, that is r.
15. **Option (A) is correct.**
Explanation: The region that is shared by circles X and Y but is outside of circle Z. So, the required region is 2.
16. **Option (B) is correct.**
Explanation: The common to all three circles regions is the necessary region. So, the required region is 3.
17. **Option (C) is correct.**
Explanation: The required region is the one that is contained within circle Y but is not a part of either circle X or circle Z. So, the required region is 6.
18. **Option (D) is correct.**
Explanation: The area outside of circle Y that is shared by circles X and Z is the one that must be considered. So, the required area is 4.
19. **Option (D) is correct.**
Explanation: The required region is the one which lies inside the circle Z but is not a part of either circle X or circle Y. So, the required region is 7.
20. **Option (D) is correct.**
Explanation: We find the teacher and student in the school.
21. **Option (A) is correct.**
Explanation: According to the Venn diagram,

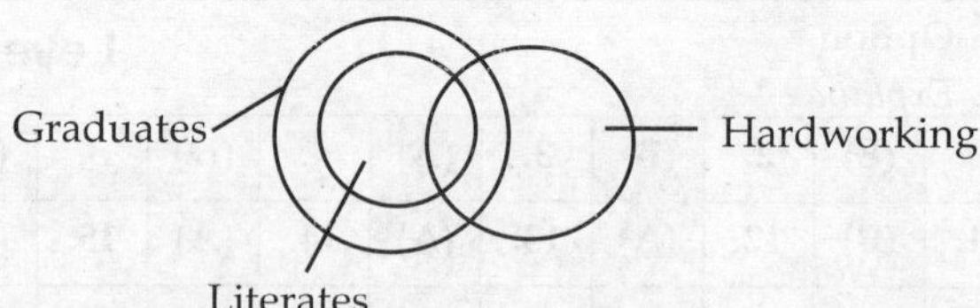

All graduates will be considered literates, but this does not imply that all hardworkers will also be graduates or literate. Consequently, the above diagram will be accurate.

22. **Option (B) is correct.**
Explanation: : According to the Venn diagram,

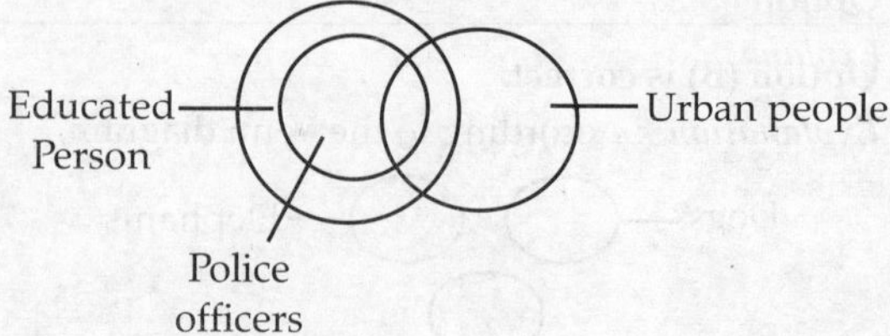

All the police officers are educated, while the urban people can be both.

23. **Option (B) is correct.**
Explanation: According to the Venn diagram,

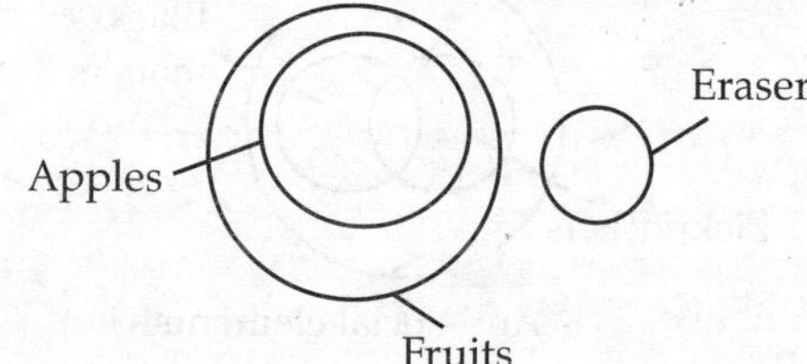

Apples are fruits but an eraser is not a fruit.

24. **Option (A) is correct.**
Explanation: The number of players who is also philosophers = 5 + 7 + 12 = 24, in which, there are 7 doctors.
So, the number of players who are philosophers but not doctors = 24 – 7 = 17
25. **Option (C) is correct.**
Explanation: There are 17 male clowns who are not acrobats but are ringmasters.
26. **Option (B) is correct.**
Explanation: : According to the Venn diagram,

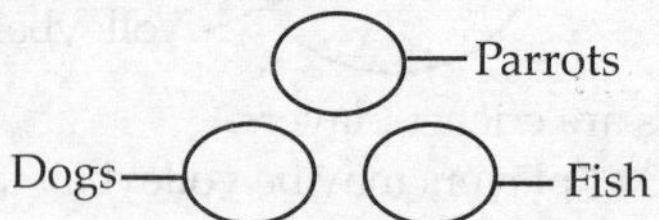

Here, all the three categories are different from each other

27. **Option (C) is correct.**
Explanation: Here

India
Haryana
Gurugram

Here, Gurugram is a city of Haryana, and Haryana is a state of India.

28. Option (A) is correct.

Explanation:

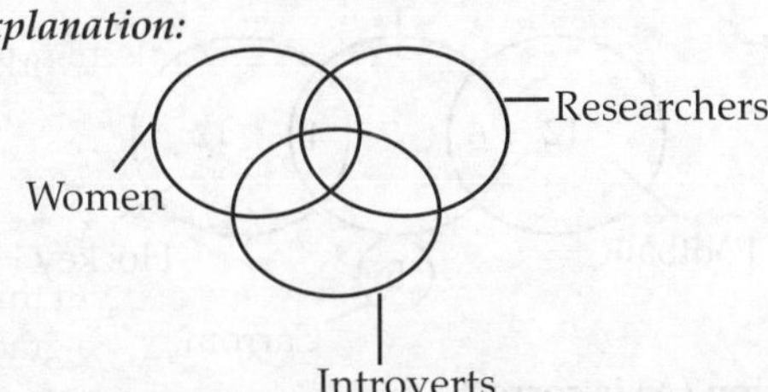

Here, some women are researchers and viceversa

Some women are introverts and viceversa.

Also, some researchers are introverts and viceversa.

29. Option (C) is correct.

Explanation:

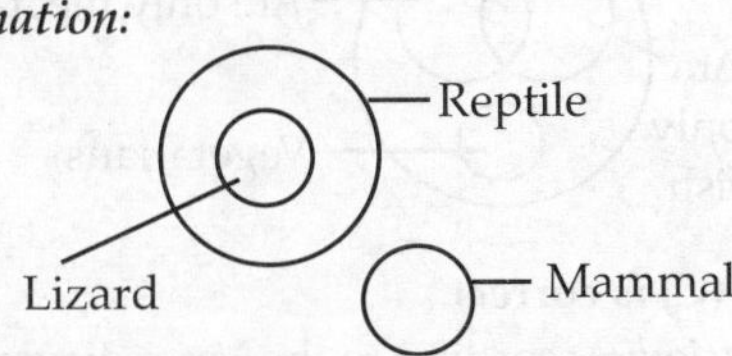

All lizards are reptiles.

Also, mammal is a different category.

30. Option (A) is correct.

Explanation:

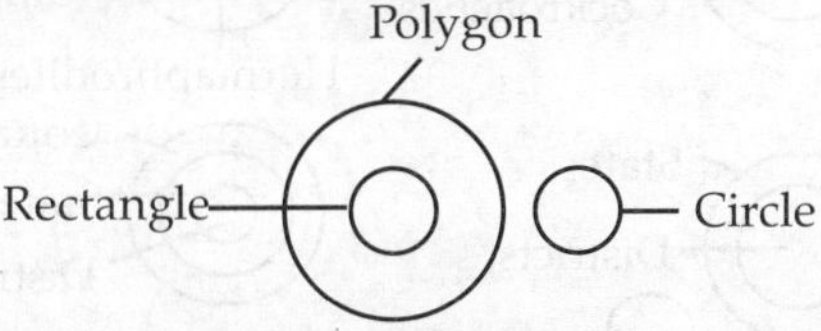

Here, all rectangles are polygons and a circle is not a polygon and is a different shape.

31. Option (B) is correct.

Explanation:

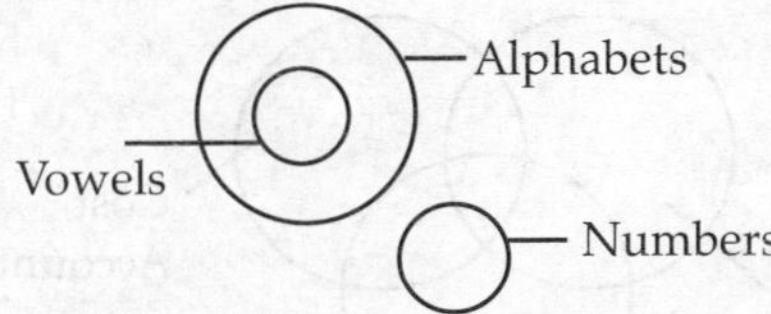

All vowels are alphabets and numbers is a different category.

32. Option (B) is correct.

Explanation:

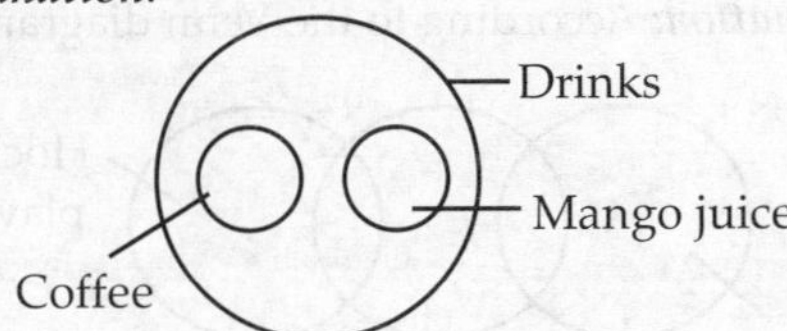

Coffee and mango juice are both drinks but are different from each other.

33. Option (A) is correct.

Explanation: :

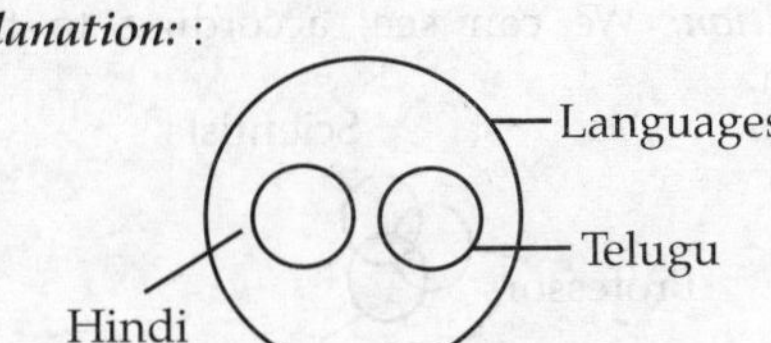

Hindi and Telugu are both languages are different from each other.

34. Option (B) is correct.

Explanation:

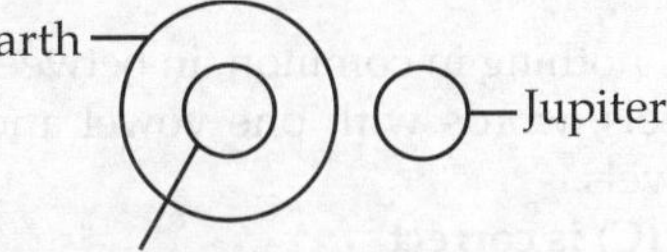

Some Chartered Accountants are females and vice-versa.

Some females are actors and vice-versa.

Some Chartered Accountants are actors and vice-versa.

35. Option (C) is correct.

Explanation:

All mountains are on earth and jupiter is a different planet.

36. Option (C) is correct.

Explanation: The number that belongs to a triangle only is 10.

37. Option (C) is correct.

Explanation: The number that belongs to a circle and rectangle but not a triangle is 18.

38. Option (A) is correct.

Explanation: The number that belongs to a triangle and rectangle but not a circle is 20.

39. Option (A) is correct.

Explanation: The number that belongs to a circle and triangle but not a rectangle is 5.

40. Option (C) is correct.

Explanation: The number that is common in a circle, rectangle and triangle is 17.

Level-2: INTERMEDIATE

1. Option (A) is correct.

Explanation: According to the Venn diagram,

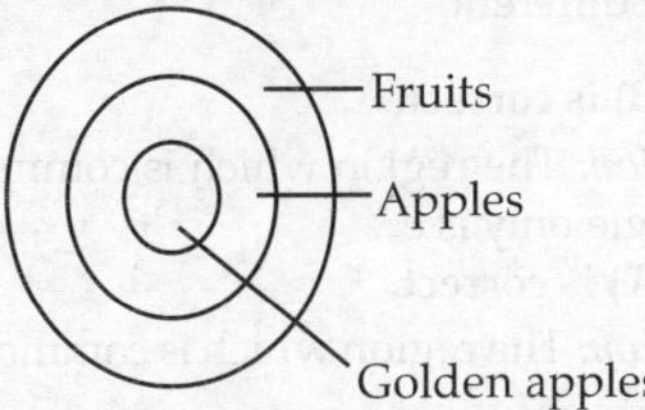

All golden apples are apples.

All apples are fruits.

2. Option (E) is correct.

Explanation: According to the Venn diagram,

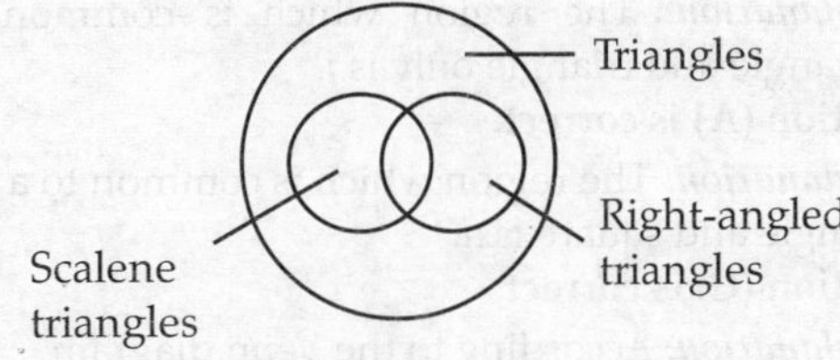

Both scalene triangles and right-angled triangles are triangles.
But some scalene triangles may be right-angled and vice versa.

3. **Option (D) is correct.**
Explanation: According to the Venn diagram,

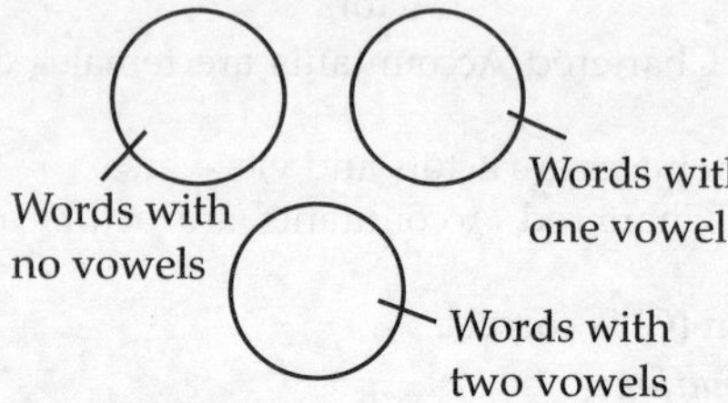

There is nothing in common in between words with no vowels, words with one vowel and words with two vowels.

4. **Option (C) is correct.**
Explanation: According to the Venn diagram,

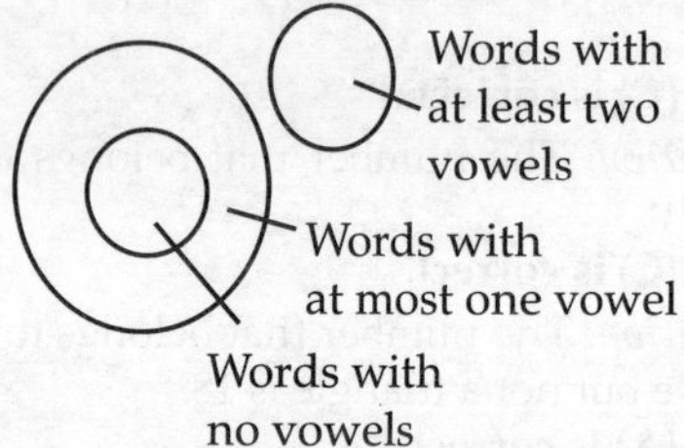

5. **Option (B) is correct.**
Explanation: According to the Venn diagram,

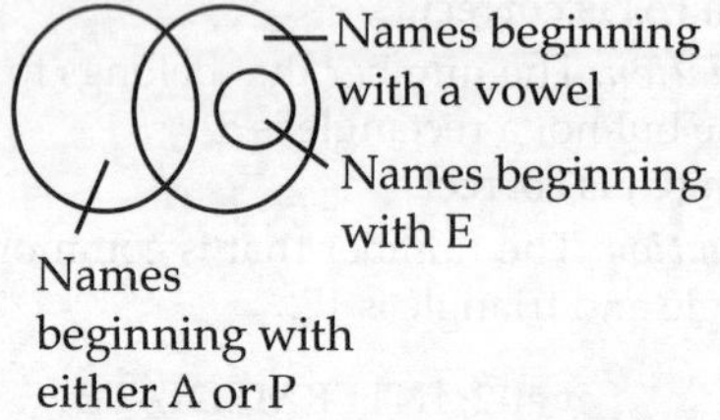

Names beginning with A shall be a part of names beginning with a vowel. But, names beginning with P shall be different.

6. **Option (B) is correct.**
Explanation: The region which is common to a circle and triangle only is e.

7. **Option (A) is correct.**
Explanation: The region which is common to a square only is e.

8. **Option (C) is correct.**
Explanation: The regions which represent the rural peoples are a + b + d + e.

9. **Option (C) is correct.**
Explanation: The region which is common to a rectangle and triangle only is *j*.

10. **Option (A) is correct.**
Explanation: The region which is common to a circle, triangle and square is *d*.

11. **Option (C) is correct.**
Explanation: According to the Venn diagram,

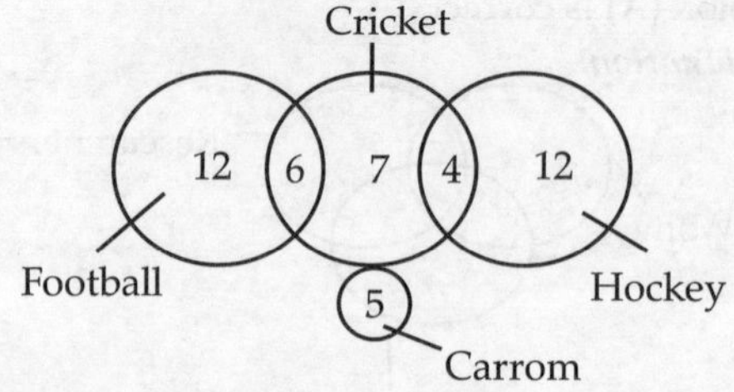

12. **Option (A) is correct.**
Explanation: According to the Venn diagram,

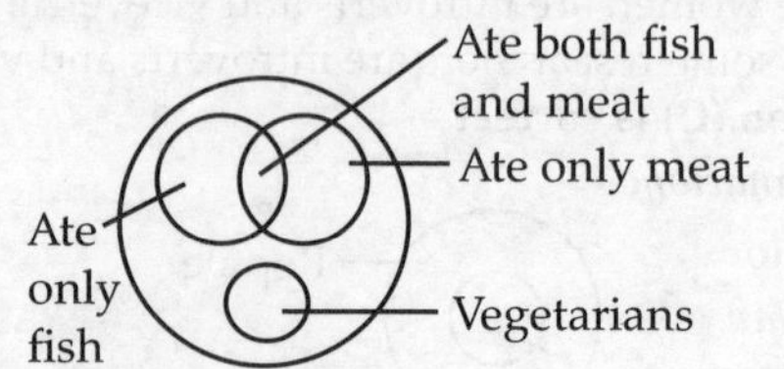

13. **Option (C) is correct.**
Explanation: According to the Venn diagram,

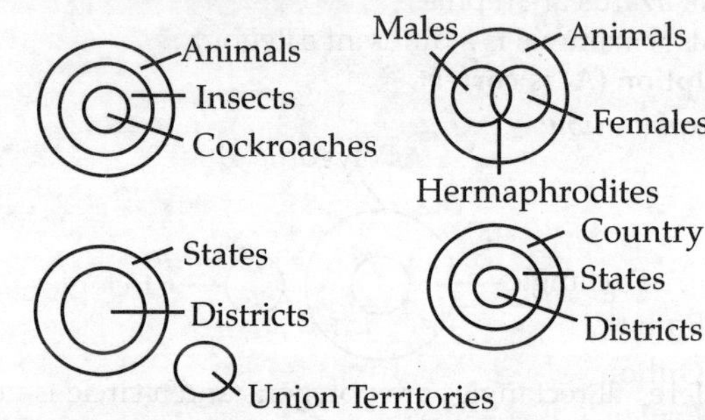

14. **Option (D) is correct.**
Explanation: According to the Venn diagram,

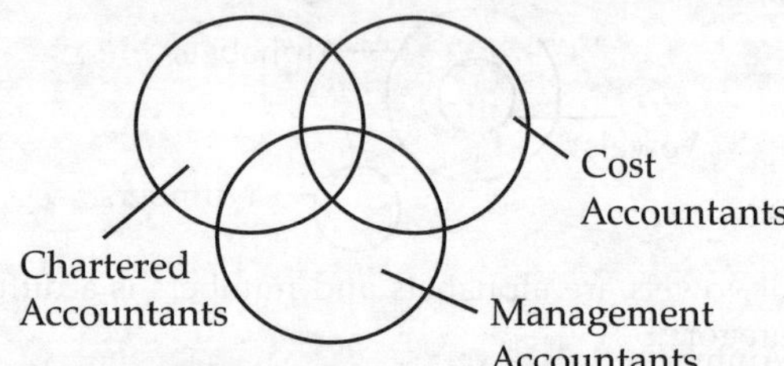

15. **Option (C) is correct.**
Explanation: According to the Venn diagram,

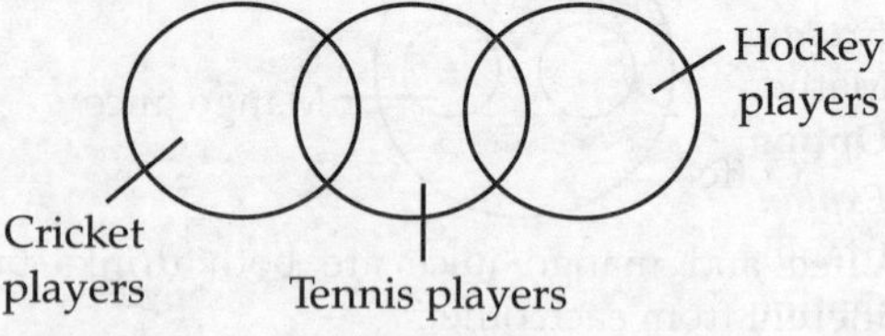

16. **Option (C) is correct.**
Explanation: We can see, according to the Venn diagram,

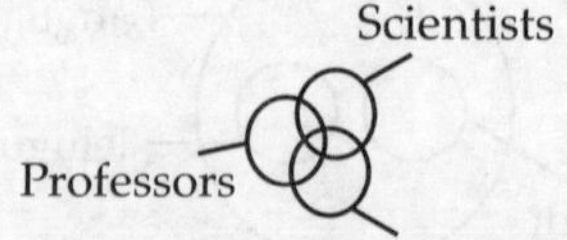

Some professors may be scientists, some scientists may be researchers and some researchers may be professors. So, option (C) is correct.

17. Option (C) is correct.

Explanation: We can see, according to the Venn diagram

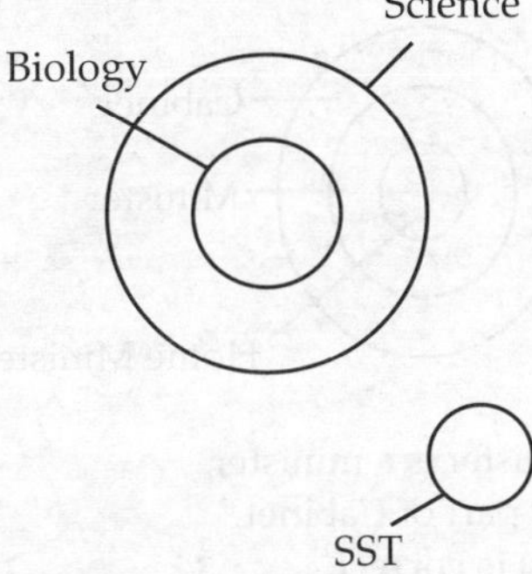

18. Option (C) is correct.

Explanation: We can see, according to the Venn diagram

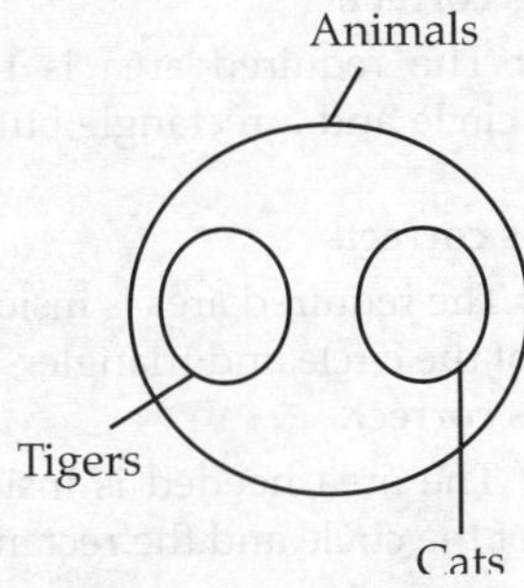

Both tigers and lions are animals.

19. Option (C) is correct.

Explanation: We can see, according to the Venn diagram.

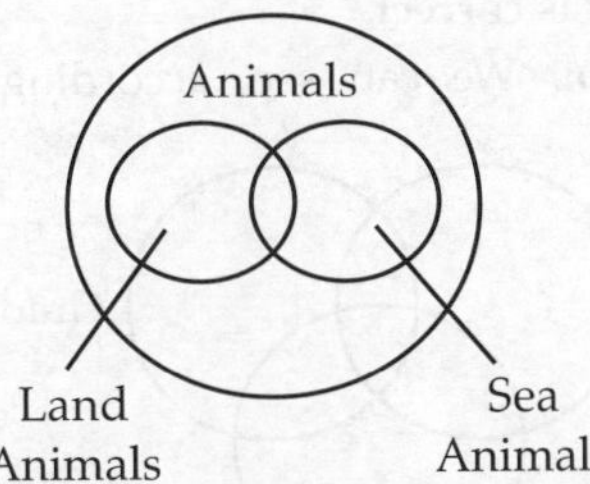

Animals include those on land and those in the sea. Some land animals can also be sea animals, and vice versa.

20. Option (B) is correct.

Explanation: Number of people who like English and Mathematics both = 17 + 15 = 32

21. Option (D) is correct.

Explanation: The only region that the circle and triangle have in common is the one that is necessary.

22. Option (D) is correct.

Explanation: The region that the triangle and rectangle share but that is outside the circle. So, Z is the required region.

23. Option (C) is correct.

Explanation: C lies inside the triangle only. So, C represents Surgical Specialists.

24. Option (C) is correct.

Explanation: B lies inside the rectangle only. So, B represents Medical Specialists who are neither Professors nor Surgical Specialists.

25. Option (B) is correct.

Explanation: The region that is needed is X, which is outside the triangle and shares the area with both the circle and the rectangle.

26. Option (B) is correct.

Explanation:

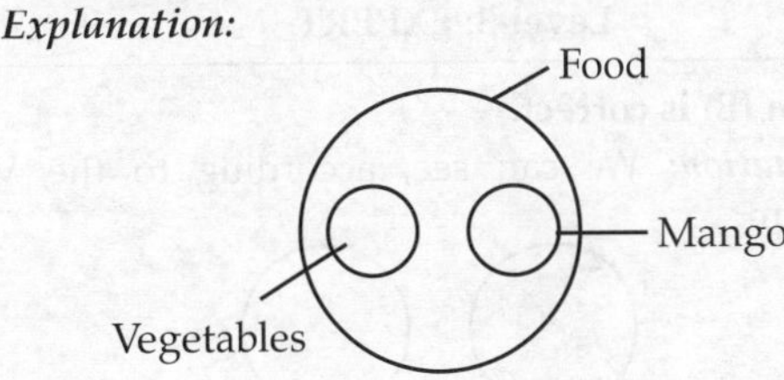

All grandmothers are mothers but grandfathers are different among the given classes.

27. Option (C) is correct.

Explanation:

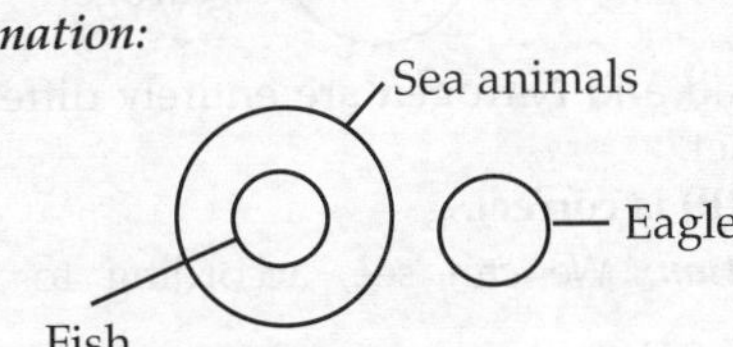

Both vegetables and mango are food items but both are totally different.

28. Option (B) is correct.

Explanation:

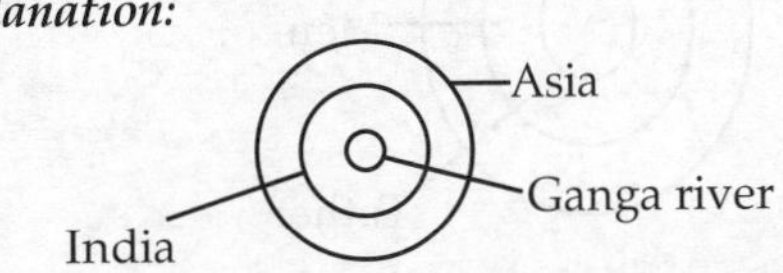

Fish are sea animals but eagle is different category.

29. Option (A) is correct.

Explanation:

India is a part of Asia. Also, Ganga river flows in India.

30. Option (B) is correct.

Explanation:

31. Option (C) is correct.

Explanation: We can see, according to the Venn diagram,

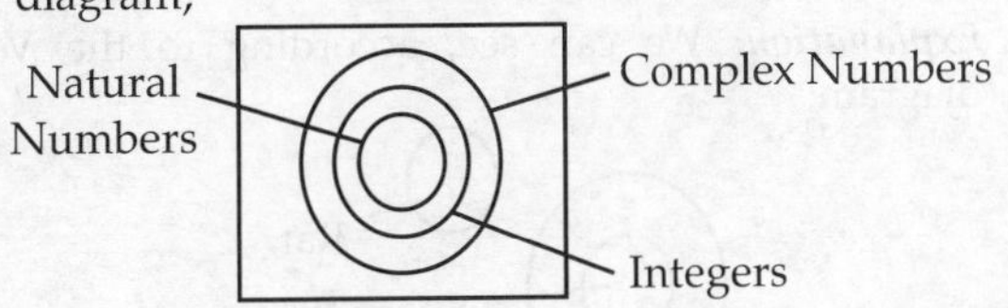

All integers are complex numbers, while all natural numbers are integers.

32. **Option (D) is correct.**
Explanation: The required region is the one which is common to the triangle and the circle but lies outside the square that is G.
33. **Option (B) is correct.**
Explanation: D is located inside the square, and the triangle but outside the circle. D therefore stands for uneducated, unemployed women in the village.
34. **Option (D) is correct.**
Explanation: The region that the triangle, circle, and square all share, namely E, is the one that is needed.
35. **Option (C) is correct.**
Explanation: The common area of the circle and square, or E and F, is the required area.

Level-3: EXPERT

1. **Option (E) is correct.**
Explanation: We can see, according to the Venn diagram.

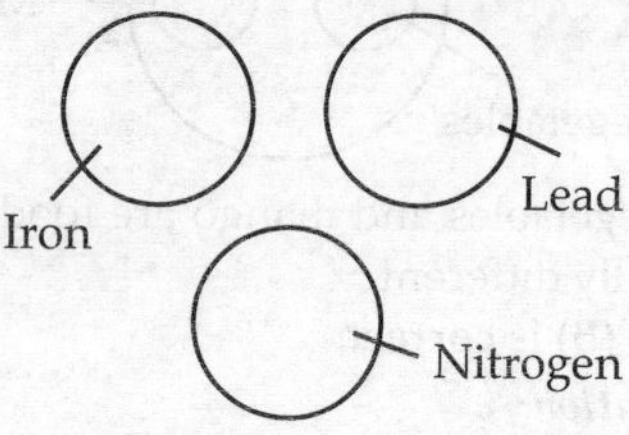

Iron, Lead and Nitrogen are entirely different from each other.
2. **Option (B) is correct.**
Explanation: We can see, according to the Venn diagram.

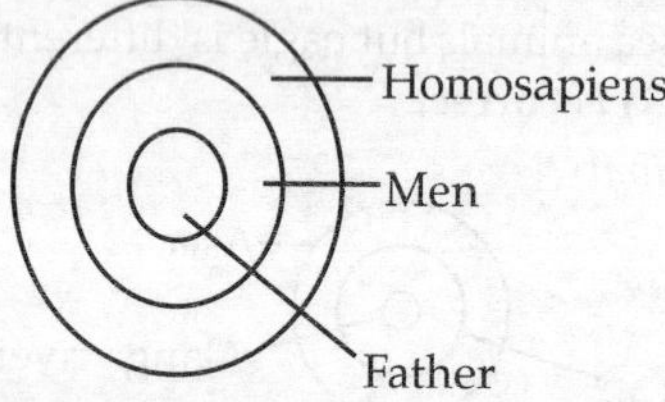

All fathers are men.
All men belong to the class of Homosapiens.
3. **Option (A) is correct.**
Explanation: We can see, according to the Venn diagram.

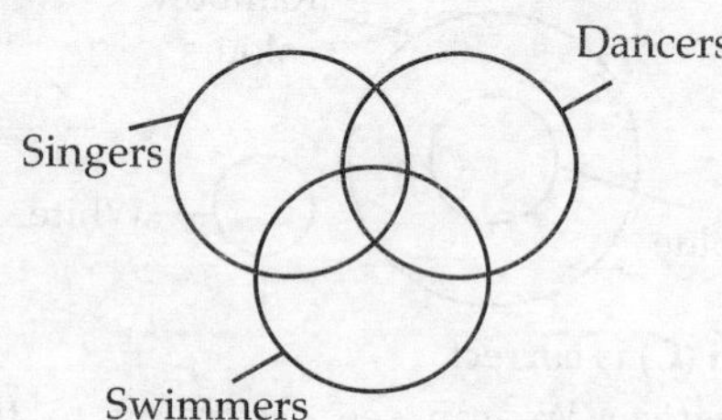

4. **Option (D) is correct.**
Explanation: We can see, according to the Venn diagram.

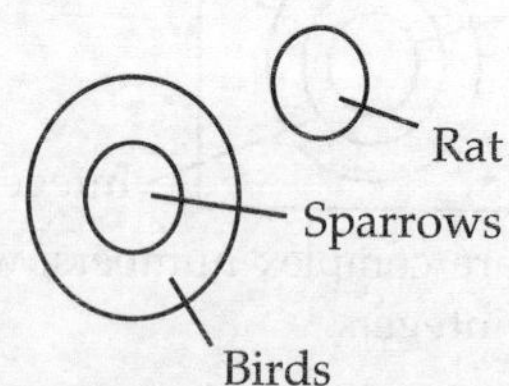

All sparrows are birds. But, rat is entirely different.
5. **Option (B) is correct.**
Explanation: We can see according, to the Venn diagram.

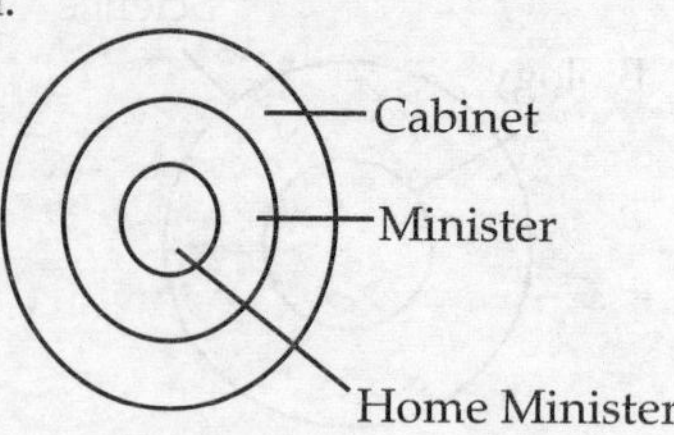

Home Minister is a minister,
Minister is part of Cabinet.
6. **Option (D) is correct.**
Explanation: The required region is the one which is common to the triangle, circle and rectangle.
7. **Option (B) is correct.**
Explanation: The required area is the one that is shared by a circle and a rectangle but is outside of a triangle.
8. **Option (A) is correct.**
Explanation: The required area is inside the rectangle but outside of the circle and triangle.
9. **Option (B) is correct.**
Explanation: The area needed is inside the triangle but outside of the circle and the rectangle.
10. **Option (D) is correct.**
Explanation: The area that is necessary must be located inside the circle but outside the triangle and rectangle.
11. **Option (B) is correct.**
Explanation: We can see, according to the Venn diagram.

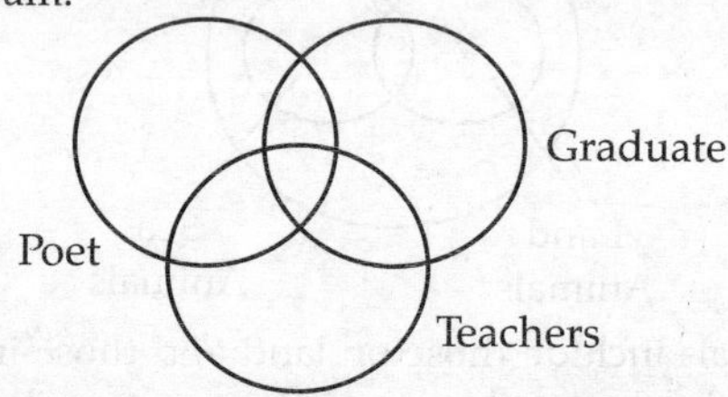

Some poets can be teachers. Some graduates can be teachers or poets.
12. **Option (A) is correct.**
Explanation: We can see, according to the Venn diagram.

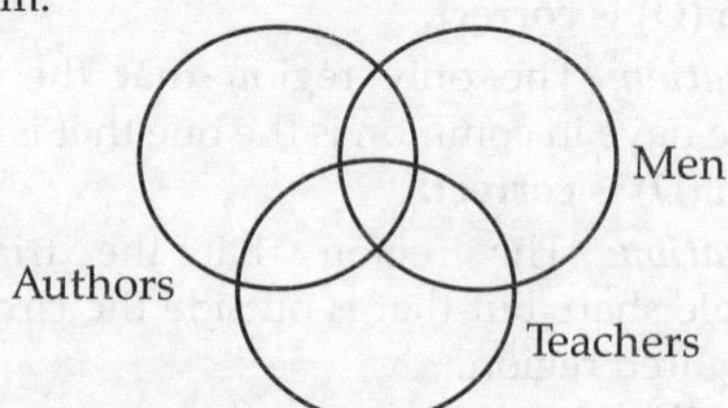

Some teachers can be authors or men.
Some authors can be men.
13. **Option (A) is correct.**
Explanation: We can see, according to the Venn diagram.

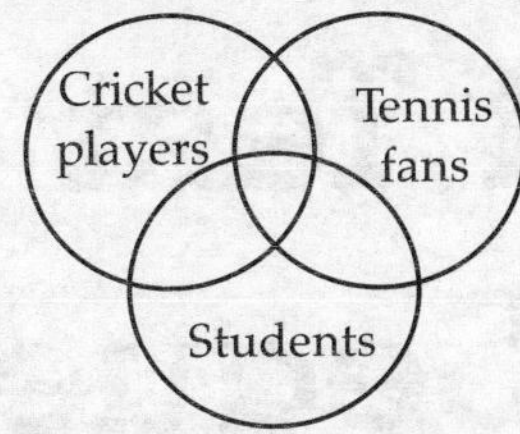

Some students can be tennis fans or cricket players.
Some cricket players can be tennis fans.

14. Option (A) is correct.

Explanation: We can see, according to the Venn diagram.

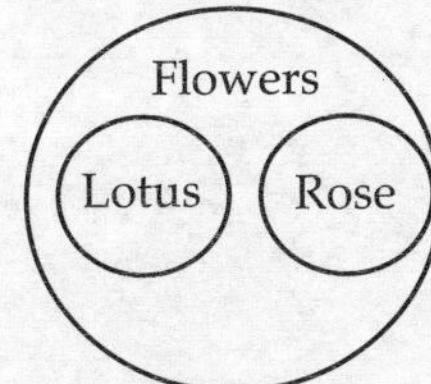

Rose and Lotus are different types of flowers.

15. Option (C) is correct.

Explanation: We can see, according to Venn diagram.

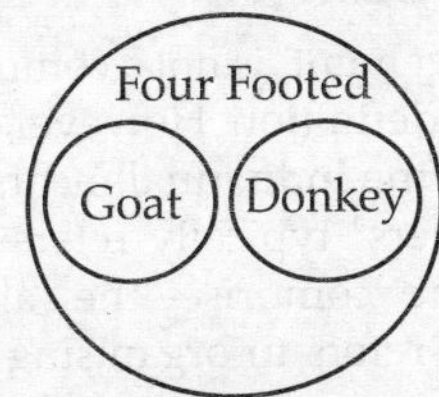

Goat and Donkey are different type of animals. But, both are four-footed.

16. Option (C) is correct.

Explanation:

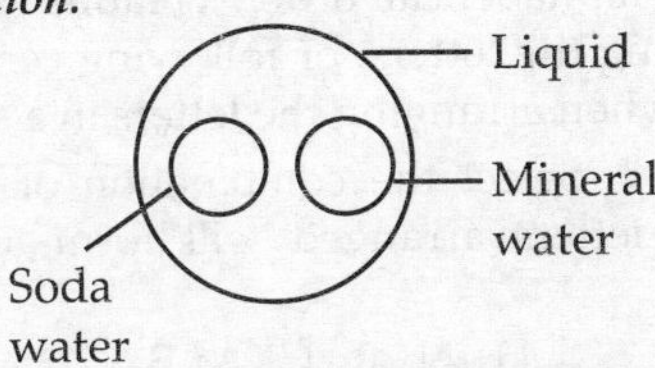

Both soda and mineral water are liquids but both are different items.

17. Option (C) is correct.

Explanation:

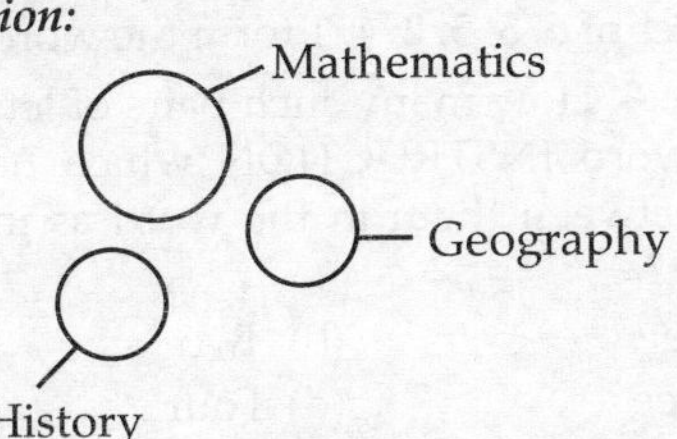

All the three subjects are different from each other.

18. Option (B) is correct.

Explanation: The number common to the triangle and circle but not the rectangle is 8.

19. Option (D) is correct.

Explanation:

Soldier
Engineer
Dentist

All the three are different professions.

20. Option (D) is correct.

Explanation:

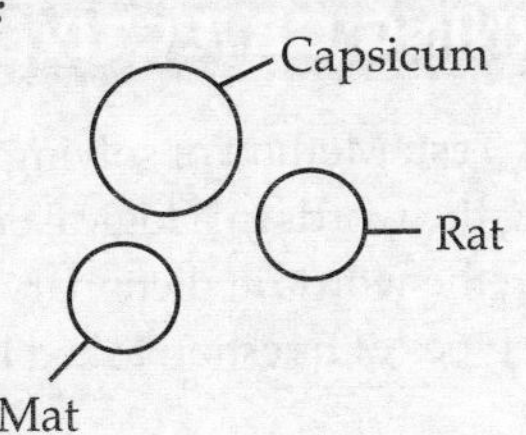

All the three are from diffferent categories.

21. Option (C) is correct.

Explanation: The region which is common to circles A and D only is y.

22. Option (B) is correct.

Explanation: The region which is common to circles A and B only is *q*.

23. Option (D) is correct.

Explanation: The region which is common to all the four given circles is *v*.

24. Option (A) is correct.

Explanation: The region which is only circle D is *m*.

25. Option (D) is correct.

Explanation: None of such region exists.

■ ■ ■

Chapter 10

Alphabet Test and Logical Sequence of Words

LEARNING OBJECTIVES:

- **Alphabet Test:** Method of solving questions based on Word Formation.
- Arranging the words in a logical Sequence
- Arranging the words in dictionary order
- Different types of question asked in competitive exams

An alphabet test is a topic in verbal reasoning that assesses your ability to comprehend and manipulate alphabetical sequences or patterns. It entails determining the pattern or rule that governs the sequence of letters and applying that pattern or rule to solve problems or answer questions.

WORD FORMATION

➢ In these tasks, a word is provided, and applicants must respond to questions such as: How many letters in the word are as far away from the beginning of the word as they are from the beginning of the English alphabet? When asked how many letters of a word would remain in the same position if the letters were arranged alphabetically, they are occasionally given the word. The question of whether a vowel or a consonant should come after a word is occasionally raised.

Example 1: Which of the following words will come second in the English dictionary?

(Bank Recruitment, 2005)

(a) Magical (b) Magnify
(c) Maternal (d) Marshal
(e) Magnetic

Sol. (e) The following words can be placed in alphabetical order: Magical, Magnetic, Magnify, Marshal, and Maternal. Magnetic is clearly in second place.

Example 2: In the given question, a word has been given, followed by four other words, one of which cannot be formed by using the letters of the given word. Find that word.

NATIONALISATION

(a) NOTATION (b) SALINATION
(c) INSTALLATION (d) SANITATION

Sol. (c) All letters except 'L' are present in the main word. Hence, 'INSTALLATION' cannot be formed form the letters of the given word 'NATIONALISATION'.

LETTERS ARRANGEMENT

➢ "Letters Arrangement" is not a commonly used phrase with a specific definition. However, we can deduce its meaning from the individual meanings of the words involved. "Letters" typically refers to the individual characters that comprise the alphabet, whereas "arrangement" refers to organising or placing things in a specific order or pattern. As a result, "Letters Arrangement" can be understood as the process or result of organising or ordering letters in a specific way. This can include arranging the letters of a word in alphabetical order, creating anagrams by rearranging the letters, or following certain patterns or rules when arranging the letters in a sequence.

Example 3: Select the combination of numbers, so that the letters arranged will form a meaningful word.

H	N	R	C	A	B
1	2	3	4	5	6

(a) 2, 5, 3, 4, 1, 6 (b) 3, 5, 6, 4, 1, 2
(c) 4, 1, 5, 6, 2, 3 (d) 6, 3, 5, 2, 4, 1

Sol. (d) Clearly, the given letters, when arranged in the order of 6, 3, 5, 2, 4, 1 form the word 'BRANCH'.

Example 4: How many such pairs of letters are there in the word INSTRUCTION which have as many letters between them in the word as in the English alphabet? **(CET 2006)**

(a) One (b) Two
(c) Three (d) Four
(e) None of these

Sol. (d) We have,

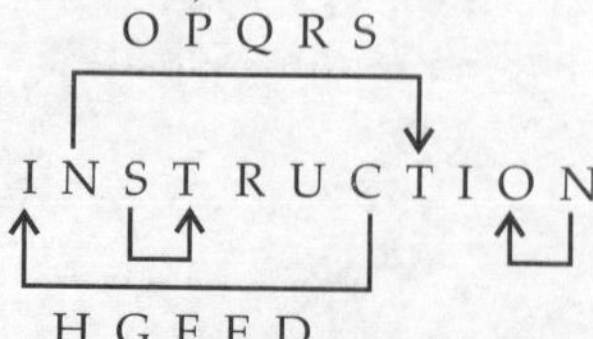

So, the pairs are: NT, NO, CI and ST. C and I are separated by five letters, as shown above. N and T are also separated by five letters, while each of the pairings (S and T) and (N and O) is separated by one letter.

LOGICAL SEQUENCE OF WORDS

➢ In this section, some different words will be given to students and they are required to arrange them in a logical order (either ascending or descending) and select the appropriate option among the given alternatives.

Example 5: Arrange the given words in a logical sequence and select the correct option.

1. Gram 2. Milligram
3. Hectogram 4. Kilogram

(a) 4, 1, 2, 3 (b) 4, 3, 1, 2
(c) 1, 2, 4, 3 (d) 2, 1, 4, 3

Sol. (b) The correct order is: Kilogram, Hectogram, Gram, Milligram.

Example 6: Arrange the given words in a logical sequence and select the correct option.

1. Desk 2. School
3. Classroom 4. City

(a) 1, 3, 2, 4 (b) 1, 2, 4, 3
(c) 1, 2, 3, 4 (d) 3, 1, 4, 2

Sol. (a) The correct order is: Desk, Classroom, School, City.

Level 1 Beginner

Directions (Qs. 1–3): In each of the following questions, five words are given. Which of them will come in the middle of all, if arranged alphabetically as in a dictionary?

1. (A) Cruisality (B) Crupper
(C) Crusade (D) Crush
(E) Crumb

2. (A) Ministry (B) Minimal
(C) Minority (D) Miniature
(E) Ministerial

3. (A) Sachet (B) Sentimental
(C) Sententious (D) Sentence
(E) Sadness

4. Arrange the given words in the sequence in which they occur in the Dictionary and locate the last word. **[SSC CPO 2012]**
(A) Frankenstein (B) Frankincense
(C) Frankalmoign (D) Frauendienst

5. Which one of the following words will appear fourth in the English Dictionary? **[SSC CPO 2012]**
(A) Encradle (B) Encourage
(C) Encroach (D) Encounter

Directions (Qs. 6–15): Each of the following questions is based on the following alphabet-series:

A B C D E F G H I J K L M N O P Q R S T U V W X Y Z

6. If the order of the English alphabet is reversed, then which letter would be exactly in the middle? **[MBA 2005]**
(A) L (B) M
(C) N (D) None of these

7. If the above alphabet is written in the reverse order, which will be the fourteenth letter to the right of W?
(A) F (B) G
(C) K (D) I
(E) None of these

8. If the above alphabet is written in the reverse order, which will be the third letter to the left of the fourth letter from the right?
(A) S (B) G
(C) D (D) K
(E) None of these

9. If the above alphabet is written in the reverse order, what will be the fourth letter to the right of the thirteenth letter from the left? **[MBA 2005]**
(A) J (B) K (C) L (D) M

10. If only the first half of the given alphabet is reversed, how many letters will be there between K and R? **[BANK PO 2002]**
(A) 6 (B) 10
(C) 14 (D) 16
(E) None of these

11. Which letter should be seventh letter to the left of seventh letter from the right, if the first half of the given alphabet is reversed?
(A) D (B) A (C) F (D) I

12. If the second half of the given alphabet is written in the reverse order, which letter will be third to the right of the eighth letter from the left end?
(A) R (B) M
(C) K (D) U
(E) None of these

13. If the last ten letters of the alphabets are written in the reverse order, which of the following will be the sixth to the right of the thirteenth letter from the left end? **[BANK PO 2002]**
(A) U (B) V
(C) W (D) X
(E) Y

14. If every alternate letter starting from A is deleted from the given alphabet, which of the following will be the fifth letter from the right end?
(A) R (B) D
(C) T (D) S
(E) None of these

15. If the alphabet is written in the reverse order and every alternate letter starting with Y is dropped, which letter will be exactly in the middle of the remaining letters of the alphabet? **[SSC 2002]**

(A) M (B) N
(C) O (D) M or O

16. In the given word 'SPLENDOR ' a consonant changed into its previous letter and the vowel into its next letter (according to the alphabetical order) and then all letters are arranged in alphabetical order from left to right. Then, which of the following letter is fifth from the left end? **[IBPS PRE Exam 2019]**
(A) R (B) O
(C) K (D) M
(E) C

17. If it is possible to make only one meaningful word with the 1st, 3rd, 5th and 11th letters of the word 'INHERITENCE', which would be the third letter of the word from the left? If more than one such word can be formed, give Y as the answer. If no such word can be formed, give 'Z' as your answer. **[SBI Clerk Exam 2020]**
(A) Y (B) R
(C) I (D) E
(E) Z

18. In the word 'GRACIOUS, how many pairs of the letters have the same number of letters between them in the word as in English alphabet?
(A) Four (B) Two
(C) One (D) None
(E) More than three

19. How many pairs of letters are there in the word "SPARKLE" which has as many letters between them as we have in the English alphabetical series (from both forward and backward direction)? **[SBI PO Exam 2021]**
(A) One (B) None
(C) Two (D) Three
(E) More than three

20. Which of the following is the second letter from the left end of the meaningful word formed by the 1st, 3rd, 5th, and 6th letter of the word "DRAWER". If more than one word is formed, mark X as your answer. If no such word is formed mark Y as your answer. **[SBI PO Exam 2021]**
(A) R (B) D
(C) E (D) X
(E) Y

Directions (Qs. 21–25): From the given words, select the word which can be formed using the letters of the given words

21. ADULTHOOD
(A) CLOTH (B) DUAL
(C) CALM (D) COULD

22. JUDGEMENTAL
(A) ANKLE (B) JUNKED
(C) JUNGLE (D) ADJUST

23. LEADERSHIP
(A) DIMPLE (B) HAMPER
(C) DEPTH (D) HELPER

24. MANAGEMENT
(A) ENGAGE (B) GAUGE
(C) AGENT (D) MUTE

25. TOURNAMENT
(A) DAMPS (B) AMOUNT
(C) MOUND (D) STUMP

Directions (Qs. 26–28): In each of the following questions, arrange the given words in the sequence in which they occur in the dictionary and then choose the correct sequence.

26. (1) wound (2) writer
(3) whiter (4) worst
(5) worked **[SSC 2000]**
(A) 1, 4, 3, 5, 2 (B) 2, 1, 3, 4, 5
(C) 3, 5, 4, 1, 2 (D) 5, 3, 2, 1, 4

27. (1) protein (2) problem
(3) proverb (4) property
(5) project **[SSC 2001]**
(A) 1, 2, 3, 4, 5 (B) 2, 1, 4, 3, 5
(C) 2, 5, 4, 1, 3 (D) 3, 4, 5, 2, 1

28. (1) eagle (2) earth
(3) eager (4) early
(5) each
(A) 1, 5, 2, 4, 3 (B) 2, 1, 4, 3, 5
(C) 1, 4, 2, 5, 3 (D) 5, 3, 1, 4, 2

Directions (Qs. 29–30): How many pairs letters are there in the given words each of which has many letters between them as in the English alphabetical series?

29. GENTLE
(A) 1 (B) 3
(C) 4 (D) 2

30. STABLE
(A) None (B) 3
(C) 2 (D) 1

31. How many such pairs of letters are there in the word "Streaming" having the same number of letters between them as they have between them according to the alphabetical order? **[IBPS PO Exam 2018]**
(A) Two (B) More than three
(C) Three (D) One
(E) None of these

32. How many words can be formed from the 1st, 5th, 7th and 8th letters of the word EMANCIPATE by using each letter once in the word?
(A) 2 (B) 1
(C) 3 (D) 4

33. If it is possible to make only one meaningful word with the 2nd, 4th, 6th and 7th letters of the word 'UNILATERAL' which would be the second letter of the word from the right end? If more than one such word can be formed, give 'Y as the answer. If no such word can be formed, give 'Z' as your answer. **[SBI CLERK Exam 2020]**
(A) Y (B) N
(C) L (D) T
(E) Z

34. How many pairs of letters are there in the word 'POPULAR', each of which has as many letters between them in the word as they have between them in the English alphabet?
(A) One (B) Two
(C) Three (D) Four
(E) Five

35. In the word 'ABSOLUTE', how many pairs of the letters have the same number of letters between them in the given word as they have in the English alphabet series?
(A) Four (B) Two
(C) One (D) Three
(E) More than four

Directions (Qs. 36–40): Arrange the given words in a logical sequence and select the correct option.

36. (1) Room (2) Window
(3) House (4) Street
(5) Locality
(A) 5, 3, 2, 1, 4 (B) 5, 4, 3, 1, 2
(C) 5, 2, 3, 1, 4 (D) 5, 1, 4, 2, 3

37. (1) Plant (2) Fruit
(3) Seed (4) Flower
[SSC 2013]
(A) 3, 2, 4, 1 (B) 3, 1, 2, 4
(C) 3, 1, 4, 2 (D) 3, 2, 1, 4

38. (1) Adult (2) Teenager
(3) Child (4) Infant
(A) 4, 1, 2, 3 (B) 4, 1, 3, 2
(C) 3, 1, 2, 4 (D) 4, 3, 2, 1

39. (1) Twilight (2) Dawn
(3) Noon (4) Night
[SSC 2013]
(A) 2, 1, 3, 4 (B) 2, 3, 1, 4
(C) 1, 2, 3, 4 (D) 1, 3, 2, 4

40. (1) Delhi (2) Qutub Minar
(3) India (4) Asia
(5) World
(A) 5, 4, 3, 1, 2 (B) 5, 4, 1, 2, 3
(C) 5, 1, 2, 3, 4 (D) 5, 3, 1, 2, 4

Level 2 Intermediate

Directions (Qs. 1–5): In each of the following questions, five words are given. Which of them will come in the middle if all of them are arranged alphabetically as in a dictionary?

1. (A) Spine (B) Spinal
(C) Spinner (D) Spinet
(E) Spindle **[Bank Recruitment 2003]**

2. (A) Prank (B) Practical
(C) Plate (D) Prayer
(E) Practice

3. (A) Hash (B) Haphazard
(C) Host (D) Hand
(E) Handkerchief

4. (A) Butterfly (B) Butler
(C) Butcher (D) Button
(E) Butter **[Bank Recruitment 2005]**

5. (A) Robot (B) Rocket
(C) Retreat (D) Restaurant
(E) Restrict

Directions (Qs. 6–15): In each of the following questions, find out which of the letter series follows the given rule.

6. Number of letters skipped in between the adjacent letters in the series is equal.
(A) HKNGSW (B) QUYCEF
(C) QUYCGK (D) SUXADF

7. Number of letters skipped in between the adjacent letters in the series are multiples of 3.
(A) BFMQA (B) DILQT
(C) CFIMO (D) LORUX

8. The group of letters should not contain more than two vowels. **[SSC 2001]**
(A) BDEJOLY (B) JKAPIXU
(C) PRAQEOS (D) ZILERAM

9. Number of letters skipped in between adjacent letters in the series is two.
(A) TWZCFIL (B) GTHKNPRT
(C) SVZJGJN (D) ZCDKMPR

10. Number of letters skipped in between adjacent letters of the series starting from behind increases by one.
(A) OIGDC (B) OMJFA
(C) OMKIG (D) ONLKJ

11. Number of letters skipped in between adjacent letters in the series is in the order of 3, 6, 8 and 10.
(A) DEGLV (B) GNKOU
(C) RVCLW (D) PSZGQ

12. Number of letters skipped in between the adjacent letters in the series are consecutive even numbers. **[SSC 2001]**
(A) ADIPY (B) CDFIM
(C) DFJPX (D) GIMSZ

13. Number of letters skipped between adjacent letters in a series increases by one. **[SSC 2000]**
(A) CIOUBK (B) HLPTXN
(C) CHMRWB (D) CEHLQW

14. Number of letters skipped in between adjacent letters in the series is odd.
(A) CEIMS (B) FJNRW
(C) FIMRX (D) NQSVY

15. Number of letters skipped in reverse order in between adjacent letters in the series is constant. **[CPO 2003]**
(A) SPMJG (B) SPNLJ
(C) SQOLJ (D) WUTRQ

Directions (Qs. 16–19): From the given alternative words, select the word which cannot be formed using the letters of the given word: **[SSC CGL Exam 2015]**

16. INCONVENIENCE
(A) CONCEIVE (B) CONSCIENCE
(C) CONCIEVE (D) CONVENE

17. DISTRIBUTION
(A) TRUST (B) SITUATION
(C) TUITION (D) DISTURB

18. SUPERINTENDENT
(A) NURSE (B) INTENSE
(C) DOCTOR (D) DENTIST

19. In the following series, how many MND occur in such a way that 'N' is in the middle and 'M' and 'D' are adjacent to it on both sides?
A K G L M N D Q K G C S N G K T G K M N D Z P U X G K E
(A) 3 (B) 5
(C) 1 (D) 2

20. In the following question, from the given alternative words, select the word which cannot be formed using the letters of the given word.
"Abandoned" **[SSC CGL Exam 2017]**
(A) Bonded (B) Banded
(C) Bland (D) Bane

21. In the following question, from the given alternative words, select the word which can be formed using the letters of the given word.
"RECAPITULATE"
(A) CAPABLE (B) RATINA
(C) PITTY (D) PLATE

22. If all the letters in the word FIGURES are arranged in alphabetical order from left to right in such a way that vowels are arranged first followed by consonants, then how many letters are there in between U and R after the arrangement? **[SBI Clerk Exam 2018]**
(A) Two (B) One
(C) None (D) Three
(E) Four

23. Arrange the given words in the sequence in they occur in the dictionary. **[SSC CGL Exam 2017]**
(1) Flinching (2) Flintlock
(3) Flinpites (4) Flintlocks
(5) Flinchers
(A) 15243 (B) 51243
(C) 51324 (D) 51342

24. Arrange the given words in the sequence in which they occur in the dictionary.
(1) Home (2) Harmony
(3) House (4) Honour
(5) Horse
(A) 12543 (B) 21453
(C) 21534 (D) 12354

25. How many letters will remain at the same position in the word 'SURFACE' when they are arranged in the alphabetical order from left to right? **[IBPS Clerk Exam, 2017]**
(A) Four (B) Three
(C) One (D) Two
(E) None of these

Directions (Qs. 26–30): Arrange the given letters in a order to form a meaningful word.

26. M, P, O, R, E, I, S
1 2 3 4 5 6 7
(A) 7, 5, 4, 6, 1, 3, 2 (B) 2, 4, 3, 1, 6, 7, 5
(C) 3, 2, 5, 1, 4, 7, 6 (D) 2, 5, 3, 1, 4, 6, 7

27. S R N E E U
1 2 3 4 5 6
(A) 2, 4, 1, 5, 3, 6 (B) 2, 4, 5, 1, 6, 3
(C) 5, 3, 1, 6, 2, 4 (D) 3, 1, 5, 2, 4, 6

28. L N U I O L S I
1 2 3 4 5 6 7 8
(A) 4, 1, 6, 3, 7, 4, 5, 2 (B) 5, 7, 6, 3, 4, 1, 2
(C) 4, 3, 1, 5, 6, 2, 7 (D) 4, 3, 5, 2, 1, 7, 6

29. A E D M N D
1 2 3 4 5 6
(A) 2, 6, 5, 1, 4, 3 (B) 3, 4, 6, 1, 2, 5
(C) 5, 1, 2, 6, 3, 4 (D) 3, 2, 4, 1, 5, 6

30. A P L R A O P S
1 2 3 4 5 6 7 8
(A) 2, 4, 6, 7, 1, 8, 5, 3 (B) 7, 5, 4, 8, 2, 3, 6, 1
(C) 4, 2, 1, 6, 8, 3, 5, 7 (D) 5, 7, 8, 2, 4, 3, 1, 6

Directions (Qs. 31–35): Study the following arrangement of the English alphabet and answer the questions given below.
F J M P O W R N B E Y C K A V L D G X U H Q I S Z T
[Bank PO 2004]

31. Which letter is tenth to the right of the letter which is exactly the middle letter between F and D?
(A) D (B) G
(C) H (D) U
(E) None of these

32. Four of the following five are alike in a certain way based on their pattern in the above arrangement and hence form a group. Which one does not be belong to that group?
(A) BRY (B) ECN
(C) HXI (D) OMR
(E) KYV

33. FMJ : TSZ in the same way as JMP : ?
(A) IZS (B) ZSI
(C) ZIS (D) ISZ
(E) SIQ

34. Which of the following pairs of letters has as many letters between them in the above arrangement as there are between them in the English alphabet?
(A) AI (B) EL
(C) LS (D) MO
(E) MR

35. If each letter is assigned a value equal to its serial number in the above arrangement starting from your left, then what will be the sum of the number attached to all the vowels in the arrangement?

(A) 50 (B) 58
(C) 63 (D) 73
(E) None of these

Directions (Qs. 36–40): Arrange the given words in a logical sequence and select the correct option.

36. (1) Toy (2) Cycle
(3) Bike (4) Car
(5) Truck
(A) 3, 1, 5, 2, 4 (B) 1, 2, 3, 4, 5
(C) 2, 1, 3, 5, 4 (D) 1, 3, 2, 5, 4

37. (1) Farmer (2) Seed
(3) Food (4) Cultivation
[SSC Multitasking 2014]
(A) 1, 2, 4, 3 (B) 2, 1, 3, 4
(C) 4, 2, 3, 1 (D) 3, 1, 4, 2

38. (1) Head (2) Waist
(3) Nose (4) Neck
(5) Legs
(A) 1, 4, 3, 2, 5 (B) 1, 2, 3, 4, 5
(C) 1, 5, 2, 3, 4 (D) 1, 3, 4, 2, 5

39. (1) Seeds (2) Plant
(3) Tree (4) Furniture
(5) Wood
(A) 3, 1, 2, 4, 5 (B) 1, 2, 3, 4, 5
(C) 1, 2, 3, 5, 4 (D) 2, 1, 4, 3, 5

40. (1) Job (2) Study
(3) Income (4) Interview
(A) 1, 3, 2, 4 (B) 2, 1, 3, 4
(C) 2, 4, 1, 3 (D) 2, 1, 4, 3

3 Level Expert

Directions (Qs. 1–3): From the given alternatives, select the word which cannot be formed using the letters of the given word.

1. MANUSCRIPT **[SSC CGL Tier 1 Exam, 2013]**
(A) PRIMUS (B) SMART
(C) RUSTIC (D) MASTER

2. SEGREGATION
(A) NATION (B) GREAT
(C) GREETINGS (D) SEATING

3. CONSTITUTIONAL **[SSC CGL Tier 1 Exam, 2013]**
(A) TUITION (B) TALENT
(C) LOCATION (D) CONSULT

4. If it is possible to make only one meaningful word with the second, the fifth, the seventh and the tenth letters of the word OMNISCIENT, which of the following will be the third letter of that word? If no such word can be made, give 'J' as the answer and if more than one such words can be made, give 'Q' as the answer. **[Management Trainees 2005]**
(A) I (B) M
(C) S (D) J
(E) Q

5. If it is possible to make a meaningful word with the second, the fifth and the eighth letters of the word NEPOTISM, which of the following will be the first letter of that word? If no such word can be made,give X as the answer. If more than one such words can be made, give 'Z' as the answer.
(A) A (B) E
(C) T (D) X
(E) M

6. From the given alternatives words, select the word which can be formed using the letters of the given word.
DEMOCRACY
(A) SECRECY (B) MICRO
(C) MARCY (D) DEMON

7. How many meaningful English words can be formed from the first, fifth, seventh and ninth letters of the word PUNCTUATE using them in different sequence only once? **[Bank Recruitment 2004]**
(A) None (B) One
(C) Two (D) Three
(E) None of these

8. If it is possible to make only one meaningful word with the fourth, the fifth, the seventh and the eleventh letters of the word PREDICTABLE, which of the following will be the first letter of that word? If only two such words can be formed, give 'W' as the answer, if three or more such words can be formed, give 'Z' as the answer and if no such word can be formed, give 'X' as the answer.
[Management Trainees 2003]
(A) D (B) T
(C) W (D) Z
(E) X

9. If with the third, fourth, fifth, seventh and tenth letters of the word PERSONALITY, a meaningful word is formed, then the first letter of the word is the answer. If no word is possible, then 'X' is the answer.
[NMAT 2005]
(A) O (B) T
(C) R (D) S
(E) X

10. If it is possible to make a meaningful word with the fourth, the eighth and the ninth letters of the word CREDULOUS, which of the following will be the last letter of that word? If no such word can be made, give X' as the answer. If more than one such words can be made, give 'M' as the answer.
(A) A (B) N
(C) T (D) X
(E) M

11. From the given alternatives words, select the word which cannot be formed using the letters of the given word. **[SSC CGL Tier 1 Exam, 2014]**
INCARCERATION

(A) RELATION (B) TERRAIN
(C) INACTION (D) CREATION

12. A meaningful word starting with A is made from the first, the second, the fourth, the fifth and the sixth letters of the word CONTRACT. Which of the following is the middle letter of that word?
(A) C (B) O
(C) R (D) T

13. If it is possible to make a meaningful word with the first, the third, the seventh and the thirteenth letters of the word PROPORTIONATE, which of the following will be the third letter of that word? If more than one such words can be made, give 'M' as the answer and if no such word can be made, give X' as the answer.
(A) I (B) R
(C) T (D) X
(E) M

14. If it is possible to make a meaningful word with the second, fourth, sixth and ninth letters of the word ATTENTION, which of the following will be the third letter of that word? If no such word can be made, give X' as the answer and if more than one such words Can be made, give 'M' as the answer.
(A) S (B) N
(C) E (D) X
(E) M

15. If a meaningful word can be formed with the third, fifth, seventh and tenth letters of the word PROJECTION, then the third letter of that word is the answer. If no such word can be formed, then 'X' is the answer and if more than one such words can be formed, then give 'M' as the answer. **[RRB 2005]**
(A) T (B) N
(C) M (D) X

Directions (Qs. 16–20): Study the following alphabetical sequence and answer the questiions following it :

A B B C D E F E I B C A F E C B B A C A O B N U V W

[IBPS Clerk 2019]

16. How many C's are there in the alphabetical series which are immediately preceeded by a vowel and immediate followed by a consonant?
(A) One (B) Two
(C) Three (D) More than three
(E) None of these

17. If all the vowels are dropped from the series, then which alphabet will be eighth from the left end?
(A) C (B) B
(C) N (D) F
(E) None of these

18. How many vowels are there in the alphabetical series which are immediately preceeded by a consonant?
(A) One (B) Two
(C) Four (D) More than four
(E) None

19. If the position of the 1st and 14th alphabets, the 2nd and the 15th alphabets and so on, up to the 13th and the 26th alphabets, are interchanged, then which alphabets will be 7th to the right of 10th alphabet from the right end?
(A) A (B) C
(C) N (D) B
(E) None of these

20. How many total vowels are there in the alphabetical series?
(A) Five (B) Ten
(C) Three (D) Nine
(E) None of these

21. If it is possible to make only one meaningful word with the 2nd, 5th, 8th and 9th letters of the word TRANSLATION, then which would be the second letter from the left? If more than one such word can be formed give Y as the answer. If no such word can be formed, give Z as your answer
(A) Y (B) S
(C) T (D) Z
(E) R

Directions (Qs. 22–25): How many pairs of letters are there in the given word which has the same number of letters between them as in the English alphabetical series?

22. UNDERTAKING
(A) 2 (B) 3
(C) 1 (D) 4

23. UNPREDICTED
(A) 5 (B) 4
(C) 3 (D) 6

24. PREFERENTIAL
(A) 2 (B) 4
(C) 3 (D) More than 4

25. ANTIBIOTIC
(A) 2 (B) 3
(C) 1 (D) 4

Directions (Qs. 26–30): Arrange the given words in a logical sequence and select the correct option.

26. (1) Postbox (2) Letter
(3) Envelope (4) Delivery
(5) Clearance **[SSC CGL 2013]**
(A) 3, 2, 4, 5, 1 (B) 3, 2, 1, 5, 4
(C) 3, 2, 1, 4, 5 (D) 2, 3, 1, 4, 5

27. (1) Birth (2) Death
(3) Funeral (4) Marriage
(5) Education **[SSC CGL 2009]**
(A) 4, 5, 3, 1, 2 (B) 2, 3, 4, 5, 1
(C) 1, 5, 4, 2, 3 (D) 1, 3, 4, 5, 2

28. (1) Collector (2) Governor
(3) Chief Secretary (4) President
(5) Clerk **[SSC 2012]**
(A) 1, 2, 3, 4, 5 (B) 5, 1, 3, 2, 4
(C) 5, 1, 3, 4, 2 (D) 5, 1, 4, 3, 2

29. (1) Weekly (2) Daily
(3) Monthly (4) Fortnightly
(5) Bimonthly **[SSC 2012]**
(A) 1, 4, 3, 2, 5 (B) 2, 1, 4, 3, 5
(C) 4, 1, 2, 3, 5 (D) 5, 1, 2, 3, 4

30. (1) Tired (2) Night
(3) Day (4) Sleep
(5) Work **[CPO 2010]**
(A) 1, 3, 5, 2, 4 (B) 3, 5, 1, 4, 2
(C) 3, 5, 1, 2, 4 (D) 3, 5, 2, 1, 4

ANSWER KEY

Level-1: Beginner

1.	(E)	2.	(E)	3.	(D)	4.	(D)	5.	(C)	6.	(D)	7.	(D)	8.	(B)	9.	(A)	10.	(C)
11.	(B)	12.	(C)	13.	(D)	14.	(A)	15.	(B)	16.	(B)	17.	(A)	18.	(D)	19.	(E)	20.	(D)
21.	(B)	22.	(C)	23.	(D)	24.	(C)	25.	(B)	26.	(C)	27.	(C)	28.	(D)	29.	(A)	30.	(C)
31.	(C)	32.	(A)	33.	(B)	34.	(D)	35.	(B)	36.	(B)	37.	(C)	38.	(D)	39.	(B)	40.	(A)

Level-2: Intermediate

1.	(A)	2.	(E)	3.	(B)	4.	(E)	5.	(C)	6.	(C)	7.	(A)	8.	(A)	9.	(A)	10.	(B)
11.	(C)	12.	(A)	13.	(D)	14.	(A)	15.	(A)	16.	(B)	17.	(B)	18.	(C)	19.	(D)	20.	(C)
21.	(D)	22.	(A)	23.	(C)	24.	(B)	25.	(C)	26.	(B)	27.	(C)	28.	(A)	29.	(D)	30.	(A)
31.	(E)	32.	(B)	33.	(B)	34.	(D)	35.	(E)	36.	(B)	37.	(A)	38.	(D)	39.	(C)	40.	(C)

Level-3: Expert

1.	(D)	2.	(A)	3.	(B)	4.	(C)	5.	(E)	6.	(C)	7.	(D)	8.	(D)	9.	(C)	10.	(D)
11.	(A)	12.	(D)	13.	(E)	14.	(B)	15.	(C)	16.	(A)	17.	(D)	18.	(D)	19.	(B)	20.	(B)
21.	(C)	22.	(A)	23.	(A)	24.	(D)	25.	(A)	26.	(C)	27.	(C)	28.	(B)	29.	(B)	30.	(C)

Solutions with Detailed Explanations

Level-1: BEGINNER

1. **Option (E) is correct.**
   Explanation: We can see the proper alphabetic sequence is:
   Crudity, Cruise. Crumb. Crupper. Crush
   So, the word 'Crumb' will come in middle.
2. **Option (E) is correct.**
   Explanation: We can see the proper alphabetic sequence is:
   Miniature, Minimal, Ministerial, Ministry, Minority
   So, word 'Ministerial' will be come in middle.
3. **Option (D) is correct.**
   Explanation: We can see the proper alphabetic sequence is:
   Sachet, Sadness, Sentence, Sententious, Sentimental
   So, word 'Sentence' will be come in middle.
4. **Option (D) is correct.**
   Explanation: We can see the proper alphabetic sequence is:
   Frankalmoign, Frankenstein, Frankincense, Frauendienst
   So, word 'Frauendienst' would be the last word.
5. **Option (C) is correct.**
   Explanation: According to the dictionary, the order of the terms is as follows:
   Encounter → Encourage → Encradle → Encroach
6. **Option (D) is correct.**
   Explanation: The new letter series acquired on reversing the order of the English alphabet is:
   ZYXWVUTSRQPONMLKJIHGF EDCBA
   Since, the series includes an even number of letters, there is no such letter that lies exactly in the middle.
7. **Option (D) is correct.**
   Explanation: The new alphabet-series is:
   Z Y X W V U T S R Q P O N M L K J I H G F E D C B A
   Clearly, the fourteenth letter to the right of W is I.
8. **Option (B) is correct.**
   Explanation: The new alphabet-series is:
   Z Y X W V U T S R Q P O N M L K J I H G F E D C B A
   The fourth letter from the right is D. The third letter to the left of D is G.
9. **Option (A) is correct.**
   Explanation: The new alphabet series is identical to that in Question 8. In the series of letters above, it is obvious that N is the thirteenth letter from the left and J is the fourth letter to the right of N.
10. **Option (C) is correct.**
    Explanation: The following letter series results from reversing just the first 13 letters:
    M L K J I H G F E D C B A N O P Q R S T U V W X Y Z
    The above series clearly has 14 letters between K and R.

11. **Option (B) is correct.**
Explanation: The new alphabet-series is:
M L K J I H G F E D C B A N O P Q R S T U V W X Y Z
The seventh letter from the right is T. The seventh letter to the left of T is A.

12. **Option (C) is correct.**
Explanation: The new alphabet-series is:
A B C D E F G H I J K L M Z Y X W V U T S R Q P O N
The eighth letter from the left is H. The third letter to the right of H is K.

13. **Option (D) is correct.**
Explanation: The new alphabet-series is:
A B C D E F G H I J K L M N O P Z Y X W V U T S R Q
The thirteenth letter from the left is M. The sixth letter to the right of M is X.

14. **Option (A) is correct.**
Explanation: The new alphabet-series is.
B D F H J L N P R T V X Z
The fifth letter from the right is R.

15. **Option (B) is correct.**
Explanation: Writing the given alphabet in reverse order,
We have:
Z Y X W V U T S R Q P O N M L K J I H G F E D C B A
Cancelling every second letter, the new series becomes: Z X V T R P N L J H F D B
There are 13 letters in the above series.
So, the middle letter is the seventh letter, that is N.

16. **Option (B) is correct.**
Explanation: We can see,
Given word = SPLENDOR
New word according to the given condition = ROKFMCPQ
Arrange word = CFKMOPQR
So, 5th letter from the left is 'O'.

17. **Option (A) is correct.**
Explanation: I, H, R, and E are the first, third, fifth, and eleventh letters of INHERITENCE, respectively. As a result, the word produced by these characters are Hire, Heir.

18. **Option (D) is correct.**
Explanation: There is no such pairs of letters.

19. **Option (E) is correct.**
Explanation: There are four such letter pairs: PR, AE, KL and LP.

20. **Option (D) is correct.**
Explanation: D, A, E, and R are the first, third, fifth, and sixth letters in the word. The three words "dear," "dare," and "read" are significant words.

21. **Option (B) is correct.**
Explanation: The letters of the word DUAL are present in the word ADULTHOOD.

22. **Option (C) is correct.**
Explanation: The letters of the word JUNGLE are present in the word JUDGEMENTAL

23. **Option (D) is correct.**
Explanation: The letters of the word HELPER are present in the word LEADERSHIP

24. **Option (C) is correct.**
Explanation: The letters of the word AGENT are present in the word MANAGEMENT.

25. **Option (B) is correct.**
Explanation: The letters of the word AMOUNT are present in the word TOURNAMENT.

26. **Option (C) is correct.**
Explanation: The correct order is : Whiter, Worked, Worst, Wound, Writer

27. **Option (C) is correct.**
Explanation: The correct order is :
Problem, Project, Property, Protein, Proverb

28. **Option (D) is correct.**
Explanation: The correct order is
Each, Eager, Eagle, Early, Earth

29. **Option (A) is correct.**
Explanation: G E N T L E
The pair is NL.

30. **Option (C) is correct.**
Explanation: S T A B L E
The pairs are : ST and AB

31. **Option (C) is correct.**
Explanation: There are three such pairs of letters: st, nt, gi.

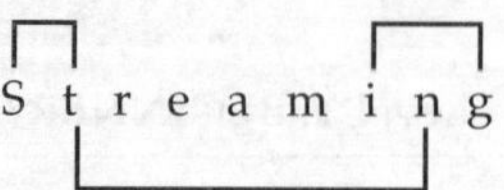

32. **Option (A) is correct.**
Explanation: The First, Fifth, Seventh and Eighth letters of the word 'EMANCIPATE' =E, C, P, A
So, two words PACE and CAPE can be formed.

33. **Option (B) is correct.**
Explanation: 2nd, 4th, 6th and 7th letters of the word 'UNILATERAL' = N, L, T, E
The word formed is LENT
Hence, the second letter from right =N.

34. **Option (D) is correct.**
Explanation: There are four such pairs of letters: OP, PL, OL and UR.

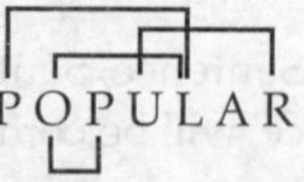

35. **Option (B) is correct.**
Explanation: There are two such pairs of letters– AB and TU.

36. **Option (B) is correct.**
Explanation: Locality, Street, House, Room, Window

37. **Option (C) is correct.**
Explanation: Seed, Plant, Flower, Fruit

38. Option (D) is correct.
Explanation: Infant, Child, Teenager, Adult

39. Option (B) is correct.
Explanation: Dawn, Noon, Twilight, Night

40. Option (A) is correct.
Explanation: World, Asia, India, Delhi, Qutub Minar

Level-2: INTERMEDIATE

1. Option (A) is correct.
Explanation: The correct alphabetical order of the given words is as shown below:
Spinal, Spindle, Spine, Spinet, Spinner
So, the word 'Spine' will come in middle.

2. Option (E) is correct.
Explanation: The correct alphabetical order of the given words is shown below:
Plate, Practical, Practice, Prank, Prayer
So, the word 'Practice' will come in middle.

3. Option (B) is correct.
Explanation: The correct alphabetical order of the given words is shown below:
Hand, Handkerchief, Haphazard, Hash, Host
So, the word 'Haphazard' will come in middle.

4. Option (E) is correct.
Explanation: The correct alphabetical order of the given words is shown below:
Butcher, Butler, Butter, Butterfly, Button
So, the word 'Butter' will come in middle.

5. Option (C) is correct.
Explanation: The correct alphabetical order of the given words is shown below:
Restaurant, Restrict, Retreat, Robot, Rocket
So, the word 'Retreat' will come in middle.

6. Option (C) is correct.
Explanation: We can see the letter series is:

[Q] R S T [U] V W X [Y] Z A B [C] D E F [G] H I J [K]
3 3 3 3 3

7. Option (A) is correct.
Explanation: We can see, according to the letter, series is:

[A] B C D [E] F G H I J K [L] M N O [P] Q R S T U V W X Y [Z]
3 6 3 9

3, 6, 3, 9 are multiples of 3.

8. Option (A) is correct.
Explanation: We can see,
B D E J O L Y has only two vowels = E and O

9. Option (A) is correct.
Explanation: We can see the letter series is,

[T] U V [W] X Y [Z] A B [C] D E [F] G H [I] J K [L]
2 2 2 2 2 2

10. Option (B) is correct.
Explanation: We can see, according to the letter series is:

[O] N [M] L K [J] I H G [F] E D C B [A]
1 2 3 4

11. Option (C) is correct.
Explanation: We can see, according to the letter series is:

Q [R] S T U [V] W X Y Z A B [C] D E F G H I J K [L] M N O P Q R [S] T U V [W]
3 6 8 10

12. Option (A) is correct.
Explanation: We can see the letter series is:

[A] B C [D] E F G H [I] J K L M N O [P] Q R S T U V W X [Y]
2 4 6 8

2, 4, 6, 8 are consecutive even numbers.

13. Option (D) is correct.
Explanation: We can see, according to the letter series is:

[C] D [E] F G [H] I J K [L] M N O P [Q] R S T U V [W]
1 2 3 4 5

14. Option (A) is correct.
Explanation: We can see the letter series is,

[C] D [E] F G H I J K L [M] N O P Q R [S]
1 2 3 5

1, 3, 5 are all odd numbers.

15. Option (A) is correct.
Explanation: We can see, according to the letter series is:

[S] R Q [P] O N [M] L K [J] I H [G]
2 2 2 2

16. Option (B) is correct.
Explanation: Letter S is not present in the given word. So, answer option (B) is correct.

17. Option (B) is correct.
Explanation: Since the letter A is absent from the supplied word, SITUATION cannot be created using the letters in the given word.

18. Option (C) is correct.
Explanation: Letters O and C are not present in the given word. So, word 'Doctor' cannot be formed by using alphabets of given word.

19. Option (D) is correct.
Explanation: We have:

A K G L [M N D] Q K G C S N G K T G K [M N D] Z P U X G K E

As shown above, there are two such groups.

20. Option (C) is correct.
Explanation: The word 'Bland' cannot be constructed because there is no "L" in word as 'ABANDONED'.

21. Option (D) is correct.
Explanation: Here "PLATE" can be created.

22. Option (A) is correct.
Explanation: We can see,
The specified word is FIGURES.
Word rearranged: EIUFGRS
So, between U and R, there are two letters (F and G).

23. Option (C) is correct.
Explanation: The order in which the terms are listed, according to the dictionary:
Flinchers → Flinching → Flinpites → Flintlock → Flintlocks
So, the correct sequence is 51324.

24. Option (B) is correct.

Explanation: The order in which the terms are listed, according to the dictionary

Harmony → Home → Honour → Horse → House

So, the correct sequence is 21453.

25. Option (C) is correct.

Explanation: We can see,

S U R F A C E

A C E F R S U

So, only one letter will remain at the same position.

26. Option (B) is correct.

Explanation: The meaningful word formed is PROMISE.

27. Option (C) is correct.

Explanation: The meaningful word formed is ENSURE.

28. Option (A) is correct.

Explanation: The meaningful word formed is ILLUSION.

29. Option (D) is correct.

Explanation: The meaningful word formed is DEMAND.

30. Option (A) is correct.

Explanation: The meaningful word formed is PROPOSAL.

31. Option (E) is correct.

Explanation: B is exactly between F and D. So, tenth to the right of letter B is letter X.

32. Option (B) is correct.

Explanation: As per the given arrangement

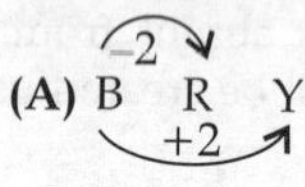

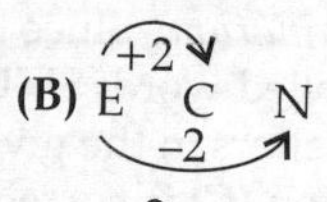

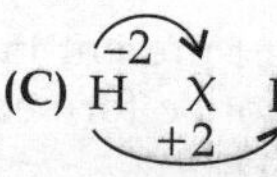

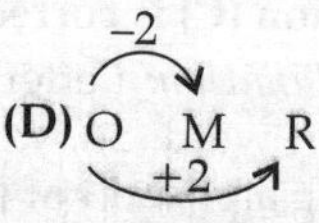

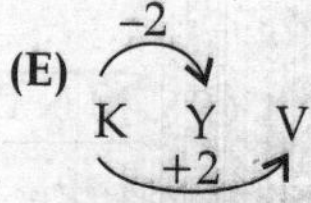

33. Option (B) is correct.

Explanation: The position of the corresponding letters are placed from the starting and from the end respectively.

34. Option (D) is correct.

Explanation: M $\xrightarrow{+2}$ O

35. Option (E) is correct.

Explanation: Sum of positions of all the vowels (O, E, A, U, I) = 5 + 10 + 14 + 20 + 23 = 72

36. Option (B) is correct.

Explanation: Toy, Cycle, Bike, Car, Truck

37. Option (A) is correct.

Explanation: Farmer, Seed, Cultivation, Food

38. Option (D) is correct.

Explanation: Head, Nose, Neck, Waist, Legs

39. Option (C) is correct.

Explanation: Seeds, Plant, Tree, Wood, Furniture

40. Option (C) is correct.

Explanation: Study, Interview, Job, Income

Level-3: EXPERT

1. Option (D) is correct.

Explanation: E is not present in the given word, so the word MASTER cannot be formed.

2. Option (A) is correct.

Explanation: The letter N only appears once in the provided word. So, the word NATION cannot be created using the letters of given word.

3. Option (B) is correct.

Explanation: E is absent from the supplied word. Therefore, TALENT cannot be created using the letters in the provided word.

4. Option (C) is correct.

Explanation: The letters M, S, I, and T are the second, fifth, seventh, and tenth letters of the word "OMNISCIENT," respectively. MIST, a word whose third letter is S, is the result.

5. Option (E) is correct.

Explanation: The letters E, T, and M are the second, fifth, and eighth letters of the word "NEPOTISM," respectively. The resultant term is MET.

6. Option (C) is correct.

Explanation: The letters provided by the word "DEMOCRACY" can be combined to generate the word "MARCY."

7. Option (D) is correct.

Explanation: The letters are P, T, A, and E, respectively, make up the first, fifth, seventh, and ninth letters of the word PUNCTUATE. The three words that result are PATE, PEAT, and TAPE.

8. Option (D) is correct.

Explanation: The word's fourth, fifth, seventh, and eleventh letters are, in order, D, I, T, and E. DIET, TIDE, TIED, and EDIT are four possible words. So, option D is correct.

9. Option (C) is correct.

Explanation: Third, fourth, fifth, seventh and tenth letters of the word PERSONALITY are R, S, O, A and T, respectively. The word formed is ROAST. So, the first letter is R.

10. Option (D) is correct.

Explanation: D, U and S, respectively, are the fourth, eighth, and ninth letters of the word CREDULOUS. No such word is formed.

11. Option (A) is correct.

Explanation: It is impossible to compose the word "RELATION" without the letter L.

12. Option (D) is correct.

Explanation: The letters C, O, T, R, and A are the first, second, fourth, fifth, and sixth letters of the word CONTRACT, respectively. The result is ACTOR, a word whose middle letter is T.

13. Option (E) is correct.

Explanation: The 1st, 3rd, 7th and 13th letters of the word PROPORTIONATE are P, O, T and E, respectively. So, the words POET and TOPE are produced.

14. Option (B) is correct.

Explanation: The letters T, E, T and N, respectively, make up the second, fourth, sixth and ninth letters of the word "ATTENTION." "TENT' is the result, and the third letter is N.

15. Option (C) is correct.

Explanation: The letters O, E, T, and N are the third, fifth, seventh, and tenth letters in the word PROJECTION. NOTE and TONE are created as a result.

16. Option (A) is correct.

Explanation:

A B B C D E F E I B C A F [E C B] B A C A O B N U V W

Only one pair exists.

17. Option (D) is correct.

Explanation: The new arrangement is:

B B C D F B C (F) C B B C B N V W

So, eighth alphabet from the left and is F.

18. Option (D) is correct.

Explanation:

A B B C [D E] [F E] I B [C A] [F E] C B [B A] [C A] O B [N U] V W

So, seven such pairs exist.

19. Option (B) is correct.

Explanation: E C B B A C A O B N U V W A B B C D E F E I B C A F

So, 10th alphabet from the right end is C and 7th to the right of C is C.

20. Option (B) is correct.

Explanation: Total number of vowels in the given arrangement = 10

21. Option (C) is correct.

Explanation: The 2nd, 5th, 8th and 9th letters of the given word TRANSLATION are: R, S, T and I. So, the word formed is STIR.

So, second letter from the left end is T.

22. Option (A) is correct.

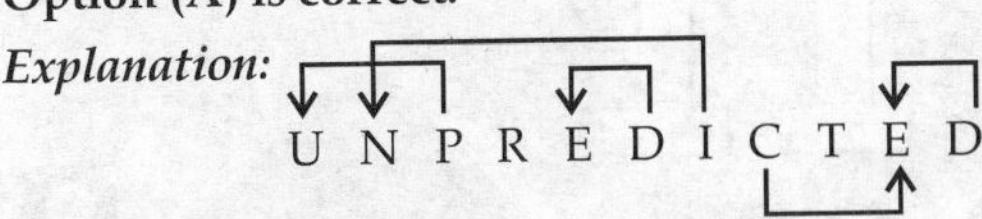

So, the pairs are DE and IG

23. Option (A) is correct.

Explanation:

U N P R E D I C T E D

The pairs are CE, ED, NI and RU

24. Option (D) is correct.

Explanation:

P R E F E R E N T I A L

The pairs are EF, EL, FE, RL, EA

25. Option (A) is correct.

Explanation: A N T I B I O T I C

So, the pairs are AI, NT

26. Option (C) is correct.

Explanation: Envelope, Letter, Postbox, Delivery, Clearance.

27. Option (C) is correct.

Explanation: Birth, Education, Marriage, Death, Funeral.

28. Option (B) is correct.

Explanation: Clerk, Collector, Chief Secretary, Governor, President.

29. Option (B) is correct.

Explanation: Daily, Weekly, Fortnightly, Monthly, Bimonthly.

30. Option (C) is correct.

Explanation: Day, Work, Tired, Night, Sleep

■ ■ ■

Alpha-Numeric Sequence Test and Number Test

LEARNING OBJECTIVES:

- Method of evaluating the questions based on Alpha-Numeric Sequence Test
- Method of evaluating the questions based on Number Test
- Different types of question asked in competitive exams

ALPHA-NUMERIC SEQUENCE TEST

This section is completely based on the positioning of letters/ numbers or symbols in a sequence. A sequence consisting of some jumbled letters/ numbers or symbols will be given to us. Students need to find the required letters/ numbers or symbols as per the requirement of the question. We need to be careful while determining the positions of letters/ numbers or symbols either from left or right side.

NOTE: If the positions from left/right side are not mentioned, students need to consider it from their left/ right side correspondingly.

Example 1: Study the following arrangement carefully and answer the following questions:

9 R £ 4 G § Q 6 & @ 5 H % E 7 # J

(i) How many symbols are there in the given arrangement each of which is immediately preceded by an even number?

(a) None (b) One
(c) Two (d) Three

Sol. (a) The given sequence is:
9 R £ 4 G § Q 6 & @ 5 H % E 7 # J
So, there is only one symbol which is immediately preceded by an even number.

(ii) Which of the following is third to the left of second element from the right end?

(a) £ (b) R
(c) @ (d) %

Sol. (d) The second element from the right end is # and third to the left of # is %.

NUMBER TEST

This section is completely based on the positioning of numbers in a sequence. A sequence consisting of some jumbled numbers will be given to us. Students need to find the required numbers as per the requirement of the question. We need to be careful while determining the positions of numbers either from left or right side.

Example 2: How many such 7s are there in the given sequence each of which is immediately preceded by 3 and immediately followed by 9?

8 5 8 5 9 2 3 7 9 4 6 1 8 2 4 3 7 9 6 4 8 5 7 2

(a) One (b) Two
(c) Three (d) Four

Sol. (b) The given sequence is:
8 5 8 5 9 2 3 7 9 4 6 1 8 2 4 3 7 9 6 4 8 5 7 2
So, there are two 7s each of which is immediately preceded by 3 and immediately followed by

Example 3: If the position of the first, third digits of the number 254789 are interchanged, similarly the positions of the second and fifth digits are interchanged and so on, which of the following will be the second digit from the left end?

(a) 9 (b) 4
(c) 8 (d) 7

Sol. (c) The new number is: 789254
Hence, the second digit from the left end is 8.

Level 1 Beginner

Directions (Qs. 1–5): Study the following information carefully and answer the questions given beside:

3 1 2 8 2 5 5 9 5 6 4 9 1 9 2 5 1 4 6 4 5 3 2 6 4 7 5 5 9 3 1 5 8 2 6

1. How many odd digits are there in the above arrangement which is immediately preceded by 2?

(A) None (B) One
(C) Two (D) Three

2. If all the even digits are deleted from the above arrangement, then which of the following will be 4th from the left end of the arrangement?
(A) 5 (B) 7
(C) 6 (D) 8

3. If all the numbers in the above arrangement are written in reverse order, then ________ is third from the right end?
(A) 8 (B) 4
(C) 1 (D) 2

4. Which of the following is 5th to the left of 9th element from the right end?
(A) 3 (B) 0
(C) 8 (D) 7

5. How many prime digits are there after the element which is 6th from the right end?
(A) 6 (B) 4
(C) 2 (D) 5

Directions (Qs. 6–10): Study the following arrangement carefully to answer these questions.

R E 5 D A P $ 3 T 1 Q 7 9 B # 2 K % U 1 M W 4 * J 8 N

[Asst. Manager 2005]

6. Which of the following is exactly in the middle between 3 and 1 in the above arrangement?
(A) B (B) K
(C) 9 (D) #
(E) None of these

7. How many such numbers are there in the above arrangement, each of which is immediately preceded by a consonant and not immediately followed by a consonant?
(A) None (B) One
(C) Two (D) Three
(E) None of these

8. How many such vowels are there in the above arrangement, each of which is immediately followed by a number and but not immediately preceded by a consonant?
(A) None (B) One
(C) Two (D) Three
(E) Four

9. Which of the following is seventh to the left of the sixteenth from the left in the above arrangement?
(A) A (B) U
(C) 4 (D) T
(E) None of these

10. Four of the following five are alike in a certain way based on their position in the above arrangement and so form a group. Which is the one that does not belong to that group?
(A) B K 7 (B) M * U
(C) D P E (D) W J 1
(E) 3 Q P

Directions (Qs. 11–15): Following questions are based on the five three-digit numbers given below:

155 364 456 857 915

11. If 2 is added to the middle digit of each of the number then ________ will be the greatest number.
(A) 456 (B) 155
(C) 857 (D) 915

12. If in each number the first and the second digits are interchanged then which will be the second highest number?
(A) 587 (B) 458
(C) 634 (D) 515

13. If all the digits in each of the numbers are arranged in ascending order, then which of the following will be the in middle in new arrangement?
(A) 155 (B) 456
(C) 857 (D) 915

14. What will be the resultant number if the second lowest number is divided by the 2?
(A) 182 (B) 154
(C) 848 (D) 456

15. If 3 is added to the middle digit of each of the numbers then which of the following numbers will be the lowest number?
(A) 915 (B) 857
(C) 364 (D) 155

Directions (Qs. 16–20): Study the following arrangement carefully and answer the questions given below.

@ E K & Y R © C A M R U L $ V Q # P % S 1 W * O T ϕ G

[SBI Clerk 2021]

16. If all consonants are replaced its next letter, then how many alphabets are repeated in the new arrangement?
(A) Four (B) One
(C) Three (D) Two
(E) None

17. How many such symbols are there in the above arrangement each of which is immediately preceded by a consonant but not immediately followed by a Vowel?
(A) None (B) Four
(C) Two (D) Three
(E) More than Four

18. Four of the following five are alike in a certain way based on their position in the above arrangement and so form a group. Which is the one that does not belong to that group?
(A) ER& (B) CUM
(C) L#V (D) PW%
(E) SOW

19. How many such alphabets are there in the above arrangement each of which is immediately preceded and immediately followed by a symbol?
(A) None (B) One
(C) Two (D) Three
(E) More than three

20. Which of the following element is 10th to the right of the element which is 18th from the right end?
(A) # (B) P
(C) % (D) S
(E) None of these

Directions (Qs. 21–25): Study the following arrangement carefully and answer the questions given below:

B 5 R I @ E K 4 F 7 © D A M 2 P 3 % 9 H I W 8 * 6 U J $ V Q #

[SBI 2018]

21. Which of the following is the fifth to the left of the seventeenth from the left end of the above arrangement?

(A) D (B) W
(C) * (D) 4
(E) None of these

22. Which of the following is exactly in the middle between D and U in the above arrangement?

(A) % (B) H
(C) 9 (D) 3
(E) None of these

23. Four of the following five are alike in a certain way based on their position in the above arrangement and so form a group. Which is the one that does not belong to that group?

(A) R1E (B) F7D
(C) M23 (D) 9HW
(E) UJ6

24. How many such symbols are there in the above arrangement each of which is immediately preceded by a number but not immediately followed by a consonant?

(A) None (B) One
(C) Two (D) Three
(E) More than three

25. Which of the following is the tenth to the left end of the thirteenth from the right end?

(A) F (B) M
(C) @ (D) %
(E) None of these

Directions (Qs. 26–30): Study the following arrangement carefully and answer the questions given below:

Z ¤ U ¥ T ¢ I § O 7 D 5 H 8 M > C @ Q # Y £
X H L & K * S % T

26. How many symbols are there in the given arrangement?

(A) 12 (B) 10
(C) 7 (D) 8

27. Which of the following element is fifth from the right end?

(A) U (B) K
(C) T (D) #

28. If all the symbols are dropped from the above arrangement, then how many numbers will be there?

(A) 4 (B) 5
(C) 3 (D) 2

29. If the above arrangement is written in reverse order, then ______ is eighth element from the left end (D)

(A) 7 (B) L
(C) U (D) ?

30. How many vowels are there in the above arrangement?

(A) 2 (B) 3
(C) 1 (D) 4

Directions (Qs. 31–35): Study the following arrangement carefully and answer the questions given below:

1 5 8 7 2 5 6 2 4 9 8 1 2 3 6 7 9 4 8 2 0 1 5 8

31. How many prime digits are there in the above arrangement?

(A) 3 (B) 4
(C) 5 (D) More than 5

32. How many odd digits are there each of which is immediately preceded by 1?

(A) 1 (B) 2
(C) 4 (D) 5

33. How many such 1 s are there which are immediately followed by an even digit?

(A) 1 (B) 5
(C) 4 (D) 2

34. Which of the following digit is ninth from the right end in the above arrangement?

(A) 9 (B) 8
(C) 5 (D) 7

35. The digit which is 3rd to the right of 5th digit from the left end is

(A) 2 (B) 8
(C) 9 (D) 5

36. In the numbers from 100 to 1000, how many times digit 1 comes at the tens place? **[RRB 2003]**

(A) 9 (B) 10
(C) 90 (D) 900

37. How many combinations of two-digit numbers having 8 can be made from the following numbers?

8, 5, 2, 1, 7, 6

[SSC 2001]

(A) 9 (B) 10
(C) 11 (D) 12

38. If each of the odd digits in the number 54638 is decreased by 1 and each of the even digits is increased by 1, then which of the following will be the sum of the digits of the new number? **[Bank Clerical 2005]**

(A) 25 (B) 26
(C) 28 (D) 29
(E) None of these

39. How many 7s immediately preceded by 6 but not immediately followed by 4 are there in the following series?

7 4 2 7 6 4 3 6 7 5 3 5 7 8 4 3 7 6 7 2 4 0 6 7 4 3

[MBA 2005]

(A) One (B) Two
(C) Four (D) Six

40. How many 9's are followed by and preceded by numbers divisible by 2?

8965359683496526973729413794173498453976153195742968532957489451 **[SSC CGL 2012]**

(A) 12 (B) 6
(C) 8 (D) 10

2 Level Intermediate

Directions (Qs. 1–5): Study the following sequence and answer the given questions.

A @ 3 % 4 E N M $ 8 & 6 L D S ♠ 9 8 6 Q Y Z 1 7 % R O G ♦ 2 I B 2 U & **[RRB Clerk 2019]**

1. Which of the following element is twelfth to the left of the twentieth element from the left end of the given arrangement?
   (A) 6 (B) &
   (C) M (D) $
   (E) None of these
2. If all the symbols are dropped from the series, which element will be fourth to the right of the one which is twelfth from the right end?
   (A) 9 (B) O
   (C) R (D) 7
   (E) None of these
3. How many such numbers are there in the given series which are immediately preceded by a symbol and followed by a letter?
   (A) None (B) One
   (C) Two (D) Three
   (E) Four
4. Four of the following five are alike in a certain way and forms a group. Find the one that does not belongs to that group?
   (A) 3E% (B) R♦2
   (C) M&$ (D) D9S
   (E) Y7Z
5. What should come in place of question mark (?) in the following series based on the above arrangement?
   34% N$M 6DL 8Q6 ?
   (A) %OR (B) 7Z%
   (C) O%R (D) R%O0
   (E) R%7

Directions (Qs. 6–10): Study the following sequence and answer the given questions.

A 7 % J 8 I 6 P R £ T 5 J ¥ 2 S 6 M © 4 L 0 £ X 8 Z 2

6. Which of the following element is third from the left end of the given arrangement?
   (A) % (B) P
   (C) £ (D) 8
7. How many such symbols are there in the arrangement, each of which is immediately followed by a vowel but not immediately preceded by a consonant?
   (A) None (B) One
   (C) Two (D) Three
8. How many such symbols are there in the given arrangement each of which is immediately preceded by a digit but not immediately followed by a vowel?
   (A) None (B) One
   (C) Two (D) Three
9. If we reverse all the elements in the given arrangement, then which of the following element is 5th from the right end?
   (A) 0 (B) J
   (C) £ (D) 8
10. If all the consonants are deleted from the above arrangement, then how many elements will be left in the arrangement?
    (A) 12 (B) 18
    (C) 17 (D) None of these

Directions (Qs. 11–15): These questions are based on the following arrangement. Study it carefully and answer the questions below it.

1 3 5 3 4 5 9 2 8 7 2 3 6 5 2 7 3 8 1 2 1 8 4 9 8 1 2 4 7 3 5 2 4 8 9 8 2 4

[IBPS Clerk 2018]

11. Which element is exactly midway between the seventh element from the left end and sixteenth from the right end?
    (A) 8 (B) 2
    (C) 5 (D) 6
    (E) 7
12. How many perfect squares are there to the right of the fourteenth element from the right end?
    (A) Two (B) One
    (C) Three (D) Four
    (E) more than four
13. How many perfect cubes are there in the above arrangement, each of which is immediately preceded by an odd number and immediately followed by an even number?
    (A) None (B) Three
    (C) Two (D) One
    (E) More than three
14. How many such odd digits are there in the given arrangement, each of which is immediately followed and preceded by an odd number?
    (A) None (B) One
    (C) Two (D) Three
    (E) More than three
15. Which of the following element is 5th to the right of 10th from the right end?
    (A) 9 (B) 8
    (C) 2 (D) 1
    (E) 4

Directions (Qs. 16–20): These questions are based on the following arrangement. Study them carefully and answer the questions that follow:

T 6 # I J 1 % L E 3 K 9 @ A H 7 B © D Z U $ R 4 ☆ 8

[SBI Clerk 2009]

16. Four of the following five are alike in a certain way on the basis of their position in the above arrangement and so form a group. Which is the one that does not belong to the group?
    (A) JI1 (B) EL3
    (C) @9A (D) 7HB
    (E) R4$

17. What will come in place of the question mark (?) in the following series based on the above arrangement?

61J %E3 9AH ?

(A) B©2 **(B)** 7©D
(C) 7BD **(D)** BD2
(E) None of these

18. If all the vowels are removed from the above arrangement, which element will be sixth to the right of fourth element from the left?

(A) 9 **(B)** K
(C) 3 **(D)** @
(C) None of these

19. How many such symbols are there in the above arrangement, each of which is immediately preceded by a number?

(A) None **(B)** One
(C) Two **(D)** Three
(E) More than three

20. Which element is fifth to the right of eleventh from the right end?

(A) $ **(B)** U
(C) 1 **(D)** 3
(E) None of these

Directions (Qs. 21–25): Study the following number sequence and answer the questions following it.

9 3 2 4 5 7 9 5 8 1 5 0 6 4 2 9 8 2 6 3 5 9 8 2 1 5 4 3 2 1

[IBPS Clerk 2017]

21. How many odd numbers are there in the numeric series which are immediately preceded by a number, which is a whole square?

(A) One **(B)** Two
(C) Three **(D)** More than three
(E) None of these

22. If all the odd numbers are dropped from the series, which number will be eighth to the left of eleventh number from the left end?

(A) 2 **(B)** 8
(C) 6 **(D)** 4
(E) None of these

23. If 1 is subtracted from all odd numbers and 2 is subtracted from all even numbers in the given number series, then which number will be sixteenth from the right end?

(A) 0 **(B)** 2
(C) 3 **(D)** 8
(E) 6

24. If the position of the 1st and the 16th numbers, the 2nd and the 17th numbers, and so on up to the 15th and the 30th numbers, are interchanged, which number will be 7th to the right of 19th number from the right end?

(A) 5 **(B)** 9
(C) 8 **(D)** 4
(E) None of these

25. How many total even numbers which is immediately preceded by a 'whole cube' or 'immediately preceded by a whole square' in the above sequence?

(A) Four **(B)** Five
(C) Three **(D)** Six
(E) None of these

Directions (Qs. 26–28): Answer these questions are based on the set of numbers given below:

738 429 156 273 894

[RBI 2004]

26. Which of the following will be the last digit of the second highest number after the positions of the digits in each number is reversed?

(A) 1 **(B)** 2
(C) 4 **(D)** 7
(E) 8

27. What will be the difference between the first digit of the highest number as well of the lowest number after the positions of the first two digits in each number is reversed?

(A) 4 **(B)** 5
(C) 6 **(D)** 7
(E) None of these

28. Which of the following will be the second digit of the third number from the top when they are arranged in descending order, after the first digit in each number is changed to the next higher digit?

(A) 2 **(B)** 3
(C) 5 **(D)** 7
(E) 9

Directions (Qs. 29–30): Study the given arrangement carefully and answer the following questions:

R @ T $ 8 % Y U 7 * P 9 Q > 4 D $ 5 U £ 2 × 0 ¤ N 7 O 9

29. If all the vowels are dropped from the above arrangement then which of the following element will be second to the left of eighth element from the right end?

(A) > **(B)** $
(C) ¤ **(D)** 8

30. If all the alphabets are arranged in alphabetical order on the places of alphabets only, then which of the following is 11th from the left end in the given arrangement?

(A) U **(B)** 4
(C) Q **(C)** %

Directions (Qs. 31–35): The following questions are based on the five three digit numbers given below:

684 512 437 385 296

[SBI 2016]

31. If 2 is added to the first digit of each of the numbers how many numbers thus formed will be divisible by three?

(A) Four **(B)** One
(C) Two **(D)** Three
(E) None of these

32. If all the digits in each of the numbers are arranged in descending order within the number, which of the following will be the highest number in the new arrangement of numbers

(A) 684 **(B)** 385
(C) 296 **(D)** 437
(E) None of these

33. What will be the resultant number if the second digit of the second lowest number is divided by the third digit of the highest number?
(A) 2 (B) 3
(C) 0 (D) 1
(E) 4

34. If 1 is added to the first digit and 2 is added to the last digit of each of the numbers then which of the following numbers will be the second highest number?
(A) 385 (B) 684
(C) 437 (D) 296
(E) 512

35. If in each number the first and the second digits are interchanged then which will be the highest number?
(A) 296 (B) 512
(C) 437 (D) 684
(E) 385

Level 3 Expert

Directions (Qs. 1–5): Study the following arrangement carefully to answer these questions.

M 1 E $ R B 3 A K 7 £ # 9 $ U D I N 4 6 % F H 2 @ 8 W

[MBA 2002]

1. How many such consonants are there in the above sequence each of which is immediately followed by a number and immediately preceded by vowel?
(A) Nil (B) One
(C) Two (D) Three
(E) Four

2. Four of the following five are alike in a certain way and so form a group, based on the above arrangement. Which is the one that does not belong to that group?
(A) %HN (B) 14$
(C) 9D£ (D) 3K$
(E) $BM

3. How many such vowels are there in the above arrangement, each of which is immediately preceded by a symbol and immediately followed by a consonant?
(A) Nil (B) One
(C) Two (D) Three
(E) None of these

4. If the order of the first fifteen elements in the above arrangement is reversed then which of the following will be the eighth to the left of twelfth letter/number/symbol from the right end?
(A) A (B) £
(C) 3 (D) K
(E) None of these

5. What should come in the place of question mark in the following series based on the above arrangement?
EBM A£B 9D£ ? H8%
(A) N%D (B) NFD
(C) 4FD (D) 16D
(E) None of these

Directions (Qs. 6–10): In each of the following questions two rows of numbers are given. The resultant number in each row is to be worked out separately based on the following rules and the question below the rows of numbers are to be answered. The operations of numbers progress from left to right.

Rules:

(i) If an odd number is followed by a two digit even number then they are to be added.

(ii) If an odd number is followed by a two digit odd number then the second number is to be subtracted from the first number.

(iii) If an even number is followed by a number which is a perfect square of a number then the second number is to be divided by the first number.

(iv) If an even number is followed by a two-digit even number then the first number is to be multiplied by the second number.

6. 13 11 4
17 13 12
If the resultant of the first set of numbers is multiplied by the resultant of the second set of numbers, what will be the outcome?
(A) 48 (B) 69
(C) 75 (D) 96
(E) None of these

7. 40 30 3600
15 24 17
What will be the sum of the two resultant numbers of the sets of numbers given above*
(A) 22 (B) 25
(C) 28 (D) 42
(E) None of these

8. 15 11 20 400
8 12 10
If the resultant of the second set of numbers is divided from the resultant of the first set of numbers, what will be the outcome?
(A) 19 (B) 92
(C) 196 (D) 200
(E) None of these

9. 19 15 12
15 12 23 16
If the resultant of the second set of numbers is subtracted from the resultant of the first set of numbers, what will be the outcome?
(A) 29 (B) 43
(C) 44 (D) 92
(E) None of these

10. 8 16 16 14
13 11 12 144
What is the difference between the resultant of the first set of numbers and the second set of numbers?
(A) 106 (B) 118
(C) 210 (D) 222
(E) None of these

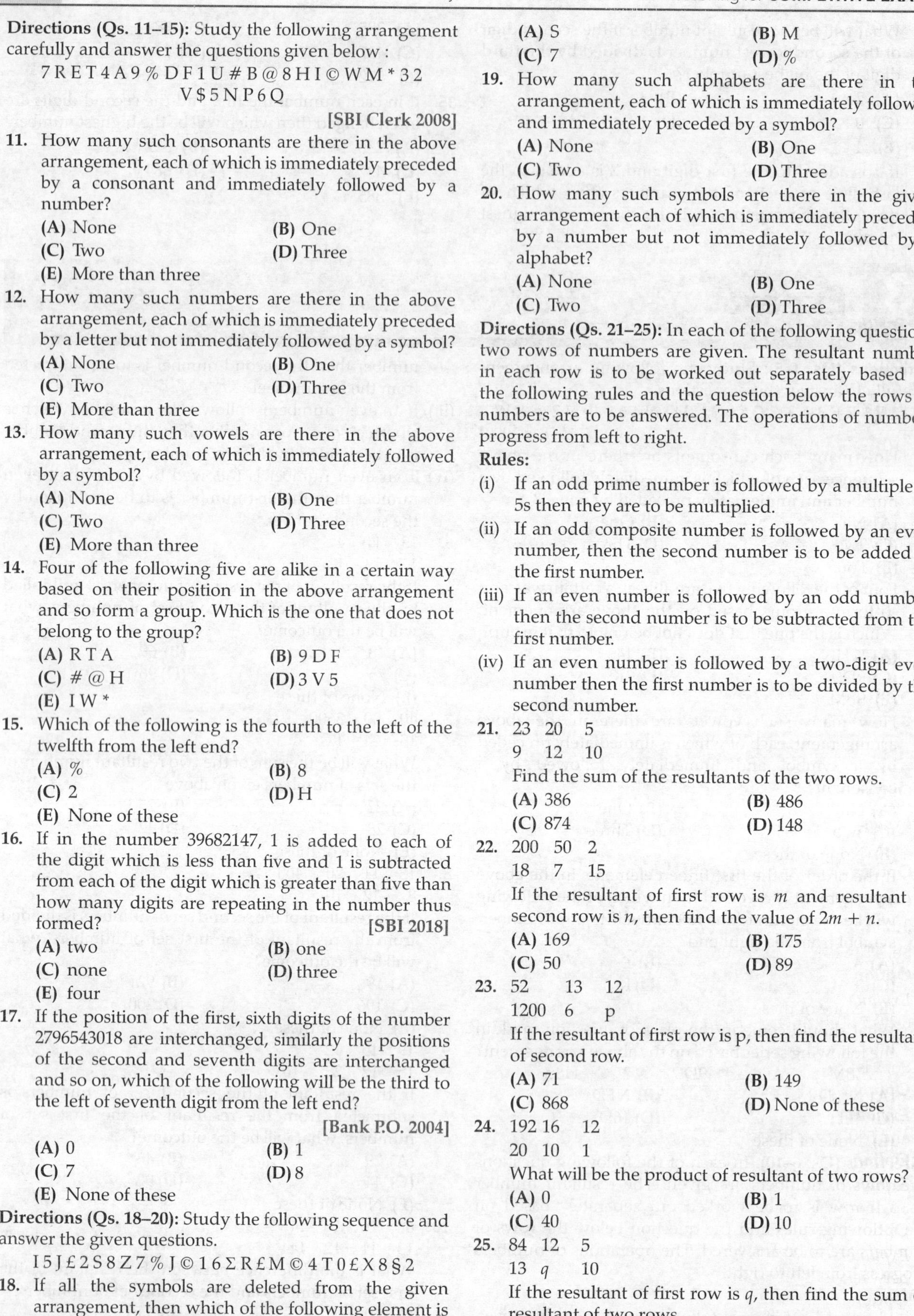

Directions (Qs. 11–15): Study the following arrangement carefully and answer the questions given below :

7 R E T 4 A 9 % D F 1 U # B @ 8 H I © W M * 3 2 V $ 5 N P 6 Q

[SBI Clerk 2008]

11. How many such consonants are there in the above arrangement, each of which is immediately preceded by a consonant and immediately followed by a number?

(A) None (B) One
(C) Two (D) Three
(E) More than three

12. How many such numbers are there in the above arrangement, each of which is immediately preceded by a letter but not immediately followed by a symbol?

(A) None (B) One
(C) Two (D) Three
(E) More than three

13. How many such vowels are there in the above arrangement, each of which is immediately followed by a symbol?

(A) None (B) One
(C) Two (D) Three
(E) More than three

14. Four of the following five are alike in a certain way based on their position in the above arrangement and so form a group. Which is the one that does not belong to the group?

(A) R T A (B) 9 D F
(C) # @ H (D) 3 V 5
(E) I W *

15. Which of the following is the fourth to the left of the twelfth from the left end?

(A) % (B) 8
(C) 2 (D) H
(E) None of these

16. If in the number 39682147, 1 is added to each of the digit which is less than five and 1 is subtracted from each of the digit which is greater than five than how many digits are repeating in the number thus formed? **[SBI 2018]**

(A) two (B) one
(C) none (D) three
(E) four

17. If the position of the first, sixth digits of the number 2796543018 are interchanged, similarly the positions of the second and seventh digits are interchanged and so on, which of the following will be the third to the left of seventh digit from the left end? **[Bank P.O. 2004]**

(A) 0 (B) 1
(C) 7 (D) 8
(E) None of these

Directions (Qs. 18–20): Study the following sequence and answer the given questions.

I 5 J £ 2 S 8 Z 7 % J © 1 6 Σ R £ M © 4 T 0 £ X 8 § 2

18. If all the symbols are deleted from the given arrangement, then which of the following element is seventh to the left of eighth element from the right end?

(A) S (B) M
(C) 7 (D) %

19. How many such alphabets are there in the arrangement, each of which is immediately followed and immediately preceded by a symbol?

(A) None (B) One
(C) Two (D) Three

20. How many such symbols are there in the given arrangement each of which is immediately preceded by a number but not immediately followed by a alphabet?

(A) None (B) One
(C) Two (D) Three

Directions (Qs. 21–25): In each of the following questions two rows of numbers are given. The resultant number in each row is to be worked out separately based on the following rules and the question below the rows of numbers are to be answered. The operations of numbers progress from left to right.

Rules:

(i) If an odd prime number is followed by a multiple of 5s then they are to be multiplied.

(ii) If an odd composite number is followed by an even number, then the second number is to be added to the first number.

(iii) If an even number is followed by an odd number, then the second number is to be subtracted from the first number.

(iv) If an even number is followed by a two-digit even number then the first number is to be divided by the second number.

21. 23 20 5
9 12 10

Find the sum of the resultants of the two rows.

(A) 386 (B) 486
(C) 874 (D) 148

22. 200 50 2
18 7 15

If the resultant of first row is m and resultant of second row is n, then find the value of $2m + n$.

(A) 169 (B) 175
(C) 50 (D) 89

23. 52 13 12
1200 6 p

If the resultant of first row is p, then find the resultant of second row.

(A) 71 (B) 149
(C) 868 (D) None of these

24. 192 16 12
20 10 1

What will be the product of resultant of two rows?

(A) 0 (B) 1
(C) 40 (D) 10

25. 84 12 5
13 q 10

If the resultant of first row is q, then find the sum of resultant of two rows.

(A) 150 (B) 480
(C) 900 (D) 500

ANSWER KEY

Level-1: Beginner

1.	(C)	2.	(A)	3.	(D)	4.	(A)	5.	(C)	6.	(E)	7.	(C)	8.	(B)	9.	(D)	10.	(C)
11.	(D)	12.	(A)	13.	(B)	14.	(A)	15.	(D)	16.	(B)	17.	(E)	18.	(D)	19.	(B)	20.	(D)
21.	(A)	22.	(C)	23.	(E)	24.	(D)	25.	(E)	26.	(A)	27.	(B)	28.	(C)	29.	(D)	30.	(A)
31.	(D)	32.	(B)	33.	(A)	34.	(D)	35.	(A)	36.	(C)	37.	(C)	38.	(E)	39.	(B)	40.	(B)

Level-2: Intermediate

1.	(C)	2.	(C)	3.	(D)	4.	(B)	5.	(A)	6.	(A)	7.	(A)	8.	(C)	9.	(D)	10.	(C)
11.	(B)	12.	(E)	13.	(C)	14.	(C)	15.	(B)	16.	(E)	17.	(B)	18.	(A)	19.	(E)	20.	(D)
21.	(D)	22.	(B)	23.	(A)	24.	(D)	25.	(E)	26.	(D)	27.	(D)	28.	(A)	29.	(B)	30.	(C)
31.	(B)	32.	(E)	33.	(A)	34.	(E)	35.	(A)										

Level-3: Expert

1.	(C)	2.	(C)	3.	(B)	4.	(A)	5.	(A)	6.	(D)	7.	(B)	8.	(E)	9.	(C)	10.	(A)
11.	(C)	12.	(D)	13.	(C)	14.	(B)	15.	(A)	16.	(B)	17.	(B)	18.	(A)	19.	(C)	20.	(A)
21.	(B)	22.	(A)	23.	(B)	24.	(B)	25.	(D)										

Solutions with Detailed Explanations

Level-1: BEGINNER

1. **Option (C) is correct.**
   Explanation: 3 1 2 8 $\boxed{25}$ 5 9 5 6 4 9 1 9 $\boxed{25}$ 1 4 6 4 5 3 2 6 4 7 5 5 9 3 1 5 8 2 6
2. **Option (A) is correct.**
   Explanation: The new arrangement is
   3 1 5 $\boxed{5}$ 9 5 9 1 9 5 1 5 3 7 5 5 9 3 1 5
   So, 4th from the left end is 5.
3. **Option (D) is correct.**
   Explanation: The new arrangement is :
   6 2 8 5 1 3 9 5 5 7 4 6 2 3 5 4 6 4 1 5 2 9 1 9 4 6 5 9 5 5 2 8 2 1 3
   So, 2 is third from the right end.
4. **Option (A) is correct.**
   Explanation: Here, 9th element from the right end is 5 and 5th to the left of 5 is 3.
5. **Option (C) is correct.**
   Explanation: Here, 6th from the right end is 3
   So, there are prime digits after 3 i.e. 5 and 2
6. **Option (E) is correct.**
   Explanation: The letter T is exactly in the middle between 3 and 1.
7. **Option (C) is correct.**
   Explanation: R E 5 D A P $ 3 T I $\boxed{Q\ 7\ 9}$ B # 2 K % U I M $\boxed{W\ 4\ A}$ J 8 N
8. **Option (B) is correct.**
   Explanation: R E S D A P $ 3 T I Q 7 9 B # 2 K $\boxed{\%\ U\ 1}$ M W 4 * J 8 N
9. **Option (D) is correct.**
   Explanation: 2 is sixteenth from the left end and then T is the seventh to the left of 2.
10. **Option (C) is correct.**
    Explanation: Except option (C), every other options have 2nd and 3rd terms like 3 right and 2nd left from first term.
11. **Option (D) is correct.**
    Explanation: The new numbers are,
    175 384 476 877 935
    So, the greatest number is 935 which comes from 915
12. **Option (A) is correct.**
    Explanation: The new numbers are,
    515 634 546 587 195
    So, second highest number is 587.
13. **Option (B) is correct.**
    Explanation: The ascending order is :
    155 364 456 857 915
    So, 456 comes in middle.
14. **Option (A) is correct.**
    Explanation: The second lowest number is 364.
    So, resulting number = 364 ÷ 2 = 182

15. **Option (D) is correct.**
Explanation: The new numbers are :
185 394 486 887 945
So, lowest number is 185 which comes from 155.

16. **Option (B) is correct.**
Explanation: The new arrangement is :
@ E L & Z S © D A N Ⓡ U M $ W R # Q % T I X A O U ϕ H

17. **Option (E) is correct.**
Explanation: @ E K & Y R © C A M Ⓡ U L $ V Q # P & % S 8 I W * O T ϕ G

18. **Option (D) is correct.**
Explanation: Except option (E), every other options have 2nd and 3rd terms like 4th right and 2nd right from first term.

19. **Option (B) is correct.**
Explanation: @ E K & Y R © C A M R U L $ V Q # P % S 1 W * O T ϕ G

20. **Option (D) is correct.**
Explanation: 18th element from the right end is M and 10th to the right of M is S.

21. **Option (A) is correct.**
Explanation: 17th element from the left end is 3 and 5th to the left of 3 is D.

22. **Option (C) is correct.**
Explanation: 9 is exactly between D and U

23. **Option (E) is correct.**
Explanation: Except option (E), every other options have 2nd and 3rd terms like 1st right and 3rd right from first term.

24. **Option (D) is correct.**
Explanation: B 5 R 1 @ E K 4 7 @ D A M 2 3 % 9 H I W 8 * 6 U J $ V Q #

25. **Option (E) is correct.**
Explanation: 13th element from the right end is 9 and 10th to the left of 9 is 4.

26. **Option (A) is correct.**
Explanation: Number of symbols in the given arrangement = 12

27. **Option (B) is correct.**
Explanation: Fifth from the right end is K.

28. **Option (C) is correct.**
Explanation: The new arrangement is
Z U T I O 7 D 5 H 8 M G Q Y X H L K S T
So, 3 numbers 7, 5 and 8 are there in new arrangement.

29. **Option (D) is correct.**
Explanation: The new arrangement is,
T % S K & L H ? X F y # Q @ C . > M 8 H 5 D 7 O § I C T Y U X Z
So, eight element from the left end is ?.

30. **Option (A) is correct.**
Explanation: Number of vowels = 2

31. **Option (D) is correct.**
Explanation:
1⑤8⑦②⑤6②4 9 8 1 2③6⑦9 4 8②0 1⑤8
Number of prime digits = 9

32. **Option (B) is correct.**
Explanation: 1 5 8 7 2 5 6 2 4 9 8 1 2 3 6 7 9 4 8 2 0 1 5 8

33. **Option (A) is correct.**
Explanation: 1 5 8 7 2 5 6 2 4 9 8 1 2 3 6 7 9 4 8 2 0 1 5 8

34. **Option (D) is correct.**
Explanation: 9th number from the right end is the given arrangement is 7.

35. **Option (A) is correct.**
Explanation: 5th digit from the left end is 2 and 3rd to the right of 2 is 2.

36. **Option (C) is correct.**
Explanation: Required number = 10 × 9 = 90

37. **Option (C) is correct.**
Explanation: Possible combinations are :
18, 28, 58, 68, 78, 81, 82, 85, 86, 87, 88, i.e. 11 is the number.

38. **Option (E) is correct.**
Explanation: The new number is 45729
So, required sum = 4 + 5 + 7 + 2 + 9 = 27

39. **Option (B) is correct.**
Explanation: 7 4 2 7 6 4 3 6 7 5 3 5 7 8 4 3 7 6 7 2 4 0 6 7 4 3

40. **Option (B) is correct.**
Explanation: 8 9 6 5 3 5 9 6 8 3 4 9 6 5 2 6 9 7 3 7 2 9 4 1 3 7 9 4 1 7 3 4 9 8 4 5 3 9 7 6 1 5 3 1 9 5 7 4 2 9 6 8 5 3 2 9 5 7 4 8 9 4 5 1

Level-2: INTERMEDIATE

1. **Option (C) is correct.**
Explanation: Here, 20th element from the left end is Q and 12th to the left of Q is M.

2. **Option (C) is correct.**
Explanation: The new arrangement becomes,
A 3 4 E N M 8 6 L D S 9 8 6 Q Y Z 1 7 R O G 2 1 B 2 U
So, 12th element from the right end is Y and 4th to the right of Y is R.

3. **Option (D) is correct.**
Explanation: A @ 3 % 4 E N M $ 8 & 6 L D S 9 8 6 Q Y Z 1 7 % R O G 2 1 B 2 U &

4. **Option (B) is correct.**

5. **Option (A) is correct.**
Explanation: Required group of terms will be % O R.

6. **Option (A) is correct.**
Explanation: Third from the left end is %.

7. **Option (A) is correct.**
Explanation: A 7 % J 8 I 6 P R £ T 5 J ¥ 2 S 6 M © 4 L O £ X 8 Z 2

8. **Option (C) is correct.**
Explanation: A 7 % J 8 J 6 P R £ T 5 J ¥ 2 S 6 M © 4 L 0 f X 8 Z 2

9. **Option (D) is correct.**
Explanation: The new arrangement is :
2 Z 8 X F O 1 4 © M 6 S 2 ¥ J S T F R P 6 I 8 J % 7 A
So, fifth element from the right end is 8.

10. Option (C) is correct.
Explanation: The new arrangement is :
A 7 % 8 1 6 £ 5 ¥ 2 6 © 4 O £ 8 2
So, number of elements left = 17

11. Option (B) is correct.
Explanation: The seventh element from the left end is 9 and sixteenth from the right end 4. So, the element which is exactly midway between 9 and 4 is 2.

12. Option (E) is correct.
Explanation: 14th element from the right end is 8. So, perfect squares to the right of 8 are : 1, 4, 4, 9 and 4 i.e. 5 in number.

13. Option (C) is correct.
Explanation: 1 3 5 3 4 5 9 2 8 7 2 3 6 5 2 7 3 8 1 2 1 8 4 9 8 1 2 4 7 3 5 2 4 8 9 8 2 4

14. Option (C) is correct.
Explanation: 1 3 5 3 4 5 9 2 8 7 2 3 6 5 2 7 3 8 1 2 1 8 4 9 8 1 2 4 7 3 5 2 4 8 9 8 2 4

15. Option (B) is correct.
Explanation: 10th element from the right end is 7 and 5th to the right of 7 is 8.

16. Option (E) is correct.

17. Option (B) is correct.

18. Option (A) is correct.
Explanation: The new arrangement is :
T 6 # Ⓙ 1 (%) L 3 K 9 @ H 7 B © D Z $ R 4 * B
So, fourth element from the left end is J and sixth to the right of J is 9.

19. Option (E) is correct.
Explanation: T 6 # 1 J 1 % L E 3 K 9 @ A H 7 B © D Z U $ R 4 * 8

20. Option (D) is correct.
Explanation: Eleventh element from the right end is 7 and fifth in the right of 7 is U.

21. Option (D) is correct.
Explanation: 9 3 2 4 5 7 9 5 8 1 5 0 6 4 2 9 8 2 6 3 5 9 8 8 1 5 4 3 2 1

22. Option (B) is correct.
Explanation: The new arrangement is
2 4 8 0 6 4 2 8 2 6 8 2 4 2
Eleventh element from the right end is 8 and eighth to the left of 8 is 8.

23. Option (A) is correct.
Explanation: The arrangement is :
8 2 0 2 4 6 8 4 6 0 4 2 4 2 0 8 6 0 4 2 4 8 6 0 0 4 2 2 0 0
So, 16th element from the right end is 0.

24. Option (D) is correct.
Explanation: The new arrangement is :
9 8 2 6 3 5 9 8 2 1 5 4 3 2 1 9 3 2 4 7 9 5 8 1 5 0 6 4 2
So, 19th number from the right end is 4 and 7th to the right of 4 is 4.

25. Option (E) is correct.
Explanation: 9 3 2 4 5 7 9 5 8 1 5 0 6 4 2 9 8 2 6 3 5 9 8 2 1 5 4 3 2 1

26. Option (D) is correct.
Explanation: The new number are :
837 924 651 372 498
Second highest number = 837
So, last digit of 837 is 7.

27. Option (D) is correct.
Explanation: The new numbers are :
378 249 516 723 984
Required difference = 9 – 2 = 7

28. Option (A) is correct.
Explanation: The new arrangement is
838 529 256 373 994
Now, the descending order is :
994 838 529 373 256
So, second digit of third number (529) is 2.

29. Option (B) is correct.
Explanation: The new arrangement is
R @ T $ 8 % 4 7 * P 9 Q > 4 D $ 5 £ 2 X O < N 7 9
So, eighth element from the right end is f and second to the left of f is $.

30. Option (C) is correct.
Explanation: The new arrangement is :
D @ N $ 8 % O P 7 * Q 9 R > 4 T $ 5 U f 2 U O ◊ U 7 Y 9
So, 11th element from the left end is Q.

31. Option (B) is correct.
Explanation: The new numbers are
884 712 637 585 496
So, number divisible by 3 is 585.

32. Option (E) is correct.
Explanation: The new numbers are
864 521 743 853 962
So, highest number = 962

33. Option (A) is correct.
Explanation: Second lowest number = 385
Highest number = 684
Required answer = 8 ÷ 4 = 2

34. Option (E) is correct.
Explanation: The new number are
786 614 539 487 398
So, second highest number 614 which comes from 512.

35. Option (A) is correct.
Explanation: The new numbers are
864 152 347 835 926
So, highest number = 926
Which comes from 296

Level-3: EXPERT

1. Option (C) is correct.
Explanation: M 1 E $ R B 3 A K 7 £ # 9 $ U D I N 4 6 % F H 2 @ 8 W

2. Option (C) is correct.

3. Option (B) is correct.
Explanation: M 1 E $ R B 3 A K 7 f # 9 $ U D I N 4 6 % F H 2 @ 8 W

4. Option (A) is correct.
Explanation: The new arrangement is
U $ 9 # f 7 K Ⓐ 3 B R $ E 1 M Ⓓ I N 4 6 % F H 2 @ 8 W
So, 12th element from the right end is D and 8th to the left of D is A.

5. **Option (A) is correct.**
Explanation: So, missing term is N % D.

6. **Option (D) is correct.**
Explanation: First row 13 11 4
= 13 11 4
= 2 4
= 4 ÷ 2 = 2
Second row 17 13 12
= 17 – 13 12
= 4 12
= 4 × 12 = 48
∴ Required answer = 2 × 48 = 96

7. **Option (B) is correct.**
Explanation: First row : 40 30 3600
= 40 × 30 3600
= 1200 3600
= 3600 ÷ 1200 = 3
Second row : 15 24 17
= 15 + 24 17
= 39 17
= 39 – 17 = 22
∴ Required sum = 3 + 22 = 25

8. **Option (E) is correct.**
Explanation: First row : 15 11 20 400
= 15 – 11 20 400
= 4 20 400
= 4 × 20 400
= 400 ÷ 80 = 5
Second row : 8 12 10
= 8 × 12 10
= 96 10
= 96 × 10 = 960
∴ Required outcome = 960 ÷ 5 = 192

9. **Option (C) is correct.**
Explanation: First row : 19 15 12
= 19 – 15 12
= 4 12
= 4 × 12 = 48
Second row : 15 12 23 16
= 15 +12 23 16
= 27 23 16
= 27 – 23 16
= 4 16
= 16 ÷ 4 = 4
∴ Required difference = 48 – 4 = 44

10. **Option (A) is correct.**
Explanation: First row : 8 16 16 14
= 16 ÷ 8 16 14
= 2 16 14
= 16 ÷ 2 14
= 8 14
= 8 × 14
= 112
Second row 13 11 12 144
= 13 – 11 12 144
= 2 12 144
= 2 × 12 144
= 24 144
= 144 ÷ 24 = 6
∴ Required difference = 112 – 6 = 106

11. **Option (C) is correct.**
Explanation: 7 R E T 4 A 9 % [D F 1] U # B @ 8 H I © W M * 3 2 V $ S [N P 6] Q

12. **Option (D) is correct.**
Explanation: 7 R E [T 4 A] 9 % D [F 1 U] # B @ 8 H I © W M * 3 2 V $ 5 N [P 6 Q]

13. **Option (C) is correct.**
Explanation: J R E T 4 A 9 % D E 1 [V #] R @ 8 H [I C] W M * 3 2 V $ 5 N P 6 Q

14. **Option (B) is correct.**

15. **Option (A) is correct.**
Explanation: 12th element from the left is U and 4th to the left of U is %.

16. **Option (B) is correct.**
Explanation: The new number is :
48573256
So, only digit 5 is repeating.

17. **Option (B) is correct.**
Explanation: The new number is :
4 3 0 1 8 2 7 9 6 5
So, 7th digit from the left end is 7, and 3rd to the left of 7 is 1.

18. **Option (A) is correct.**
Explanation: The new arrangement is :
I 5 J 2 S 8 Z 7 J I 6 R M 4 T 0 X 8 2
So, 8th element from the right end is R and 7th to the left of R is S.

19. **Option (C) is correct.**
Explanation: 5 J £ 2 S 8 Z 7 % [J] (C) I 6 Σ [R] $ M © 4 T 0 £ X 8 § 2

20. **Option (A) is correct.**
Explanation: I S J £ 2 S 8 Z 7 % J C I 6 Σ R f M © 4 T O f X 8 § 2

21. **Option (B) is correct.**
Explanation: First row 23 20 5
= 23 × 20 5
= 460 5
= 460 – 5 = 455
Second row : 9 12 10
= 9 + 12 10
= 21 10
= 21 + 10 = 31
So, resultant sum = 455 + 31 = 486

22. **Option (A) is correct.**
Explanation: First row 200 50 200
= 200 ÷ 50 2
= 4 2
= 4 ÷ 2 = 2
Second row : 18 7 15
= 18 – 7 15
= 11 15
= 11 × 15 = 165
So, $m = 2$, $n = 165$
∴ $2m + n = 4 + 165 = 169$

23. Option (B) is correct.

Explanation: First row 52 13 12
= 52 – 13 12
= 39 12
= 39 ÷ 12 = 51
Second row : 1200 6 51
= 1200 ÷ 6 51
= 200 51
= 200 – 51 = 149

24. Option (B) is correct.

Explanation: First row 192 16 12
= 192 ÷ 16 12
= 12 ÷ 12 = 1
Second row : 20 10 1
= 20 ÷ 10 1
= 2 1
= 2 – 1 = 1
∴ Required product = 1 × 1 = 1

25. Option (D) is correct.

Explanation: First row 84 12 5
= 84 ÷ 12 5
= 7 5
= 7 × 5 = 35
Second row : 13 35 10
= 13 × 35 10
= 455 + 10 = 465
∴ Required sum = 35 + 465 = 500

■ ■ ■

Chapter 12

Ranking and Time Sequence Test

LEARNING OBJECTIVES:

- Method of arrangement of people in a particular sequence
- Method of arrangement of things in a particular sequence
- Method of arrangement of things in a particular order
- Different types of question asked in competitive exams

This chapter primarily addresses issues related to the placement of individuals and objects in ascending or descending order (depending on various situations.)

Determine the position of a person or object in a row or queue using the supplied criteria (e.g., height, weight, merit, position, etc.) and solve time sequence exam problems that require the candidate to identify a specific day using the criteria provided.

Verbal reasoning tests often include questions that require ranking items or sequencing events based on given information. These questions assess your ability to understand and analyse relationships, patterns, and logical sequences. Here's an example of a ranking question and a time sequencing question:

RANKING QUESTION:

Rank the following fruits in order of their average size, from highest to lowest: apple, strawberry, watermelon.

TIME SEQUENCING QUESTION:

Arrange the following historical events in chronological order:

The signing of the Declaration of Independence.

The invention of the telephone by Alexander Graham Bell.

The fall of the Berlin Wall.

The discovery of America by Christopher Columbus.

For the ranking question, the correct order of the fruits based on their average size would be:

Watermelon (highest)

Apple

Strawberry

For the time sequencing question, the correct chronological order of the historical events would be:

The discovery of America by Christopher Columbus.

The signing of the Declaration of Independence.

The invention of the telephone by Alexander Graham Bell.

The fall of the Berlin Wall.

Verbal reasoning tests can include various types of questions, so it's important to carefully read and analyse the given information before making your rankings or sequencing choices.

ARRANGEMENT OF PEOPLE:

- In this type of question, you are provided with separate lengths or heights of different persons or objects. Your task is to arrange the given information in either ascending (from smallest to largest) or descending (from largest to smallest) order based on the given criteria. Once you have arranged the data, you can answer any related questions based on the order of the lengths or heights.

  For example, let's say you are given the heights of five people: 160 cm, 175 cm, 150 cm, 180 cm, and 165 cm. You may be asked to arrange these heights in ascending order.

  To solve this, you would compare the heights and arrange them accordingly:

  150 cm, 160 cm, 165 cm, 175 cm, 180 cm

  Now that you have arranged the heights in ascending order, you can answer any related questions. For instance, if the question asks for the third tallest person, you would find that the answer is 165 cm.

  These types of questions test your ability to compare and order numerical data. It is important to carefully read the question and organise the information correctly before answering the related questions.

Example 1: Mohan is taller than Shyam but shorter than Ramesh. Ramesh is taller than Rajat but shorter than Gautam. If Shyam is taller than Rajat, then who is the shortest among all? **(MPPSC 2018)**

(a) Gautam (b) Rajat

(c) Shyam (d) Ramesh

Sol. (b) From the given information,

Ramesh > Mohan > Shyam ...(i)

Gautam > Ramesh > Rajat ...(ii)

Shyam > Rajat ...(iii)

Combining equations (i), (ii) and (iii), we have,
Gautam > Ramesh > Mohan > Shyam > Rajat
Hence, Rajat is the shortest among all.

Example 2: D is taller than C and E. A is not as tall as E. C is taller than A. D is not as tall as B. Then, who is the 2nd tallest person? **(WBCS 2020)**

(a) B (b) C
(c) D (d) E

Sol. (c) From the information given in the question,
D > C and E; E > A; C > A; B > D
On arranging the above data, B > D > C and E > A
So, D is the 2nd tallest person.

ARRANGEMENT OF THINGS:

➤ In these type of questions, the total number of persons/objects between the original and new position of a person/object is asked which can be calculated by the given formula.

Total number of persons between two positions = New position − Old position +1

Example 3: The height of a banana tree and coconut tree is the same. The mango tree is shorter than a plum tree. A guava tree is smaller than a mango tree but bigger than a banana tree. Find out which is the tallest tree. **(UPSSSC Amin 2016)**

(a) Mango (b) Banana
(c) Coconut (d) Plum

Sol. (d) According to the question,
Plum > Mango > Guava > Banana= Coconut
So, the plum tree is the tallest.

Example 4: If Pen < Pencil, Pencil < Book and Book > Cap, then which one of the following is always true? **(UPSC Civil Services 2018)**

(a) Pen > Cap (b) Pen < Book
(c) Pencil = Cap (d) Pencil > Cap

Sol. (b) Given, Pen < Pencil ...(i)
Pencil < Book ...(ii)
Book > Cap ...(iii)
From Eqs. (i) and (ii), we can derive that
Pen < Book

ARRANGEMENT OF EVENTS:

➤ In these questions, the applicant must determine a certain day or date using a number of statements that have been given to them or are stated in the question. The questions in this part don't call for any unique techniques or formulas. The questions are fairly straightforward and call for common sense and logical thinking.

Example 5: Kamal remembers that his brother Dinu's birthday falls after 20th May but before 28th May, while Garima remembers that Dinu's birthday falls before 22nd May but after 12th May. On what date Dinu's birthday falls?

(a) 22nd May
(b) 21st May
(c) Cannot be determined
(d) None of these

Sol. (b) Dinu's birthdate falls on one of the following days in May, according to Kamal: (21st/22nd/23rd/24th/25th/26th/27th).
Garima claims that Dinu's birthday is on one of the following days in May: 13, 14, 15, 16, 17, 18, 19, 20, or 21.
21 May is the date that both groups of dates have in common.
It is obvious that Dinu's birthday is on May 21.

Example 6: Arun remembers that his mother's birthday is after April 17 but before April 21 whereas his sister Urmila remembered that their mother's birthday is after 19th but before April 24. Which of the following days in April is definitely their mother's birthday? **(MP Patwari 2017)**

(a) 21st (b) 19th
(c) 20th (d) 22nd

Sol. (c) Arun claims that his mother's birthday is on one of the following days in April: 18th, 19th, or 20th.
According to Urmila, her mother was born on April 20th, 21st, 22nd, or 23rd.
Mother's birthday is undoubtedly on April 20th, as 20th is a common date in both.

Level 1 Beginner

1. John, Aries and Joseph are brothers with different ages. **[WBCS 2020]**
Given that:
(i) Aries is the oldest.
(ii) Joseph is not the oldest.
(iii) John is not the youngest.
Who is the youngest?
(A) Aries
(B) John
(C) Joseph
(D) Cannot be determined from the given information.

2. A pole is taller than a giraffe which is taller than a tree. A signal is shorter than a pole but taller than a building which is taller than a giraffe. Which is the shortest? **[RRB NTPC 2016]**
(A) Signal (B) Giraffe
(C) Tree (D) Building

3. There are five friends–Sachin, Kunal, Mohit, Amit and Sohan. Sachin is shorter than Kunal, but taller than Sohan. Mohit is the tallest. Amit is little shorter than Kunal and little taller than Sachin. If they stand in the order of increasing heights, who will be the third? **[UPSC Assistant Commandant 2019]**

(A) Amit (B) Sohan
(C) Sachin (D) Kunal

4. The height of a banana tree and coconut tree is the same. A mango tree is shorter than the plum tree. The guava tree is smaller than the mango tree but bigger than the banana tree. Find out which is the tallest tree? **[UPSSSC Amin 2016]**
(A) Mango (B) Banana
(C) Coconut (D) Plum

5. P, Q, R and S are four males. P is the eldest in the group but he is not the poorest, R is the richest but not the eldest, Q is elder than S but he is not elder than P or R, P is richer than Q but he is not richer than S. How can the four persons be arranged in decreasing order of their age and money?
(A) PQRS, RPSQ (B) PRQS, RSPQ
(C) PRQS, RSQP (D) PRSQ, RSPQ

6. If the day before yesterday was Sunday, what day will it be three days after the day after tomorrow? **[SSC CGL 2010]**
(A) Sunday (B) Monday
(C) Wednesday (D) Saturday

7. Kartik is on the 19th position from left and on the 8th position from right in a row. How many students are there in the row?
(A) 24 (B) 25
(C) 26 (D) None of these

8. If the day after tomorrow is Sunday, what day was tomorrow's day before yesterday? **[SSC CGL 2010]**
(A) Friday (B) Thursday
(C) Monday (D) Tuesday

9. Lakshmi is elder than Meenu. Leela is elder than Meenu but younger than Lakshmi. Latha is younger than both Meenu and Hari but Hari is younger than Meenu. Who is the youngest? **[SSC 10+2 2013]**
(A) Lakshmi (B) Meenu
(C) Leela (D) Latha

10. At a public meeting, there were 8 speakers A, B, C, D, E, F, G and H. Each spoke for some time according to the following scheme:
I. 'A' spoke after 'F' and took more time than 'B'.
II. 'C' spoke before 'G' and after 'B' and took less time than E.
III. 'D' spoke after 'H' and before 'B' and took less time than 'H' but more time than 'E'.
IV. 'H' spoke after 'A' and took less time than 'B'.
Who spoke for the longest time? **[FCI 2015]**
(A) A (B) B (C) C (D) D

11. In a row of boys, Mohit is 3rd from the left and Rahul is 5th from the right end. When they interchange their places, Mohit becomes 12th from the left. How many total boys are there in the row?
(A) 16 (B) 15
(C) 18 (D) 17

12. In a row of trees, a tree is 7th from left end and 14th from the right end. How many trees are there in the row? **[SSC CGL 2011]**
(A) 18 (B) 19
(C) 20 (D) 21

13. Ashima is 15th from the left end in a row of 35 girls. What is her position from the right end?
(A) 20th (B) 21st
(C) 23rd (D) None of these

14. If Ramesh finds that he is 20th from the right in a line of boys and 5th from the left, then how many boys should be added to the line such that there are 30 boys in the line?
(A) 5 (B) 4
(C) 3 (D) 6

15. There are 45 trees in a row. The lemon tree is 20th from right end. What is the rank of lemon tree from left end? **[SSC CGL 2017]**
(A) 26 (B) 24
(C) 25 (D) 27

16. In a class of 45, Neha's rank is 15th from start, what is her rank from the last? **[SSC CHSL 2015]**
(A) 30 (B) 32
(C) 33 (D) 31

17. If the 25th of August in a year is Thursday, the number of Mondays in that month is: **[RRB 2004]**
(A) 3 (B) 4
(C) 5 (D) 6

18. Which of the following two months have the same number of days in a calendar?
(A) April, October (B) February, August
(C) August, December (D) January, June

19. If the day after tomorrow will be Monday, then what was the day before yesterday?
(A) Wednesday (B) Thursday
(C) Monday (D) None of these

20. If the 5th day of a month is Tuesday, then what day will be on 30th of the same month?
(A) Monday (B) Wednesday
(C) Sunday (D) Saturday

21. If Ramya's rank is 22nd out of 46 students. What is her rank from the last? **[SSC 10+2 2015]**
(A) 25th (B) 29th
(C) 32nd (D) 24th

22. Ravi and Kishor got 13th and 14th rank, respectively from the top in the class. If there are a total of 39 students in class, then what will be the position of both from bottom? **[UPSSC VDO 2015]**
(A) 26th and 25th (B) 27th and 26th
(C) 29th and 28th (D) 27th and 28th

23. In a line of boys, Aman is 12th from top and Baman is 18th from bottom. If there are 6 boys between Aman and Baman, then find the maximum number of boys in the row. **[SSC CPO 2017]**
(A) 34 (B) 36 (C) 35 (D) 37

24. 37 girls are standing in a row facing the school building. Ayesha is fifteenth from the left end. If she is shifted six places to the right, what is her position from the right end? **[SBI Clerk 2016]**
(A) 16th (B) 21st
(C) 20th (D) 18th
(E) None of these

25. A hawker is in the middle compartment of an interconnected train with 17 bogies. He moves six compartments backwards and gets down on the next station. Now, he enters in the third compartment next to the engine. How many compartments he is far away from his original position? **[UPSSSC Junior Assist. 2015]**
(A) 3 **(B)** 6 **(C)** 5 **(D)** 4

26. If Ramya's rank is 22nd out of 46 students. What is her rank from the last? **[SSC CHSL 2015]**
(A) 29 **(B)** 32
(C) 25 **(D)** 26

27. In a row of trees, one tree is fifth from either end of the row. How many trees are there in the row? **[Assistant Grade, 1995]**
(A) 8 **(B)** 9
(C) 10 **(D)** 11

28. Sakshi ranked 10th from the top and 26th from the bottom in a class. How many students are there in the class?
(A) 35 **(B)** 32
(C) 31 **(D)** 34

29. A remembers that B celebrated his birthday after 17 but before June 22 while B remembers that the birthday was celebrated before 24 but after the June 20. On which date was the birthday celebrated? **[CGPSC 2016]**
(A) June 23 **(B)** June 22
(C) June 21 **(D)** June 17
(E) None of these

30. Nitin correctly remembers that Nidhi's birthday is before Friday but after Tuesday. Deepak correctly remembers that Nidhi's birthday is after Wednesday but before Saturday. On which of the following days does Nidhi's birthday definitely fall? **[PNB Clerk 2009]**
(A) Monday **(B)** Tuesday
(C) Wednesday **(D)** Thursday
(E) Cannot be determined

31. Vinay remembers that his brother Anupam's birthday is after 20th of August but before 28th of August, while Rita remembers that Anupam's birthday is before 22nd of August but after 12th of August. On which date does Anupam's birthday fall? **[RRB PO 2010]**
(A) 20th August
(B) 21st August
(C) 22nd August
(D) Cannot be determined
(E) None of these

32. Ranjana correctly remembers that Kiran's birthday was after Tuesday but before Friday. Rajan correctly remembers that Kiran's birthday was after Wednesday but before Sunday. On which day of the week does Kiran's birthday definitely fall? **[CBI Clerk 2009]**
(A) Monday
(B) Thursday
(C) Saturday
(D) Cannot be determined
(E) None of these.

Directions (Qs. 33–35): Read the following information carefully and answer the questions that follow.
I. There is a group of five girls.
II. Kamini is the second in height but younger than Rupa.
III. Pooja is taller than Monika but younger in age.
IV. Rupa and Monika are of the same age but Rupa is the tallest of them.
V. Neelam is taller than Pooja and elder to Rupa.

33. If they are arranged in ascending order of height, then who will be in the third position?
(A) Monika **(B)** Monika or Rupa
(C) Rupa **(D)** None of these

34. If they are arranged in descending order of their ages, then who will be in the fourth position?
(A) Monika or Rupa **(B)** Monika
(C) Kamini **(D)** None of these

35. To answer the question, "Who is the youngest person in the group", which of the following statements is superfluous?
(A) Only I **(B)** Only V
(C) Only II **(D)** Either I or IV

Level 2 Intermediate

1. Among five people J, K, L, M and N (each running at a different speed), who ran at the third fastest speed? M ran faster than L but slower than K. J ran slower than only one person. L did not run at the slowest speed. **[NICL Assist 2015]**
(A) Cannot be determined **(B)** M
(C) N **(D)** L

2. In a row at a bus stop, A is 7th from the left and B is 9th from the right. They both interchange their positions. Now, A becomes 11th from the left. How many people are there in the row?
(A) 10 **(B)** 20 **(C)** 19 **(D)** 18

Directions (Qs. 3–5): Read the given information carefully and answer the questions.
Each of the six buildings P, Q, R, S, T and U houses different number of offices. S has more offices than only T and R. Q has more number of offices than P but less than U. R does not have the least number of offices. The building which has the least number of offices has 5 offices. The building which has second highest number of offices has 23 offices. S has 11 less number of offices than Q? **[IBPS PO 2015]**

3. Which of the following buildings has the second least number of offices?
(A) Q **(B)** U **(C)** R **(D)** P
(E) T

4. If the number of offices in P is an even number which is divisible by 2 as well as 3, how many does P have?
(A) 20 (B) 24
(C) 16 (D) 18
(E) 12

5. Which of the following is the number of offices in R?
(A) 25 (B) 12
(C) 13 (D) 1
(E) 11

6. Veni is an year older than Smith. Smith is two years older than Salim. Raju is an year older than Salim. Who is the youngest of all? [SSC CGL 2013]
(A) Raju (B) Salim
(C) Veni (D) Smith

7. Six ropes A, B, C, D, E and F each of different length are kept on a table but not necessarily in the same order. B is shorter than A but longer than F. D is longer than A. C is shorter than A but longer than B. F is not the shortest. Which is the shortest rope? [MHT MBA 2017]
(A) A (B) E
(C) C (D) B
(E) D

8. A is taller than B. D is shorter than C but taller than E. Only D is between A and B in terms of height. Who is the tallest of all? [UPSSSC Junior Assist. 2015]
(A) D (B) A (C) B (D) C

9. There is a group of seven friends Rani, Neha, Mira, Juhi, Hema, Isha and Kuku. Mira is taller than Hema and Kuku. Rani is not the tallest but taller than Mira. Neha is shorter than Hema. Juhi is taller than Hema but shorter than Kuku. If they are ranked in the ascending order of their heights, who will be ranked fifth? [MAT 2018]
(A) Kuku (B) Mira
(C) Isha (D) Juhi

10. A is 16th from the left end in a row of boys and V is 18th from the right end. G is 11th from A towards the right and 3rd from V towards the right end. How many boys are there in the row? [UPSC CSAT 2020]
(A) 40
(B) 41
(C) 42
(D) Cannot be determined due to insufficient data

Directions (Qs. 11–13): Study the following information and answer the given questions.

Each of the six stores P, Q, R, S, T and U sold different number of books in one day. Only three stores sold less books than U. P sold more books than R. T did not sell the highest number of books. S sold more books than R and P but less than U. The store which sold the second highest number of books sold 72 books. [SBI PO 2017]

11. How many books did Q probably sell?
(A) 43 (B) 58
(C) 71 (D) 65
(E) 89

12. Which of the following stores sold the second lowest number of books?
(A) T (B) P
(C) S (D) R
(E) Q

13. If the total number of books sold by P and T is 125, then how many books did P sell?
(A) 51 (B) 76
(C) 68 (D) 45
(E) 53

Directions (Qs. 14–16): Read the following information carefully and answer the questions that follow. [SBI PO 2015]

(i) A, B, C, D, E and F are six students in a class.
(ii) B and C are shorter than F but heavier than A.
(iii) D is heavier than B and taller than C.
(iv) E is shorter than D but taller than F.
(v) F is heavier than D.
(vi) A is shorter than E but taller than F.

14. Who among them is the tallest?
(A) B (B) A
(C) D (D) E
(E) None of these

15. Who is third from the top when they are arranged in descending order of their height?
(A) A (B) E
(C) B (D) C
(E) None of these

16. Which of the following statements is true for F as regarding height and weight?
(A) He is heavier than B and C but shorter than D.
(B) He is lighter than B and C but taller than D.
(C) He is heavier than B and taller than E.
(D) He is lighter than E and also shorter than E.
(E) He is lighter than E and taller than E.

17. Rashmi is 14th from the right end in a row of 40 girls. What is her position from the left end?
(A) 25th (B) 27th
(C) 21st (D) None of these

18. In a row of boys, Jeevan is 7th from the start and 11th from the end. In another row of boys, Vikas is 10th from the start and 12th from the end. How many boys are there in both the rows together?
(A) 38
(B) 40
(C) 32
(D) Cannot be determined
(E) None of these

19. In a row of thirty-seven boys facing South. 'R' is eighth to the right of 'T' who is fourteenth to the left of 'D'. How many boys are there between 'D' and 'R in the row? [UP SSC Revenue Inspector 2016]
(A) 4 (B) 5
(C) 8 (D) Data inadequate

20. In a row, 'X' is at 14th position from the beginning and 'Y' is at 17th position from the end, while 'Z' is exactly in the middle way of 'X' and 'Y'. If there are total of 48 persons in the row, then how many persons are there between 'X' and 'Z'? [UPSSSC VDO 2016]
(A) 6 (B) 7 (C) 8 (D) 9

21. In a row, 'A' is in the 11th position from the left and 'B' is in the 10th position from the right. If 'A' and 'B 'interchange, then 'A' becomes 18th from the left. How many persons are there in the row other than 'A' and 'B'? **[WBCS 2020]**

(A) 27 **(B)** 26 **(C)** 25 **(D)** 24

22. Meena correctly remembers that her father's birthday is after 18th May but before 22nd May. Her brother correctly remembers that their father's birthday is before 24th May but after 20th May. On which date in May was definitely their father's birthday? **[Andhra Bank PO 2010]**

(A) 20th
(B) 19th
(C) 18th
(D) Cannot be determined
(E) None of these

23. Mohan correctly remembers that his father's birthday is before 20th January but after 16th January whereas his sister correctly remembers that their father's birthday is after 18th January but before 23rd January. On which date in January is definitely their father's birthday? **[Syndicate Bank PO 2010]**

(A) 18th **(B)** 19th
(C) 20th **(D)** Data inadequate
(E) None of these

24. Sneha correctly remembers that her father's birthday is before 16th June but after 11th June whereas, her younger brother correctly remembers that their father's birthday is after 13th June but before 18th June and her elder brother correctly remembers that their father's birthday is on an even date. On what date in June, is definitely their father's birthday? **[Vijay Bank Clerk 2010]**

(A) Sixteenth **(B)** Twelfth
(C) Fourteenth **(D)** Data inadequate

25. Satish read a book on Sunday. Sudha read that book one day prior to Anil but 4 days after Satish. On which day did Anil read the book?

(A) Friday **(B)** Thursday
(C) Tuesday **(D)** Saturday

Directions (Qs. 26–30): Study the following information and answer the questions given below:

Nine friends - P, Q, R, S, T, U, V, W and X - live on nine different floors of a building but not necessarily in the same order. The lowermost floor of the building is numbered one, the one above that is numbered two and so on till the topmost floor is numbered nine. Only two persons live below the floor on which V lives. Only one person lives between V and P. W lives on an odd numbered floor but not on floor number 7. Only two persons live between W and Q. X does not live on the topmost floor. P does not live on the lowermost floor. S lives immediately below R but R does not live on top most floor. Neither R nor T live on floor number 6. U lives immediately above P.

26. How many persons live between the floors on which P and S live?

(A) Three **(B)** More than three
(C) None **(D)** Two
(E) One

27. Who lives on the floor immediately below V?

(A) X **(B)** T
(C) S **(D)** Q
(E) U

28. On which of the following floor numbers does X live?

(A) Four **(B)** One
(C) Two **(D)** Five
(E) Seven

29. Which of the following statements is true with respect to U as per the given arrangement?

(A) Only three persons live between U and Q.
(B) Only three persons live above U.
(C) Only one person lives between U and S.
(D) U lives on an odd numbered floor.
(E) None of the given options is true

30. Who lives on floor numbered five?

(A) U
(B) Q
(C) S
(D) P
(E) Other than those given as options

31. Ashish leaves his house at 20 minutes to seven in the morning, reaches Kunal's house in 25 minutes. They finish their breakfast in another 15 minutes and leave for their office which takes another 35 minutes. At what time do they leave Kunal's house to reach their office? **[MAT 2005]**

(A) 7:40 am **(B)** 7:20 am
(C) 7:45 am **(D)** 8:15 am
(E) 7:55 am

32. The priest told the devotee, "The temple bell is rung at regular intervals of 45 minutes. The last bell was rung five minutes ago. The next bell is due to be rung at 7.45 a.m." At what time did the priest give this information to the devotee? **[RRB 2002]**

(A) 7:40 am **(B)** 7:05 am
(C) 7:00 am **(D)** 6:55 am
(E) None of these

Directions (Qs. 33–35): Study the following information carefully and answer the questions given below it:

(I) Kamal is available at home from 12 noon to 4 p.m. on Tuesday, Thursday and Sunday.

(II) His younger brother Navin is available at home on Monday, Thursday, Friday and Sunday between 10 a.m. to 2 p.m.

(III) The eldest brother Rajiv is available between 9 a.m. to 12 noon on Monday, Wednesday and Thursday and 2 p.m. to 4 p.m. on Friday, Saturday and Sunday.

33. At a time, on which day of a week all the three brothers are available at home?

(A) None
(B) Sunday
(C) Thursday
(D) Cannot be determined
(E) None of these

34. For how many days only one brother is available at a particular time in a week ?

(A) One (B) Two
(C) Three (D) Four
(E) None of these

35. On which day(s) of a week, the youngest and the eldest brothers are available at home at the same time?
(A) Only Monday
(B) Only Thursday
(C) Only Friday
(D) Both Monday and Thursday
(E) Both Sunday and Friday

3 Level Expert

1. Priti scored more than Rahul. Yamuna scored as much as Divya. Lokita scored less than Manju. Rahul scored more than Yamuna. Manju scored less than Divva- scored to lowest?**[SSC CGL Tier 1 Exam 2013]**
(A) Manju (B) Yamuna
(C) Lokita (D) Rahul

2. There are five friends — Sachin, Kamal, Mohan, Arun and Ram. Sachin is shorter than Kamal but taller than Ram. Mohan is the tallest. Arun is a little shorter than Kamal and a little taller than Sachin. Who is the second tallest? **[SSC CGL Tier 1 Exam 2014]**
(A) Ram (B) Sachin
(C) Kamal (D) Arun

3. In a row of men, Manoj is 30th from the right and Kiran is 20th from the left. When they interchange their position, Manoj becomes 35th from the right. What is the total number of men in the row? **[SSC CGL Tier 1 Exam 2014]**
(A) 34 (B) 54 (C) 45 (D) 44

Directions (Qs. 4–9): Read the following information carefully and answer the questions that follow.

I. Seven students P, Q, R, S, T, U and V take a series of tests.
II. No two students get similar marks.
III. V always scores more than P.
IV. P always scores more than Q.
V. Each time either R scores the highest and T gets the least or alternatively S scores the highest and U or Q scores the least.

4. If V is ranked fifth, which of these must be true?
(A) S scores the highest (B) R is ranked second
(C) T is ranked third (D) Q is ranked fourth

5. If R gets the most, V should be ranked not lower than:
(A) second (B) third
(C) fourth (D) fifth

6. If S is ranked second, which of the following can be true?
(A) P gets more than R (B) V gets more than S
(C) P gets more than S (D) U gets more than V

7. If S is ranked sixth and Q is ranked fifth, which of the following can be true?
(A) V is ranked fifth or fourth
(B) R is ranked second or third
(C) P is ranked second or fourth
(D) U is ranked third or fourth

8. If R is ranked second and Q is ranked fifth, which of these must be true?
(A) S is ranked third (B) P is ranked third
(C) V is ranked fourth (D) T is ranked sixth

9. Information given in which of the statements is superfluous?
(A) Only II (B) Only I
(C) Only IV (D) All are needed

10. Six persons P, Q, R, S, T and U read a magazine one after another.
I. S was neither the first nor the last to read it.
II. There were as many readers between P and T as there were between R and P.
III. S read it sometime before Q, who read it sometime after U.
IV. The one who read it last had taken it from R.
Who were the two persons to have read the magazine first and last, respectively?
(A) T and Q (B) P and Q
(C) T and U (D) P and U

Direction (Qs. 11–15): Study the following information carefully and answer the questions given below.

Eight persons A, B, C, D, E, F, G and H were born in different years, i.e., 1991, 1995, 2002, 1998, 1985, 2018, 2015 and 2010 but not necessarily in the same order. Calculate the age of each person taking the base year 2021. B's age is a prime number. There is four years gap between B and H. Two persons were born between B and E who was born in an odd-numbered year. The number of persons born before E is the same as the number of persons born after F. G's age is a multiple of 3 but less than B. The difference between the age of A and D is neither even nor prime number. C's age is more than E's age but not less than F's age. E is older than F. **[RBI 2022]**

11. What is the sum of the ages of F and the person who was born in 2002?
(A) 25 years (B) 30 years
(C) 45 years (D) 22 years
(E) None of these

12. How many persons were born between C and the one whose age is 11 years?
(A) One (B) Four
(C) Three (D) None
(E) Two

13. Who among the following is the youngest person?
(A) A (B) D
(C) G (D) F
(E) None of these

14. Which of the following statement(s) is/are true?
(A) A was born in 1985.
(B) Two persons were born between H and B
(C) Age of E is multiple of 7
(D) C is the oldest person among all
(E) All are true

15. Four of the following five are alike in a certain way and thus form a group. Who among the following does not belong to the group?
(A) F (B) G
(C) E (D) C
(E) B

Direction (Qs. 16–20): Study the following information carefully and answer the given questions:

Eight persons P, Q, R, S, T, U, V and W, got appointments on either 10th or 15th of different months of the same year starting from March to June. Not more than two persons got the appointment in the same month. Only one person got the appointment on each date. V got the appointment in the month which has odd days. There were four persons got the appointment between V and S. P got the appointment before S but not in the month of March. Q got the appointment in the month which has even number of days. Three persons got the appointment between Q and T. R got the appointment before U and both of them got the appointment in the month which has odd number of days. W did not get the appointment in 10th of any of the month and he did not get the appointment just before S. T got the appointment in one of the months before the month in which Q got the appointment. P did not get the appointment just before S. **[RBI 2019]**

16. S got the appointment in which of the following month?
(A) March (B) April
(C) May (D) June
(E) None of these

17. P got the appointment in which of the following date?
(A) 10th March (B) 15th April
(C) 10th June (D) 15th June
(E) None of these

18. How many persons got appointments before U?
(A) one (B) three
(C) two (D) more than four
(E) four

19. Who among the following got the appointment on 10th June?
(A) V (B) U
(C) Q (D) W
(E) C

20. Which of the following combination is correct?
(A) V-April-10th (B) S-June-15th
(C) T-April-10th (D) R-March-10th
(E) W-May-15th

ANSWER KEY

Level-1: Beginner

1.	(C)	2.	(C)	3.	(A)	4.	(D)	5.	(B)	6.	(A)	7.	(C)	8.	(B)	9.	(D)	10.	(A)
11.	(A)	12.	(C)	13.	(B)	14.	(D)	15.	(A)	16.	(D)	17.	(C)	18.	(C)	19.	(B)	20.	(D)
21.	(A)	22.	(B)	23.	(B)	24.	(E)	25.	(C)	26.	(C)	27.	(B)	28.	(A)	29.	(C)	30.	(D)
31.	(B)	32.	(B)	33.	(D)	34.	(D)	35.	(A)										

Level-2: Intermediate

1.	(B)	2.	(C)	3.	(C)	4.	(D)	5.	(E)	6.	(B)	7.	(B)	8.	(D)	9.	(B)	10.	(B)
11.	(E)	12.	(B)	13.	(E)	14.	(C)	15.	(A)	16.	(A)	17.	(B)	18.	(A)	19.	(B)	20.	(C)
21.	(C)	22.	(E)	23.	(B)	24.	(C)	25.	(A)	26.	(E)	27.	(A)	28.	(C)	29.	(B)	30.	(D)
31.	(E)	32.	(B)	33.	(A)	34.	(D)	35.	(D)										

Level-3: Expert

1.	(C)	2.	(C)	3.	(B)	4.	(A)	5.	(C)	6.	(D)	7.	(D)	8.	(D)	9.	(D)	10.	(A)
11.	(A)	12.	(B)	13.	(C)	14.	(D)	15.	(E)	16.	(C)	17.	(B)	18.	(E)	19.	(C)	20.	(C)

Solutions with Detailed Explanations

Level-1: BEGINNER

1. **Option (C) is correct.**
Explanation: According to the facts, Joseph is the youngest.

2. **Option (C) is correct.**
Explanation: From given information, the descending order of height
Pole > Giraffe> Tree ...(i)
And, Pole > Signal > Building > Giraffe ...(ii)
Now, from (i) and (ii), we have
Pole > Signal > Building > Giraffe > Tree
Hence, tree is the shortest.

3. **Option (A) is correct.**
Explanation: Sohan<Sachin<Kunal ...(i)
Mohit is tallest. ...(ii)
Sachin< Amit < Kunal ...(iii)
From (i), (ii) and (iii)
Sohan < Sachin < Amit < Kunal < Mohit
So, Amit is third in increasing order of heights.

4. **Option (D) is correct.**
Explanation: From question,
Plum > Mango > Guava > Banana = Coconut
So, the plum tree is the tallest.

5. **Option (B) is correct.**
Explanation: Age-based descending order
P > R > Q > S
Decreasing financial order
R > S > P > Q
As a result, answer option (B) is correct.

6. **Option (A) is correct.**
Explanation: If day before yesterday was Sunday, then today is Tuesday. So, day after tomorrow will be Thursday and three days after Thursday will be Sunday.

7. **Option (C) is correct.**
Explanation: Number of students in the row
= 19 + 8 – 1 = 26

8. **Option (B) is correct.**
Explanation: If day after tomorrow is Sunday then today is Friday and tomorrow day before yesterday was Thursday.

9. **Option (D) is correct.**
Explanation: According to the question:
Lakshmi > Meenu, Lakshmi > Leela > Meenu
Meenu> Hari > Latha
The following order is arranged as follows:
Lakshmi > Leela > Meenu > Hari > Latha
So, Latha is the youngest as a result.

10. **Option (A) is correct.**
Explanation: There are 8 speakers A, B, C, D, E F, G and H.
According to the question,
A spoke after F and H spoke after A.
F A H
D spoke after H and before B.
F A H D B
C spoke before G and after B.
So, the sequence becomes
F A H D B C G
Now, the sequence of time taken by them:
A > B > H > D > E > C
It is clear that A spoke for the longest time.

11. **Option (A) is correct.**
Explanation:

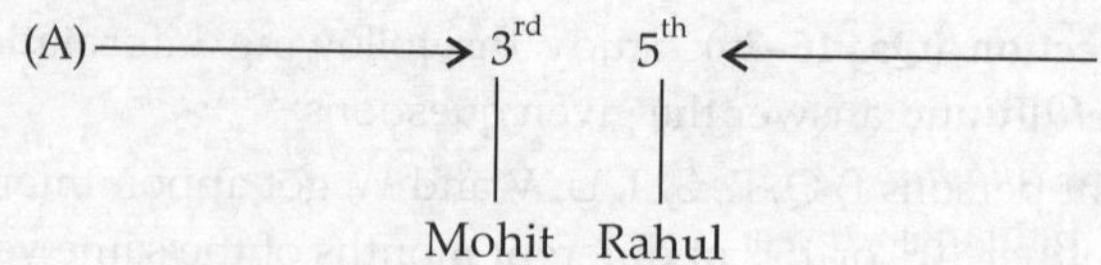

After interchanging,

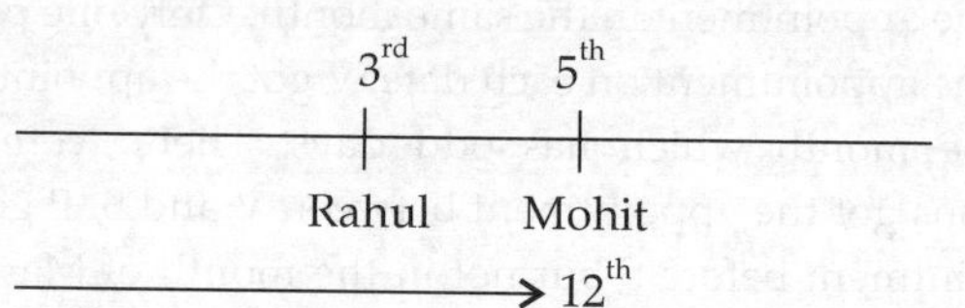

So, total number of boys
= 12 + 5 – 1 = 16

12. **Option (C) is correct.**
Explanation: Number of trees in the row
= 7 + 14 – 1 = 20

13. **Option (B) is correct.**
Explanation: Total number of girls = 35
Position of Ashima from left end = 15th
So, position of Ashima from right end
= 35 – 15 + 1 = 21st

14. **Option (D) is correct.**
Explanation: As, per Ramesh, total number of boys in the row = 20 + 5 – 1 = 24
So, number of more boys needs to be added
= 30 – 24 = 6

15. **Option (A) is correct.**
Explanation: Total number of trees = 45
So, position of the lemon tree from left end
= 45 – 20 + 1 = 26th

16. **Option (D) is correct.**
Explanation: Rank of Neha from the last
= 45 – 15 + 1 = 31st

17. **Option (C) is correct.**
Explanation: 25th August → Thursday
So, 22nd August → Monday
Hence, Mondays are : 1st, 8th, 15th, 22nd and 29th August.

18. **Option (C) is correct.**
Explanation: In August and December, the number of days are the same.

19. **Option (B) is correct.**
Explanation: If day after tomorrow will be Monday, so today is Saturday and the day before yesterday was Thursday.

20. Option (D) is correct.
Explanation: 5th day → Tuesday
⇒ 26th day → Tuesday
So, 30th day → Saturday

21. Option (A) is correct.
Explanation: Ramya's position from the bottom:
Total number of students – Ramya's position from the beginning +1 = 46 – 22 + 1 = 25th.

22. Option (B) is correct.
Explanation: Ravi's position from bottom = Total number of students– Ravi's position from top +1 = 39 –13 + 1 = 27th
Kishor's position from bottom
= Total number of students – Kishor's position from top +1
= 39 – 14 + 1 = 26th

23. Option (B) is correct.
Explanation: Number of boys between Aman and Baman = Total number of boys in row – (Aman's rank from top + Baman's rank from bottom)
6 = Total number of boys in row –(12 + 18)
So, total number of boys in row = 6 + 30 = 36

24. Option (E) is correct.
Explanation: Ayesha's current position = 15 + 6 = 21st from the left, and her position from the right is 37 – 21 + 1 = 17th.

25. Option (C) is correct.
Explanation: According to the question,

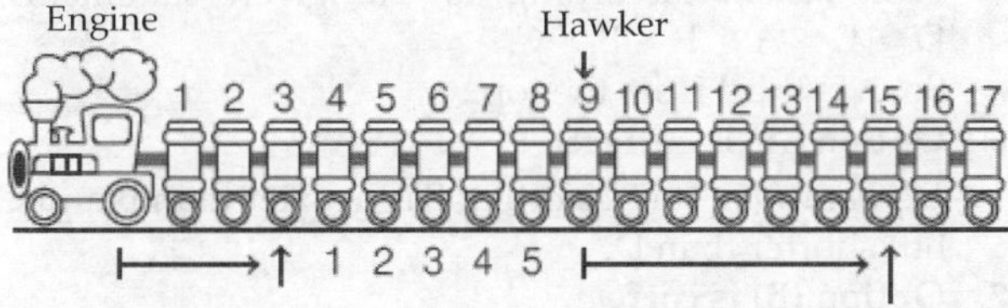

Hawker's starting position is the middle compartment of a 17-bogies train $\frac{(17+1)}{2}$, which equals $\frac{18}{2}$, or the 9th compartment.
He enters the third compartment near to the engine at the following station.
New hawker position: third compartment from the engine
Now, the distance from his starting point is (9 – 3 – 1), which equals the five compartment.
Therefore, the hawker is five compartments away from his starting point.

26. Option (C) is correct.
Explanation: Ramya's rank from the last
= 46 – 22 + 1 = 25

27. Option (B) is correct.
Explanation: Total number of trees in the row
= 5 + 5 – 1 = 9

28. Option (A) is correct.
Explanation: Total number of students
= 10 + 26 – 1 = 35

29. Option (C) is correct.
Explanation: According to A, B was born on June 18th, 19th, 20th or 21st.
B claims that her birthday is on June 21st, 22nd, or 23rd.
Here, 21st of June is the only common date.

30. Option (D) is correct.
Explanation:

According to	Nitin's birthday
Nitin	Wednesday/Thursday
Deepak	Thursday/Friday

Hence, the correct day is Thursday.

31. Option (B) is correct.
Explanation:

According to	Possibility of dates of August
Vinay	21 /22 /23/ 24/ 25/ 26/ 27
Rita	13/ 14/ 15/ 16/ 17/ 18/ 19/ 20/ 21

Hence, 21 is the answer.

32. Option (B) is correct.
Explanation:

According to	Possibility of days
Ranjana	Wednesday/(Thursday)
Rajan	(Thursday)/Friday/ Saturday

So, Thursday is the answer.

Instructions for (Qs. 33-35):
Descending order of heights and ages is as given below:
Arrangement of persons according to Height
Rupa > Kamini > Neelam > Pooja > Monika
Arrangement of persons according to Age;
Neelam > Rupa = Monika > Pooja > Kamini
or Neelam > Rupa
= Monika > Kamini > Pooja

33. Option (D) is correct.
Explanation: When the people are grouped in increasing order of height, Neelam will be at the third spot.

34. Option (D) is correct.
Explanation: If they are put in descending order of their ages, the fourth position cannot be identified.

35. Option (A) is correct.
Explanation: Just Statement I needs to be said.

Level-2: INTERMEDIATE

1. Option (B) is correct.
Explanation: According to the information, the arrangement is as follows:

K > J > (M) > L > N

Third from the left

M ran at the third-fastest pace.

2. Option (C) is correct.
Explanation:

Left ⟶ [A] ||| [B] ⟵ Right
(7th above A, 9th above B)

After interchanging the places,

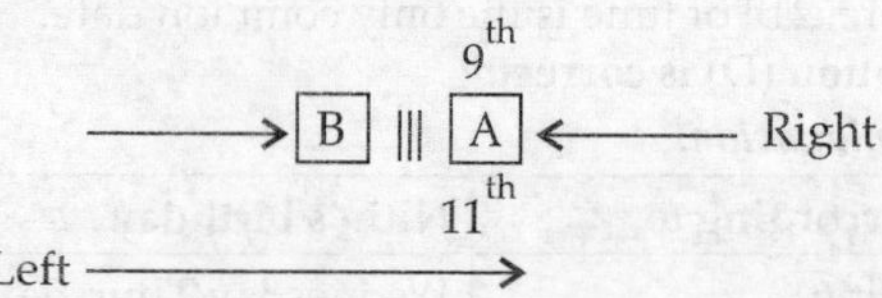

11 + 9 – 1 = 19 persons

So, total 9 persons are in the row.

(3–5). The setup is as follows in light of the provided information.

S > T / R.....(i)

U > Q > P...(ii)

The result of combining (i) and (ii) is

U > Q > P > S > R > T - Building

23 12 5 - offices.

3. **Option (C) is correct.**
Explanation: The second-least number of offices are in building R.

4. **Option (D) is correct.**
Explanation: If P has an even number of offices that is divisible by 2 and 3, then P has 18 offices.

5. **Option (E) is correct.**
Explanation: Building R should have more than 12 offices, but no fewer than 5.
Option (E) meets the criterion out of the possibilities provided.
Consequently, Building R contains 11 offices.

6. **Option (B) is correct.**
Explanation: Let the age of Salim be S years
So, age of Raju = S + 1
Age of Smith = S + 2
Age of Veni = S + 2 + 1 = S + 3
So, Salim is the youngest of all.

7. **Option (B) is correct.**
Explanation: As per the given information,we have
D > A > C > B > F > E
Therefore, E is the shortest rope.

8. **Option (D) is correct.**
Explanation: From given information, we have
A > B ...(i)
C > D > E ...(ii)
And, A > D > B ...(iii)
On combining equations, (i), (ii) and (iii),
We have,
C > A > D > B > E
Hence, C is the tallest of all.

9. **Option (B) is correct.**
Explanation: When the people are arranged according to height, we obtain,
Neha < Hema < Juhi < Kuku < Mira < Rani < Isha.
In ascending order, Mira came at fifth.

10. **Option (B) is correct.**
Explanation:

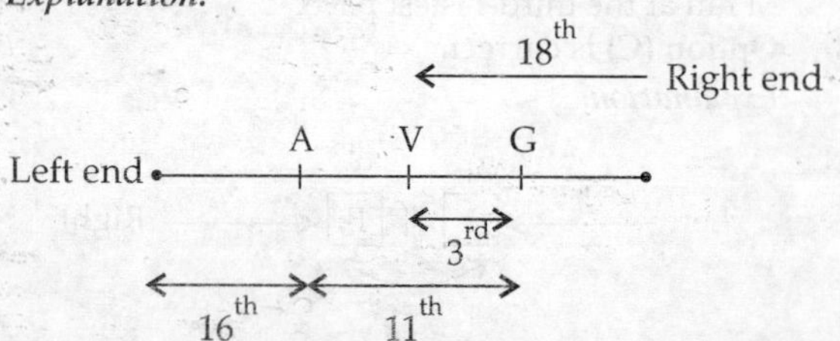

V's position from left end = (16 + 11 – 3) = 24th
The total number of boys in the row
= (18 + 24 – 1) = 41

11. **Option (E) is correct.**
Explanation: The fact that 72 books were sold by the business with the second-highest sales of books is obvious. According to the question, descending order of the stores according to their sale is
Q > T > U > S > P > R.
As a result, store Q sold the most books. By choice, we can state that store Q sold 89 books since 72 was the next-highest number.

12. **Option (B) is correct.**
Explanation: According to the question, descending order of the stores according to their sale is:
Q > T > U > S > P > R.
So, store P had sold 2nd lowest number of books.

13. **Option (E) is correct.**
Explanation: Since T = 72 and P + T = 125,
Then, P + 72 = 125
P = 125 – 72 = 53.
So, 53 books were sold at store P.

14. **Option (C) is correct.**
Explanation: According to the given statements,
D > E > A > F > B > C.
So, D is the tallest.

15. **Option (A) is correct.**
Explanation: According to the given statements,
D > E > A > F > B > C.
So, A is third from the top.

16. **Option (A) is correct.**
Explanation: It is clear that F is heavier than B and C but shorter than D.

17. **Option (B) is correct.**
Explanation: Required position
= (40 + 1 – 14) = 27th (from left.)

18. **Option (A) is correct.**
Explanation: Total number of boys
= (Number of boys in Jeevan's row)
+ (Number of boys in Vikas's row)
= (6 + 1 + 10) + (9 + 1 + 11)
= (17 + 21) = 38

19. **Option (B) is correct.**
Explanation: According to the question,

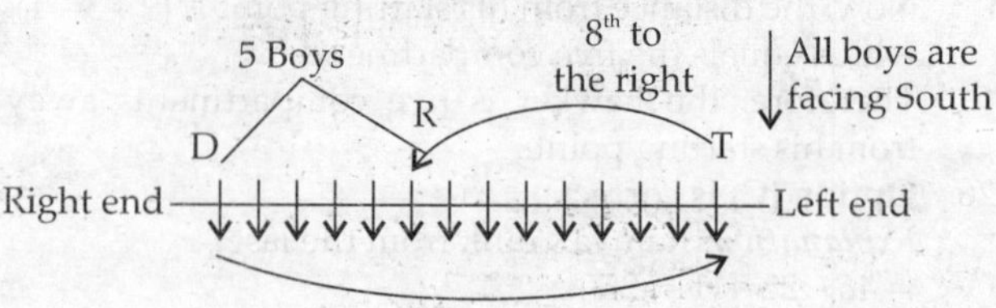

Therefore, it is evident from the above diagram that there are 5 boys between D and R.

20. **Option (C) is correct.**
Explanation: According to the question,

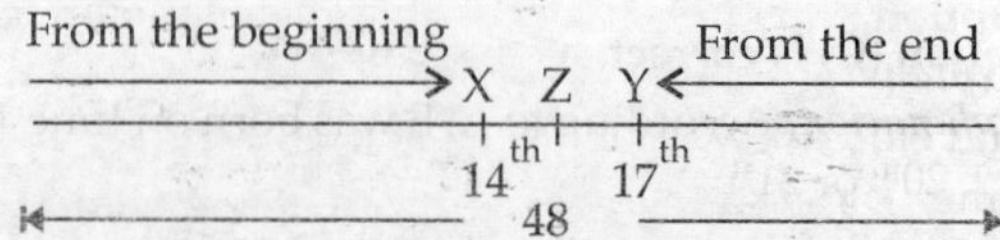

A total of 48 people are present.
Then, the number of people between X and Y
= 48 – (14 + 17) = 48 – 31= 17
Therefore, total individuals between X and Z: $\frac{17-1}{2}=8$

21. Option (C) is correct.
Explanation:

Left ⟶ 11th (A) 10th (B) ⟵ Right

If they interchange:

Left ⟶ 11 (B) 10 (A) ⟵ Right

Left ⟶ 18

Total number of persons = 18 + 10 –1 = 27
Number of persons other than A and B = 27 – 2 = 25

22. Option (E) is correct.
Explanation: Days by Meena, May 19, 20, and 21.
Days by Meena's brother, May 21, 22, and 23.
The 21st of May is undoubtedly a day that both parties share, making it the necessary day.

23. Option (B) is correct.
Explanation: Days by Mohan, January 17th, 18th, and 19th.
Days by Sister, January 19th, 20th, 21st, or 22nd.
19th of January is the required day because it is shared by both groups.

24. Option (C) is correct.
Explanation:

According to	Possibility of dates of June
Sneha	12/ 13/ 14/ 15
Younger brother	14/ 15/ 16/ 17
Elder brother	14/ 16

Hence, 14 is common in all.

25. Option (A) is correct.
Explanation: Four days after Sunday, Sudha read the book. Sudha must have finished the book on Thursday, then. So, on Friday, Anil will read the book.

(26–30):

Floor	Persons
9	T
8	R
7	S
6	U
5	P
4	Q
3	V
2	X
1	W

26. Option (E) is correct.
Explanation: There is only person who lives between the floors on which P and S live.

27. Option (A) is correct.
Explanation: X lives on the floor immediately below V.

28. Option (C) is correct.
Explanation: X lives on floor 2.

29. Option (B) is correct.
Explanation: Only three persons, i.e., T, R and S live above U.

30. Option (D) is correct.
Explanation: P lives on floor numbered S.

31. Option (E) is correct.
Explanation: Ashish leaves his house = 6:40 a.m.
Ashish reaches Kunal's house = 7:05 a.m.
They finish their breakfast at 7:20 a.m.
They leave for office at 7:55 a.m.

32. Option (B) is correct.
Explanation: Next bell will ring at 7:45 a.m.
So, previous bell rang at 7:00 a.m.
So, time at which the priest gives this information to devotee = 7:05 a.m.

(33–35):

	Mon	Tue	Wed	Thu	Fri	Sat	Sun
9 a.m. to 10 a.m.	Rajiv		Rajiv	Rajiv			
10 a.m. to 12 noon	Navin Rajiv		Rajiv	Rajiv Navin	Navin		Navin
12 noon to 2 p.m.	Navin	Kamal		Kamal Navin	Navin		Navin Kunal Kamal
2 p.m. to 4 p.m.		Kamal		Kamal	Rajiv	Rajiv	Kamal Rajiv

33. Option (A) is correct.
34. Option (D) is correct.
35. Option (D) is correct.
Explanation: On Monday and Thursday, the youngest and eldest brothers are available at home at the same time.

Level-3: EXPERT

1. Option (C) is correct.
Explanation: Priti > Rahul,
Yamuna = Divya,
Lokita < Manju,

Rahul > Yamuna,
Manju < Divya
So, Priti> Rahul> Yamuna = Divya > Manju > Lokita
Thus, it is evident that Lokita received the lowest score.

2. **Option (C) is correct.**
Explanation: According to the question,
Mohan > Kamal > Sachin > Ram ...(i)
'Kamal >Arun > Sachin ...(ii)
From (i) and (ii);
Mohan > Kamal > Arun > Sachin > Ram
So, Kamal is the second tallest.

3. **Option (B) is correct.**
Explanation: Total number of men in the given row = 20 + 35 – 1 = 54 men in the row.

4. **Option (A) is correct.**
Explanation: If V comes in fifth, P and Q will come in sixth and seventh, respectively, meaning that Q comes in last.
So, S will get the highest grade.

5. **Option (C) is correct.**
Explanation: If R receives the most, T ranks last and takes up position seven. As V always ranks higher than P and Q, P and Q will, at most, occupy the fifth and sixth positions.
So, V will therefore not come in lower than fourth.

6. **Option (D) is correct.**
Explanation: If S comes in second, R comes in first, and T comes in last. The following sequence will be used: V > P > Q. Only the arrangement specified as per option (D), i.e., R > S > U > V > P > Q > T, is possible out of all the possibilities provided.
So, choice (D) is the right one.

7. **Option (D) is correct.**
Explanation: If S is ranked sixth and Q is ranked fifth, the results are: Q > S >
In this scenario, R will be ranked highest and T will be ranked lowest.
R > - > - > - Q > S > T are the results.
Additionally, the hierarchy of V > P > Q will be upheld.
R > U > V > P > Q > S > T, R > V > U > P > Q > S > T, or R > V > P > U > Q > S > T are the conceivable arrangements.
U can be ranked third or fourth, hence option (D), which is true.

8. **Option (D) is correct.**
Explanation: If R is ranked second, S will be first, Q or U will be lowest, but Q is placed fifth.
Thus, U is ranked last.
Additionally, the progression V > P > Q will be used.
S, R, V, P, Q, T, and U are the arrangement
1 2 3 4 5 6 7
T will therefore take up position 6 as a result.

9. **Option (D) is correct.**
Explanation: All information is needed.

10. **Option (A) is correct.**
Explanation: The arrangement is :
T—S—P—U—R—Q
So, T and Q read the magazine first and last, respectively.

(11–15):

Years	Age	Person
1985	36	C
1991	30	E
1995	26	A/D
1998	23	H
2002	19	B
2010	11	D/A
2015	6	F
2018	3	G

11. **Option (A) is correct.**
Explanation: Sum = 6 + 19 = 25 years

12. **Option (B) is correct.**
Explanation: Four persons were born between C and the one whose age is 11 years.

13. **Option (C) is correct.**
Explanation: G is the youngest person.

14. **Option (D) is correct.**
Explanation: C is the oldest person among all.

15. **Option (E) is correct.**
Explanation: Except B, all others have ages, which are multiple of 3.

(16–20):

Date/ Month	10th	15th
March	V	R
April	T	P
May	U	S
June	Q	W

16. **Option (C) is correct.**
Explanation: S got in the appointment in May.

17. **Option (B) is correct.**
Explanation: P got the appointment on 15th April.

18. **Option (E) is correct.**
Explanation: Four persons got the appointment before U.

19. **Option (C) is correct.**
Explanation: Q got the appointment on 10th June.

20. **Option (C) is correct.**
Explanation: T-April - 10th is the correct combination.

■ ■ ■

Chapter 13

Mathematical Operations

LEARNING OBJECTIVES:

- ❖ Method of calculating the answer by substitution the
- ❖ Method of calculating the answer by interchanging the symbols/letters
- ❖ Different types of question asked in competitive exams

In reasoning, 'Mathematical operations' plays a vital role as this section will definitely build up the critical and analytical level of students.

In this section, two major types of questions that can be asked are :

1. By substitution
2. By Interchanging

I. By substitution

In these type of questions, we are given some substitutions for the mathematical operators or for some letters. The students are required to substitute these operators with their given substitutes and then solve the obtained expression using VBODMAS rule

V → Venicullum
B → Bracket
O → Of
D → Division
M → Multiplication
A → Addition
S → Subtraction

Example 1: If '+' denotes '×', '–' deonotes '÷', '×' denotes '+' and '÷' denotes '–' then find the value of 50 – 5 × 20 + 3 ÷ 60.

(a) 20 (b) 30
(c) 10 (d) 50

Sol. (c) Hence, first we change the symbols.

So,

$50 - 5 \times 20 + 3 \div 60 = 50 \div 5 + 20 \times 3 - 60$
$= 10 + 20 \times 3 - 60$
$= 10 + 60 - 60 = 70 - 60 = 10$

Example 2: If 'M' stands for '+', 'N' stands for '–', 'O' stands for '×' and 'P' stands for ÷, then what will be the value of 17 M 26 P 13 N 22 O 5

(a) –91 (b) 82
(c) 90 (d) None of these

Sol. (a) After changing the given letters, we get

17 M 26 P 13 N 22 O 5
$= 17 + 26 \div 13 - 22 \times 5$
$= 17 + 2 - 22 \times 5$
$= 17 + 2 - 110$
$= 19 - 110 = -91$

II. By Interchanging

In these type of questions, we have some conditions of interchanging the mathematical operator or digits. The students are required to first interchange the given operators or digits (whichever is given) and then solve further.

Example 3: If the symbols ÷ and – interchanged, then what will be the value of the following expression?

$42 \div 8 + 12 - 6 + 5$

(a) 40 (b) 41
(c) 32 (d) 27

Sol. (b) After interchanging the symbols, we get

$42 - 8 + 12 \div 6 + 5$
$= 42 - 8 + 2 + 5$
$= 49 - 8 = 41$

Example 4: If the numbers 2 and 4 interchanged then what will be the value of the following expression?

$16 \div 2 + 3 \times 8 - 4$

(a) 20 (b) 15
(c) 18 (d) 26

Sol. (d) After interchanging the numbers, we get

$16 \div 4 + 3 \times 8 - 2$
$= 4 + 3 \times 8 - 2$
$= 4 + 24 - 2 = 28 - 2 = 26$

1 Level Beginner

Direction (Qs. 1–10): If A denotes +, B denotes ×, C denotes ÷ and D denotes –, then find the value of each of the following.

1. 14 C 2 B 8 A 3 D 5
(A) 48 (B) 54 (C) 50 (D) 38

2. 180 B 90 C 10 A 3 D 2
(A) 961 (B) 541 (C) 1621 (D) 181

3. 70 A 5 B 3 D 18 C 9
(A) 83 (B) 80 (C) 84 (D) 78

4. 100 C 50 A 10 C 2 D 5
(A) 20 (B) 5 (C) 10 (D) 2

5. 4 D 4 B 4 C 4 A 4
(A) 24 (B) 10 (C) 5 (D) 4

6. 25 A 5 B 8 C 2 A 120
(A) 165 (B) 170 (C) 90 (D) 82

7. 97 A 13 B 2 D 80 C 10
(A) 125 (B) 90 (C) 115 (D) 85

8. 200 C 40 A 30 B 20 D 5
(A) 600 (B) 540 (C) 610 (D) 650

9. 90 B 5 C 5 D 3 A 1
(A) 88 (B) 80 (C) 75 (D) 70

10. 120 A 85 C 17 B 5 D 3
(A) 150 (B) 118 (C) 120 (D) 142

11. If P denotes 'multiplied by', T denotes 'subtracted from', M denotes 'added to' and B denotes 'divided by', then 28 B 7 P 8 T 6 M 4 = ? **[Asst. Manager Exam, 2005]**
(A) $\frac{-3}{2}$ (B) 30
(C) 32 (D) 34
(E) None of these

12. If M denotes ÷, N denotes –, P denotes ×, Q denotes +, then find the value of 70 M 2 N 4 P 5 Q 6 = ?
(A) 21 (B) 45 (C) 20 (D) 51

13. If × means ÷, – means ×, ÷ means + and + means –, then (3 – 15 ÷ 19) × 8 + 6 = ? **[RRB 2003]**
(A) –1 (B) 2 (C) 4 (D) 8

14. If + means ÷, ÷ means –, – means × and × means +, then 18 + 6 ÷ 6 – 2 × 10 = ?
(A) 0 (B) 5 (C) 1 (D) 8

15. If $ means +, # means –, @ means × and * means ÷, then what is the value of 16 $ 4 @ 5 # 72 * 8? **[RBI 2002]**
(A) 25 (B) 27
(C) 29 (D) 36
(E) None of these

16. If '+' means 'divided by', '–' means 'add', ' ×' means 'minus' and ÷ means 'multiplied by', then what will be the value of the following expression?
[{(32 × 24) – (4 ÷ 3)} + (3 – 2)] ÷ 3 **[SSC CHSL 2020]**
(A) 6 (B) 8 (C) 10 (D) 12

17. If + means ÷, – means ×, × means +, ÷ means –, give the value for 45 + 9 – 3 × 15 ÷ 2 **[SSC CGL 2012]**
(A) 40 (B) 36 (C) 56 (D) 28

18. If – denotes ÷, ÷ denotes –, × denotes + and + denotes ×, then 4 – 2 × 2 + 10 ÷ 2 = ?
(A) 20 (B) 10 (C) 15 (D) 18

19. If × means + , + means ÷, – means × and ÷ means –, then 7 × 9 – 5 + 20 ÷ 10 = ?
(A) 18 (B) 10
(C) 15 (D) None of these

20. After interchanging the two numbers 3 and 6, what will be the value of the given expression?
12 × 3 ÷ 6 + 8 – 2 **[MTS 2020]**
(A) 15 (B) 25 (C) 30 (D) 20

21. If P denotes '×', T denotes –, M denotes +, S denotes ÷, then 42 S6 P 4 T 3 M 2 = ?
(A) 27 (B) 30 (C) 15 (D) 22

22. If P denotes ÷. Q denotes ×, R denotes + and S denotes –, then 18 Q 12 P 4 R 5 S 6 = ? **[SSC CGL 2012]**
(A) 95 (B) 53 (C) 51 (D) 57

23. If @ denotes +, © denotes –, # denotes × and β denotes ÷, then find the value of 20 β 5 © 10 # 2 @ 5.
(A) 10 (B) –11 (C) –15 (D) 8

24. If 'A' is replaced by '+', 'B' is replaced by '–', 'C' is replaced by '÷' and 'D' is replaced by '×', then find the value of the following equation
51 C 17 D 15 A 22 B 34 **[SSC Steno 2020]**
(A) 45 (B) 55 (C) 33 (D) 65

25. If '+' means –, – means ×, ÷ means + and × means ÷, then 15 – 3 + 10 × 5 ÷ 5 = ? **[CBI 2003]**
(A) 5 (B) 22 (C) 48 (D) 52

26. If '+' means '×', '–' means '÷', '×' means '–' and ' ÷' means '+', then what will be the value of 16 ÷ 64 – 8 × 4 + 2? **[SSC CGL 2015]**
(A) 12 (B) 24 (C) 16 (D) 18

27. If P denotes '÷', Q denotes ×, R denotes + and S denotes –, then 8 Q 1 6 P 4 R 5 S 6 is equal to
(A) 68 (B) 31 (C) 53 (D) 32

28. If 'a' represents ÷, 'b' represents +, 'c' represents – and 'd' represents ×, then 24 a 6 d 4 b 9 c 8 = ? **[SSC SI 2015]**
(A) 6 (B) 17 (C) 20 (D) 19

29. If + denotes –, × denotes ÷, ÷ denotes + and – denotes ×, then find the value of
126 × 9 + 8 × 4 – 3
(A) 8 (B) 10 (C) 9 (D) 15

30. If 'A' is replaced by '+', 'B' is replaced by '–', 'C' is replaced by '÷' and D is replaced by '×', then find the value of the following equation:
20 A 15 C 3 D 8 B 9 **[SSC Steno 2018]**
(A) 65 (B) 51 (C) 55 (D) 53

31. If 'K' denotes 'X', 'L' denotes '–', 'M' denotes '+' and 'N' denotes ÷, then find the value of 36 N 4 L 10 K 2 M 5.

(A) –6 (B) –4 (C) 8 (D) 3

32. If '+' means multiplication, '–' means division, '×' means plus, '÷' means subtraction then find the value of 18 × 8 – 4 + 7 × 8

(A) 38 (B) 42 (C) 50 (D) 55

33. If '+' means minus, '–' means multiplication, '÷' means plus, and '×' means division, then 15 – 3 + 10 × 5 ÷ 5 [SSC CGL 2016]

(A) 52 (B) 48 (C) 22 (D) 5

34. If '+' stands for minus, '–' stands for multiplied by, '÷' stands for 'add' and '×' stands for 'division', then what is the value of 100 × 50 – 20 + 3 ÷ 9.

(A) 40 (B) 32 (C) 46 (D) 38

35. If '+' denotes '÷', '–' denotes '×', '×' denotes '–' and '÷' denotes '+', then 35 + 7 – 5 ÷ 5 × 6 = ? [CHSL 2013]

(A) 20 (B) 14 (C) 36 (D) 24

Level 2 Intermediate

1. If 'A' stands for 'subtraction', 'B' stands for 'multiplicaton', 'C' stands for 'addition' and 'D' stands for 'division', then what is the value of the following expression? [CGL 2020]

32 B 4 A 12 B (35 A 24) C 52 D4

(A) 47 (B) 19 (C) 9 (D) 39

2. In the following question, which mathematical operators can be used that the expression will become correct? 35 * 5 * 2 * 8 * 22

(A) ÷, ×, +, = (B) ×, ÷, =, +
(C) +, =, ×, ÷ (D) ÷, +, ×, =

3. Which of the following interchange of signs would make the given equation correct? [RRB 2020]

5 + 6 ÷ 3 – 12 × 2 = 17

(A) ÷ and × (B) + and ×
(C) + and ÷ (D) + and –

4. If I means '×, You means ÷, we means – and He means +, then what will be the value of 8 I 12 He 16 You 2 We 10 ? [SSC SI 2012]

(A) 45 (B) 94 (C) 96 (D) 112

5. 50 * 2 * 12 = 8 * 11 * 0

(A) ×, –, ×, + (B) +, –, ×, +
(C) ×, +, ×, – (D) ×, +, +, ×

6. If + stands for division, × stands for addition, – stands for multiplication, ÷ stands for 'subtraction', which of the following equation is correct? [RRB 2021]

(A) 5 – 3 + 2 × 4 ÷ 8 = 2
(B) 5 × 3 + 2 – 4 × 8 = 19
(C) 5 ÷ 3 × 2 – 4 + 8 = 8
(D) 5 + 3 × 2 ÷ 4 – 8 = 4

7. Choose the appropriate combination of signs to solve,

20 * 10 * 1 * 10

(A) =, +, – (B) –, ÷, =
(C) +, =, – (D) +, –, =

8. Which of the following interchanges of signs would make the given equation correct?

15 + 8 ÷ 3 – 10 × 2 = 34

(A) ÷ and × (B) + and ×
(C) ÷ and + (D) + and –

9. After interchanging ÷ and +, 12 and 18, which one of the following equations becomes correct? [SSC CGL 2010]

(A) (90 × 18) + 16 = 60
(B) (18 + 6) ÷ 12 = 2
(C) (72 ÷ 18) × 18 = 72
(D) (12 + 6) × 18 = 36

10. Put the correct mathematical signs in the following equation from the given options.

55 ? 11 ? 5 ? 8 = 200

(A) ÷, ×, × (B) ×, –, +
(C) –, ×, + (D) +, –, ×

11. If P means ×, Q means ÷, R means – and S means +, then find the value of 315 Q 15 S 25 P 4 R 15

(A) 106 (B) 110 (C) 90 (D) 95

12. After interchanging ÷ and =, 2 and 3, which one of the following statements becomes correct? [SSC CGL 2010]

(A) 15 = 2 ÷ 3 (B) 5 ÷ 15 = 2
(C) 2 = 15 ÷ 3 (D) 3 = 2 ÷ 15

13. If $\sqrt{\ }$ means square, Q means +, R means × and S means ÷ then $\sqrt{15}$ Q 25 R 120 S 60 = ?

(A) 275 (B) 315 (C) 280 (D) 320

14. After interchanging the given two numbers and two signs what will be values of equation (I) and (II) respectively? [CGL 2022]

× and +, 3 and 9

(I) 7 × 9 – 8 ÷ 2 + 3 (II) 4 × 9 – 3 + 8 ÷ 2

(A) 0, 1 (B) –26, –29
(C) 6, 0 (D) 12, 13

15. Which of the following interchange of signs would make the equation correct?

12 × 8 + 4 = 56

(A) + and ×, 4 and 8 (B) + and ×, 4 and 12
(C) + and ×, 4 and 12 (D) None of these

16. Select the correct set of symbols which will fit in the given equation. [SSC 2001]

5 0 3 5 = 20

(A) ×, ×, × (B) –, +, ×
(C) ×, +, × (D) +, –, ×

17. In the following question, correct the equation by interchanging two signs.

15 × 5 + 3 ÷ 2 – 7 = 20

(A) × and – (B) + and –
(C) ÷ and + (D) × and ÷

18. If '+' is denoted by @, '÷' is denoted by @, '×' is denoted by # and '–' is denoted by *, then what is the value of 80 * 40 # 4 @ 80 © 40 @ 20?

(A) –58 (B) 60 (C) –50 (D) 70

19. If the signs – and ÷ are interchanged, then which of the following equations would be correct? [MTS 2021]

(A) 12 ÷ 3 + 9 – 9 = 4 (B) 9 ÷ 9 – 9 + 9 = 9
(C) 12 + 4 – 4 ÷ 2 = 3 (D) 6 ÷ 3 + 12 – 6 = 5

20. If A mean +, B means ×, C mean ÷ and D means –, then what will be the value of (400D150 C (70D20) B 30 A 15

(A) 150 (B) 165 (C) 130 (D) 125

Direction (Qs. 21–25): In each of the following questions, the two expressions on either side of the sign (=) will have the same value of two terms on either side or on the same side are interchanged. The correct terms to be interchanged have been given as one of the four alternatives under the expressions. Find the correct alternative in each case. [CAT 1997]

21. 5 + 3 × 6 – 4 ÷ 2 = 4 × 3 – 10 ÷ 2 + 7

(A) 4, 7 (B) 5, 7 (C) 6, 4 (D) 6, 10

22. 7 × 2 – 3 + 8 ÷ 4 = 5 + 6 × 2 – 24 ÷ 3

(A) 2, 6 (B) 6, 5 (C) 3, 24 (D) 7, 6

23. 15 + 3 × 4 – 8 ÷ 2 = 8 × 5 + 16 ÷ 2 – 1

(A) 3, 5 (B) 15, 5 (C) 15, 16 (D) 3, 1

24. 6 × 3 + 8 ÷ 2 – 1 = 9 – 8 ÷ 4 + 5 × 2

(A) 3, 4 (B) 3, 5 (C) 6, 9 (D) 9, 5

25. 8 ÷ 2 × 5 – 11 + 9 = 6 × 2 – 5 + 4 ÷ 2

(A) 5, 9 (B) 8, 5 (C) 9, 6 (D) 11, 5

26. If 'W' means '×', '×' means '÷', 'Y' means '+' and 'Z' means '–', then what is the value of (176 × 11) Y (20 W 17) Z (30 Y 15)?

(A) 251 (B) 308 (C) 279 (D) 311

27. Which two signs need to be interchanged to make the following equation correct?

73 – 13 × 42 ÷ 14 + 56 = 56 [MTS 2020]

(A) + and × (B) × and ÷
(C) – and + (D) – and ×

28. If '+' means '÷', '×' means '+', '–' means '×', and '÷' means '–', then which of the following is correct? [SSC 2013]

(A) 36 + 6 – 3 × 2 = 20 (B) 36 × 6 + 3 – 2 < 20
(C) 36 × 6 + 3 × 2 > 20 (D) 36 + 6 × 3 + 2 = 20

29. If $x \times y = \frac{xy+5}{2}$ and $x \div y = \frac{x+y}{5}$, then find the value of (5 ÷ 10) × (6 ÷ 14)

(A) $\frac{17}{2}$ (B) $\frac{19}{2}$
(C) 35 (D) None of these

30. Which of the following interchanges of numbers would make the given equation correct?

8 × 20 ÷ 3 + 9 – 5 = 38 [SSC CGL 2013]

(A) 8, 9 (B) 3, 5 (C) 3, 9 (D) 3, 8

31. If 'love' means '×', 'country' means '÷', 'my' means '+" and 'I' means '–', then find the value of (150 country 50) I (40 love 3) country (10 my 5).

(A) 3 (B) –8
(C) –5 (D) None of these

32. Which two signs should be interchanged to make the given equation correct?

25 – 5 × 50 ÷ 10 + 35 = 155 [SSC SI 2021]

(A) × and ÷ (B) × and +
(C) × and – (D) + and –

33. If $p \oplus q = \frac{p+q}{3}$ and $p - q = \frac{p-q}{2}$, then find the value of (6 ⊕ 9) – (8 ⊕ 4) [SSC 2012]

(A) 2 (B) $\frac{1}{2}$ (C) 4 (D) $\frac{3}{2}$

34. If A denotes 'addition', B denotes 'multiplication' C denotes subtraction and D denotes division, then what will be the value of following expression?

43 A 22 C 15 B 4 A 72 D (10 C 2) = ? [SSC 2021]

(A) 44 (B) 18 (C) 14 (D) 32

35. Select the option by using which mathematical operators will the expression become correct?

18 ? 3 ? 5 ? 8 ? 3

(A) ×, ÷, > and $\overline{x}$ (B) ÷, ×, > and ×
(C) ÷, –, –, – (D) +, –, <, ×

Level 3 Expert

1. Select the correct combination of mathematical signs to replace the signs and balance the given equation

21 * 4 * 156 * 13 * 11= 783 [CGL 2022]

(A) –, ÷, ×, + (B) ×, +, ÷, –
(C) ×, –, ÷, + (D) +, ÷, –, ×

2. If '–' stands for '+', '+' stands for '–', '×' stands for '÷' and '÷' stands for '×, then select the correct option

(A) 40 ÷ 5 × 8 – 30 + 32 = 120
(B) 16 ÷ 8 × 2 + 40 – 30 = 11
(C) 16 ÷ 55 × 11 + 50 – 2 = 32
(D) 16 ÷ 11 × 55 + 38 + 10 = 28

3. By interchanging the given two signs which of the following equation will not be correct?

– and × [CGL 2022]

(A) 5 – 6 × 3 + 16 ÷ 4 = 31
(B) 11 + 6 × 3 – 8 ÷ 2 = 5
(C) 7 × 8 + 4 ÷ 2 – 6 = 11
(D) 7 × 2 + 27 ÷ 9 – 4 = 18

4. If 18 × 6' means '12' '15 – 3' means 18, '100 + 10' means 10 and '21 ÷ 5' means 105, then 112 + 4 ÷ 3 – 7 ÷ 10 = ?

(A) 81 (B) 89 (C) 154 (D) 72

5. Select the correct combination of mathematical sign to replace * signs and to balance the following equation:
(18 * 9 * 14) & 37 * 4 [CPO 2019]
(A) –, ÷, ×, = (B) ×, ÷, –, =
(C) ÷, –, ×, = (D) ×, –, ÷, =

6. If '25 + 5' means 125; '20 – 4' means 5; '80 × 4' means 84 and '150 ÷ 50' means 100, then 60 × 500 – 50 + 20 – 60 = ?
(A) 65 (B) 70 (C) 150 (D) 85

7. Choose the appropriate combination of signs to solve.
16 * 8 * 1 * 8 [SSC CHSL 2012]
(A) =, –, ÷ (B) –, ÷, =
(C) ÷, –, = (D) ÷, =, –

8. If '–' stands for '÷', '+' stands for '×', '÷' stands for '–' and '×' stands for '+', which one of the following equations is correct? [SSC CGL 2011]
(A) 30 – 6 + 5 × 4 ÷ 2 = 27
(B) 30 + 6 – 5 ÷ 4 × 2 = 30
(C) 30 × 6 ÷ 5 – 4 + 2 = 32
(D) 30 ÷ 6 × 5 + 4 – 2 = 40

9. If '÷' means '×', ' ×' means '+', '+' means '–' and '–1' means '÷', then select the correct option.
(A) 60 – 20 ÷ 15 × 5 + 30 = 20
(B) 60 ÷ 15 – 20 + 30 × 5 = 20
(C) 60 + 30 × 15 ÷ 3 – 20 = 41
(D) Both (A) and (B)

10. Select the correct combination of mathematical signs to replace * signs and to balance the given equation.
5 * 5 * 5 * 3 * 10 [SSC SI 2013]
(A) ×, +, =, × (B) +, –, ×, =
(C) +, ÷, =, × (D) +, ÷, ×, =

Direction (Qs. 11–16): If '+' denotes ÷ '^' denoes ×, '>' denotes '+', '<' denotes '–', '×' denotes >, '=' denotes < and '–' denotes =, then choose the correct option in the following questions.

11. (A) 16 + 8 > 2 < 5 × 10 < 5
(B) 16 > 8 + 2 > 5 × 20 + 10
(C) 8 < 16 + 2 < 5 × 5 > 2
(D) 8 < 2 < 16 + 4 × 15 + 3

12. (A) 7 + 1 < 5 > 2 = 10 + 10 > 1
(B) 7 + 7 < 5 ^ 1 × 10 < 2 > 5
(C) 7 ^ < 7 < 5 + 1 – 10 ^ 4 > 4
(D) 7 < 5 + 1 < 2 × 10 + 275

13. (A) 100 > 10 + 10 < 100 × 20 + 10 < 2
(B) 100 + 50 > 15 < 10 – 20 < 10 > 5
(C) 50 ^ 2 + 50 < 10 = 100 + 100 < 10
(D) 80 + 10 > 15 + 3 –70 < 35 + 7

14. (A) 6 + 2 – 15 + 5 < 3 ^ 2
(B) 6 ^ 2 = 15 + 3 > 2 ^ 1
(C) 6 > 2 × 30 + 3 > 2 ^ 1
(D) 6 < 2 = 10 + 2 ^ 3 ^ 1

15. (A) 8 × 4 ^ 2^ 6 + 3 > 1
(B) 8 × 2 ^ 3 ^ 4 + 2 ^ 4
(C) 38 = 2 ^ 4 + 2 ^ 3 ^ 5
(D) 8 + 4 × 4 + 2 ^ 15 + 3

16. (A) 8 > 8 < 8 + 8 = 20
(B) 8 ^ 8 > 8 + 8 = 8 ^ 8 > 1
(C) 8 < 8 + 8 = 5
(D) 8 + 8 > 8 = 3

17. In the following question, correct the equation by interchanging two signs.
9 × 3 + 8 ÷ 4 – 7 = 28 [SSC CGL 2017]
(A) × and – (B) + and –
(C) ÷ and + (D) × and ÷

18. In the given question, correct the equation by interchanging two signs.
3 × 8 – 12 ÷ 4 + 5 =3
(A) – and ÷ (B) + and ÷
(C) + and – (D) × and +

19. If '15 – 7' means 105, '55 ÷ 15' means 70; '52 × 10' means 42 and '110 + 10' means 11, then find the value of 765 + 15 – 19 ÷ 18 × 20
(A) 810 (B) 815 (C) 971 (D) 757

20. If '20 _ 20' means 400; '8 ÷ 5' means 13; '8 × 3' means 5 and '50 + 5' means 10 then find the value of
80 ÷ 8 – 20 + 10 × 17
(A) 51 (B) 39 (C) 28 (D) 47

ANSWER KEY

Level-1: Beginner

1.	(B)	2.	(C)	3.	(A)	4.	(D)	5.	(D)	6.	(A)	7.	(C)	8.	(A)	9.	(A)	10.	(D)
11.	(B)	12.	(A)	13.	(B)	14.	(C)	15.	(B)	16.	(D)	17.	(D)	18.	(A)	19.	(D)	20.	(C)
21.	(A)	22.	(B)	23.	(B)	24.	(C)	25.	(C)	26.	(C)	27.	(B)	28.	(B)	29.	(A)	30.	(B)
31.	(A)	32.	(C)	33.	(B)	34.	(C)	35.	(D)										

Level-2: Intermediate

1.	(C)	2.	(A)	3.	(A)	4.	(B)	5.	(A)	6.	(B)	7.	(B)	8.	(A)	9.	(D)	10.	(A)
11.	(A)	12.	(B)	13.	(A)	14.	(B)	15.	(D)	16.	(B)	17.	(C)	18.	(A)	19.	(D)	20.	(B)
21.	(C)	22.	(D)	23.	(A)	24.	(D)	25.	(C)	26.	(D)	27.	(C)	28.	(A)	29.	(A)	30.	(A)
31.	(C)	32.	(C)	33.	(B)	34.	(C)	35.	(B)										

Level-3: Expert

1.	(C)	2.	(C)	3.	(D)	4.	(C)	5.	(D)	6.	(A)	7.	(B)	8.	(A)	9.	(D)	10.	(A)
11.	(B)	12.	(C)	13.	(A)	14.	(D)	15.	(C)	16.	(A)	17.	(D)	18.	(A)	19.	(C)	20.	(D)

Solutions with Detailed Explanations

Level-1: BEGINNER

1. **Option (B) is correct.**
Explanation: After changing the letters,
We get,
$14 \div 2 \times 8 + 3 - 5 = 7 \times 8 + 3 - 5$
$= 56 + 3 - 5 = 59 - 5 = 54$

2. **Option (C) is correct.**
Explanation: After changing the letters, we get
$180 \times 90 \div 10 + 3 - 2$
$= 180 \times 9 + 3 - 2$
$= 1620 + 3 - 2$
$= 1623 - 2 = 1621$

3. **Option (A) is correct.**
Explanation: After changing the letters, we get
$70 + 5 \times 3 - 18 \div 9$
$70 + 5 \times 3 - 2$
$= 70 + 15 - 2$
$= 85 - 2 = 83$

4. **Option (D) is correct.**
Explanation: After changing the letters, we get
$100 \div 50 + 10 \div 2 - 5$
$= 2 + 5 - 5$
$= 7 - 5 = 2$

5. **Option (D) is correct.**
Explanation: The given expression becomes:
$4 - 4 \times 4 \div 4 + 4$
$= 4 - 4 \times 1 + 4$
$= 4 - 4 + 4$
$= 8 - 4 = 4$

6. **Option (A) is correct.**
Explanation: The given expression becomes:
$25 + 5 \times 8 \div 2 + 120$
$= 25 + 5 \times 4 + 120 = 25 + 20 + 120 = 165$

7. **Option (C) is correct.**
Explanation: The given expression becomes:
$97 + 13 \times 2 - 80 \div 10$
$= 97 + 13 \times 2 - 8$
$= 97 + 26 - 8$
$= 123 - 8 = 115$

8. **Option (A) is correct.**
Explanation: The given expression becomes:
$200 \div 40 + 30 \times 20 - 5$
$= 5 + 30 \times 20 - 5$
$= 5 + 600 - 5$
$= 605 - 5 = 600$

9. **Option (A) is correct.**
Explanation: The given expression becomes:
$90 \times 5 \div 5 - 3 + 1$
$= 90 \times 1 - 3 + 1$
$= 91 - 3 = 88$

10. **Option (D) is correct.**
Explanation: The given expression becomes:
$120 + 85 \div 17 \times 5 - 3$
$= 120 + 5 \times 5 - 3$
$= 120 + 25 - 3$
$= 145 - 3 = 142$

11. **Option (B) is correct.**
Explanation: The given expression becomes::
$28 \div 7 \times 8 - 6 + 4$
$= 4 \times 8 - 6 + 4$
$= 32 - 6 + 4$
$= 36 - 6 = 30$

12. **Option (A) is correct.**
Explanation: The given expression becomes::
$70 \div 2 - 4 \times 5 + 6$
$= 35 - 4 \times 5 + 6$
$= 35 - 20 + 6$
$= 41 - 20 = 21$

13. **Option (B) is correct.**
Explanation: The given expression becomes:
$(3 \times 15 + 19) \div 8 - 6$
$= (45 + 19) \div 8 - 6$
$= 64 \div 8 - 6$
$= 8 - 6 = 2$

14. **Option (C) is correct.**
Explanation: The given expression becomes:
$18 \div 6 - 6 \times 2 + 10$
$= 3 - 6 \times 2 + 10$
$= 3 - 12 + 10$
$= 13 - 12 = 1$

15. **Option (B) is correct.**
Explanation: $16 + 4 \times 5 - 72 \div 8$
$= 16 + 4 \times 5 - 9$
$= 16 + 20 - 9$
$= 36 - 9 = 27$

16. **Option (D) is correct.**
Explanation: According to the question,
$[\{(32 - 24) + (4 \times 3)\} \div (3 + 2)] \times 3$
$= [(8 + 12) \div 5] \times 3$
$= [20 \div 5] \times 3 = 4 \times 3 = 12$

17. **Option (D) is correct.**
Explanation: According to the question,
$45 \div 9 \times 3 + 15 - 2$
$= 5 \times 3 + 15 - 2$
$= 15 + 15 - 2$
$= 30 - 2 = 28$

18. **Option (A) is correct.**
Explanation: The given expression becomes:
$4 \div 2 + 2 \times 10 - 2$
$= 2 + 2 \times 10 - 24$
$= 2 + 20 - 2 = 20$

19. **Option (D) is correct.**
Explanation: The given expression becomes:
$7 + 9 \times 5 \div 20 - 10$
$= 7 + 9 \times \frac{1}{4} - 10$
$= 7 + \frac{9}{4} - 10 = \frac{28}{4} + \frac{9}{4} - \frac{40}{4} = \frac{-3}{4}$

20. **Option (C) is correct.**
Explanation: According to the question,
$12 \times 6 \div 3 + 8 - 2$
$= 12 \times 2 + 8 - 2$
$= 24 + 8 - 2 = 30$

21. **Option (A) is correct.**
Explanation: The given expression becomes:
$42 \div 6 \times 4 - 3 + 2$
$= 7 \times 4 - 3 + 2$
$= 28 + 2 - 3 = 30 - 3 = 27$

22. **Option (B) is correct.**
Explanation: According to the question,
$18 \times 12 \div 4 + 5 - 6$
$= 18 \times 3 + 5 - 6$
$= 54 + 5 - 6$
$= 59 - 6 = 53$

23. **Option (B) is correct.**
Explanation: The given expression becomes:
$20 \div 5 - 10 \times 2 + 5$
$= 4 - 10 \times 2 + 5$
$= 4 - 20 + 5$
$= 9 - 20 = -11$

24. **Option (C) is correct.**
Explanation: The given expression becomes:
$51 \div 17 \times 15 + 22 - 34$
$= 3 \times 15 + 22 - 34$
$= 45 + 22 - 34$
$= 67 - 34 = 33$

25. **Option (C) is correct.**
Explanation: According to the question,
$15 \times 3 - 10 \div 5 + 5$
$= 15 \times 3 - 2 + 5$
$= 45 - 2 + 5$
$= 50 - 2 = 48$

26. **Option (C) is correct.**
Explanation: The given expression becomes:
$16 + 64 \div 8 - 4 \times 2$
$= 16 + 8 - 4 \times 2$
$= 16 + 8 - 8 = 16$

27. **Option (B) is correct.**
Explanation: The given expression becomes:
$8 \times 16 \div 4 + 5 - 6$
$= 8 \times 4 + 5 - 6$
$= 32 + 5 - 6$
$= 37 - 6 = 31$

28. **Option (B) is correct.**
Explanation: The given expression becomes:
$24 \div 6 \times 4 + 9 - 8$
$= 4 \times 4 + 9 - 8$
$= 16 + 9 - 8$
$= 25 - 8 = 17$

29. **Option (A) is correct.**
Explanation: According to the questions,
$126 \div 9 - 8 \div 4 \times 3$
$= 14 - 2 \times 3$
$= 14 - 6 = 8$

30. **Option (B) is correct.**
Explanation: The given expression becomes:
$20 + 15 \div 3 \times 8 - 9$
$= 20 + 5 \times 8 - 9$
$= 20 + 40 - 9 = 60 - 9 = 51$

31. **Option (A) is correct.**
Explanation: The given expression becomes
$36 \div 4 - 10 \times 2 + 5$
$= 9 - 10 \times 2 + 5$
$= 9 - 20 + 5$
$= 14 - 20 = -6$

32. **Option (C) is correct.**
Explanation: The given expression becomes
$18 + 8 \div 4 \times 7 + 8$
$= 18 + 2 \times 7 + 8$
$= 18 + 14 + 18 = 50$

33. **Option (B) is correct.**
Explanation: The given expression becomes
$15 \times 3 - 10 \div 5 + 5$
$= 15 \times 3 - 2 + 5$
$= 45 - 2 + 5$
$= 50 - 2 = 48$

34. **Option (C) is correct.**
Explanation: The given expression becomes
$100 \div 50 \times 20 - 3 + 9$
$= 2 \times 20 - 3 + 9 = 40 - 3 + 9$
$= 49 - 3 = 46$

35. **Option (D) is correct.**
Explanation: According to question,
$35 \div 7 \times 5 + 5 - 6$
$= 5 \times 5 + 5 - 6$
$= 25 + 5 - 6$
$= 30 - 6 = 24$

Level-2: INTERMEDIATE

1. **Option (C) is correct.**
Explanation: The given expression becomes:
$32 \times 4 - 12 \times (35 - 24) + 52 \div 4$
$= 32 \times 4 - 12 \times 11 + 13$
$= 128 - 132 + 13$
$= 141 - 132 = 9$

2. **Option (A) is correct.**
Explanation: The given expression becomes:
$35 \div 5 \times 2 + 8 = 22$
$\Rightarrow 7 \times 2 + 8 = 22$
$\Rightarrow 14 + 8 = 22$
$\Rightarrow 22 = 22$ (Correct)

3. **Option (A) is correct.**
Explanation: After inter changing the signs, we get
(A) $5 + 6 \times 3 - 12 \div 2 = 17$
$\Rightarrow 5 + 6 \times 3 - 6 = 17$
$\Rightarrow 5 + 18 - 6 = 17$
$\Rightarrow 17 = 17$ (Correct)

(B) 5 × 6 ÷ 3 – 12 + 2 = 17
⇒ 5 × 2 – 12 + 2 = 17
⇒ 10 – 12 + 2 = 17
⇒ 0 = 17 (Incorrect)
(C) 5 ÷ 6 + 3 – 12 × 2 = 17

$\Rightarrow \frac{5}{6}+3-24=17$

$\Rightarrow \frac{5}{6}-21=17$

$\Rightarrow \frac{5-126}{6}=17$

$\Rightarrow -\frac{121}{6}=17$ (Incorrect)

(D) 5 – 6 ÷ 3 + 12 × 2 = 17
⇒ 5 – 2 + 12 × 2 = 17
⇒ 5 – 2 + 24 = 17
⇒ 27 = 17 (Incorrect)

4. **Option (B) is correct.**
Explanation: According to the question,
8 × 12 + 16 ÷ 2 – 10
= 8 × 12 + 8 – 10
= 96 + 8 – 10
= 104 – 10 = 94

5. **Option (A) is correct.**
Explanation: The given expression becomes
50 × 2 – 12 = 8 × 11 + 0
⇒ 100 – 12 = 88 + 0
⇒ 88 = 88

6. **Option (B) is correct.**
Explanation: After changing the symbols, we get
(A) 5 × 3 ÷ 2 + 4 – 8 = 2

$\Rightarrow 5\times\frac{3}{2}+4-8=2$

$\Rightarrow \frac{15}{2}-4=2$

$\Rightarrow -\frac{7}{2}=2$ (Incorrect)

(B) 5 + 3 ÷ 2 × 4 + 8 = 19

$\Rightarrow 5+\frac{3}{2}\times4+8=19$

⇒ 5 + 6 + 8 = 19
⇒ 19 = 19 (Correct)
(C) 5 – 3 + 2 × 4 ÷ 8 = 8

$\Rightarrow 5-3+2\times\frac{1}{2}=8$

⇒ 5 – 3 + 1 = 8
⇒ 3 = 8 (Incorrect)
(D) 5 ÷ 3 + 2 – 4 × 8 = 4

$\Rightarrow \frac{5}{3}+2-32=4$

$\Rightarrow \frac{5}{3}-30=4$

$\Rightarrow -\frac{85}{3}=4$ (Incorrect)

⇒ 7

7. **Option (B) is correct.**
Explanation: The given expression becomes:
20 – 10 ÷ 1 = 10
⇒ 20 – 10 = 10
⇒ 10 = 10

8. **Option (A) is correct.**
Explanation: After interchanging the symbols we get
(A) 15 + 8 × 3 – 10 ÷ 2 = 34
⇒ 34 = 34 (Correct)
(B) 15 × 8 ÷ 3 – 10 + 2 = 34

$\Rightarrow 15\times\frac{8}{3}-10+2=34$

⇒ 40 – 10 + 2 = 34
⇒ 32 = 34 (Incorrect)
(C) 15 ÷ 8 + 3 – 10 × 2 = 34

$\Rightarrow \frac{15}{8}+3-20=34$

$\Rightarrow \frac{15}{8}-17=34$

$\Rightarrow \frac{15-136}{8}=34$

$\Rightarrow -\frac{121}{8}=34$ (Incorrect)

(D) 15 – 8 ÷ 3 + 10 × 2 = 34

$\Rightarrow 15-\frac{8}{3}+20=34$

$\Rightarrow 35-\frac{8}{3}=34$

$\Rightarrow \frac{105-8}{3}=34$

$\Rightarrow \frac{97}{7}=34$ (Incorrect)

9. **Option (D) is correct.**
Explanation: The given expression becomes:
(18 ÷ 6) × 12 = 36
⇒ 3 × 12 = 36
⇒ 36 = 36

10. **Option (A) is correct.**
Explanation: The given expression becomes:
55 ÷ 11 × 5 × 8 = 200
⇒ 5 × 5 × 8 = 200
⇒ 200 = 200

11. **Option (A) is correct.**
Explanation: After changing the symbols, we get
315 ÷ 15 + 25 × 4 – 15
= 21 + 25 × 4 – 15
= 21 + 100 – 15= 121 – 15 = 106

12. **Option (B) is correct.**
Explanation: After interchanging the symbols and numbers we get
(A) 15 ÷ 3 = 2
⇒ 5 = 2 (Incorrect)
(B) 5 = 15 ÷ 3
⇒ 5 = 5 (Correct)
(C) 3 ÷ 15 = 2

$\Rightarrow \frac{1}{3}=2$ (Incorrect)

(D) $2 \div 3 = 15$

$\Rightarrow \frac{2}{3} = 15$ (Incorrect)

13. Option (A) is correct.

Explanation: After changing the symbols, we get

$(15)^2 + 25 \times 120 \div 60$

$= 225 + 25 \times 120 \div 60$

$= 225 + 25 \times 2$

$= 225 + 50 = 275$

14. Option (B) is correct.

Explanation: After interchanging we get

(I) $7 + 3 - 8 \div 2 \times 9$

$= 7 + 3 - 4 \times 9$

$= 7 + 3 - 36$

$= 10 - 36 = -26$

(II) $4 + 3 - 9 \times 8 \div 2$

$= 4 + 3 - 9 \times 4$

$= 4 + 3 - 36$

$= 7 - 36 = -29$

15. Option (D) is correct.

Explanation: After interchanging + and ×, 8 and 12, we get

$8 + 12 \times 4 = 8 + 48 = 56$

16. Option (B) is correct.

Explanation: (A) $5 \times 0 \times 3 \times 5 = 20$

$\Rightarrow 0 = 20$ (Incorrect)

(B) $5 - 0 + 3 \times 5 = 20$

$\Rightarrow 5 - 0 + 15 = 20$

$\Rightarrow 20 = 20$ (Correct)

(C) $5 \times 0 + 3 \times 5 = 20$

$\Rightarrow 0 + 15 = 20$

$\Rightarrow 15 = 20$ (Incorrect)

(D) $5 + 0 - 3 \times 5 = 20$

$\Rightarrow 5 + 0 - 15 = 20$

$\Rightarrow -10 = 20$ (Incorrect)

17. Option (C) is correct.

Explanation: After interchanging the signs, we get

$15 \times 5 \div 3 + 2 - 7 = 20$

$\Rightarrow 15 \times \frac{5}{3} + 2 - 7 = 20$

$\Rightarrow 25 + 2 - 7 = 20$

$\Rightarrow 20 = 20$

18. Option (A) is correct.

Explanation: After changing the symbols, we get

$80 - 40 \times 4 + 80 \div 40 + 20$

$= 80 - 40 \times 4 + 2 + 20$

$= 80 - 160 + 2 + 20$

$= 102 - 160 = -58$

19. Option (D) is correct.

Explanation: After interchanging the signs, we get

(A) $12 - 3 + 9 \div 9 = 4$

$\Rightarrow 12 - 3 + 1 = 4$

$\Rightarrow 10 = 4$ (Incorrect)

(B) $9 - 9 \div 9 + 9 = 9$

$\Rightarrow 9 - 1 + 9 = 9$

$\Rightarrow 17 = 9$ (Incorrect)

(C) $12 + 4 \div 4 - 2 = 3$

$\Rightarrow 12 + 1 - 2 = 3$

$\Rightarrow 11 = 3$ (Incorrect)

(D) $6 - 3 + 12 \div 6 = 5$

$\Rightarrow 6 - 3 + 2 = 5$

$\Rightarrow 5 = 5$ (Correct)

20. Option (B) is correct.

Explanation: After changing the symbols, we get

$(400 - 150) \div (70 - 20) \times 30 + 15$

$= 250 \div 50 \times 30 + 15$

$= 5 \times 30 + 15$

$= 150 + 15 = 165$

21. Option (C) is correct.

Explanation: $5 + 3 \times 4 - 6 \div 2 = 4 \times 3 - 10 \div 2 + 7$

$\Rightarrow 5 + 3 \times 4 - 3 = 4 \times 3 - 5 + 7$

$\Rightarrow 5 + 12 - 3 = 12 - 5 + 7$

$\Rightarrow 14 = 14$

22. Option (D) is correct.

Explanation: $6 \times 2 - 3 + 8 \div 4 = 5 + 7 \times 2 - 24 \div 3$

$\Rightarrow 6 \times 2 - 3 + 2 = 5 + 7 \times 2 - 8$

$\Rightarrow 12 - 3 + 2 = 5 + 14 - 8$

$\Rightarrow 11 = 11$

23. Option (A) is correct.

Explanation: $15 + 5 \times 4 - 8 \div 2 = 8 \times 3 + 16 \div 2 - 1$

$\Rightarrow 15 + 5 \times 4 - 4 = 8 \times 3 + 8 - 1$

$\Rightarrow 15 + 20 - 4 = 24 + 8 - 1$

$\Rightarrow 31 = 31$

24. Option (D) is correct.

Explanation: The given expression becomes

$6 \times 3 + 8 \div 2 - 1 = 5 - 8 \div 4 + 9 \times 2$

$\Rightarrow 6 \times 3 + 4 - 1 = 5 - 2 + 9 \times 2$

$\Rightarrow 18 + 4 - 1 = 5 - 2 + 18$

$\Rightarrow 21 = 21$

25. Option (C) is correct.

Explanation: The given expression becomes

$8 \div 2 \times 5 - 11 + 6 = 9 \times 2 - 5 + 4 \div 2$

$\Rightarrow 4 \times 5 - 11 + 6 = 9 \times 2 - 5 + 2$

$\Rightarrow 20 - 11 + 6 = 18 - 5 + 2$

$\Rightarrow 15 = 15$

26. Option (D) is correct.

Explanation: After interchanging the symbols, we get

$(176 \div 11) + (20 \times 17) - (30 + 15)$

$= 16 + 340 - 45$

$= 356 - 45 = 311$

27. Option (C) is correct.

Explanation: After interchanging the signs, we get

(A) $73 - 13 + 42 \div 14 \times 56 = 56$

$\Rightarrow 73 - 13 + 3 \times 56 = 56$

$\Rightarrow 73 - 13 + 168 = 56$

$\Rightarrow 228 = 56$ (Incorrect)

(B) $73 - 13 \div 42 \times 14 + 56 = 56$

$\Rightarrow 73 - \frac{13}{42} \times 14 + 56 = 56$

$\Rightarrow 73 - \frac{13}{3} + 56 = 56$

$\Rightarrow 129 - \frac{13}{3} = 56 \Rightarrow \frac{374}{3} = 56$ (Incorrect)

(C) $73 + 13 \times 42 \div 14 - 56 = 56$

$\Rightarrow 73 + 13 \times 3 - 56 = 56$

$\Rightarrow 73 + 39 - 56 = 56$

$\Rightarrow 112 - 56 = 56$

$\Rightarrow 56 = 56$ (Correct)

(D) $73 \times 13 - 42 \div 14 + 56 = 56$
$\Rightarrow 73 \times 13 - 3 + 56 = 56$
$\Rightarrow 949 - 3 + 56 = 56$
$\Rightarrow 1002 = 56$ (Incorrect)

28. Option (A) is correct.
Explanation: After interchanging the signs, we get
$36 \div 6 \times 3 + 2 = 20$
$\Rightarrow 6 \times 3 + 2 = 20$
$\Rightarrow 18 + 2 = 20$
$\Rightarrow 20 = 20$ (Correct)

29. Option (A) is correct.
Explanation: (A) $(5 \div 10) \times (6 \div 14)$
$$= \left(\frac{5+10}{5}\right) \times \left(\frac{6+14}{5}\right)$$
$$= 3 \times 4 = \frac{12+5}{2} = \frac{17}{2}$$

30. Option (A) is correct.
Explanation: (A) $9 \times 20 \div 3 + 8 - 5 = 38$
$$\Rightarrow 9 \times \frac{20}{3} + 8 - 5 = 38$$
$\Rightarrow 60 + 8 - 5 = 38$
$\Rightarrow 63 = 38$ (Incorrect)
(B) $8 \times 20 \div 5 + 9 - 3 = 38$
$\Rightarrow 8 \times 4 + 9 - 3 = 38$
$\Rightarrow 32 + 9 - 3 = 38$
$\Rightarrow 38 = 38$ (Correct)
(C) $8 \times 20 \div 9 + 3 - 5 = 38$
$$\Rightarrow 8 \times \frac{20}{9} + 3 - 5 = 38$$
$$\Rightarrow \frac{160}{9} - 2 = 38$$
$$\Rightarrow \frac{142}{9} = 38 \text{ (Incorrect)}$$
(D) $3 \times 20 \div 8 + 9 - 5 = 38$
$$\Rightarrow 3 \times \frac{5}{2} + 9 - 5 = 38$$
$$\Rightarrow \frac{15}{2} + 4 = 38$$
$$\Rightarrow \frac{23}{2} = 38 \text{ (Incorrect)}$$

31. Option (C) is correct.
Explanation: (150 country 50) I (40 love 3) country (10 my 5)
$= (150 \div 50) - (40 \times 3) \div (10 + 5)$
$= 3 - 120 \div 15$
$= 3 - 8 = -5$

32. Option (C) is correct.
Explanation: After interchanging the signs, we get
(A) $25 - 5 \div 50 \times 10 + 35 = 155$
$$\Rightarrow 25 - \frac{1}{10} \times 10 + 35 = 155$$
$\Rightarrow 25 - 1 + 35 = 155$
$\Rightarrow 59 = 155$ (Incorrect)
(B) $25 - 5 + 50 \div 10 \times 35 = 155$
$\Rightarrow 25 - 5 + 5 \times 35 = 155$
$\Rightarrow 25 - 5 + 175 = 155$
$\Rightarrow 195 = 155$ (Incorrect)
(C) $25 \times 5 - 50 \div 10 + 35 = 155$
$\Rightarrow 25 \times 5 - 5 + 35 = 155$
$\Rightarrow 125 - 5 + 35 = 155$
$\Rightarrow 155 = 155$ (Correct)
(D) $25 + 5 \times 50 \div 10 - 35 = 155$
$\Rightarrow 25 + 5 \times 5 - 35 = 155$
$\Rightarrow 25 + 25 - 35 = 155$
$\Rightarrow 15 = 155$ (Incorrect)

33. Option (B) is correct.
Explanation: $(6 \oplus 9) - (8 \oplus 4)$
$$= \left(\frac{6+9}{3}\right) - \left(\frac{8+4}{3}\right)$$
$$= 5 - 4 = \frac{5-4}{2} = \frac{1}{2}$$

34. Option (C) is correct.
Explanation: The given expression becomes
$43 + 22 - 15 \times 4 + 72 \div (10 - 2)$
$= 43 + 22 - 15 \times 4 + 72 \div 8$
$= 43 + 22 - 15 \times 4 + 9$
$= 43 + 22 - 60 + 9$
$= 74 - 60 = 14$

35. Option (B) is correct.
Explanation: On putting the signs, we get
$18 \div 3 \times 5 > 8 \times 3$
$\Rightarrow 6 \times 5 > 24$
$\Rightarrow 30 > 24$

Level-3: EXPERT

1. Option (C) is correct.
Explanation: After putting the symbols, we get
$21 \times 4 - 156 \div 13 + 11$
$= 21 \times 4 - 12 + 11$
$= 84 - 12 + 11 = 83$

2. Option (C) is correct.
Explanation: After changing the symbols, we get
(A) $40 \times 5 \div 8 + 30 - 32 = 120$
$$\Rightarrow 40 \times \frac{5}{8} + 30 - 32 = 120$$
$\Rightarrow 25 + 30 - 32 = 120$
$\Rightarrow 23 = 120$ (Incorrect)
(B) $16 \times 8 \div 2 - 40 + 30 = 11$
$\Rightarrow 16 \times 4 - 40 + 30 = 11$
$\Rightarrow 64 - 40 + 30 = 11$
$\Rightarrow 54 = 11$ (Incorrect)
(C) $16 \times 55 \div 11 - 50 + 2 = 32$
$\Rightarrow 16 \times 5 - 50 + 2 = 32$
$\Rightarrow 80 - 50 + 2 = 32$
$\Rightarrow 32 = 32$ (Correct)
(D) $16 \times 11 \div 55 - 38 - 1 = 28$
$$\Rightarrow 16 \times \frac{1}{5} - 38 - 10 = 28$$
$$\Rightarrow \frac{16}{5} - 48 = 28$$
$$\Rightarrow \frac{16-240}{5} = 28$$
$$\Rightarrow \frac{224}{5} = 28 \text{ (Incorrect)}$$

3. **Option (D) is correct.**
Explanation: After interchanging the signs, we get
(A) $5 \times 6 - 3 + 16 \div 4 = 31$
$\Rightarrow 5 \times 6 - 3 + 4 = 31$
$\Rightarrow 30 + 1 = 31$
$\Rightarrow 31 = 31$
(B) $11 + 6 - 3 \times 8 \div 2 = 5$
$\Rightarrow 11 + 6 - 3 \times 4 = 5$
$\Rightarrow 11 + 6 - 12 = 5$
$\Rightarrow 5 = 5$
(C) $7 - 8 + 4 \div 2 \times 6 = 11$
$\Rightarrow 7 - 8 + 2 \times 6 = 11$
$\Rightarrow 7 - 8 + 12 = 11$
$\Rightarrow 11 = 11$
(D) $7 - 2 + 27 \div 9 \times 4 = 18$
$\Rightarrow 7 - 2 + 3 \times 4 = 18$
$\Rightarrow 7 - 2 + 12 = 18$
$\Rightarrow 17 = 18$ (Incorrect)

4. **Option (C) is correct.**
Explanation: Here × means –, – means +, + means ÷ and ÷ means ×
The given expression becomes
$112 \div 4 \times 3 + 7 \times 10$
$= 28 \times 3 + 70$
$= 84 + 70 = 154$

5. **Option (D) is correct.**
Explanation: After putting the signs, we get
$(18 \times 9 - 14) \div 37 = 4$
$\Rightarrow (162 - 14) \div 37 = 4$
$\Rightarrow 148 \div 37 = 4$
$\Rightarrow 4 = 4$

6. **Option (A) is correct.**
Explanation: Here, + means ×, – means ÷, × means + and ÷ means –.
The given expression becomes
$60 + 500 \div 50 \times 20 \div 40$
$= 60 + 10 \times \frac{1}{2}$
$= 60 + \frac{10}{2} = 65$

7. **Option (B) is correct.**
Explanation: $16 - 8 \div 1 = 8$
$\Rightarrow 16 - 8 = 8$
$\Rightarrow 8 = 8$

8. **Option (A) is correct.**
Explanation: After changing the signs, we get
(A) $30 \div 6 \times 5 + 4 - 2 = 27$
$\Rightarrow 5 \times 5 + 4 - 2 = 27$
$\Rightarrow 25 + 4 - 2 = 27$
$\Rightarrow 27 = 27$ (Correct)
(B) $30 \times 6 \div 5 - 4 + 2 = 30$
$\Rightarrow 30 \times \frac{6}{5} - 4 + 2 = 30$
$\Rightarrow 36 - 4 + 2 = 30$
$\Rightarrow 34 = 30$ (Incorrect)
(C) $30 + 6 - 5 \div 4 \times 2 = 32$
$\Rightarrow 30 + 6 - \frac{5}{4} \times 2 = 32$
$\Rightarrow 36 - \frac{5}{2} = 32$
$\Rightarrow \frac{67}{2} = 32$ (Incorrect)
(D) $30 - 6 + 5 \times 4 \div 2 = 40$
$\Rightarrow 30 - 6 + 5 \times 2 = 40$
$\Rightarrow 30 - 6 + 10 = 40$
$\Rightarrow 34 = 40$ (Incorrect)

9. **Option (D) is correct.**
Explanation: After changing the signs, we get
(A) $60 \div 20 \times 15 + 5 - 30 = 20$
$\Rightarrow 3 \times 15 + 5 - 30 = 20$
$\Rightarrow 45 + 5 - 30 = 20$
$\Rightarrow 20 = 20$ (Correct)
(B) $60 \times 15 \div 20 - 30 + 5 = 20$
$\Rightarrow 60 \times \frac{3}{4} - 30 + 5 = 20$
$\Rightarrow 45 - 30 + 5 = 20$
$\Rightarrow 20 = 20$
(C) $60 - 30 + 15 \times 3 \div 20 = 41$
$\Rightarrow 60 - 30 + 15 \times \frac{3}{20} = 41$
$\Rightarrow 60 - 30 + \frac{9}{4} = 41$
$\Rightarrow 30 + \frac{9}{4} = 41$
$\Rightarrow \frac{129}{4} = 41$ (Incorrect)

10. **Option (A) is correct.**
Explanation: $5 \times 5 + 5 = 3 \times 10$
$\Rightarrow 25 + 5 = 30$
$\Rightarrow 30 = 30$

11. **Option (B) is correct.**
Explanation: (A) $16 \div 8 + 2 - 5 > 10 - 5$
$\Rightarrow 2 + 2 - 5 > 5$
$\Rightarrow -1 > 5$ (Incorrect)
(B) $16 + 8 \div 2 + 5 > 20 \div 10$
$\Rightarrow 16 + 4 + 5 > 2$
$\Rightarrow 25 > 2$ (Correct)
(C) $8 - 16 \div 2 - 5 > 5 + 2$
$\Rightarrow 8 - 8 - 5 > 7$
$\Rightarrow -5 > 7$ (Incorrect)
(D) $8 + 2 - 16 \div 4 = 15 \div 3$
$\Rightarrow 8 + 2 - 4 = 5$
$\Rightarrow 6 = 5$ (Incorrect)

12. **Option (C) is correct.**
Explanation: After changing the signs, we get
(A) $7 \div 1 - 5 + 2 < 10 \div 10 + 1$
$\Rightarrow 7 - 5 + 2 < 1 + 1$
$\Rightarrow 4 < 2$ (Incorrect)
(B) $7 \div 7 - 5 \times 1 > 10 - 2 + 5$
$\Rightarrow 1 - 5 > 13$
$\Rightarrow -4 > 13$ (Incorrect)
(C) $7 \times 7 - 5 = 40 + 4$
$\Rightarrow 49 - 5 = 44$
$\Rightarrow 44 = 44$ (correct)
(D) $7 - 5 \div 1 + 2 > 10 \div 2 + 5$
$\Rightarrow 7 - 5 + 2 > 5 + 5$
$\Rightarrow 4 > 10$ (Incorrect)

13. Option (A) is correct.

Explanation: After changing the signs, we get

(A) 100 + 10 ÷ 10 – 100 > 20 ÷ 10 – 2
⇒ 100 + 1 – 100 > 2 – 2
⇒ 1 > 0 (Correct)
(A) 100 + 10 ÷ 10 – 100 > 20 ÷ 10 – 2
⇒ 100 + 1 – 100 > 2 – 2
⇒ 1 > 0 (Correct)
(B) 100 ÷ 50 + 15 – 10 = 20 – 10 + 5
⇒ 2 + 15 – 10 = 25 – 10
⇒ 7 = 15 (Incorrect)
(C) 50 × 2 ÷ 50 – 10 < 100 ÷ 100 – 10

$\Rightarrow 50\times\frac{2}{50}-10<1-10$

⇒ 2 – 10 < –9
⇒ –8 < –9 (Incorrect)
(D) 80 ÷ 10 + 15 ÷ 3 = 70 – 35 ÷ 7
⇒ 8 + 5 = 70 – 5
⇒ 13 = 65 (Incorrect)

14. Option (D) is correct.

Explanation: After changing the symbols, we get

(A) 6 ÷ 2 = 15 ÷ 5 – 3 × 2
⇒ 3 = 5 – 6
⇒ 3 = –1 (Incorrect)
(B) 6 × 2 < 15 ÷ 3 + 2 × 1
⇒ 12 < 5 + 2
⇒ 12 < 7 (Incorrect)
(C) 6 + 2 > 30 ÷ 3 + 2 × 1
⇒ 8 > 10 + 2
⇒ 8 > 12 (Incorrect)
(D) 6 – 2 < 10 ÷ 2 × 3 × 1
⇒ 4 < 5 × 3 × 1
⇒ 4 < 15 (Correct)

15. Option (C) is correct.

Explanation: After changing the signs, we get

(A) 8 > 4 × 2 × 6 ÷ 3 + 1
⇒ 8 > 4 × 2 × 2 + 1
⇒ 8 > 17 (Incorrect)
(B) 8 > 2 × 3 × 4 ÷ 2 × 4
⇒ 8 > 2 × 3 × 2 × 4
⇒ 8 > 48 (Incorrect)
(C) 38 < 2 × 4 ÷ 2 × 3 × 5
⇒ 38 < 2 × 2 × 3 × 5
⇒ 38 < 60 (Correct)
(D) 8 ÷ 4 > 4 ÷ 2 × 15 ÷ 3
⇒ 2 > 2 × 5
⇒ 2 > 10 (Incorrect)

16. Option (A) is correct.

Explanation: After changing the signs, we get

(A) 8 + 8 – 8 ÷ 8 < 20
⇒ 8 + 8 – 1 < 20
⇒ 15 < 20 (Correct)
(B) 8 × 8 + 8 ÷ 8 < 8 × 8 + 1
⇒ 8 × 8 + 1 < 64 + 1
⇒ 65 < 65 (Incorrect)
(C) 8 – 8 ÷ 8 < 5
⇒ 8 – 1 < 5
⇒ 7 < 5 (Incorrect)
(D) 8 ÷ 8 + 8 < 3
⇒ 1 + 8 < 3
⇒ 9 < 3 (Incorrect)

17. Option (D) is correct.

Explanation: After interchanging the signs, we get

(A) 9 – 3 + 8 ÷ 4 × 7 = 28
⇒ 9 – 3 + 2 × 7 = 28
⇒ 9 – 3 + 14 = 28
⇒ 20 = 28 (Incorrect)
(B) 9 × 3 – 8 ÷ 4 + 7 = 28
⇒ 27 – 2 + 7 = 28
⇒ 32 = 28 (Incorrect)
(C) 9 × 3 ÷ 8 + 4 – 7 = 28

$\Rightarrow 9\times\frac{3}{8}+4-7=28$

$\Rightarrow \frac{27}{8}-3=28$

$\Rightarrow \frac{3}{8}=28$ (Incorrect)

(D) 9 ÷ 3 + 8 × 4 – 7 = 28
⇒ 3 + 32 – 7= 28
⇒ 28 = 28 (Correct)

18. Option (A) is correct.

Explanation: After interchanging the signs, we get

(A) 3 × 8 ÷ 12 – 4 + 5 = 3

$\Rightarrow 3\times\frac{8}{12}-4+5=3$

⇒ 2 – 4 + 5 = 3
⇒ 3 = 3 (Correct)
(B) 3 + 8 – 12 + 4 ÷ 5 = 3

$\Rightarrow 11-12+\frac{4}{5}=3$

$\Rightarrow \frac{-1}{5}=3$ (Incorrect)

(C) 3 × 8 + 12 ÷ 4 – 5 = 3
⇒ 24 + 3 – 5 = 3
⇒ 22 = 3 (Incorrect)
(D) 3 + 8 – 12 ÷ 4 × 5 = 3
⇒ 3 + 8 – 3 × 5 = 3
⇒ 3 + 8 – 15 = 3
⇒ – 4 = 3 (Incorrect)

19. Option (C) is correct.

Explanation: After changing the symbols, we get

765 ÷ 15 × 19 + 18 – 20
= 51 × 19 + 18 – 20
= 969 + 18 – 20 = 971

20. Option (D) is correct.

Explanation: After changing the symbols, we get

80 – 8 × 20 ÷ 10 – 17
= 80 – 8 × 2 – 17 = 80 – 16 – 17 = 47

■ ■ ■

Chapter 14

Inserting the Missing Character

LEARNING OBJECTIVES:

- ❖ Method of finding missing number in a given figure by using mathematical operations
- ❖ Method of finding missing number when a same rule is applied in multiple figures
- ❖ Different types of question asked in competitive exams

This section helps to enhance the critical learning of the students. It will helps the students to think beyond the normal situations.

In this section of logical reasoning, some figures or matrices are given to students. They need to find the connection relation between the given characters and hence using the same relation, one can find the missing character.

Example 1: Find the missing character in the given question

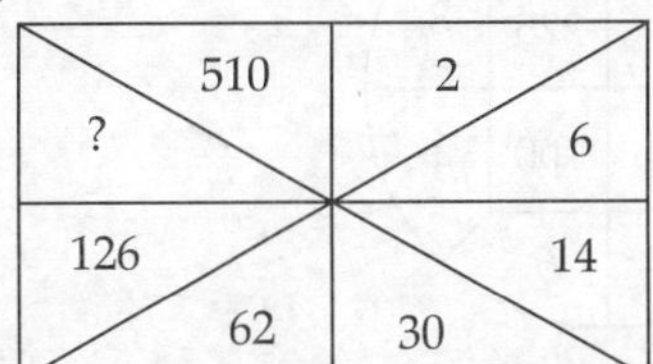

(a) 254 (b) 250

(c) 198 (d) 212

Sol. (a)

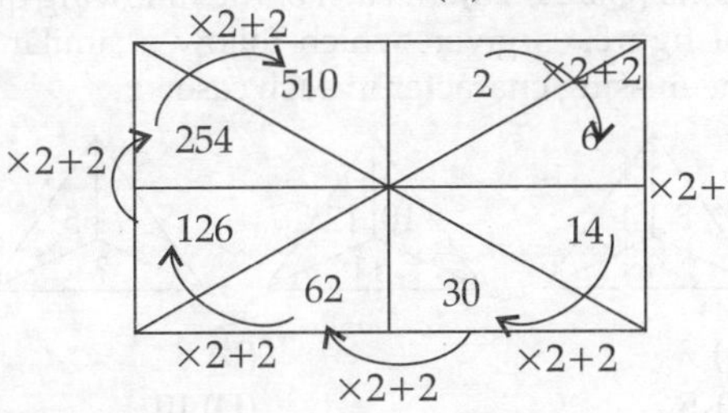

So, the missing number is 254.

Example 2: Find the missing character, if same rule is followed in all the three figures.

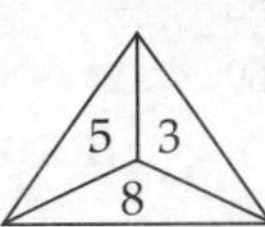

7 4 27   12 6 ?

(a) 96 (b) 216

(c) 106 (d) 116

Sol. (b) Here,

In first figure,

$(5 - 3)^3 = 2^3 = 8$;

In second figure,

$(7 - 4)^3 = 3^3 = 27$

So, $(12 - 6)^3 = 6^3 = 216$

Hence, the missing number is 216.

Example 3: Find the missing character, if a certain rule is followed either row-wise or column wise in the given matrix.

A	E	M
D	H	P
G	K	?

(a) T (b) R

(c) S (d) U

Sol. (c) Here, we have

Row 1 : $A \xrightarrow{+4} E \xrightarrow{+8} M$

Row 2 : $D \xrightarrow{+4} H \xrightarrow{+8} P$

So, $G \xrightarrow{+4} K \xrightarrow{+8} \boxed{S}$

Hence, the missing letter is S.

1 Level Beginner

Directions (Qs. 1–10): Find the missing character in each of the following.

1.

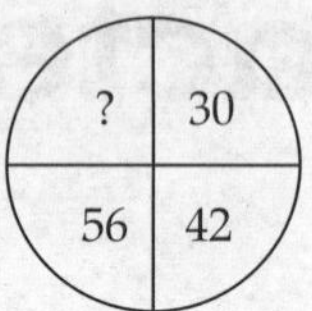

(A) 36 **(B)** 72
(C) 30 **(D)** 45

2.

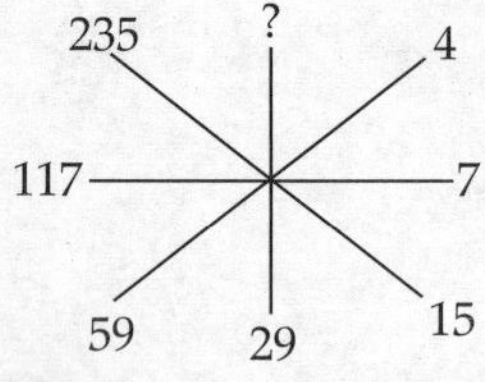

(A) 327 **(B)** 386
(C) 438 **(D)** 469

[RRB 2002]

3.

8	12
?	20

(A) 38 **(B)** 28
(C) 32 **(D)** 24

4.

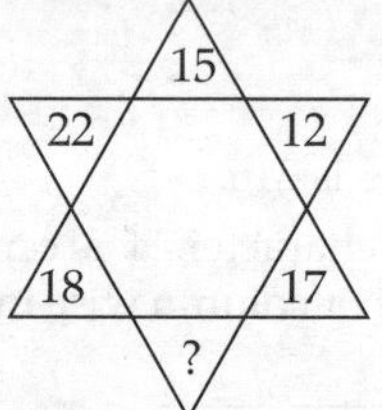

(A) 16 **(B)** 18
(C) 15 **(D)** 26

5.

[MAT 2001]

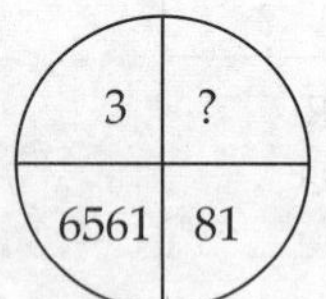

(A) 9 **(B)** 18
(C) 24 **(D)** 27

6.

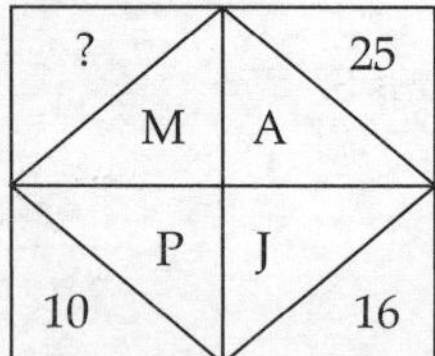

(A) 13 **(B)** 18
(C) 16 **(D)** 15

7.

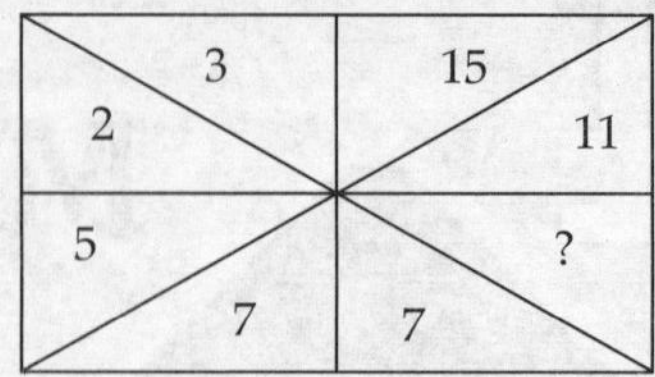

[PGDCA 2005]

(A) 5 **(B)** 12
(C) 13 **(D)** 26

8.

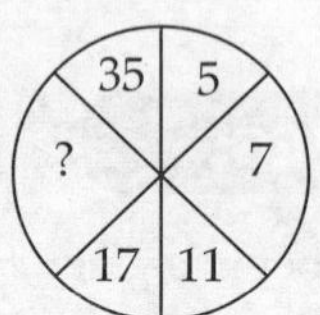

(A) 25 **(B)** 28
(C) 21 **(D)** 23

9.

[SSC 2003]

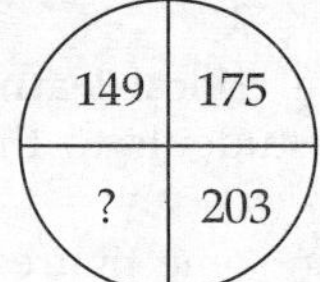

(A) 148 **(B)** 208
(C) 213 **(D)** 233

10.

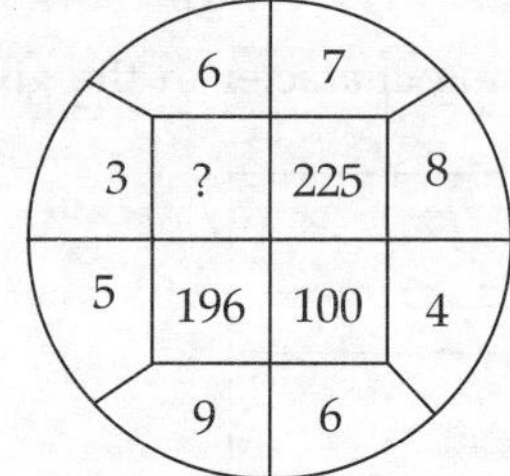

(A) 81 **(B)** 9
(C) 70 **(D)** 65

Directions (Qs. 11–20): In each of the following questions, a set of figures is given which follow a similar pattern. Find the missing character in each case.

11.

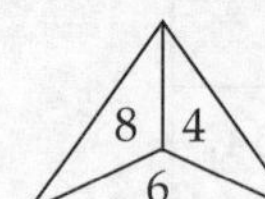

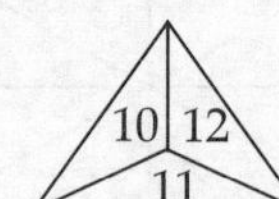

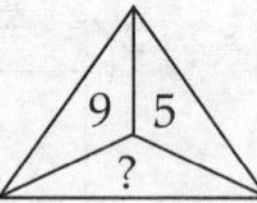

(A) 7 **(B)** 8
(C) 5 **(D)** 10

12.

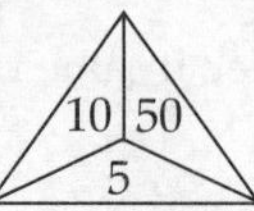

9 | 72 / 8

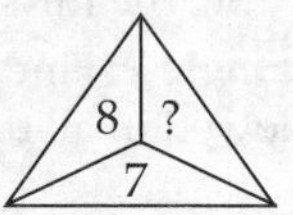

(A) 56 **(B)** 42
(C) 15 **(D)** 60

13.

2	4
20	

5	7
74	

6	10
?	

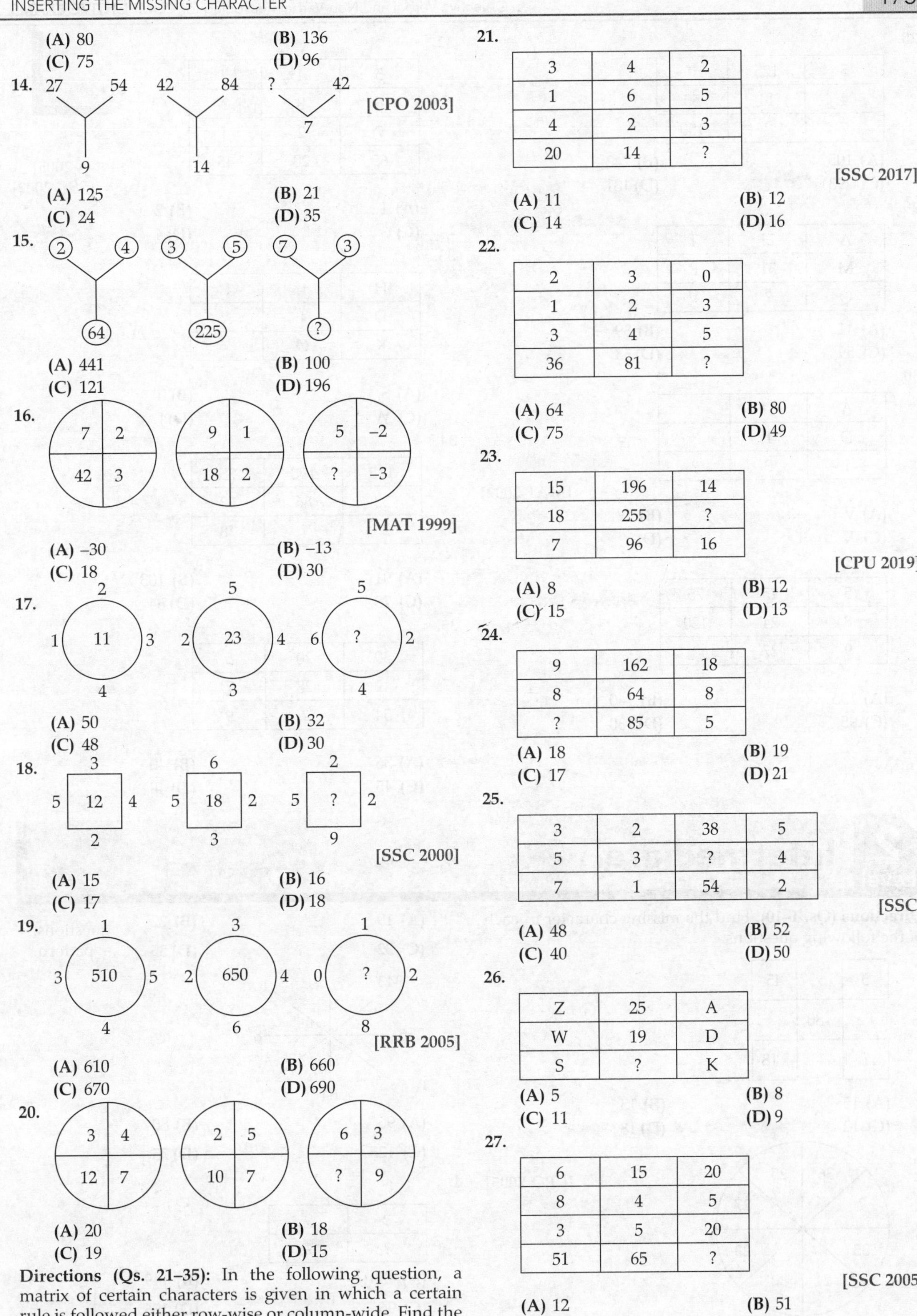

(A) 80 (B) 136
(C) 75 (D) 96

14. 27, 54, 9 | 42, 84, 14 | ?, 42, 7 **[CPO 2003]**

(A) 125 (B) 21
(C) 24 (D) 35

15. (2), (4), (64) | (3), (5), (225) | (7), (3), (?)

(A) 441 (B) 100
(C) 121 (D) 196

16. 7, 2, 42, 3 | 9, 1, 18, 2 | 5, –2, ?, –3 **[MAT 1999]**

(A) –30 (B) –13
(C) 18 (D) 30

17. 2, 1, 11, 3, 4 | 5, 2, 23, 4, 3 | 5, 6, ?, 2, 4

(A) 50 (B) 32
(C) 48 (D) 30

18. 3, 5, 12, 4, 2 | 6, 5, 18, 2, 3 | 2, 5, ?, 2, 9 **[SSC 2000]**

(A) 15 (B) 16
(C) 17 (D) 18

19. 1, 3, 510, 5, 4 | 3, 2, 650, 4, 6 | 1, 0, ?, 2, 8 **[RRB 2005]**

(A) 610 (B) 660
(C) 670 (D) 690

20. 3, 4, 12, 7 | 2, 5, 10, 7 | 6, 3, ?, 9

(A) 20 (B) 18
(C) 19 (D) 15

Directions (Qs. 21–35): In the following question, a matrix of certain characters is given in which a certain rule is followed either row-wise or column-wide. Find the missing character from the given options.

21.

3	4	2
1	6	5
4	2	3
20	14	?

[SSC 2017]

(A) 11 (B) 12
(C) 14 (D) 16

22.

2	3	0
1	2	3
3	4	5
36	81	?

(A) 64 (B) 80
(C) 75 (D) 49

23.

15	196	14
18	255	?
7	96	16

[CPU 2019]

(A) 8 (B) 12
(C) 15 (D) 13

24.

9	162	18
8	64	8
?	85	5

(A) 18 (B) 19
(C) 17 (D) 21

25.

3	2	38	5
5	3	?	4
7	1	54	2

[SSC]

(A) 48 (B) 52
(C) 40 (D) 50

26.

Z	25	A
W	19	D
S	?	K

(A) 5 (B) 8
(C) 11 (D) 9

27.

6	15	20
8	4	5
3	5	20
51	65	?

[SSC 2005]

(A) 12 (B) 51
(C) 56 (D) 120

28.

5	125	0
4	14	50
7	?	150

(A) 105 **(B)** 243
(C) 293 **(D)** 181

29.

A	21	T
M	31	R
Q	?	V

(A) 41 **(B)** 39
(C) 59 **(D)** 53

30.

A	D	G
D	I	N
I	P	?

[MAT 2002]

(A) V **(B)** W
(C) X **(D)** Y

31.

5	15	75
8	24	120
9	27	?

(A) 135 **(B)** 140
(C) 95 **(D)** 130

32.

5	4	9
6	3	?
7	2	4
65	20	45

[SSC 2002]

(A) 1 **(B)** 2
(C) 3 **(D)** 4

33.

H	L	P
D	T	X
K	O	?

(A) S **(B)** T
(C) W **(D)** J

34.

115	190	75
33	86	53
25	?	78

(A) 91 **(B)** 103
(C) 78 **(D)** 64

35.

30	20	5
42	28	7
54	?	9

(A) 36 **(B)** 40
(C) 45 **(D)** 48

Level 2 Intermediate

Directions (Qs. 1–10): Find the missing character in each of the following questions.

1.

5		45
	80	
?		18

(A) 15 **(B)** 13
(C) 12 **(D)** 18

2.

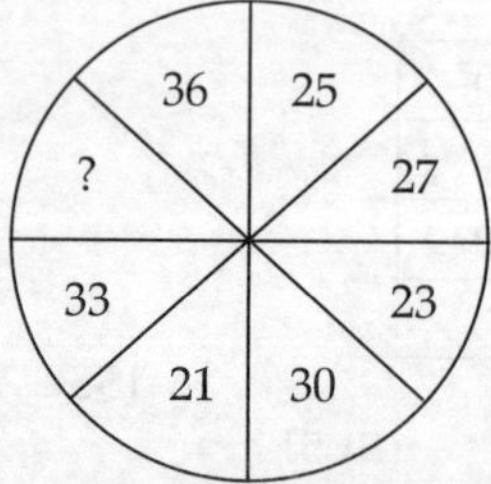

[CPO 2005]

(A) 19 **(B)** 22
(C) 32 **(D)** 35

3.

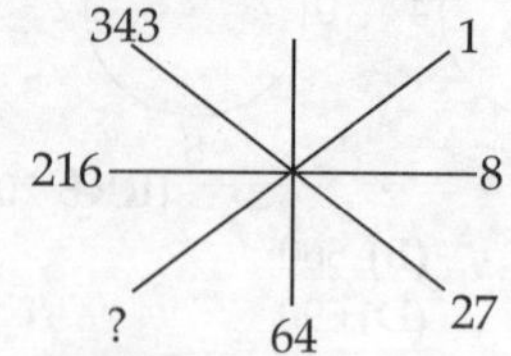

(A) 96 **(B)** 80
(C) 125 **(D)** 75

4.

2	9
?	37

(A) 130 **(B)** 149
(C) 96 **(D)** 156

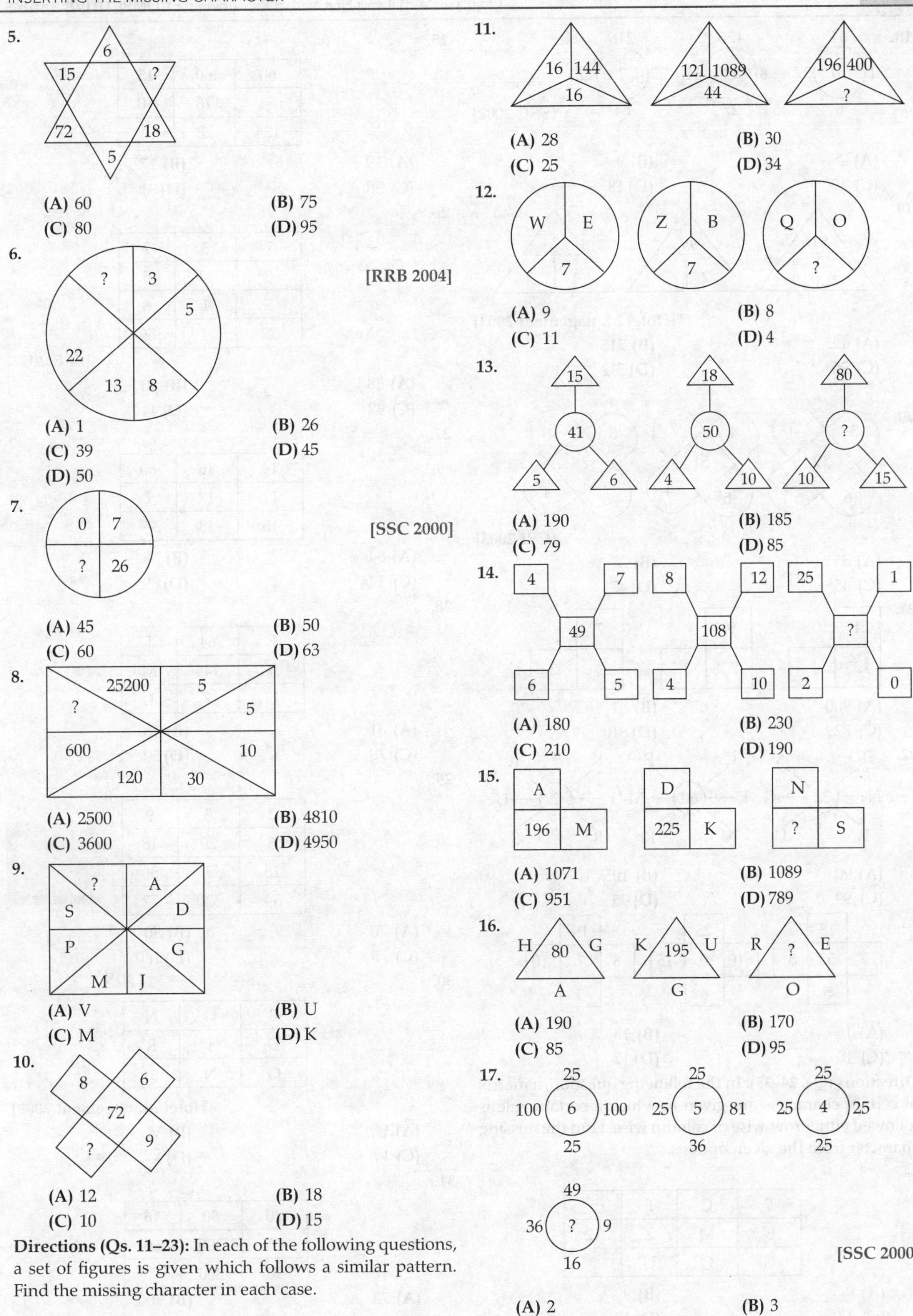

5.

6, 15, ?, 72, 18, 5

(A) 60 **(B)** 75
(C) 80 **(D)** 95

6.

?, 3, 5, 22, 13, 8

[RRB 2004]

(A) 1 **(B)** 26
(C) 39 **(D)** 45
(D) 50

7.

0, 7, ?, 26

[SSC 2000]

(A) 45 **(B)** 50
(C) 60 **(D)** 63

8.

25200, 5, ?, 5, 600, 10, 120, 30

(A) 2500 **(B)** 4810
(C) 3600 **(D)** 4950

9.

?, A, S, D, P, G, M, J

(A) V **(B)** U
(C) M **(D)** K

10.

8, 6, 72, ?, 9

(A) 12 **(B)** 18
(C) 10 **(D)** 15

Directions (Qs. 11–23): In each of the following questions, a set of figures is given which follows a similar pattern. Find the missing character in each case.

11.

16, 144, 16 | 121, 1089, 44 | 196, 400, ?

(A) 28 **(B)** 30
(C) 25 **(D)** 34

12.

W, E, 7 | Z, B, 7 | Q, O, ?

(A) 9 **(B)** 8
(C) 11 **(D)** 4

13.

15, 41, 5, 6 | 18, 50, 4, 10 | 80, ?, 10, 15

(A) 190 **(B)** 185
(C) 79 **(D)** 85

14.

4, 7, 49, 6, 5 | 8, 12, 108, 4, 10 | 25, 1, ?, 2, 0

(A) 180 **(B)** 230
(C) 210 **(D)** 190

15.

A, 196, M | D, 225, K | N, ?, S

(A) 1071 **(B)** 1089
(C) 951 **(D)** 789

16.

H, 80, G, A | K, 195, U, G | R, ?, E, O

(A) 190 **(B)** 170
(C) 85 **(D)** 95

17.

25, 100, 6, 100, 25 | 25, 25, 5, 81, 36 | 25, 25, 4, 25, 25

49, 36, ?, 9, 16

[SSC 2000]

(A) 2 **(B)** 3
(C) 4 **(D)** 5

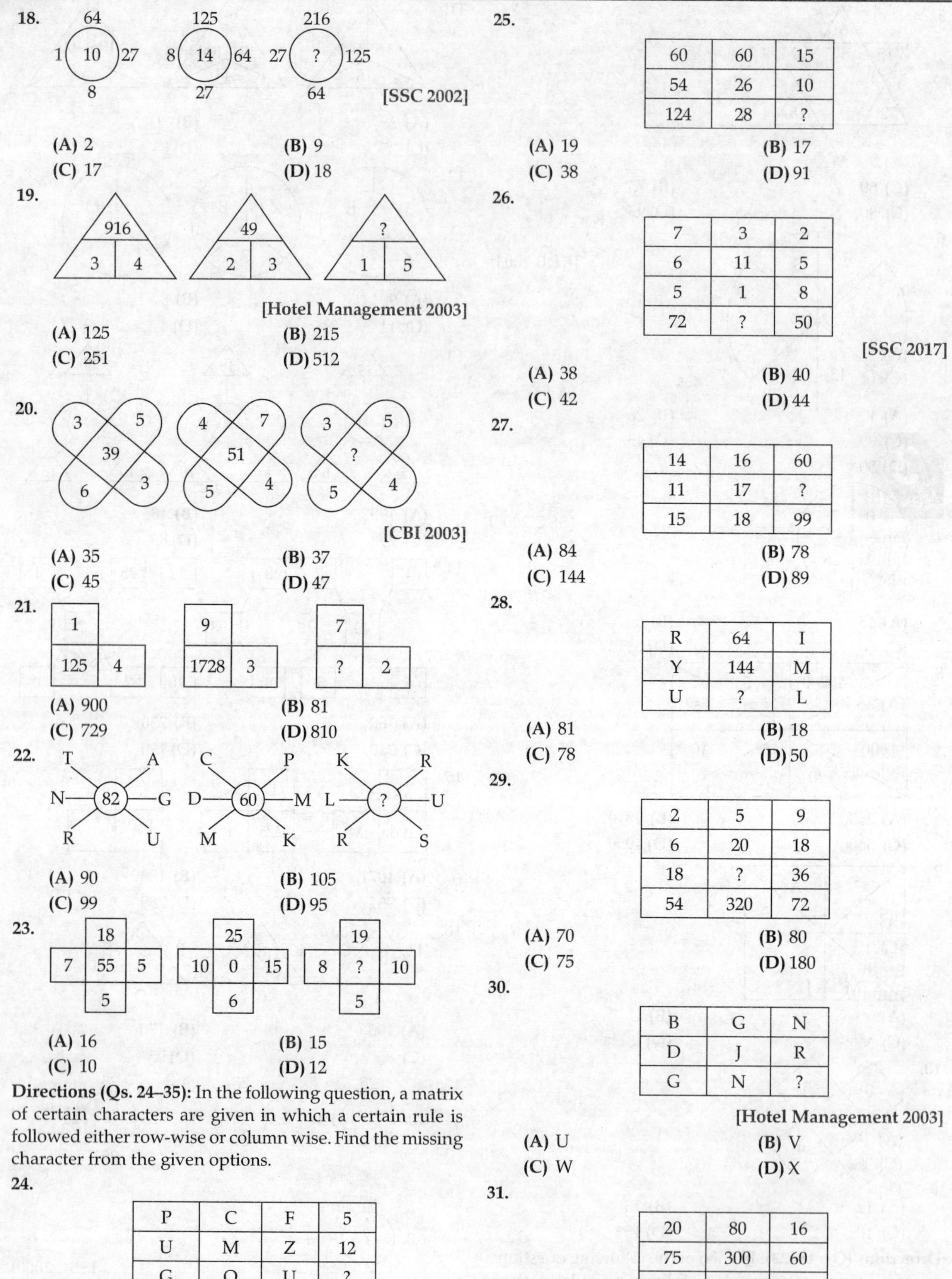

18.

[SSC 2002]

(A) 2 **(B)** 9
(C) 17 **(D)** 18

19.

[Hotel Management 2003]

(A) 125 **(B)** 215
(C) 251 **(D)** 512

20.

[CBI 2003]

(A) 35 **(B)** 37
(C) 45 **(D)** 47

21.

(A) 900 **(B)** 81
(C) 729 **(D)** 810

22.

(A) 90 **(B)** 105
(C) 99 **(D)** 95

23.

(A) 16 **(B)** 15
(C) 10 **(D)** 12

Directions (Qs. 24–35): In the following question, a matrix of certain characters are given in which a certain rule is followed either row-wise or column wise. Find the missing character from the given options.

24.

P	C	F	5
U	M	Z	12
G	Q	U	?

(A) 8 **(B)** 9
(C) 17 **(D)** 15

25.

60	60	15
54	26	10
124	28	?

(A) 19 **(B)** 17
(C) 38 **(D)** 91

26.

7	3	2
6	11	5
5	1	8
72	?	50

[SSC 2017]

(A) 38 **(B)** 40
(C) 42 **(D)** 44

27.

14	16	60
11	17	?
15	18	99

(A) 84 **(B)** 78
(C) 144 **(D)** 89

28.

R	64	I
Y	144	M
U	?	L

(A) 81 **(B)** 18
(C) 78 **(D)** 50

29.

2	5	9
6	20	18
18	?	36
54	320	72

(A) 70 **(B)** 80
(C) 75 **(D)** 180

30.

B	G	N
D	J	R
G	N	?

[Hotel Management 2003]

(A) U **(B)** V
(C) W **(D)** X

31.

20	80	16
75	300	60
90	360	?

(A) 72 **(B)** 70
(C) 80 **(D)** 75

32.

?	8	11
7	6	5
48	63	72

[CPO 2020]

(A) 7 **(B)** 4
(C) 5 **(D)** 6

33.

A	D	H
F	I	M
?	N	R

[MBA 2004]

(A) K **(B)** N
(C) O **(D)** P

34.

27	512	?
2	3	3
1	4	2
0	1	5

(A) 900 **(B)** 1000
(C) 850 **(D)** 760

35.

1	7	2
8	6	4
9	2	5
4	6	?

(A) 9 **(B)** 4
(C) 6 **(D)** 5

3 Level Expert

1. Find the missing characters, if a certain rule is followed in row-wise or column wise in the given margin.

15	256	7
19	108	13
20	?	8

(A) 864 **(B)** 4150
(C) 988 **(D)** 476

2. Find the missing number, if same rule pattern followed in each figure.

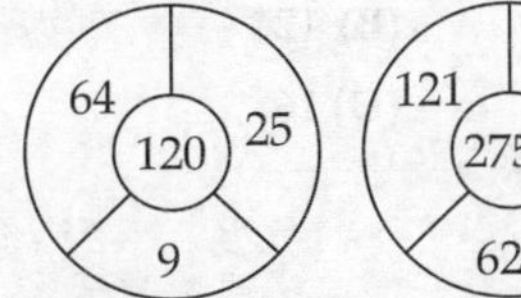

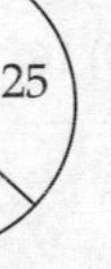
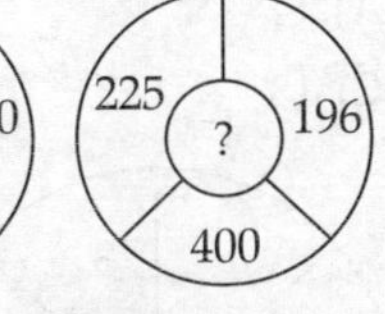

(A) 3800 **(B)** 4200
(C) 1750 **(D)** 2560

3. Study the given pattern carefully and select the number that can replace the question mark (?) in it.

28	58	118
21	44	90
47	96	?

[CPO 2020]

(A) 194 **(B)** 150
(C) 188 **(D)** 176

4. Find the missing character.

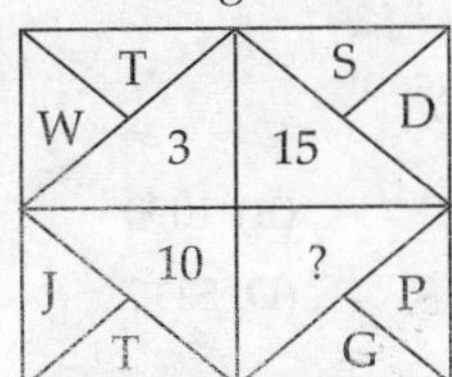

[MAT 2002]

(A) 5 **(B)** 9
(C) 11 **(D)** 13

5. Find the missing character.

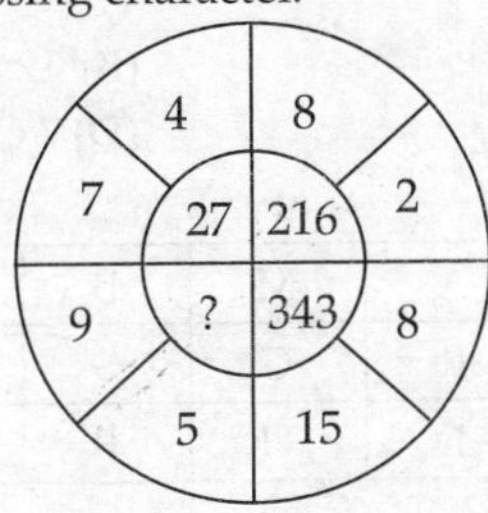

(A) 80 **(B)** 62
(C) 64 **(D)** 78

Directions (Qs. 6–10): In each of the following questions, a set of figures is given which follows a similar pattern. Find the missing character in each case.

6.

M	R
Q	B

C	H
G	R

J	O
?	Y

(A) S **(B)** R
(C) N **(D)** W

7.

5, 3, E, 4, 7

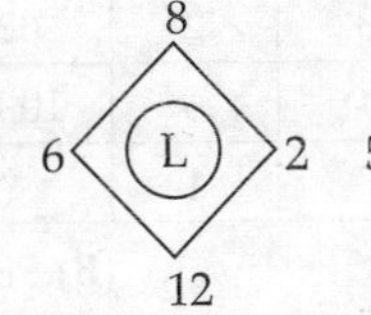

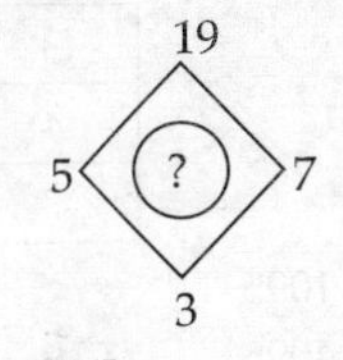

(A) H **(B)** J
(C) G **(D)** K

8.

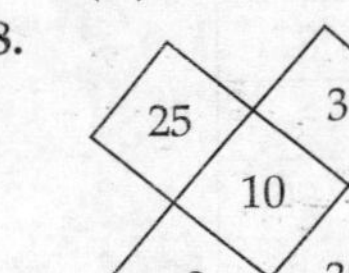

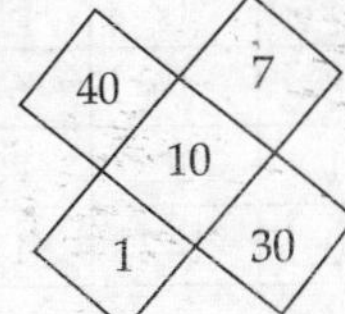

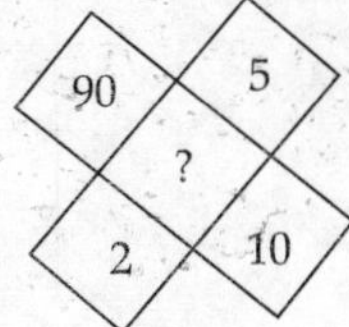

(A) 8 **(B)** 5
(C) 10 **(D)** 12

9.

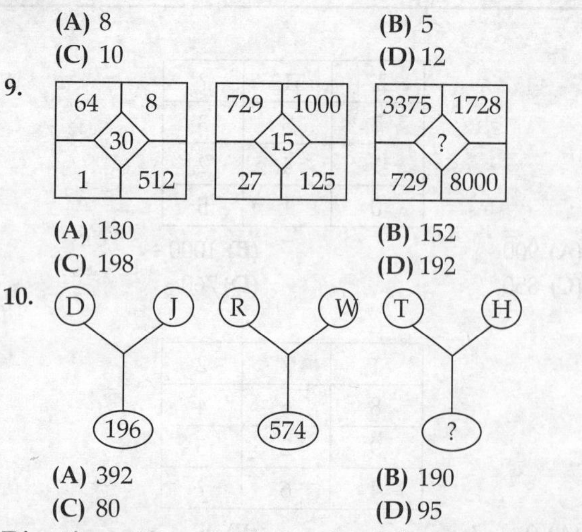

(A) 130 **(B)** 152
(C) 198 **(D)** 192

10.

(A) 392 **(B)** 190
(C) 80 **(D)** 95

Directions (Qs. 11–15): In the following questions, a matrix of certain characters is given in which a certain rule is followed on the row-wise or column wise. Find the missing character from the given options.

11.

4C	2B	3A
28A	?	15B
7C	5A	5B

[SNAP 2004]

(A) 10 C **(B)** 12 C
(C) 13 C **(D)** 7 C

12.

A	M	B	N
R	C	S	D
E	U	F	?

[MBA 2004]

(A) G **(B)** R
(C) T **(D)** V

13.

Z5	U10	P15
W6	R11	M16
Q7	L12	?

(A) G18 **(B)** G17
(C) H18 **(D)** H17

14.

3	2	625
4	6	10000
7	1	?

(A) 1095 **(B)** 981
(C) 4096 **(D)** 2085

15.

31	17	58	87
68	19	61	56
91	22	70	50
10	142	11	?

[SSC 2000]

(A) 3 **(B)** 6
(C) 7 **(D)** 9

Directions (Qs. 16–20): Find the missing character in each of the following questions.

16.

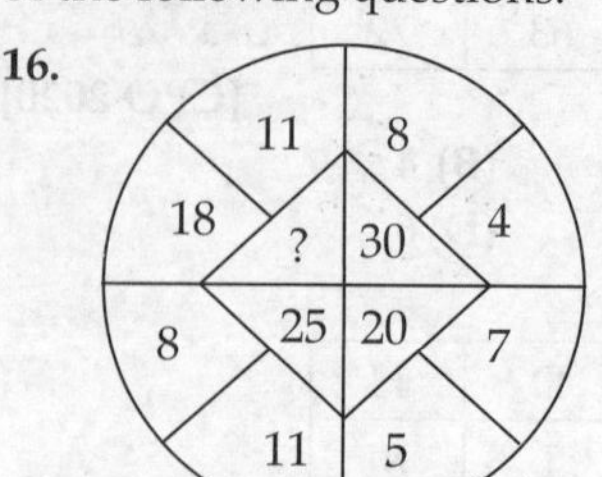

(A) 40 **(B)** 45
(C) 80 **(D)** 46

17.

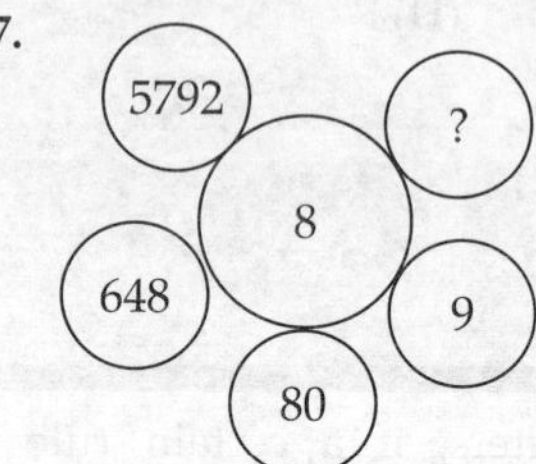

(A) 45890 **(B)** 31682
(C) 41544 **(D)** None of these

18.

15
31 ?
8400
34 41
45

(A) 14 **(B)** 12
(C) 18 **(D)** 16

19.

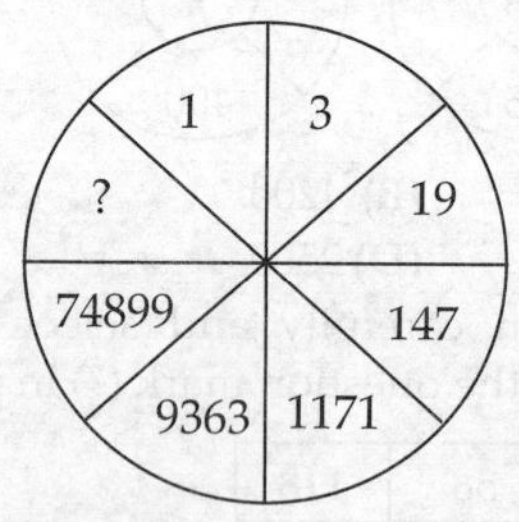

(A) 510152 **(B)** 599187
(C) 485152 **(D)** 46131

20.

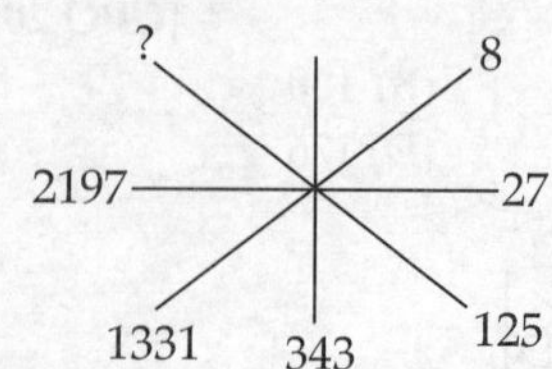

(A) 4913 **(B)** 1090
(C) 3152 **(D)** 5112

ANSWER KEY

Level-1: Beginner

1.	(B)	2.	(D)	3.	(C)	4.	(A)	5.	(A)	6.	(A)	7.	(A)	8.	(A)	9.	(D)	10.	(A)
11.	(A)	12.	(A)	13.	(B)	14.	(B)	15.	(A)	16.	(D)	17.	(B)	18.	(D)	19.	(D)	20.	(B)
21.	(D)	22.	(A)	23.	(C)	24.	(C)	25.	(D)	26.	(B)	27.	(D)	28.	(C)	29.	(B)	30.	(B)
31.	(A)	32.	(A)	33.	(A)	34.	(B)	35.	(A)										

Level-2: Intermediate

1.	(C)	2.	(A)	3.	(C)	4.	(B)	5.	(A)	6.	(C)	7.	(D)	8.	(C)	9.	(A)	10.	(A)
11.	(D)	12.	(B)	13.	(B)	14.	(C)	15.	(B)	16.	(A)	17.	(C)	18.	(D)	19.	(A)	20.	(B)
21.	(C)	22.	(C)	23.	(B)	24.	(B)	25.	(A)	26.	(D)	27.	(A)	28.	(A)	29.	(B)	30.	(C)
31.	(A)	32.	(C)	33.	(A)	34.	(B)	35.	(C)										

Level-3: Expert

1.	(A)	2.	(B)	3.	(A)	4.	(B)	5.	(C)	6.	(C)	7.	(B)	8.	(C)	9.	(D)	10.	(A)
11.	(A)	12.	(D)	13.	(B)	14.	(C)	15.	(C)	16.	(B)	17.	(C)	18.	(A)	19.	(B)	20.	(A)

Solutions with Detailed Explanations

Level-1: BEGINNER

1. **Option (B) is correct.**
Explanation: In the given figure, the rule followed in clockwise manner as:
$30 + 12 = 42; 42 + 14 = 56$
So, $56 + 16 = 72$
So, the missing number is 72.

2. **Option (D) is correct.**
Explanation: The rule followed in clockwise manner as:
$4 \times 2 - 1 = 8 - 1 = 7;$
$7 \times 2 + 1 = 15; 15 \times 2 - 1 = 29;$
$29 \times 2 + 1 = 59; 59 \times 2 - 1 = 117;$
$117 \times 2 + 1 = 235$
So, $235 \times 2 - 1 = 470 - 1 = 469$
So, the missing number is 469.

3. **Option (C) is correct.**
Explanation: In the given figure, the rule followed in clockwise manner as:
$8 + 4 = 12; 12 + 8 = 20;$
$\Rightarrow 20 + 12 = 32$
So, the missing number is 32.

4. **Option (A) is correct.**
Explanation: In each triangle, the sum of all numbers is 50.
i.e., $15 + 18 + 17 = 50$
So, $? = 50 - 22 - 12$
$= 50 - 34 = 16$
$\therefore$ The missing number is 16.

5. **Option (A) is correct.**
Explanation: The rule followed as :
$3^2 = 9; 9^2 = 81; 81^2 = 6561$
So, the missing number is 9.

6. **Option (A) is correct.**
Explanation: In each small square, the rule followed as sum of the numeric value of alphabets and numbers is 26 in each small square.
A(1) + 25 = 26
J (10) + 16 = 26
P (16) + 10 = 26
M (13) + 13 = 26
So, the missing number is 13.

7. **Option (A) is correct.**
Explanation: The rule followed in diagonally opposite parts as :
$5 \times 2 + 1 = 11; 7 \times 2 + 1 = 15$
$3 \times 2 + 1 = 7$
$\Rightarrow 2 \times 2 + 1 = 5$
So, the missing number is 5.

8. **Option (A) is correct.**
Explanation: The rule followed is:
$5 \xrightarrow{+2} 7 \xrightarrow{+4} 11 \xrightarrow{+6} 17 \xrightarrow{+8} 25 \xrightarrow{+10} 35$
So, the missing number is 25.

9. **Option (D) is correct.**
Explanation: The rule followed is:
$149 \xrightarrow{+26} 175 \xrightarrow{+28} 203 \xrightarrow{+30} 233$
So, the missing number is 233.

10. Option (A) is correct.
Explanation: The rule followed in each quadrant as :
$(7 + 8)^2 = 15^2 = 225;$
$(4 + 6)^2 = 10^2 = 100;$
$(9 + 5)^2 = 14^2 = 196;$
$\Rightarrow (3 + 6)^2 = 9^2 = 81$
So, the missing number is 81.

11. Option (A) is correct.
Explanation: The rule followed in each figure is:
$(8 + 4) \div 2 = 12 \div 2 = 6;$
$(10 + 12) \div 2 = 22 \div 2 = 11$
Hence, $(9 + 5) \div 2 = 14 \div 2 = 7$
So, the missing number is 7.

12. Option (A) is correct.
Explanation: The rule followed in each figure is:
$10 \times 5 = 50; 9 \times 8 = 72$
So, $8 \times 7 = 56$
So, the missing number is 56.

13. Option (B) is correct.
Explanation: The rule followed in each figure is:
$2^2 + 4^2 = 4 + 16 = 20;$
$5^2 + 7^2 = 25 + 49 = 74$
So, $6^2 + 10^2 = 36 + 100 = 136$
Hence, the missing number is 136.

14. Option (B) is correct.
Explanation: The rule followed is:
$9 \times 3 = 27$ and $27 \times 2 = 54;$
$14 \times 3 = 42$ and $42 \times 2 = 84$
So, $7 \times 3 = 21$ and $21 \times 2 = 42$
Hence, the missing number is 21.

15. Option (A) is correct.
Explanation: The rule followed is:
$(2 \times 4)^2 = 8^2 = 64;$
$(3 \times 5)^2 = 15^2 = 225$
So, $(7 \times 3)^2 = 21 = 441$

16. Option (D) is correct.
Explanation: The rule followed is:
$7 \times 2 \times 3 = 42;$
$9 \times 1 \times 2 = 18$
So, $5 \times (-2) \times (-3) = 30$

17. Option (B) is correct.
Explanation: The rule followed in each figure is:
$(1 \times 3) + (2 \times 4) = 3 + 8 = 11;$
$(2 \times 4) + (5 \times 3) = 8 + 15 = 23$
So, $(6 \times 2) + (5 \times 4) = 12 + 20 = 32$
So, the missing number is 32.

18. Option (D) is correct.
Explanation: The rule followed in each figure is:
$(5 \times 3 \times 4 \times 2) \div 10 = 120 \div 10 = 12;$
$(5 \times 6 \times 2 \times 3) \div 10 = 180 \div 10 = 18$
So, $(5 \times 2 \times 2 \times 9) \div 10 = 180 \div 10 = 18$
So, the missing number is 18.

19. Option (D) is correct.
Explanation: The rule followed as
$(1^2 + 5^2 + 4^2 + 3^2) \times 10 = 510;$
$(3^2 + 4^2 + 6^2 + 2^2) \times 10 = 650;$
So, $(1^2 + 2^2 + 8^2 + 0^2) \times 10 = 690;$
Hence, the missing number is 690.

20. Option (B) is correct.
Explanation: The rule followed is:
$3 + 4 = 7$ and $3 \times 4 = 12;$
$2 + 5 = 7$ and $2 \times 5 = 10$
So, $6 + 3 = 9$ and $6 \times 3 = 18$.
Hence, the missing number is 18.

21. Option (D) is correct.
Explanation: In each column the rule followed is:
$4^2 + 3 + 1 = 16 + 4 = 20;$
$2^2 + 4 + 6 = 4 + 10 = 14$
So, $3^2 + 2 + 5 = 9 + 7 = 16$
Hence, the missing number is 16.

22. Option (A) is correct.
Explanation: The rule followed in each column is:
$(2 + 1 + 3)^2 = 6^2 = 36;$
$(3 + 2 + 4)^2 = 9^2 = 81$
So, $(0 + 3 + 5)^2 = 8^2 = 64$
Hence, the missing number is 64.

23. Option (C) is correct.
Explanation: In each row, the rule followed is:
$14 \times (15 - 1) = 196;$
$16 \times (7 - 1) = 96$
So, $15 \times (18 - 1) = 255$
Hence, the missing number is 15.

24. Option (C) is correct.
Explanation: In each row, the rule followed is:
$9 \times 18 = 162; 8 \times 8 = 64$
So, $5 \times 17 = 85$
Hence, the missing number is 17.

25. Option (D) is correct.
Explanation: The rule followed as;
$3^2 + 2^2 + 5^2 = 9 + 4 + 25 = 38$
$7^2 + 1^2 + 2^2 = 49 + 1 + 4 = 54$
So, $5^2 + 3^2 + 4^2 = 25 + 9 + 16 = 50$
Hence, the missing number is 50.

26. Option (B) is correct.
Explanation: The rule followed is:
Z (26) – A (1) = 25;
W (23) – D (4) = 19
S (19) – K (11) = 8
So, the missing number is 8.

27. Option (D) is correct.
Explanation: The rule followed is:
$(6 \times 8) + 3 = 48 + 3 = 51;$
$(15 \times 4) + 5 = 60 + 5 = 65$
So, $(20 \times 5) + 20 = 100 + 20 = 120$
Hence, the missing number is 120.

28. Option (C) is correct.
Explanation: The rule followed is:
$5^3 - 0 = 125 - 0 = 125;$
$4^3 - 50 = 64 - 50 = 14$
So, $7^3 - 150 = 343 - 150 = 293$
Hence, the missing number is 293.

29. Option (B) is correct.
Explanation: Here, A = 1, B = 2, ..., Z = 26
The rule followed as
A (1) + T (20) = 21;
M (13) + R (18) = 31
So, Q (17) + V (22) = 39
Hence, the missing number is 39.

30. Option (B) is correct.

Explanation: The rule followed as;

$A \xrightarrow{+3} D \xrightarrow{+3} G$

$D \xrightarrow{+5} I \xrightarrow{+5} N$

So, $I \xrightarrow{+7} P \xrightarrow{+7} W$

Hence, the missing number is W.

31. Option (A) is correct.

Explanation: The rule followed as;

$5 \xrightarrow{\times 3} 15 \xrightarrow{\times 5} 75$

$8 \xrightarrow{\times 3} 24 \xrightarrow{\times 5} 120$

So, $9 \xrightarrow{\times 3} 27 \xrightarrow{\times 5} 135$

Hence, the missing number is 135.

32. Option (A) is correct.

Explanation: The rule followed in each column as;

$5 \times (6 + 7) = 5 \times 13 = 65;$

$4 \times (3 + 2) = 4 \times 5 = 20$

So, $9 \times (1 + 4) = 9 \times 5 = 45$

Hence, the missing number is 1.

33. Option (A) is correct.

Explanation: The rule followed as;

$H \xrightarrow{+4} L \xrightarrow{+4} P$

$P \xrightarrow{+4} T \xrightarrow{+4} X$

$K \xrightarrow{+4} O \xrightarrow{+4} \boxed{S}$

So, the missing number is S.

34. Option (B) is correct.

Explanation: The rule followed as;

$115 + 75 = 190;$

$33 + 53 = 86$

So, $181 - 78 = 103$

Hence, the missing number is 103.

35. Option (A) is correct.

Explanation: The rule followed as;

$5 \times 4 = 20$ and $5 \times 6 = 30$

$7 \times 4 = 28$ and $7 \times 6 = 42$

So, $9 \times 4 = 36$ and $9 \times 6 = 54$

Hence, the missing number is 36.

Level-2: INTERMEDIATE

1. Option (C) is correct.

Explanation: Here, we have,

$5 + 45 + 18 + ? = 80$

$\Rightarrow 68 + ? = 80$

$\Rightarrow ? = 80 - 68 = 12$

Hence, the missing number is 12.

2. Option (A) is correct.

Explanation: The rule followed as :

$25 - 4 = 21; 27 + 6 = 33$

So, $23 - 4 = 19$ and $30 + 6 = 36$

Hence, the missing number is 19.

3. Option (C) is correct.

Explanation: In clockwise way, the rule is;

$1^3 = 1; 2^3 = 8; 3^3 = 27; 4^3 = 64;$

$5^3 = 125; 6^3 = 216; 7^3 = 343$

So, the missing number is 125.

4. Option (B) is correct.

Explanation: The rule is

$2 \times 4 + 1 = 9; 9 \times 4 + 1 = 37$

So, $37 \times 4 + 1 = 148 + 1 = 149$

Hence, the missing number is 149.

5. Option (A) is correct.

Explanation: In each triangle, the rule is;

$6 \times 3 = 18; 18 \times 4 = 72$

So, $5 \times 3 = 15$ and $15 \times 4 = 60$

Hence, the missing number is 60.

6. Option (C) is correct.

Explanation: Here, we have

$3 \times 2 - 1 = 5; 5 \times 2 - 2 = 8$

$8 \times 2 - 3 = 13; 13 \times 2 - 4 = 22$

So, $22 \times 2 - 5 = 44 - 5 = 39$

Hence, the missing number is 39.

7. Option (D) is correct.

Explanation: The rule is

$1^3 - 1 = 1 - 1 = 0; 2^3 - 1 = 8 - 1 = 7;$

$3^3 - 1 = 27 - 1 = 26$

So, $4^3 - 1 = 64 - 1 = 63$

Hence, the missing number is 63.

8. Option (C) is correct.

Explanation: The rule is :

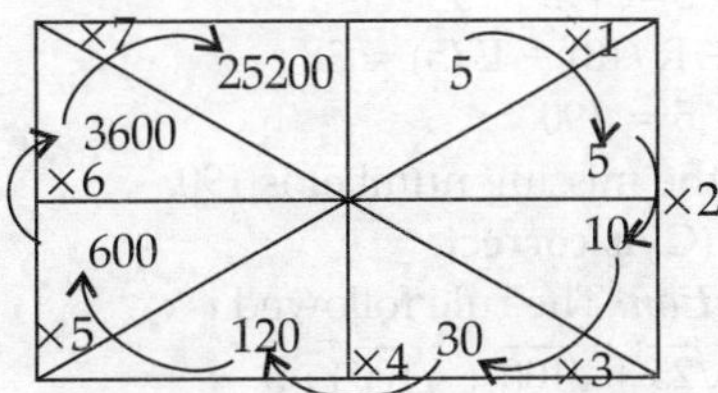

So, the missing number is 3600

9. Option (A) is correct.

Explanation: The rule is :

$A \xrightarrow{+3} D \xrightarrow{+3} G \xrightarrow{+3} J \xrightarrow{+3} M$

$\xrightarrow{+3} P \xrightarrow{+3} S \xrightarrow{+3} \boxed{V}$

So, the missing number is V.

10. Option (A) is correct.

Explanation: Here, we have

$8 \times 9 = 72$

So, $6 \times 12 = 72$

Hence, the missing number is 12.

11. Option (D) is correct.

Explanation: The rule followed as;

$\sqrt{16} + \sqrt{144} = 4 + 12 = 16;$

$\sqrt{121} + \sqrt{1089} = 11 + 33 = 44$

So, $\sqrt{196} + \sqrt{400} = 14 + 20 = \boxed{34}$

Hence, the missing number is 34.

12. Option (B) is correct.

Explanation: The rule followed as:

W (23) + E (5) = 28; 28 ÷ 4 = 7

7 (26) + B (2) = 28; 28 ÷ 4 = 7

So, Q (17) + O (15) = 32; 32 ÷ 4 = $\boxed{8}$

Hence, the missing number is 8.

13. Option (B) is correct.

Explanation: The rule is:

$(15 \times 2) + 5 + 6 = 20 + 11 = 41;$

$(18 \times 2) + 4 + 10 = 36 + 14 = 50$
So, $(80 \times 2) + 10 + 15 = 160 + 25 = 185$
Hence, the missing number is 185.

14. Option (C) is correct.
Explanation: The rule followed is :
$(4^2 + 7^2 + 6^2 + 5^2) \div 3 = (16 + 49 + 36 + 25) \div 3$
$= 126 \div 3 = 42$
$(8^2 + 12^2 + 4^2 + 10^2) \div 3 = (64 + 144 + 16 + 100) \div 3$
$= 324 \div 3 = 108$
So, $(25^2 + 1^2 + 2^2 + 0^2) \div 3 = (625 + 1 + 4 + 0) \div 3$
$= 630 \div 3 = 210$
Hence, the missing number is 210.

15. Option (B) is correct.
Explanation: Here, we have
A (1) + M (13) = 14; $14^2 = 196$
D (4) + K (11) = 15; $15^2 = 225$
So, N (14) + S (17) = 33; $33^2 = 1089$
Hence, the missing number is 1089.

16. Option (A) is correct.
Explanation: Here, we have
A (1) + H (8) + G (7) = 16
So, $16 \times 5 = 80$;
G (7) + K (11) + U (21) = 39
So, $39 \times 5 = 195$
O (15) + R (18) + E (5) = 38
So, $38 \times 5 = 190$
Hence, the missing number is 190.

17. Option (C) is correct.
Explanation: The rule followed is :
$(\sqrt{25} + \sqrt{25} + \sqrt{100} + \sqrt{100}) \div 5$
$= (5 + 5 + 10 + 10) \div 5 = 6;$
$(\sqrt{25} + \sqrt{36} + \sqrt{25} + \sqrt{81}) \div 5$
$= (5 + 6 + 5 + 9) \div 5 = 5$
$(\sqrt{25} + \sqrt{25} + \sqrt{25} + \sqrt{25}) \div 5$
$= (5 + 5 + 5 + 5) \div 5 = 4$
$(\sqrt{49} + \sqrt{16} + \sqrt{36} + \sqrt{9}) \div 5$
$= (7 + 4 + 6 + 3) \div 5 = 4$
Hence, the missing number is 4.

18. Option (D) is correct.
Explanation: We have, $\sqrt[3]{1} + \sqrt[3]{8} + \sqrt[3]{27} + \sqrt[3]{64}$
$= 1 + 2 + 3 + 4 = 10;$
$\sqrt[3]{125} + \sqrt[3]{64} + \sqrt[3]{27} + \sqrt[3]{8}$
$= 5 + 4 + 3 + 2 = 14$
So, $\sqrt[3]{216} + \sqrt[3]{125} + \sqrt[3]{64} + \sqrt[3]{27}$
$= 6 + 5 + 4 + 3 = 18$
Hence, the missing number is 18.

19. Option (A) is correct.
Explanation: Here, we have
$3^2 = 9$; $4^2 = 16$

(9)(16)

and $2^2 = 4$; $3^2 = 9$

(4)(9)

So, $1^2 = 1$; $5^2 = 25$

(1)(25)

Hence, the missing number is 125.

20. Option (B) is correct.
Explanation: The rule followed is :
$(3 \times 3) + (5 \times 6) = 9 + 30 = 39;$
$(4 \times 4) + (7 \times 5) = 16 + 35 = 51$
So, $(3 \times 4) + (5 \times 5) = 12 + 25 = 37$
Hence, the missing number is 37.

21. Option (C) is correct.
Explanation: Here, we have
$(1 + 4)^3 = 5^3 = 125;$
$(9 + 3)^3 = 12^3 = 1728$
So, $(7 + 2)^3 = 9^3 = 729$
Hence, the missing number is 729.

22. Option (C) is correct.
Explanation: Here, we have
A (1) + G (7) + U (22) + T (21) + N (14) + R (18) = 83
P (16) + M (13) + K (11) + C (3) + D (4) + M (13) = 60
So, R (18) + U (21) + S (19) + K (11) + L (12) + R (18) = 99
Hence, the missing number is 99.

23. Option (B) is correct.
Explanation: The rule is :
$(18 \times 5) - (7 \times 5) = 90 - 35 = 55;$
$(25 \times 6) - (10 \times 15) = 150 - 150 = 0$
So, $(19 \times 5) - (8 \times 10) = 95 - 80 = 15$
Hence, the missing number is 15.

24. Option (B) is correct.
Explanation: The rule followed is :
$[P(16) + C(3) + F(6)] \div 5 = 25 \div 5 = 5;$
$[U(21) + M(13) + Z(26)] \div 5 = 60 \div 5 = 12$
So, $[G(7) + Q(17) + U(21)] \div 5 = 45 \div 5 = 9$
Hence, the missing number is 9.

25. Option (A) is correct.
Explanation: The rule is :
$(60 + 60) \div 8 = 120 \div 8 = 15;$
$(54 + 26) \div 8 = 80 \div 8 = 10$
So, $(124 + 28) \div 8 = 152 \div 8 = 19$
Hence, the missing number is 19.

26. Option (D) is correct.
Explanation: The rule is
$(7 + 5) \times 6 = 12 \times 6 = 72;$
$(2 + 8) \times 5 = 10 \times 5 = 50$
So, $(3 + 1) \times 11 = 4 \times 11 = 44$
Hence, the missing number is 44.

27. Option (A) is correct.
Explanation: The rule is :
$(14 + 16) \times 3 = 30 \times 3 = 90;$
$(15 + 18) \times 3 = 33 \times 3 = 99$
So, $(11 + 17) \times 3 = 28 \times 3 = 84$
Hence, the missing number is 84.

28. Option (A) is correct.
Explanation: The rule is :
R (18) – J (10) = 8; 8 × 8 = 64
Y (25) – M (13) = 12; 12 × 12 = 1444
So, U (21) – L (12) = 9; 9 × 9 = 81
Hence, the missing number is 81.

29. Option (B) is correct.
Explanation: The rule follwed is :
$(6 \div 2) \times 18 = 3 \times 18 = 54;$
$(18 \div 9) \times 36 = 2 \times 36 = 72;$
So, $(20 \div 5) \times ? = 320$
$\Rightarrow 4 \times ? = 320$
$\Rightarrow ? = 80$
Hence, the missing number is 80.

30. Option (C) is correct.
Explanation: The rule follwed as :
$B \xrightarrow{+5} G \xrightarrow{+7} N$
$D \xrightarrow{+6} J \xrightarrow{+8} R$
$G \xrightarrow{+7} N \xrightarrow{+9} \boxed{W}$
So, the missing letter is W.

31. Option (A) is correct.
Explanation: The rule follwed as :
$20 \xrightarrow{\times 4} 80 \xrightarrow{\div 5} 16$
$75 \xrightarrow{\times 4} 300 \xrightarrow{\div 5} 60$
So, $90 \xrightarrow{\times 4} 360 \xrightarrow{\div 5} \boxed{72}$
Hence, the missing number is 72.

32. Option (C) is correct.
Explanation: We have
$(8 + 1) \times (6 + 1) = 9 \times 7 = 63$
$(11 + 1) \times (5 + 1) = 12 \times 6 = 72$
So, $(5 + 1) \times (7 + 1) = 6 \times 8 = 48$
Hence, the missing number is 5.

33. Option (A) is correct.
Explanation: The rule followed as :
$A \xrightarrow{+3} D \xrightarrow{+4} H$
$F \xrightarrow{+3} I \xrightarrow{+4} M$
So, $K \xrightarrow{+3} N \xrightarrow{+4} R$
Hence, the missing letter is K.

34. Option (B) is correct.
Explanation: The rule followed is :
$(2 + 1 + 0)^3 = 3^3 = 27;$
$(3 + 4 + 1)^3 = 8^3 = 512;$
So, $(3 + 2 + 5)^3 = 10^3 = 1000$
Hence, the missing number is 1000.

35. Option (C) is correct.
Explanation: The rule followed as :
$[(1 + 9) - 8] \times 2 = (10 - 8) \times 2 = 4$
$[(7 + 2) - 6] \times 2 = (9 - 6) \times 2 = 6$
So, $[(2 + 5) - 4] \times 2 = (7 - 4) \times 2 = 6$
Hence, the missing number is 6.

Level-3: EXPERT

1. Option (A) is correct.
Explanation: The rule followed is :
$(15 - 7)^3 \div 2 = 8^3 \div 2 = 512 \div 2 = 256$
$(19 - 13)^3 \div 2 = 6^3 \div 2 = 216 \div 2 = 108$
So, $(20 - 8)^3 \div 2 = 12^3 \div 2 = 1728 \div 2 = 864$
Hence, the missing number is 864.

2. Option (B) is correct.
Explanation: The rule followed is :
$\sqrt{64} \times \sqrt{25} \times \sqrt{9} = 8 \times 5 \times 3 = 120$
$\sqrt{121} \times \sqrt{100} \times \sqrt{625} = 11 \times 10 \times 25 = 2750$
So, $\sqrt{225} \times \sqrt{196} \times \sqrt{400} = 15 \times 14 \times 20 = 4200$
Hence, the missing number is 4200.

3. Option (A) is correct.
Explanation: The rule followed is :
$28 \times 2 + 2 = 56 + 2 = 58;$
$58 \times 2 + 2 = 116 + 2 = 118;$
$21 \times 2 + 2 = 44; 44 \times 2 + 2 = 90$
So, $47 \times 2 + 2 = 96; 96 \times 2 + 2 = 194$
Hence, the missing number is 194.

4. Option (B) is correct.
Explanation: The rule followed is :
S (19) – D (4) = 15;
T (20) – J (10) = 10;
W (23) – T (20) = 3;
So, P (16) – G (7) = 9
Hence, the missing number is 9.

5. Option (C) is correct.
Explanation: The rule is :
$(8 - 2)^3 = 6^3 = 216;$
$(15 - 8)^3 = 7^3 = 343;$
$(7 - 4)^3 = 3^3 = 27;$
So, $(9 - 5)^3 = 4^3 = 64$
Hence, the missing number is 64.

6. Option (C) is correct.
Explanation: The rule followed as :
$M \xrightarrow{+5} R \xrightarrow{+10} B \xrightarrow{+15} Q$
$C \xrightarrow{+5} H \xrightarrow{+10} R \xrightarrow{+15} G$
$J \xrightarrow{+5} O \xrightarrow{+10} Y \xrightarrow{+15} \boxed{N}$
So, the missing letter is N.

7. Option (B) is correct.
Explanation: The rule is :
(5 + 7) – (3 + 4) = 12 – 7 = 5 (E);
(8 + 12) – (6 + 2) = 20 – 8 = 12 (L);
So, (19 + 3) – (5 + 7) = 22 – 12 = 10 (J);
Hence, the missing term is J.

8. Option (C) is correct.
Explanation: The rule followed as :
$(25 + 35) \div (3 \times 2) = 60 \div 6 = 10;$
$(40 + 30) \div (1 \times 7) = 70 \div 7 = 10$
So, $(90 + 10) \div (2 \times 5) = 100 \div 10 = 10$
So, the missing number is 10.

9. Option (D) is correct.

Explanation: The rule followed as :

$(\sqrt[3]{64}\times\sqrt[3]{512})-(\sqrt[3]{8}+\sqrt[3]{1})$

$= (4 \times 8) - (2 \times 1) = 30$

$(\sqrt[3]{729}\times\sqrt[3]{125})-(\sqrt[3]{1000}\times\sqrt[3]{27})$

$= (9 \times 5) - (10 \times 3) = 45 - 30 = 15$

$(\sqrt[3]{3375}\times\sqrt[3]{8000})-(\sqrt[3]{1728}\times\sqrt[3]{729})$

$= (15 \times 20) - (12 \times 9)$

$= 300 - 108 = 192$

Hence, the missing number is 192.

10. Option (A) is correct.

Explanation: The rule followed as :

[D (4) + J (10)] = 14

So, 14 × 14 = 196

[R (18) + W (23)] = 41

So, 41 × 14 = 574

So, T (20) + H (8) = 28

So, 8 × 14 = 392

Hence, the missing number is 120.

11. Option (A) is correct.

Explanation: The rule followed as :

4 × 7 = 28; 3 × 5 = 15

2 × 5 = 10

12. Option (D) is correct.

Explanation: The rule followed as :

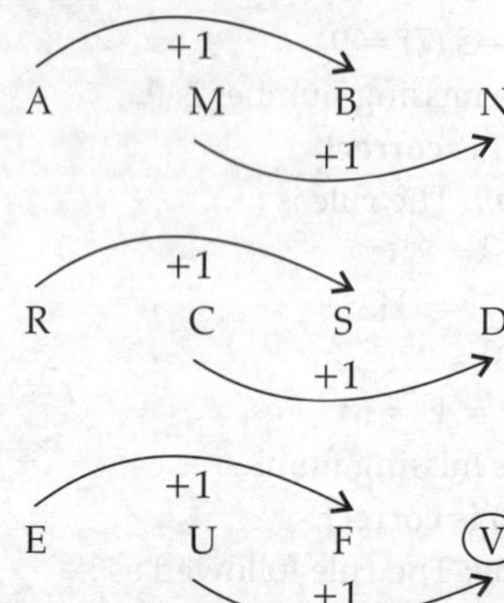

So, the missing letter is V.

13. Option (B) is correct.

Explanation: The rule followed as :

$Z \xrightarrow{-5} U \xrightarrow{-5} P$

$5 \xrightarrow{+5} 10 \xrightarrow{+5} 15;$

$W \xrightarrow{-5} R \xrightarrow{-5} M$

$6 \xrightarrow{+5} 11 \xrightarrow{+5} 16$

So,

$Q \xrightarrow{-5} L \xrightarrow{-5} \boxed{G}$

$7 \xrightarrow{+5} 12 \xrightarrow{+5} \boxed{17}$

Hence, the missing term is G17,

14. Option (C) is correct.

Explanation: The rule followed as :

$(3 + 2)^4 = 5^4 = 625;$

$(4 + 6)^4 = 10^4 = 10000;$

So, $(7 + 1)^4 = 8^4 = 4096;$

Hence, the missing number is 4096.

15. Option (C) is correct.

Explanation: The rule followed as :

31 + 68 + 91 + 10 = 200;

17 + 19 + 22 + 142 = 200;

58 + 61 + 70 + 11 = 200;

So, 87 + 56 + 50 + ? = 200

⇒ ? = 200 – 193 = 7

Hence, the missing number is 7.

16. Option (B) is correct.

Explanation: The rule followed as :

[(8 – 4) + 2] × 5 = [4 + 2] × 5 = 30;

[(7 – 5) + 2] × 5 = [2 + 2] × 5 = 20;

[(11 – 8) + 2] × 5 = [3 + 2] × 5 = 25;

So, [(18 – 11) + 2] × 5 = [7 + 2] × 5 = 45;

Hence, the missing number is 45.

17. Option (C) is correct.

Explanation: The rule is :

9 × 8 + 8 = 72 + 8 = 80;

80 × 8 + 8 = 640 + 8 = 648

648 × 8 + 8 = 5184 + 8 = 5192

So, 5192 × 8 + 8 = 41536 + 8 = 41544

Hence, the missing number is 41544.

18. Option (A) is correct.

Explanation: In each triangle,

$(15 + 34 + 41)^2 = 90^2 = 8100$

So, $(31 + ? + 45)^2 = 8100$

⇒ (76 + ?) = 90

⇒ ? = 14

Hence, the missing number is 14.

19. Option (B) is correct.

Explanation: The rule followed as :

1 × 8 – 5 = 3; 3 × 8 – 5 = 19;

19 × 8 – 5 = 147; 147 × 8 – 5 = 1171

1171 × 8 – 5 = 9363; 9363 × 8 – 5 = 74899

So, 74899 × 8 – 5 = 599187

Hence, the missing number is 599187

20. Option (A) is correct.

Explanation: The rule followed as :

$2^3 = 8; 3^3 = 27, 5^3 = 125;$

$7^3 = 343; 11^3 = 1331, 13^3 = 2197$

So, $17^3 = 4913$

Hence, the missing number is 4913.

■ ■ ■

Chapter 15

Non-Verbal Reasoning

Series

LEARNING OBJECTIVES:

- Identify the rule to find the next figure in series
- Identify the rule to find the missing figure in series
- Different types of questions asked in competitive exams

Series refers to a type of problem-solving task that involves identifying the pattern or sequence of shapes or figures and selecting the missing or next figure in the series.

Typically, series completion questions present us with a sequence of shapes, symbols, or figures arranged in a specific pattern. Our job is to analyse the pattern and figure out what logical rule governs the sequence. We must then identify the missing figure or predict the next figure in the series using this rule.

Series completion issues are frequently encountered in cognitive ability tests, aptitude tests, and entrance examinations. They evaluate our logical reasoning abilities, pattern recognition abilities, and analytical and systematic thinking abilities.

FIGURE SERIES

In this type of problem, we are given a sequence of figures or shapes, and your task is to identify the pattern or rule that governs the series. The figures can be geometric shapes, symbols, or a mix of the two. Transformations such as rotation, reflection, scaling, and translation can be used in the patterns. Changes in shape, orientation, number of elements, position, or any other relevant characteristic can also be included. The problems can be four problem or five problem figure series.

To solve such problems, we have to carefully examine the given figures and look for consistent changes or transformations that occur as you move from one figure to the next. Analysing the relationships between the elements of the figures and identifying any rules or logical patterns is critical in determining the missing or next figure in the series.

Example 1: Find the next figure from the answer figures that follows the sequence of the question figures in the following question.

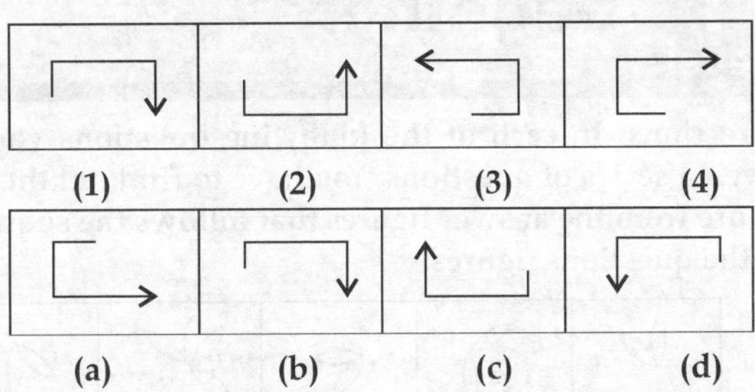

Sol. (c) In the following figure, the arrow and the small line segment turn to the other side of the larger line in one step.

Example 2: Find the next figure from the answer figures that follows the sequence of the question figures in the following question

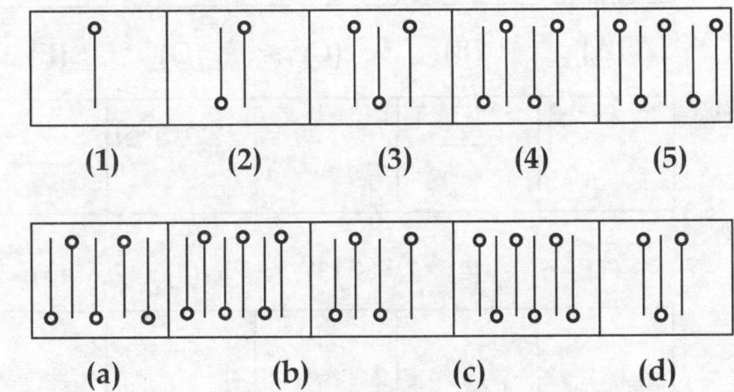

Sol. (b) In each step, a pin is added on the left side of an existing pin or pins. The pin's head is facing the opposite direction as the adjacent pin.

MIXED SERIES

A mixed series is a type of problem in non-verbal reasoning that combines multiple types of patterns or rules within a single series. Unlike other types of series, where the pattern remains consistent throughout, mixed series requires you to identify and apply different patterns or rules within the same sequence of figures or shapes.

Each part of the series follows a distinct pattern, and our task is to recognise these patterns and correctly apply them to predict or choose the missing or next figure.

Example 3: Find the next figure from the answer figures that follows the sequence of the question figures in the following question.

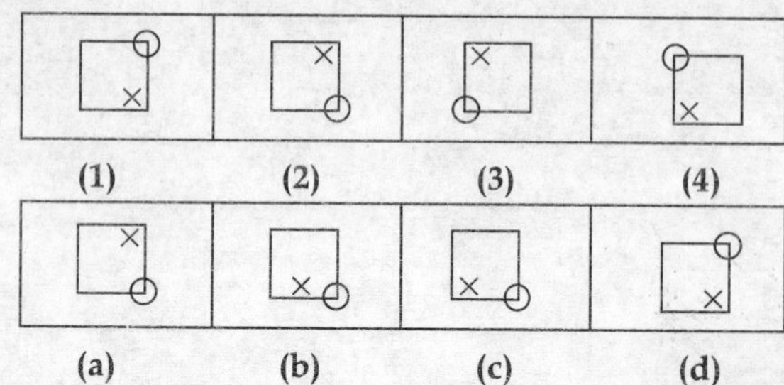

(1) (2) (3) (4)

(a) (b) (c) (d)

Sol. (d) The circle at the square's corner moves clockwise, while the cross inside the square moves anticlockwise.

Example 4: Find the missing figure from the answer figures that follows the sequence of the question figures in the following question.

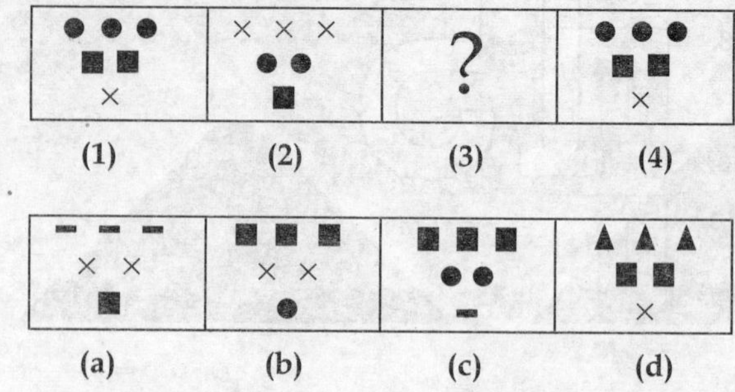

(1) (2) (3) (4)

(a) (b) (c) (d)

Sol. (b) The top row's elements are moved to the second row, the second row's elements are moved to the third row, and the third row's elements are moved to the first row.

Level 1 Beginner

Directions: In each of the following questions you are given a series of questions. You have to find out the next figure from the answer figures that follows the sequence of the questions figures.

1.

(1) (2) (3) (4) (5)

(A) (B) (C) (D) (E)

2.

(1) (2) (3) (4) (5)

(A) (B) (C) (D) (E)

3.

(1) (2) (3) (4)

(A) (B) (C) (D)

4.

(1) (2) (3) (4) (5)

(A) (B) (C) (D) (E)

5.

(1) (2) (3) (4)

?

(A) (B) (C) (D)

6.

(1) (2) (3) (4)

?

[SSC CPO Exam, 2020]

(A) (B) (C) (D)

7.

(1) (2) (3) (4) (5)

?

[SSC CPO Exam, 2018]

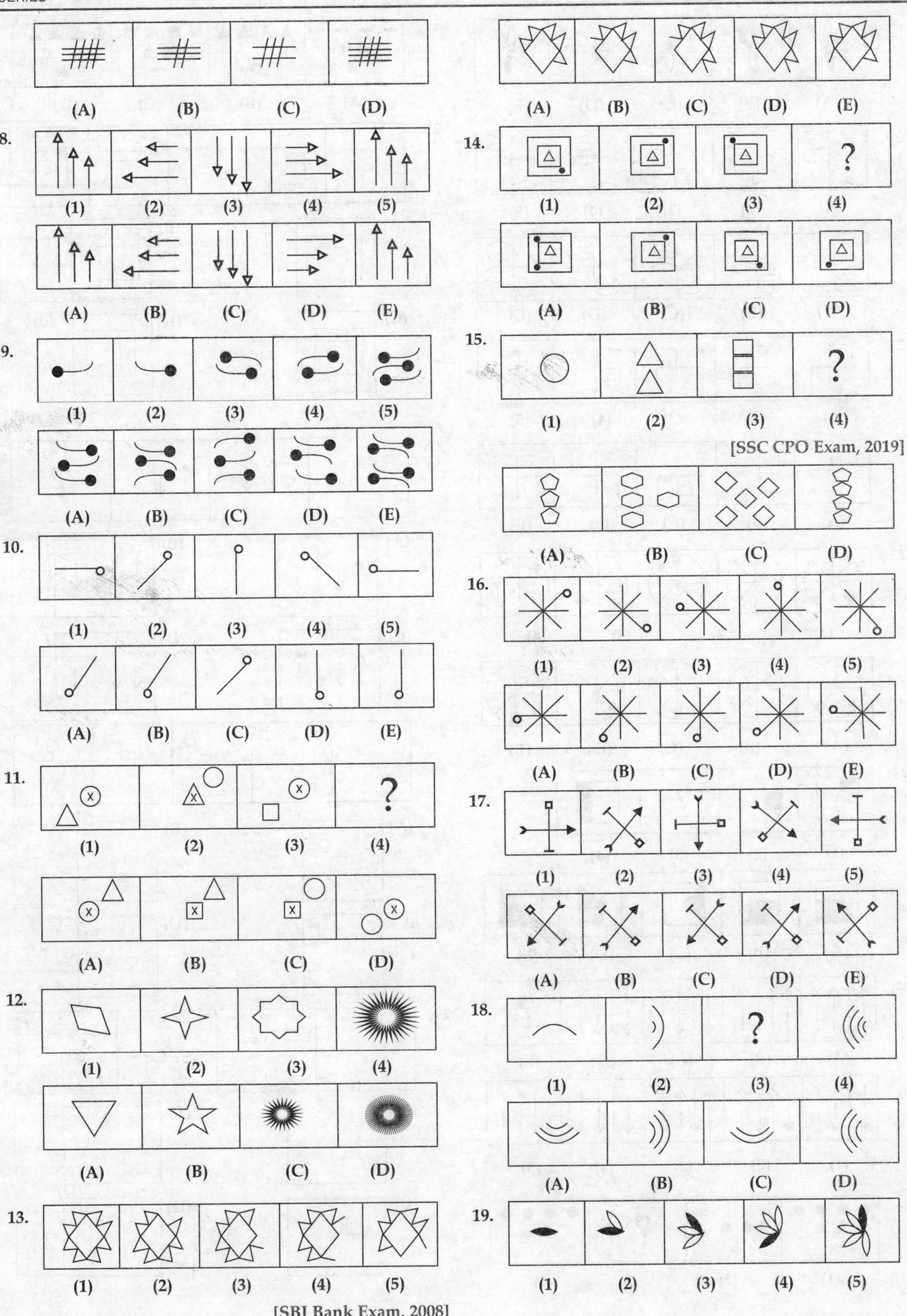

[SBI Bank Exam, 2008]

[SSC CPO Exam, 2019]

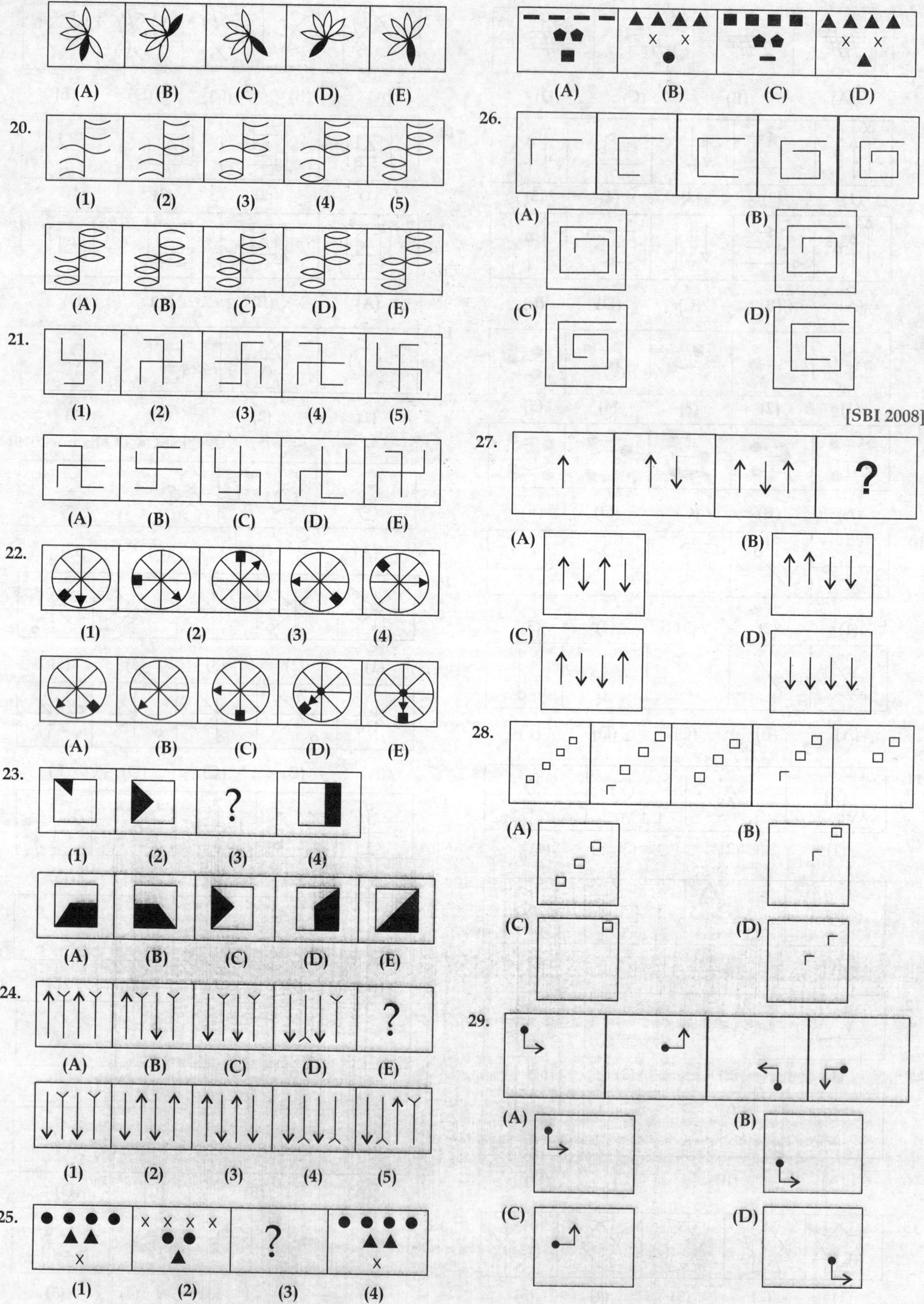
(A) (B) (C) (D) (E)
20.
(1) (2) (3) (4) (5)
(A) (B) (C) (D) (E)
21.
(1) (2) (3) (4) (5)
(A) (B) (C) (D) (E)
22.
(1) (2) (3) (4)
(A) (B) (C) (D) (E)
23.
?
(1) (2) (3) (4)
(A) (B) (C) (D) (E)
24.
?
(A) (B) (C) (D) (E)
(1) (2) (3) (4) (5)
25.
?
(1) (2) (3) (4)
(A) (B) (C) (D)
26.
(A) (B) (C) (D)
[SBI 2008]
27.
?
(A) (B) (C) (D)
28.
(A) (B) (C) (D)
29.
(A) (B) (C) (D)

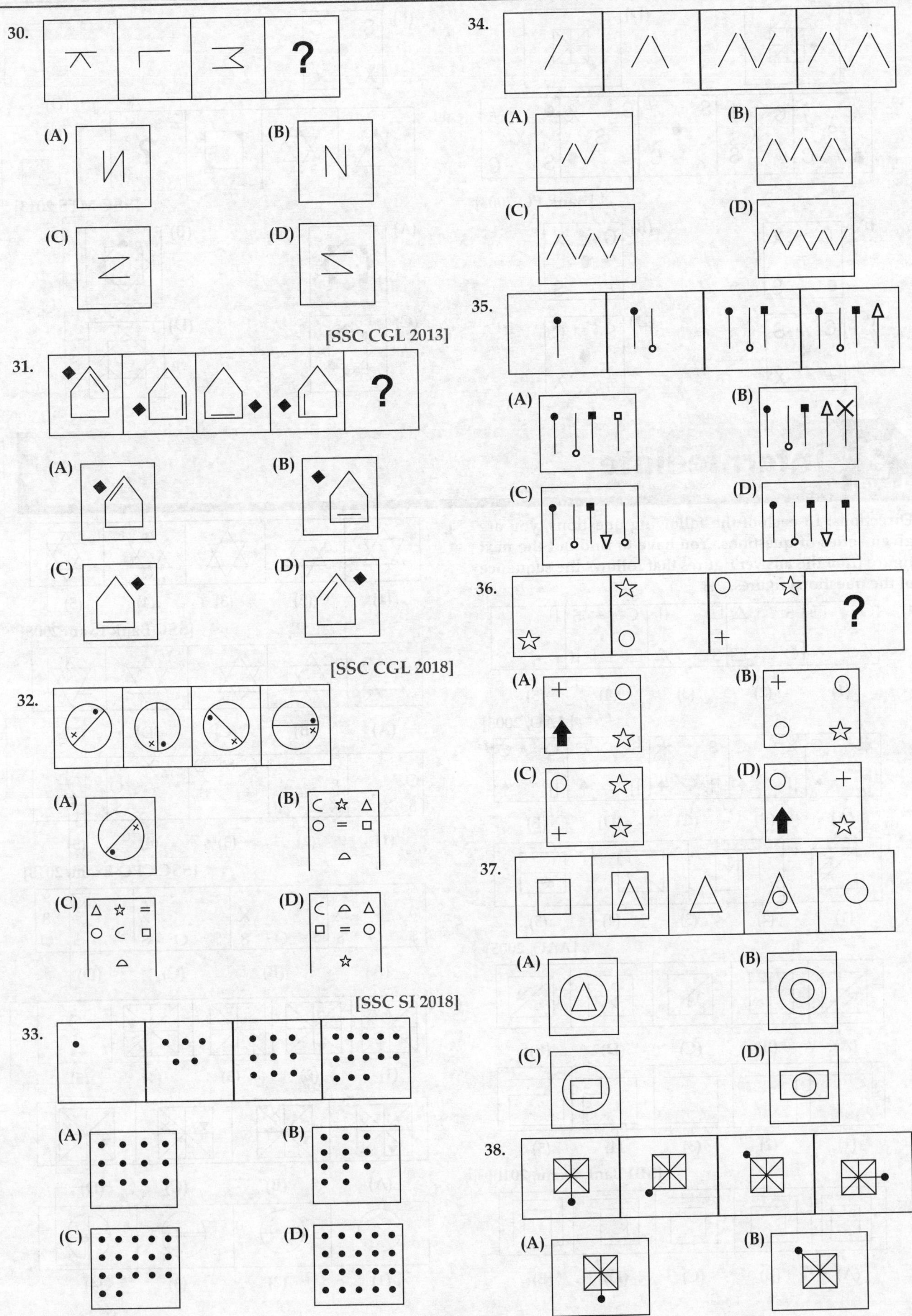
30.
(A)
(B)
(C)
(D)
[SSC CGL 2013]
31.
(A)
(B)
(C)
(D)
[SSC CGL 2018]
32.
(A)
(B)
(C)
(D)
[SSC SI 2018]
33.
(A)
(B)
(C)
(D)
34.
(A)
(B)
(C)
(D)
35.
(A)
(B)
(C)
(D)
36.
(A)
(B)
(C)
(D)
37.
(A)
(B)
(C)
(D)
38.
(A)
(B)

(C)

(D)

(E)

39.

[Bank PO 2003]

(A)

(B)

(C)

(D)

40.

[SSC MTS 2013]

(A)

(B)

(C)

(D)

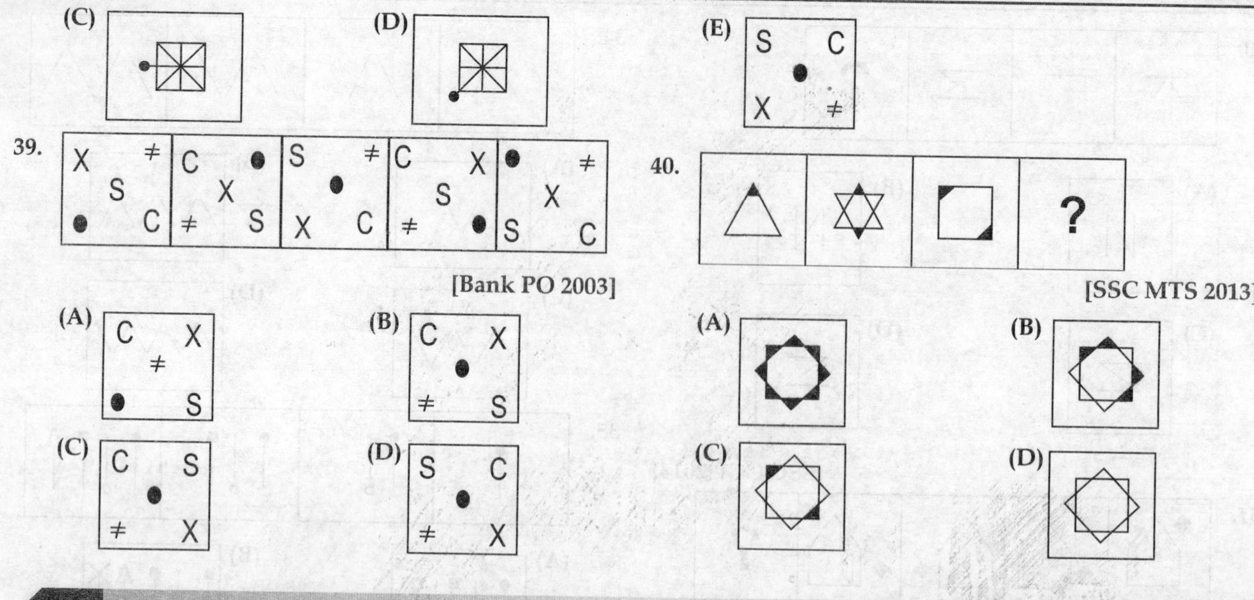

Level 2 Intermediate

Directions: In each of the following questions, you are given series of questions. You have to find out the next figure from the answer figures that follows the sequence of the questions figures.

1.

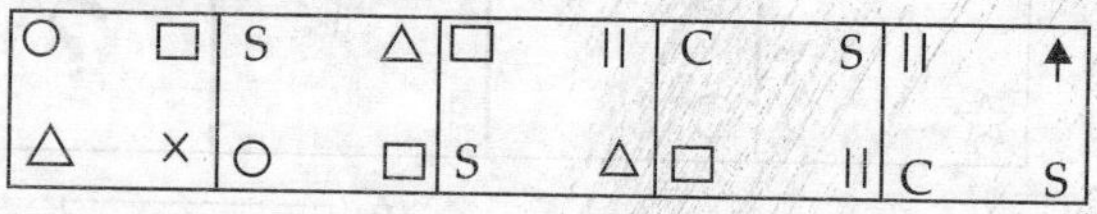

(1) (2) (3) (4) (5)

[AAO, 2005]

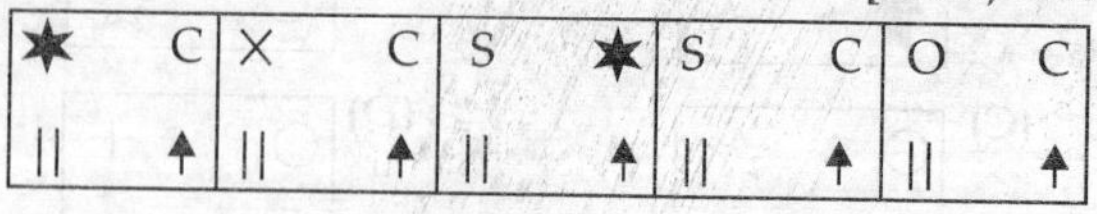

(A) (B) (C) (D) (E)

2.

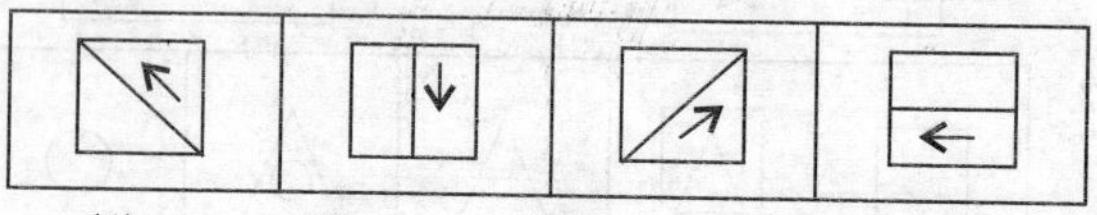

(1) (2) (3) (4) (5)

[AAO, 2005]

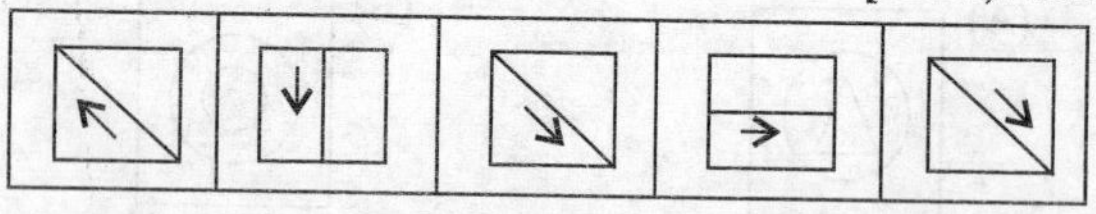

(A) (B) (C) (D) (E)

3.

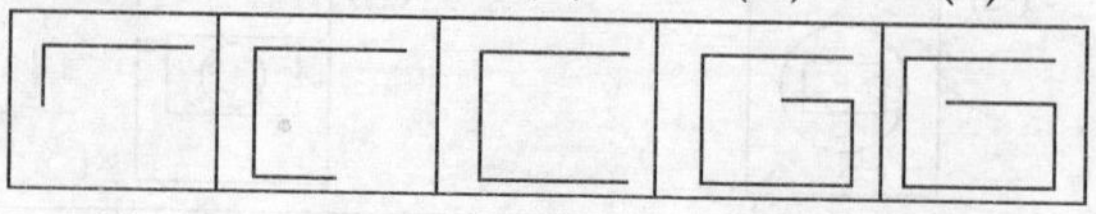

(1) (2) (3) (4) (5)

[SBI Bank Exam, 2010]

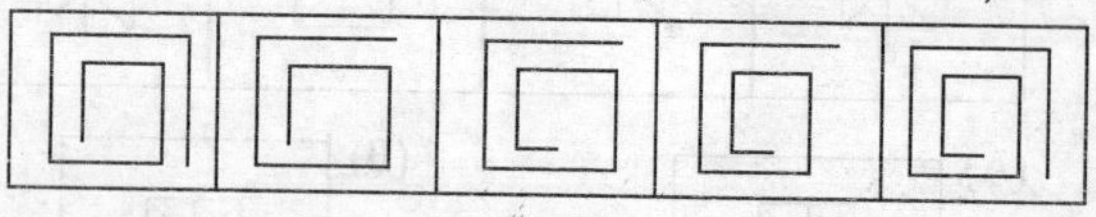

(A) (B) (C) (D) (E)

4.

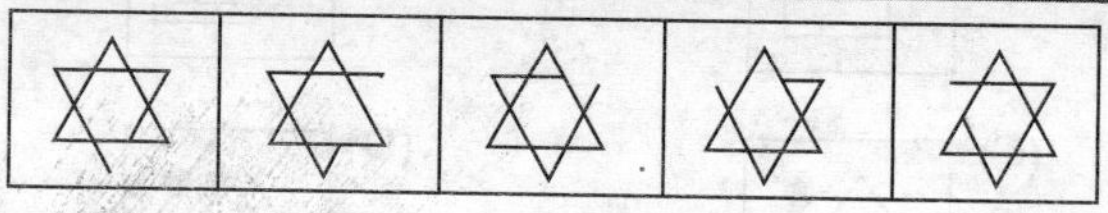

(1) (2) (3) (4) (5)

[SSC Bank Exam 2008]

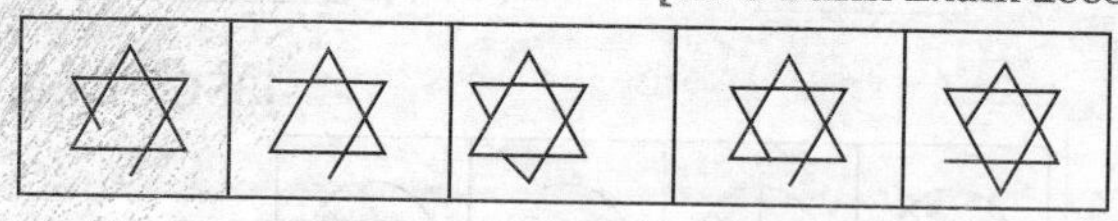

(A) (B) (C) (D) (E)

5.

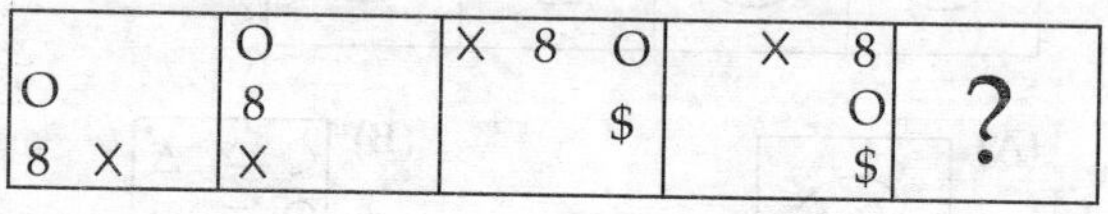

(1) (2) (3) (4) (5)

[SSC CPO Exam, 2018]

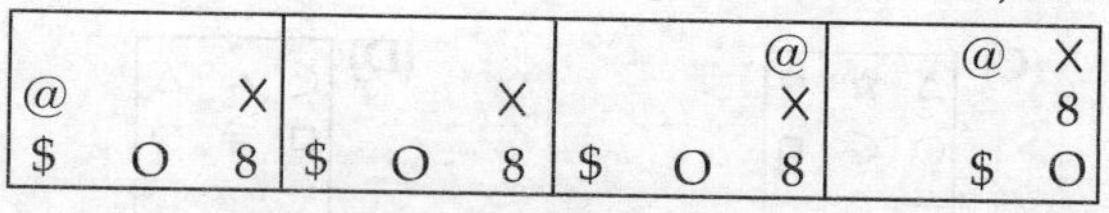

(A) (B) (C) (D)

6.

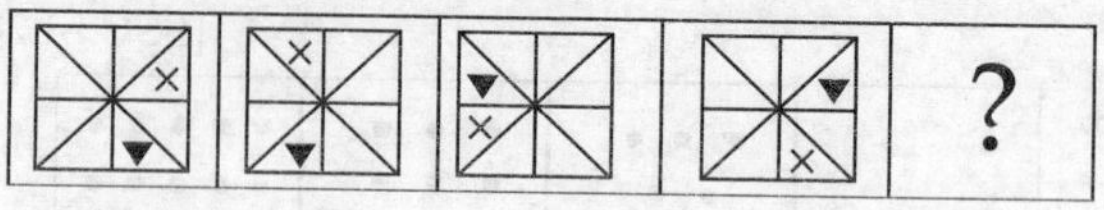

(1) (2) (3) (4) (5)

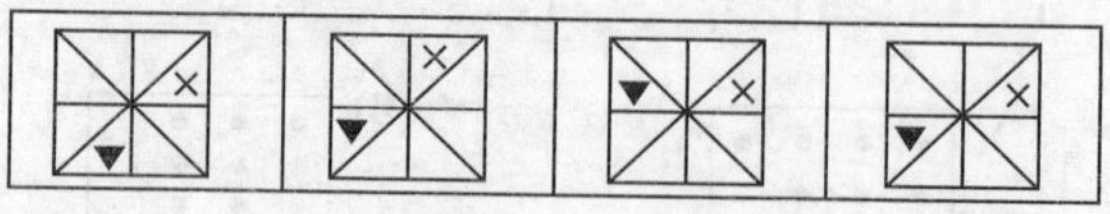

(A) (B) (C) (D)

7.

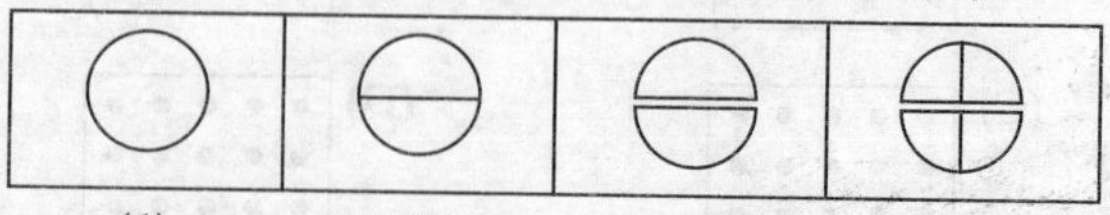

(1) (2) (3) (4)

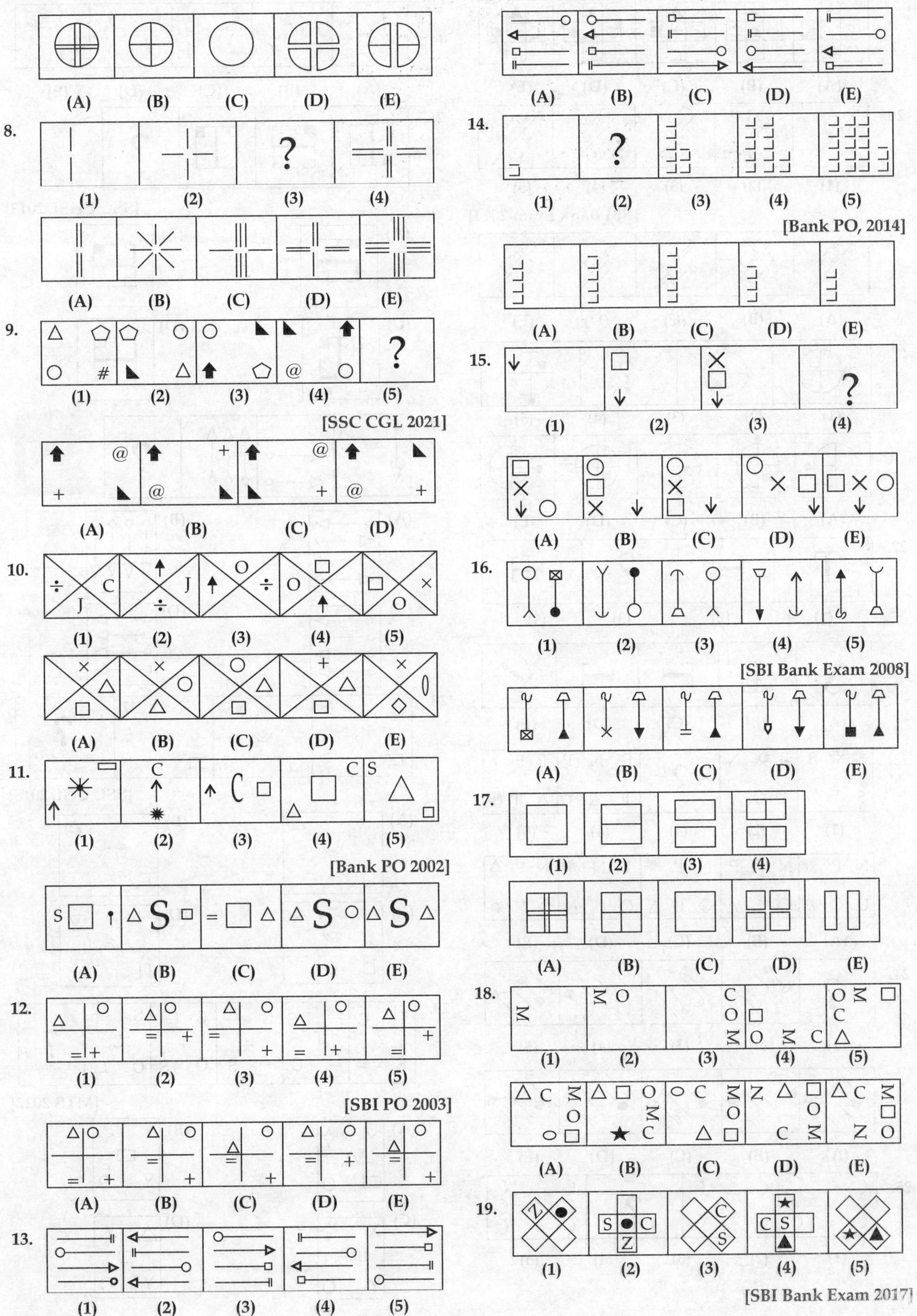
8.
9.
[SSC CGL 2021]
10.
11.
[Bank PO 2002]
12.
[SBI PO 2003]
13.
14.
[Bank PO, 2014]
15.
16.
[SBI Bank Exam 2008]
17.
18.
19.
[SBI Bank Exam 2017]

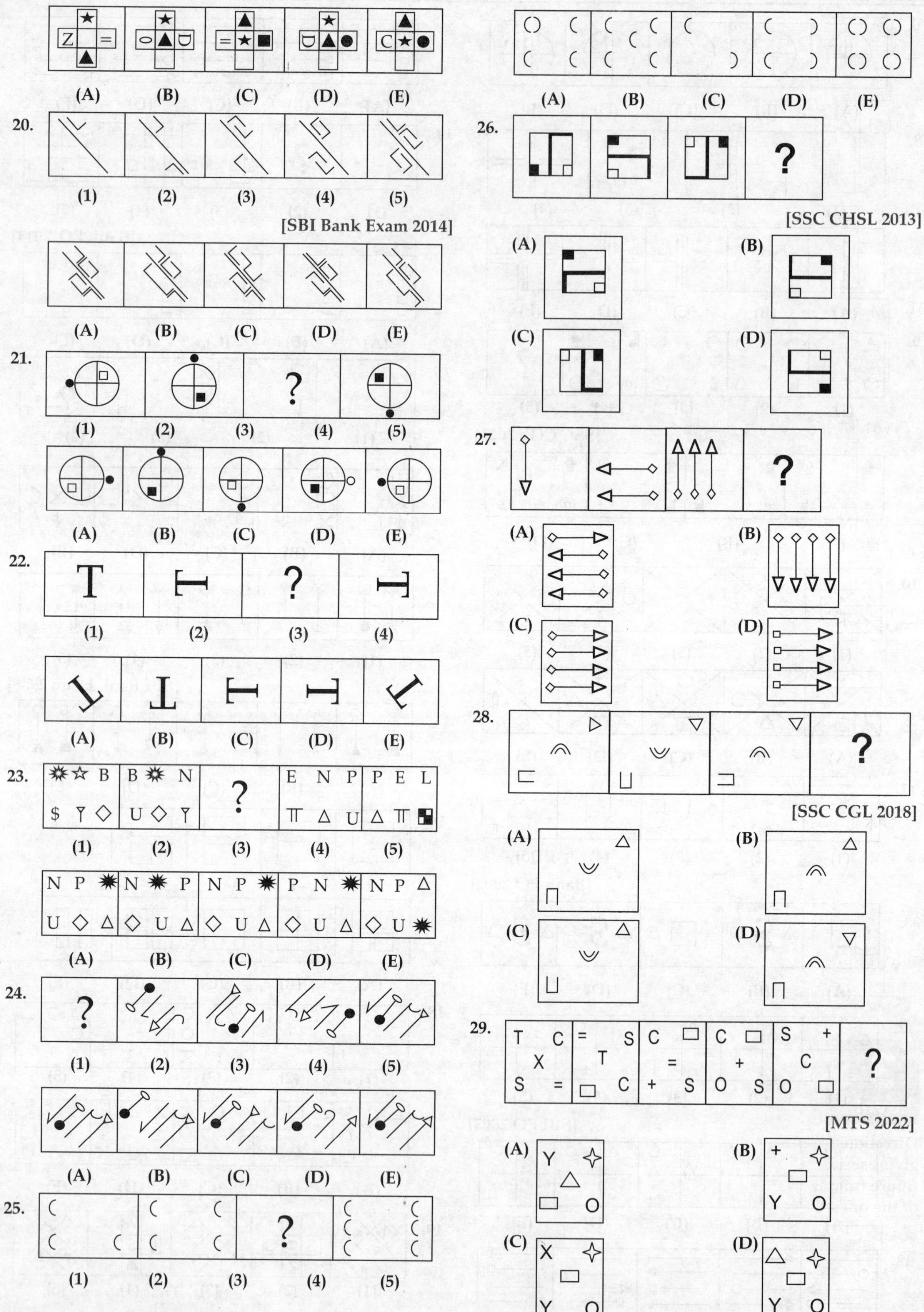
(A) (B) (C) (D) (E)
20.
(1) (2) (3) (4) (5)
[SBI Bank Exam 2014]
(A) (B) (C) (D) (E)
21.
(1) (2) (3) (4) (5)
(A) (B) (C) (D) (E)
22.
(1) (2) (3) (4)
(A) (B) (C) (D) (E)
23.
(1) (2) (3) (4) (5)
(A) (B) (C) (D) (E)
24.
(1) (2) (3) (4) (5)
(A) (B) (C) (D) (E)
25.
(1) (2) (3) (4) (5)
(A) (B) (C) (D) (E)
26.
[SSC CHSL 2013]
(A) (B) (C) (D)
27.
(A) (B) (C) (D)
28.
[SSC CGL 2018]
(A) (B) (C) (D)
29.
[MTS 2022]
(A) (B) (C) (D)

30. 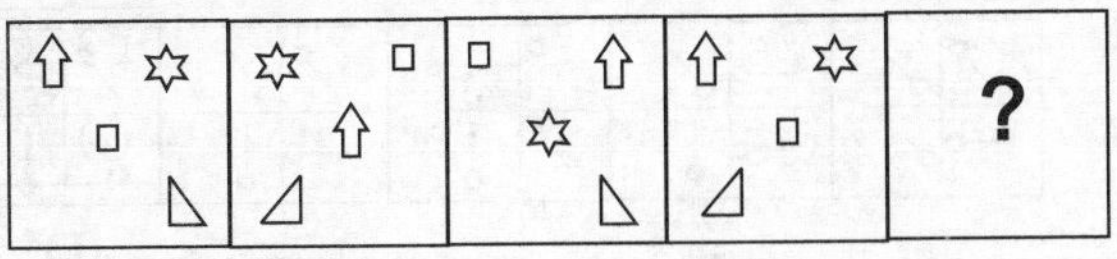 ?

(A) 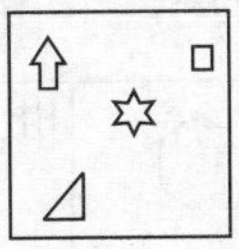 (B)

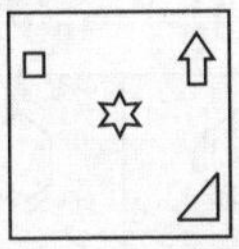

(C) 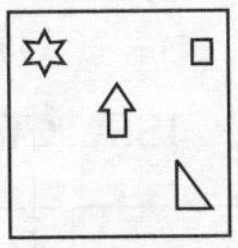 (D)

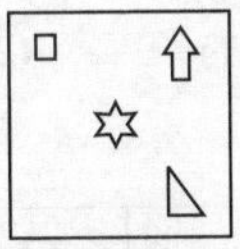

31. 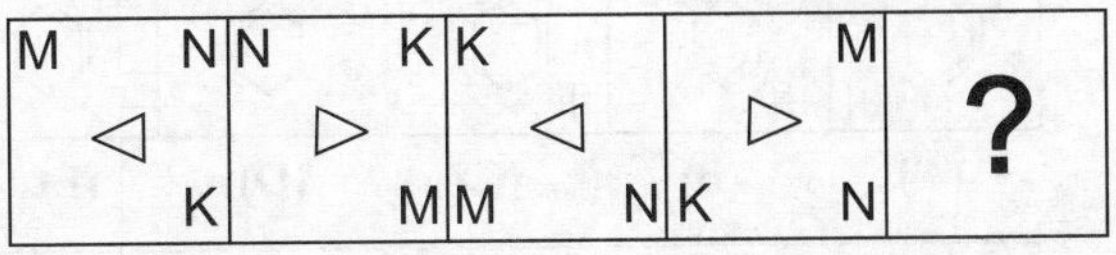 M N N K K M M N K M N ?

[MTS 2019]

(A) 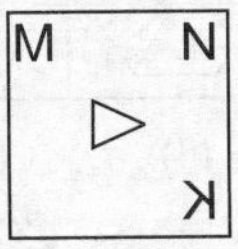 (B)

(C) 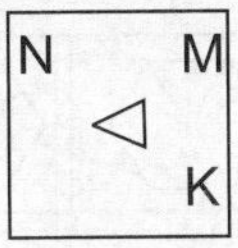 (D)

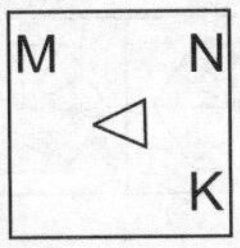

32. 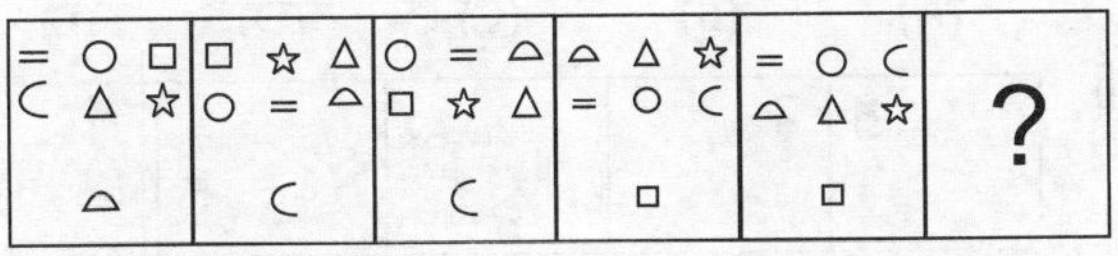 ?

(A) 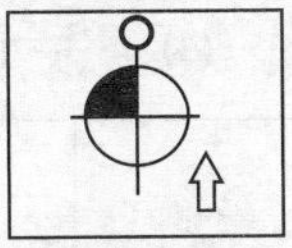 (B)

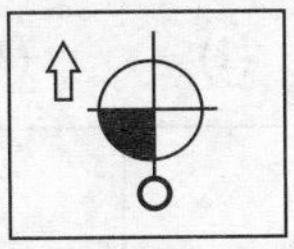

(C) 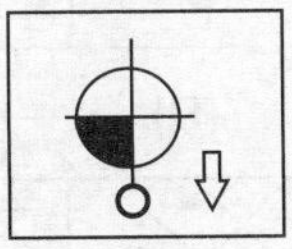 (D)

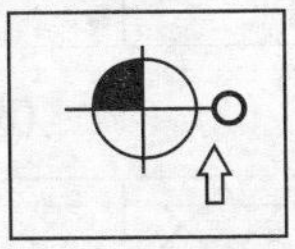

[SSC SI 2021]

33. 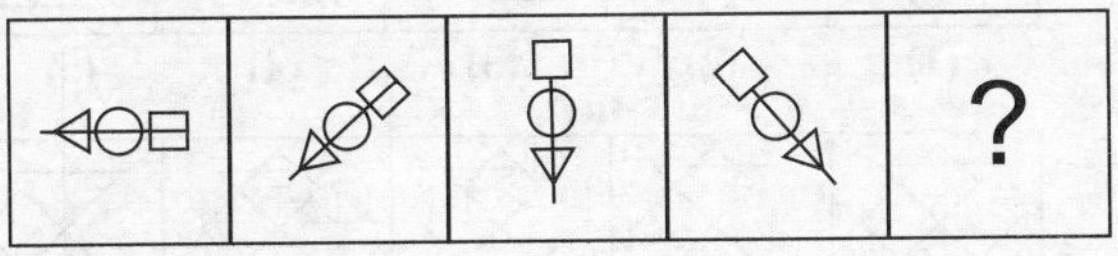 ?

(A) 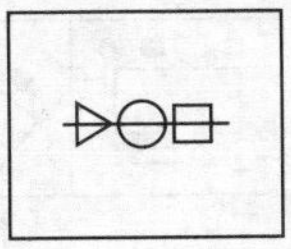 (B)

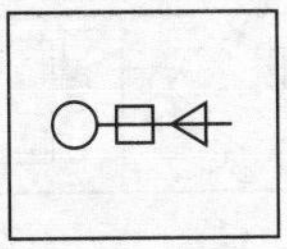

(C) 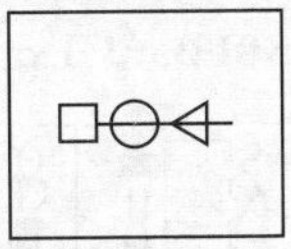 (D)

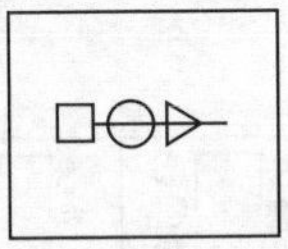

[MTS 2019]

34. 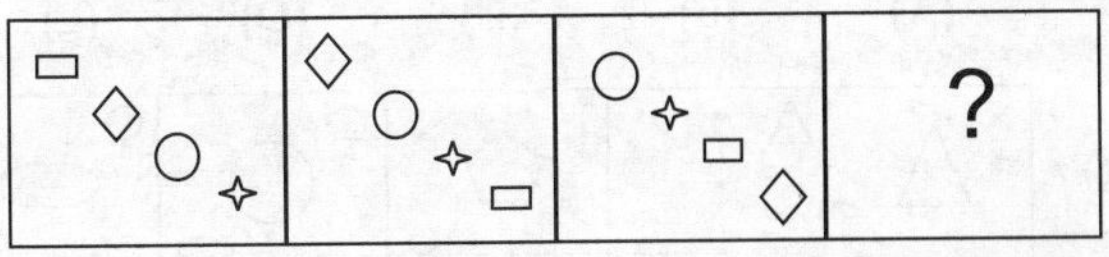 ?

[SSC SI 2021]

(A) 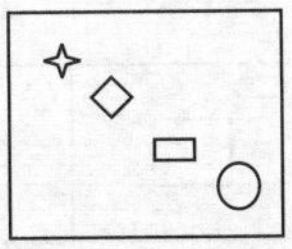 (B)

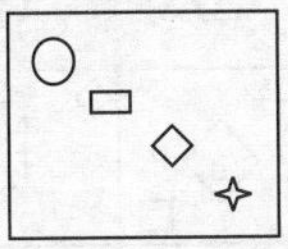

(C) 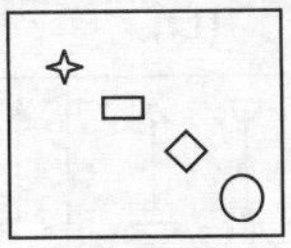 (D)

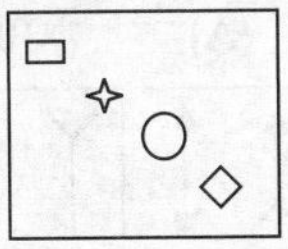

35.

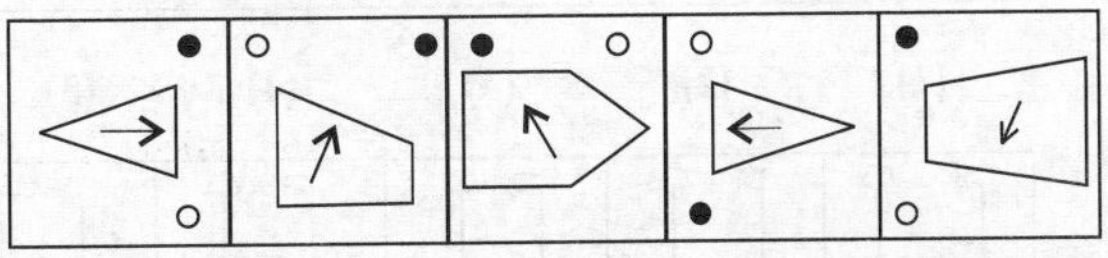

[Bank Clerical 2002]

(A) 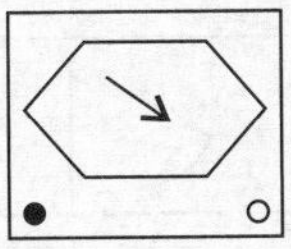 (B)

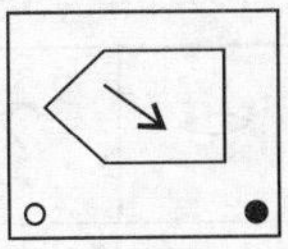

(C) 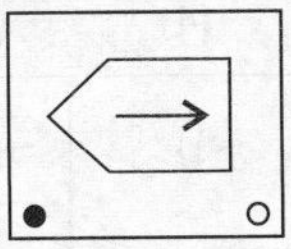 (D)

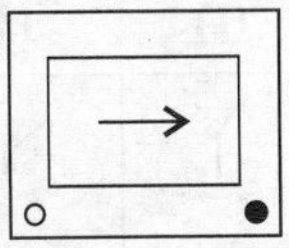

(E)

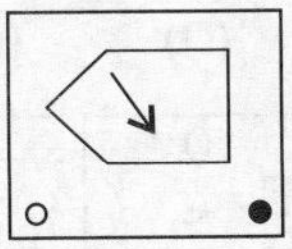

3 Level Expert

Directions: In each of the following questions, you are given series of question. you have to find out the next figure from the answer figures that follows the sequence of the questions figures.

1. 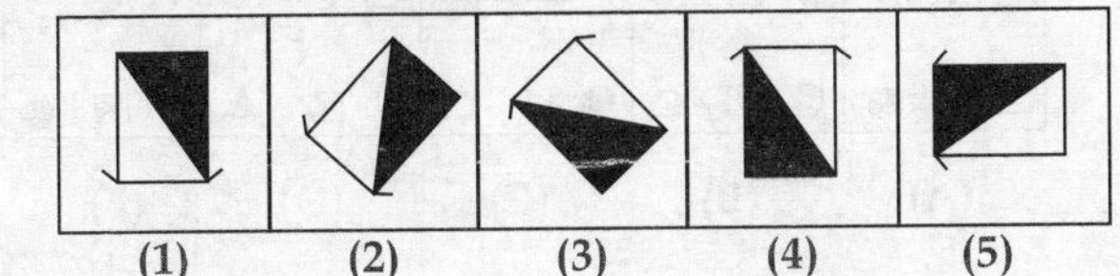

(1) (2) (3) (4) (5)

(A) 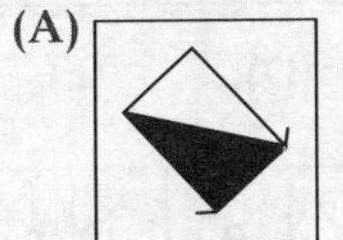

(B) 

(C) 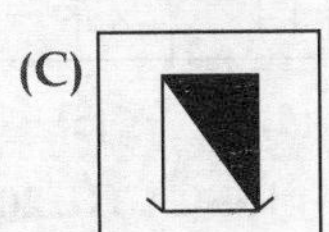

(D) 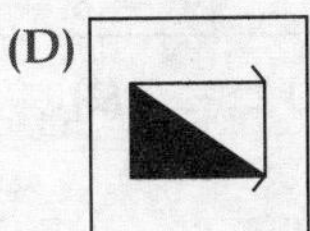

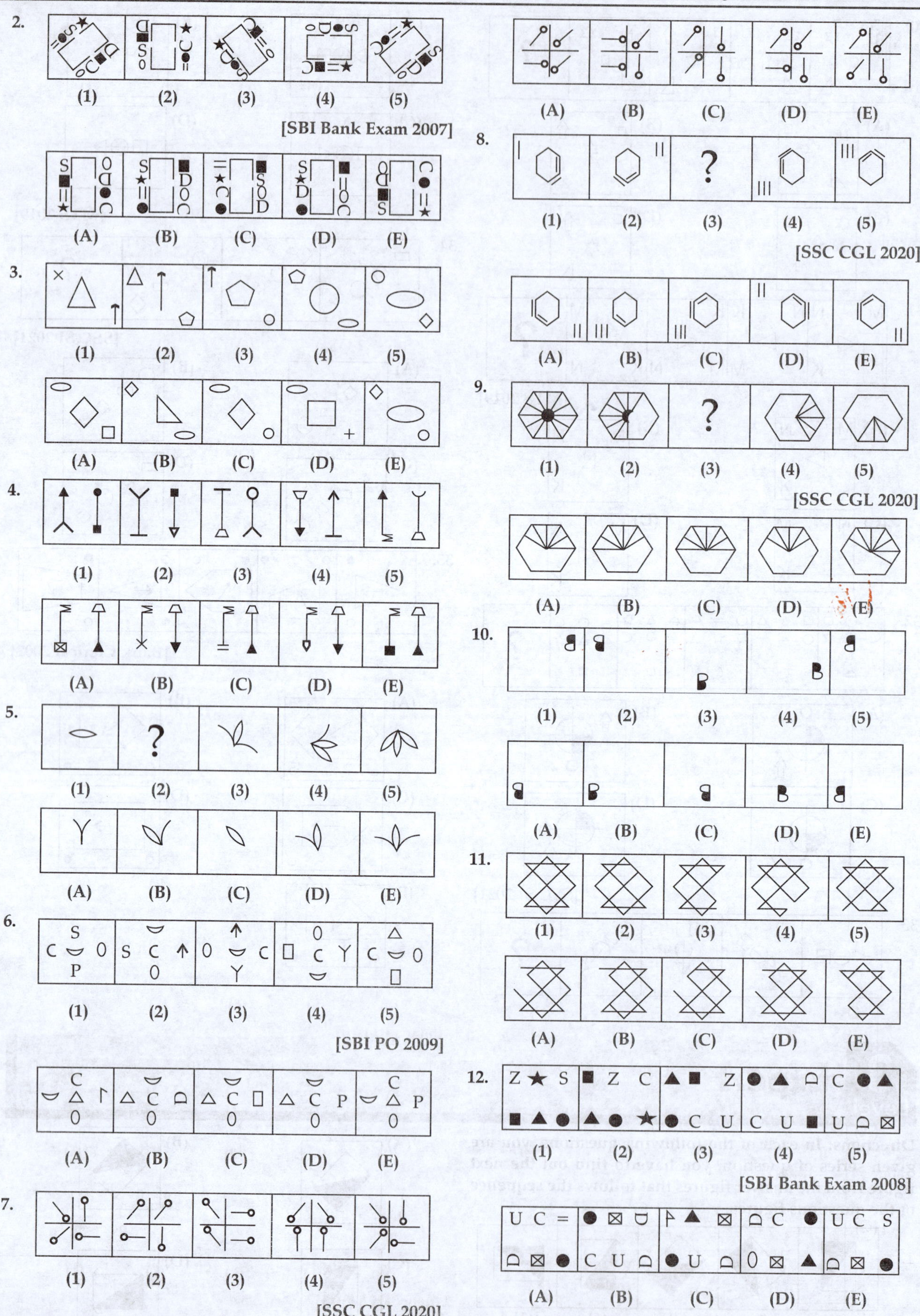

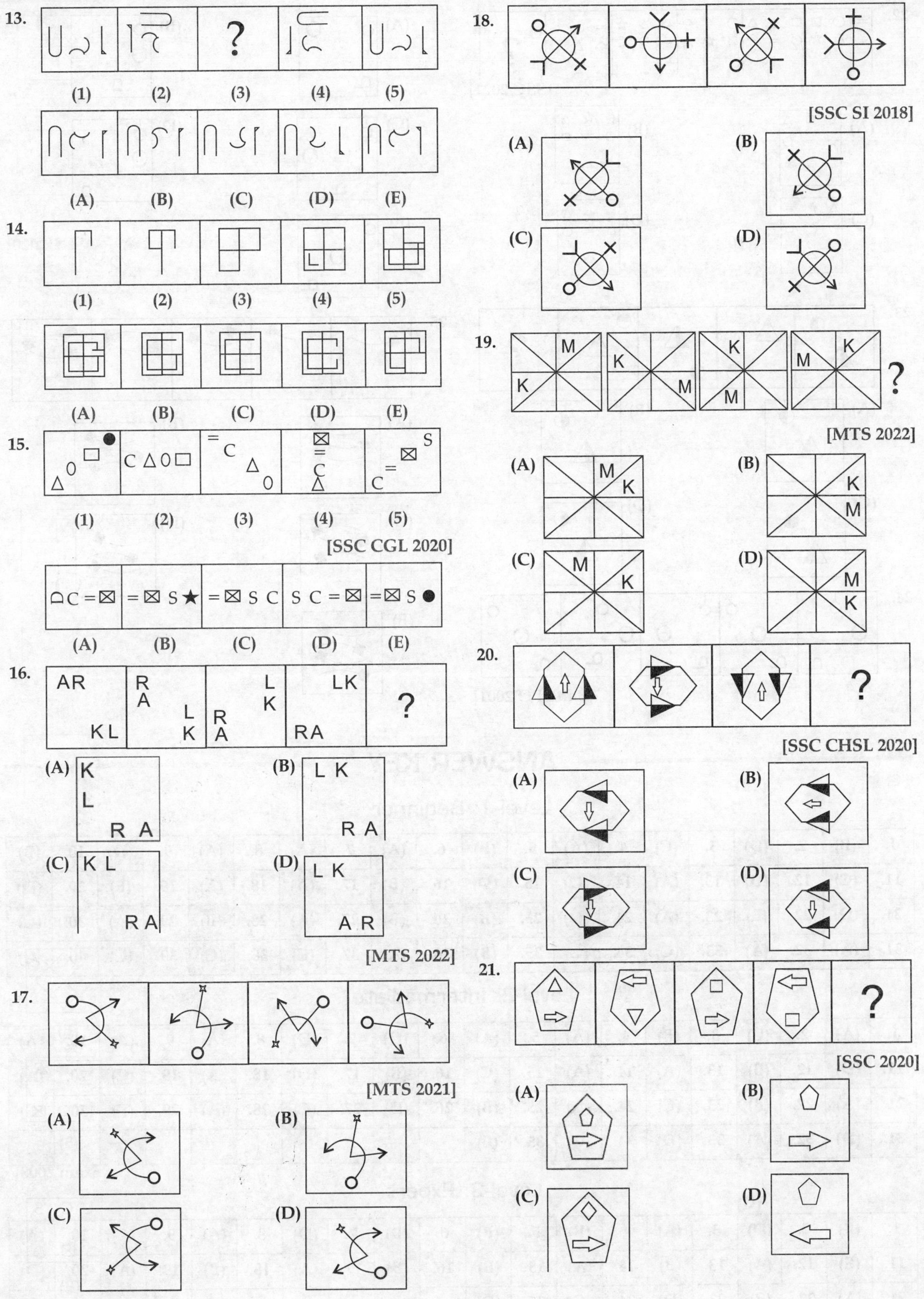
13.
(1) (2) (3) (4) (5)
(A) (B) (C) (D) (E)
14.
(1) (2) (3) (4) (5)
(A) (B) (C) (D) (E)
15.
(1) (2) (3) (4) (5)
[SSC CGL 2020]
(A) (B) (C) (D) (E)
16.
AR KL
R A L K
R A L K
LK RA
?
(A) K L R A
(B) L K R A
(C) K L R A
(D) L K A R
[MTS 2022]
17.
[MTS 2021]
(A) (B) (C) (D)
18.
[SSC SI 2018]
(A) (B) (C) (D)
19.
M K
K M
K M
M K
?
[MTS 2022]
(A) M K
(B) K M
(C) M K
(D) M K
20.
?
[SSC CHSL 2020]
(A) (B) (C) (D)
21.
?
[SSC 2020]
(A) (B) (C) (D)

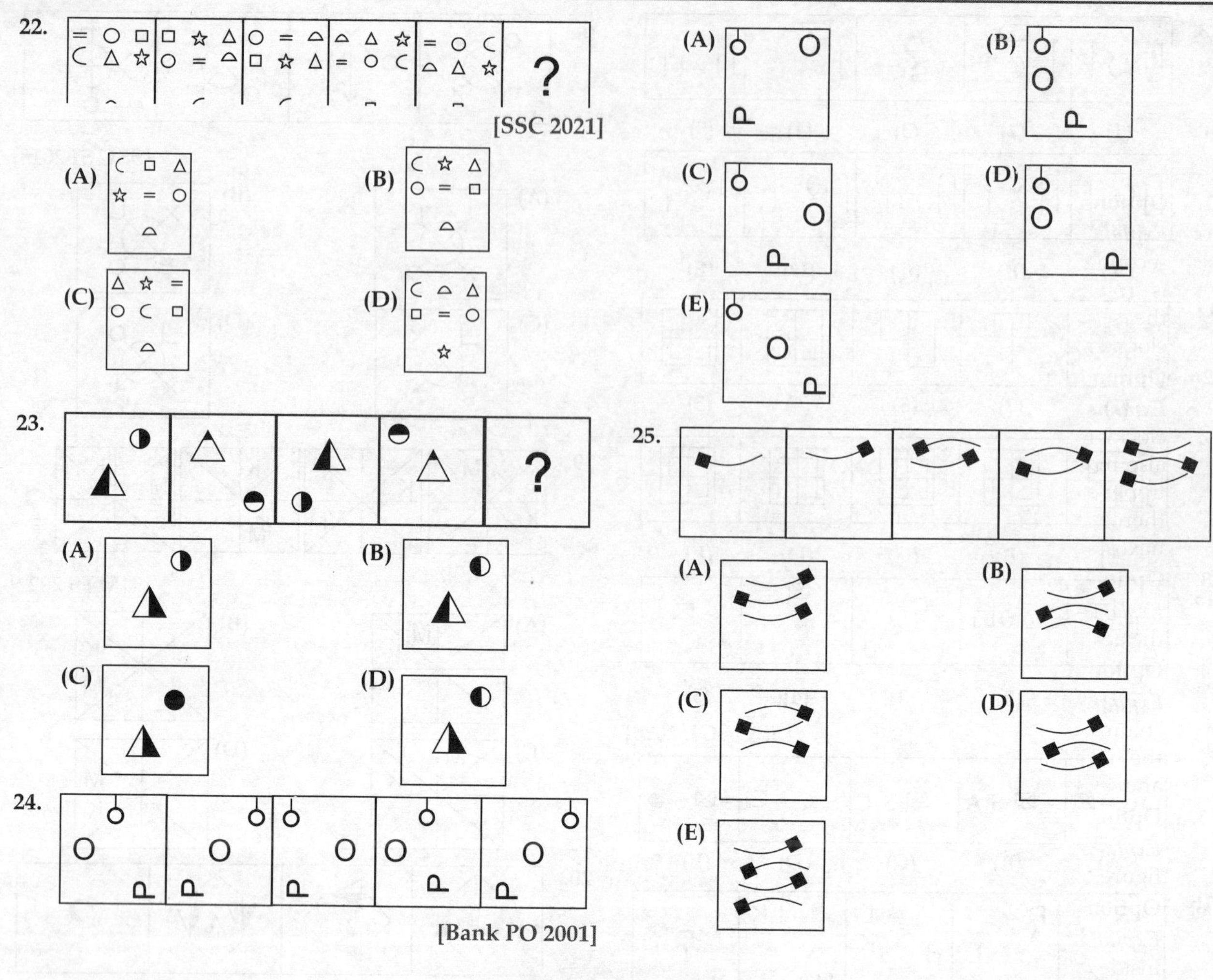

ANSWER KEY

Level-1: Beginner

1.	(B)	2.	(D)	3.	(C)	4.	(A)	5.	(B)	6.	(A)	7.	(A)	8.	(A)	9.	(D)	10.	(B)
11.	(C)	12.	(D)	13.	(A)	14.	(D)	15.	(D)	16.	(B)	17.	(A)	18.	(A)	19.	(E)	20.	(D)
21.	(D)	22.	(B)	23.	(A)	24.	(D)	25.	(B)	26.	(B)	27.	(A)	28.	(B)	29.	(A)	30.	(C)
31.	(A)	32.	(A)	33.	(C)	34.	(C)	35.	(B)	36.	(A)	37.	(C)	38.	(C)	39.	(C)	40.	(C)

Level-2: Intermediate

1.	(A)	2.	(C)	3.	(B)	4.	(A)	5.	(A)	6.	(D)	7.	(D)	8.	(A)	9.	(A)	10.	(A)
11.	(D)	12.	(B)	13.	(A)	14.	(A)	15.	(C)	16.	(B)	17.	(D)	18.	(A)	19.	(C)	20.	(A)
21.	(A)	22.	(B)	23.	(C)	24.	(A)	25.	(B)	26.	(D)	27.	(C)	28.	(A)	29.	(B)	30.	(C)
31.	(D)	32.	(A)	33.	(D)	34.	(C)	35.	(E)										

Level-3: Expert

1.	(B)	2.	(D)	3.	(A)	4.	(B)	5.	(B)	6.	(B)	7.	(D)	8.	(A)	9.	(C)	10.	(A)
11.	(E)	12.	(A)	13.	(B)	14.	(A)	15.	(B)	16.	(B)	17.	(A)	18.	(B)	19.	(A)	20.	(D)
21.	(A)	22.	(B)	23.	(D)	24.	(C)	25.	(D)										

Solutions with Detailed Explanations

Level-1: BEGINNER

1. **Option (B) is correct.**
Explanation: A similar figure is repeated at every second step. When the first figure reappears, it is rotated through 90 degrees clockwise. When the second figure reappears, it rotates 90 degrees clockwise and a new leaf is added at the CW end.

2. **Option (D) is correct.**
Explanation: The element rotates 90 degrees anti-clockwise and 45 degrees anticlockwise alternately. It also moves downwards along the diagonal from the upper-right corner to the lower-left corner, and once there, it moves back to the upper-right corner in the next step.

3. **Option (C) is correct.**
Explanation: At each step, the element is increased by the addition of a line in anticlockwise direction.

4. **Option (A) is correct.**
Explanation: The element moves up the middle column, and once it reaches the top, it moves down in the next step. It also rotates 90 degrees anticlockwise and 45 degrees anticlockwise alternately.

5. **Option (B) is correct.**
Explanation: In each step, one line segment joins the figure.

6. **Option (A) is correct.**
Explanation: The square rotates 45 degrees while the inside image rotates 90 degrees anticlockwise.

7. **Option (A) is correct.**
Explanation: In the provided sequence, the second figure is the mirror image of the first. In the third figure, there is an increase of one horizontal and one vertical line as compared to the first figure. The fourth figure is the mirror image of the third. So, in accordance with the sequence, option (1) is the next figure.

8. **Option (A) is correct.**
Explanation: The figure is rotated 90° anticlockwise in every next figure.

9. **Option (D) is correct.**
Explanation: The figure is laterally inverted in just one step. Following that, all existing bent arrows descend one space, and a new bent arrow appears at the top.

10. **Option (B) is correct.**
Explanation: A similar figure is repeated every second step. When a specific figure reappears, it is rotated 90 degrees anticlockwise.

11. **Option (C) is correct.**
Explanation: The element in the first two figures shifts diagonally, but the central figure remains unchanged.

12. **Option (D) is correct.**
Explanation: With each step, the number of projections doubles.

13. **Option (A) is correct.**
Explanation: Two line segments are eliminated from problem figures (1) to (2). Three line segments are eliminated and two line segments are reintroduced from problem figure (2) to (3). Two line segments are eliminated and one line segment is reintroduced from problem figures (3) to (4). Three line segments are eliminated and reinstated from problem figures (4) to (5). Two line segments are eliminated and one line segment is reintroduced from problem figure (5) to answer figure. As a result, the correct answer is (1).

14. **Option (D) is correct.**
Explanation: The central figure (circle at radius) rotates 90 degrees anticlockwise in every next stage.

15. **Option (D) is correct.**
Explanation: The first figure has no sides, the second has three sides, and the fourth has four sides. With each step, the number of sides and figures increases. So, according to the sequence, the next figure should have 5 sides and be 4 in number.

16. **Option (B) is correct.**
Explanation: A similar figure is repeated every second step. When a specific figure reappears, it is turned 135 degrees anticlockwise.

17. **Option (A) is correct.**
Explanation: A similar figure occurs every second step, and each time a figure reappears, it rotates 90 degrees clockwise.

18. **Option (A) is correct.**
Explanation: A new line joins the curve every time and it moves 90 degrees clockwise.

19. **Option (E) is correct.**
Explanation: The leaf arrangement is reversed in one step, and a new white leaf is added at the clockwise end next to the existing leaves. The leaf arrangement is then reversed again, and a new white leaf is added at the anticlockwise end adjacent to the existing leaves.

20. **Option (D) is correct.**
Explanation: Each step involves the addition of one half-leaf to make one of the half-leaves already present into a full leaf. As shown in the sequence below, the half-leaves are added to the figure.

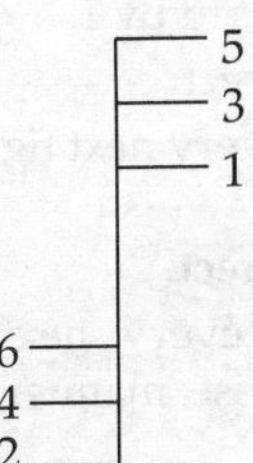

21. **Option (D) is correct.**
Explanation: At every second step, a similar figure appears, and each time it does, it is rotated 90 degrees anticlockwise.

22. **Option (B) is correct.**
Explanation: The arrow moves 1, 2, 3, 4 steps respectively in every next figure in anticlockwise direction and the square moves 1, 2, 3, 4 steps respectively in every next figure in clockwise direction.
23. **Option (A) is correct.**
Explanation: The figure rotates 45 degrees anticlockwise in a single motion, which shades an additional portion of the square (an eighth of its area) that is anticlockwise to the shaded area. The figure is then rotated 90 degrees in the opposite direction of the shaded area, resulting in the shading of one additional portion of the square.
24. **Option (D) is correct.**
Explanation: One of the figures rotates from the top to the bottom at each step. Each figure rotates downward as a result in the order listed below.
25. **Option (B) is correct.**
Explanation: The top row's elements are all moved to the second row, the second row's elements are moved to the third row, and the third row's elements are moved to the first row.
26. **Option (B) is correct.**
Explanation: In every step, one and half elements added alternately.
27. **Option (A) is correct.**
Explanation: In every next figure, one more inverse element is added towards the right side.
28. **Option (B) is correct.**
Explanation: In every next step, two sides are getting reduced.
29. **Option (A) is correct.**
Explanation: In every next step, the element rotates 90° anti-clockwise and moves to the next right corner.
30. **Option (C) is correct.**
31. **Option (A) is correct.**
Explanation: In every next figure, the line segment inside the figure moves clockwise and the element attached at corner moves anti-clockwise to next corner and after 3 steps it will move clockwise.
32. **Option (A) is correct.**
33. **Option (C) is correct.**
Explanation: The number of circles inside the figures are: 1, 1, 5, 9, 13, 17, ...
34. **Option (C) is correct.**
Explanation: The number of line segments in every next figure increased by 1.
35. **Option (B) is correct.**
Explanation: In every next figure, one new element is attached.
36. **Option (A) is correct.**
Explanation: In every next figure, the elements moved in clockwise manner and a new element is attached.
37. **Option (C) is correct.**
Explanation: From first figure to second, the element get enlarge in size and figure of side one less is placed inside it.
38. **Option (C) is correct.**
Explanation: In every next figure, the element moves, 1 step, 2 steps, 3 steps and so on.
39. **Option (C) is correct.**
Explanation: The elements moves as

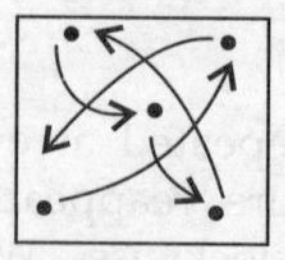 and 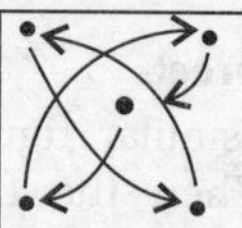

40. **Option (C) is correct.**

Level-2: INTERMEDIATE

1. **Option (A) is correct.**
Explanation: In each step, the elements moves in the sequence.

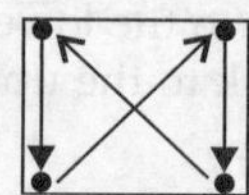

Additionally, in one step the element that reaches the upper left position is replaced by a new element, and in the following step the element that reaches the upper right position is replaced by a new element.
2. **Option (C) is correct.**
Explanation: Each time the line segment inside the quadrilateral moves 45 degrees clockwise, the arrow moves in the opposite direction.
3. **Option (B) is correct.**
Explanation: In the first step, one line segment is added. The next half-line segment is added. These two steps will alternate. So, option (B) is the correct sequence.
4. **Option (A) is correct.**
Explanation: One line segment is reintroduced and two are deleted from problem figures (1) to (2). The same procedure is followed from figure (3) to (4) and from figure (5) to the answer figure. So the correct answer is (A).
5. **Option (A) is correct.**
Explanation: The symbol in the figures moves one step, followed by two steps. One symbol is also added after every 2 steps. Answer figure is option (A).
6. **Option (D) is correct.**
Explanation: ∇ moves clockwise in each step, jumping one box, two boxes, three boxes, and so on. In addition, + moves anticlockwise with 2 box jump.
7. **Option (D) is correct.**
Explanation: The figure receives a dividing mark or line in one step, then is separated in the next, and this pattern is repeated alternately.
8. **Option (A) is correct.**
Explanation: The first two figures are doubled in the next two figures, but the position remains unchanged.
9. **Option (A) is correct.**
Explanation: At every step a new image entered in the figure at (1) and the image reached at (2) is disappeared. So, the pattern followed is as follows:

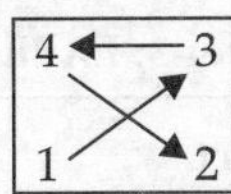

10. Option (A) is correct.

Explanation: Each element moves one space anticlockwise in each step. The anticlockwise direction end element is replaced in the first step, the middle element is replaced in the second step and the clockwise end element is replaced in the third step. The three steps are repeated to complete the series.

11. Option (D) is correct.

Explanation: The figure alternately rotates 45 degrees anticlockwise and 90 degrees anticlockwise. The central element swaps position and size with one of the side elements in a single step, and the third element is replaced by a new element. The central element then swaps positions and sizes with the other side element, and the remaining element is replaced by a new element in the following step.

12. Option (B) is correct.

Explanation: Each element moves systematically in its own quadrant.

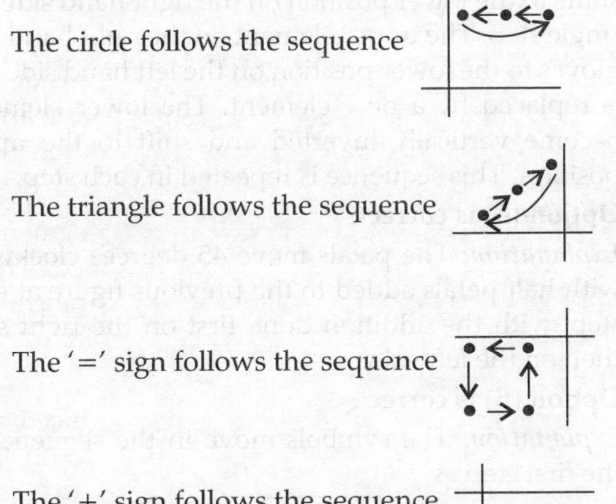

The circle follows the sequence

The triangle follows the sequence

The '=' sign follows the sequence

The '+' sign follows the sequence

13. Option (A) is correct.

Explanation: All of the elements are laterally inverted in one step and move in the sequence shown below:

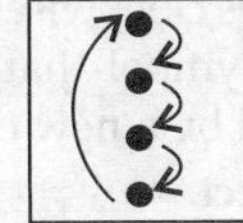

Except for the topmost element, all other elements are laterally inverted and the elements move in the sequence as follows:

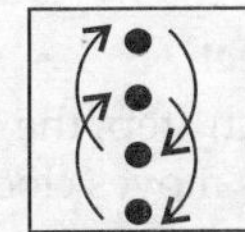

14. Option (A) is correct.

Explanation: Two and a half, three and a half, four and a half, five and a half, six and a half,....'L' shaped symbols are added to the figure sequentially.

15. Option (C) is correct.

Explanation: Each time a new figure is introduced, one unit is moved in an anti-clockwise direction.

16. Option (B) is correct.

Explanation: The top element on the left side transfers to the lower position on the right side in a single step. The top element on the right hand side moves to the lower position on the left hand side, where it is replaced by a new element. The lower parts get vertically inverted and move to the upper position. This procedure is repeated for each step.

17. Option (D) is correct.

Explanation: The figure receives a dividing mark or line in one phase, then it is separated in the next, and this pattern is repeated alternately.

18. Option (A) is correct.

Explanation: The elements move in a clockwise direction. At each step, the new element is introduced either in front of or after the existing element.

19. Option (C) is correct.

Explanation: The figure rotates through 45 degress clockwise from problem Figure (1) to (2), and one element travels two boxes while the other element moves in the middle. Two new elements are added. Similar changes occur between problem figures (3) and (4), as well as between problem figure (5) and the answer figure.

20. Option (A) is correct.

Explanation: In each consecutive figure, one L-shaped element is inserted at the upper or lower position, and an existing member is laterally inverted.

21. Option (A) is correct.

Explanation: The square in the quadrant changes position with alternating shades clockwise, while the shaded dot moves every 90° clockwise.

22. Option (B) is correct.

Explanation: The figure moves in an anticlockwise direction.

23. Option (C) is correct.

Explanation: The symbols in the figure moves alternatively in the pattern as follows:

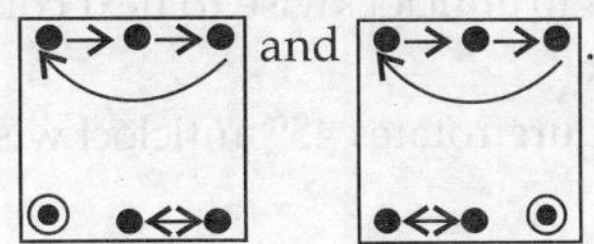

The symbol in the encircled position is replaced by a different symbol in each phase. Additionally, in the upper row, symbols that reach the RHS, middle, and LHS positions are replaced sequentially by new symbols.

24. Option (A) is correct.

Explanation: The first and second elements (numbered from the top) interchange positions in one phase, while the third and fourth elements exchange locations in another. The first and second elements are moved to the third and fourth positions, respectively, while the third and fourth elements become the first and second elements. In addition, 'the element with a circle and an ellipse at its ends' is inverted in each phase, and the half-arrow is alternately laterally and vertically inverted. Each step, the 'element with a triangle as its head' is inverted and its head is also inverted. The 'element with an arc as its head' has its head inverted in one stage and itself inverted in the next.

25. **Option (B) is correct.**
Explanation: The given figure shows an increase in arc and faces in a single direction.

26. **Option (D) is correct.**
Explanation: In every next figure, the figure rotates 90° clockwise.

27. **Option (C) is correct.**
Explanation: In every next figure, the elements rotates 90° clockwise and a similar element is attached to it.

28. **Option (A) is correct.**
Explanation: The lower left element rotates 90° anticlockwise, the center element gets flipped and upper right element rotates 90° clockwise.

29. **Option (B) is correct.**
Explanation: The element moves as

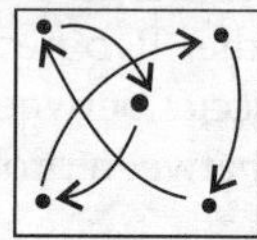

Here, the encircled element gets replaced by a new element.

30. **Option (C) is correct.**
Explanation: The element moves as

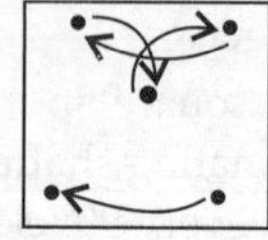

31. **Option (D) is correct.**
Explanation: The corner elements moves anticlockwise and the center element getting flipped.

32. **Option (A) is correct.**
Explanation: The shaded part moves clockwise to the next part and element at the corner moves rotates 90° clockwise and moves to anticlockwise to next corner.

33. **Option (D) is correct.**
Explanation: Each figure rotates 45° anticlockwise to get the next figure.

34. **Option (C) is correct.**
Explanation: The element moves as :

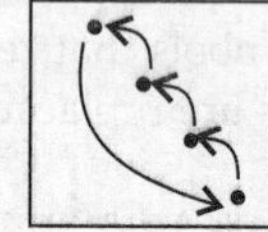

35. **Option (E) is correct.**
Explanation: The number of sides in every next figure gets increased by 1. The center element rotates 45° and 90° anticlockwise alternatively. Also, the corner elements moves anticlockwise to next corner interchanges positions alternatively.

Level-3: EXPERT

1. **Option (B) is correct.**
Explanation: Every next figure is obtained by rotating the previous figure 45 and 90 clockwise alternatively.

2. **Option (D) is correct.**
Explanation: In each subsequent step, the figure is rotated anticlockwise at an angle of 45 degrees and moves in the following sequence:

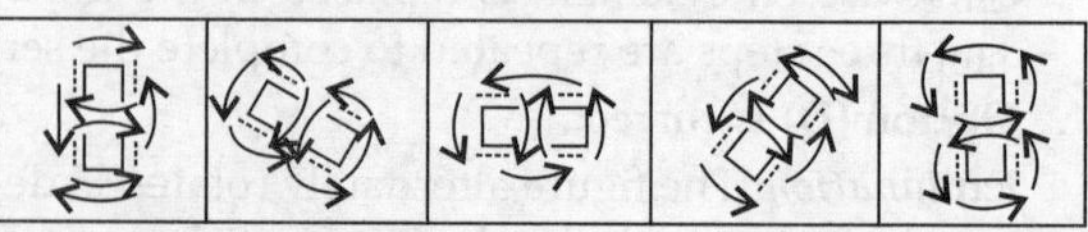

3. **Option (A) is correct.**
Explanation: Each step, the upper element is lost, the middle element shrinks and becomes the upper element, the lower element enlarges and becomes the middle element, and a new element appears at the bottom of the figure.

4. **Option (B) is correct.**
Explanation: The upper element on the left hand side shifts to the lower position on the right hand side in a single step. The upper element on the right hand side moves to the lower position on the left hand side and is replaced by a new element. The lower elements become vertically inverted and shift to the upper position. This sequence is repeated in each step.

5. **Option (B) is correct.**
Explanation: The petals move 45 degrees clockwise, with half petals added to the previous figure at each step, with the addition done first on the right side, then on the left side.

6. **Option (B) is correct.**
Explanation: The symbols move in the sequence in the first step as:

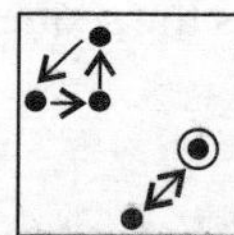

In the following steps, the symbols move in the sequence obtained by rotating the preceding sequence 90 degrees clockwise each time. In addition, at each step, the symbol that reaches the encircled position is replaced by a new one.

7. **Option (D) is correct.**
Explanation: The upper left and lower right pins revolve 90 degrees anticlockwise in each phase, whereas the upper right and lower left pins rotate 45 degrees clockwise.

8. **Option (A) is correct.**
Explanation: In each step, the line segment closest to the hexagon's sides moves clockwise, as does the line segment closest to the box's corner, and the number increases.

9. **Option (C) is correct.**
Explanation: 4, 1, 2, 1... line segments are losing sequentially from the anticlockwise end, and each remaining line segment moves two spaces clockwise.

10. **Option (A) is correct.**

Explanation: The symbol is alternately vertically and laterally inverted. It also moves anticlockwise through distances equal to two half-sides (of a square boundary) and three half sides alternately.

11. **Option (E) is correct.**

Explanation: Two line segments are eliminated in the first stage. Two line segments are reintroduced and three line segments are eliminated in the second step. Two line segments are reintroduced and two are eliminated in the third step. Two line segments are eliminated in the fourth step. Two line segments are restored and the lines are removed in the final step.

12. **Option (A) is correct.**

Explanation: The upper-left element shifts to the upper-middle position. The bottom-left piece is moved to the upper-left location. The lower-right piece reaches the lower-middle position. The upper-middle piece shifts to the lower-right location. The new element is produced in the upper-right corner. This procedure will be repeated in the following steps.

13. **Option (B) is correct.**

Explanation: In each step, the 'U' shaped element rotates 90 degrees anticlockwise and alternately moves to the left and upper positions. In one step, the half-pin rotates 180 degrees and goes to the left side position, then laterally inverts and moves to the right side position. The third element rotates 90 degrees anticlockwise and alternately gets laterally inverted.

14. **Option (A) is correct.**

Explanation: In the given figure, two elements are added in each step, whether they are two lines, two arcs, or one line and one arc.

15. **Option (B) is correct.**

Explanation: The orientation line of the four elements rotates at 45 degrees clockwise. The elements are shifted into their positions in the first step. One of the four elements transforms into a new element. This procedure is repeated in subsequent steps.

16. **Option (B) is correct.**

Explanation: In every next figure, each element moves half step in anticlockwise manner.

17. **Option (A) is correct.**

18. **Option (B) is correct.**

19. **Option (A) is correct.**

Explanation: The element K moves 1 step clockwise and the element M moves 2 steps clockwise.

20. **Option (D) is correct.**

Explanation: The outer figure moves 90° clockwise and the center element moves 180° clockwise.

21. **Option (A) is correct.**

Explanation: The outer figure rotates 180° and the upper element rotates 180° and placed at lower position and number of sides increased by 1 in 3rd figure. Also, the lower element rotates 180° and placed at upper position.

22. **Option (B) is correct.**

Explanation: The elements moves as

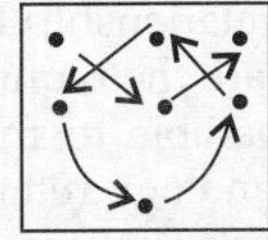

23. **Option (D) is correct.**

24. **Option (C) is correct.**

Explanation: The upper, centre and lower elements moves half step to the right.

25. **Option (D) is correct.**

Explanation: From first figure to second, element rotates 180° clockwise and a new opposite element is added from third figure.

■ ■ ■

Chapter 16

Analogy

LEARNING OBJECTIVES:

- Questions based on figure analogy
- Questions based on mixed analogy
- Different types of questions asked in competitive exams

Analogy means "resemblance of one object to another in some characteristics" in analogical reasoning. The purpose of analogy is to assess a candidate's ability to figure out the relationship between two question pairs and then locate the required pair of words that is the most comparable to that relationship. In its most basic form, analogy refers to then comprise of objects that are similar in some way.

Analogy examine a wide range of word relationships. reading comprehension, attention to detail, vocabulary, synonyms, antonyms, homophones, deductive reasoning and logic are all enhanced strengthen, and reinforced by studying them.

An analogy, two items are contrasted and conclusions are reached based on their similarities.

There are two type of analogy:

1. Figure analogy 2.Mixed analogy.

FIGURE ANALOGY

➢ In this type of problem, we have to carefully examine the given figures and look for consistent changes or transformations that occur as you move from one figure to the next. Analysing the relationships between the elements of the figures and identifying any rules or logical patterns is critical in determining the missing or next figure in the analogy.

Example 1:

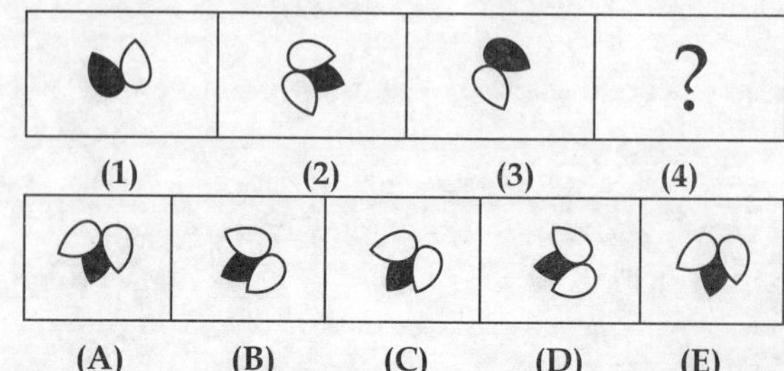

Sol. (B) In the following figure, the black leaf rotates 135 degree clockwise and while leaf rotates 45 degrees clockwise. A new white leaf attached with black leaf at 90 degrees.

Example 2:

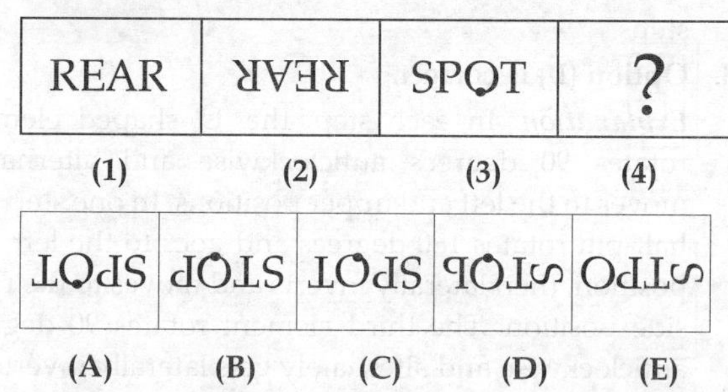

Sol. (A) The complete figures rotates through 180 degrees.

MIXED ANALOGY

➢ A mixed analogy is a type of problem in non-verbal reasoning that combines multiple types of patterns or rules within a single analogy. Unlike other types of analogy, where the pattern remains consistent throughout, mixed analogy requires you to identify and apply different patterns or rules within the same sequence of figures or shapes.

Each part of the analogy follows a distinct pattern, and our task is to recognise these patterns and correctly apply them to predict or choose the missing or next figure.

Example 3:

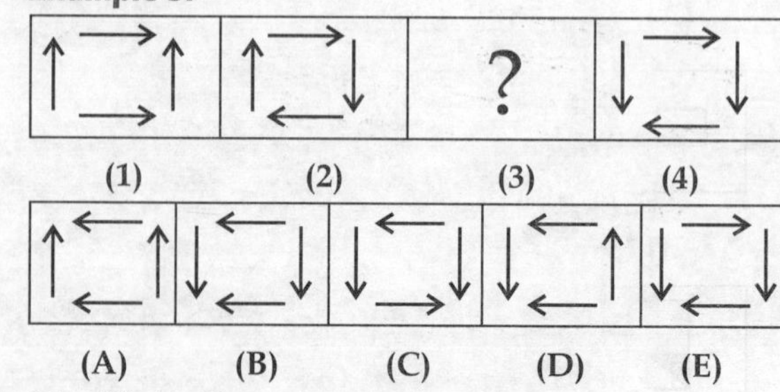

Sol. (a) All the elements rotates 180°.

1 Level Beginner

Directions: In each of the following questions, you are given analogy of questions you have to find out the missing figure.

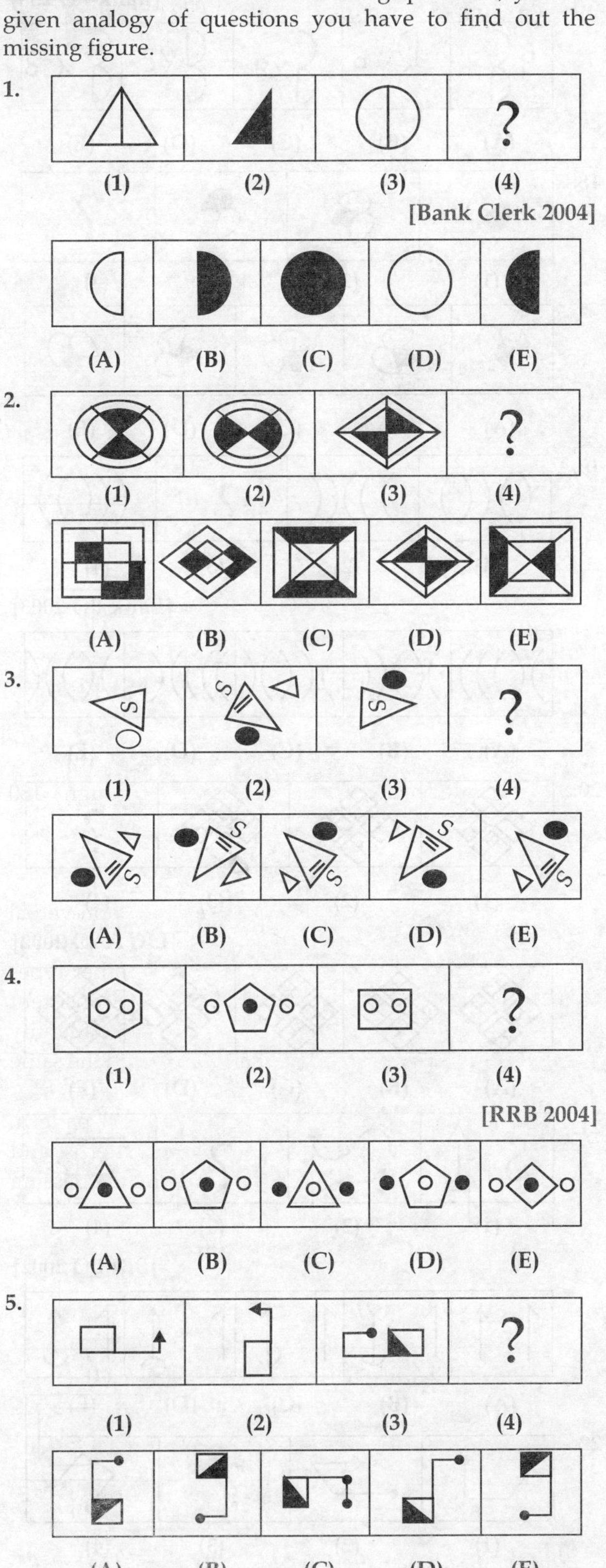

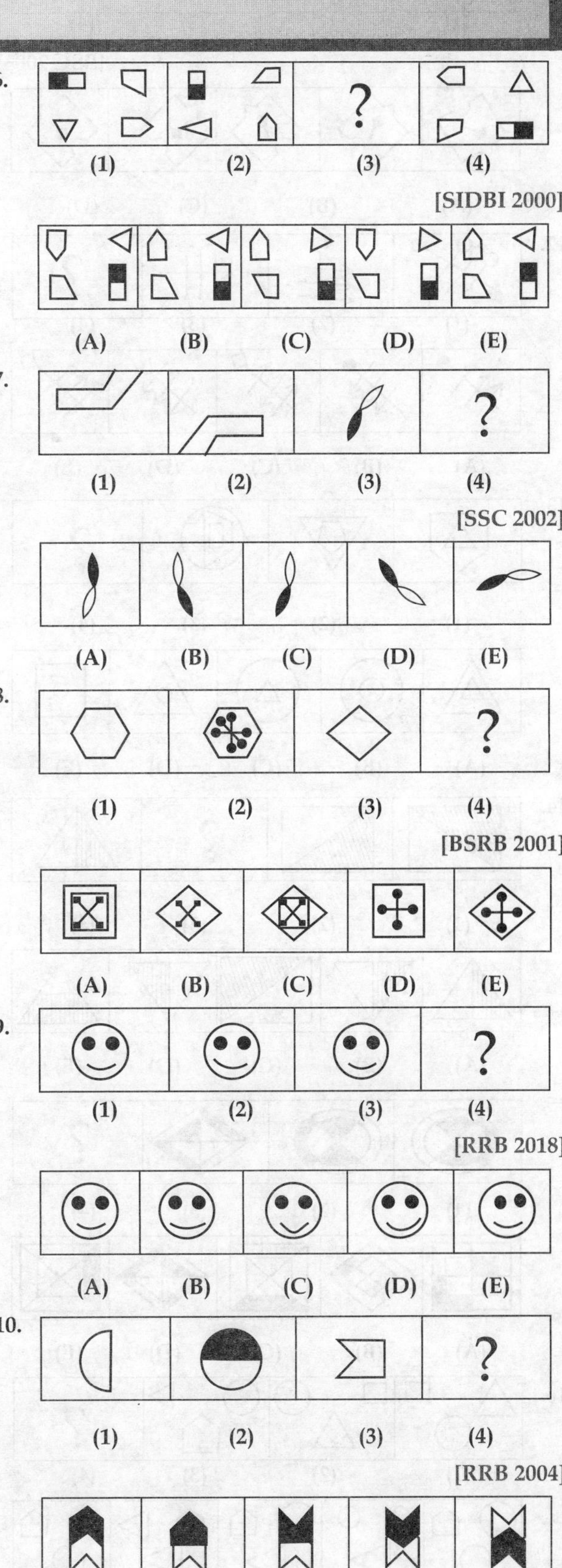

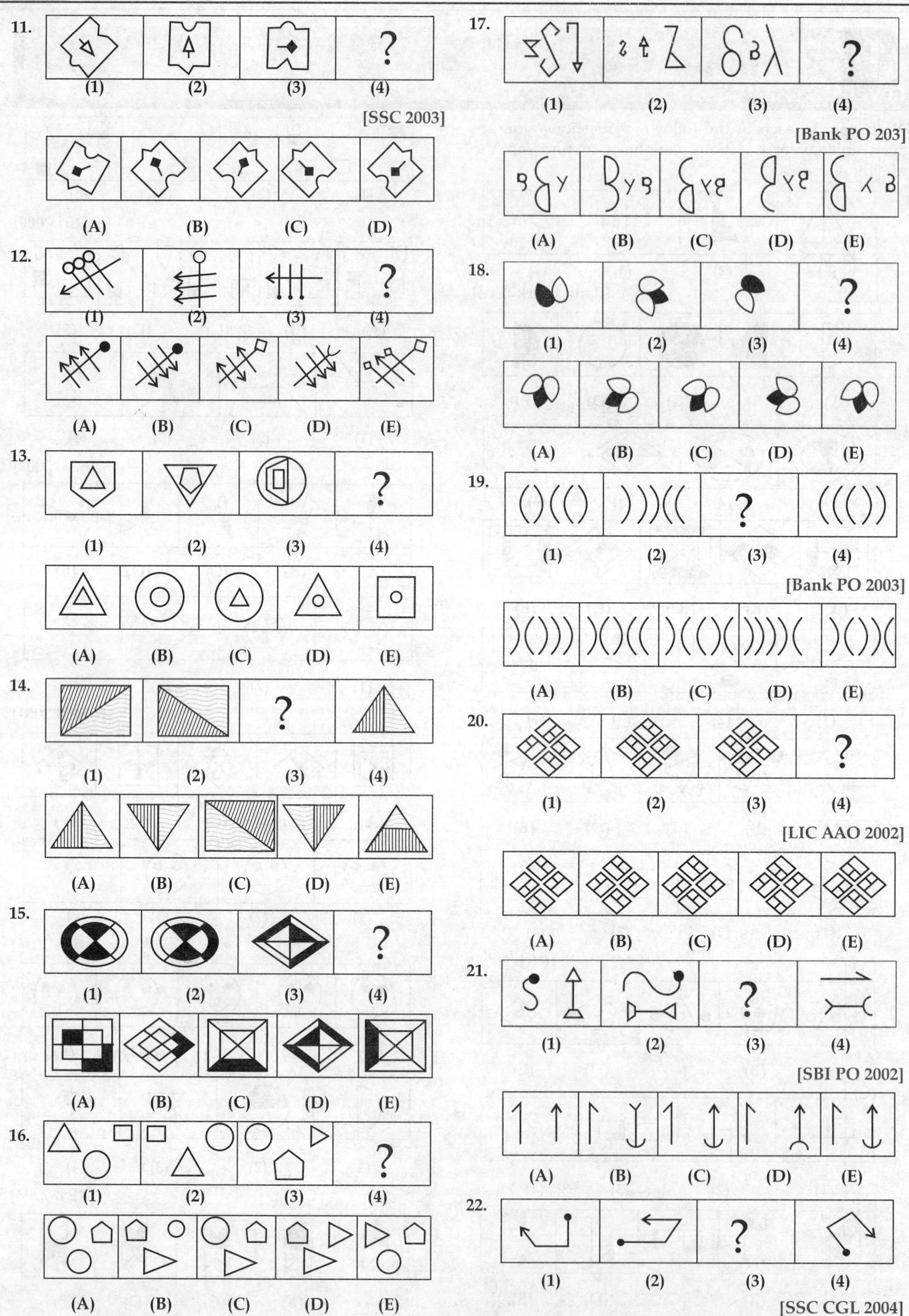
11.
[SSC 2003]
12.
13.
14.
15.
16.
17.
[Bank PO 203]
18.
19.
[Bank PO 2003]
20.
[LIC AAO 2002]
21.
[SBI PO 2002]
22.
[SSC CGL 2004]

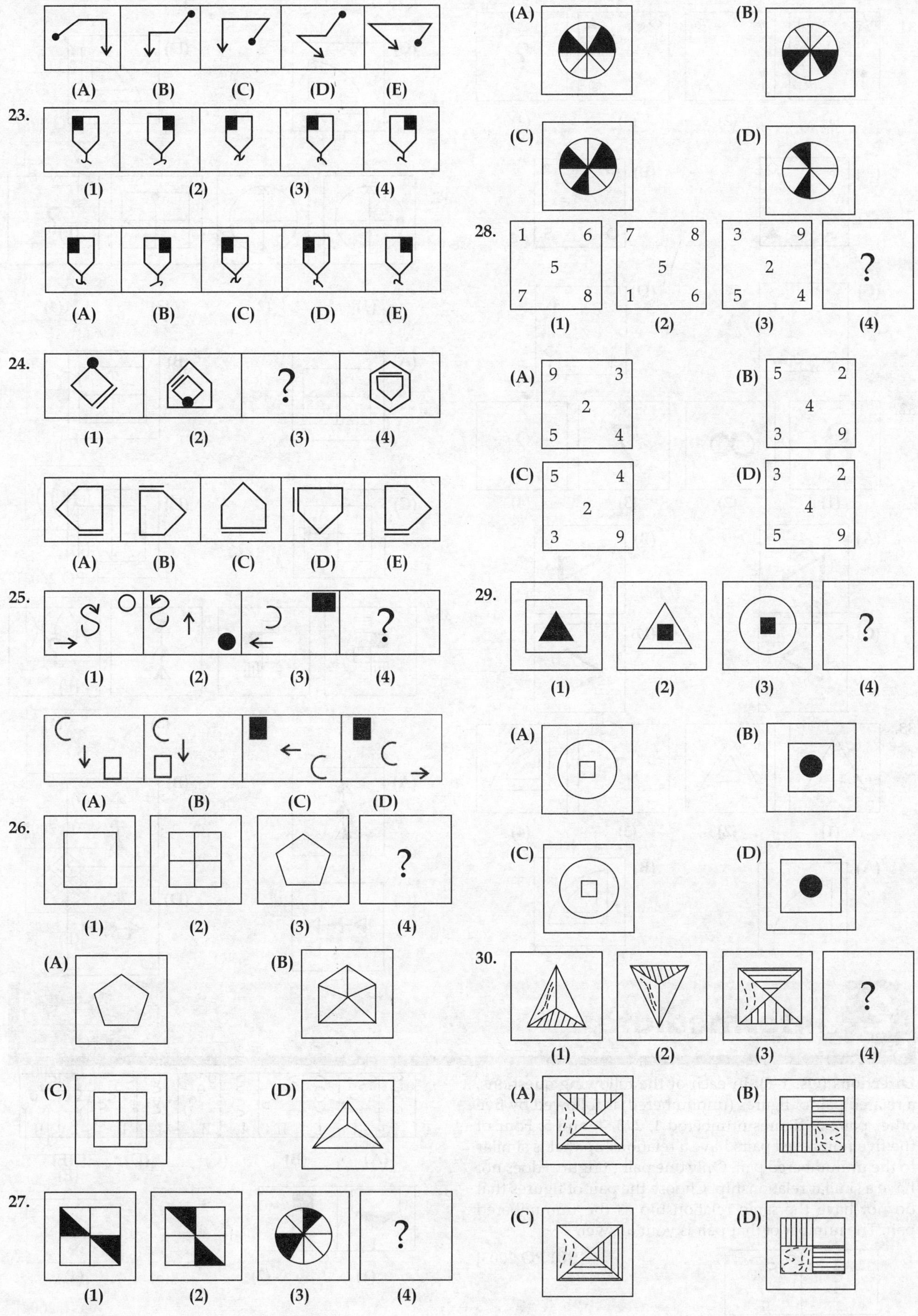
23.
24.
25.
26.
27.
28.
1 6 5 7 8
7 8 5 1 6
3 9 2 5 4
9 3 2 5 4
5 2 4 3 9
5 4 2 3 9
3 2 4 5 9
29.
30.

31. 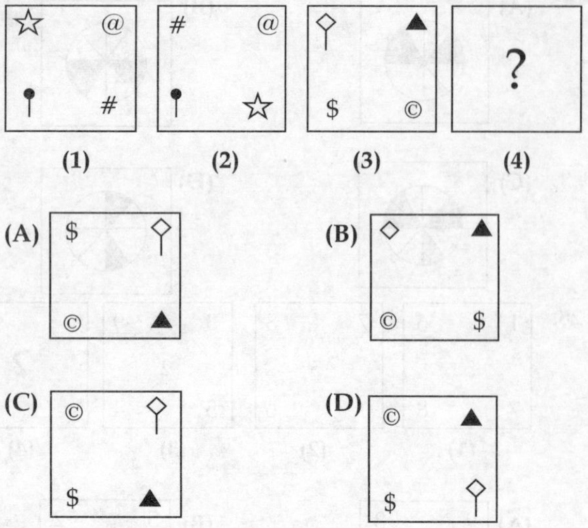 (1) (2) (3) (4)

(A) (B) (C) (D)

32. 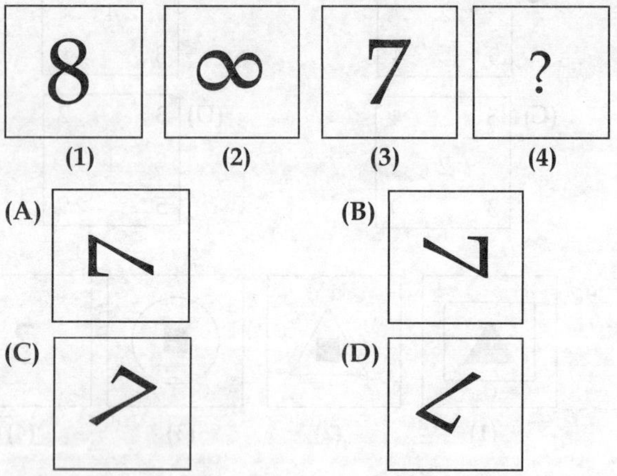 (1) (2) (3) (4)

(A) (B) (C) (D)

33. 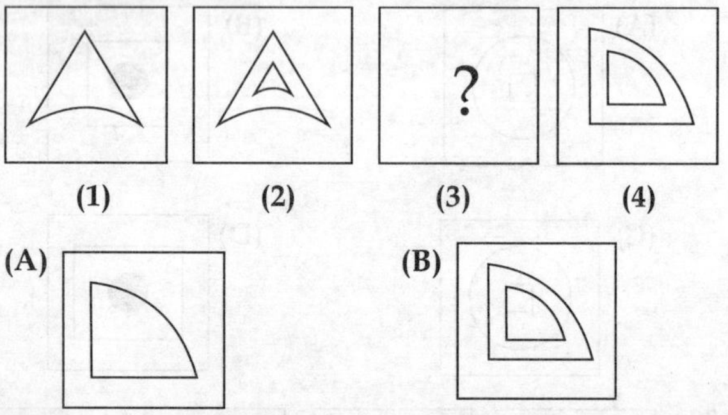 (1) (2) (3) (4)

(A) (B) (C) (D)

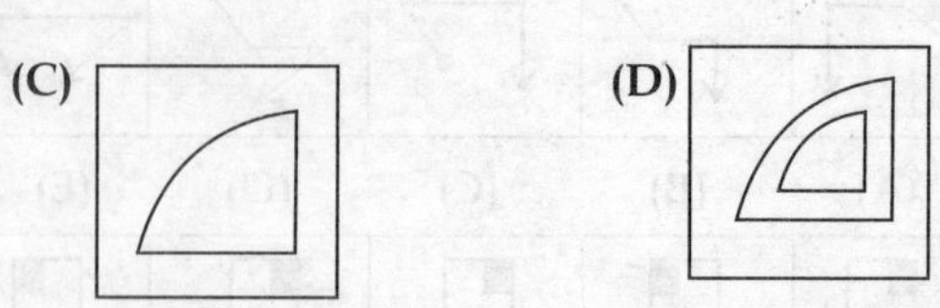

34. 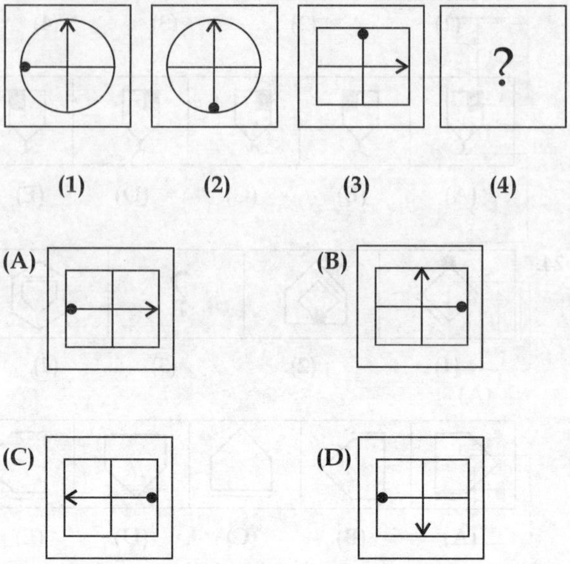 (1) (2) (3) (4)

(A) (B) (C) (D)

35. 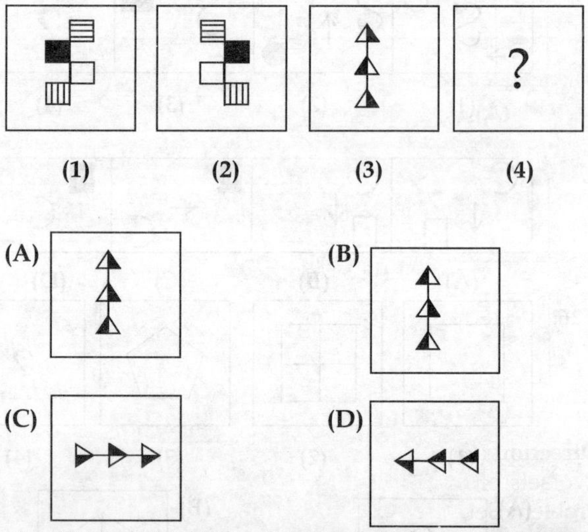 (1) (2) (3) (4)

(A) (B) (C) (D)

Level 2 Intermediate

Directions (Qs. 1–6): In each of the following questions, a related pair of figures (unnumbered) is followed by five other pairs of figures numbered 1, 2, 3, 4, and 5. Four of the five numbered pairs have a relationship that is similar to the unnumbered pair. Only one pair of figures does not have a similar relationship. Choose the pair of figures that do not have the same relationship as the unnumbered pair. The number of that pair is your answer.

1. [SBI PO 2003]

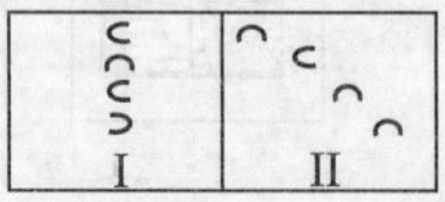

I II

I II (A) I II (B) I II (C) I II (D) I II (E)

2. I II

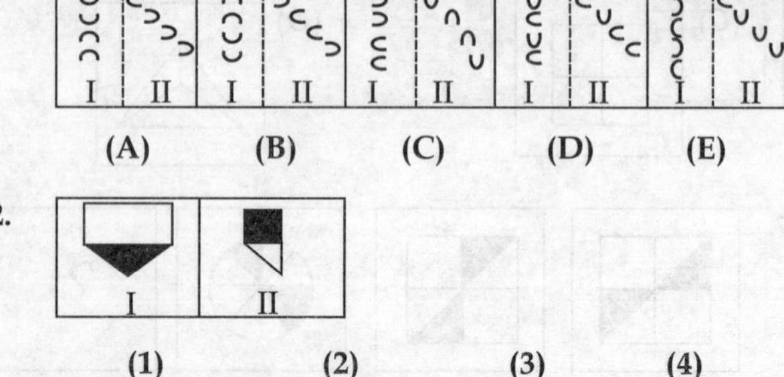

(1) (2) (3) (4)

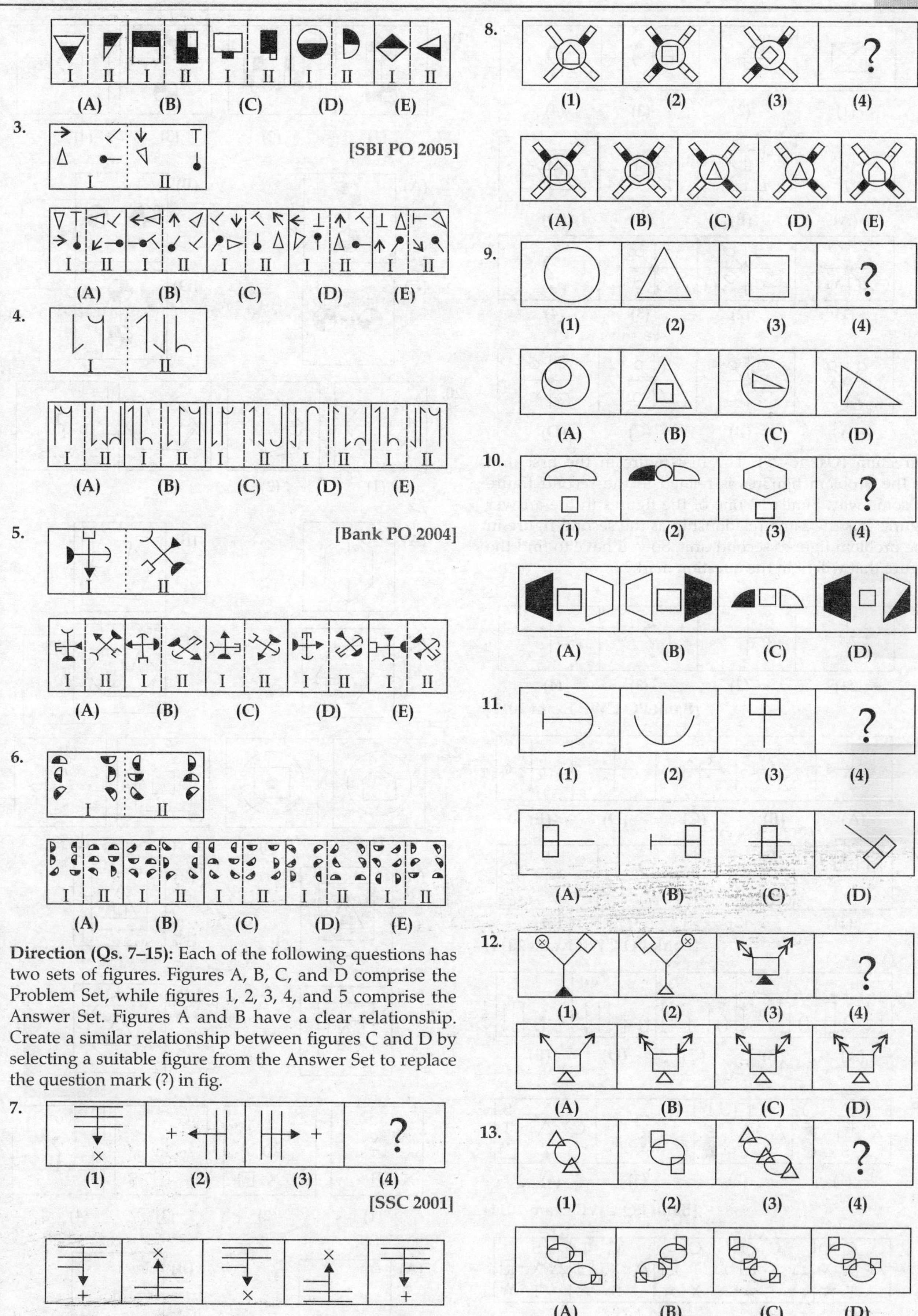

Direction (Qs. 7–15): Each of the following questions has two sets of figures. Figures A, B, C, and D comprise the Problem Set, while figures 1, 2, 3, 4, and 5 comprise the Answer Set. Figures A and B have a clear relationship. Create a similar relationship between figures C and D by selecting a suitable figure from the Answer Set to replace the question mark (?) in fig.

7.

[SSC 2001]

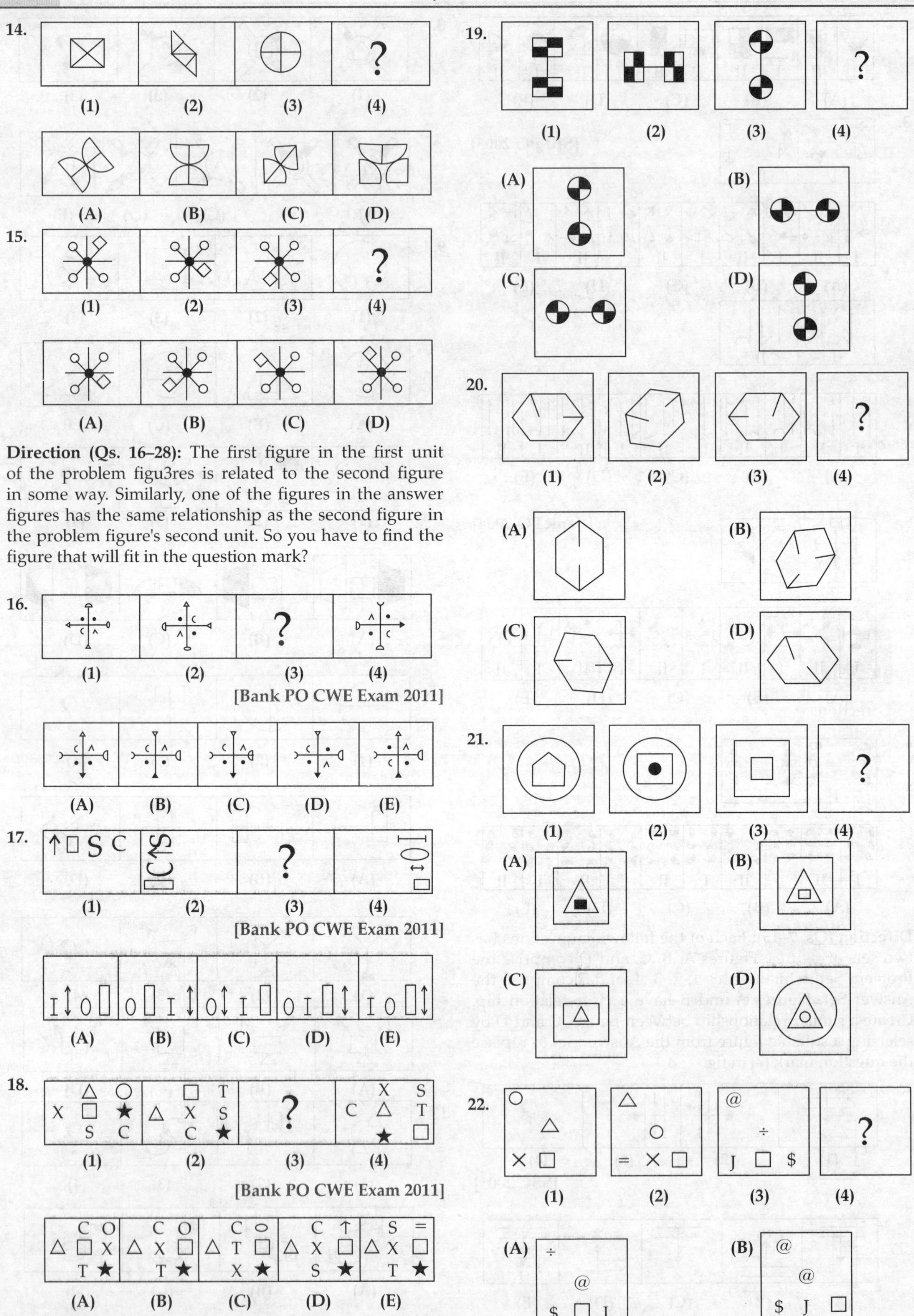

Direction (Qs. 16–28): The first figure in the first unit of the problem figu3res is related to the second figure in some way. Similarly, one of the figures in the answer figures has the same relationship as the second figure in the problem figure's second unit. So you have to find the figure that will fit in the question mark?

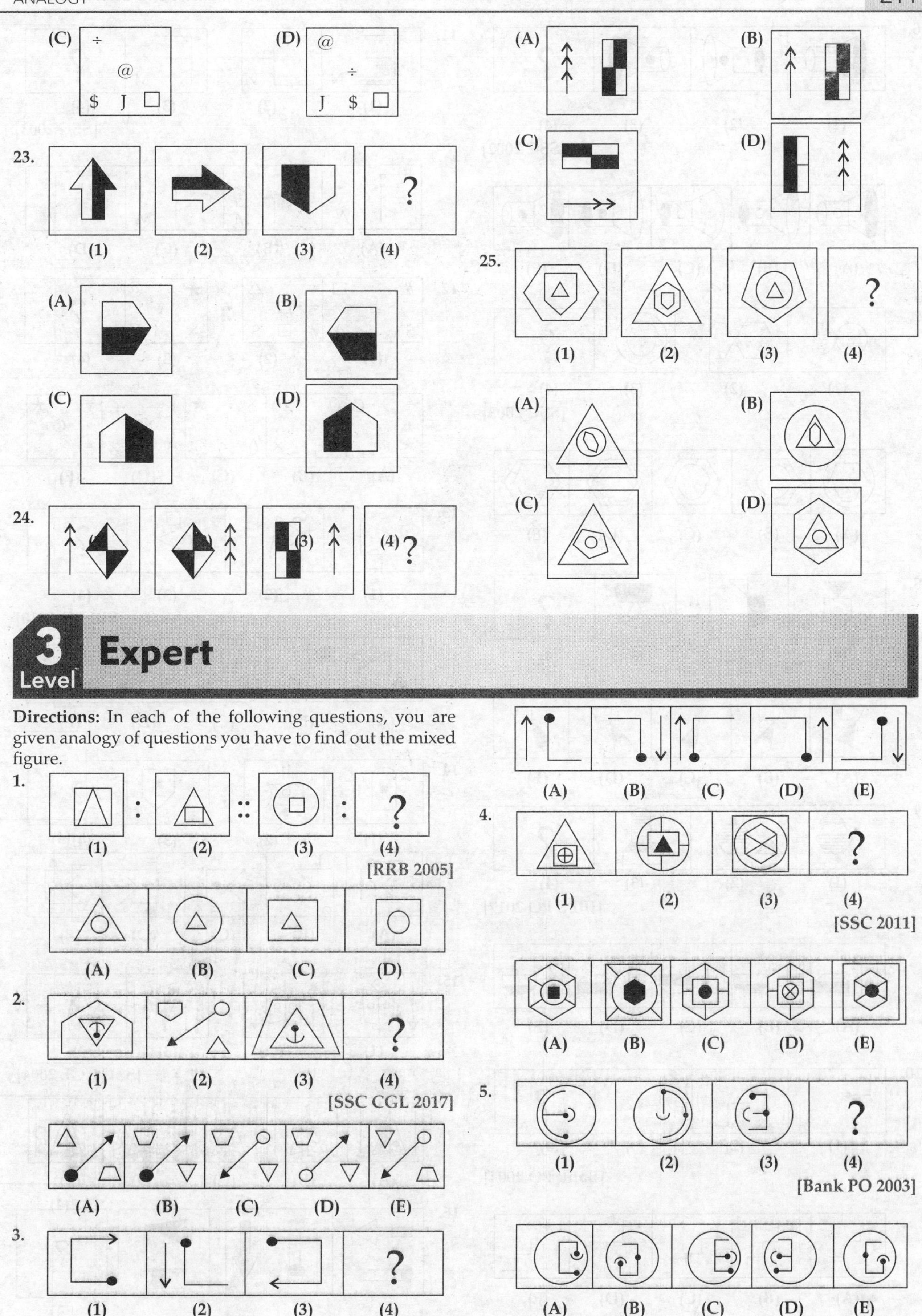

Level 3 Expert

Directions: In each of the following questions, you are given analogy of questions you have to find out the mixed figure.

1. (1) : (2) :: (3) : (4) ?

[RRB 2005]

(A) (B) (C) (D)

2. (1) (2) (3) (4) ?

[SSC CGL 2017]

(A) (B) (C) (D) (E)

3. (1) (2) (3) (4) ?

[SSC CPO 2010]

(A) (B) (C) (D) (E)

4. (1) (2) (3) (4) ?

[SSC 2011]

(A) (B) (C) (D) (E)

5. (1) (2) (3) (4) ?

[Bank PO 2003]

(A) (B) (C) (D) (E)

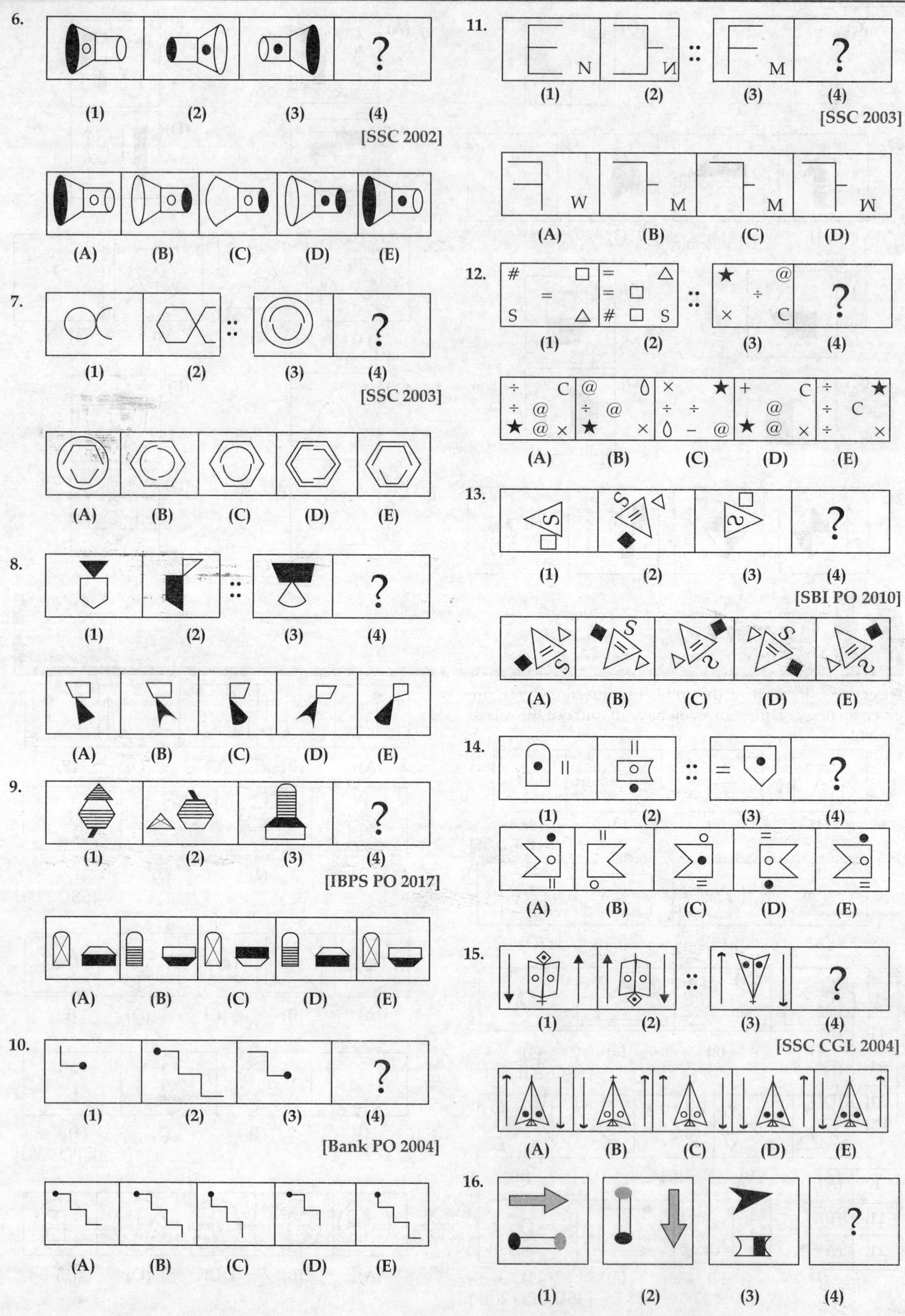
6.
(1) (2) (3) (4)
[SSC 2002]
(A) (B) (C) (D) (E)
7.
(1) (2) (3) (4)
[SSC 2003]
(A) (B) (C) (D) (E)
8.
(1) (2) (3) (4)
(A) (B) (C) (D) (E)
9.
(1) (2) (3) (4)
[IBPS PO 2017]
(A) (B) (C) (D) (E)
10.
(1) (2) (3) (4)
[Bank PO 2004]
(A) (B) (C) (D) (E)
11.
(1) (2) (3) (4)
[SSC 2003]
(A) (B) (C) (D)
12.
(1) (2) (3) (4)
(A) (B) (C) (D) (E)
13.
(1) (2) (3) (4)
[SBI PO 2010]
(A) (B) (C) (D) (E)
14.
(1) (2) (3) (4)
(A) (B) (C) (D) (E)
15.
(1) (2) (3) (4)
[SSC CGL 2004]
(A) (B) (C) (D) (E)
16.
(1) (2) (3) (4)

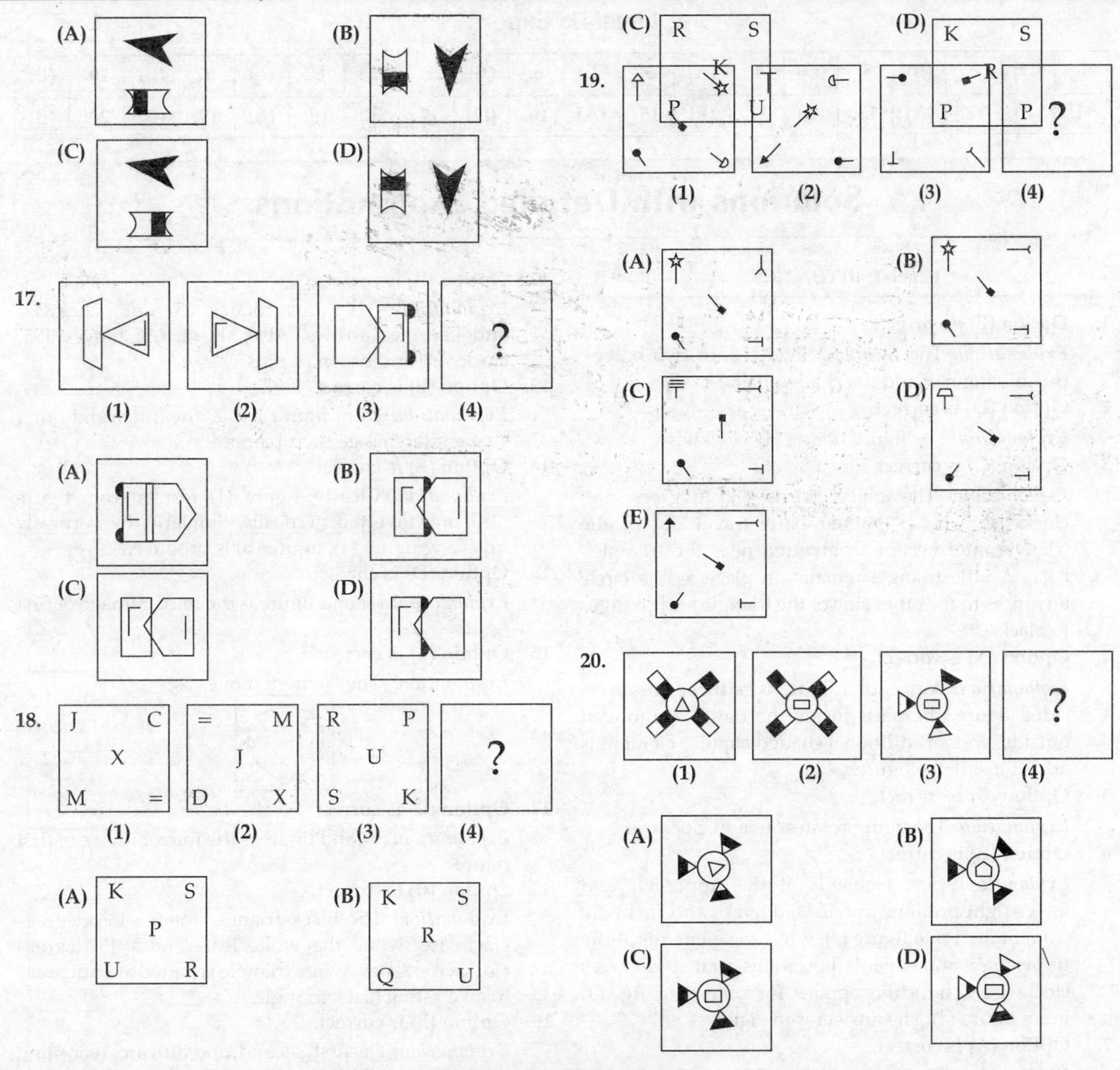

ANSWER KEY

Level-1: Beginner

1.	(E)	2.	(D)	3.	(C)	4.	(A)	5.	(B)	6.	(B)	7.	(A)	8.	(E)	9.	(B)	10.	(C)
11.	(B)	12.	(B)	13.	(E)	14.	(B)	15.	(D)	16.	(E)	17.	(C)	18.	(B)	19.	(E)	20.	(A)
21.	(D)	22.	(C)	23.	(B)	24.	(C)	25.	(A)	26.	(B)	27.	(A)	28.	(C)	29.	(B)	30.	(A)
31.	(D)	32.	(B)	33.	(A)	34.	(C)	35.	(B)										

Level-2: Intermediate

1.	(A)	2.	(D)	3.	(A)	4.	(B)	5.	(B)	6.	(E)	7.	(C)	8.	(C)	9.	(B)	10.	(A)
11.	(B)	12.	(B)	13.	(C)	14.	(B)	15.	(C)	16.	(C)	17.	(B)	18.	(B)	19.	(B)	20.	(B)
21.	(A)	22.	(C)	23.	(B)	24.	(A)	25.	(C)										

Level-3: Expert

1.	(D)	2.	(B)	3.	(D)	4.	(A)	5.	(E)	6.	(B)	7.	(E)	8.	(E)	9.	(E)	10.	(B)
11.	(B)	12.	(A)	13.	(C)	14.	(E)	15.	(A)	16.	(D)	17.	(E)	18.	(B)	19.	(B)	20.	(B)

Solutions with Detailed Explanations

Level-1: BEGINNER

1. **Option (E) is correct.**
Explanation: The figure is divided into two halves: the missing half and the shaded half.
2. **Option (D) is correct.**
Explanation: The figure rotates 90° clockwise.
3. **Option (C) is correct.**
Explanation: The object turns 135 degrees anti clockwise. The "S"-ginned parts travel out of the triangle after becoming inverted near the triangle's base. A little triangle remains in place as the circle advances to the other side of the triangle and changes to black.
4. **Option (A) is correct.**
Explanation: A six-sided figure is reduced to a five-sided figure, the parts inside the figure are moved outside, and an additional shaded circular element is added inside the figure.
5. **Option (B) is correct.**
Explanation: The figure rotates 90° anti clockwise.
6. **Option (B) is correct.**
Explanation: The elements at the upper-left and lower-right positions rotate 90 degrees anticlockwise from figure (1) to figure (2), while the elements at the upper-right and lower-left positions rotate 90 degrees clockwise. The same applies for obtaining fig. (3) From figure (4). The answer is in Figure 2.
7. **Option (A) is correct.**
Explanation: The figures rotates 180° clockwise.
8. **Option (E) is correct.**
Explanation: In 2nd figure, 6 circles are added, which is equal to the number of sides in figure 1. So, in same way 4 circles will be added in in figure 4, as the number of sides in figure 3 is four.
So, option (E) is correct answer.
9. **Option (B) is correct.**
Explanation: Figure 2 is the mirror image of figure 1
10. **Option (C) is correct.**
Explanation: The similar inverted element attached to it and shaded the upper half along with the rotation by 90 degrees in clockwise direction.
11. **Option (B) is correct.**
Explanation: The outer figure rotates 135 degrees Clockwise and the inner arrow rotates 135 degrees anticlockwise. The semicircular part of the outer figure turns inwards while the 'V-shaped part turns outwards.
12. **Option (B) is correct.**
Explanation: The pins rotates 45° anti clockwise and becomes arrows. Also, the arrow moves 135° clockwise and becomes pins.
13. **Option (E) is correct.**
Explanation: From figure 1 to 2, the inner and outer shape interchange their places.
14. **Option (B) is correct.**
Explanation: Clearly, figure (1) results from figure (2) being inverted vertically. Similarly, by vertically inverting figure (4), figure (B) is produced.
15. **Option (D) is correct.**
Explanation: Second figure is the mirror image of first figure.
16. **Option (E) is correct.**
Explanation: The element moves as

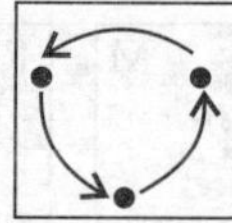

17. **Option (C) is correct.**
Explanation: Second figure is the mirror image of first figure.
18. **Option (B) is correct.**
Explanation: The black triangle rotates 135 degrees clockwise, while the white leaf rotates 45 degrees clockwise. A new white triangle is joined at 90 degrees to an existing black triangle.
19. **Option (E) is correct.**
Explanation: The first, second, and fifth arcs (counting from left to right) become laterally inverted.
20. **Option (A) is correct.**
Explanation: While the upper and lower elements rotate 90 degrees anti clockwise. The LHS and RHS elements rotate 90 degrees clockwise.
21. **Option (D) is correct.**
Explanation: The elements rotates 90° clockwise, upper element inverted and arrow head laterally inverted.
22. **Option (C) is correct.**
Explanation: The pin rotates 90 degrees clockwise, the arrow rotates 45 degrees clockwise, and the line connecting the pin and the arrow 45° degrees clockwise.
23. **Option (B) is correct.**
Explanation: The second figure is the mirror image of first figure.
24. **Option (C) is correct.**
Explanation: Both of the elements inner vertex is turn outward to create new elements. The placement of

these components changes. The pentagon expands and turns around 180 degrees.

25. **Option (A) is correct.**
Explanation: The element in the center travels to the upper-left corner and becomes laterally inverted; the element in the lower-left corner moves to the center and rotates 90 degrees anti clockwise. The element in the upper-right corner moves to the lower-right corner and changes color.

26. **Option (B) is correct.**
Explanation: From figure (1) to figure (2), the figure is divided into as many number of parts as the number of sides of the figure.

27. **Option (A) is correct.**
Explanation: The shades moves clockwise to the next part.

28. **Option (C) is correct.**
Explanation: The elements moves as follows

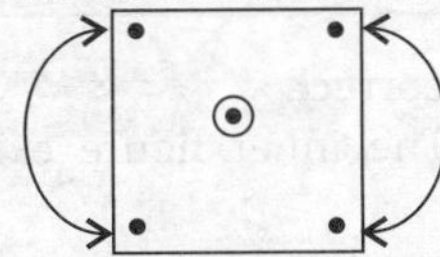

Also, the encircled element remains same.

29. **Option (B) is correct.**
Explanation: From figure (1) to (2), the elements interchanges their positions and inner part becomes shaded.

30. **Option (A) is correct.**
Explanation: Second figure is the water image of first figure.

31. **Option (D) is correct.**
Explanation: The elements moves as follows :

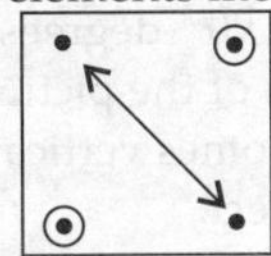

Also, the encircled elements remains same.

32. **Option (B) is correct.**
Explanation: Second figure is obtained by rotating first figure 90° clockwise.

33. **Option (A) is correct.**
Explanation: A similar figure is inserted in first figure to get the second figure.

34. **Option (C) is correct.**
Explanation: The pin rotates 90° clockwise and the arrow rotates 180° clockwise.

35. **Option (B) is correct.**
Explanation: The second figure is the mirror image of first figure.

Level-2: INTERMEDIATE

1. **Option (A) is correct.**
Explanation: From figure I to figure II, the line of orientation of the arcs rotates 45 degrees anticlockwise. Furthermore, the first (uppermost) and third arcs rotate 90 degrees clockwise, while the other two arcs rotate 90 degrees anticlockwise.

2. **Option (D) is correct.**
Explanation: Figures 1–2: Figure 1 is divided into two equal halves along the vertical line of symmetry; the right-hand side section is gone, and in the remaining area, the black portion becomes white and the white portion becomes black.

3. **Option (A) is correct.**
Explanation: From figure I to figure II, the upper-left element rotates 90 degrees clockwise; the upper-right and lower-left elements revolve 135 degrees clockwise; and the lower-right element rotates 90 degrees anticlockwise.

4. **Option (B) is correct.**
Explanation: Between Figures 1 and 2, the left-side component of Figure 1 rotates through 180 degrees to become the left-side component of Figure 2, and it also undergoes lateral inversion to become the middle component of Figure 2. The right-side element in Figure 1 rotates through 180 degrees to become Figure 2's right-side element.

5. **Option (B) is correct.**
Explanation: The parts that reach the upper-right and upper-left positions are inverted when the entire figure rotates 135 degrees anticlockwise from figure I to figure II.

6. **Option (E) is correct.**
Explanation: Each of the half-shaded semicircles in Figures I and II rotates through 90 degrees in the opposite direction of clockwise rotation.

7. **Option (C) is correct.**
Explanation: The figure turns 90 degrees clockwise. A single line segment on one side of the arrow vanishes. The symbol rotates through 45 degrees and advances in a clockwise manner to the opposite side of the square's boundary.

8. **Option (C) is correct.**
Explanation: The inner element is replaced by a new element with one fewer number of sides. The remaining (outer) figure is the mirror image.

9. **Option (B) is correct.**
Explanation: The existing figure becomes the inner figure and a new figure is attached outside it.

10. **Option (A) is correct.**
Explanation: The upper element is divided into two equal parts along the vertical line of symmetry; the two parts are separated; the left hand side part is shaded; and the lower element is introduced between the two parts.

11. **Option (B) is correct.**
Explanation: The figure has been turned 90 degrees. If there is a short line segment that is perpendicular to the longer line, it is removed; otherwise, it is added. This is a situation with an inverted relationship.

12. **Option (B) is correct.**
Explanation: The black triangle at the bottom of the illustration changes to white and figure is laterally inverted.

13. **Option (C) is correct.**
Explanation: A parallelogram is created out of each triangle.

14. Option (B) is correct.

Explanation: As illustrated below, the picture is divided into two equal pieces along one of the diagonals depicted in it, with the lower half positioned above the parts:

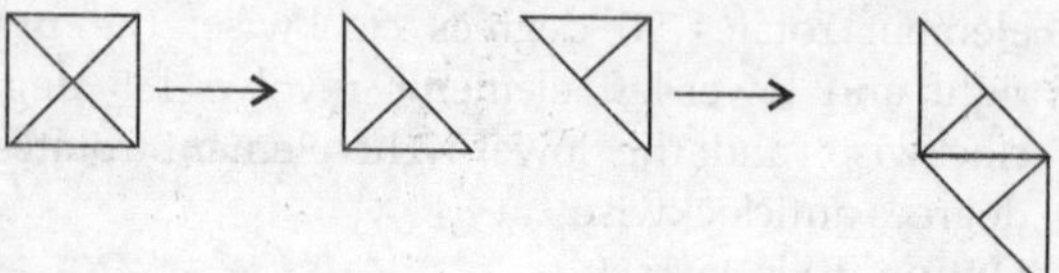

Similarly,

15. Option (C) is correct.

Explanation: The figure turns 90 degrees in the clockwise direction.

16. Option (C) is correct.

Explanation: The horizontal line's design becomes vertical and the vertical line's design becomes horizontal in the second figure from the top. Its middle slide contains four designs, as follows:

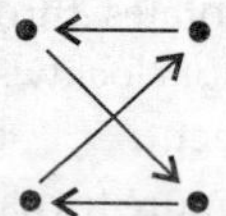

17. Option (B) is correct.

Explanation: In the first figure from the second, the four various patterns placed in a line slide one side clockwise, and the design slide in it as follows:

The greater element transforms into the smaller element during this shifting, and vice versa.

18. Option (B) is correct.

Explanation: In the second figure from the top, the design slide is as follows and new design forms are used in place of encircled element.

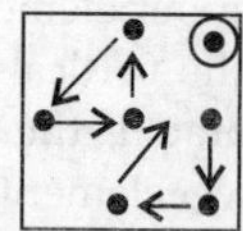

19. Option (B) is correct.

Explanation: Second figure is obtained by rotating the first figure 90° clockwise.

20. Option (B) is correct.

Explanation: Second figure is obtained by rotating the first figure 45° anti clockwise.

21. Option (A) is correct.

Explanation: From figure first to second figure, outer figure remains same, number of sides of inner figure reduced by 1 and a shaded outer figure get inserted in the middle.

22. Option (C) is correct.

Explanation: The elements moves as follows :

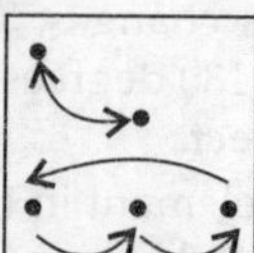

23. Option (B) is correct.

Explanation: The figure rotates 90° clockwise and shaded & unshaded get interchanged.

24. Option (A) is correct.

Explanation: Second figure in the mirror image of first figure and number of arrow head increases by one.

25. Option (C) is correct.

Explanation: From first figure to second figure, the outer figure becomes middle figure, middle figure becomes inner figure and inner figure becomes outer figure.

Level-3: EXPERT

1. Option (D) is correct.

Explanation: The inner figure exits and the outer figure enters.

2. Option (B) is correct.

Explanation: The outermost element shrinks in size, becomes vertically inverted, and moves to the upper-left position. The middle element shrinks in size, becomes vertically inverted, and moves to the lower-right corner. The innermost element expands and rotates 45 degrees clockwise. Its arc becomes a circle, and the dot becomes a blank triangle.

3. Option (D) is correct.

Explanation: The arrow separates from the figure when it turns 90 degrees anticlockwise. The remaining portion of the picture is laterally reversed, and the arrow becomes vertically inverted.

4. Option (A) is correct.

Explanation: The outermost element shrinks, turns black, and transforms into the innermost element as the former grows to become the latter.

5. Option (E) is correct.

Explanation: The entire image is laterally reversed. The dot advances to the centre of the huge element (the arc or the incomplete rectangle).To get to the end of the big element, turn the pin and the arc anticlockwise. The pin becomes inverted vertically.

6. Option (B) is correct.

Explanation: The circles and ellipses that were black change to white, while those that were white change to black when the figure is laterally inverted.

7. Option (E) is correct.

Explanation: Both a full circle and a semicircle can be transformed into hexagons.

8. Option (E) is correct.

Explanation: As we progress from the problem figure first to the second, the right-half section of the lower figure and the left-half portion of the higher figure have been erased. The bottom part, as a result, is black, and the top part, which was black, has been rendered white.

9. Option (E) is correct.

Explanation: The pentagon and the pin both get inverted. The upper section of the picture separates, becomes unshaded, and turns into the LHS as the arrow and clamp spin 90 degrees anticlockwise.

10. Option (B) is correct.

Explanation: Three additional line segments are added to the lower end of the figure, which is then rotated 180 degrees.

11. Option (B) is correct.

Explanation: Mirror image of F and take the middle line to outside. Mirror image of M as well without changing it's place.

12. Option (A) is correct.

Explanation: The movement rotated as

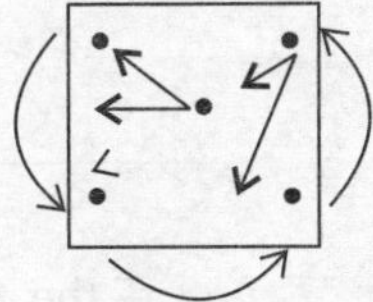

13. Option (C) is correct.

Explanation: The figure revolves 135 degrees anticlockwise. The "S"-shaped pieces are inverted at the triangle base and move away. A little triangle is initially present when the square is moved to the other side of the triangle and turned into a black. The major figure (the big triangle) has an = symbol inside of it.

14. Option (E) is correct.

Explanation: The protruding part of the figure is pushed in as the figure turns 90 degrees clockwise. A shady dot emerges from the figure. The sign of = rotates 90° degrees anticlockwise, forming a blank dot inside the figure.

15. Option (A) is correct.

Explanation: A line segment from the figure's head is deleted, the entire figure's arrows are reversed.

16. Option (D) is correct.

Explanation: The top element rotates 90° clockwise and moves to the right position. Also, the lower element rotates 90° anti clockwise and moves to the left position.

17. Option (E) is correct.

Explanation: The figure get laterally inverted and a small line segment inserted in it.
Also, the element inside the figure rotates 180°.

18. Option (B) is correct.

Explanation: The element moves as.

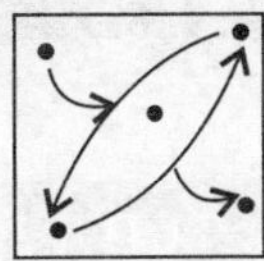

The encircled element replaced by a new element.

19. Option (B) is correct.

Explanation: The upper left corner element rotates 135° anticlockwise and shift to lower left corner. The upper right corner element rotates 90° anticlockwise and shift to centre position. The lower left corner element rotates 90° anti clockwise and move to the lower right position. The lower right corner element rotates 135° clockwise and moves to the upper right position.
Also, a new element added to upper left position.

20. Option (B) is correct.

Explanation: From first figure to second, the shaded part becomes unshaded and vice-versa. Also, the number of sides of middle element increased by 1.

■ ■ ■

Chapter 17 Classification

LEARNING OBJECTIVES:

- ❖ Questions based on figure classification
- ❖ Questions based on mixed classification
- ❖ Different types of questions asked in competitive exams

The classification chapter focuses on recognising the odd-one-out figure in a set of figures where all but one share similar attributes. Furthermore, the chapter digs into numerous different forms of classification issues, which are thoroughly defined and explored.

Classification is a process linked to classification that involves the recognition, differentiation, and comprehension of ideas and objects. Classification is the classification of related facts.

FIGURE CLASSIFICATION

➢ The goal of this type of problem is to find the rule or pattern that governs the classification of a given set of shapes or figures. The figures may be made up of symbols, geometric shapes, or a combination of the two, and may undergo transformations such as scaling, reflection, translation, and rotation. Changes in relevant characteristics such as orientation, shape, position, and number of elements can also be incorporated. These problems may involve groups of four or five figures, and in order to solve them, one must carefully examine the figures and identify consistent transformations or changes. The task entails analysing the relationships between the figures and selecting the figure that stands out. The chapter includes several examples of figure classification.

Example 1: Here, we have five set of figures. Four are similar in a certain way. One figure is not like the other four. Find out the figure which does not belong to the group.

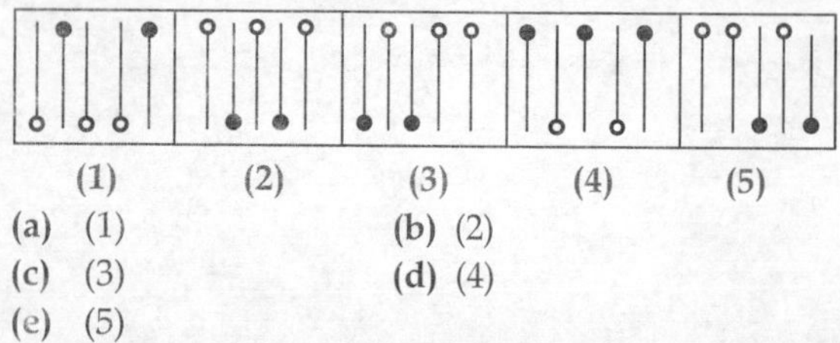

(1) (2) (3) (4) (5)

(a) (1) (b) (2)
(c) (3) (d) (4)
(e) (5)

Sol. (d) In all the figure except (4), there are two shaded pins and three unshaded pins. In figure (4) there are three shaded pins and two unshaded pins. Thus, it is different from the others.

MIXED CLASSIFICATION

➢ Mixed classification is a non-verbal reasoning problem that incorporates multiple types of patterns or rules within a single pattern. In contrast to other classification problems where the pattern remains consistent throughout, mixed classification requires the identification and application of different patterns or rules within the same sequence of shapes or figures. Each part of the problem has a distinct pattern, and the goal is to recognise these patterns and accurately apply them to select or predict the different element.

Example 2: There are five letters are given. Four are similar in a certain way. One is different from others. Choose the different one.

J	K	T	I	W
(1)	(2)	(3)	(4)	(5)

(a) 3 (b) 2
(c) 5 (d) 4

Sol. (d) As in the figure, all are consonant, except (d) as it is vowel.

Example 3: Find the different one.

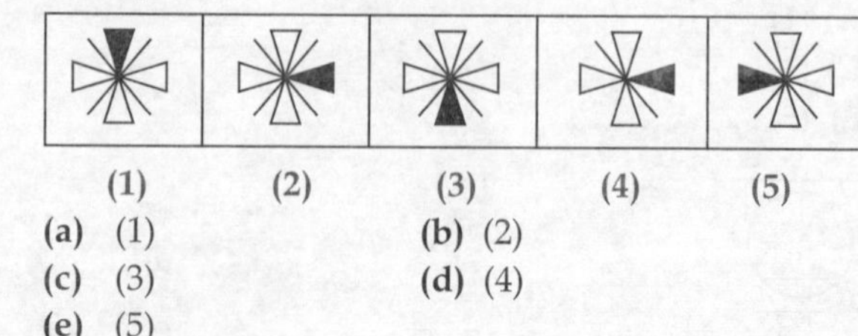

(1) (2) (3) (4) (5)

(a) (1) (b) (2)
(c) (3) (d) (4)
(e) (5)

Sol. (d) In all other figures, the appearance of a black triangle in either of the two areas between the line segment.

Level 1 Beginner

Directions: In the given problems, we are given a set of figures. Out of which one all except one are alike in some manner. Select the exclusively different figure in the given set.

1. 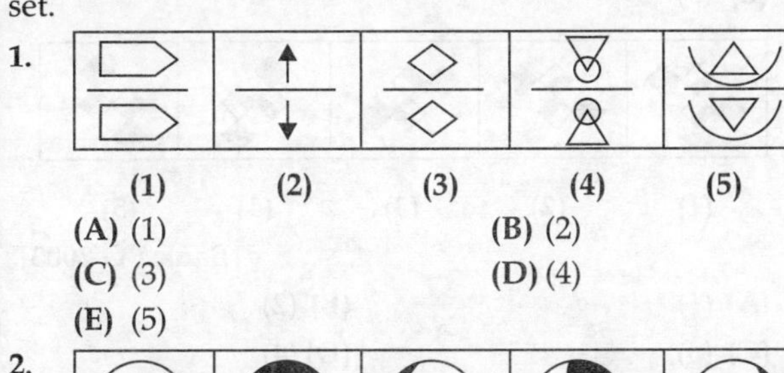

(1) (2) (3) (4) (5)

(A) (1) **(B)** (2)
(C) (3) **(D)** (4)
(E) (5)

2. 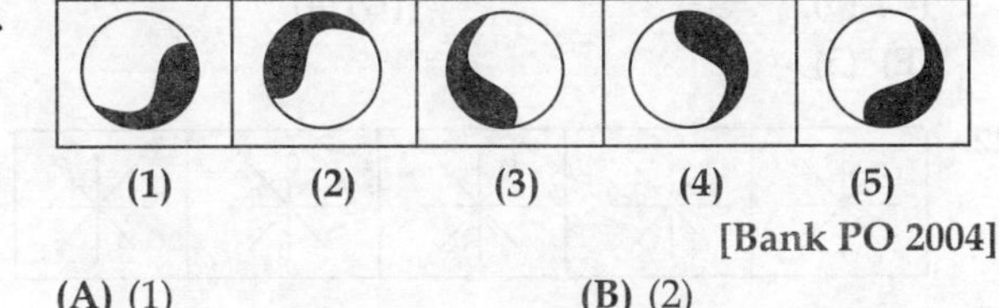

(1) (2) (3) (4) (5)

[Bank PO 2004]

(A) (1) **(B)** (2)
(C) (3) **(D)** (4)
(E) (5)

3. 

(1) (2) (3) (4) (5)

[Bank PO 2005]

(A) (1) **(B)** (2)
(C) (3) **(D)** (4)
(E) (5)

4. 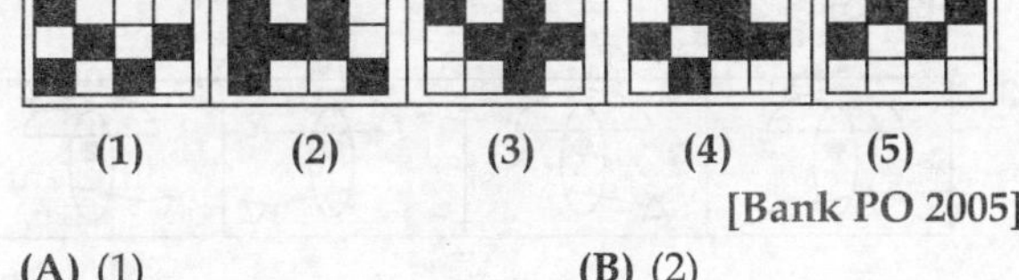

(1) (2) (3) (4)

[SSC 2002]

(A) (1) **(B)** (2)
(C) (3) **(D)** (4)

5. 

(1) (2) (3) (4) (5)

[SBI Clerk 2007]

(A) (1) **(B)** (2)
(C) (3) **(D)** (4)
(E) (5)

6. 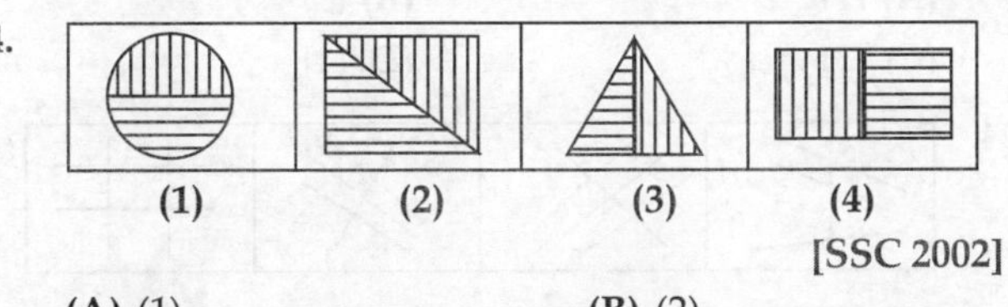
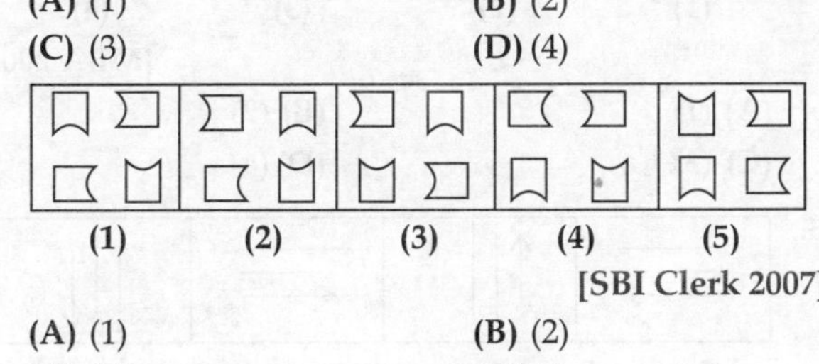

(1) (2) (3) (4) (5)

(A) (1) **(B)** (2)
(C) (3) **(D)** (4)
(E) (5)

7. 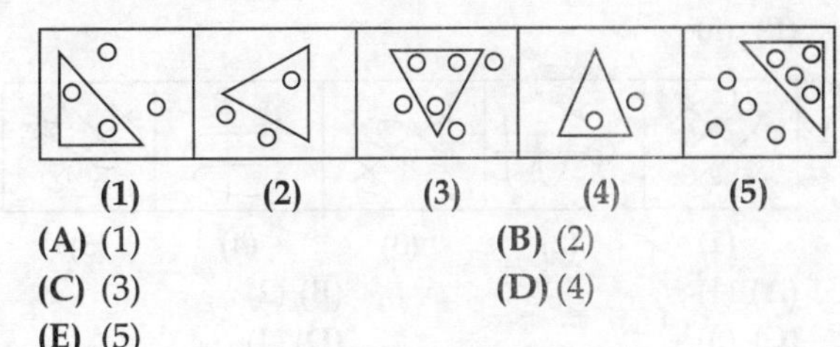

(1) (2) (3) (4) (5)

(A) (1) **(B)** (2)
(C) (3) **(D)** (4)
(E) (5)

8. 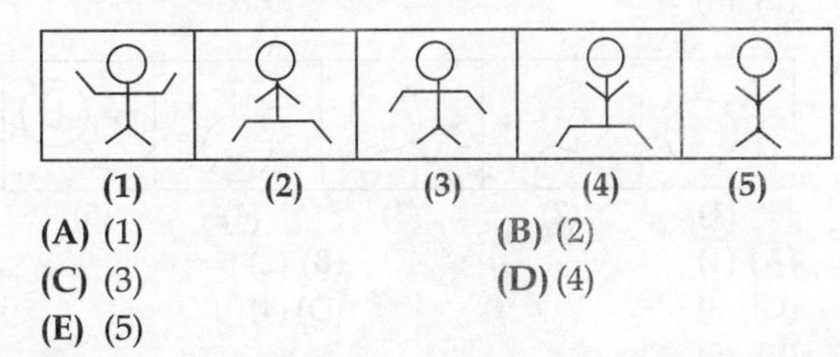

(1) (2) (3) (4) (5)

(A) (1) **(B)** (2)
(C) (3) **(D)** (4)
(E) (5)

9. 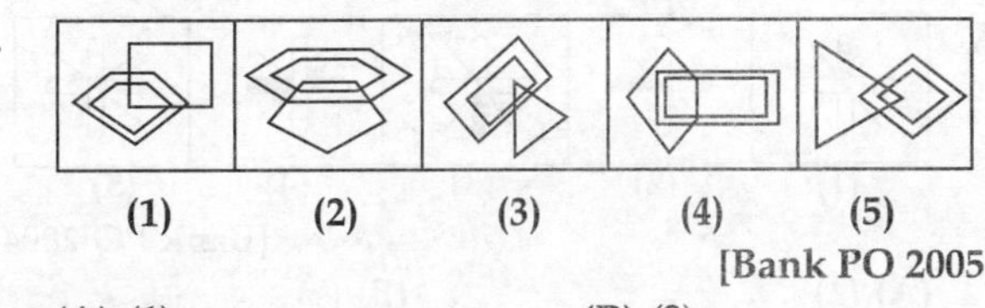

(1) (2) (3) (4) (5)

[Bank PO 2005]

(A) (1) **(B)** (2)
(C) (3) **(D)** (4)
(E) (5)

10. 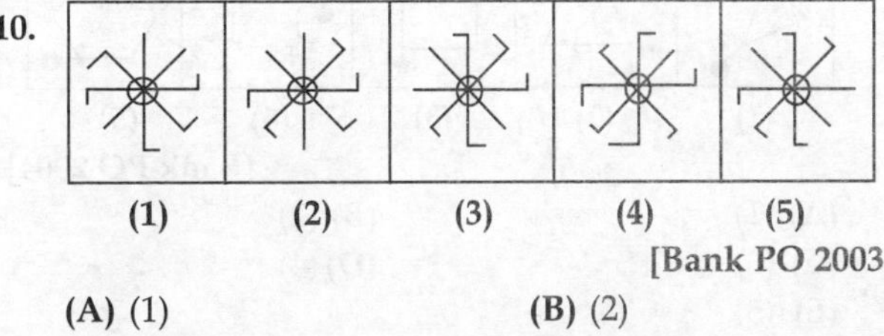

(1) (2) (3) (4) (5)

[Bank PO 2003]

(A) (1) **(B)** (2)
(C) (3) **(D)** (4)
(E) (5)

11. 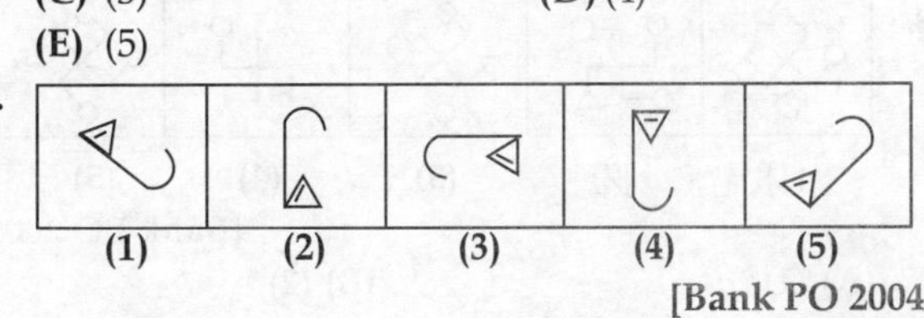
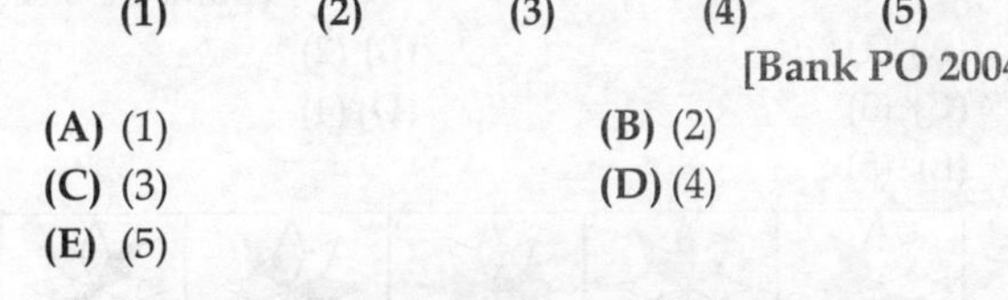

(1) (2) (3) (4) (5)

[Bank PO 2004]

(A) (1) **(B)** (2)
(C) (3) **(D)** (4)
(E) (5)

12. 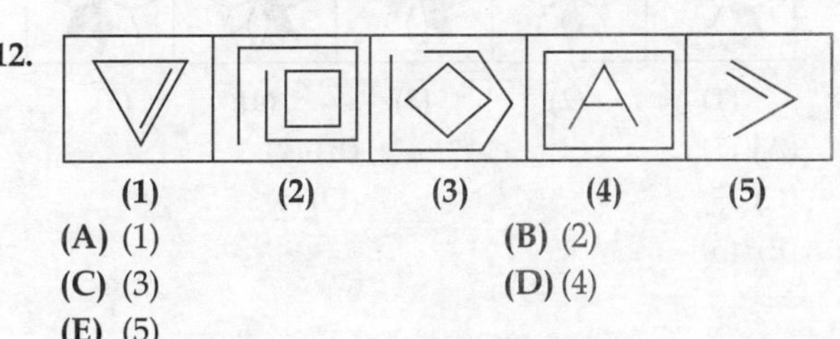

(1) (2) (3) (4) (5)

(A) (1) **(B)** (2)
(C) (3) **(D)** (4)
(E) (5)

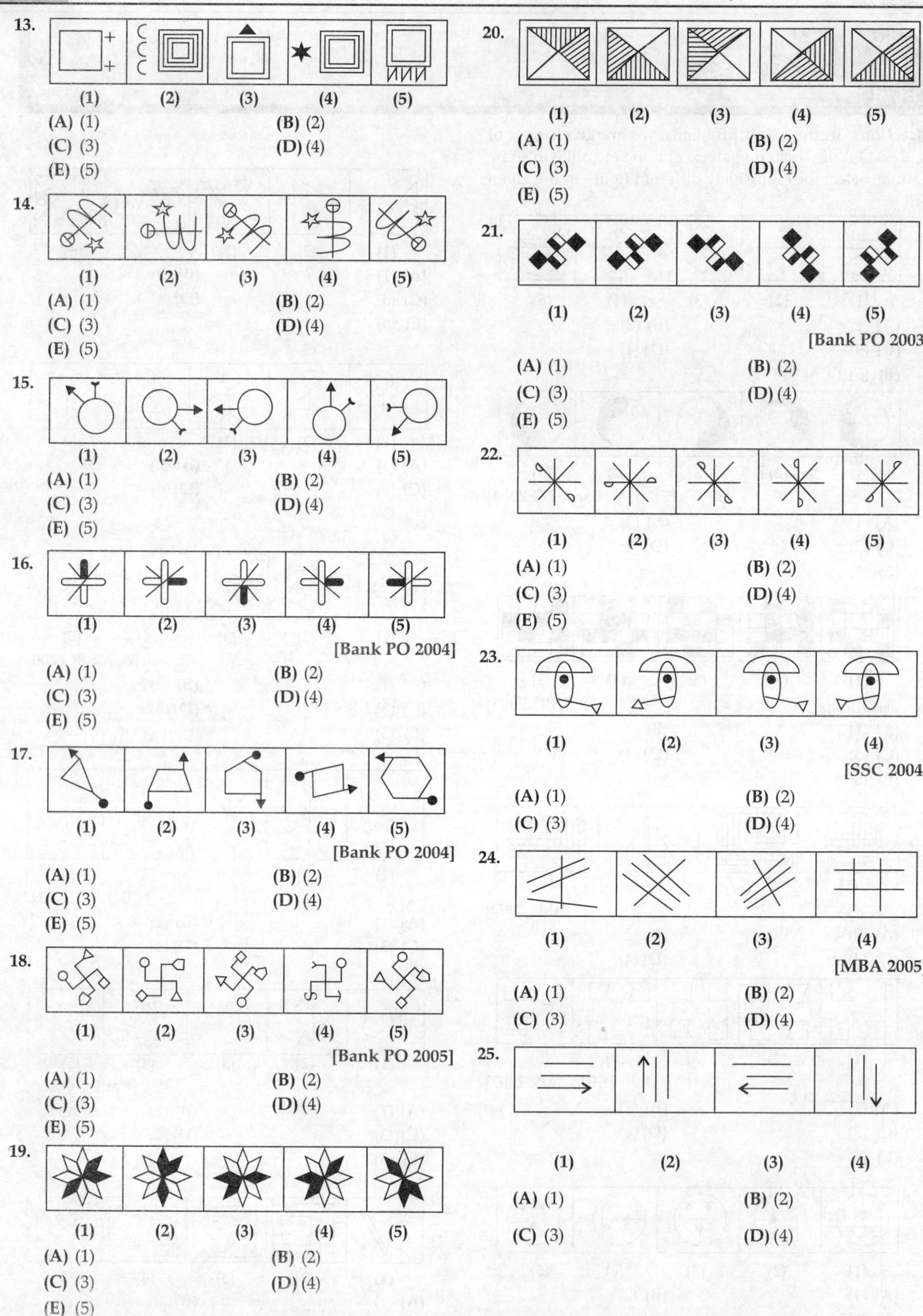

13. (1) (2) (3) (4) (5)
(A) (1) (B) (2)
(C) (3) (D) (4)
(E) (5)

14. (1) (2) (3) (4) (5)
(A) (1) (B) (2)
(C) (3) (D) (4)
(E) (5)

15. (1) (2) (3) (4) (5)
(A) (1) (B) (2)
(C) (3) (D) (4)
(E) (5)

16. (1) (2) (3) (4) (5)
[Bank PO 2004]
(A) (1) (B) (2)
(C) (3) (D) (4)
(E) (5)

17. (1) (2) (3) (4) (5)
[Bank PO 2004]
(A) (1) (B) (2)
(C) (3) (D) (4)
(E) (5)

18. (1) (2) (3) (4) (5)
[Bank PO 2005]
(A) (1) (B) (2)
(C) (3) (D) (4)
(E) (5)

19. (1) (2) (3) (4) (5)
(A) (1) (B) (2)
(C) (3) (D) (4)
(E) (5)

20. (1) (2) (3) (4) (5)
(A) (1) (B) (2)
(C) (3) (D) (4)
(E) (5)

21. (1) (2) (3) (4) (5)
[Bank PO 2003]
(A) (1) (B) (2)
(C) (3) (D) (4)
(E) (5)

22. (1) (2) (3) (4) (5)
(A) (1) (B) (2)
(C) (3) (D) (4)
(E) (5)

23. (1) (2) (3) (4)
[SSC 2004]
(A) (1) (B) (2)
(C) (3) (D) (4)

24. (1) (2) (3) (4)
[MBA 2005]
(A) (1) (B) (2)
(C) (3) (D) (4)

25. (1) (2) (3) (4)
(A) (1) (B) (2)
(C) (3) (D) (4)

2 Level Intermediate

Directions (Qs. 1–13): In each the following questions, there are two problem figures, followed by five answer figures. There are certain common properties between the two problem figures. Select the answer figure which shows similar properties.

1. Problem figure

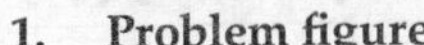

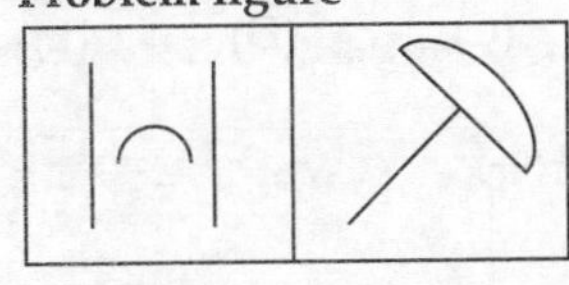

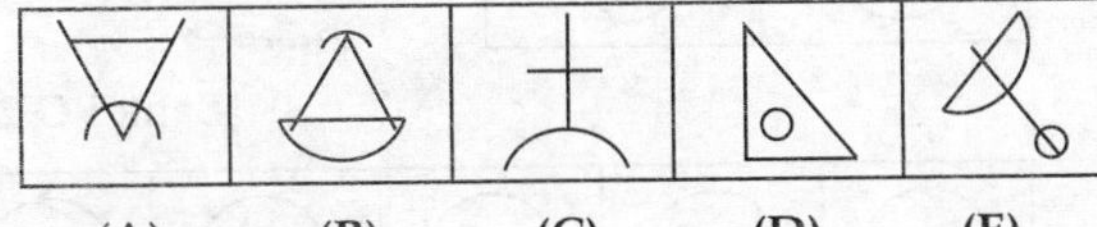

(A) (B) (C) (D) (E)

2. Problem figure

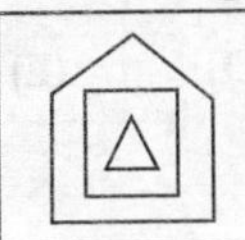

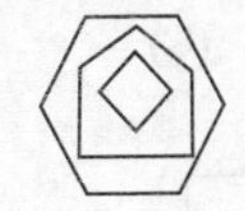

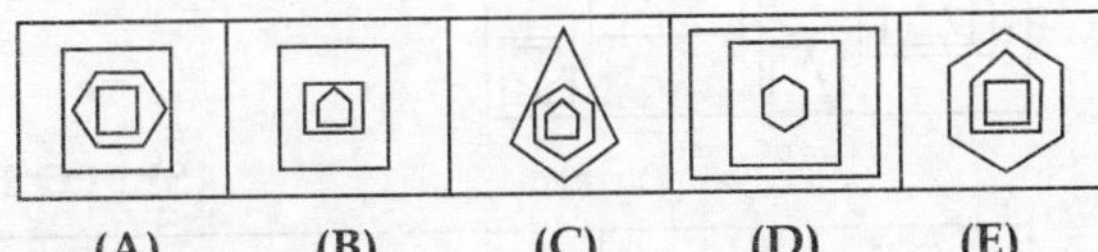

(A) (B) (C) (D) (E)

3. Problem figure

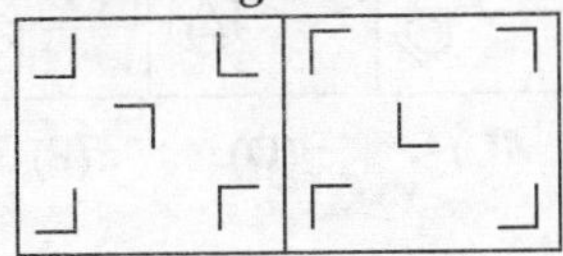

[Bank PO 2004]

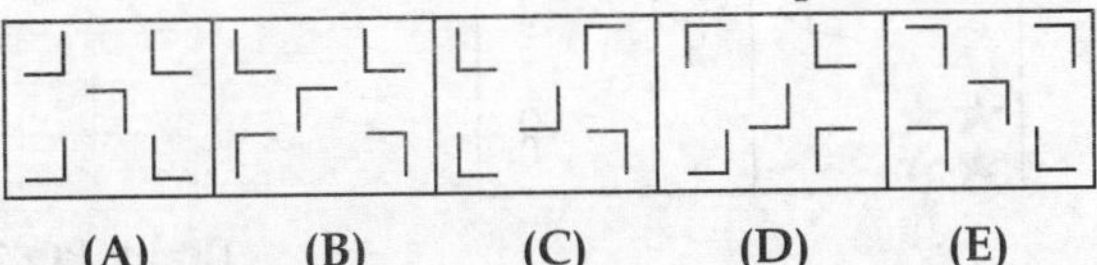

(A) (B) (C) (D) (E)

4. Problem figure

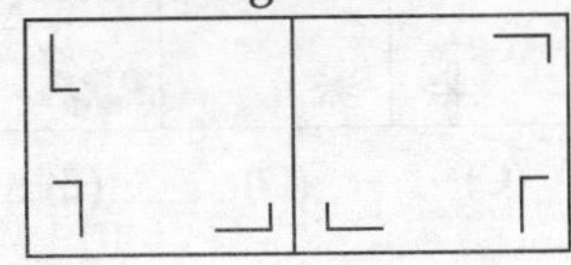

[Bank PO 2002]

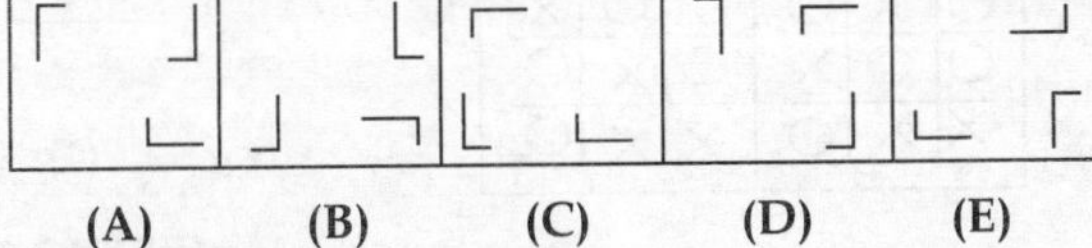

(A) (B) (C) (D) (E)

5. Problem figure

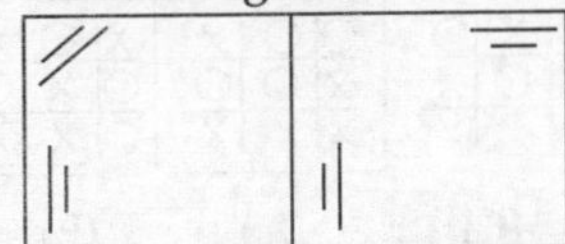

[SSC CPO Exam 2018]

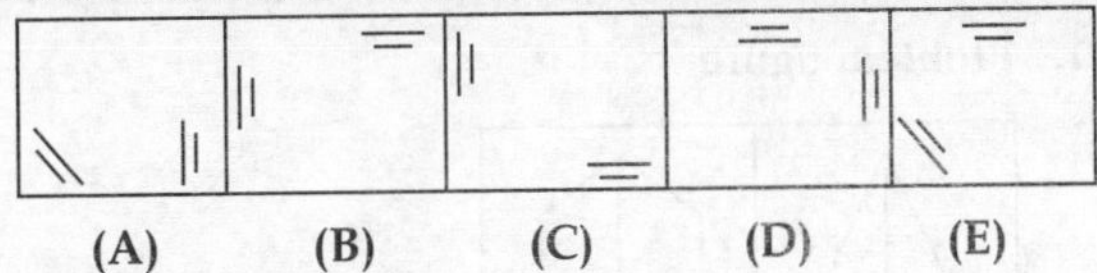

(A) (B) (C) (D) (E)

6. Problem figure

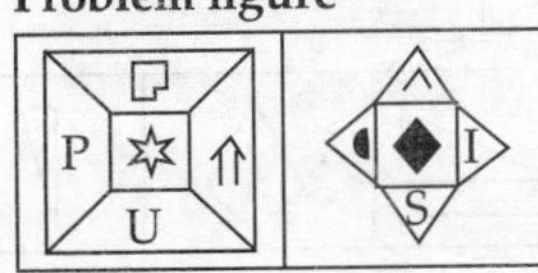

[Bank PO 2001]

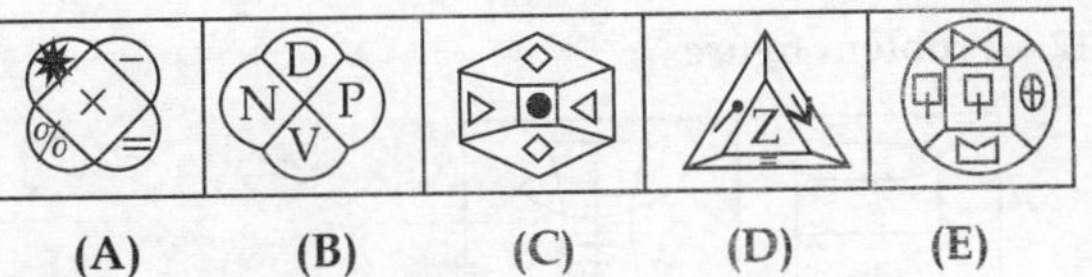

(A) (B) (C) (D) (E)

7. Problem figure

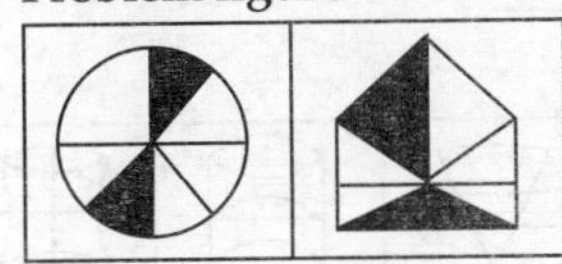

[Bank PO 2005]

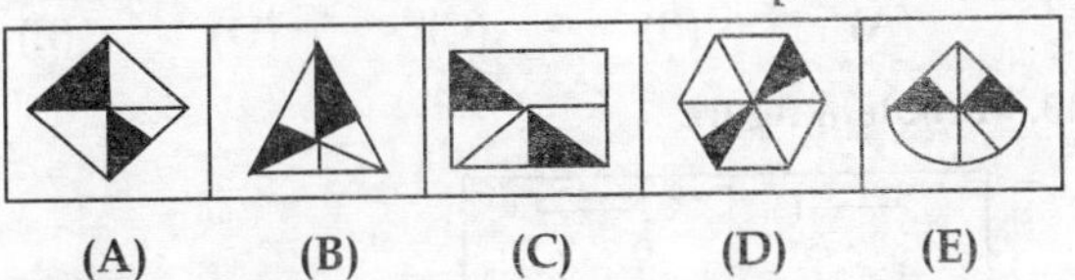

(A) (B) (C) (D) (E)

8. Problem figure

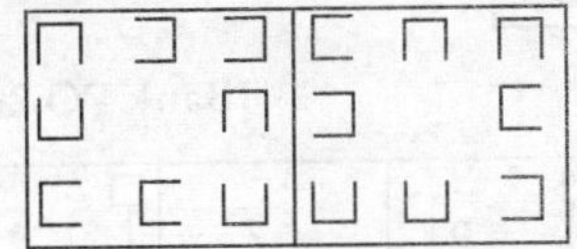

[Bank PO 2003]

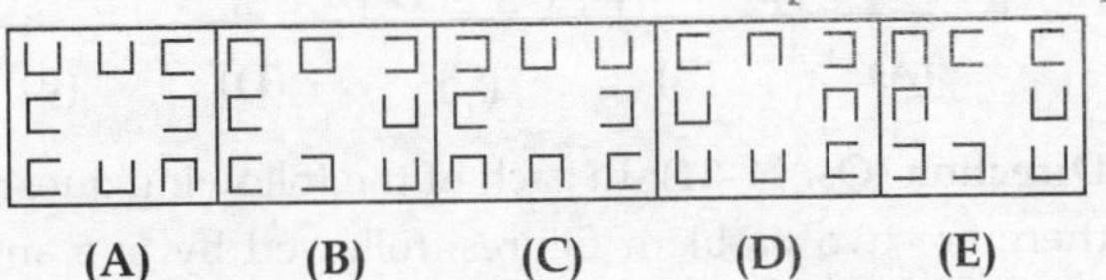

(A) (B) (C) (D) (E)

9. Problem figure

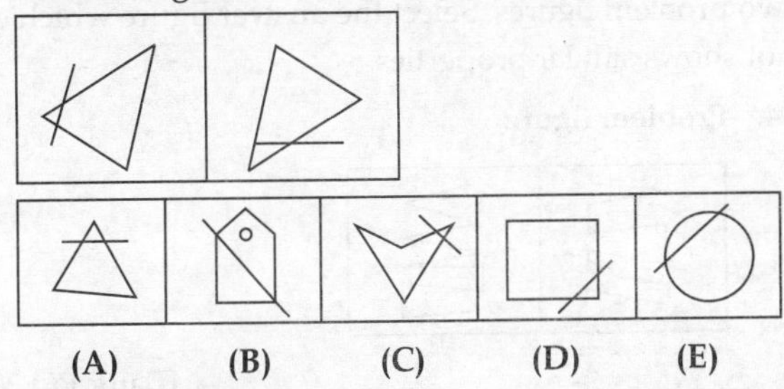

(A) (B) (C) (D) (E)

10. Problem figure

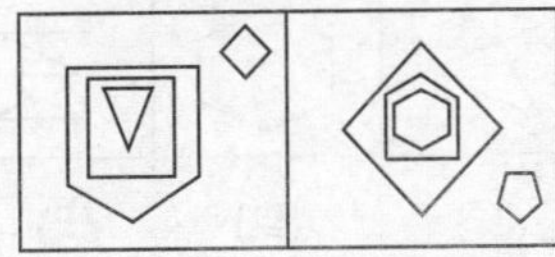

[SBI PO 2002]

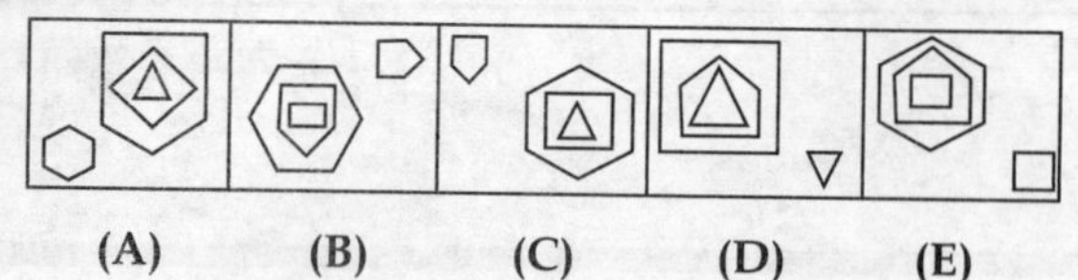

(A) (B) (C) (D) (E)

11. Problem figure

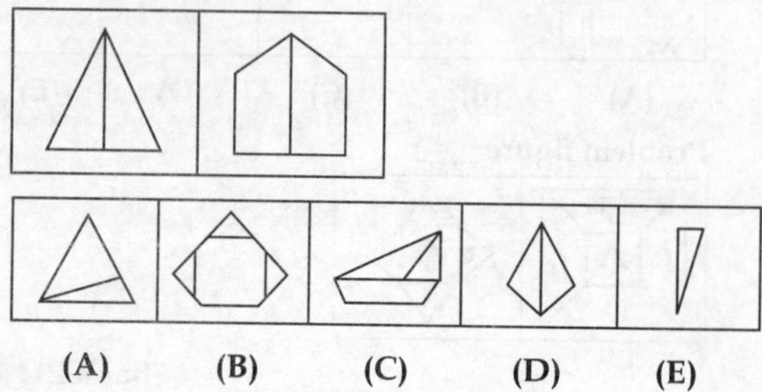

(A) (B) (C) (D) (E)

12. Problem figure

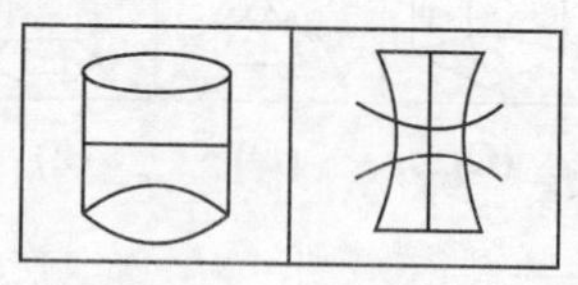

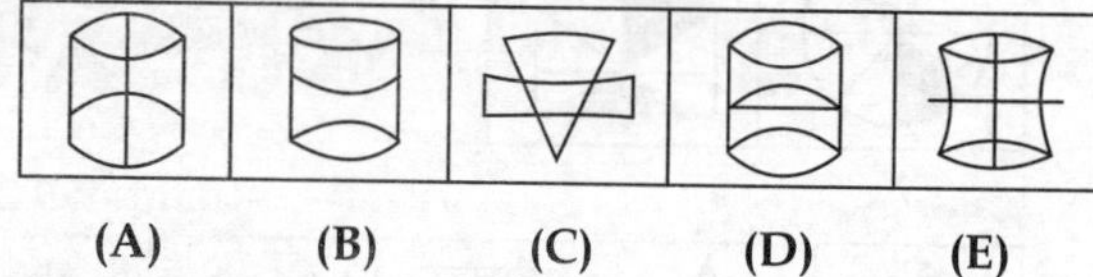

(A) (B) (C) (D) (E)

13. Problem figure

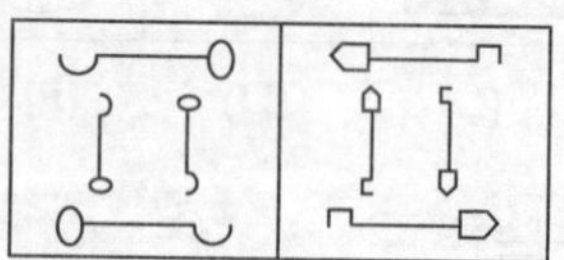

[Bank PO 2004]

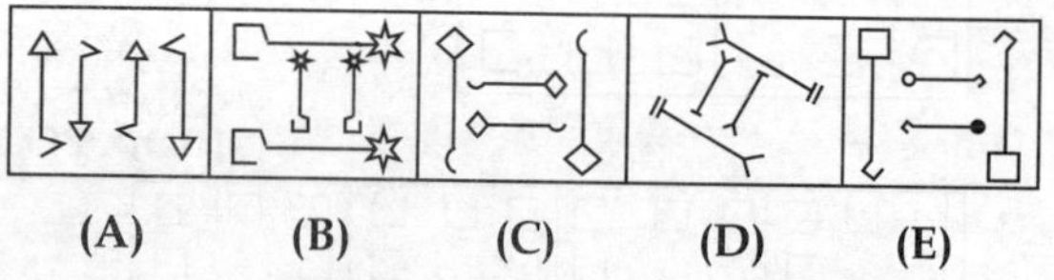

(A) (B) (C) (D) (E)

Direction (Qs. 14–21): In each of the following questions, there are two problem figures, followed by five answer figures. There are certain common properties between the two problem figures. Select the answer figure which does not shows similar properties.

14. Problem figure

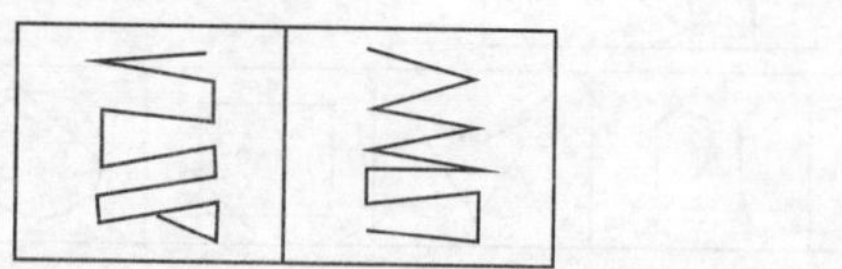

[Bank PO 2004]

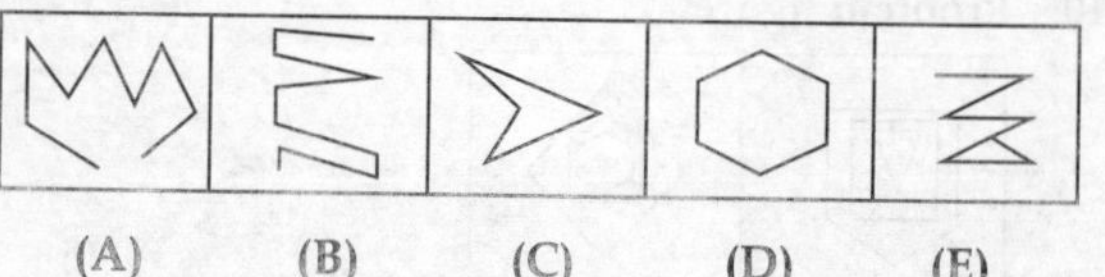

(A) (B) (C) (D) (E)

15. Problem figure

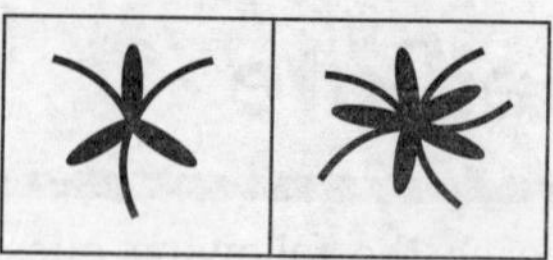

[SBI PO 2002]

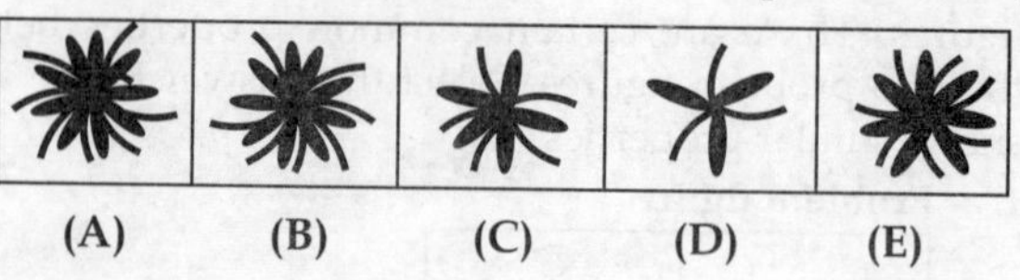

(A) (B) (C) (D) (E)

16. Problem figure

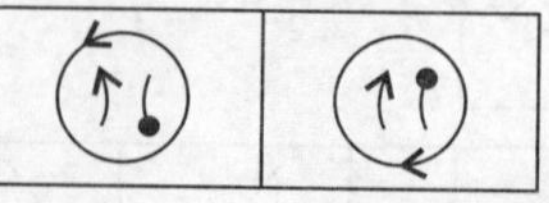

[Bank PO 2003]

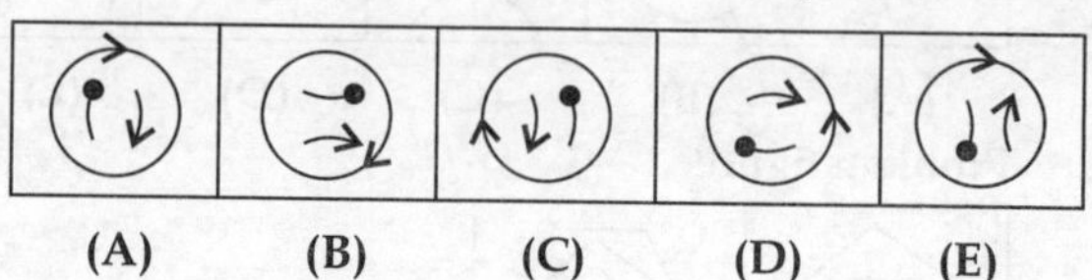

(A) (B) (C) (D) (E)

17. Problem figure

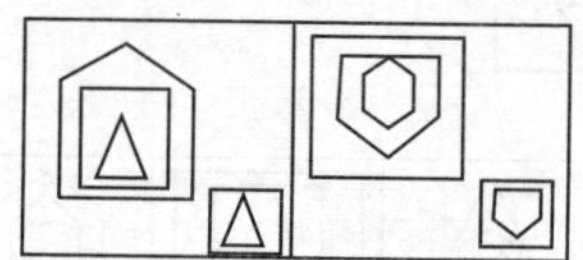

[SBI PO 2002]

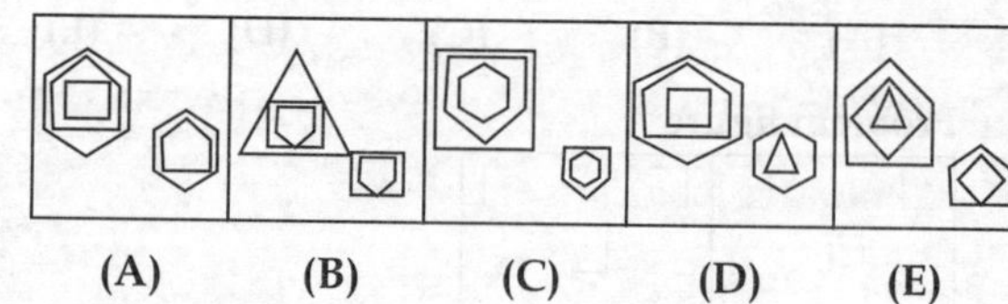

(A) (B) (C) (D) (E)

18. Problem figure

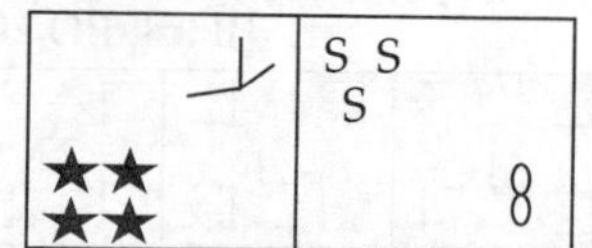

[Bank PO 2002]

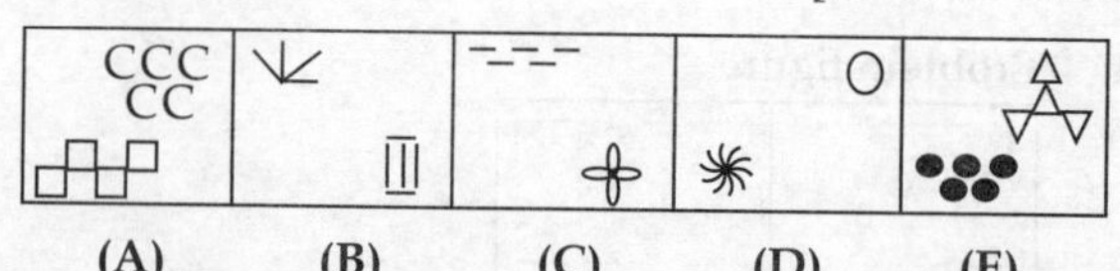

(A) (B) (C) (D) (E)

19. Problem figure

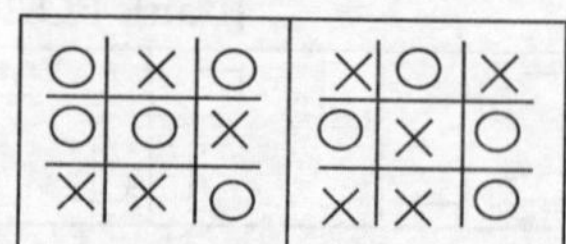

[SBI PO 2002]

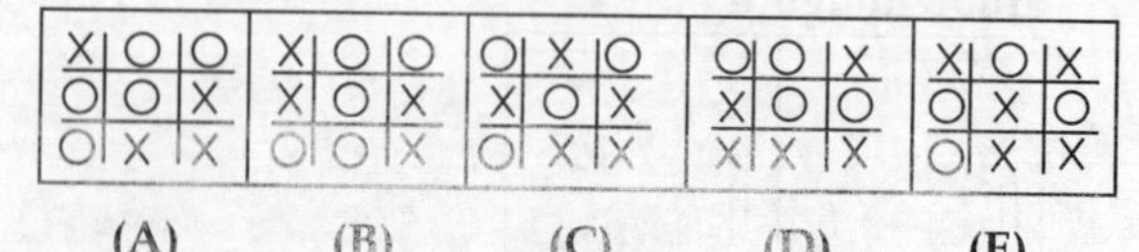

(A) (B) (C) (D) (E)

20. Problem figure

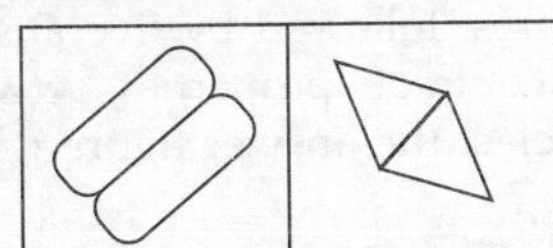

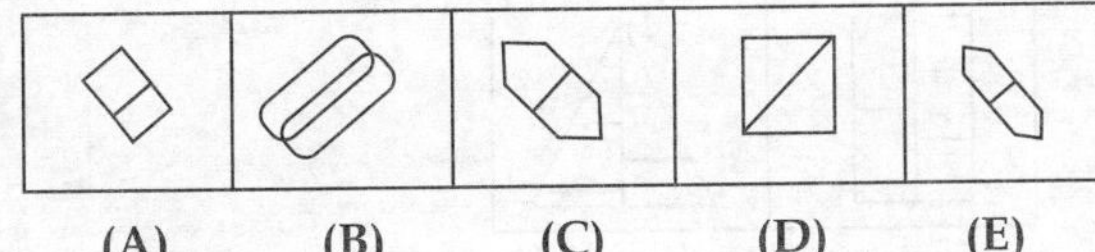

(A) (B) (C) (D) (E)

21. Problem figure

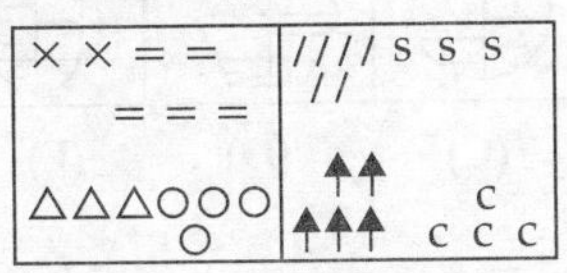

(A) (B) (C) (D) (E)

Directions (Qs. 22–24): In the given problems, we are given a set of figures. Out of which one all except one are alike in some manner. Select the exclusively different figure in the given set.

22. Problem figure

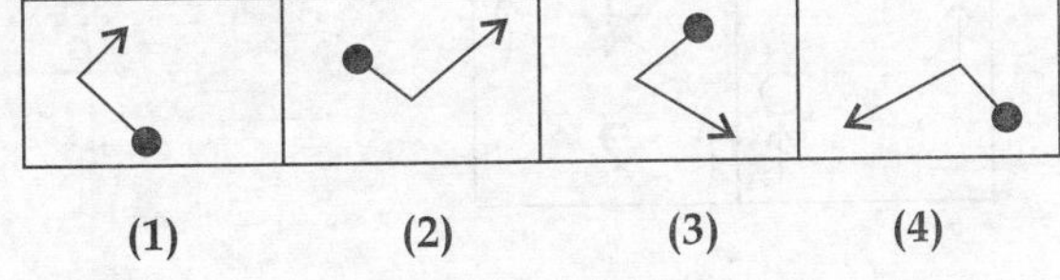

(1) (2) (3) (4)

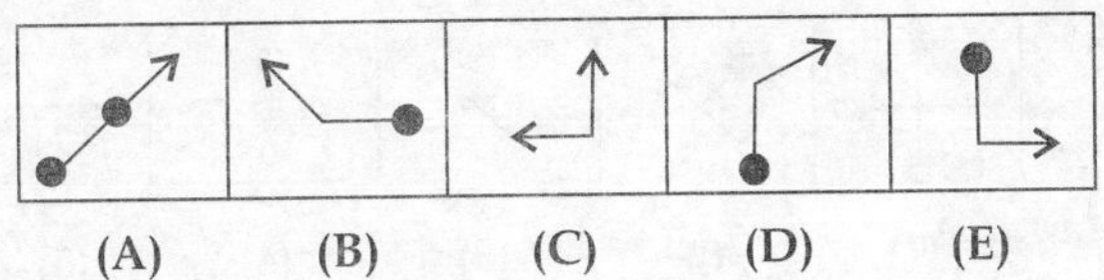

(A) (B) (C) (D) (E)

23. Problem figure

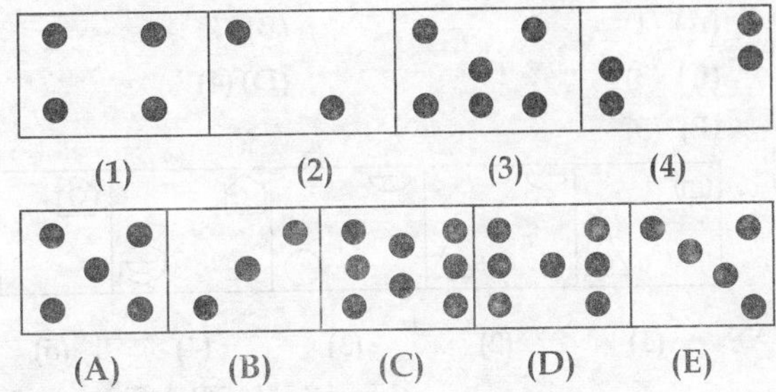

(1) (2) (3) (4)

(A) (B) (C) (D) (E)

24. Problem figure

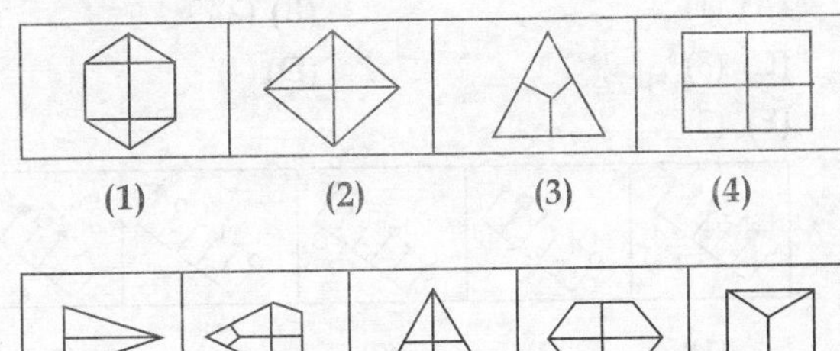

(1) (2) (3) (4)

(A) (B) (C) (D) (E)

25. Find the different one.

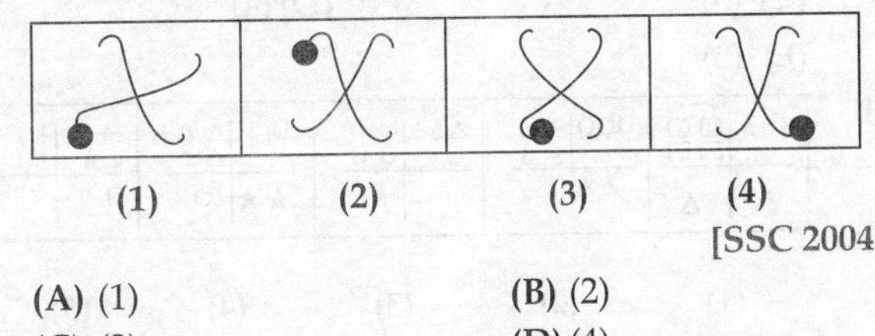

(1) (2) (3) (4)

[SSC 2004]

(A) (1) (B) (2)
(C) (3) (D) (4)

Level 3 Expert

Directions: In each question, five figures are given. Four are similar in a certain way. One is different from others. Find the different one.

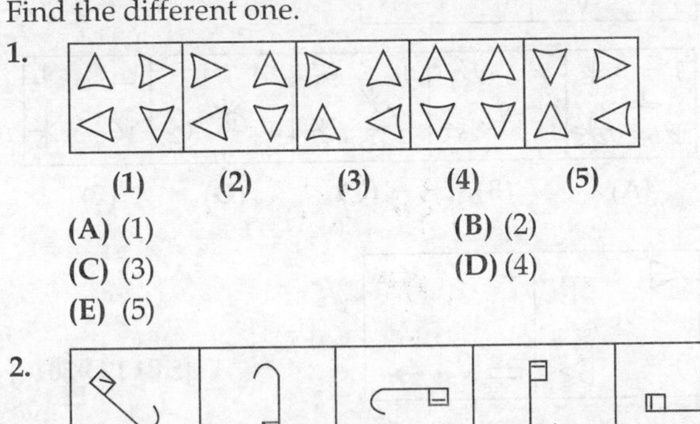

1. (1) (2) (3) (4) (5)

(A) (1) (B) (2)
(C) (3) (D) (4)
(E) (5)

2. (1) (2) (3) (4) (5)

(A) (1) (B) (2)
(C) (3) (D) (4)
(E) (5)

3. The following figure follows a series. One figure not fit in the series. Find the odd one.

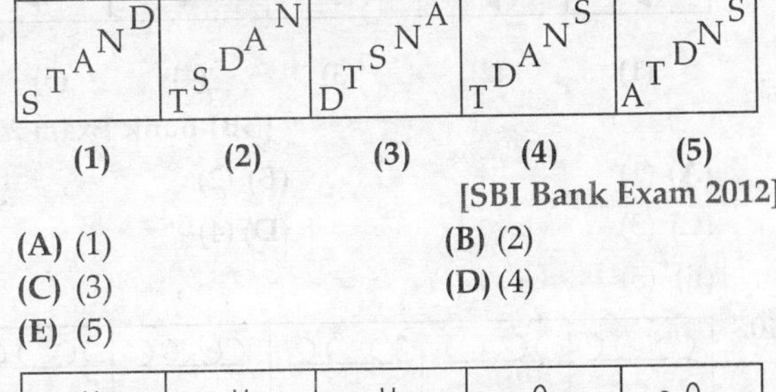

(1) (2) (3) (4) (5)

[SBI Bank Exam 2012]

(A) (1) (B) (2)
(C) (3) (D) (4)
(E) (5)

4.

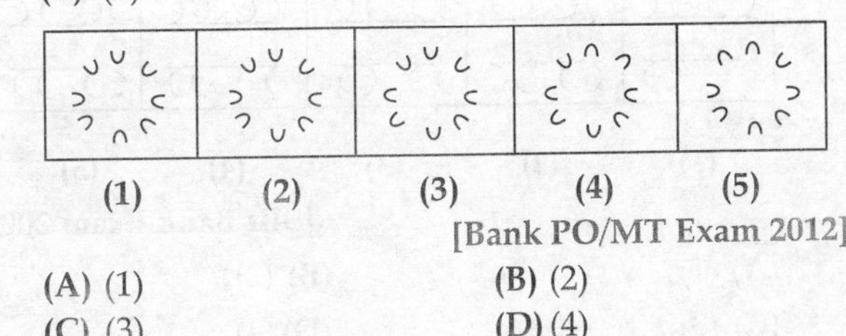

(1) (2) (3) (4) (5)

[Bank PO/MT Exam 2012]

(A) (1) (B) (2)
(C) (3) (D) (4)
(E) (5)

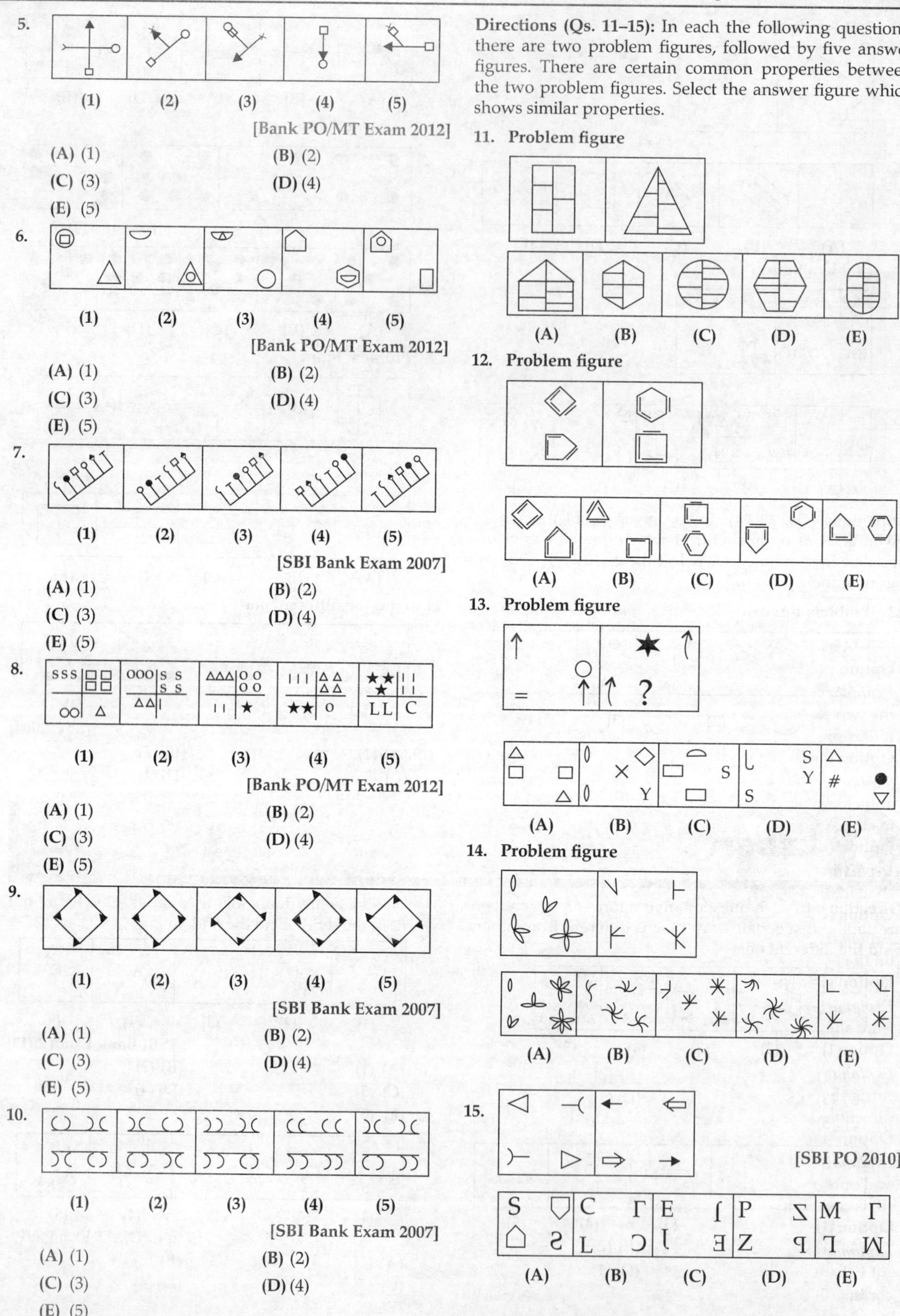

5. (1) (2) (3) (4) (5)

[Bank PO/MT Exam 2012]

(A) (1) (B) (2)
(C) (3) (D) (4)
(E) (5)

6. (1) (2) (3) (4) (5)

[Bank PO/MT Exam 2012]

(A) (1) (B) (2)
(C) (3) (D) (4)
(E) (5)

7. (1) (2) (3) (4) (5)

[SBI Bank Exam 2007]

(A) (1) (B) (2)
(C) (3) (D) (4)
(E) (5)

8. (1) (2) (3) (4) (5)

[Bank PO/MT Exam 2012]

(A) (1) (B) (2)
(C) (3) (D) (4)
(E) (5)

9. (1) (2) (3) (4) (5)

[SBI Bank Exam 2007]

(A) (1) (B) (2)
(C) (3) (D) (4)
(E) (5)

10. (1) (2) (3) (4) (5)

[SBI Bank Exam 2007]

(A) (1) (B) (2)
(C) (3) (D) (4)
(E) (5)

Directions (Qs. 11–15): In each the following questions, there are two problem figures, followed by five answer figures. There are certain common properties between the two problem figures. Select the answer figure which shows similar properties.

11. **Problem figure**

(A) (B) (C) (D) (E)

12. **Problem figure**

(A) (B) (C) (D) (E)

13. **Problem figure**

(A) (B) (C) (D) (E)

14. **Problem figure**

(A) (B) (C) (D) (E)

15. [SBI PO 2010]

(A) (B) (C) (D) (E)

ANSWER KEY

Level-1: Beginner

1.	(E)	2.	(E)	3.	(C)	4.	(C)	5.	(C)	6.	(E)	7.	(B)	8.	(E)	9.	(D)	10.	(D)
11.	(B)	12.	(A)	13.	(D)	14.	(B)	15.	(C)	16.	(B)	17.	(C)	18.	(D)	19.	(C)	20.	(E)
21.	(A)	22.	(C)	23.	(B)	24.	(D)	25.	(A)										

Level-2: Intermediate

1.	(C)	2.	(E)	3.	(C)	4.	(A)	5.	(C)	6.	(A)	7.	(E)	8.	(C)	9.	(D)	10.	(B)
11.	(D)	12.	(A)	13.	(C)	14.	(B)	15.	(A)	16.	(D)	17.	(D)	18.	(D)	19.	(D)	20.	(B)
21.	(B)	22.	(E)	23.	(C)	24.	(B)	25.	(A)										

Level-3: Expert

1.	(D)	2.	(B)	3.	(D)	4.	(E)	5.	(E)	6.	(E)	7.	(A)	8.	(D)	9.	(D)	10.	(C)
11.	(C)	12.	(E)	13.	(D)	14.	(B)	15.	(D)										

Solutions with Detailed Explanations

Level-1: BEGINNER

1. **Option (E) is correct.**
Explanation: It is obvious that in every other figure, the two elements on either side of the line are mirror reflections of one another.

2. **Option (E) is correct.**
Explanation: In figure 5, the pattern is revolving in anti-clockwise direction, while in others it's revolving in clockwise direction.

3. **Option (C) is correct.**
Explanation: Only figure 3 has even number of shaded blocks. So, option (C) is correct.

4. **Option (C) is correct.**
Explanation: Each figure features horizontal shading on the bottom half of the figure.

5. **Option (C) is correct.**
Explanation: Only two of the four elements in figure 3 are aligned in the same direction.

6. **Option (E) is correct.**
Explanation: A series of figures are present. Each step turns the entire figure 90 degrees in the clockwise direction except figure 5.

7. **Option (B) is correct.**
Explanation: There are equal number of circles inside and outside of the triangle except figure 2. So, option (B) is correct.

8. **Option (E) is correct.**
Explanation: In figure 5, there are two arrow symbols. All other figures have only one. So, option (E) is correct.

9. **Option (D) is correct.**
Explanation: All double sided figure have one more side than single sided figure. So, option (D) is correct.

10. **Option (D) is correct.**
Explanation: Every other figure can be turned around one another.

11. **Option (B) is correct.**
Explanation: The main figure can be rotated into each other in any other situations. However, the triangle's sides can all have the small line segment.

12. **Option (A) is correct.**
Explanation: In every other figure, the number of line segments constituting the inner element is one less.

13. **Option (D) is correct.**
Explanation: In all other figures, there are either one or two more or one less squares than there are symbols along the boundary.

14. **Option (B) is correct.**
Explanation: It is possible to rotate all other figures into one another.

15. **Option (C) is correct.**
Explanation: Each of the other figures may rotate into the others.

16. **Option (B) is correct.**
Explanation: The black leaf may be seen in either of the two areas between the line segments in all other representations.

17. **Option (C) is correct.**
Explanation: The pin and arrow are pointed in the opposite directions in the other figures.

18. **Option (D) is correct.**
Explanation: The four minor components are connected to the end of the major element in all other figures.
19. **Option (C) is correct.**
Explanation: It is possible to rotate all other figures into one another.
20. **Option (E) is correct.**
Explanation: All other figures, with the exception of fig. (5), have the same shading pattern when rotated to the same position. Additionally, we may state that every other figure can be turned into itself.
21. **Option (A) is correct.**
Explanation: The two half-shaded squares only have comparable half sections in Fig. (1).
22. **Option (C) is correct.**
Explanation: It is possible to rotate all other figures into one another.
23. **Option (B) is correct.**
Explanation: The triangle in the lower portion of figure (2) is upside down.
24. **Option (D) is correct.**
Explanation: No sets of parallel lines are only present in fig. (4).
25. **Option (A) is correct.**
Explanation: It is possible to rotate all other figures into one another.

Level-2: INTERMEDIATE

1. **Option (C) is correct.**
Explanation: Two straight and one curved line compose the figure.
2. **Option (E) is correct.**
Explanation: From the innermost to the outermost polygons, the number of sides increases successively.
3. **Option (C) is correct.**
Explanation: The core element is rotated 90 degrees in clockwise direction to produce the identical upper-left and lower-left components. The core element is rotated via 180 degrees and 90 degrees in anti-clockwise direction to produce the upper-right and lower-right components, respectively.
4. **Option (A) is correct.**
Explanation: Any of the other two elements can be rotated through 180 degrees to produce one of the elements.
5. **Option (C) is correct.**
Explanation: One of the line pairs has a shorter outer line and a longer interior line, while the other pair has a longer other line and a shorter interior line.
6. **Option (A) is correct.**
Explanation: The primary figure is broken into five sections, each of which contains a symbol different from the other four.
7. **Option (E) is correct.**
Explanation: The figure is split into seven pieces, which may or may not be equal, and two of those parts are shaded.
8. **Option (C) is correct.**
Explanation: The middle-right and upper-left elements are identical. The upper-left element is generated by rotating it through 90 degrees clockwise to produce the upper-middle and upper-right components, which are both identical. By 180° rotating the upper-left element, we may get the middle-left and lower-right components, which are both identical.
The upper-left element is rotated through 90 degrees anti-clockwise manner to produce the lower-left and lower-middle components, which are both identical.
9. **Option (D) is correct.**
Explanation: The three-sided convex object features a straight line cutting through one of its corners.
10. **Option (B) is correct.**
Explanation: The number of sides in three figures are in decreasing or increasing order. Also the corner figure is the middle figure of three figures.
11. **Option (D) is correct.**
Explanation: A line in the middle of each figure divides it in half.
12. **Option (A) is correct.**
Explanation: Each figure is made up of three straight lines and four arcs.
13. **Option (C) is correct.**
Explanation: By turning one of the smaller pieces 90 degrees clockwise and increasing it, one of the bigger elements may be created. The other bigger element is created in a similar manner from the other smaller element.
14. **Option (B) is correct.**
Explanation: The open figure must have an even number of line segments.
15. **Option (A) is correct.**
Explanation: The number of petals and arcs is equal. The number of arcs that bend in the two directions varies by 1, or 1. i.e., there should be one more arcs that leave the centre and curve in an anti-clockwise manner than arcs that curve in a CW direction.
16. **Option (D) is correct.**
Explanation: The circle's boundary is marked with an arrowhead that points in the same direction (clockwise or anti-clockwise).
17. **Option (D) is correct.**
Explanation: The lower figure is created by removing one of the pieces from the above image, while also reducing the size of the remaining figure.
18. **Option (D) is correct.**
Explanation: The number of components in the composite design in one corner is either one more or one less than the number of elements in the opposite corner.
19. **Option (D) is correct.**
Explanation: At least one of the diagonal elements are same in every figure.
20. **Option (B) is correct.**
Explanation: All the given figures are symmetrical around their mid lines. So, option (B) is correct.

21. Option (B) is correct.

Explanation: With the exception of Figure B, we discover that the numbers of the various types (four types) of elements are all in sequential order in the remaining response figures. This is a quality that two difficult figure out as well. Since Figure B does not possible this characteristic. So, Figure B is the correct answer.

22. Option (E) is correct.

Explanation: The pin and the arrow are perpendicular to one another.

23. Option (C) is correct.

Explanation: Each figure has an even number of dots.

24. Option (B) is correct.

Explanation: The number of pieces that make up the figure equals the number of its sides.

25. Option (A) is correct.

Explanation: One can rotate all other figures into one another.

Level-3: EXPERT

1. Option (D) is correct.

Explanation: All four curves on each line segment in figure (D) face the same way. It is therefore an oddity.

2. Option (B) is correct.

Explanation: All other figures, with the exception of figure (2), have a line segment within a square that is parallel to one of the square's sides.

3. Option (D) is correct.

Explanation: The designs slide as follows in the figures that follow:

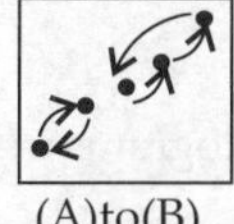
(A)to(B)

(B)to(C)

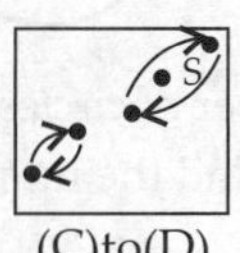

(C)to(D)

(D)to(E)

So, D is the not fit in the series.

4. Option (E) is correct.

Explanation: Following that, the design 'U' reverses 1, 2, 3, and 4 in turn, clockwise, in each of the following figures. So, the odd one out is option (E).

5. Option (E) is correct.

Explanation: The design '↑' rotates 45 degrees and 90 degrees anticlockwise, the design '⚲' rotates 45 degrees, 90 degrees, 135 degrees, and 180 degrees clockwise, the design '⚲' rotates 45 degrees and 90 degrees clockwise, the design T rotates 45 degrees anticlockwise rotates 45 degrees, 90 degrees, and 135 degrees, respectively. Option (E) is the correct answer.

6. Option (E) is correct.

Explanation: One new design is created in the top left and lower right places, respectively, from (1) to (2) and (3) to (4). So, the odd one out is option (E).

7. Option (A) is correct.

Explanation: The element (◆) always comes before the adjacent to white square.

8. Option (D) is correct.

Explanation: The lower-right location of the next figure forms a new design, and all succeeding designs move into the following portion clockwise to merge into one another. So, the odd one out is option (D).

9. Option (D) is correct.

Explanation: Each of the four triangles on a line segment in figure (D) is facing a different direction. It is therefore an oddity.

10. Option (C) is correct.

Explanation: The arcs in image C are facing the opposite way. This makes it unusual.

11. Option (C) is correct.

Explanation: In the gaps between the lines from the other side, the lines on each side of the centre vertical line contact this line.

12. Option (E) is correct.

Explanation: Each of the two components has two line segments that occur along two consecutive sides.

13. Option (D) is correct.

Explanation: At the diagonally opposite corners, there are two identical symbols, and there are also two additional distinct symbols.

14. Option (B) is correct.

Explanation: The amount of components that make up any composite design in a certain order.

15. Option (D) is correct.

Explanation: Mirror representations of the components are found in the diagonally opposite corners.

■ ■ ■

Chapter 18 Analytical Reasoning

LEARNING OBJECTIVES:

- ❖ Counting the number of different types of shapes
- ❖ Different types of questions asked in competitive exams

This section plays an important role in increasing the thinking level of students. In this section, geometrical figures are divided into some parts. A student need to identify the differents parts by using the tagging and hence count the number of shapes so formed.

Example 1: Find the number of triangles in the given figure.

(a) 6 (b) 7 (c) 8 (d) 5

Sol. (b)

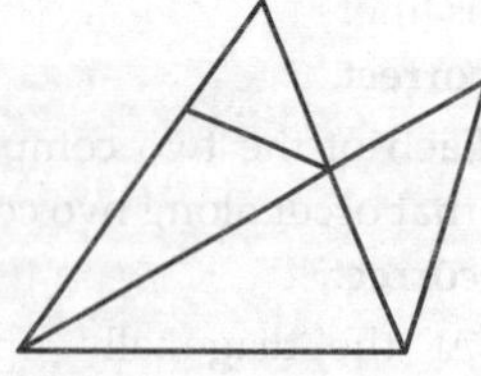

Triangles formed are:
a, b, c, d, ab, cd, abd

∴ Number of triangles = 7

Example 2: Find the number of circles in the given figure.

(a) 6 (b) 5 (c) 4 (d) 7

Sol. (a)

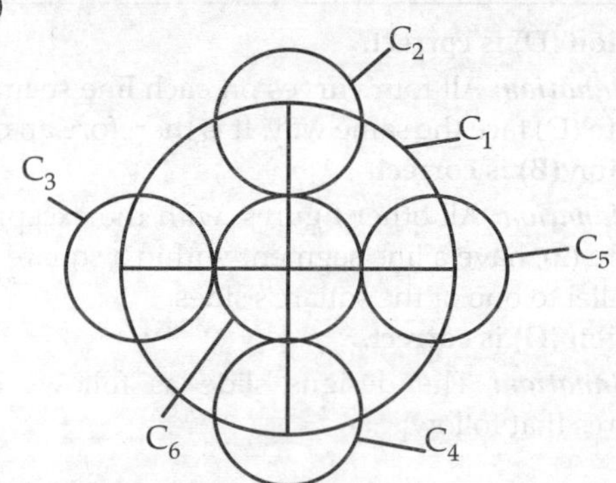

∴ Number of circles = 6

Example 3: Find the number of parallelograms in the given figure.

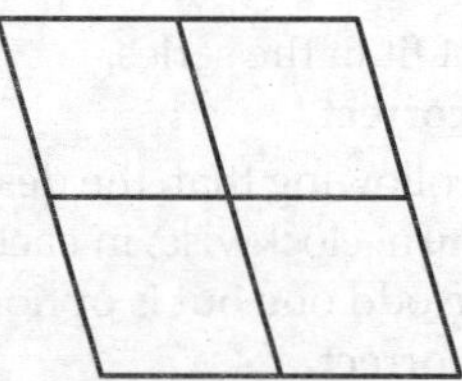

(a) 7 (b) 10 (c) 8 (d) 9

Sol. (d)

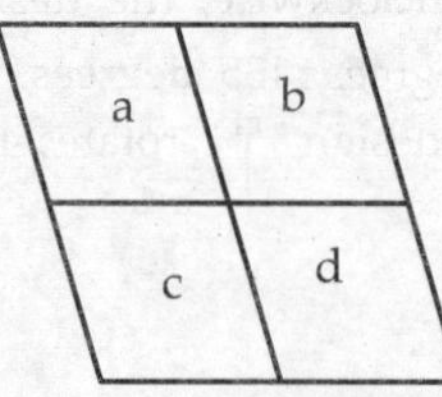

Parallelograms formed are :
a, b, c, d, ab, cd, ac, bd, abcd

∴ Number of parallelograms = 9

Level 1 Beginner

Directions (Qs. 1–10): Find the number of triangles in each of the given figure.

1.

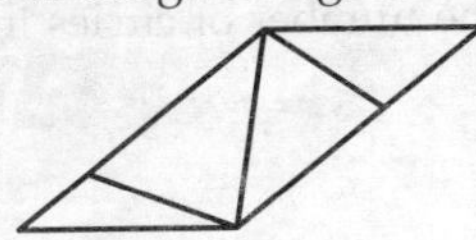

(A) 6 **(B)** 7 **(C)** 5 **(D)** 8

2.

(A) 9 **(B)** 8 **(C)** 10 **(D)** 7

3.

(A) 11 **(B)** 13 **(C)** 14 **(D)** 12

4.

(A) 5 **(B)** 6 **(C)** 7 **(D)** 8

5.

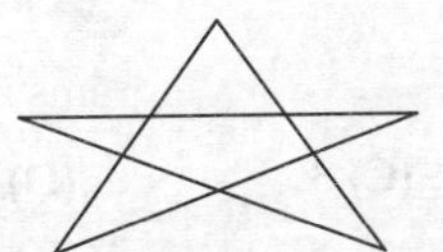

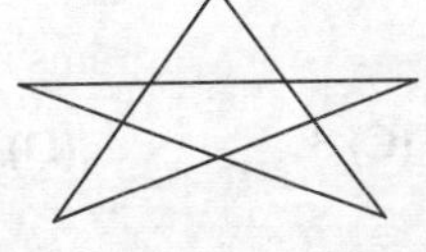

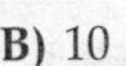

(A) 5 **(B)** 10 **(C)** 7 **(D)** 8

6.

(A) 6 **(B)** 8 **(C)** 7 **(D)** 10

7.

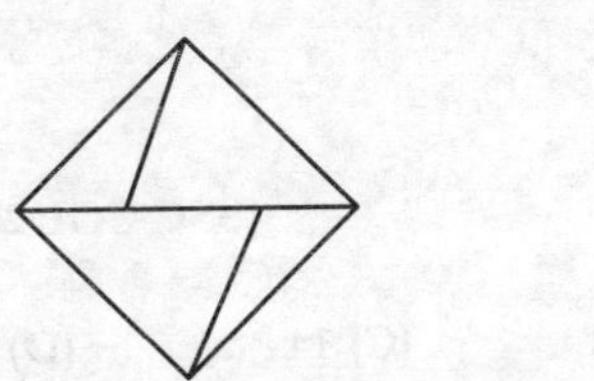

(A) 7 **(B)** 8 **(C)** 6 **(D)** 5

8.

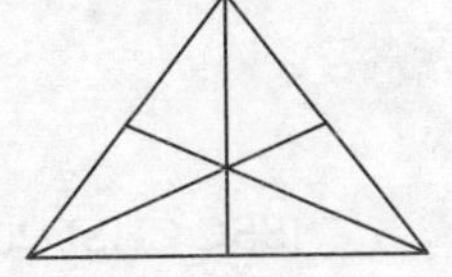

[SSC 2004]

(A) 16 **(B)** 13 **(C)** 9 **(D)** 7

9.

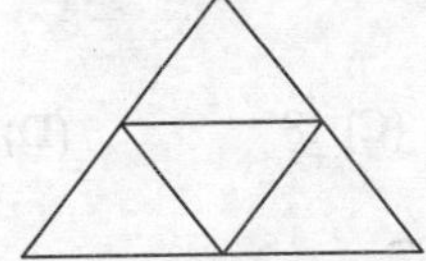

[RRB 2003]

(A) 4 **(B)** 5 **(C)** 6 **(D)** 7

10.

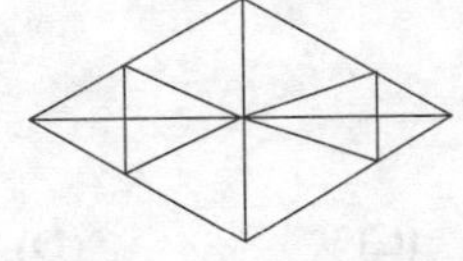

[AAO 2009]

(A) 16 **(B)** 22 **(C)** 28 **(D)** 32

Directions (Qs. 11–18): Find the number of squares in the given figures.

11.

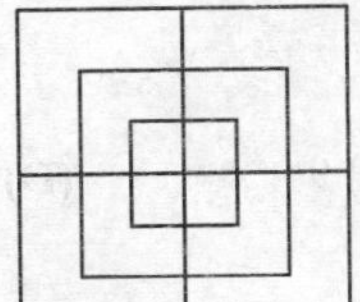

[RRB 2006]

(A) 8 **(B)** 12 **(C)** 15 **(D)** 18

12.

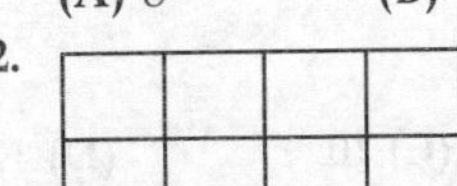

(A) 11 **(B)** 10 **(C)** 12 **(D)** 15

13.

(A) 4 **(B)** 6 **(C)** 5 **(D)** 8

14.

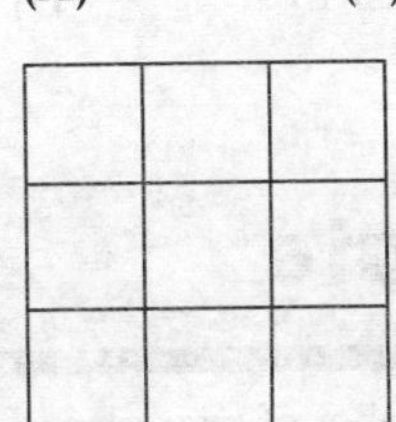

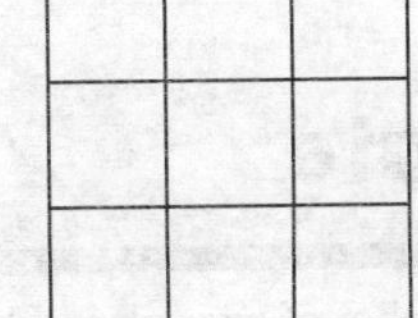

(A) 10 **(B)** 4 **(C)** 8 **(D)** 12

15.

(A) 7 **(B)** 5 **(C)** 8 **(D)** 6

16.

(A) 9 **(B)** 8 **(C)** 10 **(D)** 12

17.

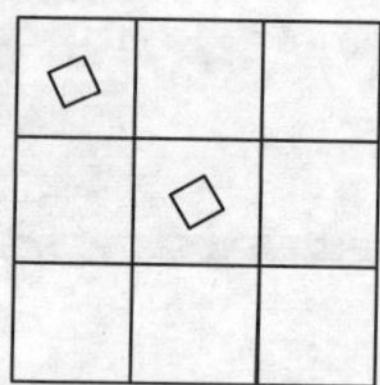

[SSC CHSL 2018]

(A) 12 **(B)** 14 **(C)** 18 **(D)** 16

18.

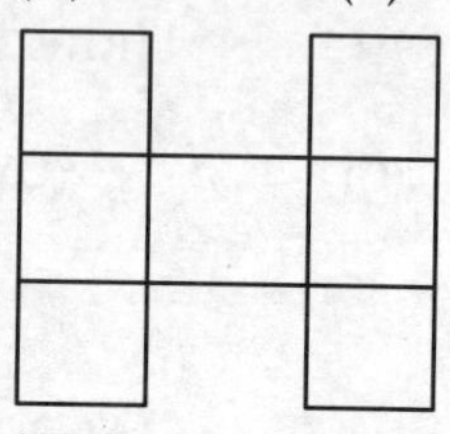

(A) 8 **(B)** 7 **(C)** 9 **(D)** 6

Directions (Qs. 19–22): Find the number of rectangles in the given figures.

19.

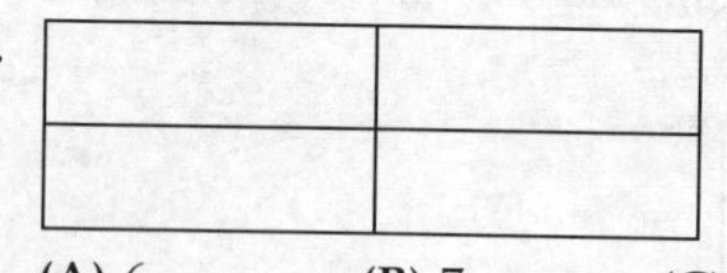

(A) 6 **(B)** 7 **(C)** 9 **(D)** 8

20.

(A) 9 **(B)** 8 **(C)** 10 **(D)** 12

21.

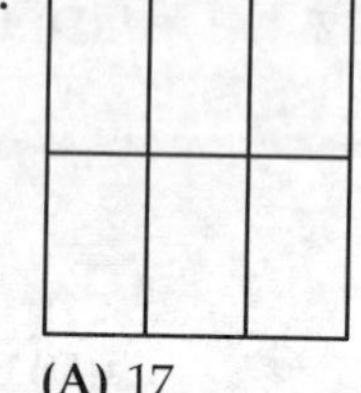

(A) 17 **(B)** 16 **(C)** 15 **(D)** 18

22.

(A) 4 **(B)** 3 **(C)** 2 **(D)** 5

Directions (Qs. 23–25): Find the number of circles in the given figures.

23.

(A) 6 **(B)** 8 **(C)** 9 **(D)** 7

24.

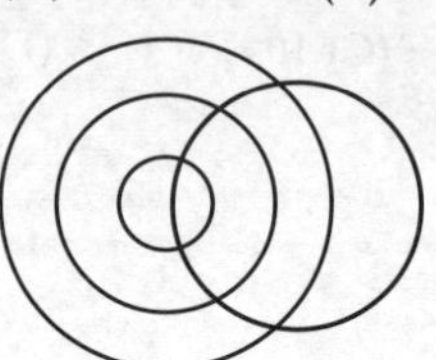

(A) 4 **(B)** 5 **(C)** 3 **(D)** 6

25.

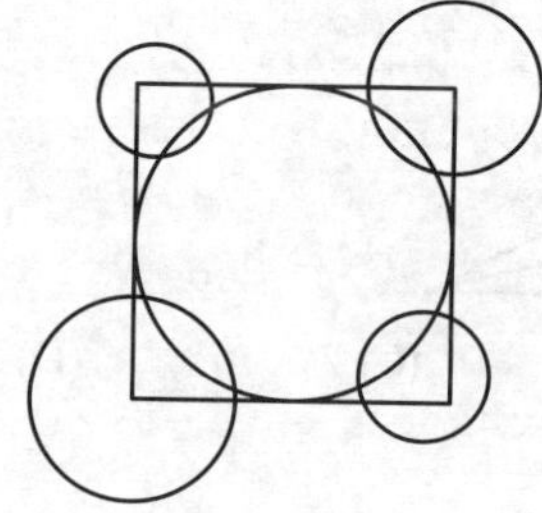

(A) 4 **(B)** 2 **(C)** 3 **(D)** 5

2 Level Intermediate

Directions (Qs. 1–10): Find the number of triangles in the given figures.

1.

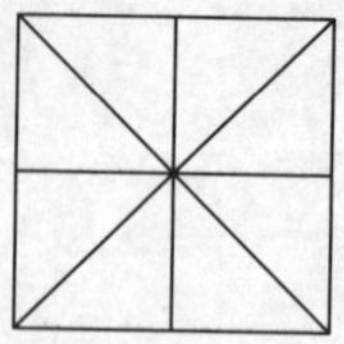

[SSC CGL 2011]

(A) 16 **(B)** 14 **(C)** 8 **(D)** 12

2.

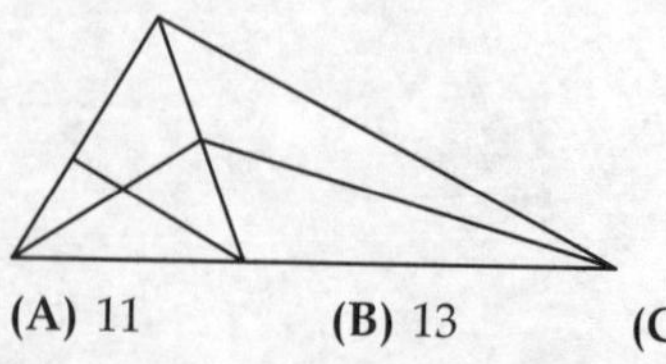

[SSC CGL 2010]

(A) 11 **(B)** 13 **(C)** 9 **(D)** 15

3.

[SSC CGL 2013]

(A) 10 **(B)** 12 **(C)** 14 **(D)** 11

4.

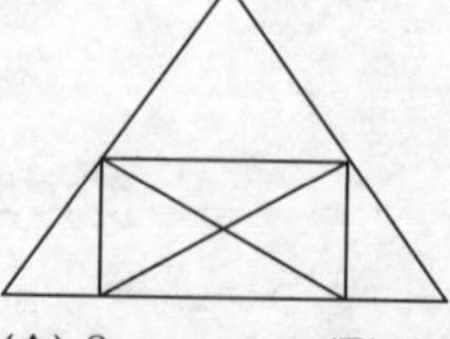

[SSC CHSL 2015]

(A) 8 **(B)** 14 **(C)** 10 **(D)** 12

5.

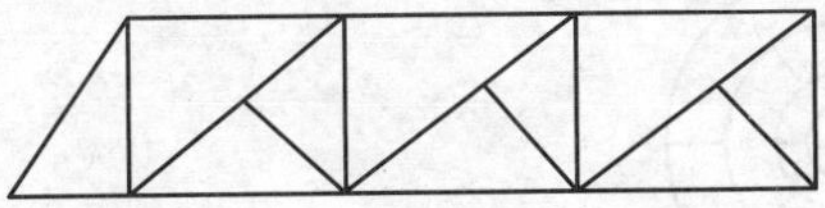

(A) 13 (B) 15 (C) 12 (D) 16

6.

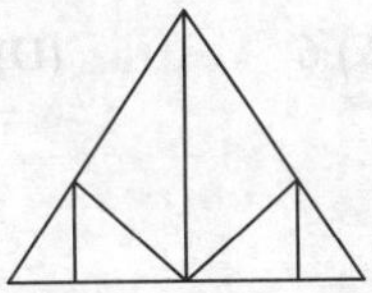

[SSC CGL 2017]

(A) 10 (B) 11 (C) 12 (D) 13

7.

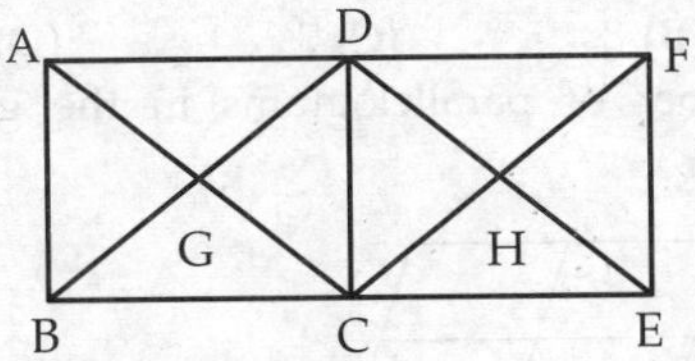

A D F

G H

B C E

[SSC MTS 2017]

(A) 16 (B) 18 (C) 8 (D) 12

8.

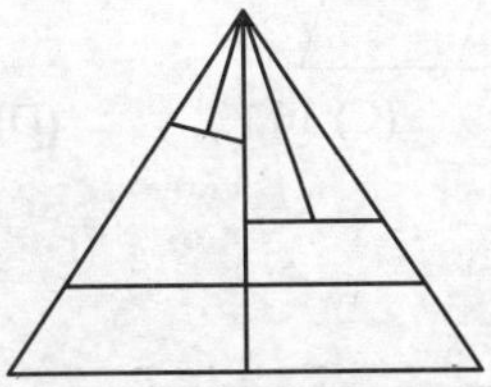

[SSC CGL 2021]

(A) 12 (B) 8 (C) 11 (D) 15

9.

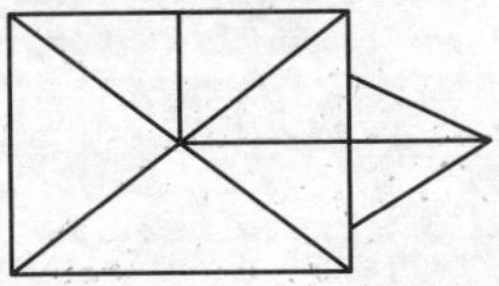

[SSC CHSL 2021]

(A) 16 (B) 15 (C) 17 (D) 14

10.

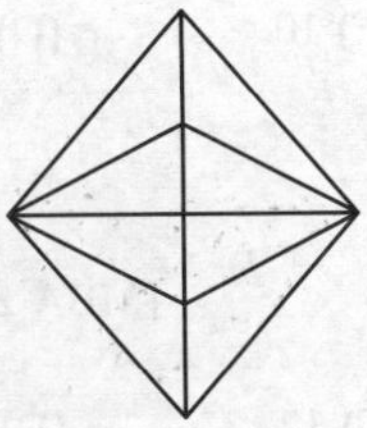

(A) 20 (B) 18 (C) 21 (D) 24

Directions (Qs. 11–15): Find the number of squares in the given figures.

11.

(A) 3 (B) 6 (C) 4 (D) 5

12.

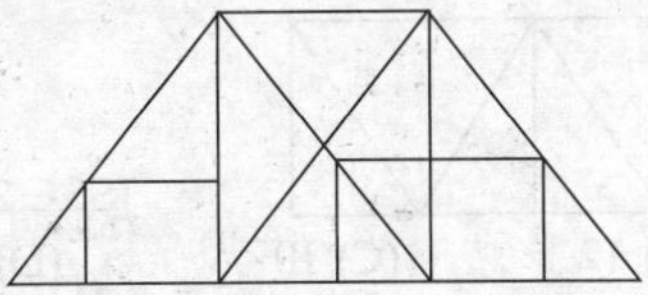

(A) 5 (B) 3 (C) 4 (D) 6

13.

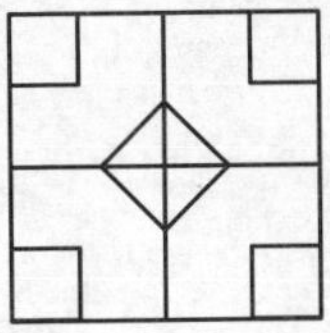

(A) 9 (B) 8 (C) 12 (D) 10

14.

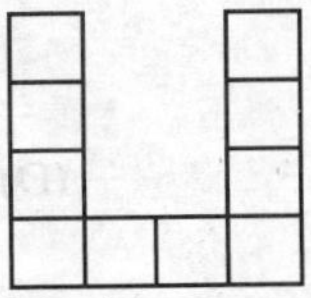

(A) 10 (B) 9 (C) 8 (D) 7

15.

(A) 12 (B) 10 (C) 11 (D) 15

Directions (Qs. 16–20): Find the number of rectangles in the given figures.

16.

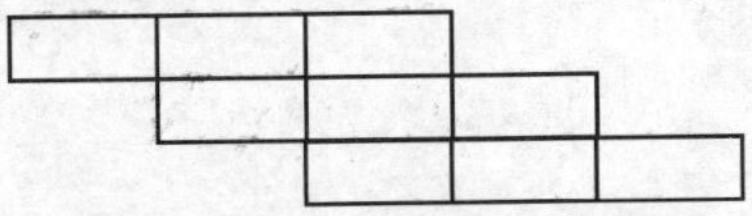

(A) 20 (B) 25 (C) 24 (D) 23

17.

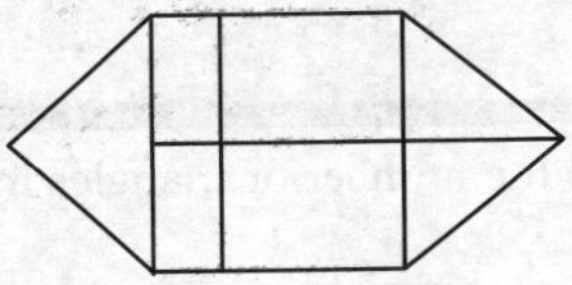

[SSC 2004]

(A) 10 (B) 9 (C) 8 (D) 7

18.

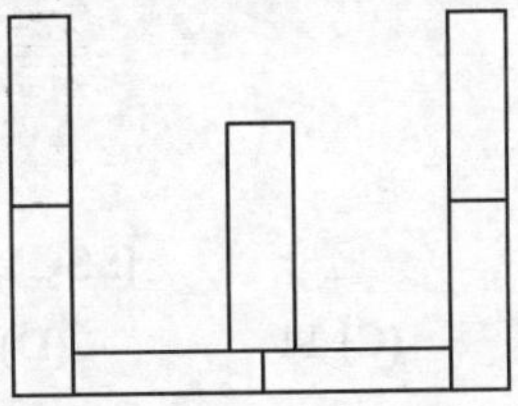

(A) 12 (B) 11 (C) 10 (D) 9

19.

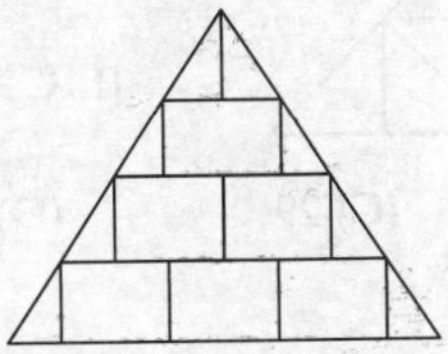

(A) 10 (B) 9 (C) 8 (D) 12

20.

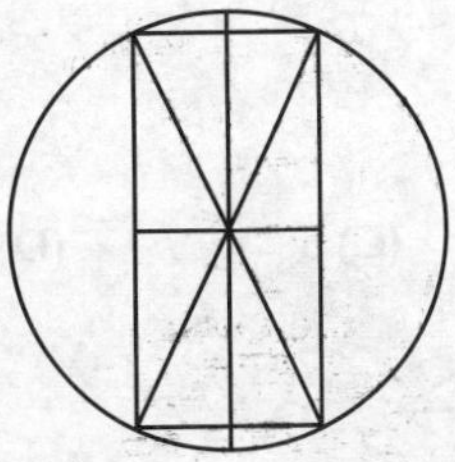

(A) 12 (B) 8 (C) 9 (D) 10

Directions (Qs. 21–24): Find the number of circles in the given figure.

21.

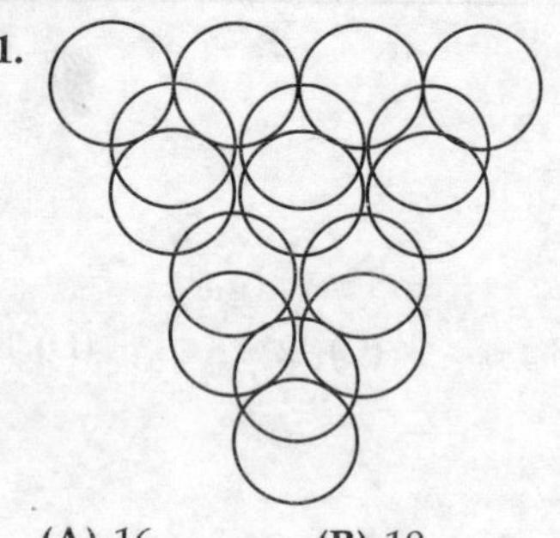

(A) 16 **(B)** 10 **(C)** 15 **(D)** 8

22.

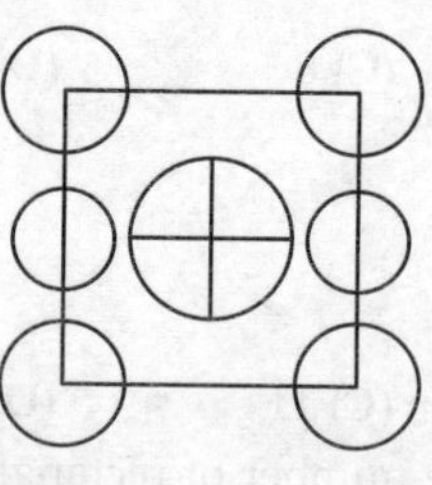

(A) 5 **(B)** 7 **(C)** 8 **(D)** 10

23.

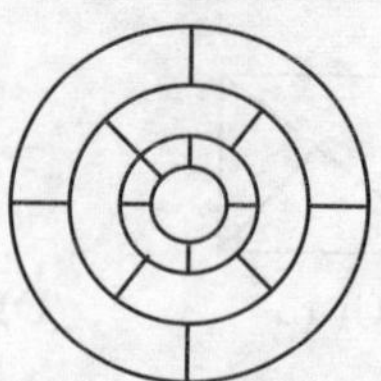

(A) 4 **(B)** 5 **(C)** 6 **(D)** 3

24.

(A) 11 **(B)** 8 **(C)** 7 **(D)** 10

25. Find the number of parallelograms in the given figure.

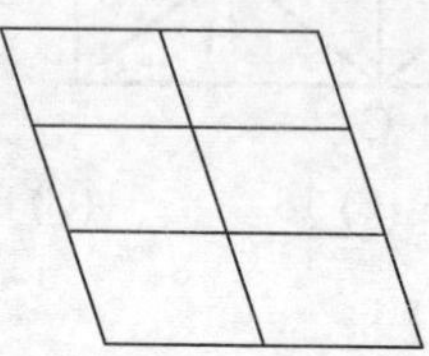

(A) 17 **(B)** 18 **(C)** 16 **(D)** 15

Level 3 Expert

Directions (Qs. 1–8): Find the number of triangles in the given figures.

1.

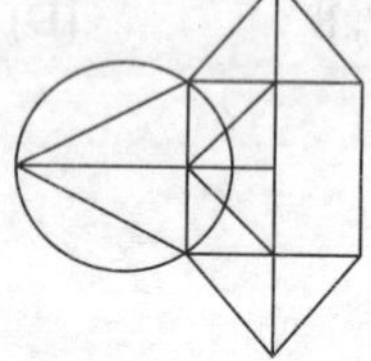

[SSC 2002]

(A) 10 **(B)** 12 **(C)** 14 **(D)** 16

2.

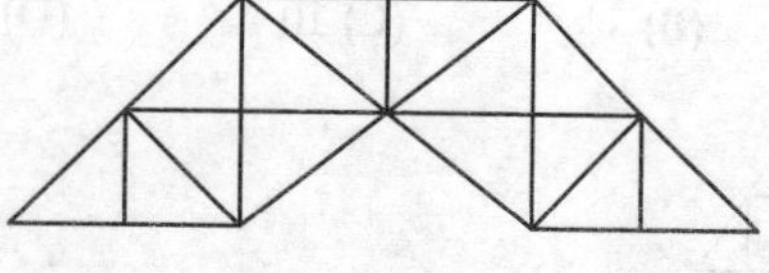

[LIC 2005]

(A) 23 **(B)** 27 **(C)** 29 **(D)** 31

3.

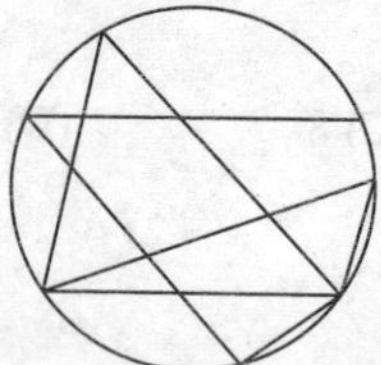

(A) 12 **(B)** 9 **(C)** 8 **(D)** 10

4.

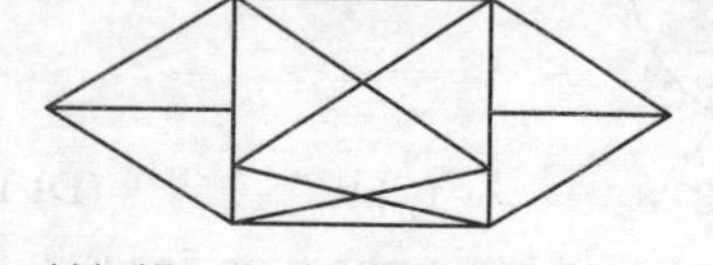

(A) 15 **(B)** 18 **(C)** 16 **(D)** 17

5.

[SSC CHSL 2019]

(A) 14 **(B)** 13 **(C)** 10 **(D)** 12

6.

[MBA 2005]

(A) 8 **(B)** 10 **(C)** 12 **(D)** 14

7.

(A) 23 **(B)** 22
(C) 25 **(D)** None of these

8.

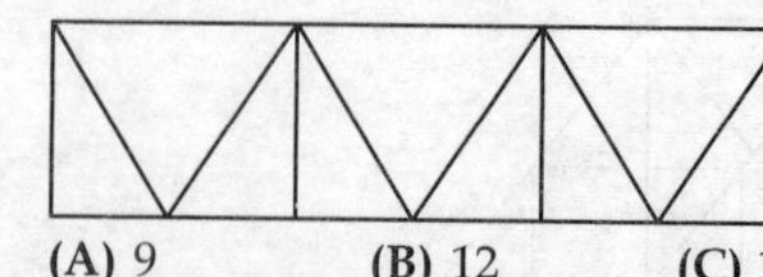

[SSC 2022]

(A) 9 **(B)** 12 **(C)** 10 **(D)** 11

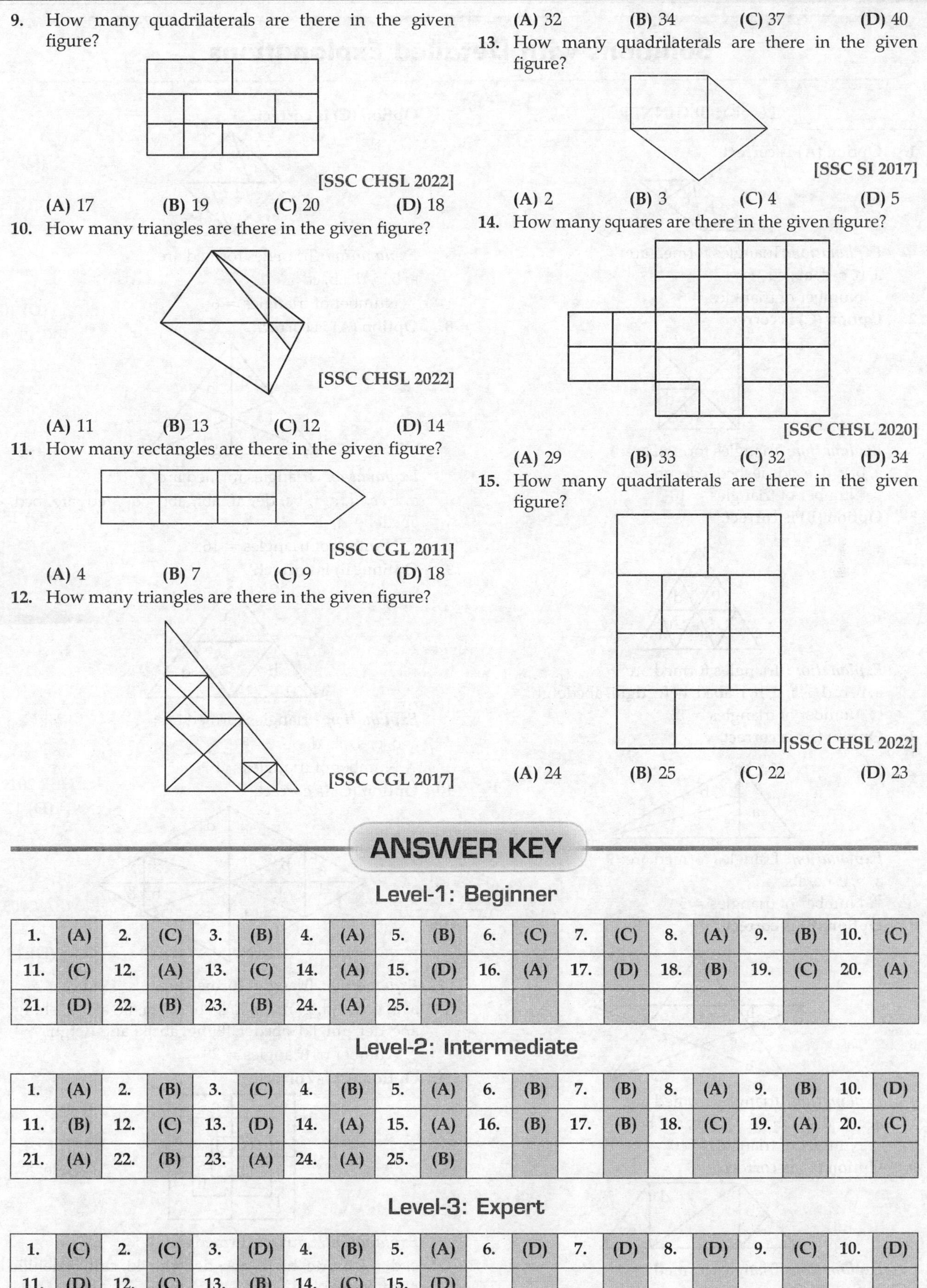

9. How many quadrilaterals are there in the given figure?

[SSC CHSL 2022]

(A) 17 (B) 19 (C) 20 (D) 18

10. How many triangles are there in the given figure?

[SSC CHSL 2022]

(A) 11 (B) 13 (C) 12 (D) 14

11. How many rectangles are there in the given figure?

[SSC CGL 2011]

(A) 4 (B) 7 (C) 9 (D) 18

12. How many triangles are there in the given figure?

[SSC CGL 2017]

(A) 32 (B) 34 (C) 37 (D) 40

13. How many quadrilaterals are there in the given figure?

[SSC SI 2017]

(A) 2 (B) 3 (C) 4 (D) 5

14. How many squares are there in the given figure?

[SSC CHSL 2020]

(A) 29 (B) 33 (C) 32 (D) 34

15. How many quadrilaterals are there in the given figure?

[SSC CHSL 2022]

(A) 24 (B) 25 (C) 22 (D) 23

ANSWER KEY

Level-1: Beginner

1.	(A)	2.	(C)	3.	(B)	4.	(A)	5.	(B)	6.	(C)	7.	(C)	8.	(A)	9.	(B)	10.	(C)
11.	(C)	12.	(A)	13.	(C)	14.	(A)	15.	(D)	16.	(A)	17.	(D)	18.	(B)	19.	(C)	20.	(A)
21.	(D)	22.	(B)	23.	(B)	24.	(A)	25.	(D)										

Level-2: Intermediate

1.	(A)	2.	(B)	3.	(C)	4.	(B)	5.	(A)	6.	(B)	7.	(B)	8.	(A)	9.	(B)	10.	(D)
11.	(B)	12.	(C)	13.	(D)	14.	(A)	15.	(A)	16.	(B)	17.	(B)	18.	(C)	19.	(A)	20.	(C)
21.	(A)	22.	(B)	23.	(A)	24.	(A)	25.	(B)										

Level-3: Expert

1.	(C)	2.	(C)	3.	(D)	4.	(B)	5.	(A)	6.	(D)	7.	(D)	8.	(D)	9.	(C)	10.	(D)
11.	(D)	12.	(C)	13.	(B)	14.	(C)	15.	(D)										

Solutions with Detailed Explanations

Level-1: BEGINNER

1. **Option (A) is correct.**

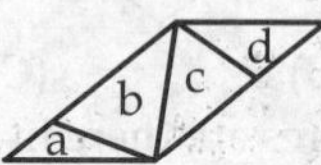

Explanation: Triangles formed are:
a, b, c, d, ab, cd
∴ Number of triangles = 6

2. **Option (C) is correct.**

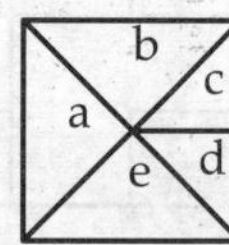

Explanation: Triangles formed are:
a, b, c, d, e, cd, ae, bcd, cde, ab
∴ Number of triangles = 10

3. **Option (B) is correct.**

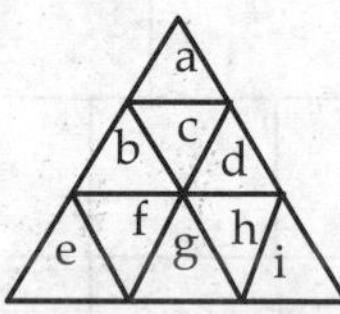

Explanation: Triangles formed are:
a, b, c, d, e, f, g, h, i, abcd, befg, dghi, abcdefghi
∴ Number of triangles = 13

4. **Option (A) is correct.**

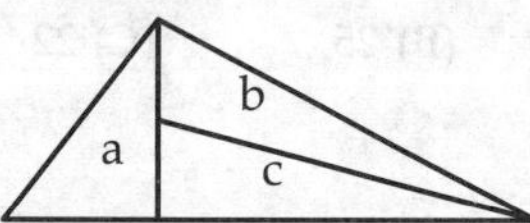

Explanation: Triangles formed are:
a, b, c, bc, abc
∴ Number of triangles = 5

5. **Option (B) is correct.**

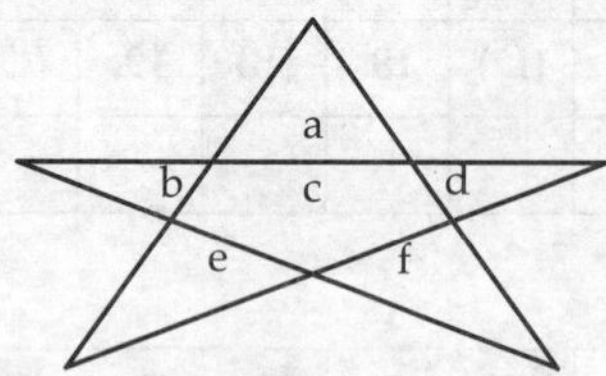

Explanation: Triangles formed are:
a, b, c, d, e, f, bcf, ecd, ace, acf, bcd
∴ Number of triangles = 10

6. **Option (C) is correct.**

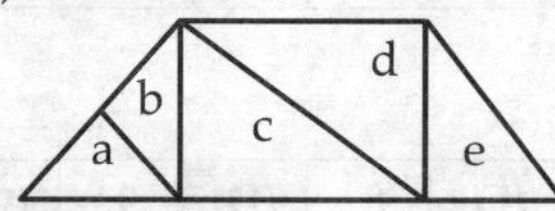

Explanation: Triangles formed are:
a, b, c, d, e, ab, abc
∴ Number of triangles = 7

7. **Option (C) is correct.**

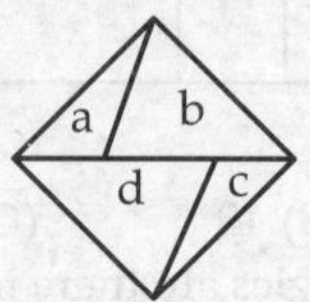

Explanation: Triangles formed are:
a, b, c, d, ab, cd
∴ Number of triangles = 6

8. **Option (A) is correct.**

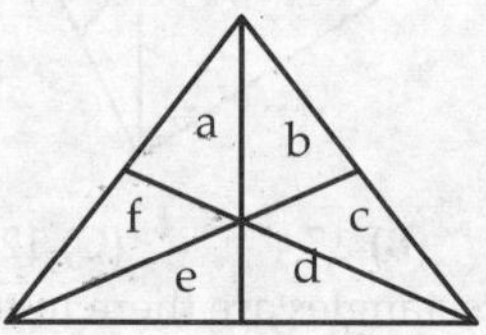

Explanation: Triangles formed are:
a, b, c, d, e, f, bc, de, af, abf, abc, cde, fed, afe, bcd, abcdef
∴ Number of triangles = 16

9. **Option (B) is correct.**

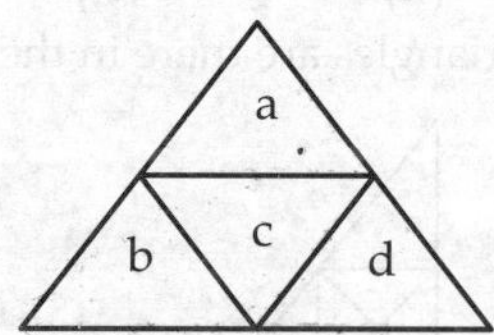

Explanation: Triangles formed are:
a, b, c, d, abcd
∴ Number of triangles = 5

10. **Option (C) is correct.**

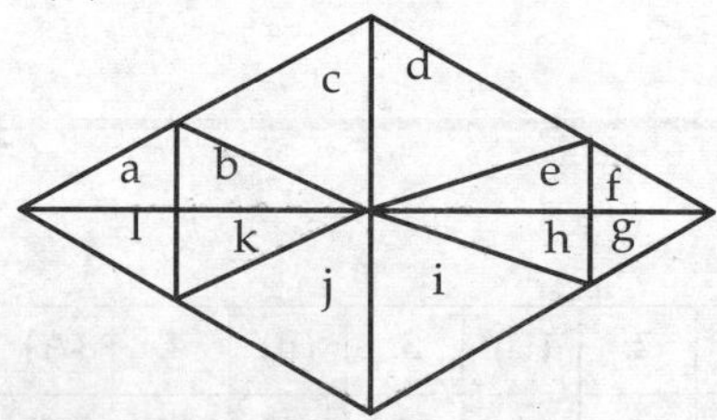

Explanation: Triangles formed are:
a, b, c, d, e, f, g, h, i, j, k, l, ab, ef, gh, lk, al, bk, eh, fg, abc, def, ghi, jkl, abcdef, lkjihg, abclkj and defghi
∴ Number of triangles = 28

11. **Option (C) is correct.**

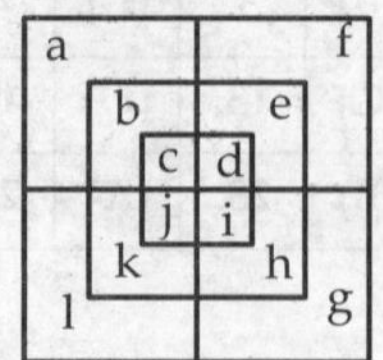

Explanation: Squares formed are:
c, d, i, j, bc, de, hi, jk, abc, def, ghi, jkl, cdji, bcdehijk, abcdefghijkl
∴ Number of squares = 15

12. **Option (A) is correct.**

a	b	c	d
h	g	f	e

Explanation: Squares formed are:
a, b, c, d, e, f, g, h, abgh, bcgf, cdef
∴ Number of squares = 11

13. **Option (C) is correct.**

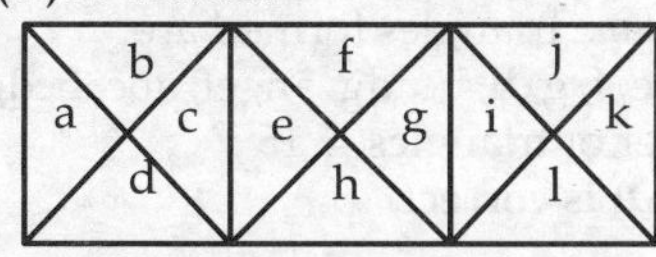

Explanation: Squares formed are:
abcd, efgh, ijkl, ce, gi
∴ Number of squares = 5

14. **Option (A) is correct.**

a b c
f e d
g h

Explanation: Squares formed are:
a, b, c, d, e, f, g, h, abef, bcde
∴ Number of squares = 10

15. **Option (D) is correct.**

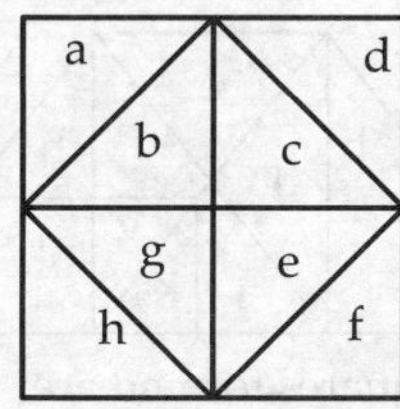

Explanation: Squares formed are:
ab, cd, ef, gh, bceg and abcdefgh
∴ Number of squares = 6

16. **Option (A) is correct.**

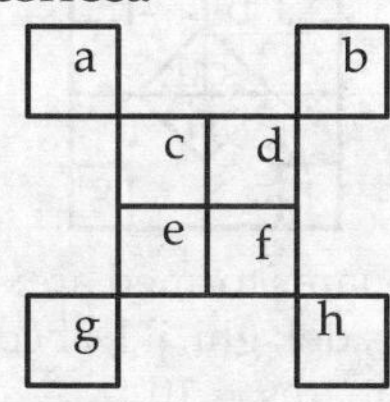

Explanation: Squares formed are:
a, b, c, d, e, f, g, h, cdfe
∴ Number of squares = 9

17. **Option (D) is correct.**

a b c d
e g f h
i j k

Explanation: Squares formed are:
b, f, ab, c, d, h, gf, e, i, j, k, abcegf, cdgfh, egfij, gfhjk, abcdefghijk
∴ Number of squares = 16

18. **Option (B) is correct.**

a e
b d f
c g

Explanation: Squares formed are:
a, b, c, d, e, f and g
∴ Number of squares = 7

19. **Option (C) is correct.**

a	b
c	d

Explanation: Rectangles formed are:
a, b, c, d, ab, cd, ac, bd and abcd
∴ Number of rectangles = 9

20. **Option (A) is correct.**

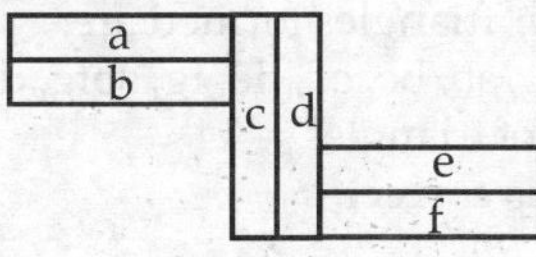

Explanation: Rectangles formed are:
a, b, c, d, e, f, ab, cd and ef
∴ Number of rectangles = 9

21. **Option (D) is correct.**

a b c
f e d

Explanation: Rectangles formed are:
a, b, c, d, e, f, ab, bc, fe, ed, af, be, cd, abc, def, abfe, bced, abcdef
∴ Number of rectangles = 18

22. **Option (B) is correct.**
Explanation:
∴ Number of rectangles = 3

23. **Option (B) is correct.**
Explanation:
∴ Number of circles = 8

24. **Option (A) is correct.**
Explanation:
∴ Number of circles = 4

25. **Option (D) is correct.**
Explanation:
∴ Number of circles = 5

Level-2: INTERMEDIATE

1. **Option (A) is correct.**

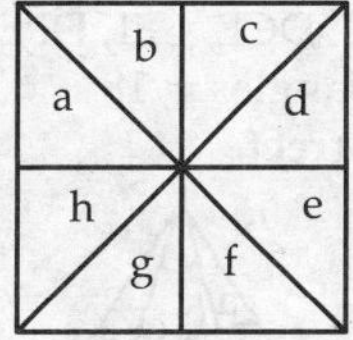

Explanation: Triangles formed are:
a, b, c, d, e, f, g, h, bc, de, gf, ah, abch, bcde, defg, ahgf,
∴ Number of triangles = 16

2. Option (B) is correct.

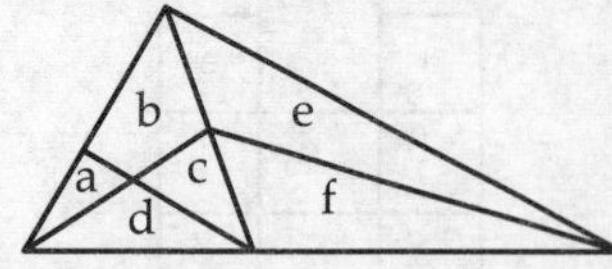

Explanation: Triangles formed are:
a, d, c, e, f, ab, bc, ad, cd, ef, dcf, abcd, abcdef
∴ Number of triangles = 13

3. Option (C) is correct.

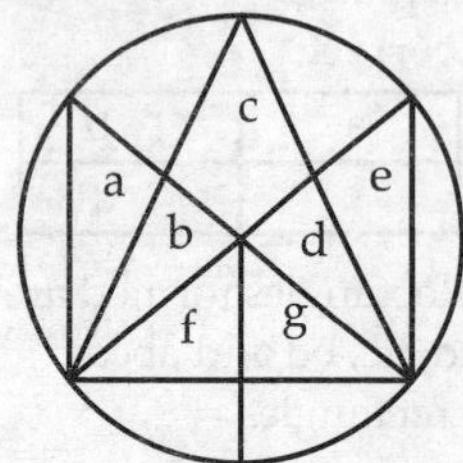

Explanation: Triangles formed are:
a, b, d, e, f, g, ab, bc, cd, de, fg, abfg, defg, bcdgf
∴ Number of triangles = 14

4. Option (B) is correct.

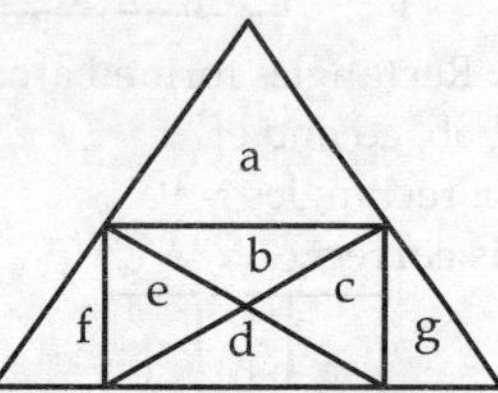

Explanation: Triangles formed are:
a, b, c, d, e, f, g, be, bc, cd, de, fed, dcg, abcdefg
∴ Number of triangles = 14

5. Option (A) is correct.

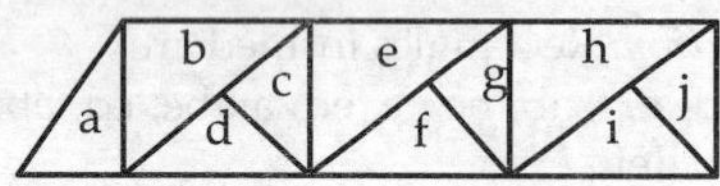

Explanation: Triangles formed are:
a, b, c, d, e, f, g, h, i, j, cd, gf, ji
∴ Number of triangles = 13

6. Option (B) is correct.

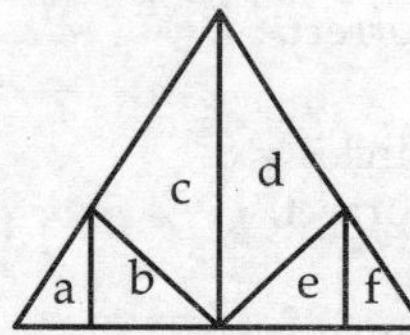

Explanation: Triangles formed are:
a, d, c, d, e, f, ab, ef, abc, def, abcdef
∴ Number of triangles = 11

7. Option (B) is correct.

Explanation: Triangles formed are:
ABG, AGD, GDC, BGC, DHC, FHE, CHE, DHF, ABC, DAB, DBC, ADC, DCE, CEF, DFE, DCF, ACF, DBE
∴ Number of triangles = 18

8. Option (A) is correct.

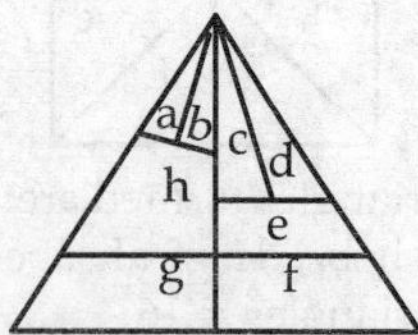

Explanation: Triangles formed are:
a, b, c, d, ab, cd, abh, cde, abhg, cdef, abcdeh, abcdefgh
∴ Number of triangles = 12

9. Option (B) is correct.

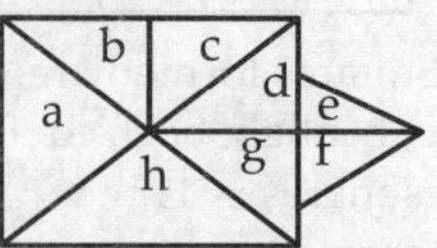

Explanation: Triangles formed are:
a, b, c, d, e, f, g, h, bc, dg, ah, ef, abc, bcdg, dhg
∴ Number of triangles = 15

10. Option (D) is correct.

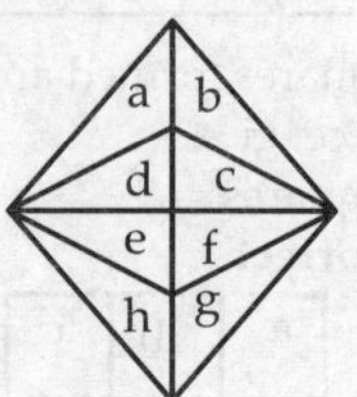

Explanation: Triangles formed are:
a, b, c, d, e, f, g, h, ad, bc, eh, fg, dc, ef, de, cf, ade, deh, bcf, cfg, adeh, bcfg, abcd, efgh
∴ Number of triangles = 24

11. Option (B) is correct.

Explanation:
∴ Number of squares = 6

12. Option (C) is correct.

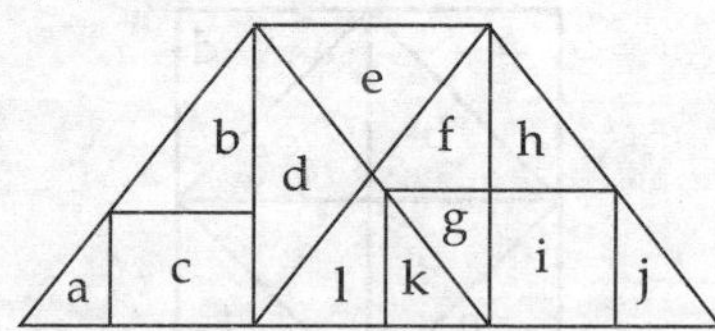

Explanation: Squares formed are:
c, gk, i, defgkl
∴ Number of squares = 4

13. Option (D) is correct.

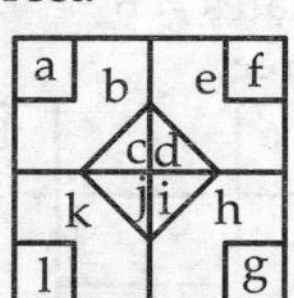

Explanation: Squares formed are:
a, f, g, l, cdij, abc, def, ghi, jkl, abcdefghijkl
∴ Number of squares = 10

14. Option (A) is correct.

a			j
b			i
c			h
d	e	f	g

Explanation: Squares formed are:
a, b, c, d, e, f, g, h, i, j
∴ Number of squares = 10

15. Option (A) is correct.

a	b	c	d
	e	f	
g	h	i	j

Explanation: Squares formed are:
a, b, c, d, e, f, g, h, i, j, bcef, efhi
∴ Number of squares = 12

16. **Option (B) is correct.**

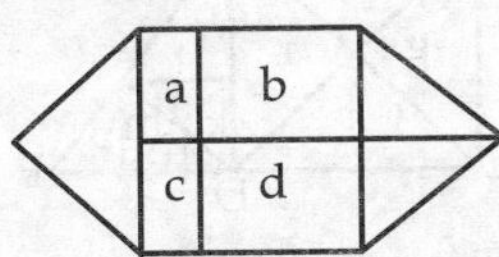

Explanation: Rectangles formed are:
a, b, c, d, e, f, g, h, i, ab, bc, bd, de, ce, ef, eg, gh, fh, hi, ceg, abc, def, ghi, bcde, efgh
∴ Number of rectangles = 25

17. **Option (B) is correct.**

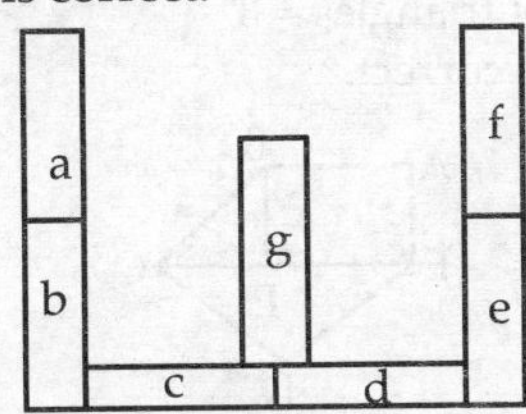

Explanation: Rectangles formed are:
a, b, c, d, ab, bd, cd, ac, abcd
∴ Number of rectangles = 9

18. **Option (C) is correct.**

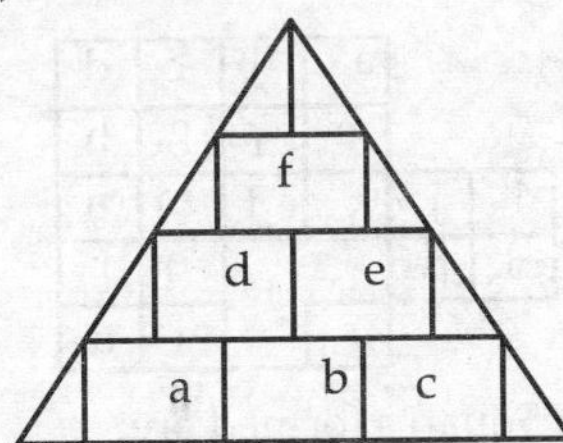

Explanation: Rectangles formed are:
a, b, c, d, e, f, g, ab, cd, ef
∴ Number of rectangles = 10

19. **Option (A) is correct.**

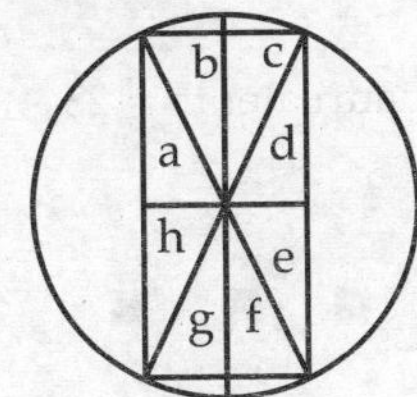

Explanation:
Rectangles formed are:
a, b, c, d, e, f, ab, bc, de, abc
∴ Number of rectangles = 10

20. **Option (C) is correct.**

Explanation: Rectangles formed are:
ab, cd, ef, gh, abcd, efgh, abgh, cdef, abcdefgh
∴ Number of rectangles = 9

21. **Option (A) is correct.**
Explanation:
∴ Number of circles = 16

22. **Option (B) is correct.**
Explanation:
∴ Number of circles = 7

23. **Option (A) is correct.**
Explanation:
∴ Number of circles = 4

24. **Option (A) is correct.**
Explanation:
∴ Number of circles = 11

25. **Option (B) is correct.**

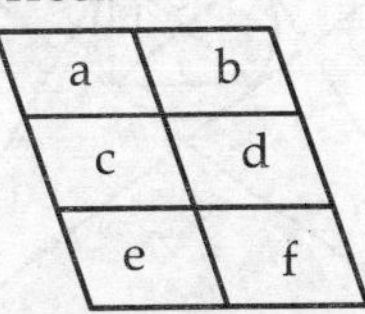

Explanation: Parallelograms formed are:
a, b, c, d, e, f, ab, cd, ef, ac, bd, ce, df, ace, bdf, abcd, cdef, abcdef
∴ Number of parallelograms= 18

Level-3: EXPERT

1. **Option (C) is correct.**

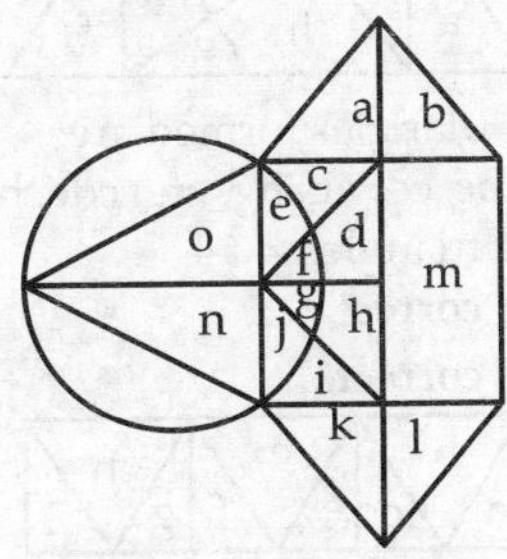

Explanation: Triangles formed are:
a, b, ce, df, gh, ji, k, l, o, n, ab, kl, on, fgdh
∴ Number of triangles = 14

2. **Option (C) is correct.**

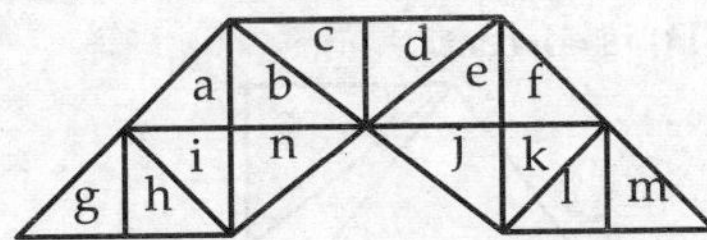

Explanation: Triangles formed are:
a, b, c, d, e, f, g, h, i, j, k, l, m, n, gh, in, bn, ai, ab, cd, ef, jk, ej, fk, lm, aghi, bcnd, cdej, fklm
∴ Number of triangles = 29

3. **Option (D) is correct.**

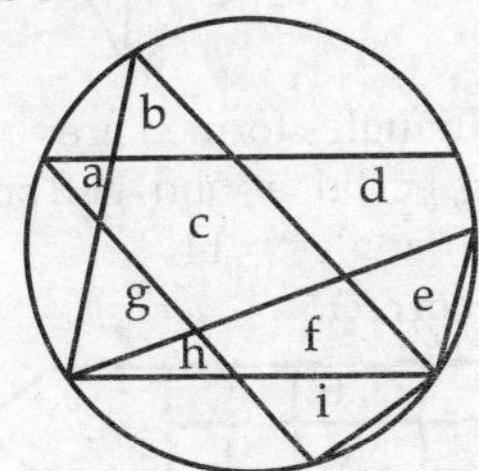

Explanation: Triangles formed are:
a, b, e, g, h, i, gh, hf, hfe, bcg
∴ Number of triangles = 10

4. **Option (B) is correct.**

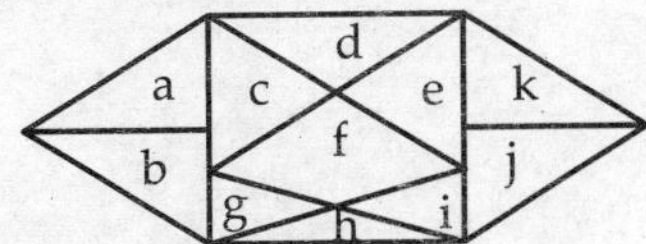

Explanation: Triangles formed are:
a, b, c, d, e, g, h, i, k, j, ab, cd, de, gh, hi, kj, cfg, efi
∴ Number of triangles = 18

5. Option (A) is correct.

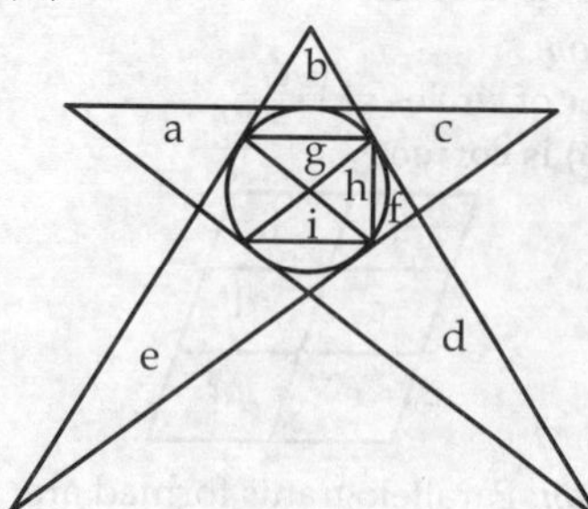

Explanation: Triangles formed are:
a, b, c, d, e, afc, cfe, bfe, afd, g, h, l, gh, hi
∴ Number of triangles = 14

6. Option (D) is correct.

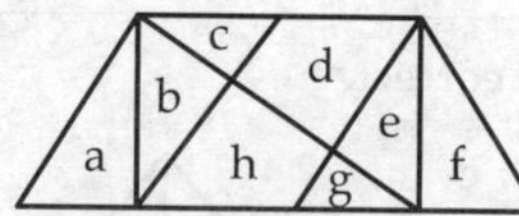

Explanation: Triangles formed are:
a, b, c, e, f, g, bc, cd, eg, hg, efg, cde, bhg, abhg
∴ Number of triangles = 14

7. Option (D) is correct.

8. Option (D) is correct.

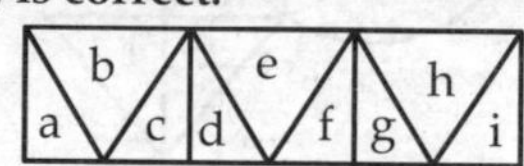

Explanation: Triangles formed are:
a, b, c, d, e, f, g, h, i, cd, fg
∴ Number of triangles = 11

9. Option (C) is correct.

10. Option (D) is correct.

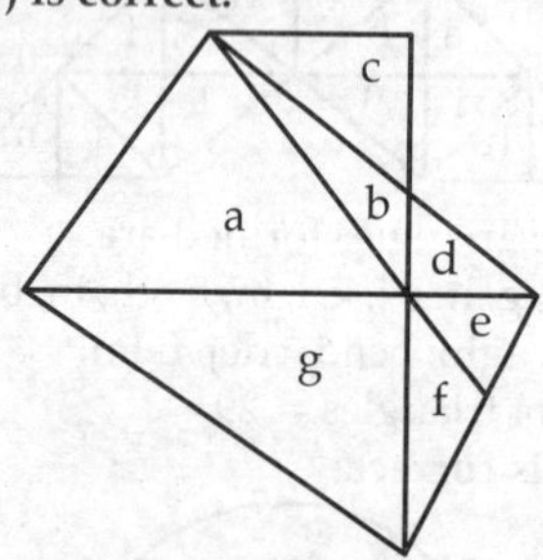

Explanation: Triangles formed are:
a, d, c, d, e, f, g, bc, bd, ef, abd, gef, bde, def
∴ Number of triangles = 14

11. Option (D) is correct.

Explanation: Rectangles formed are:
a, b, c, d, e, f, ab, bc, de, ef, ad, be, cf, abc, def, abde, bcef, abcdef
∴ Number of rectangles= 18

12. Option (C) is correct.

Explanation: Triangles formed are:
a, b, c, d, e, f, g, h, i, j, k, l, m, n, o, p, bc, be, cd, de, gh, hi, gj, ji, kl, lm, mn, kn, abc, def, klo, mnp, ABF, CFE, ACF, FDE, ACE
∴ Number of triangles= 37

13. Option (B) is correct.

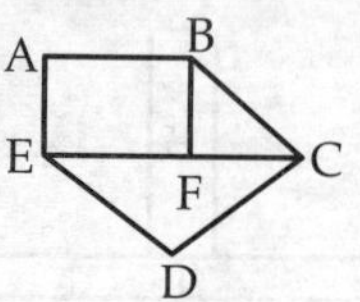

Explanation: Quadrilaterals formed are:
ABEF, ABCE, BCDEF
∴ Number of quadrilaterals= 3

14. Option (C) is correct.

Explanation: Squares formed are:
a, b, c, d, e, f, g, h, i, j, k, l, m, n, o, p, q, r, s, t, u, abef, bcfg, cdgh, efkl, fglm, ghmn, ijop, mnqr, qrtu, abcefgklm, bcdfghlmn
∴ Number of triangles= 32

15. Option (D) is correct.

Explanation:
∴ Number of quadrilaterals= 23

■ ■ ■

Chapter 19

Mirror and Water Images

LEARNING OBJECTIVES:

- ❖ Identifying the mirror image of given figure/combination
- ❖ Identifying the water image of given figure/combination
- ❖ Different types of questions asked in competitive exams

Non-verbal reasoning frequently employs water and mirror images as concepts to assess an individual's capacity to mentally manipulate and identify patterns. Now, let's analyse each concept in detail.

MIRROR IMAGES

➢ Mirror images involve the reflection of a shape or pattern as if it were seen in a mirror. These questions test your ability to visualise the mirror reflection of a given figure.

Keep the following points in mind when dealing with mirror image problems:

The mirror image will appear exactly opposite the original image, as if it were reflected along a vertical axis.

The mirror image has the left and right directions reversed.

Straight lines will remain straight in the mirror image.

You can find the correct mirror image by mentally flipping the figure horizontally and visualising its reflection in the mirror.

In both water and mirror images, it is critical to carefully examine the given figures and understand how they will appear when transformed or reflected. Practice and familiarisation with various patterns will improve your ability to solve these types of non-verbal reasoning problems effectively.

Letters	Mirror Images	Letters	Mirror Images	Letters	Mirror Images
A	A	J	Ⴑ	S	Ƨ
B	ᙠ	K	ꓘ	T	T
C	Ɔ	L	⅃	U	U
D	ᗡ	M	M	V	V
E	Ǝ	N	И	W	W
F	ꟻ	O	O	X	X
G	Ә	P	ꟼ	Y	Y
H	H	Q	Ϙ	Z	Ƹ
I	I	R	Я		

Mirror Images of Numbers	
1	Ɩ
2	ᘔ
3	Ɛ
4	ᔨ
5	ᘕ
6	∂
7	ᒣ
8	8
9	ϱ

Example 1: Find the correct mirror image of the given word : GLOBE

(A) ƎᗺO⅃Ә (B) ƎᗺOLӘ (C) ƎBO⅃Ә (D) ƎᗺOΓӘ

Sol. (A) GLOBE | ƎᗺO⅃Ә

Example 2: Find the correct mirror image of the given figure.

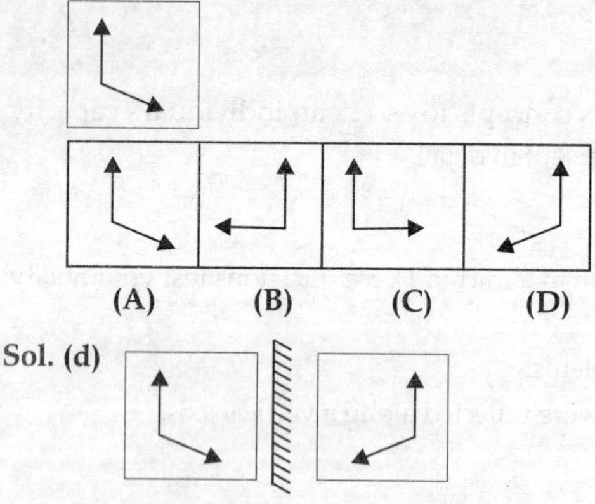

WATER IMAGES

➢ Water images are the reflection or transformation of a specific shape or pattern, simulating its appearance when viewed through the surface of water. These questions present the original figure and ask you to imagine it reflected or distorted as seen through water. To effectively solve water image problems, it is critical to follow the following guidelines:
The image will be inverted, with the top becoming the bottom and vice versa.
Horizontal symmetry is maintained, which means that the left side of the original figure corresponds to the left side of the water image, and vice-versa.
Slanted or diagonal lines will also appear slanted or diagonal in the water image.
Understanding these rules and mentally flipping or inverting the given figure will allow you to determine the correct water image.

Water Images of Alphabets																									
A	B	C	D	E	F	G	H	I	J	K	L	M	N	O	P	Q	R	S	T	U	V	W	X	Y	Z
∀	B	C	D	E	Ⅎ	⅁	H	I	ſ	K	Γ	W	И	O	b	Ό	ᴚ	Ƨ	⊥	∩	Λ	M	X	⅄	Z

Water Images of Numbers								
1	2	3	4	5	6	7	8	9
I	ᘔ	3	ᔭ	ᘕ	ϱ	ㄥ	8	∂

Directions: In the following question given a combination of alphabets followed by four alternatives.Choose the alternatives which is closely resembles the water image of the given combination.

Example 1: REASONING

(A) ꓘEVSOИIИC (B) ꓘƎVSONINC (C) ꓘƎVSONING (D) ЯEASONING

Sol. (A) REASONING

....

ꓘEVSOИIИC

Example 2:

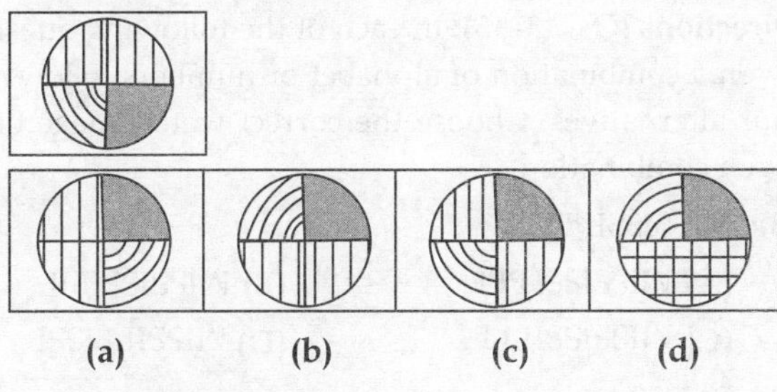

(a) (b) (c) (d)

Sol. (b)

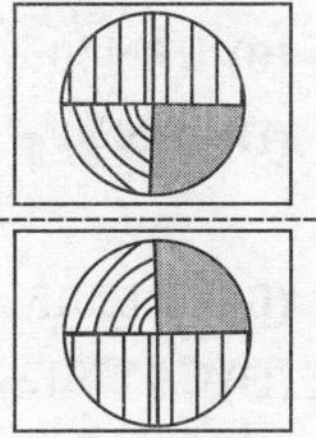

1 Level Beginner

1. If a mirror is placed on the line MN, then which of the answer figures is the right image of the given problem figure?

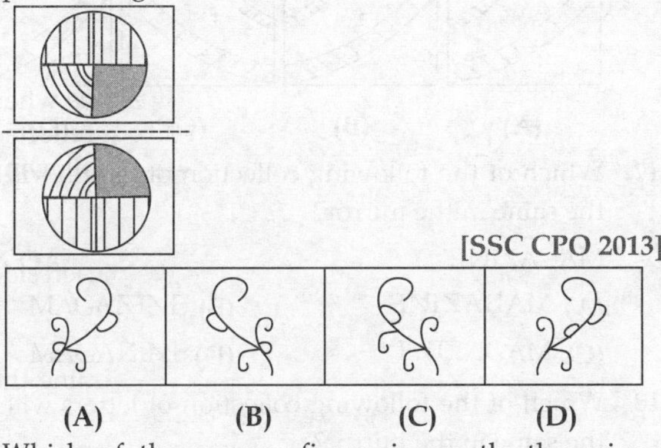

[SSC CPO 2013]

(A) (B) (C) (D)

2. Which of the answer figure is exactly the mirror image of the given figure, when the mirror is held on the line MN?

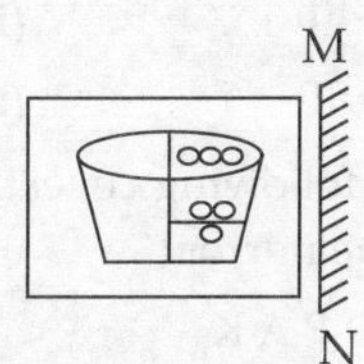

[SSC FCI 2012]

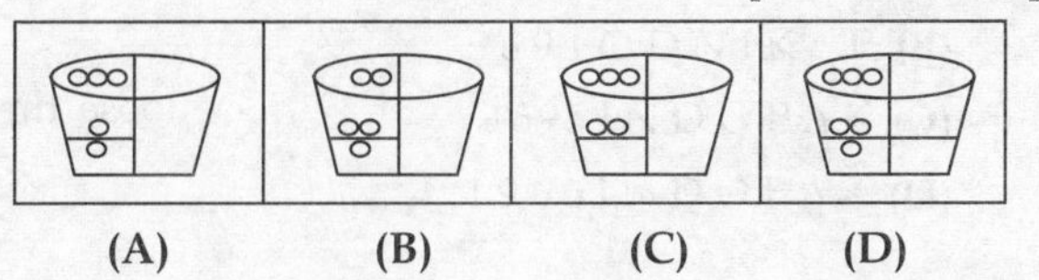

(A) (B) (C) (D)

3. If a mirror is placed on the line MN, then which of the answer figure is the right image of the given figure?

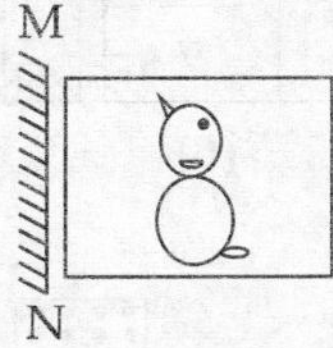

[SSC Multitasking 2013]

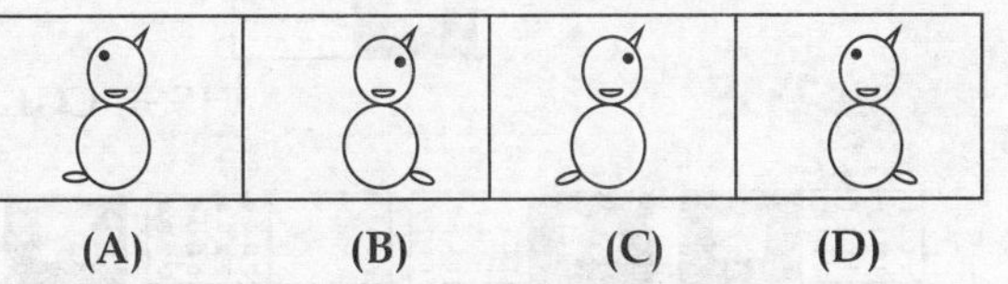

(A) (B) (C) (D)

4. If a mirror is placed on the line XY, then which of the answer figure is the right image of the given figure?

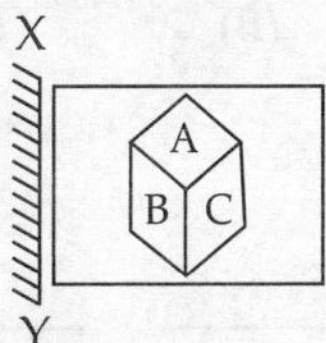

[SSC CGL 2013]

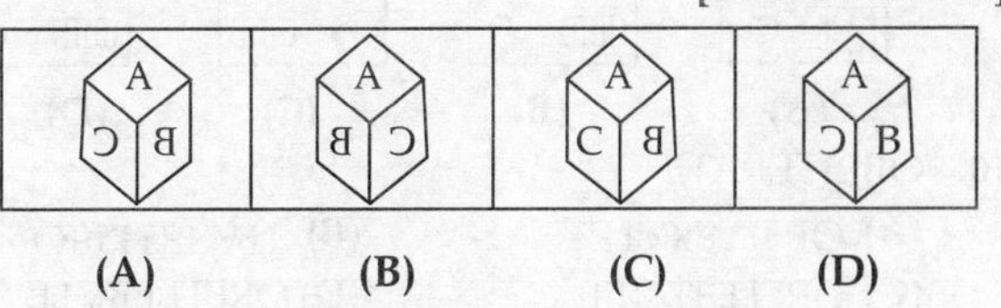

(A) (B) (C) (D)

5. If a mirror is placed on the line AB, then which of the answer figures is the right image of the given figure?

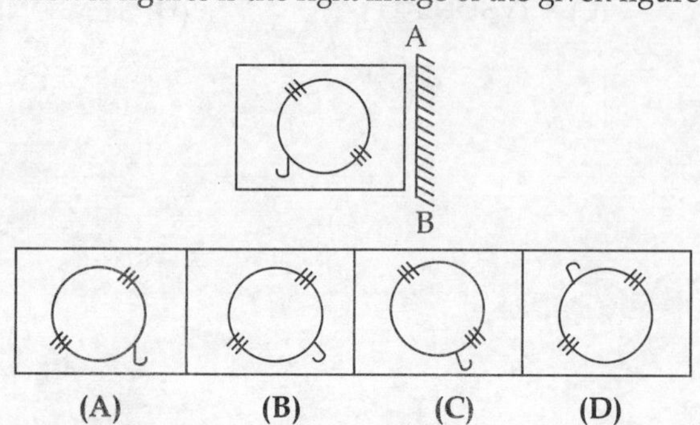

Directions: From question 6-10 related to water image. Select the answer figure of given question.

6.

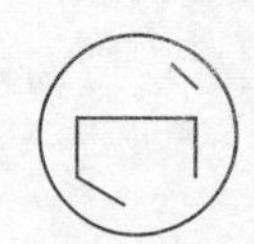

[RRB 2005]

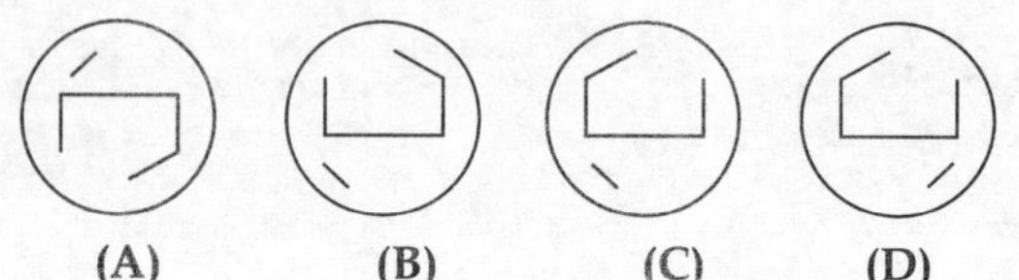

7.

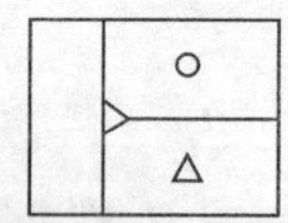

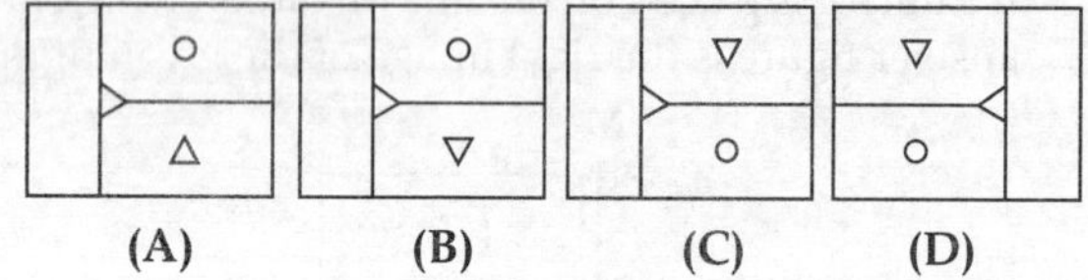

8.

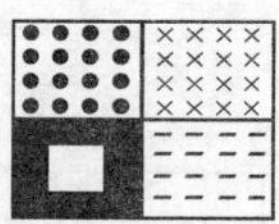

[SSC CGL 2013]

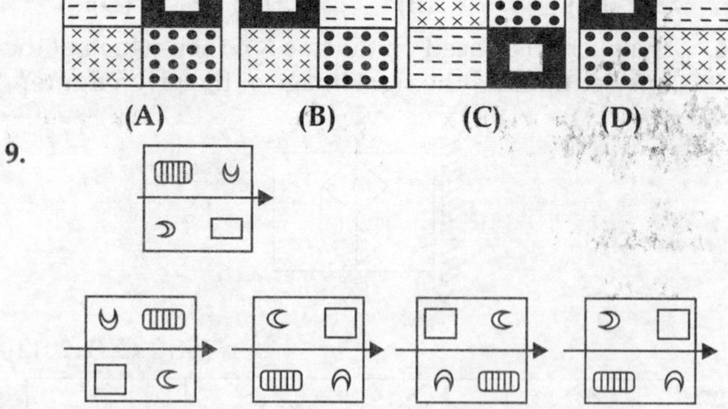

10. OBLITERATE

(A) OBLITERATE (B) ETARETILBO

(C) OBLITETARE (D) OBLITERATE

11. MUNDANE

(A) MUИEИAD (B) MUИDAИE

(C) MUИDAИE (D) ƎИADИUM

12. D6Z7F4

(A) D6Z7F4 (B) D6CZ7F4

(C) D6Z7F4 (D) D6ZF47

Directions (Qs. 13–15): In each of the following questions given a combination of alphabet or numbers followed by four alternatives. Choose the correct water image of the given combination.

13. MISSISSIPPI

(A) MISSISSIPPI (B) MISSISSIPP

(C) MISSISSIPPI (D) MISSIPPISSI

14. PAN20

(A) PAИ20 (B) PAN20

(C) PAN 20 (D) PAN20

15. CAT2015

(A) CAT2015 (B) CAT2015

(C) CAT2015 (D) CAT2015

16. Choose the alternatives which is closely resembles the water image of the given combination.

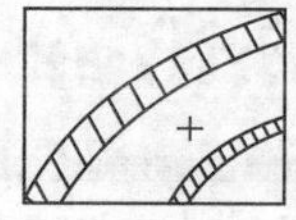

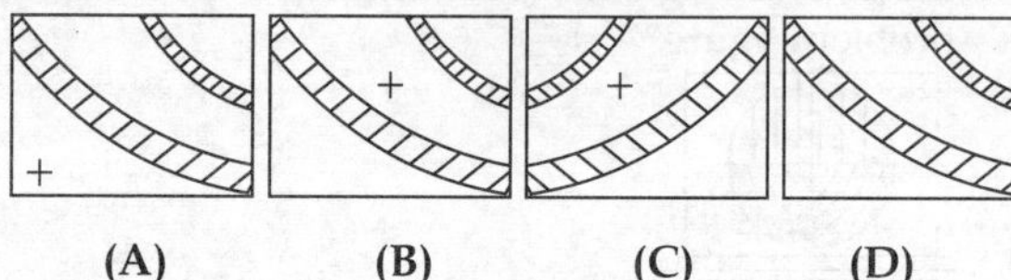

17. Which of the following collection of letters will look the same in the mirror?

MAGAZINE [AAO 2005]

(A) MAGAZIИE (B) ƎИIZAGAM

(C) MAGAZIИƎ (D) ƎИIZAGAM

18. Which of the following collection of letters will look the same in the mirror?

BR4AQ16HI [AAO 2005]

(A) IH61QA4RB (B) IH61QA4RB

(C) IH61QA4RB (D) IH91QA4RB

19. Which of the following collection of letters will look the same in the mirror?

1965INDOPAK [AAO 2005]

(A) KAPODNI5691

(B) 5691DNIKAP

(C) KAPODNI5691

(D) KAPODNI5691

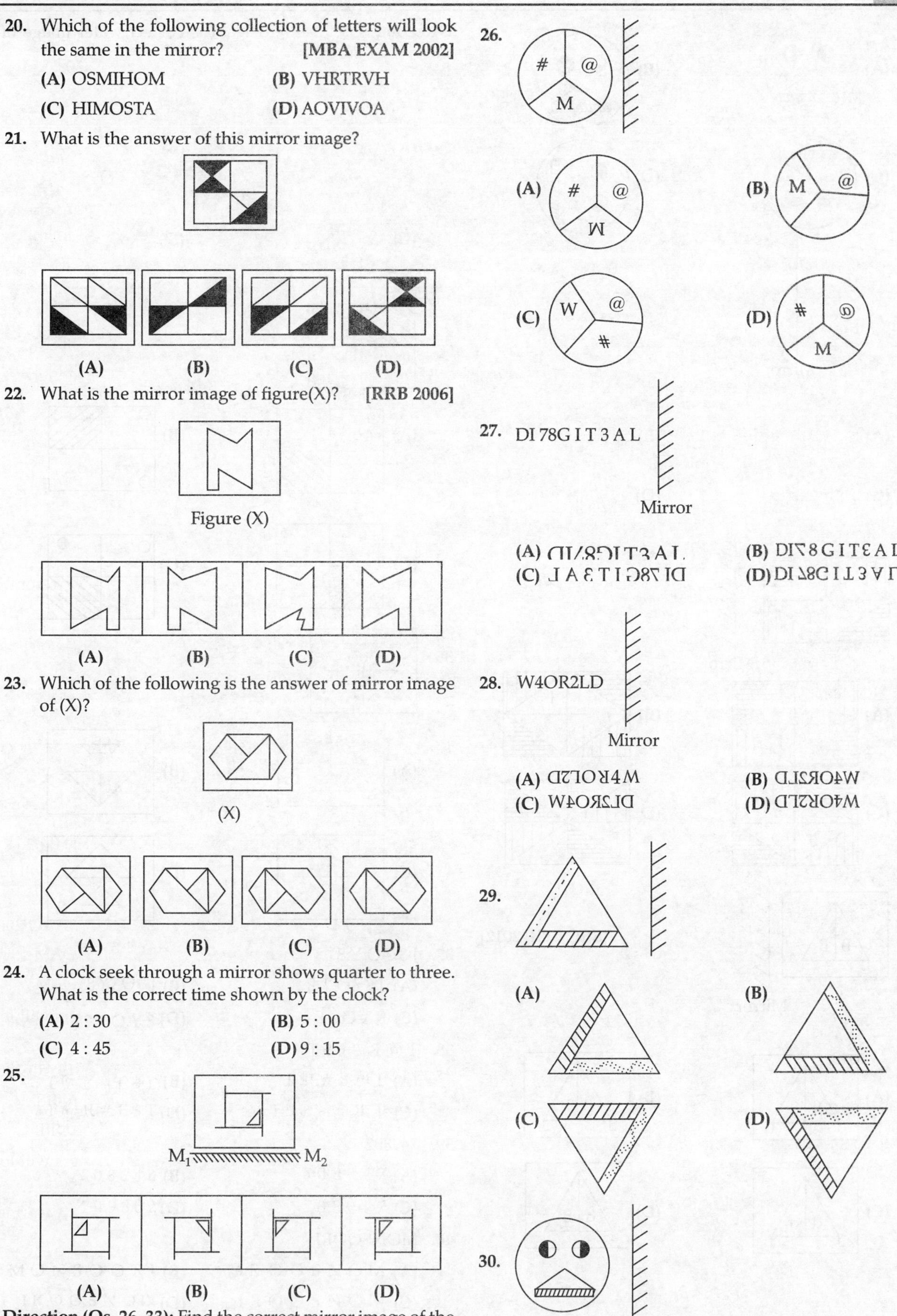

20. Which of the following collection of letters will look the same in the mirror? **[MBA EXAM 2002]**

(A) OSMIHOM **(B)** VHRTRVH

(C) HIMOSTA **(D)** AOVIVOA

21. What is the answer of this mirror image?

(A) **(B)** **(C)** **(D)**

22. What is the mirror image of figure(X)? **[RRB 2006]**

Figure (X)

(A) **(B)** **(C)** **(D)**

23. Which of the following is the answer of mirror image of (X)?

(X)

(A) **(B)** **(C)** **(D)**

24. A clock seek through a mirror shows quarter to three. What is the correct time shown by the clock?

(A) 2 : 30 **(B)** 5 : 00

(C) 4 : 45 **(D)** 9 : 15

25.

M_1 M_2

(A) **(B)** **(C)** **(D)**

Direction (Qs. 26–33): Find the correct mirror image of the given figures.

26.

(A) **(B)** **(C)** **(D)**

27. DI 78G I T 3 A L

Mirror

(A) **(B)** **(C)** **(D)**

28. W4OR2LD

Mirror

(A) **(B)** **(C)** **(D)**

29.

(A) **(B)** **(C)** **(D)**

30.

Mirror

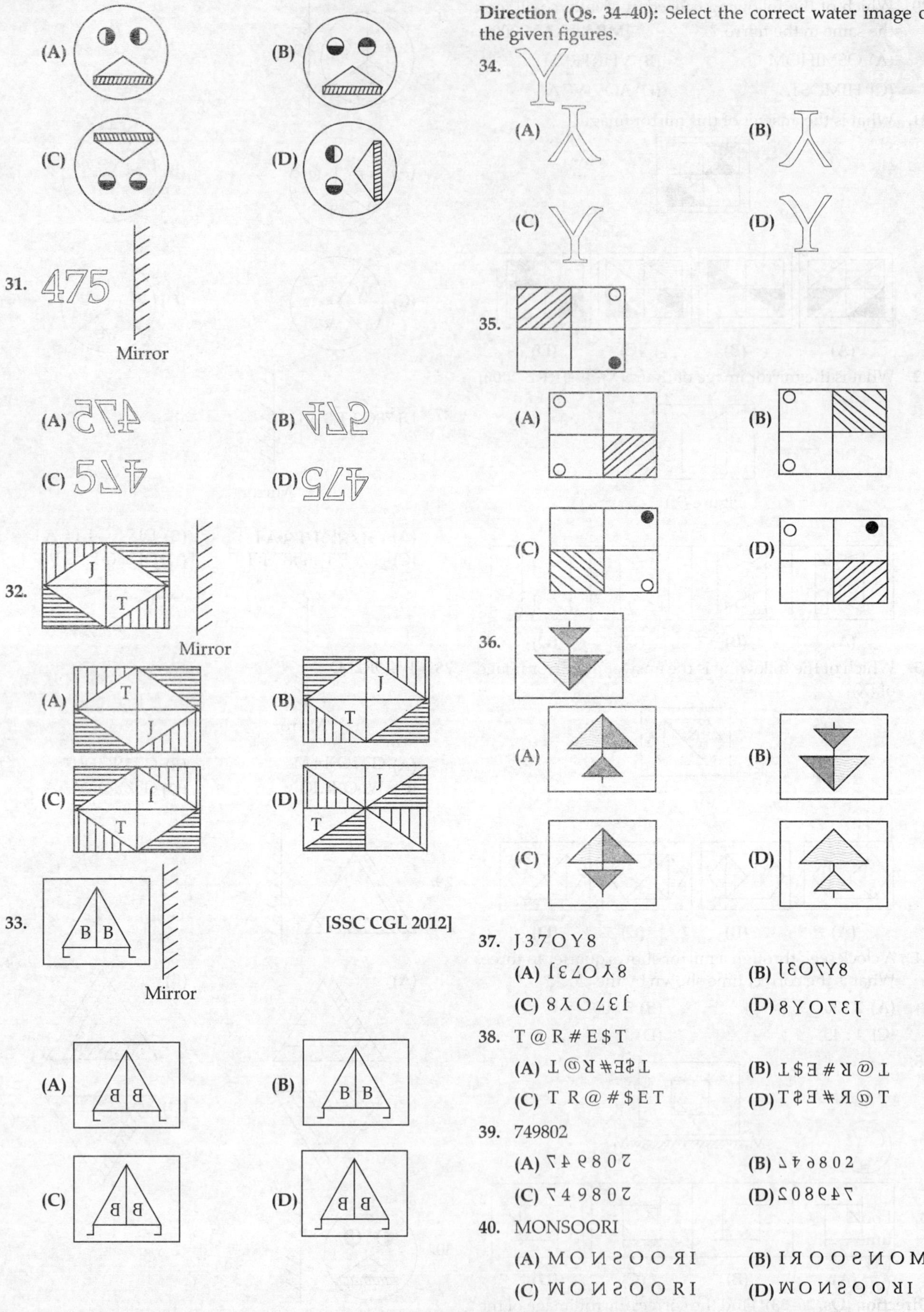
(A)
(B)
(C)
(D)
31. 475
Mirror
(A)
(B)
(C)
(D)
32.
J
T
Mirror
(A)
(B)
(C)
(D)
33.
B B
Mirror
[SSC CGL 2012]
(A)
(B)
(C)
(D)
Direction (Qs. 34–40): Select the correct water image of the given figures.
34.
(A)
(B)
(C)
(D)
35.
(A)
(B)
(C)
(D)
36.
(A)
(B)
(C)
(D)
37. J37OY8
38. T@R#E$T
39. 749802
40. MONSOORI

2 Level Intermediate

Directions: In each of the following question, choose the correct water image of the figure (X) from amongst the four alternatives given along with it?

1. 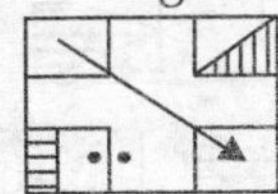

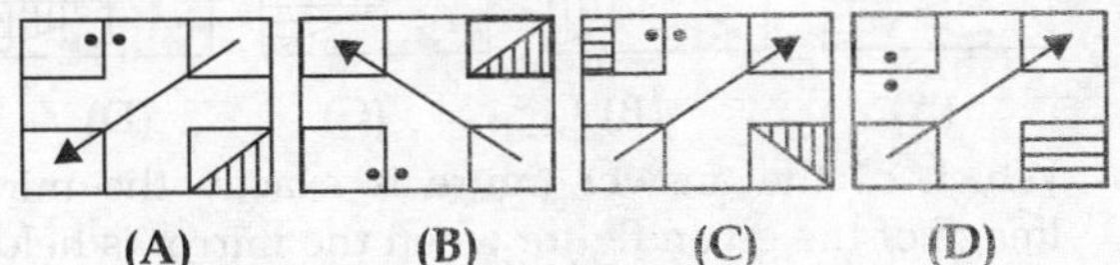

(A) (B) (C) (D)

2. 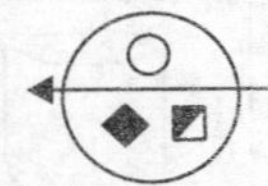

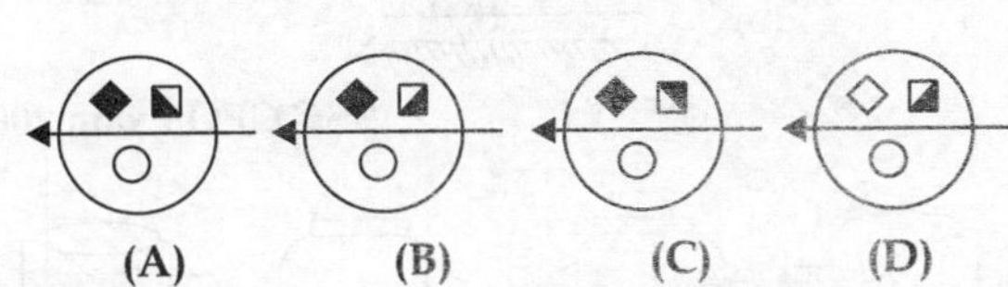

(A) (B) (C) (D)

3. 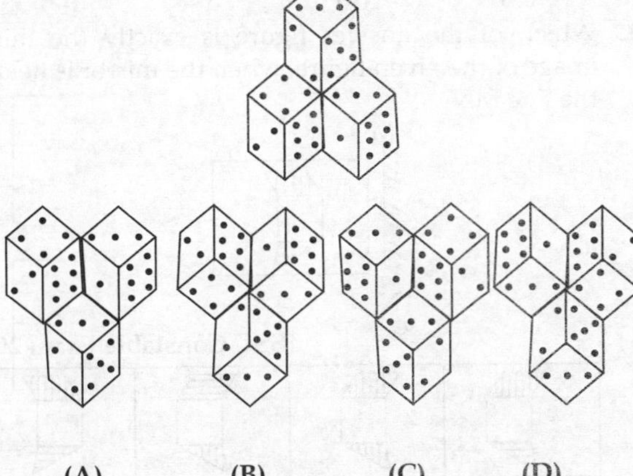

(A) (B) (C) (D)

4. 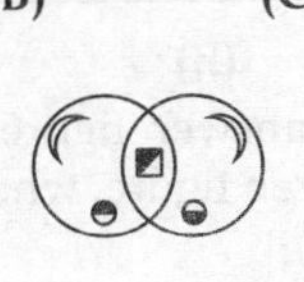

[SSC Bank Exam 2008]

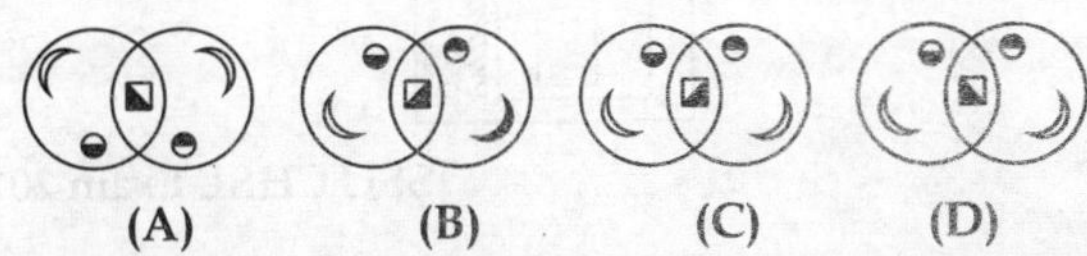

(A) (B) (C) (D)

5. Looking into a mirror, the clock shows 9:30 as the time. The actual time is **[RRB 2004]**
   (A) 2 : 30 (B) 3 : 30 (C) 4 : 30 (D) 6 : 30
6. When seen through a mirror, a clock shows 8:30. Then what is the correct time? **[Hotel Management 2004]**
   (A) 2 : 30 (B) 3 : 30
   (C) 5 : 30 (D) 8 : 30
7. By looking in a mirror, it appears that it is 6:30 in the clock. What is the real time? **[Investigator Exam 2005]**
   (A) 6 : 30 (B) 5 : 00\
   (C) 6 : 00 (D) 5 : 30
8. A clock seen through a mirror, shows quarter past three. What is the correct time shows by the clock? **[MBA 2002]**
   (A) 9 : 45 (B) 9 : 15
   (C) 8 : 45 (D) 3 : 15
9. What is the answer of this mirror image of figure (X)?

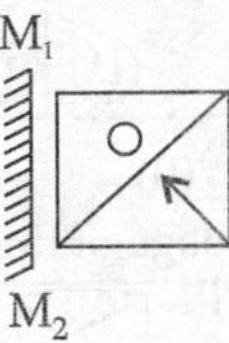

[SSC 2002]

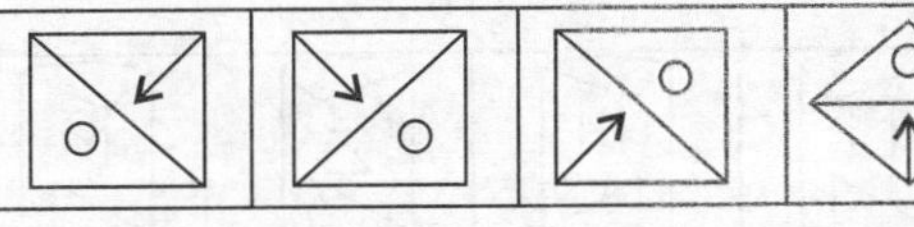

(A) (B) (C) (D)

10. What is the answer of figure (X), when mirror is put in MN place?

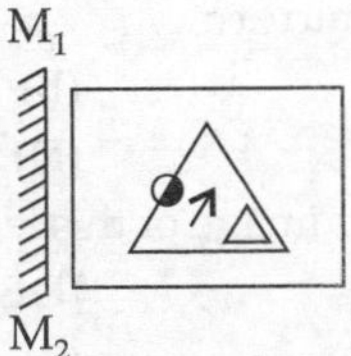

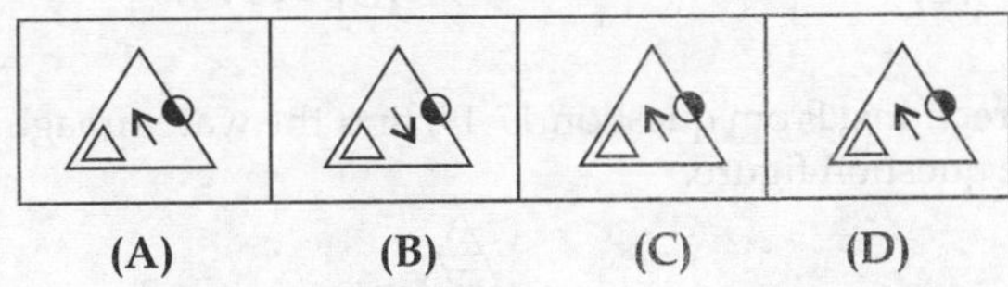

(A) (B) (C) (D)

11. What is the mirror image of this question figure, when mirror is put on MN?

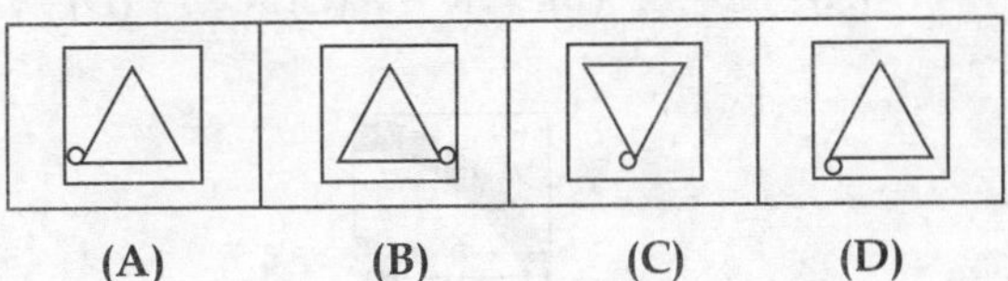

(A) (B) (C) (D)

12. What is the answer of the figure when mirror is represented by MN? **[SSC 2012]**

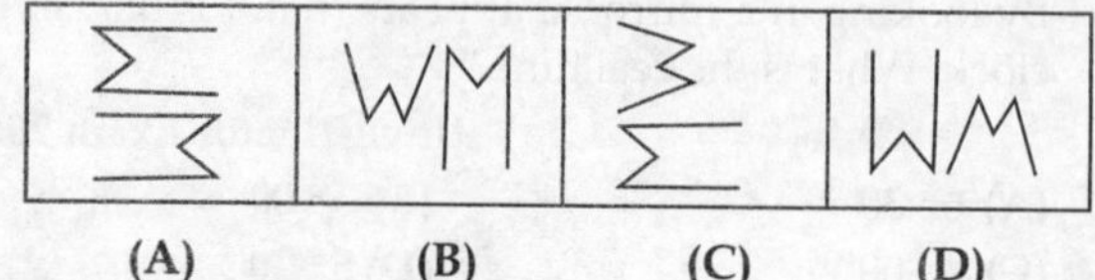

(A) (B) (C) (D)

13. Find the correct mirror image of this question figure?

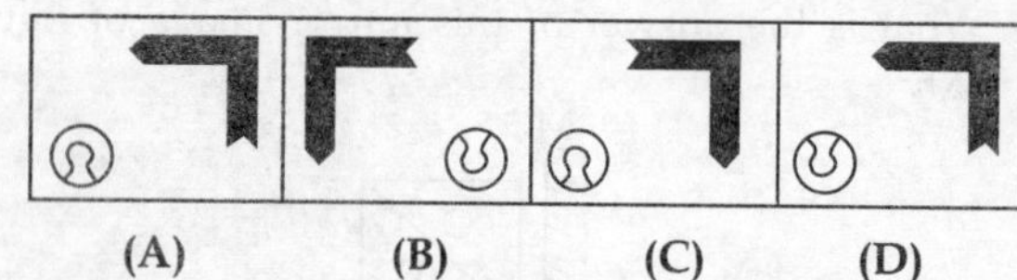

(A) (B) (C) (D)

14. Find the mirror image of this question figure.

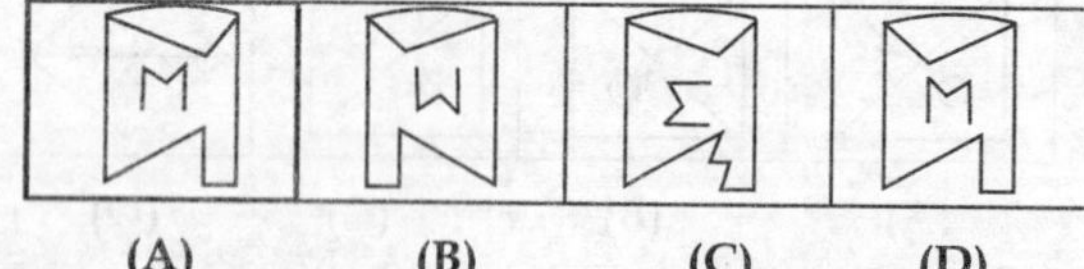

(A) (B) (C) (D)

15. Which of the following collection of letters will look the same in the mirror?

(A) OKLRMUI **(B)** HJGHRSTA

(C) JKMRSTU **(D)** AOVIVOA

16. What is the water image of this letters?

A1M3b **[DELHI POLICE 2005]**

(A) ∀ꞁƜ3P **(B)** ∀IƜ3P

(C) ∀ɿƜ3P **(D)** ∀ɿƜƐP

Directions: From question 17-19, find the water image for the question figure.

17.

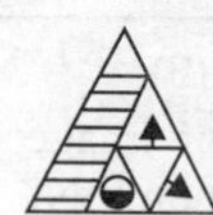

(A) (B) (C) (D)

18.

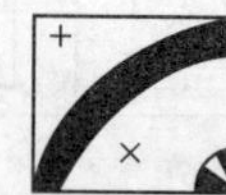

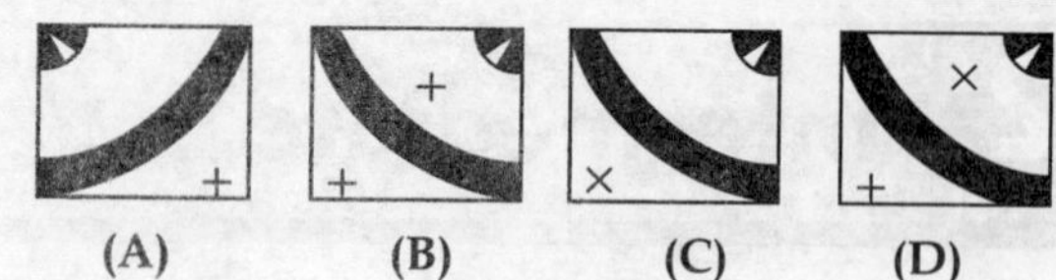

(A) (B) (C) (D)

19.

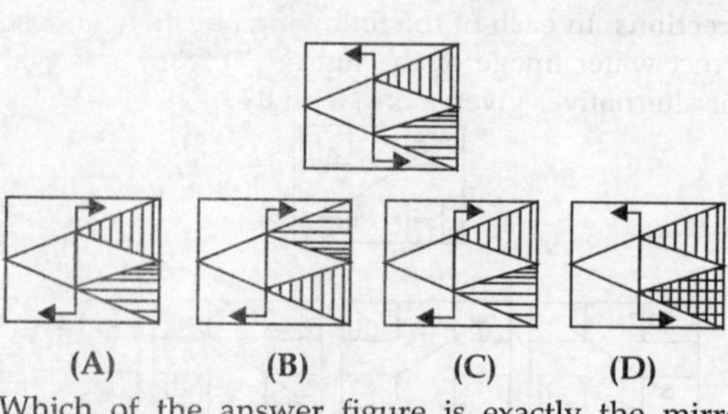

(A) (B) (C) (D)

20. Which of the answer figure is exactly the mirror image of the given figure when the mirror is held at MN?

[SSC CPO Exam 2006]

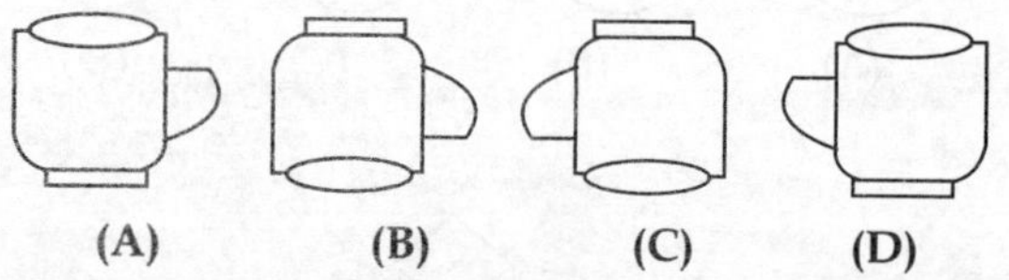

(A) (B) (C) (D)

21. Which of the answer figure is exactly the mirror image of the given figure. when the mirror is held on the line MN?

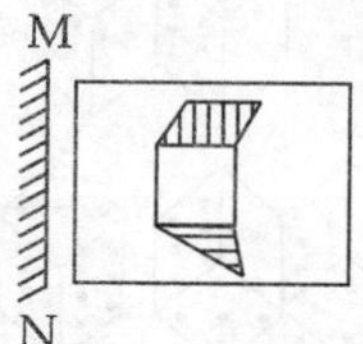

[SSC Constable Exam 2012]

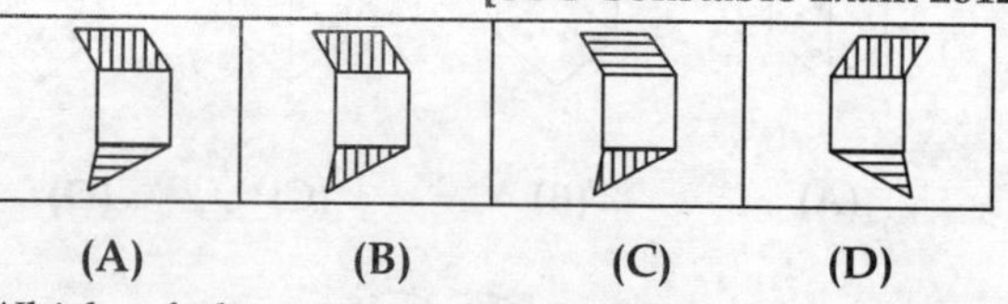

(A) (B) (C) (D)

22. Which of the answer figure is exactly the mirror image of the given figure, when the mirror is held on the line AB?

[SSC CHSL Exam 2011]

(A) (B) (C) (D)

Directions (Qs. 23–25): Find the water image of question figure.

23.

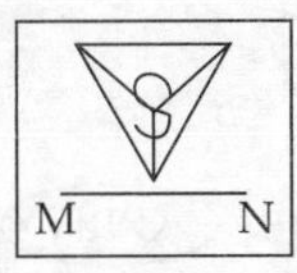

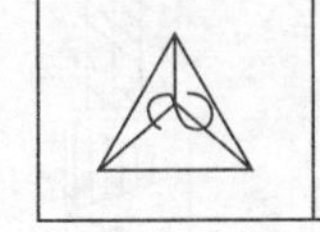

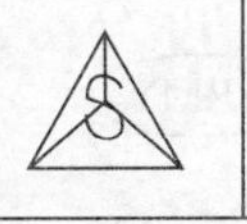

(A) (B) (C) (D)

24.

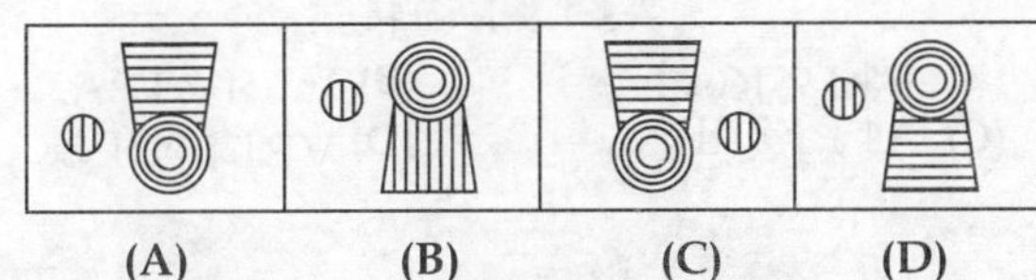

(A) (B) (C) (D)

25.

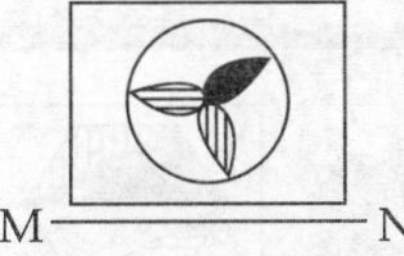

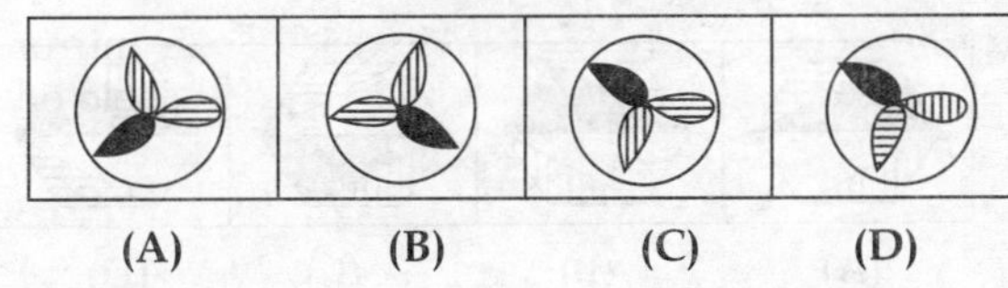

(A) (B) (C) (D)

26. Which answer figure is the exact mirror image of the given question figure when the mirror is held from the right at PQ? **[SSC CGL 2010]**

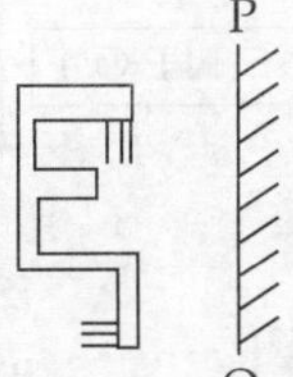

(A) 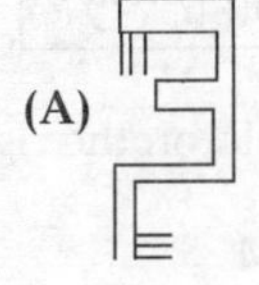

(B) 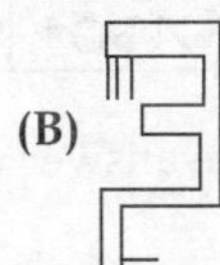

(C) 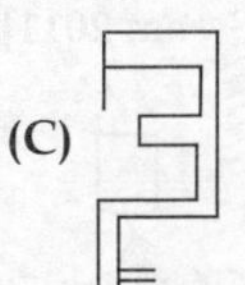

(D) 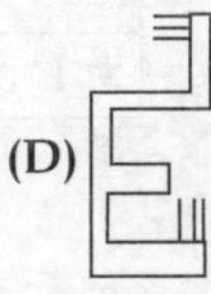

27. Find the mirror image of the following figure if the mirror is placed at line MN. **[RRB 2018]**

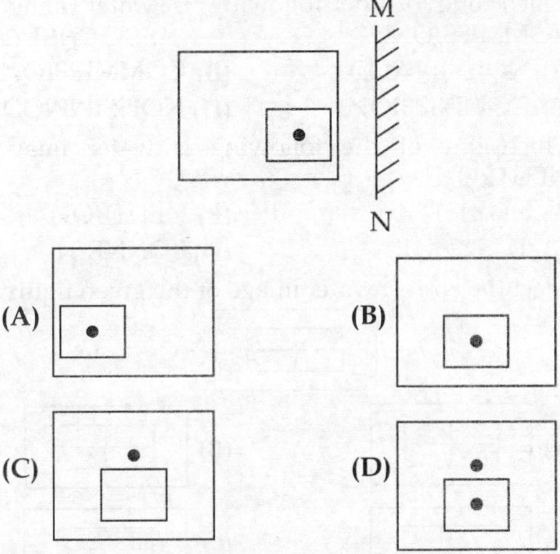

28. Select the correct mirror image of the given figure when the mirror is placed at right side. **[MTS 2022]**

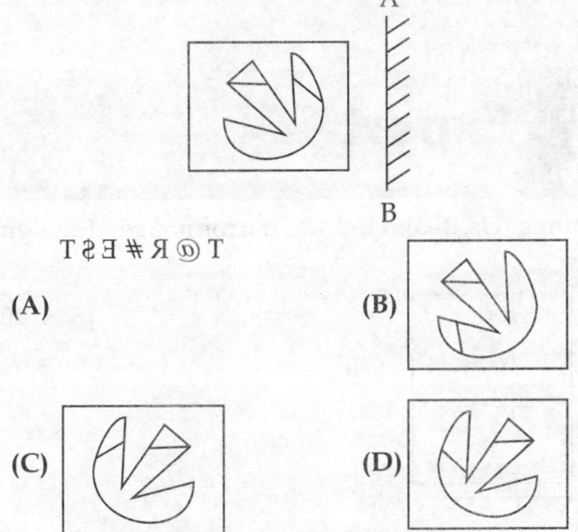

TƧƎ⋕ЯⓌT

(A) (B) (C) (D)

29. Select the correct mirror image of the given figure. **[MTS 2022]**

TY6L452

M N

(A) ⊥⅄ϱΓ⫩ƧƧ (B) ⊥⅄ϱΓ⫩ƧƧ

(C) ⊥⅄9⅂⫩ƧƧ (D) ⊥⅄ϱΓ⫩ƧƧ

30. Select the correct option that will be the mirror reflection of the problem figure. **[SSC CGL 2012]**

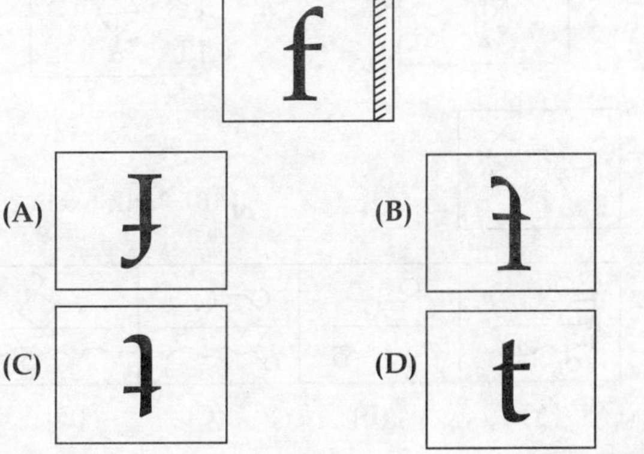

(A) (B) (C) (D)

31. Which one of the following is water image of "COMMISSION"? **[SSC CHSL 2015]**

(A) NOISSIMMOϽ (B) COMMIꙄꙄIOИ

(C) COWWISSIOИ (D) NOISSIMMOϽ

32. Which one of the following is water image of "NEUTRON"?

(A) ИOЯTUƎИ (B) ИEUTЯOИ

(C) TUƎИИOЯ (D) ЯONNEUT

33. Select the correct water image of the given figure.

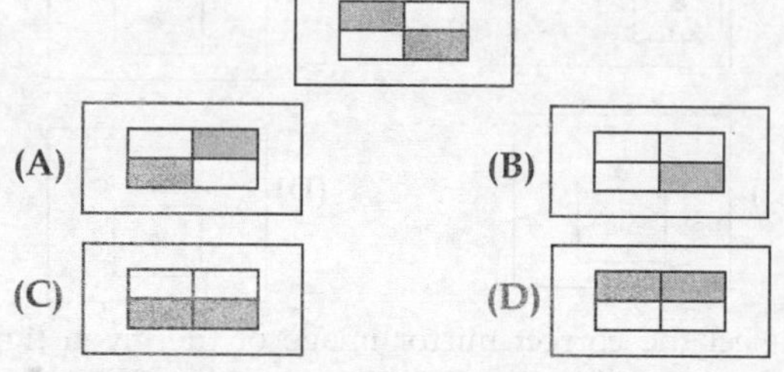

34. Select the correct water image of the given figure.

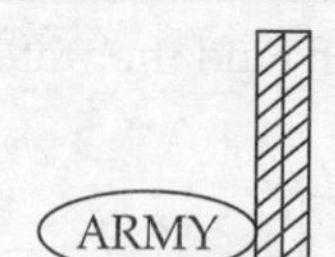

(A) 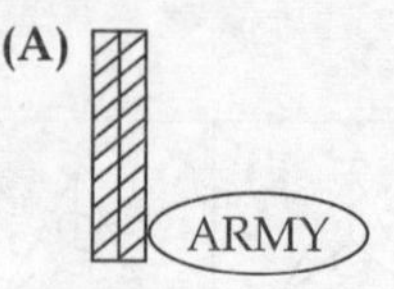

(B) 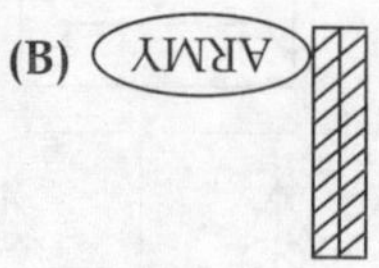

(C) 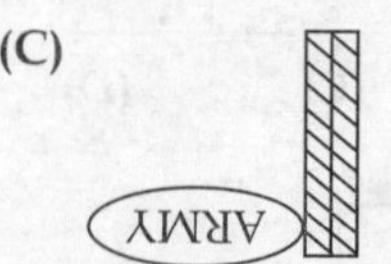

(D) 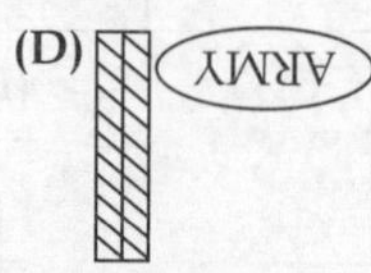

35. Select the correct water image of the given figure.

A $ T & R @ J

(A) A$T&R@J (B) J@R&T$A

(C) A$T J@R& (D) A$TJ@R&

3 Level Expert

Directions (Qs. 1–3): Find the mirror image of the given figure.

1. **[SSC 2010]**

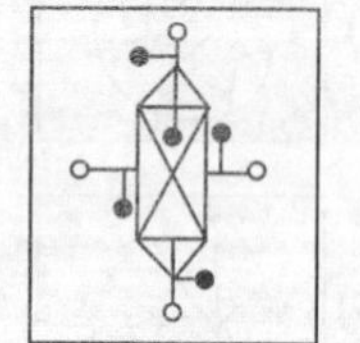
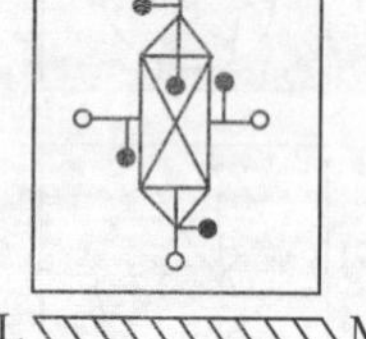

(A) 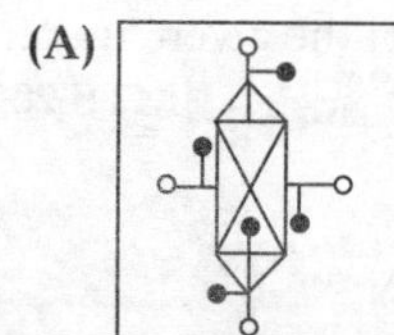

(B) 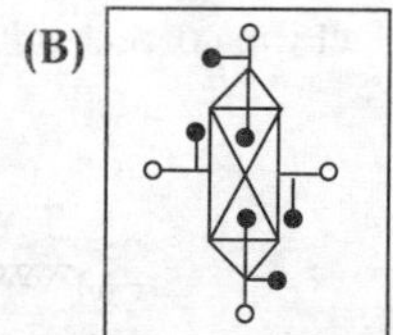

(C) 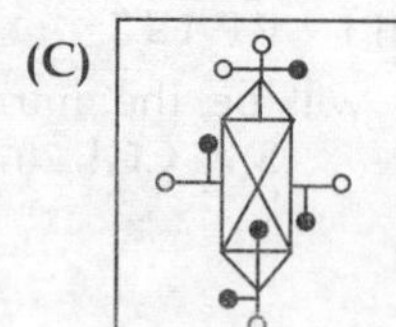

(D) 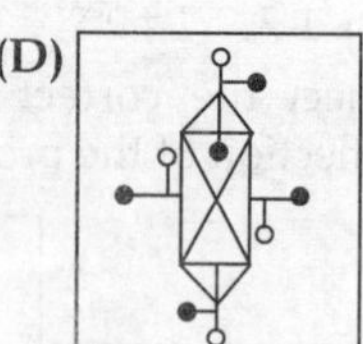

2. **[SBI Bank Exam 2007]**

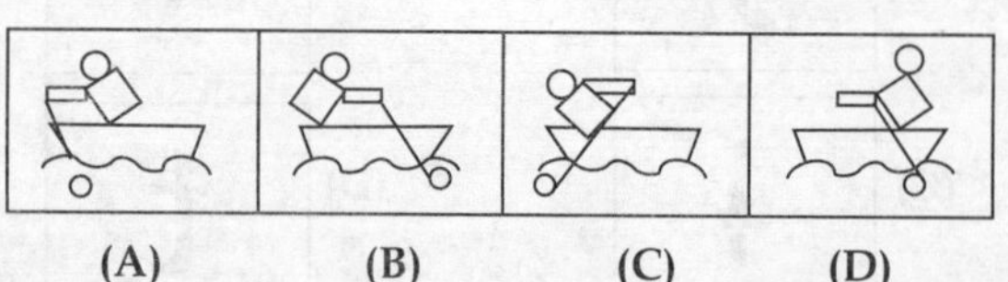

(A) (B) (C) (D)

3.

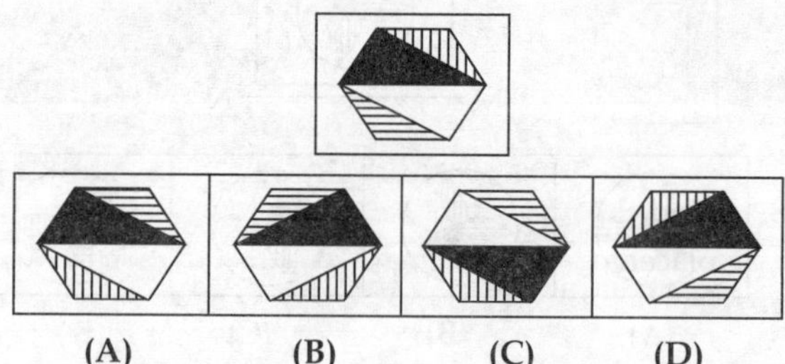

(A) (B) (C) (D)

4. What is the answer when mirror is placed on MN?

[SSC CGL Exam 2020]

(A) 4QPN7G5 (B) 4QPN7G5

(C) 5G7NPQ4 (D) 4QPN7G5

5. What is the answer when mirror is held on the right side?

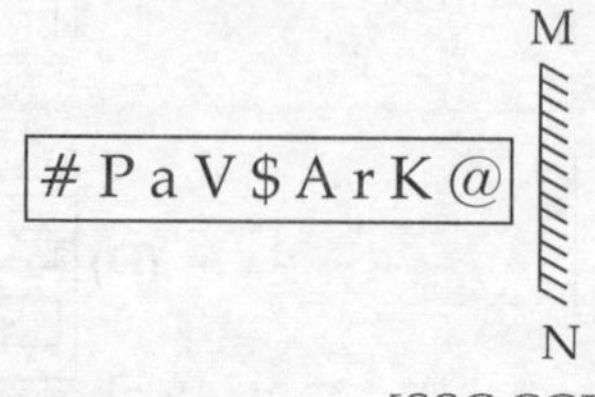

[SSC CGL Exam 2020]

(A) @ K r A $ V a P #

(B) @ K r A $ V a P #

(C) 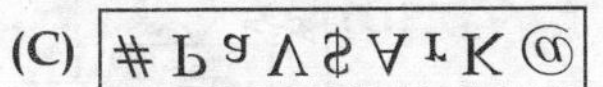

(D)

6. What is the answer when mirror is placed on MN?

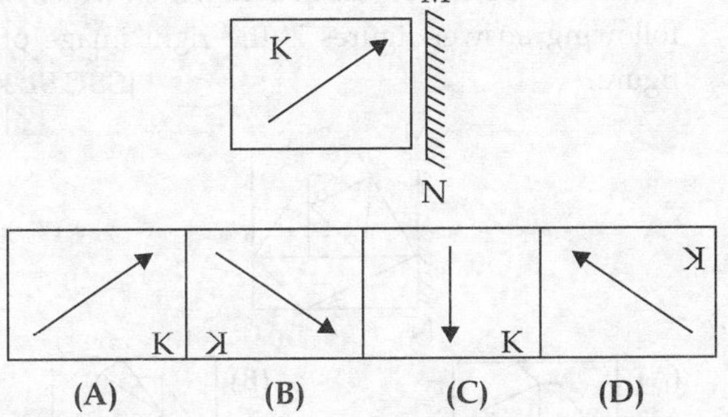

7. What is the answer when mirror is placed right side of this figure?

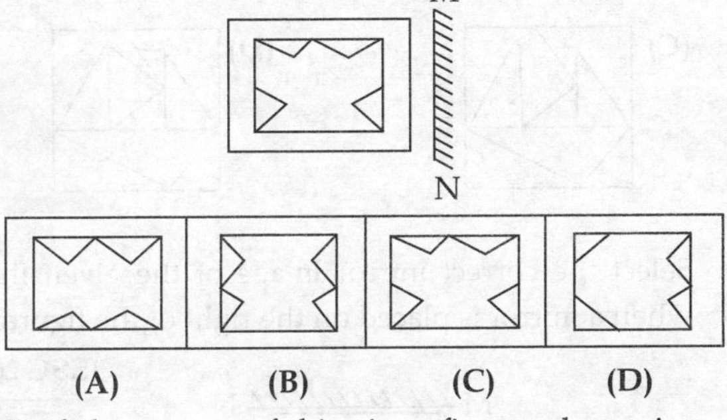

8. Find the answer of this given figure when mirror is placed on MN.

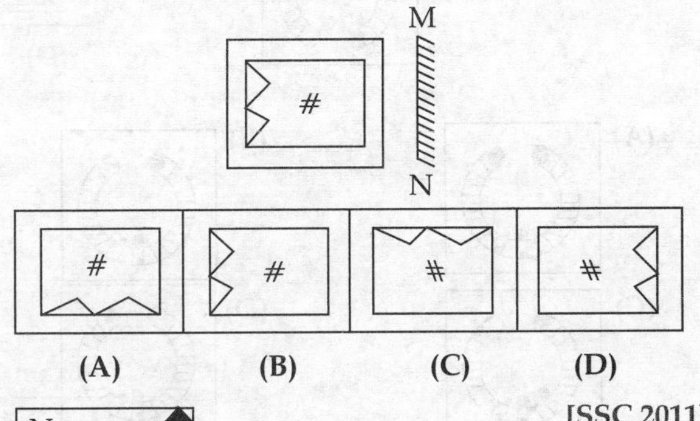

9. [SSC 2011]

(A) 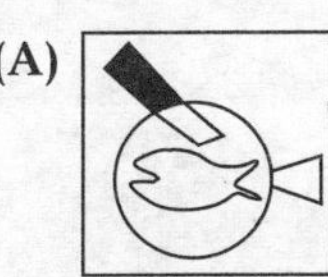

(B) 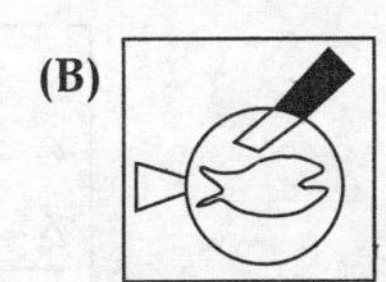

(C) 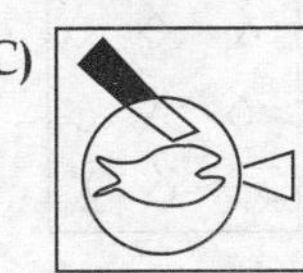

(D) 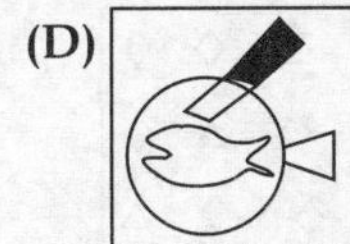

10. 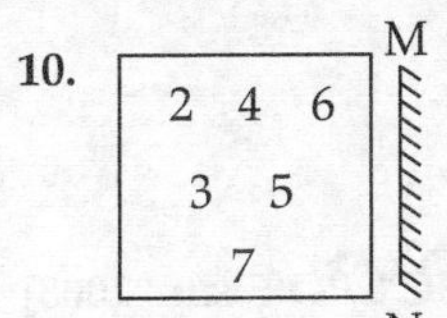

[SSC 2013]

(A) 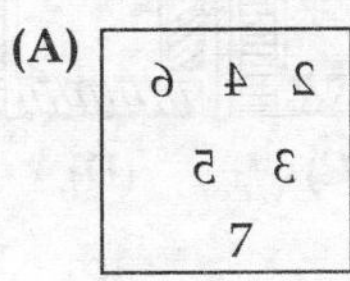

(B)

(C) 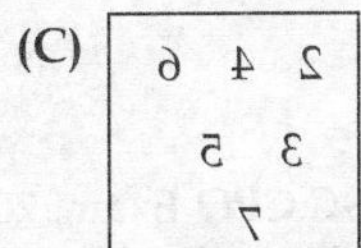

(D)

11. What is the answer when mirror is placed on XY?

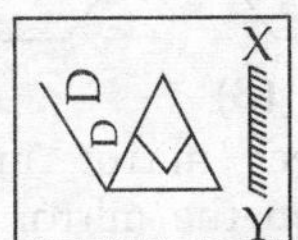

[SSC CPO Exam, 2009]

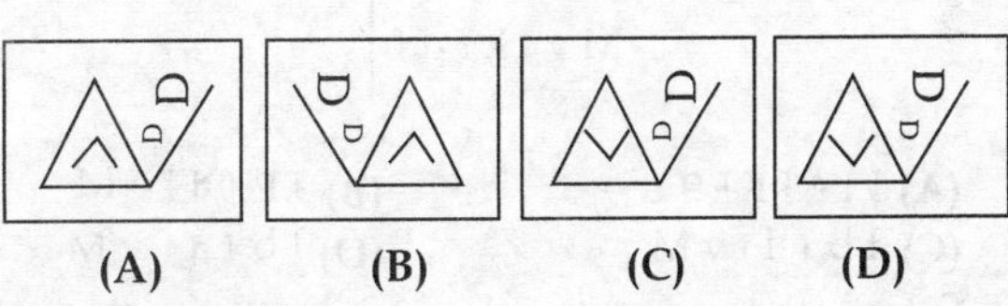

12. [SSC 2013]

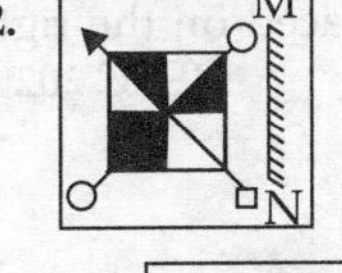

(A) 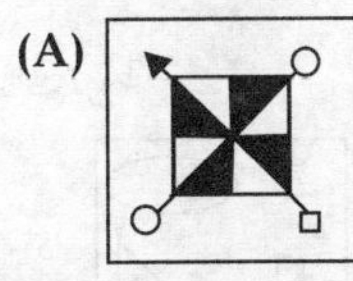

(B) 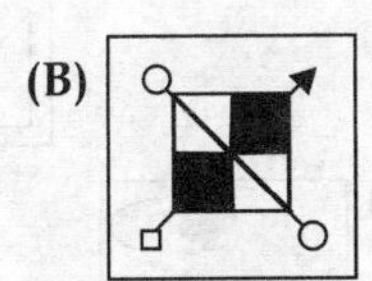

(C) 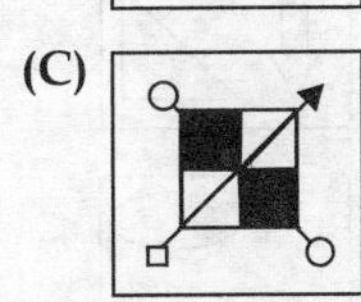

(D) 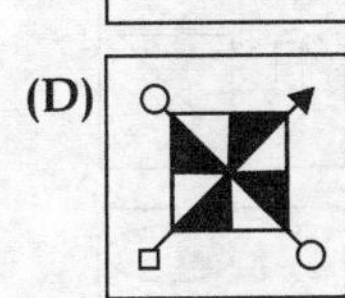

Directions: Find the water image of the question 13-15, from the answer figure.

13.

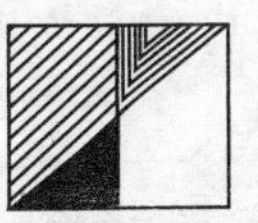

[SSC CPO Exam, 2008]

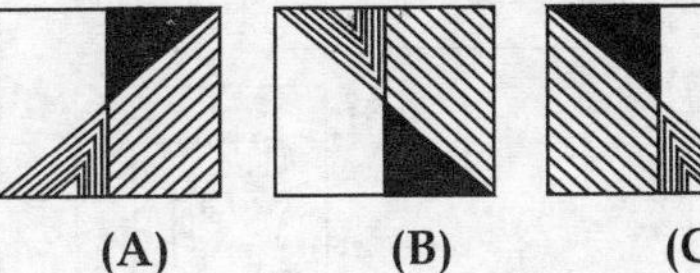

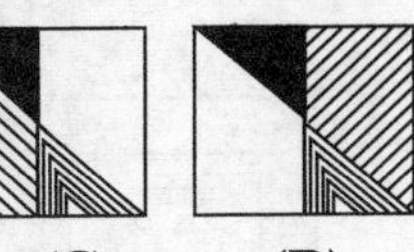

(A) (B) (C) (D)

14.

[SSC CPO Exam, 2008]

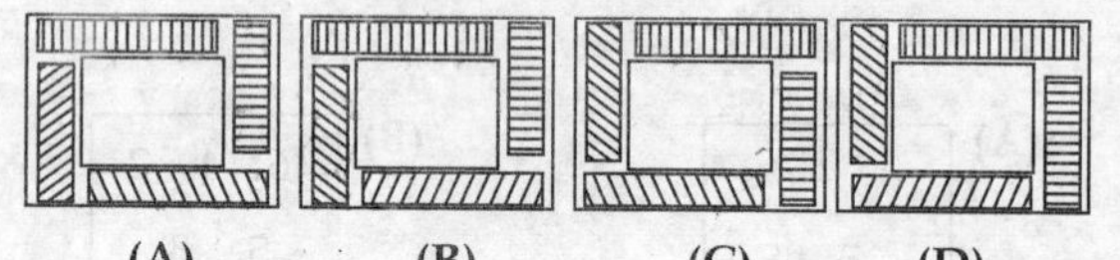

(A) (B) (C) (D)

15.

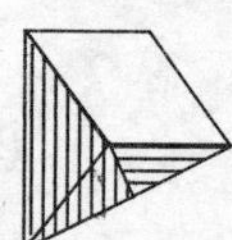

[SSC CPO Exam, 2008]

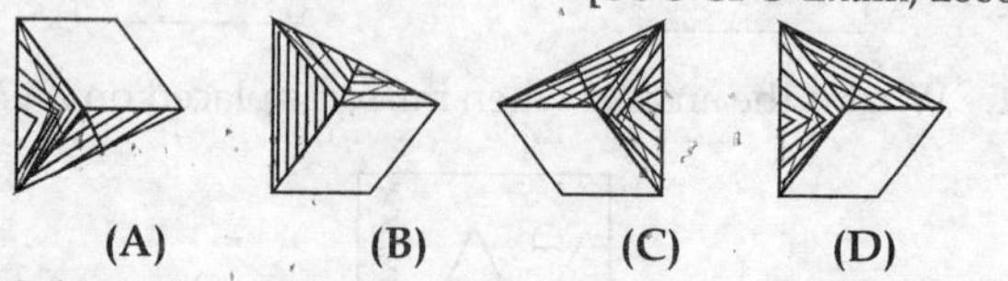

(A) (B) (C) (D)

16. Select the correct mirror image of the given combination when the mirror is placed at MN as shown. **[SSC 2021]**

(A) Mvtkrdf (B) fdrktvM

(C) fdrktvM (D) fdrktv M

17. Select the correct mirror image of the given combination when the mirror is placed on the right of the figure. **[SSC 2020]**

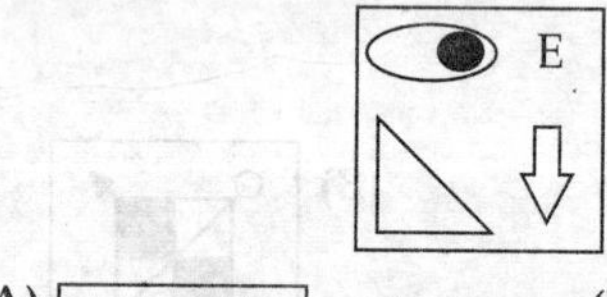

(A) 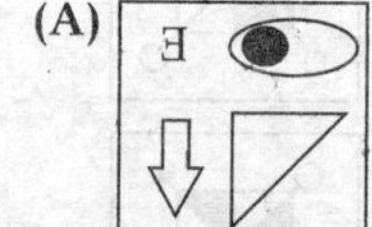

(B) 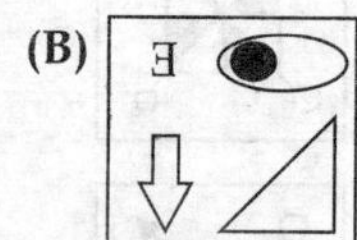

(C) 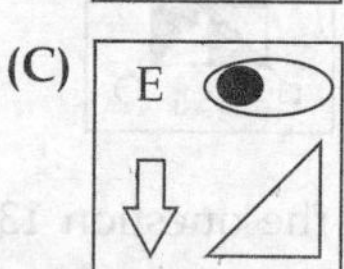

(D) 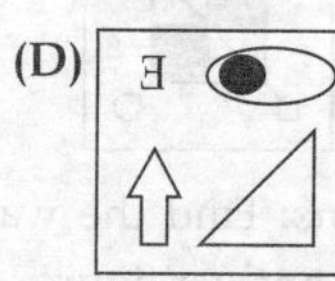

18. If a mirror is place on the line MN, then which of the following answer figures is the right image of the figure? **[SSC CGL 2016]**

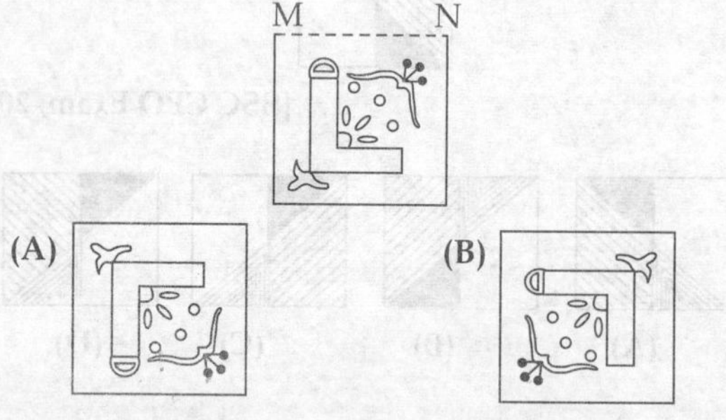

(C) 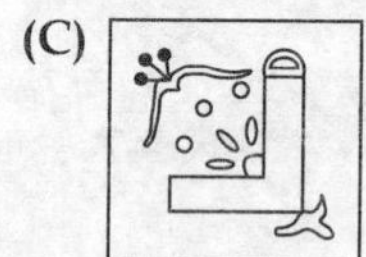

(D) 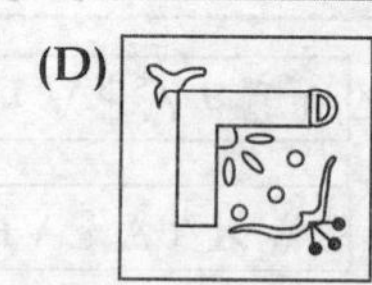

19. If a mirror is place on the line MN, then which of the following answer figures is the right image of the figure? **[SSC SI 2015]**

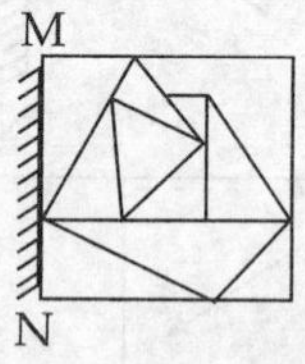

(A) 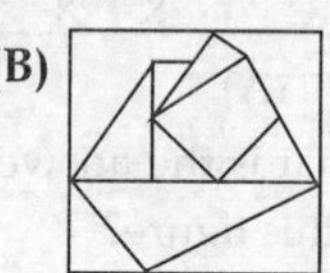

(B) 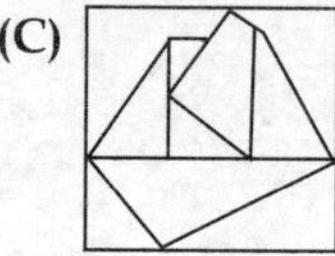

(C) 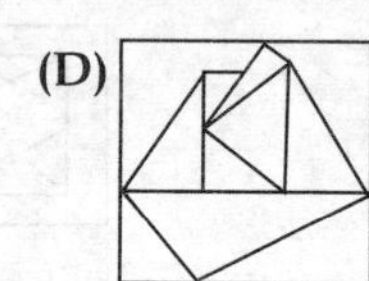

(D)

20. Select the correct mirror image of the given figure when a mirror is placed on the right of the figure. **[SSC 2012]**

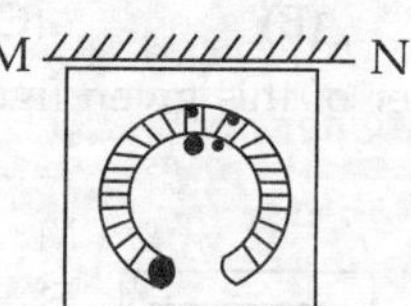

(A)

(B) 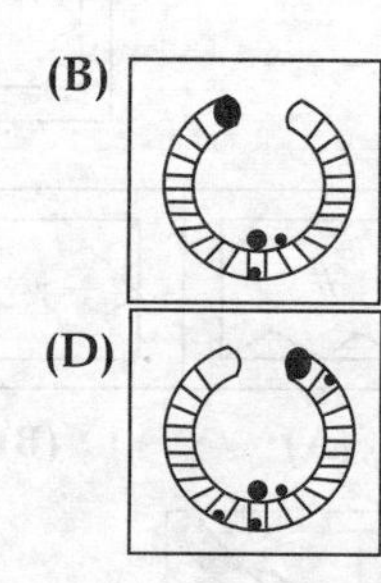

(C)

(D)

21. Which of the answer figures is exactly the mirror image of the given figure when the mirror is held at MN? **[SSC CGL 2013]**

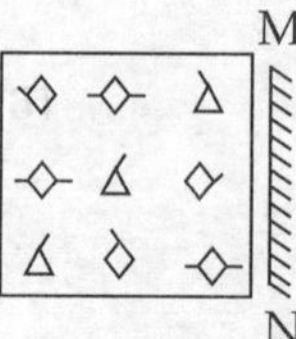

(A) 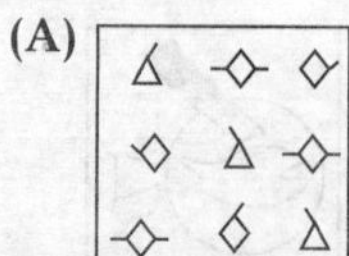

(B) 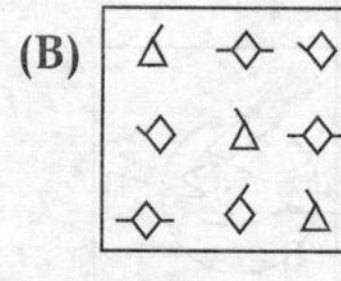

(C) 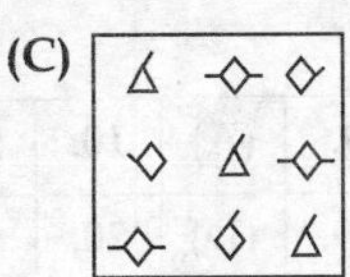 (D)

22. Select the correct water image of the given figure.

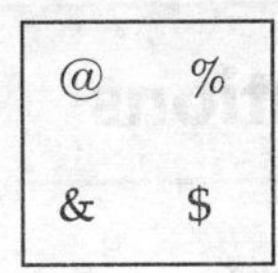

(A) (B) 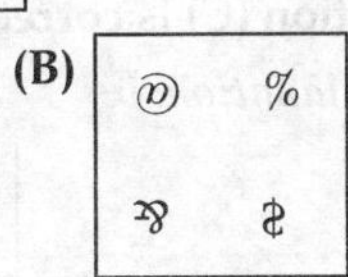

(C) (D) 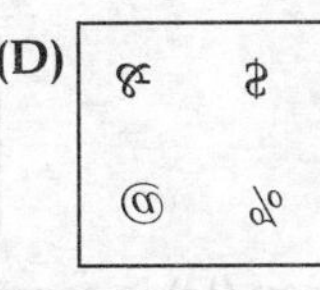

23. Select the correct water image of the given figure.

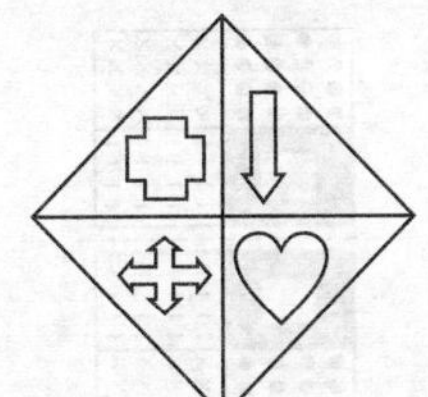

(A) 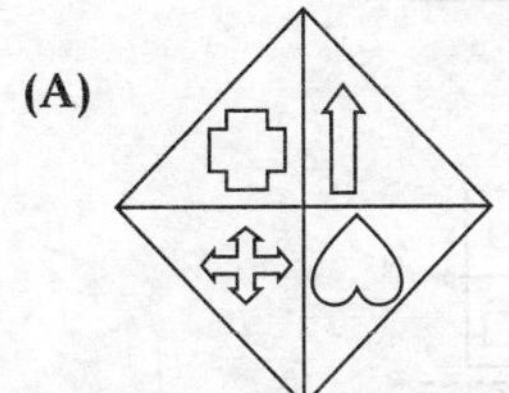 (B) 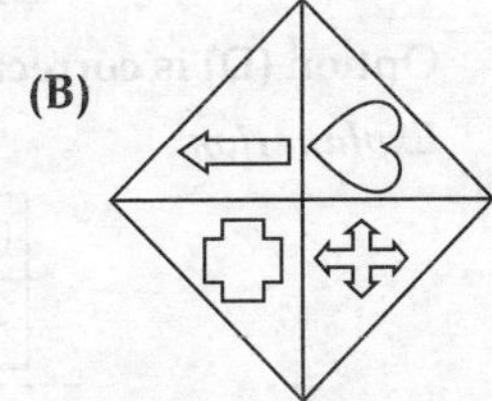

(C) 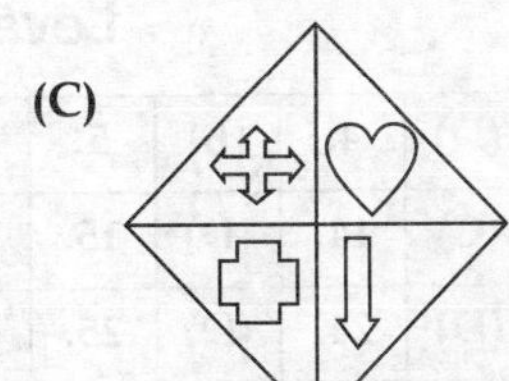 (D) 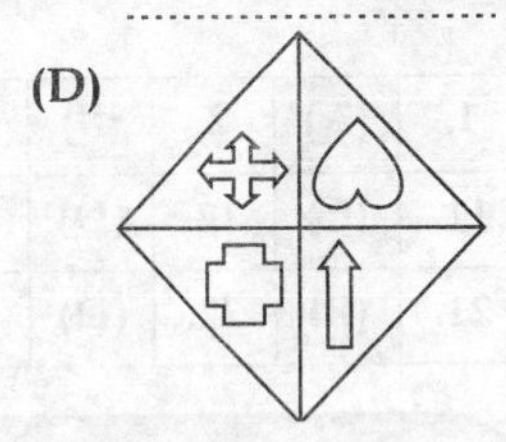

24. Select the correct water image of the given figure.

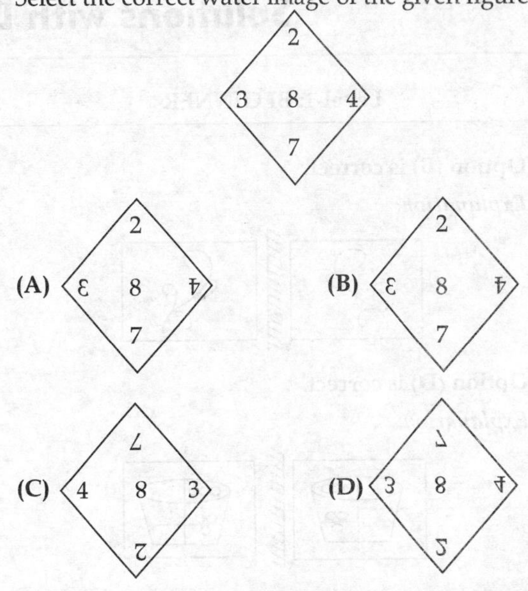

25. Select the correct water image of the given figure.

MISSION

(A) NOISSIM (B) IONWISS

(C) MISSION (D) IONMISS

ANSWER KEY

Level-1: Beginner

1.	(B)	2.	(D)	3.	(A)	4.	(A)	5.	(A)	6.	(D)	7.	(C)	8.	(D)	9.	(D)	10.	(D)
11.	(C)	12.	(A)	13.	(C)	14.	(A)	15.	(C)	16.	(B)	17.	(D)	18.	(A)	19.	(D)	20.	(D)
21.	(D)	22.	(D)	23.	(D)	24.	(D)	25.	(B)	26.	(D)	27.	(C)	28.	(B)	29.	(B)	30.	(A)
31.	(A)	32.	(C)	33.	(D)	34.	(A)	35.	(C)	36.	(A)	37.	(C)	38.	(B)	39.	(B)	40.	(D)

Level-2: Intermediate

1.	(C)	2.	(A)	3.	(B)	4.	(D)	5.	(A)	6.	(B)	7.	(D)	8.	(C)	9.	(C)	10.	(A)
11.	(C)	12.	(D)	13.	(A)	14.	(D)	15.	(D)	16.	(A)	17.	(B)	18.	(D)	19.	(B)	20.	(C)
21.	(A)	22.	(B)	23.	(D)	24.	(C)	25.	(B)	26.	(A)	27.	(A)	28.	(C)	29.	(B)	30.	(B)
31.	(C)	32.	(B)	33.	(A)	34.	(C)	35.	(A)										

Level-3: Expert

1.	(A)	2.	(B)	3.	(D)	4.	(B)	5.	(A)	6.	(D)	7.	(C)	8.	(D)	9.	(A)	10.	(C)
11.	(C)	12.	(D)	13.	(C)	14.	(D)	15.	(B)	16.	(C)	17.	(B)	18.	(A)	19.	(D)	20.	(A)
21.	(B)	22.	(D)	23.	(D)	24.	(D)	25.	(C)										

Solutions with Detailed Explanations

Level-1: BEGINNER

1. **Option (B) is correct.**

Explanation:

2. **Option (D) is correct.**

Explanation:

3. **Option (A) is correct.**

Explanation:

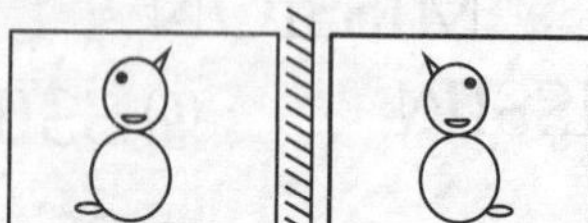

4. **Option (A) is correct.**

Explanation:

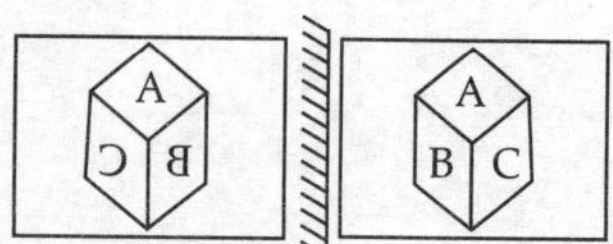

5. **Option (A) is correct.**

Explanation:

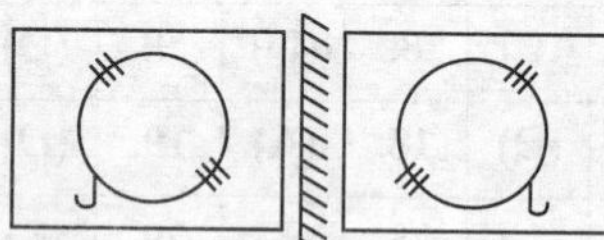

6. **Option (D) is correct.**

Explanation:

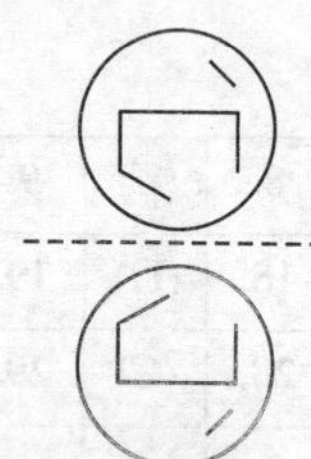

7. **Option (C) is correct.**

Explanation:

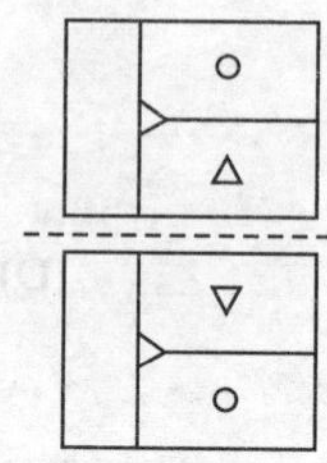

8. **Option (D) is correct.**

Explanation:

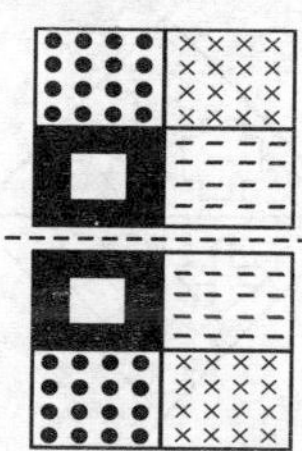

9. **Option (D) is correct.**

Explanation:

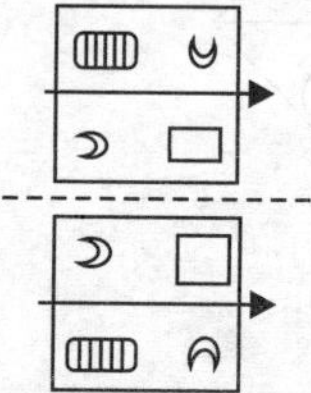

10. **Option (D) is correct.**

Explanation:

OBLITERATE

11. **Option (C) is correct.**

Explanation:

MUNDANE

12. **Option (A) is correct.**

Explanation:

D6Z7F4

13. **Option (C) is correct.**

Explanation:

MISSISSIPPI

14. Option (A) is correct.

Explanation:

PAN20
- - - - - - - - -
ꟼ∀ИZ0

15. Option (C) is correct.

Explanation:

CAT2015
- - - - - - - - -
C∀TZ01Ƨ

16. Option (B) is correct.

Explanation:

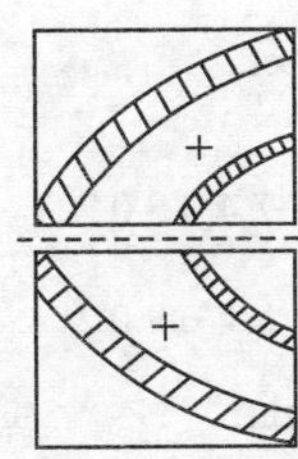

17. Option (D) is correct.

Explanation:

MAGAZINE ||| ƎИIZAGAM

18. Option (A) is correct.

Explanation:

BR4AQ16HI ||| IH61QA4ЯB

19. Option (D) is correct.

Explanation:

1965INDOPAK ||| KAPODNI5691

20. Option (D) is correct.

Explanation:

AOVIVOA
- - - - - - - - -
ⱯOΛIΛOⱯ

21. Option (D) is correct.

Explanation:

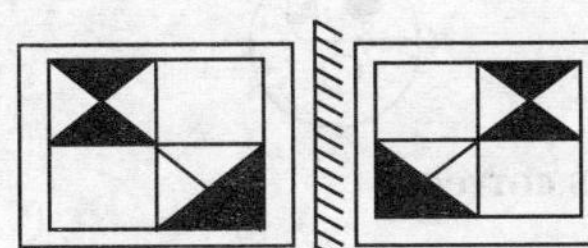

22. Option (D) is correct.

Explanation:

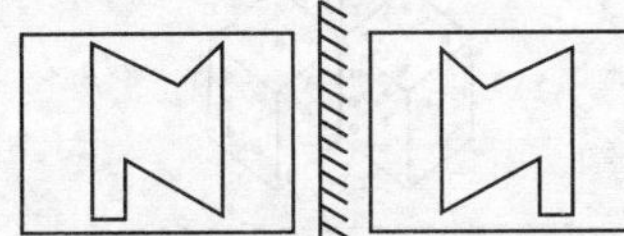

23. Option (D) is correct.

Explanation:

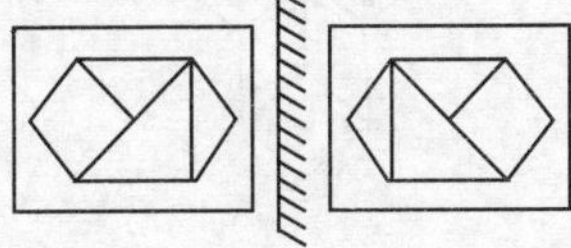

24. Option (D) is correct.

Explanation:

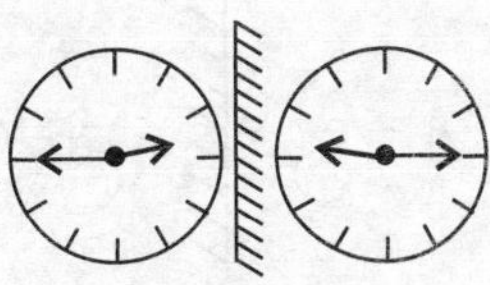

25. Option (B) is correct.

Explanation:

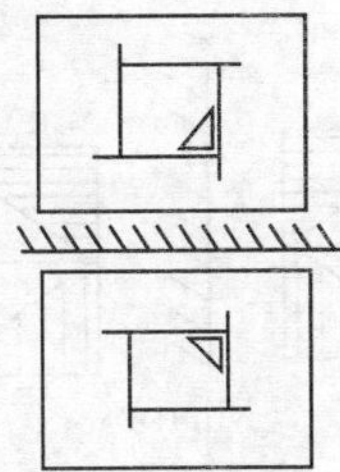

26. Option (D) is correct.

Explanation:

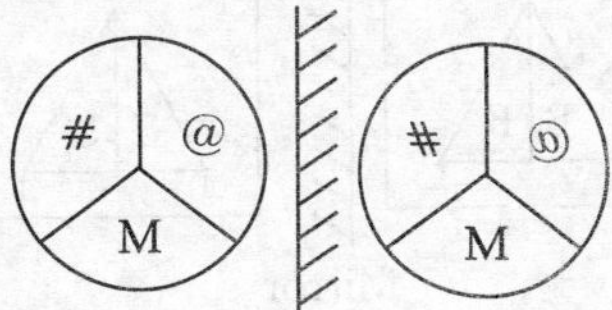

27. Option (C) is correct.

Explanation:

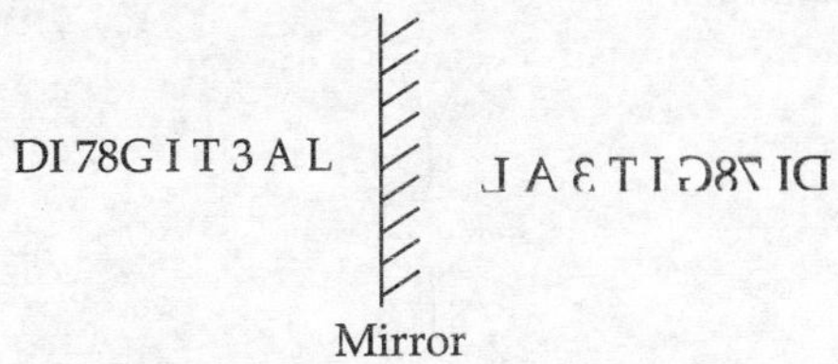

28. Option (B) is correct.

Explanation:

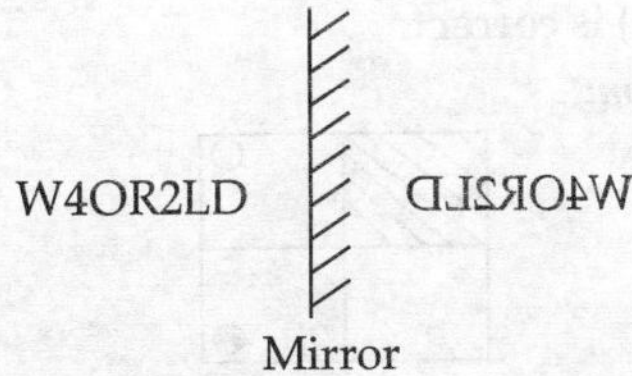

29. Option (B) is correct.

Explanation:

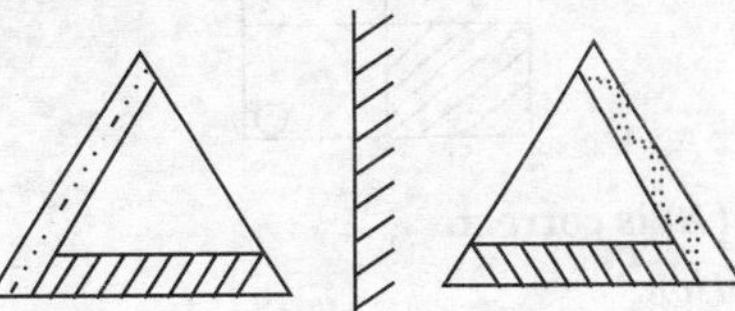

30. Option (A) is correct.

Explanation:

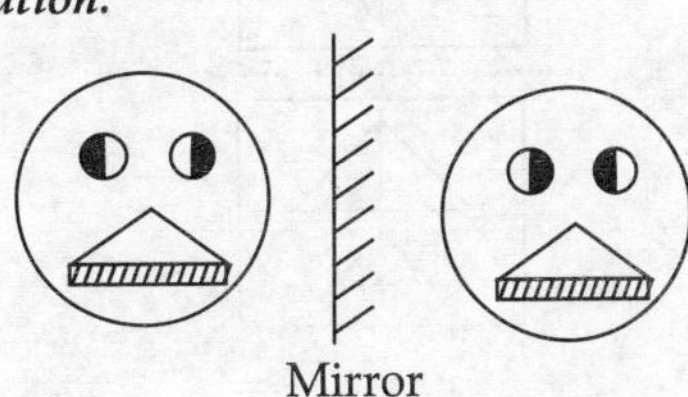

31. Option (A) is correct.

Explanation:

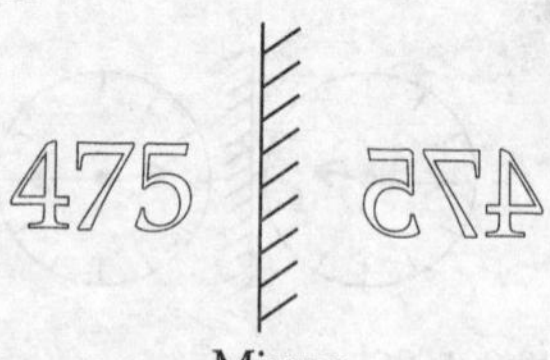

32. Option (C) is correct.

Explanation:

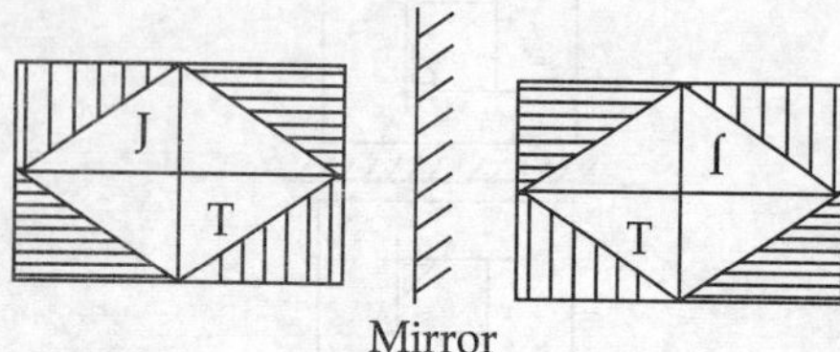

33. Option (D) is correct.

Explanation:

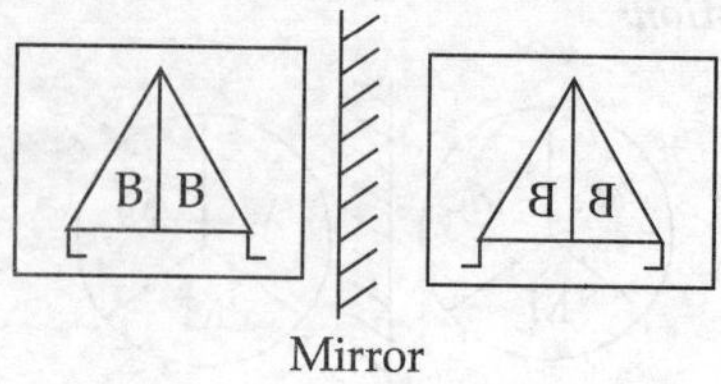

34. Option (A) is correct.

Explanation:

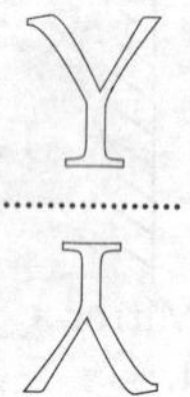

35. Option (C) is correct.

Explanation:

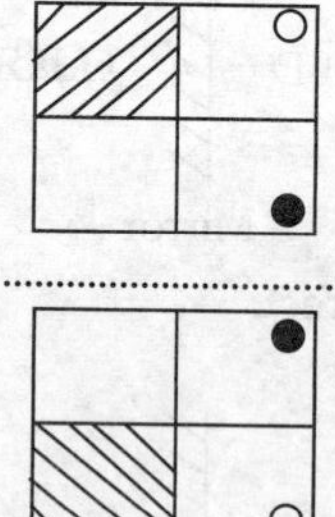

36. Option (A) is correct.

Explanation:

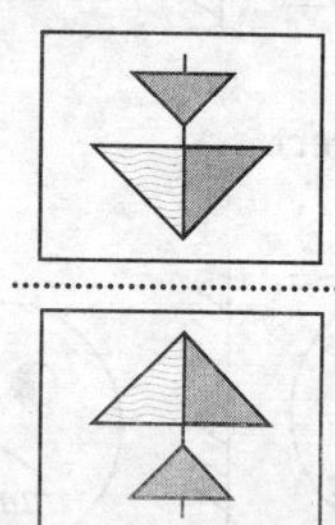

37. Option (C) is correct.

Explanation:

J37OY8

....

J37OY8

38. Option (B) is correct.

Explanation:

T@R#E$T

....

T@R#E$T

39. Option (B) is correct.

Explanation:

749802

....

749802

40. Option (D) is correct.

Explanation:

MONSOORI

....

MONSOORI

Level-2: INTERMEDIATE

1. Option (C) is correct.

Explanation:

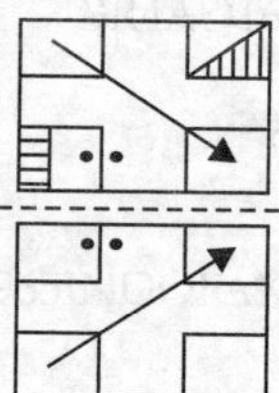

2. Option (A) is correct.

Explanation:

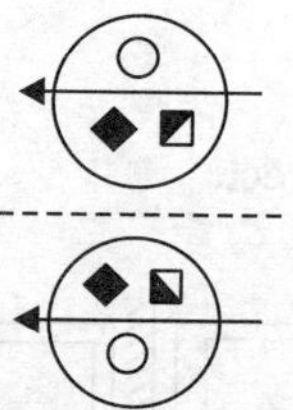

3. Option (B) is correct.

Explanation:

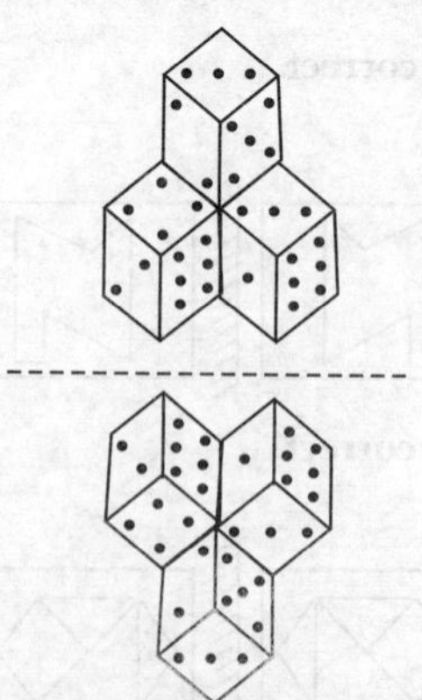

4. **Option (D) is correct.**
Explanation:

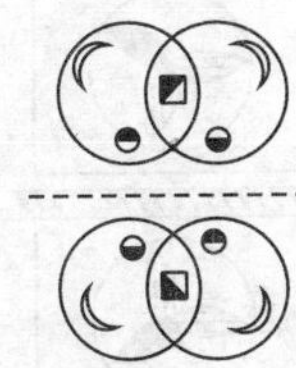

5. **Option (A) is correct.**
Explanation:

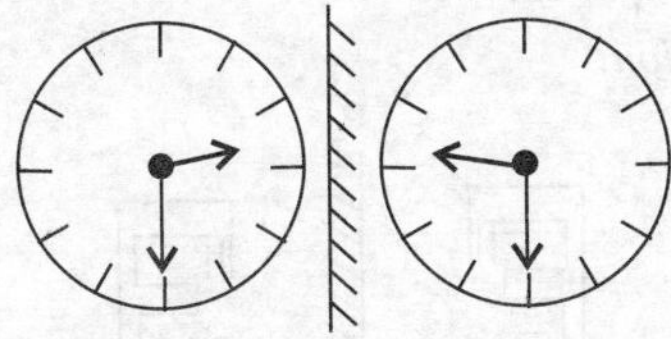

6. **Option (B) is correct.**
Explanation:

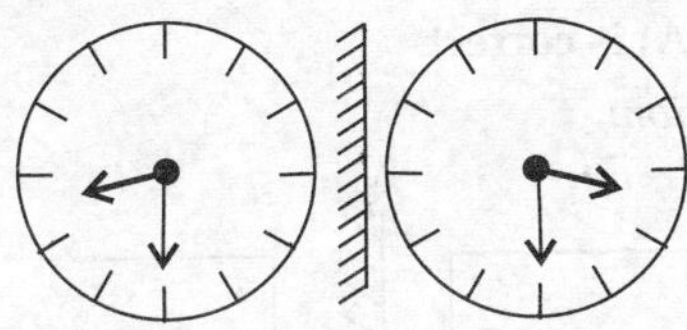

7. **Option (D) is correct.**
Explanation:

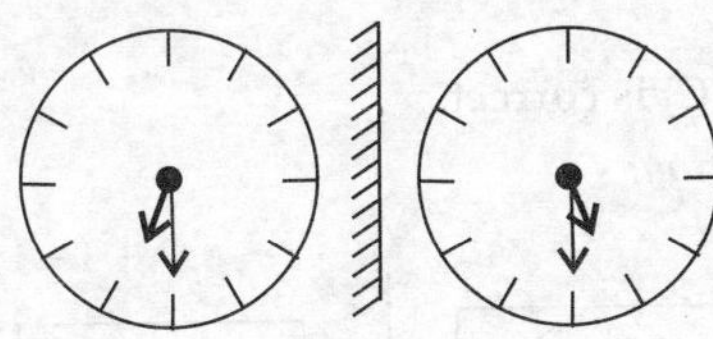

8. **Option (C) is correct.**
Explanation:

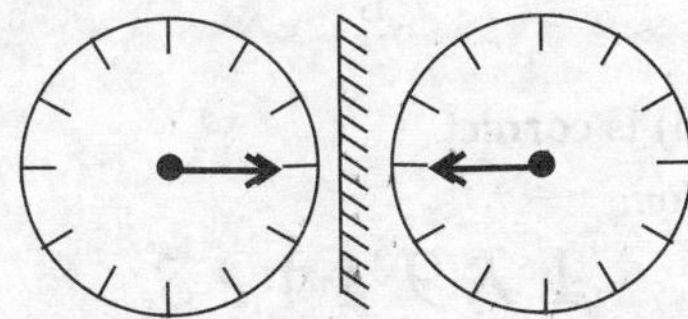

9. **Option (C) is correct.**
Explanation:

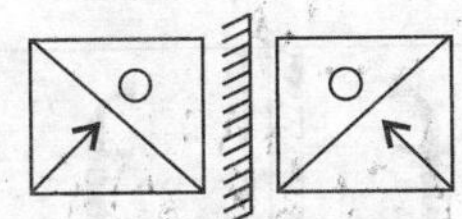

10. **Option (A) is correct.**
Explanation:

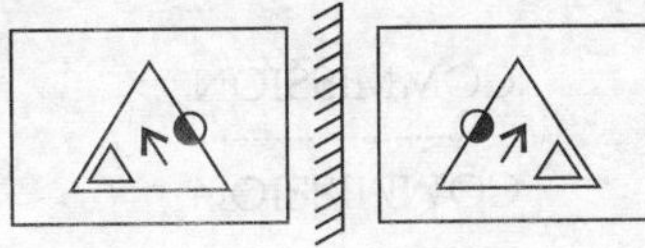

11. **Option (C) is correct.**
Explanation:

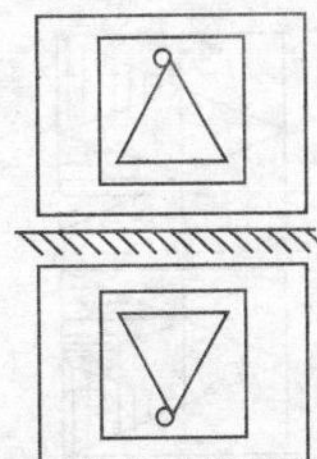

12. **Option (D) is correct.**
Explanation:

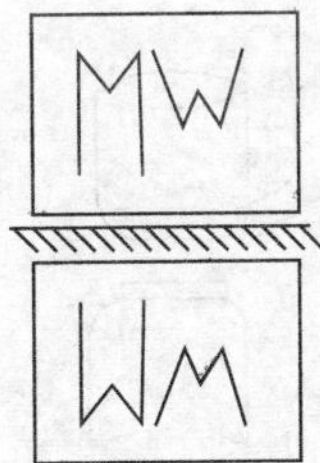

13. **Option (A) is correct.**
Explanation:

14. **Option (D) is correct.**
Explanation:

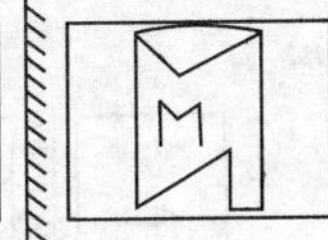

15. **Option (D) is correct.**
Explanation:

AOVIVOA | AOVIVOA

16. **Option (A) is correct.**
Explanation:

A1M3b

17. **Option (B) is correct.**
Explanation:

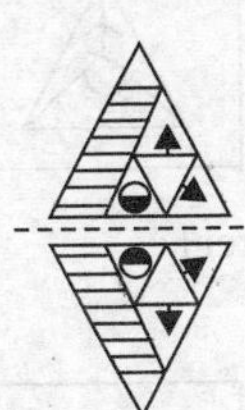

18. **Option (D) is correct.**
Explanation:

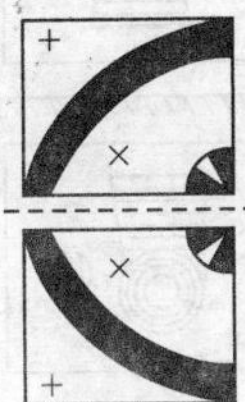

19. Option (B) is correct.

Explanation:

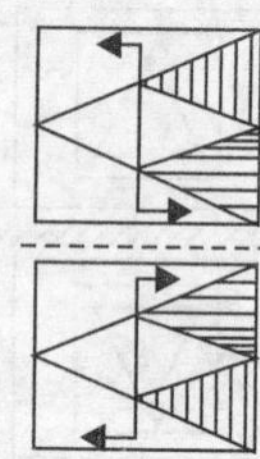

20. Option (C) is correct.

Explanation:

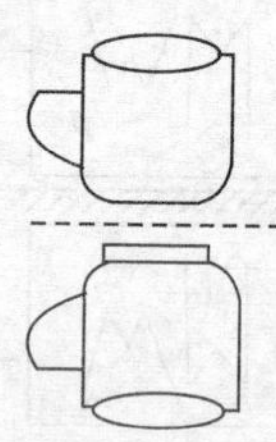

21. Option (A) is correct.

Explanation:

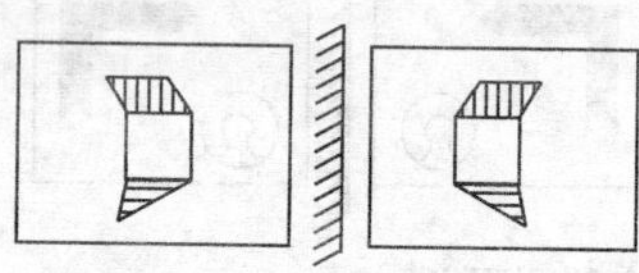

22. Option (B) is correct.

Explanation:

23. Option (D) is correct.

Explanation:

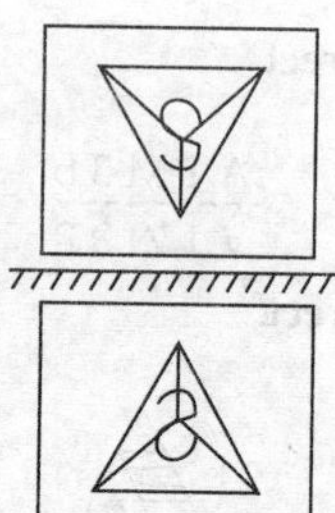

24. Option (C) is correct.

Explanation:

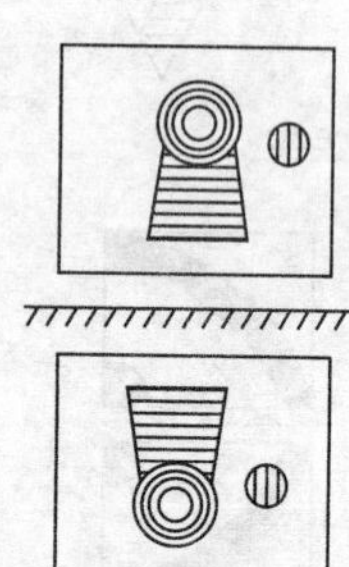

25. Option (B) is correct.

Explanation:

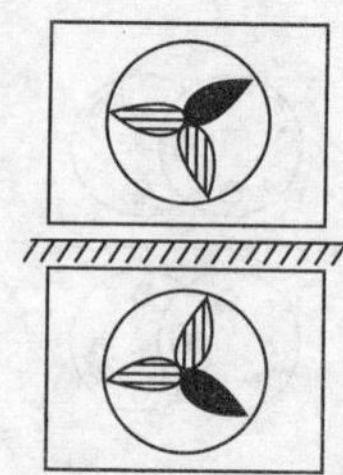

26. Option (A) is correct.

Explanation:

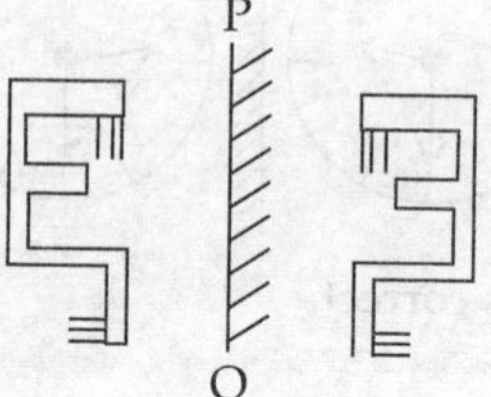

27. Option (A) is correct.

Explanation:

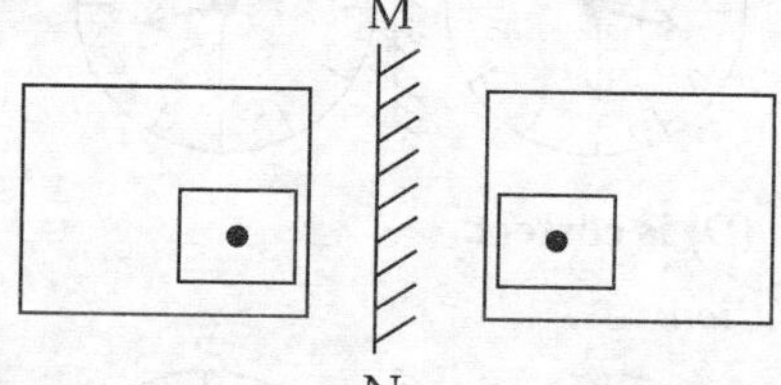

28. Option (C) is correct.

Explanation:

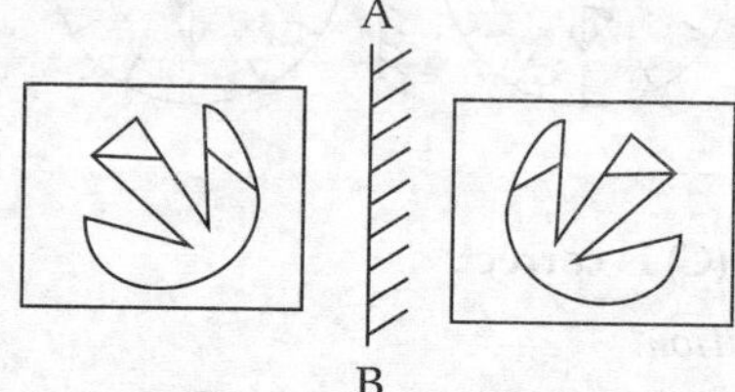

29. Option (B) is correct.

Explanation:

⊥⅄9⇂ᔭϛᘔ

30. Option (B) is correct.

Explanation:

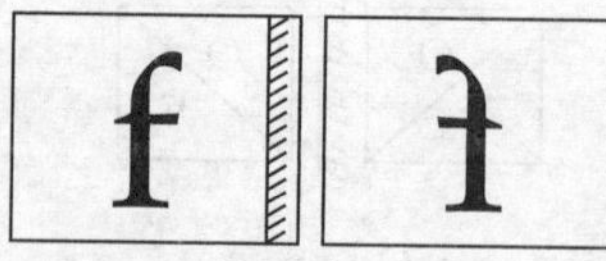

31. Option (C) is correct.

Explanation:

COMMISSION
....
COWWIƧƧIOИ

32. Option (B) is correct.

Explanation:

NEUTRON

....

33. Option (A) is correct.

Explanation:

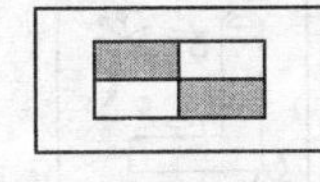

....

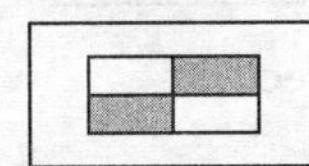

34. Option (C) is correct.

Explanation:

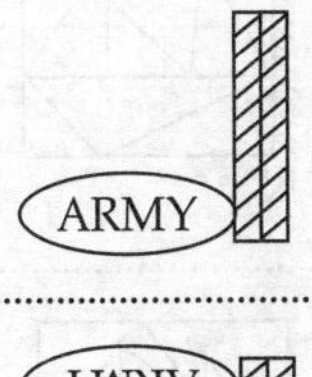

....

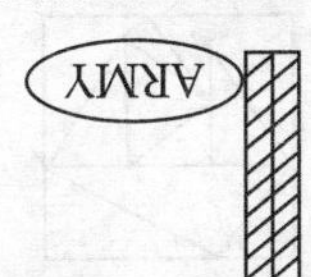

35. Option (A) is correct.

Explanation:

Level-3: EXPERT

1. Option (A) is correct.

Explanation:

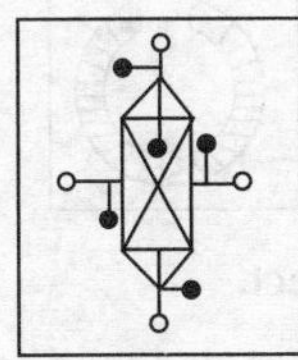

....

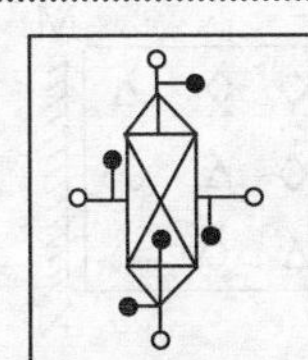

2. Option (B) is correct.

Explanation:

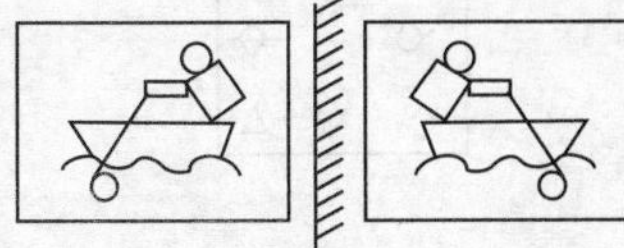

3. Option (D) is correct.

Explanation:

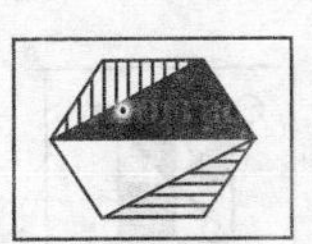

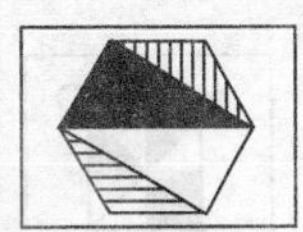

4. Option (B) is correct.

Explanation:

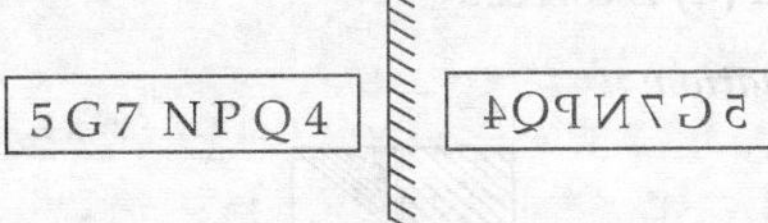

5. Option (A) is correct.

Explanation:

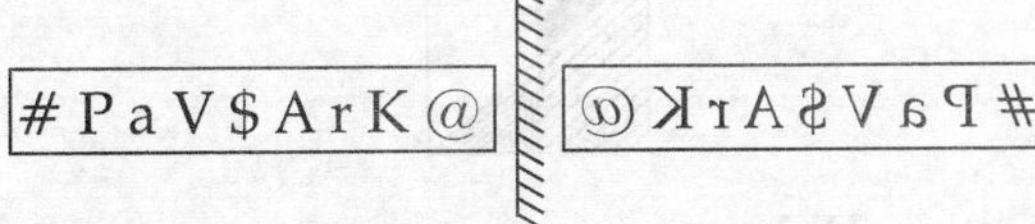

6. Option (D) is correct.

Explanation:

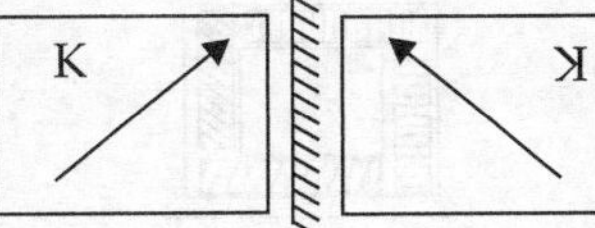

7. Option (C) is correct.

Explanation:

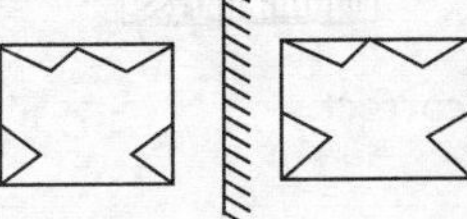

8. Option (D) is correct.

Explanation:

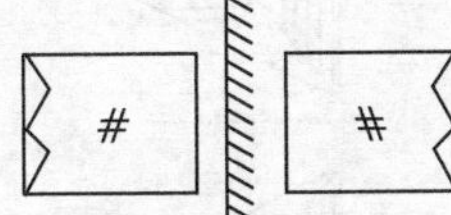

9. Option (A) is correct.

Explanation:

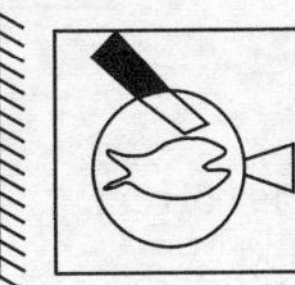

10. Option (C) is correct.

Explanation:

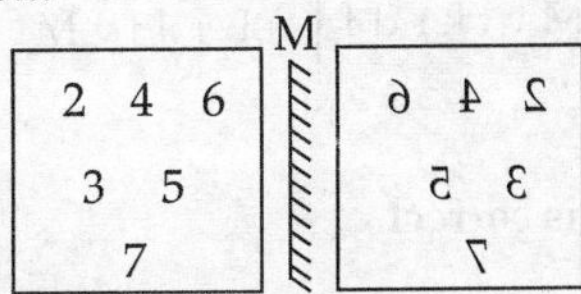

11. Option (C) is correct.

Explanation:

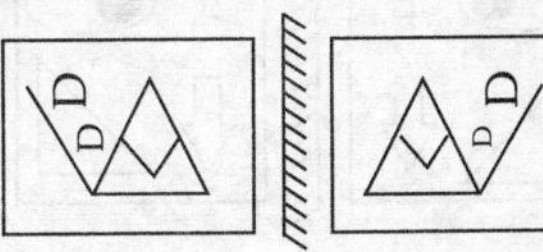

12. Option (D) is correct.

Explanation:

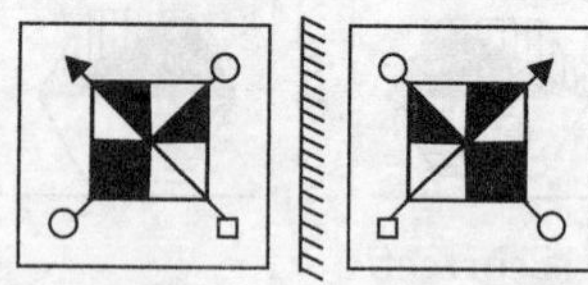

13. Option (C) is correct.

Explanation:

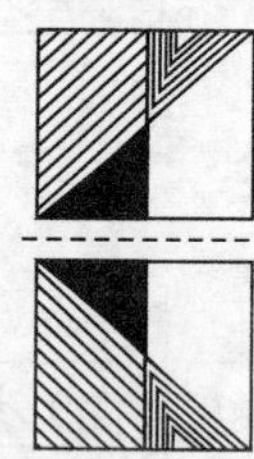

14. Option (D) is correct.

Explanation:

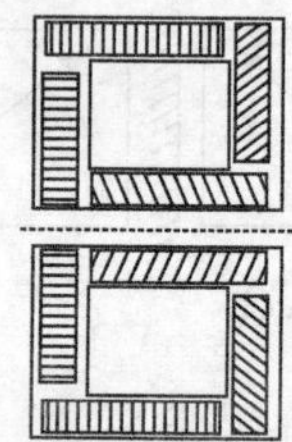

15. Option (B) is correct.

Explanation:

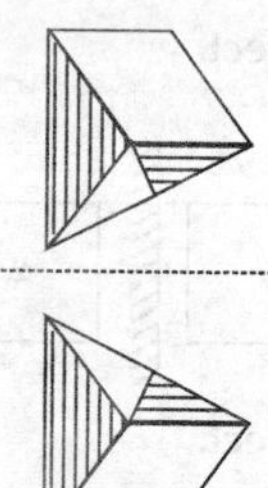

16. Option (C) is correct.

Explanation:

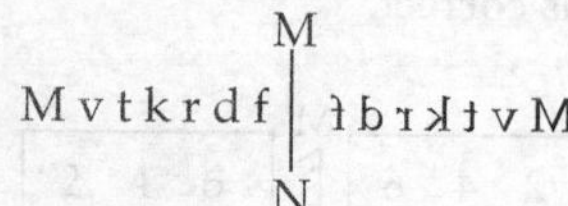

17. Option (B) is correct.

Explanation:

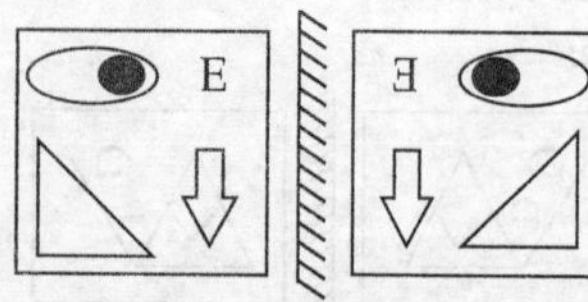

18. Option (A) is correct.

Explanation:

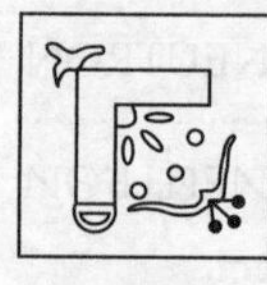

19. Option (D) is correct.

Explanation:

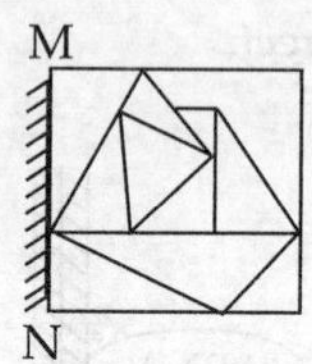

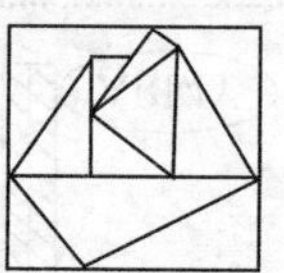

20. Option (A) is correct.

Explanation:

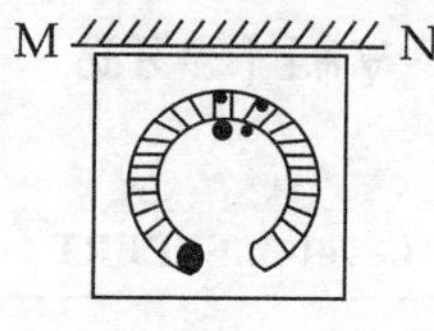

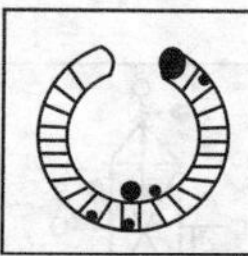

21. Option (B) is correct.

Explanation:

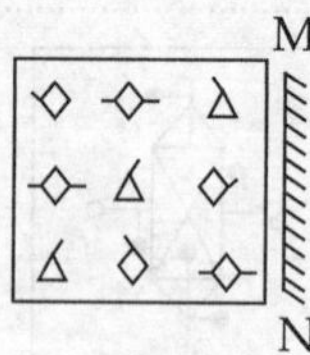

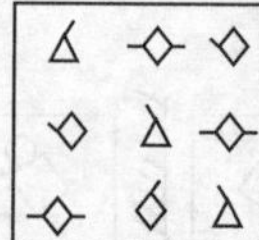

22. Option (D) is correct.

Explanation:

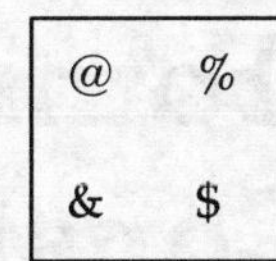

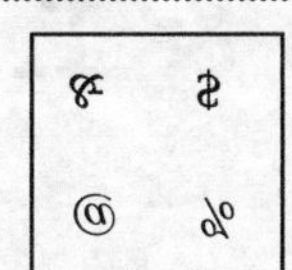

23. Option (D) is correct.

Explanation:

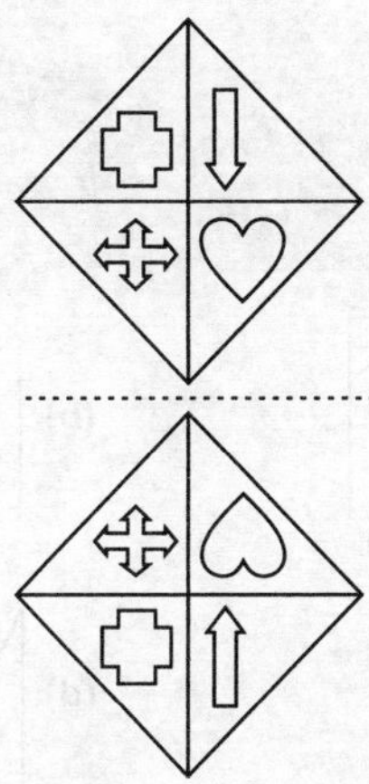

24. Option (D) is correct.

Explanation:

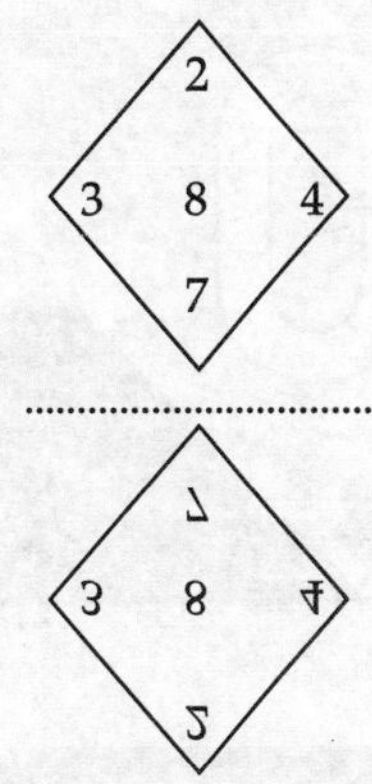

25. Option (C) is correct.

Explanation:

MISSION

Chapter 20 Embedded Figures, Figure Formation & Analysis and Construction of Squares & Triangles

LEARNING OBJECTIVES:

- ❖ Identifying the part hidden in the question figure
- ❖ Identifying the part not hidden in the question figure
- ❖ Different types of questions asked in competitive exams

1. **Embedded figures:** This section will helps the students to enhance their logical and critical ability. Here, some of the option figures and a question figure will be given. We have to find the option figure in which the question figure will be hidden as one of its part.

Example 1: Select a figure from the options in which the question figure is hidden.

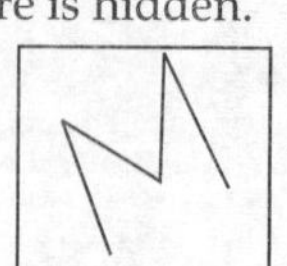

(a) 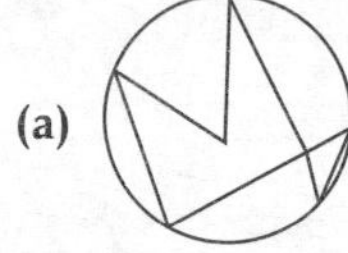

(b) 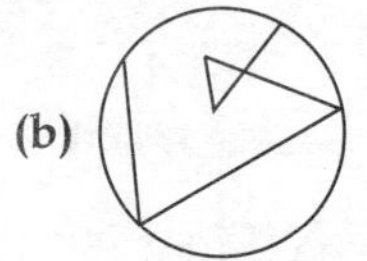

(c) 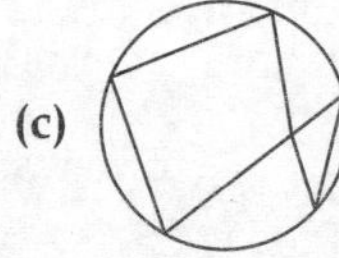

(d) 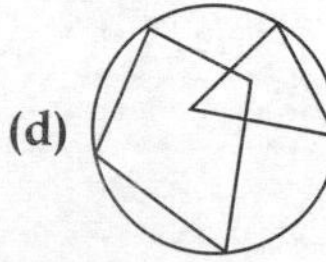

Sol. (a)

2. **Figure formation:** In this section, we are given some different types of pieces and we need to join these pieces to form a complete figure.

Example 2: Select a figure from the option which will be formed by using the given pieces.

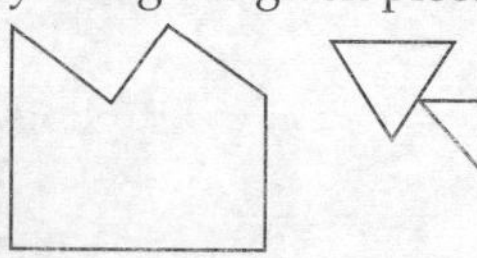

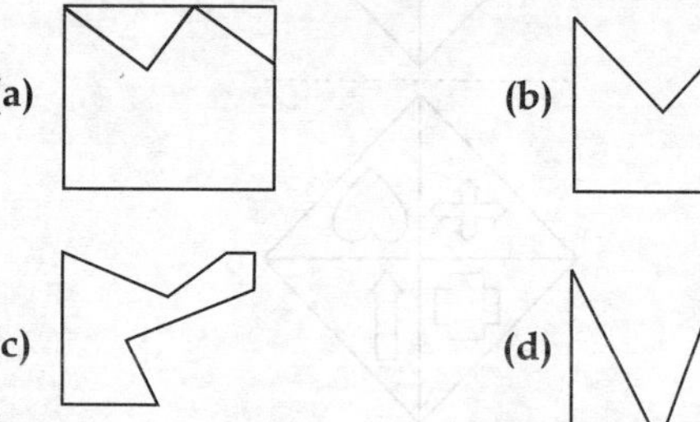

Sol. (a)

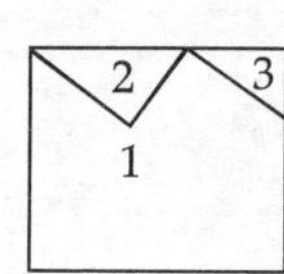

3. **Construction of squares and triangles:** In this section, we are given types of pieces which will be used to form either square or triangle.

Example 3: Select a figure from the options which when joined with question figure will form a complete square.

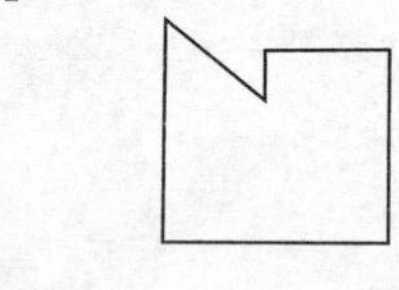

(a)

(b) 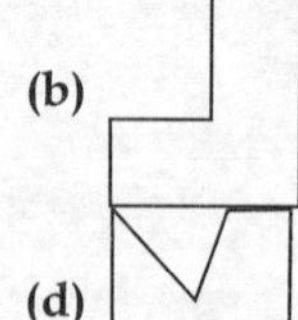

(c)

(d) 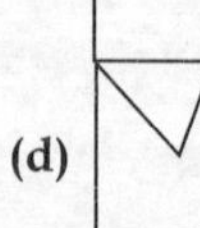

Sol. (a)

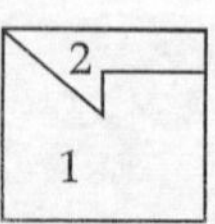

Example 4: Select a figure from the options which when joined with question figure will form a complete triangle.

a b c d e

(a) ABC (b) BCE
(c) ACD (d) ACE

Sol. (a)

Level 1 Beginner

Direction (Qs. 1–8): Select a figure from the options which is exactly embedded in the given figure as one of its part.

1.

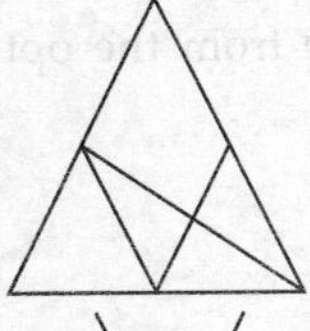

(A) 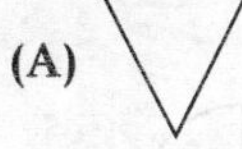 **(B)**

(C)  **(D)**

2.

(A) 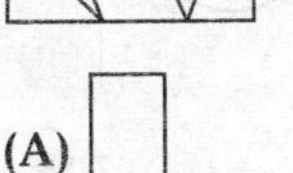 **(B)**  **(C)** 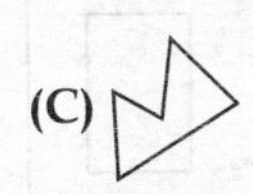 **(D)**

3.

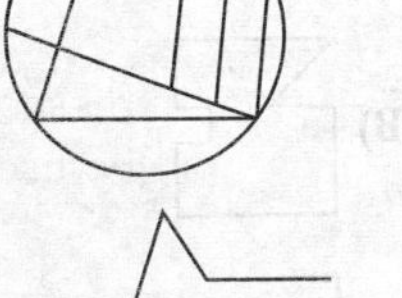

(A) 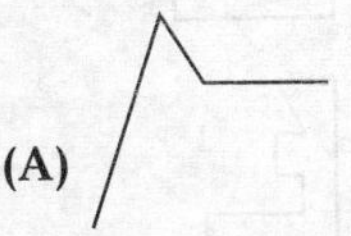 **(B)**

(C) 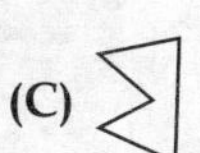 **(D)**

4.

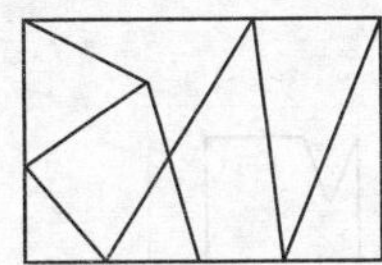

(A) 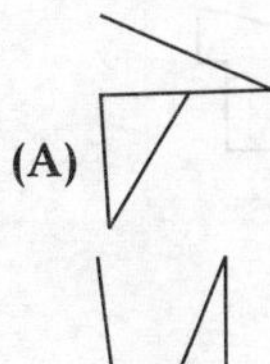 **(B)** 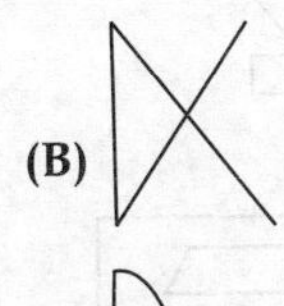

(C) **(D)** 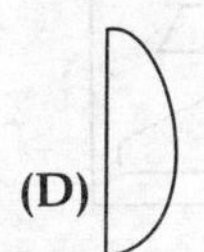

5.

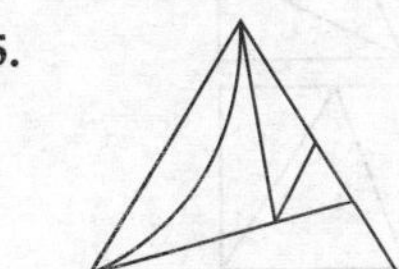

(A) 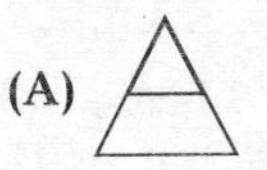 **(B)**

(C) 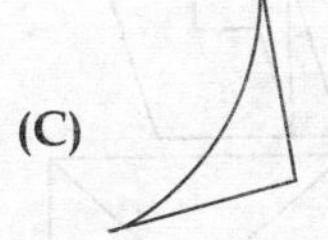 **(D)**

6.

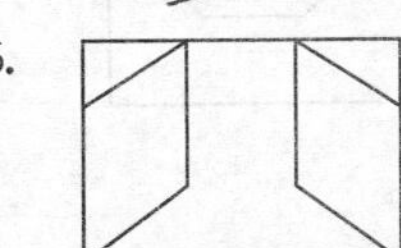

(A)  **(B)**

(C) 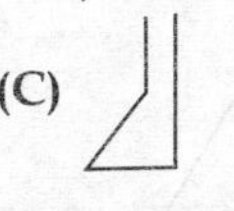 **(D)**

7.

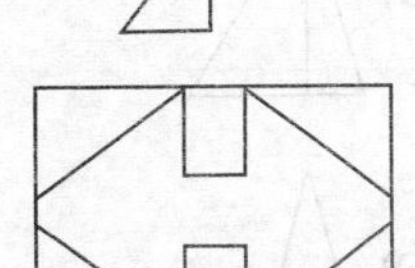

(A) 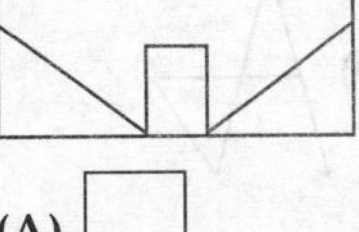 **(B)**

(C) 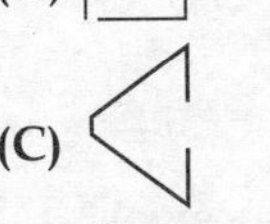 **(D)** 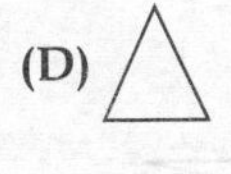

8.

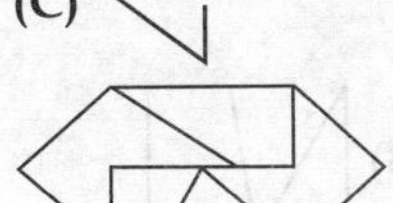

(A) 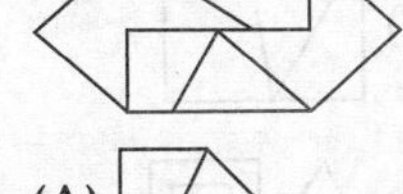 **(B)** 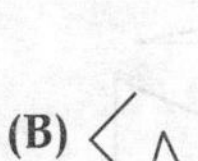

(C) 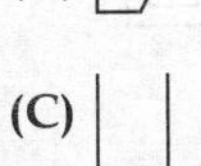 **(D)** 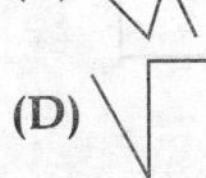

Direction (Qs. 9–15): Select a figure from the options in which the given figure is exactly embedded as one of its part.

9.

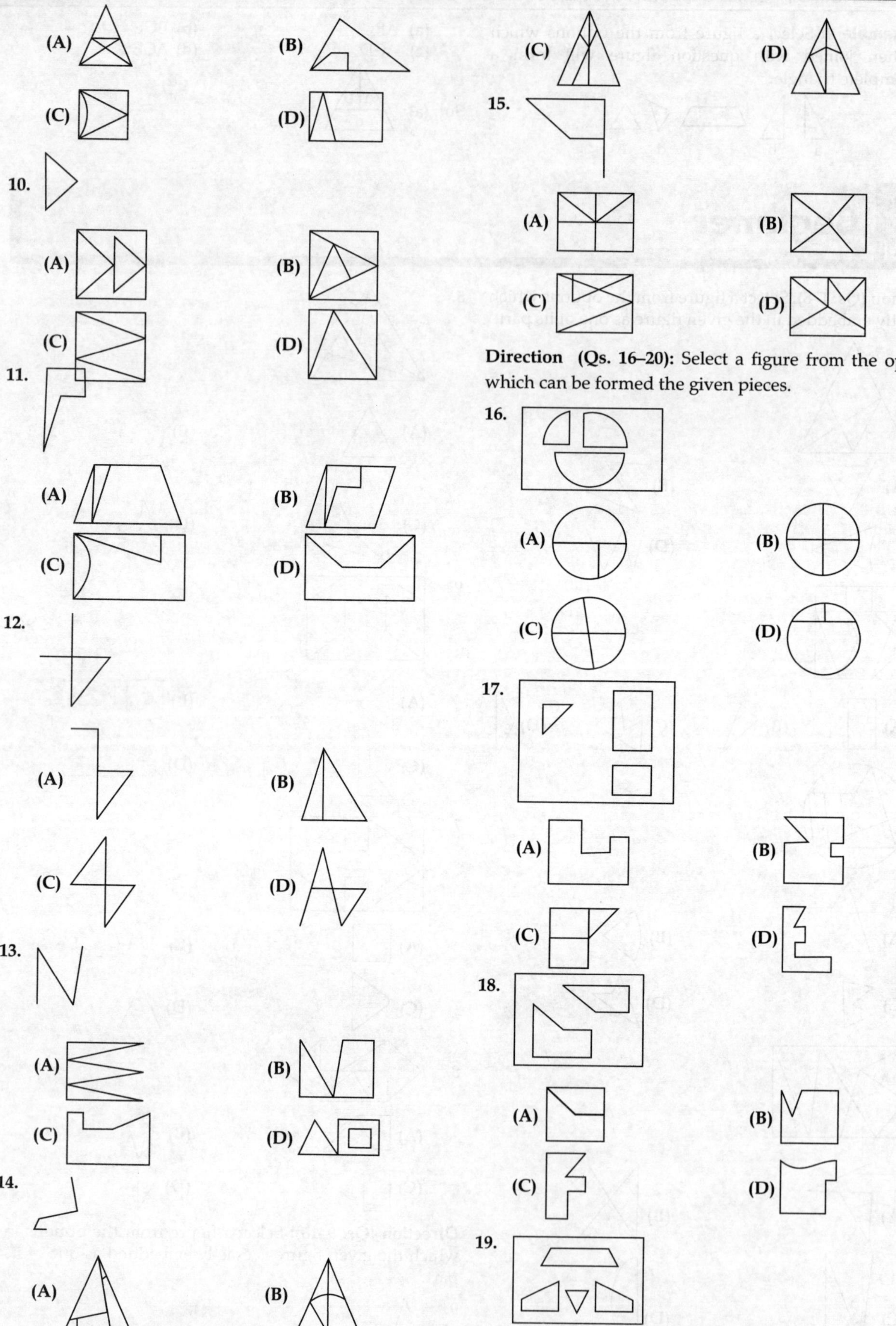

Direction (Qs. 16–20): Select a figure from the options which can be formed the given pieces.

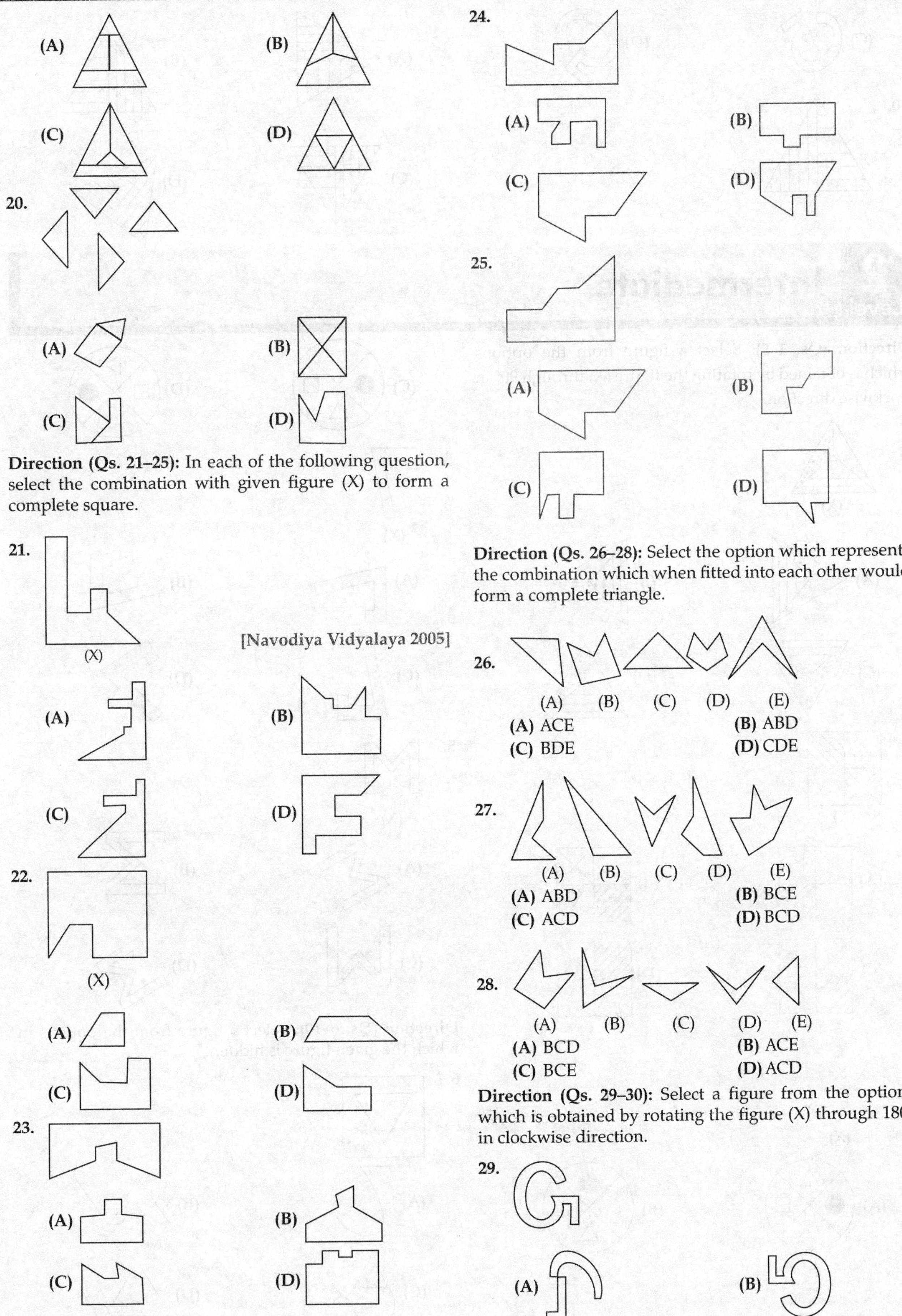

(A) (B)

(C) (D)

20.

(A) (B)

(C) (D)

Direction (Qs. 21–25): In each of the following question, select the combination with given figure (X) to form a complete square.

21. (X)

[Navodiya Vidyalaya 2005]

(A) (B)

(C) (D)

22. (X)

(A) (B)

(C) (D)

23.

(A) (B)

(C) (D)

24.

(A) (B)

(C) (D)

25.

(A) (B)

(C) (D)

Direction (Qs. 26–28): Select the option which represents the combination which when fitted into each other would form a complete triangle.

26.

(A) (B) (C) (D) (E)

(A) ACE **(B)** ABD

(C) BDE **(D)** CDE

27.

(A) (B) (C) (D) (E)

(A) ABD **(B)** BCE

(C) ACD **(D)** BCD

28.

(A) (B) (C) (D) (E)

(A) BCD **(B)** ACE

(C) BCE **(D)** ACD

Direction (Qs. 29–30): Select a figure from the options which is obtained by rotating the figure (X) through 180° in clockwise direction.

29.

(A) (B)

(C) 

(D) 

30.

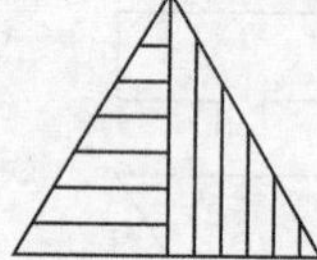

(A) 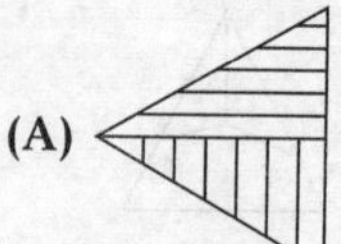

(B) 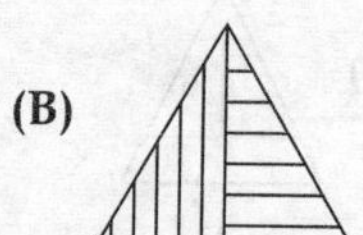

(C) 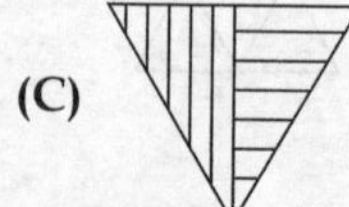

(D) 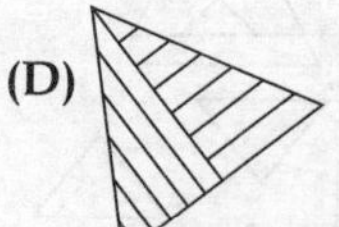

Level 2 Intermediate

Direction (Qs. 1–5): Select a figure from the options which is obtained by rotating the figure (X) through 90° in clockwise direction.

1.

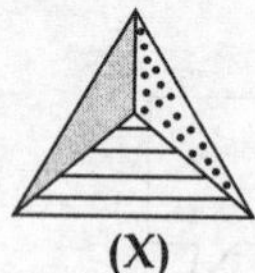

(X)

(A) 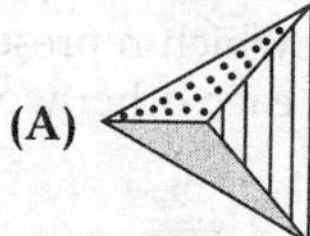

(B) 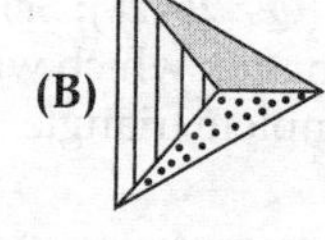

(C) 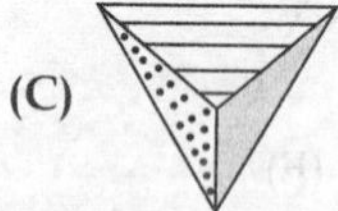

(D) 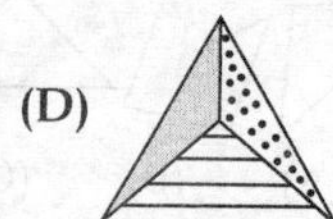

2.

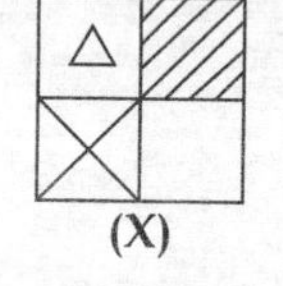

(X)

(A) 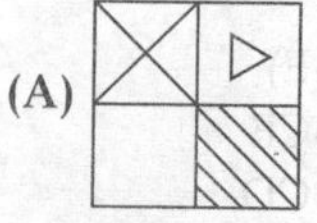

(B)

(C) 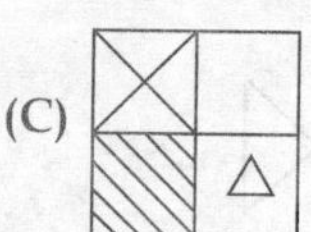

(D)

3.

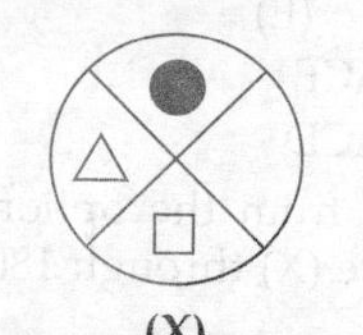

(X)

(A) 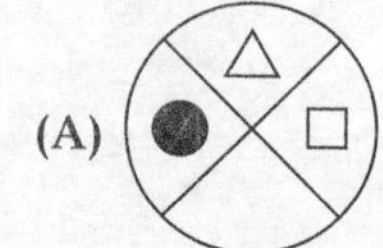

(B) 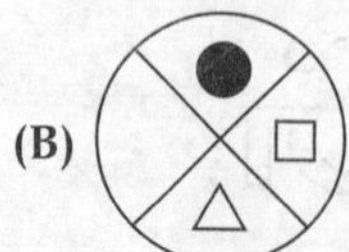

(C) 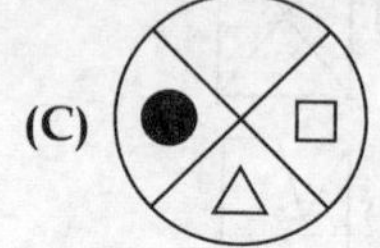

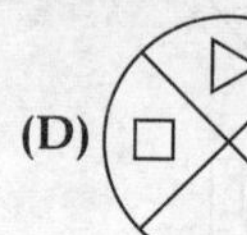

(D) 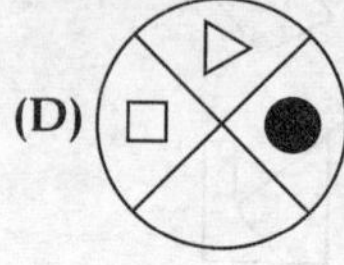

4.

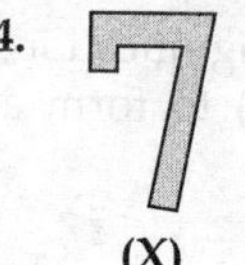

(X)

(A) 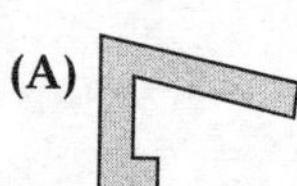

(B) 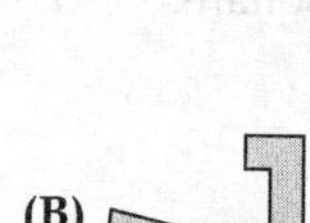

(C) 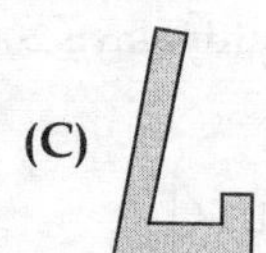

(D) 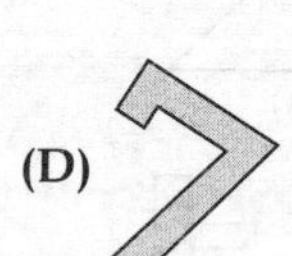

5.

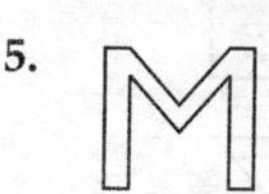

(X)

(A) 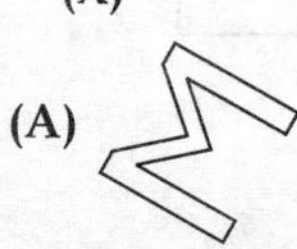

(B) 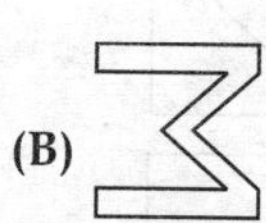

(C) 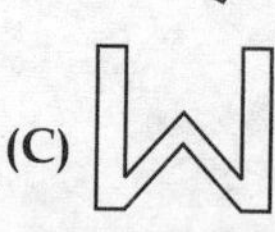

(D) 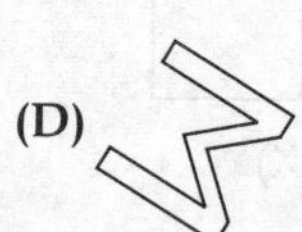

Direction (Qs. 6–10): Select a figure from the options in which the given figure is hidden.

6.

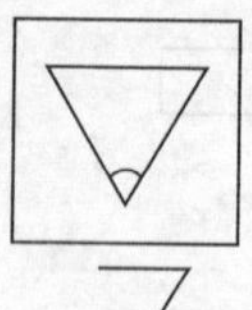

(A) 

(B) 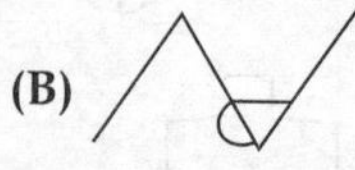

(C) 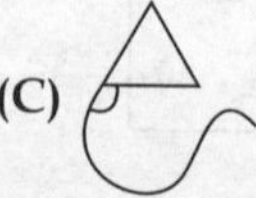

(D) 

7.

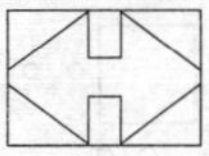

(A) (B)

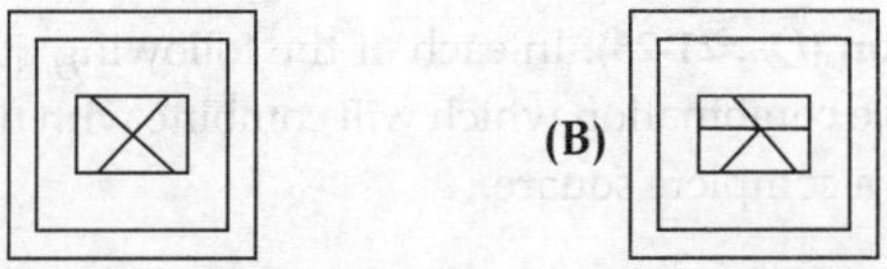

(C) (D)

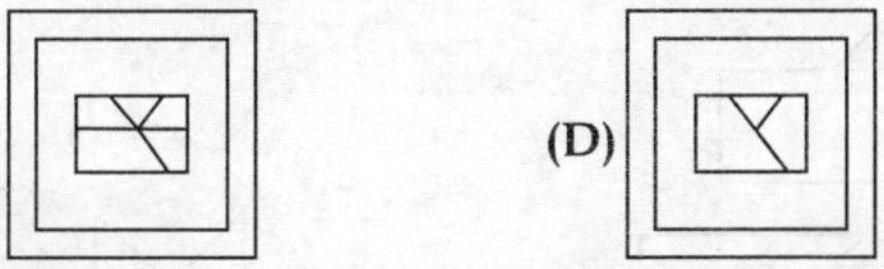

8.

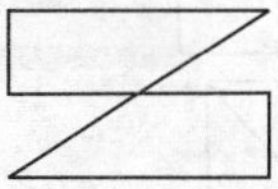

(A) (B)

(C) (D)

9.

(A) (B)

(C) (D)

10.

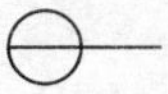

(A) (B)

(C) (D)

Direction (Qs. 11–15): Select a figure from the options which is exactly embedded in the question figure as one of its part.

11.

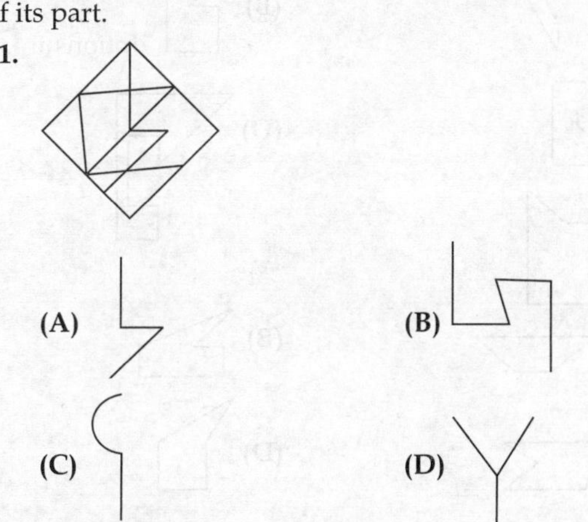

(A) (B)

(C) (D)

12.

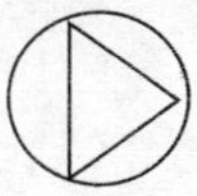

(A) (B)

(C) (D)

13.

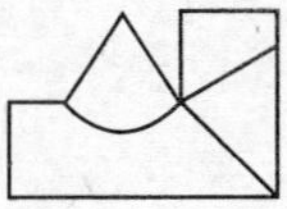

(A) (B)

(C) (D)

14.

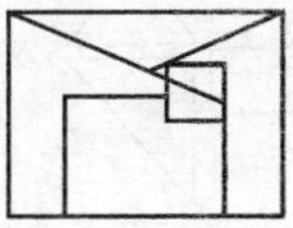

(A) (B)

(C) (D)

15.

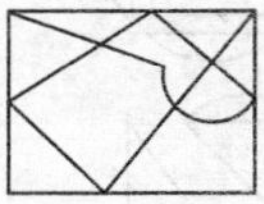

(A) (B)

(C) (D)

Direction (Qs. 16–20): Select a figure from the option which when combined will look like the given figure.

16.

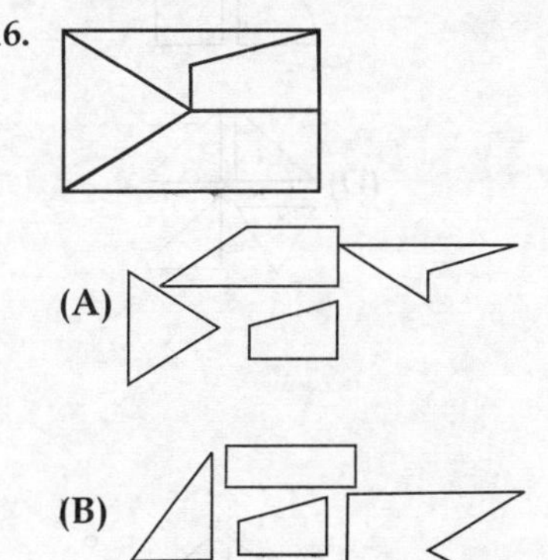

(A)

(B)

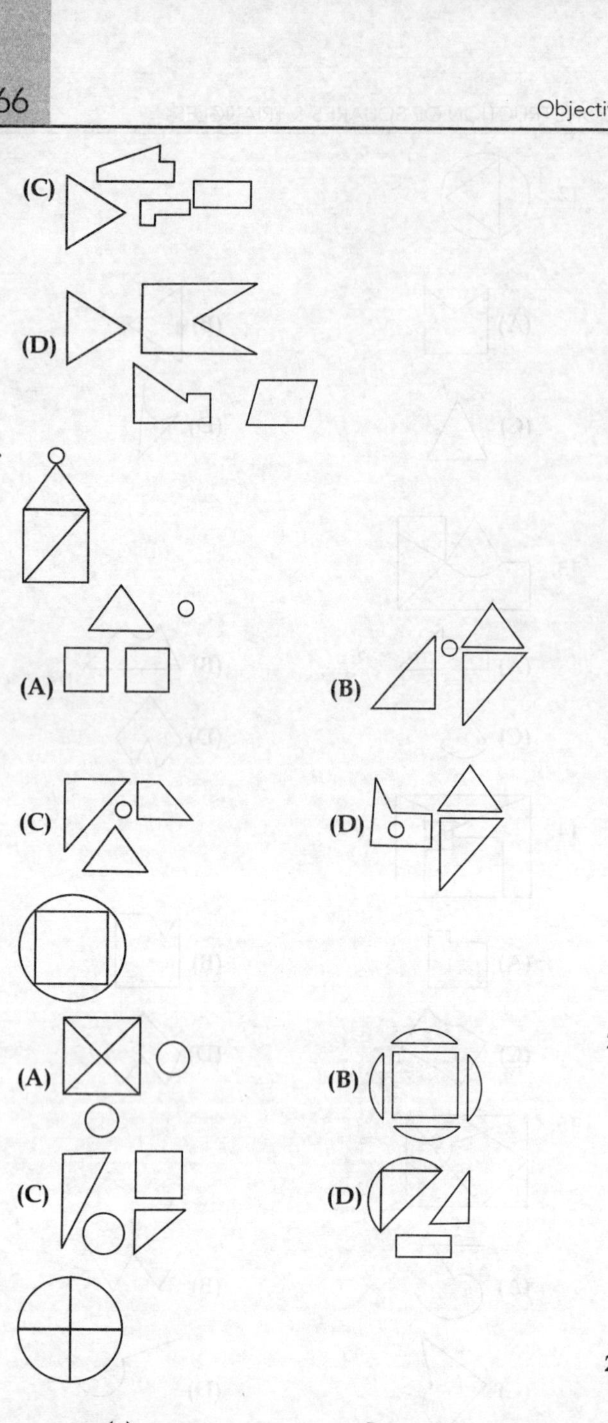

(C) (D)

19.

(A) (B)

(C) (D)

20.

(A) (B)

(C)

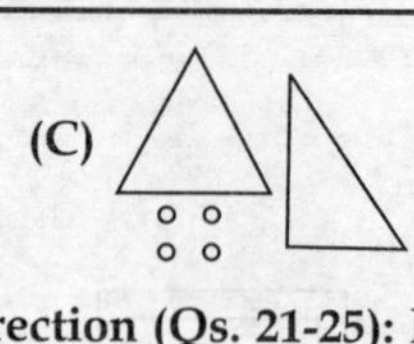

(D)

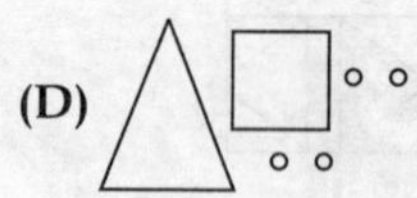

Direction (Qs. 21-25): In each of the following questions, select the combination which will combine with figure (X) to form a complete square.

21.

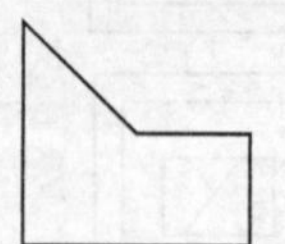

(A) (B)

(C) (D)

22.

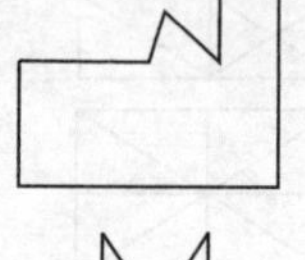

(A) (B)

(C) (D)

23.

(A) (B)

(C) (D)

24.

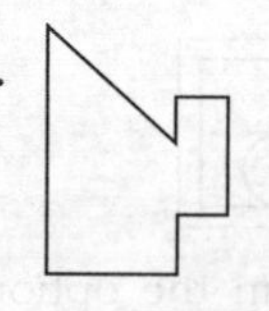

(A) (B)

(C) (D)

25.

(A) (B)

(C) (D)

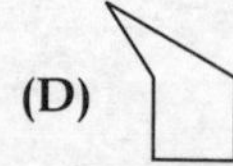

3 Level Expert

Direction (Qs. 1–5): Select a figure from the options in which the given figure is exactly embedded.

1. 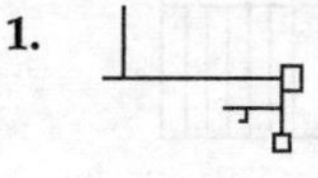

[SSC CHSL 2020]

(A) 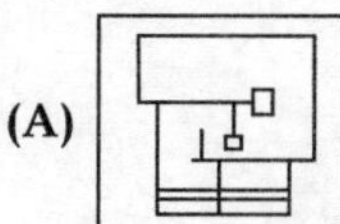 (B) 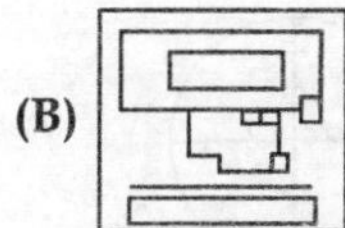

(C) (D) 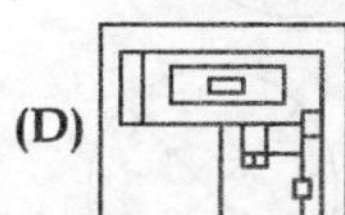

2.

[SSC 2018]

(A) 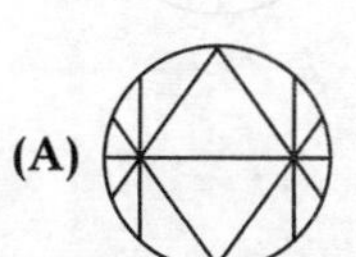 (B) 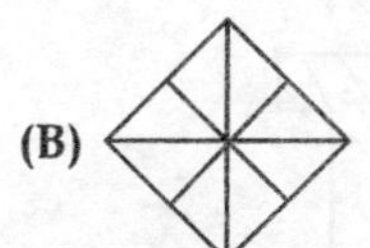

(C) 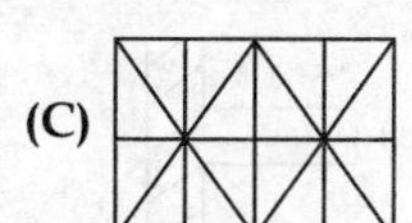 (D) 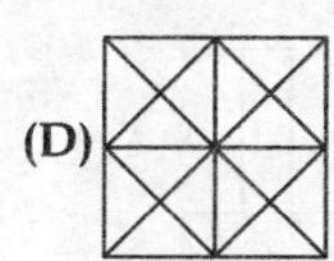

3. 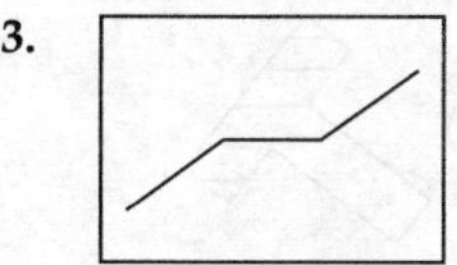

[SSC CGL 2019]

(A) 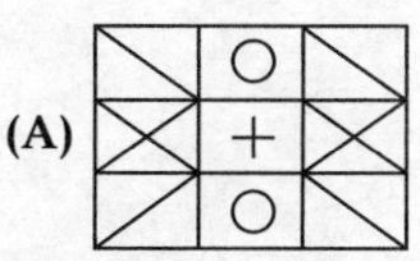 (B) 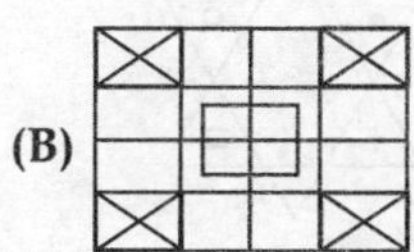

(C) 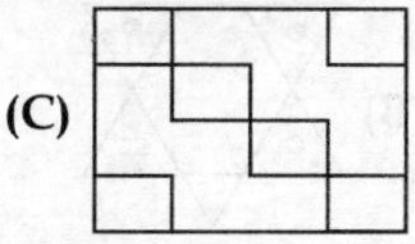 (D) 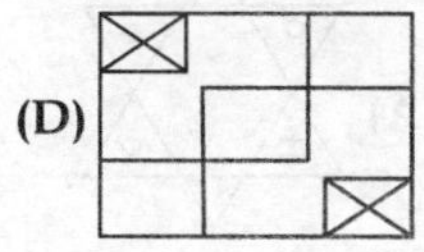

4. 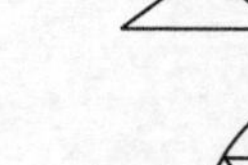

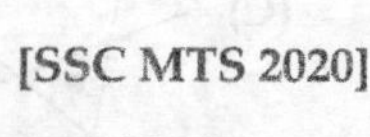

[SSC MTS 2020]

(A) 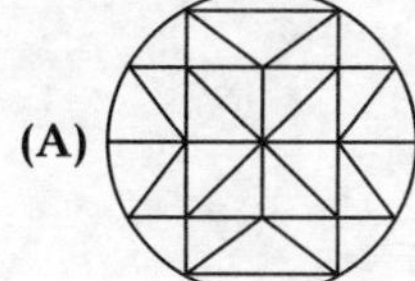 (B) 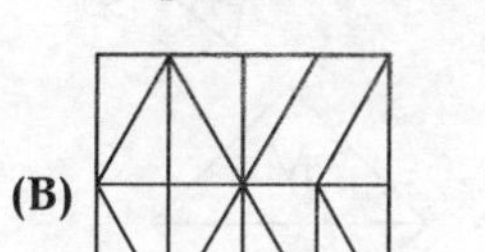

(C) 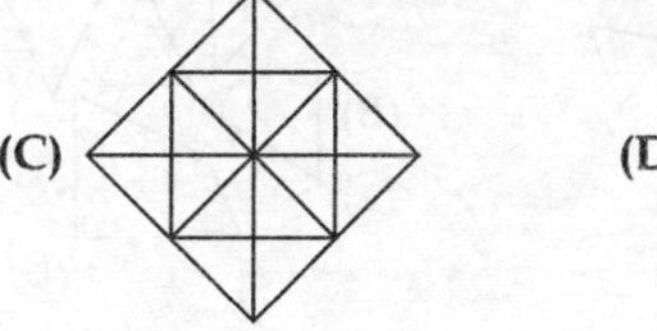 (D) 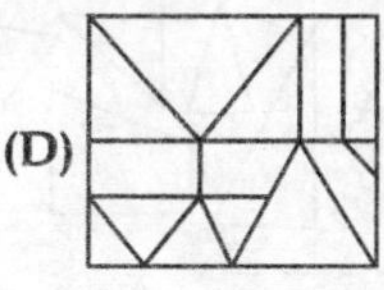

5.

[SSC CGL 2017]

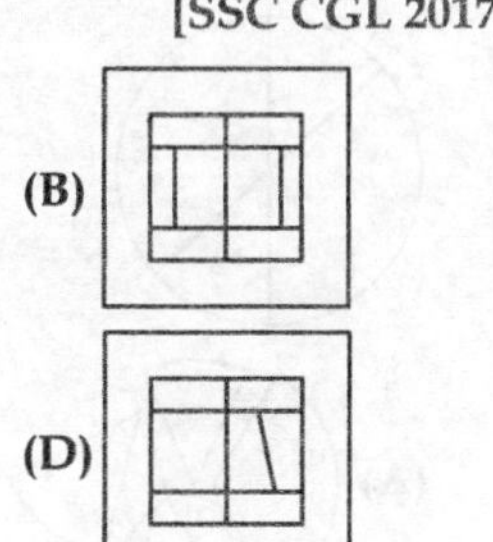

(A) (B)

(C) (D)

Direction (Qs. 6–10): Select a figure from the options which when combined will look like the given figure.

6. 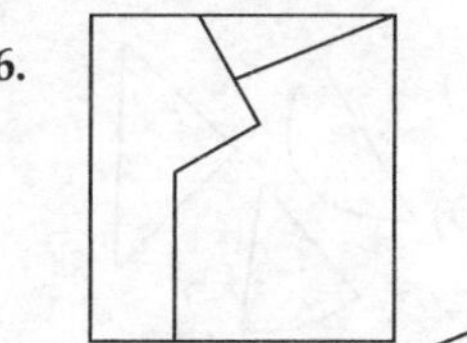

(A) (B) 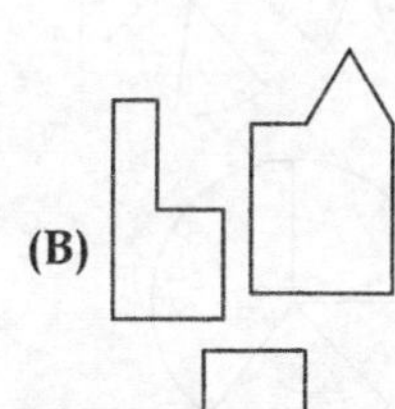

(C) 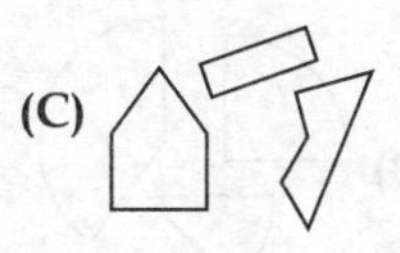 (D) 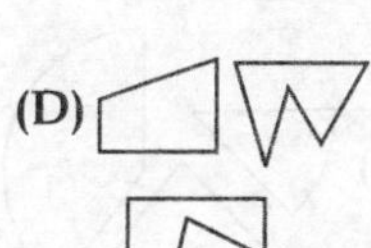

7. 

(A) (B) 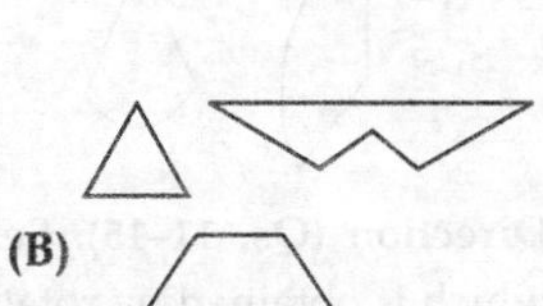

(C) 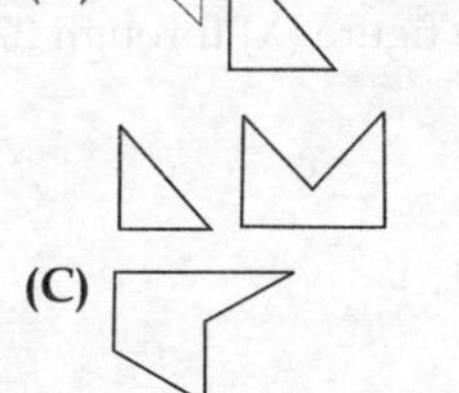 (D) 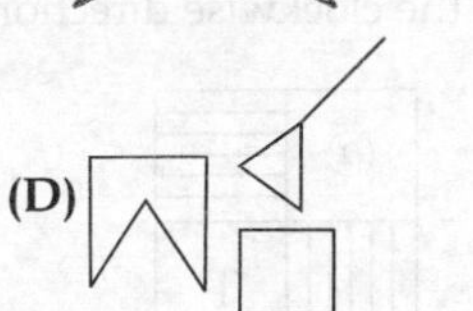

8.

(A) **(B)**

(C) **(D)**

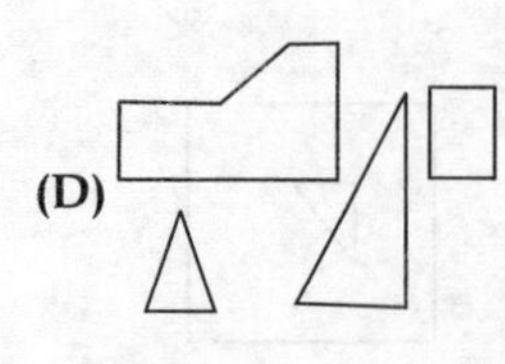

9.

(A) **(B)**

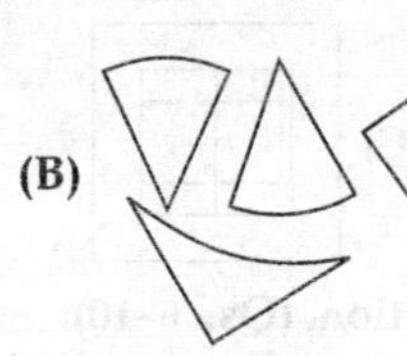

(C)

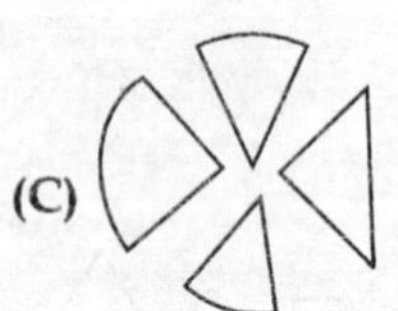

(D)

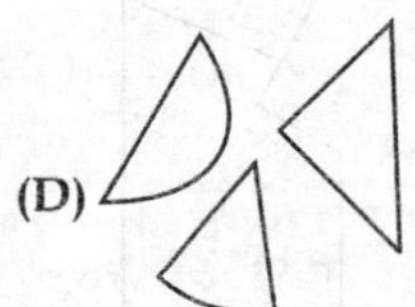

10.

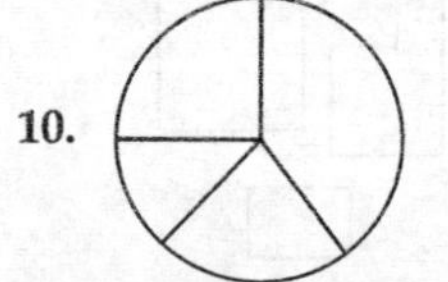

(A)

(B)

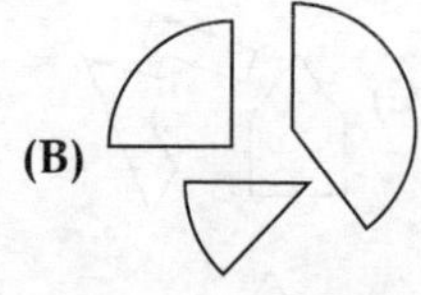

(C)

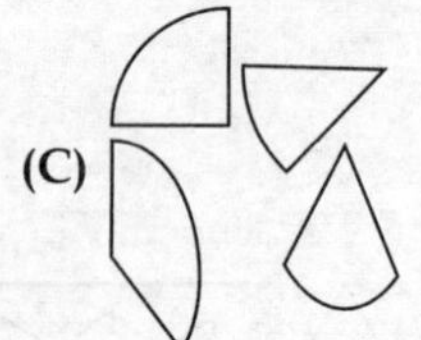

(D)

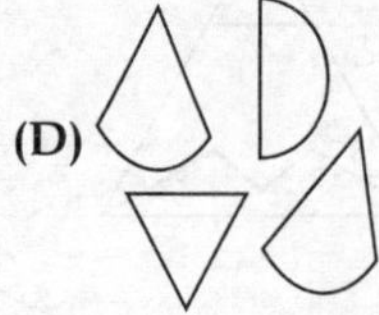

Direction (Qs. 11–15): Select a figure from the options which is obtained by rotating the figure (X) through 270° in the clockwise direction.

11.

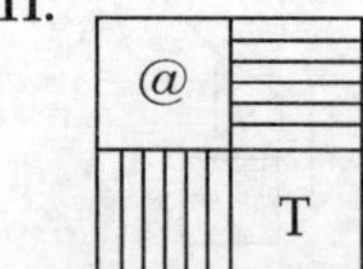

(A) **(B)**

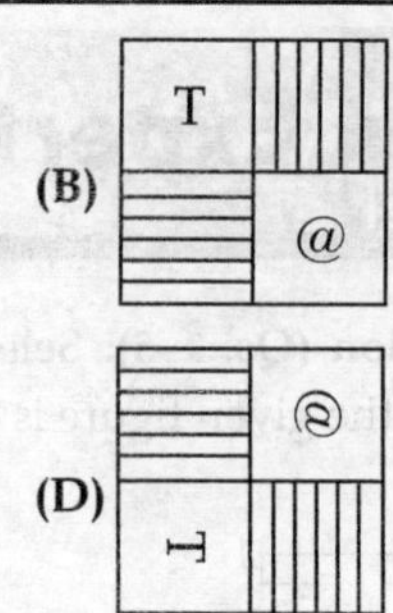

(C)

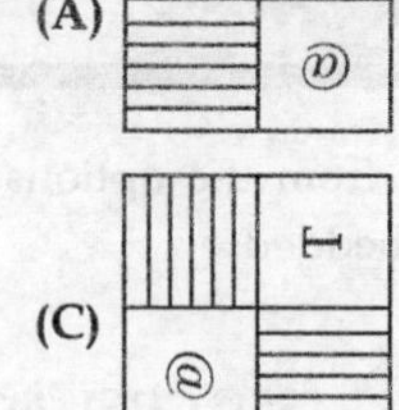

(D)

12.

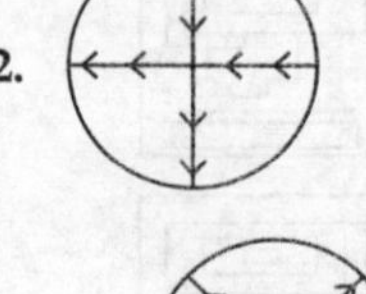

(A) **(B)**

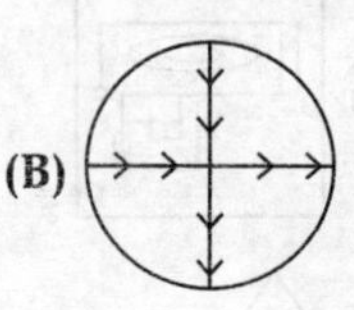

(C)

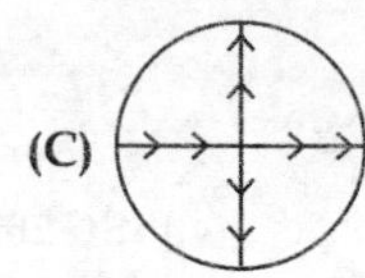

(D)

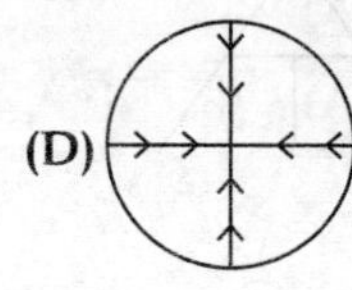

13.

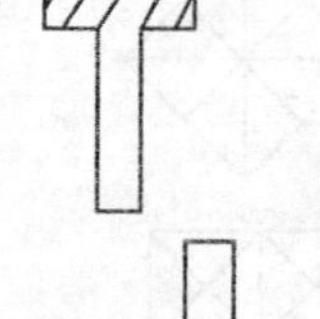

(A) **(B)**

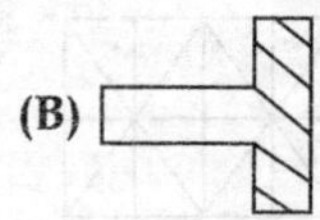

(C)

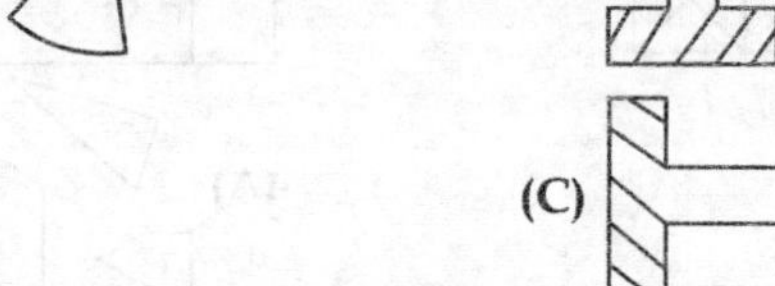

(D)

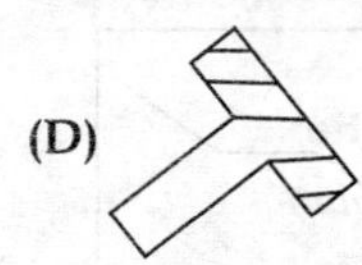

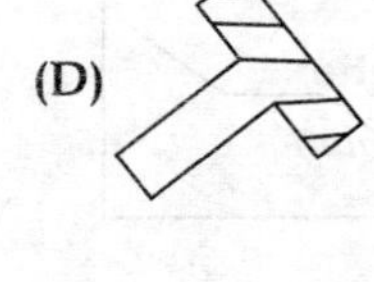

14.

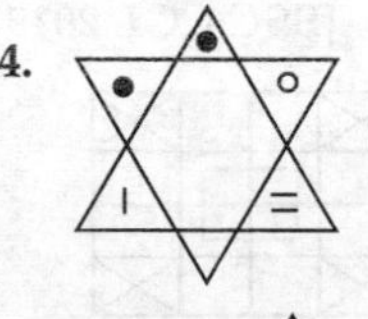

(A)

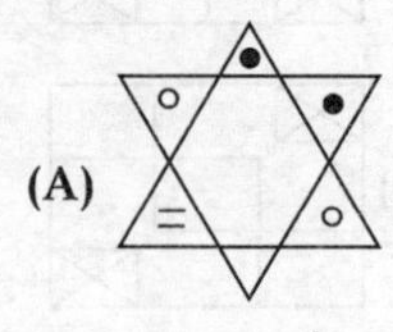

(B)

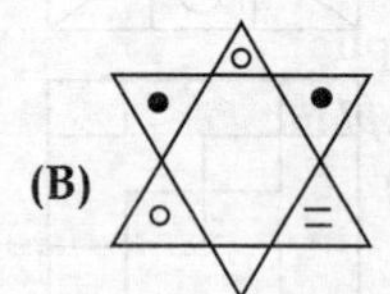

(C)

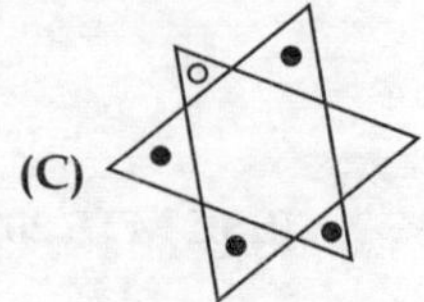

(D)

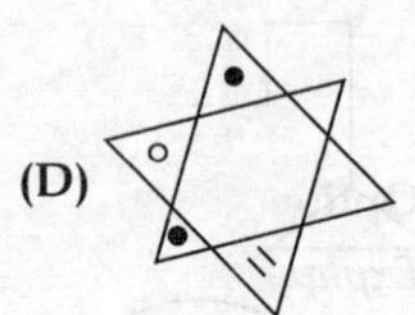

15.

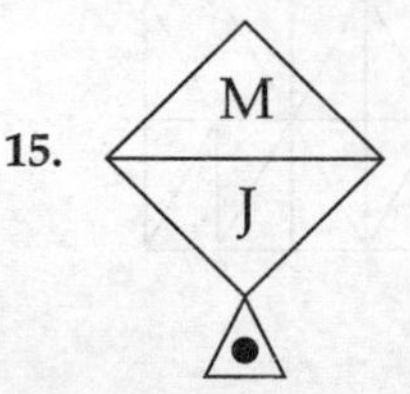

(A) 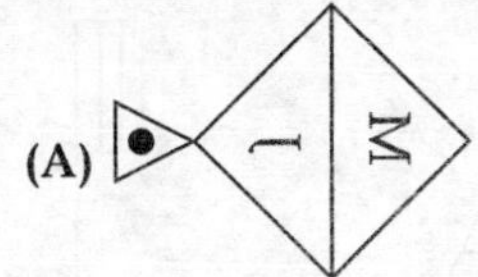 (B) 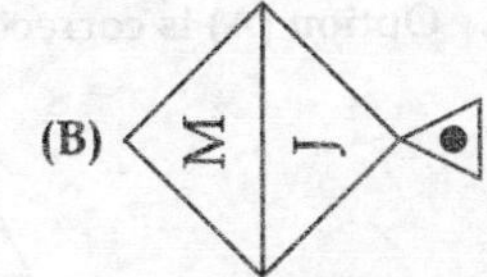 (C) 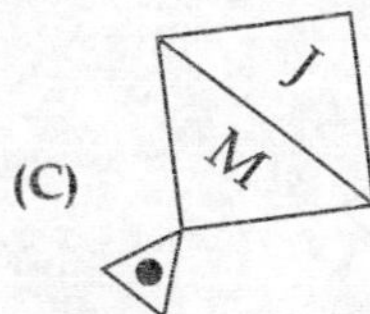 (D) 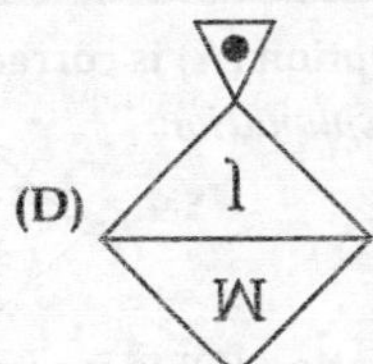

ANSWER KEY

Level-1: Beginner

1.	(A)	2.	(B)	3.	(A)	4.	(C)	5.	(C)	6.	(D)	7.	(C)	8.	(A)	9.	(D)	10.	(A)
11.	(A)	12.	(C)	13.	(B)	14.	(A)	15.	(A)	16.	(A)	17.	(C)	18.	(A)	19.	(A)	20.	(B)
21.	(D)	22.	(A)	23.	(B)	24.	(C)	25.	(A)	26.	(D)	27.	(A)	28.	(A)	29.	(B)	30.	(C)

Level-2: Intermediate

1.	(B)	2.	(A)	3.	(D)	4.	(B)	5.	(B)	6.	(D)	7.	(A)	8.	(D)	9.	(D)	10.	(B)
11.	(A)	12.	(B)	13.	(C)	14.	(A)	15.	(D)	16.	(A)	17.	(B)	18.	(B)	19.	(C)	20.	(B)
21.	(A)	22.	(C)	23.	(A)	24.	(D)	25.	(A)										

Level-3: Expert

1.	(D)	2.	(C)	3.	(A)	4.	(A)	5.	(A)	6.	(A)	7.	(B)	8.	(B)	9.	(A)	10.	(C)
11.	(C)	12.	(B)	13.	(C)	14.	(C)	15.	(B)										

Solutions with Detailed Explanations

Level-1: BEGINNER

1. **Option (A) is correct.**
   Explanation:

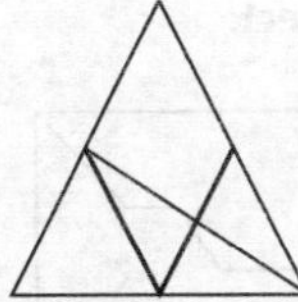

2. **Option (B) is correct.**
   Explanation:

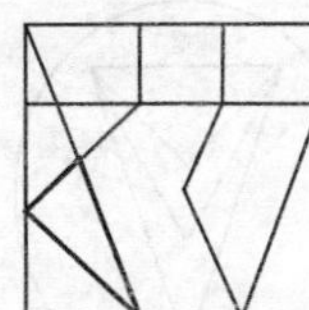

3. **Option (A) is correct.**
   Explanation:

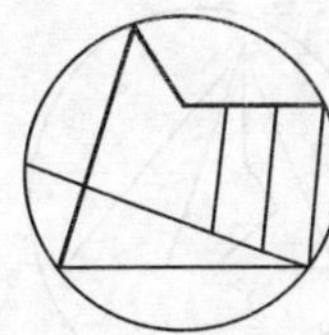

4. **Option (C) is correct.**
   Explanation:

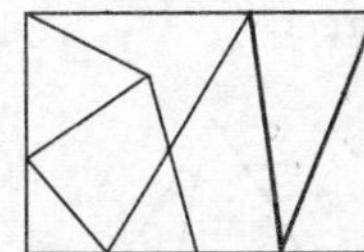

5. **Option (C) is correct.**
   Explanation:

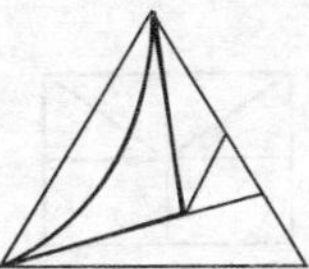

6. **Option (D) is correct.**
   Explanation:

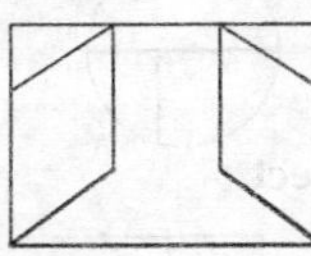

7. **Option (C) is correct.**
   Explanation:

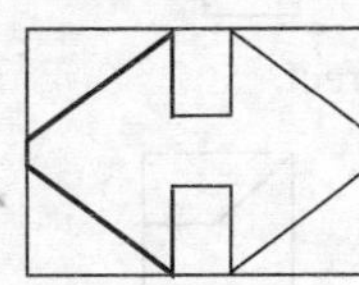

8. **Option (A) is correct.**
Explanation:

9. **Option (D) is correct.**
Explanation:

10. **Option (A) is correct.**
Explanation:

11. **Option (A) is correct.**
Explanation:

12. **Option (C) is correct.**
Explanation:

13. **Option (B) is correct.**
Explanation:

14. **Option (A) is correct.**
Explanation:

15. **Option (A) is correct.**
Explanation:

16. **Option (A) is correct.**

17. **Option (C) is correct.**

18. **Option (A) is correct.**

19. **Option (A) is correct.**

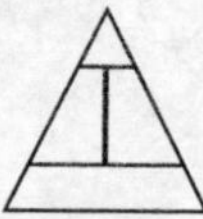

20. **Option (B) is correct.**

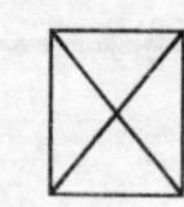

21. **Option (D) is correct.**

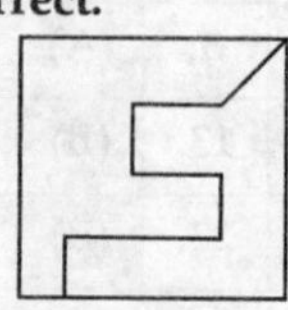

22. **Option (A) is correct.**
Explanation:

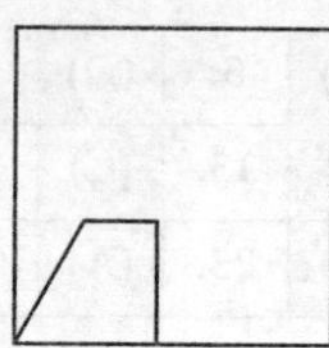

23. **Option (B) is correct.**
Explanation:

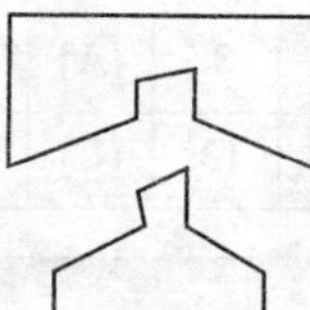

24. **Option (C) is correct.**
Explanation:

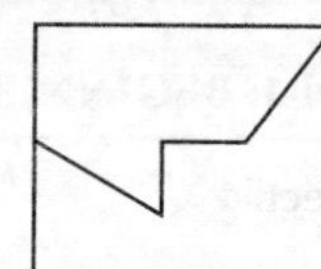

25. **Option (A) is correct.**
Explanation:

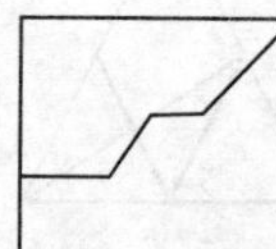

26. **Option (D) is correct.**

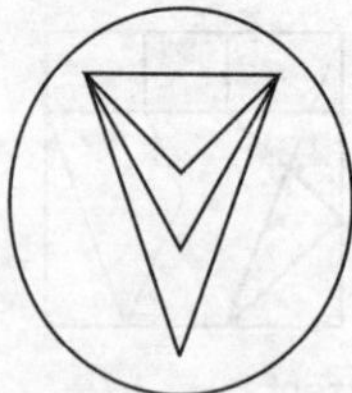

27. **Option (A) is correct.**

28. Option (A) is correct.

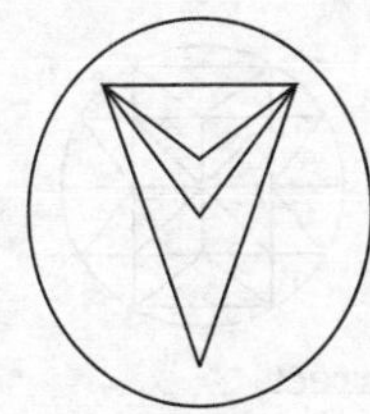

29. Option (B) is correct.

Explanation:

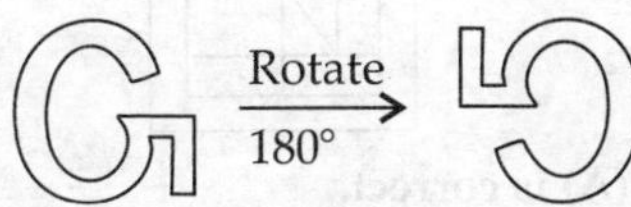

30. Option (C) is correct.

Explanation:

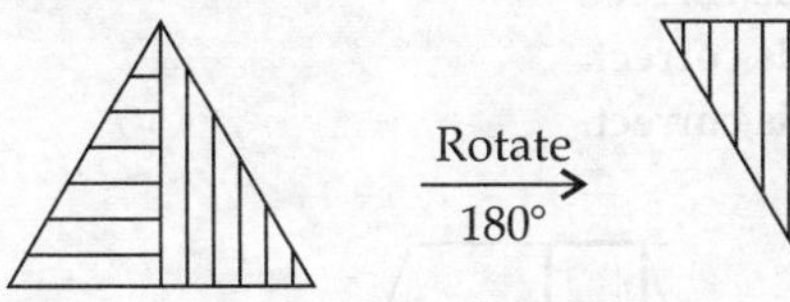

Level-2: INTERMEDIATE

1. Option (B) is correct.

Explanation:

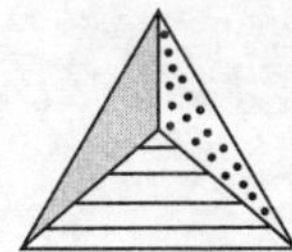

Rotate 90°

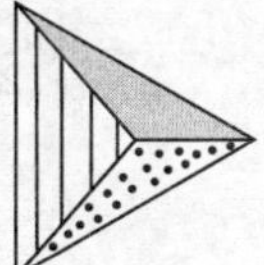

2. Option (A) is correct.

Explanation:

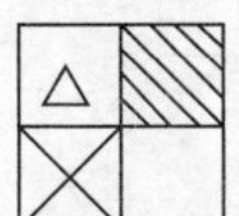

Rotate 90°

3. Option (D) is correct.

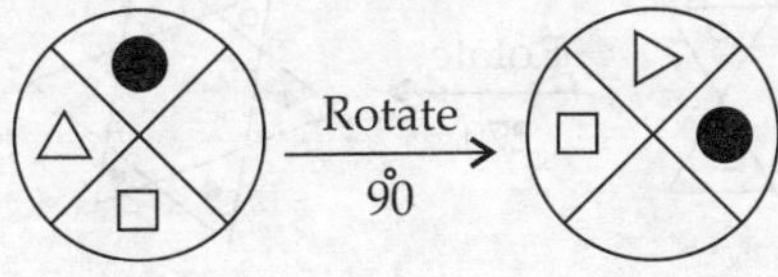

4. Option (B) is correct.

Explanation:

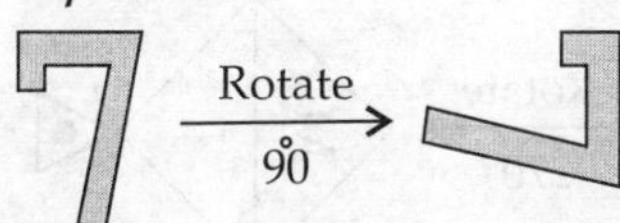

5. Option (B) is correct.

Explanation:

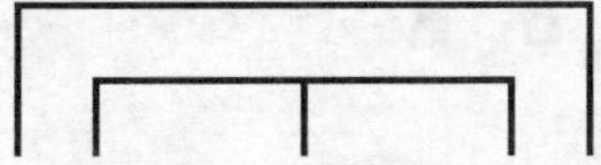

6. Option (D) is correct.

Explanation:

7. Option (A) is correct.

Explanation:

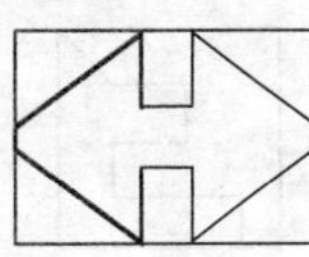

8. Option (D) is correct.

Explanation:

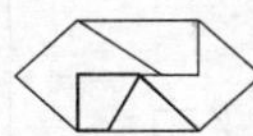

9. Option (D) is correct.

Explanation:

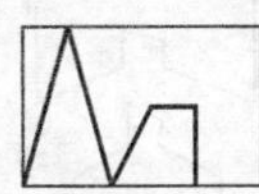

10. Option (B) is correct.

Explanation:

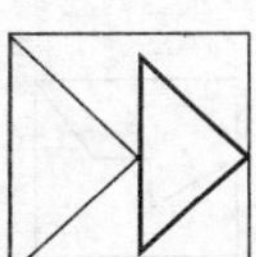

11. Option (A) is correct.

Explanation:

12. Option (B) is correct.

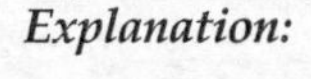

Explanation:

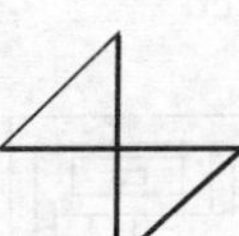

13. Option (C) is correct.

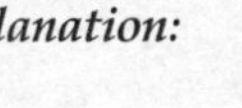

Explanation:

14. Option (A) is correct.

Explanation:

15. Option (D) is correct.

Explanation:

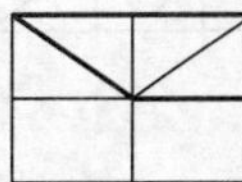

16. **Option (A) is correct.**
17. **Option (B) is correct.**
18. **Option (B) is correct.**
19. **Option (C) is correct.**
20. **Option (B) is correct.**
21. **Option (A) is correct.**
Explanation:

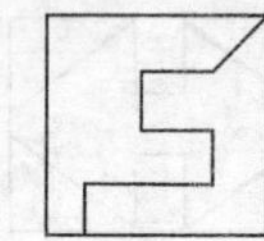

22. **Option (C) is correct.**
Explanation:

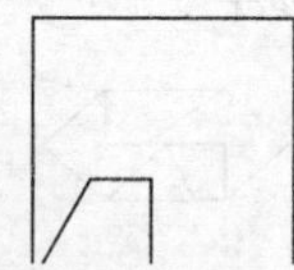

23. **Option (A) is correct.**
Explanation:

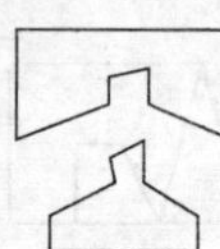

24. **Option (D) is correct.**
Explanation:

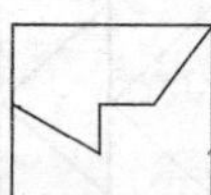

25. **Option (A) is correct.**

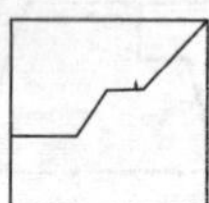

Level-3: EXPERT

1. **Option (D) is correct.**
Explanation:

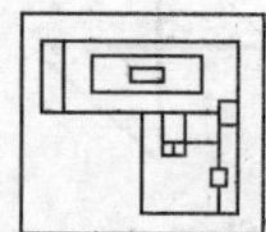

2. **Option (C) is correct.**
Explanation:

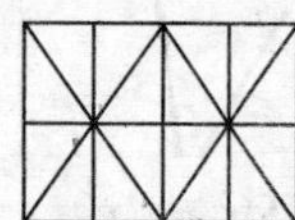

3. **Option (A) is correct.**
Explanation:

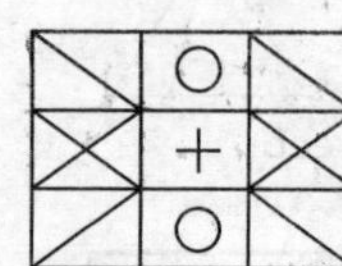

4. **Option (A) is correct.**
Explanation:

5. **Option (A) is correct.**
Explanation:

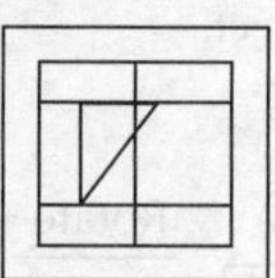

6. **Option (A) is correct.**
7. **Option (B) is correct.**
8. **Option (B) is correct.**
9. **Option (A) is correct.**
10. **Option (C) is correct.**
11. **Option (C) is correct.**
Explanation:

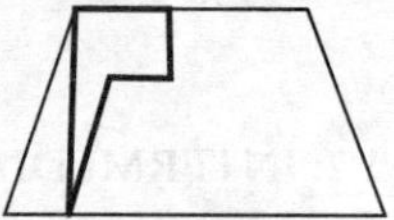

12. **Option (B) is correct.**
Explanation:

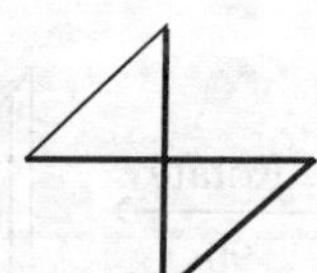

13. **Option (C) is correct.**
Explanation:

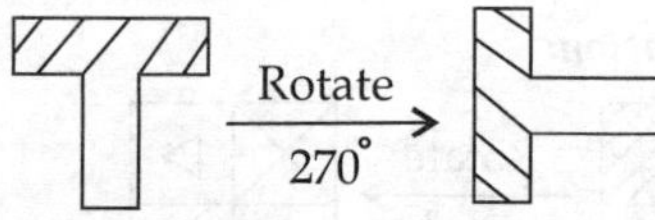

14. **Option (C) is correct.**
Explanation:

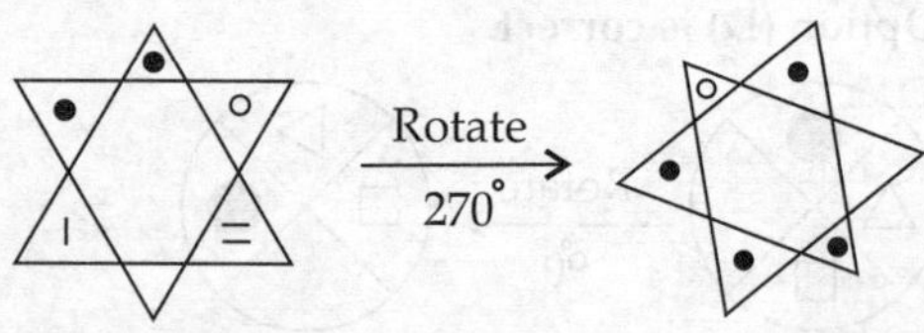

15. **Option (B) is correct.**
Explanation:

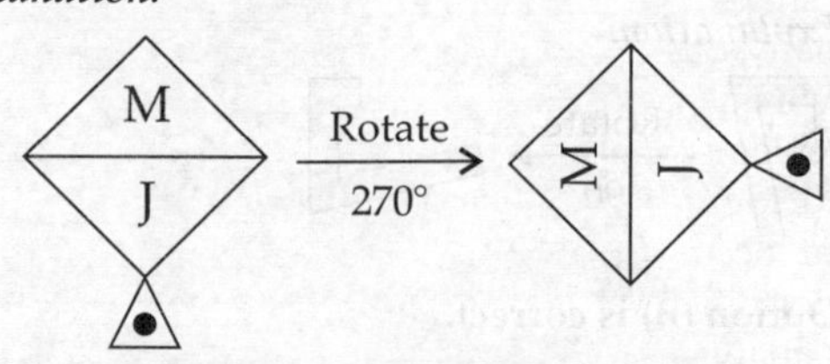

■ ■ ■

Chapter 21

Completion of Incomplete Pattern

LEARNING OBJECTIVES:

- Identifying the missing part to complete the given figure
- Different types of questions asked in competitive exams

Visual pattern recognition tests or puzzles often feature a problem type known as completion problems. In this type of problem, a figure or matrix is displayed with a missing quarter, and the objective is to identify the figure that completes the pattern. To solve these problems, one must first analyse the given figures or matrices to detect any underlying patterns or sequences. Relationships between the figures, such as the orientation, shape, size, position, or color of their elements should be examined. Next, the missing part should be imagined, and the available alternative figures should be compared to select the one that best matches the original pattern. Various factors such as symmetry, direction of gradients or sequences, and other relevant visual characteristics that contribute to the pattern should be considered. This problem type is commonly encountered in visual pattern recognition tests or puzzles.

You can improve your ability to recognise and complete visual patterns and successfully solve these types of problems by carefully observing and analysing the given figures.

IDENTIFYING THE MISSING PART:

The missing part problem is a type of problem in which a series of shapes or figures is presented, with the goal of identifying the missing part. The figures may be made up of symbols, geometric shapes, or a combination of the two, and may include changes in shape, orientation, position, number of elements, or any other relevant feature. These problems may involve a series of four or five figures. To solve such problems, carefully examine the provided figures and identify consistent changes or transformations that occur as the missing portion of the figure is determined. It is critical to identify the missing figure by analysing the relationships between the elements of the figures and identifying any rules or logical patterns.

Example 1: Find the missing figure from the answer figures that follows the sequence of the question figures in the following question.

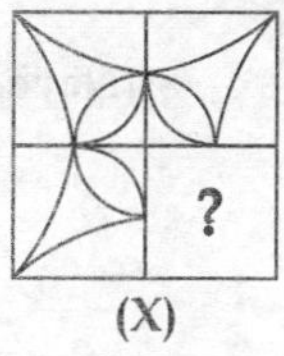

(X)

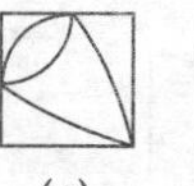 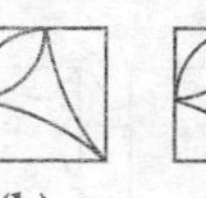  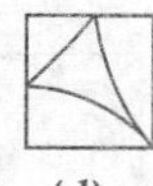

(a) (b) (c) (d)

Sol. (b) Clearly, figure (B) will complete the pattern when placed in the blank space.

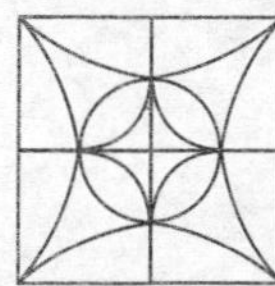

Example 2: Find the missing part from the answer figures that follows the answer of the question figures in the following question.

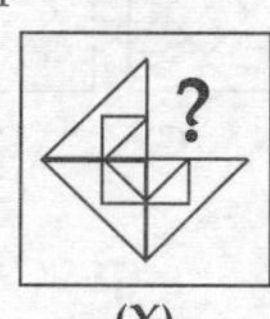

(X)

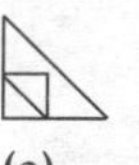 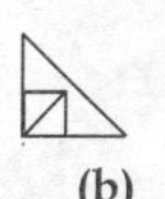  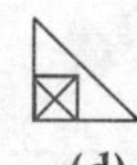

(a) (b) (c) (d)

Sol. (a) If we will fit the figure (A) in the figure (X) then the figure is completed.

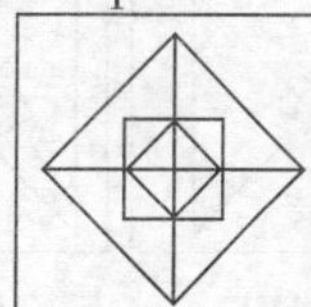

1 Level Beginner

Directions: In each of the following questions you are given a pattern. You have to find out the missing figure from the answer figures that will complete the question figure.

1. [MBA 2006]

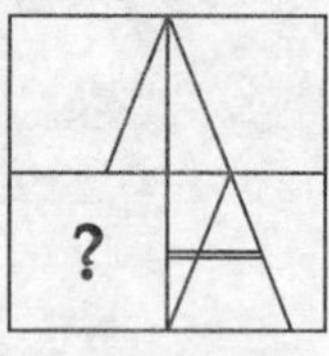

(X)

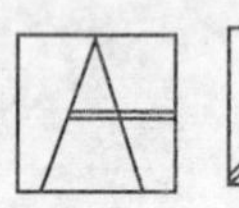 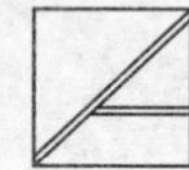 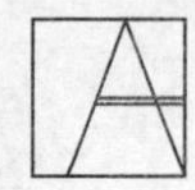 

(A) (B) (C) (D)

2. [Navodaya Vidyalaya 2005]

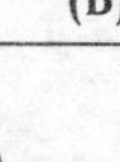

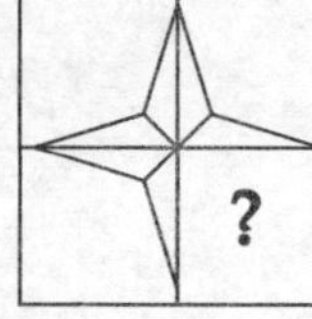

(X)

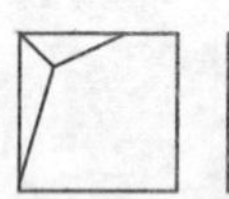  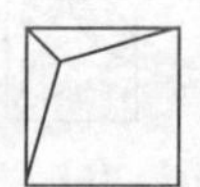 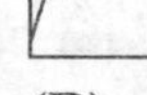

(A) (B) (C) (D)

3.

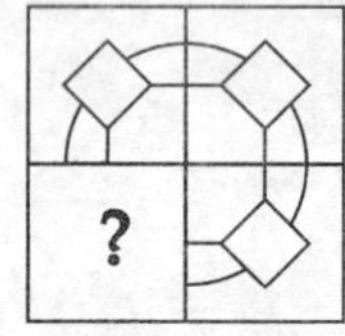

(X)

   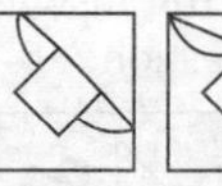 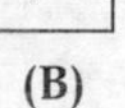 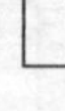 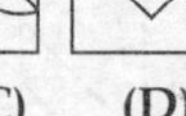

(A) (B) (C) (D)

4. [SSC 2004]

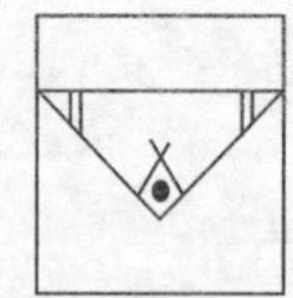 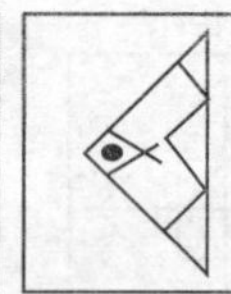 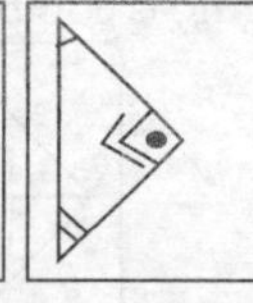 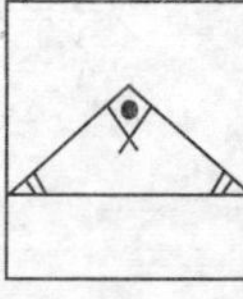

(A) (B) (C) (D)

5.

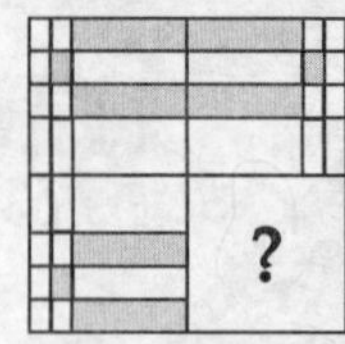

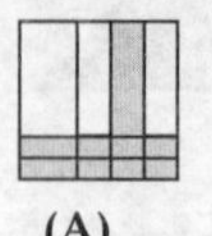 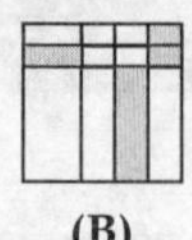 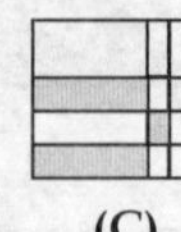 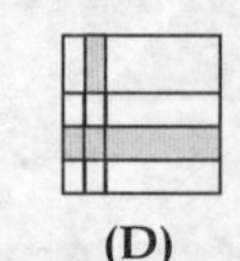

(A) (B) (C) (D)

6. [RRB 2005]

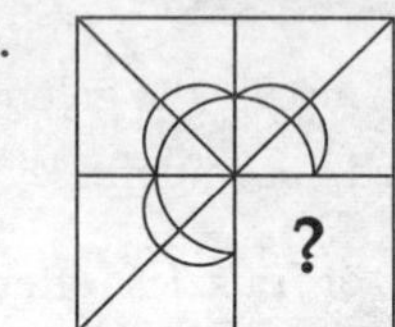

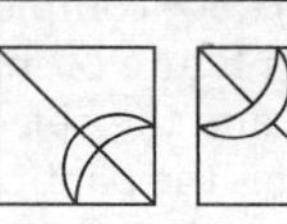 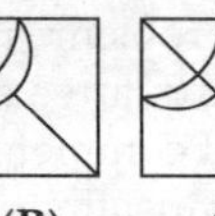 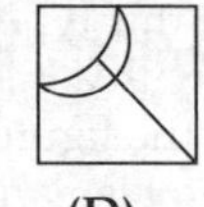

(A) (B) (C) (D)

7.

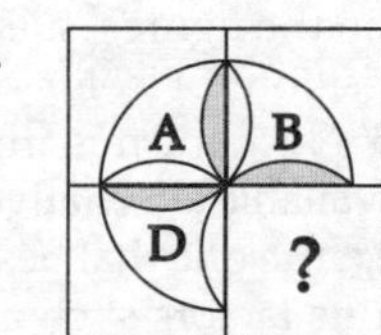

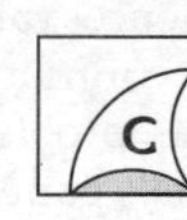 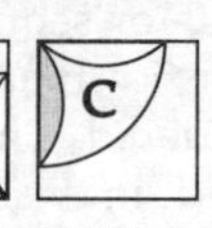 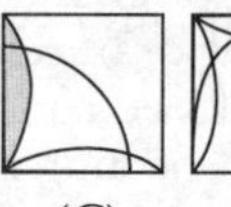 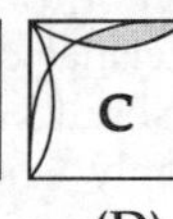

(A) (B) (C) (D)

8. [Investigator's Exam 2005]

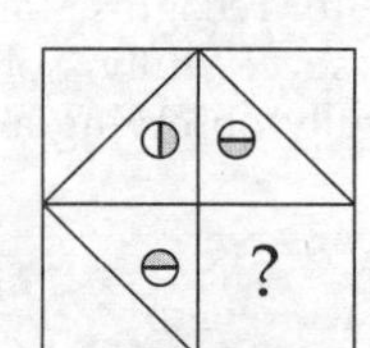

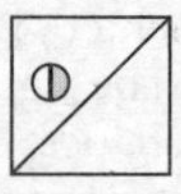 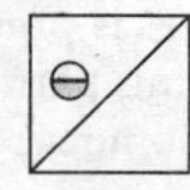 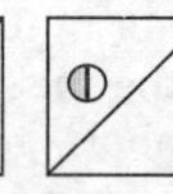 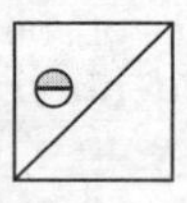 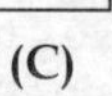 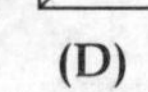

(A) (B) (C) (D)

9.

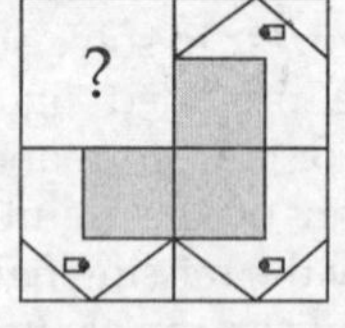

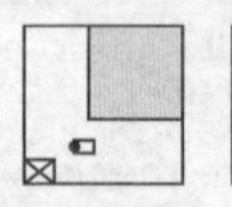 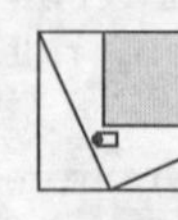  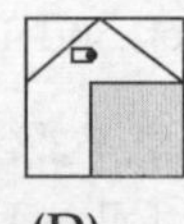

(A) (B) (C) (D)

10. 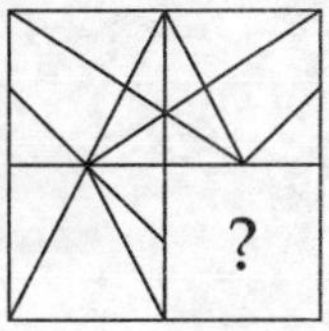 ? [MBA 2006]

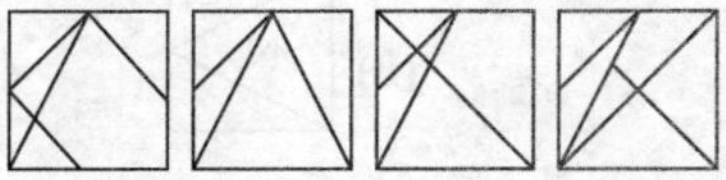

(A) (B) (C) (D)

11.  ?

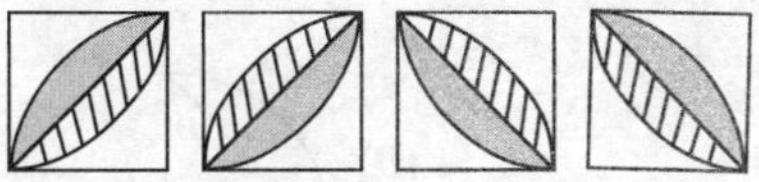

(A) (B) (C) (D)

12.  ?

(A) (B) (C) (D)

13. 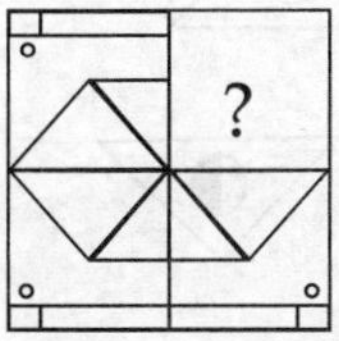 ? [SSC 2002]

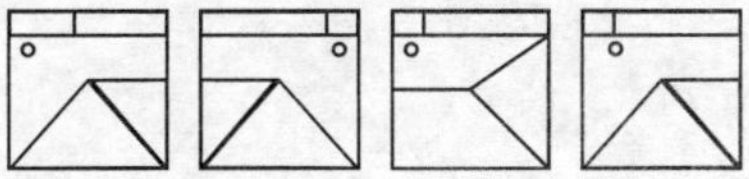

(A) (B) (C) (D)

14. 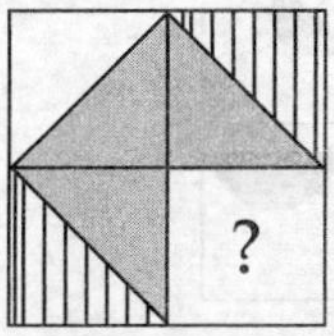 ?

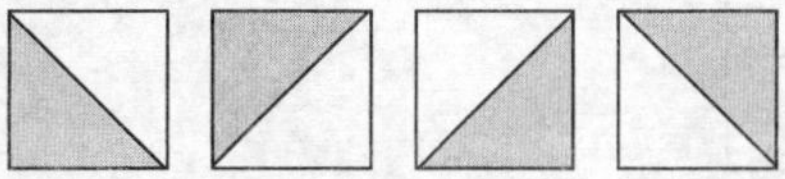

(A) (B) (C) (D)

15. 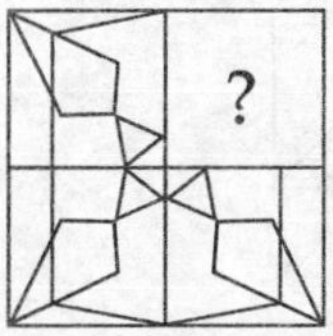 ? [Navodaya Vidyalaya 2006]

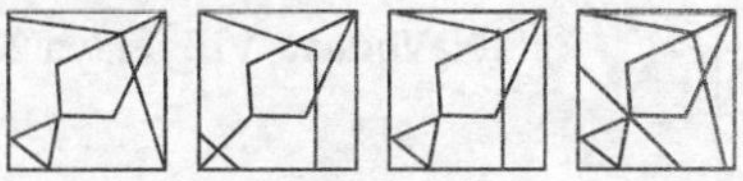

(A) (B) (C) (D)

16. 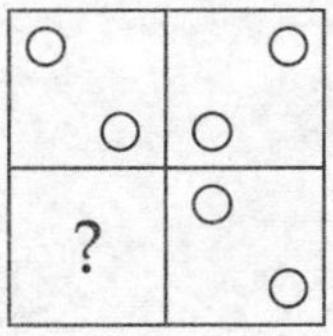 ?

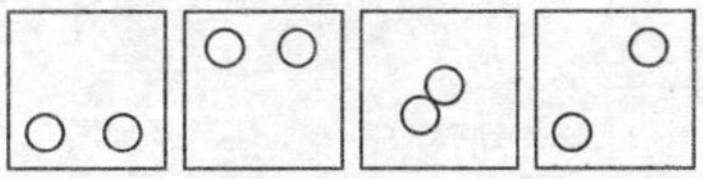

(A) (B) (C) (D)

17. 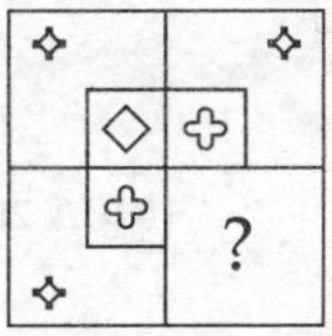 ? [RRB 2004]

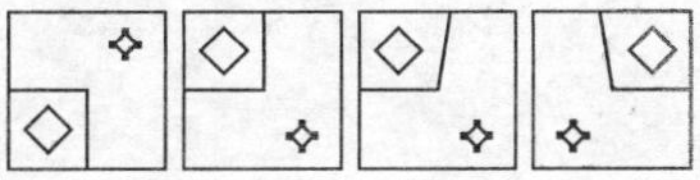

(A) (B) (C) (D)

18. 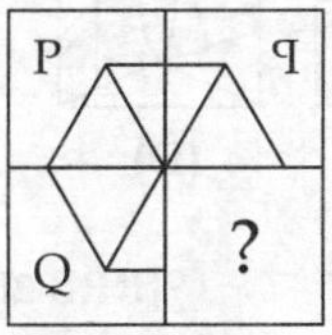 P P Q ?

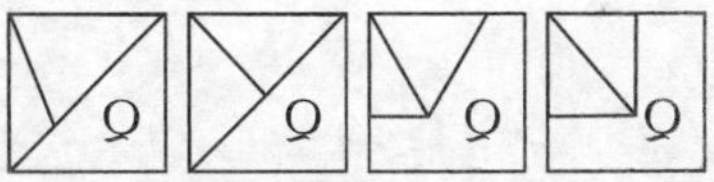

(A) (B) (C) (D)

19. 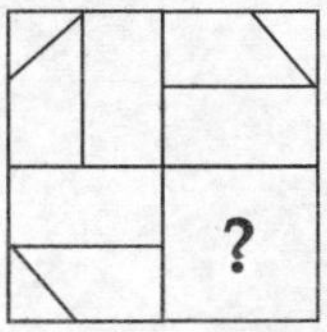 ?

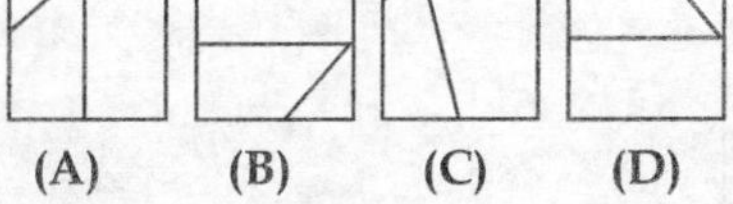

(A) (B) (C) (D)

20. 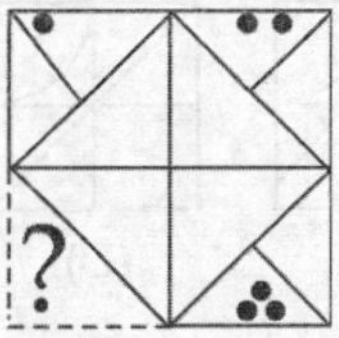 ? [SSC 2005]

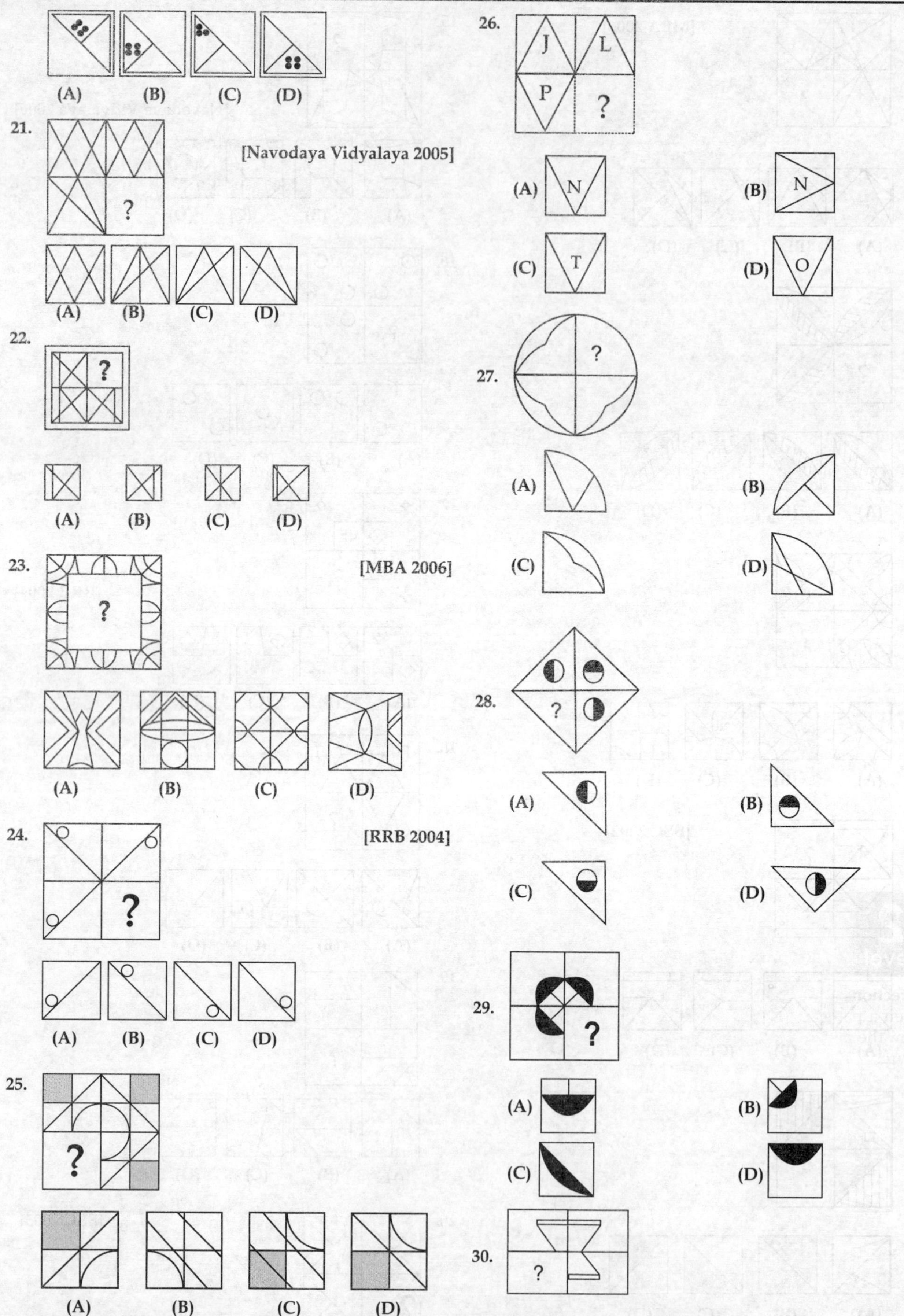
(A) (B) (C) (D)
21.
[Navodaya Vidyalaya 2005]
?
(A) (B) (C) (D)
22.
?
(A) (B) (C) (D)
23.
[MBA 2006]
?
(A) (B) (C) (D)
24.
[RRB 2004]
?
(A) (B) (C) (D)
25.
?
(A) (B) (C) (D)
26.
J
L
P
?
(A) N
(B) N
(C) T
(D) O
27.
?
(A) (B) (C) (D)
28.
?
(A) (B) (C) (D)
29.
?
(A) (B) (C) (D)
30.
?

(A) 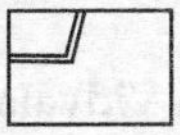 (B)

(C)  (D)

31. 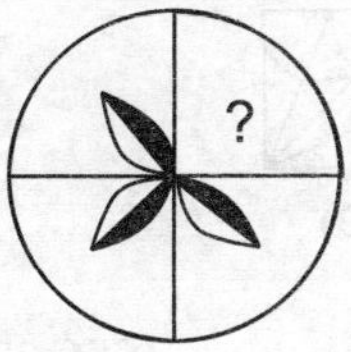 ?

(A)  (B)

(C)  (D)

32. 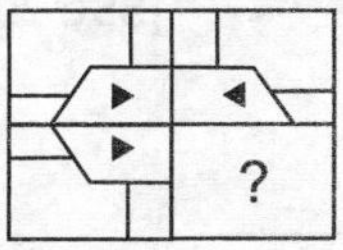 ?

(A) 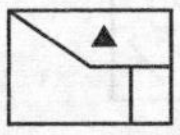 (B)

(C) 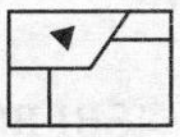 (D)

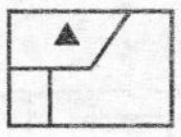

33. 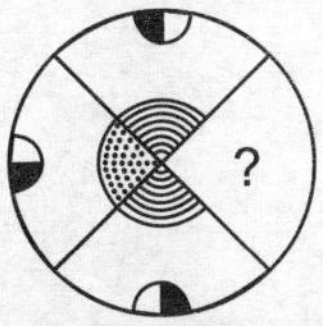 ?

(A) 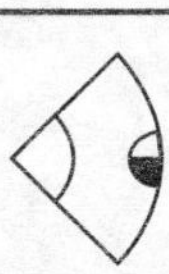 (B)

(C)  (D)

34. 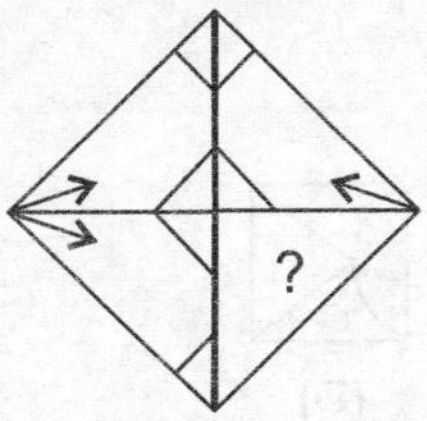 ?

(A) 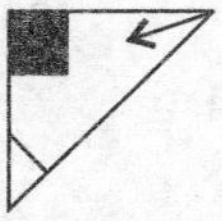 (B)

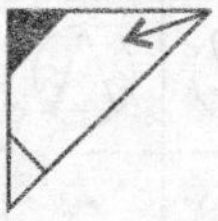

(C) 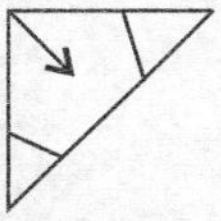 (D)

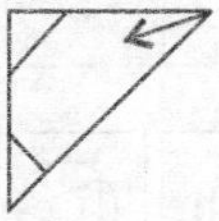

35.  ?

(A) 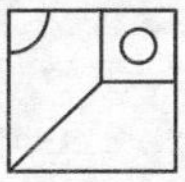 (B)

(C) 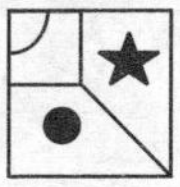 (D)

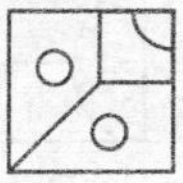

2 Level Intermediate

Directions: In each of the following questions you are given a pattern. You have to find out the missing figure from the answer figures that will complete the question figure.

1.

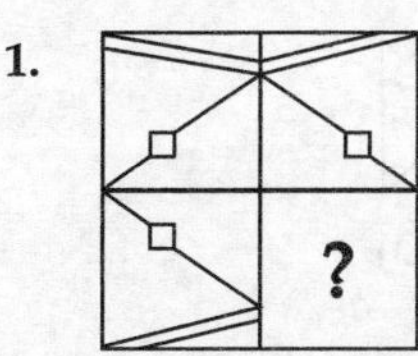

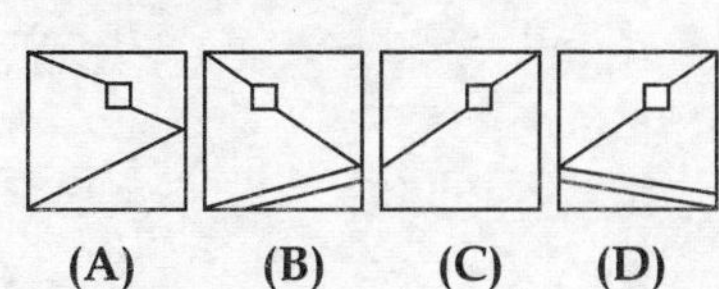

(A) (B) (C) (D)

2.

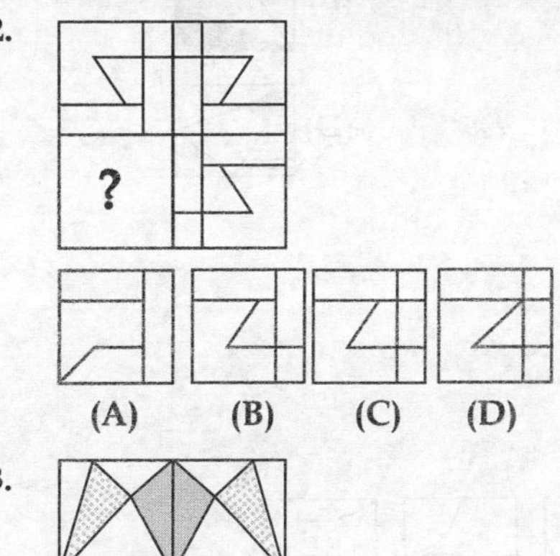

(A) (B) (C) (D)

3.

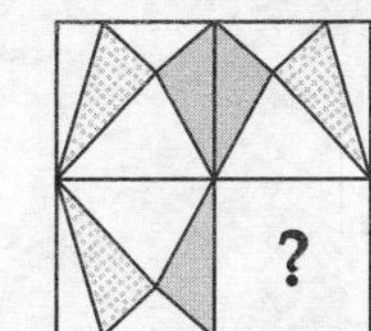

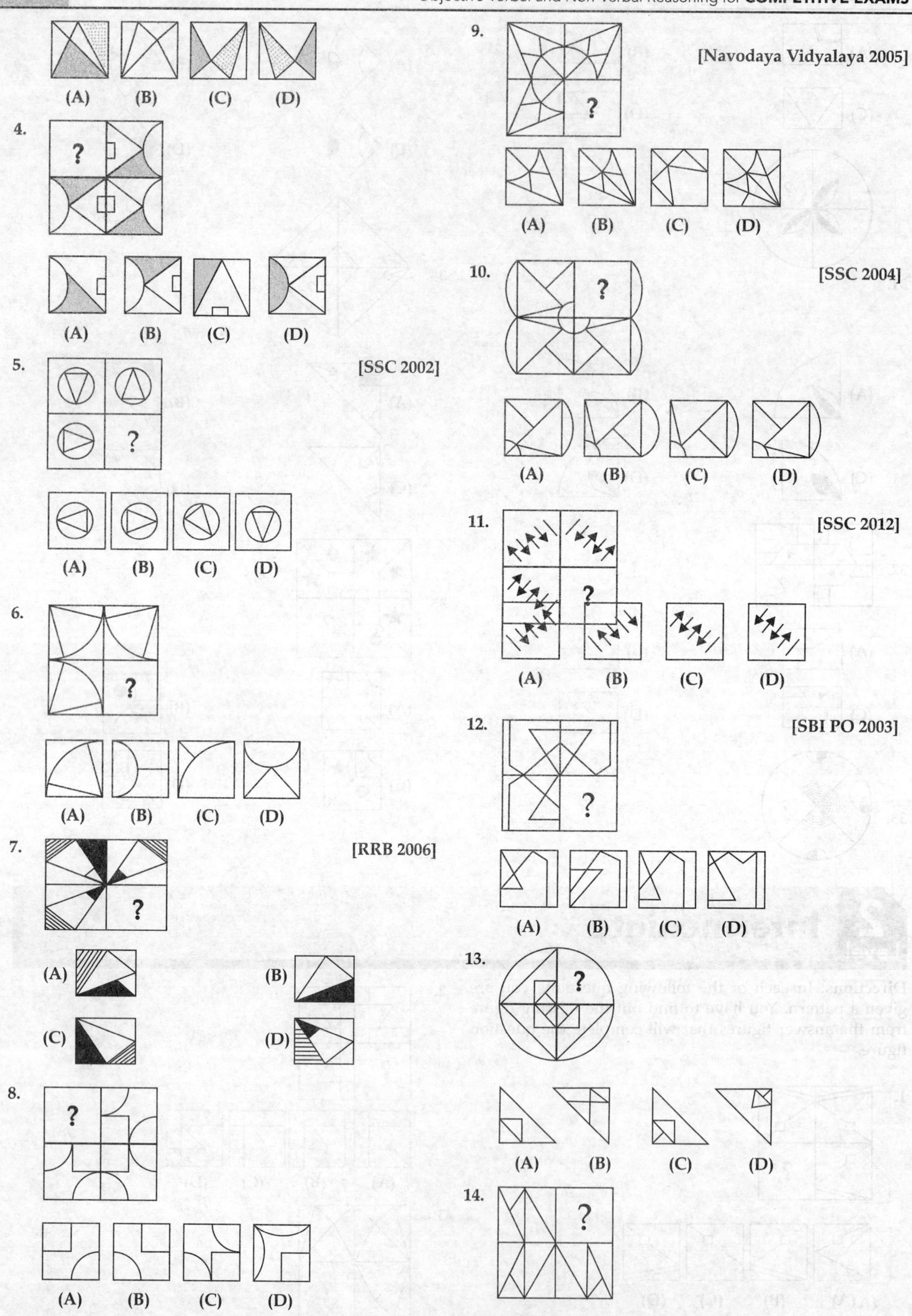
(A) (B) (C) (D)
4.
?
(A) (B) (C) (D)
5.
[SSC 2002]
?
(A) (B) (C) (D)
6.
?
(A) (B) (C) (D)
7.
[RRB 2006]
?
(A) (B) (C) (D)
8.
?
(A) (B) (C) (D)
9.
[Navodaya Vidyalaya 2005]
?
(A) (B) (C) (D)
10.
[SSC 2004]
?
(A) (B) (C) (D)
11.
[SSC 2012]
?
(A) (B) (C) (D)
12.
[SBI PO 2003]
?
(A) (B) (C) (D)
13.
?
(A) (B) (C) (D)
14.
?

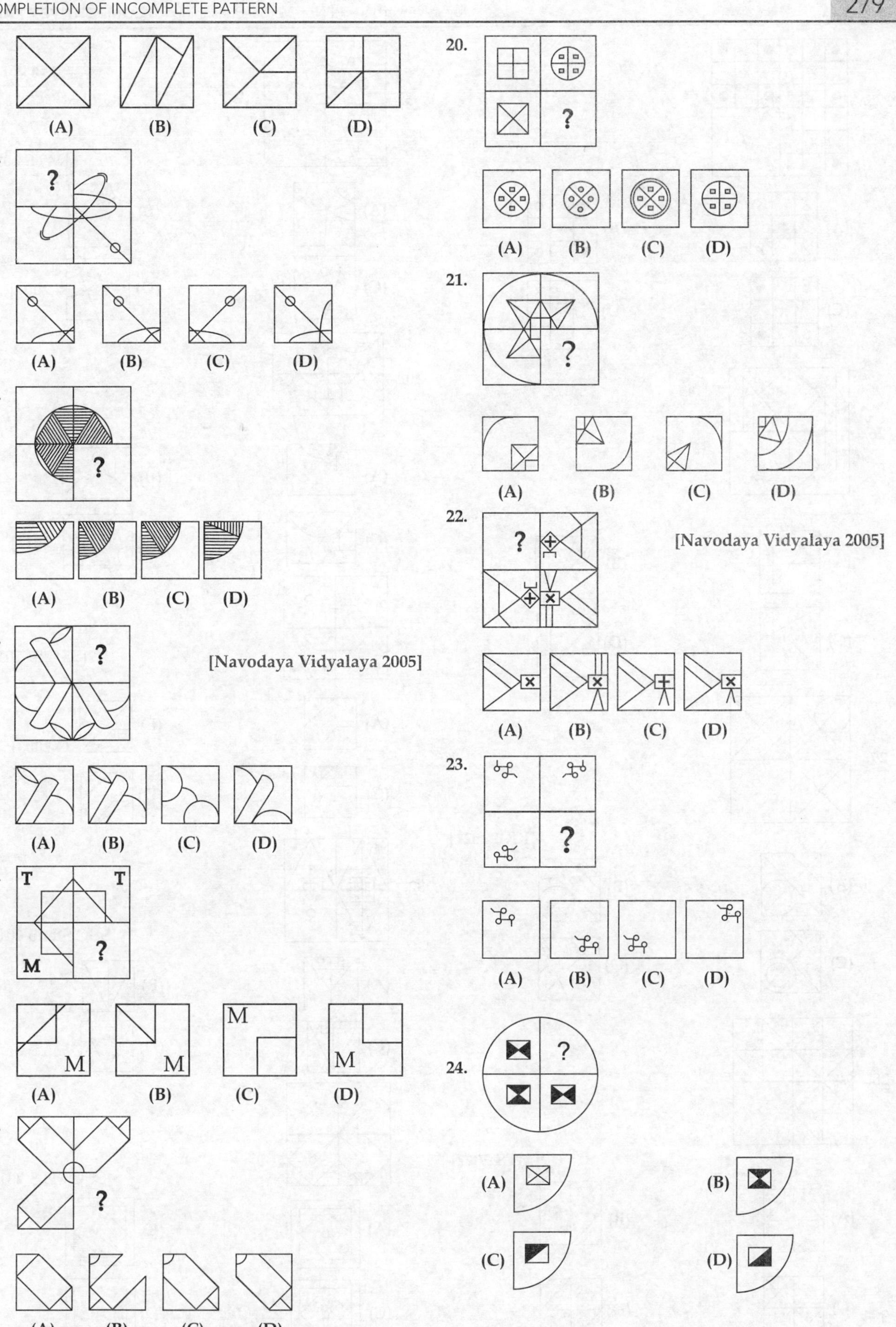

(A) (B) (C) (D)
15.
?
(A) (B) (C) (D)
16.
?
(A) (B) (C) (D)
17.
?
[Navodaya Vidyalaya 2005]
(A) (B) (C) (D)
18.
T T
M ?
M M M M
(A) (B) (C) (D)
19.
?
(A) (B) (C) (D)
20.
?
(A) (B) (C) (D)
21.
?
(A) (B) (C) (D)
22.
?
[Navodaya Vidyalaya 2005]
(A) (B) (C) (D)
23.
?
(A) (B) (C) (D)
24.
?
(A) (B) (C) (D)

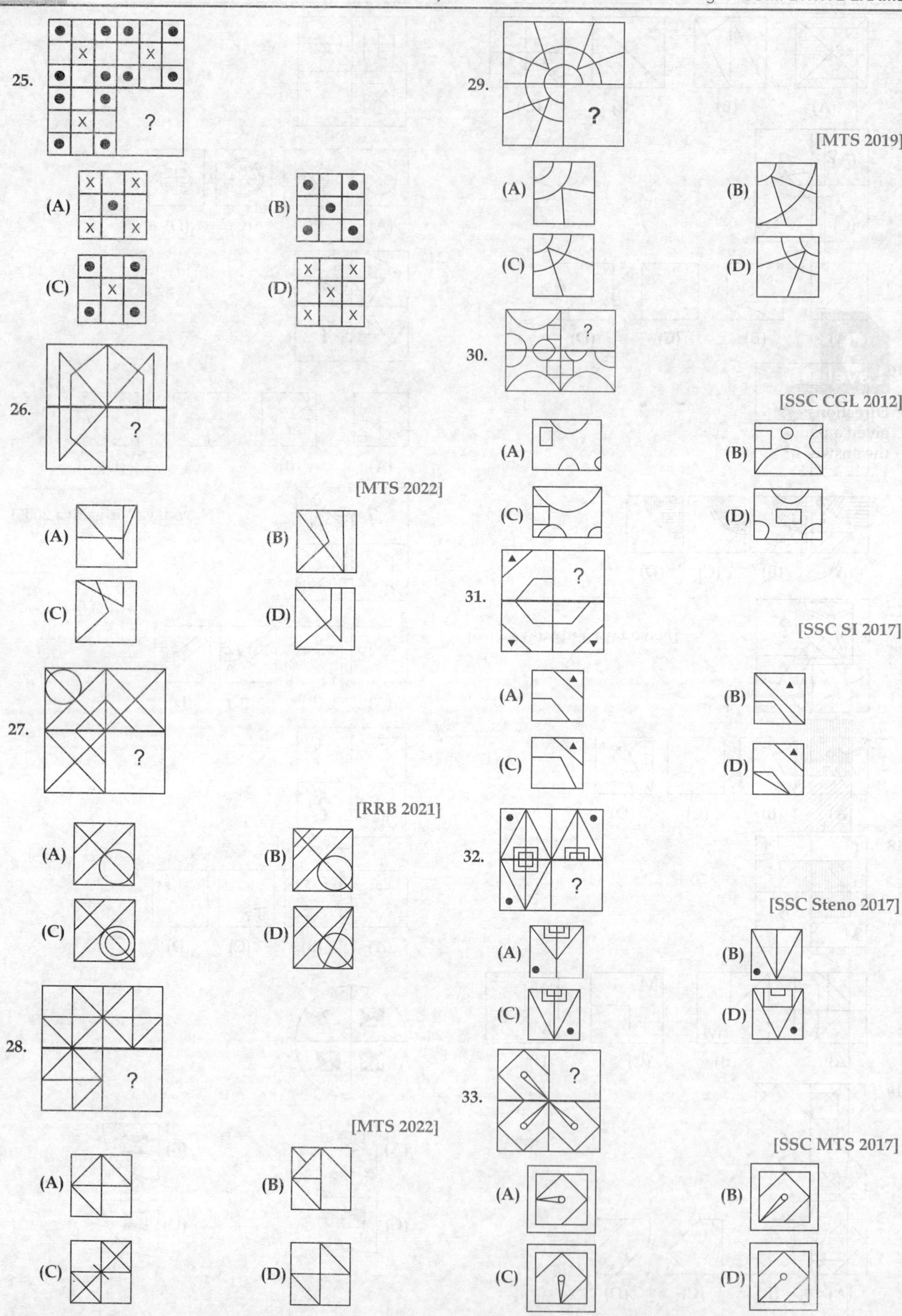
25.
?
(A)
(B)
(C)
(D)
26.
?
[MTS 2022]
(A)
(B)
(C)
(D)
27.
?
[RRB 2021]
(A)
(B)
(C)
(D)
28.
?
[MTS 2022]
(A)
(B)
(C)
(D)
29.
?
[MTS 2019]
(A)
(B)
(C)
(D)
30.
?
[SSC CGL 2012]
(A)
(B)
(C)
(D)
31.
?
[SSC SI 2017]
(A)
(B)
(C)
(D)
32.
?
[SSC Steno 2017]
(A)
(B)
(C)
(D)
33.
?
[SSC MTS 2017]
(A)
(B)
(C)
(D)

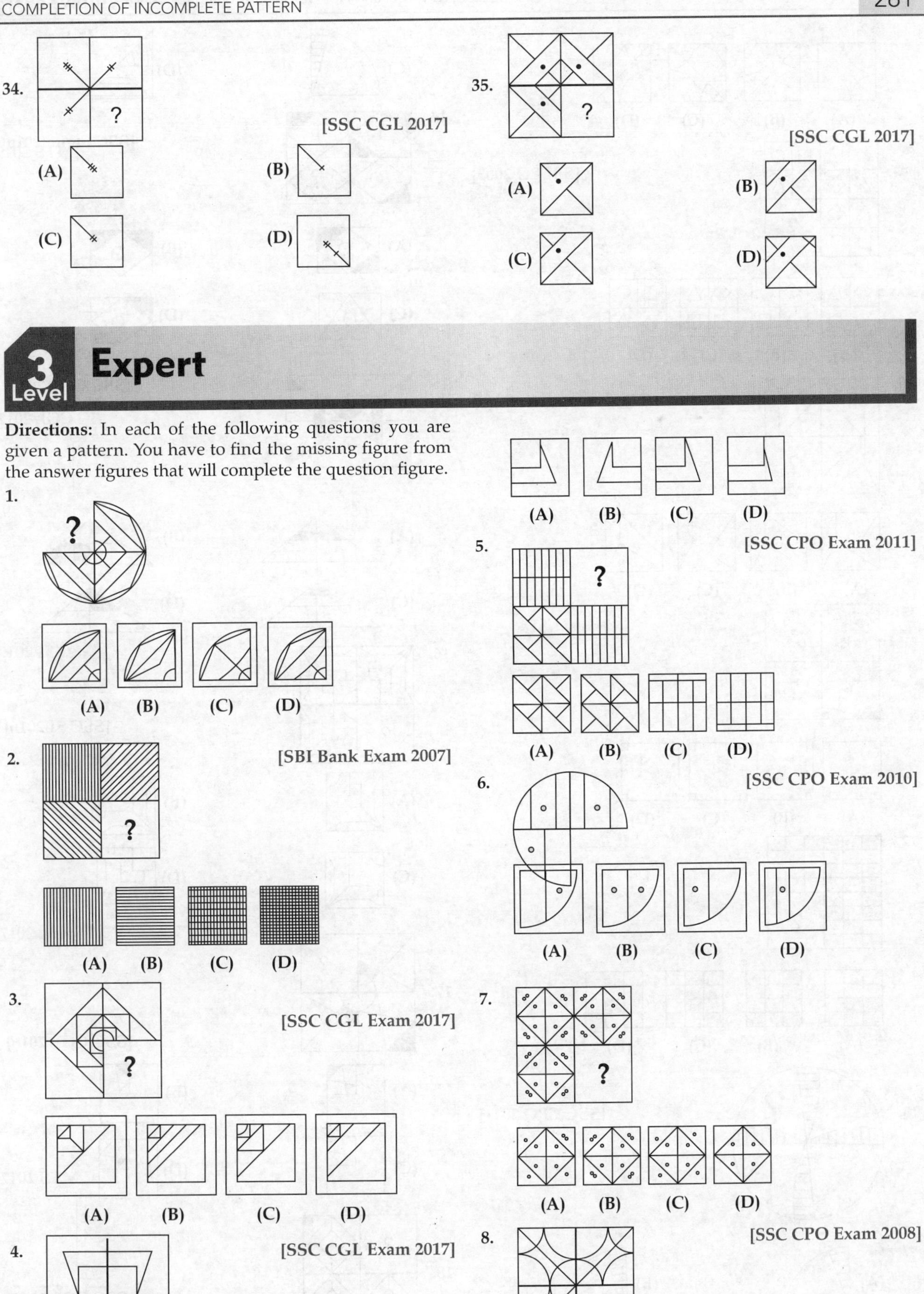

3 Level Expert

Directions: In each of the following questions you are given a pattern. You have to find the missing figure from the answer figures that will complete the question figure.

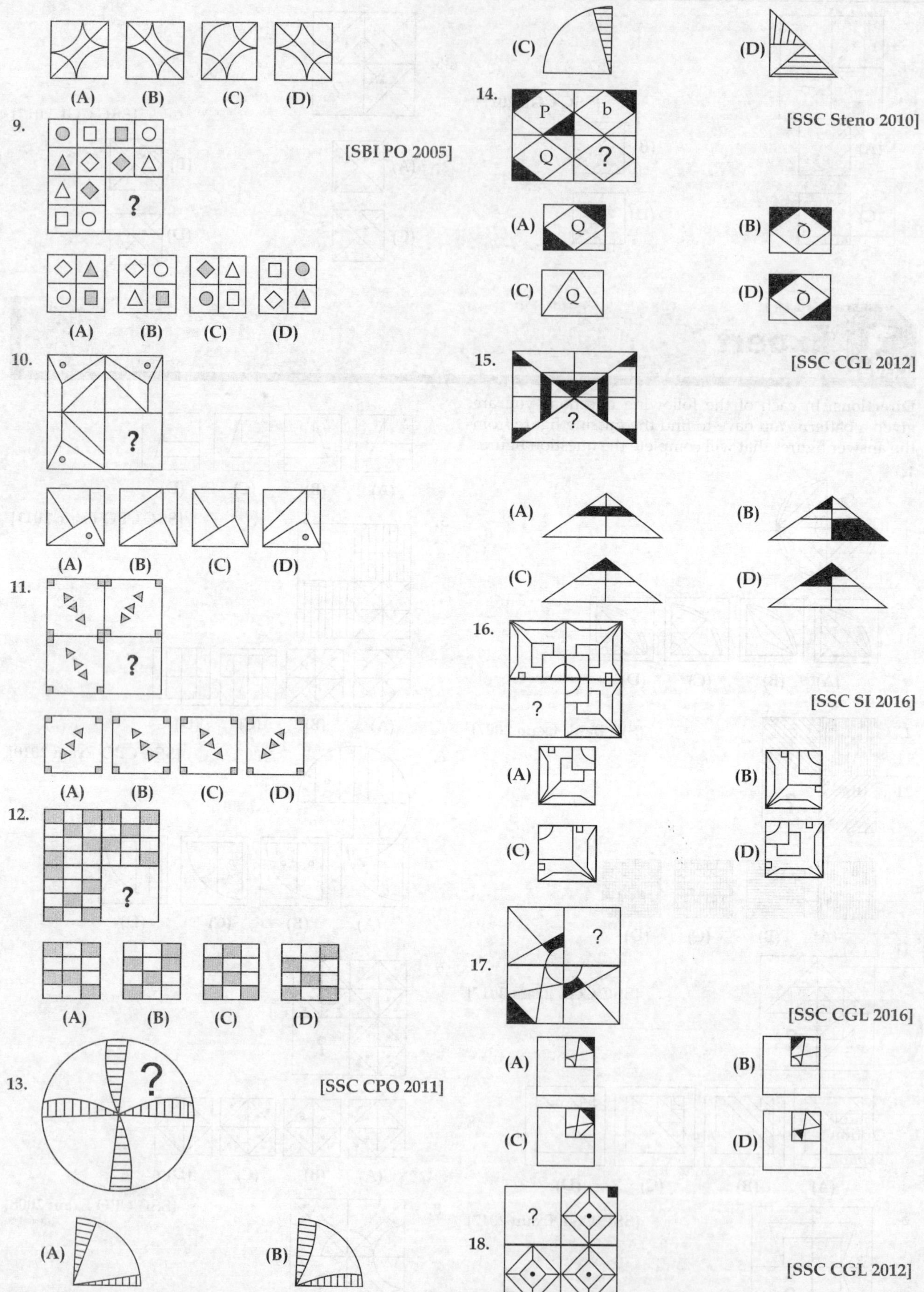

(A) (B) (C) (D)
9.
[SBI PO 2005]
?
(A) (B) (C) (D)
10.
?
(A) (B) (C) (D)
11.
?
(A) (B) (C) (D)
12.
?
(A) (B) (C) (D)
13.
?
[SSC CPO 2011]
(A) (B) (C) (D)
14.
P
b
Q
?
[SSC Steno 2010]
(A) Q
(B) Q
(C) Q
(D) Q
15.
?
[SSC CGL 2012]
(A) (B) (C) (D)
16.
?
[SSC SI 2016]
(A) (B) (C) (D)
17.
?
[SSC CGL 2016]
(A) (B) (C) (D)
18.
?
[SSC CGL 2012]

(A) 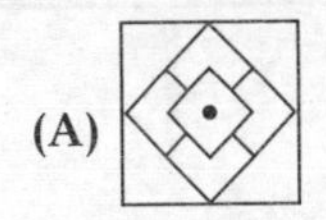 (B) 

(C) 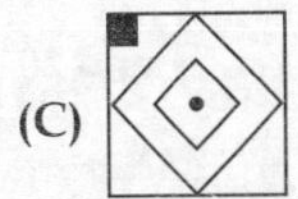 (D) 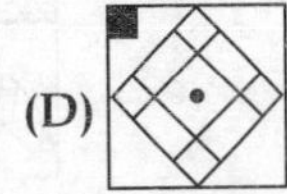

19. 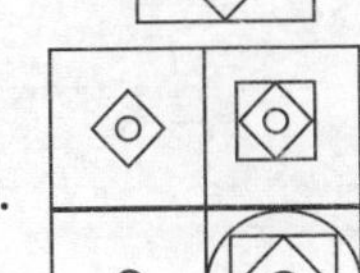

[SSC SI 2013]

(A)  (B) 

(C) 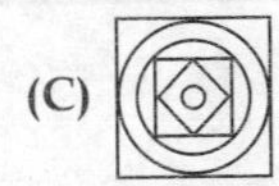 (D) 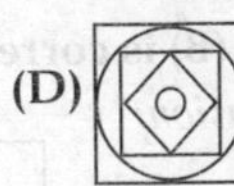

20. 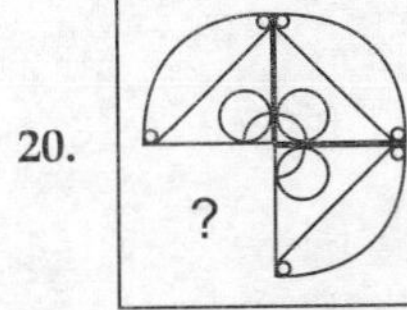

[SSC CGL 2016]

(A) (B) 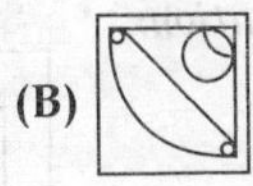

(C) 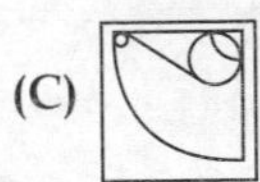 (D) 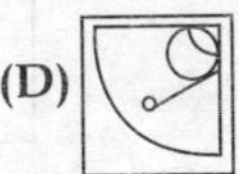

ANSWER KEY

Level-1: Beginner

1.	(C)	2.	(D)	3.	(B)	4.	(A)	5.	(C)	6.	(C)	7.	(B)	8.	(C)	9.	(D)	10.	(B)
11.	(B)	12.	(A)	13.	(B)	14.	(B)	15.	(C)	16.	(D)	17.	(B)	18.	(C)	19.	(A)	20.	(D)
21.	(C)	22.	(B)	23.	(C)	24.	(C)	25.	(D)	26.	(A)	27.	(C)	28.	(C)	29.	(B)	30.	(D)
31.	(A)	32.	(C)	33.	(B)	34.	(D)	35.	(B)										

Level-2: Intermediate

1.	(D)	2.	(B)	3.	(C)	4.	(A)	5.	(A)	6.	(A)	7.	(C)	8.	(C)	9.	(A)	10.	(D)
11.	(A)	12.	(C)	13.	(B)	14.	(B)	15.	(A)	16.	(C)	17.	(A)	18.	(A)	19.	(C)	20.	(A)
21.	(B)	22.	(B)	23.	(B)	24.	(B)	25.	(C)	26.	(D)	27.	(A)	28.	(A)	29.	(C)	30.	(C)
31.	(A)	32.	(C)	33.	(B)	34.	(A)	35.	(C)										

Level-3: Expert

1.	(A)	2.	(B)	3.	(C)	4.	(C)	5.	(B)	6.	(A)	7.	(B)	8.	(B)	9.	(A)	10.	(D)
11.	(A)	12.	(D)	13.	(B)	14.	(D)	15.	(C)	16.	(A)	17.	(A)	18.	(B)	19.	(C)	20.	(B)

Solutions with Detailed Explanations

Level-1: BEGINNER

1. **Option (C) is correct.**

Explanation:

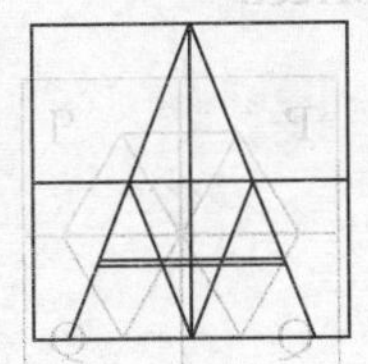

2. **Option (D) is correct.**

Explanation:

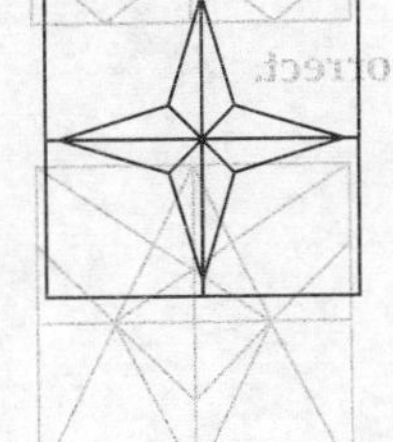

3. **Option (B) is correct.**
Explanation:

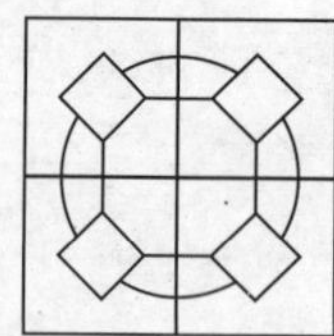

4. **Option (A) is correct.**
Explanation:

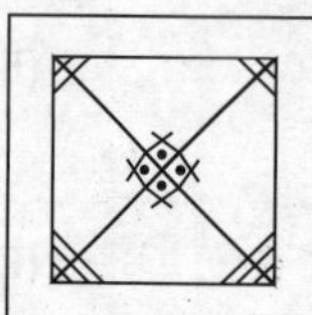

5. **Option (C) is correct.**
Explanation:

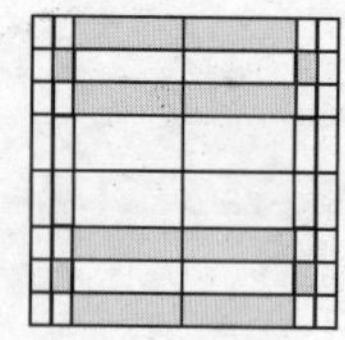

6. **Option (C) is correct.**
Explanation:

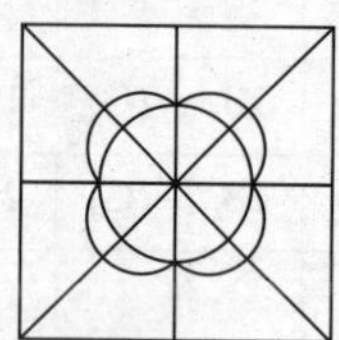

7. **Option (B) is correct.**
Explanation:

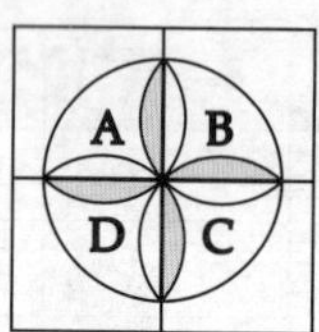

8. **Option (C) is correct.**
Explanation:

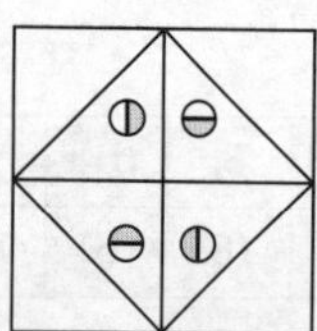

9. **Option (D) is correct.**
Explanation:

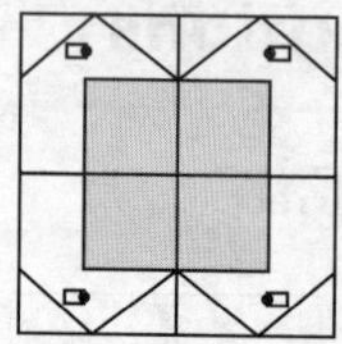

10. **Option (B) is correct.**
Explanation:

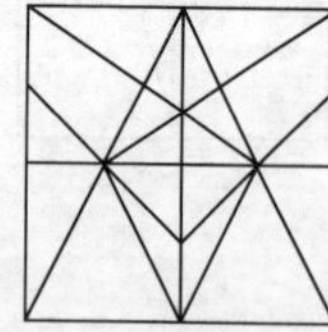

11. **Option (B) is correct.**
Explanation:

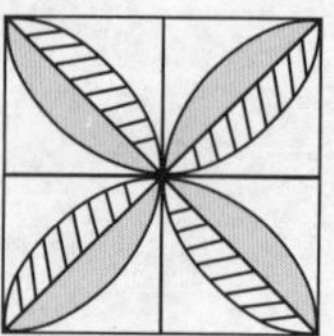

12. **Option (A) is correct.**
Explanation:

13. **Option (B) is correct.**
Explanation:

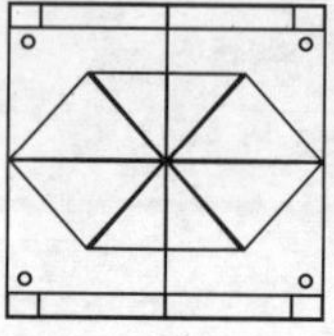

14. **Option (B) is correct.**
Explanation:

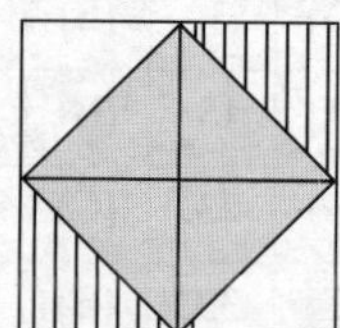

15. **Option (C) is correct.**
Explanation:

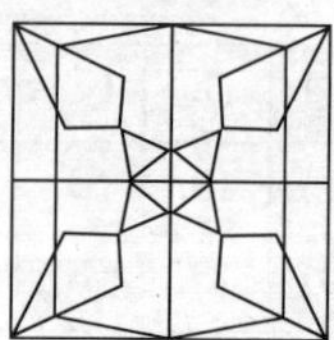

16. **Option (D) is correct.**
Explanation:

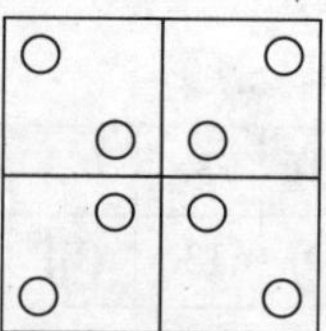

17. **Option (B) is correct.**
Explanation:

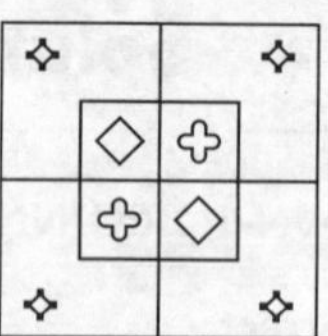

18. **Option (C) is correct.**
Explanation:

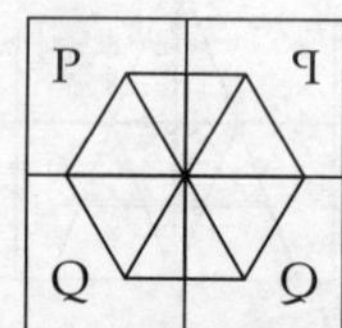

19. **Option (A) is correct.**
Explanation:

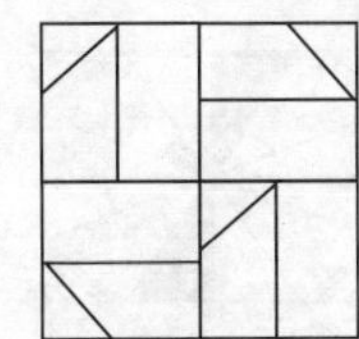

20. **Option (D) is correct.**
Explanation:

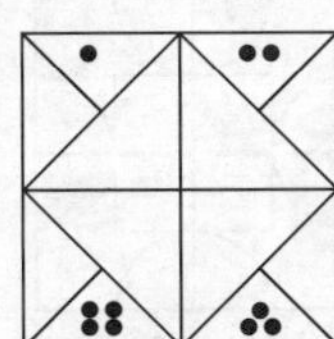

21. **Option (C) is correct.**
Explanation:

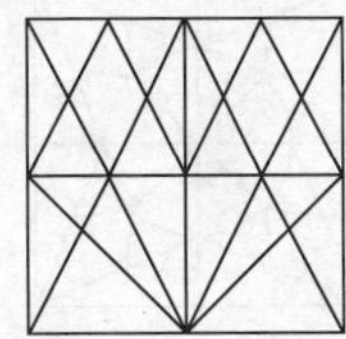

22. **Option (B) is correct.**
Explanation:

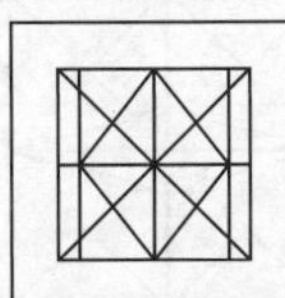

23. **Option (C) is correct.**
Explanation:

24. **Option (C) is correct.**
Explanation:

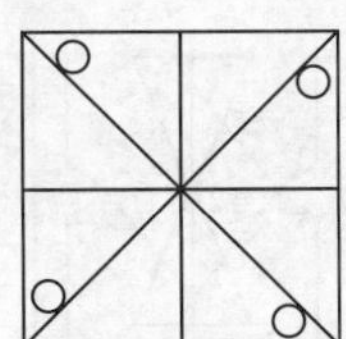

25. **Option (D) is correct.**
Explanation:

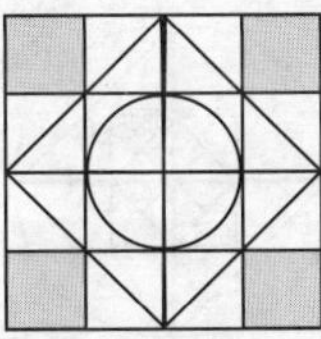

26. **Option (A) is correct.**
Explanation:

27. **Option (C) is correct.**
Explanation:

28. **Option (C) is correct.**
Explanation:

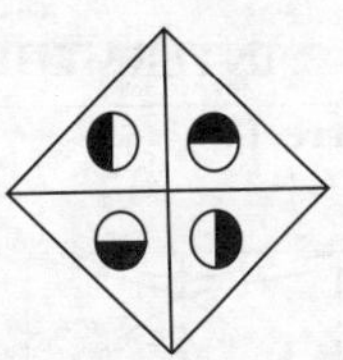

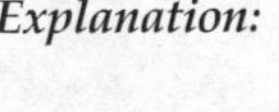

29. **Option (B) is correct.**
Explanation:

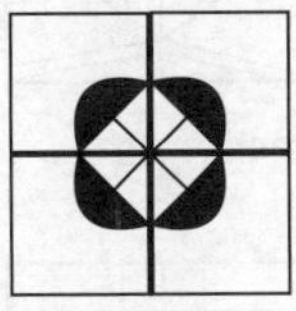

30. **Option (D) is correct.**
Explanation:

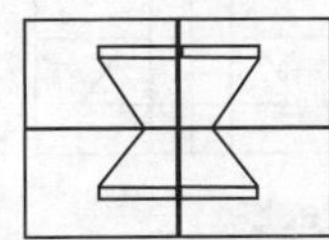

31. **Option (A) is correct.**
Explanation:

32. **Option (C) is correct.**
Explanation:

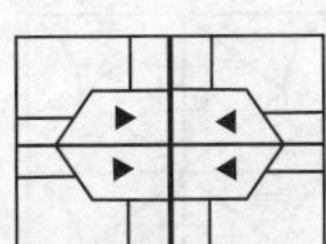

33. **Option (B) is correct.**
Explanation:

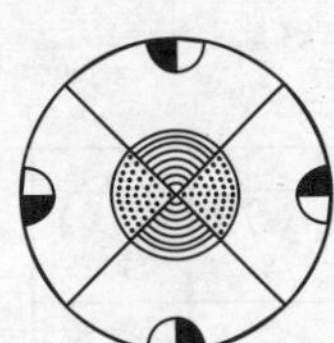

34. **Option (D) is correct.**
Explanation:

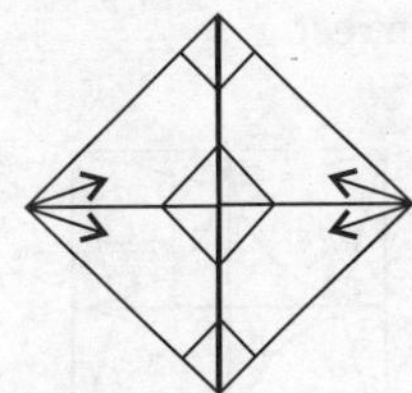

35. **Option (B) is correct.**
Explanation:

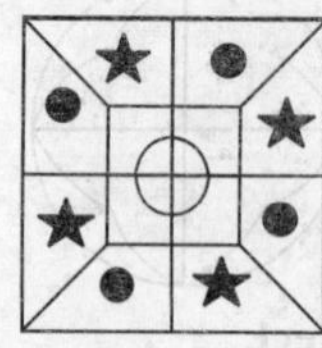

Level-2: INTERMEDIATE

1. **Option (D) is correct.**
Explanation:

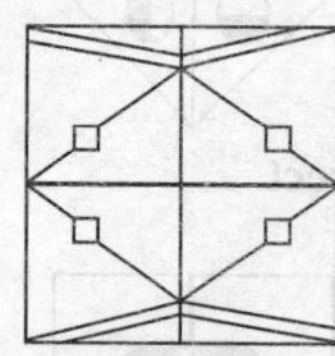

2. **Option (B) is correct.**
Explanation:

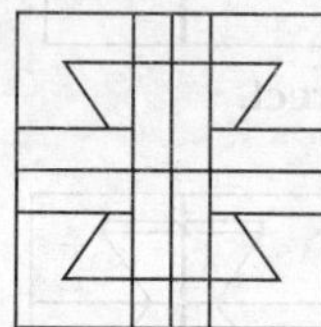

3. **Option (C) is correct.**
Explanation:

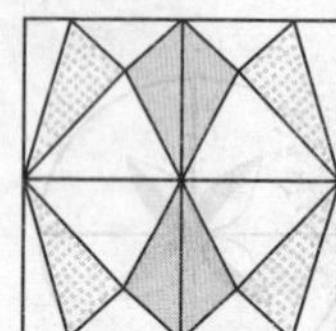

4. **Option (A) is correct.**
Explanation:

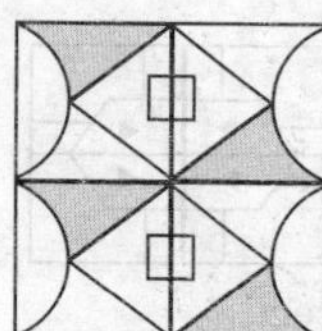

5. **Option (A) is correct.**
Explanation:

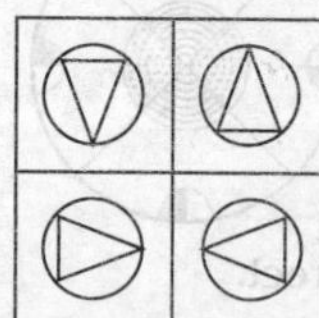

6. **Option (A) is correct.**
Explanation:

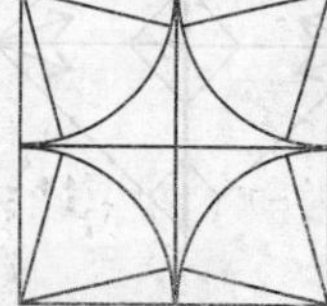

7. **Option (C) is correct.**
Explanation:

8. **Option (C) is correct.**
Explanation:

9. **Option (A) is correct.**
Explanation:

10. **Option (D) is correct.**
Explanation:

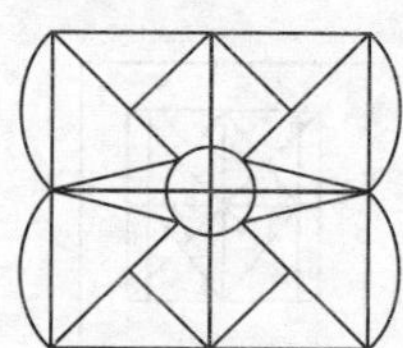

11. **Option (A) is correct.**
Explanation:

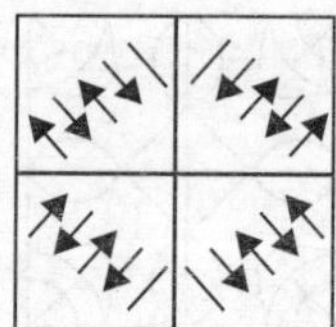

12. **Option (C) is correct.**
Explanation:

13. **Option (B) is correct.**
Explanation:

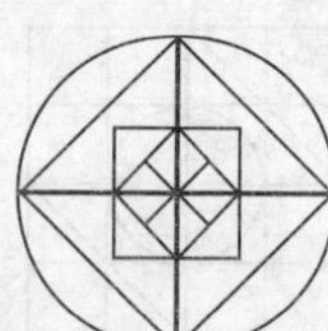

14. **Option (B) is correct.**
Explanation:

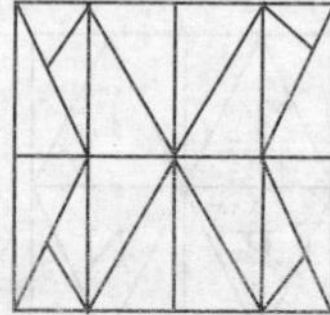

15. Option (A) is correct.
Explanation:

16. Option (C) is correct.
Explanation:

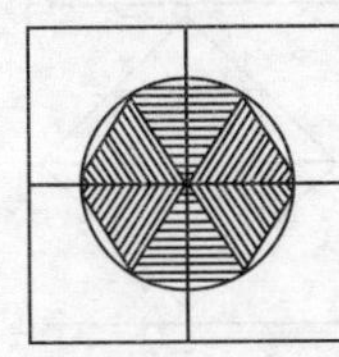

17. Option (A) is correct.
Explanation:

18. Option (A) is correct.
Explanation:

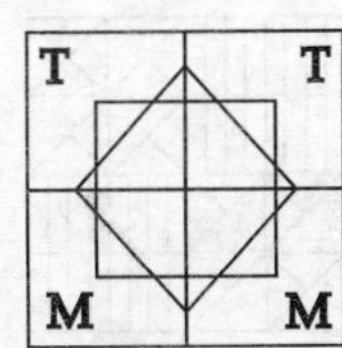

19. Option (C) is correct.
Explanation:

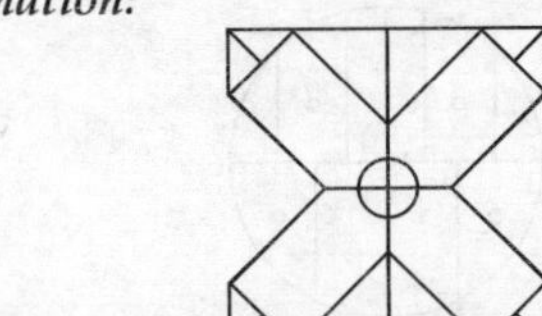

20. Option (A) is correct.
Explanation:

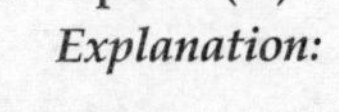

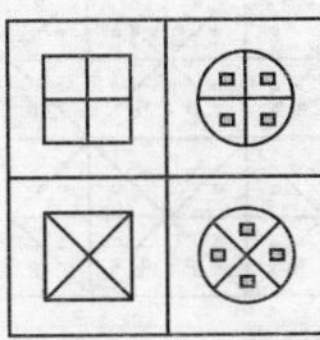

21. Option (B) is correct.
Explanation:

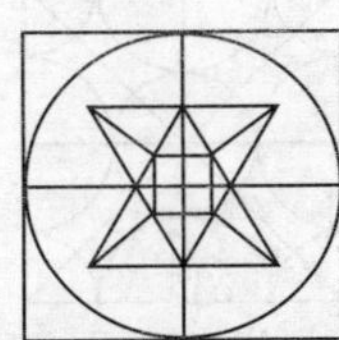

22. Option (B) is correct.
Explanation:

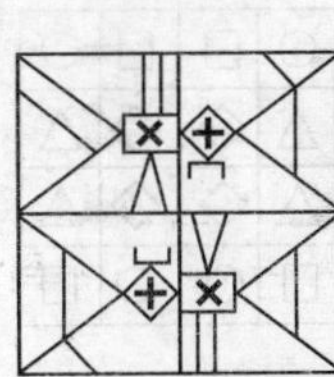

23. Option (B) is correct.
Explanation:

24. Option (B) is correct.
Explanation:

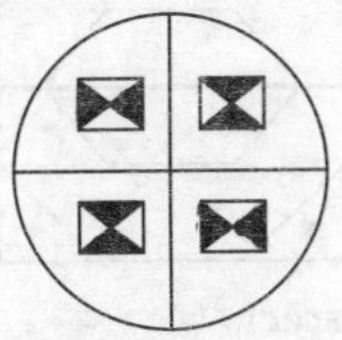

25. Option (C) is correct.
Explanation:

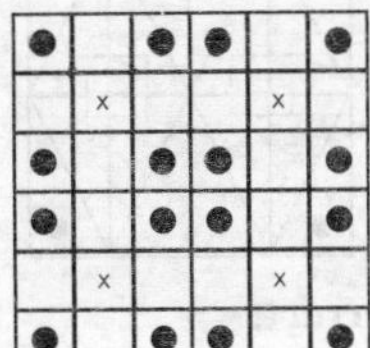

26. Option (D) is correct.
Explanation:

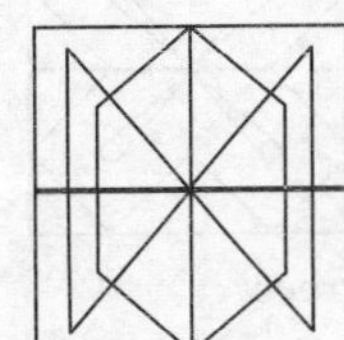

27. Option (A) is correct.
Explanation:

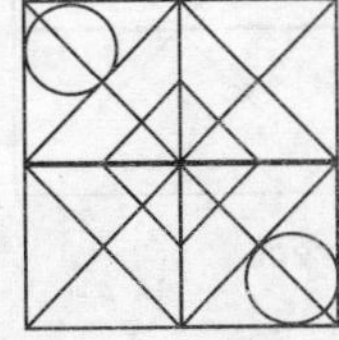

28. Option (A) is correct.
Explanation:

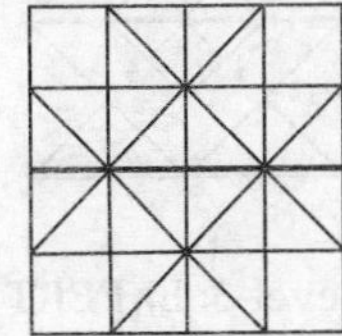

29. Option (C) is correct.
Explanation:

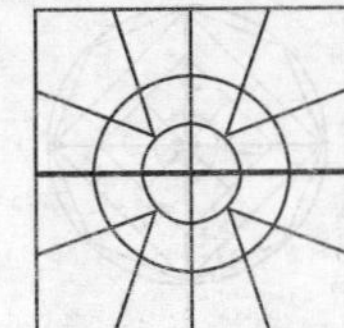

30. Option (C) is correct.
Explanation:

31. Option (A) is correct.
Explanation:

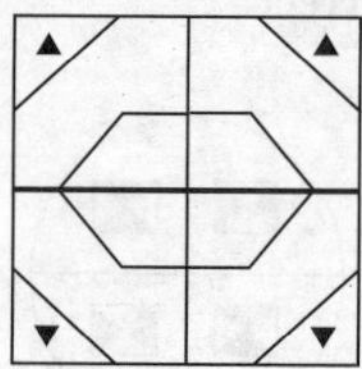

32. Option (C) is correct.
Explanation:

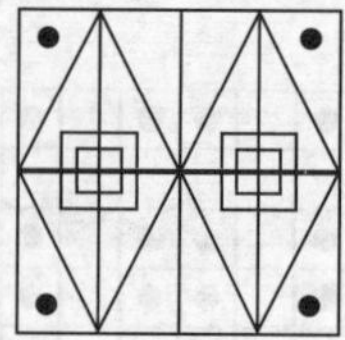

33. Option (B) is correct.
Explanation:

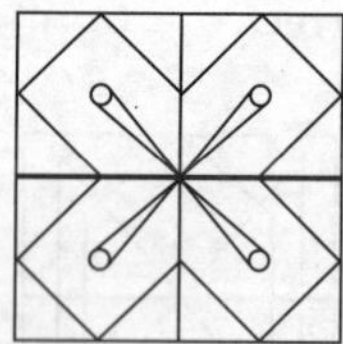

34. Option (A) is correct.
Explanation:

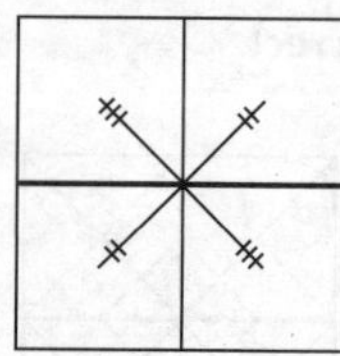

35. Option (C) is correct.
Explanation:

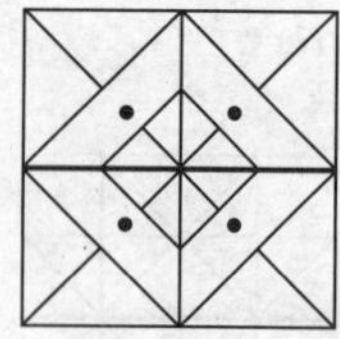

Level-3: EXPERT

1. Option (A) is correct.
Explanation:

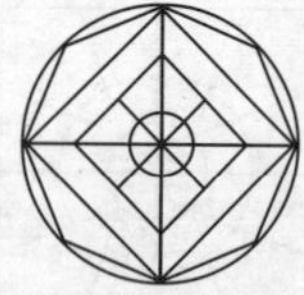

2. Option (B) is correct.
Explanation:

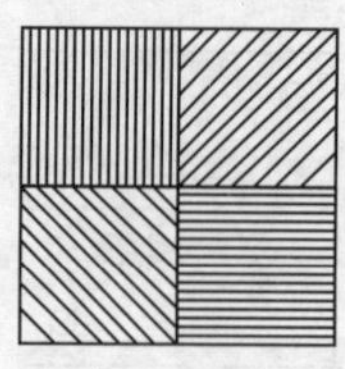

3. Option (C) is correct.
Explanation:

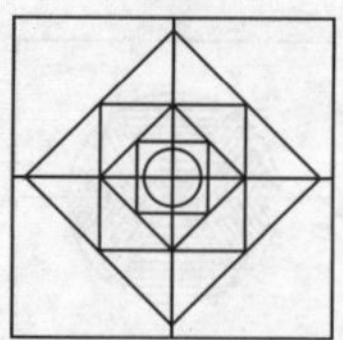

4. Option (C) is correct.
Explanation:

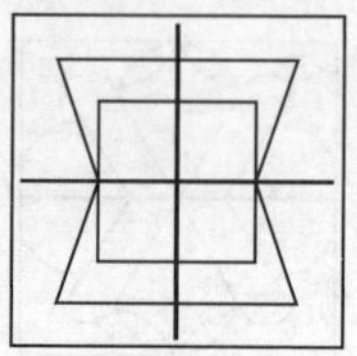

5. Option (B) is correct.
Explanation:

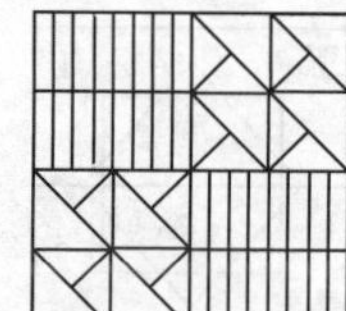

6. Option (A) is correct.
Explanation:

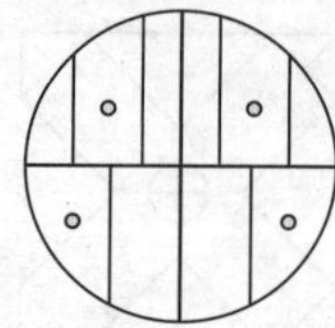

7. Option (B) is correct.
Explanation:

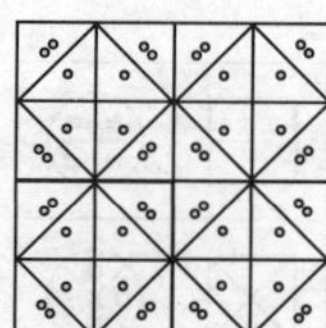

8. Option (B) is correct.
Explanation:

9. Option (A) is correct.
Explanation:

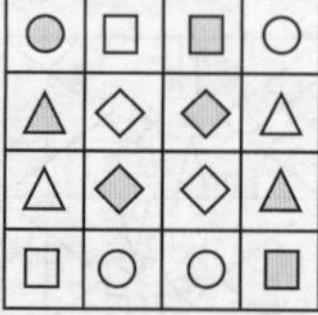

10. Option (D) is correct.
Explanation:

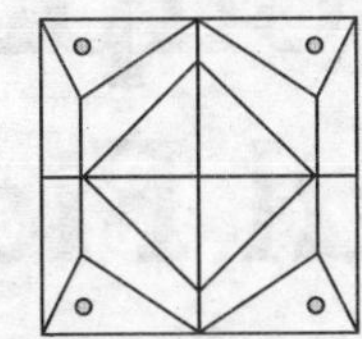

11. Option (A) is correct.
Explanation:

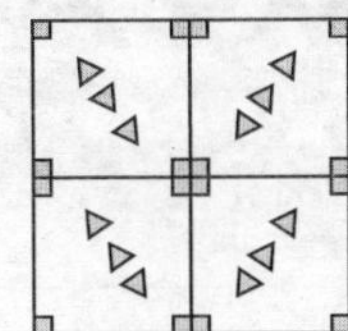

12. Option (D) is correct.
Explanation:

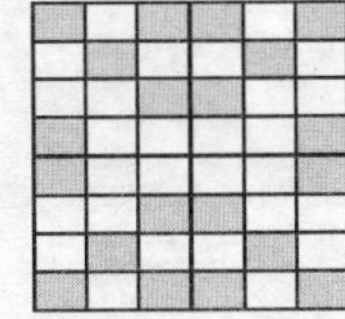

13. Option (B) is correct.
Explanation:

14. Option (D) is correct.
Explanation:

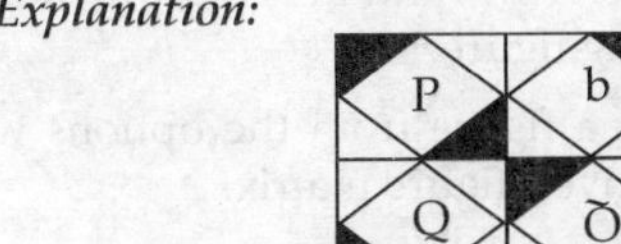

15. Option (C) is correct.
Explanation:

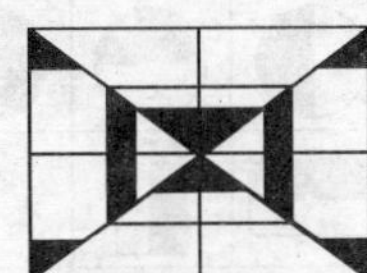

16. Option (A) is correct.
Explanation:

17. Option (A) is correct.
Explanation:

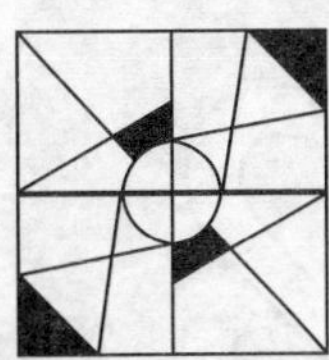

18. Option (B) is correct.
Explanation:

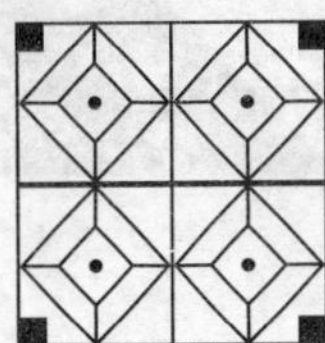

19. Option (C) is correct.
Explanation:

20. Option (B) is correct.
Explanation:

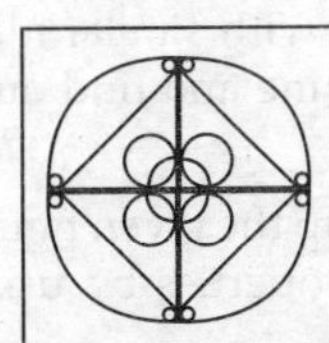

■ ■ ■

Chapter 22

Grouping of Identical Figures and Figure Matrix

LEARNING OBJECTIVES:

- Identifying the rule to group the given figures
- Identifying the rule to find the missing figure in matrix
- Different types of questions asked in competitive exams

GROUPING OF FIGURES

In this section, we are given some different figures (shapes) having each of three with similar/identical properties. A student need to examine and find out the groups having similar properties.

Example 1: Group the given figures into three classes with identical properties by using each figure only once.

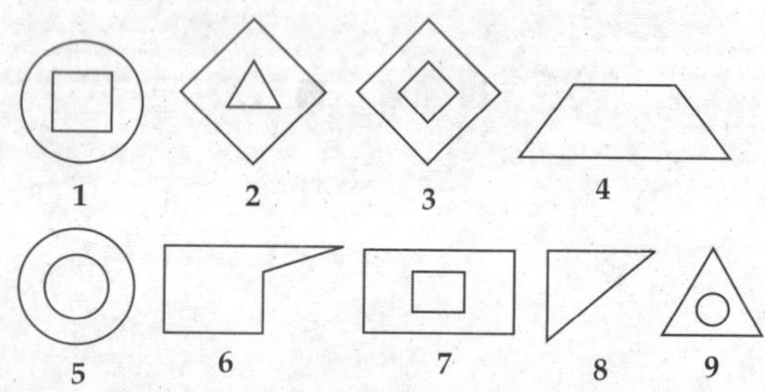

(a) 1, 2, 3; 4, 5, 6; 7, 8, 9

(b) 1, 4, 5; 2, 3, 8; 6, 7, 9

(c) 1, 2, 8; 3, 4, 7; 5, 6, 9

(d) 1, 2, 9; 3, 5, 7; 4, 6, 8

Sol. (d) 1, 2, 9 – Contains two different figures one inside the other.

3, 5, 7 – Contains two similar figures one inside the other.

4, 6, 8 – Contains polygons.

FIGURE MATRIX

In this section, a square matrix having figures given inside it, where a certain rule will be followed in each row. A student need to examine the rule followed among the given figures in the given rows and hence using the same rule, find out the missing figure.

Example 2: Select a figure from the options which will complete the given figure matrix.

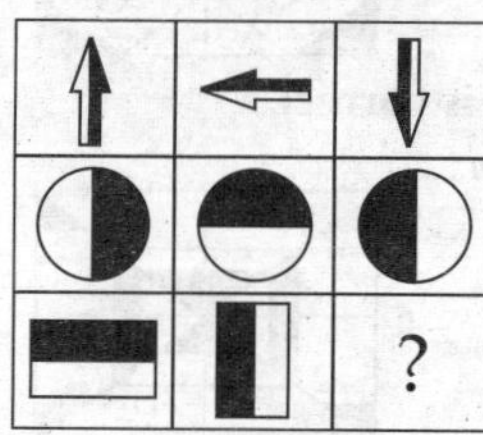

(a) 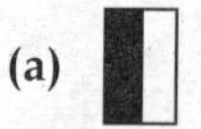

(b) 

(c) 

(d) 

Sol. (d) In each row, the figure rotates 90° anti clockwise to get the next figure. So, the missing figure is [figure].

Level 1 Beginner

Directions (Qs. 1–10): In each of the given question, group the given figures into three classes using each figure only once.

1.

5	8	3
1	2	3
9	10	16
4	5	6
25	32	21
7	8	9

(A) 1, 2, 3; 4, 5, 8; 6, 7, 9 **(B)** 1, 5, 7; 3, 4, 9; 2, 6, 8
(C) 1, 4, 5; 2, 3, 6; 7, 8, 9 **(D)** 1, 5, 7; 2, 4, 9; 3, 6, 8

2.

(A) 1, 8, 9; 2, 6, 7; 3, 4, 5 **(B)** 1, 2, 4; 3, 5, 8; 6, 7, 9
(C) 1, 3, 5; 2, 6, 8; 4, 7, 9 **(D)** 1, 7, 8; 2, 3, 5; 4, 6, 9

3.

A	M	E
1	2	3
W	F	L
4	5	6
X	V	H
7	8	9

(A) 1, 4, 9; 2, 3, 8; 5, 6, 7 **(B)** 1, 2, 4; 3, 5, 8; 6, 7, 9
(C) 1, 5, 9; 2, 3, 4; 6, 7, 8 **(D)** 1, 2, 8; 3, 4, 5; 6, 7, 9

4.

(A) 1, 3, 6; 2, 4, 8; 5, 7, 9 **(B)** 1, 2, 7; 3, 5, 9; 4, 6, 8
(C) 1, 2, 9; 4, 6, 8; 3, 5, 7 **(D)** 1, 2, 4; 3, 6, 9; 5, 7, 8

5.

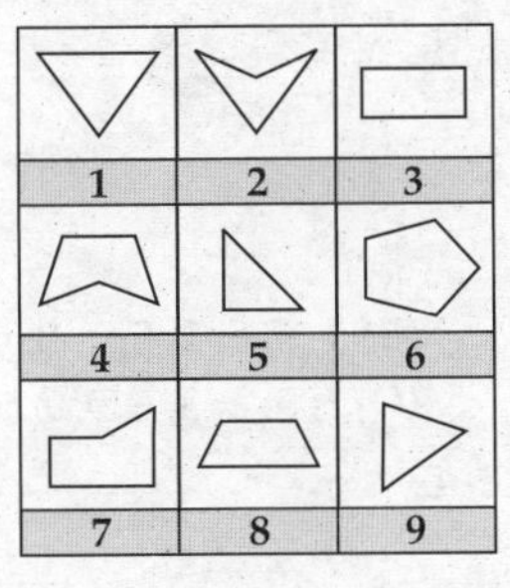

(A) 1, 3, 4; 2, 5, 8; 6, 7, 9 **(B)** 1, 2, 5; 3, 6, 9; 4, 7, 8
(C) 1, 5, 9; 2, 3, 8; 4, 6, 7 **(D)** 1, 4, 7; 2, 3, 5; 6, 8, 9

6.

(A) 1, 6, 8; 2, 4, 9; 3, 5, 7 **(B)** 1, 2, 6; 3, 5, 9; 4, 7, 8
(C) 1, 3, 5; 2, 4, 6; 7, 8, 9 **(D)** 1, 3, 8; 2, 4, 6; 5, 7, 9

7.

3	2	5
1	2	3
4	7	25
4	5	6
8	35	11
7	8	9

(A) 1, 2, 5; 3, 7, 9; 4, 6, 8 **(B)** 1, 3, 4; 2, 5, 8; 6, 7, 9
(C) 1, 5, 9; 2, 4, 7; 3, 6, 8 **(D)** 1, 4, 8; 2, 3, 9; 5, 6, 7

8.

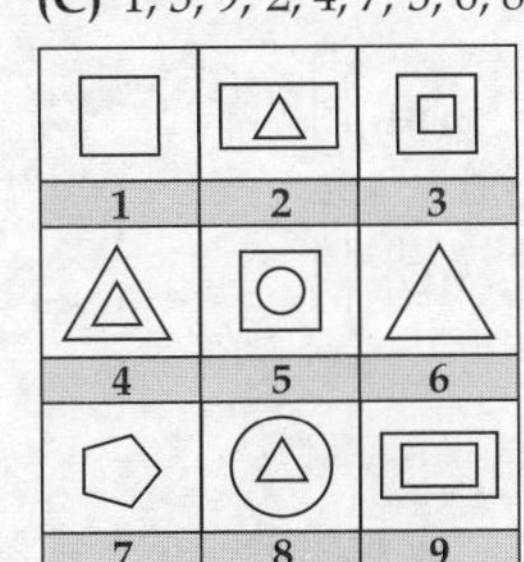

(A) 1, 2, 9; 3, 5, 8; 4, 6, 7 **(B)** 1, 3, 8; 2, 4, 6; 5, 7, 9
(C) 1, 2, 5; 3, 4, 8; 6, 7, 9 **(D)** 1, 6, 7; 2, 5, 8; 3, 4, 9

9.

1	2	3
4	5	6
7	8	9

(A) 1, 2, 5; 3, 6, 9; 4, 7, 8 **(B)** 1, 6, 8; 2, 5, 7; 3, 4, 9
(C) 1, 3, 5; 2, 6, 9; 4, 7, 8 **(D)** 1, 5, 4; 3, 6, 9; 2, 7, 8

10.

1	2	3
4	5	6
7	8	9

(A) 1, 2, 7; 3, 4, 8; 5, 6, 9 **(B)** 1, 3, 5; 2, 6, 7; 4, 8, 9
(C) 1, 2, 5; 3, 6, 9; 4, 7, 8 **(D)** 1, 6, 9; 2, 4, 8; 3, 5, 7

Directions (Qs. 11–20): Select a figure from the options which will complete the given figure matrix.

11.

?

(A) **(B)**
(C) **(D)**

12.

?

(A) **(B)**
(C) **(D)**

13.

3	5	7
5	7	9
7	9	?

(A) 10 **(B)** 11 **(C)** 8 **(D)** 12

14.

?

(A) **(B)**
(C) **(D)**

15.

?

(A) **(B)**
(C) **(D)**

16.

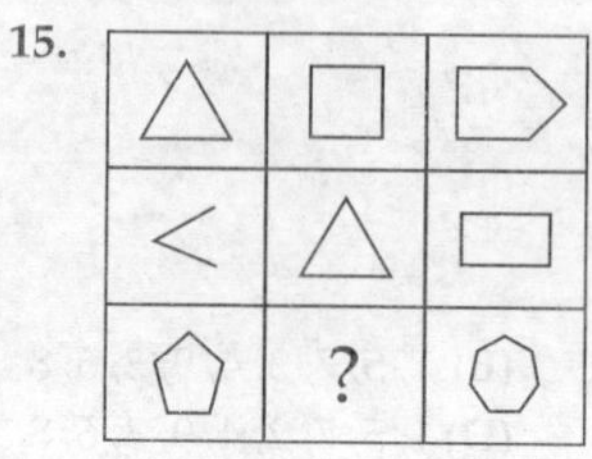

?

(A) **(B)**
(C) **(D)**

17.

?

(A) **(B)**
(C) **(D)**

18.

A	D	G
C	F	I
J	?	P

(A) L **(B)** M
(C) G **(D)** H

19.

(A) (B) (C) (D)

20.

(A) (B) (C) (D)

2 Level Intermediate

Directions (Qs. 1–10): In each of the given question, group the given figures into three classes using each figure only once.

1.

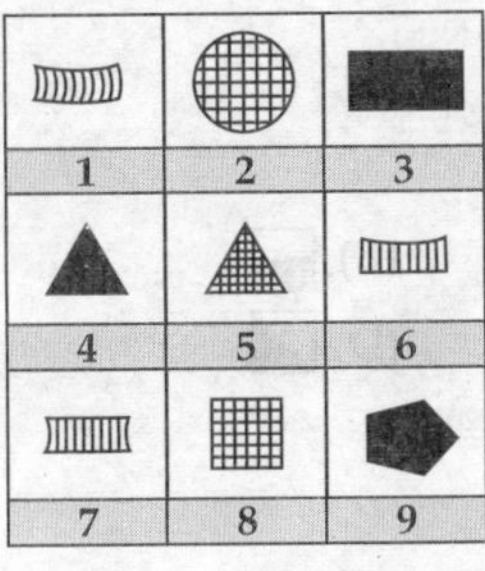

(A) 1, 6, 7; 2, 5, 8; 3, 4, 9 **(B)** 1, 5, 6; 2, 3, 8; 4, 7, 9
(C) 1, 3, 5; 2, 6, 8; 4, 7, 9 **(D)** 1, 2, 5; 3, 6, 9; 4, 7, 8

2.

(A) 1, 2, 5; 3, 6, 9; 4, 7, 8 **(B)** 1, 3, 5; 2, 4, 7; 6, 8, 9
(C) 1, 4, 5; 3, 6, 9; 2, 7, 8 **(D)** 1, 5, 8; 2, 4, 9; 3, 6, 7

3.

(A) 1, 2, 4; 3, 5, 8; 6, 7, 9 **(B)** 1, 5, 9; 2, 6, 7; 3, 4, 8
(C) 1, 2, 5; 3, 6, 8; 4, 7, 9 **(D)** 1, 3, 4; 2, 5, 6; 7, 8, 9

4.

(A) 1, 2, 3; 4, 6, 8; 5, 7, 9 **(B)** 1, 3, 5; 2, 6, 7; 4, 8, 9
(C) 1, 2, 5; 3, 6, 9; 4, 7, 8 **(D)** 1, 6, 7; 3, 4, 9; 2, 5, 8

5.

(A) 1, 7, 9; 2, 4, 8; 3, 5, 6 **(B)** 1, 2, 8; 3, 4, 5; 6, 7, 9
(C) 1, 3, 5; 2, 6, 9; 4, 7, 8 **(D)** 1, 2, 7; 3, 5, 8; 4, 6, 9

6.

(A) 1, 5, 9; 2, 4, 8; 3, 6, 7 **(B)** 1, 2, 5; 3, 6, 9; 4, 7, 8
(C) 1, 2, 5; 3, 6, 8; 4, 7, 9 **(D)** 1, 2, 7; 3, 4, 8; 5, 6, 9

7.

(A) 1, 2, 9; 3, 5, 8; 4, 6, 7 **(B)** 1, 3, 5; 2, 4, 8; 6, 7, 9
(C) 1, 2, 4; 3, 5, 8; 6, 7, 9 **(D)** 1, 5, 9; 3, 6, 7; 2, 4, 8

8.

(A) 1, 2, 9; 3, 5, 8; 4, 6, 7 **(B)** 1, 3, 8; 2, 4, 7; 5, 8, 9
(C) 1, 7, 9; 2, 3, 8; 4, 5, 6 **(D)** 1, 2, 5; 3, 6, 9; 4, 7, 8

9.

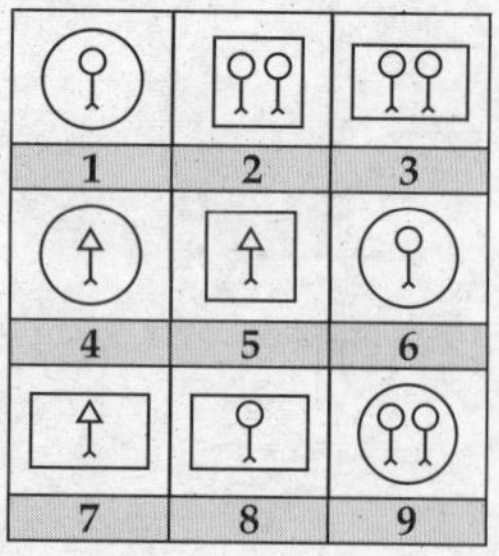

1 2 3
4 5 6
7 8 9

(A) 1, 6, 8; 2, 3, 9; 4, 5, 7 **(B)** 1, 2, 5; 3, 6, 8; 4, 7, 9
(C) 1, 2, 3; 4, 5, 6; 7, 8, 9 **(D)** 1, 2, 5; 3, 6, 9; 4, 7, 8

10.

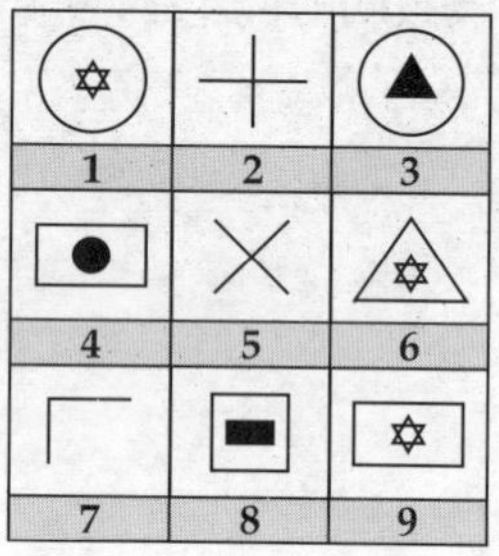

1 2 3
4 5 6
7 8 9

(A) 1, 5, 6; 2, 3, 8; 4, 7, 9 **(B)** 1, 2, 5; 3, 6, 8; 4, 7, 9
(C) 1, 6, 9; 2, 5, 7; 3, 4, 8 **(D)** 1, 3, 4; 2, 5, 6; 7, 8, 9

Directions (Qs. 11–20): Select a figure from the options which will complete the given figure matrix.

11. ?

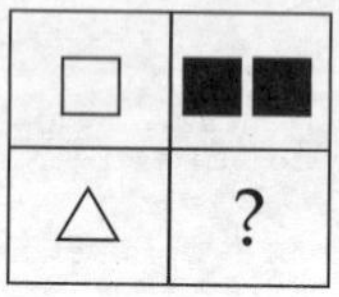

(A)  **(B)** 
(C)  **(D)**

12. ?

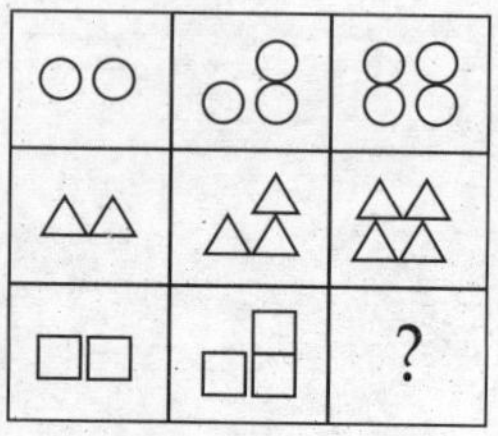

(A) **(B)** 
(C)  **(D)**

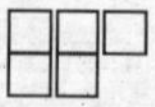

13. ?

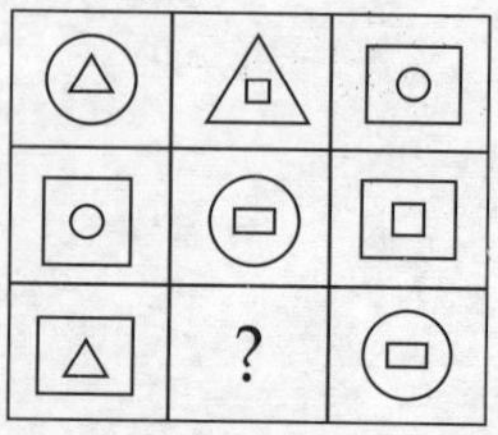

(A)  **(B)**  **(C)**  **(D)**

14. ?

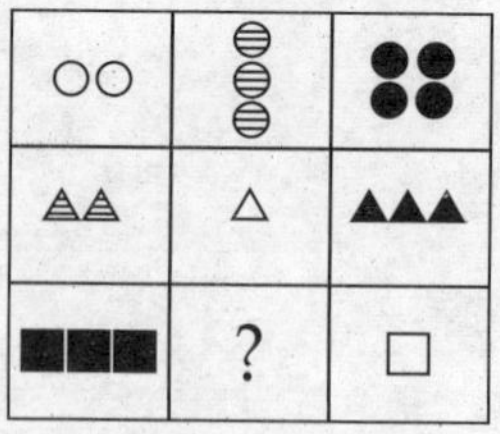

(A) 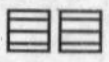 **(B)**
(C) **(D)**

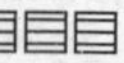

15. ?

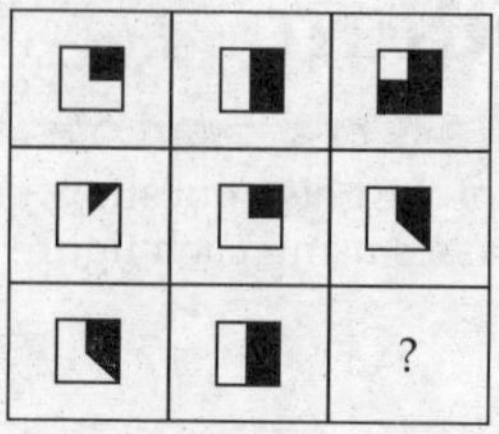

(A) **(B)**
(C) **(D)**

16. ?

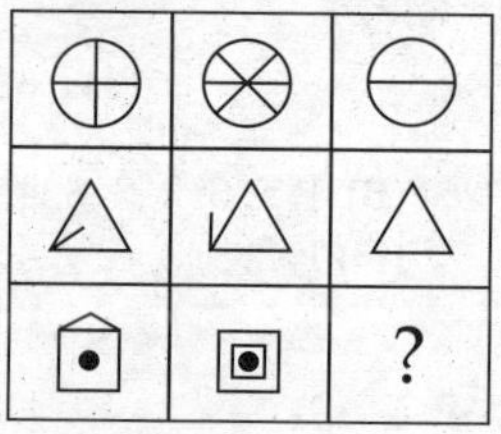

(A) **(B)**
(C) **(D)**

17. ?

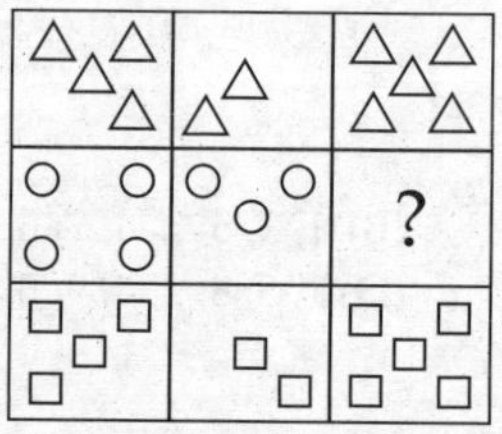

(A) 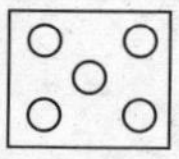 **(B)** 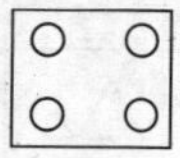
(C) 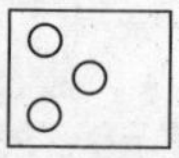 **(D)**

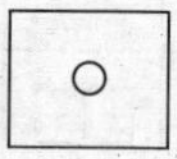

18.

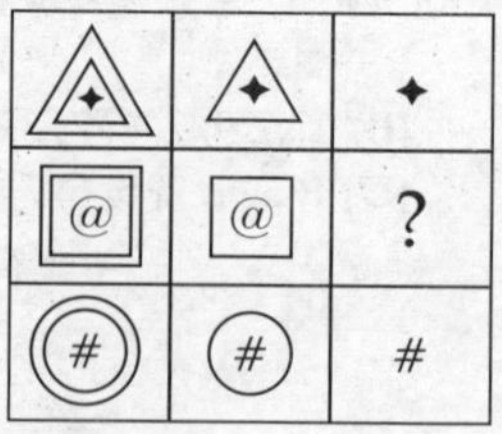

✦	✦	✦
@	@	?
#	#	#

(A) **(B)** @
(C)  @ **(D)**

19.

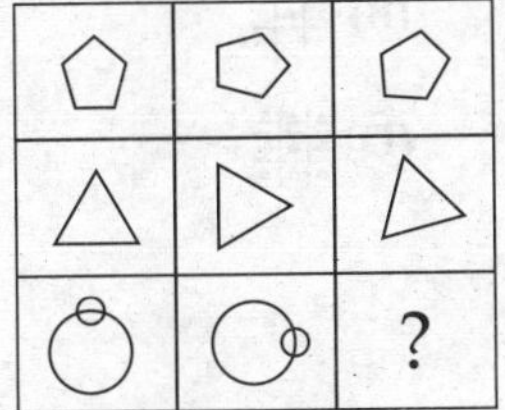

(A)

(B)

(C)

(D)

20.

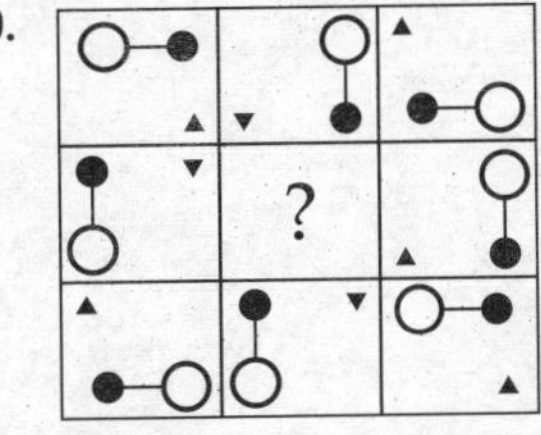

(A)

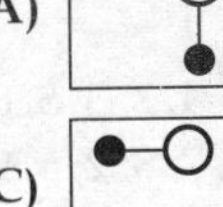

(B)

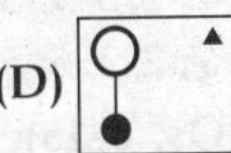

(C)

(D)

3 Level Expert

Directions (Qs. 1–7): In each of the following questions, group the given figures into three classes using each figure only once.

1.

[SSC 2003]

(A) 1, 5, 8; 2, 6, 7; 3, 4, 9
(B) 1, 5, 7; 2, 6, 8; 3, 4, 5
(C) 1, 5, 8; 2, 4, 7; 3, 6, 9
(D) 1, 5, 8; 2, 6, 9; 3, 4, 7

2.

(A) 1, 6, 8; 2, 3, 4; 7, 8, 9
(B) 1, 2, 3; 4, 5, 7; 6, 8, 9
(C) 1, 6, 8; 3, 4, 7; 2, 5, 9
(D) 1, 6, 9; 3, 4, 7; 2, 5, 8

3.

(A) 1, 6, 8; 2, 4, 7; 3, 5, 9
(B) 1, 2, 5; 3, 6, 8; 4, 7, 9
(C) 1, 2, 5; 3, 4, 8; 6, 7, 9
(D) 1, 2, 5; 3, 7, 8; 4, 6, 9

4.

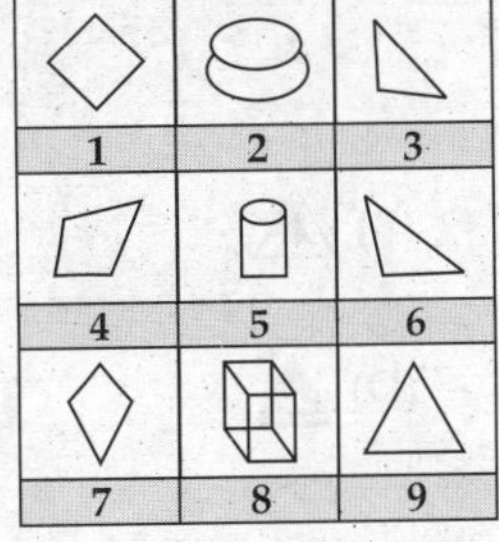

[SSC 2007]

(A) 1, 4, 7; 2, 5, 8; 3, 6, 9
(B) 1, 4, 7; 2, 5, 9; 3, 6, 8
(C) 1, 3, 4; 2, 5, 8; 6, 7, 9
(D) 1, 2, 3; 4, 5, 6; 7, 8, 9

5.

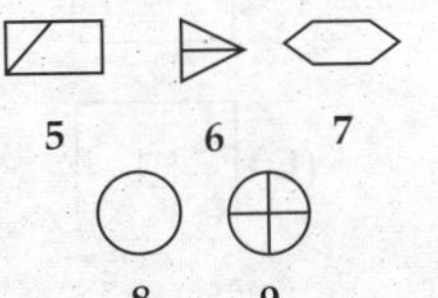

[SSC 2004]

(A) 1, 2, 4; 3, 5, 6; 7, 8, 9
(B) 1, 7, 8; 3, 5, 6; 2, 4, 9
(C) 1, 3, 4; 2, 8, 9; 5, 6, 7
(D) 1, 7, 8; 2, 3, 6; 4, 5, 9

6.

(A) 1, 6, 7; 2, 4, 9; 3, 5, 8
(B) 1, 2, 3; 4, 5, 6; 7, 8, 9
(C) 1, 3, 5; 2, 6, 8; 4, 7, 9
(D) 1, 2, 8; 3, 4, 7; 5, 6, 9

7.

1	2	3
4	5	6
7	8	9

(A) 1, 4, 7; 2, 5, 9; 3, 8, 6 (B) 2, 6, 9; 1, 4, 7; 3, 5, 8
(C) 1, 4, 7; 2, 3, 6; 5, 8, 9 (D) 1, 3, 5; 4, 7, 8; 2, 6, 9

Directions (Qs. 8–15): Select a figure from the options which will complete the given figure matrix.

8.

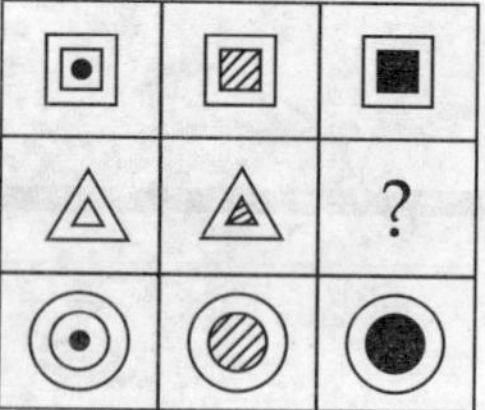

(A) (B) (C) (D)

9.

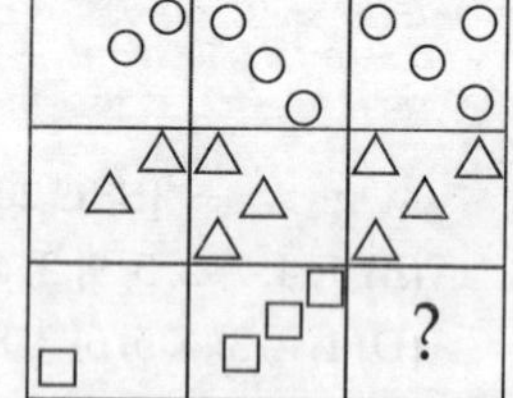

(A) 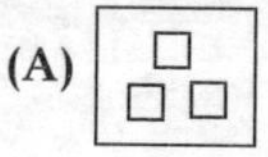

(B) 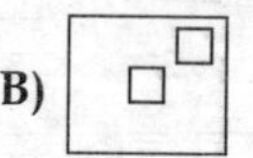

(C) 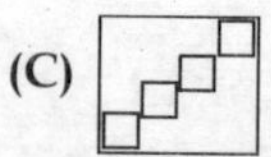

(D) 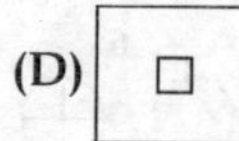

10.

Z	X	U
M	K	H
R	P	?

(A) O (B) M
(C) N (D) Q

11.

(A) (B)
(C) (D)

12.

(A) (B)
(C) (D)

13.

(A) (B)
(C) (D)

14.

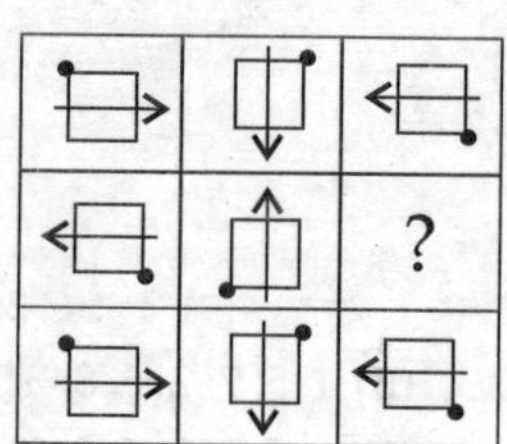

(A) (B)
(C) (D)

15.

(A)

(B) 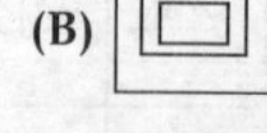

(C)

(D) 

ANSWER KEY

Level-1: Beginner

1.	(B)	2.	(A)	3.	(C)	4.	(C)	5.	(C)	6.	(A)	7.	(C)	8.	(D)	9.	(B)	10.	(D)
11.	(A)	12.	(C)	13.	(B)	14.	(C)	15.	(B)	16.	(A)	17.	(D)	18.	(B)	19.	(B)	20.	(D)

Level-2: Intermediate

1.	(A)	2.	(D)	3.	(B)	4.	(D)	5.	(A)	6.	(A)	7.	(D)	8.	(C)	9.	(A)	10.	(C)
11.	(C)	12.	(C)	13.	(A)	14.	(A)	15.	(C)	16.	(D)	17.	(A)	18.	(B)	19.	(D)	20.	(B)

Level-3: Expert

1.	(C)	2.	(D)	3.	(A)	4.	(A)	5.	(B)	6.	(A)	7.	(C)	8.	(B)	9.	(C)	10.	(B)
11.	(A)	12.	(C)	13.	(C)	14.	(C)	15.	(D)										

Solutions with Detailed Explanations

Level-1: BEGINNER

1. **Option (B) is correct.**
   Explanation:
   1, 5, 7 – Numbers are multiples of 5.
   3, 4, 9 – Numbers are multiples of 3.
   2, 6, 8 – Numbers are multiples of 8.
2. **Option (A) is correct.**
   Explanation:
   1, 8, 9 – Contains closed curves.
   2, 6, 7 – Contains polygons.
   3, 4, 5 – Contains open figures.
3. **Option (C) is correct.**
   Explanation:
   1, 5, 9 – Alphabets made up of three segments.
   2, 3, 4 – Alphabets made up of four line segments.
   6, 7, 8 – Alphabets made up of two line segments.
4. **Option (C) is correct.**
   Explanation:
   1, 2, 9 – Figures divided into 2 equal parts.
   4, 6, 8 – Figures divided into 3 equal parts.
   3, 5, 7 – Contains two similar figures one inside the other.
5. **Option (C) is correct.**
   Explanation:
   1, 5, 9 – Figures made up of 3 line segments.
   2, 3, 8 – Figures made up of 4 line segments.
   4, 6, 7 – Figures made up of 5 line segments.
6. **Option (A) is correct.**
   Explanation:
   1, 6, 8 – Contains 2-D shapes.
   2, 4, 9 – Contains half figures.
   3, 5, 7 – Contains 3-D shapes.
7. **Option (C) is correct.**
   Explanation:
   1, 5, 9 – Contains prime numbers.
   2, 4, 7 – Contains multiples of 2.
   3, 6, 8 – Contains multiples of 5.
8. **Option (D) is correct.**
   Explanation:
   1, 6, 7 – Contains single figure.
   2, 5, 8 – Contains two different figures one inside the other.
   3, 4, 9 – Contains two similar figures one inside the other.
9. **Option (B) is correct.**
   Explanation:
   1, 6, 8 – Contains figures with horizontal lines.
   2, 5, 7 – Contains figures with slanting lines.
   3, 4, 9 – Contains figures with vertical lines.
10. **Option (D) is correct.**
    Explanation:
    1, 6, 9 – Figures divided into 3 equal parts.
    2, 4, 8 – Contains open figures.
    3, 5, 7 – Figures divided into 4 equal parts.
11. **Option (A) is correct.**
    Explanation: In each row, the third figure is the combination of first two figures. So, the missing figure is .
12. **Option (C) is correct.**
    Explanation: In each row, every next figure is obtained by rotating the previous figure 45° clockwise. So, the missing figure is .
13. **Option (B) is correct.**
    Explanation: In each row, the next number is obtained by adding 2 to previous number. So, the missing number is 11.
14. **Option (C) is correct.**
    Explanation: In each row, every next figure is obtained by rotating the previous figure 90° clockwise. So, the missing figure is .

15. **Option (B) is correct.**
Explanation: In each row, the number of sides in every next figure increased by 1. So, the missing figure is .

16. **Option (A) is correct.**
Explanation: In each row, the inside figure is getting removed in every next figure. So, the missing figure is .

17. **Option (D) is correct.**
Explanation: In each row, the figure rotates 90° clockwise to get the next figure. So, the missing figure is .

18. **Option (B) is correct.**
Explanation: In each row, the next letter is obtained by moving three lettes forward in an alphabetical series. So, the missing letter is M.

19. **Option (B) is correct.**
Explanation: In each row, third figure is the uncommon part of first two figures So, the missing figure is .

20. **Option (D) is correct.**
Explanation: In each row, the number of sides in every next figure decreased by 1. So, the missing figure is .

Level-2: INTERMEDIATE

1. **Option (A) is correct.**
Explanation:
1, 6, 7 – Contains figures with horizontal lines.
2, 5, 8 – Contains figures with horizontal and vertical lines.
3, 4, 9 – Contains shaded polygons.

2. **Option (D) is correct.**
Explanation:
1, 5, 8 – Contains figures with curve and straight lines.
2, 4, 9 – Contains two similar figures one inside the other.
3, 6, 7 – Contains polygons.

3. **Option (B) is correct.**
Explanation:
1, 5, 9 – Contains two similar figures attached to each other.
2, 6, 7 – Contains two different figures one inside the other.
3, 4, 8 – Figures divided into four equal parts.

4. **Option (D) is correct.**
Explanation:
1, 6, 7 – Contains figures with 1 line attached.
3, 4, 9 – Contains figures with 2 lines attached.
2, 5, 8 – Contains figures with 3 lines attached.

5. **Option (A) is correct.**
Explanation:
1, 7, 9 – Contains figures having two line segments and 1 circle.
2, 4, 8 – Contains figures having four line segments and 1 circle.
3, 5, 6 – Contains figures having three lines segments and 2 circles.

6. **Option (A) is correct.**
Explanation:
1, 5, 9 – Two slanting lines drawn of the figure.
2, 4, 8 – One rectangle line drawn of the figure.
3, 6, 7 – One slanting line drawn of the figure.

7. **Option (D) is correct.**
Explanation:
1, 5, 9 – Figures divided into 4 parts
3, 6, 7 – Contains figures with two opposite parts shaded among 4 equal parts.
2, 4, 8 – Figures divided into 2 equal parts.

8. **Option (C) is correct.**
Explanation: In each combination, three different types of corners attached with the arrow.

9. **Option (A) is correct.**
Explanation: In each combination, one type of element is placed inside three different types of figures.

10. **Option (C) is correct.**
Explanation:
1, 6, 9 – Contains figures having ✡ inside them.
2, 5, 7 – Contains open figures.
3, 4, 8 – Contains two different figure and inside the others and inside figure shaded.

11. **Option (C) is correct.**
Explanation: In each row, the number of elements in the next figure increased by 1 and becomes shaded. So, the missing figure is ▲▲.

12. **Option (C) is correct.**
Explanation: In each row, the number of elements in every next figure increased by 1. So, the missing figure is .

13. **Option (A) is correct.**
Explanation: In each row, from left row, the inner figure becomes the outer figure of next one and a new figure is placed in it. So, the missing number is .

14. **Option (A) is correct.**

15. **Option (C) is correct.**
Explanation: In each row, the shaded part increased clockwise. So, the missing figure is .

16. **Option (D) is correct.**
Explanation: In each row, the third figure is the common part of first two figures. So, the missing figure is .

17. **Option (A) is correct.**
Explanation: In each row, the third figure is the combination of first two figures. So, the missing figure is 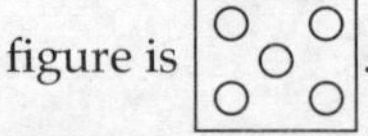.

18. Option (B) is correct.

Explanation: In each row, the outer figure getting removed in every next figure. So, the missing figure is @.

19. Option (D) is correct.

Explanation: In each row, the figure rotates 90° and 135° clockwise respectively. So, the missing figure is .

20. Option (B) is correct.

Explanation: In each row, the elements move right to next part. So, the missing figure is 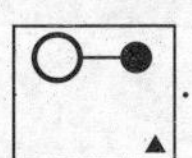.

Level-3: EXPERT

1. **Option (C) is correct.**
2. **Option (D) is correct.**

Explanation:
1, 6, 9 – Contains three sided figures.
3, 4, 7 – Contains four sided figures.
2, 5, 8 – Contains five sided figures.

3. **Option (A) is correct.**

Explanation:
1, 6, 8 – Figures divided into two parts and having dots inside it.
2, 4, 7 – Contains two similar shapes attached to each other.
3, 5, 9 – Contains figure having same number of line segments inside them as the number of sides of the figure.

4. **Option (A) is correct.**

Explanation:
1, 4, 7 – Contains 4 sided figure.
2, 5, 8 – Contains 3-D shapes.
3, 6, 9 – Contains 3 sided figure.

5. **Option (B) is correct.**

Explanation:
1, 7, 8 – Contains 2-D shapes.
3, 5, 6 – Contains figures divided into 2 parts.
2, 4, 9 – Contains figures divided into 4 parts.

6. **Option (A) is correct.**

Explanation:
1, 6, 7 – Contains Two similar figures one inside the other.
2, 4, 9 – Contains figures divided into 4 equal parts.
3, 5, 8 – Contains Two different figures one inside the other.

7. **Option (C) is correct.**
8. **Option (B) is correct.**
9. **Option (C) is correct.**

Explanation: In each row, the third figure is the combination of first two figures. So, the missing figure is 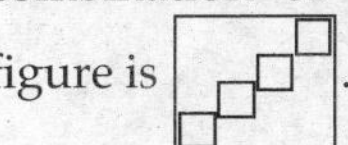.

10. **Option (B) is correct.**

Explanation: In each row, $Z \xrightarrow{-2} X \xrightarrow{-3} U$

$M \xrightarrow{-2} K \xrightarrow{-3} H$

So, $R \xrightarrow{-2} P \xrightarrow{-3} M$

So, the missing alphabet is M.

11. **Option (A) is correct.**

Explanation: In each row, the third figure is the combination of first two figures. So, the missing figure is .

12. **Option (C) is correct.**

Explanation: The number of elements get increased by 1 in every next figure. So, the missing figure is .

13. **Option (C) is correct.**

Explanation: In each row, the third figure is the uncommon part of first two figures. So, the missing number is .

14. **Option (C) is correct.**

Explanation: In each row, the next figure is obtained by rotating 90° clockwise. So, the missing figure is 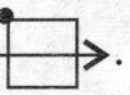.

15. **Option (D) is correct.**

Explanation: In each row, the number of elements in every next figure is decreased by 1. So, the missing figure is 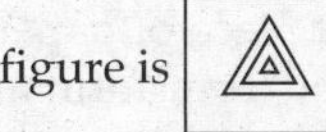.

■ ■ ■

Paper Folding and Cutting

LEARNING OBJECTIVES:

- ❖ Identifying the figure after unfolding the given patterns
- ❖ Identifying the figure after folding the given pattern
- ❖ Different types of questions asked in competitive exams

Paper cutting and paper folding can also be used as visual aids in reasoning exercises or puzzles. Here's how they can be applied in a reasoning context:

PAPER CUTTING IN REASONING

Paper cutting can be used to create visual puzzles or challenges that require logical reasoning to solve. For example, a sheet of paper with a specific pattern can be cut into pieces, and the task is to rearrange the pieces to form a particular shape or solve a puzzle. The challenge may involve understanding spatial relationships, symmetry, and pattern recognition. It requires logical thinking and problem-solving skills to determine how the pieces fit together to achieve the desired outcome.

PAPER FOLDING IN REASONING

Paper folding, particularly in the context of origami, can be utilized to illustrate and explore geometric and mathematical concepts. Folding a piece of paper can help to visualize and understand transformations, angles, proportions, and spatial relationships.

We will talk about issues involving paper folding and cutting in this chapter.

PAPER CUTTING

➢ In this type of problem, a set of three figures showing in which a piece of paper is folded first and followed by a cut than the examinee has to select one of the figures from the set of four alternative figures which would must closely resemble the pattern when the paper is unfolded.

Directions (for example 1–2): What will be the answer figure, when the given piece of problem figure is opened?

Example (1-2):

What will be the answer figure, when the given piece of prblem figure is opened?

1. 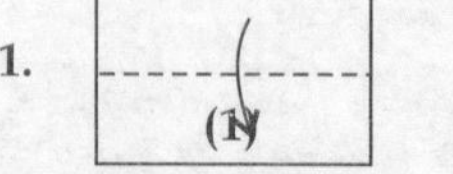 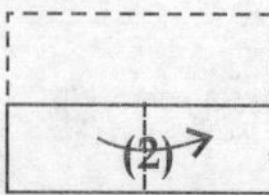 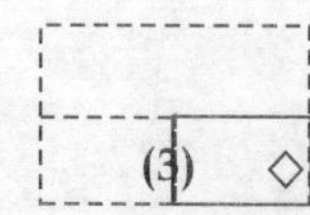

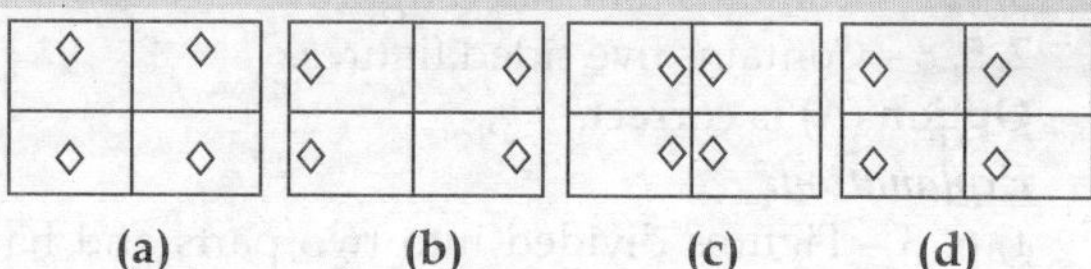

(a) (b) (c) (d)

Sol. (b) As the paper is folded to one fourth of the portion and a cut (in the shape of diamond) is present to the middle of the right most corner. Once it open, option (b) figure follows the pattern.

Example 2:

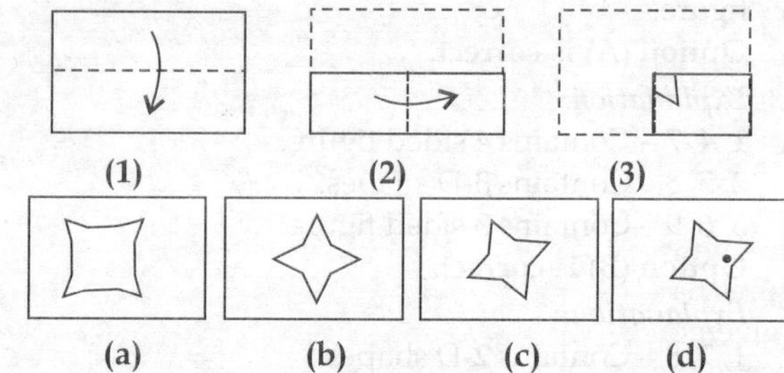

(a) (b) (c) (d)

Sol. (c) If we will fold the next figure looks like option (c).

PAPER FOLDING

➢ The problem based on paper folding are such that the examine has to select a figure from the four alternative which will be closely resemble the pattern that would be formed when a sheet (basically a transparent sheet) is folded along a dotted line carrying any design or figure.

Directions (for example 3–4): A square transparent sheet is given. Select a figure from the options which will look like when the given sheet is folded along the dotted line.

Example (3-4)

A square transparent sheet is given. Select a figure from the options which will look like when the given sheet is folded along the dotted line.

3.

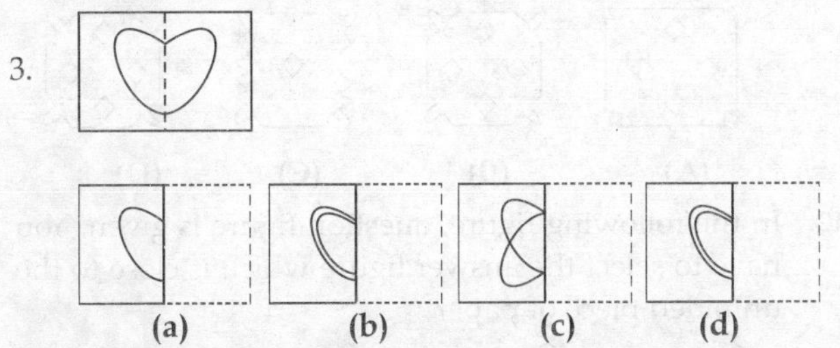

Sol. (a) Option (a) as the transparent figure consists a diagram of heart shape, when folded along the dotted line, the lines of the heart overlapped with each other and appears as a single line figure. So, option (a) is the answer.

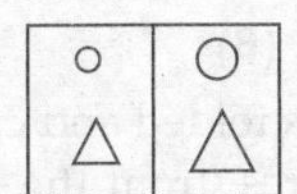

Example 4:

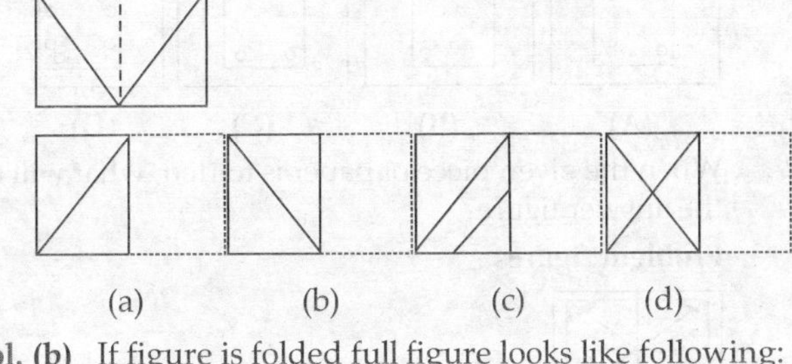

Sol. (b) If figure is folded full figure looks like following:

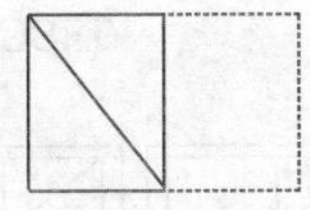

Level 1 Beginner

1. A square transparent sheet with a pattern is given. Figure out from the four alternatives as to how the pattern would appear when the transparent sheet is folded at the middle line shown?

[SSC (10+2) 2011]

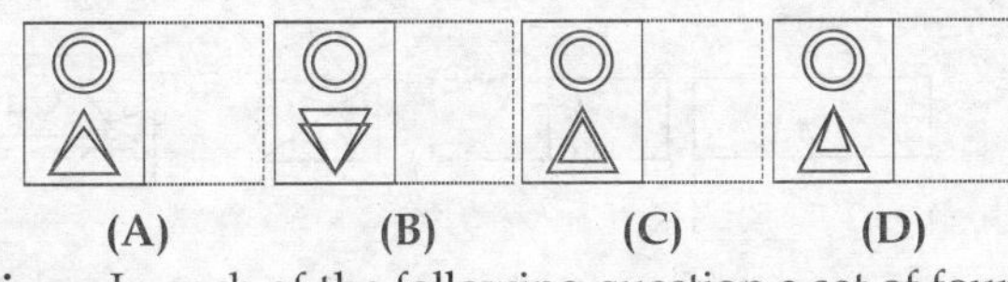

Directions: In each of the following question a set of four figures have been given. Below these figure answer figure is given. You have to select the answer figure which is close to the unfolded piece of paper.

2.

3.

[SSC FCI 2012]

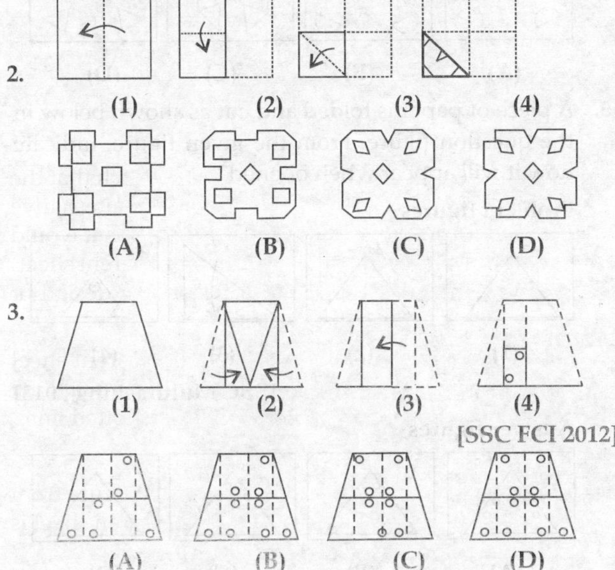

4. A piece of paper is folded and cut as shown below in the question figure. From the given answer figure, indicate how it will appear when opened?

[SSC Steno 2013]

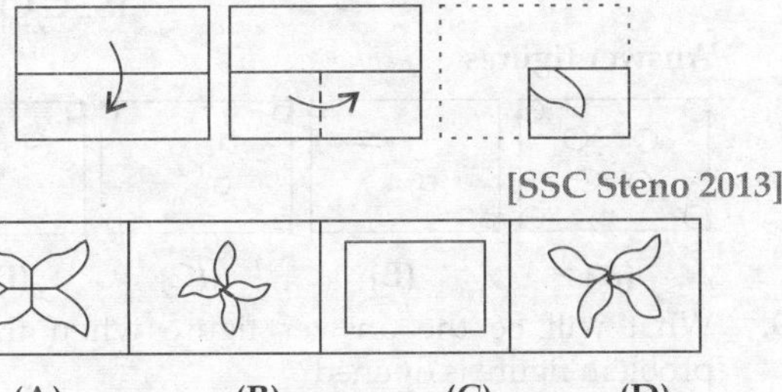

5. A piece of paper is folded and punched as shown below in the question figure. From the given answer figure, indicate how it will appear when opened?

[SSC CGL 2013]

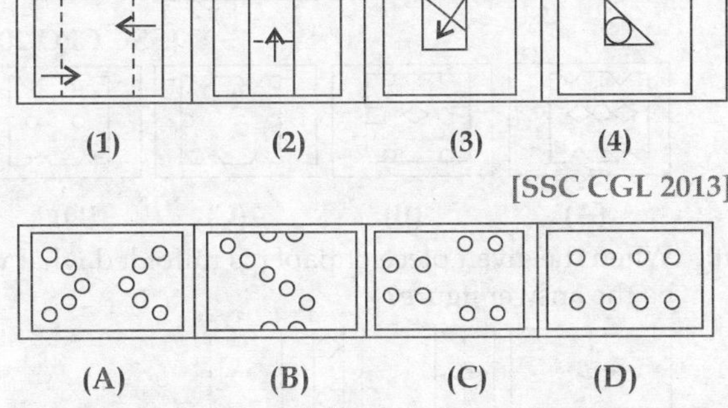

6. A piece of paper is folded and punched as shown below in the question figure. From the given answer figure, indicate how it will appear when opened?

Problem figures

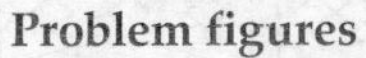

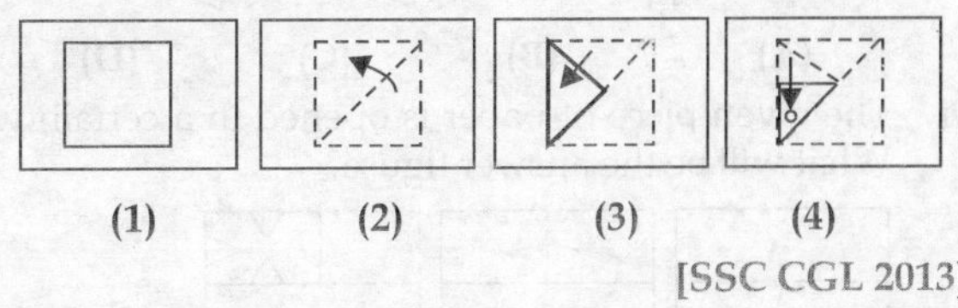

[SSC CGL 2013]

Answer figures

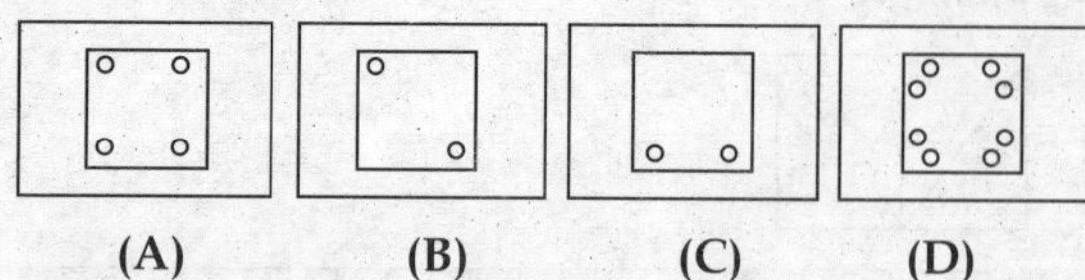

(A) (B) (C) (D)

7. When the given piece of paper is folded, what will be the answer figure?

Problem figures

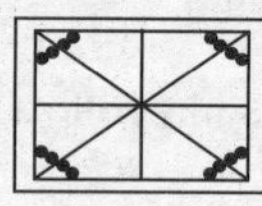

[SSC Multitasking, 2013]

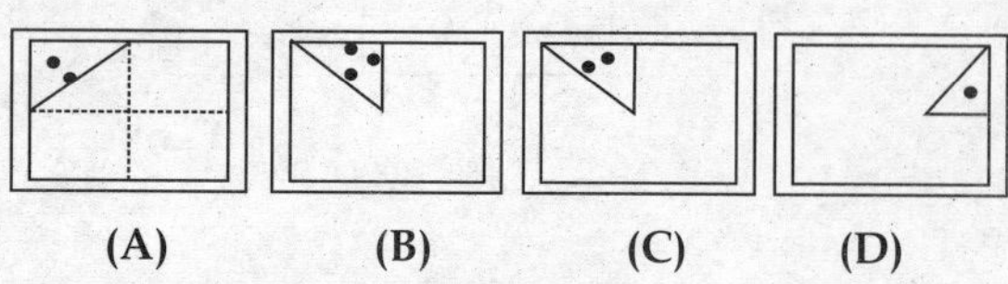

(A) (B) (C) (D)

8. What will be the answer figure, when the given piece of problem figure is opened?

Problem figures

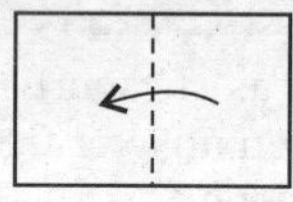
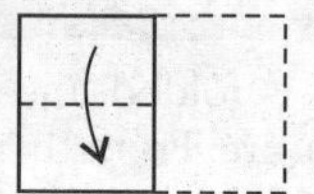
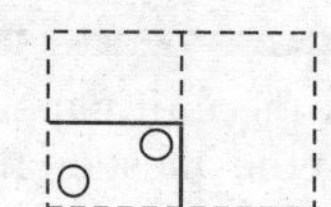

[SSC CPO 2013]

Answer figures

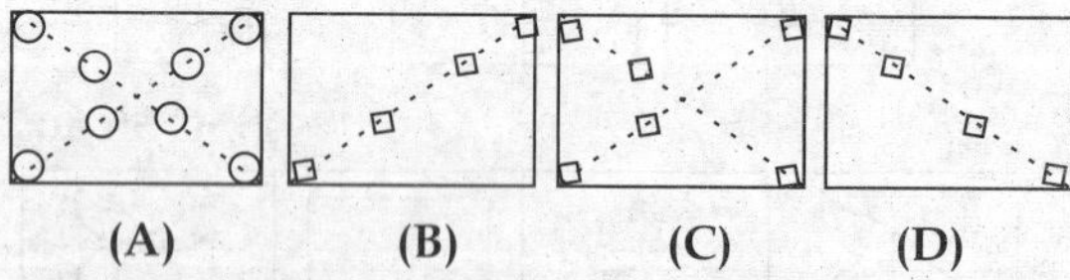

(A) (B) (C) (D)

9. What will be the answer figure when the given problem figure is opened?

Problem figures

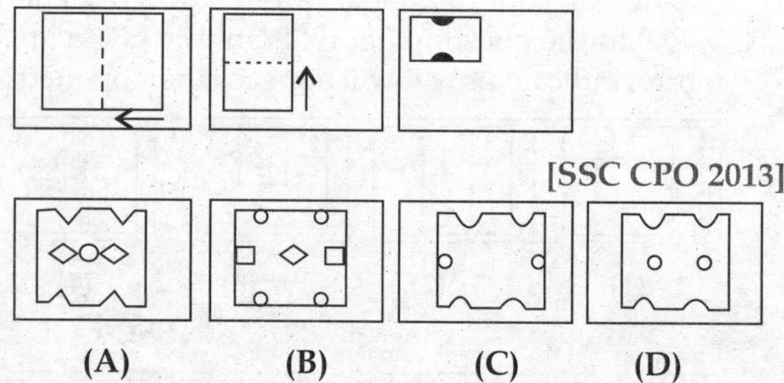

[SSC CPO 2013]

(A) (B) (C) (D)

10. When the given piece of paper is unfolded what will be the answer figure?

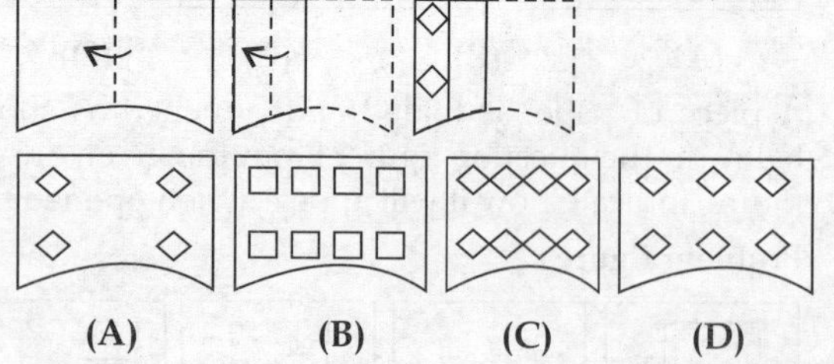

(A) (B) (C) (D)

11. The given piece of paper is opened in a certain way. What will be the answer figure?

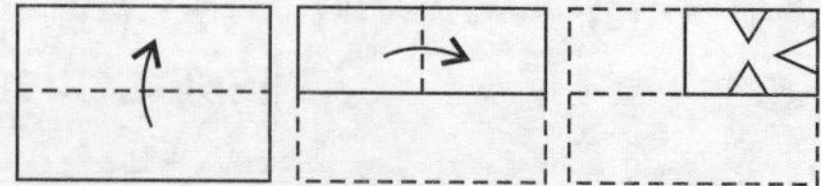

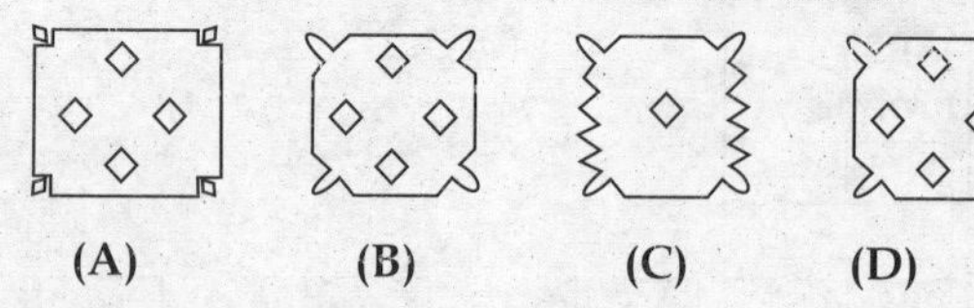

(A) (B) (C) (D)

12. In the following figure, question figure is given. You have to select the answer figure which is close to the unfolded piece of paper.

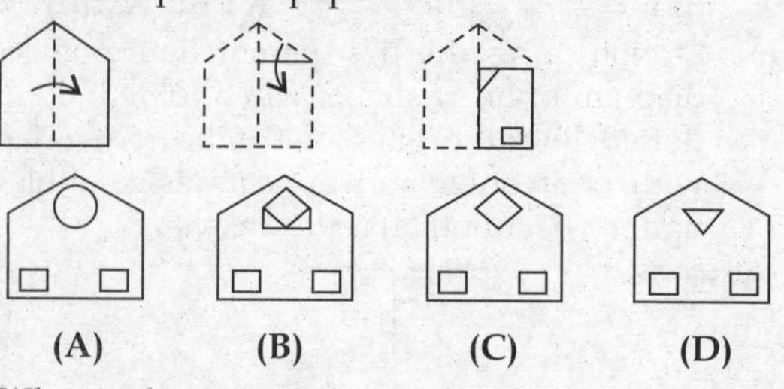

(A) (B) (C) (D)

13. What is the answer figure of given figure when it is opened?

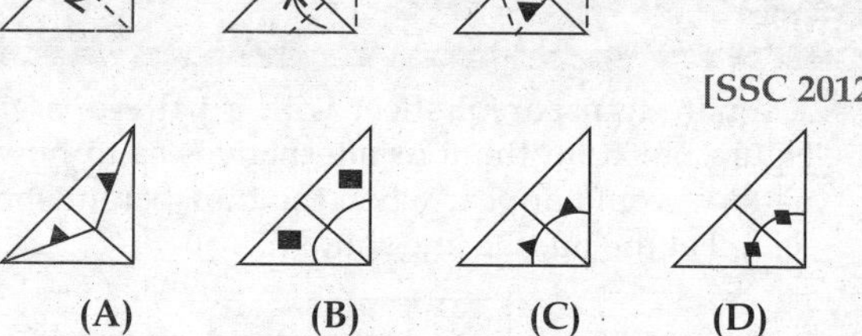

[SSC 2012]

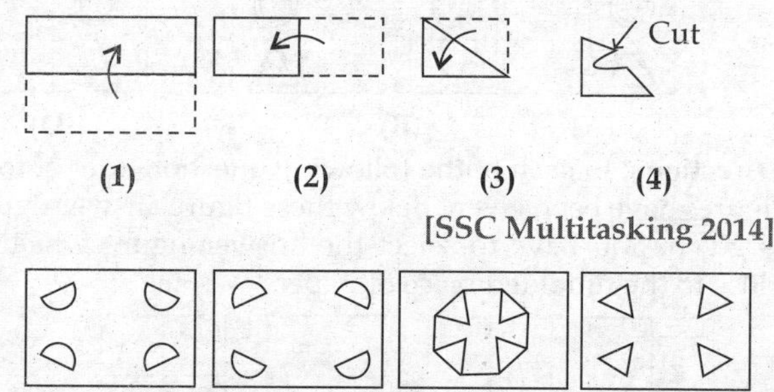

(A) (B) (C) (D)

14. A piece of paper is folded and cut as shown below in the question figures, from the given answer figure, indicate how it will appear when opened?

(1) (2) (3) (4)

[SSC Multitasking 2014]

(A) (B) (C) (D)

15. A piece of paper is folded and cut as shown below in the question figure. From the given figure, indicate how it will appear when opened?

Problem figures

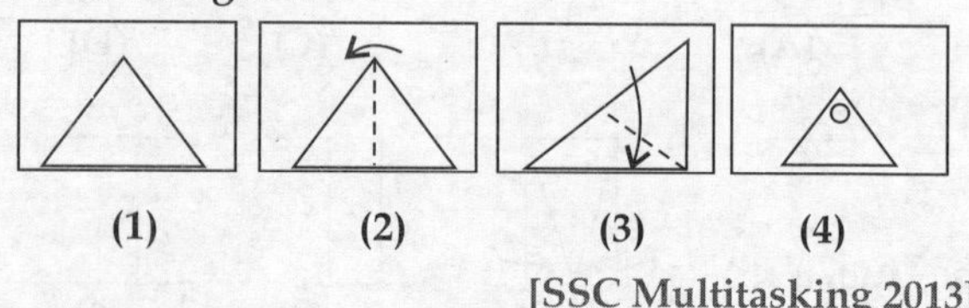

(1) (2) (3) (4)

[SSC Multitasking 2013]

Answer figures

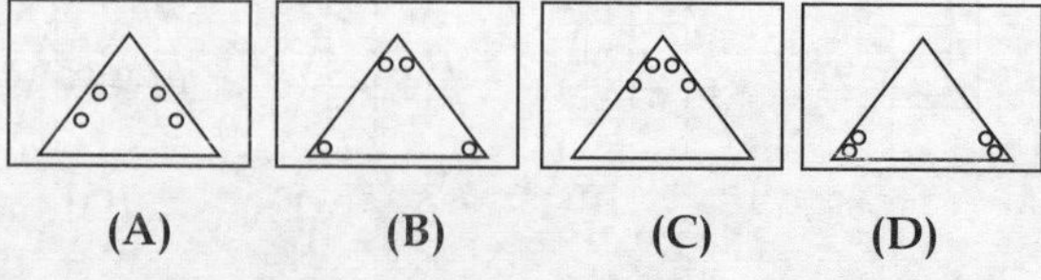

(A) (B) (C) (D)

16. What will be the answer when it opened?

Problem figures

(1) (2) (3) (4)

[SSC 2012]

Answer figures

(A) (B) (C) (D)

17. A paper is folded and cut as shown below. From the given answer figure, indicate how it will appear when opened?

Problem figures

(1) (2) (3) (4)

[SSC (10 + 2) 2013]

Answer figures

(A) (B) (C) (D)

18. What will be the answer figure, when it is opened?

Problem figures

[SSC (10 + 2) 2013]

Answer figures

(A) (B) (C) (D)

19. What is unfolded figure?

(A) (B) (C) (D)

20. What is unfolded figure?

(A) (B) (C) (D)

Directions (21-25): In each of the following question a set of four figures have been given. Below these figure answer figure is given. You have to select the answer figure which is close to the unfolded piece of paper.

21.

[RRB 2007]

(A) (B) (C) (D)

22.

[SSC 2012]

(1) (2) (3) (4)

23.

[RRB 2009]

(A) (B) (C) (D)

24.

(A) (B) (C) (D)

25.

(A) (B) (C) (D)

2 Level Intermediate

Directions: In each of the following question, a square transparent sheet with a pattern is given. Figure out from amongst the four alternatives as to how the pattern would appear when the transparent sheet is folded along the dotted line.

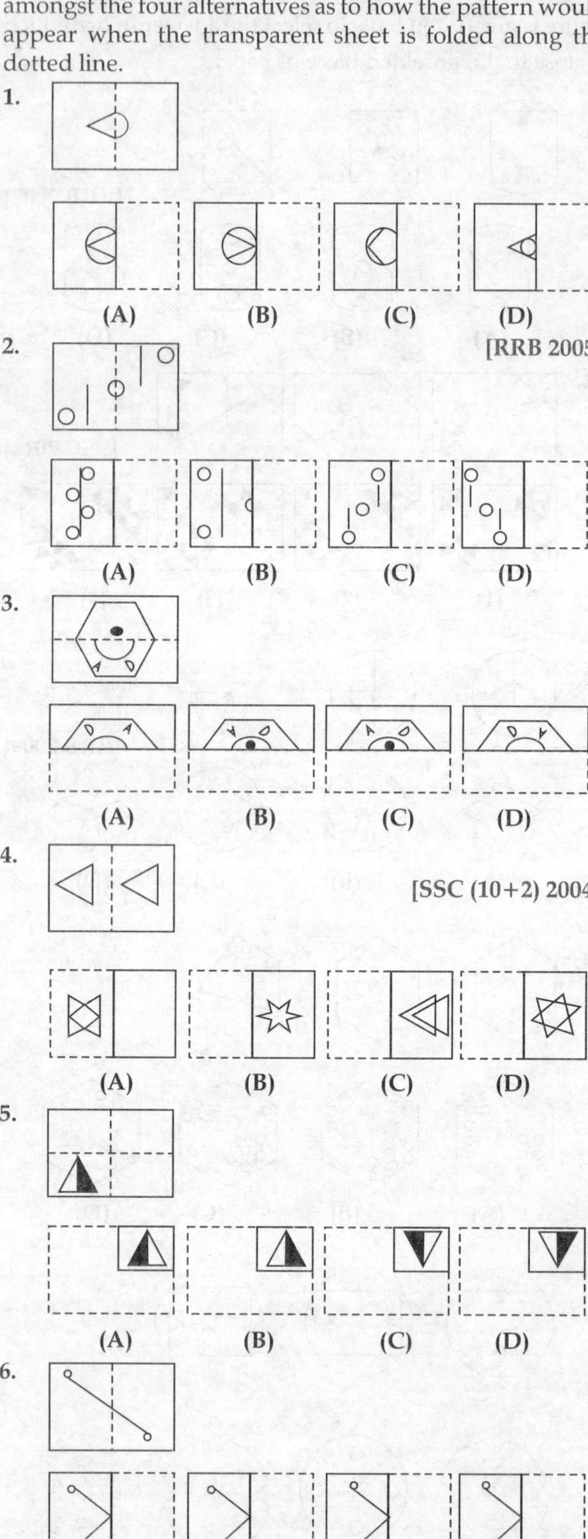

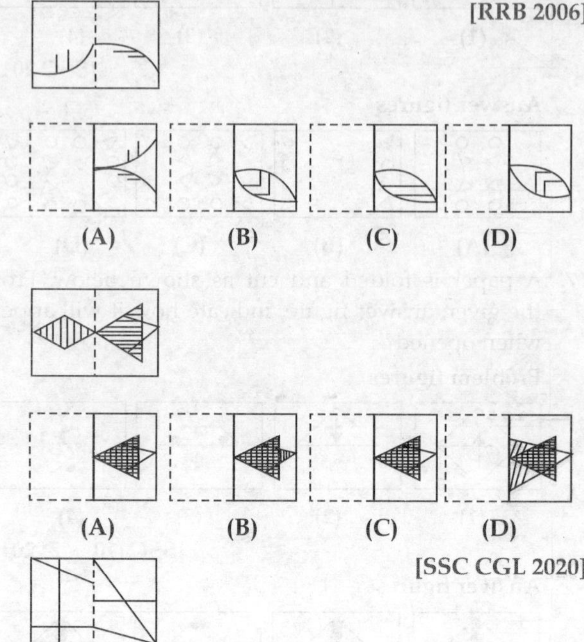

10. [SSC CGL 2020]

(A) (B) (C) (D)

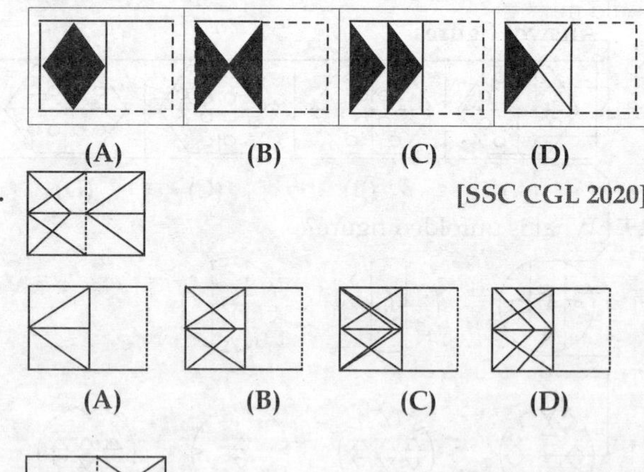

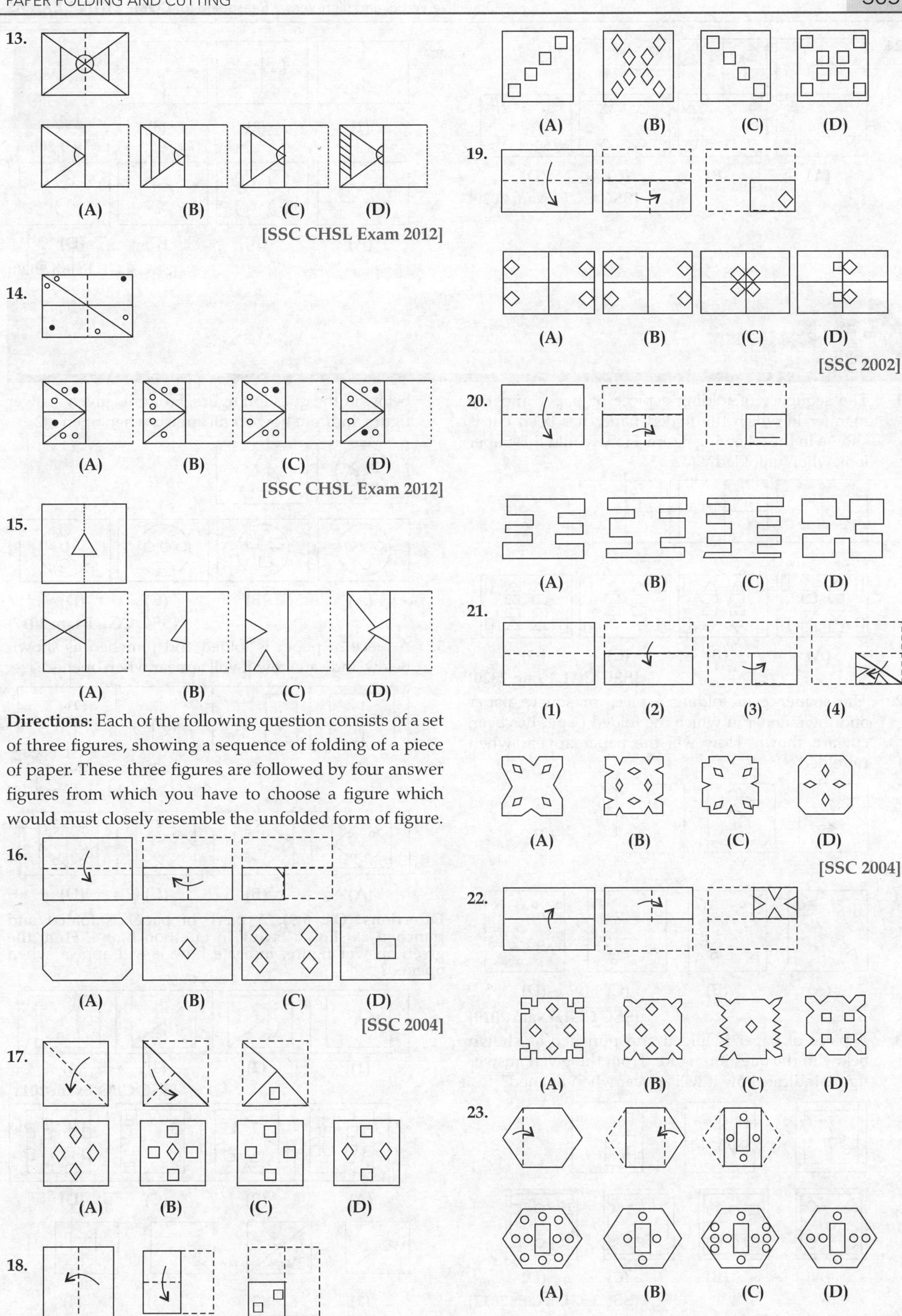

Directions: Each of the following question consists of a set of three figures, showing a sequence of folding of a piece of paper. These three figures are followed by four answer figures from which you have to choose a figure which would must closely resemble the unfolded form of figure.

24.

25.

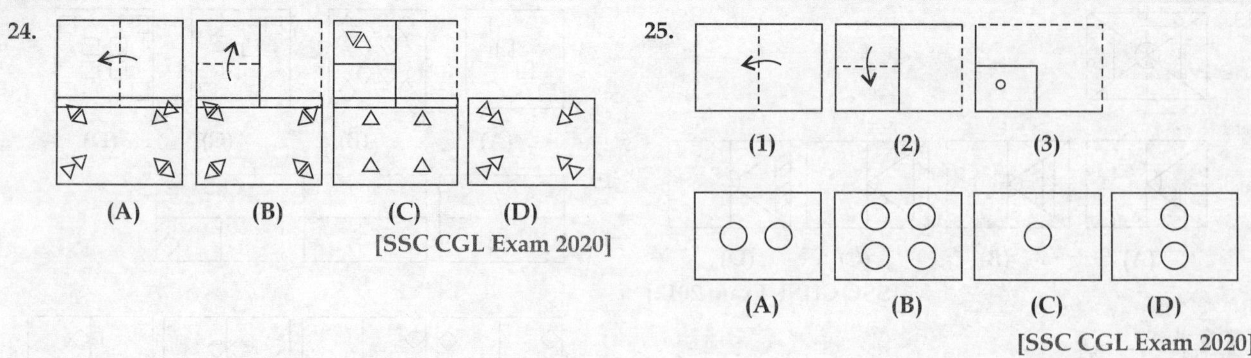

[SSC CGL Exam 2020]

[SSC CGL Exam 2020]

3 Level Expert

1. The sequence of folding a piece of paper and the manner in which the folded paper has been cut is shown in the following figure. How would this paper look when unfolded?

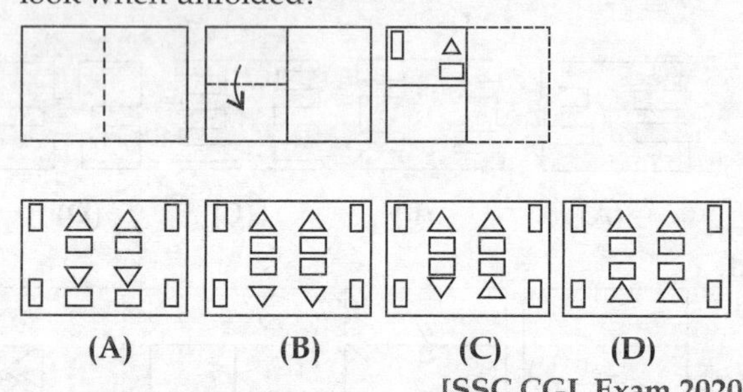

[SSC CGL Exam 2020]

2. The sequence of folding a piece of square paper and the manner in which the folded paper has been cut are shown. How will the paper appear when unfolded?

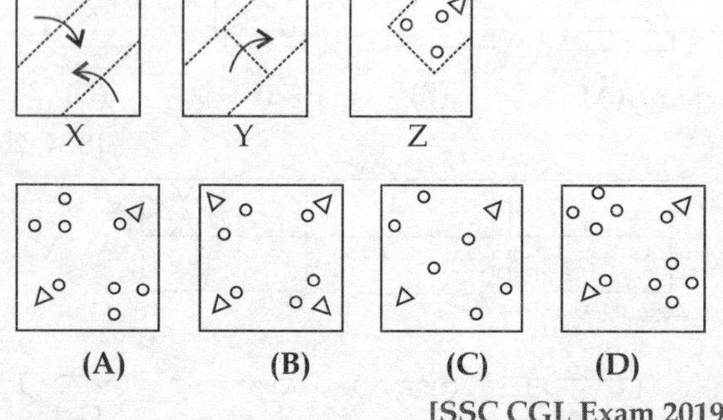

[SSC CGL Exam 2019]

3. A piece of paper is folded and punched as shown below in the question figure. From the given answer figure indicate how it will appear when opened?

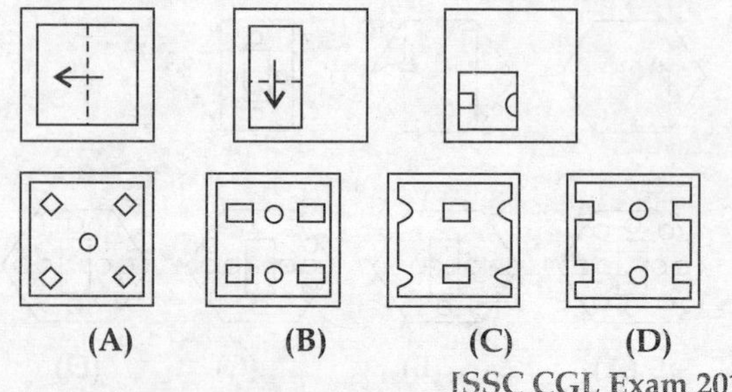

[SSC CGL Exam 2017]

4. A piece of paper is folded and punched as shown below in the question figure. From the given answer figure, indicate how it will appear when opened?

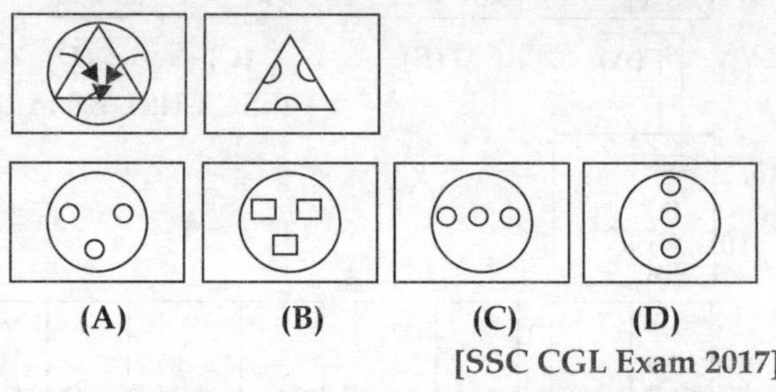

[SSC CGL Exam 2017]

5. A piece of paper is folded and punched as shown below. Indicate how it will appear when opened?

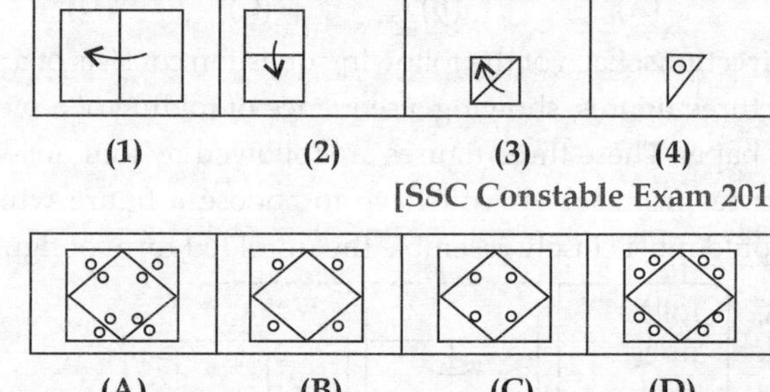

[SSC Constable Exam 2012]

Directions (Qs. 6-9): A piece of paper is folded and punched as shown below in question figure. From the given answer figure, indicate how it will appear when opened?

6.

7.

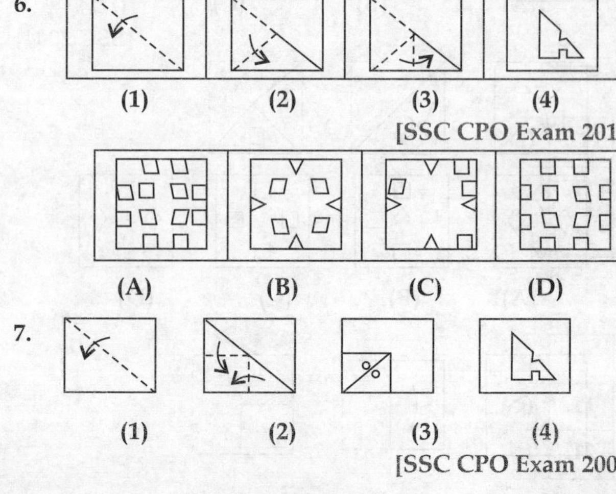

[SSC CPO Exam 2011]

[SSC CPO Exam 2009]

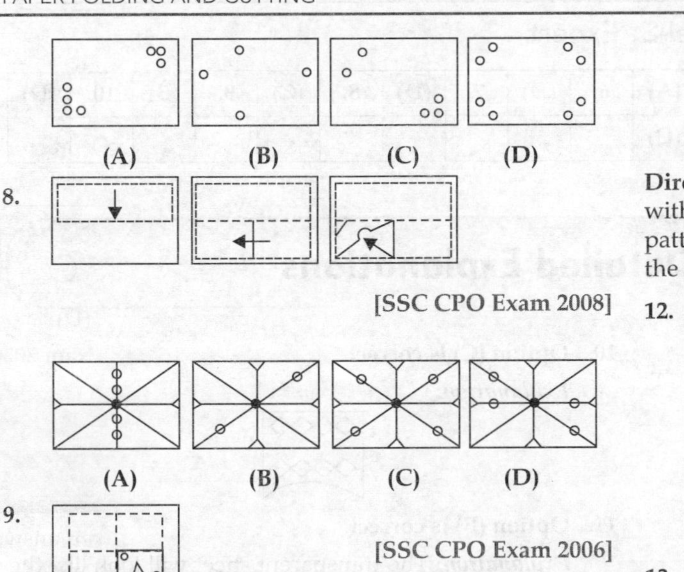

(A) (B) (C) (D)

8.

[SSC CPO Exam 2008]

(A) (B) (C) (D)

9.

[SSC CPO Exam 2006]

(A) (B) (C) (D)

10. A piece of paper is folded and cut into a manner way. What will be the answer when it opened?

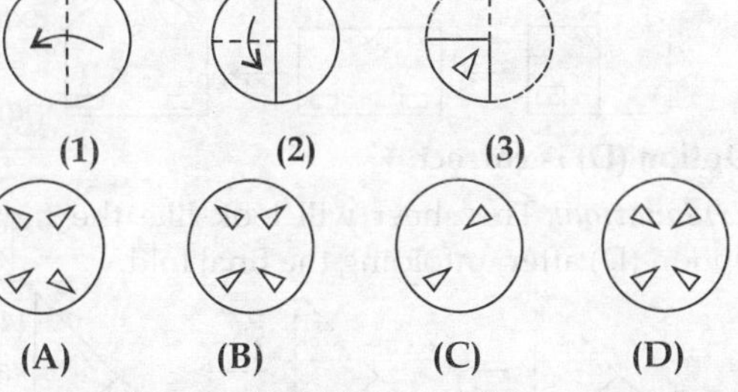

(1) (2) (3)

(A) (B) (C) (D)

11. A piece of paper is folded and the manner in which the folded paper has been cut is shown in the following figures. How would this paper look when unfolded?

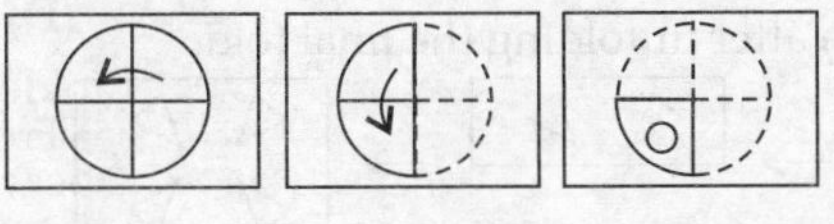

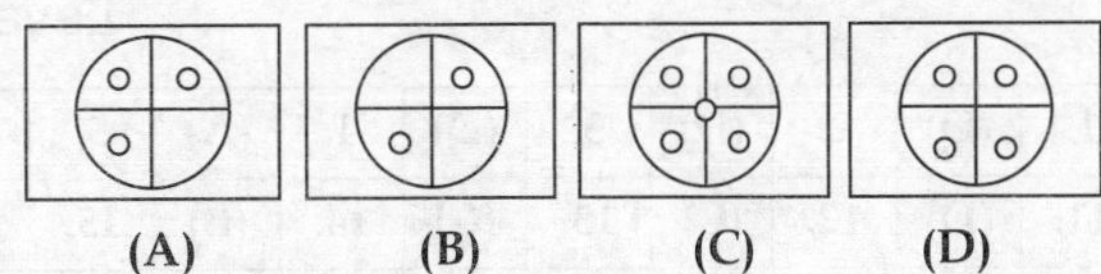

(A) (B) (C) (D)

Directions: Given below is a transparent sheet of paper with a pattern on the left and right side. How will the pattern appear when the transparent sheet is folded on the dotted line?

12. [SSC CGL 2019]

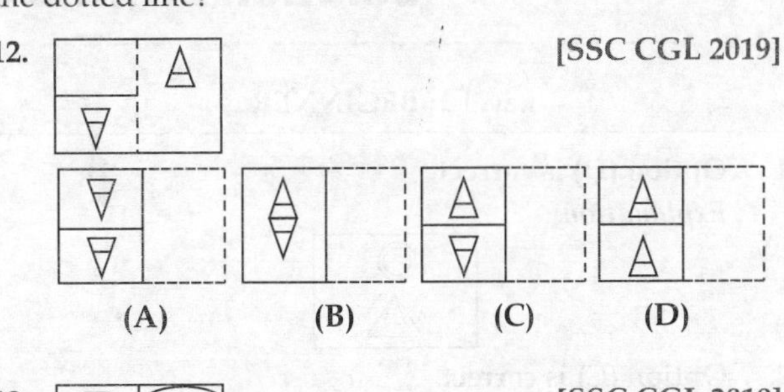

(A) (B) (C) (D)

13. [SSC CGL 2019]

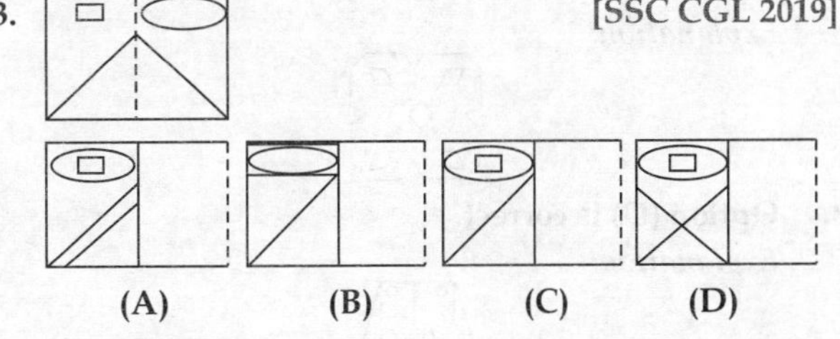

(A) (B) (C) (D)

14. [SSC CGL 2018]

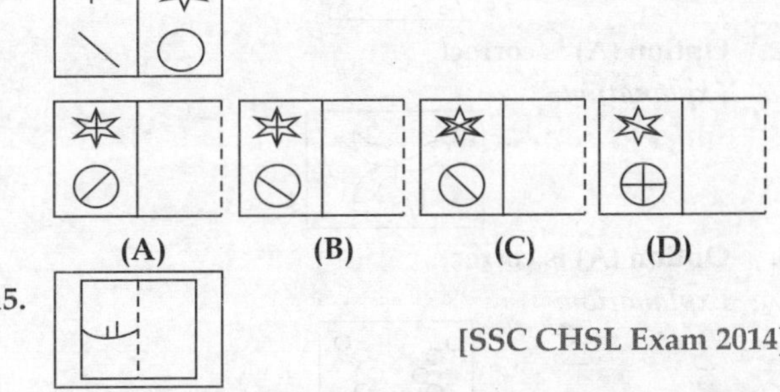

(A) (B) (C) (D)

15. [SSC CHSL Exam 2014]

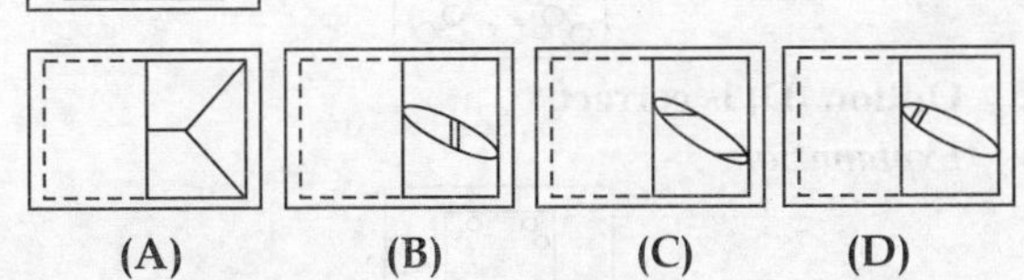

(A) (B) (C) (D)

ANSWER KEY

Level-1: Beginner

1.	(D)	2.	(C)	3.	(D)	4.	(A)	5.	(A)	6.	(D)	7.	(C)	8.	(A)	9.	(D)	10.	(C)
11.	(B)	12.	(A)	13.	(D)	14.	(D)	15.	(A)	16.	(D)	17.	(D)	18.	(B)	19.	(D)	20.	(C)
21.	(D)	22.	(B)	23.	(B)	24.	(C)	25.	(B)										

Level-2: Intermediate

1.	(A)	2.	(B)	3.	(B)	4.	(A)	5.	(C)	6.	(C)	7.	(D)	8.	(B)	9.	(A)	10.	(D)
11.	(C)	12.	(C)	13.	(C)	14.	(D)	15.	(C)	16.	(B)	17.	(C)	18.	(D)	19.	(A)	20.	(B)
21.	(B)	22.	(B)	23.	(D)	24.	(B)	25.	(B)										

Level-3: Expert

1.	(D)	2.	(D)	3.	(D)	4.	(A)	5.	(A)	6.	(D)	7.	(D)	8.	(C)	9.	(B)	10.	(D)
11.	(D)	12.	(C)	13.	(C)	14.	(B)	15.	(D)										

Solutions with Detailed Explanations

Level-1: BEGINNER

1. Option (D) is correct.
Explanation:

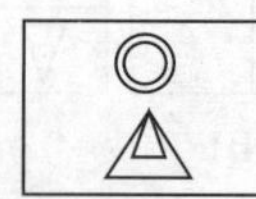

2. Option (C) is correct.
Explanation:

3. Option (D) is correct.
Explanation:

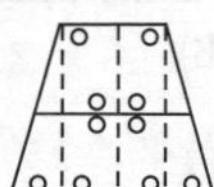

4. Option (A) is correct.
Explanation:

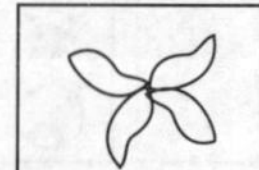

5. Option (A) is correct.
Explanation:

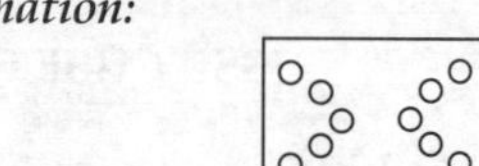

6. Option (D) is correct.
Explanation:

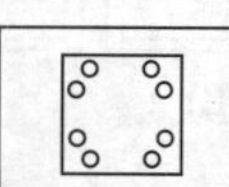

7. Option (C) is correct.
Explanation:

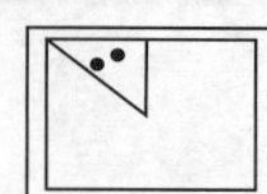

8. Option (A) is correct.
Explanation:

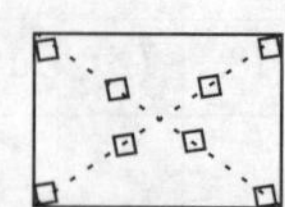

9. Option (D) is correct.
Explanation:

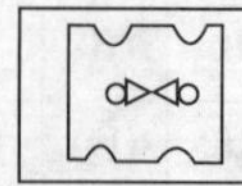

10. Option (C) is correct.
Explanation:

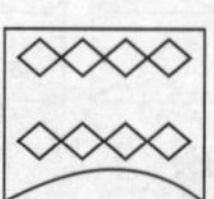

11. Option (B) is correct.
Explanation: The transparent sheet will look like the figure in option (B) after unfolding the final fold.

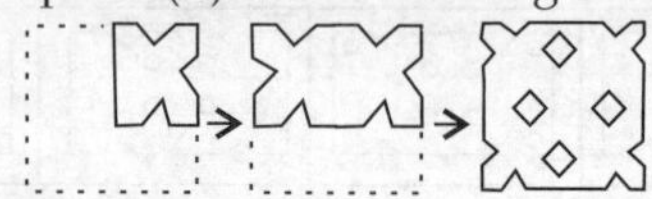

12. Option (C) is correct.
Explanation: The transparent sheet will look like the figure in option (A) after unfolding the final fold.

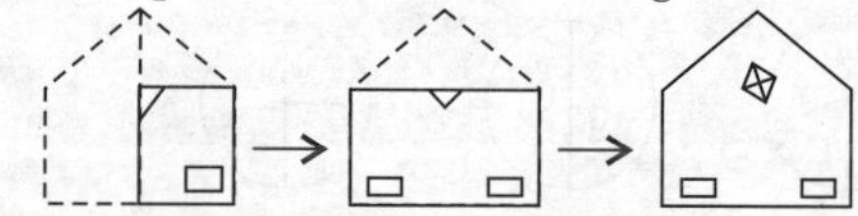

13. Option (D) is correct.
Explanation: The sheet will look like the figure in option (D) after unfolding the final fold.

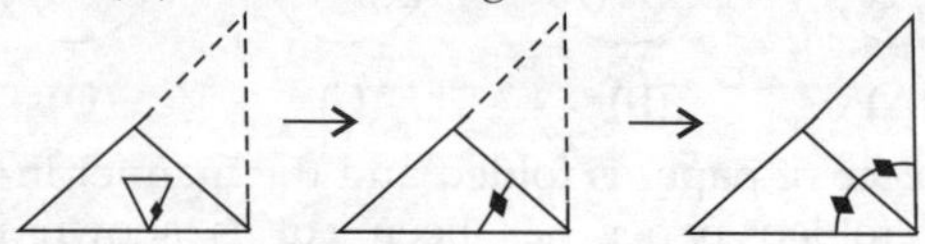

14. Option (D) is correct.
Explanation: The sheet will look like the figure in option (D) after unfolding the final fold.

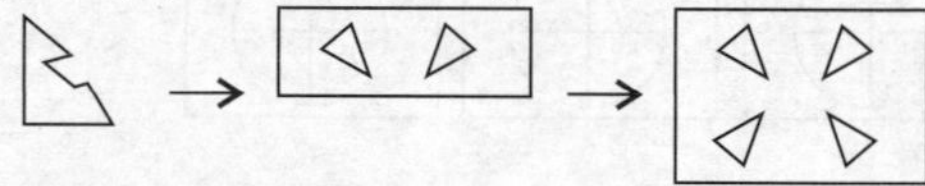

15. Option (A) is correct.
Explanation: The sheet will look like the figure in option (A) after unfolding the final fold.

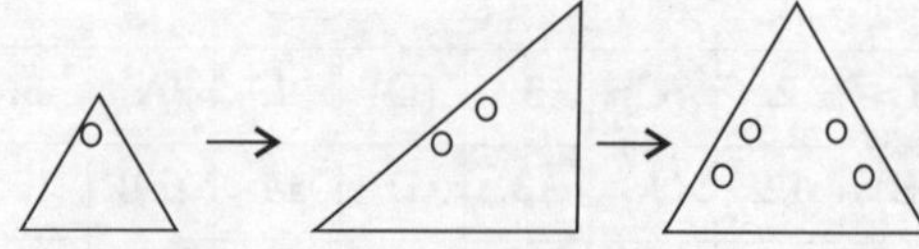

16. Option (C) is correct.
Explanation:

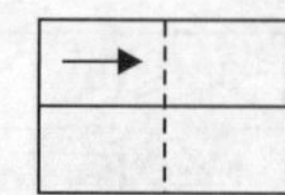

17. Option (D) is correct.

Explanation: The sheet will look like the figure in option (D) after unfolding the final fold.

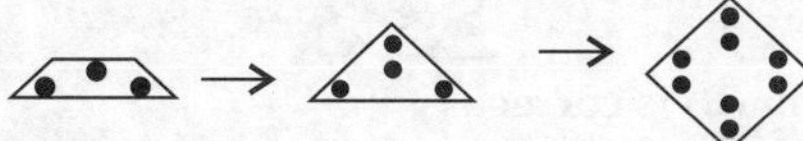

18. Option (B) is correct.

Explanation: The sheet will look like the figure in option (B) after unfolding the final fold.

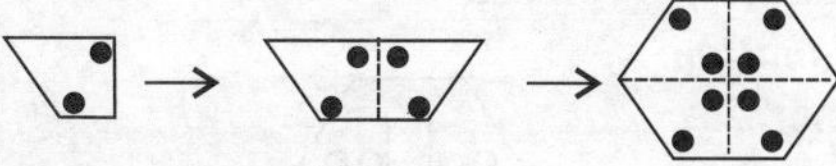

19. Option (D) is correct.

Explanation: The transparent sheet will look like the figure in option (D) after unfolding the last fold.

20. Option (C) is correct.

Explanation: The transparent sheet will look like the figure in option (C) after unfolding the last fold.

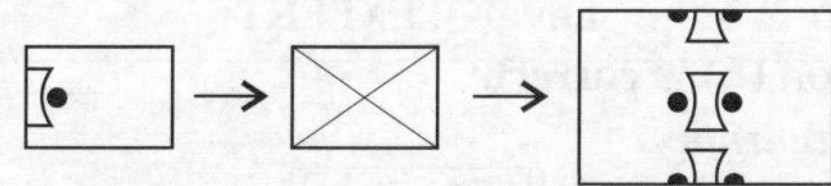

21. Option (D) is correct.

Explanation: The transparent sheet will look like the figure in option (D) after unfolding the last fold.

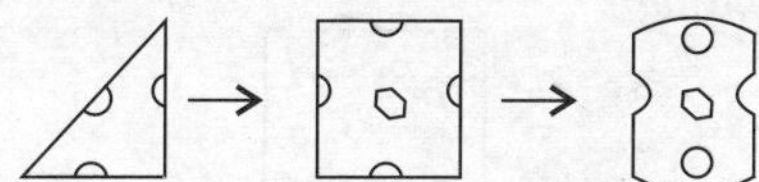

22. Option (B) is correct.

Explanation: The transparent sheet will look like the figure in option (2) after unfolding the last fold.

23. Option (B) is correct.

Explanation: The transparent sheet will look like the figure in option (B) after unfolding the last fold.

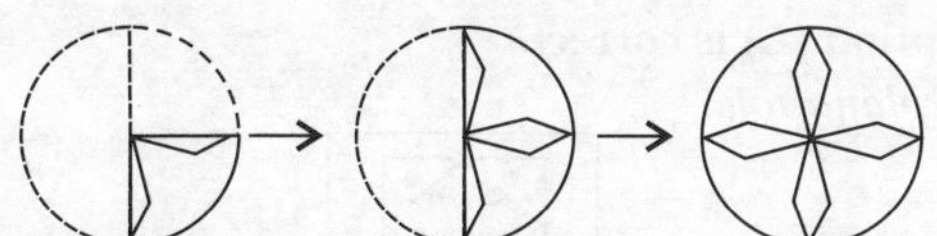

24. Option (C) is correct.

Explanation: The transparent sheet will look like the figure in option (C) after unfolding the last fold.

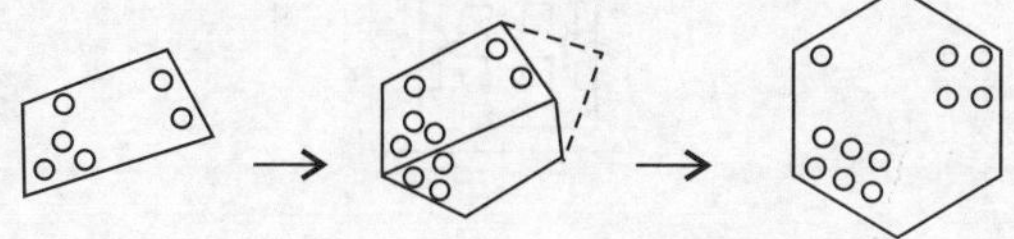

25. Option (B) is correct.

Explanation: The transparent sheet will look like the figure in option (B) after unfolding the last fold.

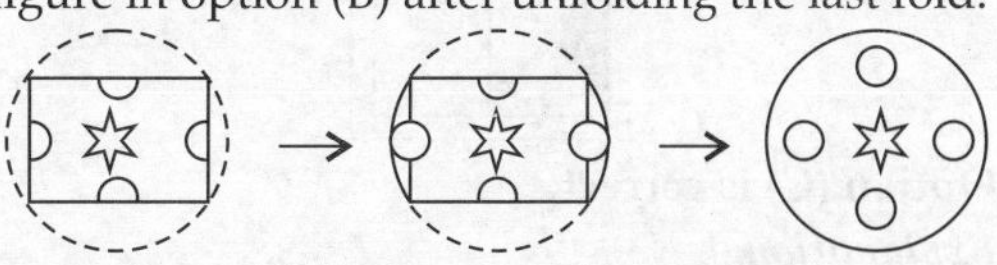

Level-2: INTERMEDIATE

1. Option (A) is correct.

Explanation:

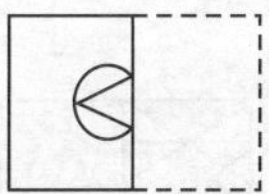

2. Option (B) is correct.

Explanation:

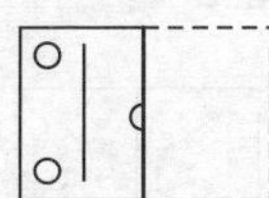

3. Option (B) is correct.

Explanation:

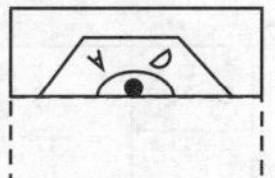

4. Option (A) is correct.

Explanation:

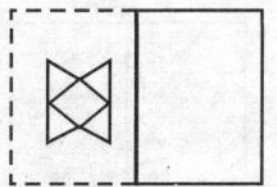

5. Option (C) is correct.

Explanation:

6. Option (C) is correct.

Explanation:

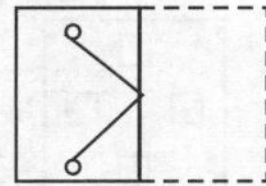

7. Option (D) is correct.

Explanation:

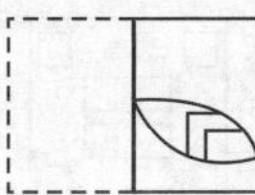

8. Option (B) is correct.

Explanation:

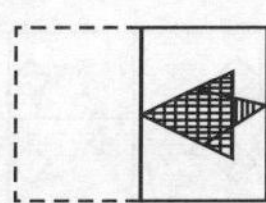

9. Option (A) is correct.

Explanation:

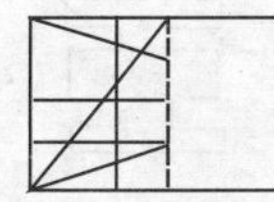

10. **Option (D) is correct.**
Explanation:

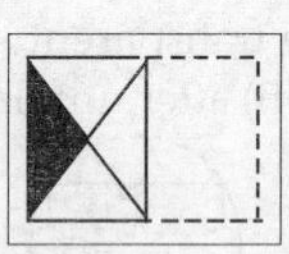

11. **Option (C) is correct.**
Explanation:

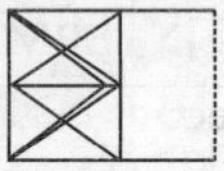

12. **Option (C) is correct.**
Explanation:

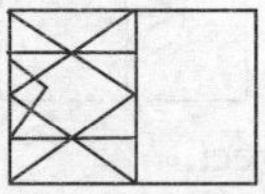

13. **Option (C) is correct.**
Explanation:

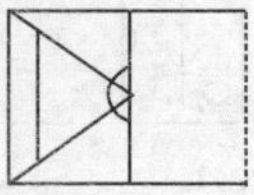

14. **Option (D) is correct.**
Explanation:

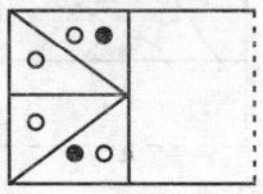

15. **Option (B) is correct.**
Explanation:

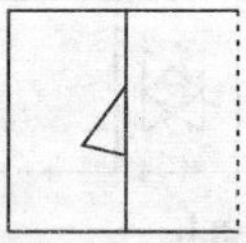

16. **Option (B) is correct.**
Explanation:

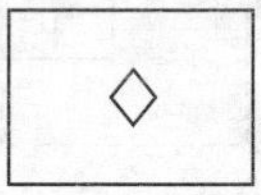

17. **Option (C) is correct.**
Explanation:

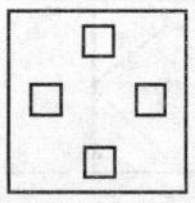

18. **Option (D) is correct.**
Explanation:

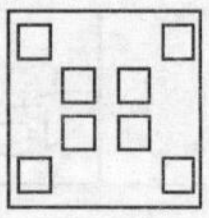

19. **Option (A) is correct.**
Explanation:

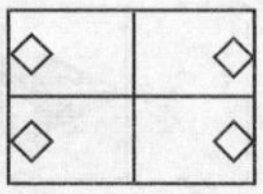

20. **Option (B) is correct.**
Explanation:

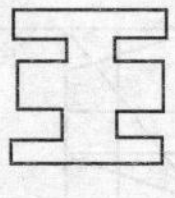

21. **Option (B) is correct.**
Explanation:

22. **Option (B) is correct.**
Explanation:

23. **Option (D) is correct.**
Explanation:

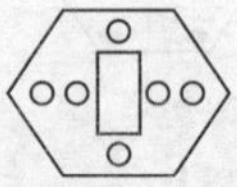

24. **Option (B) is correct.**
Explanation:

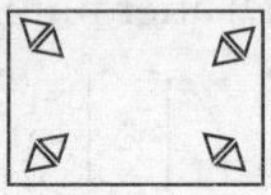

25. **Option (B) is correct.**
Explanation:

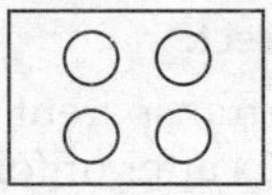

Level-3: EXPERT

1. **Option (B) is correct.**
Explanation:

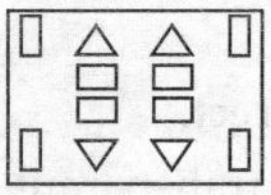

2. **Option (D) is correct.**
Explanation:

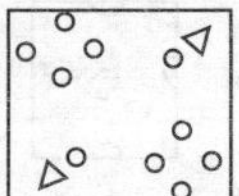

3. **Option (D) is correct.**
Explanation:

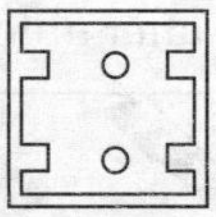

4. **Option (A) is correct.**
Explanation:

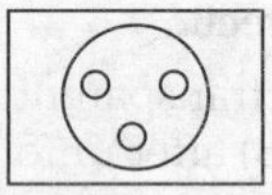

5. **Option (A) is correct.**
Explanation:

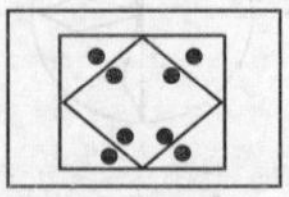

6. **Option (D) is correct.**
Explanation:

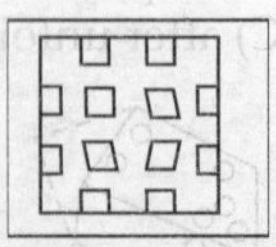

7. **Option (D) is correct.**
Explanation:

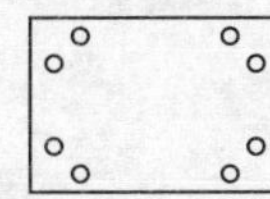

8. **Option (C) is correct.**
Explanation:

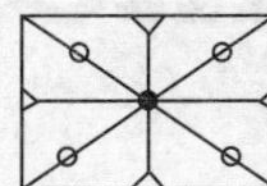

9. **Option (B) is correct.**
Explanation:

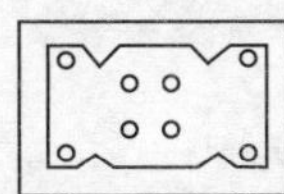

10. **Option (D) is correct.**
Explanation:

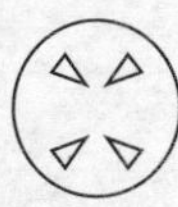

11. **Option (D) is correct.**
Explanation:

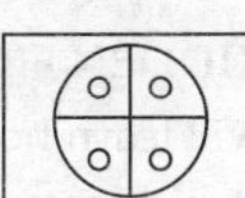

12. **Option (C) is correct.**
Explanation:

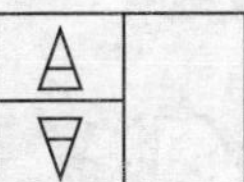

13. **Option (C) is correct.**
Explanation:

14. **Option (B) is correct.**
Explanation:

15. **Option (D) is correct.**
Explanation:

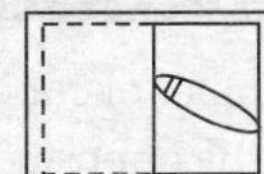

Chapter 24

Cubes and Dice

LEARNING OBJECTIVES:

- Counting the number of cubes
- Methods to find the opposite faces of cubes and dice
- Different types of questions asked in competitive exams

In this chapter, we will look at the ideas and concepts of handling and visualising three-dimensional objects, with a specific emphasis on cubes and dice. The ability to analyse and handle three-dimensional objects is essential in many professions, including engineering, architecture, and design. The study of cubes and dice in non-verbal reasoning can help you to build spatial reasoning skills, which will be useful in these subjects and beyond.

This chapter will go over the many viewpoints of a cube or a dice and how to establish their relationship. You will also learn about the principles of rotation, reflection, and folding of these objects, as well as how to apply these ideas to solve issues.

A cube is a three-dimensional object with six square faces that are identical, 12 edges, and eight vertices. It is a basic geometric shape that is used in mathematics, engineering, architecture, and graphic design.

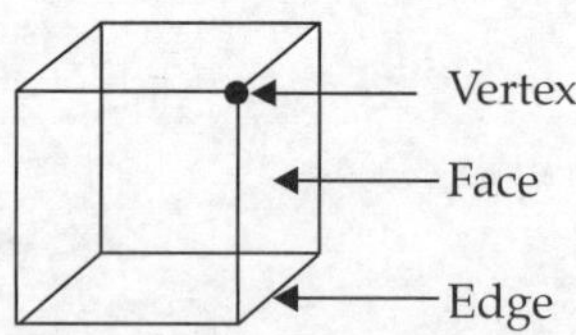

Dice are small, cubical objects that are used in games and gambling. They are typically made of plastic or other materials and have a different number of dots on each face, ranging from one to six. The dots are arranged in a specific pattern on each face, so that the sum of the dots on any two opposite faces is always seven.

IDENTIFYING THE HIDDEN FIGURES

➢ In this topic, you will learn how to recognise a three-dimensional object hidden within a set of cubes or dice.

The task of identifying the hidden figure entails viewing the object from various angles and determining the relationship between the cubes or dice that form it. This necessitates a combination of spatial reasoning and visualisation abilities, as well as an understanding of the principles of rotation, reflection, and folding of three-dimensional objects.

Example 1: Choose one of the four alternatives that can be the same boxes as the question figure.

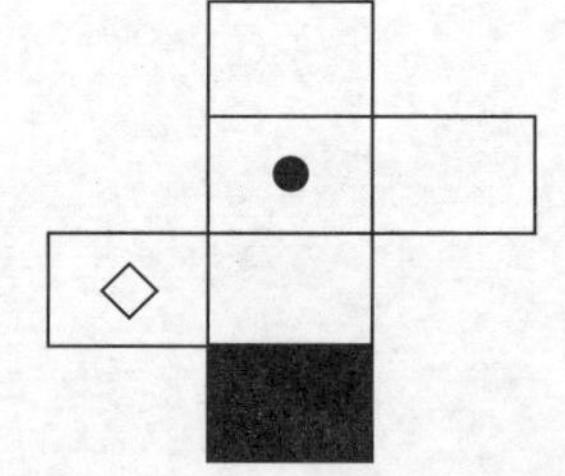

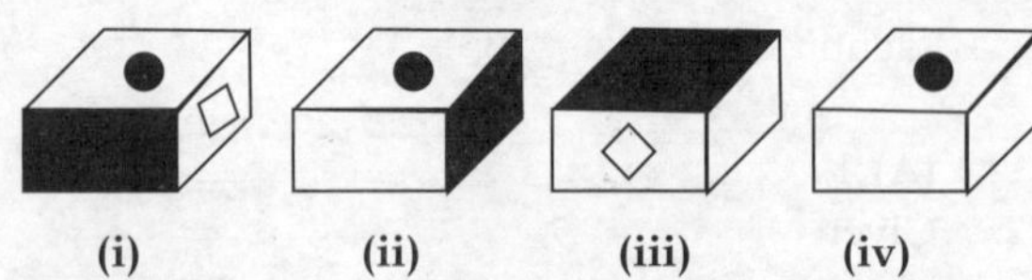

(a) Only (i) (b) Only (ii)

(c) Both (i) and (ii) (d) Both (iii) and (iv)

Sol. (d) Figures (i) and (ii) are not possible because the shaded face will not be adjacent to the dotted face.

Example 2: In the figure below, how many cubes/blocks are there?

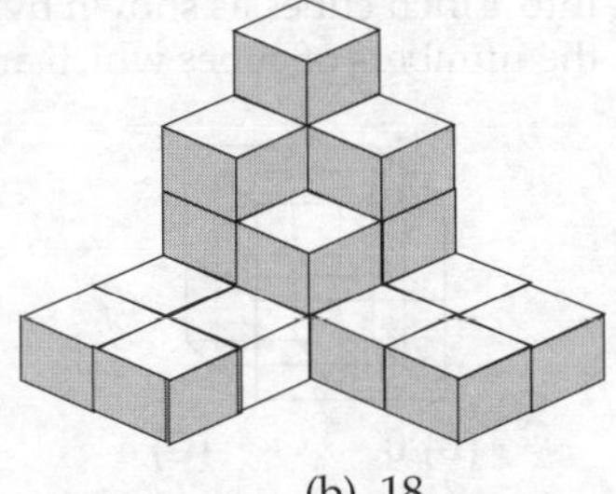

(a) 15 (b) 18
(c) 20 (d) 22

Sol. (c) When we count the above figures by counting columns.

8 columns: 1 cube each
1 column: 2 cubes each
2 columns: 3 cubes each
1 column: 4 cube each
Hence, total number of cubes
= (8 × 1) + (1 × 2) + (2 × 3) + (4 × 4)
= 8 + 2 + 6 + 4 = 20

RELATIONSHIP BETWEEN CUBES AND DICE

- In this topic, you will learn how to analyse the patterns and relationships between a set of cubes and dice in order to identify the underlying rules and relationships that govern them.
  The task of determining the relationship between the cubes and dice requires you to examine the configuration of the cubes and dice, including the number of faces, the arrangement of dots or pips, and the orientation of the objects. By analysing these characteristics, you can discover the hidden relationships that govern the object's configuration.

Example 3: Two different positions of the same dice are given below. Find the number on the face opposite the face showing 3.

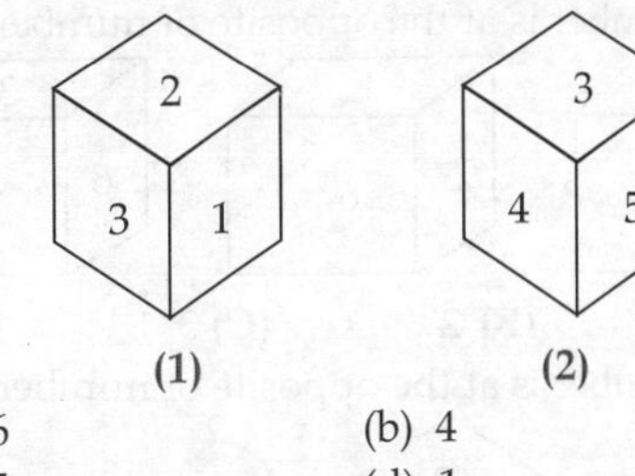

(a) 6 (b) 4
(c) 5 (d) 1

Sol. (a) We shall first find the number which occurs must often in the given figures. Clearly, from the first and second figure we find that the adjacent numbers of 3 be 1, 2, 4, and 5. So, the number which face number 3 will be opposite to 6.

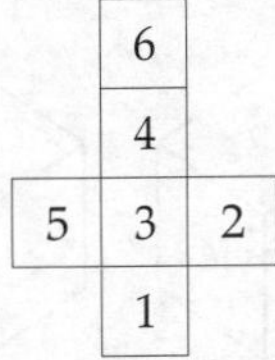

Example 4: How many dots are there on the dice face opposite the one with three dots?

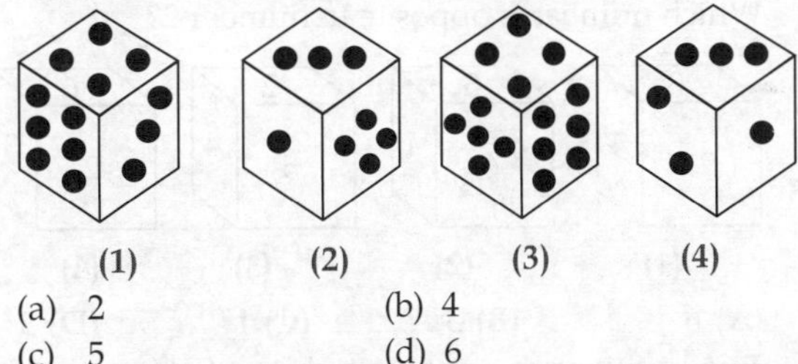

(a) 2 (b) 4
(c) 5 (d) 6

Sol. (c) From figure 1, 2, and 4 we get that 1,2,4, and 6 are adjacent to 3 dots. Hence, 5 dots on the face opposite the face with 3 dots. So, option (c) is the answer.

1 Level Beginner

1. Three positions of a dice are given below:

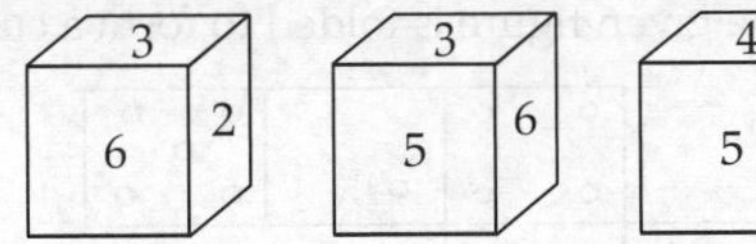

Identify the number on the face opposite to 6.
[SSC Steno 2011]

(A) 1 **(B)** 4 **(C)** 5 **(D)** 7

2. Given below are the different positions of a dice.

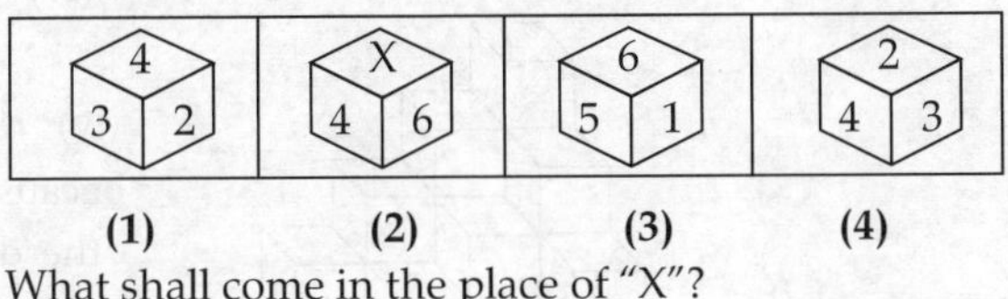

What shall come in the place of "X"?
[SSC FCI 2012]

(A) 3 **(B)** 5 **(C)** 2 **(D)** 1

3. Four position of dice is given below:

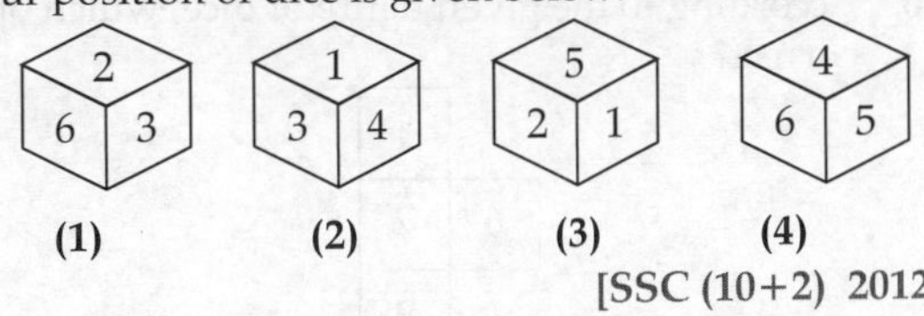

[SSC (10+2) 2012]

Identify the number at the bottom where the top is 3.

(A) 5 **(B)** 1 **(C)** 2 **(D)** 6

4. Which number is on the face opposite to the face having 1?

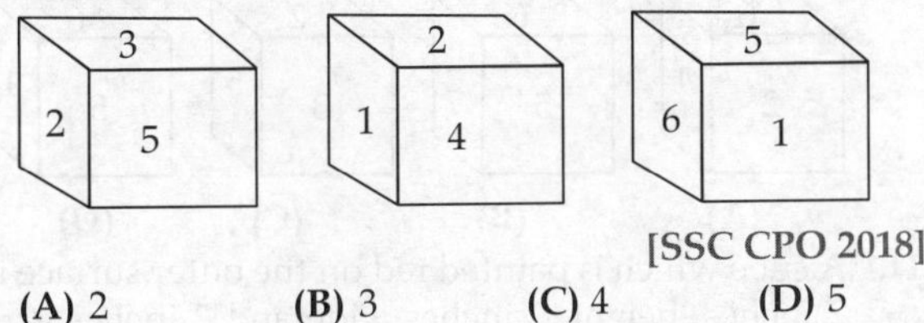

[SSC CPO 2018]

(A) 2 **(B)** 3 **(C)** 4 **(D)** 5

5. Which number is at the opposite of number 6?

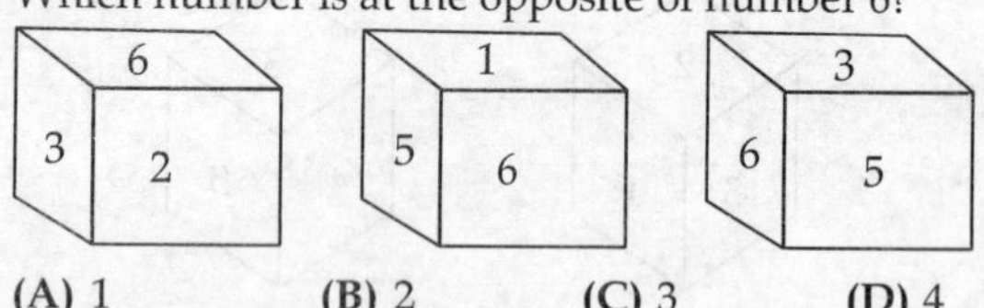

(A) 1 **(B)** 2 **(C)** 3 **(D)** 4

6. Which number is at the opposite of number 1?

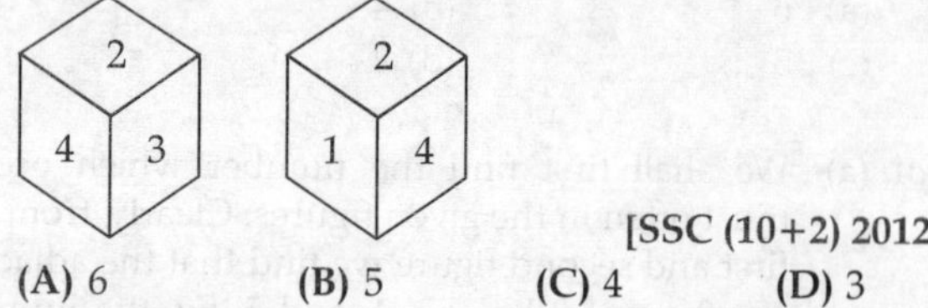

[SSC (10+2) 2012]

(A) 6 **(B)** 5 **(C)** 4 **(D)** 3

7. A dice is thrown 4 times and its different positions are shown below. What number is opposite to face showing 2? **[CPO 2013]**

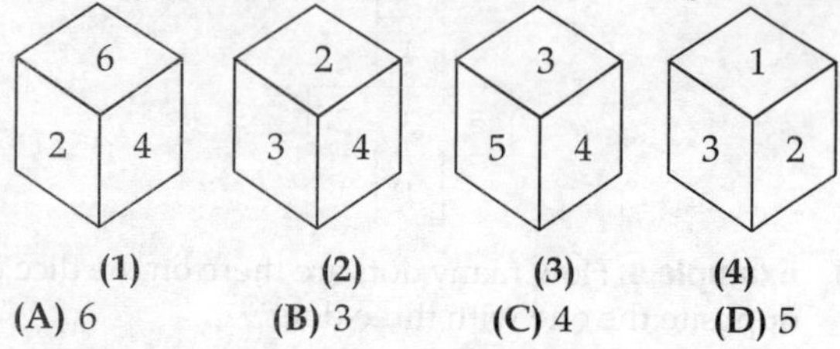

(A) 6 **(B)** 3 **(C)** 4 **(D)** 5

8. Which number is opposite to number 2?

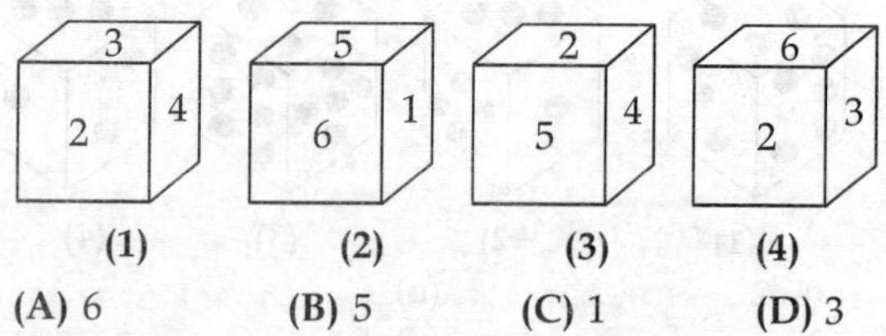

(A) 6 **(B)** 5 **(C)** 1 **(D)** 3

9. Two positions of a cube are shown below. When the number 4 will be at the bottom, then which number will come at the top?

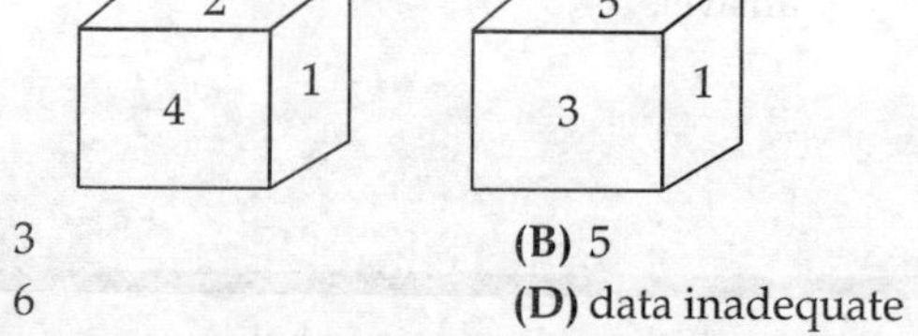

(A) 3 **(B)** 5
(C) 6 **(D)** data inadequate

10. According to the given figure of dice, which option is correct?

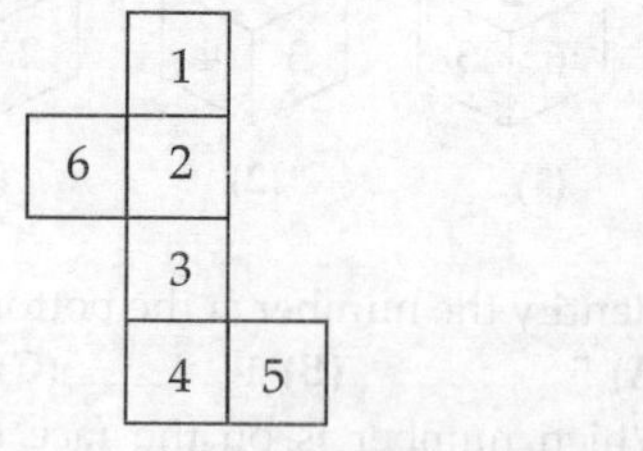

[SSC Mutitasking 2011]

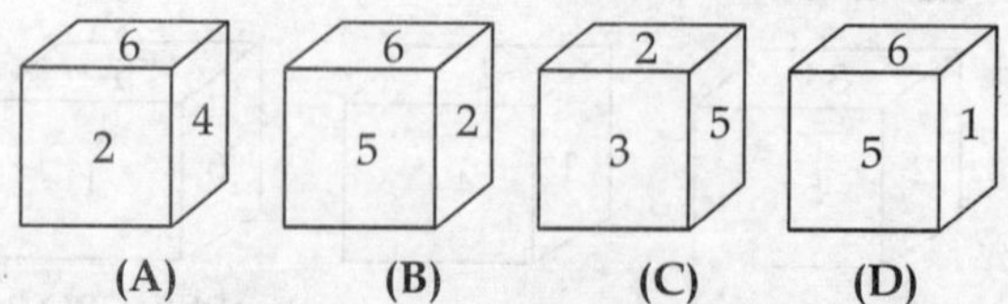

11. A cube which is painted red on the outer surface is of 2 inches' height, 2 inches wide and 2 inches across. If it is cut into 1 inch cubes as shown by dotted lines, then find the numbers of cubes which are red on two sides.

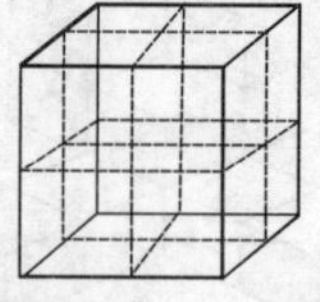

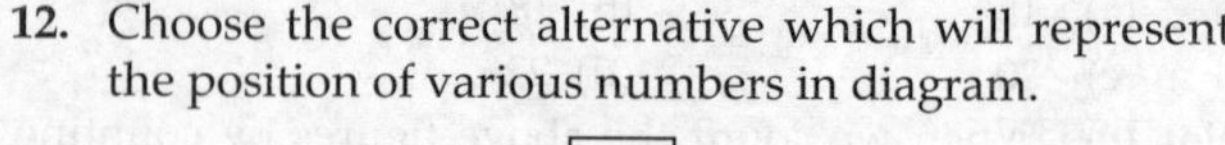

(A) 8 **(B)** 0 **(C)** 4 **(D)** 6

12. Choose the correct alternative which will represent the position of various numbers in diagram.

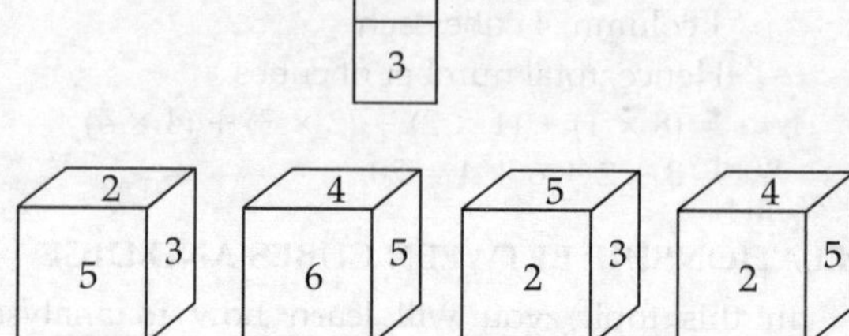

13. Choose the correct alternative which will represent the position of various letters in the diagram.

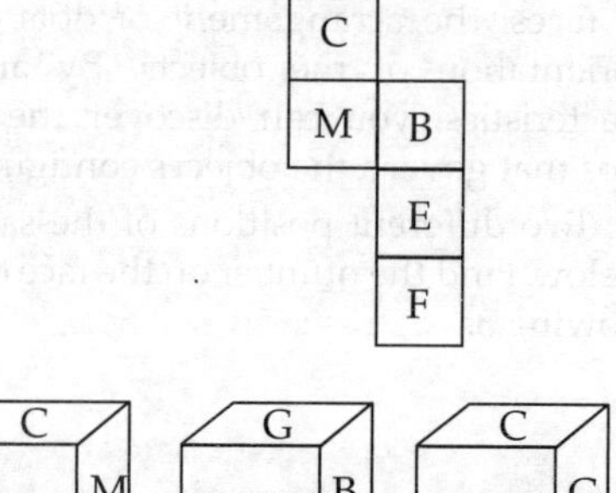

14. How many dots lie opposite to the face having three dots. When the given figure is folded to form a cube?

(A) 2 **(B)** 4 **(C)** 5 **(D)** 6

15. How many cubes are there in the group?

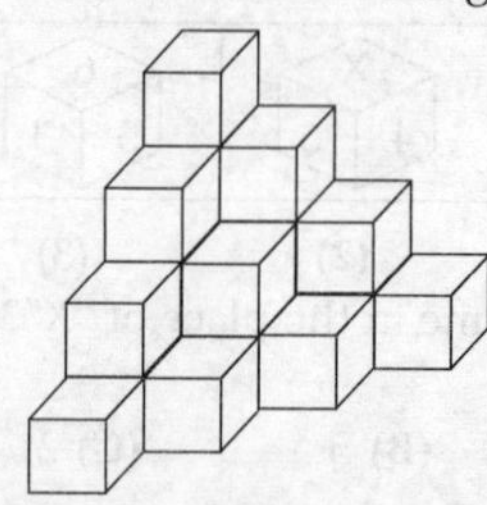

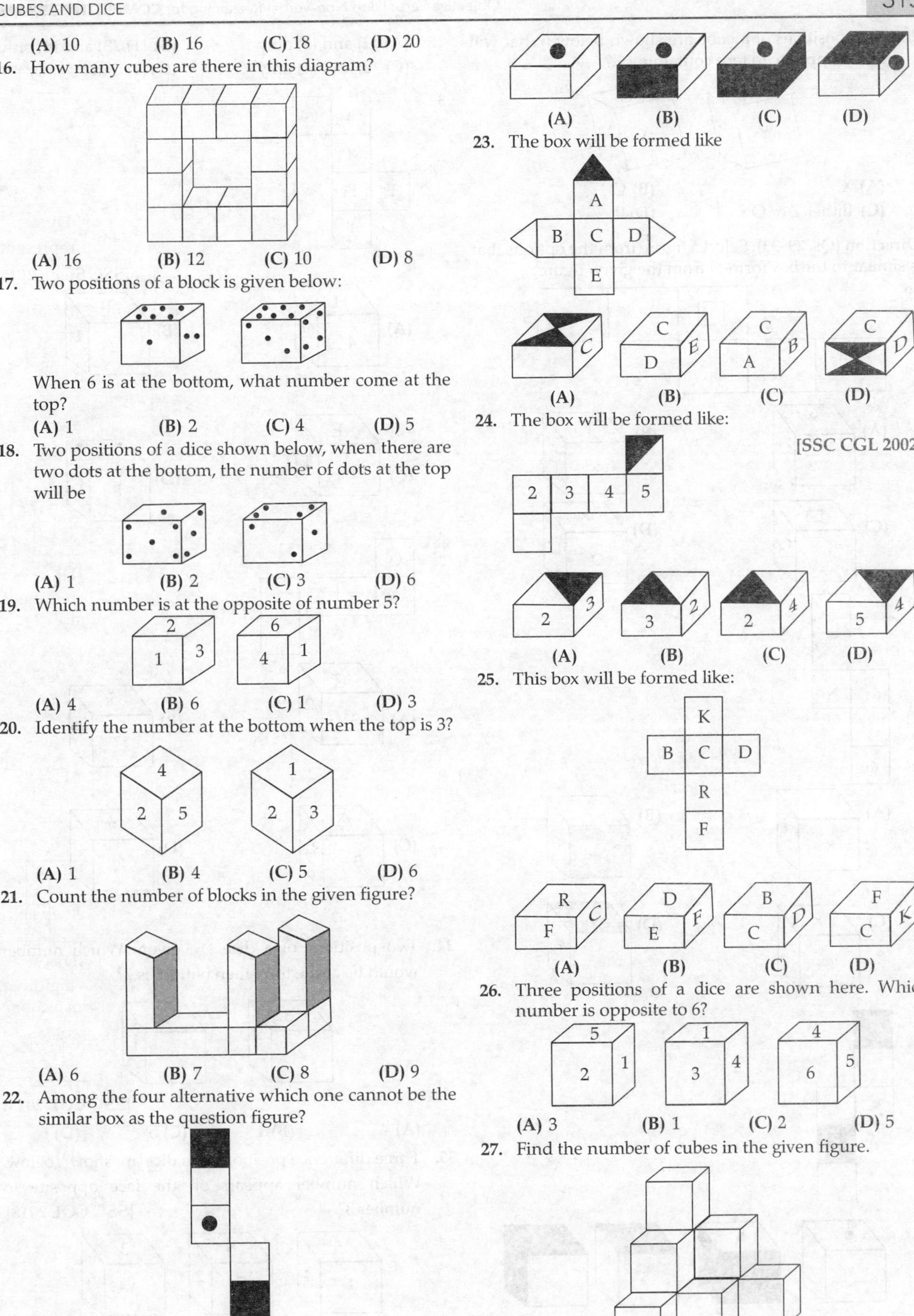

(A) 10 (B) 16 (C) 18 (D) 20

16. How many cubes are there in this diagram?

(A) 16 (B) 12 (C) 10 (D) 8

17. Two positions of a block is given below:

When 6 is at the bottom, what number come at the top?

(A) 1 (B) 2 (C) 4 (D) 5

18. Two positions of a dice shown below, when there are two dots at the bottom, the number of dots at the top will be

(A) 1 (B) 2 (C) 3 (D) 6

19. Which number is at the opposite of number 5?

(A) 4 (B) 6 (C) 1 (D) 3

20. Identify the number at the bottom when the top is 3?

(A) 1 (B) 4 (C) 5 (D) 6

21. Count the number of blocks in the given figure?

(A) 6 (B) 7 (C) 8 (D) 9

22. Among the four alternative which one cannot be the similar box as the question figure?

(A) (B) (C) (D)

23. The box will be formed like

(A) (B) (C) (D)

24. The box will be formed like: [SSC CGL 2002]

(A) (B) (C) (D)

25. This box will be formed like:

(A) (B) (C) (D)

26. Three positions of a dice are shown here. Which number is opposite to 6?

(A) 3 (B) 1 (C) 2 (D) 5

27. Find the number of cubes in the given figure.

(A) 10 (B) 6 (C) 8 (D) 9

28. Two positions of a cube are shown below. What will come opposite to face containing Z?

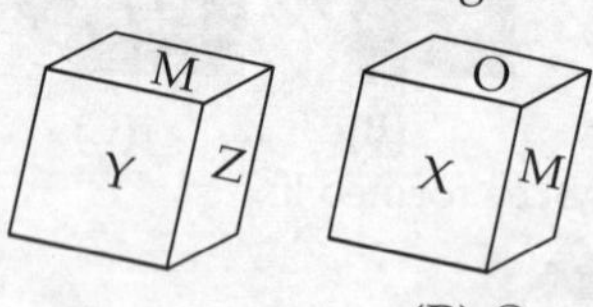

(A) X **(B)** O
(C) Either Z or O **(D)** P

Direction (Qs. 29–33): Select a figure from the options that is similar to the box formed from the given figure.

29.

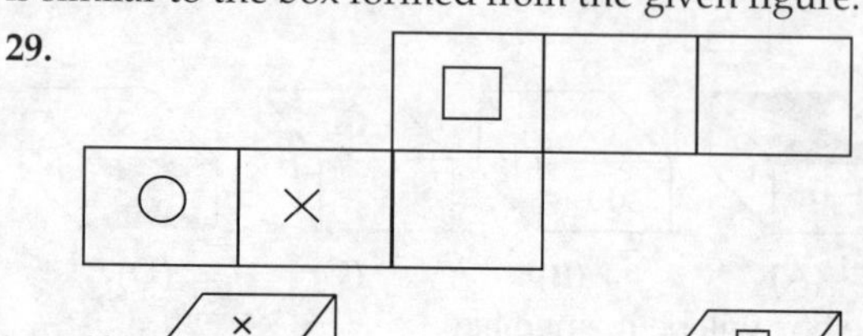

(A) 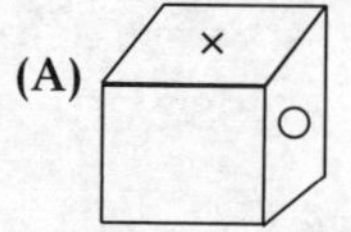 **(B)** 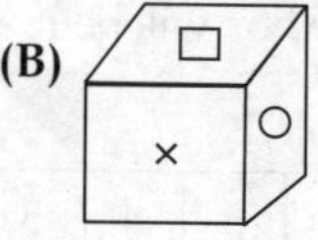

(C) 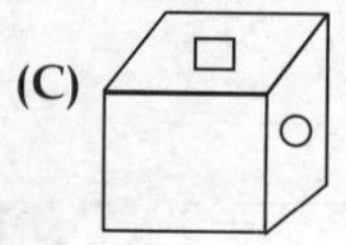 **(D)** 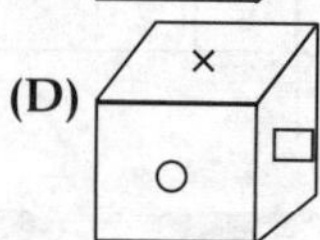

30.

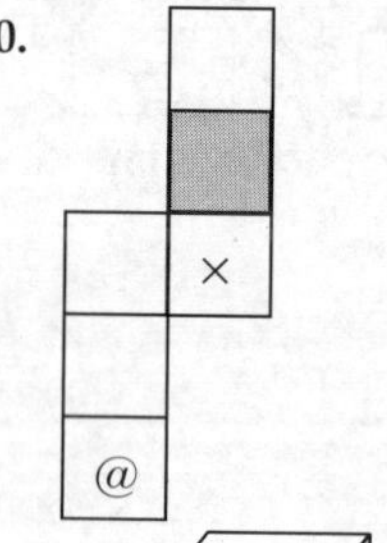

(A) 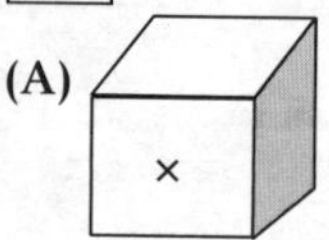 **(B)** 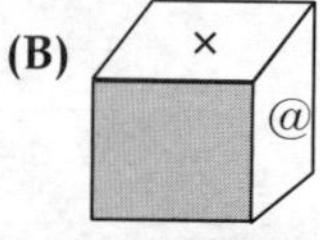

(C) 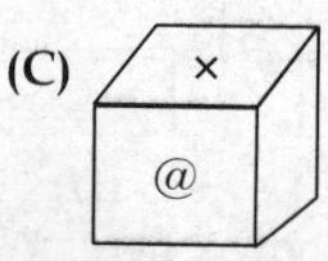

(D) 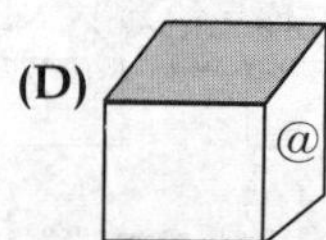

31.

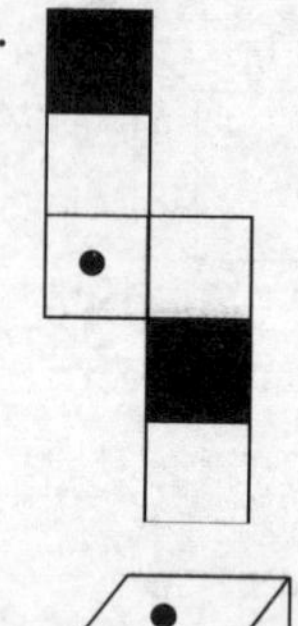

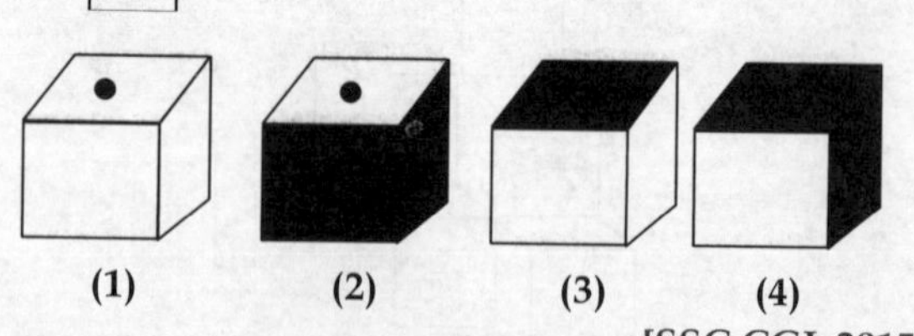

[SSC CGL 2015]

(A) (2) and (3) only **(B)** (1), (3) and (4) only
(C) (2) and (4) only **(D)** (1) and (4) only

32.

4 @
1
E H
8

[SSC Steno 2018]

(A) 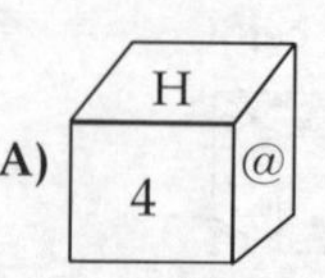

(B) 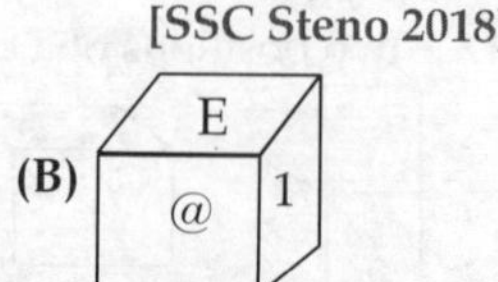

(C) 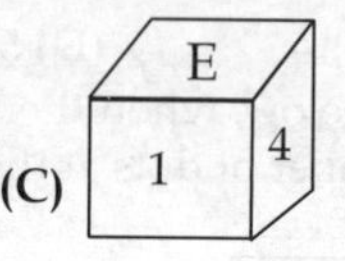

(D) 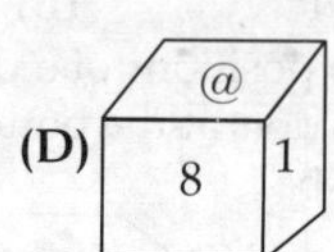

33.

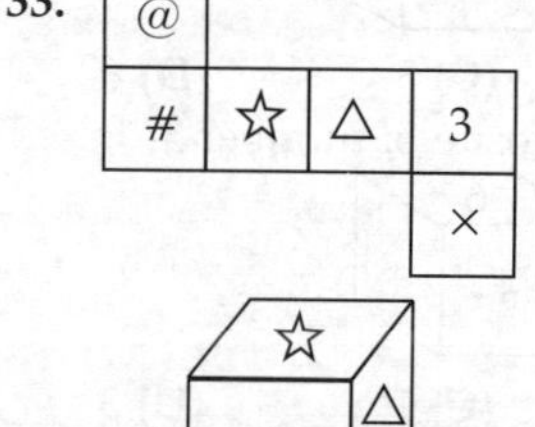

(A) 3

(B) 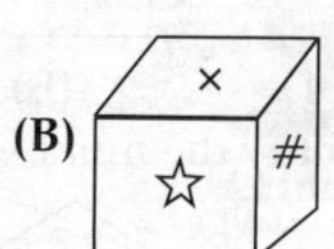

(C) 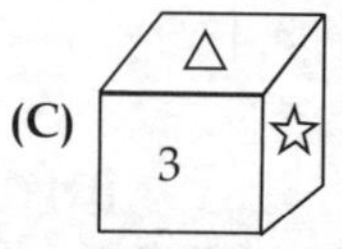

(D) 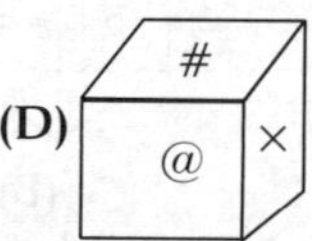

34. Two positions of a dice are given. Which number would be at the top when bottom is 2?

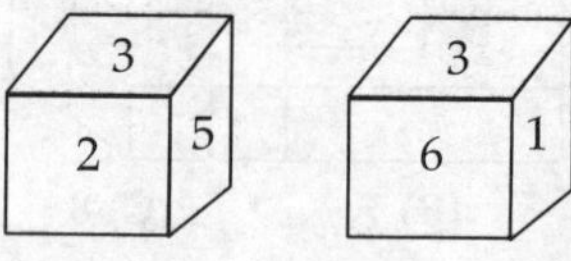

[SSC CGL 2013]

(A) 4 **(B)** 1 **(C)** 5 **(D)** 6

35. Three difference positions of a dice are shown below. Which number appears on the face opposite to number 3? [SSC CGL 2018]

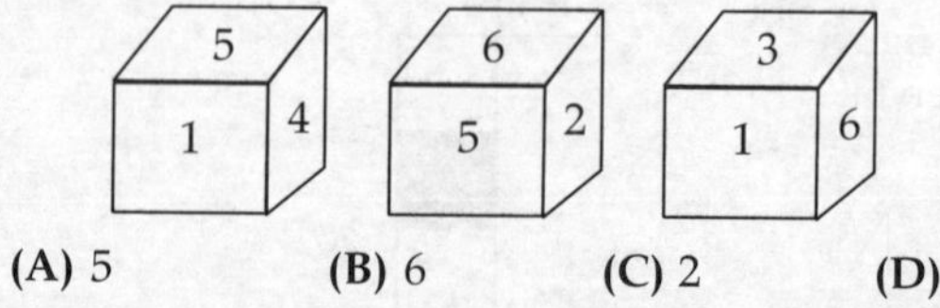

(A) 5 **(B)** 6 **(C)** 2 **(D)** 4

Directions (Qs. 36–38): Count the number of cubes in the given figures.

36.

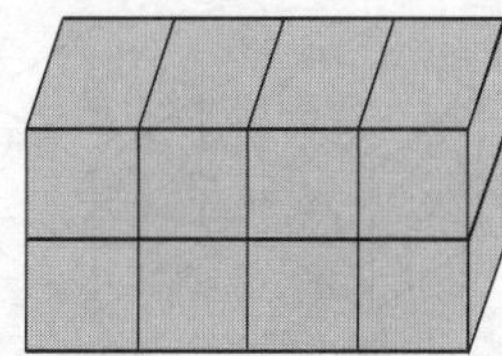

(A) 8 **(B)** 7 **(C)** 6 **(D)** 5

37.

(A) 5 **(B)** 6 **(C)** 7 **(D)** 8

38.

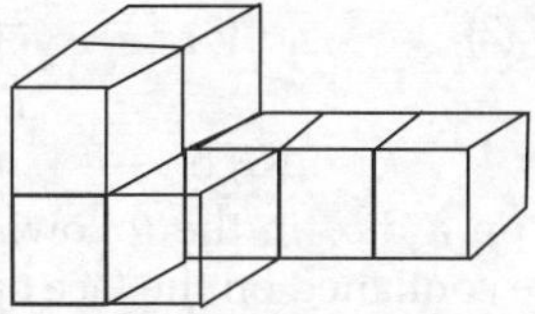

(A) 5 **(B)** 8 **(C)** 7 **(D)** 9

39. Two positions of the same dice are shown. Select the number that will be on the face opposite to the one showing 6. **[SSC CGL 2020]**

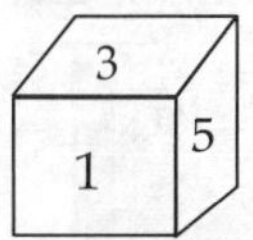

(A) 1 **(B)** 4 **(C)** 3 **(D)** 5

40. Select a figure from the options that is similar to the box formed from the given figure.

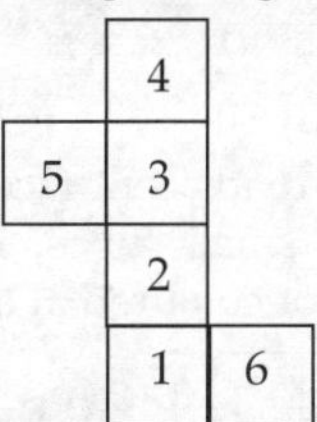

(A)

(B)

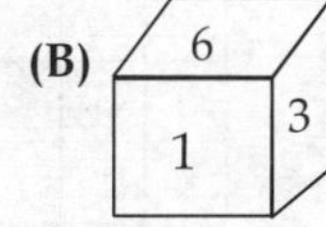

(C)

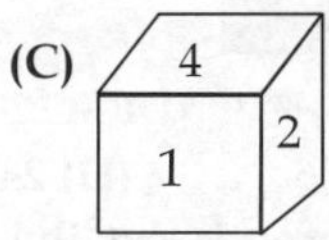

(D)

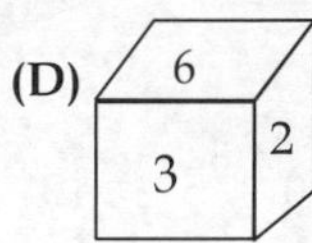

2 Level Intermediate

1. Count the number of blocks in the given figure:

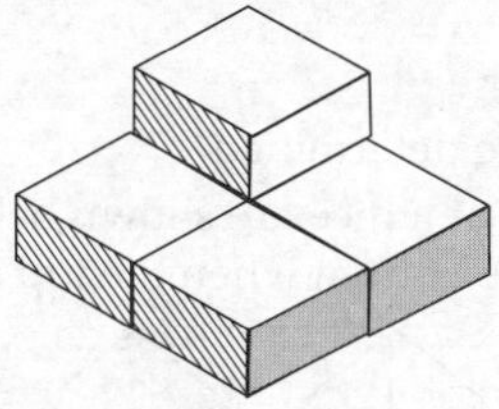

[SSC 2002]

(A) 3 **(B)** 4 **(C)** 5 **(D)** 6

2. Count the number of cubes in the given figure:

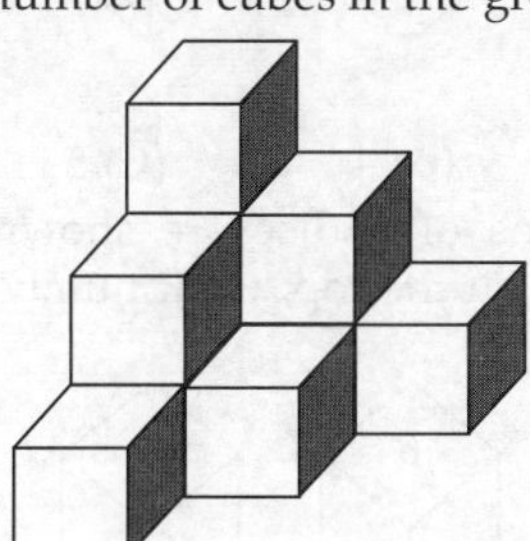

[Invigilator Exam 2005/RRB 2006]

(A) 14 **(B)** 12 **(C)** 10 **(D)** 8

3. The figure given below is a drawing of pile of blocks. When taken apart, how many blocks would there be?

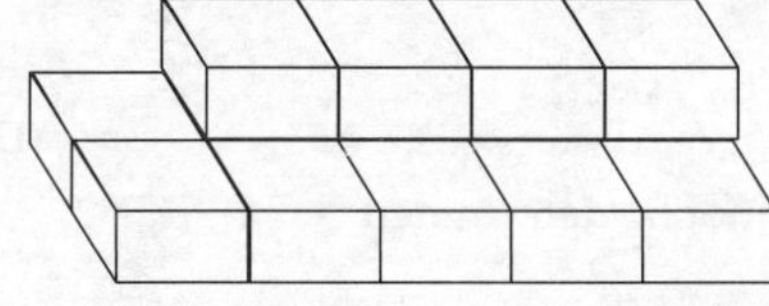

[SSC 2002]

(A) 10 **(B)** 14 **(C)** 18 **(D)** 20

4. Count the number of blocks in the given figure.

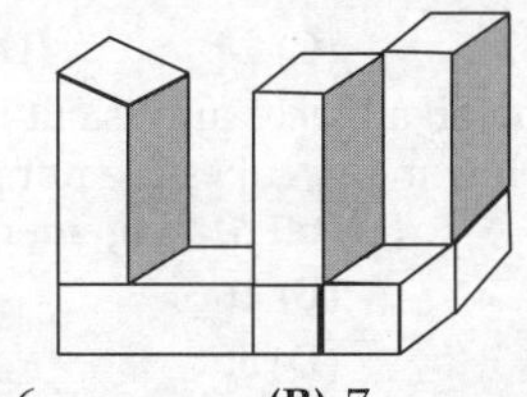

[SSC 2004]

(A) 6 **(B)** 7 **(C)** 8 **(D)** 9

5. Count the number of cubes in the given figure?

(A) 6 **(B)** 8 **(C)** 11 **(D)** 12

6. Count the number of cubes in the given figure.

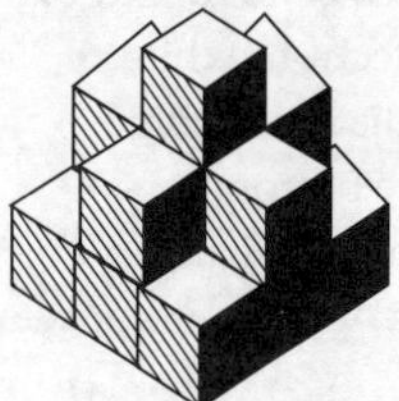

[AAO EXAM 2003]

(A) 8 (B) 9 (C) 12 (D) 15

7. Count the number of cubes in the given figure?

(A) 25 (B) 30 (C) 32 (D) 34

8. A cube whose two adjacent faces are coloured is cut into 64 identical small cubes. How many of these small cubes are not coloured at all?

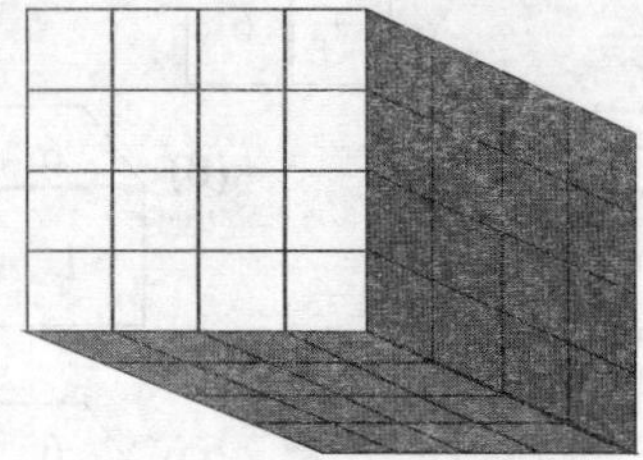

[UPSC 2005]

(A) 60 (B) 48 (C) 36 (D) 24

9. A cube painted yellow on all faces is cut into 27 small cubes of equal size. How many small cubes are painted on one face only? **[RRB 2004]**

(A) 1 (B) 6 (C) 8 (D) 12

10. All surfaces of a cube are coloured. If a number of smaller cube are taken out from it, each side ¼ the size of original cube's side, and then indicate the number of cubes with only one side painted. **[MBA 2006]**

(A) 60 (B) 32 (C) 24 (D) 16

11. A cube is painted blue on all faces and is cut into 125 cubes of equal size. How many cubes are not painted on any face? **[Hotel Management 2002]**

(A) 8 (B) 16
(C) 27 (D) 36
(E) 54

12. A cube of white material is painted black on all its surface. If it is cut into 125 smaller cubes of the same size, then how many cubes will have two sides painted black? **[RRB 2005]**

(A) 8 (B) 16
(C) 22 (D) 44
(E) None of these

13. The 6 faces of a cube are coloured black, brown, green, red, white and blue. Such that
(A) Red is opposite to black.
(B) Green is between red and black.
(C) Blue is adjacent to white.
(D) Brown is adjacent to blue.
(E) Red is at the bottom.
Then answer the following:
Which colour is opposite to brown? **[RRB 2003]**

(A) white (B) red
(C) green (D) blue

14. The four different positions of a dice are given below; which number is opposite to 6?

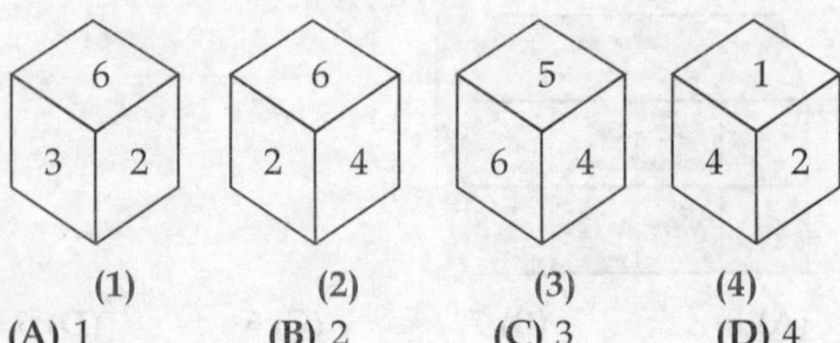

(A) 1 (B) 2 (C) 3 (D) 4

15. How many dots are there on the dice face opposite the one with three dots?

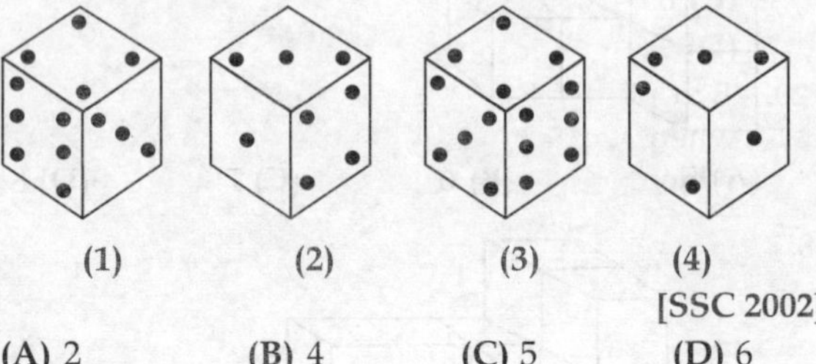

[SSC 2002]

(A) 2 (B) 4 (C) 5 (D) 6

16. Observe the dots on a dice in the following figure, how many dots are contained on the face opposite to that containing four dot?

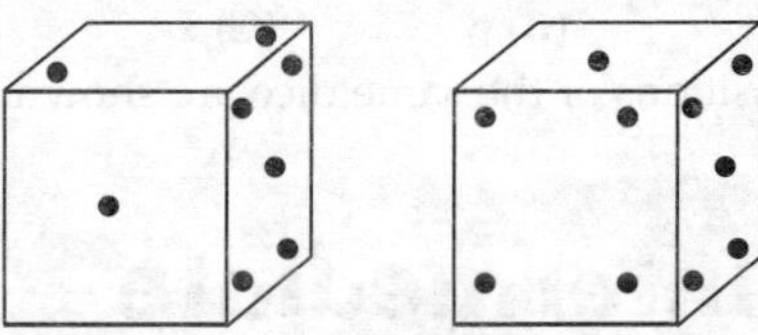

[Tax and Central Excise 1996]

(A) 2
(B) 3
(C) 6
(D) Cannot be determined

17. Two position of a dice are shown below. Identify the number at the bottom when the top is 3.

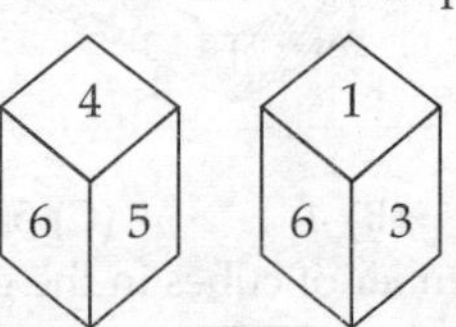

[SSC 2004]

(A) 2 (B) 4 (C) 5 (D) 6

18. Two positions of a dice are shown below. When number 1 is on the top, what number will be at the bottom?

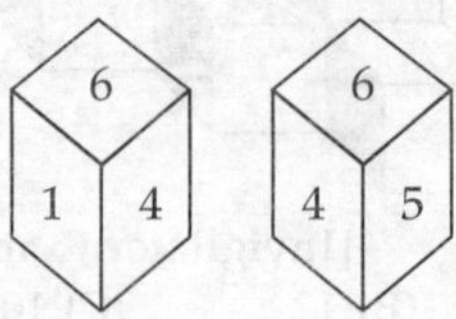

[RRB 2004]

(A) 2
(B) 3
(C) 5
(D) Cannot be determined

19. Two position of a dice is given below. When 2 is at the bottom, which number will be at the top?

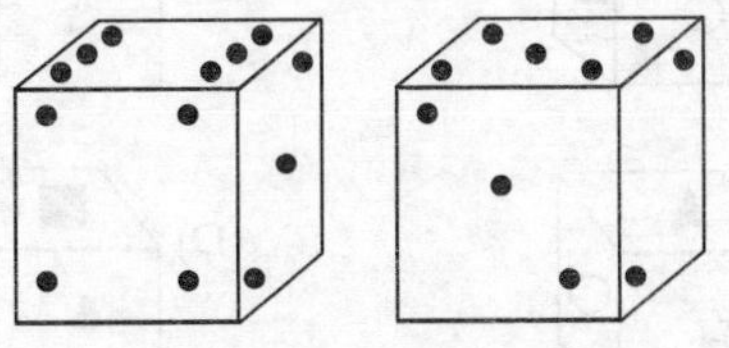

[UDS 1995]

(A) 1
(B) 4
(C) 6
(D) Cannot be determined

20. Two position of a parallelepiped are shown below. when the number 3 will be on the top side, then which number will be at the bottom?

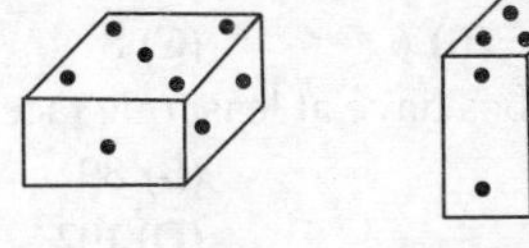

(A) 1 **(B)** 4 **(C)** 5 **(D)** 6

21. In the following block 6 is at the bottom, what number will be at the top?

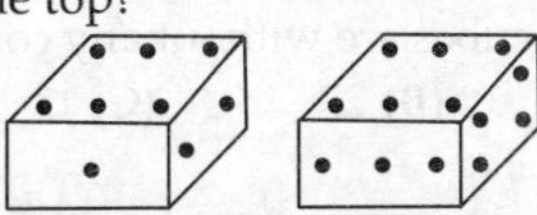

[UDC 1995]

(A) 1 **(B)** 2 **(C)** 4 **(D)** 5

22. In a dice a, b, c and d are written on the adjacent faces in a clockwise order and e and f at the top and bottom. when c is at the top, what will be at the bottom?

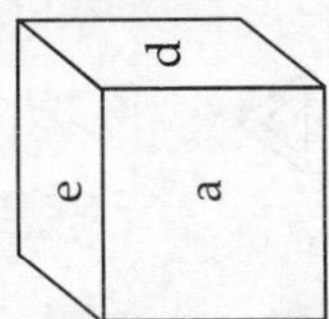

[Asst. Grade 1995]

(A) a
(B) b
(C) c
(D) Cannot be determined

23.

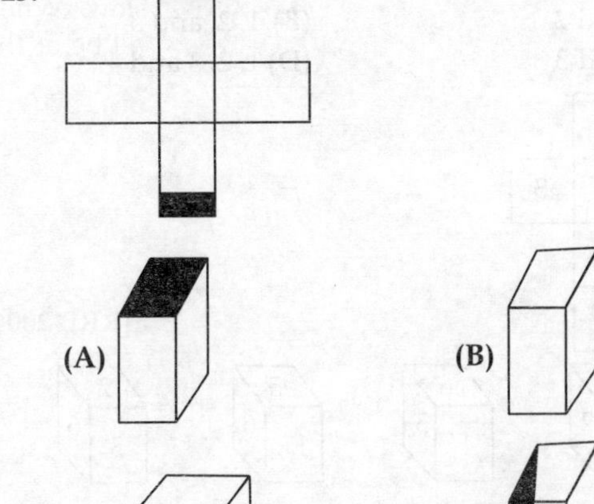

24.

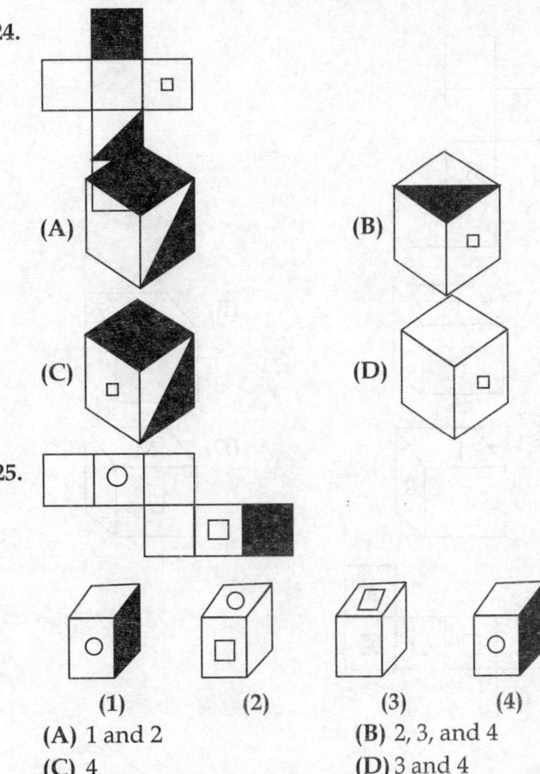

(A) 1 and 2 **(B)** 2, 3, and 4
(C) 4 **(D)** 3 and 4

26. Two different positions of the same dice are shown, the faces of which are marked with the letters E, F, G, H, I and J. Select the letter that will be on the face opposite to the face having the letter 'J'.

[SSC CGL 2021]

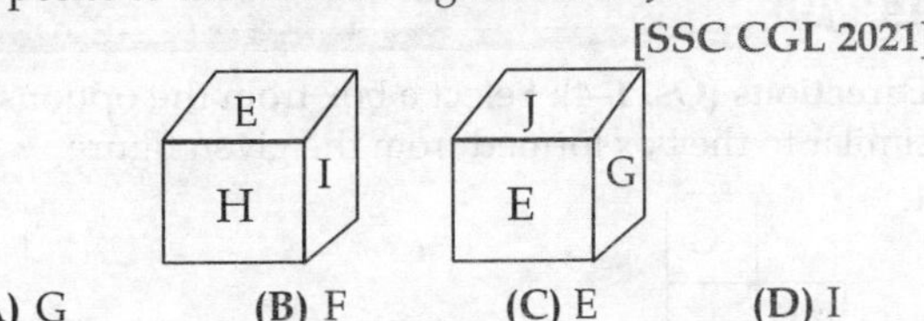

(A) G **(B)** F **(C)** E **(D)** I

27. Two positions of the same dice are given. Which number will be at the bottom if '4' is at the top?

[SSC SI 2018]

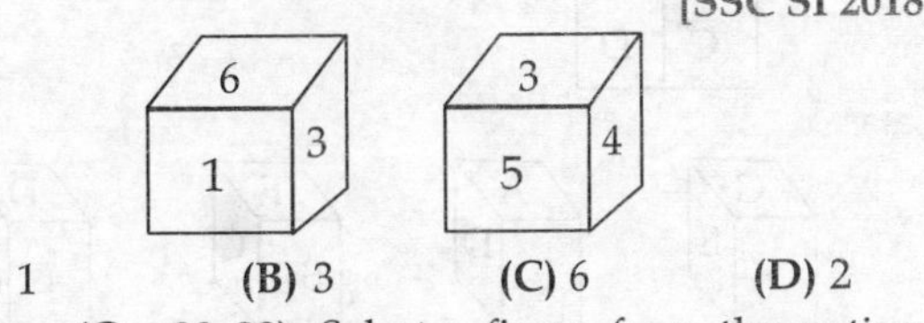

(A) 1 **(B)** 3 **(C)** 6 **(D)** 2

Directions (Qs. 28–30): Select a figure from the options that is similar to the box formed the given options.

28.

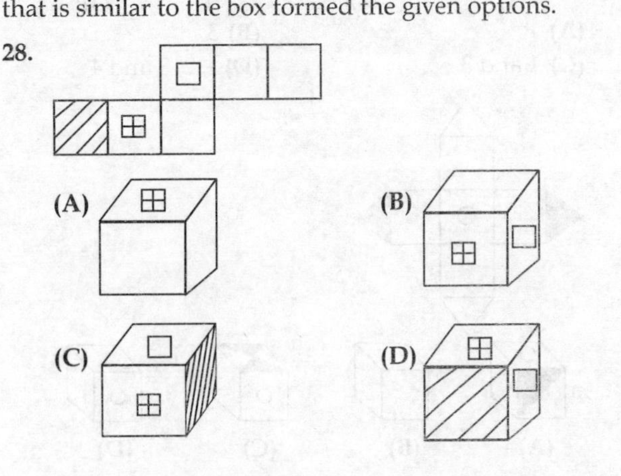

29.

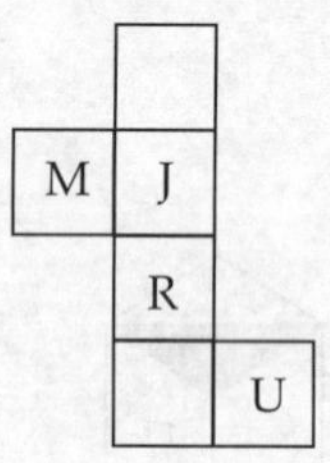

(A)
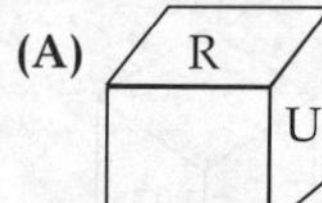

(B) J

(C)
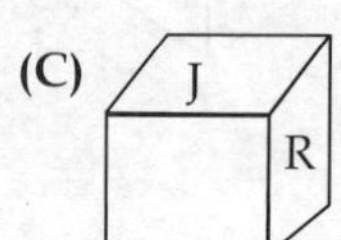

(D)
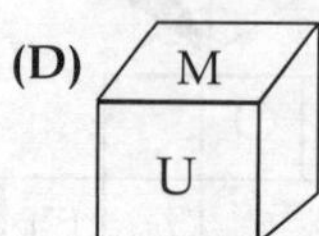

30.

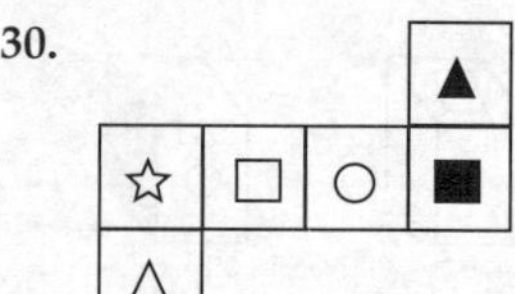

(A)
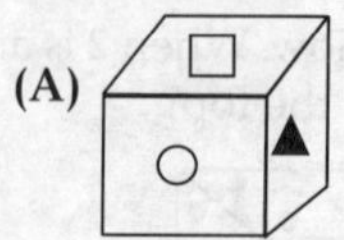

(B)
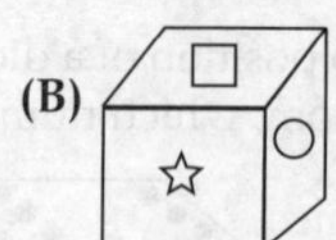

(C)
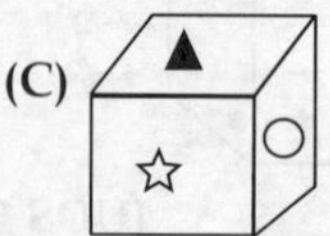

(D)
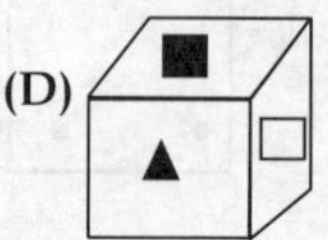

Directions (Qs. 31–35): A cube of side 10 cm is coloured red with a 2 cm wide green strip along all the faces. The cube is cut into 125 smaller cubes of equal size. Answer the following questions based on this statement. **[AAO 2002]**

31. How many cubes have three green faces each?

(A) 0 **(B)** 4 **(C)** 8 **(D)** 16

32. How many cubes have one face red and an adjacent face green?

(A) 0 **(B)** 6 **(C)** 8 **(D)** 16

33. How many cubes have at least one face coloured?

(A) 76 **(B)** 89
(C) 98 **(D)** 102

34. How many cubes have at least two green faces each?

(A) 8 **(B)** 27 **(C)** 44 **(D)** 63

35. How many cubes are without any colour?

(A) 64 **(B)** 27 **(C)** 12 **(D)** 0

Level 3 Expert

Directions (Qs. 1–4): Select a box from the options that is similar to the box formed from the given figure.

1.

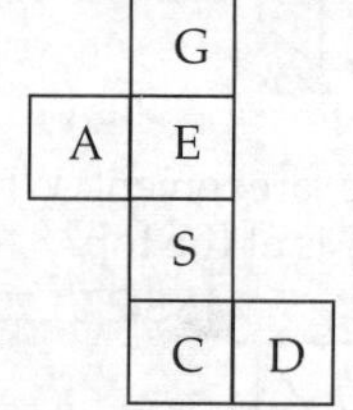

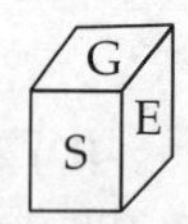

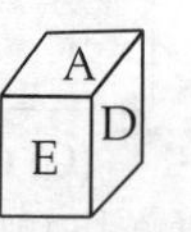

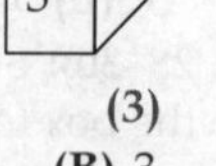

D E A

(1) (2) (3) (4)

(A) 1 **(B)** 3
(C) 1 and 3 **(D)** 1, 2, 3 and 4

2.

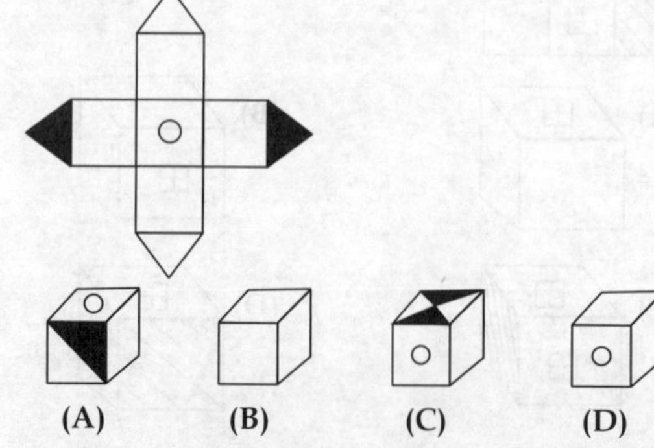

3.

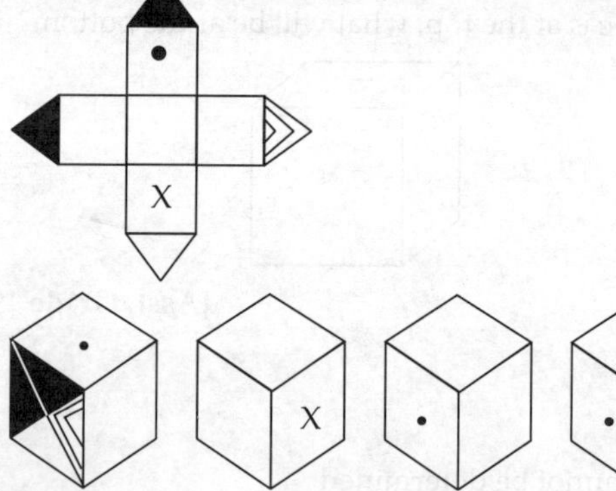

(A) 1 and 2 **(B)** 1, 2, and 3
(C) 1 and 3 **(D)** 1, 2, 3 and 4

4.

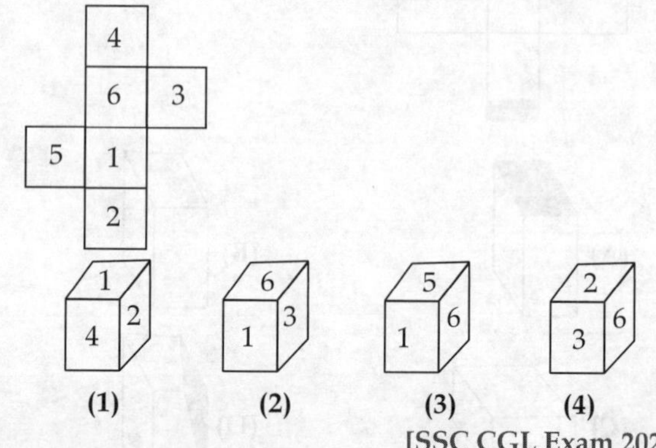

[SSC CGL Exam 2020]

(A) 2, 3, and 4 **(B)** 2 and 3
(C) 2 and 4 **(D)** 1 and 2

5. Select a box from the options that is similar to the box formed from the given figure.

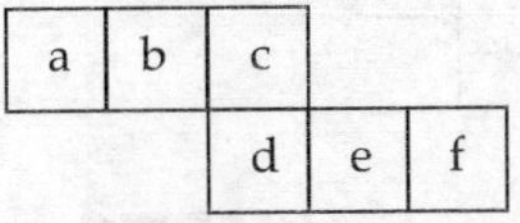

[SSC CGL Exam 2020]

(A) 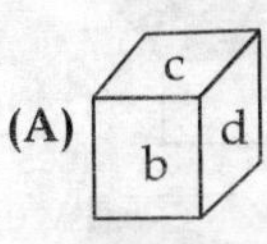

(B) 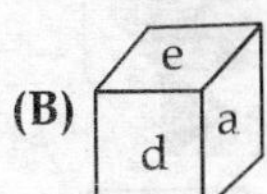

(C) 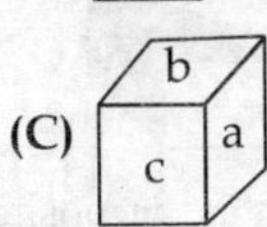

(D) 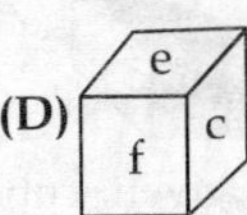

6. Which number will be at the top if 3 is at the bottom in the following figure?

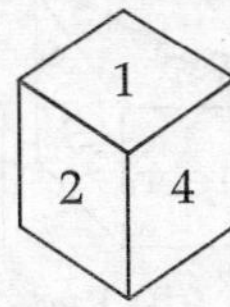

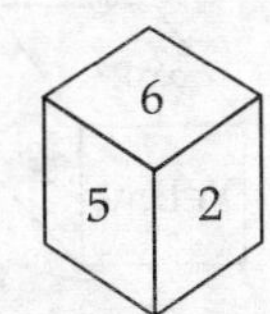

[SSC CGL Exam 2019]

(A) 4 **(B)** 1 **(C)** 2 **(D)** 6

7. Select a box from the options that is similar to the box formed from the given figure.

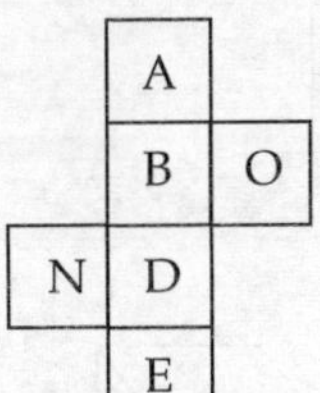

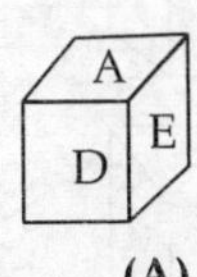

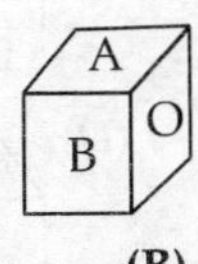

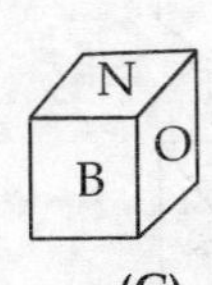

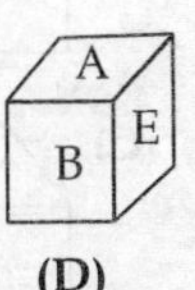

(A) **(B)** **(C)** **(D)**

8. Select a box from the options that is similar to the box formed from the given figure.

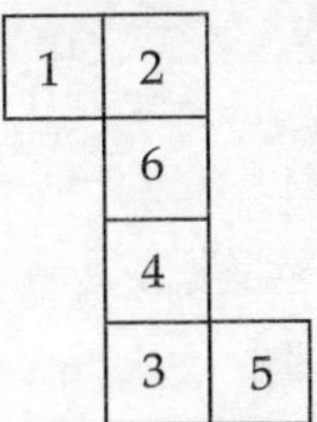

[SSC CPO Exam 2011]

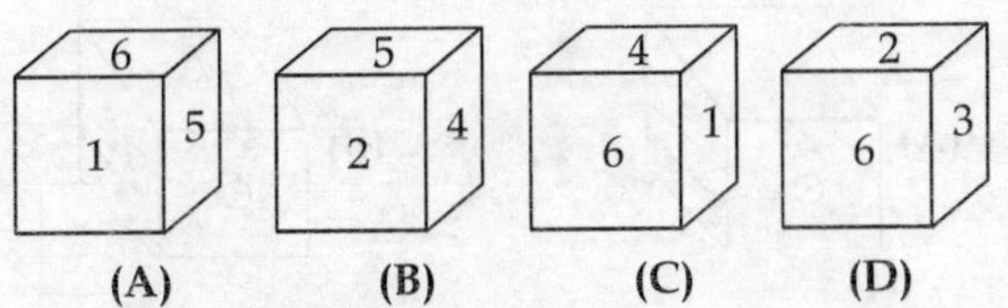

(A) **(B)** **(C)** **(D)**

9. Two positions of a cubical block are given below, each face having a number of small triangles. In another positions of the cube, if there is one triangle at the bottom, how many triangles will be there on the top face?

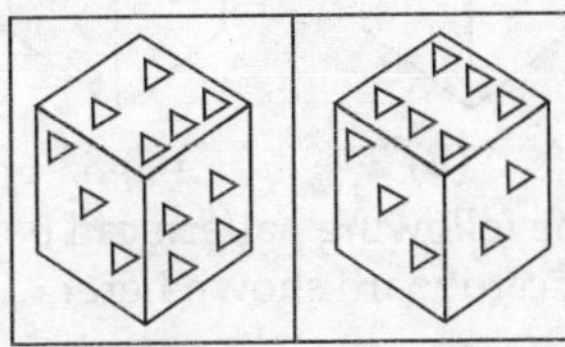

[SSC CPO Exam 2011]

(A) 4 **(B)** 3 **(C)** 2 **(D)** 5

10. Which number will be at the top , when 2 is at the bottom in the following figure?

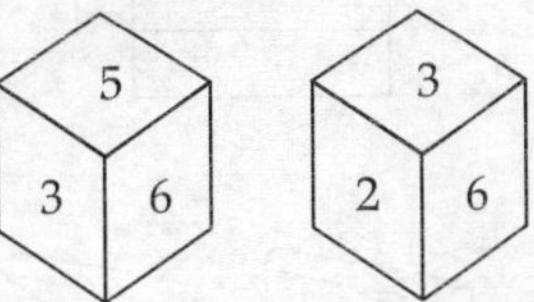

[SSC CPO Exam 2010]

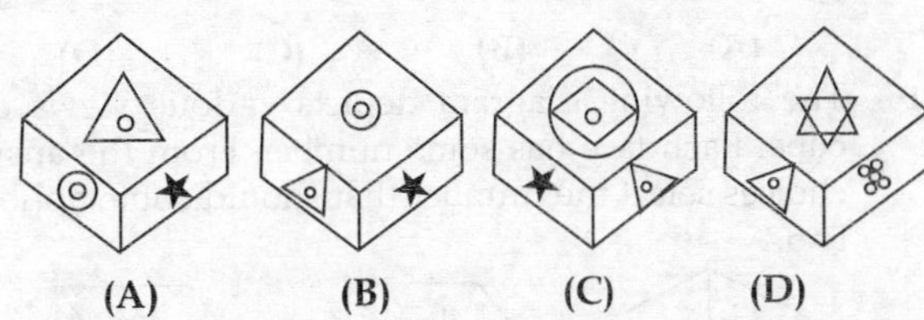

(A) **(B)** **(C)** **(D)**

11. The following diagram shows the different view of same cube. Find out how many spots are on face directly opposite to the face of the cube having 6 spots?

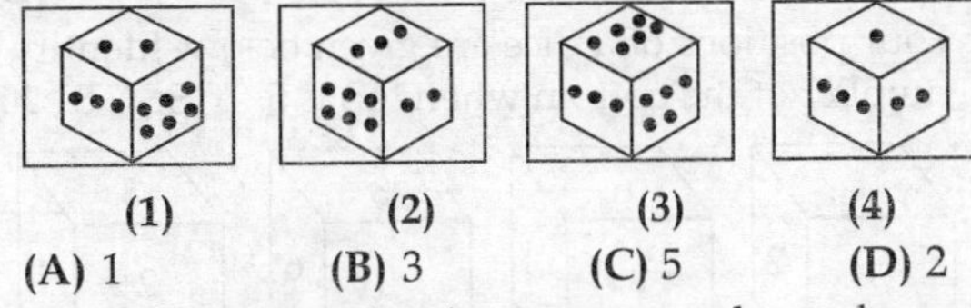

(1) **(2)** **(3)** **(4)**

(A) 1 **(B)** 3 **(C)** 5 **(D)** 2

12. The following cubes has some number, whereas in cube 4, one is blank. From the answer choices select the number that should come in the blank space.

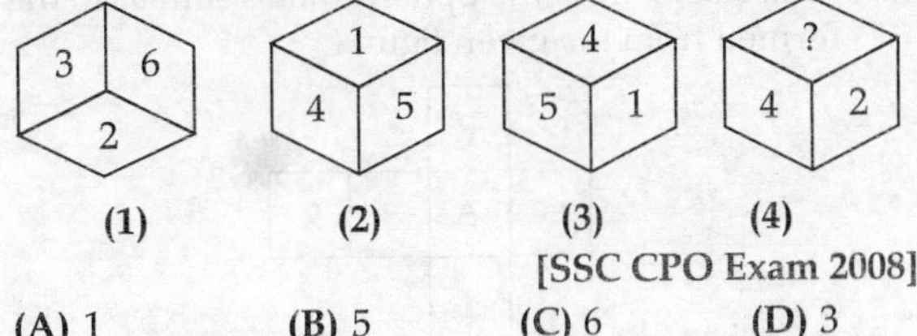

(1) **(2)** **(3)** **(4)**

[SSC CPO Exam 2008]

(A) 1 **(B)** 5 **(C)** 6 **(D)** 3

13. Two positions of a dice are shown below, If the face with 1 dot is at the bottom, then the number of dots on the top is:

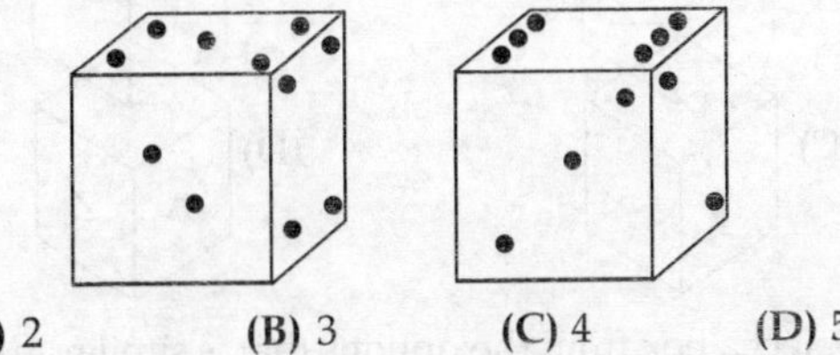

(A) 2 **(B)** 3 **(C)** 4 **(D)** 5

14. What will be the number at the bottom, if 5 is at the top?

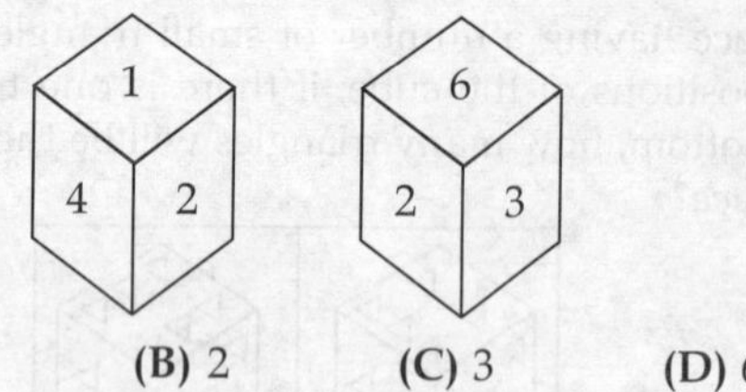

(A) 1 **(B)** 2 **(C)** 3 **(D)** 6

15. Which of the following pattern can be obtained from the piece of cardboard shown here?

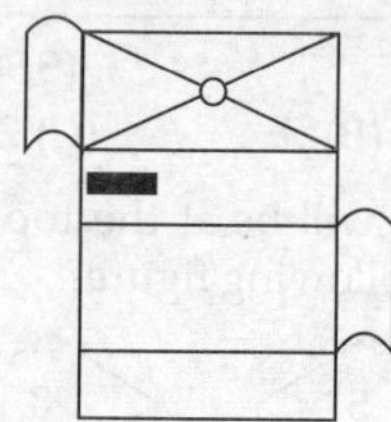

[RRB 2009]

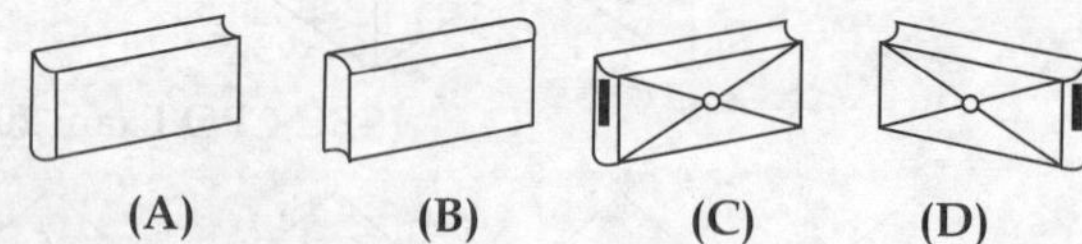

(A) **(B)** **(C)** **(D)**

16. The following diagram depicts various views of a cube. Each face has some number. From the answer choices select the number that should come opposite to 5.

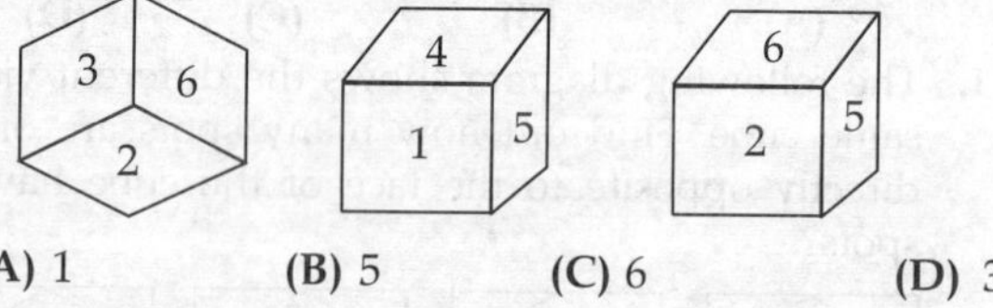

(A) 1 **(B)** 5 **(C)** 6 **(D)** 3

17. Four positions of a dice are given below. Identify the number at the bottom when top is 5. **[SSC SI 2016]**

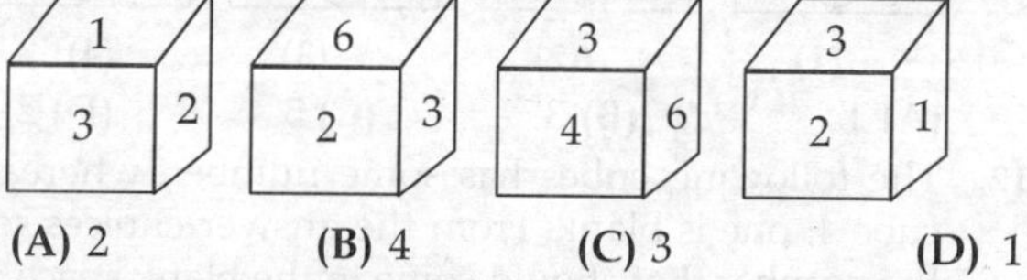

(A) 2 **(B)** 4 **(C)** 3 **(D)** 1

18. Select a box from the options that is similar to the box formed from the given figure.

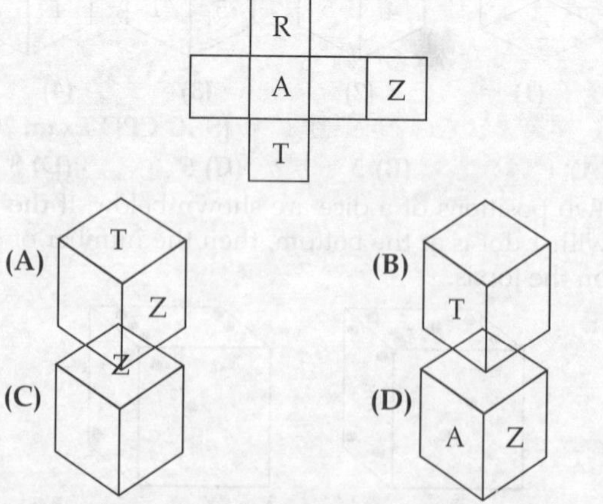

19. Select a box from the options that is similar to the box formed from the given figure.

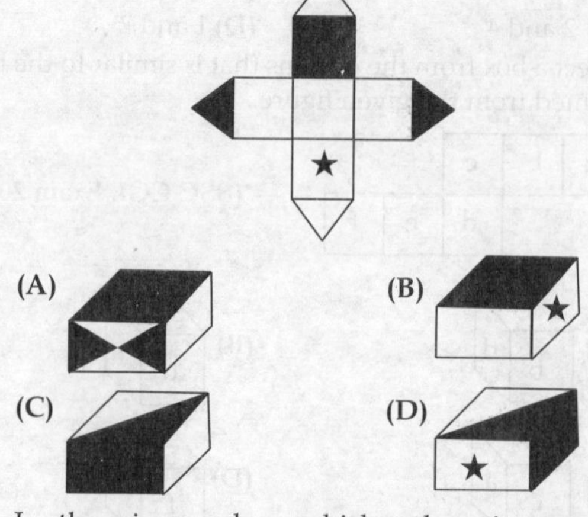

20. In the given cubes, which colour is opposite to purple? **[SSC CGL 2016]**

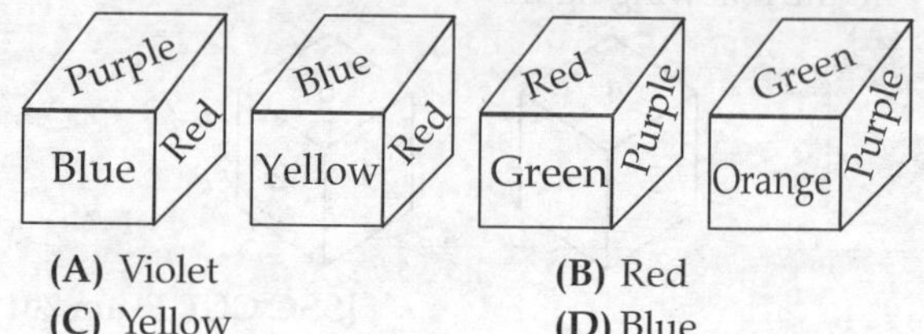

(A) Violet **(B)** Red
(C) Yellow **(D)** Blue

21. Which of the four cubes pictured below are correct view when the six squares are folded (in clockwise directioin) into a cube? **[SSC CGL 2013]**

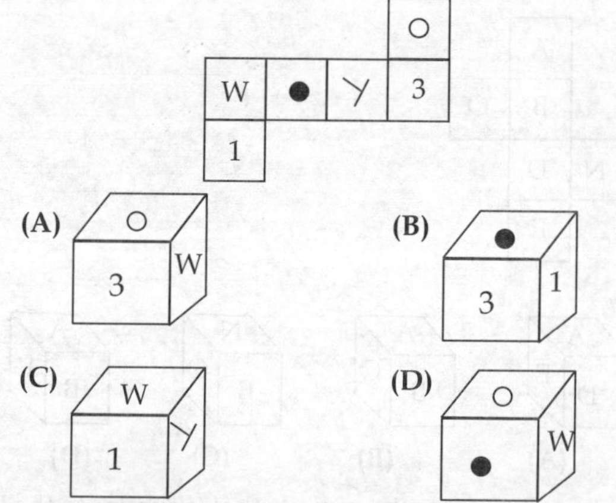

22. Select a box from the options that is similar to the box formed from the given figure.

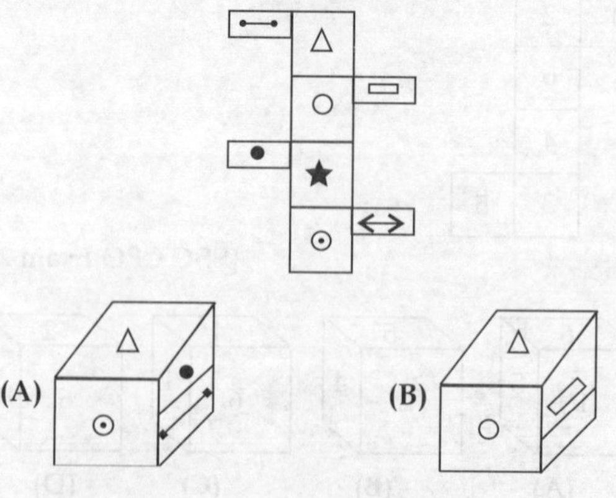

(C) 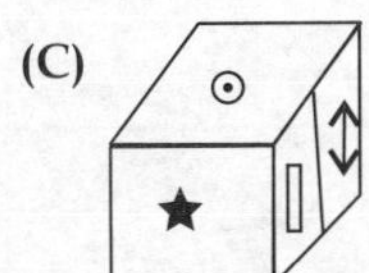

(D) 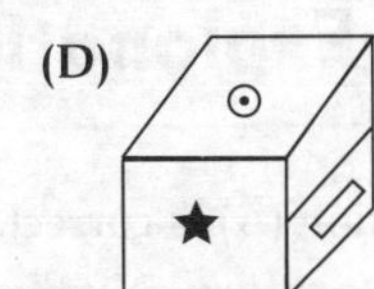

23. Select a box from the options that is similar to the box formed the given figure

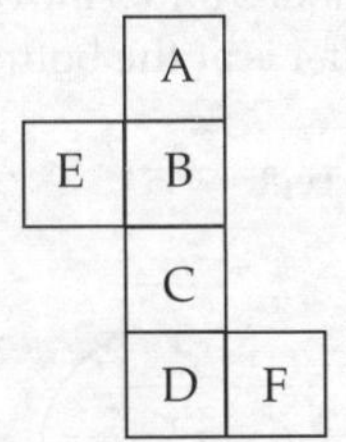

(A) 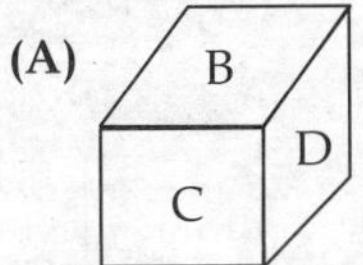

(B) 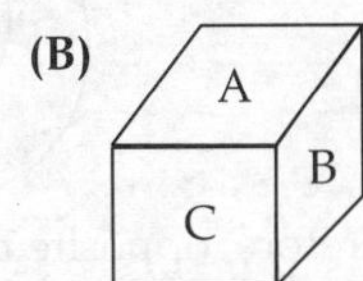

(C) 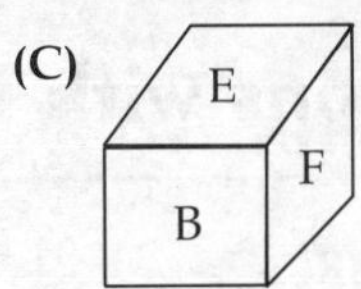

(D) 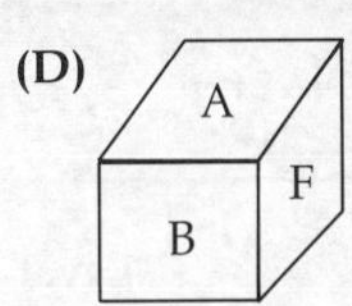

24. A dice is thrown four times and its four different positions are given below. Find the number on the face opposite the face showing 2? **[SSC CHSL 2012]**

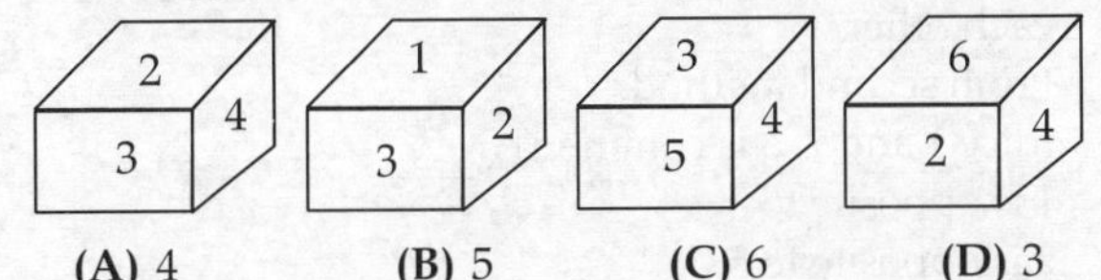

(A) 4 (B) 5 (C) 6 (D) 3

25. The following figure is folded to form a block. Which symbol will appear on the opposite of ▲? **[SSC 2016]**

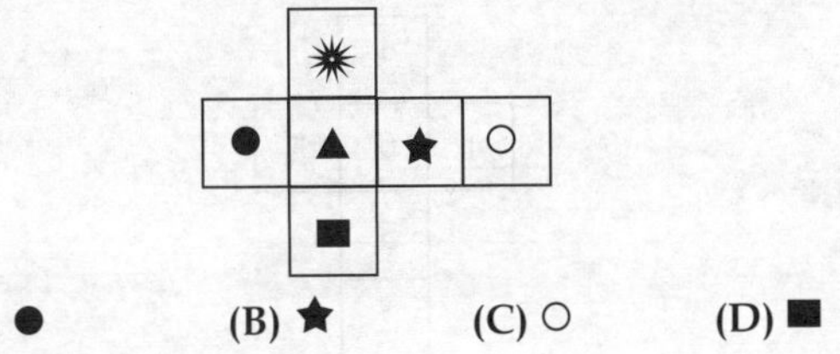

(A) ● (B) ★ (C) ○ (D) ■

ANSWER KEY

Level-1: Beginner

1.	(B)	2.	(A)	3.	(A)	4.	(B)	5.	(D)	6.	(D)	7.	(D)	8.	(C)	9.	(A)	10.	(C)
11.	(B)	12.	(D)	13.	(B)	14.	(D)	15.	(D)	16.	(B)	17.	(D)	18.	(C)	19.	(C)	20.	(C)
21.	(B)	22.	(C)	23.	(C)	24.	(A)	25.	(B)	26.	(B)	27.	(A)	28.	(A)	29.	(C)	30.	(A)
31.	(B)	32.	(C)	33.	(B)	34.	(D)	35.	(A)	36.	(A)	37.	(B)	38.	(B)	39.	(A)	40.	(D)

Level-2: Intermediate

1.	(C)	2.	(C)	3.	(B)	4.	(B)	5.	(C)	6.	(D)	7.	(B)	8.	(C)	9.	(B)	10.	(C)
11.	(C)	12.	(E)	13.	(A)	14.	(A)	15.	(C)	16.	(A)	17.	(C)	18.	(C)	19.	(C)	20.	(C)
21.	(D)	22.	(A)	23.	(A)	24.	(B)	25.	(D)	26.	(D)	27.	(A)	28.	(A)	29.	(A)	30.	(A)
31.	(C)	32.	(A)	33.	(C)	34.	(C)	35.	(B)										

Level-3: Expert

1.	(B)	2.	(D)	3.	(B)	4.	(B)	5.	(B)	6.	(C)	7.	(B)	8.	(C)	9.	(B)	10.	(B)
11.	(A)	12.	(C)	13.	(B)	14.	(B)	15.	(A)	16.	(D)	17.	(C)	18.	(A)	19.	(A)	20.	(C)
21.	(A)	22.	(B)	23.	(D)	24.	(B)	25.	(C)										

Solutions with Detailed Explanations

Level-1: BEGINNER

1. **Option (B) is correct.**
Explanation: From dice 2 and 3. 3 and 5 are two common numbers. Hence, 6 and 4 are opposite to each other.
From second method
(dice 1 and 2, 3 is common)
1 is opposite to 3
2 is opposite to 5
4 is opposite to 6

2. **Option (A) is correct.**
Explanation: Expanded form of the dice is

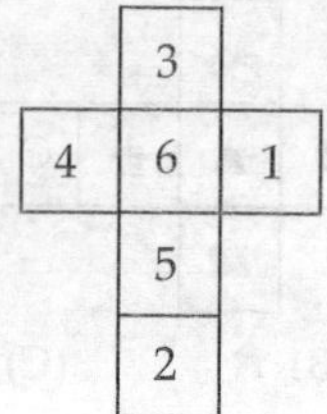

Thus, X = 3

3. **Option (A) is correct.**
Explanation: Form the question, expanded form of the dice is

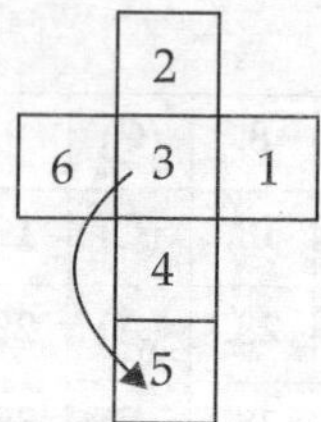

So, opposite of 3 is 5.

4. **Option (B) is correct.**
Explanation: The number 2, 4, 5, and 6 are on the surface adjacent to 1. So, 3 is on the surface opposite to number 1.

5. **Option (D) is correct.**
Explanation: The number 1, 2, 3 and 5 are adjacent faces of 6. Hence, 4 is opposite to 6.

6. **Option (D) is correct.**
Explanation: Dice 1: 2 3 4
Dice 2 : 2 1 4
So, opposite of 1 is 3.

7. **Option (D) is correct.**
Explanation: From 1st and 2nd dice: 6 is opposite to 3.
From 2nd and 4th dice : 1 is opposite to 4.
So, 2 is opposite to 5.
Thus, opposite faces of 2 is 5.

8. **Option (C) is correct.**
Explanation: From 1st and 4th dice : 6 is opposite to 4.
From 2nd and 3rd dice : Adjacent faces of 5 are 1, 4, 2 and 6. So, 3 is opposite to 5.
Hence, 1 is opposite to 2.

9. **Option (A) is correct.**
Explanation: Number 1 is common to both the positions of the dice. Let us assume figure second to be rotated. So that 1 remains on the right hand side face and the number 5 and 3 move to the faces hidden behind 2 and 4. If 4 is at the bottom, 3 must lie on the top.

10. **Option (C) is correct.**
Explanation:

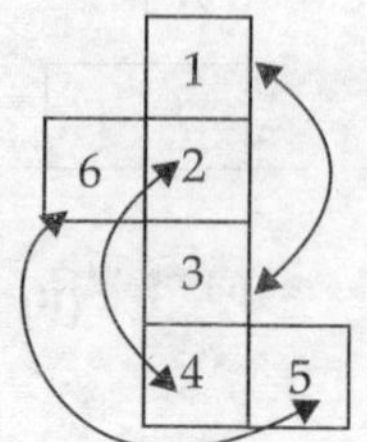

Therefore, opposite faces are
1 – 3
2 – 4
6 – 5
Figure (A), (B), and (D) will not be identical to question figure because number forming the opposite pairs appear on the adjacent surfaces.
So, figure (C) is correct.

11. **Option (B) is correct.**
Explanation: From the figure there are no such cube which is painted red only on two sides.

12. **Option (D) is correct.**
Explanation: From the question figure,
4 is opposite to 6.
1 is opposite to 2.
3 is opposite to 5.
Figure (A), (B), and (C) will not be identical to question figure because number forming the opposite pairs appear on the adjacent surfaces.

13. **Option (B) is correct.**
Explanation: From the question figure, it is clear that
G is opposite to M.
C is opposite to E.
B is opposite to F.
Hence, figure (A), (C) and (D) is not identical to question figure.

14. **Option (D) is correct.**
Explanation: When the figure is folded to form a cube. Then the face 6 dots will be opposite to 3 dots.

15. **Option (D) is correct.**
Explanation: From the given figure,
Cube in first row = 1
Cubes in second row = 3
Cubes in third row = 6
Cubes in fourth row = 10
Total number of cubes = 1 + 3 + 6 + 10 = 20

16. Option (B) is correct.

Explanation: From figure it is clear that figure having 12 cubes.

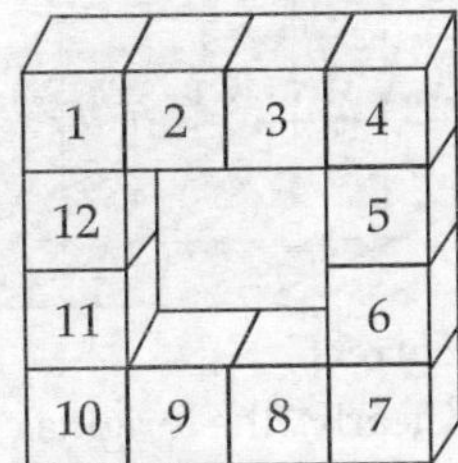

17. Option (D) is correct.

Explanation: From figure first and second, we conclude that when 6 is at the bottom, then 5 will be at the top.

18. Option (C) is correct.

Explanation: From figure it is clear that number 3 is opposite to number 2.

	3	
4	1	5
	2	
	6	

19. Option (C) is correct.

Explanation: From figure 1 and 2: Adjacent faces of 1 are 2, 3, 4 and 6. So, 1 is opposite to 5.

20. Option (C) is correct.

Explanation: Using both figures, we conclude that 1,3, 4, and 5 are adjacent side of number 2. So, 2 is opposite to 6.

4 and 2 are adjacent of 5. So, either 1 or 3 is opposite to 5. So, 3 is opposite to 5.

21. Option (B) is correct.

Explanation: It is clear from the figure, four block in the lower layer. Three blocks standing over the lower layer. Hence, total number of block is 7.

22. Option (C) is correct.

Explanation: As the dot face cannot be adjacent to both the dark shaded faces. Hence, option (C) cannot possible.

23. Option (C) is correct.

Explanation: From the figure, we can see that option (A), (B), and (D) will not be answer. So, answer is option (C).

24. Option (A) is correct.

25. Option (B) is correct.

Explanation: From the question figure:

K is opposite to R.

C is opposite to F.

B is opposite to D.

So, answer figure is as shown below,

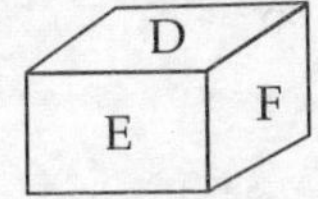

26. Option (B) is correct.

Explanation: 2, 3, 4 and 5 are adjacent to 1. So, 6 is opposite to 1.

27. Option (A) is correct.

Explanation: Number of cubes in bottom layer = 6

Number of cubes in middle layer = 3

Number of cubes in top layer = 1

So, total number of cubes in the given figure = 6 + 3 + 1 = 10

28. Option (A) is correct.

Explanation: The letter on opposite faces are : (O, Y) and (X, Z).

29. Option (C) is correct.

Explanation: Box in option (C) can be formed from the given figure.

30. Option (A) is correct.

Explanation: The opposite faces are: (@, □), (×, □), (■, □)

31. Option (B) is correct.

Explanation: The opposite faces are : (□, □), (■, □) and (●, ■)

32. Option (C) is correct.

Explanation: The opposite faces are (H, 4), (E, @) and (8, 1). So, box in option (C) can be formed.

33. Option (B) is correct.

Explanation: The opposite faces are (☆, 3), (@, X) and (#, △). So, box in option (B) can be formed.

34. Option (D) is correct.

Explanation: The numbers on opposite faces are: (2, 6), (1, 5)

35. Option (A) is correct.

Explanation: The numbers on opposite faces are: (4, 6), (1, 2) and (3, 5)

36. Option (A) is correct.

Explanation: Total number of cubes = 4 + 4 = 8

37. Option (B) is correct.

Explanation: Number of cubes in bottom layer = 4

Number of cubes in top layer = 2

So, total number of cubes = 4 + 2 = 6

38. Option (B) is correct.

Explanation: Number of cubes in bottom layer = 6

Number of cubes in top layer = 2

So, total number of cubes = 6 + 2 = 8

39. Option (A) is correct.

Explanation: 3 and 5 both are adjacent to 1 and 6. So, 1 and 6 are on the opposite faces.

40. Option (D) is correct.

Explanation: The numbers on the opposite faces are (1, 3), (2, 4) and (5, 6). So, box in option (D) can be formed.

Level-2: INTERMEDIATE

1. Option (C) is correct.

Explanation: In the figure, there are 1 row containing 4 blocks and 1 row containing 1 block each. Therefore, total number of blocks = 5

2. Option (C) is correct.

Explanation: Clearly, in the figure, there are– 1 column containing

3 cubes, 2 columns containing 2 cubes each and 3 columns containing 1 cube each.
Number of cubes in columns of 3 cubes; $1 \times 3 = 3$
Number of cubes in columns of 2 cubes; $2 \times 2 = 4$
Number of cubes in columns of 1 cube; $3 \times 1 = 3$
Therefore, total number of cubes $= 3 + 4 + 3 = 10$
Hence, the answer is (C).

3. Option (B) is correct.
Explanation: Clearly, there are 4 columns containing 2 cubes each and 6 columns containing 1 cube each.
Number of cubes in columns of 2 cubes $= 4 \times 2 = 8$;
Number of cubes in columns of 1 cube $= 6 \times 1 = 6$,
Therefore, total number of cubes $= 8 + 6 = 14$,
Hence, the answer is (B).

4. Option (B) is correct.
Explanation: There are 4 blocks in the lower layer close to the ground. Also, there are 3 blocks standing over the lower layer of blocks.
Thus, there are $4 + 3 = 7$ blocks in the given figure.

5. Option (C) is correct.
Explanation: Clearly, there are 1 column containing 4 cubes, 2 columns containing 2 cubes each and 3 columns containing 1 cube each.
So, total number of cubes
$= (1 \times 4) + (2 \times 2) + (3 \times 1)$
$= 4 + 4 + 3 = 11$

6. Option (D) is correct.
Explanation: Clearly, there are 4 columns containing 1 cube each, 4 columns containing 2 cubes each and 1 column containing 3 cubes,
Hence, total number of cubes $= (4 \times 1) + (4 \times 2) + (1 \times 3) = 4 + 8 + 3 = 15$.

7. Option (B) is correct.
Explanation: Total number of cubes
$= (1 \times 3) + (7 \times 2) + (13 \times 1) = 3 + 14 + 13 = 30$.

8. Option (C) is correct.
Explanation: As shown in the adjoining figure, let the upper face and the RHS face of the cube be coloured. Then, clearly, the rows of smaller cubes (formed by cutting the large cube into 64 parts) which are indicated by dots, have none of their sides coloured. Since there are 9 such rows and each row consists of 4 cubes. So, there are 36 cubes which are not coloured at all.
Hence, the answer is (C).

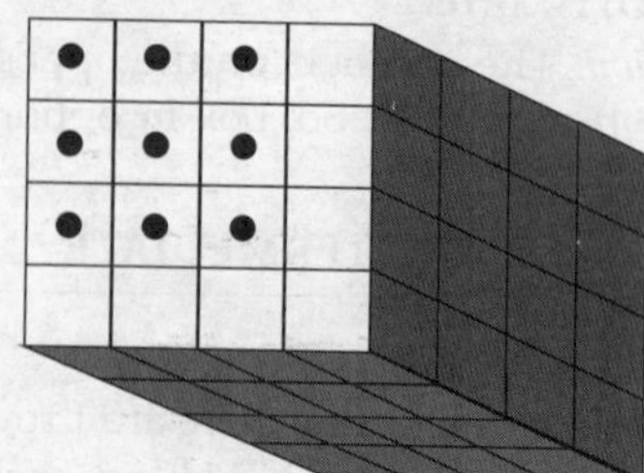

9. Option (B) is correct.
Explanation: The big cube can be cut into 27 small cubes as shown. Clearly, out of these 27 small cubes, cubes having only one side painted are those which lie the center of each face of the big cube. Since, there are 6 faces of a cube, therefore, the required number of cubes is 6.

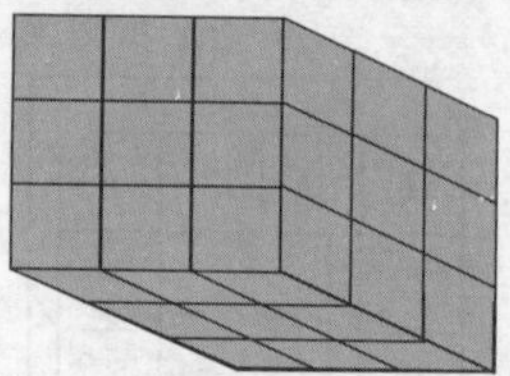

10. Option (C) is correct.
Explanation: Clearly, the original (colored) cube is divided into 64 smaller cubes as shown in the figure. The four central cubes on each face of the larger cube, have only one side painted. Since, there are six faces, therefore total number of such cubes $4 \times 6 = 24$.

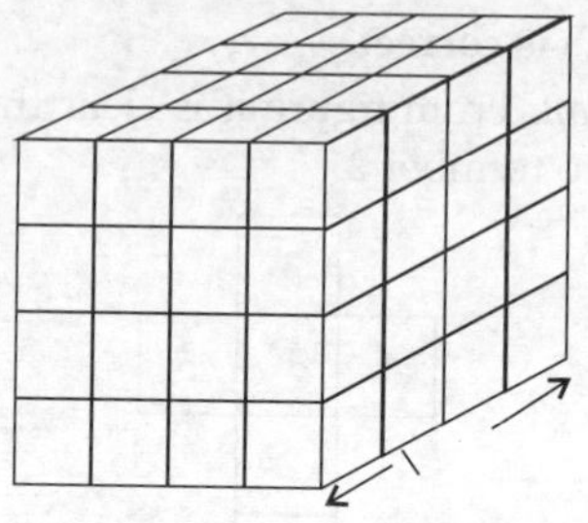

11. Option (C) is correct.
Explanation: The following figure shows the cubes painted blue on all faces and divided into 125 smaller cubes as:

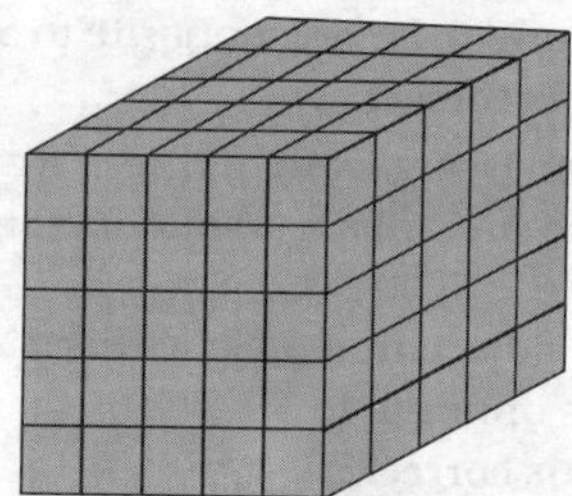

There are 9 central cubes in each of the layers II, III and IV which have no face painted are $9 \times 3 = 27$ such cubes.

12. Option (E) is correct.
Explanation: The following figure shows the cubes painted black on all faces and then divided into 125 smaller cubes:

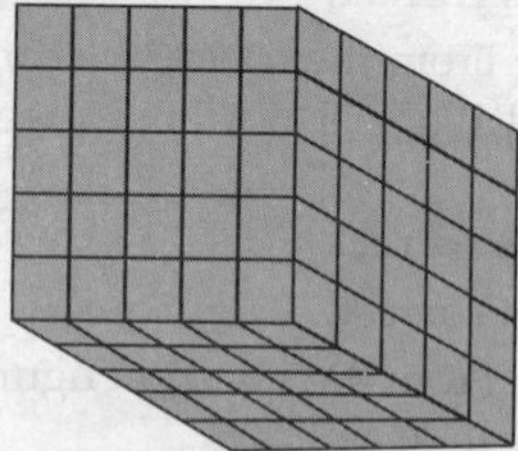

Clearly, at each edge, there are 3 such cubes with two sides painted.
So, total number of cubes with two sides painted black $= 12 \times 3 = 36$

13. Option (A) is correct.

Explanation:

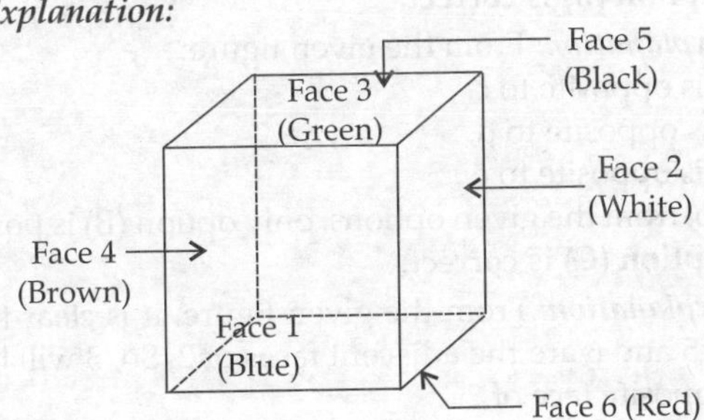

From the figure, it is clear that white is opposite to brown.

14. Option (A) is correct.

Explanation: From figures (i), (ii) and (iii), we conclude that the numbers 2, 3, 4 and 5 appear adjacent, to 6. Clearly, the remaining number i.e., 1 will appear on the face opposite 6.

15. Option (C) is correct.

Explanation: From figures (i), (ii) and (iv), we conclude that 6, 4, 1 and 2 dots appear to 3 dots. Clearly, there will be 5 dots on the face opposite the face with 3 dots.

16. Option (A) is correct.

Explanation: We are assuming the dice in fig. (ii) to be rotated so that the 5 dots appear at the same position as in fig. (i) i.e., on RHS face (i.e., on face 2 as per activity 1) and 1 dot appears at the same position as in fig. (i) i.e., on front face (i.e., on face 1). Then, from the two figures, 2 dots appear on the top face (i.e., on face 5) and 4 dots appear on the bottom face (i.e., on face 6). Since, these two faces are opposite to each other, therefore, two dots are contained on the face opposite to that containing four dots.

17. Option (C) is correct.

Explanation: The number 6 is common to both the positions of the dice. We assume the dice in fig. (ii) to be rotated so that 6 remains on the FR-LH face and the numbers 1 and 3 move to the faces hidden behind 4 and 5 respectively [in fig. (i)]. Then, 5 lies on FR-RH face (i.e., face 1), 4 lies on top face (i.e., face 5), 3 lies on RR-LH face i.e., face 3) and 1 lies on bottom face (i.e., face 6). Thus, 3 lies opposite 5. Hence, when the top is 3, then the number at the bottom is 5.

18. Option (C) is correct.

Explanation: Number 6 is common to both the positions of the dice. We assume the dice in fig. (ii) to be rotated so that 6 remains on the top face and the number 4 in fig. (ii) moves to the FR-RH face (i.e., face 1) as in fig. (i), then 5 will move to the RR-RH face (i.e.,, face 2). Clearly, 5 (which lies on face 2) and 1 (which lies on face 4) will be opposite to each other. So, when 1 is on the top, then 5 will be at the bottom.

SHORTCUT: Two numbers 6 and 4 are common to both the given dices. So, 1 is opposite to 5.

19. Option (C) is correct.

Explanation: Number 3 is common to the two positions of the block. We assume the block in fig. (ii) to be rotated so that 3 appears at the same position as in fig. (i) i.e., on RHS face and the numbers 5 and 2 move to the faces hidden behind the numbers 4 and 6 respectively [in fig. (i)]. Thus, the combined figure will have 3 on RHS face (i.e., face 2), 4 on the front face (i.e., face 1), 6 on the top face (i.e., face 5), 5 on the rear face (i.e., face 3) and 2 on the bottom face (i.e., face 6). Clearly, when 2 is at the bottom, then 6 is at the top.

20. Option (C) is correct.

Explanation:

Dice 1: Clockwise numbers starting from 2 = 2, 1, 5

Dice 2: Clockwise numbers starting from 2 = 2, 6, 3

So, 1 is opposite to 6 and 5 is opposite to 3.

21. Option (D) is correct.

Explanation:

Dice 1: Clockwise numbers starting from 6 = 6, 2, 1

Dice 2: Clockwise numbers starting from 6 = 6, 4, 3

So, 2 is opposite to 4 and 1 is opposite to 3.

Hence, 6 will be opposite to 5.

22. Option (A) is correct.

Explanation: Clearly, the six faces of the dice are labelled as

Adjacent faces : a, b, c, d

and opposite faces : e, f

Therefore, 'a' appears opposite c.

Hence, when 'c' is at the top, then 'a' will be at the bottom.

23. Option (A) is correct.

Explanation: When the sheet is folded , then one of the faces of the cube formed will be of the form ◨

Thus, a cube of the type as shown in fig. (a) will be formed.

24. Option (B) is correct.

Explanation: When the sheet is folded to form a cube, then the completely shaded face lies opposite to the half shaded face. Therefore, the cubes shown in figures (A) and (C) which have the completely shaded face adjacent to the half-shaded face cannot be formed. Hence, only the cubes in figures (B) can be formed.

25. Option (D) is correct.

Explanation: When the sheet is folded to form a cube, then the face bearing a square lie opposite to the face bearing a circle.

26. Option (D) is correct.

Explanation: The letters on the opposite faces are: (I, J), (G, H).

27. Option (A) is correct.

Explanation: The numbers on the opposite faces are: (1, 4), (5, 6)

28. Option (A) is correct.

Explanation: The opposite faces are: (▨, □), (⊞, □), (□, □)

29. Option (A) is correct.

Explanation: The opposite faces are: (U, M), (R, □), (J, □)

30. Option (A) is correct.
Explanation: The opposite faces are: (▲, △), (■, □), (O, ☆)

(31-35) :

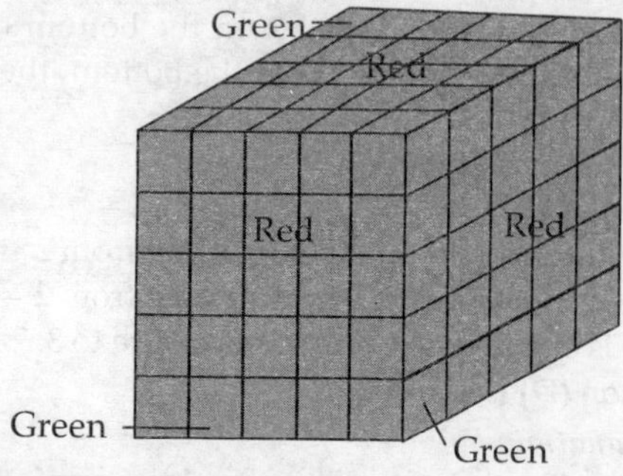

31. Option (C) is correct.
Explanation: Number of cubes having 3 green faces = 8

32. Option (A) is correct.
Explanation: Number of cubes = 0

33. Option (C) is correct.
Explanation: Number of cubes = 25 + 25 + 15 + 15 + 9 + 9 = 98

34. Option (C) is correct.
Explanation: Number of cubes = 16 + 16 + 6 + 6 = 44

35. Option (B) is correct.
Explanation: Number of cubes with no color = 125 – 98 = 27

Level-3: EXPERT

1. **Option (B) is correct.**
Explanation: The question figure is similar to the answer figure (3). So, when the sheet in figure is folded to form a cube, then G opposite to S, E opposite to C, and A opposite to D. Hence, only the cube in figure (3) can be formed.

2. **Option (D) is correct.**
Explanation: When the sheet folded to create a cube, then blank faces will be opposite to each other and circle will be opposite to the combined faces of four triangles given at end.
In figure (A) and (C), circle and shaded part are adjacent, So, these are not possible. In figure (B), three blank faces are visible. So, here also circle and triangle faces are adjacent and this is also not possible.
Hence, only figure (D) is possible.

3. **Option (B) is correct.**
Explanation: A face with a circle on it is located across from a face with a dot.
This cube obviously lacks the faces that can be seen on the cubes in pictures (4). Only the cubes depicted in figures (1), (2) and (3) can so be created.

4. **Option (B) is correct.**
Explanation: From the given figure:
1 is opposite to 4.
2 is opposite to 6.
3 is opposite to 5.
So. from given options, only option (2) and (3) are possible.
Hence, option (B) is correct.

5. **Option (B) is correct.**
Explanation: From the given figure:
a is opposite to c.
f is opposite to d.
b is opposite to e.
So, from the given options, only option (B) is possible.

6. **Option (C) is correct.**
Explanation: From the given figure, it is clear that 1, 4, 5 and 6 are the adjacent faces of 2. So, 3 will be the opposite face of 2.

7. **Option (B) is correct.**
Explanation: From the given figure:
A will be opposite to D.
B will be opposite to E.
N will be opposite to O.
So, from given options, only option (B) is possible.

8. **Option (C) is correct.**
Explanation: From the given figure:
2 will be opposite to 4.
6 will be opposite to 3.
1 will be opposite to 5.
So, from given options, only option (C) is possible.

9. **Option (B) is correct.**
Explanation:
Dice 1: Clockwise numbers starting from 3 (triangles) = 3, 5, 4 (triangles)
Dice 2: Clockwise numbers starting from 3 (triangles) = 3, 6, 2 (triangles)
So, 5 triangles face is opposite to 6 triangle of face and 4 triangle face is opposite to 2 triangle face.
Hence, when 1 triangle at the bottom then 3 triangles will be at top.
So, option (B) is correct.

10. **Option (B) is correct.**

11. **Option (A) is correct.**
Explanation: In cube (1) and (4), face having 2 dots and 3 dots are common. So, face having 1 dot will be opposite to face having 6 dots.
Hence, option (A) is correct.

12. **Option (C) is correct.**
Explanation: From the given cubes , 6 will replace the question mark in given cube.

13. **Option (B) is correct.**
Explanation: From figure first and second, we conclude that 5, 4, 6 and 2 dots appear adjacent to 3 dots. Therefore 1 dot must appear opposite 3 dot. Thus, if the face with 1 dot is at the bottom then the face with 3 dot will appear on the top.
SHORTCUT:
Dice 1: Clockwise numbers starting from 3 = 3, 5, 4
Dice 2: Clockwise numbers starting from 3 = 3, 6, 2
So, 5 is opposite to 6 and 4 is opposite to 2.
Hence, 3 will be at top when 1 is at the bottom.

14. **Option (B) is correct.**
Explanation: From figure first and second, it is clear that 4, 1, 3 and 6 lie adjacent to 2. So, 5 must lie opposite 2. If 5 is at the top then 2 must be at the bottom.

15. Option (A) is correct.

Explanation: The pattern and also the fact is rectangle, indicate that only fig (A) can be obtained by folding the pattern.

16. Option (D) is correct.

Explanation: The numbers on the opposite faces are : (3, 5), (1, 6), (4, 2).

17. Option (C) is correct.

Explanation: The numbers on the opposite faces are : (1, 6), (2, 4) and (3, 5). So, 3 is opposite to 5.

18. Option (A) is correct.

Explanation: The opposite faces are :
(□, □), (A, Z) and (R, T)
So, box in option (A) can be formed.

19. Option (A) is correct.

20. Option (C) is correct.

Explanation: The colors on the opposite faces are : (Purple, Yellow), (Blue, Green) and (Red, Orange)

21. Option (A) is correct.

Explanation: The opposite faces are : (●, 3), (W, Y) and (0, 1)

22. Option (B) is correct.

23. Option (D) is correct.

Explanation: The letters on the opposite faces are : (A, C), (B, D) and (E, F)

24. Option (B) is correct.

Explanation: The numbers on the opposite faces are : (2, 5), (1, 4), (3, 6)

25. Option (C) is correct.

Explanation: The opposite faces are : (●, ★), (▲, O) and (✷, ■)

■ ■ ■

Chapter 25 Dot Situations

LEARNING OBJECTIVES:

- Identifying the figure similar to dot situations as in question figure
- Identifying the figure different to dot situations as in question figure
- Different types of questions asked in competitive exams

This section of reasoning helps the students to enhance the critical learning. It increase the visual learning of students. Here, the questions includes three or more geometrical figures having dots inside them. The students needs to find out the similar situation of dots among the given options.

Example 1: Select a figure from the options which satisfies the same conditions of placements of dots as in the question figure.

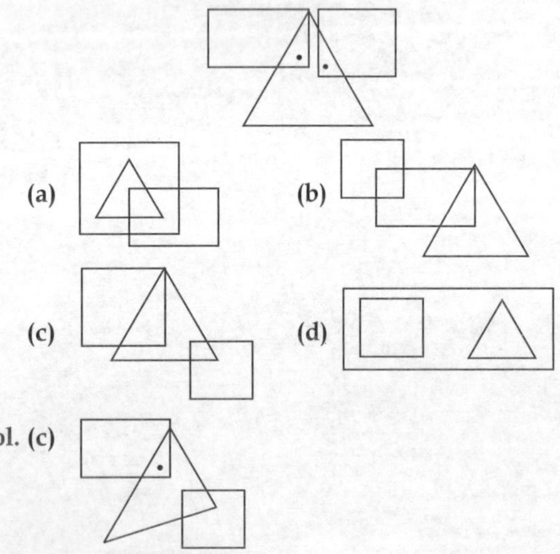

Sol. (c)

Example 2: Which of the following option figure does not satisfy the same conditions of placement of dots as in the question figure?

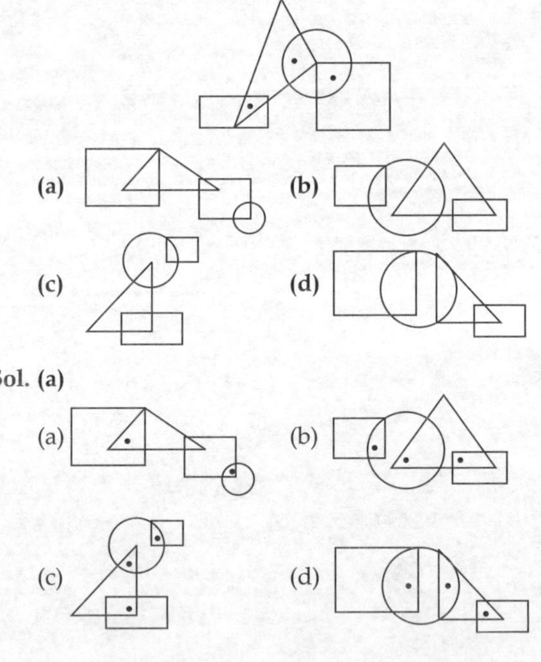

Sol. (a)

1 Level Beginner

Directions (Qs. 1–25): Which of the following option figure will satisfy the conditions of dots as in question figure?

1. 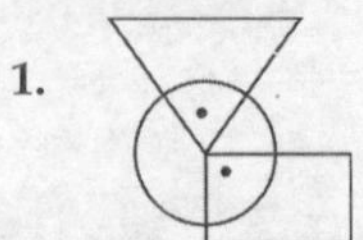

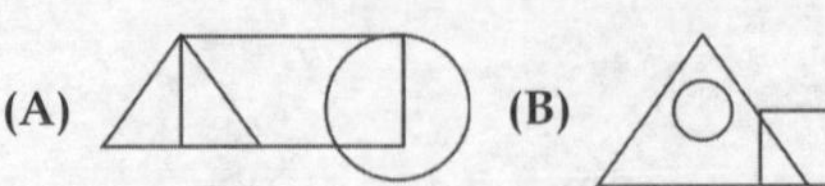

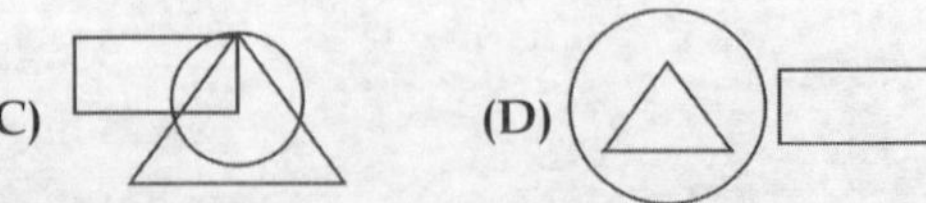

2.

(A) (B)

(C) (D)

3.

(A) (B)

(C) (D)

4.

(A)

(B)

(C)

(D)

5.

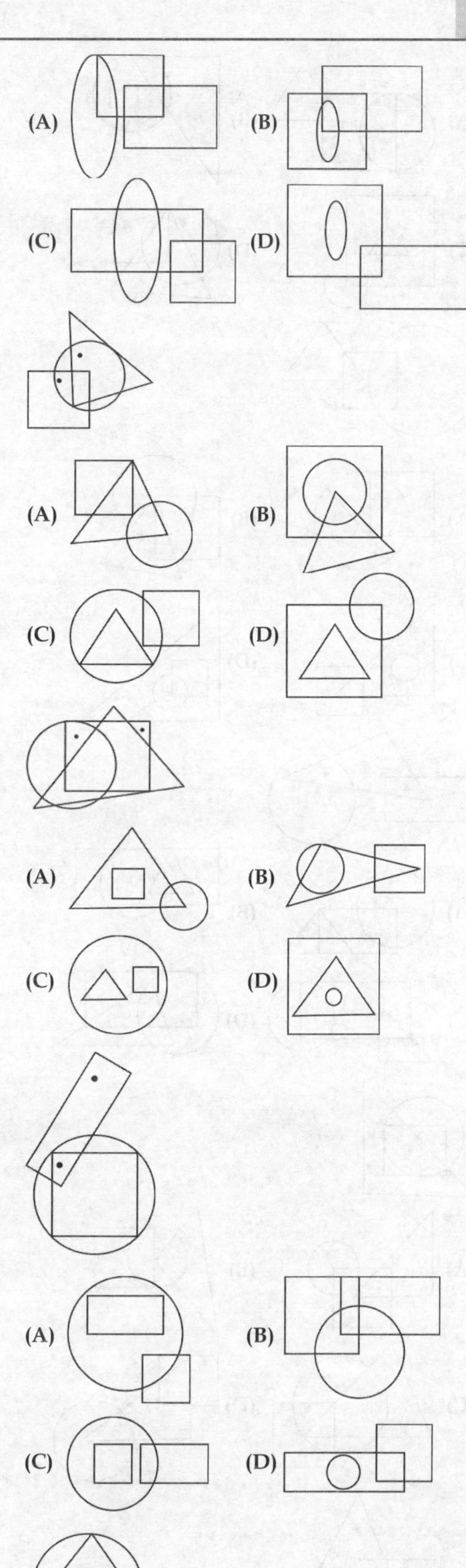

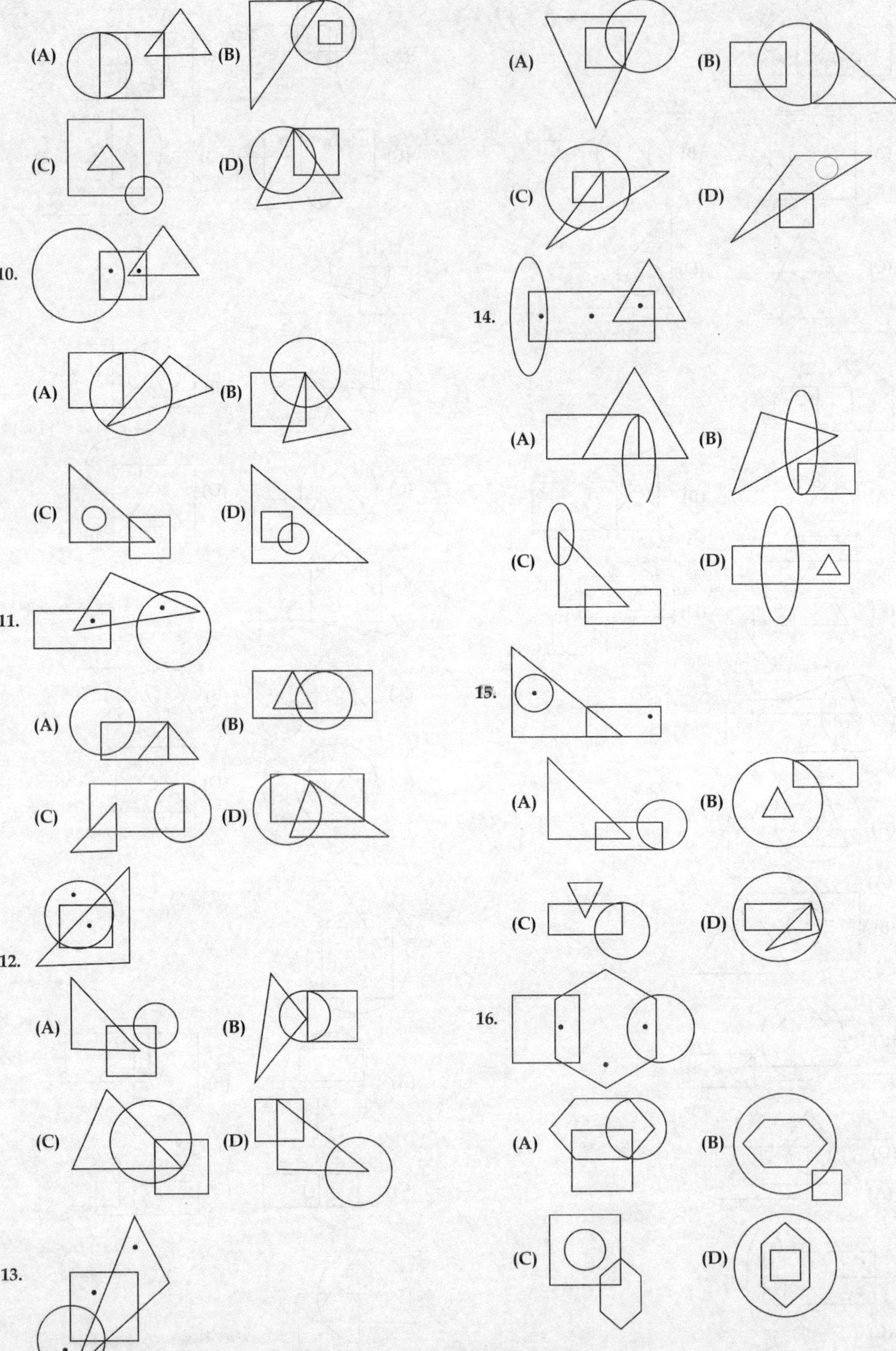
(A)
(B)
(C)
(D)
10.
(A)
(B)
(C)
(D)
11.
(A)
(B)
(C)
(D)
12.
(A)
(B)
(C)
(D)
13.
(A)
(B)
(C)
(D)
14.
(A)
(B)
(C)
(D)
15.
(A)
(B)
(C)
(D)
16.
(A)
(B)
(C)
(D)

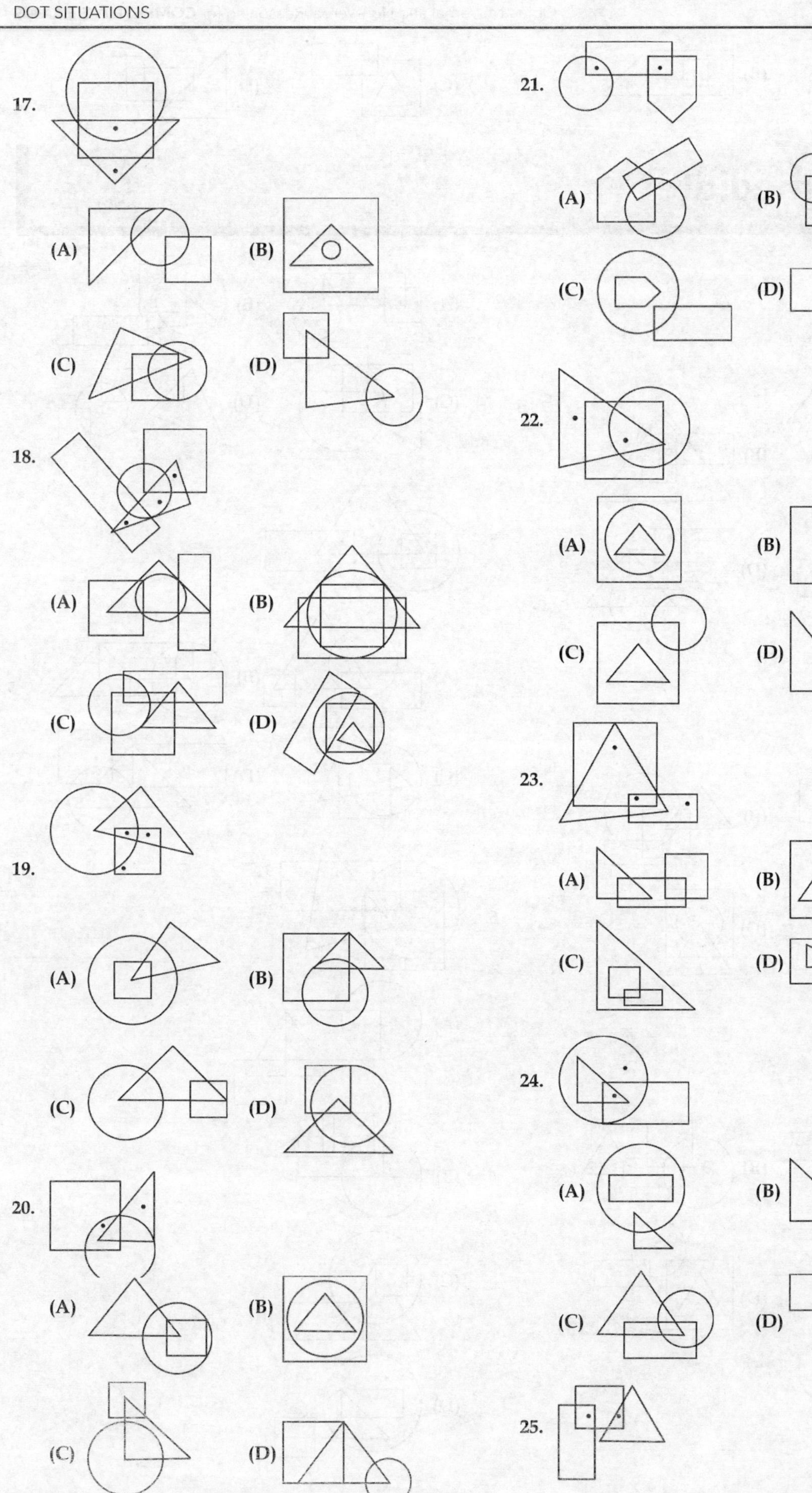
17.
(A)
(B)
(C)
(D)
18.
(A)
(B)
(C)
(D)
19.
(A)
(B)
(C)
(D)
20.
(A)
(B)
(C)
(D)
21.
(A)
(B)
(C)
(D)
22.
(A)
(B)
(C)
(D)
23.
(A)
(B)
(C)
(D)
24.
(A)
(B)
(C)
(D)
25.

(A) 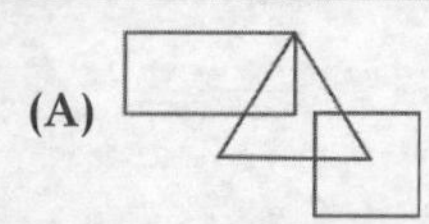 (B) 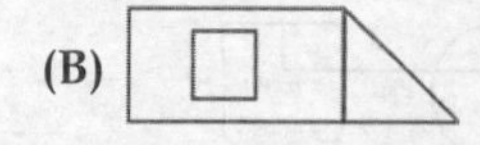 (C) 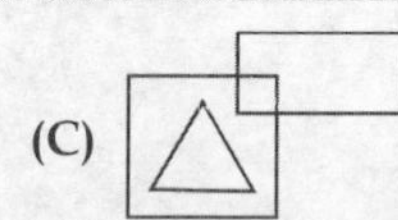 (D) 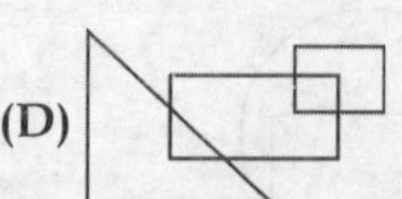

Level 2 Intermediate

1.  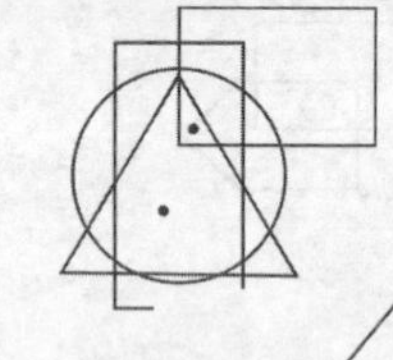

(A) 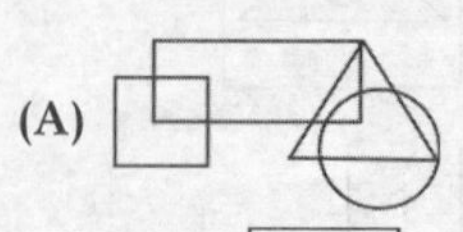 (B) 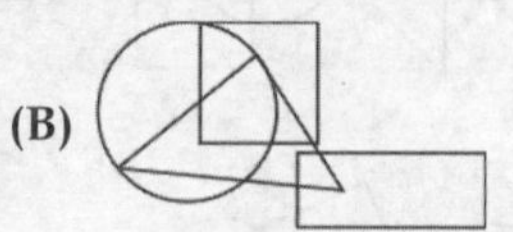

(C) 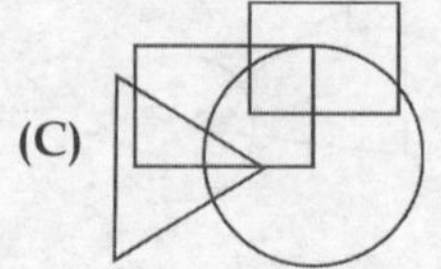 (D) 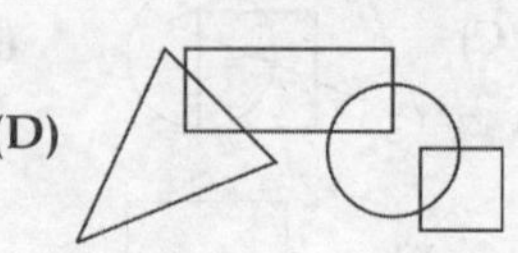

(A) 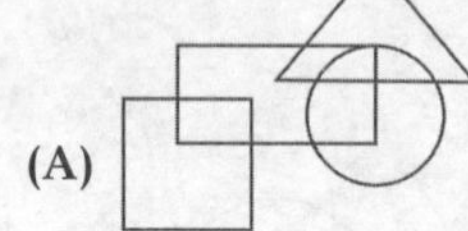 (B) 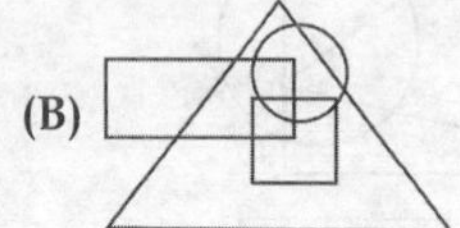

(C) 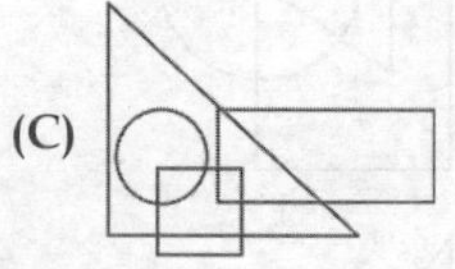 (D) 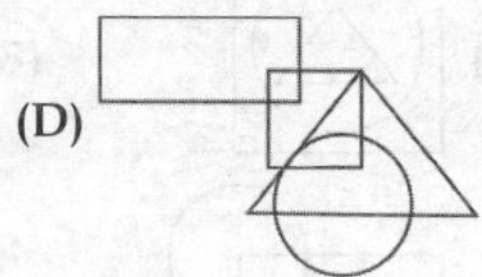

2. 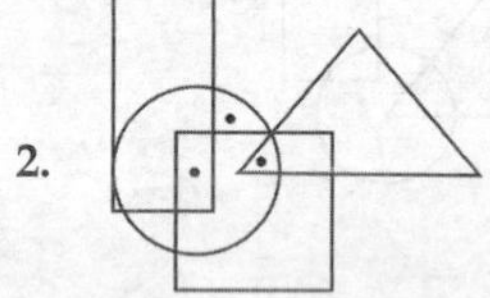

(A) 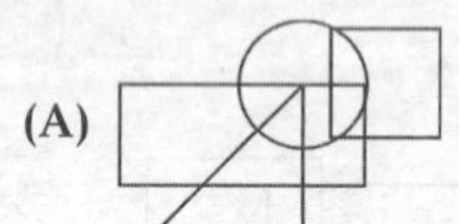 (B) 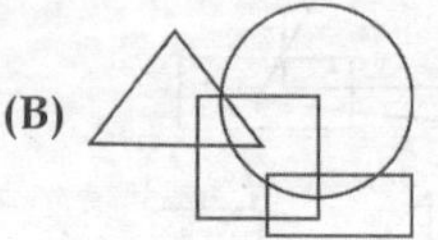

(C) 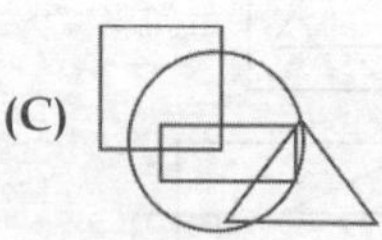 (D) 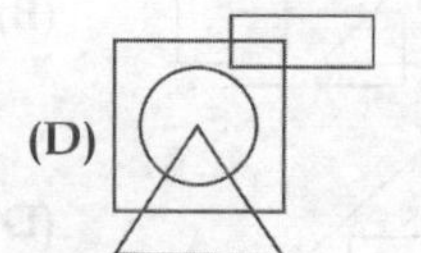

3. 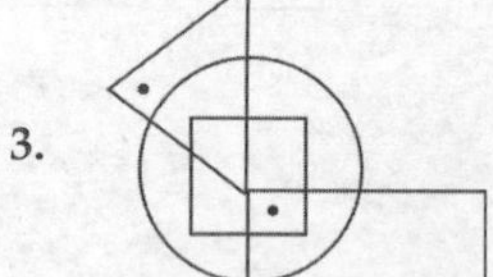

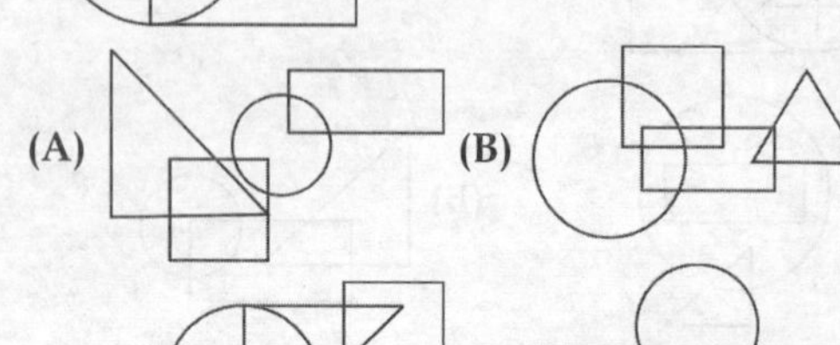

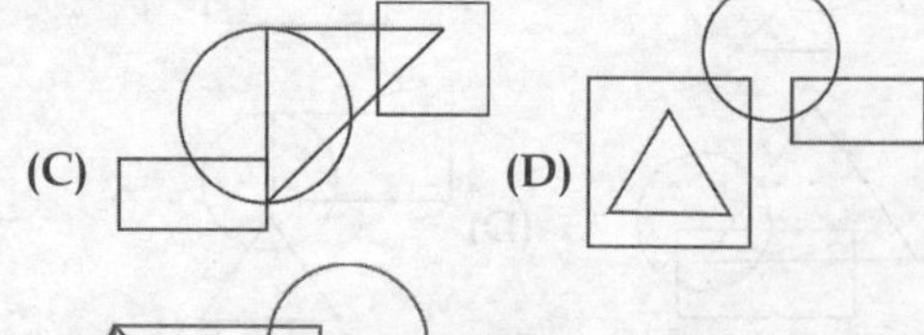

4. 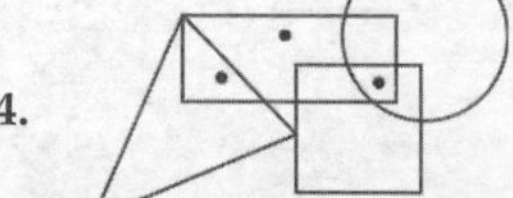

5. 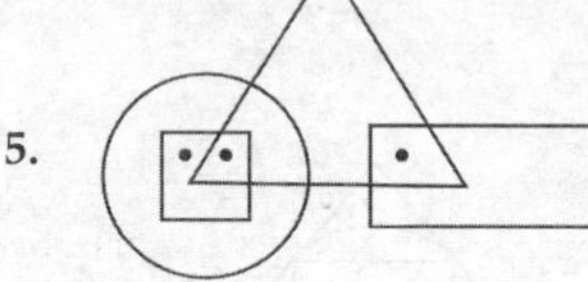

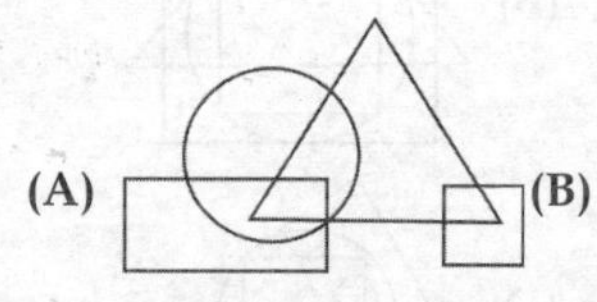

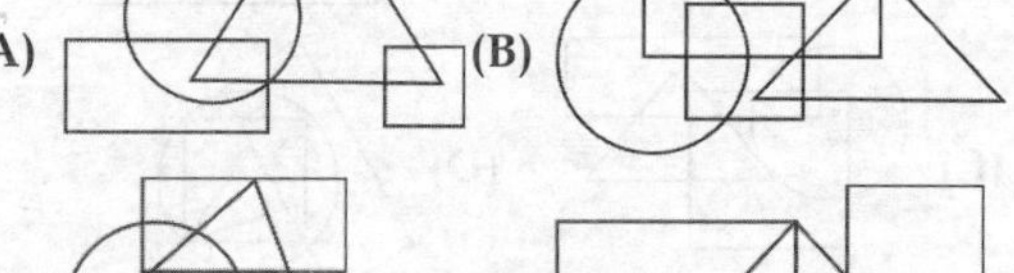

(C) 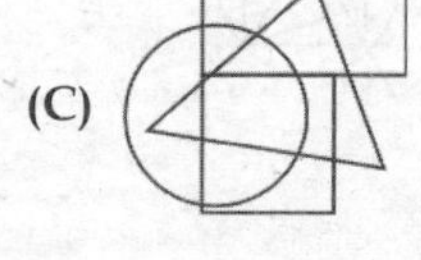 (D) 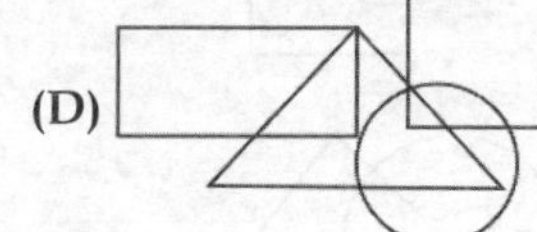

6. 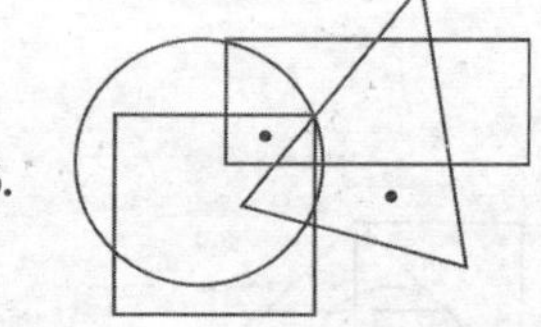

(A) 

(B) 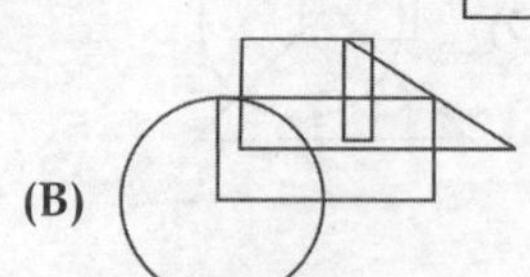

(C) 

(D) 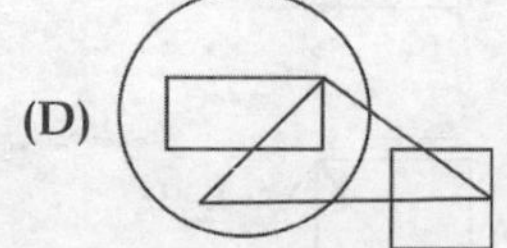

7.

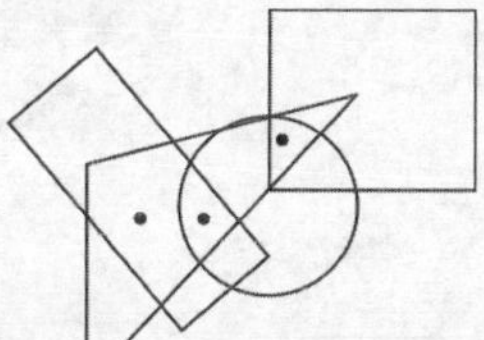

(A) 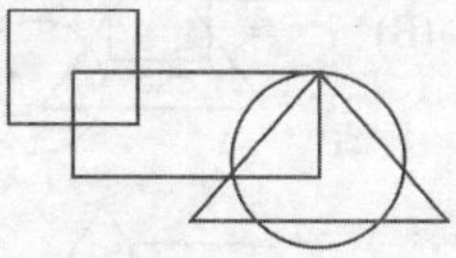 (B)

(C) 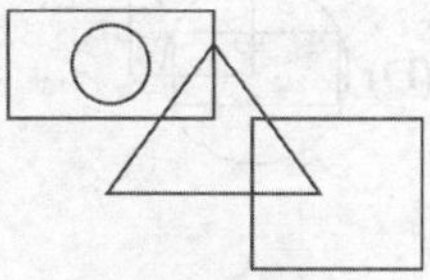 (D)

8.

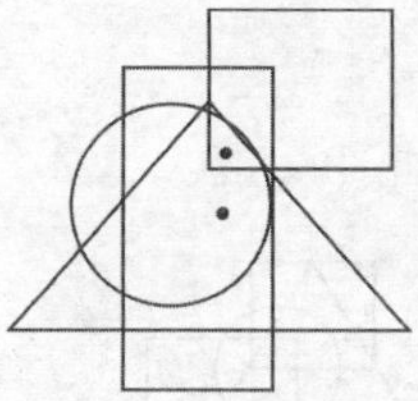

(A)

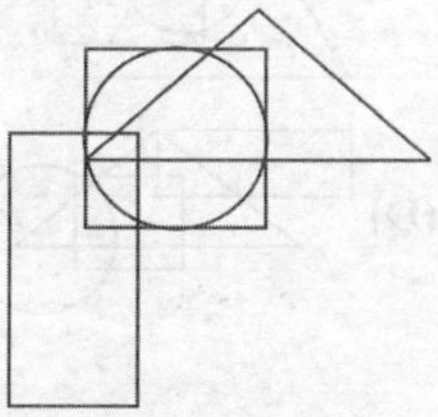

(B)

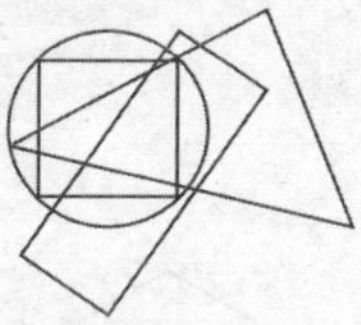

(C)

(D)

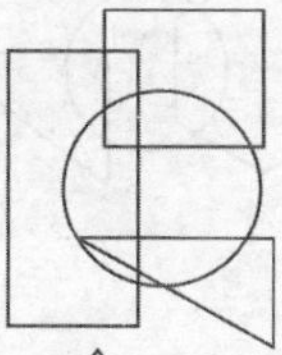

9.

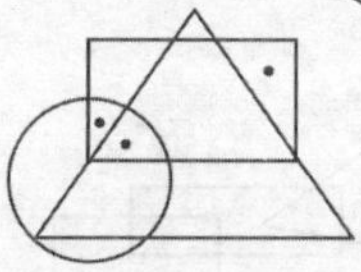

(A) 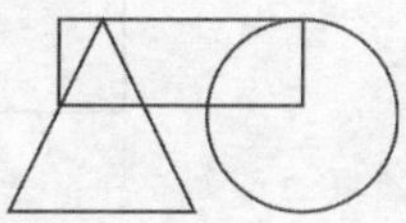 (B)

(C) 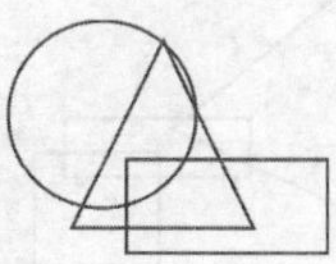 (D)

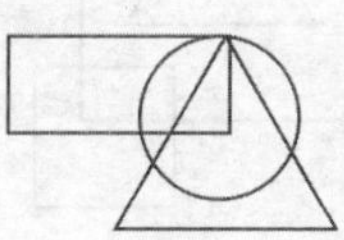

10.

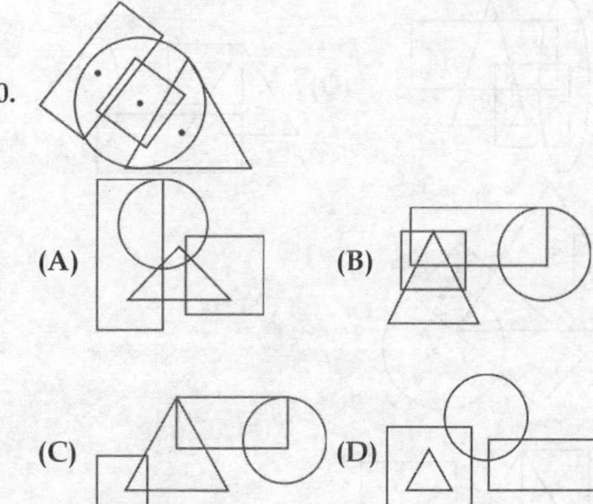

(A) (B)

(C) (D)

11.

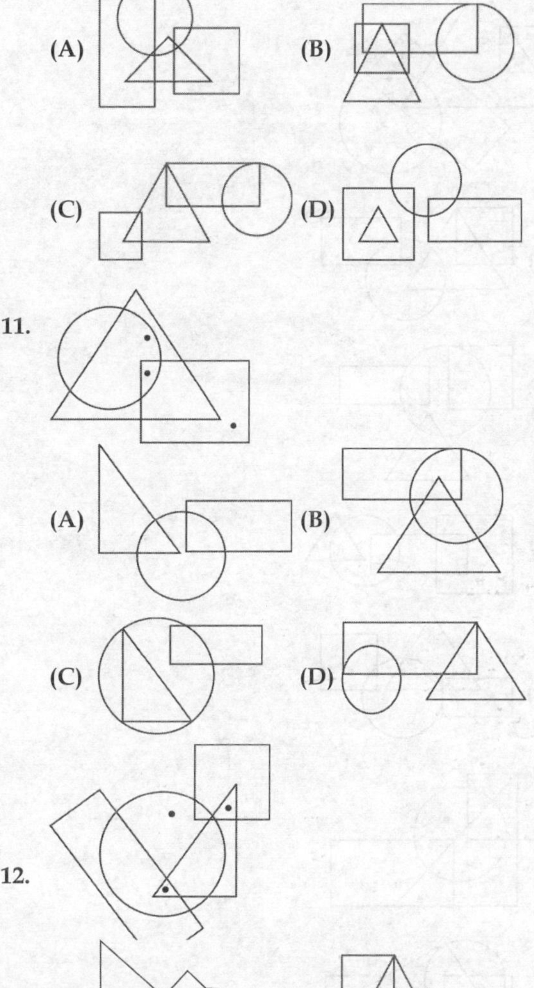

(A) (B)

(C) (D)

12.

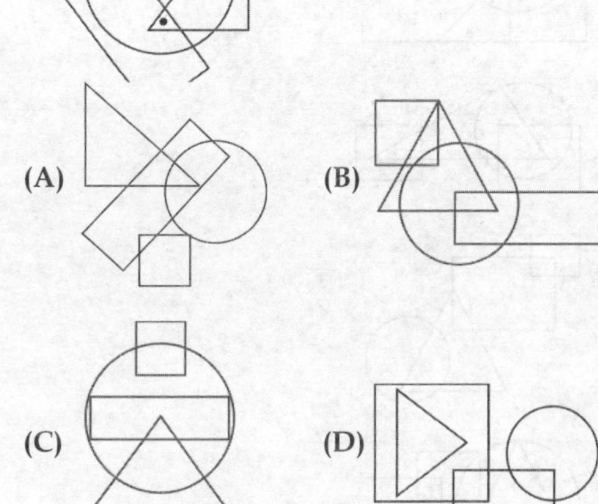

(A) (B)

(C) (D)

13.

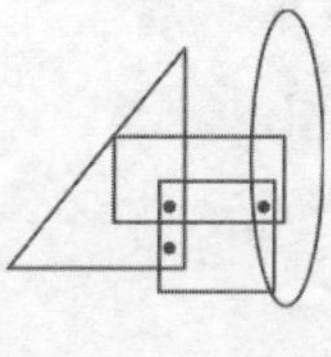

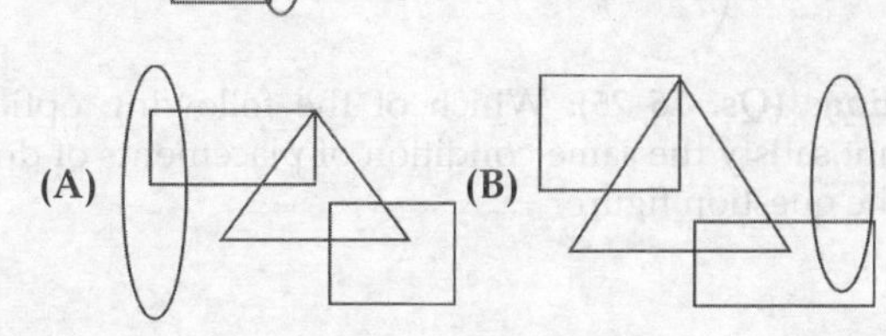

(A) (B)

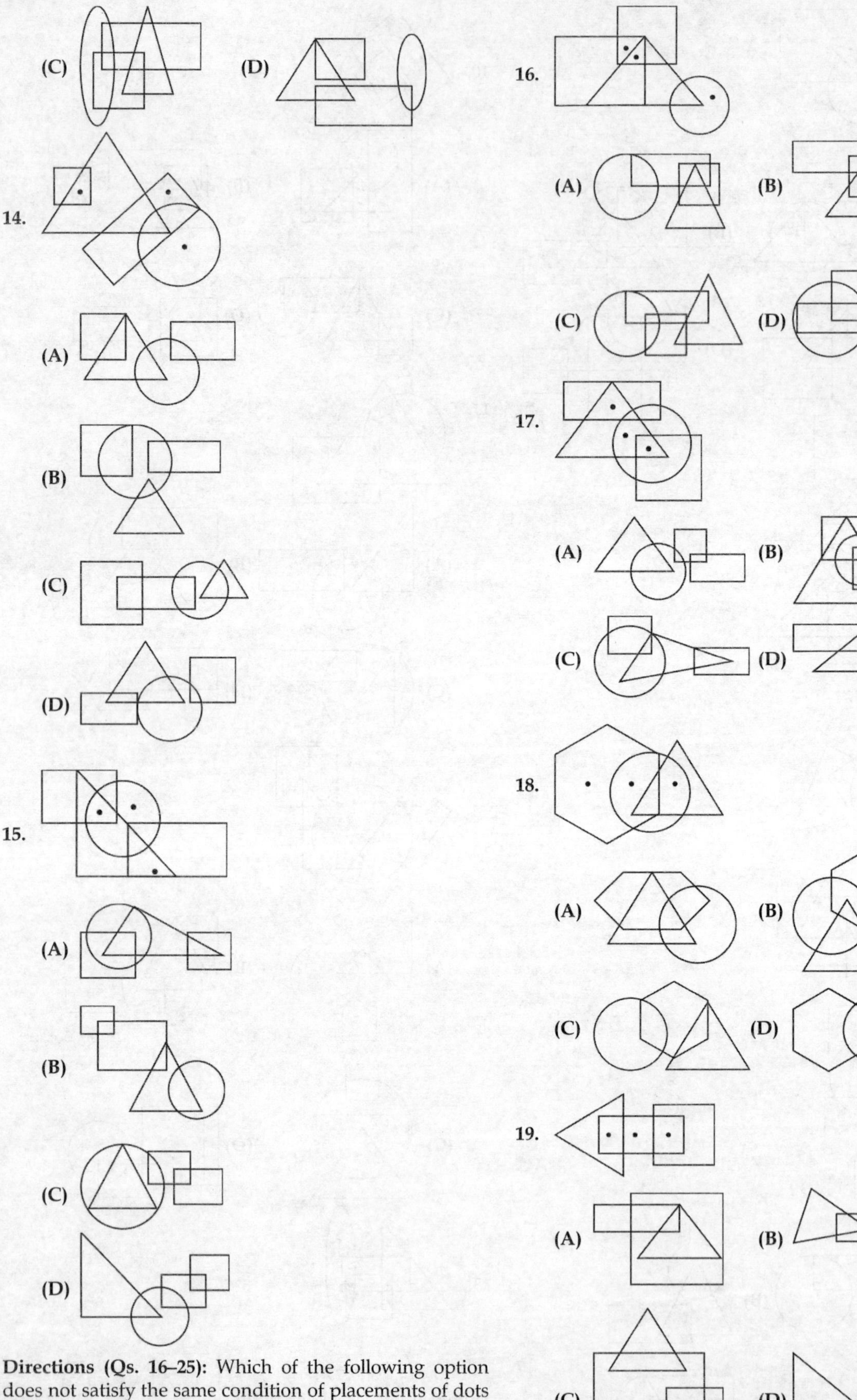

Directions (Qs. 16–25): Which of the following option does not satisfy the same condition of placements of dots as in the question figure?

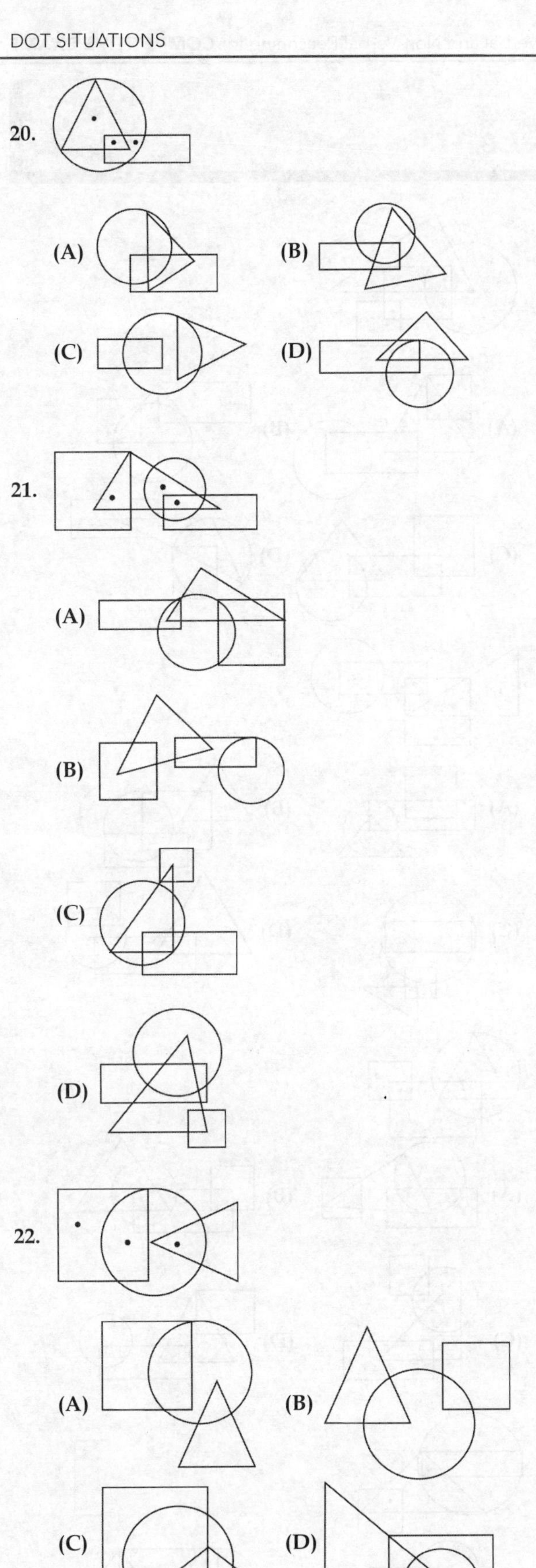
20.
(A)
(B)
(C)
(D)
21.
(A)
(B)
(C)
(D)
22.
(A)
(B)
(C)
(D)

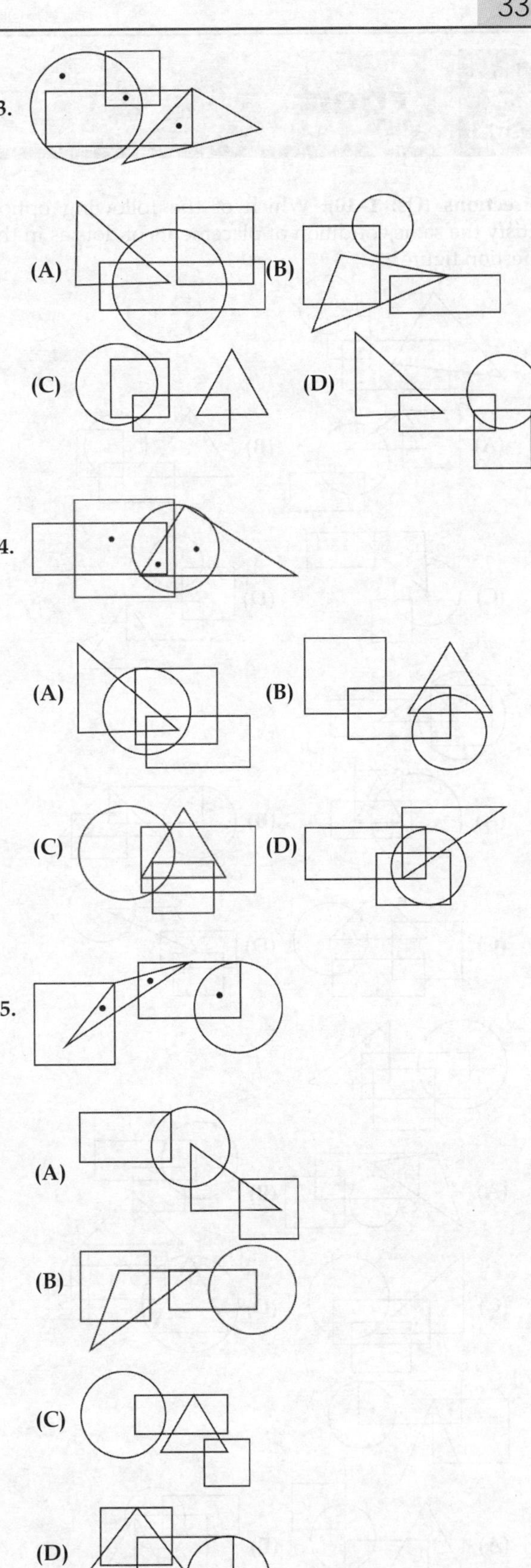
23.
(A)
(B)
(C)
(D)
24.
(A)
(B)
(C)
(D)
25.
(A)
(B)
(C)
(D)

3 Level Expert

Directions (Qs. 1–10): Which of the following option satisfy the same condition of placements of dots as in the question figure?

1. 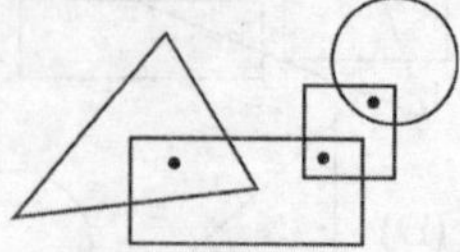

(A) 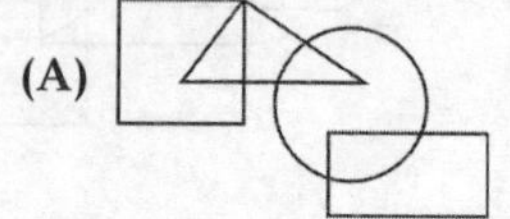 (B) 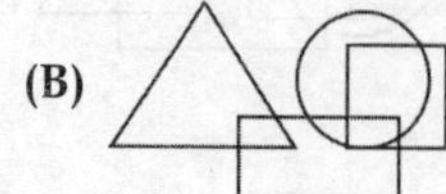

(C) 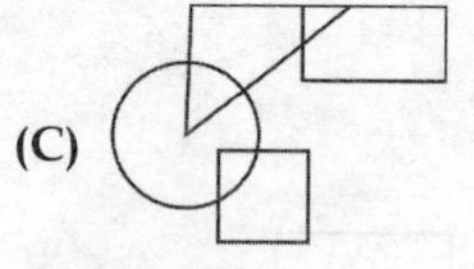 (D) 

2. 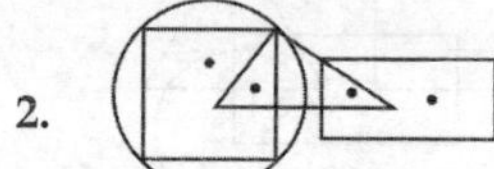

(A) 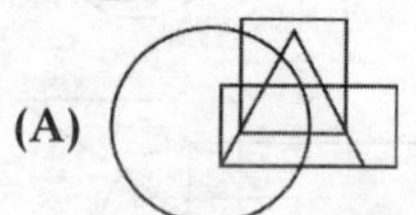 (B) 

(C) 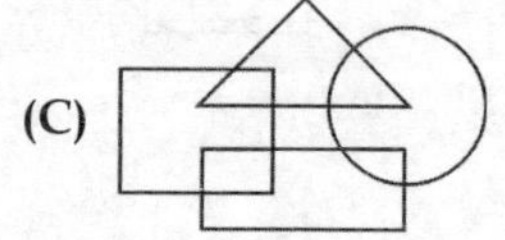 (D) 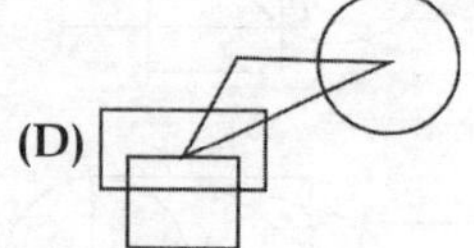

3. 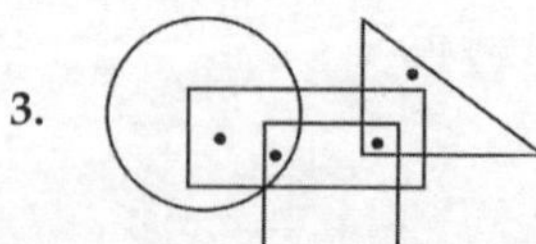

(A)  (B) 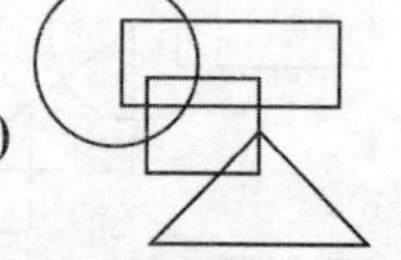

(C) 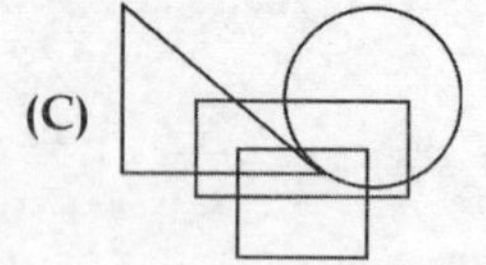 (D) 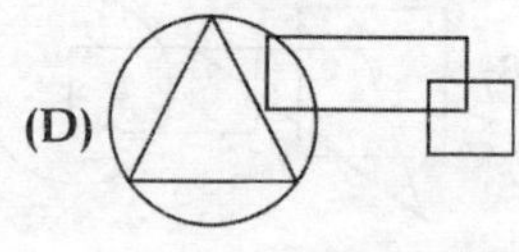

4. 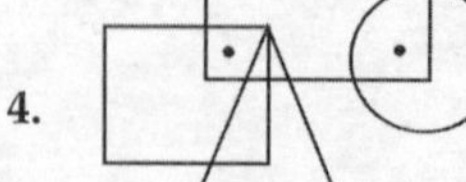

(A) 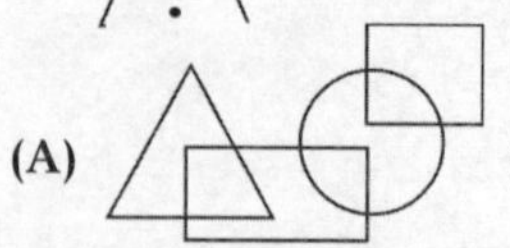 (B) 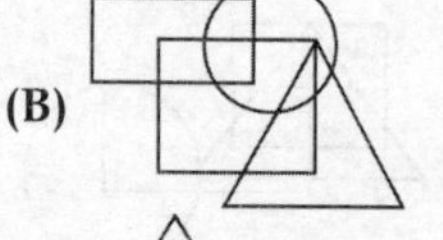

(C) 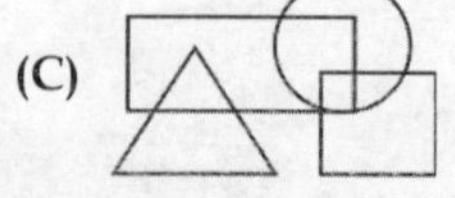 (D) 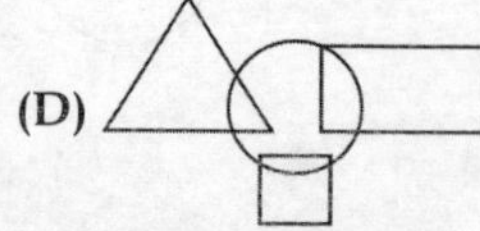

5. 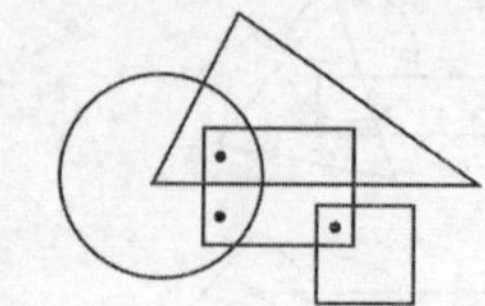

(A) (B) 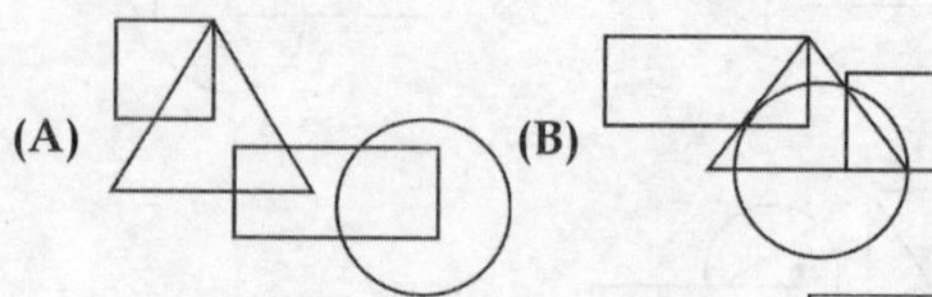

(C) (D) 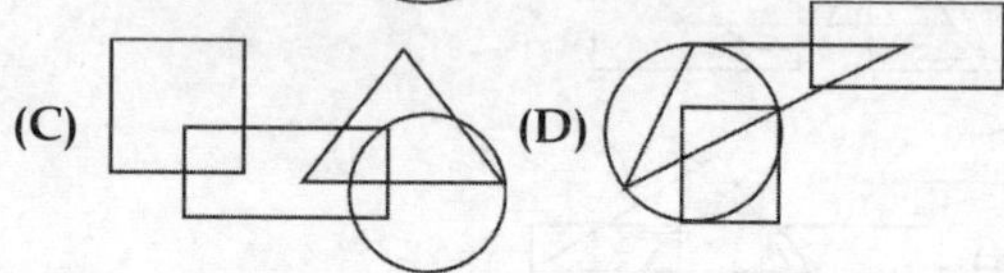

6. 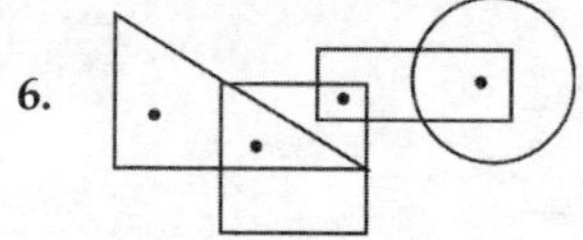

(A) 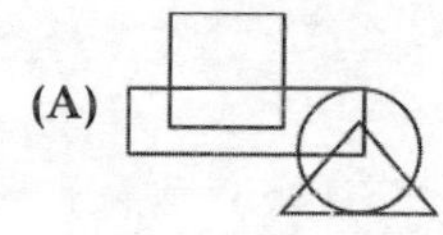 (B) 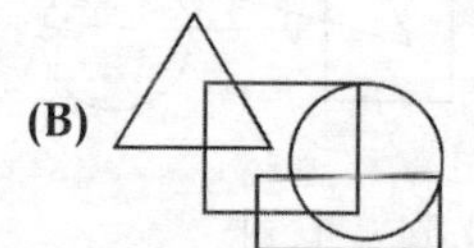

(C) 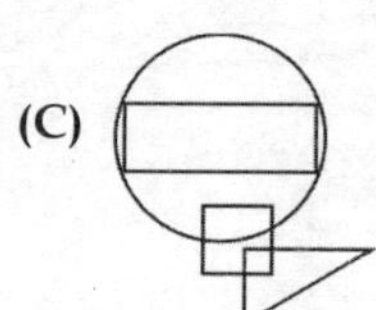 (D) 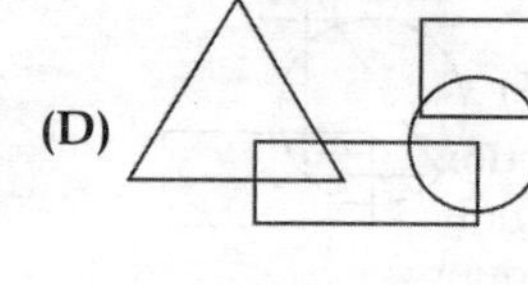

7.

(A) 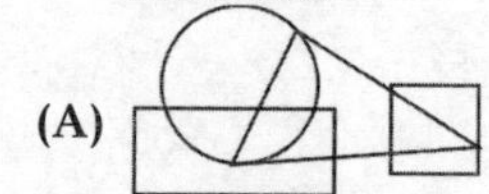 (B) 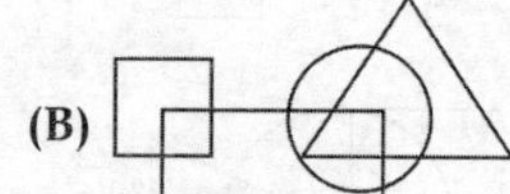

(C) 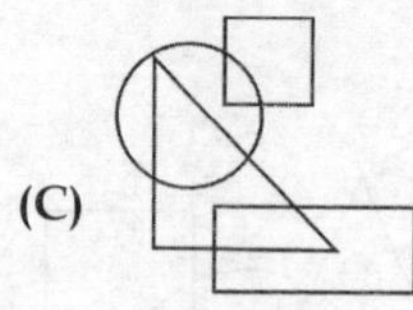 (D) 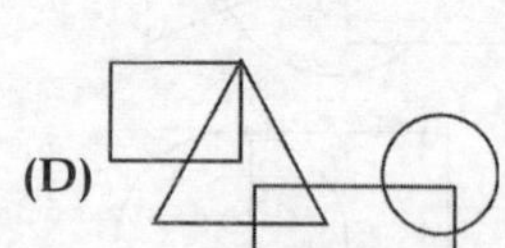

8. 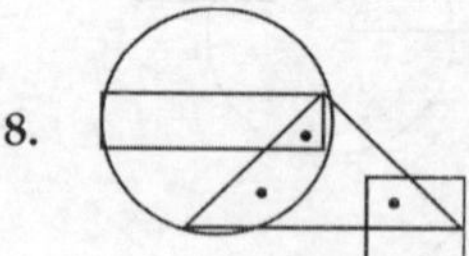

(A) 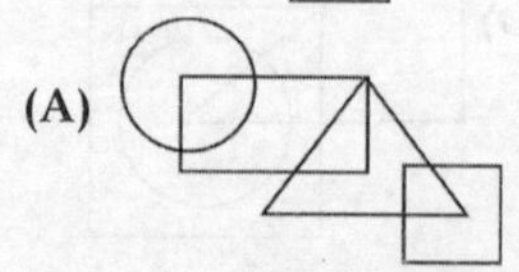 (B) 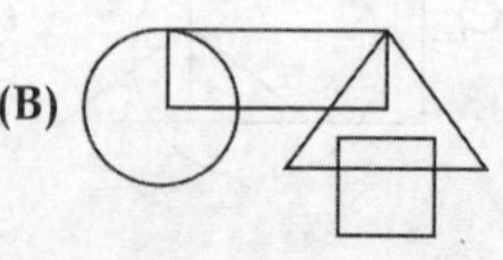

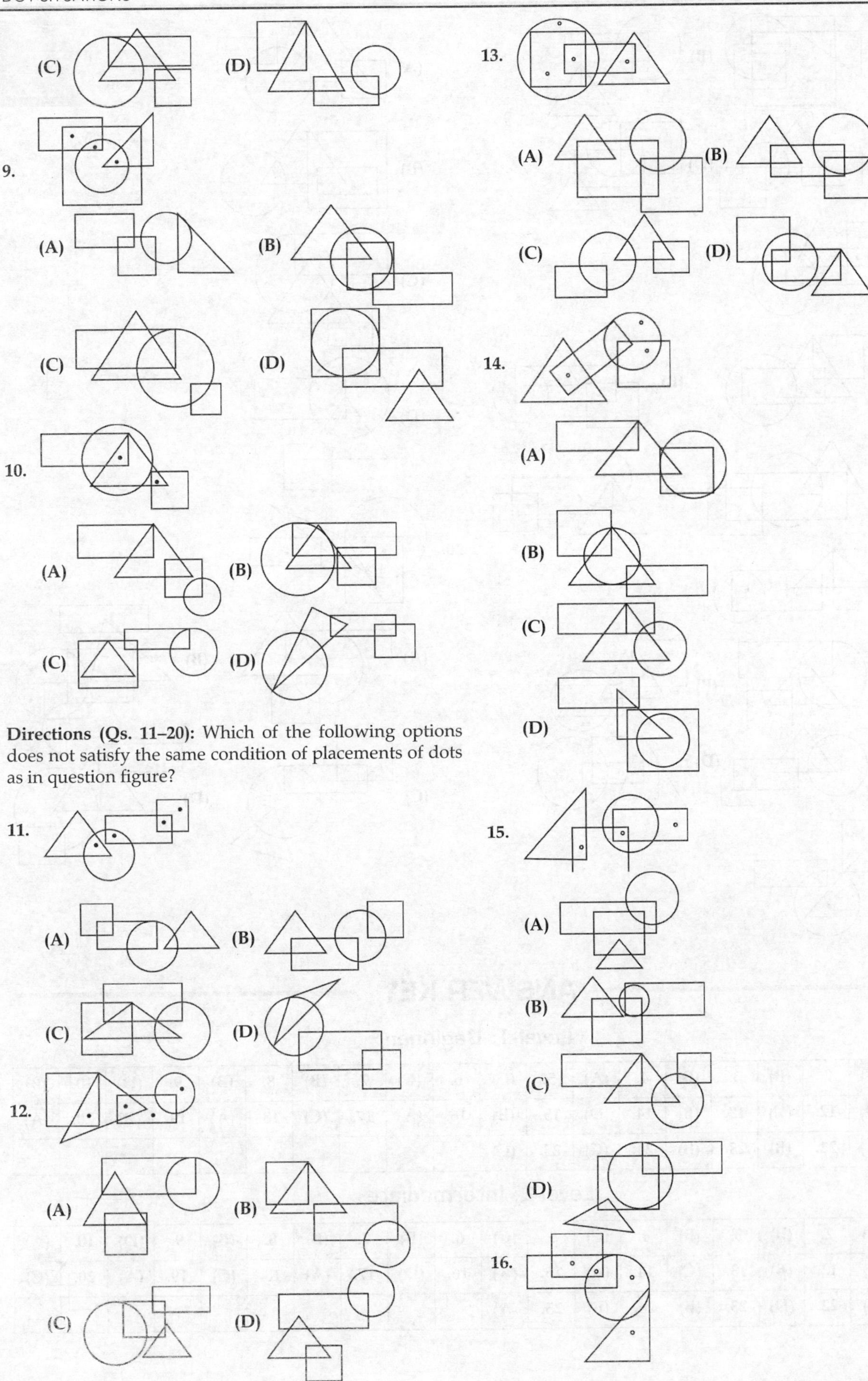

Directions (Qs. 11–20): Which of the following options does not satisfy the same condition of placements of dots as in question figure?

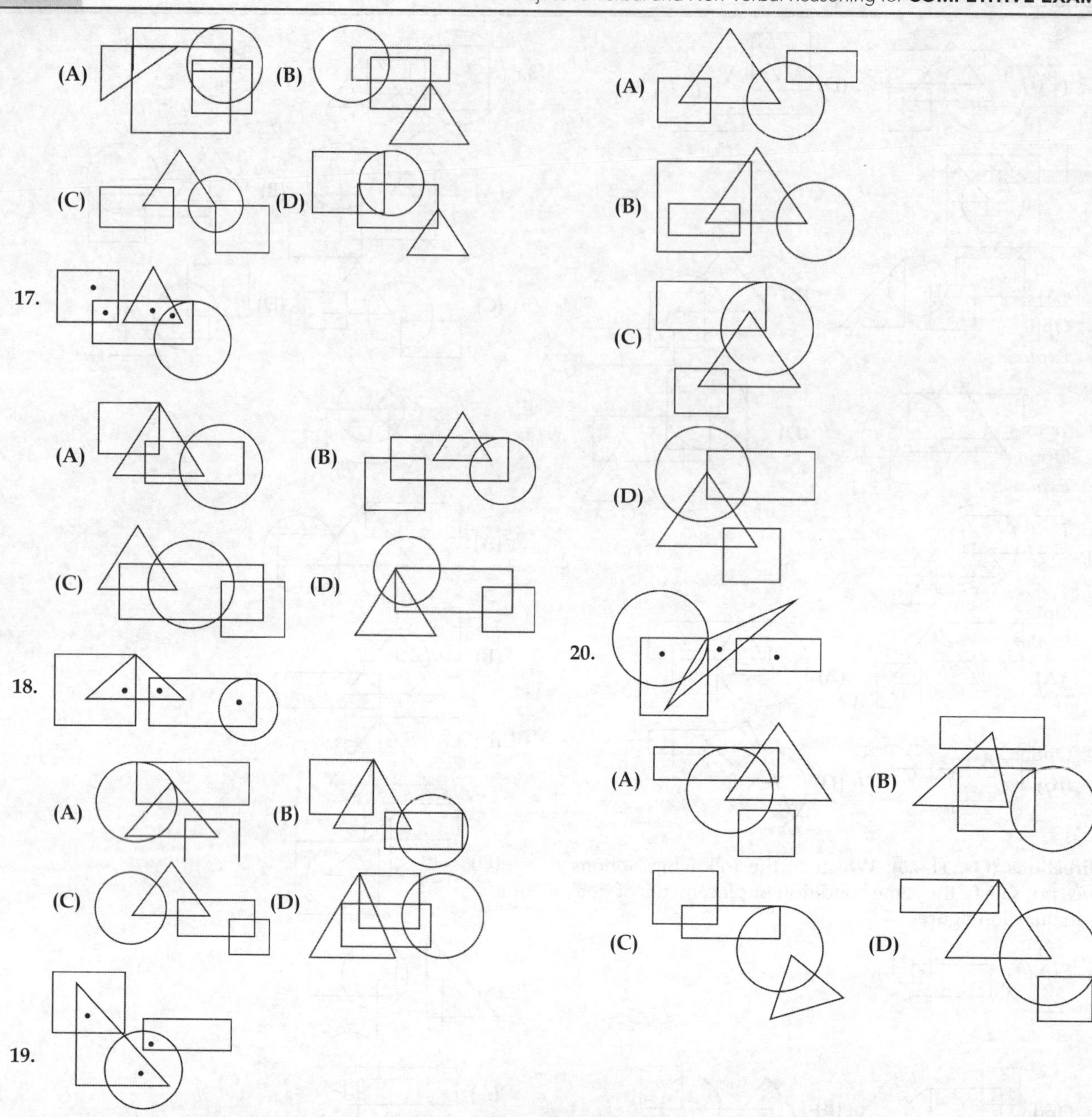

ANSWER KEY

Level-1: Beginner

1.	(C)	2.	(B)	3.	(B)	4.	(A)	5.	(C)	6.	(C)	7.	(B)	8.	(B)	9.	(D)	10.	(B)
11.	(D)	12.	(C)	13.	(B)	14.	(D)	15.	(B)	16.	(A)	17.	(C)	18.	(A)	19.	(B)	20.	(A)
21.	(A)	22.	(B)	23.	(B)	24.	(C)	25.	(C)										

Level-2: Intermediate

1.	(B)	2.	(B)	3.	(B)	4.	(C)	5.	(C)	6.	(B)	7.	(B)	8.	(B)	9.	(D)	10.	(A)
11.	(B)	12.	(B)	13.	(C)	14.	(A)	15.	(A)	16.	(D)	17.	(A)	18.	(C)	19.	(A)	20.	(C)
21.	(B)	22.	(D)	23.	(B)	24.	(B)	25.	(A)										

Level-3: Expert

1.	(D)	2.	(A)	3.	(C)	4.	(B)	5.	(C)	6.	(B)	7.	(B)	8.	(C)	9.	(B)	10.	(B)
11.	(B)	12.	(C)	13.	(C)	14.	(D)	15.	(C)	16.	(C)	17.	(A)	18.	(C)	19.	(B)	20.	(C)

Solutions with Detailed Explanations

Level-1: BEGINNER

1. **Option (C) is correct.**
Explanation:

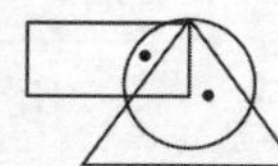

2. **Option (B) is correct.**
Explanation:

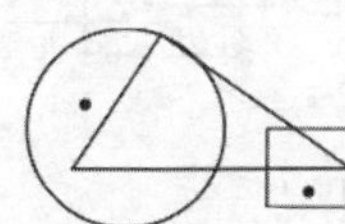

3. **Option (B) is correct.**
Explanation:

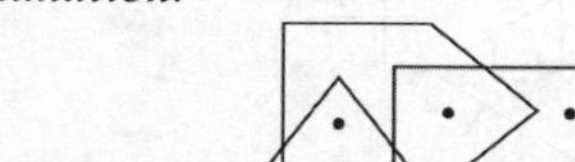

4. **Option (A) is correct.**
Explanation:

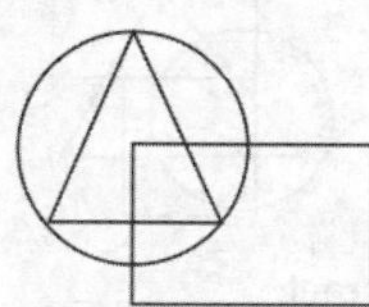

5. **Option (C) is correct.**
Explanation:

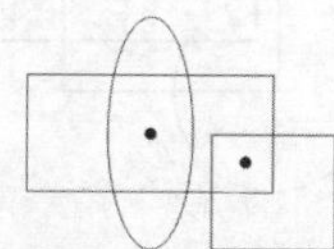

6. **Option (C) is correct.**
Explanation:

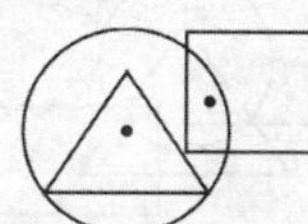

7. **Option (B) is correct.**
Explanation:

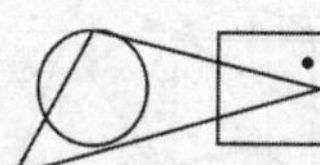

8. **Option (B) is correct.**
Explanation:

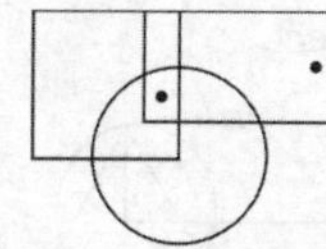

9. **Option (D) is correct.**
Explanation:

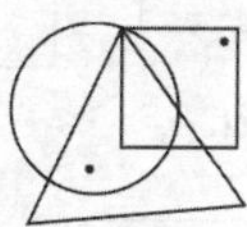

10. **Option (B) is correct.**
Explanation:

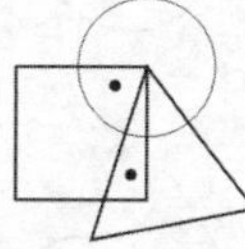

11. **Option (D) is correct.**
Explanation:

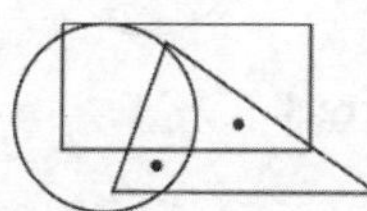

12. **Option (C) is correct.**
Explanation:

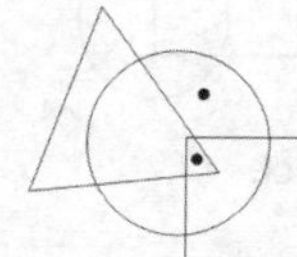

13. **Option (B) is correct.**
Explanation:

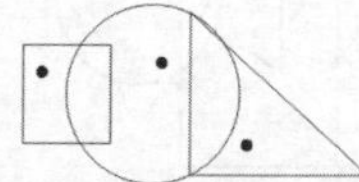

14. **Option (D) is correct.**
Explanation:

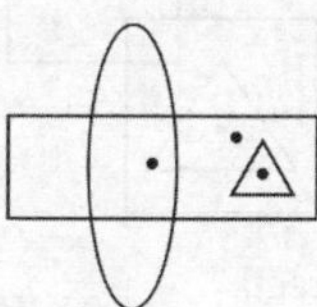

15. **Option (B) is correct.**
Explanation:

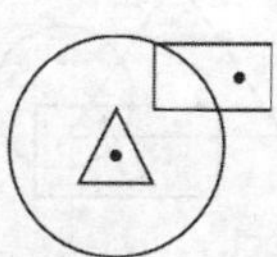

16. **Option (A) is correct.**
Explanation:

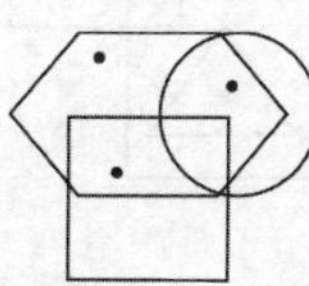

17. Option (C) is correct.
Explanation:

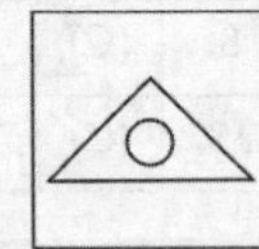

18. Option (A) is correct.
Explanation:

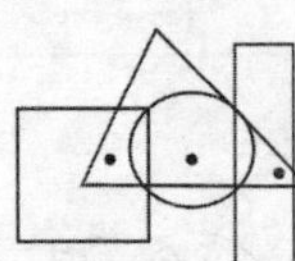

19. Option (B) is correct.
Explanation:

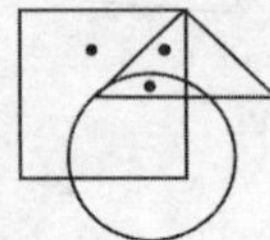

20. Option (A) is correct.
Explanation:

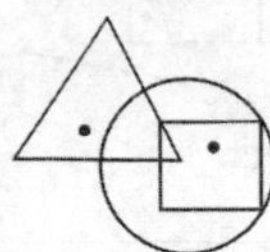

21. Option (A) is correct.
Explanation:

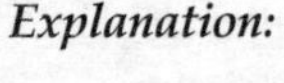

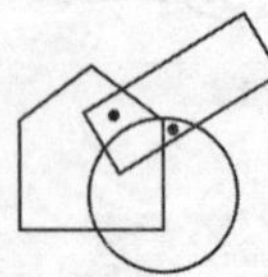

22. Option (B) is correct.
Explanation:

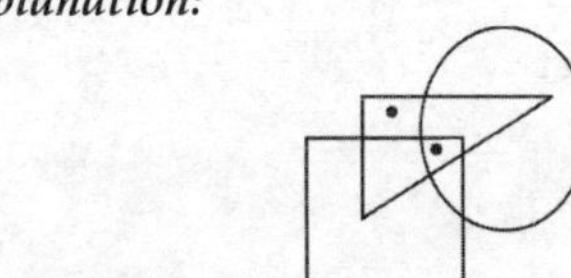

23. Option (B) is correct.
Explanation:

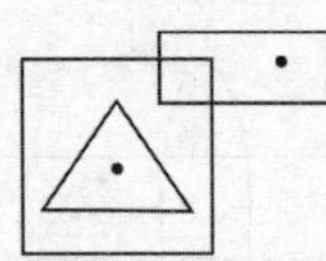

24. Option (C) is correct.
Explanation:

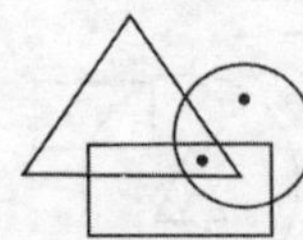

25. Option (C) is correct.
Explanation:

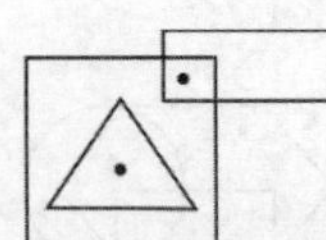

Level-2: INTERMEDIATE

1. Option (B) is correct.
Explanation:

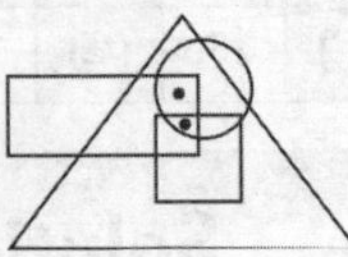

2. Option (B) is correct.
Explanation:

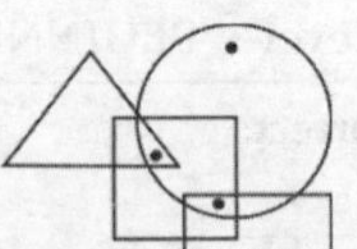

3. Option (B) is correct.
Explanation:

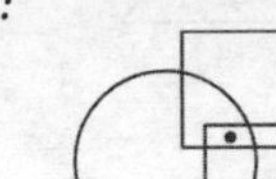

4. Option (C) is correct.
Explanation:

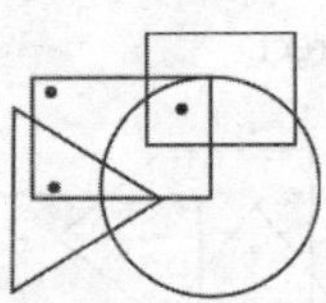

5. Option (C) is correct.
Explanation:

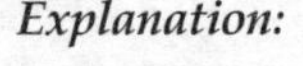

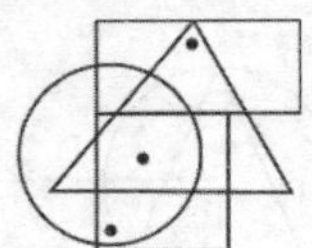

6. Option (B) is correct.
Explanation:

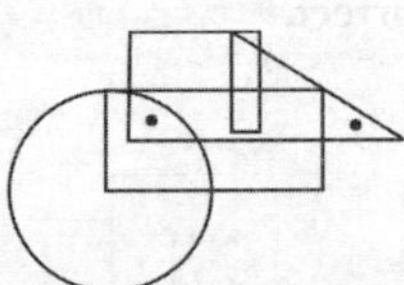

7. Option (B) is correct.
Explanation:

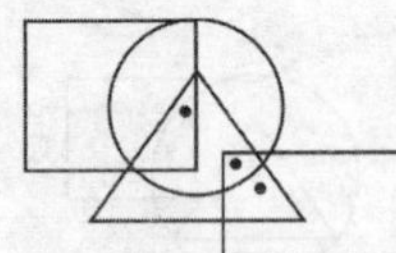

8. Option (B) is correct.
Explanation:

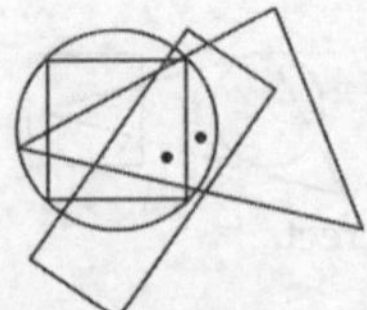

9. Option (D) is correct.
Explanation:

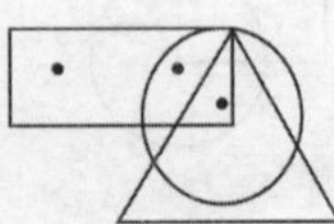

10. Option (A) is correct.
Explanation:

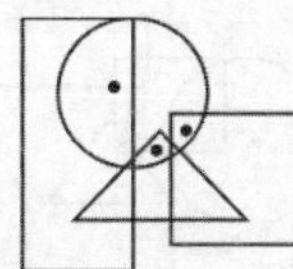

11. Option (B) is correct.
Explanation:

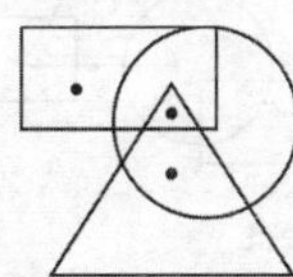

12. Option (B) is correct.
Explanation:

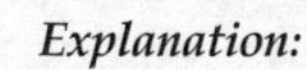

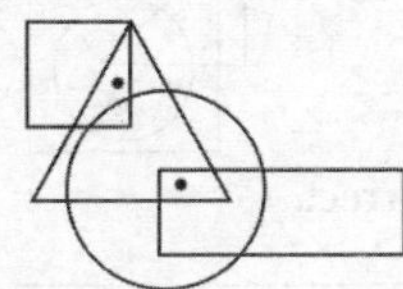

13. Option (C) is correct.
Explanation:

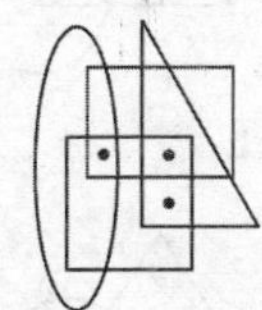

14. Option (A) is correct.
Explanation:

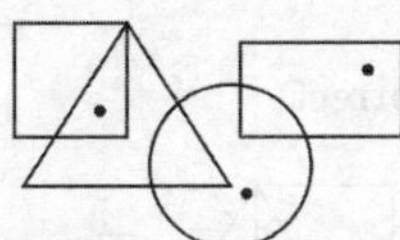

15. Option (A) is correct.
Explanation:

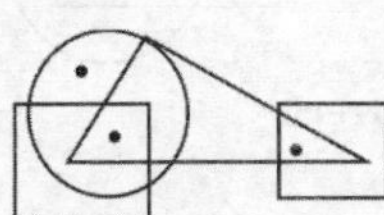

16. Option (D) is correct.
Explanation:

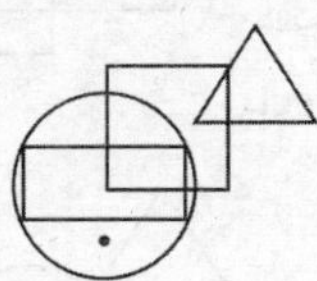

17. Option (A) is correct.
Explanation:

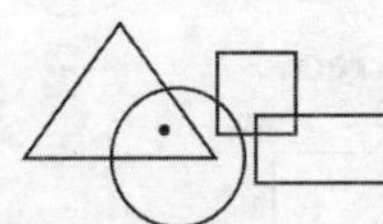

18. Option (C) is correct.
Explanation:

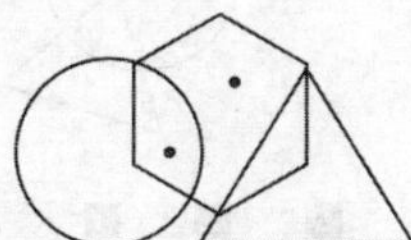

19. Option (A) is correct.
Explanation:

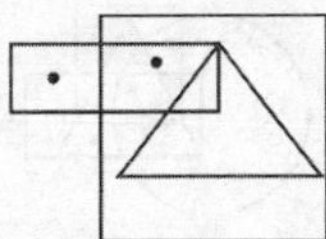

20. Option (C) is correct.
Explanation:

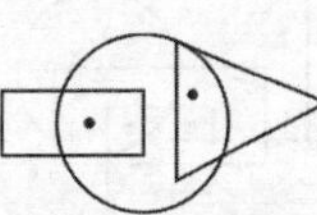

21. Option (B) is correct.
Explanation:

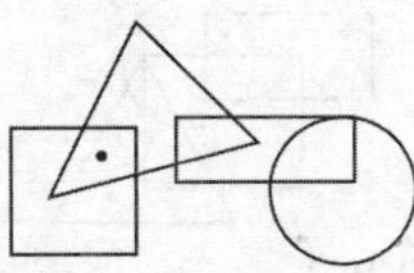

22. Option (D) is correct.
Explanation:

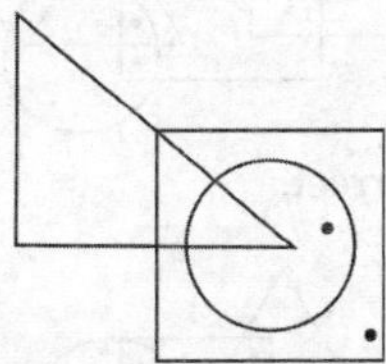

23. Option (B) is correct.
Explanation:

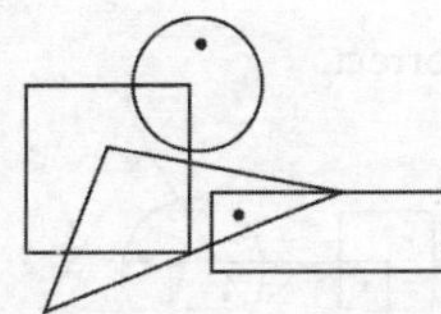

24. Option (B) is correct.
Explanation:

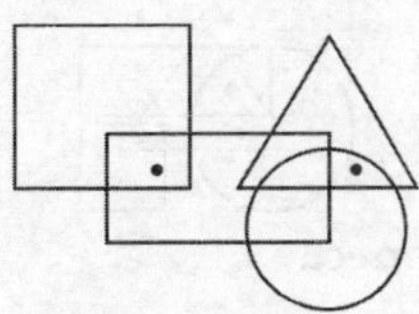

25. Option (A) is correct.
Explanation:

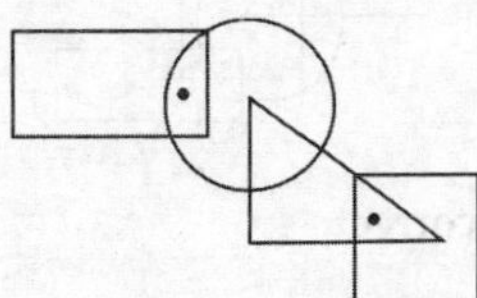

Level-3: EXPERT

1. Option (D) is correct.
Explanation:

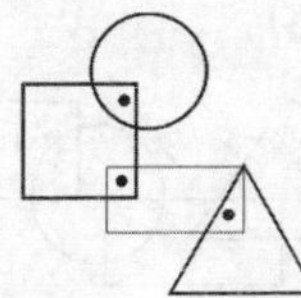

2. **Option (A) is correct.**
Explanation:

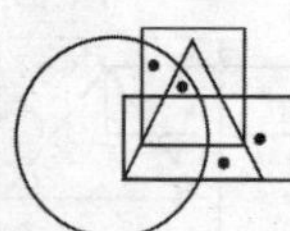

3. **Option (C) is correct.**
Explanation:

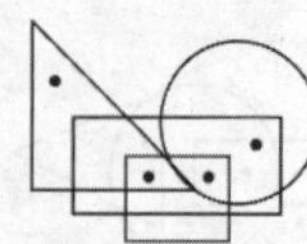

4. **Option (B) is correct.**
Explanation:

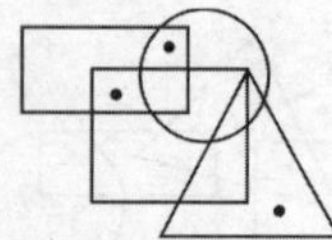

5. **Option (C) is correct.**
Explanation:

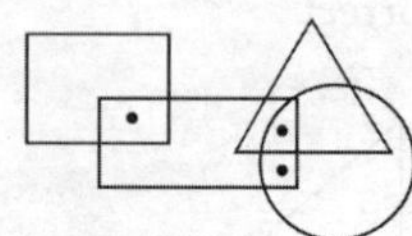

6. **Option (B) is correct.**
Explanation:

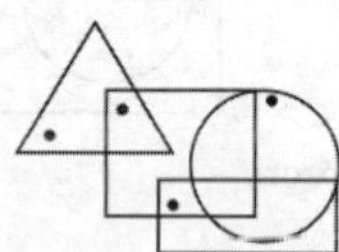

7. **Option (B) is correct.**
Explanation:

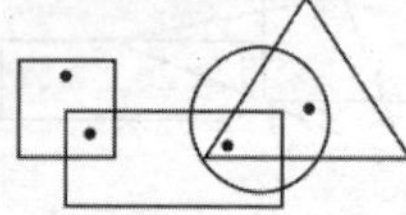

8. **Option (C) is correct.**
Explanation:

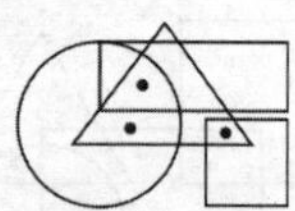

9. **Option (B) is correct.**
Explanation:

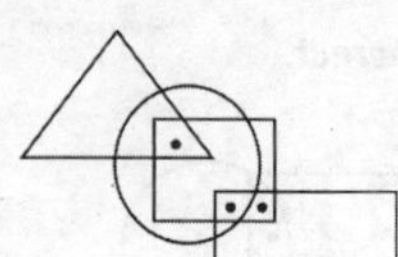

10. **Option (B) is correct.**
Explanation:

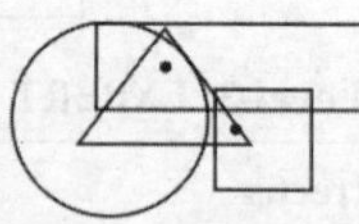

11. **Option (B) is correct.**
Explanation:

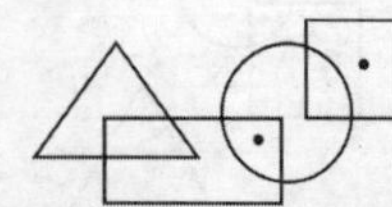

12. **Option (C) is correct.**
Explanation:

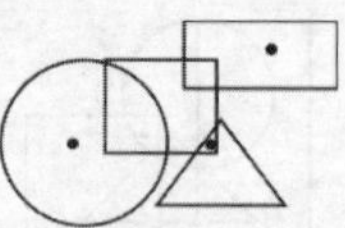

13. **Option (C) is correct.**
Explanation:

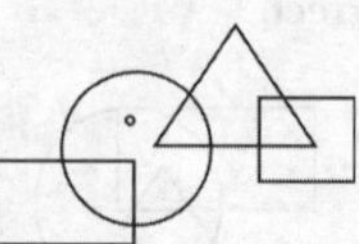

14. **Option (D) is correct.**
Explanation:

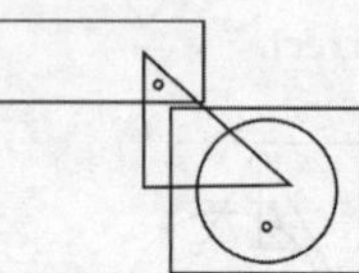

15. **Option (C) is correct.**
Explanation:

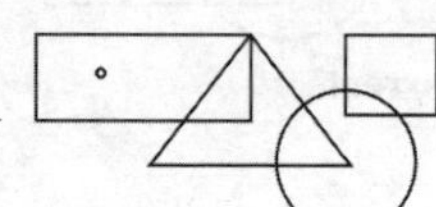

16. **Option (C) is correct.**
Explanation:

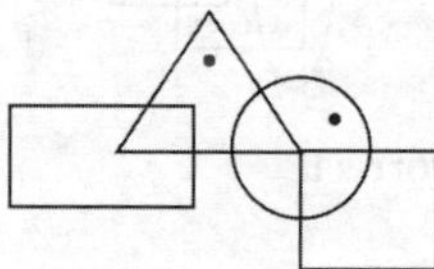

17. **Option (A) is correct.**
Explanation:

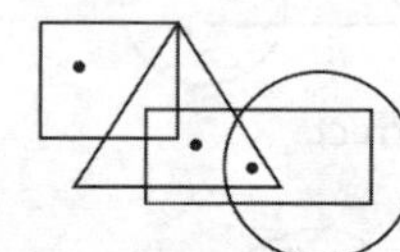

18. **Option (C) is correct.**
Explanation:

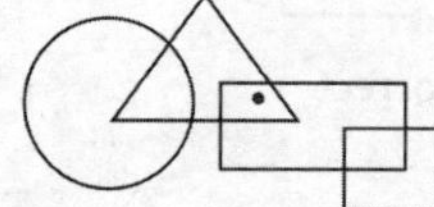

19. **Option (B) is correct.**
Explanation:

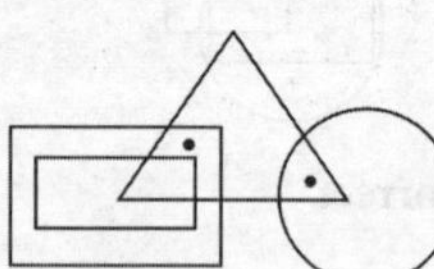

20. **Option (C) is correct.**
Explanation:

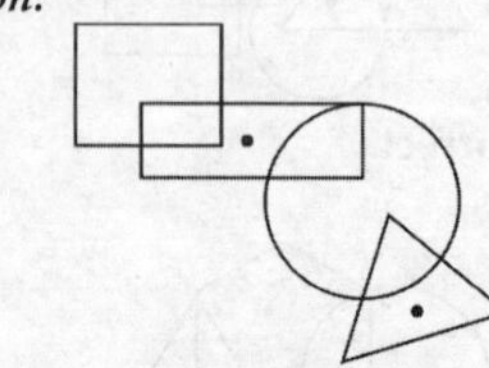

■ ■ ■